OXFORD PAPERBACK REFERENCE

The Oxford
Spelling
Dictionary

KT-434-054

Maurice Waite is an Associate Editor in the
Dictionaries department at Oxford University Press,
currently working on a thesaurus. He is the editor of
The Little Oxford Dictionary, *The Oxford Colour Spelling
Dictionary*, and *The Oxford MiniDictionary of Spelling*, and
has contributed to many works, including *The New
Oxford Thesaurus of English*, *The New Oxford Dictionary of
English*, and *The Oxford–Duden German Dictionary*.

Oxford Paperback Reference

The most authoritative and up-to-date reference books for both students and the general reader.

The Oxford

Spelling
Dictionary

EDITED BY

Maurice Waite

OXFORD
UNIVERSITY PRESS

OXFORD

UNIVERSITY PRESS

Great Clarendon Street, Oxford OX2 6DP

Oxford University Press is a department of the University of Oxford.
It furthers the University's objective of excellence in research, scholarship,
and education by publishing worldwide in

Oxford New York

Athens Auckland Bangkok Bogotá Buenos Aires Calcutta
Cape Town Chennai Dar es Salaam Delhi Florence Hong Kong Istanbul
Karachi Kuala Lumpur Madrid Melbourne Mexico City Mumbai
Nairobi Paris São Paulo Singapore Taipei Tokyo Toronto Warsaw

with associated companies in Berlin Ibadan

Oxford is a registered trade mark of Oxford University Press
in the UK and in certain other countries

Published in the United States
by Oxford University Press Inc., New York

© Oxford University Press 1986, 1995, 1996

Database right Oxford University Press (maker)

First published in 1986 as *The Oxford Spelling Dictionary*
Second edition 1995
Published in paperback as *The Oxford Colour Spelling Dictionary* 1996
Reissued in new covers as *The Oxford Spelling Dictionary* 2000

British Library Cataloguing in Publication Data

Data available

Library of Congress Cataloging in Publication Data

Data available

ISBN 0-19-280110-4

10 9 8 7 6 5 4 3 2 1

Printed in Great Britain by
Cox & Wyman Ltd,
Reading, Berkshire

Preface

This volume contains the full text of the second edition of the *Oxford Spelling Dictionary*, which has been completely re-edited and considerably enlarged by the addition of not only more headwords but also all inflections. The coverage is based on that of the *Concise Oxford Dictionary* (Ninth Edition, 1995) and the *Oxford English Reference Dictionary* (1995), with further items included on grounds of spelling difficulty or possible confusion. This edition also includes a large number of compounds written as two words (see the Introduction for the categories covered).

American spellings are now included, and both they and their British equivalents are labelled and cross-referred to each other to enable the book to be used for adapting texts to either British or American usage.

Another major innovation in this edition is the use of computerized collections of English (the British National Corpus and the Oxford Dictionary Department's own body of citations) in identifying new words for inclusion and in comparing the frequencies of variant spellings. The recommended spelling of a word is not always simply that found most frequently, because other factors are also taken into account, such as the number and type of sources using each variant.

The recommended word divisions shown have been completely revised in the light of modern practice and represent an attempt to find the most unobtrusive solutions. They are based on a combination of etymological and phonological considerations, since overstrict adherence to either principle can result in misleading or inelegant divisions, such as *auto-nomous* and *lung-ing* or *profi-teer* and *overwa-ter*.

I am indebted to Rosamund Moon for her contribution to the planning of the project before I became involved.

M. J. W.

Editorial Staff

Editor
Maurice Waite

Adviser on word division
Judith Scott

Assistant editor and keyboarder
Susan Wilkin

Chief Editor, Current English Dictionaries
Patrick Hanks

Contents

Introduction

I. SPELLING

Indicators

Various indicators are given to help the reader spell a word correctly, especially when there are others with which it could be confused. These are referred to after the symbol △, which can be taken to mean 'Do not confuse with…'. The indicators are of the following types:

1. Sense indicators, e.g.

> **hare** (animal. △ **hair**)
> **hair** (on head etc. △ **hare**)

These are not complete definitions, nor do they always cover all parts of speech, as they are intended to be merely enough to enable the reader to choose the correct spelling of a word, often giving no more than a single quality or feature which distinguishes one thing from another.

2. Word-class (or part-of-speech) labels, e.g.

> **double fault** *noun*
> **double-fault** *verb*

3. Subject-field labels, e.g.

> **bailor** (*Law.* △ **bailer, baler**)

4. Brief descriptions of people, places, institutions, etc., e.g.

> **Pavarotti, Luciano** (Italian tenor)
> **Delhi** (capital of India)

Spelling recommendations

When there is variation in the spelling of a word, e.g. *judg(e)ment*, the use of one spelling is normally recommended, thus:

> **judgment** (use judgement)

No preference is normally given among variants which differ more than slightly in pronunciation and are therefore treated as synonyms, e.g. *brontosaur/brontosaurus* or *archil/orchil*.

A non-recommended spelling is normally entered with a cross-reference to the recommended spelling, as with *judgment* above, but if it is also the recommended or only spelling of a different word, it is not mentioned as being a non-recommended variant, since the purpose of this book is not to provide a record of all existing variants. For example, although *weepy*, besides meaning 'tearful', is a non-recommended spelling of *weepie*, meaning 'a sentimental or emotional film, play, etc.', the two words are simply entered thus:

> **weepie** (film etc. △ **weepy**)
> **weepy** (tearful. △ **weepie**)

Variants which differ only in the matter of accents, apostrophes, or capital letters, or whether they are written hyphenated, as two words, or as one, e.g. *fete*, *Holarctic*, and *back-up* (as opposed to the recommended *fête*, *holarctic*, and *backup*) are not normally shown, since they would almost always be adjacent to the recommended forms and there are very large numbers of particularly the last type.

When an inflection has different spellings which are pronounced identically, the first one given is recommended. For example, in

> **cue**
> cues
> cued
> cueing *or* cuing

cueing is recommended, and in

> **bureau**
> bureaux *or* bureaus

bureaux is recommended.

Capital initial letters

Many pairs of words with capital and lower-case initials are given if each refers to a very different person or thing, e.g.

> **Balaclava** (battlefield, Crimea)
> **balaclava** (helmet)
>
> **Felicity** (name)
> **felicity** (happiness)
>
> **Pentagon** (US defence HQ)
> **pentagon** (five-sided figure)

However, when the capitalized form refers merely to a particular example of the person or thing in question, e.g. *the Queen* or *the Renaissance*, it is not normally entered.

Compounds

This dictionary contains large numbers of compound expressions written as one word or with a hyphen, so that the reader is left in no doubt as to the recommended form. ('Syntactic' hyphenated compounds, such as *mud-spattered* or *assembly-line* in *assembly-line workers*, being almost unlimited in number, are only given if they are extremely common, e.g. *high-street* in *high-street shops*, or if there could be doubt about another aspect of their spelling.)

In addition, compounds that are written as separate words are given if

1. there is evidence of variation in their use, as with, e.g., *street lamp*, which is also, but not so frequently, written as *street-lamp*;

2. they are of a construction that might suggest that they are written as one word or with a hyphen, e.g. *chess player*;

3. they could be confused with particular single-word or hyphenated compounds, e.g. *all together* (compare *altogether*) or *way in* (compare *weigh-in*); or

4. the predominant form has recently changed, resulting in a different recommendation from that in earlier Oxford publications, e.g. *horse race*.

In this book, hyphens introduced because a word is divided at the end of a line are printed sloping (-), while 'permanent' hyphens, as in *eighty-first*, are always printed horizontally, even at the end of a line.

British and American spellings

The labels *Br.* and *Am.* are recommendations as to which spelling to use in British and American English respectively, e.g.

> **pretence** *Br.* (*Am.* **pretense**)
> **pretense** *Am.* (*Br.* **pretence**)

They are not to be taken as indications of the currency of the different spellings; *pretence* is in fact used in both British and American English but is labelled *Br.* as it is the only British spelling and is not the predominant American spelling.

Words that are found only in British or American English, such as *blowlamp* and *preppy*, are not labelled as such.

-ise and *-ize*

The verbal ending *-ize* has been in general use since the 16th century; it is favoured in American use, while, in Britain, both *-ize* and *-ise* are acceptable, provided that their use is consistent. The preferred style of Oxford University Press in academic and general books published in Britain is *-ize*, and this book therefore lists words showing such variation thus:

> **nationalise** *Br.* (use **nationalize**)
> **nationalize**
>
> **organiser** *Br.* (use **organizer**)
> **organizer**

Note that a number of verbs ending in *-ise* or *-ize* do not have alternative spellings, such as *televise* and *capsize*.

Transliterations

Alternative transliterations of foreign names are entered thus:

> **Tsinghai** (= Qinghai)

indicating that they are acceptable but at the same time showing which spelling to use to ensure consistency with other names.

Inflections

Inflections are given in the order:

> noun plural and/or 3rd person singular of the present tense
> past tense
> present participle
> past participle
> comparative adjective
> superlative adjective

If the noun plural and the 3rd person singular of a word that is both a noun and a verb have the same form, it is given only once, e.g.

> **break**
>   breaks
>   broke
>   breaking
>   broken

(If it is different, the noun and the verb are given separate entries for the sake of clarity.)

If the past tense and the past participle have the same form, it is given only once, in the position for the past tense, e.g.

> **deal**
>   deals
>   dealt
>   dealing

If all the inflections of a word are regular, e.g. *calms, calmed, calming, calmer, calmest*, then only the endings are given, thus:

> **calm** +s +ed +ing +er +est
> **claim** +s +ed +ing
> **cold** +s +er +est

II. WORD DIVISION

'Word division' means the splitting of a word at the end of a line of print or writing, with a hyphen added at the end of the first part, and the second part taken over to the next line. (It is often called 'hyphenation', but that term is also used to refer to the use of 'permanent' hyphens in compounds such as *pay-bed* and *over-abundant*.)

In handwriting and typing, it is safest (and often neatest) not to divide words at all; however, in word-processing and typesetting that is justified (i.e., with the lines expanded to make the right-hand ends align vertically, as in this Introduction), the overall appearance may well be better if a word is divided than if it is taken over to the next line and the remaining words are spaced out.

Where to divide

The vertical bar (|) indicates a 'preferred' division point, at which a word can be divided under almost any circumstances, while a broken vertical bar (¦) indicates a 'secondary' division point, at which a word is best divided only in narrow-measure work (i.e., narrow columns of type, as, for example, in newspapers and some dictionaries). A word containing both kinds should be divided at a preferred point if possible.

The division indicators have both relative and absolute value: for instance, a secondary division point in a word which also contains a preferred point, such as **con¦tent|ment** (*con-tentment*), may be a better division than that indicated by a secondary point that is the only point in a short word, such as **hag¦gle**, but it is given secondary status because it is not as good as the preferred division (*content-ment*).

Every word division should, ideally, be vetted by eye as a check that it is both the best division possible and better than not dividing at all: for instance, even a 'preferred' division may be quite unnecessary at the end of a wide line if the word spaces are not too large. Furthermore, the recommendations in this or any other book should not be regarded as inviolable rules; the typesetter or proof-reader should occasionally feel free to depart from them if the circumstances warrant it.

Division of regular inflections

In regular inflections (shown as **+ing** etc.—see p. xii), the endings are separable as follows:

+ed: only in narrow-measure work and then only if the word is of at least six letters and the ending is pronounced as a separate syllable, e.g. *bleat-ed* or *part-ed*; compare *ended* and *calmed*.

+ing: always, if the word is of more than six letters, e.g. *calm-ing* or *sharpen-ing*, but otherwise only in narrow-measure work, e.g. *buy-ing*.

+er: only in narrow-measure work and then only if the word is of at least six letters, e.g. *calm-er* or *sharp-er*; compare *odder*.

+est: always, if the word is of more than six letters, as in *calm-est* or *shallow-est*, but otherwise only in narrow-measure work, e.g. *odd-est*.

The above rules are all qualified by those for the division of hyphenated compounds given on p. xiv; thus, e.g., *self-seeded* and *self-seeding* should not normally be divided before *-ed* and *-ing* respectively, and *co-presented* and *co-presenting* should be divided at those points normally only in narrow-measure work.

Division of hyphenated compounds

A hyphenated compound, such as *after-effect*, can be divided at the hyphen under almost any circumstances; the only proviso is that, because it could then appear to be a divided solid word, care should be taken that no confusion can arise as a result, as it might with, e.g., *re-cover* (meaning 'cover again'), which could be mistaken for *recover* (meaning 'reclaim' etc.).

Additionally, hyphenated compounds are shown with secondary division points at least six letters after the hyphen, e.g. **self-govern¦ment**. Finally, in order to avoid very bad spacing, one could divide either (*a*) the second element at a point fewer than six letters after the hyphen or (*b*) the first element, in each case following, whenever possible, the recommendations for the elements as words on their own. The most important consideration in doing so would be to avoid producing an unacceptably obtrusive or misleading result, such as *scab-bard-fish*.

Personal names

Some writers and typesetters prefer not to divide personal names at all, and some prefer to do so only in narrow-measure work. The personal names included in this dictionary are shown with both preferred and secondary division points so that, if they are divided, the best point at which to do so can be chosen, but they are identified as the names of people, e.g.

Mac¦ken¦zie, Alex¦an¦der (Scottish explorer)

so that it is possible to avoid dividing them if one wishes.

Note on Proprietary Terms

This dictionary includes some words which are, or are asserted to be, proprietary names or trade marks. Their inclusion does not imply that they have acquired for legal purposes a non-proprietary or general significance, nor is any other judgement implied concerning their legal status. In cases where the editor has some evidence that a word is used as a proprietary name or trade mark this is indicated by the label *Propr.*, but no judgement concerning the legal status of such words is made or implied thereby.

Aa

a *indefinite article*
aa (lava)
Aachen (city,
　Germany)
Aal|borg (city,
　Denmark)
Aalst (town,
　Belgium)
Aalto, Alvar
　(Finnish architect)
aard|vark +s
aard|wolf
　aard|wolves
Aar|gau (canton,
　Switzerland)
Aar|hus (city,
　Denmark)
Aaron (*Bible*; name)
Aaron's beard
Aaron's rod
aas|vogel +s
Ab (Jewish month)
aba +s
abac +s
abaca +s
aback
aba|cus
　aba|cuses *or*
　abaci
Aba|dan (port,
　Iran)
Abad|don
abaft
Aba|kan (city,
　Russia)
aba|lone +s
aban|don +s +ed
　+ing
aban|don|ee +s
aban|don|er +s
aban|don|ment +s
abase
　abases
　abased
　abas|ing
abase|ment
abash
　abashes
　abashed
　abash|ing
abash|ment
abask
abat|able
abate
　abates
　abated
　abat|ing
abate|ment

aba|tis
　plural aba|tis *or*
　aba|tises
aba|tised
abat|tis (use
　abatis)
　plural abat|tis *or*
　abat|tises
ab|at|toir +s
ab|ax|ial
abaya +s
Abba (Swedish pop
　group)
abba +s (garment;
　use aba)
ab|bacy
ab|ba|cies
Abbas, Fer|hat
　(Algerian
　nationalist leader)
Ab|basid +s
ab|ba|tial
Abbe, Ernst
　(German
　physicist)
abbé +s
ab|bess
　ab|besses
　(nun. △ abyss)
Abbe|vil|lian
abbey +s
abbot +s
ab|bot|ship +s
ab|bre|vi|ate
　ab|bre|vi|ates
　ab|bre|vi|ated
　ab|bre|vi|at|ing
ab|bre|vi|ation +s
ab|bre|vi|atory
ABC Is|lands
　(Aruba, Bonaire,
　and Curaçao,
　Netherlands
　Antilles)
ab|dic|able
ab|di|cate
　ab|di|cates
　ab|di|cated
　ab|di|cat|ing
ab|di|ca|tion +s
ab|di|ca|tor +s
ab|do|men +s
ab|dom|inal +s
ab|dom|in|al|ly
ab|dom|in|ous
ab|duct +s +ed
　+ing
ab|duc|tion +s
ab|duct|or +s
Abduh,
　Mu|ham|mad

Abduh (*cont.*)
　(Egyptian
　reformer)
Abdul Hamid II
　(Sultan of Turkey)
Ab|dul|lah, Sheikh
　Mu|ham|mad
　(Kashmiri leader)
Ab|dul|lah ibn
　Hus|sein
　(Jordanian king,
　1946–51)
Abdul Rah|man,
　Tunku (Malayan
　statesman)
Abe
abeam
abe|ce|dar|ian +s
abed
Abel (*Bible*; name)
Abel, Niels
　Hen|rik
　(Norwegian
　mathematician)
Abel|ard, Peter
　(French scholar)
abele +s
abelia +s
abel|ian
Abeo|kuta (city,
　Nigeria)
Aber|deen (city,
　Scotland)
Aber|deen, Lord
　(British prime
　minister)
Aber|deen Angus
　Aber|deen
　An|guses
Aber|deen|shire
　(former county,
　Scotland)
Aber|do|nian +s
Aber|fan (town,
　Wales)
Aber|nethy
　Aber|neth|ies
ab|er|rance
ab|er|rancy
ab|er|rant
ab|er|ra|tion +s
Aber|yst|wyth
　(city, Wales)
abet
　abets
　abet|ted
　abet|ting
abet|ment
abet|ter +s
abet|tor +s *Law*
abey|ance
abey|ant

abhor
　ab|hors
　ab|horred
　ab|hor|ring
ab|hor|rence
ab|hor|rent
ab|hor|rent|ly
ab|hor|rer +s
abid|ance
abide
　abides
　abided *or* abode
　abid|ing
abid|ing|ly
Abi|djan (port, the
　Ivory Coast)
Abi|gail (name)
abi|gail +s
abil|ity
　abil|ities
ab ini|tio
abio|gen|esis
abio|gen|ic
abio|gen|ic|al|ly
abi|ogen|ist +s
Abi|ola, Mos|hood
　(Nigerian
　politician)
abi|ot|ic
ab|ject
ab|jec|tion
ab|ject|ly
ab|ject|ness
ab|jur|ation +s
ab|jure
　ab|jures
　ab|jured
　ab|jur|ing
Ab|khaz
　plural Ab|khaz
Ab|khazi
　plural Ab|khazi *or*
　Ab|kha|zis
Ab|khazia
　(territory,
　Georgia)
Ab|khaz|ian +s
ab|late
　ab|lates
　ab|lated
　ab|lat|ing
ab|la|tion
ab|la|tival
ab|la|tive +s
ab|la|tive|ly
ab|laut +s
ablaze
able
　abler
　ablest
able-bodied

abled
able|ism
ablism (use
  ableism)
abloom
ablush
ab|lu|tion +s
ab|lu|tion|ary
ably
ab|neg|ate
  ab|neg|ates
  ab|neg|ated
  ab|neg|at|ing
ab|neg|ation +s
ab|neg|ator +s
Abner
ab|nor|mal
ab|nor|mal|ity
  ab|nor|mal|ities
ab|nor|mal|ly
ab|nor|mity
  ab|nor|mities
ABO (blood-group
  system)
Abo +s (offensive;
  use Aborigine or
  Aboriginal)
aboard
abode +s
abol|ish
  abol|ishes
  abol|ished
  abol|ish|ing
abol|ish|able
abol|ish|er +s
abol|ish|ment
abo|li|tion
abo|li|tion|ism
abo|li|tion|ist +s
abo|ma|sum
  abo|masa
A-bomb +s
Abo|mey (town,
  Benin)
abom|in|able
abom|in|able|ness
abom|in|ably
abom|in|ate
  abom|in|ates
  abom|in|ated
  abom|in|at|ing
abom|in|ation +s
abom|in|ator +s
ab|oral
Abo|ri|ginal +s
  (indigenous
  Australian;
  language; *may
  cause offence* when
  used of one
  person; use
  Aborigine)

abo|ri|ginal +s
  (indigenous;
  person)
abo|ri|gin|al|ity
abo|ri|gin|al|ly
Abo|ri|gine +s
  (indigenous
  Australian; *may
  cause offence* in
  plural; use
  Aboriginals)
abo|ri|gine +s
  (indigenous
  person)
aborn|ing
abort +s +ed +ing
abor|ti|fa|cient +s
abor|tion +s
abor|tion|ist +s
abort|ive
abort|ive|ly
abort|ive|ness
Abou|kir Bay (off
  Egypt)
abou|lia
aboulic
abound +s +ed
  +ing
about
about-face
  about-faces
  about-faced
  about-facing
about-turn +s +ed
  +ing
above
above-mentioned
ab ovo
abra|ca|dabra
ab|rade
  ab|rades
  ab|raded
  ab|rad|ing
ab|rader +s
Abra|ham (*Bible*;
  name)
Abra|hams,
  Har|old (British
  sprinter)
Abram
abra|sion +s
abra|sive
abra|sive|ly
abra|sive|ness
ab|re|act +s +ed
  +ing
ab|re|ac|tion +s
ab|re|act|ive
abreast
abridg|able
abridge
  abridges

abridge (*cont.*)
  abridged
  abridg|ing
abridge|ment +s
abridger +s
abroach
abroad
ab|ro|gate
  ab|ro|gates
  ab|ro|gated
  ab|ro|gat|ing
ab|ro|ga|tion +s
ab|ro|ga|tor +s
ab|rupt
ab|rup|tion
ab|rupt|ly
ab|rupt|ness
Ab|ruzzi (region,
  Italy)
ab|scess
  ab|scesses
ab|scessed
ab|scisic
ab|scissa
  ab|scis|sas *or*
  ab|scis|sae
ab|scis|sion +s
ab|scond +s +ed
  +ing
ab|scond|er +s
ab|seil +s +ed
  +ing
ab|seil|er +s
ab|sence +s
ab|sent
ab|sen|tee +s
ab|sen|tee|ism
ab|sent|ly
absent-minded
absent-minded|ly
absent-
  minded|ness
ab|sent|ness
ab|sinth (plant)
ab|sinthe +s
  (drink)
absit omen
ab|so|lute +s
ab|so|lute|ly
ab|so|lute|ness
ab|so|lu|tion
ab|so|lut|ism
ab|so|lut|ist +s
ab|solve
  ab|solves
  ab|solved
  ab|solv|ing
ab|solver +s
ab|sorb +s +ed
  +ing
ab|sorb|abil|ity
ab|sorb|able

ab|sorb|ance
ab|sorb|ed|ly
ab|sorb|ency
ab|sorb|en|cies
ab|sorb|ent +s
ab|sorb|er +s
ab|sorb|ing|ly
ab|sorp|tion
ab|sorp|tive
ab|sorp|tive|ness
ab|squatu|late
  ab|squatu|lates
  ab|squatu|lated
  ab|squatu|lat|ing
ab|stain +s +ed
  +ing
ab|stain|er +s
ab|ste|mi|ous
ab|ste|mi|ous|ly
ab|ste|mi|ous|ness
ab|sten|tion +s
ab|sten|tion|ism
ab|ster|gent +s
ab|ster|sion +s
ab|ster|sive
ab|stin|ence +s
ab|stin|ency
ab|stin|ent
ab|stin|ent|ly
ab|stract +s +ed
  +ing
ab|stract|ed|ly
ab|stract|ed|ness
ab|strac|tion +s
ab|strac|tion|ism
ab|strac|tion|ist +s
ab|stract|ly
ab|stract|ness
ab|stract|or +s
ab|struse
ab|struse|ly
ab|struse|ness
ab|surd
ab|surd|ism
ab|surd|ist +s
ab|surd|ity
  ab|surd|ities
ab|surd|ly
ab|surd|ness
ABTA (Association
  of British Travel
  Agents)
Abu Dhabi (state
  and capital, UAE)
Abuja (capital of
  Nigeria)
Abu|kir Bay (use
  Aboukir Bay)
abu|lia (use
  aboulia)
Abu Musa (island,
  Persian Gulf)

abun|dance +s
abun|dant
abun|dant|ly
abuse
  ab|uses
  ab|used
  ab|us|ing
ab|user +s
Abu Sim|bel
  (ancient site,
  Egypt)
abu|sive
abu|sive|ly
abu|sive|ness
abut
  abuts
  abut|ted
  abut|ting
abut|ment +s
abut|ter +s
abuzz
abysm +s
abys|mal
abys|mal|ly
abyss
  abysses
  (chasm.
  △ abbess)
abys|sal
Abys|sinia (former
  name of Ethiopia)
ab|zyme +s
aca|cia +s
Aca|deme (in
  'groves of
  Academe')
aca|deme +s (the
  world of learning)
aca|demia
aca|dem|ic +s
aca|dem|ic|al +s
aca|dem|ic|al|ly
acad|em|ician +s
aca|demi|cism
Acad|émie
  fran|çaise
acad|em|ism
Acad|emy (of
  Plato)
acad|emy
  acad|emies
  (place of study)
Aca|dia (Nova
  Scotia, Canada)
Aca|dian +s (of
  Nova Scotia.
  △ Akkadian,
  Arcadian)
acan|tho|
      ceph|alan +s
acan|tho|ceph|alid
  +s

acan|thus
  acan|thuses
a cap|pella
Aca|pulco (resort,
  Mexico)
acari|cide +s
aca|rid +s
acar|ology
acarp|ous
ACAS (Advisory,
  Conciliation, and
  Arbitration
  Service)
acata|lec|tic +s
acaus|al
Ac|ca|dian +s (use
  Akkadian.
  △ Acadian,
  Arcadian)
ac|cede
  ac|cedes
  ac|ceded
  ac|ced|ing
  (take up office;
  agree. △ exceed)
ac|cel|er|ando
  ac|cel|er|andos or
  ac|cel|er|andi
ac|cel|er|ate
  ac|cel|er|ates
  ac|cel|er|ated
  ac|cel|er|at|ing
ac|cel|er|ation +s
ac|cel|era|tive
ac|cel|er|ator +s
ac|cel|er|om|eter
  +s
ac|cent +s +ed
  +ing
ac|cent|or +s
ac|cen|tual
ac|cen|tual|ly
ac|cen|tu|ate
  ac|cen|tu|ates
  ac|cen|tu|ated
  ac|cen|tu|at|ing
ac|cen|tu|ation +s
ac|cept +s +ed
  +ing (receive.
  △ except)
ac|cept|abil|ity
ac|cept|able
ac|cept|able|ness
ac|cept|ably
ac|cept|ance +s
ac|cept|ant
ac|cep|ta|tion +s
ac|cept|er +s
  (generally)
ac|cept|or +s
  Commerce and
  Science

ac|cess
  ac|cesses
  ac|cessed
  ac|cess|ing
ac|ces|sary (use
  accessory)
ac|ces|sar|ies
ac|ces|si|bil|ity
  ac|ces|si|bil|ities
ac|cess|ible
ac|cess|ibly
ac|ces|sion +s +ed
  +ing
ac|ces|sit (in
  'proxime
  accessit')
ac|ces|sor|ial
ac|ces|sor|ise Br.
  (use accessorize)
  ac|ces|sor|ises
  ac|ces|sor|ised
  ac|ces|sor|is|ing
ac|ces|sor|ize
  ac|ces|sor|izes
  ac|ces|sor|ized
  ac|ces|sor|iz|ing
ac|ces|sory
  ac|ces|sor|ies
ac|ciac|ca|tura
  ac|ciac|ca|turas
  or ac|ciac|ca|ture
ac|ci|dence +s
ac|ci|dent +s
ac|ci|den|tal +s
ac|ci|den|tal|ly
accident-prone
ac|ci|die
ac|cip|iter +s
ac|claim +s +ed
  +ing
ac|claim|er +s
ac|clam|ation +s
ac|climat|ation
ac|cli|mate
  ac|cli|mates
  ac|cli|mated
  ac|cli|mat|ing
ac|cli|ma|tion
ac|cli|ma|tisa|tion
  Br. +s (use
  acclimatization)
ac|cli|ma|tise Br.
  (use acclimatize)
  ac|cli|ma|tises
  ac|cli|ma|tised
  ac|cli|ma|tis|ing
ac|cli|ma|tiza|tion
  +s
ac|cli|ma|tize
  ac|cli|ma|tizes
  ac|cli|ma|tized
  ac|cli|ma|tiz|ing

ac|clivi|tous
ac|cliv|ity
  ac|cliv|ities
ac|col|ade +s
ac|com|mo|date
  ac|com|mo|dates
  ac|com|mo|dated
  ac|com|
      mo|dat|ing
ac|com|
      mo|dat|ing|ly
ac|com|mo|da|tion
  +s
ac|com|
  mo|da|tion|ist +s
ac|com|pani|ment
  +s
ac|com|pan|ist +s
ac|com|pany
  ac|com|pan|ies
  ac|com|pan|ied
  ac|com|pany|ing
ac|com|plice +s
ac|com|plish
  ac|com|plishes
  ac|com|plished
  ac|com|plish|ing
ac|com|plish|ment
  +s
ac|cord +s +ed
  +ing
ac|cord|ance
ac|cord|ant
ac|cord|ant|ly
ac|cord|ing|ly
ac|cor|dion +s
ac|cor|dion|ist +s
ac|cost +s +ed
  +ing
ac|couche|ment +s
ac|couch|eur +s
  male
ac|couch|euse +s
  female
ac|count +s +ed
  +ing
ac|count|abil|ity
ac|count|
      abil|ities
ac|count|able
ac|count|able|ness
ac|count|ably
ac|count|ancy
ac|count|ant +s
ac|cou|ter Am. +s
  +ed +ing
ac|cou|ter|ment
  Am. +s
ac|coutre Br.
  ac|coutres
  ac|coutred
  ac|cout|ring

ac|coutre|ment *Br.*
+s
Accra (capital of
Ghana)
ac|credit +s +ed
+ing
ac|credit|ation +s
ac|crete

ac|cretes
ac|creted
ac|cret|ing
ac|cre|tion +s
ac|cre|tive
ac|crual +s
ac|crue

ac|crues
ac|crued
ac|cru|ing
ac|cul|tur|ate

ac|cul|tur|ates
ac|cul|tur|ated
ac|cul|tur|at|ing
ac|cul|tur|ation
ac|cul|tur|ative
ac|cu|mu|late

ac|cu|mu|lates
ac|cu|mu|lated
ac|cu|mu|lat|ing
ac|cu|mu|la|tion
+s
ac|cu|mu|la|tive
ac|cu|mu|la|tive|ly
ac|cu|mu|la|tor +s
ac|cur|acy

ac|cur|acies
ac|cur|ate
ac|cur|ate|ly
ac|cur|sed
ac|curst (*archaic*
accursed)
ac|cusal
ac|cus|ation +s
ac|cusa|tival
ac|cusa|tive +s
ac|cusa|tive|ly
ac|cusa|tor|ial
ac|cusa|tory
ac|cuse

ac|cuses
ac|cused
ac|cus|ing
ac|cuser +s
ac|cus|ing|ly
ac|cus|tom +s +ed
+ing
ace

aces
aced
acing
acedia

Acel|dama (field
near ancient
Jerusalem)
acel|lu|lar
aceph|al|ous
acer +s
acerb
acerb|ic
acerb|ic|al|ly
acerb|ity

acerb|ities
aces|cence
aces|cent
acet|abu|lum

acet|abula
acetal
acet|al|de|hyde
acet|amino|phen
acet|ate +s
acet|ic
acet|one +s
acet|ous
acetyl
acetyl|chol|ine
acetyl|ene
acetyl|ide
acetyl|sali|cyl|ic
Achaea (district,
ancient Greece)
Achaean +s
Achae|men|ian +s
Achae|menid +s
acharne|ment
Acha|tes

plural **Acha|tes**
ache

aches
ached
ach|ing
Achebe, Chinua
(Nigerian writer)
achene +s
Acher|nar (star)
Ache|son, Dean
(American
statesman)
Acheu|lean +s
Acheu|lian +s (use
Acheulean)
achiev|able
achieve

achieves
achieved
achiev|ing
achieve|ment +s
achiever +s
achil|lea
Achil|les *Greek
Mythology*
Achil|les heel +s
Achil|les ten|don
+s

Achi|nese

plural **Achi|nese**
ach|ing|ly
achiral
achon|dro|pla|sia
achon|dro|pla|sic
+s
achon|dro|plas|tic
+s
achro|mat +s
achro|mat|ic
achro|mat|ic|al|ly
achro|ma|ti|city
achro|ma|tism
achron|ical (use
acronychal)
achron|ic|al|ly
(use
acronychally)
achy
acid +s
acid-free *attributive*
acid head +s
acid house
acid|ic
acid|ifi|ca|tion
acid|ify

acid|ifies
acid|ified
acid|ify|ing
acid|im|eter +s
acid|im|etry
acid|ity
acid|ly
acid|ness
acido|phil +s
acido|phile +s
acido|phil|ic
acid|oph|ilus
acid|osis

acid|oses
acid|otic
acid test +s
acidu|late

acidu|lates
acidu|lated
acidu|lat|ing
acidu|la|tion
acidu|lous
aci|nus

acini
ack
ack-ack
ackee +s
ack emma
ac|know|ledge

ac|know|ledges
ac|know|ledged
ac|know|ledg|ing
ac|know|ledge|
         able

ac|know|ledge|
        ment +s
ac|know|ledg|
        ment +s (use
acknowledge-
ment)
aclin|ic
acme +s
acne
acned
aco|lyte +s
Ac|on|cagua
(volcano, Andes)
acon|ite +s
acon|it|ic
acon|it|ine
acorn +s
acoty|ledon +s
acoty|led|on|ous
acous|tic
acous|tic|al
acous|tic|al|ly
acous|ti|cian +s
acous|tics
ac|quaint +s +ed
+ing
ac|quaint|ance +s
ac|quaint|ance|
         ship

ac|quest +s
ac|qui|esce

ac|qui|esces
ac|qui|esced
ac|qui|es|cing
ac|qui|es|cence
ac|qui|es|cent
ac|qui|es|cing|ly
ac|quir|able
ac|quire

ac|quires
ac|quired
ac|quir|ing
ac|quire|ment
ac|quirer +s
ac|qui|si|tion +s
ac|quisi|tive
ac|quisi|tive|ly
ac|quisi|tive|ness
ac|quit

ac|quits
ac|quit|ted
ac|quit|ting
ac|quit|tal +s
ac|quit|tance +s
Acre (town, Israel)
acre +s
acre|age +s
acred
acrid
ac|rid|ine
ac|rid|ity
ac|rid|ly

acri|fla|vine
acri|mo|ni|ous
acri|mo|ni|ous|ly
acri|mony
acro|bat +s
acro|bat|ic
acro|bat|ic|al|ly
acro|bat|ics
acro|gen +s
ac|rogen|ous
ac|ro|meg|al|ic +s
ac|ro|meg|aly
acrony|cal (use
acronychal)
acrony|cal|ly (use
acronychally)
acrony|chal
acrony|chal|ly
acro|nym +s
acrop|etal
acrop|et|al|ly
acro|pho|bia
acro|pho|bic +s
Acrop|olis (in
Athens)
acrop|olis
(generally)
acrop|olises or
acrop|oles
across
ac|ros|tic +s
Acrux (star)
acryl|ic +s
acrylo|ni|trile
act +s +ed +ing
act|abil|ity
act|able
Ac|taeon Greek
Mythology
actin
ac|tinia
ac|tiniae
ac|tin|ic
ac|tin|ide +s
ac|tin|ism
ac|tin|ium
ac|tin|oid +s
ac|tin|om|eter +s
ac|tino|morph|ic
Ac|tino|
my|cet|ales
ac|tino|my|cete +s
ac|tion +s +ed
+ing
ac|tion|able
ac|tion|ably
Ac|tion Di|recte
action-packed
Ac|tium (battle off
Greece)
ac|ti|vate
ac|ti|vates

ac|ti|vate (cont.)
ac|ti|vated
ac|ti|vat|ing
ac|ti|vation
ac|ti|va|tor +s
ac|tive
ac|tive|ly
ac|tive|ness
ac|tiv|ism
ac|tiv|ist +s
ac|tiv|ity
ac|tiv|ities
actor +s
actor-manager +s
ac|tress
ac|tresses
ac|tressy
ac|tual +s
ac|tu|al|isa|tion Br.
(use
actualization)
ac|tu|al|ise Br. (use
actualize)
ac|tu|al|ises
ac|tu|al|ised
ac|tu|al|is|ing
ac|tu|al|ity
ac|tu|al|ities
ac|tu|al|iza|tion
ac|tu|al|ize
ac|tu|al|izes
ac|tu|al|ized
ac|tu|al|iz|ing
ac|tu|al|ly
ac|tu|ar|ial
ac|tu|ari|al|ly
ac|tu|ary
ac|tu|ar|ies
ac|tu|ate
ac|tu|ates
ac|tu|ated
ac|tu|at|ing
ac|tu|ation
ac|tu|ator +s
acu|ity
acu|leate +s
acu|men
acu|min|ate
acu|min|ates
acu|min|ated
acu|min|at|ing
acu|pres|sure
acu|punc|ture
acu|punc|tur|ist +s
acushla +s
acu|tance
acute
acuter
acut|est
acute|ly
acute|ness
acyclo|vir

acyl +s
ad +s
(advertisement.
△ add)
Ada (computer
language; name)
adage +s
ada|gio +s
Adam (Bible; name)
Adam, Rob|ert
(Scottish
architect)
ad|am|ance
ad|am|ant +s
ad|am|ant|ine
ad|am|ant|ly
Ad|am|ite +s
Adams, Ansel
(American
photographer)
Adams, John
(American
president)
Adams, John
Couch (English
astronomer)
Adams, John
Quincy
(American
president)
Adam's ale
Adam's apple +s
Adam's Bridge
(series of shoals
between Sri Lanka
and India)
Adam's Peak
(mountain, Sri
Lanka)
Adana (town,
Turkey)
adapt +s +ed +ing
adapt|abil|ity
adapt|able
adapt|able|ness
adapt|ably
adap|ta|tion +s
adapt|er Am. +s
(Br. adaptor)
adap|tive
adap|tive|ly
adap|tive|ness
adap|tor Br. +s
(Am. adapter)
Adar (Jewish
month)
adat
ad|ax|ial
ad cap|tan|dum
vul|gus

add +s +ed +ing
(put together.
△ ad)
Ad|dams, Jane
(American
reformer)
addax
ad|daxes
ad|den|dum
ad|denda
adder +s
adder's tongue +s
ad|dict +s +ed
+ing
ad|dic|tion +s
ad|dict|ive
Ad|ding|ton,
Henry (British
prime minister)
Addis Ababa
(capital of
Ethiopia)
Ad|di|son, Jo|seph
(English writer)
Ad|di|son,
Thomas (English
physician)
Ad|di|son's
dis|ease
add|ition +s
(adding;
something added.
△ edition)
add|ition|al
add|ition|al|ity
add|ition|al|ly
add|itive +s
addle
ad|dles
ad|dled
ad|dling
Addo (national
park, South Africa)
add-on +s noun and
adjective
ad|dress
ad|dresses
ad|dressed
ad|dress|ing
ad|dress|ee +s
ad|dress|er +s
Ad|dresso|graph
+s Propr.
ad|duce
ad|duces
ad|duced
ad|du|cing
ad|du|cible
ad|duct +s +ed
+ing
ad|duc|tion +s
ad|duct|or +s

Adel|aide (city, Australia; name)
Adele
Ad|élie Coast (= Adélie Land)
Ad|élie Land (part of Antarctica)
Adel|ine
Aden (port, South Yemen)
Aden, Gulf of (part of Arabian Sea)
Aden|auer, Kon|rad (German statesman)
ad|en|ine
ad|en|oid|al
ad|en|oid|al|ly
ad|en|oids
ad|en|oma
   ad|en|omas *or*
   ad|en|omata
adeno|sine
adept +s
adept|ly
adept|ness
ad|equacy
ad|equate
ad|equate|ly
ad eun|dem
à deux
ad fin.
ad|here
   ad|heres
   ad|hered
   ad|her|ing
ad|her|ence
ad|her|ent +s
ad|he|sion +s
ad|he|sive
ad|he|sive|ly
ad|he|sive|ness
ad|hibit +s +ed +ing
ad|hib|ition +s
ad hoc
ad hom|inem
adia|bat|ic +s
adia|bat|ic|al|ly
adi|an|tum +s
adieu
   adieus *or* adieux
Adi Granth (Sikh scripture)
ad in|fin|itum
ad in|terim
adios
adi|po|cere
adi|pose
adi|pos|ity

Adi|ron|dack Moun|tains (in USA)
Adi|ron|dacks (= Adirondack Mountains)
Adis Abeba (use Addis Ababa)
adit +s
Adi|vasi +s
ad|ja|cency
ad|ja|cent
ad|jec|tival
ad|jec|tival|ly
ad|jec|tive +s
ad|join +s +ed +ing
ad|journ +s +ed +ing
ad|journ|ment +s
ad|judge
   ad|judges
   ad|judged
   ad|judg|ing
ad|judge|ment +s
ad|judg|ment +s (use adjudgement)
ad|ju|di|cate
   ad|ju|di|cates
   ad|ju|di|cated
   ad|ju|di|cat|ing
ad|ju|di|ca|tion +s
ad|ju|di|ca|tive
ad|ju|di|ca|tor +s
ad|junct +s
ad|junct|ive +s
ad|junct|ive|ly
ad|jur|ation +s
ad|jura|tory
ad|jure
   ad|jures
   ad|jured
   ad|jur|ing
ad|just +s +ed +ing
ad|just|abil|ity
ad|just|able
ad|just|er +s
ad|just|ment +s
ad|ju|tage +s
ad|ju|tancy
   ad|ju|tan|cies
ad|ju|tant +s
Ad|ju|tant Gen|eral +s
ad|ju|vant +s
Adlai
Adler, Al|fred (Austrian psychologist and psychiatrist)

Ad|ler|ian +s
ad lib
   ad libs
   ad libbed
   ad lib|bing
ad lib|itum
ad litem
adman
   admen
ad|mass
ad|meas|ure
   ad|meas|ures
   ad|meas|ured
   ad|meas|ur|ing
ad|meas|ure|ment +s
admin
ad|min|icle +s
ad|min|icu|lar
ad|min|is|ter +s +ed +ing
ad|min|is|trable
ad|min|is|trate
   ad|min|is|trates
   ad|min|is|trated
   ad|min|is|trat|ing
ad|min|is|tra|tion +s
ad|min|is|tra|tive
ad|min|is| tra|tive|ly
ad|min|is|tra|tor +s
ad|min|is|tra|tor| ship +s
ad|min|is|tra|trix *female*
   ad|min|is| tra|trixes *or*
   ad|min|is| tra|tri|ces
ad|mir|able
ad|mir|ably
ad|miral +s
Ad|miral's Cup
ad|miral|ship +s
Ad|mir|alty (department)
ad|mir|alty *Law*
Ad|mir|alty Is|lands (part of Papua New Guinea)
ad|mir|ation
ad|mire
   ad|mires
   ad|mired
   ad|mir|ing
ad|mir|er +s
ad|mir|ing|ly
ad|mis|si|bil|ity
ad|mis|sible

ad|mis|sion +s
ad|mis|sive
admit
   ad|mits
   ad|mit|ted
   ad|mit|ting
ad|mit|table
ad|mit|tance
ad|mit|ted|ly
admix
   ad|mixes
   ad|mixed
   ad|mix|ing
ad|mix|ture +s
ad|mon|ish
   ad|mon|ishes
   ad|mon|ished
   ad|mon|ish|ing
ad|mon|ish|ment +s
ad|mon|ition +s
ad|moni|tory
ad nau|seam
ad|nom|inal
Ad|nya|matha|nha
ado
adobe
ado|les|cence
ado|les|cent +s
Ado|nis *Greek Mythology*
Ado|nis blue +s
adopt +s +ed +ing
adopt|ee +s
adopt|er +s
adop|tion +s
adop|tive
adop|tive|ly
ador|able
ador|ably
ad|or|ation
adore
   adores
   adored
   ador|ing
ador|er +s
ador|ing|ly
adorn +s +ed +ing
adorn|ment +s
Adorno, Theo|dor (German philosopher)
adown
ad per|sonam
Adrar des Iforas (massif, Sahara)
ad rem
ad|renal
ad|rena|lin
ad|rena|line (use adrenalin)

ad¦reno|cor¦tico|
    troph¦ic
ad¦reno|cor¦tico|
    troph¦in
ad¦reno|cor¦tico|
    trop¦ic
Adrian (man's
    name)
Adrian IV (born
    Nicholas
    Breakspear,
    English pope)
Adri|anne
    (woman's name)
Adri|at¦ic
Adri|at¦ic Sea (part
    of Mediterranean)
Adri|enne
adrift
adroit
adroit¦ly
adroit|ness
ad¦sci|ti¦tious
ad¦sorb +s +ed
    +ing
ad¦sorb|able
ad¦sorb|ate +s
ad¦sorb|ent +s
ad¦sorb|tion (use
    adsorption)
ad|sorp¦tion
ad|sorp¦tive
ad¦suki +s (use
    adzuki)
adsum
aduki +s
adu|late
    adu|lates
    adu|lated
    adu|lat¦ing
adu|la¦tion
adu|la¦tor +s
adu|la¦tory
Adul¦lam|ite +s
adult +s
adul¦ter|ant +s
adul¦ter|ate
    adul¦ter|ates
    adul¦ter|ated
    adul¦ter|at¦ing
adul¦ter|ation
adul¦ter|ator +s
adul¦ter|er +s
adul¦ter|ess
    adul¦ter|esses
adul¦ter|ine
adul¦ter|ous
adul¦ter|ous¦ly
adul¦ter|ous|ness
adul¦tery
    adul|ter¦ies
adult|hood

adult¦ly
ad¦um|brate
    ad¦um|brates
    ad¦um|brated
    ad¦um|brat¦ing
ad¦um|bra¦tion
ad¦um|bra¦tive
ad val|orem
ad|vance
    ad|vances
    ad|vanced
    ad|van¦cing
ad|vance|ment +s
ad|van¦cer +s
ad|van¦tage
    ad|van¦tages
    ad|van¦taged
    ad|van¦ta¦ging
ad|van¦ta¦geous
ad|van¦ta¦geous¦ly
ad|vect +s +ed
    +ing
ad|vec¦tion
ad|vec¦tive
Ad¦vent (of Christ;
    season)
ad|vent +s
    (generally)
Ad¦vent|ism
Ad¦vent|ist +s
ad|ven¦ti¦tious
ad|ven¦ti¦tious¦ly
ad|ven¦ture
    ad|ven¦tures
    ad|ven¦tured
    ad|ven¦tur|ing
ad|ven¦turer +s
ad|ven¦ture|some
ad|ven¦tur|ess
    ad|ven¦tur|esses
ad|ven¦tur|ism
ad|ven¦tur|ist +s
ad|ven¦tur|ous
ad|ven¦tur|ous¦ly
ad|ven¦tur|ous|
                ness
ad|verb +s
ad|ver¦bial +s
ad|ver¦bi|al¦ly
ad ver¦bum
ad|ver¦sar¦ial
ad|ver¦sary
    ad|ver¦sar¦ies
ad|ver¦sa|tive +s
ad|ver¦sa|tive¦ly
ad|verse
ad|verse¦ly
ad|verse|ness
ad|ver¦sity
    ad|ver¦sities
ad¦vert +s +ed
    +ing

ad¦ver|tise
    ad¦ver|tises
    ad¦ver|tised
    ad¦ver|tis¦ing
ad¦ver|tise|ment
    +s
ad¦ver|tiser +s
ad¦ver|tor¦ial +s
ad¦vice +s noun
ad|vis|abil¦ity
ad¦vis|able
ad¦vis|ably
ad¦vise
    ad¦vises
    ad¦vised
    ad¦vis¦ing
    verb
ad|vised¦ly
ad|viser +s
ad|visor +s (use
    adviser)
ad|vis¦ory
ad¦vo|caat +s
ad¦vo|cacy
ad¦vo|cate
    ad¦vo|cates
    ad¦vo|cated
    ad¦vo|cat¦ing
ad¦vo|cate|ship +s
ad¦vo|ca¦tory
ad¦vow|son
Ady¦gea (republic,
    Russia)
ady¦tum
    adyta
adz (use adze)
    adzes
    adzed
    adz¦ing
adze
    adzes
    adzed
    adz¦ing
ad¦zuki +s
ae¦dile +s
ae¦dile|ship +s
Ae¦gean
Ae¦gean Sea (part
    of Mediterranean)
aegis
    ae|gises
Ae¦gis|thus Greek
    Mythology
aegro|tat +s
Aelf|ric (Anglo-
    Saxon monk and
    writer)
Ae¦neas Greek and
    Roman Mythology
Ae¦neid (epic
    poem)

ae|olian Br. (Am.
    eolian)
Ae|olian Is¦lands
    (ancient name for
    the Lipari
    Islands)
Ae|ol¦ic Br. (Am.
    Eolic)
Ae¦olus Greek
    Mythology
aeon +s
aepy|or¦nis
    aepy|or¦nises
aer¦ate
    aer¦ates
    aer¦ated
    aer¦at¦ing
aer¦ation
aer¦ator +s
aer¦en|chyma
aer¦ial +s (radio
    etc.; in the air.
    △ areal, ariel)
aer¦ial|ist +s
aeri|al¦ity
aeri|al¦ly
aerie +s (use eyrie)
aeri|form
aero|batic
aero|bat¦ics
aer|obe +s
aer|ob¦ic
aer|ob¦ic|al¦ly
aer|obics
aero|biolo¦gist +s
aero|biol¦ogy
aero|drome +s
aero|dy¦nam¦ic
aero|dy¦nam¦ic|
                al¦ly
aero|dy¦nami|cist
    +s
aero|dy¦nam¦ics
aero-engine +s
aero|foil +s
aero|gram +s (use
    aerogramme)
aero|gramme +s
aero|lite +s
aero|logic¦al
aer|olo¦gist +s
aer|ology
aero|mag¦net¦ic
aero|naut +s
aero|naut¦ic
aero|naut¦ic|al
aero|naut¦ic|al¦ly
aero|naut¦ics
aer|onomy
aero|plane Br. +s
aero|sol +s
aero|space

aero|stat +s
aero|tow +s +ed
+ing
aero|train +s
Aer|tex Propr.
aer|ugin|ous
Aes|chi|nes
(Athenian orator
and statesman)
Aes|chyl|ean
Aes|chylus (Greek
dramatist)
Aes|cu|la|pian
Aesir Norse
Mythology
Aesop (Greek
storyteller)
aes|thete Br. +s
(Am. esthete)
aes|thet|ic Br. (Am.
esthetic)
aes|thet|ic|al|ly Br.
(Am. esthetically)
aes|thet|ician Br.
+s (Am.
esthetician)
aes|theti|cism Br.
(Am. estheticism)
aes|thet|ics Br.
(Am. esthetics)
aes|tival Br. (Am.
estival)
aes|tiv|ate Br.
aes|tiv|ates
aes|tiv|ated
aes|tiv|at|ing
(Am. estivate)
aes|tiv|ation Br.
(Am. estivation)
ae|ta|tis
ae|ther (use ether)
aetio|logic Br. (Am.
etiologic)
aetio|logic|al Br.
(Am. etiological)
aetio|logic|al|ly Br.
(Am.
etiologically)
aeti|ology Br. (Am.
etiology)
Afar
plural Afar or
Afars
(people; language)
afar (at or to a
distance)
af|fa|bil|ity
af|fable
af|fably
af|fair +s
af|faire (busy)

af|faire (de cœur)
af|faires (de cœur)
af|fect +s +ed +ing
(have an effect on;
feign. △effect)
af|fect|ation +s
af|fect|ed|ly
af|fect|ing|ly
af|fec|tion +s
af|fec|tion|al
af|fec|tion|al|ly
af|fec|tion|ate
af|fec|tion|ate|ly
af|fect|ive
(concerning
emotion.
△effective)
af|fect|ive|ly (as
regards emotion.
△effectively)
af|fect|iv|ity
(emotional
susceptibility.
△effectivity)
af|fen|pin|scher +s
af|fer|ent
af|fi|ance
af|fi|ances
af|fi|anced
af|fi|an|cing
af|fi|ant +s
af|fiche +s
af|fi|da|vit +s
af|fili|ate
af|fili|ates
af|fili|ated
af|fili|at|ing
af|fili|ation +s
af|fined
af|fin|ity
af|fin|ities
af|firm +s +ed
+ing
af|firm|able
af|firm|ation +s
af|firma|tive
af|firma|tive|ly
af|firma|tory
af|firm|er +s
affix
af|fixes
af|fixed
af|fix|ing
af|fix|ture
af|fla|tus
af|flict +s +ed +ing
af|flic|tion +s
af|flict|ive
af|flu|ence
af|flu|ent
af|flu|en|tial
af|flu|ent|ly

af|flux
af|fluxes
af|force
af|forces
af|forced
af|for|cing
af|ford +s +ed
+ing
af|ford|abil|ity
af|ford|able
af|ford|ably
af|for|est +s +ed
+ing
af|for|est|ation
af|fran|chise
af|fran|chises
af|fran|chised
af|fran|chis|ing
af|fray +s
af|freight|ment
af|fri|cate +s
af|fright +s +ed
+ing
af|front +s +ed
+ing
af|fu|sion
Af|ghan +s (of
Afghanistan;
hound)
af|ghan +s
(blanket; shawl)
af|ghani +s
(Afghan currency)
Af|ghani|stan
afi|cion|ado +s
afield
afire
aflame
af|la|toxin +s
afloat
afoot
afore
afore|men|tioned
afore|said
afore|thought
a for|ti|ori
afoul
afraid
A-frame +s
afreet +s
afresh
afric
Af|rica
Af|ri|can +s
Af|ri|cana
African-American
+s
Af|ri|can|der +s
Af|ri|can|ise Br.
(use Africanize)
Af|ri|can|ises

Af|ri|can|ise (cont.)
Af|ri|can|ised
Af|ri|can|is|ing
Af|ri|can|ism
Af|ri|can|ist +s
Af|ri|can|ize
Af|ri|can|izes
Af|ri|can|ized
Af|ri|can|iz|ing
Af|ri|kaans
Af|rika Korps
(German army
force)
Af|ri|kan|der +s
(use Africander)
Af|ri|kaner +s
(person)
af|ri|kaner +s
(sheep; cattle;
gladiolus)
afrit +s (use afreet)
Afro +s
Afro-American +s
Afro-Asian +s
Afro-Asiat|ic
Afro-Caribbean +s
Afro|cen|tric
Afro-Indian +s
af|ror|mo|sia +s
aft
after
after|birth +s
after|burn|er +s
after|care
after|damp
after|deck +s
after-dinner
attributive
after-effect +s
after|glow +s
after|grass
after-hours
attributive
after-image +s
after|life +s
after|light
after|mar|ket +s
after|math +s
after|most
after|noon +s
after|pains
af|ters
after-sales
after-school
attributive
after|shave +s
after|shock +s
after|taste +s
after|thought +s
after|ward
after|wards
after|word +s

Aga+s (stove)
Propr.
aga+s (Muslim
chief)
Aga¦dir(port,
Morocco)
again
against
Aga Khan+s
agal+s
agama+s
Aga¦mem¦non
(Mycenaean king)
aǥam¦ic
agamo|gen¦esis
agamo|gen¦et¦ic
agamo|spermy
ag¦am¦ous
aga|pan¦thus
aga|pan¦thuses
agape+s (gaping;
fellowship; feast)
aga|pem¦one
agar
agar-agar
agar¦ic
Agar¦tala(city,
India)
Agas|siz, Louis
(Swiss-born
zoologist etc.)
agate+s
Aga¦tha
agave+s
agaze
agba
age
ages
aged
age¦ing
age group+s
age¦ism
age¦ist+s (showing
age-discrimination;
person. △ agist)
age|less
age-long
agency
agen|cies
agenda+s
agen|dum
agenda
agent+s
agent-general
agents-general
agen|tial
agent
pro|voca|teur
agents
pro|voca|teurs
age-old

age range+s
age-related
Aggie
ag¦giorna|mento
ag¦glom¦er¦ate
ag¦glom¦er¦ates
ag¦glom¦er¦ated
ag¦glom¦er¦at¦ing
ag¦glom¦er¦ation
+s
ag¦glom¦era|tive
ag¦glu¦tin|ate
ag¦glu¦tin|ates
ag¦glu¦tin|ated
ag¦glu¦tin|at¦ing
ag¦glu¦tin|ation+s
ag¦glu¦tin|ative
ag¦glu¦tinin+s
ag¦grand¦ise*Br.*
(use **aggrandize**)
ag¦grand¦ises
ag¦grand¦ised
ag¦grand¦is¦ing
ag¦grand¦ise|ment
Br. (use
aggrandizement)
ag¦grand¦iser*Br.*
+s (use
aggrandizer)
ag¦grand¦ize
ag¦grand¦izes
ag¦grand¦ized
ag¦grand¦iz¦ing
ag¦grand¦ize|ment
+s
ag¦grand¦izer+s
ag¦gra|vate
ag¦gra|vates
ag¦gra|vated
ag¦gra|vat¦ing
ag¦gra|vat¦ing|ly
ag¦gra|va¦tion+s
ag¦gre|gate
ag¦gre|gates
ag¦gre|gated
ag¦gre|gat¦ing
ag¦gre|ga¦tion+s
ag¦gre|ga¦tive
ag¦gres|sion+s
ag¦gres|sive
ag¦gres|sive¦ly
ag¦gres|sive|ness
ag¦gres|sor+s
ag¦grieve
ag¦grieves
ag¦grieved
ag¦griev|ing
ag¦griev|ed¦ly
aggro
aghast
Aghios Niko|laos
(port, Crete)

agile
agile¦ly
agil|ity
agin
Agin|court(battle
site, France)
aging(use **ageing**)
agio+s
agio|tage
agism(use **ageism**)
agist+s +ed +ing
(feed livestock.
△ ageist)
agist|ment
agi|tate
agi|tates
agi|tated
agi|tat¦ing
agi|tated¦ly
agi|ta|tion+s
agi|tato
agi|ta¦tor+s
agit|prop
aglet+s
agley
aglow
agma+s
ag¦nail+s
ag¦nate+s
ag¦nat¦ic
ag¦na¦tion
Agnes(Roman
saint; patron saint
of Bohemia;
name)
**Agnesi, Maria
Gae|tana**(Italian
mathematician)
Agni *Hinduism*
agno|lotti
ag¦no¦men+s
ag¦no¦sia
ag¦nos¦tic+s
ag¦nos¦ti|cism
Agnus Dei
ago
agog
agogic
ago¦gics
à gogo
agon¦ic
ag¦on|ise *Br.* (use
agonize)
ag¦on|ises
ag¦on|ised
ag¦on|is¦ing
ag¦on|is¦ing|ly *Br.*
(use **agonizingly**)
agon|ist+s
ag¦on|is¦tic
ag¦on|is¦tic|al¦ly

ag¦on|ize
ag¦on|izes
ag¦on|ized
ag¦on|iz¦ing
ag¦on|iz¦ing|ly
agony
ag|onies
agora|phobe+s
agora|pho¦bia
agora|pho¦bic+s
agouti+s
Agra(city, India)
ag¦ra|phon
ag¦ra|pha
agrar¦ian+s
agree
agrees
agreed
agree|ing
agree|able
agree|able|ness
agree|ably
agree|ment+s
agri|busi¦ness
agri|busi¦ness|
man
agri|busi¦ness|
men
agri|chem¦ical+s
Agric¦ola, Ju¦lius
(Roman general)
agri|cul¦tural
agri|cul¦tur|al¦ly
agri|cul¦ture+s
agri|cul¦tur|ist+s
agri|mony
agri|monies
**Agrippa, Mar¦cus
Vip|san|ius**
(Roman general)
agro|chem¦ical+s
agro|for¦est¦ry
agro|nom¦ic
agro|nom¦ic|al
agro|nom¦ic|al¦ly
agro|nom¦ics
agrono|mist+s
agron|omy
aground
Aguas|cali¦en|tes
(state and state
capital, Mexico)
ague+s
agued
aguish
Agul|has, Cape(in
South Africa)
Agul|has Cur|rent
(off E. Africa)
aguti +s (use
agouti)
ah *interjection.* △ **are**

aha

Ahag|gar
  Moun|tains (in
  Algeria)
ahead
ahem
ahimsa
ahis|tor|ic
ahis|tor|ic|al
Ah|mada|bad (city,
  India)
ahoy
Ah|ri|man
  (Zoroastrian evil
  spirit)
à huis clos
ahull
Ahura Mazda
  (Zoroastrian god)
Ahvaz (town, Iran)
Ahwaz (use Ahvaz)
ai +s
aid +s +ed +ing
  (help)
Aidan (Irish
  missionary and
  saint; name)
aide +s (assistant)
aide-de-camp
  aides-de-camp
aide-mémoire
  aides-mémoires
  or aides-mémoire
Aids (= acquired
  immune
  deficiency
  syndrome)
Aids-related
aig|let +s (use
  aglet)
aig|rette +s
Aigues-Mortes
  (town, France)
ai|guille +s
ai|guill|ette +s
ai|kido
ail +s +ed +ing (be
  ill. △ ale)
ai|lan|thus
  ai|lan|thuses
Ai|leen
ail|eron +s
ail|ment +s
Ailsa
ai|luro|phile +s
ai|luro|phobe +s
ai|luro|pho|bia
ai|luro|pho|bic
aim +s +ed +ing
Aimée
aim|less
aim|less|ly

aim|less|ness
Ains|ley
ain't
Ain|tab (former
  name of
  Gaziantep)
Ain|tree
  (racecourse,
  England)
Ainu
  plural Ainu or
  Ainus
aioli
air +s +ed +ing
  (gas; tune; breeze
  etc. △ e'er, ere,
  heir)
air bag +s
air|base +s
air-bed +s
air|borne
air brake +s
air|brick +s
air bridge +s
air|brush
  air|brushes
  air|brushed
  air|brush|ing
Air|bus Propr.
Air Chief Mar|shal
  +s
Air Com|mo|dore
  +s
air-conditioned
air-condition|er +s
air-condition|ing
air-cooled
air|craft
  plural air|craft
air|craft car|rier
  +s
air|craft|man
  air|craft|men
air|craft|woman
  air|craft|women
air|crew +s
air cush|ion +s
air|drop
  air|drops
  air|dropped
  air|drop|ping
Aire|dale +s
airer +s
air fare +s
air|field +s
air|flow +s
air|foil +s
air force +s
air|frame +s
air|freight
air|glow
air|gun +s

air|head +s
air host|ess
  air host|esses
air|ily
airi|ness
air-jacket +s
air|less (lacking air.
  △ heirless)
air|less|ness
air|lift +s +ed +ing
air|line +s
air|liner +s
air|lock +s
air|mail +s +ed
  +ing
air|man
  air|men
Air Mar|shal +s
air mile +s (unit of
  distance)
Air Miles (points
  exchangeable for
  free air travel)
  Propr.
air|miss
  air|misses
air|mo|bile +s
Air Of|ficer +s
air|plane +s
air|play +s
air|port +s
air raid +s
air-raid shel|ter
  +s
air|screw +s
air-sea rescue +s
air|ship +s
  (aircraft.
  △ heirship)
air show +s
air|sick
air|sick|ness
air|side
air|space
air|speed
air|stream +s
air|strip +s
air|tight
air|time
Air Vice-Marshal
  +s
air|wave attributive
air|waves noun
air|way +s
air|woman
  air|women
air|worthi|ness
air|worthy
Airy, George
  Bid|dell (English
  astronomer and
  geophysicist)

airy
  air|ier
  airi|est
airy-fairy
aisle +s (passage.
  △ I'll, isle)
aisled
ait +s (island.
  △ ate, eight)
aitch
  aitches
aitch|bone +s
Ait|ken, Max
  (Lord
  Beaverbrook)
Aix-en-Provence
  (city, France)
Aix-la-Chapelle
  (French name for
  Aachen)
Aiz|awl (city, India)
Ajac|cio (city,
  Corsica)
Aj|anta Caves (in
  India)
ajar
Ajax Greek
  Mythology
Ajman (emirate
  and city, UAE)
Ajmer (city, India)
Akbar the Great
  (Mogul emperor
  of India)
akee +s (use
  ackee)
Akela +s
Akhe|na|ten
  (pharaoh)
Akhe|na|ton (use
  Akhenaten)
Akhe|taten
  (ancient capital of
  Egypt)
Akh|mat|ova,
  Anna (Russian
  poet)
ak|hund +s
akimbo
akin
Akkad (city and
  ancient kingdom,
  Mesopotamia)
Ak|ka|dian +s (of
  Akkad.
  △ Acadian,
  Arcadian)
Akko (port, Israel)
Ak-Mechet (former
  name of
  Simferopol)
Akron (city, USA)

Aksai Chin(region,
Himalayas)
Aksum(town,
Ethiopia)
Akur|eyri(city,
Iceland)
akva|vit(use
aquavit)
Al(name)
à la
Ala|bama(state,
USA)
Ala|baman+s
ala|bas|ter
ala|bas|trine
à la carte
alack
alack-a-day
alac|rity
Alad|din
Alad|din's cave+s
Alad|din's lamp
+s
Ala|goas(state,
Brazil)
Alain-Fournier
(French novelist)
Ala|mein in full El
Ala|mein
(battle site, Egypt)
Alamo, the
(mission and
siege, USA)
à la mode
Alan also Allan,
Allen, Alun
Alana also Al|anna,
Alan|nah
Åland Is|lands(in
Gulf of Bothnia)
ala|nine
Al|anna also Alana,
Alan|nah
Alan|nah also
Alana, Al|anna
Alar(plant growth
regulator) Propr.
alar(of wings)
Alar|cón, Pedro
An|tonio de
(Spanish writer)
Alar|cón y
Men|doza, Juan
Ruiz de (Spanish
playwright)
Al|aric(king of
Visigoths)
alarm+s +ed +ing
alarm clock+s
alarm|ing|ly
alarm|ism
alarm|ist+s

al|arum+s
alas
Alas|dair also
Alas|tair,
Alis|dair, Alis|tair
Al|aska(state,
USA; in 'baked
Alaska')
Al|aska, Gulf of
(part of NE
Pacific)
Alas|tair also
Alas|dair,
Alis|dair, Alis|tair
Al|as|tor+s
alate
alb+s
Al|ba|cete
(province and city,
Spain)
al|ba|core
plural al|ba|core
Alba Iulia(city,
Romania)
Alban(British
saint)
Al|ba|nia
Al|ba|nian+s
Al|bany(city, USA)
al|bata
al|ba|tross
al|ba|trosses
al|bedo+s
Albee, Ed|ward
(American
dramatist)
al|beit
Al|bena(resort,
Bulgaria)
Al|bers, Josef
(German-born
artist)
Al|bert(name)
Al|bert, Lake
(former name of
Lake Mobutu
Sese Seko)
Al|bert, Prince
(husband of
Queen Victoria)
al|bert+s (watch-
chain)
Al|berta(province,
Canada)
Al|berti, Leon
Bat|tista(Italian
architect, painter,
etc.)
Al|ber|tus
Mag|nus
(medieval saint)
al|bes|cent

Albi(town, France)
Al|bi|gen|ses
Al|bi|gen|sian+s
al|bin|ism
al|bino+s
Al|bi|noni,
Tom|aso(Italian
composer)
al|bin|ot|ic
Al|bi|nus
(alternative name
for Alcuin)
Al|bion(England;
Britain)
alb|ite
Ål|borg(use
Aalborg)
Al|bu|feira(town,
Portugal)
album+s
al|bu|men(white of
egg)
al|bu|min(protein)
al|bu|min|oid
al|bu|min|ous
al|bu|min|uria
Al|bu|quer|que
(city, USA)
Al|bu|quer|que,
Al|fonso de
(Portuguese
statesman)
al|bur|num
Al|caeus(Greek
poet)
al|ca|hest(use
alkahest)
al|caic
Al|calá de
He|nares(city,
Spain)
al|calde+s
Al|ca|traz(island,
USA)
Al|ces|tis Greek
Mythology
al|chem|ic
al|chem|ic|al
al|chem|ise Br.
(use alchemize)
al|chem|ises
al|chem|ised
al|chem|is|ing
al|chem|ist+s
al|chem|ize
al|chem|izes
al|chem|ized
al|chem|iz|ing
al|chemy
al|cher|inga

Al|ci|bi|ades
(Athenian general
and statesman)
alcid+s
Al|cock, John
Wil|liam(English
aviator)
al|co|hol+s
alcohol-free
al|co|hol|ic+s
al|co|hol|ism
al|co|hol|om|eter
+s
al|co|hol|om|etry
Al|cott, Lou|isa
May(American
novelist)
al|cove+s
Al|cuin(English
theologian)
Al|dabra(island
group, Indian
Ocean)
Al|deb|aran(star)
Alde|burgh(town,
England)
al|de|hyde+s
al|de|hydic
al dente
alder+s
al|der|man
al|der|men
al|der|man|ic
al|der|man|ry
al|der|man|ship
Al|der|mas|ton
(village, England)
Al|der|ney
(Channel Island;
cattle)
al|der|per|son+s
Al|der|shot(town,
England)
al|der|woman
al|der|women
Al|dine
Aldis lamp+s
Al|diss, Brian
(English writer)
al|dos|ter|one
Al|dous
al|drin
Aldus Manu|tius
(Italian printer)
ale+s (beer. △ ail)
alea|tor|ic
alea|tory
Alec also Alick
(name)
alec+s (in 'smart
alec')
ale|cost

Alecto *Greek Mythology*

alee

ale¦gar

ale|house +s

Ale|khine, Alex|an¦der (Russian-born chess player)

Alek|san|dro|pol (former name of Gyumri)

Alek|san|drovsk (former name of Zaporizhzhya)

Alem|bert, Jean le Rond d' (French philosopher and mathematician)

alem|bic +s

alem|bi|cated

alem|bi|ca¦tion

Alen|tejo (region and former province, Portugal)

aleph +s

Al¦eppo (city, Syria)

alert +s +ed +ing

alert¦ly

alert|ness

Aletsch|horn (mountain, Switzerland)

aleuron

aleur|one

Aleut +s

Aleu|tian Is¦lands (off Alaska)

Aleu|tians (=Aleutian Islands)

A level +s

ale|wife
  ale|wives

Alex *also* Alix

Alexa

Alex|an¦der (Russian emperors and Scottish kings)

Alex|an¦der, Har¦old (British field marshal)

Alex|an¦der Archi|pel¦ago (island off Alaska)

Alex|an¦der Nev¦sky (Russian hero)

alex|an¦ders (plant)

Alex|an¦der tech|nique

Alex|an¦der the Great (Macedonian king)

Alex|an¦dra

Alex|an¦dretta (former name of Iskenderun)

Alex|an¦dria (port, Egypt; name)

Alex|an¦drian +s

alex|an¦drine +s (line of verse)

alex|an¦drite (mineral)

Alex|an¦dro|pol (former name of Gyumri)

alexia

alexin

alex|ine (use alexin)

alexi|phar¦mic

Alexis

al|fal¦fa

Al Fatah (Palestinian organization)

Al|fonso (Spanish kings)

Al¦fred

Al¦fred the Great (king of Wessex)

al|fresco

Alf¦vén, Hannes Olof Gösta (Swedish theoretical physicist)

alga
  algae

algal

Al|garve (province, Portugal)

al¦ge|bra +s

al¦ge|bra¦ic

al¦ge|bra¦ic¦al

al¦ge|bra¦ic¦al¦ly

al¦ge|bra¦ist +s

Al¦ge|ciras (port and resort, Spain)

Alger

Al|geria

Al|ger¦ian +s

Al¦ger|non

al¦gi|cide

algid

al¦gid|ity

Al|giers (capital of Algeria)

al¦gin|ate +s

al|gin¦ic

alg|oid

Algol (star; computing language)

al¦go|lag|nia

al¦go|lag¦nic

al¦go|logic¦al

al¦golo|gist +s

al|gology

Al¦gon|quian +s

Al¦gon|quin +s

al¦go|rithm +s

al¦go|rith¦mic

al¦go|rith¦mic|al¦ly

al¦gua|cil +s

al¦gua|zil +s (use alguacil)

Al¦ham|bra (palace, Granada)

Al¦ham|bresque

Ali, Mu¦ham|mad (American boxer)

alias
  aliases

Ali Baba

alibi
  ali¦bis
  ali|bied
  alibi|ing

Ali|cante (port, Spain)

Alice

Alice-in-Wonder¦land *attributive*

Alice Springs (town, Australia)

Ali¦cia

Alick *also* Alec

ali|cyc¦lic

al¦id|ade +s

alien +s

alien|abil¦ity

alien|able

alien|age

alien|ate
  alien|ates
  alien|ated
  alien|at¦ing

alien|ation

alien|ator +s

alien|ism

alien|ist +s

alien|ness

ali|form

Ali|garh (city, India)

Ali|ghieri, Dante (Italian poet)

alight +s +ed +ing

align +s +ed +ing

align|ment +s

alike

ali|ment +s

ali|men¦tal

ali|men¦tary

ali|men|ta¦tion

ali|mony

Alinda

Aline (name)

A-line (flared)

ali|phat¦ic

ali|quot +s

Alis|dair *also* Alas|dair, Alas|tair, Alis|tair

Ali¦son *also* Al|lison

Al|issa

Alis|tair *also* Alas|dair, Alas|tair, Alis|dair

alive

alive|ness

Alix *also* Alex

aliz|arin

Al Jizah (Arabic name for Giza)

al|ka|hest

al¦kali
  al¦ka|lis *Br.*
  al¦ka|lies *Am.*

al¦kal|ify
  al¦kali|fies
  al¦kali|fied
  al¦kali|fy|ing

al¦kal|im¦eter +s

al¦kal|im¦etry

al¦ka|line

al¦ka|lin|ity

al¦kal|oid +s

al¦kal|osis
  al¦kal|oses

al¦kane +s

al¦ka|net +s

al¦kene +s

alkie +s (use alky)

alky
  alk¦ies

alkyd +s

alkyl +s

al¦kyl|ate
  al¦kyl|ates
  al¦kyl|ated
  al¦kyl|at¦ing

al¦kyne +s

all (everything, everyone, etc.
  △awl ,orle)

alla breve

alla cap|pella
Allah *Islam*
Al'lah|abad (city,
India)
all-America +s
all-American
Allan *also* Alan,
Allen, Alun
al'lan|toic
al'lan|tois
al'lan|to|ides
all-around
attributive
allay +s +ed +ing
All Blacks
all-clear +s *noun*
all comers
all-day *attributive*
Al'lecto (use
Alecto)
al'le|ga'tion +s
al'lege
al|leges
al|leged
al|leging
al|leged'ly
Al'le|ghen'ies
(= Allegheny
Mountains)
Al'le|gheny
Moun|tains (in
USA)
al'le|giance +s
al'le|gor'ic
al'le|gor'ic|al
al'le|gor'ic'al'ly
al'le|gor'isa'tion
Br. (use
allegorization)
al'le|gor'ise *Br.*
(use allegorize)
al'le|gor'ises
al'le|gor'ised
al'le|gor'is'ing
al'le|gor'ist +s
al'le|gor'iza'tion
al'le|gor'ize
al'le|gor'izes
al'le|gor'ized
al'le|gor'iz'ing
al'le|gory
al'le|gor'ies
al'le|gretto +s
al|legro +s
allel +s
al'lele +s
al'lel'ic
al'lelo|morph +s
al'lelo|morph'ic
al'le|luia +s
alle|mande +s
all-embracing

Allen *also* Alan,
Allan, Alun
Allen (key, screw)
Propr.
Allen, Woody
(American film
director, writer,
and actor)
Al|lenby, Vis|count
(British soldier)
all-encompass'ing
Al|lende,
Sal'va'dor
(Chilean
statesman)
Al'len|stein
(German name for
Olsztyn)
al'ler|gen +s
al'ler|gen'ic
al'ler|gic
al'ler|gist +s
al'lergy
al'ler|gies
al'le'vi'ate
al'le'vi'ates
al'le'vi'ated
al'le'vi'at'ing
al'le'vi'ation
al'le'via'tive
al'le'vi'ator +s
al'le'vi'atory
alley +s
alley cat +s
al'ley|way +s
All Fools' Day
All Hal|lows
al'li|aceous
al'li|ance +s
al'li|cin
Allie *also* Ally
al'lied
Al'lier (river,
France)
al'li|ga'tor +s
all-import'ant
all in (tired)
all-in (complete)
all-inclusive
all-in-one +s
adjective and noun
all-in wrest|ling
Al|lison *also*
Ali'son
al'lit'er|ate
al'lit'er|ates
al'lit'er|ated
al'lit'er|at'ing
al'lit'er|ation +s
al'lit'era|tive
al'lium +s
all-night *attributive*

Alloa (town,
Scotland)
al'loc|able
al'lo|cate
al'lo|cates
al'lo|cated
al'lo|cat'ing
al'lo|ca'tion +s
al'lo|ca'tor +s
al'loch|thon|ous
al'lo|cu'tion +s
al'lo|dial +s
al'lo|dium +s
al'logamy
allo|graft +s
allo|morph +s
allo|morph'ic
allo|path +s
allo|path'ic
al'lop'ath'ist +s
al'lop'athy
al'lo|pat'ric
allo|phone +s
allo|phon'ic
allo|poly|ploid +s
all-or-nothing
attributive
allo|saur +s
allo|saurus
allo|saur'uses
allot
al'lots
al'lot|ted
al'lot|ting
al'lot|ment +s
allo|trope +s
allo|trop'ic
allo|trop'ic'al
al'lot|ropy
al'lot|tee +s
all-out *attributive*
all-over *attributive*
allow +s +ed +ing
al'low|able
al'low|ably
al'low|ance +s
al'low|ed'ly
alloy +s +ed +ing
all-party *attributive*
all-pervad'ing
attributive
all-pervasive
all-powerful
all-purpose
all ready (entire
number of people
or things in a state
of readiness.
△ already)
all right *adjective,
adverbial, and
interjection*

all-right *attributive*
all-round *attributive*
all-rounder +s
All Saints' Day
all-seater *attributive*
all|seed
all-share *attributive*
All Souls' Day
all|spice
All|ston,
Wash|ing|ton
(American
painter)
all-ticket *attributive*
all-time
all to|gether (all at
once; all in one.
△ altogether)
al'lude
al|ludes
al|luded
al|lud'ing
(refer indirectly.
△ elude, illude)
all-up *attributive*
al'lure
al|lures
al|lured
al'lur|ing
al'lure|ment +s
al'lu'sion +s
(indirect
reference.
△ illusion)
al'lu'sive
(containing an
allusion.
△ elusive,
illusive)
al'lu'sive'ly (in an
allusive way.
△ elusively,
illusively)
al'lu'sive|ness
(allusive nature.
△ elusiveness,
illusiveness)
al'lu'vial
al'lu'vion
al'lu'vium
al'lu'via *or*
al'lu'vi'ums
all-weather
attributive
all-wheel
Ally (name)
ally
al'lies
al'lied
ally|ing
allyl +s
Alma

Alma-Ata (former name of Almaty)
al¦ma¦can¦tar +s (use almucantar)
Al¦ma¦gest (Ptolemy's treatise)
al¦ma¦gest +s (generally)
Alma Mater +s
al¦manac +s
Al¦man¦ach de Gotha
Al¦man¦ack (in 'Oxford Almanack', 'Whittaker's Almanack')
al¦man¦dine +s
Alma-Tadema, Law¦rence (Dutch-born British painter)
Al¦maty (capital of Kazakhstan)
Al¦mería (town, Spain)
al¦mighty
al¦mirah +s
Al¦mir¦ante Brown (city, Argentina)
Al¦mo¦had +s
Al¦mo¦hade +s (use Almohad)
al¦mond +s
al¦mon¦er +s
al¦mon¦ry
Al¦mora¦vid +s
Al¦mora¦vide +s (= Almoravid)
al¦most
alms (charity. △ arms)
alms¦house +s
alms¦man
alms¦men
al¦mu¦can¦tar +s
aloe +s
alo¦et¦ic
aloe vera
aloft
alogic¦al
alogic¦al¦ly
aloha
alone
alone¦ness
along
along¦shore
along¦side
aloof
aloof¦ly
aloof¦ness

alo¦pe¦cia
Alor Setar (city, Malaysia)
Alost (French name for Aalst)
aloud (audibly. △ allowed)
alow (below, in a ship)
Aloy¦sius
alp +s (mountain)
al¦paca +s
al¦par¦gata +s
al¦pen¦horn +s
al¦pen¦stock +s
alpha +s
al¦pha¦bet +s
al¦pha¦bet¦ic
al¦pha¦bet¦ic¦al
al¦pha¦bet¦ic¦al¦ly
al¦pha¦bet¦isa¦tion Br. (use alphabetization)
al¦pha¦bet¦ise Br. (use alphabetize)
al¦pha¦bet¦ises
al¦pha¦bet¦ised
al¦pha¦bet¦is¦ing
al¦pha¦bet¦iza¦tion
al¦pha¦bet¦ize
al¦pha¦bet¦izes
al¦pha¦bet¦ized
al¦pha¦bet¦iz¦ing
Alpha Cen¦tauri (star)
alpha¦numer¦ic
alpha¦numer¦ic¦al
alpha test +s +ed +ing
Al¦pine (of Alps or downhill skiing)
al¦pine (of high mountains)
Al¦pin¦ist +s
Alps (mountain range, Europe; also in names of other ranges)
al¦ready (beforehand; as early or as soon as this. △ all ready)
al¦right (use all right or all-right)
Al¦sace (region, France)
Al¦sa¦tian +s
al¦sike
also
also-ran +s
al¦stroe¦me¦ria +s

Altai (territory, Russia)
Al¦taic
Altai Moun¦tains (central Asia)
Al¦tair (star)
Al¦ta¦mira (site of cave paintings, Spain; town, Brazil)
altar +s (table in church. △ alter)
al¦tar¦piece +s
Altay (use Altai)
alt¦azi¦muth +s
Alt¦dor¦fer, Al¦brecht (German painter)
Alte Pi¦na¦ko¦thek (museum, Munich)
alter +s +ed +ing (change. △ altar)
al¦ter¦able
al¦ter¦ation +s
al¦tera¦tive
al¦ter¦cate
al¦ter¦cates
al¦ter¦cated
al¦ter¦cat¦ing
al¦ter¦ca¦tion +s
alter ego +s
al¦ter¦nance
al¦ter¦nant +s
al¦ter¦nate
al¦ter¦nates
al¦ter¦nated
al¦ter¦nat¦ing
al¦ter¦nate¦ly
al¦ter¦na¦tion +s
al¦ter¦na¦tive +s
al¦ter¦na¦tive¦ly
al¦ter¦na¦tor +s
Al¦thea
alt¦horn +s
al¦though
Al¦thus¦ser, Louis (French philosopher)
Al¦thus¦ser¦ean +s (use Althusserian)
Al¦thus¦ser¦ian +s
al¦tim¦eter +s
al¦ti¦plano +s
al¦ti¦tude +s
al¦ti¦tud¦inal
alto +s
alto¦cumu¦lus
alto¦cumuli

al¦together (totally; in total. △ all together)
alto-relievo +s
alto-rilievo +s (use alto-relievo)
alto¦stra¦tus
al¦tri¦cial
al¦tru¦ism
al¦tru¦ist +s
al¦tru¦is¦tic
al¦tru¦is¦tic¦al¦ly
alum
alu¦mina
alu¦min¦isa¦tion Br. (use aluminization)
alu¦min¦ise Br. (use aluminize)
alu¦min¦ises
alu¦min¦ised
alu¦min¦is¦ing
alu¦min¦ium Br.
alu¦min¦iza¦tion
alu¦min¦ize
alu¦min¦izes
alu¦min¦ized
alu¦min¦iz¦ing
alu¦mino¦sili¦cate +s
alu¦mi¦num Am.
alumna
alum¦nae female
alum¦nus
alumni male
Alun also Alan, Allan, Allen
Alvar
Al¦varez, Luis Wal¦ter (American physicist)
al¦veo¦lar +s
al¦veo¦late
al¦veo¦lus
al¦veoli
Alvin
al¦ways
alys¦sum +s
Alz¦heim¦er's dis¦ease
am
ama¦da¦vat +s
ama¦dou
amah +s (maid. △ armor, armour)
amain
Amal +s
Amalfi (resort, Italy)

amal|gam +s
amal|gam|ate
  amal|gam|ates
  amal|gam|ated
  amal|gam|at|ing
amal|gam|ation
  +s
Amal|thea (*Greek Mythology*; moon of Jupiter)
Amanda
amanu|en|sis
  amanu|en|ses
Amapá (state, Brazil)
am|ar|anth
am|ar|anth|ine
am|ar|etto
  am|ar|etti
  (liqueur; biscuit.
  △ *amoretto*)
Amarna, Tell el- (site of Akhetaten, Egypt)
amar|yl|lis
  amar|yl|lises
amass
  amasses
  amassed
  amass|ing
amass|er +s
Ama|ter|asu
ama|teur +s
ama|teur|ish
ama|teur|ish|ly
ama|teur|ish|ness
ama|teur|ism
Amati +s
ama|tive
ama|tory
am|aur|osis
  am|aur|oses
am|aur|ot|ic
amaze
  amazes
  amazed
  amaz|ing
amaze|ment
amaz|ing|ly
amaz|ing|ness
Amazon +s (region, S. America; legendary female warrior)
amazon +s (strong, athletic woman)
amazon ant +s
Ama|zo|nas (state, Brazil)
Ama|zonia (region, S. America)

Ama|zon|ian
am|bas|sador +s
ambassador-at-large
  ambassadors-at-large
am|bas|sador|ial
am|bas|sa|dor|ship +s
am|bas|sadress
  am|bas|sadresses
am|batch
  am|batches
Am|bato (town, Ecuador)
amber
am|ber|gris
am|ber|jack
  plural am|ber|jack
  or am|ber|jacks
am|bi|ance +s (use ambience)
ambi|dex|ter|ity
ambi|dex|trous
ambi|dex|trous|ly
ambi|dex|trous|ness
am|bi|ence +s
am|bi|ent
am|bi|gu|ity
  am|bi|gu|ities
am|bigu|ous
am|bigu|ous|ly
am|bigu|ous|ness
ambi|son|ics
ambit +s
am|bi|tion +s
am|bi|tious
am|bi|tious|ly
am|bi|tious|ness
am|biva|lence +s
am|biva|lency
am|biva|lent
am|biva|lent|ly
ambi|ver|sion
ambi|vert +s
amble
  am|bles
  am|bled
  am|bling
am|bler +s
am|bly|opia
am|bly|opic
ambo
  ambos *or*
  am|bo|nes
Am|boina (= Ambon)
Am|boi|nese
  plural
  Am|boi|nese

Ambon (island and port, Indonesia)
am|boyna
Am|brose (Roman saint; name)
am|bro|sia
am|bro|sial
am|bro|sian
ambry
  am|bries
ambs-ace
am|bu|lance +s
am|bu|lant
am|bu|la|tory
  am|bu|la|tor|ies
am|bus|cade
  am|bus|cades
  am|bus|caded
  am|bus|cad|ing
am|bush
  am|bushes
  am|bushed
  am|bush|ing
ameba *Am.*
  amebas *or*
  amebae
  (*Br.* amoeba)
ame|bean *Am.* (*Br.* amoebean)
ameb|ia|sis *Am.*
  ameb|ia|ses
  (*Br.* amoebiasis)
ameb|ic *Am.* (*Br.* amoebic)
ameb|oid *Am.* (*Br.* amoeboid)
ameer +s (use amir)
Am|elia
ameli|or|ate
  ameli|or|ates
  ameli|or|ated
  ameli|or|at|ing
ameli|or|ation
ameli|ora|tive +s
ameli|or|ator +s
amen +s
amen|abil|ity
amen|able
amen|able|ness
amen|ably
amend +s +ed +ing (improve. △ emend)
amend|able
amende
  hon|or|able
  amendes
  hon|or|ables
amend|er +s
amend|ment +s

Amen|ho|tep (pharaohs)
amen|ity
  amen|ities
Ameno|phis (Greek name for Amenhotep)
amen|or|rhea *Am.*
amen|or|rhoea *Br.*
ament +s
amen|tia
amen|tum
amenta
Amer|asian +s
amerce
  amerces
  amerced
  amer|cing
amerce|ment +s
amer|ci|able
Amer|ica +s
Ameri|can +s
Ameri|cana
Ameri|can|isa|tion *Br.* (use Americanization)
Ameri|can|ise *Br.* (use Americanize)
  Ameri|can|ises
  Ameri|can|ised
  Ameri|can|is|ing
Ameri|can|ism +s
Ameri|can|iza|tion
Ameri|can|ize
  Ameri|can|izes
  Ameri|can|ized
  Ameri|can|iz|ing
Amer|ica's Cup
ameri|cium
Amer|ind +s
Amer|in|dian +s
Amer|in|dic
Ames|lan (= American sign language)
ameth|yst +s
ameth|yst|ine
Amex (= American Stock Exchange)
Amex (= American Express) *Propr.*
Am|har|ic
ami|abil|ity
ami|able
ami|able|ness
ami|ably
ami|an|thus
am|ic|abil|ity
am|ic|able
am|ic|able|ness
am|ic|ably

amice +s
ami|cus curiae
  amici curiae
amid
amide +s
amid|done
amid|ship
amid|ships
amidst
Am|iens (city,
  France)
amigo +s
Amin, Idi
  (Ugandan soldier
  and head of state)
Am|in|divi
  Is|lands (now
  part of
  Lakshadweep
  Islands)
amine +s
amino +s
amino acid +s
amir +s (title of
  some Muslim
  rulers. △ emir)
Amir|ante Is|lands
  (in Indian Ocean)
amir|ate +s
  (position or
  territory of an
  amir. △ emirate)
Amis, Kings|ley
  and Mar|tin
  (British writers)
Amish
amiss
ami|tosis
ami|trip|tyl|ine
amity
Amman (capital of
  Jordan)
am|meter +s
ammo
Ammon (= Amun)
am|mo|nia
am|mo|niac
am|mo|ni|ac|al
am|mo|ni|ated
am|mon|ite +s
am|mo|nium
am|mu|ni|tion +s
am|nesia
am|nesiac +s
am|nesic +s
am|nesty
  am|nes|ties
  am|nes|tied
  am|nesty|ing
amnio +s
  (= amniocentesis)

am|nio|cen|tesis
  am|nio|cen|teses
am|nion
  amnia or
  am|nions
am|ni|ote +s
am|ni|ot|ic
amoeba Br.
  amoe|bas or
  amoe|bae
  (Am. ameba)
amoe|bean Br.
  (Am. amebean)
amoeb|ia|sis Br.
  amoeb|ia|ses
  (Am. amebiasis)
amoeb|ic Br. (Am.
  amebic)
amoeb|oid Br. (Am.
  ameboid)
amok
among
amongst
amon|til|lado +s
amoral
amor|al|ism
amor|al|ist +s
amor|al|ity
amor|al|ly
amor|etto
  amor|etti
  (Cupid.
  △ amaretto)
am|or|ist +s
Am|or|ite +s
amor|oso +s
am|or|ous
am|or|ous|ly
am|or|ous|ness
amorph|ous
amorph|ous|ly
amorph|ous|ness
amort|isa|tion Br.
  (use
  amortization)
amort|ise Br. (use
  amortize)
amort|ises
amort|ised
amort|is|ing
amort|iza|tion
amort|ize
  amort|izes
  amort|ized
  amort|iz|ing
Amos Bible
amount +s +ed
  +ing
amour +s
amour|ette +s
amour propre

Amoy (alternative
  name for Xiamen)
amp +s
am|pel|op|sis
  plural
  am|pel|op|sis
am|per|age +s
Am|père, André-
  Marie (French
  physicist)
am|pere +s (unit)
am|per|sand +s
am|phet|amine +s
Am|phibia
am|phib|ian +s
am|phibi|ous
am|phibi|ous|ly
amphi|bole +s
am|phibo|lite +s
amphi|bology
  amphi|bolo|gies
amphi|brach +s
amphi|brach|ic
am|phic|tyon +s
am|phic|ty|on|ic
am|phic|ty|ony
am|phig|am|ous
amphi|gouri +s
amphi|mic|tic
amphi|mixis
  amphi|mixes
amphi|oxus
  amphi|oxi
amphi|path|ic
amphi|pod +s
am|phip|ro|style
  +s
am|phis|baena +s
amphi|theater Am.
  +s
amphi|theatre Br.
  +s
Amphi|trite Greek
  Mythology
am|phit|ryon
am|phora
  am|phorae or
  am|phoras
ampho|ter|ic
ampi|cil|lin
ample
amp|ler
amp|lest
ample|ness
amp|li|fi|ca|tion
amp|li|fier +s
amp|lify
  amp|li|fies
  amp|li|fied
  amp|li|fy|ing
amp|li|tude
amply

am|poule +s
amp|ster +s
am|pulla
am|pul|lae
am|pu|tate
  am|pu|tates
  am|pu|tated
  am|pu|tat|ing
am|pu|ta|tion +s
am|pu|ta|tor +s
am|pu|tee +s
Am|rit|sar (city,
  India)
amster +s (use
  ampster)
Am|ster|dam
  (capital of the
  Netherlands)
am|trac +s
  (amphibious
  vehicle)
Am|track (use
  Amtrak)
Am|trak (US
  railway) Propr.
am|trak +s
  (amphibious
  vehicle; use
  amtrac)
amuck (use amok)
Amu Darya (river,
  central Asia)
amu|let +s
Amun Egyptian
  Mythology
Amund|sen, Roald
  (Norwegian
  explorer)
Amur (river, NE
  Asia)
amuse
  amuses
  amused
  amus|ing
amuse|ment +s
amus|ing|ly
Amy
amyg|dale +s
amyg|dal|oid +s
amyl
amyl|ase
amyl|oid
amyl|op|sin
Amy|tal Propr.
an indefinite article
ana +s
Ana|bap|tism
Ana|bap|tist +s
ana|bas
ana|basis
  ana|bases
ana|bat|ic

ana|bi|osis
  ana|bi|oses
ana|bi|ot|ic
ana|bol|ic
an|ab|ol|ism
ana|branch
  ana|branches
ana|chron|ic
an|achron|ism +s
ana|chron|is|tic
ana|chron|is|tic
    al|ly
ana|co|lu|thic
ana|co|lu|thon
  ana|co|lu|tha
ana|conda +s
Anac|reon (Greek
  poet)
anac|re|on|tic
ana|cru|sis
  ana|cru|ses
anad|ro|mous
an|aemia Br. (Am.
  anemia)
an|aemic Br. +s
  (Am. anemic)
an|aer|obe +s
an|aer|obic
an|aes|the|sia Br.
  (Am. anesthesia)
an|aes|the|si|ology
  Br. (Am.
  anesthesiology)
an|aes|thet|ic Br.
  +s (Am.
  anesthetic)
an|aes|thet|ic|al|ly
  Br. (Am.
  anesthetically)
an|aes|the|tisa|
  tion Br. (use
  anaesthetization .
  Am.
  anesthetization)
an|aes|the|tise Br.
  (use
  anaesthetize)
  an|aes|the|tises
  an|aes|the|tised
  an|aes|the|tis|ing
  (Am. anesthetize)
an|aes|the|tist Br.
  +s (Am.
  anesthetist)
an|aes|the|tiza|
  tion Br. (Am.
  anesthetization)
an|aes|the|tize Br.
  an|aes|the|tizes
  an|aes|the|tized
  an|aes|the|tiz|ing
  (Am. anesthetize)

ana|glyph +s
ana|glyph|ic
Ana|glypta +s
  Propr.
an|ag|nor|isis
  an|ag|nor|ises
ana|goge +s
ana|gogic
ana|gogic|al
ana|gram +s
ana|gram|mat|ic
ana|gram|
    mat|ic|al
ana|gram|ma|tise
  Br. (use
  anagrammatize)
  ana|gram|
    ma|tises
  ana|gram|
    ma|tised
  ana|gram|
    ma|tis|ing
ana|gram|ma|tize
  ana|gram|
    ma|tizes
  ana|gram|
    ma|tized
  ana|gram|
    ma|tiz|ing
Ana|heim (city,
  USA)
anal
ana|lecta
ana|lects
ana|lep|tic +s
an|al|gesia
an|al|gesic +s
anal|ly
ana|log +s
  Computing
ana|log Am. (Br.
  analogue)
ana|logic
ana|logic|al
ana|logic|al|ly
analo|gise Br. (use
  analogize)
  analo|gises
  analo|gised
  analo|gis|ing
analo|gist +s
analo|gize
  analo|gizes
  analo|gized
  analo|giz|ing
analo|gous
analo|gous|ly
ana|logue Br. +s
  (Am. analog)
ana|logy
  ana|lo|gies
anal re|ten|tion

anal-retentive +s
anal
  re|ten|tive|ness
ana|lys|able Br.
  (Am. analyzable)
an|aly|sand +s
ana|lyse Br.
  ana|lyses
  ana|lysed
  ana|lys|ing
  (Am. analyze)
ana|lyser Br. +s
  (Am. analyzer)
an|aly|sis
  an|aly|ses
ana|lyst +s (person
  who analyses.
  △annalist)
ana|lyt|ic
ana|lyt|ic|al
ana|lyt|ic|al|ly
ana|lyz|able Am.
  (Br. analysable)
ana|lyze Am.
  ana|lyzes
  ana|lyzed
  ana|lyz|ing
  (Br. analyse)
ana|lyzer Am. +s
  (Br. analyser)
an|am|nesis
  an|am|neses
ana|morph|ic
ana|mor|phosis
  ana|mor|phoses
ana|nas
an|an|drous
An|angu
  plural An|angu
Ananias Bible
ana|paest +s
ana|paes|tic
ana|phase +s
anaph|ora +s
ana|phor|ic
an|aphro|dis|iac
  +s
ana|phyl|actic
ana|phyl|axis
  ana|phyl|axes
anap|tyc|tic
anap|tyxis
  anap|tyxes
an|arch +s
an|arch|ic
an|arch|ic|al
an|arch|ic|al|ly
an|arch|ism
an|arch|ist +s
an|arch|is|tic
an|archy
Ana|sazi

Ana|sta|sia
ana|stig|mat +s
ana|stig|mat|ic
anas|to|mose
  anas|to|moses
  anas|to|mosed
  anas|to|mos|ing
anas|to|mosis
  anas|to|moses
anas|tro|phe +s
anath|ema +s
anath|ema|tise Br.
  (use
  anathematize)
  anath|ema|tises
  anath|ema|tised
  anath|ema|tis|ing
anath|ema|tize
  anath|ema|tizes
  anath|ema|tized
  anath|ema|tiz|ing
Ana|to|lia
  (peninsula forming
  most of Turkey)
Ana|to|lian +s
ana|tom|ical
ana|tom|ic|al|ly
anato|mise Br. (use
  anatomize)
  anato|mises
  anato|mised
  anato|mis|ing
anato|mist +s
anato|mize
  anato|mizes
  anato|mized
  anato|miz|ing
anat|omy
  anat|omies
anatta
anatto (use
  annatto)
An|ax|ag|oras
  (Greek
  philosopher)
Anaxi|man|der
  (Greek
  philosopher and
  astronomer)
An|ax|im|enes
  (Greek
  philosopher)
an|bury
  an|bur|ies
an|ces|tor +s
an|ces|tral
an|ces|tral|ly
an|ces|tress
  an|ces|tresses
an|ces|try
  an|ces|tries

An|chises *Greek and Roman Mythology*
an|chor +s +ed +ing
An|chor|age (city, USA)
an|chor|age +s
an|chor|ess
an|chor|esses
an|choret +s
an|chor|et|ic
an|chor|ite +s (recluse. ⚠ ankerite)
an|chor|it|ic
an|chor|man
an|chor|men
an|chor|per|son
an|chor|per|sons *or* an|chor|people
an|chor plate +s
an|chor|woman
an|chor|women
an|cho|veta +s
an|chovy
an|cho|vies
an|chusa +s
an|chy|lose (use ankylose)
an|chy|loses
an|chy|losed
an|chy|los|ing
an|chy|losis (use ankylosis)
an|cien ré|gime
an|ciens ré|gimes
an|cient +s
an|cient|ly
an|cient|ness
an|cil|lary
an|cil|lar|ies
ancon
an|co|nes *or* an|cons
An|cona (port, Italy)
An|cyra (ancient name for Ankara)
and
An|da|lu|cia (Spanish name for Andalusia)
An|da|lu|sia (region, Spain)
An|da|lu|sian +s
An|da|man and Nico|bar Is|lands (off India)
an|dante +s
an|dan|tino +s
An|dean

An|der|sen, Hans Chris|tian (Danish writer)
An|der|son, Carl David (American physicist)
An|der|son, Eliza|beth Gar|rett (English physician and feminist)
An|der|son, Mar|ian (American contralto)
Andes (mountain range, S. America)
an|des|ite +s
An|dhra Pra|desh (state, India)
and|iron +s
An|dorra
An|dor|ran +s
Andre, Carl (American sculptor)
André
An|drea
An|drea del Sarto (Italian painter)
An|dreas
An|drew (name, but merry andrew)
An|drew (Apostle and saint)
An|drew, Prince (Duke of York)
An|drews, Julie (English actress and singer)
An|drews, Thomas (Irish chemist)
An|drić, Ivo (Yugoslav writer)
an|dro|cen|tric
an|dro|cen|trism
An|dro|cles (legendary Roman slave)
an|droe|cium
an|droe|cia
an|dro|gen +s
an|dro|gen|ic
an|dro|gyne +s
an|drogy|nous
an|drogyny
an|droid +s
An|drom|ache *Greek Mythology*

An|drom|eda (*Greek Mythology*; constellation)
An|dro|pov (former name of Rybinsk)
An|dro|pov, Yuri (Soviet statesman)
an|ec|dot|age
an|ec|dotal
an|ec|dotal|ist +s
an|ec|dot|al|ly
an|ec|dote +s
an|ec|dot|ic
an|echo|ic
An|eirin *also* An|eurin
anele
aneles
aneled
anel|ing (anoint. ⚠ anneal)
an|emia *Am.* (*Br.* anaemia)
an|emic *Am.* +s (*Br.* anaemic)
anemo|graph +s
anemo|graph|ic
an|emom|eter +s
anemo|met|ric
an|emom|etry
anem|one +s
an|emoph|il|ous
anen|ceph|al|ic +s
anen|ceph|aly
anent
an|er|oid +s
an|es|the|sia *Am.* (*Br.* anaesthesia)
an|es|the|si|ology *Am.* (*Br.* anaesthesiology)
an|es|thet|ic *Am.* +s (*Br.* anaesthetic)
an|es|thet|ic|al|ly *Am.* (*Br.* anaesthetically)
an|es|the|tist *Am.* +s (*Br.* anaesthetist)
an|es|the|tiza|tion *Am.* (*Br.* anaesthetization)
an|es|the|tize *Am.* an|es|the|tizes an|es|the|tized an|es|the|tiz|ing (*Br.* anaesthetize)
An|eurin *also* An|eirin
an|eurin (vitamin)
an|eur|ysm +s

an|eur|ys|mal
anew
an|frac|tu|os|ity
an|frac|tu|ous
an|gary
Angel (name)
angel +s
An|gela
An|gel|eno +s
Angel Falls (in Venezuela)
angel|fish *plural* angel|fish *or* angel|fishes
an|gel|ic
An|gel|ica (name)
an|gel|ica
an|gel|ic|al
an|gel|ic|al|ly
An|gel|ico, Fra (Italian painter)
An|gel|ina
An|ge|lou, Maya (American writer)
angel-shark +s
angels-on-horseback
an|gelus
anger +s +ed +ing
An|gers (city, France)
An|ge|vin +s
An|gharad
Angie
an|gina
an|gio|gram +s
an|gi|og|raphy
an|gi|oma an|gi|omas *or* an|gi|omata
angio|plasty
angio|sperm +s
angio|sperm|ous
Ang|kor (ancient city, Cambodia)
Angle +s (people)
angle
an|gles
an|gled
an|gling (*Geometry*; fish)
angle|dozer +s
angle-iron +s
angle|poise +s *Propr.*
an|gler +s
angler-fish *plural* angler-fish
Angle|sey (island, Wales)
An|glian +s
An|gli|can +s

An|gli|can|ism
an|glice
An|gli|cisa|tion *Br.*
  (use
  Anglicization)
An|gli|cise *Br.* (use
  Anglicize)
An|gli|cises
An|gli|cised
An|gli|cis|ing
An|gli|cism +s
An|gli|ciza|tion
An|gli|cize
An|gli|cizes
An|gli|cized
An|gli|ciz|ing
An|glist +s
An|glis|tics
Anglo +s
Anglo-American
  +s
Anglo-Catholic +s
Anglo-
  Catholi|cism
Anglo|cen|tric
Anglo-French
Anglo-Indian +s
Anglo-Irish
Anglo-Latin
Anglo|mania
Anglo|maniac +s
Anglo-Norman +s
Anglo|phile +s
Anglo|phobe +s
Anglo|pho|bia
anglo|phone +s
Anglo-Saxon +s
An|gola
An|gora (former
  name of Ankara)
an|gora +s (goat;
  wool)
An|gos|tura
  (former name of
  Ciudad Bolívar)
an|gos|tura (plant;
  Angostura Bitters)
An|gos|tura
  Bit|ters *Propr.*
an|grily
angry
  an|grier
  an|gri|est
angst
angst-ridden
Ång|ström,
  An|ders Jonas
  (Swedish
  physicist)
ang|strom +s (unit)
An|guilla (island,
  West Indies)

an|guine
an|guish
  an|guishes
  an|guished
  an|guish|ing
an|gu|lar
an|gu|lar|ity
an|gu|lar|ly
Angus (former
  county, Scotland;
  name)
an|gwan|tibo +s
an|he|dral
an|hinga +s
Anhui (province,
  China)
An|hwei (= Anhui)
an|hyd|ride +s
an|hyd|rite
an|hyd|rous
ani +s (bird)
an|icon|ic
ani|cut +s
anile
an|il|ine
anil|ity
anima
an|im|ad|ver|sion
  +s
an|im|ad|vert +s
  +ed +ing
ani|mal +s
ani|mal|cu|lar
ani|mal|cule +s
ani|mal|isa|tion
  Br. (use
  animalization)
ani|mal|ise *Br.* (use
  animalize)
ani|mal|ises
ani|mal|ised
ani|mal|is|ing
ani|mal|ism
ani|mal|ist +s
ani|mal|is|tic
ani|mal|ity
ani|mal|iza|tion
ani|mal|ize
ani|mal|izes
ani|mal|ized
ani|mal|iz|ing
anima mundi
ani|mate
  ani|mates
  ani|mated
  ani|mat|ing
ani|mated|ly
ani|ma|teur +s
ani|ma|tion +s
ani|ma|tor +s
anima|tron +s
anima|tron|ic

anima|tron|ics
animé
ani|mism
ani|mist +s
ani|mis|tic
ani|mos|ity
  ani|mos|ities
ani|mus
anion +s
an|ion|ic
anise
ani|seed
an|is|ette
an|iso|trop|ic
an|iso|trop|ic|al|ly
an|isot|ropy
Anita
Anjou (former
  province, France;
  wine)
An|kara (capital of
  Turkey)
an|ker|ite (mineral.
  △ anchorite)
ankh +s
ankle +s
ankle-biter +s
ankle-bone +s
ankle-deep
ankle sock +s
ank|let +s
an|ky|lo|saur +s
an|ky|lose
  an|ky|loses
  an|ky|losed
  an|ky|los|ing
an|ky|losis
  an|ky|loses
Ann *also* Anne
Anna (name)
anna +s (former
  Indian and
  Pakistani
  currency)
An|naba (port,
  Algeria)
annal +s
an|nal|ist +s
  (writer of annals.
  △ analyst)
an|nal|is|tic
an|nal|is|tic|al|ly
An|nap|olis (city,
  USA)
An|na|purna
  (mountain ridge,
  Himalayas)
an|nates
an|natto
Anne *also* Ann

Anne (saint; mother
  of the Virgin
  Mary)
Anne (queen of
  England and
  Scotland)
Anne, Prin|cess
  (the Princess
  Royal)
Anne of Cleves
  (wife of Henry
  VIII of England)
an|neal +s +ed
  +ing (toughen.
  △ anele)
an|neal|er +s
an|nect|ent
an|nelid +s
an|nel|id|an
An|nette
annex
  an|nexes
  an|nexed
  an|nex|ing
  verb
an|nex|ation +s
an|nexe +s *noun*
an|ni|cut +s (use
  anicut)
Annie
An|ni|goni, Pietro
  (Italian painter)
an|ni|hi|late
  an|ni|hi|lates
  an|ni|hi|lated
  an|ni|hi|lat|ing
an|ni|hi|la|tion
an|ni|hi|la|tion|
           ism
an|ni|hi|la|tor +s
an|ni|ver|sary
  an|ni|ver|sar|ies
Anno|bón (island,
  Gulf of Guinea)
Anno Dom|ini
an|no|tat|able
an|no|tate
  an|no|tates
  an|no|tated
  an|no|tat|ing
an|no|ta|tion +s
an|no|ta|tive
an|no|ta|tor +s
an|nounce
  an|nounces
  an|nounced
  an|noun|cing
an|nounce|ment
  +s
an|noun|cer +s
annoy +s +ed +ing
an|noy|ance +s

an|noy|er +s
an|noy|ing|ly
an|noy|ing|ness
an|nual +s
an|nu|al|ise *Br.*
(use annualize)
an|nu|al|ises
an|nu|al|ised
an|nu|al|is|ing
an|nu|al|ize
an|nu|al|izes
an|nu|al|ized
an|nu|al|iz|ing
an|nu|al|ly
an|nu|it|ant +s
an|nu|ity
an|nu|ities
annul
an|nuls
an|nulled
an|null|ing
an|nu|lar
an|nu|lar|ly
an|nu|late
an|nu|lated
an|nu|la|tion
an|nu|let +s
an|nul|ment +s
an|nu|lus
an|nuli
an|nun|ci|ate
an|nun|ci|ates
an|nun|ci|ated
an|nun|ci|at|ing
An|nun|ci|ation (of
birth of Christ;
festival)
an|nun|ci|ation +s
(generally)
an|nun|ci|ator +s
annus hor|ri|bilis
annus mira|bilis
anoa +s
an|odal
anode +s
an|odic
ano|dise *Br.* (use
anodize)
ano|dises
ano|dised
ano|dis|ing
ano|diser *Br.* +s
(use anodizer)
ano|dize
ano|dizes
ano|dized
ano|diz|ing
ano|dizer +s
ano|dyne +s
ano|esis
ano|eses
ano|etic

anoint +s +ed
+ing
anoint|er +s
anole +s
anom|al|is|tic
anom|al|ous
anom|al|ous|ly
anom|al|ous|ness
anom|al|ure +s
anom|aly
anom|al|ies
anom|ic
an|omie
anomy (use
anomie)
anon (soon)
anon.
(= anonymous)
an|on|aceous
ano|nym +s
ano|nym|ity
an|onym|ous
an|onym|ous|ly
anoph|eles
plural anoph|eles
an|oph|thal|mia
ano|rak +s
an|or|ec|tic +s
an|or|exia
(ner|vosa)
an|or|exic +s
an|or|ex|ic|al|ly
an|ortho|site +s
an|ortho|sit|ic
an|os|mia
an|os|mic +s
an|other
an|otherie (use
anothery)
an|othery
Anouilh, Jean
(French writer)
ANOVA (= analysis
of variance)
an|ovu|lant +s
an|ox|ae|mia
an|oxia
an|oxic
An|schluss (of
Austria)
an|schluss (other
unification)
An|selm (Italian-
born saint)
an|ser|ine
An|shan (city,
China)
an|swer +s +ed
+ing
an|swer|abil|ity
an|swer|able
an|swer|phone +s

ant +s +ed +ing
(insect)
an't (= am not;
have not.
⚠ aren't, aunt)
ant|acid +s
An|taeus *Greek
Mythology*
an|tag|on|isa|tion
Br. (use
antagonization)
an|tag|on|ise *Br.*
(use antagonize)
an|tag|on|ises
an|tag|on|ised
an|tag|on|is|ing
an|tag|on|ism +s
an|tag|on|ist +s
an|tag|on|is|tic
an|tag|on|is|tic|
al|ly
an|tag|on|iza|tion
an|tag|on|ize
an|tag|on|izes
an|tag|on|ized
an|tag|on|iz|ing
An|takya (Turkish
name for Antioch)
An|tall, Jo|zsef
(Hungarian
statesman)
An|talya (port,
Turkey)
An|tana|na|rivo
(capital of
Madagascar)
Ant|arc|tic
Ant|arc|tica
ant-bear +s
ante
antes
anted
ante|ing
(stake. ⚠ anti)
ant|eat|er +s
ante-bellum
ante|ce|dence
ante|ce|dent +s
ante|ce|dent|ly
ante|cham|ber +s
ante|chapel +s
ante|date
ante|dates
ante|dated
ante|dat|ing
ante|di|lu|vian +s
ante|lope +s
ante-mortem
ante|mun|dane
ante|natal

an|tenna
an|ten|nae
Zoology
an|tenna +s
(aerial)
an|ten|nal
an|ten|nary
ante|nup|tial
ante|pen|dium
ante|pen|dia
ante|pen|ult +s
ante|pen|ul|ti|
mate +s
ante-post
ante|pran|dial
an|ter|ior
an|ter|ior|ity
an|teri|or|ly
ante-room +s
An|thea
ant|heap +s
ant|he|lion
ant|he|lia
an|thel|min|thic
+s
an|thel|min|tic +s
an|them +s
an|the|mion
an|the|mia
An|the|mius of
Tralles (Greek
mathematician,
engineer, and
artist)
an|ther +s
an|ther|al
an|ther|id|ium
an|ther|idia
ant|hill +s
an|tholo|gise *Br.*
(use anthologize)
an|tholo|gises
an|tholo|gised
an|tholo|gis|ing
an|tholo|gist +s
an|tholo|gize
an|tholo|gizes
an|tholo|gized
an|tholo|giz|ing
an|thol|ogy
an|tholo|gies
An|thony *also*
An|tony
An|thony (Egyptian
saint)
An|thony of
Padua
(Portuguese saint)
an|tho|zoan +s
an|thra|cene
an|thra|cite
an|thra|cit|ic

an|thrac|nose
an|thrax
an|thro|po|cen|tric
an|thro|po|cen|tric|
   al|ly
an|thro|po|
   cen|trism
an|thro|po|
   gen|esis
an|thro|po|gen|ic
an|thro|pogeny
an|thro|pog|raphy
an|thro|poid +s
an|thro|po|logic|al
an|thro|po|logic|
   al|ly
an|thro|polo|gist
   +s
an|thro|pol|ogy
an|thro|po|met|ric
an|thro|pom|etry
an|thro|po|
   morph|ic
an|thro|po|
   morph|ic|al|ly
an|thro|po|morph|
   ise *Br.* (use
   anthropomorph-
   ize)
an|thro|po|morph|
   ises
an|thro|po|morph|
   ised
an|thro|po|morph|
   is|ing
an|thro|po|morph|
   ism
an|thro|po|morph|
   ize
an|thro|po|morph|
   izes
an|thro|po|morph|
   ized
an|thro|po|morph|
   iz|ing
an|thro|po|
   morph|ous
an|thro|ponymy
an|thro|
   popha|gous
an|thro|poph|agy
an|thro|poso|phy
anti +s (against;
   opposer. △ ante)
anti-abortion
   attributive
anti-abortion|ist
   +s
anti-aircraft
anti-apartheid
   attributive
an|tiar +s

anti|bac|ter|ial
An|tibes (resort
   and port, France)
anti|bi|osis
anti|bi|oses
anti|bi|ot|ic +s
anti|body
anti|bodies
antibody-negative
antibody-positive
antic +s
anti|cath|ode +s
anti-choice
Anti|christ +s
anti|chris|tian
an|tici|pate
an|tici|pates
an|tici|pated
an|tici|pat|ing
an|tici|pa|tion
an|tici|pa|tive
an|tici|pa|tor +s
an|tici|pa|tory
anti|cler|ic|al
anti|cler|ic|al|ism
anti|cli|mac|tic
anti|cli|mac|tic|
   al|ly
anti|cli|max
anti|cli|maxes
anti|clinal
anti|cline +s
anti|clock|wise
anti|coagu|lant +s
anti|codon +s
anti-commun|ist
   +s
anti|con|sti|
   tu|tion|al
anti|con|vul|sant
   +s
anti|cyc|lone +s
anti|cyc|lon|ic
anti|depres|sant
   +s
anti|diur|et|ic +s
anti|dotal
anti|dote +s
anti-
   establish|ment
   attributive
anti-fascist +s
anti|freeze +s
anti-g
anti|gen +s
anti|gen|ic
An|tig|one *Greek*
   Mythology
anti-govern|ment
   attributive
anti-gravity

An|tigua (town,
   Guatemala)
An|tigua
   Gua|te|mala
   (= Antigua)
An|ti|guan +s
anti-hero
anti-heroes
anti|his|ta|mine
anti-
   inflam|ma|tory
anti-inflation
   attributive
anti-Jacobin +s
anti|knock
Anti-Lebanon
   Moun|tains (in
   Near East)
An|til|lean +s
An|til|les (islands,
   Caribbean)
anti-lock
anti|log +s
anti|log|ar|ithm +s
an|tilogy
an|tilo|gies
anti|macas|sar +s
anti|mal|ar|ial
anti|masque +s
anti|mat|ter
anti|metab|ol|ite
   +s
anti|mon|arch|
   ic|al
anti|monial
anti|mon|ic
anti|moni|ous
an|tim|ony
   (chemical
   element.
   △ antinomy)
anti|node +s
anti|nomian +s
anti|nomian|ism
anti|nomy
   anti|nomies
   (contradiction
   between laws.
   △ antimony)
anti|novel +s
anti-nuclear
An|tioch (city,
   Turkey)
An|tioch (city,
   ancient Phrygia)
An|tio|chus
   (Seleucid kings)
anti|oxi|dant +s
anti|par|ticle +s
anti|pasto
   anti|pasti *or*
   anti|pas|tos

anti|path|et|ic
anti|path|et|ic|al
anti|path|et|ic|
   al|ly
anti|path|ic
an|tip|athy
   an|tip|athies
anti-person|nel
anti|per|spir|ant
   +s
anti|phlo|gis|tic
anti|phon +s
an|tiph|on|al
an|tiph|on|al|ly
an|tiph|on|ary
an|tiph|on|ar|ies
an|tiph|ony
an|tiph|on|ies
anti|podal
anti|pode
An|tipo|dean +s
   (Australasian)
an|tipo|dean +s
   (generally)
An|tipo|des
   (Australasia)
an|tipo|des
   (generally)
anti|pole +s
anti|pope +s
anti|pro|ton +s
anti|prur|it|ic
anti|pyr|et|ic +s
anti|quar|ian +s
anti|quar|ian|ism
anti|quary
   anti|quar|ies
anti|quated
an|tique
an|tiques
an|tiqued
an|tiquing
an|tiquity
   an|tiqui|ties
anti-racism
anti-racist +s
anti-roll bar +s
an|tir|rhinum +s
anti|sab|bat|ar|ian
   +s
Anti|sana (volcano,
   Ecuador)
anti|scor|bu|tic +s
anti|scrip|tural
anti-Semite +s
anti-Semitic
anti-Semitism
anti|sep|sis
anti|sep|tic +s
anti|sep|tic|al|ly
anti|serum
   anti|sera

anti|social
anti|social|ly
anti|stat|ic
anti|stat|ic|al|ly
an|tis|tro|phe
anti|stroph|ic
anti-tank *attributive*
anti-terror|ist
  attributive
anti|tet|anus
anti|the|ism
anti|the|ist +s
an|tith|esis
  an|tith|eses
anti|thet|ic
anti|thet|ic|al
anti|thet|ic|al|ly
anti|toxic
anti|toxin +s
anti|trade +s
anti|trini|tar|ian
anti|trust *attributive*
anti|type +s
anti|typ|ical
anti|ven|ene +s
anti|venin +s
anti|viral
anti|virus
  anti|viruses
anti|vivi|sec|tion|
    ism
anti|vivi|sec|tion|
    ist +s
ant|ler +s
ant|lered
ant-lion +s
An|to|fa|gasta
  (port and region,
  Chile)
An|toine
An|toin|ette
Anton
An|tonia
An|to|nine +s
An|to|ni|nus Pius
  (Roman emperor)
an|tono|ma|sia
An|tony *also*
  An|thony
An|tony of Padua
  (use Anthony of
  Padua)
ant|onym +s
ant|onym|ous
an|tral
An|trim (district,
  Northern Ireland)
an|trum
  antra
antsy

An|tung (former
  name of
  Dandong)
Ant|werp (port and
  province,
  Belgium)
Anu|bis *Egyptian
  Mythology*
Anura|dha|pura
  (city, Sri Lanka)
anur|an +s
anus
  anuses
anvil +s
anx|iety
  anx|ieties
anxio|lyt|ic
anx|ious
anx|ious|ly
anx|ious|ness
any
Anya|oku,
  Elea|zar
  (Nigerian
  diplomat)
any|body
any|how
any|more *Am.
  adverb (Br.* any
  more)
any more *Br.
  adverb (Am.*
  anymore)
any|one (anybody)
any one (any single
  one)
any|place
  (anywhere)
any road (anyway)
any|thing
any|time *Am.
  adverb (Br.* any
  time)
any time *Br. adverb
  (Am.* anytime)
any|way
any|ways
any|where
any|wise
Anzac +s
  (Australian or
  New Zealander,
  especially a
  soldier)
Anzus (= Australia,
  New Zealand, and
  United States)
ao dai +s
A-OK (= all systems
  OK)
A-okay (use A-OK)

Aor|angi (region
  and mountain,
  New Zealand)
aor|ist +s
aor|is|tic
aorta +s
aor|tic
Aosta (city, Italy)
Aotea|roa (Maori
  name for New
  Zealand)
aou|dad +s
à ou|trance
Aou|zou Strip
  (region, Chad)
apace
Apa|che +s
  (American Indian)
apa|che +s (street
  ruffian)
ap|an|age +s
apart
apart|heid
apart|ment +s
apart|ness
apa|thet|ic
apa|thet|ic|al|ly
ap|athy
apa|tite +s
apato|saurus
  apato|saur|uses
ape
  apes
  aped
  aping
apeak
Apel|doorn (town,
  the Netherlands)
ape|like
Apel|les (painter to
  Alexander the
  Great)
ape|man
  ape|men
Ap|en|nines
  (mountain range,
  Italy)
ap|erçu +s
aperi|ent +s
aperi|odic
aperi|od|icity
aperi|tif +s
aper|ture +s
apery
  aper|ies
apet|al|ous
APEX (Association
  of Professional,
  Executive,
  Clerical, and
  Computer Staff)

Apex (airline ticket
  system)
apex
  apexes *or* api|ces
  (point)
ap|fel|stru|del +s
aphaer|esis
  aphaer|eses
apha|sia
apha|sic +s
ap|he|lion
ap|he|lia
aph|esis
  aph|eses
aphet|ic
aphet|ic|al|ly
aphid +s
aphis
  aphi|des
apho|nia
aph|ony
aph|or|ise *Br.* (use
  aphorize)
aph|or|ises
aph|or|ised
aph|or|is|ing
aph|or|ism +s
aph|or|ist +s
aph|or|is|tic
aph|or|is|tic|al|ly
aph|or|ize
  aph|or|izes
  aph|or|ized
  aph|or|iz|ing
aph|ro|dis|iac +s
Aph|ro|dis|ias
  (ancient city,
  Turkey)
Aph|ro|dite *Greek
  Mythology*
aphyl|lous
Apia (capital of
  Western Samoa)
apian
api|ar|ian
api|ar|ist +s
api|ary
  api|ar|ies
ap|ical
ap|ic|al|ly
api|ces
api|cul|tural
api|cul|ture
api|cul|tur|ist
apiece
Apis *Egyptian
  Mythology*
apish
apish|ly
ap|ish|ness
ap|la|nat +s
ap|la|nat|ic

apla|sia
aplas|tic
aplenty
aplomb
apnea *Am.*
ap|noea *Br.*
Apoca|lypse *Bible*
apoca|lypse +s
 (generally)
apoca|lyp|tic
apoca|lyp|tic|al
apoca|lyp|tic|al|ly
apo|carp|ous
apo|chro|mat +s
apo|chro|mat|ic
apoc|ope +s
apo|crine
Apoc|rypha *Bible*
apoc|rypha
 (spurious writings)
apoc|ryph|al
apoc|ryph|al|ly
apo|dal
apo|dic|tic
apo|dict|ic|al|ly
apo|dosis
 apo|doses
apo|dous
apo|gean
apo|gee +s
apo|laus|tic
apol|it|ical
apol|it|ic|al|ly
Apol|lin|aire,
 Guil|laume
 (French writer)
Apol|lin|ar|ian +s
Apol|lin|aris (early
 bishop)
Apollo (*Greek
 Mythology*;
 American space
 programme)
Apol|lo|nian
Apol|lon|ius of
 Perga (Greek
 mathematician)
Apol|lon|ius of
 Rhodes (Greek
 poet)
Apol|lyon (the
 Devil)
apolo|get|ic
apolo|get|ic|al|ly
apolo|get|ics
apo|lo|gia +s
apolo|gise *Br.* (use
 apologize)
 apolo|gises
 apolo|gised
 apolo|gis|ing
apolo|gist +s

apolo|gize
 apolo|gizes
 apolo|gized
 apolo|giz|ing
apo|logue +s
apol|ogy
 apolo|gies
apo|lune +s
apo|mic|tic
apo|mixis
apo|phat|ic
apoph|thegm *Br.*
 +s (*Am.*
 apothegm.
 maxim.
 △ apothem)
apoph|theg|mat|ic
 Br. (*Am.*
 apothegmatic)
apoph|theg|mat|ic|
 al|ly *Br.* (*Am.*
 apothegmatic-
 ally)
apo|plec|tic
apo|plec|tic|al|ly
apo|plexy
 apo|plex|ies
apop|tosis
apop|totic
aporia +s
apo|sem|at|ic
apo|sio|pesis
 apo|sio|peses
apos|tasy
 apos|tas|ies
apos|tate +s
apos|tat|ical
apos|ta|tise *Br.*
 (use apostatize)
 apos|ta|tises
 apos|ta|tised
 apos|ta|tis|ing
apos|ta|tize
 apos|ta|tizes
 apos|ta|tized
 apos|ta|tiz|ing
a pos|teri|ori
 *adjective and
 adverb*
Apos|tle +s *Bible*
apos|tle +s (leader;
 representative)
apostle-bird +s
Apos|tles' Creed
apostle|ship +s
Apos|tle spoon +s
apos|to|late +s
apos|tol|ic +s
apos|tol|ic|al
apos|tol|ic|al|ly
apos|tro|phe +s
apos|troph|ic

apos|tro|phise *Br.*
 (use
 apostrophize)
apos|tro|phises
apos|tro|phised
apos|tro|phis|ing
apos|tro|phize
 apos|tro|phizes
 apos|tro|phized
 apos|tro|phiz|ing
apoth|ecar|ies'
 measure +s
apoth|ecar|ies'
 weight +s
apoth|ecary
 apoth|ecar|ies
apo|thegm *Am.* +s
 (*Br.* apophthegm.
 maxim.
 △ apothem)
apo|theg|mat|ic
 Am. (*Br.*
 apophthegmatic)
apo|theg|mat|ic|
 al|ly *Am.* (*Br.*
 apophthegmatic-
 ally)
apo|them +s
 (*Geometry.*
 △ apophthegm,
 apothegm)
apothe|osis
 apothe|oses
apotheo|sise *Br.*
 (use apotheosize)
 apotheo|sises
 apotheo|sised
 apotheo|sis|ing
apotheo|size
 apotheo|sizes
 apotheo|sized
 apotheo|siz|ing
apo|tro|paic
app +s
 (= application)
appal *Br.*
 ap|pals
 ap|palled
 ap|pal|ling
 (*Am.* appall)
Ap|pa|lach|ian +s
Ap|pa|lach|ian
 Moun|tains (in
 USA)
Ap|pa|lach|ians
 (= Appalachian
 Mountains)
ap|pall *Am.*
 ap|palls
 ap|palled
 ap|pall|ing
 (*Br.* appal)

ap|pal|ling|ly
Ap|pa|loosa +s
ap|pan|age +s (use
 apanage)
ap|parat +s
ap|par|at|chik
 ap|par|at|chiks *or*
 ap|par|at|chiki
ap|par|atus
 plural ap|par|atus
 or ap|par|atuses
ap|par|atus
 criti|cus
ap|parel
 ap|parels
 ap|par|elled *Br.*
 ap|par|eled *Am.*
 ap|parel|ling *Br.*
 ap|parel|ing *Am.*
ap|par|ent
ap|par|ent|ly
ap|par|ition +s
ap|pari|tor +s
ap|peal +s +ed
 +ing
ap|peal|able
ap|peal|er +s
ap|peal|ing|ly
ap|pear +s +ed
 +ing
ap|pear|ance +s
ap|pease
 ap|peases
 ap|peased
 ap|peas|ing
ap|pease|ment
ap|peaser +s
Appel, Karel
 (Dutch painter)
ap|pel|lant +s
ap|pel|late
ap|pel|la|tion +s
*ap|pel|la|tion
 con|trôlée*
*ap|pel|la|tion
 d'ori|gine
 con|trôlée*
ap|pel|la|tive +s
ap|pend +s +ed
 +ing
ap|pend|age +s
ap|pend|ant +s
ap|pend|ec|tomy
 ap|pend|
     ec|tomies
ap|pen|di|
     cec|tomy
ap|pen|di|
     cec|tomies
ap|pen|di|citis

ap|pen|dix
  ap|pen|di|ces *or*
  ap|pen|dixes
ap|per|ceive
  ap|per|ceives
  ap|per|ceived
  ap|per|ceiv|ing
ap|per|cep|tion +s
ap|per|cep|tive
ap|per|tain +s +ed
  +ing
ap|pe|tence +s
ap|pe|tency
  ap|pe|ten|cies
ap|pe|tent
ap|pe|tise *Br.* (use
  appetize)
  ap|pe|tises
  ap|pe|tised
  ap|pe|tis|ing
ap|pe|tiser *Br.* +s
  (use appetizer)
ap|pe|tis|ing|ly *Br.*
  (use appetizingly)
ap|pe|tite +s
ap|pe|ti|tive
ap|pe|tize
  ap|pe|tizes
  ap|pe|tized
  ap|pe|tiz|ing
ap|pe|tizer +s
ap|pe|tiz|ing|ly
Ap|pian Way
  (road, Roman
  Italy)
ap|plaud +s +ed
  +ing
ap|plause
apple +s
apple-cart +s
apple-cheeked
apple|jack +s
apple juice +s
apple-pie bed +s
apple-pie order
Apple|ton,
  Ed|ward (English
  physicist)
apple tree +s
ap|pli|ance +s
ap|plic|abil|ity
ap|plic|able
ap|plic|ably
ap|pli|cant +s
ap|pli|ca|tion +s
ap|pli|ca|tor +s
ap|plier +s
ap|pli|qué
  ap|pli|qués
  ap|pli|quéd
  ap|pli|qué|ing

apply
  ap|plies
  ap|plied
  ap|ply|ing
ap|pog|gia|tura +s
ap|point +s +ed
  +ing
ap|point|ee +s
ap|point|er +s
ap|point|ive
ap|point|ment +s
ap|port +s +ed
  +ing
ap|por|tion +s +ed
  +ing
ap|por|tion|able
ap|por|tion|ment
ap|po|site
ap|po|site|ly
ap|po|site|ness
ap|pos|ition +s
ap|pos|ition|al
ap|prais|able
ap|prais|al +s
ap|praise
  ap|praises
  ap|praised
  ap|prais|ing
ap|praisee +s
ap|praise|ment +s
ap|praiser +s
ap|prais|ing|ly
ap|prais|ive
ap|pre|ciable
ap|pre|ciably
ap|pre|ci|ate
  ap|pre|ci|ates
  ap|pre|ci|ated
  ap|pre|ci|at|ing
ap|pre|ci|ation +s
ap|pre|cia|tive
ap|pre|cia|tive|ly
ap|pre|cia|tive|
          ness
ap|pre|ci|ator +s
ap|pre|ci|atory
ap|pre|hend +s
  +ed +ing
ap|pre|hen|si|
         bil|ity
ap|pre|hen|sible
ap|pre|hen|sion +s
ap|pre|hen|sive
ap|pre|hen|sive|ly
ap|pre|hen|sive|
         ness
ap|pren|tice
  ap|pren|tices
  ap|pren|ticed
  ap|pren|ticing
ap|pren|tice|ship
  +s

ap|prise
  ap|prises
  ap|prised
  ap|pris|ing
  (inform)
ap|prize
  ap|prizes
  ap|prized
  ap|priz|ing
  (esteem highly;
  praise)
appro
ap|proach
  ap|proaches
  ap|proached
  ap|proach|ing
ap|proach|abil|ity
ap|proach|able
ap|pro|bate
  ap|pro|bates
  ap|pro|bated
  ap|pro|bat|ing
ap|pro|ba|tion
ap|pro|ba|tive
ap|pro|ba|tory
ap|pro|pri|ate
  ap|pro|pri|ates
  ap|pro|pri|ated
  ap|pro|pri|at|ing
ap|pro|pri|ate|ly
ap|pro|pri|ate|ness
ap|pro|pri|ation +s
ap|pro|pri|ation|ist
  +s
ap|pro|pria|tive
ap|pro|pri|ator +s
ap|prov|al +s
ap|prove
  ap|proves
  ap|proved
  ap|prov|ing
ap|prov|ing|ly
ap|proxi|mate
  ap|proxi|mates
  ap|proxi|mated
  ap|proxi|mat|ing
ap|proxi|mate|ly
ap|proxi|ma|tion
  +s
ap|proxi|ma|tive
ap|pur|ten|ance +s
ap|pur|ten|ant
après-ski
apri|cot +s
April (month;
  name)
April Fool +s
April Fool's Day
a pri|ori
apri|or|ism
apron +s
ap|roned

apron|ful +s
apron strings
apro|pos
apse +s
ap|sidal
apsis
  ap|si|des
apt +er +est
ap|ter|ous
ap|teryx
  ap|ter|yxes
ap|ti|tude +s
aptly
apt|ness
Apu|leius (Roman
  writer)
Apu|lia (region,
  Italy)
Aqaba (port,
  Jordan)
Aqaba, Gulf of
  (part of Red Sea)
aqua
aqua|cul|ture
aqua for|tis
aqua|lung +s
aqua|mar|ine +s
aqua|naut +s
aqua|plane
  aqua|planes
  aqua|planed
  aqua|plan|ing
aqua regia
aqua|relle +s
Aquar|ian +s
aqua|rist +s
aquar|ium
  aqua|ria *or*
  aquar|iums
Aquar|ius
  (constellation;
  sign of zodiac)
aqua|tic +s
aqua|tics
aqua|tint +s
aqua|vit
aqua vitae
aque|duct +s
aque|ous
aqui|fer +s
Aquila
  (constellation)
aqui|le|gia +s
aquil|ine
Aqui|nas, Thomas
  (Italian saint)
Aqui|taine (region,
  France)
Arab +s
Ara|bella
ar|ab|esque
ar|ab|esques

ar¦ab¦esque (*cont.*)
ar¦ab¦esqued
ar¦ab¦esquing
Ara¦bia
Ara|bian +s
Arab¦ic (language)
arab¦ic (numerals;
 in 'gum arabic')
arab¦ica +s
Arabi¦cise *Br.* (use
 Arabicize)
Arabi¦cises
Arabi¦cised
Arabi¦cis¦ing
Arabi¦cism +s
Arabi¦cize
Arabi¦cizes
Arabi¦cized
Arabi¦ciz¦ing
ar¦abis
Ar¦ab|ism +s
Arab-Israeli
 attributive
Arab|ist +s
ar¦able
Araby (Arabia)
Ara|cajú (port,
 Brazil)
Arachne *Greek
 Mythology*
arach|nid +s
arach|nid¦an +s
arach|noid +s
arach¦no|phobe +s
arach¦no|pho¦bia
Ara¦fat, Yas¦ser
 (Palestinian
 leader)
Ara¦fura Sea (north
 of Australia)
Ara¦gon (region,
 Spain)
arak (use arrack)
Ara¦kan (former
 name of Rakhine)
Ar¦al|dite *Propr.*
Aral Sea (in central
 Asia)
Ara|maean +s
Ara|maic
Aran (knitwear.
 △ Arran)
Ar¦anda
 plural Ar¦anda *or*
 Ar¦an|das
Aran Is¦lands (off
 the Republic of
 Ireland. △ Arran)
Ara|nyaka +s
 Hinduism
ara|paima +s

Ara¦rat, Mount
 (two volcanic
 peaks, Turkey)
aration|al
Arau|can¦ian +s
arau|caria +s
Ara¦wak
 plural Ara¦wak
arb +s
ar¦ba|lest +s
ar¦bi|ter +s
ar¦bi|ter
 ele¦gan¦tiae
ar¦bi|ter
 ele¦gan¦ti|arum
ar¦bi|trage
ar¦bi|trages
ar¦bi|traged
ar¦bi|tra¦ging
ar¦bi|trager +s (use
 arbitrageur)
ar¦bi|tra¦geur +s
ar¦bi|tral
ar¦bi|tra|ment +s
ar¦bi|trar¦ily
ar¦bi|trari|ness
ar¦bi|trary
ar¦bi|trate
ar¦bi|trates
ar¦bi|trated
ar¦bi|trat¦ing
ar¦bi|tra¦tion +s
ar¦bi|tra¦tor +s
ar¦bi|tra¦tor|ship
 +s
ar¦bi|tress
 ar¦bi|tresses
arb¦last +s
arbor +s (spindle.
 △ arbour)
arbor *Am.* +s
 (bower. *Br.*
 arbour)
ar¦bor|aceous
Arbor Day
ar¦bor|eal
ar¦bored *Am.* (*Br.*
 arboured)
ar¦bor|eous
ar¦bor|es¦cence
ar¦bor|es¦cent
ar¦bor|etum
 ar¦bor|eta *or*
 ar¦bor|etums
ar¦bori|cul¦tural
ar¦bori|cul¦ture
ar¦bori|cul¦tur|ist
 +s
ar¦bor|isa¦tion *Br.*
 (use arborization)
ar¦bor|iza¦tion
arbor vitae

ar¦bour *Br.* +s (*Am.*
 arbor. bower.
 △ arbor)
ar|boured *Br.* (*Am.*
 arbored)
arbo|virus
 arbo|viruses
Arbus, Diane
 (American
 photographer)
Ar¦buth|not, John
 (Scottish
 physician and
 writer)
ar¦bu|tus
 ar¦bu|tuses
arc +s +ed +ing
 (curve. △ ark)
ar¦cade +s
ar¦caded
Ar¦ca|dia (district,
 Greece; pastoral
 paradise)
Ar¦ca|dian +s (of
 Arcadia.
 △ Acadian,
 Akkadian)
Ar¦ca¦dian|ism
ar¦cad¦ing
Ar¦cady (pastoral
 paradise)
ar¦cane
ar¦cane¦ly
ar¦canum
 ar¦cana
Arc de Tri|omphe
 (in Paris)
arch
 arches
 arched
 arch|ing
Ar|chaean *Br.* (*Am.*
 Archean)
arch¦aeo|logic
arch¦aeo|logic¦al
arch¦aeo|logic|
 al¦ly
archae|olo¦gise *Br.*
 (use
 archaeologize)
archae|olo¦gises
archae|olo¦gised
archae|olo¦gis¦ing
archae|olo¦gist +s
archae|olo¦gize
 archae|olo¦gizes
 archae|olo¦gized
 archae|olo¦giz¦ing
archae|ology
arch¦aeo|mag¦net|
 ism

archae|op¦teryx
 archae|
 op¦ter¦yxes
ar|chaic
ar¦cha¦ic¦al¦ly
ar¦cha|ise *Br.* (use
 archaize)
ar¦cha|ises
ar¦cha|ised
ar¦cha|is¦ing
archa|ism +s
archa|ist +s
archa|is¦tic
archa|is¦tic|al¦ly
ar¦cha|ize
 ar¦cha|izes
 ar¦cha|ized
 ar¦cha|iz¦ing
Arch|an¦gel (port,
 Russia)
arch|an¦gel +s
arch|an¦gel¦ic
arch|bishop +s
arch|bish¦op|ric
 +s
arch|deacon +s
arch|deacon¦ry
 arch|deacon¦ries
arch|deacon|ship
 +s
arch|dio¦cesan
arch|dio¦cese +s
arch|ducal
arch|duch¦ess
 arch|duch¦esses
arch|duchy
 arch|duch¦ies
arch|duke +s
Ar|chean *Am.* (*Br.*
 Archaean)
arche|go¦nium
 arche|go¦nia
arch-enemy
 arch-enemies
archeo|logic *Am.*
 (*Br.*
 archaeologic)
archeo|logic¦al
 Am. (*Br.*
 archaeological)
archeo|logic|al¦ly
 Am. (*Br.*
 archaeologically)
arche|olo¦gist *Am.*
 +s (*Br.*
 archaeologist)
arche|olo¦gize *Am.*
 arche|olo¦gizes
 arche|olo¦gized
 arche|olo¦giz¦ing
 (*Br.*
 archaeologize)

arche|ology *Am.*
(*Br.* archaeology)
Arch|er, Jef|frey
(British writer and
politician)
Arch|er, the
(constellation;
sign of zodiac)
arch|er +s
arch|er fish
plural arch|er fish
arch|ery
arche|typal
arche|typ|al|ly
arche|type +s
arche|typ|ical
Archi|bald
archi|diac|onal
archi|diac|on|ate
+s
Ar|chie *also* Archy
archi|epis|copal
archi|epis|cop|ate
+s
ar|chil +s
Ar|chilo|chus
(Greek poet)
archi|man|drite +s
Archi|me|dean +s
Archi|me|des
(Greek
mathematician
and inventor)
Archi|me|des'
principle
archi|pel|ago +s
Archi|penko,
Alex|an|der
Por|fir|ye|vich
(Russian-born
American
sculptor)
Archi|piél|ago de
Colón (official
Spanish name for
the Galapagos
Islands)
archi|tect +s +ed
+ing
archi|tec|ton|ic
archi|tec|ton|ics
archi|tec|tural
archi|tec|tur|al|ly
archi|tec|ture +s
archi|trave +s
arch|ival
arch|ive +s
arch|iv|ist +s
archi|volt +s
arch|lute +s
arch|ly

arch|ness
ar|chon +s
ar|chon|ship +s
arch-rival +s
arch|way +s
Archy *also* Ar|chie
arc lamp +s
arc light +s
ar|cology
ar|colo|gies
Arc|tic (north polar
region)
arc|tic +s (very
cold; overshoe)
Arc|turus (star)
ar|cu|ate
arcus sen|ilis
arc weld|ing
Arden, Eliza|beth
(Canadian-born
American
businesswoman)
ar|dency
Ar|dennes (region,
NW Europe)
ar|dent
ar|dent|ly
Ard|na|mur|chan
(peninsula,
Scotland)
ardor *Am.* +s
ar|dour *Br.* +s
ar|du|ous
ar|du|ous|ly
ar|du|ous|ness
are +s (in 'we are'
etc.; unit. △ ah)
area +s
areal (pertaining to
area. △ aerial,
ariel)
area|way +s
areca +s
areg (plural of erg,
'sand dunes')
arena +s
ar|en|aceous
Ar|endt, Han|nah
(German-born
American
philosopher)
aren't (are not.
△ an't, aunt)
areola
areo|lae
areo|lar
Are|opa|gus (hill;
ancient Athenian
council)
Are|quipa (city,
Peru)

Ares (*Greek
Mythology.*
△ Aries)
arête +s
ar|gala +s
ar|gali
plural ar|gali
(sheep)
ar|gent
ar|gent|ifer|ous
Ar|gen|tina
Ar|gen|tine +s (of
Argentina;
Argentinian)
ar|gen|tine
(containing silver)
Ar|gen|tin|ian +s
argil
ar|gil|la|ceous
ar|gin|ine +s
Ar|give
Argo (constellation)
Argo (Jason's ship)
argol +s
argon
Ar|go|naut +s
(companion of
Jason)
ar|go|naut +s (sea
animal)
Argos (city, ancient
Greece. △ Argus)
ar|gosy
ar|gos|ies
argot +s
ar|gu|able
ar|gu|ably
argue
ar|gues
ar|gued
ar|gu|ing
ar|guer +s
ar|gufy
ar|gu|fies
ar|gu|fied
ar|gu|fy|ing
ar|gu|ment +s
ar|gu|men|ta|tion
ar|gu|men|ta|tive
ar|gu|
    men|ta|tive|ly
ar|gu|men|ta|tive|
            ness
ar|gu|men|tum e
    si|len|cio
Argus (*Greek
Mythology.*
△ Argos)
argus
ar|guses
(butterfly;
pheasant)

Argus-eyed
ar|gute
ar|gute|ly
argy-bargy
argy-bargies
argy-bargied
argy-bargying
Ar|gyll|shire
(former county,
Scotland)
Århus (use Aarhus)
aria +s
Ari|adne (name;
Greek Mythology)
Arian +s (of Arius.
△ Aryan)
Ar|ian|ism
arid
arid|ity
arid|ly
arid|ness
Ariel (spirit in *The
Tempest*; moon of
Uranus; name)
ariel +s (gazelle.
△ areal, aerial)
Ari|elle
Aries
(constellation;
sign of zodiac.
△ Ares)
aright
aril +s
aril|late
Arion (Greek poet
and musician)
ari|oso +s
Ari|osto,
Ludo|vico (Italian
poet)
arise
arises
arose
aris|ing
arisen
aris|ings
Ar|is|tar|chus
(Greek
astronomer; Greek
librarian and
commentator)
Ar|is|ti|des
(Athenian
statesman and
general)
Ar|is|tip|pus (two
Greek
philosophers)
ar|is|toc|racy
ar|is|toc|ra|cies
ar|is|to|crat +s
ar|is|to|crat|ic

ar¦is¦to¦crat¦ic¦
    al¦ly
Ar¦is¦topha¦nes
  (Greek dramatist)
Ar¦is¦to¦tel¦ian +s
Ar¦is¦totle (Greek
  philosopher)
Arita
arith¦met¦ic
arith¦met¦ic¦al
arith¦met¦ic¦al¦ly
arith¦met¦ician +s
Arius (Christian
  theologian and
  heretic)
Ari¦zona (state,
  USA)
Ar¦juna *Hinduism*
ark +s (*Judaism*;
  also in 'Noah's
  Ark'. △ arc)
Ar¦kan¦sas (state,
  USA)
Ark¦wright,
  Rich¦ard (English
  inventor and
  industrialist)
Ar¦lene
Arles (city, France)
Ar¦lette
Ar¦ling¦ton
  (national
  cemetery,
  Virginia; city,
  Texas)
Arlon (town,
  Belgium)
arm +s +ed +ing
ar¦mada +s
ar¦ma¦dillo +s
Ar¦ma¦ged¦don
Ar¦magh (district,
  Northern Ireland)
Ar¦mag¦nac +s
  (area, France;
  brandy)
ar¦ma¦ment +s
ar¦ma¦ment¦arium
  ar¦ma¦ment¦aria
Ar¦mani, Gior¦gio
  (Italian couturier)
ar¦ma¦ture +s
arm¦band +s
arm¦chair +s
Armco +s (crash
  barrier) *Propr.*
arme blanche
  armes blanches
Ar¦menia
Ar¦me¦nian +s (of
  Armenia.
  △ Arminian)

arm¦ful +s
arm¦hole +s
ar¦mi¦ger +s
ar¦mi¦ger¦ous
ar¦mil¦lary
  ar¦mil¦lar¦ies
arm in arm
Ar¦mi¦nian +s (of
  Arminius.
  △ Armenian)
Ar¦mi¦nian¦ism
Ar¦mi¦nius (Dutch
  theologian)
ar¦mis¦tice +s
arm¦less
arm¦let +s
arm¦load +s
arm¦lock +s +ed
  +ing
ar¦moire +s
armor *Am.* +s +ed
  +ing (*Br.* armour.
  △ amah)
ar¦mor¦er *Am.* +s
  (*Br.* armourer)
ar¦mor¦ial +s
ar¦mor¦ist +s
armor-plate *Am.*
  (*Br.* armour-
  plate)
armor-plated *Am.*
  (*Br.* armour-
  plated)
armor-plating *Am.*
  (*Br.* armour-
  plating)
ar¦mory
  ar¦mor¦ies
  (heraldry.
  △ armoury)
ar¦mory *Am.*
  ar¦mor¦ies
  (arsenal; weapons.
  Br. armoury)
ar¦mour *Br.* +s +ed
  +ing (*Am.* armor.
  △ amah)
ar¦mour¦er *Br.* +s
  (*Am.* armorer)
armour-plate *Br.*
  (*Am.* armor-plate)
armour-plated *Br.*
  (*Am.* armor-
  plated)
armour-plating *Br.*
  (*Am.* armor-
  plating)
ar¦moury *Br.*
  ar¦mour¦ies
  (*Am.* armory.
  arsenal.
  △ armory)

arm¦pit +s
arm¦rest +s
arms (weapons.
  △ alms)
Arm¦strong,
  Edwin How¦ard
  (American
  electrical
  engineer)
Arm¦strong, Louis
  (American jazz
  musician)
Arm¦strong, Neil
  (American
  astronaut)
arm-twisting
arm-wrestling
army
  ar¦mies
Arne, Thomas
  (English
  composer)
Arn¦hem (town, the
  Netherlands)
Arn¦hem Land
  (peninsula,
  Australia)
ar¦nica
Arno (river, Italy)
Ar¦nold
Ar¦nold, Mat¦thew
  (English writer)
aroid +s
aroma +s
aroma¦thera¦
      peut¦ic
aroma¦ther¦ap¦ist
  +s
aroma¦ther¦apy
aro¦mat¦ic +s
aro¦mat¦ic¦al¦ly
aroma¦ti¦city
aroma¦tisa¦tion *Br.*
  (use
  aromatization)
aroma¦tise *Br.* (use
  aromatize)
aroma¦tises
aroma¦tised
aroma¦tis¦ing
aroma¦tiza¦tion
aroma¦tize
aroma¦tizes
aroma¦tized
aroma¦tiz¦ing
arose
around
arous¦able
arousal
arouse
  arouses

arouse (*cont.*)
  aroused
  arous¦ing
arouser +s
Arp, Jean *also*
  Hans
  (French painter,
  sculptor, and
  poet)
ar¦peg¦gio +s
arque¦bus
  arque¦buses
ar¦rack
ar¦raign
  ar¦raigns
  ar¦raigned
  ar¦raign¦ing
ar¦raign¦ment +s
Arran (island,
  Scotland. △ Aran)
ar¦range
  ar¦ranges
  ar¦ranged
  ar¦ran¦ging
ar¦range¦able
ar¦range¦ment +s
ar¦ran¦ger +s
ar¦rant
ar¦rant¦ly
Arras (town,
  France)
arras
  ar¦rases
  (tapestry. △ arris)
Arrau, Clau¦dio
  (Chilean pianist)
array +s +ed +ing
ar¦rear +s
ar¦rear¦age +s
ar¦rest +s +ed +ing
ar¦rest¦able
ar¦rest¦ation
ar¦rest¦er +s
ar¦rest¦ing¦ly
ar¦rest¦ment +s
Ar¦rhen¦ius,
  Svante Au¦gust
  (Swedish chemist)
ar¦rhyth¦mia +s
arrière-pensée
  +s
arris
  ar¦rises
  (*Architecture*.
  △ arras)
ar¦rival +s
ar¦rive
  ar¦rives
  ar¦rived
  ar¦riv¦ing
ar¦riv¦isme
ar¦riv¦iste +s

ar¦ro|gance
ar¦ro|gancy
ar¦ro|gant
ar¦ro|gant¦ly
ar¦ro|gate
ar¦ro|gates
ar¦ro|gated
ar¦ro|gat¦ing
ar¦ro|ga¦tion
ar¦ron|disse|ment +s
Arrow, Ken|neth Jo|seph (American economist)
arrow +s +ed +ing
arrow-grass
ar¦row|head +s
ar¦row|root
arrow slit +s
arrow-worm +s
ar¦rowy
ar¦royo +s
arse Br. +s (coarse slang; Am. ass)
arse|hole Br. +s (coarse slang; Am. asshole)
arse-licker Br. +s (coarse slang; Am. ass-licker)
arse-licking Br. (coarse slang; Am. ass-licking)
ar¦senal +s
ar¦senic
ar¦sen|ic¦al
ar¦seni|ous
arses (plural of arse and arsis)
ars¦ine
arsis
arses
arson
ar¦son|ist +s
ars|phen|am¦ine +s
arsy-versy
Art (name)
art +s (creative skill etc.; in 'thou art')
Ar¦taud, An|tonin (French actor etc.)
Ar¦ta|xer¦xes (Persian kings)
art deco
arte|fact +s
arte|fac¦tual
artel
ar¦tels or ar¦teli
Ar¦te|mis (Greek Mythology; name)

ar¦te|misia +s
ar¦ter¦ial
ar¦teri|al|isa¦tion Br. (use arterialization)
ar¦teri|al|ise Br. (use arterialize)
ar¦teri|al|ises
ar¦teri|al|ised
ar¦teri|al|is¦ing
ar¦teri|al|iza¦tion
ar¦teri|al|ize
ar¦teri|al|izes
ar¦teri|al|ized
ar¦teri|al|iz¦ing
ar¦teri|ole +s
ar¦terio|scler|osis
ar¦terio|scler|oses
ar¦terio|scler|ot¦ic
ar¦ter|itis
ar¦tery
ar¦ter|ies
ar¦te|sian
Artex Propr.
art form +s
art¦ful
art¦ful¦ly
art¦ful|ness
art his|tor|ian +s
art-historical
art his¦tory
arth|rit¦ic +s
arth|ritis
arthro|pod +s
Ar¦thur
Ar¦thur (legendary king of Britain)
Ar¦thur, Ches¦ter Alan (American president)
Ar¦thur|ian +s
artic +s
ar¦ti|choke +s
art|icle
art|icles
art|icled
art|ic|ling
ar¦ticu|lacy
ar¦ticu|lar
ar¦ticu|late
ar¦ticu|lates
ar¦ticu|lated
ar¦ticu|lat¦ing
ar¦ticu|late¦ly
ar¦ticu|late|ness
ar¦ticu|la¦tion +s
ar¦ticu|la¦tor +s
ar¦ticu|la¦tory
ar¦ti|fact +s (use artefact)
ar¦ti|fac¦tual (use artefactual)

ar¦ti|fice +s
ar¦tifi|cer +s
ar¦ti|fi¦cial
ar¦ti|fi¦cial|ise Br. (use artificialize)
ar¦ti|fi¦cial|ises
ar¦ti|fi¦cial|ised
ar¦ti|fi¦cial|is¦ing
ar¦ti|fi¦ci¦al|ity
ar¦ti|fi¦ci¦al|ities
ar¦ti|fi¦cial|ize
ar¦ti|fi¦cial|izes
ar¦ti|fi¦cial|ized
ar¦ti|fi¦cial|iz¦ing
ar¦ti|fi¦cial|ly
ar¦til¦ler|ist +s
ar¦til|lery
ar¦til|ler|ies
ar¦til|lery|man
ar¦til|lery|men
arti|ness
artio|dac¦tyl +s
ar¦ti|san +s
ar¦ti|san|ate
art¦ist +s (painter)
ar¦tiste +s (performer)
art|is¦tic
art|is¦tic|al¦ly
art|is¦try
art|less
art|less¦ly
art|less|ness
art nou|veau
Ar¦tois (region, France)
artsy-fartsy
art|work +s
arty
art¦ier
arti|est
arty-crafty
arty-farty
Aruba (island, Caribbean)
aru|gula
arum +s
Ar¦un|achal Pra|desh (state, India)
Ar¦unta (= Aranda) plural Ar¦unta or Ar¦un|tas
arvo +s
Arya|bhata I (Indian astronomer and mathematician)
Aryan +s (peoples; language. △ Arian)
aryl +s

as preposition and conjunction
as
asses (Roman coin)
Asa
asa|foe¦tida
Asan|sol (city, India)
As¦ante (Twi name for Ashanti)
as¦best|ine
as¦bes¦tos
as¦bes¦tos|ine
as¦bes¦tosis
As¦ca|llon (ancient city, Israel, site of Ashqelon)
as¦carid +s
as¦caris
as¦cari|des (worm. △ askari)
as¦cend +s +ed +ing
as¦cend|ancy
as¦cend|an|cies
as¦cend|ant +s
as¦cend|er +s
As¦cen|sion (of Christ)
as¦cen|sion (generally)
as¦cen|sion|al
As¦cen|sion|tide
as¦cent +s (climb. △ assent)
as¦cen|tion|ist +s
as¦cer|tain +s +ed +ing
as¦cer|tain|able
as¦cer|tain|ment
as|cesis
as|ceses
as¦cet|ic +s
as¦cet|ic|al¦ly
as¦ceti|cism
As¦cham, Roger (English scholar)
as¦cid|ian +s
ASCII (= American Standard Code for Information Interchange)
as¦ci|tes plural as|ci¦tes
As|cle¦piad +s
As|cle¦pius Greek Mythology
as¦cor|bic
Ascot (racecourse, England)
ascrib|able

ascribe
ashes
ashed
ascribing
ascrip|tion +s
asdic
ASEAN
(= Association of
South East Asian
Nations)
ase|ity
asep|sis
asep|tic
asex|ual
a..exu|al|ity
asexu|al|ly
As|gard *Norse
Mythology*
ASH (= Action on
Smoking and
Health)
ash
ashes
ashamed
ashamed|ly
Ash|anti (region,
Ghana)
Ash|anti
plural Ash|anti
(people)
ash blonde +s
ash|can +s
Ash|croft, Peggy
(English actress)
Ash|dod (port,
Israel)
Ash|down, Paddy
(British politician)
Ashe, Ar|thur
(American tennis
player)
ashen
ashen-faced
Asher *Bible*
ashet +s
Ash|ga|bat (capital
of Turkmenistan)
Ash|ke|lon (ancient
Philistine city, site
of modern
Ashqelon)
Ash|ken|azi
Ash|ken|azim
Ash|ken|az|ic
Ash|ken|azy,
Vlad|imir
(Russian-born
Icelandic pianist)
ash-key +s
Ash|kha|bad
(use
Ashgabat)

ash|lar
ash|lar|ing
Ash|ley (name)
Ash|ley, Laura
(Welsh fashion
and textile
designer)
Ash|molean
Mu|seum (in
Oxford)
Ash|more and
Car|tier Is|lands
(in Indian Ocean)
ashore
ash|pan
ash|plant +s
Ash|qe|lon (resort,
Israel)
ash|ram +s
ash|rama +s
Hinduism
Ash|ton,
Fred|erick
(British dancer
and
choreographer)
ash|tray +s
Ashur (alternative
name for Assur)
Ashur|bani|pal
(Assyrian king)
ash|wood
ashy
ash|ier
ashi|est
Asia
Asia Minor
Asian +s
Asi|at|ic +s
(*offensive* when
used of people;
prefer Asian)
A-side +s
aside +s
Asi|mov, Isaac
(Russian-born
American writer)
as|in|ine
as|in|in|ity
Asir Moun|tains
(in Saudi Arabia)
ask +s +ed +ing
askance
as|kari
plural as|kari *or*
as|karis
(E. African soldier
or policeman.
⚠ ascaris)
asker +s
askew
aslant

asleep
Aslef (= Associated
Society of
Locomotive
Engineers and
Firemen)
AS level +s
aslope
As|mara (capital of
Eritrea)
As|mera
(alternative name
for Asmara)
aso|cial
aso|cial|ly
Asoka (Indian
emperor)
asp +s
as|para|gine
as|para|gus
as|par|tame
as|par|tic
as|pect +s
as|pect|ed
as|pect|ual
Aspen (city, USA)
aspen +s (tree)
as|per|gil|lum
as|per|gilla *or*
as|per|gil|lums
as|per|ity
as|perse
as|perses
as|persed
as|pers|ing
as|per|sion +s
as|per|sor|ium
as|per|soria
as|phalt
as|phalt|er +s
as|phal|tic
as|pho|del +s
as|phyxia
as|phyx|ial
as|phyxi|ant +s
as|phyxi|ate
as|phyxi|ates
as|phyxi|ated
as|phyxi|at|ing
as|phyxi|ation
as|phyxi|ator +s
aspic
as|pi|dis|tra +s
as|pir|ant +s
as|pir|ate
as|pir|ates
as|pir|ated
as|pir|at|ing
as|pir|ation +s
as|pir|ation|al
as|pir|ator +s

as|pire
as|pires
as|pired
as|pir|ing
as|pirin
plural as|pirin *or*
as|pir|ins
as|plen|ium
asquint
As|quith, Her|bert
Henry (British
prime minister)
ass
asses
(donkey)
ass *Am.*
asses
(*coarse slang*
buttocks; *Br.* arse)
Assad, Hafiz al-
(Syrian Baath
statesman)
as|sa|gai +s (use
assegai)
assai
as|sail +s +ed +ing
as|sail|able
as|sail|ant +s
Assam (state, India;
tea)
As|sam|ese
plural As|sam|ese
as|sas|sin +s
as|sas|sin|ate
as|sas|sin|ates
as|sas|sin|ated
as|sas|sin|at|ing
as|sas|sin|ation +s
as|sas|sin|ator +s
as|sault +s +ed
+ing
as|sault|er +s
as|sault|ive
assay +s +ed +ing
as|say|able
as|se|gai +s
as|sem|blage
as|sem|ble
as|sem|bles
as|sem|bled
as|sem|bling
as|sem|bler +s
as|sem|bly
as|sem|blies
as|sem|bly line +s
as|sem|bly|man
as|sem|bly|men
as|sent +s +ed
+ing (agree.
⚠ ascent)

as|sent|er +s
  (person who
  assents)
as|sen|tient
as|sent|or +s (in
  nomination of
  candidate)
as|sert +s +ed
  +ing
as|sert|er +s (use
  assertor)
as|ser|tion +s
as|sert|ive
as|sert|ive|ly
as|sert|ive|ness
as|sert|or +s
asses (plural of as
  and ass)
asses' bridge
as|sess
  as|sesses
  as|sessed
  as|sess|ing
as|sess|able
as|sess|ment +s
as|ses|sor +s
as|ses|sor|ial
asset +s
asset-strip
  asset-strips
  asset-stripped
  asset-stripping
asset-stripper +s
as|sev|er|ate
  as|sev|er|ates
  as|sev|er|ated
  as|sev|er|at|ing
as|sev|er|ation +s
ass|hole Am. +s
  (coarse slang; Br.
  arsehole)
as|sibi|late
  as|sibi|lates
  as|sibi|lated
  as|sibi|lat|ing
as|sibi|la|tion
as|si|du|ity
as|sidu|ous
as|sidu|ous|ly
as|sidu|ous|ness
as|sign +s +ed
  +ing
as|sign|able
as|sig|na|tion +s
as|sign|ee +s
as|sign|er +s
as|sign|ment +s
as|sign|or +s Law
as|sim|il|able
as|simi|late
  as|simi|lates

as|simi|late (cont.)
  as|simi|lated
  as|simi|lat|ing
as|simi|la|tion +s
as|simi|la|tion|ist
  +s
as|simi|la|tive
as|simi|la|tor +s
as|simi|la|tory
As|sisi (town, Italy)
as|sist +s +ed +ing
as|sist|ance
as|sist|ant +s
as|sist|er +s
as|size +s
ass-kissing Am.
ass-licker Am. +s
  (coarse slang; Br.
  arse-licker)
ass-licking Am.
  (coarse slang; Br.
  arse-licking)
as|so|ci|abil|ity
as|so|ci|able
as|so|ci|ate
  as|so|ci|ates
  as|so|ci|ated
  as|so|ci|at|ing
as|so|ci|ate|ship
  +s
as|so|ci|ation +s
as|so|ci|ation|al
As|so|ci|ation
  Foot|ball
as|so|ci|ation|ist
  +s
as|so|cia|tive
as|so|cia|tor +s
as|so|cia|tory
as|soil +s +ed +ing
as|son|ance +s
as|son|ant +s
as|son|ate
  as|son|ates
  as|son|ated
  as|son|at|ing
as|sort +s +ed
  +ing
as|sorta|tive
as|sort|ment +s
as|suage
  as|suages
  as|suaged
  as|sua|ging
as|suage|ment
as|sua|ger +s
As
  Su|lay|man|iyah
  (full name of
  Sulaymaniyah)
as|sum|able

as|sume
  as|sumes
  as|sumed
  as|sum|ing
as|sumed|ly
As|sump|tion (of
  Virgin Mary)
as|sump|tion +s
  (act of assuming
  etc.)
as|sump|tive
Assur (ancient city-
  state of
  Mesopotamia)
as|sur|able
as|sur|ance +s
as|sure
  as|sures
  as|sured
  as|sur|ing
as|sured|ly
as|sured|ness
as|surer +s
As|syria
As|syr|ian +s
As|syri|olo|gist +s
As|syri|ology
astable
As|taire, Fred
  (American dancer
  etc.)
As|tarte Semitic
  Mythology
astat|ic
as|ta|tine
aster +s
as|ter|isk
  as|ter|isks
  as|ter|isked
  as|ter|isk|ing
as|ter|ism
As|terix (cartoon
  character)
astern
as|ter|oid +s
as|ter|oid|al
as|the|nia
as|then|ic +s
as|theno|sphere
asthma
asth|mat|ic +s
asth|mat|ic|al|ly
Asti +s (wine)
astig|matic
astig|ma|tism
as|tilbe +s
astir
Asti spu|mante
Aston, Fran|cis
  Wil|liam (British
  physicist)

as|ton|ish
  as|ton|ishes
  as|ton|ished
  as|ton|ish|ing
as|ton|ish|ing|ly
as|ton|ish|ment +s
Astor, Nancy
  (Lady Astor,
  American-born
  British politician)
as|tound +s +ed
  +ing
as|tound|ing|ly
astrad|dle
As|traea (Roman
  Mythology;
  asteroid)
as|tra|gal +s
as|trag|alus
  as|trag|ali
As|tra|khan (city,
  Russia)
as|tra|khan (fleece)
as|tral
astray
As|trid
astride
astrin|gency
  astrin|gen|cies
astrin|gent +s
astrin|gent|ly
astro|biol|ogy
astro|bot|any
astro|chem|is|try
astro|dome +s
astro|hatch
  astro|hatches
as|troid +s
astro|labe +s
as|trol|oger +s
astro|logic
astro|logic|al
astro|logic|al|ly
as|trol|ogy
astro|naut +s
astro|naut|ic|al
astro|naut|ics
as|tron|omer +s
astro|nom|ic
astro|nom|ic|al
astro|nom|ic|al|ly
as|tron|omy
astro|phys|ic|al
astro|physi|cist +s
astro|phys|ics
Astro|Turf Propr.
As|tur|ias (region,
  Spain)
As|tur|ias,
  Ma|nuel Ángel
  (Guatemalan
  writer)

as¦tute
as¦tute¦ly
as¦tute¦ness
Asun|ción (capital of Paraguay)
asun|der
Asur (use Assur)
asura +s
Aswan (city and dam, Egypt)
asy¦lum +s
asym|met¦ric
asym|met¦ric|al
asym|met¦ric|al¦ly
asym|metry
asym|met¦ries
asymp¦tom|at¦ic
asymp|tote +s
asymp|tot¦ic
asymp|tot¦ic|al¦ly
asyn|chron|ous
asyn|chron|ous¦ly
asyn|det¦ic
asyn|deton
asyn|deta
at
At¦ab|rine Propr.
Ata|cama Des¦ert (in Chile)
Ata|lanta Greek Mythology
at¦ar|ac¦tic
at¦ar|axia
at¦ar|axic
at¦ar|axy
Ata|türk, Kemal (Turkish general and statesman)
at¦av|ism
at¦av|is¦tic
at¦av|is¦tic|al¦ly
ataxia
ataxic
ataxy
at bat +s Baseball
ate (past tense of eat. △ ait, eight)
A-team +s
At¦eb|rin Propr.
atel|ier +s
a tempo
Aten Egyptian Mythology
Atha|basca, Lake (in Canada)
Atha|bas|can +s (use Athapaskan)
Atha|na¦sian +s
Athan¦as|ius
Atha|pas|kan +s
Atharva-veda Hinduism

athe|ism
athe|ist +s
athe|is¦tic
athe|is¦tic|al
athel|ing +s
Athel|stan (Anglo-Saxon king)
athem|at¦ic
Athen|aeum (temple; London club)
athen|aeum Br. +s (institution; library. Am. atheneum)
Athe¦ne Greek Mythology
athen|eum Am. +s (institution; library. Br. athenaeum)
Athen|ian +s
Ath¦ens (capital of Greece)
ath¦ero|scler|osis
ath¦ero|scler|oses
ath¦ero|scler|ot¦ic
Ather|ton Table|land (in Australia)
athirst
ath|lete +s
ath|lete's foot
ath|let¦ic
ath|let¦ic|al¦ly
ath|leti|cism
ath|let¦ics
at-home +s noun
Athos, Mount (in Greece)
athwart
atilt
At¦kin|son, Harry (New Zealand prime minister)
At|lanta (city, USA)
At|lan|tean +s
at|lan|tes
At|lan|tic (Ocean)
At|lan|ti|cism
At|lan|ti|cist +s
At|lan|tis (legendary island)
Atlas Greek Mythology
atlas
at¦lases (book; bone)
Atlas Moun|tains (in N. Africa)
atman

at¦mos|phere +s
at¦mos|pher¦ic
at¦mos|pher¦ic|al
at¦mos|pher¦ic| al¦ly
at¦mos|pher¦ics
atoll +s
atom +s
atom bomb +s
atom¦ic
atom¦ic|al¦ly
atom¦ic|ity
atom|isa¦tion Br. (use atomization)
atom|ise Br. (use atomize)
atom|ises
atom|ised
atom|is¦ing
atom|iser Br. +s (use atomizer)
atom|ism
atom|ist +s
atom|is¦tic
atom|is¦tic|al¦ly
atom|iza¦tion
atom|ize
atom|izes
atom|ized
atom|iz¦ing
atom|izer +s
atom smash¦er +s
atomy
atom|ies
Aton (use Aten)
atonal
aton|al|ity
aton|al¦ly
atone
atones
atoned
aton¦ing
atone|ment +s
atonic
atony
atop
atra|bili¦ous
At¦reus Greek Mythology
at¦rial
at¦rium
atria or at|riums
atro|cious
atro|cious¦ly
atro|cious|ness
atro¦city
atro¦ci|ties
at¦ro|phy
at¦ro|phies
at¦ro|phied
at¦ro|phy|ing
at¦ro|pine

At¦ro|pos Greek Mythology
at¦ta|boy
at¦tach
at|taches
at|tached
at|tach|ing
at|tach|able
at|taché +s
at|taché case +s
at|tach¦er +s
at|tach|ment +s
at¦tack +s +ed +ing
at|tack¦er +s
at¦tain +s +ed +ing
at¦tain|abil¦ity
at¦tain|able
at¦tain|able|ness
at¦tain|der +s
at¦tain|ment +s
at¦taint
At¦ta|lid +s
attar +s
at¦tem|per +s +ed +ing
at¦tempt +s +ed +ing
at¦tempt|able
At¦ten|bor|ough, David (British naturalist)
At¦ten|bor|ough, Rich|ard (British film director etc.)
at¦tend +s +ed +ing
at¦tend|ance +s
at¦tend|ant +s
at¦tend|ee +s
at¦tend¦er +s
at¦ten|tion +s
at¦ten|tion|al
at¦ten|tive
at¦ten|tive¦ly
at¦ten|tive|ness
at¦tenu|ate
at¦tenu|ates
at¦tenu|ated
at¦tenu|at¦ing
at¦tenu|ation
at¦tenu|ator +s
at¦test +s +ed +ing
at|test|able
at|test|ation
at|test|or +s
Attic (of Attica; language)
attic +s (room in roof)

At¦tica
(promontory,
Greece)
at¦ti¦cism
At¦tila (king of the
Huns)
at¦tire
at¦tires
at¦tired
at¦tir¦ing
Attis *Anatolian
Mythology*
at¦ti¦tude +s
at¦ti¦tu¦dinal
at¦ti¦tu¦din¦ise *Br.*
(use attitudinize)
at¦ti¦tu¦din¦ises
at¦ti¦tu¦din¦ised
at¦ti¦tu¦din¦is¦ing
at¦ti¦tu¦din¦ize
at¦ti¦tu¦din¦izes
at¦ti¦tu¦din¦ized
at¦ti¦tu¦din¦iz¦ing
Att¦lee, Clem¦ent
(British prime
minister)
atto¦meter *Am.* +s
atto¦metre *Br.* +s
at¦tor¦ney +s
Attorney-General
Attorneys-
General *or*
Attorney-
Generals
at¦torney¦ship +s
at¦tract +s +ed
+ing
at¦tract¦able
at¦tract¦ant +s
at¦trac¦tion +s
at¦tract¦ive
at¦tract¦ive¦ly
at¦tract¦ive¦ness
at¦tract¦or +s
at¦trib¦ut¦able
at¦trib¦ut¦able¦
        ness
at¦trib¦ut¦ably
at¦tri¦bute +s *noun*
at¦trib¦ute
at¦trib¦utes
at¦trib¦uted
at¦trib¦ut¦ing
verb
at¦tri¦bu¦tion +s
at¦tribu¦tive
at¦tribu¦tive¦ly
at¦trit
at¦trits
at¦trit¦ted
at¦trit¦ting
at¦tri¦tion

at¦tri¦tion¦al
at¦tune
at¦tunes
at¦tuned
at¦tun¦ing
At¦wood,
Mar¦ga¦ret
(Canadian writer)
atyp¦ical
atyp¦ic¦al¦ly
au¦bade +s
au¦berge +s
au¦ber¦gine +s
Au¦beron
Aub¦rey (name)
Aub¦rey, John
(English
antiquarian and
writer)
au¦brie¦tia +s
au¦burn +s
Au¦bus¦son +s
(town, France;
tapestry)
Auck¦land (city,
New Zealand)
au cour¦ant
auc¦tion +s +ed
+ing
auc¦tion¦eer +s
auc¦tion¦eer¦ing
auc¦tion house +s
au¦da¦cious
au¦da¦cious¦ly
au¦da¦cious¦ness
au¦da¦city
Auden, W. H.
(British poet)
Au¦den¦arde
(French name for
Oudenarde)
Audh (use Oudh)
audi¦bil¦ity
aud¦ible
aud¦ible¦ness
aud¦ibly
audi¦ence +s
aud¦ile +s
audio +s
audio-animatron
+s
audio-
animatron¦ic
Propr.
Audio-
Animatron¦ics
Propr.
audio cas¦sette +s
audi¦olo¦gist +s
audi¦ology
audi¦om¦eter +s
audi¦om¦etry

audio¦phile +s
audio¦tape +s
audio typ¦ist +s
audio-visual
audit +s +ed +ing
au¦di¦tion +s +ed
+ing
audi¦tive
au¦dit¦or +s
audi¦tor¦ial
audi¦tor¦ium
audi¦tor¦iums *or*
  audi¦toria
audi¦tory
Audra
Aud¦rey
Au¦du¦bon, John
James (American
naturalist and
artist)
Auer von
Wels¦bach, Carl
(Austrian chemist)
au fait
au fond
Au¦gean
Au¦geas *Greek
Mythology*
auger +s (tool.
  △ augur)
aught (anything.
  △ ought)
aug¦ite +s
aug¦ment +s +ed
+ing
aug¦men¦ta¦tion +s
aug¦men¦ta¦tive
aug¦ment¦er +s
Au¦gra¦bies Falls
(in South Africa)
au grand séri¦eux
au gra¦tin
Augs¦burg (city,
Germany)
augur +s +ed +ing
(portend;
interpreter of
omens. △ auger)
au¦gural
au¦gury
au¦gur¦ies
Au¦gust +s (month)
au¦gust (venerable)
Au¦gusta (cities,
USA; name)
Au¦gust¦an +s
Au¦gust¦ine (Italian
saint)
Au¦gust¦ine +s
(friar)

Au¦gust¦ine of
Hippo (N. African-
born saint)
Au¦gust¦in¦ian +s
au¦gust¦ly
au¦gust¦ness
Au¦gus¦tus (Roman
emperor; name)
auk +s (bird. △ orc)
auk¦let +s
auld
auld lang syne
aulic
aum¦bry
aum¦bries
au nat¦urel
Aung San
(Burmese
nationalist leader)
Aung San Suu Kyi
(Burmese political
leader, daughter of
Aung San)
aunt +s (parent's
sister. △ an't,
aren't)
Auntie (= BBC)
auntie +s (aunt)
Aunt Sally
Aunt Sal¦lies
(game)
aunty (use auntie)
aunt¦ies
au pair +s
aura
auras *or* aurae
aural (of the ear.
  △ oral)
aur¦al¦ly
Aur¦ang¦zeb
(Mogul emperor
of Hindustan)
aure¦ate
Aur¦elia
Aur¦elian (Roman
emperor)
aur¦elian +s
(lepidopterist)
Aur¦elius, Mar¦cus
(Roman emperor)
aure¦ola +s
aure¦ole +s
aureo¦my¦cin
au re¦voir +s
Auric, Georges
(French
composer)
auric (of trivalent
gold)
aur¦icle +s
aur¦ic¦ula +s
aur¦icu¦lar

aur|icu|lar|ly
aur|icu|late
aur|if|er|ous
Aur|iga
(constellation)
Aur|ig|na|cian +s
auri|scope +s
aur|ist +s
aur|ochs
  plural aur|ochs
Aur|ora (Roman
  Mythology; name)
aur|ora
  aur|oras or
  aur|orae
  (atmospheric
  lights)
aur|ora aus|tralis
aur|ora bor|ealis
aur|oral
Ausch|witz
  (concentration
  camp, Poland)
aus|cul|ta|tion
aus|cul|ta|tory
au séri|eux
aus|pi|cate
  aus|pi|cates
  aus|pi|cated
  aus|pi|cat|ing
aus|pice +s
aus|pi|cious
aus|pi|cious|ly
aus|pi|cious|ness
Aus|sie +s
Aus|ten, Jane
  (English novelist)
aus|tere
  aus|terer
  aus|terest
aus|tere|ly
aus|ter|ity
  aus|ter|ities
Aus|ter|litz (battle
  site, Czech
  Republic)
Aus|tin (city, USA;
  name)
Aus|tin +s (friar)
Aus|tin, Her|bert
  (British car maker)
Aus|tin, John
  (English jurist)
Aus|tin, John
  Lang|shaw
  (English
  philospher)
Aus|tral (of
  Australia or
  Australasia)
aus|tral (southern)
Austra|lasia

Austra|la|sian +s
Aus|tra|lia
Aus|tra|lian +s
Aus|tra|li|ana
Aus|tra|lian|ise Br.
  (use
  Australianize)
Aus|tra|lian|ises
Aus|tra|lian|ised
Aus|tra|lian|is|ing
Aus|tra|lian|ism
  +s
Aus|tra|lian|ize
  Aus|tra|lian|izes
  Aus|tra|lian|ized
  Aus|tra|lian|iz|ing
Aus|tra|lian Rules
Austral|oid +s
aus|tralo|
    pith|ecine +s
*Aus|tralo|pith|ecus
Aus|tria
Austria–Hungary
Aus|trian +s
Austro-Hungar|ian
Austro|nes|ian +s
aut|arch|ic
aut|arch|ic|al
aut|archy (absolute
  sovereignty.
  ⚠ autarky)
aut|ark|ic
aut|ark|ic|al
aut|ark|ist +s
aut|arky (self-
  sufficiency.
  ⚠ autarchy)
au|teur +s
au|teur|ism
au|teur|ist
au|then|tic +s
au|then|tic|al|ly
au|then|ti|cate
  au|then|ti|cates
  au|then|ti|cated
  au|then|ti|cat|ing
au|then|ti|ca|tion
  +s
au|then|ti|ca|tor
  +s
au|then|ti|city
author +s +ed
  +ing
author|ess
  author|esses
au|thor|ial
au|thor|isa|tion Br.
  (use
  authorization)
au|thor|ise Br. (use
  authorize)
au|thor|ises

au|thor|ise (cont.)
  au|thor|ised
  au|thor|is|ing
au|thori|tar|ian +s
au|thori|tar|ian|
                ism
au|thori|ta|tive
au|thori|ta|tive|ly
au|thori|ta|tive|
                ness
au|thor|ity
  au|thor|ities
au|thor|iza|tion
au|thor|ize
  au|thor|izes
  au|thor|ized
  au|thor|iz|ing
author|ship
aut|ism
aut|is|tic
auto +s
auto|bahn +s
auto|biog|raph|er
  +s
auto|bio|graph|ic
auto|bio|graph|
              ic|al
auto|biog|raphy
auto|
      biog|raph|ies
auto|cade +s
auto|car +s
auto|cata|lyst +s
auto|ceph|al|ous
au|toch|thon
  au|toch|thons or
  au|toch|thones
au|toch|thon|al
au|toch|thon|ic
au|toch|thon|ous
auto|clave +s
auto|code +s
au|toc|racy
  au|toc|ra|cies
auto|crat +s
auto|crat|ic
auto|crat|ic|al|ly
auto|cross
auto|cue +s Propr.
auto|cycle +s
auto-da-fé +s
auto|didact +s
auto|didac|tic
auto-erotic
auto-eroticism
auto-erotism
auto|focus
au|tog|am|ous
au|tog|amy
auto|gen|ic
au|togen|ous
auto|giro +s

auto|graft +s
auto|graph +s +ed
  +ing
auto|graph|ic
aut|og|raphy
auto|gyro +s (use
  autogiro)
auto|harp +s
auto|immune
auto|immun|ity
auto|intoxi|ca|tion
au|toly|sis
auto|lyt|ic
auto|mat +s
auto|mate
  auto|mates
  auto|mated
  auto|mat|ing
auto|mat|ic +s
auto|mat|ic|al|ly
auto|ma|ti|city
auto|ma|tion
au|toma|tisa|tion
  Br. (use
  automatization)
au|toma|tise Br.
  (use automatize)
  au|toma|tises
  au|toma|tised
  au|toma|tis|ing
au|toma|tism
au|toma|tiza|tion
auto|ma|tize
  auto|ma|tizes
  auto|ma|tized
  auto|ma|tiz|ing
au|toma|ton
  au|toma|tons or
  au|tom|ata
auto|mo|bile +s
auto|mo|tive
auto|nomic
au|tono|mist +s
au|tono|mous
au|tono|mous|ly
au|ton|omy
  au|ton|omies
auto|pilot +s
auto|pista +s
auto|poly|ploid +s
auto|poly|ploidy
aut|opsy
  aut|op|sies
  aut|op|sied
  aut|opsy|ing
auto|radio|graph
auto|radio|
          graph|ic
auto|radi|og|raphy
auto|rotate
  auto|rotates

auto|rotate (*cont.*)
auto|rotated
auto|rotat|ing
auto|rota'tion +s
auto|route +s
auto|strada
auto|stra|das
auto-suggestion
auto|tel|ic
au|tot|omy
auto|toxic
auto|toxin +s
auto|troph|ic
auto|type +s
aut|oxi|da'tion
au'tumn +s
au'tum|nal
Au|vergne (region, France)
aux|an|ometer +s
aux|il'iary
aux|il'iar|ies
auxin +s
Av (alternative name for Ab)
Ava
ava|da|vat +s
avail +s +ed +ing
avail|abil'ity
avail|abil'ities
avail|able
avail|able|ness
avail|ably
ava|lanche
ava|lanches
ava|lanched
ava|lanch|ing
Ava'lon (in Arthurian Legend)
avant-garde +s
avant-gardism
avant-gardist +s
Avar +s
avar|ice
avar|icious
avar|icious|ly
avar|icious|ness
avast
ava'tar +s
avaunt
Ave +s (prayer)
ave +s (welcome; farewell)
Ave|bury (village and ancient monument, England)
avenge
avenges
avenged
aven|ging
aven|ger +s

avens
plural avens
aven'tur|ine
av'enue +s
aver
avers
averred
aver|ring
aver|age
aver|ages
aver|aged
aver|aging
aver|age|ly
aver|ment
Aver|nus (lake, Italy)
Aver|roës (Islamic philosopher)
averse
aver|sion +s
aver|sive
avert +s +ed +ing
avert|able (use avertible)
avert|ible
Avery
Avesta
Aves|tan
Aves|tic +s
av'go|lem'ono
avian +s
avi'ary
avi|ar|ies
avi'ate
avi|ates
avi|ated
avi|at|ing
avi|ation
avi|ator +s
avia|trix
avi|at|ri|ces
female
Avi|cenna (Islamic philosopher and physician)
avi|cul'ture
avi|cul'tur|ist +s
avid
avid|ity
avid|ly
Avie|more (resort, Scotland)
avi|fauna
avi|faunal
Avi|gnon (city, France)
Ávila, Ter'esa of (Spanish saint)
avi|on'ics
avit|amin|osis
avit|amin|oses
aviz|an|dum

avo|cado +s
avo|ca'tion
avo'cet +s
Avo|gadro, Ama|deo (Italian physicist)
avoid +s +ed +ing
avoid|able
avoid|ably
avoid|ance
avoid|er +s
avoir|du'pois
Avon (county and rivers, England)
avouch
avouches
avouched
avouch|ing
avouch|ment +s
avow +s +ed +ing
avow|able
avow'al +s
avow|ed|ly
Avril
avul|sion +s
avun'cu|lar
AWACS
plural AWACS
(= airborne warning and control system)
Awadh (= Oudh)
await +s +ed +ing
awake
awakes
awoke
awak|ing
awoken
awaken +s +ed +ing
award +s +ed +ing
award'er +s
award-winning
attributive
aware
aware|ness
aware|nesses
awash
away
awe
awes
awed
awing
aweary
aweigh
awe-inspir|ing
awe|some
awe|some|ly
awe|some|ness
awe|stricken
awe|struck
awful

aw|ful|ly
aw'ful|ness
awheel
awhile
awk|ward
awk|ward|ly
awk|ward|ness
awk|ward|nesses
awl +s (tool. △ all, orle)
awn +s
awned
awn|ing +s
awoke
awoken
AWOL (= absent without leave)
aw-shucks
adjective
ax *Am.*
axes
axed
axing
axe *Br.*
axes
axed
axing
axe-breaker +s
axel +s (skating movement. △ axil, axle)
axe|man *Br.*
axe|men
(*Am.* axman)
axes (plural of ax, axe, and axis)
axial
axi|al'ity
axi|al'ly
axil +s (angle between leaf and stem. △ axel, axle)
ax'illa
ax'il|lae
ax'il|lary
axio|logic'al
axi|olo|gist +s
axi|ology
axiom +s
axio|mat'ic
axio|mat'ic|al'ly
Axis (German alliance)
axis
axes
axle +s (spindle connecting wheels. △ axel, axil)
axled

axle-tree +s
axman *Am.*
  axmen
  (*Br.* axeman)
Ax¦min|ster +s
  (town, England;
  carpet)
axo|lotl +s
axon +s
axono|met¦ric
Axum (use Aksum)
ay +s (yes; vote;
  use aye. △ eye, I)
Aya|cucho (city,
  Peru)
ayah +s (nurse.
  △ ire)
aya¦tol|lah +s
Aya¦tol|lah
  Kho|meini
  (Iranian Shiite
  Muslim leader)
Ayck|bourn, Alan
  (English
  playwright)
aye +s (yes; vote.
  △ eye, I)
aye (always. △ eh)
aye aye (*Nautical*
  yes)
aye-aye +s (lemur)
Ayer, A. J. (English
  philosopher)
Ayers Rock (in
  Australia)
Ayles|bury +s
  (town, England;
  duck)
Ay¦mara
  plural Ay¦mara *or*
  Ay|maras
Ayr (town,
  Scotland)
Ayr|shire +s
  (former county,
  Scotland; cattle)
Ayub Khan,
  Mu¦ham|mad
  (Pakistani soldier
  and president)
ayur|veda
ayur|vedic
Azad Kash|mir
  (state, Pakistan)
aza¦lea +s
Aza¦nia (South
  Africa)
azeo|trope +s
azeo|trop¦ic
Azer|bai|jan
Azer|bai|jani +s
Azeri +s

azide +s
azido|thy¦mid¦ine
Azi|kiwe, Nnamdi
  (Nigerian
  statesman)
Azil|ian
azi|muth +s
azi|muth¦al
azine +s
azo dye +s
azoic
Azores (island
  group, N. Atlantic)
Azov, Sea of
  (north of Black
  Sea)
Az¦rael
Aztec +s
azuki +s
azure +s
azy|gous
Az Zarqa
  (alternative name
  for Zarqa)

Bb

baa
  baas
  baaed *or* baa'd
  baa¦ing
  (bleat. △ bah, bar,
  barre)
Baade, Wal¦ter
  (German-born
  physicist)
Baader-Meinhof
  (terrorist group)
Baa¦gan|dji
Baal (ancient god)
baa-lamb +s
Baal|bek (town,
  Lebanon)
Baal|ism
baas
  baases
baas|skap
Baath|ism
Baath|ist +s
Baath Party (Arab
  political party.
  △ Bath)
baba +s (in 'rum
  baba')
baba|coote +s
Bab|bage, Charles
  (English
  mathematician)
Bab|bitt +s (metal;
  complacent
  business man)
Bab|bitt, Mil¦ton
  (American
  composer)
bab|bitt +s
  (bearing-lining)
Bab|bitt¦ry
bab|ble
  bab|bles
  bab|bled
  bab|bling
babble|ment
bab|bler +s
bab|bling +s
babe +s
Babel, Tower of
  Bible
babel (scene of
  confusion)
Babi +s
babi|roussa +s
  (use babirusa)
babi|rusa +s
Bab|ism

Bab¦ist +s
  (adherent of
  Babism. △ Barbie)
ba¦boon +s
Ba|bru¦isk (city,
  Belarus)
Babs
babu +s
Babur (Mogul
  emperor of India)
ba|bushka +s
Babu|yan Is¦lands
  (in Philippines)
baby
  ba¦bies
  ba¦bied
  baby|ing
baby blue +s *noun
  and adjective*
baby-blue
  attributive
baby boom +s
baby boom¦er +s
baby boun|cer +s
baby buggy
  baby bug|gies
  Propr.
baby-doll *adjective*
baby face +s
baby-faced
Baby|gro +s *Propr.*
baby|hood
baby|ish
baby|ish|ness
Baby|lon (ancient
  city, Middle East;
  white society)
Baby|lonia
  (ancient region,
  Middle East)
Baby|lon|ian +s
baby's breath
  (plant)
baby|sit
  baby|sits
  baby|sat
  baby|sit¦ting
baby|sit¦ter +s
baby-snatch¦er +s
baby talk
baby walk¦er +s
Ba¦call, Lauren
  (American
  actress)
Ba|cardi +s *Propr.*
bac|ca|laur¦eate
  +s
bac|carat
bac|cate
Bac|chae *Greek
  Mythology*
bac|chanal +s

Bac|chan|alia
(Roman festival)
bac|chan|alia
(general revelry)
Bac|chan|al|ian +s
bac|chant
bac|chants or
bac|chan|tes
male
bac|chante +s
female
bac|chan|tic
Bac|chic
Bac|chus Greek
Mythology
baccy
bac|cies
Bach, Jo|hann
Se|bas|tian
(German
composer)
bach|elor +s
bach|elor|hood
bach|elor's
but|tons
bach|elor|ship
ba|cil|lary
ba|cil|li|form
ba|cil|lus
ba|cilli
back +s +ed +ing
back|ache +s
back|bar +s
back|beat +s
back|bench
back|benches
back|bench|er +s
back|bite
back|bites
back|bit
back|bit|ing
back|bit|ten
back|biter +s
back|blocks
back|board +s
back boil|er +s
back|bone +s
back-breaking
back-channel
adjective
back|chat
back|cloth +s
back|comb +s +ed
+ing
back|coun|try
back-crawl
back cross
back crosses
back crossed
back cross|ing
back|date
back|dates

back|date (cont.)
back|dated
back|dat|ing
back door +s noun
back-door adjective
back|down +s
back|draft +s
back|drop +s
back|er +s
back|field
back|fill +s +ed
+ing
back|fire
back|fires
back|fired
back|fir|ing
back|flip +s
back-formation +s
back|gam|mon
back|ground +s
back|hand +s
back|hand|ed
back|hand|er +s
back|hoe +s
back|ing +s
back|lash
back|lashes
back|less
back|light
back|list +s
back|lit
back|log +s
back|mark|er +s
back|most
back num|ber +s
back|pack +s +ed
+ing
back|pack|er +s
back pas|sage +s
back-pedal
back-pedals
back-pedalled Br.
back-pedaled Am.
back-pedalling
Br.
back-pedaling
Am.
back-projec|tion
back|rest +s
back room +s noun
back-room
attributive
Backs (in
Cambridge)
back|scat|ter|ing
back-scratch|er +s
back-scratch|ing
back seat +s
back-seat driver
+s
back|sheesh (use
baksheesh)

back|side +s
back|sight +s
back slang
back|slap|ping
back|slash
back|slashes
back|slide
back|slides
back|slid
back|slid|ing
back|slid|den or
back|slid
back|slider +s
back|space
back|spaces
back|spaced
back|spa|cing
back|spin
back|stage
back|stair
back|stairs
back|stay +s
back|stitch
back|stitches
back|stitched
back|stitch|ing
back|stop +s
back|street +s
back|stroke
back talk
back to back
adverbial
back-to-back +s
adjective and noun
back to front
back-to-nature
back|track +s +ed
+ing
back-up +s
back|veld +s
back|veld|er +s
back|ward
back|ward|ation
back|ward|ness
back|wards
back|wash
back|water +s
back|woods
back|woods|man
back|woods|men
backy
back|ies
(use baccy)
back|yard +s
bac|lava (use
baklava)
Ba|co|lod (city,
Philippines)
Bacon, Fran|cis
(English
statesman and
philosopher)

Bacon, Fran|cis
(Irish painter)
Bacon, Roger
(English
philosopher etc.)
bacon +s
Ba|con|ian +s
bac|teria (plural of
bacterium)
bac|ter|ial
bac|teri|cidal
bac|teri|cide +s
bac|terio|logic|al
bac|terio|logic|
al|ly
bac|teri|olo|gist +s
bac|teri|ology
bac|teri|oly|sis
bac|teri|oly|ses
bac|terio|lyt|ic
bac|terio|phage +s
bac|terio|stasis
bac|terio|stases
bac|terio|stat +s
bac|terio|stat|ic
bac|ter|ium
bac|teria
Bac|tria (region,
central Asia)
Bac|trian
bad
worse
worst
(inferior; harmful;
etc. ⚠ bade)
bad
bad|der
bad|dest
(slang excellent.
⚠ bade)
bad|ass
bad|asses
bad|die +s (use
baddy)
bad|dish
baddy
bad|dies
bade (archaic past
tense of bid.
⚠ bad)
Baden (town,
Austria)
Baden-Baden
(town, Germany)
Baden-Powell,
Rob|ert (English
soldier and
founder of the Boy
Scouts)
Baden-
Württem|berg
(state, Germany)

Bader, Doug¦las
(British airman)
badge
ba¦dges
badged
. badg¦ing
badger +s +ed +ing
Ba¦dian +s
bad¦in¦age
Bad Lands (region, USA)
bad¦lands
(generally)
badly
bad¦min¦ton
bad mouth *noun*
bad-mouth +s +ed +ing *verb*
bad¦ness
Badon Hill
(battlefield, England)
bad-tempered
bad-tempered¦ly
Bae¦deker +s
Baer, Karl von
(German biologist)
Bae¦yer, Adolph von (German chemist)
Baez, Joan
(American folk singer)
Baf¦fin, Wil¦liam
(English explorer)
Baf¦fin Bay
(between Canada and Greenland)
Baf¦fin Is¦land (off Canada)
baf¦fle
baf¦fles
baf¦fled
baf¦fling
baf¦fle board +s
baffle¦ment
baffle-plate +s
baf¦fler +s
baf¦fling¦ly
BAFTA (= British Association of Film and Television Arts)
bag
bags
bagged
bag¦ging
Ba¦ganda (people)
ba¦garre +s
ba¦gasse
baga¦telle +s

Bage¦hot, Wal¦ter
(English economist and political journalist)
bagel +s
bag¦ful +s
bag¦gage +s
bag¦gily
bag¦gi¦ness
baggy
bag¦gier
bag¦gi¦est
Bagh¦dad (capital of Iraq)
bag lady
bag la¦dies
bag¦man
bag¦men
bagnio +s
bag¦pipe +s
bag¦piper +s
bag¦pip¦ing
ba¦guette +s
bag¦wash
bag¦washes
bag¦worm +s
bah (*interjection*.
△ baa, bar, barre)
Baha'i +s
Ba¦ha'ism
Ba¦ha'ist +s
Ba¦ha'ite +s
Ba¦ha¦mas
Ba¦ha¦mian +s
Ba¦hasa In¦do¦nesia
Baha Ullah
(Persian founder of Baha'ism)
Ba¦ha¦wal¦pur
(city, Pakistan)
Bahia (state, Brazil; former name of Salvador)
Bahía Blanca
(port, Argentina)
Bah¦rain
Bah¦raini +s
baht
plural baht
Ba¦hutu (plural of Hutu)
baign¦oire +s
Bai¦kal, Lake (in Siberia)
Bai¦ko¦nur (space launch site, Kazakhstan)
bail +s +ed +ing
(security for prisoner; secure release of;

bail (*cont.*)
crosspiece on cricket stumps; bar on typewriter; bar in stable; hold up to rob; scoop water. △ bale)
bail¦able
bail¦ee +s *Law*
bail¦er +s (scoop for water.
△ bailor, baler)
Bai¦ley (shipping area)
Bai¦ley, David
(English photographer)
bai¦ley +s (part of castle)
Bai¦ley bridge +s
bai¦lie +s (Scottish magistrate)
bail¦iff +s
baili¦wick +s
bail¦ment
bail¦or +s (*Law*.
△ bailer, baler)
bail¦out +s *noun*
bails¦man
bails¦men
bain-marie
bains-marie
Bai¦ram (Muslim festival)
Baird, John Logie
(Scottish pioneer of television)
bairn +s
Bair¦rada (region, Portugal)
bait +s +ed +ing
(in hunting or fishing; harass; torment. △ bate)
baize +s
Baja Cali¦for¦nia
(peninsula, Mexico)
Bajan +s
bajra
bake
bakes
baked
bak¦ing
bake¦house +s
Bake¦lite *Propr.*
Baker, Janet
(English mezzo-soprano)
Baker, Jo¦seph¦ine
(American dancer)
baker +s

Baker day +s
baker's dozen +s
bakery
baker¦ies
Bake¦well, Rob¦ert
(English livestock expert)
Bake¦well tart +s
Bakh¦tin, Mikh¦ail
(Russian critic)
bak¦ing pow¦der
bak¦ing soda
bak¦lava
bak¦sheesh
Bakst, Léon
(Russian painter and designer)
Baku (capital of Azerbaijan)
Ba¦ku¦nin, Mikh¦ail (Russian revolutionary)
Bala (lake, Wales)
Bala¦clava
(battlefield, Crimea)
bala¦clava +s
(helmet)
bala¦laika +s
Bal¦ance, the
(constellation; sign of zodiac)
bal¦ance
bal¦ances
bal¦anced
bal¦an¦cing
bal¦ance¦able
bal¦an¦cer +s
bal¦ance sheet +s
bal¦ance wheel +s
Bal¦an¦chine, George (Russian-born American ballet dancer and choreographer)
bal¦anda +s (use balander)
bal¦an¦der +s
balas-ruby
balas-rubies
bal¦ata +s
Bala¦ton, Lake (in Hungary)
Bal¦boa (port, Panama)
Bal¦boa, Vasco de
(Spanish explorer)
bal¦boa +s
(Panamanian currency)
Bal¦brig¦gan
(fabric)

Bal¦con, Mi¦chael
(film producer)
bal¦con¦ied
bal¦cony
  bal¦con¦ies
bald +s +ed +ing
  +er +est
bal¦da¦chin +s
bal¦da¦quin +s (use
  baldachin)
Bal¦der *Norse
  Mythology*
bal¦der¦dash
bald-faced
bald¦head +s
bald-headed
baldie +s (use
  baldy)
bald¦ish
bald¦ly
bald¦money +s
bald¦ness
bald¦pate +s
bal¦dric +s
Bald¦win (name)
Bald¦win, James
  (American
  novelist)
Bald¦win, Stan¦ley
  (British prime
  minister)
baldy
  bald¦ies
Bâle (French name
  for Basle)
bale
  bales
  baled
  bal¦ing
  (bundle; evil,
  destruction, etc.;
  in 'bale out' (of
  aircraft). ▲bail)
Ba¦le¦ar¦ic Is¦lands
  (off E. Spain)
Ba¦le¦ar¦ics
  (=Balearic
  Islands)
ba¦leen
bale¦ful
bale¦ful¦ly
bale¦ful¦ness
Ba¦len¦ciaga,
  Cris¦tó¦bal
  (international
  couturier)
baler +s (machine
  for making bales.
  ▲bailer, bailor)
Bal¦four, Ar¦thur
  (British prime
  minister)

Bali (island,
  Indonesia)
Bali¦nese
  plural Bali¦nese
balk +s +ed +ing
  (use baulk)
Bal¦kan
Bal¦kan¦isa¦tion
  Br. (use
  Balkanization)
Bal¦kan¦ise *Br.* (use
  Balkanize)
  Bal¦kan¦ises
  Bal¦kan¦ised
  Bal¦kan¦is¦ing
Bal¦kan¦iza¦tion
Bal¦kan¦ize
  Bal¦kan¦izes
  Bal¦kan¦ized
  Bal¦kan¦iz¦ing
Bal¦kans, the
  (group of
  countries, SE
  Europe)
Bal¦khash, Lake
  (use Balqash)
Bal¦kis (queen of
  Sheba)
balky
  balk¦ier
  balki¦est
  (use baulky)
ball +s +ed +ing
  (sphere; dance.
  ▲bawl)
bal¦lad +s
bal¦lade +s
bal¦lad¦eer +s
ballad-monger +s
bal¦lad¦ry
  bal¦lad¦ries
Bal¦la¦dur,
  Édou¦ard (French
  statesman)
ball-and-socket
  attributive
Bal¦la¦rat (town,
  Australia)
bal¦last +s
ball-bearing +s
ball¦boy +s
ball¦cock +s
bal¦ler¦ina +s
Bal¦le¦steros,
  Sev¦eri¦ano
  (Spanish golfer)
bal¦let +s
bal¦let dan¦cer +s
bal¦let¦ic
bal¦leto¦mane +s
bal¦leto¦mania

Bal¦lets Russes
  (ballet company)
ball-flower +s
ball game +s
ball¦girl +s
ball gown +s
bal¦lista
  bal¦lis¦tae
bal¦lis¦tic
bal¦lis¦tic¦al¦ly
bal¦lis¦tics
bal¦locks (*coarse
  slang*; use
  bollocks)
bal¦lon d'essai
  bal¦lons d'essai
bal¦loon +s +ed
  +ing
bal¦loon¦ist +s
bal¦lot +s +ed +ing
bal¦lot box
  bal¦lot boxes
bal¦lot paper +s
ball¦park +s
ball-pen +s
ball¦point +s
ball-race +s
ball¦room +s
ball¦room
  dan¦cing
balls-up +s *noun*
  (*coarse slang*)
ballsy
ball valve +s
bally
bally¦hoo
Bally¦mena (town,
  Northern Ireland)
bally¦rag
  bally¦rags
  bally¦ragged
  bally¦rag¦ging
balm +s (ointment;
  plant. ▲barm)
balm¦ily
balmi¦ness
bal¦moral +s (cap;
  boot)
Bal¦moral Cas¦tle
  (in Scotland)
balmy
  balm¦ier
  balmi¦est
  (soothing.
  ▲barmy)
bal¦ne¦ary
bal¦neo¦logic¦al
bal¦ne¦olo¦gist +s
bal¦ne¦ology
ba¦lo¦ney +s

BALPA (= British
  Air Line Pilots
  Association)
Bal¦qash, Lake (in
  Kazakhstan)
balsa
bal¦sam +s
bal¦sam¦ic
bal¦sam¦ifer¦ous
balsa wood
Balt +s
Bal¦tha¦sar (one of
  the Magi; name)
Balti +s
Bal¦tic (sea, N.
  Europe)
Bal¦ti¦more (city,
  USA)
Bal¦ti¦stan (region,
  Himalayas)
Ba¦luchi +s
Ba¦luchi¦stan
  (region, W. Asia;
  province,
  Pakistan)
bal¦us¦ter +s
bal¦us¦trade +s
bal¦us¦traded
bal¦us¦trad¦ing
Bal¦zac, Hon¦oré
  de (French
  novelist)
bama +s
Bam¦ako (capital of
  Mali)
bam¦bino
  bam¦bi¦nos *or*
  bam¦bini
bam¦boo +s
bam¦boo¦zle
  bam¦boo¦zles
  bam¦boo¦zled
  bam¦booz¦ling
bam¦boozle¦ment
bam¦booz¦ler +s
Ba¦mian (province
  and city,
  Afghanistan)
ban
  bans
  banned
  ban¦ning
  (prohibit;
  prohibition; curse.
  ▲banns)
Ba¦naba (in W.
  Pacific)
banal
ban¦al¦ity
  ban¦al¦ities
ban¦al¦ly
ba¦nana +s

ban|ausic
Ban|bury cake +s
banc (*Law* in 'in banc'. △ bank)
band +s +ed +ing
Banda, Hast|ings (Malawian statesman)
ban|dage
  ban|dages
  ban|daged
  ban|da|ging
Band-Aid +s *Propr.*
ban|danna +s
Ban|da|ra|naike, Siri|mavo (Sri Lankan prime minister)
Ban|dar Lam|pung (city, Indonesia)
Ban|dar Seri Be|ga|wan (capital of Brunei)
Banda Sea (in Indonesia)
band|box
  band|boxes
ban|deau
  ban|deaux
ban|der|illa +s
ban|derol +s (use banderole)
ban|der|ole +s
bandi|coot +s
ban|dit
  ban|dits *or* ban|ditti
ban|dit|ry
Band|jar|masin (use Banjarmasin)
band|lead|er +s
band|mas|ter +s
ban|dog +s
ban|do|leer +s (use bandolier)
ban|do|lier +s
band|pass
  band|passes
band|saw +s
bands|man
  bands|men
band|stand +s
Ban|dung (city, Indonesia)
band|wagon +s
band|width +s
bandy
  ban|dies
  ban|died
  bandy|ing

bandy (*cont.*)
  ban|dier
  ban|di|est
bandy-legged
bane +s
bane|berry
  bane|berries
bane|ful
bane|ful|ly
Banff (towns, Scotland and Canada)
Banff|shire (former county, Scotland)
bang +s +ed +ing (sound; fringe; strike; etc. △ bhang)
Banga|lore (city, India)
bang|er +s
Bang|kok (capital of Thailand)
Ban|gla|desh
Ban|gla|deshi +s
ban|gle +s
Ban|gor (towns, Wales and Northern Ireland)
bang|tail +s
Ban|gui (capital of the Central African Republic)
bang-up *adjective*
ban|ian +s (use banyan)
ban|ish
  ban|ishes
  ban|ished
  ban|ish|ing
ban|ish|ment +s
ban|is|ter +s
Ban|jar|masin (port, Indonesia)
banjo +s
ban|jo|ist +s
Ban|jul (capital of the Gambia)
bank +s +ed +ing
bank|abil|ity
bank|able
bank bill +s
bank book +s
bank card +s
bank|er +s
bank|er's card +s
bank|er's order +s
bank|note +s
bank|roll +s +ed +ing
bank|rupt +s +ed +ing

bank|rupt|cy
  bank|rupt|cies
Banks, Jo|seph (English naturalist)
bank|sia +s
ban|ner +s
ban|nered
ban|neret +s
Ban|nis|ter, Roger (English athlete)
ban|nis|ter +s (use banister)
ban|nock +s
Ban|nock|burn (battlefield, Scotland)
banns (of marriage)
ban|quet +s +ed +ing
ban|quet|er +s
ban|quette +s
ban|shee +s
ban|tam +s
ban|tam|weight +s
ban|ter +s +ed +ing
ban|ter|er +s
Ban|ting, Fred|erick (Canadian surgeon)
Bantu
  plural Bantu *or* Ban|tus
Ban|tu|stan +s
ban|yan +s
ban|zai
bao|bab +s
Bao|tou (city, China)
bap +s
bap|tise *Br.* (use baptize)
  bap|tises
  bap|tised
  bap|tis|ing
bap|tism +s
bap|tis|mal
Bap|tist +s (denomination)
bap|tist +s (person who baptizes)
bap|tist|ery
  bap|tist|er|ies
bap|tist|ry (use baptistery)
  bap|tist|ries
bap|tize
  bap|tizes
  bap|tized
  bap|tiz|ing

Bar, the (barristers collectively)
bar
  bars
  barred
  bar|ring
(rod; counter; room in pub; obstruction; section of music; unit of pressure; fasten; prohibit; except. △ baa, bah, barre)
Bar|ab|bas *Bible*
bara|thea +s
Barb (= Broadcasters' Audience Research Council)
barb +s +ed +ing (projection; hurtful remark)
Bar|ba|dian +s
Bar|ba|dos (state, Caribbean)
Bar|bara
bar|bar|ian +s
bar|bar|ic
bar|bar|ic|al|ly
bar|bar|isa|tion *Br.* (use barbarization)
bar|bar|ise *Br.* (use barbarize)
  bar|bar|ises
  bar|bar|ised
  bar|bar|is|ing
bar|bar|ism +s
bar|bar|ity
  bar|bar|ities
bar|bar|iza|tion
bar|bar|ize
  bar|bar|izes
  bar|bar|ized
  bar|bar|iz|ing
Bar|ba|rossa, Fred|erick (German king)
bar|bar|ous
bar|bar|ous|ly
bar|bar|ous|ness
Bar|bary
Bar|bary Coast (area, NW Africa)
bar|ba|stelle +s
bar|be|cue
  bar|be|cues
  bar|be|cued
  bar|be|cu|ing
barbed wire *Br.* (*Am.* barbwire)

bar¦bel +s (fish;
part of fish)
bar¦bell +s
(weights)
Bar¦ber, Sam¦uel
(American
composer)
bar¦ber +s
bar¦berry
bar¦berries
barber-shop
(singing)
bar¦ber's pole +s
bar¦ber's shop +s
(place)
bar¦bet +s (bird)
bar¦bette +s (gun
platform)
bar¦bi¦can +s
bar¦bie +s
(= barbecue)
Bar¦bie doll +s
(doll; young
woman. △ Babi)
Propr.
Bar¦bi¦rolli, John
(English
conductor)
bar¦bi¦tal
bar¦bi¦tone
bar¦bit¦ur¦ate +s
bar¦bi¦tur¦ic
Bar¦bi¦zon School
(French painters)
barb¦less
bar¦bola
Bar¦bour +s
(jacket) Propr.
Bar¦bour, John
(Scottish poet)
Bar¦buda (island,
West Indies)
Bar¦budan +s
barb¦ule +s
barb¦wire Am. (Br.
barbed wire)
Barca, Pedro
Cal¦derón de la
(Spanish writer)
bar¦car¦ole +s
bar¦car¦olle +s (use
barcarole)
Bar¦ce¦lona (city,
Spain)
bar¦chan +s
Bar¦clay (name.
△ Barkly,
Berkeley)
Bar-Cochba
(Jewish rebel)
bar code +s noun

bar-code
bar-codes
bar-coded
bar-coding
verb
Bar¦coo
bard +s
bard¦ic
bard¦ol¦atry
Bar¦dot, Bri¦gitte
(French actress)
bardy
bar¦dies
bare
bares
bared
bar¦ing
barer
bar¦est
(naked; mere;
uncover; etc.
△ bear)
bare¦back
Bare¦bones
Par¦lia¦ment
bare¦faced
bare¦faced¦ly
bare¦faced¦ness
bare¦foot
bare¦foot¦ed
bar¦ège +s
bare¦head¦ed
Ba¦reilly (city,
India)
bare-knuckle
adjective
bare-knuckled
bare¦ly
bare¦ness
Bar¦ents, Wil¦lem
(Dutch explorer)
Bar¦ents Sea (part
of Arctic Ocean)
barf +s +ed +ing
bar¦fly
bar¦flies
bar¦fly jump¦ing
bar¦gain +s +ed
+ing
bar¦gain
base¦ment +s
bar¦gain¦er +s
barge
barges
barged
bar¦ging
barge¦board +s
bar¦gee +s
Bar¦gello
barge¦man
barge¦men
barge¦pole +s

Bari (city, Italy)
bar¦illa +s
Bari¦sal (port,
Bangladesh)
bar¦ite Am. (Br.
barytes)
bari¦tone +s
bar¦ium
bark +s +ed +ing
(cry of dog; on
tree trunk.
△ barque)
bar¦keep +s
bar¦keep¦er +s
bar¦ken¦tine Am.
+s (Br.
barquentine)
Bark¦er, George
(English poet)
bark¦er +s
Barkly Table¦land
(plateau,
Australia)
bar¦ley +s
bar¦ley¦corn +s
bar¦ley¦mow +s
bar¦ley sugar
bar¦ley water
bar¦ley wine
bar¦line +s
barm (froth; yeast.
△ balm)
bar¦maid +s
bar¦man
bar¦men
barm¦brack +s
Bar¦me¦cide +s
bar¦mily
barmi¦ness
bar mitz¦vah +s
barmy
bar¦mier
bar¦mi¦est
(crazy. △ balmy)
barn +s
Bar¦na¦bas
(Apostle and saint;
name)
Bar¦naby
bar¦nacle +s
bar¦nacled
Bar¦nard,
Chris¦tiaan
(South African
surgeon)
Bar¦nardo,
Thomas (English
philanthropist,
founder of 'Dr
Barnardo's
homes')

Bar¦naul (city,
Russia)
barn¦brack +s
Bar¦ney (name)
bar¦ney +s
(quarrel)
barn owl +s
Barns¦ley (town,
England)
barn¦storm +s +ed
+ing
barn¦storm¦er +s
Bar¦num, Phin¦eas
T. (American
showman)
barn¦yard +s
Bar¦oda (former
state, India;
former name of
Vadodara)
baro¦graph +s
bar¦om¦eter +s
baro¦met¦ric
baro¦met¦ric¦al
baro¦met¦ric¦al¦ly
bar¦om¦etry
baron +s
(nobleman.
△ barren)
bar¦on¦age
bar¦on¦ess
bar¦on¦esses
bar¦onet +s
bar¦on¦et¦age
bar¦on¦et¦cy
bar¦on¦et¦cies
bar¦on¦ial
bar¦ony
bar¦on¦ies
bar¦oque
baro¦recep¦tor +s
bar¦ouche +s
bar per¦son +s
bar¦quan¦tine +s
(use barquentine)
barque +s (ship.
△ bark)
bar¦quen¦tine Br.
+s (Am.
barkentine)
Bar¦qui¦si¦meto
(city, Venezuela)
Barra (Scottish
island)
bar¦rack +s +ed
+ing
barrack-room
attributive
bar¦racks
bar¦rack square +s
bar¦ra¦couta
plural

bar¦ra|couta (cont.)
bar¦ra|couta or
bar¦ra|cou¦tas
(long thin food
fish; loaf)
bar¦ra|cuda +s
(large voracious
fish)
bar¦rage +s
bar¦ra|mundi
plural
bar¦ra|mundi or
bar¦ra|mun¦dis
Bar¦ran|quilla
(city, Colombia)
bar¦ra|tor +s
bar¦ra|trous
bar¦ra|try
barre +s (Ballet.
△ baa, bah, bar)
barré Music
bar¦rel
bar¦rels
bar¦relled Br.
bar¦reled Am.
bar¦rel|ling Br.
bar¦rel|ing Am.
barrel-chested
bar¦rel|ful +s
bar¦rel organ +s
barrel-vaulted
bar¦ren +er +est
(infertile.
△ baron)
bar¦ren|ly
bar¦ren|ness
bar¦ret +s (cap)
Bar¦rett,
Eliza|beth
(English poet, wife
of Robert
Browning)
bar¦rette +s
(hairslide)
bar¦ri|cade
bar¦ri|cades
bar¦ri|caded
bar¦ri|cad|ing
Bar¦rie, James M.
(Scottish writer.
△ Barry)
bar¦rier +s
bar¦rio +s
bar¦ris|ter +s
barrister-at-law
barristers-at-law
bar room +s
bar¦row +s
bar¦row boy +s
Barrow-in-
Furness (town,
England)

bar¦row|load +s
Barry (name)
Barry, Charles
(English architect.
△ Barrie)
Barry|more
(American
theatrical family)
Bar¦sac +s (region,
France; wine)
bar stool +s
Bart (name)
Bart. (= Baronet)
bar|tend¦er +s
bar¦ter +s +ed
+ing
bar¦ter|er +s
Barth, John
(American writer)
Barth, Karl (Swiss
theologian)
Barthes, Ro|land
(French
semiotician)
Bar|tholo|mew
(Apostle and
saint)
bar¦ti|zan +s
bar¦ti|zaned
Bar¦tók, Béla
(Hungarian
composer)
Bar|to|lom|meo,
Fra (Florentine
painter)
Bart's (St
Bartholomew's
Hospital, London)
Bar¦uch Bible
baryon +s
bary|on¦ic
Bar¦ysh|nikov,
Mikh|ail (Latvian-
born American
ballet dancer)
bary|sphere +s
ba¦ryta
bar¦yte (use barite)
ba|ry¦tes
ba|ryt¦ic
basal
bas¦alt +s
bas|alt¦ic
bas|cule +s
(bridge)
base
bases
based
bas¦ing
baser
bas¦est
(foundation;

base (cont.)
establish;
cowardly; impure.
△ bass)
base|ball +s
base|ball play¦er
+s
base|board +s
base|born
base camp +s
base|head +s
BASE jump +s +ed
+ing
BASE jump¦er +s
Basel (German
name for Basle)
base|less
base|less|ness
base|line +s
base|load +s
base|man
base|men
base|ment +s
base metal +s
base|ness
bas|enji +s
base|plate +s
base rate +s
bases (plural of
base and basis)
bash
bashes
bashed
bash|ing
bash|ful
bash|ful|ly
bash|ful|ness
bashi-bazouk +s
Bash|kir
plural Bash|kir or
Bash|kirs
Bash|kiria
(republic, Russia)
Bash|kor|to|stan
(alternative name
for Bashkiria)
basho
plural basho or
bashos
BASIC Computing
basic +s
ba|sic|ally
Basic Eng|lish
bas|icity
bas|ici|ties
ba|sid|ium
ba|sidia
Basie, Count
(American jazz
musician)
Basil (early saint;
name)

basil +s (herb)
basi|lar
Bas|il|don (town,
England)
ba|sil|ica +s
ba|sili|can
Ba|sili|cata (region,
Italy)
basi|lisk +s
basin +s
basi|net +s
(headpiece.
△ bassinet)
basin|ful +s
ba|sip|etal
ba|sip|et|al¦ly
basis
bases
bask +s +ed +ing
(laze in the sun
etc. △ basque)
Bas|ker|ville, John
(English printer)
bas|ket +s
bas|ket|ball +s
bas|ket case +s
(offensive)
bas|ket|ful +s
Bas¦ket Maker +s
(American Indian)
basket-maker +s
(maker of baskets)
basket-making
bas|ket¦ry
bas|ket weave
bas|ket|work
Basle (city,
Switzerland)
bas|mati
baso|phil +s
baso|phile +s
baso|phil¦ic
Ba|so|tho
Basque +s (people;
language)
basque +s (bodice.
△ bask)
Basra (port, Iraq)
bas-relief +s
bass
basses
(voice; double
bass; low pitch.
△ base)
bass
plural bass or
basses
(fish. △ base)
Bas|sein (port,
Burma)
Basse-Norman|die
(region, France)

bas¦set +s
Basse¦terre (capital of St Kitts and Nevis)
Basse-Terre (island and city, Guadeloupe)
basset-horn +s
basset-hound +s
bassi (plural of basso)
bas¦sinet +s (cradle; pram. △ basinet)
bass¦ist +s
basso
bas¦sos *or* bassi
bas¦soon +s
bas¦soon¦ist +s
basso pro¦fundo
basso pro¦fun¦dos *or* bassi pro¦fundi
basso-relievo +s
basso-rilievo +s (use basso-relievo)
bass play¦er +s
Bass Strait (channel between Australia and Tasmania)
bass¦wood
bast
bas¦tard +s
bas¦tard¦isa¦tion *Br.* (use bastardization)
bas¦tard¦ise *Br.* (use bastardize)
bas¦tard¦ises
bas¦tard¦ised
bas¦tard¦is¦ing
bas¦tard¦iza¦tion
bas¦tard¦ize
bas¦tard¦izes
bas¦tard¦ized
bas¦tard¦iz¦ing
bas¦tardy
baste
bastes
basted
bast¦ing
Bas¦tet *Egyptian Mythology*
Bas¦tia (port, Corsica)
Bas¦tille (in Paris)
bas¦tille +s (fortress)
bas¦tin¦ado +s *noun*

bas¦tin¦ado
bas¦tin¦adoes
bas¦tin¦adoed
bas¦tin¦ado¦ing *verb*
bas¦tion +s
ba¦suco
Ba¦su¦to¦land (former name of Lesotho)
bat
bats
bat¦ted
bat¦ting
Bata (town, Equatorial Guinea)
Batan Is¦lands (part of the Philippines)
ba¦tata +s
Bat¦avia (former name of Djakarta)
Bat¦avian +s
batch
batches
batched
batch¦ing
Bat¦dam¦bang (use Battambang)
bate +s (rage. △ bait)
bat¦eau
bat¦eaux
bated (in 'with bated breath')
bat¦el¦leur +s
Bates, Alan (English actor)
Bates, Henry (English naturalist)
Bates, H. E. (English writer)
Bates¦ian
Bate¦son, Wil¦liam (English geneticist)
Bath (city, England. △ Baath)
bath +s +ed +ing
Bath bun +s
bath chair +s
Bath chap +s
bath cube +s
bathe
bathes
bathed
bath¦ing
bather +s
bath¦et¦ic
bath¦house +s

bath¦ing cos¦tume +s
bath¦ing suit +s
bath mat +s
batho¦lith +s
Bath Oli¦ver +s *Propr.*
bath¦om¦eter +s
bathos
bath¦ot¦ic
bath¦robe +s
bath¦room +s
bath salts
Bath¦sheba *Bible*
bath¦tub +s
Bath¦urst (former name of Banjul)
bath¦water
ba¦thym¦eter +s
bathy¦met¦ric
ba¦thym¦etry
bathy¦scaphe +s
bathy¦sphere +s
batik +s
Bat¦ista, Ful¦gen¦cio (Cuban soldier and dictator)
bat¦iste +s
Bat¦man (fictional character)
bat¦man
bat¦men (military attendant)
baton +s (stick used by conductor, relay runner, or drum major or as symbol of authority; truncheon. △ batten)
Baton Rouge (city, USA)
baton round +s
bat¦ra¦chian +s
bats¦man
bats¦men
bats¦man¦ship
Ba¦tswana (plural of Tswana)
bat¦tal¦ion +s
Bat¦tam¦bang (region and city, Cambodia)
bat¦tels (college account at Oxford University. △ battles)

Bat¦ten, Jean (New Zealand aviator)
bat¦ten +s +ed +ing (strip of wood used for fastening. △ baton)
Bat¦ten¦berg +s (cake)
bat¦ter +s +ed +ing
bat¦ter¦er +s
bat¦ter¦ing ram +s
bat¦tery
bat¦ter¦ies
battery-operated
battery-powered
Bat¦ti¦ca¦loa (city, Sri Lanka)
bat¦tily
bat¦ti¦ness
bat¦tle
bat¦tles
bat¦tled
bat¦tling (fight. △ battels)
battle¦axe +s
battle¦bus
battle¦buses
battle¦cruiser +s
battle-cry
battle-cries
battle¦dore +s
battle¦dress
battle¦field +s
battle¦ground +s
battle¦group +s
battle-hardened
battle¦ment +s
battle¦ment¦ed
bat¦tler +s
bat¦tle royal
bat¦tles royal
battle-scarred
battle¦ship +s
battle-weary
bat¦tue +s
batty
bat¦tier
bat¦ti¦est
Batwa (plural of Twa)
bat¦wing *attributive*
bat¦woman
bat¦women
bau¦ble +s
Bau¦cis *Greek Mythology*
baud
plural baud *or* bauds

baud (*cont.*)
(*Computing* unit of
speed. △ **bawd**,
board, bored)
**Baude|laire,
Charles** (French
poet)
Bau|haus
baulk +s +ed +ing
baulk|er +s
baulki|ness
baulky
baulk|ier
baulki|est
baux|ite
baux|it|ic
bav|ard|age
Bav|aria (state,
Germany)
Bav|ar|ian +s
bawd +s
(prostitute.
△ baud, board,
bored)
bawd|ily
bawdi|ness
bawdy
bawd|ier
bawdi|est
bawdy house +s
bawl +s +ed +ing
(yell. △ ball)
bawl|er +s
Bax, Ar|nold
(English
composer)
Bax|ter (name)
Bax|ter, James
(New Zealand
poet)
bay +s +ed +ing
(inlet of sea; tree;
window; recess;
compartment;
colour; horse;
howl. △ **bey**)
bay|ad|ère
Bay|ard, Pierre
(French soldier)
bay|berry
bay|berries
Bay|eux (town,
France; tapestry)
Bay|kal, Lake (use
Baikal)
Bay|ko|nur (use
Baikonur)
bay leaf
bay leaves
Bay|lis, Lil|ian
(English theatre
manager)

bay|onet
bay|on|ets
bay|on|et|ed *or*
bay|on|et|ted
bay|on|et|ing *or*
bay|on|et|ting
bayou +s
Bay|reuth (town,
Germany)
bay tree +s
bay win|dow +s
Baz
ba|zaar +s
bazoo +s
ba|zooka +s
ba|zuco (use
basuco)
B-cell +s
bdel|lium
be
am
are
is
was
were
being
been
Bea (name)
beach
beaches
beached
beach|ing
(shore. △ **beech**)
beach ball +s
Beach Boys, the
(American pop
group)
beach|comb|er +s
beach|front
beach|head +s
Beach-la-mar
beach|side
beach|wear
Beachy Head
(headland,
England)
bea|con +s
bead +s +ed +ing
bead|ily
beadi|ness
bea|dle +s
beadle|ship +s
bead-moulding
beads|man
beads|men
bead|work
beady
bead|ier
beadi|est
beady-eyed

bea|gle
bea|gles
bea|gled
beag|ling
Bea|gle Chan|nel
(off S. America)
beag|ler +s
beak +s
beaked
Bea|ker (people)
bea|ker +s
(drinking vessel)
beaky
Beale, Doro|thea
(English
educationist)
be-all and end-all
beam +s +ed +ing
beam-compass
beam-compasses
beam-ends
beam|er +s
Bea|mon, Bob
(American athlete)
beamy
beam|ier
beami|est
bean +s (vegetable.
△ **been**)
bean|bag +s
bean-counter +s
bean curd
bean|ery
bean|er|ies
bean|feast +s
beanie +s
beano +s
bean|pole +s
bean sprout +s
bean|stalk +s
bear +s (animal.
△ **bare**)
bear
bears
bore
bear|ing
borne
(carry; exert;
tolerate; etc.
△ **bare**)
bear
bears
bore
bear|ing
born
(give birth to.
△ **bare**)
bear|abil|ity
bear|able
bear|ably
bear-baiting

bear|berry
bear|berries
beard +s +ed +ing
beardie +s
beard|less
**Beard|more
Gla|cier** (in
Antarctica)
**Beards|ley,
Aub|rey** (English
painter)
bear|er +s
bear|gar|den +s
bear-hug +s
bear|ing +s
bearing-rein +s
bear|ish
bear mar|ket +s
Béarn|aise
bear|pit +s
bear's breech
bear's ear +s
bear's foot +s
bear|skin +s
Beas (river, India)
beast +s
beastie +s
beast|ings (use
beestings)
beast|li|ness
beast|ly
beast|lier
beast|li|est
beat
beats
beat
beat|ing
beaten
(hit; rhythm; etc.
△ **beet**)
beat|able
beat|er +s (person
or thing that beats.
△ **beta**)
bea|tif|ic
bea|tif|ic|al|ly
be|ati|fi|ca|tion
be|atify
be|ati|fies
be|ati|fied
be|ati|fy|ing
be|ati|tude +s
Beatles, the
(British pop
group)
beat|nik +s
Bea|ton, Cecil
(English
photographer)
Bea|trice (woman
loved by Dante;
name)

Bea|trix

Beatty, David
(British admiral)

Beatty, War|ren
(American actor)

beat-up adjective

Beau (man's name.
△ Bo)

beau

beaux or beaus
(dandy. △ bo,
bow)

Beau|bourg
(building, Paris)

Beau|fort scale

Beau|fort Sea (part
of Arctic Ocean)

beau geste

beaux gestes

beau idéal

beaux idéals

Beau|jo|lais
plural Beau|jo|lais
(district, France;
wine)

Beau|jo|lais
Nou|veau

Beau|mar|chais,
Pierre de (French
dramatist)

Beau|maris (town,
Wales)

beau monde

Beau|mont,
Fran|cis (English
dramatist)

Beaune +s (town,
France; wine)

beaut +s (excellent;
beautiful. △ butte)

beaut|eous

beaut|ician +s

beau|ti|fi|ca|tion

beau|ti|fier +s

beau|ti|ful

beau|ti|ful|ly

beaut|ify

beau|ti|fies
beau|ti|fied
beau|ti|fy|ing

beauty

beaut|ies

beauty spot +s

Beau|voir,
Sim|one de
(French writer)

beaux (plural of
beau)

beaux arts

Bea|ver +s (junior
Scout)

bea|ver
plural bea|ver or
bea|vers
(animal)

bea|ver +s +ed
+ing (armour;
bearded man;
work)

bea|ver|board

Bea|ver|brook,
Lord (Canadian-
born British
politician and
newspaper
proprietor)

bebop

be|bop|per +s

be|calm +s +ed
+ing

be|came

be|cause

béch|amel

bêche-de-mer
plural bêche-de-
mer or bêche-de-
mers

Bech|stein,
Fried|rich
(German piano-
builder)

Bech|uana|land
(former name of
Botswana)

Beck, Jeff (English
rock musician)

beck +s

Beck|en|bauer,
Franz (German
footballer)

Becker, Boris
(German tennis
player)

Becket, St
Thomas à
(English
archbishop)

becket +s

Beck|ett, Sam|uel
(Irish writer)

Beck|ford,
Wil|liam (English
writer)

Beck|mann, Ernst
Otto (German
chemist)

Beck|mann, Max
(German painter)

beckon +s +ed
+ing

Becky

be|cloud +s +ed
+ing

be|come

be|comes

be|came

be|com|ing

be|come

be|com|ing|ly

be|com|ing|ness

Bec|querel,
Antoine-Henri
(French physicist)

bec|querel +s
(unit)

bed

beds

bed|ded

bed|ding

be|dab|ble

be|dab|bles
be|dab|bled
be|dab|bling

bedad

bed and
break|fast +s
noun

bed-and-breakfast
+s +ed +ing verb

be|daub +s +ed
+ing

be|daz|zle

be|daz|zles
be|daz|zled
be|daz|zling

be|dazzle|ment

bed|bug +s

bed|cham|ber +s

bed|clothes

bed|cover +s

bed-covering +s

bed|dable

bed|der +s

beddy-byes

Bede, The
Ve|ner|able
(English monk and
writer)

be|deck +s +ed
+ing

bed|eguar

bedel +s

bed|ell +s (use
bedel)

be|devil

be|devils
be|dev|illed Br.
be|dev|iled Am.
be|dev|il|ling Br.
be|dev|il|ing Am.

be|devil|ment

bedew +s +ed
+ing

bed|fast

bed|fel|low +s

Bed|ford (town,
England)

Bed|ford|shire
(county, England)

bed|head +s

bed-hop

bed-hops

bed-hopped

bed-hopping

be|dight

bedim

be|dims

be|dimmed

be|dim|ming

be|dizen +s +ed
+ing

bed|jacket +s

bed|lam +s

bed|linen

Bed|ling|ton
(terrier)

bed|maker +s

Bed|ouin
plural Bed|ouin

bed|pan +s

bed|plate +s

bed|post +s

be|drag|gle

be|drag|gles
be|drag|gled
be|drag|gling

bed|rest

bed|rid|den

bed|rock +s

bed|roll +s

bed|room +s

Beds.
(= Bedfordshire)

bed|side +s

bed|sit +s

bed|sit|ter +s

bed-sitting room
+s

bed|skirt +s

bed|sock +s

bed|sore +s

bed|spread +s

bed|stead +s

bed|straw

bed|table +s

bed|time +s

Bed|uin (use
Bedouin)
plural Beduin

bed-wetter +s

bed-wetting

bee +s

Beeb

bee-bread

beech

beeches
(tree. △ beach)

Beecham,
  Thomas (English
  conductor)
beech-fern +s
beech mar|ten +s
beech|mast
  plural beech|mast
beech|wood
beechy
bee-eater +s
beef
  plural beef *or*
  beeves
  (meat; cattle)
beef +s +ed +ing
  (complaint;
  complain)
beef|alo
  plural beef|alo *or*
  beef|aloes
beef|bur|ger +s
beef|cake +s
beef cat|tle
beef|eater +s
beef|heart
beef|ily
beefi|ness
beef|steak +s
beef tea
beef|wood +s
beefy
  beef|ier
  beefi|est
bee|hive +s
bee-keeper +s
bee-keeping
bee|line +s
Be|el|ze|bub *Bible*
bee-master +s
been (past
  participle of be.
  ⚠ bean)
beep +s +ed +ing
beep|er +s
beer +s (drink.
  ⚠ bier)
Beer|bohm, Max
  (English writer)
beer cel|lar +s
beer en|gine +s
beer gar|den +s
beer hall +s
beer|house +s
beer|ily
beeri|ness
beer mat +s
Beer|sheba (town,
  Israel)
beery
  beeri|er
  beeri|est
beest|ings

bees|wax
bees|wing
beet +s (vegetable.
  ⚠ beat)
Beet|hoven,
  Lud|wig van
  (German
  composer)
Bee|tle +s
  (Volkswagen)
  Propr.
bee|tle
  bee|tles
  bee|tled
  beet|ling
  (insect; game;
  scurry; tool;
  projecting; to
  project. ⚠ betel)
beetle-browed
beetle-crusher +s
Bee|ton, Mrs
  (Isa|bella)
  (English cookery
  writer)
beet|root
  plural beet|root *or*
  beet|roots
beeves
be|fall
  be|falls
  be|fell
  be|fall|ing
  be|fallen
befit
  be|fits
  be|fit|ted
  be|fit|ting
be|fit|ting|ly
befog
  be|fogs
  be|fogged
  be|fog|ging
be|fool +s +ed
  +ing
be|fore
Be|fore Christ
be|fore|hand
be|foul +s +ed
  +ing
be|friend +s +ed
  +ing
be|fud|dle
  be|fud|dles
  be|fud|dled
  be|fud|dling
be|fuddle|ment
beg
  begs
  begged
  beg|ging
begad

began
beget
  be|gets
  begot
  or begat *archaic*
  be|get|ting
  be|got|ten
be|get|ter +s
beg|gar +s
beg|gar|li|ness
beg|gar|ly
beggar-my-
  neighbour
beg|gary
Begin,
  Men|achem
  (Israeli prime
  minister)
begin
  be|gins
  began
  be|gin|ning
  begun
be|gin|ner +s
be|gin|ner's luck
be|gin|ning +s
be|gird
  be|girds
  be|girt
  be|gird|ing
be|gone *interjection*
be|go|nia +s
be|gorra
begot
be|got|ten
be|grime
  be|grimes
  be|grimed
  be|grim|ing
be|grudge
  be|grudges
  be|grudged
  be|grudg|ing
be|grudg|ing|ly
be|guile
  be|guiles
  be|guiled
  be|guil|ing
be|guile|ment
be|guiler +s
be|guil|ing|ly
be|guine +s
Begum (title of
  Muslim woman)
begum +s (high-
  ranking Muslim
  lady)
begun
be|half
Behan, Bren|dan
  (Irish dramatist)

be|have
  be|haves
  be|haved
  be|hav|ing
be|hav|ior *Am.* +s
be|hav|ior|al *Am.*
be|hav|ior|al|ist
  Am. +s
be|hav|ior|al|ly
  Am.
be|hav|ior|ism *Am.*
be|hav|ior|ist *Am.*
  +s
be|hav|ior|is|tic
  Am.
be|hav|iour *Br.* +s
be|hav|iour|al *Br.*
be|hav|iour|al|ist
  Br. +s
be|hav|iour|al|ly
  Br.
be|hav|iour|ism *Br.*
be|hav|iour|ist *Br.*
  +s
be|hav|iour|is|tic
  Br.
be|head +s +ed
  +ing
be|head|ing +s
be|held
be|he|moth +s
be|hest +s
be|hind
be|hind|hand
behind-the-scenes
  attributive
Behn, Aphra
  (English writer)
be|hold
  be|holds
  be|held
  be|hold|ing
be|holden
be|hold|er +s
be|hoof
be|hoove *Am.*
  be|hooves
  be|hooved
  be|hoov|ing
be|hove *Br.*
  be|hoves
  be|hoved
  be|hov|ing
Behr|ens, Peter
  (German
  architect)
Behr|ing, Emil
  von (German
  immunologist)
Bei|der|becke, Bix
  (American jazz
  musician)

beige +s
bei¦gel +s (use
  bagel)
Bei¦jing (capital of
  China)
being +s
Beira (region,
  Portugal; port,
  Mozambique)
Bei¦rut (capital of
  Lebanon)
be¦jab|bers
be¦ja¦bers
Bé¦jart, Maur¦ice
  (French
  choreographer)
be¦jew¦eled Am.
be¦jew¦elled Br.
Bekaa (valley,
  Lebanon)
Bel (= Baal)
bel +s (10 decibels.
  △ bell, belle)
be¦la¦bor Am. +s
  +ed +ing
be¦la¦bour Br. +s
  +ed +ing
Bela¦fonte, Harry
  (American singer)
Bela¦rus
Bela¦rus¦sian +s
  (use Belorussian)
be¦lated
be¦lated¦ly
be¦lated|ness
Belau (= Pelau)
belay +s +ed +ing
belaying-pin +s
bel canto
belch
  belches
  belched
  belch|ing
belch¦er +s
bel¦dam +s
bel¦dame +s (use
  beldam)
be¦lea¦guer +s +ed
  +ing
Belém (city, Brazil)
bel¦em|nite +s
bel es¦prit
  beaux es¦prits
Bel¦fast (capital of
  Northern Ireland)
bel¦fry
  bel|fries
Bel¦gae
Bel¦gaum (city,
  India)
Bel¦gian +s

Bel¦gian Congo
  (former name of
  Zaire)
Bel¦gic
Bel¦gium
Bel¦gorod (city,
  Russia)
Bel¦grade (capital
  of Serbia)
Bel¦gra¦via (area,
  London)
Bel¦gra¦vian +s
Be¦lial
belie
  be¦lies
  be¦lied
  bely¦ing
be¦lief +s
be¦liev|abil¦ity
be¦liev|able
be¦liev|ably
be¦lieve
  be¦lieves
  be¦lieved
  be¦liev¦ing
be¦liever +s
Be¦linda
Beli¦sar¦ius
  (Roman general)
Be¦li¦sha (beacon)
be¦lit¦tle
  be¦lit¦tles
  be¦lit¦tled
  be¦lit¦tling
be¦little|ment
be¦lit¦tler +s
be¦lit¦tling¦ly
Be¦li¦tung (island,
  Indonesia)
Be¦lize
Be¦lize City (city,
  Belize)
Be¦li¦zian +s
Bell, Alex|an¦der
  Gra¦ham
  (Scottish inventor
  of the telephone)
Bell, Ger¦trude
  (English traveller
  and scholar)
bell +s +ed +ing
  (object that rings;
  cry of stag; etc.
  △ bel, belle)
Bella
bella|donna
bell|bird +s
bell-bottom +s
bell-bottomed
bell|boy +s (page
  in hotel or club)

bell-buoy +s
  (warning device)
Belle (name)
belle +s (woman.
  △ bel, bell)
belle époque
  belles époques
belle laide
  belles laides
Bel¦ler|ophon
  Greek Mythology
belles-lettres
bel|let¦rism
bel|let¦rist +s
bel|let¦ris¦tic
bell|flower +s
bell-founder +s
bell-glass
  bell-glasses
bell|hop +s
bel¦li|cose
bel¦li|cos¦ity
bel¦li|ger|ence
bel¦li|ger|ency
bel¦li|ger|ent
bel¦li|ger|ent¦ly
Bel¦lings|hau¦sen
  Sea (part of SE
  Pacific)
Bel|lini, Gen|tile,
  Gio|vanni, and
  Ja¦copo
  (Venetian
  painters)
Bel|lini, Vin|cenzo
  (Italian composer)
bell jar +s
bell|man
  bell|men
bell metal
Bel¦loc, Hil|aire
  (British humorist)
Bel¦low, Saul
  (American
  novelist)
bel¦low +s +ed
  +ing
bell pull +s
bell push
  bell pushes
bell-ringer +s
bell-ringing
Bell Rock (off
  Scotland)
Bell's palsy
bell tent +s
bell tower +s
bell-wether +s
belly
  bel¦lies
  bel¦lied
  belly|ing

belly|ache
  belly|aches
  belly|ached
  belly|ach¦ing
belly|acher +s
belly|band +s
belly but¦ton +s
belly dance +s
belly dan¦cer +s
belly dan¦cing
belly|flop
  belly|flops
  belly|flopped
  belly|flop|ping
belly|ful +s
belly land¦ing
belly laugh +s
Bel|mondo, Jean-
  Paul (French
  actor)
Bel¦mo|pan
  (capital of Belize)
Belo Hori|zonte
  (city, Brazil)
be¦long +s +ed
  +ing
be¦long|ing|ness
be¦long|ings
Belo¦rus¦sia
  (alternative name
  for Belarus)
Belo¦rus¦sian +s
Belo|stok (Russian
  name for
  Białystok)
be¦loved
below (under.
  △ billow)
below-the-line
  attributive
Bel Paese Propr.
Bel¦sen
  (concentration
  camp, Germany)
Bel¦shaz¦zar
  (Babylonian king)
belt +s +ed +ing
belt and braces
Bel¦tane
belt drive +s
belt¦er +s
belt|man
  belt|men
belt|way +s
be¦luga +s
bel¦ve¦dere +s
be¦ly¦ing (present
  participle of belie)
be¦med¦aled Am.
be¦med¦alled Br.
be¦mire
  be¦mires

be¦mire (*cont.*)
 be¦mired
 be¦mir¦ing
be¦moan +s +ed
 +ing
be¦muse
 be¦muses
 be¦mused
 be¦mus¦ing
be¦mused¦ly
be¦muse¦ment
Ben
Ben¦ares (former
 name of
 Varanasi)
Ben¦bec¦ula
 (Scottish island)
Ben Bella, Ahmed
 (Algerian
 statesman)
bench
 benches
 benched
 bench¦ing
bench¦er +s
bench¦mark +s
 +ed +ing
bench seat +s
bench war¦rant +s
bend
 bends
 bent
 bend¦ing
bend¦able
bend¦ed
bend¦er +s
Ben¦digo (town,
 Australia)
bendi¦ness
bend sin¦is¦ter
 bends sin¦is¦ter
bendy
 bend¦ier
 bendi¦est
be¦neath
Bene¦di¦cite
 (canticle)
bene¦di¦cite +s
 (blessing; grace)
Bene¦dict
Bene¦dic¦tine +s
 (monk or nun)
Bene¦dic¦tine
 (liqueur) *Propr.*
bene¦dic¦tion +s
bene¦dic¦tory
Bene¦dic¦tus
bene¦fac¦tion +s
bene¦fac¦tor +s
bene¦fac¦tress
 bene¦fac¦tresses
bene¦fice +s

bene¦ficed
bene¦fi¦cence
be¦nefi¦cent
be¦nefi¦cent¦ly
bene¦fi¦cial
bene¦fi¦cial¦ly
bene¦fi¦ciary
 bene¦fi¦ciar¦ies
bene¦fici¦ation
bene¦fit
 bene¦fits
 bene¦fit¦ed *or*
 bene¦fit¦ted
 bene¦fit¦ing *or*
 bene¦fit¦ting
Bene¦lux
 (= Belgium, the
 Netherlands, and
 Luxembourg)
Ben¦en¦den
 (school, England)
Beneš, Ed¦vard
 (Czechoslovak
 statesman)
Benet¦ton,
 Lu¦ciano and
 Giuli¦ana (Italian
 clothing store
 founders)
be¦nevo¦lence
be¦nevo¦lent
be¦nevo¦lent¦ly
Ben¦gal (region,
 India)
Ben¦gali +s
Ben¦ghazi (port,
 Libya)
Ben¦guela (port,
 Angola)
Ben¦guela
 Cur¦rent (off SW
 Africa)
Ben-Gurion,
 David (Israeli
 statesman)
Beni¦dorm
 (Spanish resort)
be¦night¦ed
be¦night¦ed¦ness
be¦nign
be¦nig¦nancy
be¦nig¦nant
be¦nig¦nant¦ly
be¦nig¦nity
 be¦nig¦nities
be¦nign¦ly
Benin
Benin, Bight of
 (off W. Africa)
Be¦nin¦ese
 plural Be¦nin¦ese
beni¦son +s

Ben¦ja¦min (*Bible*;
 name)
Ben¦late *Propr.*
Ben¦nett, Alan
 (English writer)
Ben¦nett, Ar¦nold
 (English writer)
Ben Nevis
 (mountain,
 Scotland)
benni
Be¦noni (city, South
 Africa)
bent +s
Ben¦tham,
 Jer¦emy (English
 philosopher)
Ben¦tham¦ism
Ben¦tham¦ite +s
ben¦thic
ben¦thos
ben¦ton¦ite
ben tro|*vato*
bent¦wood
be¦numb +s +ed
 +ing
Benxi (city, China)
Benz, Karl
 (German car
 maker)
Ben¦ze¦drine *Propr.*
ben¦zene
 (substance
 obtained from
 coal tar)
ben¦zene ring +s
ben¦zen¦oid
ben¦zin (use
 benzine)
ben¦zine
 (substance
 obtained from
 petroleum)
benzo¦di¦azep¦ine
 +s
ben¦zoic
ben¦zoin
ben¦zol
ben¦zole (use
 benzol)
benzo¦quin¦one
ben¦zoyl
ben¦zyl
Beo¦wulf
 (legendary
 Scandinavian
 hero)
be¦queath +s +ed
 +ing
be¦queather +s
be¦quest +s

be¦rate
 be¦rates
 be¦rated
 be¦rat¦ing
Ber¦ber +s
Ber¦bera (port,
 Somalia)
ber¦beris
ber ceuse +s
Berch¦tes¦gaden
 (town, Germany)
be¦reave
 be¦reaves
 be¦reaved *or*
 be¦reft
 be¦reav¦ing
be¦reave¦ment +s
be¦reft
Bere¦nice (Egyptian
 queen; name)
beret +s (cap.
 △ berry, bury)
Berg, Alban
 (Austrian
 composer)
berg +s (ice.
 △ burg)
ber¦ga¦masque +s
Ber¦gamo (city,
 Italy)
ber¦ga¦mot +s
Ber¦gen (city,
 Norway)
Ber¦ger, Hans
 (German
 psychiatrist)
Ber¦gerac +s
 (region, France;
 wine)
Ber¦gerac, Cyr¦ano
 de (French soldier
 and writer)
Ber¦gius,
 Fried¦rich
 (German industrial
 chemist)
Berg¦man,
 Ing¦mar (Swedish
 film and theatre
 director)
Berg¦man, Ing¦rid
 (Swedish actress)
berg¦schrund +s
Berg¦son, Henri
 (French
 philosopher)
berg wind +s
Beria, Lav¦renti
 (head of Soviet
 secret police)
be¦rib¦boned
beri¦beri

Ber¦ing, Vitus
(Danish navigator
and explorer)
Ber¦ing Sea (part of
N. Pacific)
Ber¦ing Strait
(between Siberia
and Alaska)
Berio, Lu¦ciano
(Italian composer)
berk +s
Berke¦leian +s
Berke¦ley (city and
university, USA.
△ Barkly)
Berke¦ley, Busby
(American
choreographer.
△ Barclay)
Berke¦ley, George
(Irish philosopher
and bishop.
△ Barclay)
ber¦ke¦lium
Berks.
(= Berkshire)
Berk¦shire (county,
England)
Ber¦lin (capital of
Germany)
Ber¦lin, Ir¦ving
(American song
writer)
ber¦lin +s
(carriage)
Ber¦lin¦er +s
Ber¦lioz, Hec¦tor
(French
composer)
berm +s
Ber¦muda (country;
rig; shorts)
Ber¦mudan +s
Ber¦mu¦das
(= Bermuda
shorts)
Ber¦mu¦das, the
(= Bermuda)
**Ber¦muda
Tri¦angle** (area of
W. Atlantic)
Ber¦mu¦dian +s
Bern (German
name for Berne)
Ber¦na¦dette *also*
Ber¦nar¦dette
(name)
Ber¦na¦dette
(French saint)
**Ber¦na¦dotte,
Folke** (Swedish
statesman)

Ber¦na¦dotte, Jean
(French soldier)
Ber¦nard (French
saint; name)
Ber¦nard, Claude
(French
physiologist)
Ber¦nar¦dette *also*
Ber¦na¦dette
**Ber¦nard of
Clair¦vaux**
(French saint)
Berne (capital of
Switzerland)
Bern¦hardt, Sarah
(French actress)
Ber¦nice
**Ber¦nini,
Gian¦lor¦enzo**
(Italian sculptor)
Ber¦noulli (Swiss
family of
mathematicians
and scientists)
Bern¦stein, Basil
(English
sociologist and
educationist)
**Bern¦stein,
Leon¦ard**
(American
composer etc.)
Berra, Yogi
(American
baseball player)
Berry (former
province, France)
Berry, Chuck
(American singer
and songwriter)
berry
ber¦ries
ber¦ried
berry¦ing
(fruit. △ beret,
bury)
ber¦serk
ber¦serk¦er +s
Bert *also* Burt
berth +s +ed +ing
(bed; place for
ship. △ birth)
Ber¦tha (name)
ber¦tha +s (collar;
cape)
**Ber¦til¦lon,
Al¦phonse**
(French
criminologist)
**Ber¦to¦lucci,
Ber¦nardo** (Italian
film director)

Ber¦tram
Ber¦trand
Ber¦wick¦shire
(former county,
Scotland)
**Berwick-upon-
Tweed** (town,
England)
Beryl (name)
beryl +s (precious
stone)
beryl¦lium
Ber¦ze¦lius, Jöns
(Swedish chemist)
Bes *Egyptian
Mythology*
Be¦san¦çon (city,
France)
Bes¦ant, Annie
(English writer
and politician)
be¦seech
be¦seeches
be¦seeched *or*
be¦sought
be¦seech¦ing
beset
be¦sets
beset
be¦set¦ting
be¦set¦ment
be¦side
be¦sides
be¦siege
be¦sieges
be¦sieged
be¦sieging
be¦sieger +s
be¦slaver +s +ed
+ing
be¦slob¦ber +s +ed
+ing
be¦smear +s +ed
+ing
be¦smirch
be¦smirches
be¦smirched
be¦smirch¦ing
besom +s
be¦sot¦ted
be¦sought
be¦span¦gle
be¦span¦gles
be¦span¦gled
be¦span¦gling
be¦spat¦ter +s +ed
+ing
be¦speak
be¦speaks
be¦spoke
be¦speak¦ing
be¦spoken

be¦spec¦tacled
be¦sprin¦kle
be¦sprin¦kles
be¦sprin¦kled
be¦sprink¦ling
Bess
Bess¦arabia
(region, Moldova
and Ukraine)
Bess¦arab¦ian +s
**Bes¦sel, Fried¦rich
Wil¦helm**
(German
astronomer)
Bes¦semer, Henry
(English engineer
and inventor;
process;
converter)
Bes¦sie *also* Bessy
Bessy *also* Bes¦sie
**Best, Charles
Her¦bert**
(Canadian
physiologist)
Best, George (Irish
footballer)
best
bests
best¦ed
best¦ing
(superlative of
good)
bes¦tial
bes¦tial¦ise *Br.* (use
bestialize)
bes¦tial¦ises
bes¦tial¦ised
bes¦tial¦is¦ing
bes¦ti¦al¦ity
bes¦ti¦al¦ities
bes¦tial¦ize
bes¦tial¦izes
bes¦tial¦ized
bes¦tial¦iz¦ing
bes¦ti¦al¦ly
bes¦tiary
bes¦tiar¦ies
be¦stir
be¦stirs
be¦stirred
be¦stir¦ring
best-known
be¦stow +s +ed
+ing
be¦stow¦al +s
be¦stow¦ment
be¦strew
be¦strews
be¦strewed
be¦strew¦ling

be|strew (cont.)
  be|strewed or
  be|strewn
be|stride
  be|strides
  be|strode
  be|strid|ing
  be|strid|den
best-seller +s
best-selling
Bet also Bette
  (name)
bet
  bets
  bet or bet|ted
  bet|ting
  (wager)
beta +s (Greek
  letter. △ beater)
beta block|er +s
beta decay
be|take
  be|takes
  be|took
  be|tak|ing
  be|taken
Beta|max *Propr.*
beta par|ticle +s
beta ray +s
beta rhythm +s
beta test +s +ed
  +ing
be|ta|tron +s
beta waves
betel +s (leaf.
  △ beetle)
Betel|geuse (star)
betel-nut +s
bête noire
  bêtes noires
Beth
Bethan
Beth|any
bethel +s
be|think
  be|thinks
  be|thought
  be|think|ing
Beth|le|hem (town,
  Israel)
Beth|une, Henry
  Nor|man
  (Canadian
  surgeon)
be|tide
be|times
bêt|ise +s
Betje|man, John
  (English poet)
be|token +s +ed
  +ing

bet|ony
  bet|onies
be|took
be|tray +s +ed
  +ing
be|tray|al +s
be|tray|er +s
be|troth +s +ed
  +ing
be|troth|al +s
Betsy
Bette also Bet
bet|ter +s +ed
  +ing
bet|ter|ment
better-off *attributive*
Bet|ter|ton,
  Thomas (English
  actor)
Betti, Ugo (Italian
  writer)
Bet|tina
bet|ting shop +s
bet|tor +s (use
  better)
Betty
be|tween
be|twixt
Beu|lah
Beu|then (German
  name for Bytom)
Bevan, An|eurin
  (Nye) (British
  politician. △ Bevin)
beva|tron
bevel
  bevels
  bev|elled *Br.*
  bev|eled *Am.*
  bev|el|ling *Br.*
  bev|el|ing *Am.*
bev|er|age +s
Bev|er|idge,
  Wil|liam (British
  economist)
Bev|er|ley also
  Bev|erly
  (name)
Bev|er|ley (town,
  England)
Bev|erly also
  Bev|er|ley
  (name)
Bev|erly Hills (city,
  USA)
Bevin, Er|nest
  (British
  statesman.
  △ Bevan)
bevvy
  bev|vies
  (drink)

bevy
  bev|ies
  (flock)
be|wail +s +ed
  +ing
be|wail|er +s
be|ware
be|whis|kered
Bew|ick, Thomas
  (English artist and
  engraver)
Bew|ick's swan +s
be|wigged
be|wil|der +s +ed
  +ing
be|wil|der|ing|ly
be|wil|der|ment
be|witch
  be|witches
  be|witched
  be|witch|ing
be|witch|ing|ly
bey +s (Ottoman
  governor. △ bay)
be|yond
bez|ant +s
bezel +s
be|zique +s
be|zoar +s
B-film +s
Bhag|avad|gita
bhaji +s
bhakti
bhang (drug.
  △ bang)
bhangra
bharal +s
Bha|rat|pur (bird
  sanctuary, India)
Bhav|nagar (port,
  India)
Bhoj|puri
Bho|pal (city,
  India)
Bhu|ba|nes|war
  (city, India)
Bhu|tan
Bhu|tan|ese
  plural Bhu|tan|ese
Bhutto, Bena|zir
  and Zul|fikar
  (Pakistani prime
  ministers)
bi +s (= bisexual.
  △ buy, by, bye)
Bi|afra
Bi|af|ran +s
Bia|łys|tok (city,
  Poland)
Bi|anca

bi|an|nual (half-
  yearly.
  △ biennial)
bi|an|nu|al|ly (half-
  yearly.
  △ biennially)
Biar|ritz (resort,
  France)
bias
  biases
  biased or biassed
  bias|ing or
  bias|sing
bias-ply
bi|ath|lete +s
bi|ath|lon +s
bi|axial
bib
  bibs
  bibbed
  bib|bing
bib|ber +s
bib-cock +s
bibe|lot +s
Bible (Christian or
  Jewish scriptures)
bible +s (generally)
Bible-basher +s
Bible-bashing
Bible belt
Bible-puncher +s
Bible-punching
Bible-thumper +s
Bible-thumping
bib|lical
bib|lic|al|ly
bibli|og|raph|er +s
bib|lio|graph|ic
bib|lio|graph|ic|al
bib|lio|graph|ic|
  al|ly
bibli|og|ra|phise
  Br. (use
  bibliographize)
  bibli|og|ra|phises
  bibli|og|ra|phised
  bibli|
    og|ra|phis|ing
bibli|og|ra|phize
  bibli|og|ra|phizes
  bibli|og|ra|phized
  bibli|
    og|ra|phiz|ing
bibli|og|raphy
  bibli|og|raph|ies
bib|lio|mancy
bib|lio|mania
bib|lio|maniac +s
bib|lio|phil +s
bib|lio|phile +s
bib|lio|phil|ic
bibli|oph|ily

bib|lio|pole +s
bibli|op|oly
bibu|lous
bibu|lous|ness
bi|cam|eral
bi|cam|eral|ism
bi|carb
bi|car|bon|ate +s
bice +s
bi|cen|ten|ary
  bi|cen|ten|ar|ies
bi|cen|ten|nial +s
bi|ceph|al|ous
bi|ceps
  plural bi|ceps
bicker +s +ed +ing
bick|er|er +s
bicky
  bick|ies
bi|color Am. +s
bi|col|ored Am.
bi|col|our Br. +s
bi|col|oured Br.
bi|con|cave
bi|con|vex
bi|cul|tural
bi|cus|pid +s
bi|cus|pi|date
bi|cycle
  bi|cycles
  bi|cycled
  bi|cyc|ling
bi|cyc|ler +s
bi|cyc|lic
bi|cyc|list +s
bid
  bids
  bid
  or bade archaic
  bid|ding
  bid
  or bid|den archaic
bid|dabil|ity
bid|dable
bid|der +s
bid|ding prayer +s
Biddy (name)
biddy
  bid|dies
  (woman)
bide
  bides
  bided
  bid|ing
bidet +s
bi|dir|ec|tion|al
bid|on|ville +s
Bie|der|meier
Biele|feld (city,
  Germany)
bi|en|nia

bi|en|nial +s (two-
  yearly.
  △ biannual)
bi|en|ni|al|ly (two-
  yearly.
  △ biannually)
bi|en|nium
  bi|en|ni|ums or
  bi|en|nia
bier +s (coffin-
  stand. △ beer)
Bierce, Am|brose
  (American writer)
bier|wurst
biff +s +ed +ing
bif|fin +s
bifid
bif|ida (in 'spina
  bifida')
bi|focal +s
bi|fur|cate
  bi|fur|cates
  bi|fur|cated
  bi|fur|cat|ing
bi|fur|ca|tion
big
  big|ger
  big|gest
bigam|ist +s
bigam|ous
big|amy
Big Dip|per
  (constellation)
big dip|per +s
  (switchback)
Big|foot
  Big|feet
  (creature)
big|gie +s
big|gish
big-head +s
big-headed
big-headed|ness
big-hearted
big|horn +s
bight +s (inlet;
  loop. △ bite, byte)
big-league
  attributive
big-name attributive
big|ness
bigot +s
big|ot|ed
big|ot|ry
  big|ot|ries
big-timer +s
big|wig +s
Bihar (state, India)
Bi|hari +s
bijou (small and
  elegant)

bijou
  bi|joux
  (jewel)
bi|jou|terie
bike
  bikes
  biked
  bik|ing
biker +s
bikie +s
Bi|kini (atoll, W.
  Pacific)
bi|kini +s
  (garment)
bikky (use bicky)
  bik|kies
Biko, Steve (South
  African black
  activist)
bi|la|bial
bi|lat|eral
bi|lat|eral|ism
bi|lat|eral|ly
Bil|bao (city, Spain)
bill|berry
  bill|berries
bilbo
  bil|bos or bil|boes
  (sword)
bil|boes (ankle
  shackles)
Bil|dungs|roman
  Bil|dungs|romane
bile
bile duct +s
bilge
  bilges
  bilged
  bil|ging
bilge keel +s
bilge water
bil|har|zia
bil|har|zia|sis
bill|iary
bi|lin|gual +s
bi|lin|gual|ism
bili|ous
bili|ous|ness
bili|ru|bin
bilk +s +ed +ing
bilk|er +s
Bill (name)
bill +s +ed +ing
bill|able
billa|bong +s
bill|board +s
bil|let +s +ed +ing
billet-doux
  billets-doux
bil|let|ee +s
bil|let|er +s
bill|fold +s

bill|head +s
bill|hook +s
bil|liard
bil|liards
Bil|lings|gate
  (market, London)
bil|lion +s
bil|lion|aire +s
bil|lion|air|ess
  bil|lion|air|esses
bil|lionth +s
Bil|li|ton
  (= Belitung)
Bill of Rights
bil|lon
bil|low +s +ed
  +ing (wave.
  △ below)
bil|lowy
bill|post|er +s
bill|post|ing
bill|stick|er +s
Billy (name)
billy
  bil|lies
  (billycan; billy
  goat)
billy|can +s
billy|cart +s
billy goat +s
billy-o
billy-oh (use
  billy-o)
bi|lob|ate
bi|lobed
bil|tong
bi|manal
bim|an|ous
bim|bashi +s
bimbo +s
bi-media
bi|met|al|lic
bi|met|al|lism
bi|met|al|list +s
bi|mil|len|ary
  bi|mil|len|ar|ies
bi|modal
bi|month|ly
  bi|month|lies
bin
  bins
  binned
  bin|ning
bin|ary
  bin|ar|ies
bin|ate
bin|aural
bind
  binds
  bound
  bind|ing
bind|er +s

bind|ery
  bind|er|ies
bindi-eye
bind|ing+s
bind|weed+s
bine+s
bin-end+s
Binet, Al|fred
  (French
  psychologist)
Binet–Simon (test)
binge
  binges
  binged
  binge|ing or
  bin|ging
bin|gie+s (use
  bingy)
bin|gle+s
bingo+s
bingy
  bin|gies
bin liner+s
bin|man
  bin|men
bin|nacle+s
Bin|nie
bin|ocu|lar
bin|ocu|lars
bi|no|mial+s
bi|no|mi|al|ly
bi|nom|inal
bint+s
bin|tur|ong+s
bio|assay+s
bio|cen|ology Am.
  (Br.
  biocoenology)
bio|cen|osis Am.
  bio|cen|oses
  (Br. biocoenosis)
bio|cen|ot|ic Am.
  (Br. biocoenotic)
bio|ceram|ic+s
bio|chem|ical+s
bio|chem|ist+s
bio|chem|is|try
bio|chip+s
bio|cide+s
bio|coen|ology Br.
  (Am.
  biocenology)
bio|coen|osis Br.
  bio|coen|oses
  (Am. biocenosis)
bio|coen|ot|ic Br.
  (Am. biocenotic)
bio|com|pati|
    bil|ity
bio|com|pat|ible
bio|com|put|ing
bio|con|trol

bio|degrad|abil|ity
bio|degrad|able
bio|deg|rad|ation
bio|diver|sity
bio|ener|get|ic
bio|ener|get|ics
bio|energy
bio|engin|eer+s
bio|engin|eer|ing
bio|eth|cist+s
bio|eth|ics
bio|feed|back
bio|flavon|oid
bio|gas
bio|gen|esis
bio|gen|et|ic
bio|gen|ic
bio|geo|graph|ic
bio|geo|graph|ic|al
bio|geog|raphy
biog|raph|er+s
biog|raph|ic
biog|raph|ic|al
biog|raphy
  biog|raph|ies
bio|haz|ard+s
Bioko (island,
  Equatorial Guinea)
bio|logic|al
bio|logic|al|ly
biolo|gist+s
biol|ogy
  biol|ogies
bio|lu|min|
    es|cence
bio|lu|min|es|cent
bio|mass
  bio|masses
bio|mater|ial+s
bio|mathe|mat|ics
biome+s
bio|mech|an|ics
bio|med|ical
bio|medi|cine
bio|met|ric
bio|met|ric|al
bio|met|ri|cian+s
bio|met|rics
bi|om|etry
bio|morph+s
bio|morph|ic
bi|onic
bi|on|ic|al|ly
bi|on|ics
bio|nomic
bio|nom|ics
bio|phys|ic|al
bio|physi|cist+s
bio|phys|ics
bio|pic+s
bi|opsy
  bi|op|sies

bio|rhythm
bio|rhyth|mic
bio|rhyth|mic|
    al|ly
bio|scope+s
bio|sen|sor+s
bio|sphere+s
bio|syn|thesis
  bio|syn|theses
bio|syn|thet|ic
biota
bio|tech|nolo|gist
  +s
bio|tech|nol|ogy
  bio|tech|nolo|gies
bi|ot|ic
bio|tin
bio|tite+s
bi|par|tisan
bi|par|tisan|ship
bi|part|ite
biped+s
bi|pedal
bi|pedal|ism
bi|pedal|ity
bi|phenyl+s
bi|pin|nate
bi|plane+s
bi|po|lar
bi|po|lar|ity
birch
  birches
birch-bark
birch|en
birch-rod+s
birch|wood
bird+s +ed +ing
bird bath+s
bird|brain+s
bird|brained
bird|cage+s
bird call+s
bird|er+s
bird-fancier+s
bir|die
  bir|dies
  bir|died
  birdy|ing
bird|lime
bird-nesting
bird|seed
Birds|eye,
  Clar|ence
  (American
  inventor of frozen
  food)
bird's-eye (plant)
bird's-eye view
bird's-foot+s
  (plant)
bird's-nesting
bird's nest soup

bird|song
bird-strike+s
bird table+s
bird|watch|er+s
bird|watch|ing
bi|refrin|gence
bi|refrin|gent
bi|reme+s
bi|retta+s
Bir|gitta (Swedish
  name for St
  Bridget)
biri|ani+s
Bir|ken|head (port,
  England)
Bir|ming|ham
  (cities, England
  and USA)
biro+s Propr.
birth+s +ed +ing
  (being born.
  △ berth)
birth con|trol
birth|day+s
birth|mark+s
birth|place+s
birth rate+s
birth|right+s
birth|stone+s
birth|weight
Birt|wistle,
  Har|ri|son
  (English
  composer)
biry|ani+s (use
  biriani)
Bis|cay (shipping
  area)
Bis|cay, Bay of
  (between France
  and Spain)
bis|cotti
bis|cuit+s
bis|cuity
bise+s (wind)
bi|sect+s +ed
  +ing
bi|sec|tion+s
bi|sect|or+s
bi|sex|ual+s
bi|sexu|al|ity
bish
  bishes
Bish|kek (capital of
  Kyrgyzstan)
Bisho (town, South
  Africa)
bishop+s
bish|op|ric+s
bisk+s (use
  bisque)
Bis|lama

Bis|marck (city, USA)

Bis|marck, Otto, Prince of (German statesman)

Bis|marck Archi|pel|ago (Papua New Guinea)

Bis|marck Sea (part of W. Pacific)

bis|muth

bison
  plural bison

bisque +s

Bis|sa|gos Is|lands (off W. Africa)

Bis|sau (capital of Guinea-Bissau)

bis|sex|tile +s

bi|stable

bis|ter *Am.* +s (*Br.* bistre)

bis|tort

bis|toury
  bis|tour|ies

bistre *Br.* +s (*Am.* bister)

bis|tro +s

bi|sul|fate *Am.* +s

bi|sul|phate *Br.* +s

bit
  bits
  bit|ted
  bit|ting
  (small part; tool; part of bridle; *Computing*; past tense of **bite**.
  △ bitts)

bitch
  bitches
  bitched
  bitch|ing

bitch|ily

bitchi|ness

bitchy
  bitch|ier
  bitchi|est

bite
  bites
  bit
  bit|ing
  bit|ten
  (cut with teeth; etc. △ **bight, byte**)

biter +s

bite-size

bite-sized

Bi|thynia (ancient region, Asia Minor)

bit|ing|ly

bit|map
  bit|maps
  bit|mapped
  bit|map|ping

bit part +s

bit|ser +s (use bitzer)

bit|ter +s +er +est

bitter-apple +s

bit|ter|ling +s

bit|ter|ly

bit|tern +s

bit|ter|ness

bitter-sweet

bit|tily

bit|ti|ness

bitts (*Nautical.*
  △ bit)

bitty
  bit|tier
  bit|ti|est

bitu|men

bi|tu|min|isa|tion
  Br. (use bituminization)

bi|tu|min|ise *Br.*
  (use bituminize)
  bi|tu|min|ises
  bi|tu|min|ised
  bi|tu|min|is|ing

bi|tu|min|iza|tion

bi|tu|min|ize
  bi|tu|min|izes
  bi|tu|min|ized
  bi|tu|min|iz|ing

bi|tu|min|ous

bit|zer +s

bi|va|lent *Chemistry*

biva|lent +s
  Biology

bi|valve +s

biv|ouac
  biv|ouacs
  biv|ou|acked
  biv|ou|ack|ing

bivvy
  biv|vies

bi|week|ly
  bi|week|lies

bi|year|ly

biz

bi|zarre

bi|zarre|ly

bi|zarre|ness

bi|zar|rerie

Bi|zerta (port, Tunisia)

Bi|zerte (use Bizerta)

Bizet, Georges (French composer)

Bjerk|nes, Vil|helm (Norwegian geophysicist and meteorologist)

blab
  blabs
  blabbed
  blab|bing

blab|ber +s +ed +ing

blab|ber|mouth +s

Black, Jo|seph (Scottish chemist)

black +s +ed +ing +er +est (colour; person)

black|amoor +s

black and blue

Black and Tans

black and white

black|ball +s +ed +ing

black|berry
  black|berries

black|berry|ing

black|bird +s

black|board +s

black|boy +s (tree)

black|buck
  plural black|buck

Black|burn (town, England)

black|cap +s (bird)

black|cock
  plural black|cock
  or black|cocks

black|cur|rant +s

black|en +s +ed +ing

Black|ett, Pat|rick (English physicist)

black-eye bean +s

black-eyed bean +s

black-eyed Susan +s

black|face (sheep; make-up)

black|fel|low +s

black|fish
  plural black|fish

black|fly
  plural black|fly *or* black|flies

Black|foot
  plural Black|foot
  or Black|feet

Black For|est gat|eau
  Black For|est gat|eaus *or* Black For|est gat|eaux

black|guard +s

black|guard|ly

black|head +s

black|ish

black|jack +s

black|lead +s +ed +ing

black|leg
  black|legs
  black|legged
  black|leg|ging

black|list +s +ed +ing

black|ly

black|mail +s +ed +ing

black|mail|er +s

Black Maria +s

black mar|ket +s

black mar|ket|eer +s

black mar|ket|eer|ing

black mass
  black masses

Black|more, R. D. (English writer)

black|ness

black|out +s

Black|pool (city, England)

black power

black|shirt +s (fascist)

black|smith +s

black spot +s

Black|stone, Wil|liam (English jurist)

black|thorn +s

black|top +s

black|water fever

blad|der +s

blad|der|wort

blad|der|wrack

blade +s

blade-bone +s

bladed

blae|berry
  blae|berries

blag
  blags
  blagged
  blag|ging

blag|ger +s
blague
bla|gueur +s
blah
blah-blah
blain +s
Blair (name)
Blair, Tony
(Scottish
politician)
Blaise
Blake (name)
Blake, Peter
(English painter)
Blake, Wil|liam
(English artist and
poet)
blakey +s
blam|able *Am.* (*Br.*
blameable)
blame
blames
blamed
blam|ing
blame|able *Br.*
(*Am.* blamable)
blame|ful
blame|ful|ly
blame|less
blame|less|ness
blame|worthi|ness
blame|worthy
blanch
blanches
blanched
blanch|ing
Blan|chard, Jean
(French
balloonist)
Blanche
blanc|mange +s
blanco
blan|coes
blan|coed
blanco|ing
bland +er +est
bland|ish
bland|ishes
bland|ished
bland|ish|ing
bland|ish|ment +s
bland|ly
bland|ness
blank +s +ed +ing
+er +est
blan|ket +s +ed
+ing
blan|ket|weed
blank|ety
blank|ness
blanky
blan|quette +s

Blan|tyre (city,
Malawi)
blare
blares
blared
blar|ing
blar|ney
blasé
blas|pheme
blas|phemes
blas|phemed
blas|phem|ing
blas|phemer +s
blas|phem|ous
blas|phem|ous|ly
blas|phemy
blas|phemies
blast +s +ed +ing
blast|er +s
blast-furnace +s
blast-hole +s
blast-off +s *noun*
blas|tula
blas|tu|lae *or*
blas|tu|las
bla|tancy
bla|tant
bla|tant|ly
blather +s +ed
+ing
blather|skite +s
Blaue Reit|er, Der
(German painters)
Bla|vat|sky,
Ma|dame
(Russian
spiritualist)
blax|ploit|ation
blaze
blazes
blazed
blaz|ing
blazer +s
blaz|ing|ly
blazon +s +ed
+ing
blaz|on|ment
blaz|on|ry
bleach
bleaches
bleached
bleach|ing
bleach|er +s
bleach|ing
pow|der +s
bleak +er +est
bleak|ly
bleak|ness
blear
blear|ily
bleari|ness

bleary
blear|ier
bleari|est
bleary-eyed
bleat +s +ed +ing
bleat|ing|ly
bleb +s
bleed
bleeds
bled
bleed|ing
bleed|er +s (*coarse
slang*)
bleep +s +ed +ing
bleep|er +s
blem|ish
blem|ishes
blem|ished
blem|ish|ing
blench
blenches
blenched
blench|ing
blend +s +ed +ing
(mix; mixture)
blende +s (metal
sulphide)
blend|er +s
Blen|heim
(battlefield,
Germany)
Blen|heim Or|ange
+s (apple)
Blen|heim Pal|ace
(in England)
blenny
blen|nies
blent
bleph|ar|itis
Blér|iot, Louis
(French aviator)
bles|bok
plural bles|bok
bles|buck +s
bless
blesses
blessed
bless|ing
bless|ed|ly
bless|ed|ness
bless|ing +s
blest (*poetic
= blessed*)
blether +s +ed
+ing
blether|skate +s
(use blatherskite)
blew (past tense of
blow. △ blue)
blew|its
plural blew|its

Bligh, Wil|liam
(captain of *The
Bounty*)
blight +s +ed +ing
blight|er +s
Blighty
(= England)
bli|mey
Blimp (in 'Colonel
Blimp')
blimp +s (airship;
barrage balloon;
camera cover)
blimp|ery
blimp|ish
blind +s +ed +ing
+er +est
blind|er +s
blind|fold +s +ed
+ing
blind|ing|ly
blind|ly
blind man's buff
blind|ness
blind side
blind stitch *noun*
blind-stitch
blind-stitches
blind-stitched
blind-stitch|ing
verb
blind|worm +s
blink +s +ed +ing
blink|er +s +ed
+ing
blip
blips
blipped
blip|ping
Bliss, Ar|thur
(English
composer)
bliss
blisses
blissed
bliss|ing
bliss|ful
bliss|ful|ly
bliss|ful|ness
blis|ter +s +ed
+ing
blis|tery
blithe
blither
blith|est
blithe|ly
blithe|ness
blith|er|ing
blithe|some
Blitz, the (on
London in 1940)

blitz
  blitzes
  blitzed
  blitz|ing
  (generally)
blitz|krieg +s
Blixen, Karen
  (Danish writer)
bliz|zard +s +ing
bloat +s +ed +ing
bloat|er +s
blob
  blobs
  blobbed
  blob|bing
bloc +s (group of
  governments etc.
  △ block)
Bloch, Er|nest
  (Swiss-born
  composer)
block +s +ed +ing
block|ade
  block|ades
  block|aded
  block|ad|ing
block|ader +s
blockade-runner
  +s
block|age +s
block|board +s
block|bust|er +s
block|bust|ing
block|er +s
block|head +s
block|head|ed
block|head|ing
block|house +s
block|ish
block|ish|ly
block|ish|ness
block|ship +s
bloc vote +s (use
  block vote)
Blod|wen
Bloem|fon|tein
  (judicial capital of
  South Africa)
Blok, Alex|an|der
  (Russian poet)
bloke +s *male*
blond +s *male*
blonde +s *female*
Blon|del (minstrel)
Blon|din, Charles
  (French tightrope-
  walker)
blond|ness
Blood
  plural Blood *or*
  Bloods
  (American Indian)

blood +s +ed +ing
  (body fluid)
**blood-and-
  thunder**
blood bank +s
blood|bath +s
blood-borne
blood brother +s
blood cell +s
blood clot +s
blood-curdling
blood donor +s
blood-heat
blood|hound +s
blood|ily
bloodi|ness
blood|less
blood|less|ly
blood|less|ness
blood|let|ting
blood|line +s
blood|lust
blood money
blood poi|son|ing
blood pres|sure
blood red +s *noun
  and adjective*
blood-red
  attributive
blood|shed
blood|shot
blood sport +s
blood|stain +s
blood|stained
blood|stock
blood|stone +s
blood|stream +s
blood|suck|er +s
blood|suck|ing
blood sugar
blood test +s
blood|thirst|ily
blood|thirsti|ness
blood|thirsty
  blood|thirst|ier
  blood|thirsti|est
blood ves|sel +s
blood|worm +s
blood-wort +s
bloody
  blood|ies
  blood|ied
  bloody|ing
  blood|ier
  bloodi|est
Bloody Mary +s
bloody-minded
bloody-minded|ly
**bloody-
  minded|ness**
bloom +s +ed +ing
bloom|er +s

bloom|ery
  bloom|er|ies
**Bloom|field,
  Leon|ard**
  (American
  linguist)
Blooms|bury
  (district, London;
  group of writers)
bloop|er +s
Blos|som (name)
blos|som +s +ed
  +ing (flower)
blos|somy
blot
  blots
  blot|ted
  blot|ting
blotch
  blotches
  blotched
  blotch|ing
blotchy
  blotch|ier
  blotchi|est
blot|ter +s
blot|ting paper
blotto
blouse
  blouses
  bloused
  blous|ing
blouson +s
blow
  blows
  blew
  blow|ing
  blown
  (all senses except
  'curse')
blow
  blows
  blowed
  blow|ing
  (curse)
blow-ball +s
blow-by-blow
  attributive
blow-drier +s (use
  blow-dryer)
blow-dry
  blow-dries
  blow-dried
  blow-drying
blow-dryer +s
blow|er +s
blow|fish
  plural blow|fish
blow|fly
  blow|flies
blow|gun +s
blow|hard +s

blow|hole +s
blowi|ness
blow job +s (*coarse
  slang*)
blow|lamp +s
blown
blow-out +s *noun*
blow|pipe +s
blow|torch
  blow|torches
blow-up +s *noun*
blowy
  blow|ier
  blowi|est
blowz|ily
blowzi|ness
blowzy
  blowz|ier
  blowzi|est
blub
  blubs
  blubbed
  blub|bing
blub|ber +s +ed
  +ing
blub|ber|ing|ly
blub|bery
blu|chers
bludge
  bludges
  bludged
  bludg|ing
bludg|eon +s +ed
  +ing
bludger +s
blue
  blues
  blued
  blu|ing *or* blue|ing
  bluer
  blu|est
  (colour;
  depressed.
  △ blew)
Blue|beard
  (fictional wife-
  murderer)
blue|bell +s
blue|berry
  blue|berries
blue|bird +s
blue-black
blue-blooded
blue|bot|tle +s
blue-chip *attributive*
blue-collar
  attributive
blue-eyed
Blue|fields (port,
  Nicaragua)
blue|fish
  plural blue|fish

blue|grass
blue-green +s
blue|gum
blue|ish (use
   bluish)
blue|jacket +s
Blue John
   (mineral)
Blue|man|tle
blue|ness
blue-pencil
   blue-pencils
   blue-pencilled Br.
   blue-penciled Am.
   blue-pencil|ling
   Br.
   blue-pencil|ing
   Am.
   verb
blue|print +s +ed
   +ing
blue|stock|ing +s
blue|stone +s
bluesy
bluet +s
blue|throat +s
blue tit +s
Blue Vin|ney
bluey +s
bluff +s +ed +ing
bluff|er +s
bluff|ly
bluff|ness
blu|ish
Blum, Léon
   (French
   statesman)
Blu|men|bach,
   Jo|hann (German
   physiologist)
Blun|den,
   Ed|mund
   (English writer)
blun|der +s +ed
   +ing
blun|der|buss
   blun|der|busses
blun|der|ing|ly
blunge
   blunges
   blunged
   blun|ging
blun|ger +s
Blunt, An|thony
   (English art
   historian and
   Soviet spy)
blunt +s +ed +ing
   +er +est
blunt|ly
blunt|ness

blur
   blurs
   blurred
   blur|ring
blurb +s
blurry
   blur|rier
   blur|ri|est
blurt +s +ed +ing
blush
   blushes
   blushed
   blush|ing
blush|er +s
blush|ful
blus|ter +s +ed
   +ing
blus|tery
B-lympho|cyte +s
Bly|ton, Enid
   (English writer)
B-movie +s
B.Mus. (= Bachelor
   of Music)
B'nai B'rith
   (Jewish
   organization)
Bo (woman's name.
   ∆ Beau)
bo +s (interjection;
   form of address to
   man. ∆ beau,
   bow)
boa +s (snake;
   feather stole.
   ∆ Boer)
Boa|di|cea (use
   Boudicca)
boar
   plural boar or
   boars
   (pig. ∆ Boer,
   boor, bore)
board +s +ed +ing
   (timber; go on
   board ship, train,
   etc. ∆ baud,
   bawd, bored)
board|er +s
   (person who
   boards. ∆ border)
board game +s
board|ing house
   +s
board|ing ken|nel
   +s
board|ing school
   +s
board|room +s
board|sail|er +s
   (use boardsailor)
board|sail|ing +s

board|sail|or +s
board|walk +s
boart +s (use bort
   diamond.
   ∆ bought)
Boas, Franz
   (American
   anthropologist)
boast +s +ed +ing
boast|er +s
boast|ful
boast|ful|ly
boast|ful|ness
boast|ing|ly
boat +s +ed +ing
boat|build|er +s
boat-building
boatel +s (use
   botel)
boat|er +s
boat|ful +s
boat-hook +s
boat|house +s
boatie +s
boat|load +s
boat|man
   boat|men
boat people
boat race +s
boat|swain +s
boat|swain's chair
   +s
boat-train +s
boat|yard +s
Boa Vista (town,
   Brazil)
Boaz
Bob (name, but
   'bob's your uncle')
bob
   bobs
   bobbed
   bob|bing
bob|ber +s
Bob|bie also Bobby
bob|bin +s
bob|binet +s
bob|bin lace
bob|ble +s
bob|bly
Bobby also Bobbie
   (name)
bobby
   bob|bies
bobby-dazzler +s
bobby-pin +s
bobby socks Br.
bobby sox Am.
bobby-soxer +s
bob|cat +s
bobo|link +s

Bo|bru|isk (use
   Babruisk)
bob|sled +s
bob|sled|ding
bob|sleigh +s
bob|stay +s +ed
   +ing
bob|tail +s
boc|age
Boc|cac|cio,
   Gio|vanni (Italian
   writer and
   humanist)
Boc|cher|ini, Luigi
   (Italian composer)
Boche +s (offensive
   German soldier.
   ∆ bosh)
Bochum (city,
   Germany)
bock +s
bod +s
bo|da|cious
bode
   bodes
   boded
   bod|ing
bode|ful
bo|dega +s
bode|ment +s
Bode's law
bodge
   bodges
   bodged
   bodg|ing
bodgie +s
Bodh|gaya (village,
   India)
Bodhi|sat|tva +s
bod|ice +s
bodice-ripper +s
bodice-ripping
bodi|less
bod|ily
bod|kin +s
Bod|leian Lib|rary
   (in Oxford)
Bod|ley
   (= Bodleian
   Library)
Bo|doni,
   Giam|bat|tista
   (Italian painter)
Bod|rum (town,
   Turkey)
body
   bod|ies
   bod|ied
   body|ing
body bag +s
body blow +s
body|build|er +s

body-building
body-check
　body-checks
　body-checked
　body-checking
body color *Am.* +s
body col|our *Br.*
　+s
body|guard +s
body lan|guage
body-line *attributive*
body louse
　body lice
body pier|cing
body-popping
body scan|ner +s
body-snatch|er +s
body-snatch|ing
body stock|ing +s
body|suit +s
body wall +s
body warm|er +s
body wave +s
body weight
body|work
Boe|otia (region,
　Greece)
Boe|otian +s
Boer +s (Afrikaner.
　△ boa, boar,
　boor, bore)
Bo|eth|ius (Roman
　statesman and
　philosopher)
bof|fin +s
Bo|fors gun +s
bog
　bogs
　bogged
　bog|ging
bogan +s
Bo|garde, Dirk
　(British actor)
Bo|gart,
　Hum|phrey
　(American actor)
bog|bean +s
bogey +s +ed +ing
　(in golf; evil spirit;
　nasal mucus.
　△ bogie)
bo|gey|man
　bo|gey|men
bog|gi|ness
bog|gle
　bog|gles
　bog|gled
　bog|gling
boggy
　bog|gier
　bog|gi|est

bogie +s (wheeled
　undercarriage.
　△ bogey)
bogle +s
Bo|gotá (capital of
　Colombia)
bog|trot|ter +s
　(*offensive*)
bogus
bogus|ness
bogy (use bogey)
　bogies
bogy|man (use
　bogeyman)
　bogy|men
Bo Hai (inlet,
　China)
bohea +s
Bo|he|mia (region,
　Czech Republic)
Bo|he|mian +s
　(from Bohemia)
bo|he|mian +s
　(unconventional)
bo|he|mian|ism
boho +s
Bohol (island,
　Philippines)
Bohr, Niels
　(Danish physicist)
boil +s +ed +ing
Boi|leau, Nico|las
　in full Boileau-
　Despré|aux
　(French critic and
　writer)
boil|er +s
boiler|maker +s
boiler-plate +s
boil|ing point +s
Boise (city, USA)
bois|ter|ous
bois|ter|ous|ly
bois|ter|ous|ness
Bo|kassa, Jean
　(Central African
　dictator)
Bo|khara
　(= Bukhoro)
Bok|mål
boko +s
bolas
　plural bolas
　(missile. △ bolus)
bold +er +est
bold|face *Printing*
bold|ly
bold|ness
Boldre|wood, Rolf
　(Australian writer)

bole +s (trunk of
　tree; clay. △ boll,
　bowl)
bo|lec|tion +s
bol|ero +s
bol|etus
　bol|eti *or*
　bol|etuses
Bo|leyn, Anne
　(wife of Henry
　VIII of England)
Bol|ger, James
　(New Zealand
　prime minister)
Bol|ing|broke
　(surname of
　Henry IV of
　England)
Bol|in|ger, Dwight
　(American
　linguist)
Boli|var, Simón
　(Venezuelan
　patriot and
　statesman)
boli|var +s
　(Venezuelan
　currency)
Bo|livia
Bo|liv|ian +s
bo|liv|iano +s
Böll, Hein|rich
　(German writer)
boll (seed-vessel.
　△ bole, bowl)
Bol|land|ist +s
bol|lard +s
Bol|lin|ger +s
　(champagne)
　Propr.
boll|lock +s +ed
　+ing (*coarse slang*)
boll|lock|ing +s
　(*coarse slang*)
boll|locky (*coarse
　slang*)
boll-weevil +s
Bol|ogna (city,
　Italy)
bol|ogna
　(= Bologna
　sausage)
Bol|ogna saus|age
　+s
Bol|ognese
bol|om|eter +s
bolo|met|ric
bol|om|etry
bo|lo|ney +s (use
　baloney)
Bol|shevik +s
Bol|shev|ism

Bol|shev|ist +s
Bol|shie +s
　(Bolshevik)
bol|shie (rebellious;
　left-wing)
bol|shi|ness
Bol|shoi (Ballet;
　Theatre)
Bol|shy
　Bol|shies
　(use Bolshie)
bol|shy (use
　bolshie)
bol|ster +s +ed
　+ing
bol|ster|er +s
bolt +s +ed +ing
bolt|er +s
bolt-hole +s
Bol|ton (town,
　England)
bolt-on +s *noun
　and adjective*
Boltz|mann,
　Lud|wig
　(Austrian
　physicist)
bolus
　bol|uses
　(ball of food etc.
　△ bolas)
Bol|zano (province
　and city, Italy)
bomb +s +ed +ing
　(explosive device.
　△ bombe)
bom|bard +s +ed
　+ing (attack)
bom|barde +s
　(musical
　instrument)
bom|bard|ier +s
bom|bard|ment +s
bom|bardon +s
bom|bas|ine +s
　(use bombazin)
bom|bast
bom|bas|tic
bom|bas|tic|al|ly
Bom|bay (city,
　India)
bom|baz|ine +s
bombe +s (dessert.
　△ bomb)
bombed-out
　adjective
bomb|er +s
bomb|ing +s
bomb-maker +s
bomb-making
bom|bora +s
bomb|proof

bomb|shell +s
bomb|sight +s
 (device in aircraft)
bomb-site +s (area
 destroyed by
 bomb)
Bon, Cape (in
 Tunisia)
bona fide
bona fides
 plural bona fides
Bon|aire (island,
 Netherlands
 Antilles)
bon|anza +s
Bona|parte,
 Na|po|leon
 (French emperors)
bona va|can|tia
Bona|ven|tura
 (Italian saint)
bon-bon +s
bonce +s
Bond, James
 (fictional British
 agent)
bond +s +ed +ing
bond|age
bond|ager +s
bond|hold|er +s
Bondi (resort,
 Australia)
bondi +s (weapon)
bonds|man
 bonds|men
bond|stone +s
bond-washing
Bône (former name
 of Annaba)
bone
 bones
 boned
 bon|ing
bone china
bone dry
bone|fish
 plural bone|fish
bone|head +s
bone|head|ed
bone idle
bone lazy
bone|less
bone|meal
bone-oil
boner +s
bone-setter +s
bone|shaker +s
bone-yard +s
bon|fire +s
Bon|fire Night
bongo
 plural bongo *or*

bongo (*cont.*)
 bon|gos
 (antelope)
bongo +s (drum)
Bon|hoef|fer,
 Diet|rich
 (German
 theologian)
bon|homie
bon|hom|ous
boni|er
 (comparative of
 bony)
boni|est
 (superlative of
 bony)
Boni|face (Anglo-
 Saxon saint)
boni|ness
Bon|ing|ton, Chris
 (English
 mountaineer)
bon|ism
bon|ist +s
Bon|ita
bon|ito +s
bonk +s +ed +ing
bonk|er +s
bonk|ers
bon mot
 bons mots
Bonn (city,
 Germany)
Bon|nard, Pierre
 (French artist)
bonne bouche
 bonne bouches or
 bonnes bouches
bon|net +s
bon|net|ed
bon|net|head +s
Bon|nie (name)
Bon|nie Prince
 Char|lie (Charles
 Edward Stuart, the
 'Young
 Pretender')
bon|nily
bon|ni|ness
bonny
 bon|nier
 bon|ni|est
 (attractive etc.)
bon|sai +s
bon|spiel +s
bont|bok
 plural bont|bok *or*
 bont|boks
bon|te|bok
 plural bon|te|bok
 or bon|te|boks

bonus
 bo|nuses
bon viv|ant
 bon viv|ants *or*
 bons viv|ants
bon viv|eur
 bon viv|eurs *or*
 bons viv|eurs
bon voy|age
bony
 boni|er
 boni|est
bonze +s
bon|zer
boo +s +ed +ing
boob +s +ed +ing
boo|boo +s
boo|book +s
booby
 boo|bies
booby-hatch
 booby-hatches
booby trap +s
 noun
booby-trap
 booby-traps
 booby-trapped
 booby-trapping
 verb
boo|dle
boof|head +s
boo|gie
 boo|gies
 boo|gied
 boo|gie|ing
boogie-woogie
boo|hoo +s +ed
 +ing
book +s +ed +ing
book|able
book|bind|er +s
book|bind|ing +s
book|case +s
book|end +s
book|er +s
Book|er Prize +s
book|ie +s
book|ing +s
book|ing clerk +s
book|ing hall +s
book|ing of|fice +s
book|ish
book|ish|ness
book|keep|er +s
book|keep|ing
book|land
book|let +s
book|list +s
book-louse
 book-lice
book|maker +s
book|mak|ing

book|man
 book|men
book|mark +s
book|mark|er +s
book|mobile +s
book|plate +s
book-rest +s
book|sell|er +s
book|shelf
 book|shelves
book|shop +s
book|stall +s
book|store +s
booksy
book-trough +s
book|work
book|worm +s
Boole, George
 (English
 mathematician)
Bool|ean +s
boom +s +ed +ing
boom|er +s
boom|er|ang +s
 +ed +ing
boom|let +s
boom|slang +s
boom town +s
boon +s
boon|dock +s
boon|dog|gle
 boon|dog|gles
 boon|dog|gled
 boon|dog|gling
Boone, Dan|iel
 (American
 pioneer)
boong +s (*offensive*)
boon|ies, the
boor +s (rude
 person. △ Boer)
boor|ish
boor|ish|ly
boor|ish|ness
boost +s +ed +ing
boost|er +s
boot +s +ed +ing
boot|black +s
boot|boy +s
bootee +s (shoe.
 △ booty)
Bo|ötes
 (constellation)
boot-faced
Booth, Wil|liam
 and Cath|er|ine
 (founders of the
 Salvation Army)
booth +s
Boothia, Gulf of
 (off Canada)

Boothia
  Pen|in|sula (in
  Canada)
boot|jack +s
boot|lace +s
Boo|tle (town,
  England)
boot|leg
  boot|legs
  boot|legged
  boot|leg|ging
boot|leg|ger +s
boot|less
boot|lick|er +s
boot|maker +s
boot|strap
  boot|straps
  boot|strapped
  boot|strap|ping
boot-tree +s
booty (plunder.
  △ bootee)
booze
  boozes
  boozed
  booz|ing
boozer +s
booze-up +s
booz|ily
boozi|ness
boozy
  booz|ier
  boozi|est
bop
  bops
  bopped
  bop|ping
bo-peep
Bophu|tha|tswana
  (former homeland,
  South Africa)
bop|per +s
bora +s
Bora-Bora (island,
  French Polynesia)
bor|acic
bor|age
borak
bor|ane +s
Borås (city,
  Sweden)
bor|ate +s
borax
Bor|azon
bor|bo|ryg|mic
bor|bo|ryg|mus
  bor|bo|rygmi
Bor|deaux
  plural Bor|deaux
  (city, France;
  wine)
bor|del +s

bor|dello +s
Bor|der, Allan
  (Australian
  cricketer)
bor|der +s +ed
  +ing (edge.
  △ boarder)
Bor|der col|lie +s
bor|der|er +s
bor|der|land +s
bor|der|line +s
Bor|ders (region,
  Scotland)
Bor|der ter|rier +s
Bor|det, Jules
  (Belgian
  bacteriologist and
  immunologist)
Bor|done, Paris
  (Venetian painter)
bord|ure +s
bore
  bores
  bored
  bor|ing
  (make hole; hole;
  wave; past tense
  of bear. △ boar,
  Boer)
bor|eal
bor|ea|lis (in
  'aurora borealis')
bored (fed up.
  △ baud, bawd,
  board)
bore|dom
bore|hole +s
borer +s
Borg, Björn
  (Swedish tennis
  player)
Bor|ges, Jorge
  Luis (Argentinian
  writer)
boric
bor|ing +s
bor|ing|ly
bor|ing|ness
Boris
Born, Max
  (German
  physicist)
born (in 'to be born'
  etc. △ borne,
  bourn)
born-again
  attributive
borne (past
  participle of bear.
  △ born, bourn)
borné (narrow-
  minded)

Born|ean +s
Bor|neo (island,
  Malay
  archipelago)
Born|holm (island,
  Baltic Sea)
Born|holm
  dis|ease
Boro|bu|dur
  (monument, Java)
Boro|din,
  Alek|sandr
  (Russian
  composer)
Boro|dino (battle
  site, Russia)
boro|fluor|ide
boron
bo|ro|nia +s
boro|sili|cate
bor|ough +s
  (British town; US
  municipal
  corporation;
  division of New
  York; Alaskan
  county. △ burgh)
Boro|vets (resort,
  Bulgaria)
Bor|ro|mini,
  Fran|cesco
  (Italian architect)
Bor|row, George
  (English writer)
bor|row +s +ed
  +ing
bor|row|er +s
bor|row|ing +s
borsch
Bor|stal +s
bort +s (diamond.
  △ bought)
bortsch
bor|zoi +s
Bosan|quet,
  Ber|nard (English
  cricketer)
bosc|age
Bosch,
  Hier|ony|mus
  (Dutch painter)
Bose, Sat|yen|dra
  Nath (Indian
  physicist)
Bose, Jag|dis
  Chan|dra (Indian
  physicist and plant
  physiologist)
bosh (nonsense.
  △ Boche)
bosie +s

bosk|age (use
  boscage)
Bos|kop (town,
  South Africa)
bosky
  bosk|ier
  boski|est
bo's'n +s (use
  bosun)
Bos|nia (region,
  Bosnia–Herzegovina)
Bosnia–Herzegov|ina
Bos|nian +s
bosom +s
bos|omy
boson +s
Bos|phorus
  (= Bosporus)
Bos|porus
  (between Black
  Sea and Sea of
  Marmara)
BOSS (= Bureau of
  State Security)
boss
  bosses
  bossed
  boss|ing
bossa nova +s
boss-eyed
boss|ily
bossi|ness
boss-shot +s
bossy
  boss|ier
  bossi|est
bossy-boots
Bos|ton (town,
  England; city,
  USA)
bosun +s
Bos|well, James
  (biographer of Dr
  Johnson)
Bos|well|ian +s
Bos|worth Field
  (battlefield,
  England)
bot +s
bo|tan|ic
bo|tan|ic|al
bo|tan|ic|al|ly
bot|an|ise *Br.* (use
  botanize)
  bot|an|ises
  bot|an|ised
  bot|an|is|ing
bot|an|ist +s
bot|an|ize
  bot|an|izes
  bot|an|ized
  bot|an|iz|ing

Bot¦any (wool)
bot¦any
  bot¦anies
  (study of plants)
Bot¦any Bay (on
  SE coast of
  Australia)
bo¦targo
  bo¦tar¦goes
botch
  botches
  botched
  botch¦ing
botch¦er +s
botel +s
bot¦fly
  bot¦flies
both
Botha, Louis
  (South African
  soldier and
  statesman)
Botha, P. W.
  (South African
  statesman)
Botham, Ian
  (English cricketer)
bother +s +ed
  +ing
both¦er¦ation
both¦er¦some
bothie +s (use
  bothy)
Both¦nia, Gulf of
  (part of Baltic Sea)
Both¦well, James
  (Earl of Bothwell,
  husband of Mary
  Queen of Scots)
bothy
  both¦ies
bo tree +s
botry¦oid¦al
Bot¦swana
bott +s (use bot)
bott-fly (use
  botfly)
  bott-flies
Bot¦ti¦celli,
  San¦dro
  (Florentine
  painter)
bot¦tle
  bot¦tles
  bot¦tled
  bot¦tling
bot¦tle bank +s
bottle-brush
  bottle-brushes
bottle-feed
  bottle-feeds

bottle-feed (cont.)
  bottle-fed
  bottle-feeding
bottle¦ful +s
bot¦tle green +s
  noun and adjective
bottle-green
  attributive
bottle¦neck +s
bottle¦nose
  plural bottle¦nose
bottle-nosed
bot¦tler +s
bottle-washer +s
bot¦tom +s +ed
  +ing
bot¦tom¦less
bot¦tom¦most
bot¦tom¦ry
  bot¦tom¦ries
  bot¦tom¦ried
  bot¦tom¦ry¦ing
bottom-up
  attributive
botu¦lism
Bou¦cher,
  Fran¦çois (French
  artist)
Bou¦cher de
  Perthes, Jacques
  (French
  archaeologist)
bou¦clé
Bou¦dicca (queen
  of the Iceni)
bou¦doir +s
bouf¦fant +s
Bou¦gain¦ville
  (island, Solomon
  Islands)
Bou¦gain¦ville,
  Louis de (French
  explorer)
bou¦gain¦vil¦lea
  +as
Bou¦gain¦vil¦lian
  +s
bough +s (limb of
  tree. △ bow)
bought (past tense
  and past participle
  of buy. △ bort)
bought¦en
bou¦gie +s
bouil¦la¦baisse
bouilli
bouil¦lon +s
boul¦der +s (rock.
  △ bolder)
boul¦der clay
boul¦dery

boule (French
  bowls)
boule +s (Greek
  council)
boule (inlay; use
  buhl)
boules (French
  bowls; use boule)
boule¦vard +s
Bou¦lez, Pierre
  (French composer
  and conductor)
Boulle, André-
  Charles (French
  cabinet-maker)
boulle (inlay; use
  buhl)
Bou¦logne *in full*
  Boulogne-sur-
  Mer
  (port, France)
Boult, Ad¦rian
  (English
  conductor)
boult +s +ed +ing
  (use bolt)
Boult¦ing, John
  and Roy (British
  film producers and
  directors)
Boul¦ton,
  Mat¦thew
  (English engineer)
bounce
  bounces
  bounced
  boun¦cing
bounce-back +s
  *noun and
  attributive*
boun¦cer +s
boun¦cily
boun¦ci¦ness
bouncy
  boun¦cier
  boun¦ci¦est
bound +s +ed +ing
bound¦ary
  bound¦ar¦ies
bound¦en
bound¦er +s
bound¦less
bound¦less¦ness
boun¦teous
boun¦teous¦ness
boun¦ti¦ful
boun¦ti¦ful¦ly
Bounty (mutiny
  ship)
bounty
  boun¦ties
bounty hunt¦er +s

bou¦quet +s
bou¦quet garni
  bou¦quets gar¦nis
Bour¦baki
Bour¦bon +s
  (French dynasty;
  biscuit;
  reactionary)
bour¦bon +s
  (whisky)
Bour¦bon¦nais
  (former province,
  France)
bour¦don +s
bour¦geois
  plural bour¦geois
bour¦geoisie +s
Bour¦guiba, Habib
  ben Ali (Tunisian
  statesman)
Bourke-White,
  Mar¦ga¦ret
  (American
  photojournalist)
bourn +s (stream;
  goal; limit.
  △ born, borne)
bourne +s (goal;
  limit; use bourn)
Bourne¦mouth
  (resort, England)
bour¦rée +s
Bourse (Paris Stock
  Exchange)
bourse +s (money
  market)
bous¦tro¦phedon
bout +s
bou¦tique +s
bou¦ton¦nière +s
Bou¦vet Is¦land (in
  S. Atlantic)
bou¦zouki +s
bo¦vate +s
bo¦vine
bo¦vine¦ly
Bov¦ril *Propr.*
bov¦ver
Bow, Clara
  (American
  actress)
bow +s +ed +ing
  (incline head or
  body; front of
  ship. △ bough)
bow +s +ed +ing
  (knot; ribbon; in
  archery; for violin
  etc. △ beau, bo)
bow-compass
  bow-compasses

bowd¦ler¦isa¦tion
Br. (use
  bowdlerization)
bowd¦ler¦ise *Br.*
  (use bowdlerize)
bowd¦ler¦ises
bowd¦ler¦ised
bowd¦ler¦is¦ing
bowd¦ler¦ism
bowd¦ler¦iza¦tion
bowd¦ler¦ize
bowd¦ler¦izes
bowd¦ler¦ized
bowd¦ler¦iz¦ing
bowel +s
Bowen, Eliza¦beth
  (Irish-born writer)
bower +s +ed +ing
bower-anchor +s
bower¦bird +s
bower-cable +s
bow¦ery
  bow¦er¦ies
bow¦fin +s
bow¦head +s
Bowie, David
  (English rock
  singer and actor)
bowie +s
bowl +s +ed +ing
  (basin; ball; etc.
  △ bole, boll)
bow-legged
bow-legs
bowl¦er +s
bowl¦er hat +s
  noun
bowler-hat
  bowler-hats
  bowler-hatted
  bowler-hatting
  verb
bowl¦ful +s
bow¦line +s
bowl¦ing alley +s
bowl¦ing crease
  +s
bowl¦ing green +s
bow¦man
  bow¦men
bow¦saw +s
bow¦ser +s
bow¦shot
bow¦sprit +s
Bow Street (in
  London)
bow¦string
  bow¦strings
  bow¦stringed *or*
  bow¦strung
  bow¦string¦ing
bow tie +s

bow win¦dow +s
bow-wow +s
bow¦yang +s
bow¦yer +s
box
  boxes
  boxed
  box¦ing
Box and Cox
box-bed +s
box¦calf
  box¦calves
box¦car +s
Boxer +s (member
  of Chinese secret
  society)
boxer +s (in
  boxing; dog)
box file +s
box¦ful +s
box-haul +s +ed
  +ing
Box¦ing Day
box¦ing glove +s
box kite +s
box of¦fice +s *noun*
box-office *adjective*
box pleat +s
box¦room +s
box spring +s
box¦wood +s
boxy
  box¦ier
  boxi¦est
boy +s (male child.
  △ buoy)
boyar +s
Boyce, Wil¦liam
  (English
  composer)
Boy¦cott,
  Geof¦frey
  (English cricketer)
boy¦cott +s +ed
  +ing
Boyd, Ar¦thur
  (Australian artist)
Boyer, Charles
  (French actor)
boy¦friend +s
boy¦hood
boy¦ish
boy¦ish¦ly
boy¦ish¦ness
Boyle, Rob¦ert
  (Irish scientist)
Boyle's law
Boyne (river,
  Republic of
  Ireland)
boyo +s
Boys' Bri¦gade

Boy Scout +s
  (former name for
  a Scout)
boy¦sen¦berry
  boy¦sen¦berries
Boz (pseudonym of
  Charles Dickens)
bozo +s
B.Phil. (= Bachelor
  of Philosophy)
B-picture +s
bra +s
Bra¦bant (former
  duchy, NW
  Europe)
Brab¦ham, Jack
  (Australian racing
  driver)
brace
  braces
  braced
  bra¦cing
brace¦let +s
bracer +s
bra¦chial
bra¦chi¦ate
  bra¦chi¦ates
  bra¦chi¦ated
  bra¦chi¦at¦ing
bra¦chi¦ation
bra¦chi¦ator +s
bra¦chio¦pod +s
bra¦chio¦saurus
  bra¦chio¦
  saur¦uses *or*
  bra¦chio¦sauri
bra¦chis¦to¦chrone
  +s
bra¦chy¦ceph¦al¦ic
bra¦chy¦ceph¦al¦
        ous
bra¦chy¦ceph¦aly
bra¦chyl¦ogy
  bra¦chylo¦gies
bra¦cing¦ness
brack +s
bracken +s
bracket +s +ed
  +ing
brack¦ish
brack¦ish¦ness
bract +s
brac¦teal
brac¦te¦ate +s
Brad (name)
brad +s (nail)
brad¦awl +s
Brad¦bury,
  Mal¦colm
  (English novelist)

Brad¦bury, Ray
  (American science
  fiction writer)
Bra¦den
Brad¦ford (city,
  England)
Brad¦ley (name)
Brad¦ley, James
  (English
  astronomer)
Brad¦man,
  Don¦ald
  (Australian
  cricketer)
Brad¦shaw +s
Brady
brady¦car¦dia
brae +s (hill.
  △ bray)
Brae¦mar (town,
  Scotland)
brag
  brags
  bragged
  brag¦ging
Braga (city,
  Portugal)
Bra¦ganza (city,
  Portugal; dynasty)
Bragg, Wil¦liam
  and Law¦rence
  (English
  physicists)
brag¦ga¦do¦cio
brag¦gart +s
brag¦ger +s
brag¦ging¦ly
Brahe, Tycho
  (Danish
  astronomer)
Brahma *Hinduism*
brahma +s (fowl)
Brah¦man +s
  (Hindu supreme
  being; member of
  highest Hindu
  class. △ Brahmin)
Brah¦mana
Brah¦man¦ic
Brah¦man¦ic¦al
Brah¦man¦ism
Brah¦ma¦putra
  (river, S. Asia)
brah¦ma¦putra +s
  (fowl)
Brah¦min +s
  (superior person.
  △ Brahman)
Brahms,
  Jo¦han¦nes
  (German
  composer)

braid +s +ed +ing
braid¦er +s
brail +s +ed +ing
  (haul up)
Bräila (city,
  Romania)
Braille (writing for
  the blind)
Brain, Den¦nis
  (English horn
  player)
brain +s +ed +ing
brain|box
  brain|boxes
brain|child
  brain|chil¦dren
brain-damaged
brain-dead
brain death
brain drain +s
Braine, John
  (English writer)
brain fever
braini|ness
brain|less
brain|pan +s
brain|power
brain|stem +s
brain|storm +s
  +ed +ing
brains trust +s
brain-teaser +s
brain trust +s
brain|wash
  brain|washes
  brain|washed
  brain|wash|ing
brain|wave +s
brain|work
brainy
  brain|ier
  braini|est
braise
  braises
  braised
  brais|ing
  (cook. △ braze)
brake
  brakes
  braked
  brak¦ing
  (slow down;
  device for
  slowing; estate
  car; crushing
  instrument;
  thicket; bracken;
  archaic past tense
  of **break**.
  △ **break**)
brake block +s
brake drum +s

brake|less
brake|man
  brake|men
brake shoe +s
brakes|man
  brakes|men
brake|van +s
Bra¦mah, Jo¦seph
  (English inventor)
Bra|mante,
  Do|nato (Italian
  architect)
bram¦ble
  bram¦bles
  bram¦bled
  bram|bling
bram|bling +s
bram¦bly
Bram|ley +s
Bram|ley's
  seed|ling +s
bran
Bran|agh,
  Ken|neth (English
  actor and director)
branch
  branches
  branched
  branch|ing
bran|chia
bran|chiae
bran|chial
bran|chi|ate
branch|let +s
branch|like
branchy
Bran|cusi,
  Con|stan|tin
  (Romanian
  sculptor)
brand +s +ed +ing
Bran|den|burg
  (state, Germany)
brand|er +s
bran|dish
  bran|dishes
  bran|dished
  bran|dish|ing
bran|dish|er +s
brand|ling +s
brand new
Brando, Mar¦lon
  (American actor)
Bran|don
Brands Hatch
  (motor-racing
  circuit, England)
Brandt, Bill
  (British
  photographer)

Brandt, Willy
  (German
  statesman)
brandy
  bran|dies
brandy ball +s
brandy but¦ter
brandy snap +s
brank-ursine
Bran|son,
  Rich|ard (English
  entrepreneur)
brant +s
bran tub +s
Braque, Georges
  (French painter)
Brase|nose (Oxford
  college)
brash
brash¦ly
brash|ness
Bra|silia (city,
  Brazil)
Bra¦şov (city,
  Romania)
brass
  brasses
  brassed
  brass|ing
brass|age
bras|sard +s
brassed off
bras|serie +s
Bras|sey, Thomas
  (English engineer)
bras|sica +s
brassie +s (golf
  club)
bras|siere +s
brass|ily
brassi|ness
Brassó (Hungarian
  name for Braşov)
brass-rubbing
brass|ware
brassy
  brass|ier
  brassi|est
  (like brass)
brassy (golf club;
  use **brassie**)
  brass|ies
brat +s
Brati|slava (capital
  of Slovakia)
brat pack +s
brat pack¦er +s
brat|tice +s
bratty
brat|wurst +s

Braun, Karl
  (German
  physicist)
Braun, Wern|her
  von (German
  rocket designer)
Braun|schweig
  (city, Germany)
bra|vado
brave
  braves
  braved
  brav¦ing
  braver
  brav¦est
brave¦ly
brave|ness
bravery
bravo +s (cry of
  approval)
bravo
  bra|voes *or*
  bra¦vos
  (desperado)
bra|vura
braw
brawl +s +ed +ing
brawl¦er +s
brawn
brawni|ness
brawny
  brawn|ier
  brawni|est
Bray (in '*The Vicar
  of Bray*')
bray +s +ed +ing
  (cry of donkey;
  crush. △ brae)
braze
  brazes
  brazed
  braz|ing
  (solder. △ braise)
bra|zen +s +ed
  +ing
brazen-faced
bra|zen|ly
bra|zen|ness
bra|zier +s
bra|ziery
  bra|zier|ies
Bra¦zil
bra|zil +s (nut;
  wood)
Bra¦zil|ian +s
Bra¦zil nut +s
Bra¦zil wood +s
Braz¦za|ville
  (capital of the
  Republic of the
  Congo)

breach
  breaches
  breached
  breach|ing
  (break; failure; etc.
  ⚠ breech)
bread +s +ed +ing
  (loaf etc.; coat
  with breadcrumbs.
  ⚠ bred)
bread-and-butter
  attributive
bread|bas|ket +s
bread bin +s
bread|board +s
bread|crumb +s
bread|fruit
  plural bread|fruit
  or bread|fruits
bread|line
breadth +s
breadth|ways
breadth|wise
bread|win|ner +s
break
  breaks
  broke
  break|ing
  broken
  (shatter; make or
  become
  inoperative; etc.
  ⚠ brake)
break|able +s
break|age +s
break|away +s
  noun and
  attributive
break-dancing
break|down +s
  noun
break|er +s
break|fast +s +ed
  +ing
break|fast|er +s
break-in +s *noun*
break|ing point +s
break-line +s
break|neck
break-off +s *noun*
  and attributive
break|out +s *noun*
break|point +s
  Computing
break point +s
  (*Tennis*;
  interruption)
Break|spear,
  Nich|olas
  (English pope,
  Adrian IV)

break|through +s
  noun
break-up +s *noun*
  and attributive
break|water +s
Bream, Ju|lian
  (English classical
  guitarist and
  lutenist)
bream
  plural bream
  (fish)
breast +s +ed +ing
breast|bone +s
breast|feed
  breast|feeds
  breast|fed
  breast|feed|ing
breast-high
breast|less
breast-pin +s
breast|plate +s
breast pocket +s
breast|stroke
breast|sum|mer
  +s
breast|work +s
breath +s *noun*
breath|able
breath|alyse *Br.*
  breath|alyses
  breath|alysed
  breath|alys|ing
breath|alyser *Br.*
  +s
breath|alyze *Am.*
  breath|alyzes
  breath|alyzed
  breath|alyz|ing
breath|alyzer *Am.*
  +s *Propr.*
breathe
  breathes
  breathed
  breath|ing
  verb
breather +s
breath|ily
breathi|ness
breathing-space
  +s
breath|less
breath|less|ly
breath|less|ness
breath|tak|ing
breath|tak|ing|ly
breath test +s
breathy
  breath|ier
  breathi|est
brec|cia +s

brec|ci|ate
  brec|ci|ates
  brec|ci|ated
  brec|ci|at|ing
brec|ci|ation
Brecht, Ber|tolt
  (German
  dramatist)
Breck|nock|shire
  (alternative name
  for Breconshire)
Brecon (town,
  Wales)
Brecon Bea|cons
  (hills, Wales)
Brecon|shire
  (former county,
  Wales)
bred (past tense
  and past participle
  of breed.
  ⚠ bread)
Breda (town, the
  Netherlands)
breech
  breeches
  breeched
  breech|ing
  (part of gun;
  buttocks; put into
  breeches.
  ⚠ breach)
breech birth +s
breech-block +s
breeches (trousers)
Breeches Bible
breeches-buoy +s
breech-loader +s
breech-loading
breed
  breeds
  bred
  breed|ing
breed|er +s
breed|ing ground
  +s
breeks
breeze
  breezes
  breezed
  breez|ing
breeze-block +s
breeze|less
breeze|way +s
breez|ily
breezi|ness
breezy
  breez|ier
  breezi|est
Bre|genz (city,
  Austria)

Bre|men (state and
  city, Germany)
brems|strahl|ung
Bren +s (= gun)
Brenda
Bren|dan (Irish
  saint)
Bren|del, Al|fred
  (Austrian pianist)
Bren gun +s
Bren|nan
Bren|ner Pass (in
  the Alps)
Brent (name)
brent +s (goose)
brent-goose
  brent-geese
Brescia (city, Italy)
Bres|lau (German
  name for
  Wrocław)
Bres|son, Rob|ert
  (French film
  director)
Brest (port, France;
  city, Belarus)
Brest-Litovsk
  (former name of
  Brest, Belarus)
breth|ren
Bre|ton +s
Bre|ton, André
  (French writer)
Brett
bret|zel +s
Breu|ghel (use
  Bruegel or
  Brueghel)
Breuil, Henri
  (French
  archaeologist)
breve +s
brevet
  brev|ets
  brev|et|ed *or*
  brev|et|ted
  brev|et|ing *or*
  brev|et|ting
bre|vi|ary
  bre|vi|ar|ies
brev|ity
  brev|ities
brew +s +ed +ing
brew|er +s
brew|ery
  brew|er|ies
Brew|ster, David
  (Scottish
  physicist)
brew|ster +s
brew-up +s *noun*

**Brezh|nev,
Leo|nid** (Soviet
statesman)
Brian *also* **Bryan**
Brian Boru (Irish
king)
Bri|and, Aris|tide
(French
statesman)
Bri|ansk (use
Bryansk)
briar +s (use **brier**)
Bri|ard +s
brib|able
bribe
bribes
bribed
brib|ing
briber +s
brib|ery
brib|er|ies
bric-a-brac
brick +s +ed +ing
brick|bat +s
brick-built
brick-field +s
brick|field|er +s
brickie +s
(bricklayer.
△ **bricky**)
brick|lay|er +s
brick|lay|ing
brick red +s *noun
and adjective*
brick-red *attributive*
brick|work +s
bricky (made of
many bricks.
△ **brickie**)
brick|yard +s
bri|dal (of bride.
△ **bridle**)
bri|dal|ly
Bride (Irish saint)
bride +s
bride|groom +s
bride price +s
brides|maid +s
bride|well +s
Bridge, Frank
(English
composer)
bridge
bridges
bridged
bridg|ing
bridge|able
bridge-builder +s
bridge-building
bridge-deck +s
bridge|head +s

Bridge of Sighs (in
Venice)
Bridges, Rob|ert
(English poet)
Bridget *also* **Brigid,
Brigit**
Bridget (Irish and
Swedish saints)
Bridge|town
(capital of
Barbados)
bridge|work
**Bridg|man, Percy
Wil|liams**
(American
physicist)
bri|die +s
bridle
bridles
bridled
brid|ling
(for horse; bring
under control.
△ **bridal**)
bridle path +s
bridle|way +s
bri|doon +s
Brie (cheese)
brief +s +ed +ing
+er +est
brief|case +s
brief|less
brief|ness
brier +s
brier rose +s
bri|ery
brig +s
bri|gade
bri|gades
bri|gaded
bri|gad|ing
briga|dier +s
briga|dier gen|eral
+s
briga|low +s
brig|and +s
brig|and|age
brig|an|dine +s
brig|and|ish
brig|and|ism
brig|and|ry
brig|an|tine +s
Briggs, Henry
(English
mathematician)
Brig|ham
Bright, John
(English political
reformer)
bright +er +est
bright|en +s +ed
+ing

bright-eyed
bright|ish
bright|ly
bright|ness
Brighton (town,
England)
Bright's dis|ease
bright|work
Brigid *also* **Bridget,
Brigit**
Brigit *also* **Bridget,
Brigid**
Bri|gitte
brill
plural **brill**
(fish; brilliant)
bril|liance
bril|liancy
bril|liant +s
bril|liant|ine
bril|li|ant|ly
brim
brims
brimmed
brim|ming
brim|ful (use **brim-
full**)
brim-full
brim|less
brim|stone
brim|stony
brin|dle
brin|dled
Brind|ley, James
(British canal
builder)
brine
brines
brined
brin|ing
bring
brings
brought
bring|ing
bring-and-buy +s
bring|er +s
brini|ness
brin|jal +s
Brink, André
(South African
writer)
brink
brink|man|ship
brinks|man|ship
briny
brini|er
brini|est
brio
bri|oche +s
Bri|ony *also*
Bry|ony

bri|quet +s (use
briquette)
bri|quette +s
Bris|bane (city,
Australia)
brisk +er +est
brisk|en +s +ed
+ing
bris|ket +s
brisk|ness
bris|ling (fish)
bris|tle
bris|tles
bris|tled
brist|ling
(stiff hair etc.)
bristle|cone pine
+s
bristle|tail +s
bristle|worm +s
brist|ly
Bris|tol (city,
England)
Bris|tol fash|ion
bris|tols
Brit +s
Brit|ain
Bri|tan|nia
Bri|tan|nic
Briti|cism +s
Brit|ish
**Brit|ish
Col|um|bia**
(province,
Canada)
Brit|ish|er +s
Brit|ish Hon|duras
(former name of
Belize)
Brit|ish|ism +s
(use **Briticism**)
Brit|ish|ness
Briton +s
Brit|tany (region,
France; name)
**Brit|ten,
Ben|ja|min**
(English
composer)
brit|tle
**brittle-bone
disease**
brittle|ly
brittle|ness
brittle-star +s
brit|tly
Brit|ton|ic
britzka +s
Brno (city, Czech
Republic)
bro (= brother)

broach
broaches
broached
broach|ing
(pierce; raise
subject; spire; a
spit. △ brooch)
broad +s +er +est
broad|band
broad-based
broad bean +s
broad-brush
broad|cast
broad|casts
broad|cast or
broad|cast|ed
broad|cast|ing
broad|cast|er +s
Broad Church
broad|cloth
broad|en +s +ed
+ing
broad|leaved
broad|loom +s
broad|ly
broad-minded
broad-minded|ly
broad-
minded|ness
Broad|moor
(secure hospital,
England)
Broads, the
(region, England)
broad|sheet +s
broad|side +s
broad|sword +s
broad|tail +s
Broad|way (in New
York)
broad|way +s
(broad road)
broad|wise
Brob|ding|nag
(imaginary
country)
Brob|ding|nag|ian
+s
bro|cade
bro|cades
bro|caded
bro|cad|ing
broc|coli
broch +s (tower.
△ brock)
bro|chette +s
bro|chure +s
brock +s (badger.
△ broch)
Brocken
(mountain,
Germany)

brocket +s
bro|derie an|glaise
Brod|sky, Jo|seph
(Russian-born
American poet)
brogue +s
broil +s +ed +ing
broil|er +s
broil|er house +s
broke
broken
broken-down
adjective
broken-hearted
Broken Hill (town,
Australia; former
name of Kabwe)
broken|ness
broken-winded
broker +s
broker|age +s
broker-dealer +s
brok|ing
brolga +s
brolly
brol|lies
bro|mate +s
Brom|berg
(German name for
Bydgoszcz)
brome +s
bro|melia +s
bro|meliad +s
bro|mic
brom|ide +s
brom|ine
brom|ism
bronc +s
bron|chi
bron|chia
bron|chial
bron|chi|olar
bron|chi|ole +s
bron|chit|ic +s
bron|chitis
bron|cho|cele +s
bron|cho|di|la|tor
+s
bron|cho|
pneu|mo|nia
bron|cho|scope +s
bron|chos|copy
bron|chus
bron|chi
bronco +s
bronco|bust|er +s
Brontë, Anne,
Char|lotte, and
Emily (English
writers)
bron|to|saur +s

bron|to|saurus
bron|to|saur|uses
or bron|to|sauri
Bron|wen
Bronx, the
(borough, New
York)
bronze
bronzes
bronzed
bronz|ing
Bronze Age
bronzy
brooch
brooches
(ornamental
fastening.
△ broach)
brood +s +ed +ing
brood|er +s
brood|ily
broodi|ness
brood|ing|ly
brood mare +s
broody
brood|ier
broodi|est
Brook, Peter
(English stage and
film director)
brook +s +ed +ing
Brooke (name)
Brooke, Ru|pert
(English poet)
Brook|lands
(motor-racing
circuit, England)
brook|let +s
brook|lime
Brook|lyn
(borough, New
York)
Brook|ner, Anita
(English novelist)
brook|weed
broom +s +ed
+ing (brush;
shrub. △ brume)
broom|rape +s
broom|stick +s
brose
broth +s
brothel +s
brother
broth|ers or in
religious use
breth|ren
brother ger|man
broth|ers ger|man
brother|hood +s
brother-in-law
brothers-in-law

broth|er|li|ness
broth|er|ly
brother uter|ine
broth|ers uter|ine
brougham +s
brought
brou|haha +s
Brou|wer,
Adri|aen (Flemish
painter)
brow +s
brow|beat
brow|beats
brow|beat
brow|beat|ing
brow|beat|en
brow|beat|er +s
browed
Brown, Ar|thur
Whit|ten
(Scottish aviator)
Brown,
Cap|abil|ity
(English landscape
gardener)
Brown, Ford
Madox (British
painter)
Brown, George
Mac|kay
(Scottish writer)
Brown, James
(American singer)
Brown, John
(American
abolitionist)
brown +s +ed
+ing +er +est
brown-bagger +s
Browne, Thomas
(English
physician)
browned off
brown|field
attributive
Brown|ian +s
Brownie +s
(former name for
a Brownie Guide)
brownie +s
(goblin; cake)
Brownie Guide +s
Brownie Guider
+s
brownie point +s
Brown|ing,
Eliza|beth
Bar|rett and
Rob|ert (English
poets)
Brown|ing +s
(gun)

brown|ish
brown|ness
brown-nose
  brown-noses
  brown-nosed
  brown-nosing
Brown Owl +s
  (Brownie Guide
  leader)
brown owl +s
  (bird)
Brown|shirt +s
brown|stone +s
browny
browse
  browses
  browsed
  brows|ing
browser +s
Bruce
Bruce, Rob|ert the
  (Scottish king)
Bruce, James
  (Scottish explorer)
Bruce, James (Earl
  of Elgin)
bru|cel|losis
bru|cite
Bruck|ner, Anton
  (Austrian
  composer)
Brue|gel, Pieter
  ('the Elder' and
  'the Younger',
  Flemish artists)
Brue|gel, Jan
  (Flemish artist)
Brue|ghel (use
  Bruegel)
Bruges (city,
  Belgium)
Bruin (bear)
bruise
  bruises
  bruised
  bruis|ing
bruiser +s
bruit +s +ed +ing
  (spread rumour.
  △ brut, brute)
Brum
  (= Birmingham)
brumby
  brum|bies
brume (mist.
  △ broom)
Brum|ma|gem
Brum|mell, Beau
  (English dandy)
Brum|mie +s

Brummy (use
  Brummie)
Brum|mies
bru|mous
brunch
  brunches
  brunched
  brunch|ing
Brundt|land, Gro
  Har|lem
  (Norwegian
  stateswoman)
Bru|nei (sultanate,
  Borneo)
Bru|neian +s
Bru|nel, Marc
  Isam|bard and
  Isam|bard
  King|dom
  (English
  engineers)
Bru|nel|les|chi,
  Fi|lippo
  (Florentine
  architect)
bru|net +s (use
  brunette)
bru|nette +s
Brun|hild Germanic
  Legend
Bruno (German-
  born French saint;
  name)
Bruno, Gior|dano
  (Italian
  philosopher)
Bruns|wick
  (English name for
  Braunschweig)
brunt
brush
  brushes
  brushed
  brush|ing
brush|fire +s
brush|less
brush|like
brush-off +s noun
brush stroke +s
brush-up +s noun
brush|wood
brush|work
brushy
brusque
  brusquer
  brusquest
brusque|ly
brusque|ness
brus|querie
Brus|sels (capital of
  Belgium)
Brus|sels sprout
  +s

brut (of wine.
  △ bruit, brute)
bru|tal
bru|tal|isa|tion Br.
  (use
  brutalization)
bru|tal|ise Br. (use
  brutalize)
  bru|tal|ises
  bru|tal|ised
  bru|tal|is|ing
bru|tal|ism
bru|tal|ist
bru|tal|ity
  bru|tal|ities
bru|tal|iza|tion
bru|tal|ize
  bru|tal|izes
  bru|tal|ized
  bru|tal|iz|ing
bru|tal|ly
brute +s (brutal
  person; etc.
  △ bruit, brut)
brute force
bru|tish
bru|tish|ly
bru|tish|ness
Bru|tus (supposed
  ancestor of the
  British)
Bru|tus, Lu|cius
  Jun|ius
  (legendary
  founder of the
  Roman Republic)
Bru|tus, Mar|cus
  Jun|ius (Roman
  senator)
brux|ism
Bryan also Brian
Bry|ansk (city,
  Russia)
Bryl|creem Propr.
Bryl|creemed
Bryn|ner, Yul
  (American actor)
bryo|logic|al
bry|olo|gist +s
bry|ology
Bry|ony also
  Bri|ony (name)
bry|ony
  bry|onies
  (plant)
bryo|phyte +s
bryo|phyt|ic
bryo|zoan +s
bryo|zo|ology
Bry|thonic
B side +s (second
  team)

B-side +s (of
  record etc.)
bub +s
bubal
bub|ble
  bub|bles
  bub|bled
  bub|bling
bub|ble bath +s
bubble|gum
bub|bly
  bub|blier
  bub|bli|est
bubbly-jock +s
Buber, Mar|tin
  (Austrian-born
  Israeli
  philosopher)
bubo
  bu|boes
bu|bon|ic
bu|bono|cele +s
buc|cal (of the
  cheek or mouth.
  △ buckle)
buc|can|eer +s
  +ed +ing
buc|can|eer|ish
buc|cin|ator +s
Bu|ce|las (region,
  Portugal)
Bu|ceph|alus
  (Alexander the
  Great's horse)
Buchan,
  Alex|an|der
  (Scottish
  meteorologist)
Buchan, John
  (Scottish writer
  and statesman)
Bu|chanan, James
  (American
  president)
Bu|cha|rest (capital
  of Romania)
Buchen|wald
  (concentration
  camp, Germany)
Buch|man|ism
Buch|man|ite +s
Buch|ner, Ed|uard
  (German organic
  chemist)
buck +s +ed +ing
buck|bean +s
buck|board +s
buck|er +s
bucket +s +ed
  +ing
bucket|ful +s
bucket shop +s

buck|eye +s
buck-horn
buck-hound +s
Buck|ing|ham
  Pal|ace (in
  London)
Buck|ing|ham|
  shire (county,
  England)
Buck|land,
  Wil|liam (English
  geologist)
buckle
  buckles
  buckled
  buck|ling
  (fastener; fasten;
  crumple; make an
  effort. △ buccal)
buck|ler +s
Buck|ley's
  (chance)
buck|ling +s
buck|min|ster|
  ful|ler|ene
bucko
  buck|oes
buck-passing
buck|ram
buck rare|bit
Bucks.
  (= Buckingham-
  shire)
Buck's Fizz
buck|shee
buck|shot
buck|skin +s
buck|thorn +s
buck-tooth
  buck-teeth
buck-toothed
buck|wheat
bucky|ball +s
bu|col|ic
bu|col|ic|al|ly
bud
  buds
  bud|ded
  bud|ding
Buda|pest (capital
  of Hungary)
Bud|dha (founder
  of Buddhism)
Buddh Gaya
  (= Bodhgaya)
Bud|dhism
Bud|dhist +s
Bud|dhis|tic|al
bud|dleia +s
buddy
  bud|dies

buddy (cont.)
  bud|died
  buddy|ing
Budge, Don
  (Australian tennis
  player)
budge
  budges
  budged
  budg|ing
budg|eri|gar +s
budget +s +ed
  +ing
budget|ary
budgie +s
Bud|weis (German
  name for České
  Budějovice)
Buena|ven|tura
  (port, Colombia)
Bue|nos Aires
  (capital of
  Argentina)
buff +s +ed +ing
Buf|falo (city, USA)
buf|falo
  plural buf|falo or
  buf|fa|loes
Buf|falo Bill
  (nickname of
  William Cody,
  American
  showman)
buf|fer +s
buf|fet +s +ed
  +ing
buffle|head +s
buffo +s
Buf|fon, Georges-
  Louis, Comte de
  (French naturalist)
buf|foon +s
buf|foon|ery
buf|foon|ish
buff-stick +s
bug
  bugs
  bugged
  bug|ging
bug|aboo +s
Bu|ganda (former
  kingdom, E.
  Africa)
bug|bear +s
bug-eyed
bug|ger +s +ed
  +ing (coarse slang)
bugger-all (coarse
  slang)
bug|gery
Bug|gins's turn

buggy
  bug|gies
  bug|gier
  bug|gi|est
bugle
  bu|gles
  bu|gled
  bu|gling
bugle call +s
bugle-horn +s
bu|gler +s
bu|glet +s (small
  bugle)
bug|let +s (small
  bug in program)
bu|gloss
  bu|glosses
buhl +s (inlay.
  △ boule)
build
  builds
  built
  build|ing
build|er +s
build|ers'
  mer|chant +s
build|ing +s
build-up +s noun
built-in +s adjective
  and noun
built-up adjective
Bu|jum|bura
  (capital of
  Burundi)
Bu|khara
  (= Bukhoro)
Bu|kha|rin,
  Niko|lai (Soviet
  political leader)
Bu|khoro (city,
  Uzbekistan)
Buko|vina (region,
  SE Europe)
Bu|kow|ski,
  Charles
  (American writer)
Bula|wayo (city,
  Zimbabwe)
bulb +s
bul|bil +s (small
  bulb)
bulb|ous
bul|bul +s (bird)
Bul|ga|kov,
  Mikh|ail (Russian
  writer)
Bul|ga|nin,
  Niko|lai (Soviet
  political leader)
Bul|gar +s
bul|gar (wheat)
Bul|garia

Bul|gar|ian +s
bulge
  bulges
  bulged
  bul|ging
bul|ghur (use
  bulgar)
bul|gur (use
  bulgar)
bulgy
  bul|gier
  bul|gi|est
bu|lima|rexia
bu|lima|rex|ic +s
bu|limia
  (ner|vosa)
bu|lim|ic +s
bulk +s +ed +ing
bulk-buy +s +ed
  +ing verb
bulk buy|ing noun
bulk|head +s
bulk|ily
bulki|ness
bulky
  bulk|ier
  bulki|est
Bull, the
  (constellation;
  sign of zodiac)
bull +s +ed +ing
bull|ace +s
bull|ate
bull|dog +s
bull|dog clip +s
bull|doze
  bull|dozes
  bull|dozed
  bull|doz|ing
bull|dozer +s
bul|let +s
bullet-headed
bul|letin +s
bul|letin board +s
bul|let|proof
bull-fiddle +s
bull|fight +s
bull|fight|er +s
bull|fight|ing
bull|finch
  bull|finches
bull|frog +s
bull|head +s
bull-headed
bull-headed|ness
bull|horn +s
bull|ion
bull|ish
bull|ish|ly
bull|ish|ness
bull mar|ket +s
bull-nose

bull-nosed
bul|lock +s
bul|locky
  bul|lock|ies
bull|ring +s
Bull Run (river and
  battlefield, USA)
bull-running
bull's-eye +s
bull|shit (*coarse
  slang*)
bull|shit|ter +s
  (*coarse slang*)
bull-terrier +s
bull|trout +s
bully
  bul|lies
  bul|lied
  bully|ing
bully boy +s
bully|rag
  bully|rags
  bully|ragged
  bully|rag|ging
bul|rush
  bul|rushes
Bult|mann,
  Ru|dolf (German
  theologian)
bul|wark +s
Bulwer-Lytton,
  Ed|ward (English
  writer and
  statesman)
bum
  bums
  bummed
  bum|ming
bum|bag +s
bum-bailiff +s
bum|ble
  bum|bles
  bum|bled
  bum|bling
bumble-bee +s
bumble|dom
bumble-puppy
  bumble-puppies
bum|bler +s
bum|boat +s
bum|boy +s
bumf
bumi|putra
  plural bumi|putra
  or bumi|pu|tras
bum|malo
  plural bum|malo
bum|mer +s
bump +s +ed +ing
bump|er +s
bumph (use bumf)
bump|ily

bumpi|ness
bump|kin +s
bump-start +s +ed
  +ing
bump|tious
bump|tious|ly
bump|tious|ness
bumpy
  bump|ier
  bumpi|est
bum's rush
bum-sucker +s
  (*coarse slang*)
bum-sucking
  (*coarse slang*)
bun +s
Buna *Propr.*
Bun|bury (town,
  Australia)
bunch
  bunches
  bunched
  bunch|ing
bunchy
bunco
  bun|coes
  bun|coed
  bunco|ing
bun|combe (use
  bunkum)
bun|der +s
Bun|des|bank
Bun|des|rat
Bun|des|tag
bun|dle
  bun|dles
  bun|dled
  bund|ling
bund|ler +s
bundo|bust
bun fight +s
bung +s +ed +ing
bun|ga|low +s
bun|gee +s
bun|gee jump|ing
bung-hole +s
bun|gle
  bun|gles
  bun|gled
  bun|gling
bun|gler +s
Bunin, Ivan
  (Russian poet)
bun|ion +s
bunk +s +ed +ing
bunk bed +s
bun|ker +s +ed
  +ing
Bun|ker Hill
  (battlefield, USA)
bunk|house +s
bun|kum

bunny
  bun|nies
Bun|sen, Rob|ert
  (German chemist;
  burner)
bunt +s +ed +ing
bun|tal +s
Bun|ter, Billy
  (fictional
  schoolboy)
bunt|ing
bunt|line +s
Bunty
Bu|ñuel, Luis
  (Spanish film
  director)
bunya +s
bunya bunya +s
Bun|yan, John
  (English religious
  writer)
bun|yip +s
Buona|parte
  (Italian name for
  Bonaparte)
Buon|ar|roti,
  Mi|chel|an|gelo
  (Italian artist)
buoy +s +ed +ing
  (float; etc. ⚠ boy)
buoy|age
buoy|ancy
  buoy|an|cies
buoy|ant
buoy|ant|ly
bup|pie +s
bur +s (clinging
  seed case; catkin.
  ⚠ burr)
burb +s
Bur|bage,
  Rich|ard (English
  actor)
Bur|bank (city,
  USA)
Bur|berry
  Bur|berries
  Propr.
bur|ble
  bur|bles
  bur|bled
  burb|ling
bur|bler +s
bur|bot +s
bur|den +s +ed
  +ing
bur|den|some
bur|dock +s
bur|eau
  bur|eaux *or*
  bur|eaus

bur|eau|cracy
  bur|eau|cra|cies
bur|eau|crat +s
bur|eau|crat|ic
bur|eau|crat|ic|
  al|ly
bur|eau|crat|
  isa|tion *Br.* (use
  bureaucrat-
  ization)
bur|eau|crat|ise
  Br. (use
  bureacratize)
  bur|eau|crat|ises
  bur|eau|crat|ised
  bur|eau|crat|
    is|ing
bur|eau|crat|
  iza|tion
bur|eau|crat|ize
  bur|eau|crat|izes
  bur|eau|crat|ized
  bur|eau|crat|
    iz|ing
buret *Am.* +s
bur|ette *Br.* +s
burg +s (town.
  ⚠ berg)
bur|gage +s
Bur|gas (port,
  Bulgaria)
bur|gee +s
Bur|gen|land
  (state, Austria)
bur|geon +s +ed
  +ing
bur|ger +s (food.
  ⚠ burgher)
Bur|gess,
  An|thony
  (English novelist
  and critic)
Bur|gess, Guy
  (British Soviet
  spy)
bur|gess
  bur|gesses
  (citizen; governor)
burgh +s (former
  Scottish borough.
  ⚠ borough)
bur|ghal (of a
  burgh. ⚠ burgle)
bur|gher +s
  (citizen. ⚠ burger)
Burgh|ley,
  Wil|liam Cecil
  (English
  statesman)
burg|lar +s
burg|lari|ous

burg|lar|ise *Br.*
(use **burglarize**)
  burg|lar|ises
  burg|lar|ised
  burg|lar|is|ing
burg|lar|ize
  burg|lar|izes
  burg|lar|ized
  burg|lar|iz|ing
burg|lary
  burg|lar|ies
bur|gle
  bur|gles
  bur|gled
  burg|ling
  (commit burglary.
  △ **burghal**)
burgo|mas|ter +s
Bur|gos (town,
  Spain)
Bur|goyne, John
  (English general
  and writer)
bur|grave +s
Bur|gundy (region,
  France)
bur|gundy
  bur|gun|dies
  (wine; colour)
bur|hel +s (use
  bharal)
bur|ial +s
bur|ial ground +s
burin +s
burk +s (use berk)
burka +s
Burke, Ed|mund
  (British writer and
  politican)
Burke, John (Irish
  genealogist)
Burke, Rob|ert
  O'Hara (Irish
  explorer)
Burke, Wil|liam
  (Irish body-
  snatcher)
Bur|kina (Faso) (in
  W. Africa)
Bur|kinan +s
Bur|kin|ese
  plural Bur|kin|ese
Bur|kitt's
  lymph|oma
burl +s
bur|lap
bur|lesque
  bur|lesques
  bur|lesqued
  bur|lesquing
bur|lesquer +s
bur|li|ness

Bur|ling|ton (city,
  Canada)
burly
  bur|lier
  bur|li|est
Burma
Bur|man +s
Burm|ese
  plural Burm|ese
burn
  burns
  burned *or* burnt
  burn|ing
Burne-Jones,
  Ed|ward (English
  painter and
  designer)
burn|er +s
bur|net +s
Bur|nett, Fran|ces
  Hodg|son
  (English-born
  American
  novelist)
Bur|ney, Fanny
  (English novelist)
Burn|ham (scale)
burning-ghat +s
burning-glass
  burning-glasses
burn|ing|ly
bur|nish
  bur|nishes
  bur|nished
  bur|nish|ing
bur|nish|er +s
Burn|ley (town,
  Lancashire)
bur|noose *Am.* +s
bur|nous *Br.*
  bur|nouses
burn-out *noun*
Burns, Rob|ert
  (Scottish poet)
burnt
burnt-out *adjective*
bur oak +s
burp +s +ed +ing
bur|pee +s
Burr, Aaron
  (American
  statesman)
burr +s +ed +ing
  (rough edge;
  rough sounding of
  r; drill; rock; on
  antler. △ **bur**)
Burra, Ed|ward
  (English painter
  and designer)
burra|wang +s

Bur|ren, the
  (region, Republic
  of Ireland)
bur|rito +s
burro +s (donkey.
  △ **burrow**)
Bur|roughs, Edgar
  Rice (American
  writer)
Bur|roughs,
  Wil|liam
  (American writer)
bur|row +s +ed
  +ing (hole; dig.
  △ **burro**)
bur|row|er +s
Bursa (city,
  Turkey)
bursa
  bur|sae *or* bur|sas
bur|sal
bur|sar +s
bur|sar|ial
bur|sar|ship
bur|sary
  bur|sar|ies
bur|sitis
burst
  bursts
  burst
  burst|ing
burst|proof
Burt *also* Bert
bur|then +s
Bur|ton, Rich|ard
  (Welsh actor;
  English explorer)
bur|ton +s
Burton-upon-
  Trent (town,
  England)
Bur|undi
Bur|und|ian +s
bur wal|nut
Bury (town,
  England)
bury
  bur|ies
  bur|ied
  bury|ing
  (inter. △ **beret,**
  berry)
Bur|yat
Burya|tia (republic,
  Russia)
Bury St Ed|munds
  (town, England)
bus
  buses
  (vehicle;
  Computing.
  △ **buss**)

bus
  bus|ses *or* buses
  bussed *or* bused
  buss|ing *or*
  bus|ing
  (convey by bus.
  △ **buss**)
bus|bar +s
bus|boy +s
busby
  bus|bies
bus driver +s
Bush, George
  (American
  president)
bush
  bushes
  bushed
  bush|ing
bush|baby
  bush|babies
bush basil
bush|buck +s
bushel +s
bushel|ful +s
bush|fire +s
bu|shido
bush|ily
bushi|ness
Bush|man
  Bush|men
  (in South Africa)
bush|man
  bush|men
  (in Australia)
bush|mas|ter +s
bush|ran|ger +s
bush|veld
bush|whack +s
  +ed +ing
bush|whack|er +s
bushy
  bush|ies
  bush|ier
  bushi|est
busily
busi|ness
  busi|nesses
  (trade; work; etc.
  △ **busyness**)
busi|ness|like
busi|ness|man
  busi|ness|men
busi|ness per|son
  busi|ness people
busi|ness|woman
  busi|ness|women
busk +s +ed +ing
busk|er +s
bus|kin +s
bus|kined
busk|ing

bus¦man
  bus¦men
bus¦man's
  holi¦day +s
Bu¦soni,
  Fer¦ruc¦cio
  (Italian composer
  and conductor)
Buss, Fran¦ces
  (English
  educationist)
buss
  busses
  bussed
  buss¦ing
  (kiss. △ bus)
bus shel¦ter +s
bus sta¦tion +s
bus stop +s
bust
  busts
  bust¦ed or bust
  bust¦ing
bus¦tard +s
bus¦tee +s
bust¦er +s
bus¦tier +s (bodice)
bust¦ier
  (comparative of
  busty)
busti¦ness
bus¦tle
  bus¦tles
  bus¦tled
  bust¦ling
bust¦ler +s
bust-up +s noun
busty
  bust¦ier
  busti¦est
busy
  busies
  busied
  busy¦ing
  busier
  busi¦est
busy bee +s
busy¦body
  busy¦bod¦ies
busy Liz¦zie +s
busy¦ness (being
  busy. △ business)
but +s
  (conjunction,
  preposition,
  and adverb;
  room; also in 'but
  me no buts'.
  △ butt, butte)
bu¦ta¦di¦ene

but and ben
  (rooms in house)
bu¦tane
butch
  butches
butcher +s +ed
  +ing
butcher-bird +s
butcher¦ly
butcher meat
butcher's (look)
butcher's broom
  +s
butcher's meat
butch¦ery
  butch¦er¦ies
Bute (island,
  Scotland)
Bute, Earl of
  (Scottish
  statesman)
Bu¦the¦lezi,
  Man¦go¦su¦thu
  (Zulu leader and
  politican)
butle (use buttle)
  butles
  butled
  but¦ling
But¦ler, Reg
  (English sculptor)
But¦ler, Sam¦uel
  (English poet;
  English novelist)
but¦ler +s
But¦lin's (holiday
  camp)
butt +s +ed +ing
  (push; cask;
  target; end;
  buttocks; fish.
  △ but, butte)
butte +s (hill.
  △ beaut, but,
  butt)
butt-end +s
but¦ter +s +ed
  +ing
butter-and-eggs
but¦ter¦ball +s
butter-bean +s
but¦ter¦bur +s
butter-cream
but¦ter¦cup +s
but¦ter¦fat
butter-fingers
  plural butter-
  fingers
but¦ter¦fish
  plural but¦ter¦fish
  or but¦ter¦fishes

but¦ter¦fly
  but¦ter¦flies
butter-icing
but¦teri¦ness
but¦ter knife
  but¦ter knives
but¦ter¦milk
but¦ter¦nut +s
but¦ter¦scotch
but¦ter¦wort +s
but¦tery
  but¦ter¦ies
but¦tie +s
but¦tle
  but¦tles
  but¦tled
  but¦tling
but¦tock +s
but¦ton +s +ed
  +ing
button-back
  adjective
but¦ton¦ball tree
  +s
button-down
  adjective
but¦ton¦hole
  but¦ton¦holes
  but¦ton¦holed
  but¦ton¦hol¦ing
but¦ton¦hook +s
but¦ton¦less
but¦tons (page-
  boy)
button-through
  adjective
but¦ton¦wood +s
but¦tony
but¦tress
  but¦tresses
  but¦tressed
  but¦tress¦ing
butts (shooting
  range)
butt weld
butty
  but¦ties
butty-gang +s
butyl
bu¦tyr¦ate +s
bu¦tyr¦ic
buxom
bux¦om¦ly
bux¦om¦ness
Bux¦te¦hude,
  Diet¦rich (Danish
  musician and
  composer, in N.
  Germany)
buy
  buys
  bought

buy (cont.)
  buy¦ing
  (purchase. △ bi,
  by, bye)
buy-back +s noun
  and adjective
buyer +s
  (purchaser.
  △ byre)
buyer's mar¦ket
  +s
buy-in +s noun
buy¦out +s noun
buzz
  buzzes
  buzzed
  buzz¦ing
buz¦zard +s
buzz¦er +s
buzz-saw +s
buzz¦word +s
bwana +s
by (preposition and
  adverb. △ bi, buy,
  bye)
Byatt, A. S.
  (English writer)
Byb¦los (ancient
  port, Lebanon)
by-blow +s
Byd¦goszcz (port,
  Poland)
bye +s (Sport;
  goodbye. △ bi,
  buy, by)
bye-bye interjection
bye-byes (sleep)
bye-law +s (use by-
  law)
by-election +s
Byelo¦rus¦sia (use
  Belorussia)
Byelo¦rus¦sian (use
  Belorussian)
by-form +s
by¦gone +s
by-lane +s
by-law +s
by¦line +s
by¦name +s
by¦pass
  by¦passes
  by¦passed
  by¦pass¦ing
by¦path +s
by¦play +s
by-product +s
Byrd, Rich¦ard
  (American
  explorer)

Byrd, Wil|liam
(English
composer)
Byrds, the
(American rock
group)
byre +s (barn.
△ buyer)
by|road +s
Byron (name)
Byron, Lord
(English poet)
Byron|ic
bys|sin|osis
bys|sus
bys|suses *or* byssi
by|stand|er +s
by-street +s
byte +s (*Computing*.
△ bight, bite)
Bytom (city,
Poland)
byway +s
by|word +s
by-your-leave
noun
By|zan|tine +s
By|zan|tin|ism
By|zan|tin|ist +s
By|zan|tium
(ancient Istanbul)

Cc

Caaba (use Kaaba)
cab +s
cabal +s
Ca|bala (*Judaism*;
use Kabbalah)
ca|bala +s
(generally; use
cabbala)
Cab|al|ism
(*Judaism*; use
Kabbalism)
cab|al|ism
(generally; use
cabbalism)
Cab|al|ist +s
(*Judaism*; use
Kabbalist)
cab|al|ist +s
(generally; use
cabbalist)
Cab|al|is|tic
(*Judaism*; use
Kabbalistic)
cab|al|is|tic
(generally; use
cabbalistic)
ca|bal|lero +s
ca|bana +s
caba|ret +s
cab|bage +s
cab|bage palm +s
cab|bage white +s
cab|bagy
Cab|bala (*Judaism*;
use Kabbalah)
cab|bala +s
(generally)
Cab|bal|ism
(*Judaism*; use
Kabbalism)
cab|bal|ism
(generally)
Cab|bal|ist +s
(*Judaism*; use
Kabbalism)
cab|bal|ist +s
(generally)
Cab|bal|is|tic
(*Judaism*; use
Kabbalistic)
cab|bal|is|tic
(generally)
cab|bie +s (use
cabby)
cabby
cab|bies
cab driver +s
caber +s

Cab|er|net +s
Cab|er|net Franc
+s
**Cab|er|net
Sau|vi|gnon** +s
cabin +s +ed +ing
cabin boy +s
Cab|inda (enclave,
Angola)
Cab|inet +s
(government)
cab|inet +s
(furniture)
cab|inet|maker +s
cab|inet|mak|ing
cab|in|et|ry
cable
cables
cabled
cab|ling
cable car +s
cable|gram +s
cable-laid
cable-laying
cable tele|vi|sion
cable TV
cable|way +s
cab|man
cab|men
cabo|chon +s (but
en cabochon)
ca|boo|dle
ca|boose +s
Ca|bora Bassa
(lake,
Mozambique)
Cabot, John and
Se|bas|tian
(Venetian
explorers)
cab|ot|age
cabo|tin +s *male*
cabo|tine +s *female*
cab|ri|ole +s
cab|ri|olet +s
ca'|canny
cacao +s
cacha|lot +s
cache
caches
cached
cach|ing
(store. △ cash)
cach|ec|tic
cache pot +s
cachet +s
cach|exia
cach|exy
cach|in|nate
cach|in|nates
cach|in|nated
cach|in|nat|ing

cach|in|na|tion
cach|in|na|tory
cacho|long +s
cachou +s
(lozenge.
△ cashew)
ca|chu|cha +s
ca|cique +s
ca|ciqu|ism
cack-handed
cack-handed|ly
cack-handed|ness
cackle
cackles
cackled
cack|ling
caco|dae|mon +s
(use cacodemon)
caco|demon +s
caco|dyl
caco|dyl|ic
caco|epy
caco|ethes
cac|og|raph|er +s
caco|graph|ic
caco|graph|ic|al
cac|og|raphy
cac|ology
cac|olo|gies
caco|mis|tle +s
cac|oph|on|ous
cac|oph|ony
cac|oph|onies
cac|ta|ceous
cac|tal
cac|tus
cacti *or* cac|tuses
ca|cu|min|al
cad +s
ca|das|tral
ca|da|ver +s
ca|da|ver|ic
ca|da|ver|ous
Cad|bury, George
and **Rich|ard**
(British
manufacturers and
reformers)
cad|die
cad|dies
cad|died
caddy|ing
(in golf. △ caddy)
cad|dis
cad|dises
caddis-fly
caddis-flies
cad|dish
(dishonourable.
△ Kaddish)
cad|dish|ly
cad|dish|ness

caddis-worm +s
caddy
  cad¦dies
  (box for tea.
  △ **caddie**)
ca¦dence +s
ca¦denced
ca¦dency
ca¦den¦tial
ca¦denza +s
cadet +s
ca¦det¦ship +s
cadge
  cadges
  cadged
  cadg¦ing
cadger +s
cadi +s (Muslim
  judge. △ **cardy**)
Cadiz (city, Spain)
Cad|mean (victory)
cad|mium
Cad¦mus *Greek*
  Mythology
cadre +s
ca¦du|ceus
  ca¦du|cei
  Greek and Roman
  Mythology
ca¦du¦city
ca¦du|cous
cae¦cal *Br.* (*Am.*
  cecal)
cae¦cil|ian +s
cae¦citis *Br.* (*Am.*
  cecitis)
cae¦city *Br.* (*Am.*
  cecity)
cae¦cum *Br.*
  caeca
  (*Am.* cecum)
Caed|mon (English
  poet)
Caen (city, France)
Cae¦no|zoic (use
  Cenozoic)
Caer|nar¦fon (city,
  Wales)
Caer|nar¦von
  (English spelling
  of Caernarfon)
Caer¦nar|von|shire
  (former county,
  Wales)
Caer|philly (town,
  Wales; cheese)
Cae¦sar +s (Roman
  emperor)
Cae¦sa|rea (ancient
  port, Israel)

Cae¦sa|rea
  Maz¦aca (former
  name of Kayseri)
Cae¦sar|ean *Br.* +s
  (*Am.* Cesarean)
Cae¦sa|rea
  Phil|ippi (city,
  ancient Palestine)
Cae¦sar|ian *Br.* +s
  (use Caesarean.
  Am. Cesarean)
Cae¦sar's wife
cae¦si|ous
cae¦sium *Br.* (*Am.*
  cesium)
caes¦ura +s
caes¦ural
ca¦fard
café +s
café au lait
café-bar +s
café noir
cafe¦teria +s
cafe|tière +s
caff +s
caf|feine
Cafod (= Catholic
  Fund for Overseas
  Development)
caf¦tan +s (use
  kaftan)
Ca¦gayan Is¦lands
  (in the
  Philippines)
Cage, John
  (American
  composer)
cage
  cages
  caged
  ca¦ging
cage bird +s
cagey
  cagi¦er
  cagi|est
ca¦gey|ness (use
  caginess)
cagi¦ly
cagi|ness
Cagli|ari (capital of
  Sardinia)
Cag¦ney, James
  (American actor)
ca¦goule +s
cagy
  cagi¦er
  cagi|est
ca|hoots
cai¦man +s (use
  cayman)

Cain (*Bible*; in 'raise
  Cain'. △ **cane**)
Caine, Mi¦chael
  (English actor)
Caino|zoic (use
  Cenozoic)
ca¦ique +s
cairn +s
cairn¦gorm +s
  (mineral)
Cairn|gorm
  Moun|tains (in
  Scotland)
Cairn|gorms
  (= Cairngorm
  Mountains)
Cairo (capital of
  Egypt)
cais|son +s
Caith|ness (former
  county, Scotland;
  glass)
cai¦tiff +s
Cait|lin
ca¦jole
  ca|joles
  ca|joled
  ca|jol¦ing
ca¦jole|ment
ca|joler +s
ca|jolery
Cajun +s
cake
  cakes
  caked
  cak¦ing
cake-hole +s
cake|walk +s
Cala|bar (port,
  Nigeria; bean)
cala|bash
  cala|bashes
cala|boose +s
cala|brese
Ca¦lab|ria (region,
  Italy)
Ca¦lab|rian +s
Cal|ais (port,
  France)
cala|manco
  cala|man¦coes
cala|man¦der +s
cala|mares (Greek
  dish)
cala|mari (Italian
  dish)
cala|mary
  cala|mar¦ies
  (animal)
cala|mine
cala|mint +s
ca¦lami|tous

ca¦lami|tous¦ly
ca¦lam|ity
  ca¦lam|ities
Ca¦lam|ity Jane
  (American horse-
  rider and
  markswoman)
ca|lando
ca¦lash
  ca|lashes
cal¦ca|neum
  cal¦ca|nea
cal¦ca|neus
  cal¦ca|nei
cal¦car|eous
cal¦ceo|laria
  plural
  cal¦ceo|laria *or*
  cal¦ceo|lar¦ias
cal¦ceo|late
cal¦ces (plural of
  calx)
cal¦ci|cole +s
cal¦cif|erol
cal¦cif¦er|ous
cal¦cif¦ic
cal¦ci|fi|ca¦tion
cal¦ci|fuge +s
cal¦cify
  cal¦ci|fies
  cal¦ci|fied
  cal¦ci|fy|ing
cal¦cin|ation
cal¦cine
  cal|cines
  cal|cined
  cal|cin¦ing
cal¦cite
cal¦cium
cal|crete
calc-sinter
calc|spar
calc-tuff +s
cal¦cul|abil¦ity
cal¦cul|able
cal¦cul|ably
cal¦cu|late
  cal¦cu|lates
  cal¦cu|lated
  cal¦cu|lat¦ing
  cal¦cu|lated¦ly
  cal¦cu|lat¦ing¦ly
cal¦cu|la¦tion +s
cal¦cu|la¦tive
cal¦cu|la¦tor +s
cal¦cu|lous
  Medicine adjective
cal¦cu|lus
  cal|culi
  Medicine noun

cal|cu|lus
  cal|cu|luses
  Mathematics
Cal|cutta (port,
  India)
cal|dar|ium
  cal|dar|iums *or*
  cal|daria
Cal|de|cott, Ralph
  (English artist)
Cal|der,
  Alex|an|der
  (American artist
  and sculptor)
cal|dera +s
Cal|derón de la
  Barca, Pedro
  (Spanish writer)
cal|dron +s (use
  cauldron)
Caleb
Cale|do|nian +s (of
  Scotland; Scottish
  person; geology)
cale|fa|cient +s
cale|fac|tory
  cale|fac|tor|ies
cal|en|dar +s
  (almanac)
cal|en|der +s
  (press)
ca|len|dric
ca|len|dric|al
cal|ends
cal|en|dula +s
cal|en|ture
calf
  calves
calf|hood
calf|ish
calf-length
  adjective
calf|like
calf love
calf|skin
Cal|gary (city,
  Canada)
Cali (city,
  Colombia)
Cali|ban (in *The
  Tempest*)
cali|ber *Am.* +s (*Br.*
  calibre)
cali|bered *Am.* (*Br.*
  calibred)
cali|brate
  cali|brates
  cali|brated
  cali|brat|ing
cali|bra|tion +s
cali|bra|tor +s

cali|bre *Br.* +s (*Am.*
  caliber)
cali|bred *Br.* (*Am.*
  calibered)
ca|li|ces (plural of
  calix)
ca|li|che
cal|icle +s
cal|ico
cali|coes *Br.*
cali|cos *Am.*
Cali|cut (port,
  India)
Cali|for|nia (state,
  USA)
Cali|for|nian +s
cali|for|nium
Ca|lig|ula (Roman
  emperor)
cali|pash
  cali|pashes
cali|pee +s
cali|per +s (use
  calliper)
ca|liph +s
ca|liph|ate +s
cal|is|then|ic (use
  callisthenic)
cal|is|then|ics (use
  callisthenics)
calix (use calyx)
ca|lixes *or*
ca|li|ces
calk *Am.* +s +ed
  +ing (*Br.* caulk.
  stop up. △ cork)
calk|er +s *Am.* (*Br.*
  caulker. person
  who calks.
  △ corker)
call +s +ed +ing
  (shout; telephone;
  visit; name; etc.
  △ caul)
calla +s
Cal|laghan, James
  (British prime
  minister)
Cal|lao (port, Peru)
Cal|las, Maria
  (American-born
  Greek soprano)
call box
  call boxes
call-boy +s
call|er +s
call-girl +s
cal|lig|raph|er +s
cal|lig|raph|ic
cal|lig|raph|ist +s
cal|lig|raphy

Cal|lil, Car|men
  (Australian
  publisher)
Cal|lima|chus
  (Hellenistic poet)
call|ing +s
call|ing card +s
Cal|liope *Roman
  Mythology*
cal|liope +s
cal|li|per +s
cal|li|py|gian
cal|li|py|gous
cal|lis|then|ic
cal|lis|then|ics
Cal|listo (*Greek
  Mythology*; moon
  of Jupiter)
cal|lop
  plural cal|lop
cal|los|ity
  cal|los|ities
cal|lous *adjective*
  (unfeeling.
  △ callus)
cal|lous *noun* (use
  callus)
  cal|louses
cal|lous|ly
cal|lous|ness
call-out +s *noun*
call-over +s *noun*
cal|low
cal|low|ly
cal|low|ness
call sign +s
cal|luna +s
call-up +s
cal|lus
  cal|luses
  (hard skin.
  △ callous)
calm +s +ed +ing
  +er +est
calma|tive +s
calm|er +s (person
  who calms.
  △ Kama, karma)
calm|ly
calm|ness
calo|mel +s
Calor gas *Propr.*
cal|oric +s
cal|orie +s
calorie-free
  adjective
cal|or|if|ic
cal|or|if|ic|al|ly
cal|or|im|eter +s
cal|ori|met|ric
cal|or|im|etry

cal|ory (use
  calorie)
  cal|or|ies
ca|lotte +s
calque +s
cal|trap +s (use
  caltrop)
cal|trop +s
Calum
calu|met +s
ca|lum|ni|ate
  ca|lum|ni|ates
  ca|lum|ni|ated
  ca|lum|ni|at|ing
ca|lum|ni|ation
ca|lum|ni|ator +s
ca|lum|ni|atory
ca|lum|ni|ous
cal|umny
  cal|um|nies
cal|um|nied
cal|um|ny|ing
Cal|va|dos (region,
  France)
cal|va|dos (drink)
Cal|vary
  (Jerusalem)
calve
  calves
  calved
  calv|ing
  (give birth to a
  calf. △ carve)
calves (plural of
  calf)
Cal|vin (name)
Cal|vin, John
  (French Protestant
  theologian)
Cal|vin, Mel|vin
  (American
  biochemist; cycle)
Cal|vin|ise *Br.* (use
  Calvinize)
  Cal|vin|ises
  Cal|vin|ised
  Cal|vin|is|ing
Cal|vin|ism
Cal|vin|ist +s
Cal|vin|is|tic
Cal|vin|is|tic|al
Cal|vin|ize
  Cal|vin|izes
  Cal|vin|ized
  Cal|vin|iz|ing
Cal|vino, Italo
  (Italian writer)
calx
  cal|ces
  (metal oxide.
  △ calques)
Ca|lypso

ca|lypso +s
calyx
  ca|ly|ces *or*
  ca|lyxes
cal|zone
  cal|zoni or
  cal|zones
Cam (river,
  England)
cam +s (device)
cama|rad|erie
Cam|argue, the
  (region, France)
cama|rilla +s
cama|ron +s
Cam|bay, Gulf of
  (Arabian Sea)
cam|ber +s
Cam|ber|well
  Beauty
  Cam|ber|well
  Beau|ties
cam|bial
cam|bist +s
cam|bium
  cam|bia *or*
  cam|biums
Cam|bo|dia
Cam|bo|dian +s
Cam|brian +s
  (Welsh; *Geology*)
cam|bric +s
Cam|bridge (cities,
  England and USA)
Cam|bridge blue
  +s *noun and*
  adjective
Cambridge-blue
  attributive
Cam|bridge|shire
  (county, England)
Cam|by|ses
  (Persian king and
  soldier)
cam|cord|er +s
came (past tense of
  come. △ kame)
camel +s
cam|el|back
cam|el|eer +s
camel-hair +s
cam|el|lia +s
cam|elo|pard +s
Cam|elot
  Arthurian Legend
cam|el|ry
  cam|el|ries
camel's-hair +s
Cam|em|bert +s
  (village, France;
  cheese)
cameo +s

cam|era +s
cam|era lu|cida +s
cam|era|man
  cam|era|men
cam|era ob|scura
  +s
camera-ready
cam|era-work
cam|er|lingo +s
Cam|eron
Cam|eron, Julia
  Mar|ga|ret
  (English
  photographer)
Cam|eron
  High|lands
  (resort, Malaysia)
Cam|er|oon (in W.
  Africa)
Cam|er|oon|ian +s
Cam|er|oun
  (French name for
  Cameroon)
cami|knick|ers
Cam|illa
cam|ion +s
cami|sole +s
Cam|ões, Luis de
  (Portuguese poet)
camo|mile
Cam|orra
cam|ou|flage
  cam|ou|flages
  cam|ou|flaged
  cam|ou|fla|ging
camp
  camps
  camped
  camp|ing
  camp|er
  camp|est
cam|paign +s +ed
  +ing
cam|paign|er +s
Cam|pa|nia
  (region, Italy)
Cam|pa|nian +s
cam|pa|nile +s
cam|pan|olo|ger
  +s
cam|pano|logic|al
cam|pan|olo|gist
  +s
cam|pan|ology
cam|pan|ula +s
cam|panu|late
camp bed +s
Camp|bell,
  Don|ald (English
  holder of water-
  speed record)

Camp|bell,
  Mal|colm
  (English racing
  driver)
Camp|bell, Mrs
  Pat|rick (English
  actress)
Camp|bell, Roy
  (South African
  poet)
Camp|bell,
  Thomas (Scottish
  poet)
Campbell-
  Banner|man,
  Henry (British
  statesman)
Camp David (in
  USA)
Cam|peachy wood
Cam|peche (state,
  Mexico)
camp|er +s
camp|fire +s
camp fol|low|er +s
camp|ground +s
cam|phor
cam|phor|ate
  cam|phor|ates
  cam|phor|ated
  cam|phor|at|ing
cam|phor|ic
camp|ily
Cam|pi|nas (city,
  Brazil)
campi|ness
Cam|pion,
  Ed|mund
  (English saint)
cam|pion +s
Campo|basso (city,
  Italy)
Campo Grande
  (city, Brazil)
camp-on *noun*
camp|site +s
cam|pus
  cam|puses
campy
  camp|ier
  campi|est
cam|pylo|bacter
  +s
CAMRA
  (= Campaign for
  Real Ale)
cam|shaft +s
Camu|lo|dunum
  (Roman name for
  Colchester)
Camus, Al|bert
  (French writer)

cam|wood
can (*auxiliary verb*
  be able)
can
  cans
  canned
  can|ning
  (tin; put in tin)
Cana (town,
  Galilee)
Ca|naan
  (= Palestine)
Ca|naan|ite +s
Can|ada (in N.
  America.
  △ Kannada)
Can|adian +s
ca|naille
canal +s
Cana|letto,
  Gio|vanni
  (Venetian painter)
can|al|isa|tion *Br.*
  (use canalization)
can|al|ise *Br.* (use
  canalize)
can|al|ises
can|al|ised
can|al|is|ing
can|al|iza|tion
can|al|ize
can|al|izes
can|al|ized
can|al|iz|ing
canal|side
can|apé +s
can|ard +s
Can|ar|ese (use
  Kanarese)
  plural Can|ar|ese
Can|ar|ies
  (= Canary
  Islands)
can|ary
  can|ar|ies
canary-colored
  Am.
canary-coloured
  Br.
can|ary creep|er
  +s
can|ary grass
Can|ary Is|lands
  (off African coast)
can|ary yel|low +s
  noun and adjective
canary-yellow
  attributive
can|asta +s (card
  game)
can|as|ter +s
  (tobacco)

Can|av|eral, Cape
(US space centre)
Can|berra (capital
of Australia)
can|can +s
can|cel
can|cels
can|celled *Br.*
can|celed *Am.*
can|cel|ling *Br.*
can|cel|ing *Am.*
can|cel|ler *Am.* +s
can|cel|late
can|cel|lated
can|cel|la|tion +s
can|cel|ler *Br.* +s
can|cel|lous
Can|cer
(constellation;
sign of zodiac)
can|cer +s
Can|cer|ian +s
can|cer|ous
can|croid +s
Can|cún (resort,
Mexico)
Can|dace *also*
Can|dice
can|dela +s
can|de|la|brum
can|de|la|bra
can|des|cence
can|des|cent
Can|dice *also*
Can|dace
can|did
Can|dida (name)
can|dida +s
(fungus)
can|di|dacy
can|di|da|cies
can|di|date +s
can|di|da|ture +s
can|did|ly
can|did|ness
can|dle
can|dles
can|dled
cand|ling
candle|hold|er +s
candle|light
candle|lit
Candle|mas
candle|power
cand|ler +s
candle|stick +s
candle|wick +s
can-do *adjective*
Can|dolle,
Augustin-
Pyramus de
(Swiss botanist)

can|dor *Am.*
cand|our *Br.*
Candy (name)
candy
candies
can|died
candy|ing
(confectionery)
candy|floss
candy stripe +s
candy-striped
candy|tuft
plural candy|tuft
cane
canes
caned
can|ing
(stick; to hit with a
cane. △ Cain)
cane-brake +s
caner +s
cane sugar
Canes Ve|nat|ici
(constellation)
cane toad +s
cane-trash
ca|nine +s
can|ing +s
Canis Major
(constellation)
Canis Minor
(constellation)
can|is|ter +s
(container.
△ canaster)
can|ker +s +ed
+ing
can|ker|ous
can|ker|worm +s
Can|more,
Mal|colm
(Malcolm III of
Scotland)
canna +s (plant.
△ canner)
can|na|binol
can|na|bis
can|na|bis resin
can|nel
can|nel|loni
can|nel|ure +s
can|ner +s (person
who cans.
△ canna)
can|nery
can|ner|ies
Cannes (resort,
France)
can|ni|bal +s
can|ni|bal|isa|tion
Br. (use
cannibalization)

can|ni|bal|ise *Br.*
(use cannibalize)
can|ni|bal|ises
can|ni|bal|ised
can|ni|bal|is|ing
can|ni|bal|ism
can|ni|bal|is|tic
can|ni|bal|is|tic|
al|ly
can|ni|bal|iza|tion
can|ni|bal|ize
can|ni|bal|izes
can|ni|bal|ized
can|ni|bal|iz|ing
can|ni|kin +s
can|nily
can|ni|ness
Can|ning, George
(British prime
minister)
Can|niz|zaro,
Stan|is|lao
(Italian chemist)
can|non +s +ed
+ing (gun;
Billiards;
Mechanics.
△ canon)
can|non|ade
can|non|ades
can|non|aded
can|non|ad|ing
can|non ball +s
cannon-bit +s
cannon-bone +s
can|non fod|der
can|not
can|nula
can|nu|lae *or*
can|nu|las
can|nu|late
can|nu|lates
can|nu|lated
can|nu|lat|ing
canny
can|nier
can|ni|est
canoe
ca|noes
ca|noed
ca|noe|ing
ca|noe|ist +s
canon +s (rule;
member of
cathedral chapter;
Music. △ cannon)
cañon +s (use
canyon)
ca|non|ess
ca|non|esses
ca|non|ic
ca|non|ic|al +s

ca|non|ic|al|ly
ca|noni|cate +s
can|on|icity
can|on|isa|tion *Br.*
+s (use
canonization)
can|on|ise *Br.* (use
canonize)
can|on|ises
can|on|ised
can|on|is|ing
can|on|ist +s
can|on|iza|tion
can|on|ize
can|on|izes
can|on|ized
can|on|iz|ing
canon law
canon regu|lar
canons regu|lar
can|on|ry
can|on|ries
ca|noo|dle
ca|noo|dles
ca|noo|dled
ca|nood|ling
can-opener +s
Ca|no|pic
Ca|no|pus (*Greek
Mythology*; star)
can|opy
can|opies
can|opied
can|opy|ing
can|or|ous
Ca|nova, An|tonio
(Italian sculptor)
canst
cant +s +ed +ing
can't (= cannot)
can|ta|bile +s
Can|tab|ria
(region. Spain)
Can|tab|rian +s
Can|ta|bri|gian +s
(of Cambridge or
Cambridge
University)
can|tal
can|ta|loup +s (use
cantaloupe)
can|ta|loupe +s
can|tan|ker|ous
can|tan|ker|ous|ly
can|tan|ker|ous|
ness
can|tata +s
can|ta|trice +s
cant-dog +s
can|teen +s
can|ter +s +ed
+ing

Can|ter|bury (city,
England)
Can|ter|bury
can|ter|buries
(furniture)
Can|ter|bury bell
+s (plant)
Can|ter|bury
Plains (region,
New Zealand)
can|thari|des
cant-hook +s
can|thus
can|thi
can|ticle +s
can|ti|lena +s
can|ti|lever
can|ti|levers
can|ti|levered
can|ti|lever|ing
can|til|late
can|til|lates
can|til|lated
can|til|lat|ing
can|til|la|tion
can|tina +s
cant|ing arms
can|tle +s
canto +s
Can|ton (city,
China)
can|ton +s +ed
+ing (subdivision
of country;
Heraldry)
can|ton|al
Can|ton|ese
plural Can|ton|ese
can|ton|ment +s
Can|tor, Georg
(Russian-born
mathematician)
can|tor +s
can|tor|ial
can|toris
cant|rail +s
can|trip +s
Can|tuck +s (*usually
offensive*)
Can|ute (use Cnut)
can|vas
can|vases
(cloth. △ canvass)
canvas-back
can|vass
can|vasses
can|vassed
can|vass|ing
(solicit. △ canvas)
can|vass|er +s
can|yon +s
can|zonet +s

can|zon|etta +s
caou|tchouc +s
cap
caps
capped
cap|ping
cap.
caps.
(= capital letter)
cap|abil|ity
cap|abil|ities
Capa|blanca, José
(Cuban chess
player)
cap|able
cap|ably
cap|acious
cap|acious|ly
cap|acious|ness
cap|aci|tance +s
cap|aci|tate
cap|aci|tates
cap|aci|tated
cap|aci|tat|ing
cap|aci|ta|tive
cap|aci|tive (use
capacitative)
cap|aci|tor +s
cap|acity
cap|aci|ties
ca|pari|son +s +ed
+ing
cape +s
Cape ... (see
Agulhas, Bon,
etc.)
Cape Bre|ton
Is|land (in
Canada)
Cape Col|ony
(former name of
Cape Province)
Cape Col|ored *Am.*
+s
Cape Col|oured *Br.*
+s
caped
Cape doc|tor +s
Cape Dutch
Cape goose|berry
Cape
goose|berries
Cape John|son
Depth (in W.
Pacific)
Čapek, Karel
(Czech writer)
cap|elin +s
Ca|pella (star)
caper +s +ed +ing
cap|er|cail|lie +s

cap|er|cail|zie +s
(use capercaillie)
caper|er +s
cape|skin
Capet, Hugh
(French king)
Cap|etian +s
Cape Town
(legislative capital
of South Africa)
Cape Ver|dean +s
Cape Verde
Is|lands (off coast
of Senegal)
cap|ful +s
cap|ias
ca|pil|lar|ity
ca|pil|lary
ca|pil|lar|ies
cap|ital +s
cap|ital gain +s
cap|ital gains tax
capital-intensive
cap|it|al|isa|tion
Br. (use
capitalization)
cap|it|al|ise *Br.*
(use capitalize)
cap|it|al|ises
cap|it|al|ised
cap|it|al|is|ing
cap|it|al|ism
cap|it|al|ist +s
cap|it|al|is|tic
cap|it|al|is|tic|
    al|ly
cap|it|al|iza|tion
cap|it|al|ize
cap|it|al|izes
cap|it|al|ized
cap|it|al|iz|ing
cap|it|al|ly
capi|ta|tion +s
Cap|itol (in ancient
Rome or
Washington DC)
Ca|pit|ol|ine (hill,
ancient Rome)
ca|pitu|lar
ca|pitu|lary
ca|pitu|lar|ies
ca|pitu|late
ca|pitu|lates
ca|pitu|lated
ca|pitu|lat|ing
ca|pitu|la|tion +s
ca|pitu|la|tor +s
ca|pitu|la|tory
ca|pit|ulum
ca|pit|ula
cap|lin +s (use
capelin)

cap'n (= captain)
capo +s
Capo di Monte
(porcelain)
capon +s
Ca|pone, Al
(American
gangster)
ca|pon|ier +s
ca|pon|ise *Br.* (use
caponize)
ca|pon|ises
ca|pon|ised
ca|pon|is|ing
ca|pon|ize
ca|pon|izes
ca|pon|ized
ca|pon|iz|ing
capot
ca|pots
ca|pot|ted
ca|pot|ting
capo tasto +s
Ca|pote, Tru|man
(American writer)
ca|pote +s
Cap|pa|do|cia
(ancient name of
region of Asia
Minor)
Cap|pa|do|cian +s
cap|ping +s
cap|puc|cino +s
Capra, Frank
(Italian-born
American film
director)
Capri (island, Italy)
cap|ric
ca|pric|cio +s
ca|pric|ci|oso +s
Music
ca|price +s
ca|pri|cious
ca|pri|cious|ly
ca|pri|cious|ness
Cap|ri|corn
(constellation;
sign of zodiac)
Cap|ri|corn|ian +s
Cap|ri|cor|nus
(constellation; use
Capricorn)
cap|rine
cap|ri|ole
cap|ri|oles
cap|ri|oled
cap|ri|ol|ing
Capri pants
Ca|pris
Ca|privi Strip (in
Namibia)

cap rock
cap|roic
caps. (= capital
   letters)
Cap|sian +s
cap|sicum +s
cap|sid +s
cap|sizal
cap|size
   cap|sizes
   cap|sized
   cap|siz|ing
cap sleeve +s
cap|stan +s
cap|stone +s
cap|su|lar
cap|su|late
cap|sule +s
cap|su|lise Br. (use
   capsulize)
   cap|su|lises
   cap|su|lised
   cap|su|lis|ing
cap|su|lize
   cap|su|lizes
   cap|su|lized
   cap|su|liz|ing
cap|tain +s +ed
   +ing
Cap|tain Cook|er
   +s
cap|tain|cy
   cap|tain|cies
captain-general
   +s
cap|tain|ship +s
cap|tion +s +ed
   +ing
cap|tious
cap|tious|ly
cap|tious|ness
cap|tiv|ate
   cap|tiv|ates
   cap|tiv|ated
   cap|tiv|at|ing
cap|tiv|at|ing|ly
cap|tiv|ation
cap|tive +s
cap|tiv|ity
   cap|tiv|ities
cap|tor +s
cap|ture
   cap|tures
   cap|tured
   cap|tur|ing
cap|turer +s
Capu|chin +s
   (friar; cloak and
   hood)
capu|chin +s
   (monkey; pigeon)
capy|bara +s

car +s (vehicle.
   △ carr, ka)
Cara
cara|bin|eer +s
   (soldier.
   △ karabiner)
cara|bin|iere
   cara|bin|ieri
cara|cal +s (lynx.
   △ karakul)
Cara|calla (Roman
   emperor)
cara|cara +s
Ca|ra|cas (capital
   of Venezuela)
cara|cole
   cara|coles
   cara|coled
   cara|col|ing
Ca|ract|acus (use
   Caratacus)
cara|cul +s (use
   karakul)
ca|rafe +s
Cara|jás (region,
   Brazil)
ca|ram|bola +s
cara|mel +s
cara|mel|isa|tion
   Br. (use
   caramelization)
cara|mel|ise Br.
   (use caramelize)
   cara|mel|ises
   cara|mel|ised
   cara|mel|is|ing
cara|mel|iza|tion
cara|mel|ize
   cara|mel|izes
   cara|mel|ized
   cara|mel|iz|ing
ca|ran|gid +s
cara|pace +s
carat +s (unit of
   weight for jewels.
   △ caret, carrot,
   karat)
carat Br. +s
   (measure of purity
   for gold. Am.
   karat. △ caret,
   carrot)
Ca|rat|acus (British
   chieftain)
Cara|vag|gio
   (Italian painter)
cara|van
   cara|vans
   cara|vanned
   cara|van|ning
cara|van|ette +s
cara|van|ner +s

cara|van|sary (use
   caravanserai)
   cara|van|sar|ies
cara|van|serai +s
cara|vel +s
cara|way
carb +s
car|ba|mate +s
car|bide +s
car|bie +s
car|bine +s
carbo|hy|drate +s
car|bol|ic
car bomb +s
car|bon +s
car|bon|aceous
car|bon|ade +s
   (use carbonnade)
car|bon|ado +s
car|bon|ara
car|bon|ate
   car|bon|ates
   car|bon|ated
   car|bon|at|ing
car|bon|ation
car|bon black
car|bon copy
   car|bon cop|ies
car|bon cycle +s
car|bon dat|ing
car|bon fiber Am.
   +s
car|bon fibre Br.
   +s
carbon-14
car|bon|ic
Car|bon|ifer|ous
   Geology
car|bon|ifer|ous
car|bon|isa|tion Br.
   (use
   carbonization)
car|bon|ise Br. (use
   carbonize)
   car|bon|ises
   car|bon|ised
   car|bon|is|ing
car|bon|iza|tion
car|bon|ize
   car|bon|izes
   car|bon|ized
   car|bon|iz|ing
car|bon|nade +s
car|bon paper
carbon-12
car|bonyl +s
car-boot sale +s
car|bor|un|dum
carb|oxyl +s
carb|ox|yl|ate +s
carb|ox|yl|ic
car|boy +s

car|bun|cle +s
car|bun|cu|lar
car|bur|ation
car|buret
   car|bur|ets
car|bur|et|ted Br.
   car|bur|et|ed Am.
   car|bur|et|ting Br.
   car|bur|et|ing Am.
car|bur|etor Am.
   +s
car|bur|et|tor Br.
   +s
car|bur|isa|tion Br.
   (use
   carburization)
car|bur|ise Br. (use
   carburize)
   car|bur|ises
   car|bur|ised
   car|bur|is|ing
car|bur|iza|tion
car|bur|ize
   car|bur|izes
   car|bur|ized
   car|bur|iz|ing
carby (use carbie)
   car|bies
car|ca|jou +s
car|case +s (use
   carcass)
car|cass
   car|casses
Car|cas|sonne
   (city, France)
Car|chem|ish
   (ancient city,
   Syria)
car|cino|gen +s
car|cino|gen|esis
car|cino|gen|ic
car|cino|gen|ic|
   al|ly
car|cino|gen|icity
car|cin|oma
   car|cin|omata or
   car|cin|omas
car|cin|omat|ous
card +s +ed +ing
car|da|mom
Car|da|mom
   Moun|tains (in
   Cambodia)
car|dan joint +s
car|dan shaft +s
card|board +s
card-carrying
card|er +s
card game +s
card|hold|er +s
car|diac

car¦die +s (use
cardy. cardigan.
△ cadi)
Car¦diff (capital of
Wales)
car¦di¦gan +s
Car¦di¦gan Bay (off
Wales)
Car¦di¦gan¦shire
(former county,
Wales)
Car¦din, Pierre
(French couturier)
car¦din¦al +s
car¦din¦al¦ate +s
car¦din¦al flower
+s
car¦din¦al¦ly
car¦din¦al¦ship +s
card index
card in¦dexes
card¦ing wool
car¦dio|gram +s
car¦dio|graph +s
car¦di|og¦raph¦er
+s
car¦di|og¦raphy
car¦di|oid +s
car¦di|olo¦gist +s
car¦di|ology
car¦dio|
⠀⠀⠀⠀my¦op¦athy
car¦dio|
⠀⠀⠀⠀my¦op¦athies
car¦dio|
⠀⠀⠀⠀pul¦mon¦ary
car¦dio|vas¦cu¦lar
car¦doon +s
card|phone +s
card-playing
card-sharp +s
card-sharper +s
card table +s
card vote +s
cardy
⠀⠀car¦dies
⠀⠀(cardigan. △ cadi)
care
⠀⠀cares
⠀⠀cared
⠀⠀car¦ing
car¦een +s +ed
⠀⠀+ing
car¦een|age
car¦eer +s +ed
⠀⠀+ing
career-best +s
car¦eer|ism
car¦eer|ist +s
care|free
care|free|ness

care|ful
care|ful¦ly
care|ful|ness
care|giver +s
care|less
care|less¦ly
care|less|ness
carer +s
ca¦ress
⠀⠀ca¦resses
⠀⠀ca¦ressed
⠀⠀ca¦ress|ing
ca¦ress|ing¦ly
caret (omission
⠀⠀mark. △ carat,
⠀⠀carrot, karat)
care|taker +s
Carew, Thomas
⠀⠀(English poet)
care|worn
Carey also Cary
⠀⠀(name)
Carey, George
⠀⠀(English
⠀⠀archbishop)
car¦ezza (use
⠀⠀karezza)
car¦fare +s
car¦fax
⠀⠀car¦faxes
car¦ful +s
cargo
⠀⠀car¦goes
car¦hop +s
Caria (ancient
⠀⠀region, SW Asia)
cari|ama +s
Car¦ian +s
Carib +s
Carib|bean +s
Carib|bean Sea
cari|bou
⠀⠀plural cari|bou
cari¦ca|tural
cari¦ca|ture
⠀⠀cari¦ca|tures
⠀⠀cari¦ca|tured
⠀⠀cari¦ca|tur|ing
cari¦ca|tur|ist +s
CARICOM
⠀⠀(= Caribbean
⠀⠀Community and
⠀⠀Common Market)
car¦ies
⠀⠀plural car¦ies
car¦il|lon +s
Ca¦rina (name)
ca¦rina +s Biology
car¦in¦al
car¦in¦ate
Car¦in¦thia (state,
⠀⠀Austria)

Car¦in|thian +s
cari|oca +s
cario|gen¦ic
cari|ole +s (use
⠀⠀carriole)
cari|ous
car¦jack +s +ed
⠀⠀+ing
car¦jack¦er +s
cark|ing
⠀⠀(burdensome)
Carl also Karl
⠀⠀(name)
carl +s (man)
Carla
carl|ine +s
Car¦lisle (city,
⠀⠀England)
car¦load +s
Car¦lo|vin|gian †
Car¦low (county
⠀⠀and city, Republic
⠀⠀of Ireland)
Carls|bad (German
⠀⠀name for Karlovy
⠀⠀Vary)
Carl|ton
Carly
Car¦lyle, Thomas
⠀⠀(Scottish writer)
car maker +s
car¦man
⠀⠀car¦men
Car¦mar|then
⠀⠀(town, Wales)
Car¦mar|then|
⠀⠀shire (former
⠀⠀county, Wales)
Car¦mel (name)
Car¦mel, Mount
⠀⠀(group of
⠀⠀mountains, Israel)
Car¦mel|ite +s
Car¦men
Car¦michael,
⠀⠀Hoagy (American
⠀⠀jazz musician)
Car¦mina Bur¦ana
car¦mina|tive +s
car¦mine +s
Car¦naby Street
⠀⠀(in London)
Car¦nac (village,
⠀⠀France.
⠀⠀△ Karnak)
carn|age
car¦nal
car¦nal|ise Br. (use
⠀⠀carnalize)
⠀⠀car¦nal|ises

car¦nal|ise (cont.)
⠀⠀car¦nal|ised
⠀⠀car¦nal|is|ing
car¦nal|ity
car¦nal|ize
⠀⠀car¦nal|izes
⠀⠀car¦nal|ized
⠀⠀car¦nal|iz|ing
car¦nal|ly
Car¦nap, Ru¦dolf
⠀⠀(German-
⠀⠀American
⠀⠀philosopher)
car¦nas|sial +s
car¦na|tion +s
car¦nauba +s
Carné, Mar¦cel
⠀⠀(French film
⠀⠀director)
Car¦negie,
⠀⠀An¦drew (Scottish
⠀⠀entrepreneur and
⠀⠀philanthropist)
r¦nel|ian +s
r¦net +s
ar¦ni|val +s
Car¦niv¦ora
car¦ni|vore +s
car¦niv¦or¦ous
car¦niv¦or¦ous¦ly
car¦niv¦or¦ous|
⠀⠀⠀⠀⠀⠀⠀⠀ness
Car¦not, Nico¦las
⠀⠀(French scientist)
car¦no|tite
carny
⠀⠀car¦nies
⠀⠀car¦nied
⠀⠀carny|ing
carob +s
carob tree +s
Carol also Car¦ole,
⠀⠀Caryl
⠀⠀(name)
carol
⠀⠀carols
⠀⠀car¦olled Br.
⠀⠀car¦oled Am.
⠀⠀car¦ol|ling Br.
⠀⠀car¦ol|ing Am.
⠀⠀(song. △ carrel)
Car¦ole also Carol,
⠀⠀Caryl
⠀⠀(name)
Caro¦lean +s
car¦ol¦er Am. +s
⠀⠀(Br. caroller)
Caro¦lina, North
⠀⠀and South (states,
⠀⠀USA)
Caro¦line (of the
⠀⠀time of Charles I

Caro|line (*cont.*)
   or II of England;
   name)
Caro|line Is|lands
   (in W. Pacific)
Caro|lines
   (= Caroline
   Islands)
Caro|lin|gian +s
car|ol|ler *Br.* +s
   (*Am.* caroler)
Caro|lyn
carom +s +ed +ing
car|ot|ene
ca|rot|en|oid
Ca|roth|ers,
   Wal|lace
   (American
   chemist)
ca|rotid +s
ca|rousal +s
   (drinking party)
ca|rouse
   ca|rouses
   ca|roused
   ca|rous|ing
car|ou|sel *Br.* +s
   (merry-go-round;
   conveyor. *Am.*
   carrousel)
ca|rouser +s
carp +s +ed +ing
   (find fault)
.carp
   plural carp
   (fish)
Car|pac|cio,
   Vit|tore (Italian
   painter)
car|pac|cio (food)
car|pal +s (bone.
   △ carpel)
car park +s
Car|pa|thian
   Moun|tains (in E.
   Europe)
car|pel +s (part of
   flower. △ carpal)
car|pel|lary
Car|pen|taria,
   Gulf of (on N
   coast of Australia)
car|pen|ter +s
car|pen|try
carp|er +s
car|pet +s +ed
   +ing
carpet-bag +s
carpet-bagger +s
car|pet bomb|ing
car|pet|ing +s
car|pet slip|per +s

car|pet sweep|er
   +s
car|phol|ogy
car phone +s
car|pol|ogy
car|port +s
car|pus
   carpi
Carr, Emily
   (Canadian painter)
carr +s (marsh.
   △ car, ka)
Car|racci (Italian
   family of painters)
car|rack +s
car|ra|geen
car|ra|geenan
car|ra|gheen (use
   carrageen)
Car|rara (town,
   Italy)
Car|rel, Alexis
   (French surgeon
   and biologist)
car|rel +s (cubicle.
   △ carol)
Car|reras, José
   (Spanish tenor)
car|riage +s
car|riage clock +s
carriage-dog +s
car|riage|way +s
car|rick bend +s
Carrick-on-
   Shannon (town,
   Republic of
   Ireland)
Car|rie
car|rier +s
car|rier bag +s
car|rier pi|geon +s
car|ri|ole +s
car|rion
car|rion crow +s
carrion-eater +s
carrion-eating
Car|roll, Lewis
   (English writer)
car|ron|ade +s
car|rot +s
   (vegetable.
   △ carat, caret,
   karat)
car|roty
car|rou|sel *Am.* +s
   (*Br.* carousel)
carry
   car|ries
   car|ried
   carry|ing
   (convey. △ karri)
carry-all +s

carry|cot +s
carrying-on
   carryings-on
   noun
carrying trade
carry-on +s noun
carry-out +s
carry-over +s
carry-through
   adjective
carse +s
car|sick
car|sick|ness
Car|son, Kit
   (American
   frontiersman)
Car|son, Ra|chel
   (American
   zoologist)
Car|son City (city,
   USA)
cart +s +ed +ing
   (unpowered
   vehicle; convey.
   △ kart, khat,
   quart)
cart|age
Car|ta|gena (ports,
   Spain and
   Colombia)
carte (*Fencing*; use
   quart. △ cart,
   kart, khat)
carte blanche
car|tel +s
car|tel|isa|tion *Br.*
   (use
   cartelization)
car|tel|ise *Br.* (use
   cartelize)
   car|tel|ises
   car|tel|ised
   car|tel|is|ing
car|tel|iza|tion
car|tel|ize
   car|tel|izes
   car|tel|ized
   car|tel|iz|ing
Car|ter, An|gela
   (English writer)
Car|ter, El|li|ott
   Cook (American
   composer)
Car|ter, Jimmy
   (American
   president)
car|ter +s
Car|te|sian +s
Car|tes|ian|ism
cart|ful +s
Car|thage (ancient
   city, Africa)

Car|tha|gin|ian +s
cart|horse +s
Car|thu|sian +s
Car|tier, Jacques
   (French explorer)
Cartier-Bresson,
   Henri (French
   photographer)
Car|tier Is|lands
   (in Indian Ocean)
car|til|age +s
car|ti|la|gin|oid
car|ti|la|gin|ous
Cart|land,
   Bar|bara (English
   writer)
cart|load +s
carto|gram +s
car|tog|raph|er +s
carto|graph|ic
carto|graph|ic|al
carto|graph|ic|
      al|ly
car|tog|raphy
carto|mancy
car|ton +s
car|toon +s
car|toon|ing
car|toon|ish
car|toon|ist +s
car|toon strip +s
car|toony
car|touche +s
cart|ridge +s
cart|ridge belt +s
cart|ridge paper
cart road +s
cart track +s
car|tu|lary
   car|tu|lar|ies
cart|wheel +s +ed
   +ing
Cart|wright,
   Ed|mund
   (English inventor)
cart|wright +s
car|uncle +s
car|un|cu|lar
Ca|ruso, En|rico
   (Italian tenor)
carve
   carves
   carved
   carv|ing
   (cut; slice.
   △ calve)
car|vel +s
carvel-built
car|ven
Car|ver *Am.* +s
   (rush-seated chair)

car¦ver +s (person
who carves; knife;
dining chair with
arms. △ cava,
kava)
car¦very
car¦ver¦ies
carve-up +s noun
carv¦ing +s
carv¦ing fork +s
carv¦ing knife
carv¦ing knives
car wash
car washes
C¦ary also Carey
(name)
Cary, Joyce
(English novelist)
cary¦atid
cary¦atides or
cary¦atids
Caryl also Carol,
Car¦ole
cary¦op¦sis
cary¦op¦ses
Casa¦blanca (city,
Morocco)
Ca¦sals, Pablo
(Spanish cellist
and composer)
Casa¦nova +s
(philanderer)
cas¦bah +s (use
kasbah)
cas¦cade
cas¦cades
cas¦caded
cas¦cad¦ing
Cas¦cade Range
(mountains, N.
America)
Cas¦cais (resort,
Portugal)
cas¦cara
(sag¦rada)
case
cases
cased
cas¦ing
case¦book +s
case-bound
case-harden +s
+ed +ing
case his¦tory
case his¦tor¦ies
ca¦sein
ca¦sein¦ogen
case knife
case knives
case law
case¦load +s
case¦mate +s

Case¦ment, Roger
(Irish nationalist)
case¦ment +s
ca¦se¦ous
case-shot
case study
case studies
case¦work
case¦work¦er +s
Casey also Casy
Cash, Johnny
(American singer)
cash
cashes
cashed
cash¦ing
(money. △ cache)
cash¦able
cash and carry
cash book +s
cash box
cash boxes
cash card +s
cash crop +s
cash desk +s
cash dis¦pen¦ser
+s
cashew +s (nut.
△ cachou)
cashew apple +s
cashew nut +s
cash flow +s
cash¦ier +s +ed
+ing
cash-in +s noun
cash¦less
cash¦mere (wool.
△ Kashmir)
cash¦point +s
cash regis¦ter +s
cas¦ing +s
ca¦sino +s
cask +s (box.
△ casque)
cas¦ket +s
Cas¦lon, Wil¦liam
(English
typographer)
Cas¦par also
Cas¦per
(name)
Cas¦par (one of the
Magi)
Cas¦per also
Cas¦par
(name)
Cas¦pian Sea (in
central Asia)
casque +s (helmet;
helmet-like
structure. △ cask)

Cas¦san¦dra (Greek
Legend; name)
cas¦sata +s
cas¦sa¦tion +s
cas¦sava +s
Casse¦grain
(telescope)
cas¦ser¦ole
cas¦ser¦oles
cas¦ser¦oled
cas¦ser¦ol¦ing
cas¦sette +s
cas¦sette play¦er
+s
cas¦sia +s
Cas¦sie
cas¦sin¦gle +s
Propr.
Cas¦sini (moon of
Saturn)
Cas¦sini,
Gio¦vanni
Do¦men¦ico
(Italian-born
astronomer)
Cas¦sio¦peia
(constellation)
cas¦sis
cas¦sit¦er¦ite +s
Cas¦sius (Roman
general)
cas¦sock +s
cas¦socked
cas¦sou¦let +s
cas¦so¦wary
cas¦so¦war¦ies
cast
casts
cast
cast¦ing
(throw etc.
△ caste, karst)
Cas¦talia (sacred
spring, Mount
Parnassus)
Cas¦ta¦lian
cas¦ta¦net +s
cast¦away +s
caste +s (social
class. △ cast,
karst)
caste¦ism
Cas¦tel Gan¦dolfo
(in Italy)
cas¦tel¦lan +s
cas¦tel¦lated
cas¦tel¦la¦tion +s
caste mark +s
cast¦er +s (person
or machine that
casts. △ castor)
cast¦er sugar

cas¦ti¦gate
cas¦ti¦gates
cas¦ti¦gated
cas¦ti¦gat¦ing
cas¦ti¦ga¦tion
cas¦ti¦ga¦tor +s
cas¦ti¦ga¦tory
Cas¦tile (region,
Spain)
Cas¦tile soap
Cas¦til¦ian +s
Castilla-La
Mancha
(province, Spain)
Castilla-León
(region, Spain)
cast¦ing +s
cast iron noun
cast-iron adjective
cas¦tle
cas¦tles
cas¦tled
cast¦ling
Castle¦bar (town,
Republic of
Ireland)
Castle¦reagh,
Rob¦ert (British
statesman)
cast net +s
cast-off +s adjective
and noun
Cas¦tor (Greek
Mythology; star)
cas¦tor +s
(perforated jar;
wheel; oily
substance.
△ caster)
cas¦tor ac¦tion
cas¦tor oil
cas¦tor oil plant
cas¦tor sugar (use
caster sugar)
cas¦trate
cas¦trates
cas¦trated
cas¦trat¦ing
cas¦tra¦tion +s
cas¦tra¦tive
cas¦trato
cas¦trati
cas¦tra¦tor +s
cas¦tra¦tory
Cas¦tries (capital of
St Lucia)
Cas¦tro, Fidel
(Cuban
statesman)
Cas¦tro¦ism
cas¦ual +s
casu¦al¦ly

casu|al|ness
casu|alty
  casu|al|ties
casu|ar|ina +s
casu|ist +s
casu|is|tic
casu|is|tic|al
casu|is|tic|al|ly
casu|is|try
casus belli
Casy *also* Casey
cat
  cats
  cat|ted
  cat|ting
cata|bol|ic
cata|bol|ic|al|ly
ca|tab|ol|ism
cata|chre|sis
  cata|chre|ses
cata|chres|tic
cata|chres|tic|al
cata|clasis
  cata|clases
cata|clasm +s
cata|clas|tic
cata|clysm +s
cata|clys|mal
cata|clys|mic
cata|clys|mic|al|ly
cata|comb +s
cata|di|op|tric
ca|tad|rom|ous
cata|falque +s
Cata|lan +s
cata|lase +s
cata|lec|tic
cata|lepsy
  cata|lep|sies
cata|lep|tic
cata|log *Am.* +s
  +ed +ing
cata|log|er *Am.* +s
cata|logue *Br.*
  cata|logues
  cata|logued
  cata|loguing
cata|loguer *Br.* +s
cata|logue
  rai|sonné
  cata|logues
  rai|son|nés
Cata|lo|nia (region,
  Spain)
cat|alpa +s
cata|lyse *Br.*
  cata|lyses
  cata|lysed
  cata|lys|ing
cata|lyser *Br.* +s
cata|ly|sis
  cata|ly|ses

cata|lyst +s
cata|lyt|ic
cata|lyze *Am.*
  cata|lyzes
  cata|lyzed
  cata|lyz|ing
cata|ma|ran +s
cata|mite +s
cata|moun|tain +s
cata|nan|che +s
cat-and-dog
  adjective
Cat|ania (port,
  Sicily)
cata|plec|tic
cata|plexy
  cata|plex|ies
cata|pult +s +ed
  +ing
cat|ar|act +s
ca|tarrh +s
ca|tar|rhal
cat|ar|rhine
ca|tas|trophe +s
cata|stroph|ic
cata|stroph|ic|
  al|ly
ca|tas|troph|ism
ca|tas|troph|ist +s
cata|to|nia
cata|ton|ic +s
ca|tawba +s
cat|bird +s
cat|boat +s
cat burg|lar +s
cat|call +s
catch
  catches
  caught
  catch|ing
catch|able
catch-all +s
catch-as-catch-
  can
catch crop +s
catch|er +s
catch|fly
  catch|flies
catch|ily
catchi|ness
catch|line +s
catch|ment
catch|penny
  catch|pen|nies
catch|phrase +s
catch-points
catch|pole +s
catch-22
catchup +s (sauce)
catch-up *noun and
  attributive*
catch|weight +s

catch|word +s
catchy
  catch|ier
  catchi|est
cat door +s
cate +s
cat|ech|et|ic
cat|ech|et|ic|al
cat|ech|et|ic|al|ly
cat|ech|et|ics
cat|ech|ise *Br.* (use
  catechize)
  cat|ech|ises
  cat|ech|ised
  cat|ech|is|ing
cat|ech|iser *Br.* +s
  (use catechizer)
cat|ech|ism +s
cat|ech|is|mal
cat|ech|ist +s
cat|ech|ize
  cat|ech|izes
  cat|ech|ized
  cat|ech|iz|ing
cat|ech|izer +s
cat|echol|amine
  +s
cat|echu +s
cat|echu|men +s
cat|egor|ial
cat|egoric
cat|egor|ic|al
cat|egor|ic|al|ly
cat|egor|isa|tion
  Br. +s (use
  categorization)
cat|egor|ise *Br.*
  (use categorize)
  cat|egor|ises
  cat|egor|ised
  cat|egor|is|ing
cat|egor|iza|tion
  +s
cat|egor|ize
  cat|egor|izes
  cat|egor|ized
  cat|egor|iz|ing
cat|egory
  cat|egor|ies
ca|tena
  ca|tenae
ca|ten|ary
  ca|ten|ar|ies
cat|en|ate
  cat|en|ates
  cat|en|ated
  cat|en|at|ing
cat|en|ation +s
cater +s +ed +ing
cat|eran +s
cater-cornered
cater|er +s

cat|er|pil|lar +s
  (larva)
cat|er|pil|lar track
  +s *Propr.*
cat|er|waul +s +ed
  +ing
cat|fish
  plural cat|fish
cat flap +s
cat|gut
Cath *also* Kath
Cathar
  Cath|ars *or*
  Cath|ari
Cath|ar|ine *also*
  Cath|er|ine,
  Cath|ryn,
  Kath|ar|ine,
  Kath|er|ine,
  Kath|ryn
Cath|ar|ism
Cath|ar|ist +s
cath|ar|sis
  cath|ar|ses
cath|ar|tic +s
cath|ar|tic|al|ly
Ca|thay (poetic or
  historical name of
  China)
cat|head +s
cath|ec|tic
cath|edra (in 'ex
  cathedra')
cath|edral +s
Cather, Willa
  (American
  novelist)
Cath|er|ine *also*
  Cath|ar|ine,
  Cath|ryn,
  Kath|ar|ine,
  Kath|er|ine,
  Kath|ryn
Cath|er|ine
  (Russian empress)
Cath|er|ine de'
  Med|ici (French
  queen)
Cath|er|ine of
  Alex|an|dria
  (early saint)
Cath|er|ine of
  Ara|gon (wife of
  Henry VIII of
  England)
Cath|er|ine wheel
  +s
cath|eter +s
cath|et|er|ise *Br.*
  (use catheterize)
  cath|et|er|ises

cath¦et¦er¦ise
(cont.)
  cath¦et¦er¦ised
  cath¦et¦er¦is¦ing
cath¦et¦er¦ize
  cath¦et¦er¦izes
  cath¦et¦er¦ized
  cath¦et¦er¦iz¦ing
cath¦etom¦eter +s
cath¦exis
  cath¦exes
Cathie *also* Cathy,
  Kathie, Kathy
Cath¦leen *also*
  Kath¦leen
cath¦odal
cath¦ode +s
cath¦ode ray +s
cath¦ode ray tube
  +s
cath¦od¦ic
Cath¦olic +s (in
  religious senses)
cath¦olic (universal
  etc.)
cath¦olic¦al¦ly (use
  catholicly)
Cath¦oli¦cise *Br.*
  (use Catholicize)
  Cath¦oli¦cises
  Cath¦oli¦cised
  Cath¦oli¦cis¦ing
  (make or become
  a Roman Catholic)
cath¦oli¦cise *Br.*
  (use catholicize)
  cath¦oli¦cises
  cath¦oli¦cised
  cath¦oli¦cis¦ing
  (make or become
  catholic)
Cath¦oli¦cism
cath¦ol¦icity
Cath¦oli¦cize
  Cath¦oli¦cizes
  Cath¦oli¦cized
  Cath¦oli¦ciz¦ing
  (make or become
  a Roman Catholic)
cath¦oli¦cize
  cath¦oli¦cizes
  cath¦oli¦cized
  cath¦oli¦ciz¦ing
  (make or become
  catholic)
cath¦olic¦ly
cath¦oli¦con +s
Cath¦ryn *also*
  Cath¦ar¦ine,
  Cath¦er¦ine,
  Kath¦ar¦ine,

Cath¦ryn (*cont.*)
  Kath¦er¦ine,
  Kath¦ryn
Cathy *also* Cathie,
  Kathie, Kathy
cat-ice
Cati¦line (Roman
  nobleman and
  conspirator)
cat¦ion +s
cat¦ion¦ic
cat¦kin +s
cat-lap
cat¦lick +s
cat¦like
cat¦mint
cat¦nap
  cat¦naps
  cat¦napped
  cat¦nap¦ping
cat¦nip
Cato (Roman
  statesman and
  orator)
cat-o'-nine-tails
  plural cat-o'-nine-
  tails
cat¦op¦tric
cat¦op¦trics
Cat¦rin
Ca¦tri¦ona
cat's cra¦dle +s
Cats¦eye +s (on
  road) *Propr.*
cat's-eye +s
  (precious stone;
  marble)
cat's-foot +s
Cats¦kill
  Moun¦tains (in
  USA)
cat's-paw +s
cat's py¦ja¦mas
cat's-tail +s
cat¦suit +s
cat¦sup +s
cat's whis¦ker +s
cat¦tery
  cat¦ter¦ies
cat¦tily
cat¦ti¦ness
cat¦tish
cat¦tish¦ly
cat¦tish¦ness
cat¦tle
cat¦tle cake +s
cattle-dog +s
cat¦tle grid +s
cat¦tle guard +s
cattle¦man
  cattle¦men
cattle-plague

cat¦tle stop +s
catt¦leya +s
catty
  cat¦tier
  cat¦ti¦est
catty-cornered
Ca¦tul¦lus (Roman
  poet)
cat¦walk +s
Cau¦ca¦sian +s
Cau¦cas¦oid +s
Cau¦casus
  (mountain range,
  Georgia)
Cauchy,
  Au¦gus¦tin Louis
  (French
  mathematician)
cau¦cus
  cau¦cuses
cau¦dal (of or like a
  tail. △ chordal)
caud¦al¦ly
caud¦ate (having a
  tail. △ chordate,
  cordate)
cau¦dillo +s
caught (past tense
  and past participle
  of catch. △ court)
caul +s (amnion.
  △ call)
caul¦dron +s
cauli¦flower +s
caulk *Br.* +s +ed
  +ing (*Am.* calk.
  stop up. △ cork)
caulk¦er +s *Br.*
  (*Am.* calker.
  person who
  caulks. △ corker)
caus¦able
causal
caus¦al¦ity
caus¦al¦ly
caus¦ation
causa¦tive +s
causa¦tive¦ly
cause
  causes
  caused
  caus¦ing
'cause (= because)
cause and ef¦fect
cause cé¦lèbre
  causes cé¦lèbres
cause¦less
causer +s
caus¦erie +s
cause¦way +s
causey +s
caus¦tic

caus¦tic¦al¦ly
caus¦ti¦cise *Br.* (use
  causticize)
  caus¦ti¦cises
  caus¦ti¦cised
  caus¦ti¦cis¦ing
caus¦ti¦city
caus¦ti¦cize
  caus¦ti¦cizes
  caus¦ti¦cized
  caus¦ti¦ciz¦ing
caus¦tic soda
caut¦er¦isa¦tion *Br.*
  (use
  cauterization)
caut¦er¦ise *Br.* (use
  cauterize)
  caut¦er¦ises
  caut¦er¦ised
  caut¦er¦is¦ing
caut¦er¦iza¦tion
caut¦er¦ize
  caut¦er¦izes
  caut¦er¦ized
  caut¦er¦iz¦ing
caut¦ery
  caut¦er¦ies
cau¦tion +s +ed
  +ing
cau¦tion¦ary
cau¦tious
cau¦tious¦ly
cau¦tious¦ness
Cau¦very (river,
  India)
cava +s (wine.
  △ carver, kava)
Ca¦vafy,
  Con¦stan¦tine
  (modern Greek
  poet)
cav¦al¦cade +s
Cava¦lier +s (in
  English Civil War)
cava¦lier +s
cava¦lier¦ly
cav¦alry
  cav¦al¦ries
cav¦al¦ry¦man
  cav¦al¦ry¦men
Cavan (county,
  Republic of
  Ireland)
cava¦tina +s
cave
  caves
  caved
  cav¦ing
  (hollow; explore
  caves; collapse)
cave (beware)
cav¦eat +s

cav|eat emp|tor
cave bear +s
cave dwell|er +s
cave-in +s
cave|like
Cav|ell, Edith
(English nurse)
cave|man
cave|men
Cav|en|dish,
Henry (English
scientist)
cave paint|ing +s
caver +s
cav|ern +s
cav|erned
cav|ern|ous
cav|ern|ous|ly
cav|es|son +s
ca|vetto
ca|vetti
cav|iar +s
cavi|are +s (use
caviar)
cavil
cavils
cav|illed
cav|il|ling
cav|il|ler +s
cavi|ta|tion
cav|ity
cav|ities
cav|ity wall +s
ca|vort +s +ed
+ing
Ca|vour, Cam|illo
di (Italian
statesman)
cavy
cavies
caw +s +ed +ing
(bird's cry. △ cor,
core, corps)
Caw|ley, Evonne
(Australian tennis
player)
Cawn|pore (former
name of Kanpur)
Cax|ton, Wil|liam
(English printer)
cay +s
Cay|enne (capital
of French Guiana)
cay|enne +s
(pepper)
Cay|ley, Ar|thur
(English
mathematician)
Cay|ley, George
(British
aeronautics
pioneer)

cay|man +s
(alligator)
Cay|man Is|lands
(in Caribbean)
Cay|mans
(= Cayman
Islands)
Ca|yuga
plural Ca|yuga or
Ca|yu|gas
CD play|er +s
CD-ROM +s
cea|no|thus
Ceará (state, Brazil)
cease
ceases
ceased
ceas|ing
cease|fire +s
cease|less
cease|less|ly
Ceau|şescu,
Nico|lae
(Romanian
statesman)
Cebu (island and
city, Philippines)
cecal Am. (Br.
caecal)
Cecil
Ce|ci|lia (Roman
saint; name)
Cecily
ce|citis Am. (Br.
caecitis)
ce|city Am. (Br.
caecity)
cecum Am.
ceca
(Br. caecum)
cedar +s (tree.
△ seeder)
ce|darn
cedar|wood
cede
cedes
ceded
ced|ing
(give up. △ seed)
cedi +s (Ghanaian
currency.
△ seedy)
ce|dilla +s
Ced|ric
Cee|fax Propr.
cei|lidh +s
ceil|ing +s (upper
surface of room.
△ sealing)
cela|don +s
cel|an|dine +s
celeb +s

Cel|ebes (former
name of
Sulawesi)
cele|brant +s
cele|brate
cele|brates
cele|brated
cele|brat|ing
cele|bra|tion +s
cele|bra|tor +s
cele|bra|tory
ce|leb|rity
ce|leb|rities
ce|ler|iac
ce|ler|ity
cel|ery
cel|er|ies
cel|esta +s
Cé|leste
cel|leste +s
ce|les|tial
ce|les|ti|al|ly
Celia
ce|liac Am. (Br.
coeliac)
celi|bacy
celi|bate +s
cell +s (prison;
Biology. △ sell)
cel|lar +s
(basement.
△ seller)
cel|lar|age
cel|lar|er +s
cel|laret +s
cel|lar|man
cel|lar|men
cell block +s
celled
Cel|lini,
Ben|ve|nuto
(Florentine
goldsmith and
sculptor)
cell|ist +s
cell-like
Cell|net Propr.
cello +s
cel|lo|phane Propr.
cell|phone +s
cel|lu|lar
cel|lu|lar|ity
cel|lu|late
cel|lu|la|tion
cel|lule +s
cel|lu|lite
cel|lu|litis
cel|lu|loid +s
cel|lu|lose
cel|lu|los|ing
cel|lu|los|ic
cel|lu|lous

celom Am. (Br.
coelom)
Cel|sius
(temperature
scale)
Cel|sius, An|ders
(Swedish
astronomer)
Celt +s (people.
△ kelt)
celt +s (implement.
△ kelt)
Cel|tic
Cel|ti|cism +s
cem|balo +s
ce|ment +s +ed
+ing
ce|men|ta|tion
ce|ment|er +s
ce|men|ti|tious
ce|ment mixer +s
ce|men|tum
cem|et|ery
cem|et|er|ies
ceno|bite Am. +s
(Br. coenobite)
ceno|bit|ic|al Am.
(Br. coenobitical)
ceno|taph +s
Ceno|zoic
cense
censes
censed
cens|ing
(to perfume.
△ sense)
cen|ser +s (vessel
for incense.
△ censor, sensor)
cen|sor +s +ed
+ing (cut film etc.;
Roman
magistrate.
△ censer, sensor)
cen|sor|ial
cen|sori|al|ly
cen|sori|ous
cen|sori|ous|ly
cen|sori|ous|ness
cen|sor|ship
cen|sur|able
cen|sure
cen|sures
cen|sured
cen|sur|ing
(criticize;
criticism)
cen|sus
cen|suses
cen|sused
cen|sus|ing

cent +s (monetary unit (not of Estonia); in 'per cent'. △ scent, sent)

cen|tal +s

cen|taur +s

Cen|taurus (constellation)

cen|taury
cen|taur|ies (plant)

cen|tavo +s

Cent|com

cen|ten|ar|ian +s

cen|ten|ary
cen|ten|ar|ies

cen|ten|nial +s

cen|ter Am. +s +ed +ing (Br. centre)

cen|ter back Am. +s (Br. centre back)

cen|ter bit Am. +s (Br. centre bit)

cen|ter|board Am. +s (Br. centreboard)

cen|ter|fold Am. +s (Br. centrefold)

cen|ter for|ward Am. +s (Br. centre forward)

cen|ter half Am. cen|ter halves (Br. centre half)

cen|ter line Am. +s (Br. centre line)

cen|ter|most Am. (Br. centremost)

cen|ter|piece Am. +s (Br. centrepiece)

cen|ter spread Am. +s (Br. centre spread)

cen|ter stage Am. (Br. centre stage)

cen|tes|im|al

cen|tes|im|al|ly

cen|tésimo +s

centi|grade

centi|gram +s

centi|liter Am. +s

centi|litre Br. +s

cent|ime +s

centi|meter Am. +s

centi|metre Br. +s

centimetre-gram-second (system)

cen|timo +s

centi|pede +s

cento +s

cen|tral

cen|tral|isa|tion Br. (use centralization)

cen|tral|ise Br. (use centralize)

cen|tral|ises

cen|tral|ised

cen|tral|is|ing

cen|tral|ism

cen|tral|ist +s

cen|tral|ity

cen|tral|iza|tion

cen|tral|ize

cen|tral|izes

cen|tral|ized

cen|tral|iz|ing

cen|tral|ly

Centre (region, France)

centre Br.
centres
centred
cen|tring or centre|ing (Am. center)

centre-back Br. +s (Am. center back)

centre bit Br. +s (Am. center bit)

centre|board Br. +s (Am. centerboard)

centre|fold Br. +s (Am. centerfold)

centre for|ward Br. +s (Am. center forward)

centre half Br. centre halves (Am. center half)

centre|ing Br. +s (use centring Am. centering)

centre line Br. +s (Am. center line)

centre|most Br. (Am. centermost)

centre|piece Br. +s (Am. centerpiece)

centre spread Br. +s (Am. center spread)

centre stage Br. (Am. center stage)

cen|tric

cen|tric|al

cen|tri|city

cen|tri|fu|gal

cen|tri|fu|gal|ly

cen|tri|fu|ga|tion

cen|tri|fuge
cen|tri|fuges
cen|tri|fuged
cen|tri|fu|ging

cen|tring Br. +s (Am. centering)

cen|tri|ole +s

cen|tri|pet|al

cen|tri|pet|al|ly

cen|trism

cen|trist +s

cen|tro|mere +s

cen|tro|some +s

cen|tu|ple
cen|tu|ples
cen|tu|pled
cen|tu|pling

cen|tur|ion +s

cen|tury
cen|tur|ies

cep +s

ceph|al|ic

ceph|al|isa|tion (use cephalization)

ceph|al|iza|tion

Cepha|lonia (island, Greece)

ceph|alo|pod +s

ceph|alo|thorax
ceph|alo|thor|aces or
ceph|alo|thor|axes

ce|pheid +s

Ce|pheus (Greek Mythology; constellation)

cer|am|ic +s

cer|ami|cist +s

cer|am|ics

cer|am|ist +s

Ceram Sea (part of W. Pacific)

cer|as|tes
plural cer|as|tes

cer|as|tium +s

Cer|berus Greek Mythology

cer|caria
cer|cariae

cer|cus
cerci
(Zoology.
△ circus)

cere +s (swelling at base of bird's beak. △ sear, seer, sere)

cer|eal +s (grain used for food. △ serial)

ce|re|bel|lar

ce|re|bel|lum
ce|re|bel|lums or
ce|re|bella

cere|bral

cere|bral|ly

cere|brate
cere|brates
cere|brated
cere|brat|ing

cere|bra|tion

cere|bro|spinal

cere|bro|vas|cu|lar

cere|brum
ce|re|bra

cere|cloth +s

cere|ment +s

cere|mo|nial +s

cere|mo|ni|al|ism

cere|mo|ni|al|ist +s

cere|mo|ni|al|ly

cere|mo|ni|ous

cere|mo|ni|ous|ly

cere|mo|ni|ous|ness

cere|mony
cere|monies

Cer|en|kov, Pavel (Soviet physicist)

Cer|en|kov ra|di|ation

Ceres (Roman Mythology; asteroid)

cer|esin

cer|ise +s

cer|ium

cer|met

CERN (European Council (or Organization) for Nuclear Research)

cer|og|raphy

cero|plas|tic

cert +s

cer|tain

cer|tain|ly

cer|tainty
cer|tain|ties

Cert. Ed. (= Certificate in Education)

cer|ti|fi|able

cer|ti|fi|ably

cer|tifi|cate
cer|tifi|cates
cer|tifi|cated
cer|tifi|cat|ing

cer¦ti¦fi¦ca¦tion +s
cer¦tify
  cer¦ti¦fies
  cer¦ti¦fied
  cer¦ti¦fy¦ing
cer¦ti¦or¦ari
cer¦ti¦tude +s
ceru¦lean
ceru¦men
ceru¦min¦ous
cer¦use
Cer¦van¦tes,
  Mi¦guel (Spanish
  writer)
cer¦velat +s
cer¦vical
cer¦vine
cer¦vix
  cer¦vi¦ces
Ce¦sar¦ean Am. +s
  (Br. Caesarean)
ce¦sar¦evitch
  (eldest son of
  Russian emperor;
  use tsarevich)
Ce¦sar¦ewitch
  (horse race)
Ce¦sar¦ian Am. +s
  (use Cesarean. Br.
  Caesarean)
ces¦ium
České
  Budě¦jo¦vice
  (city, Czech
  Republic)
cess
  cesses
  (tax, levy; also in
  'bad cess to')
ces¦sa¦tion +s
cess¦er
ces¦sion (ceding;
  territory ceded.
  △ session)
ces¦sion¦ary
  ces¦sion¦ar¦ies
cess¦pit +s
cess¦pool +s
cest¦ode +s
cest¦oid +s
cet¦acean +s
cet¦aceous
ce¦tane
cet¦eris pari¦bus
Cetus
  (constellation)
Ceuta (enclave,
  Morocco)
Cé¦vennes
  (mountain range,
  France)

Cey¦lon (former
  name of Sri
  Lanka)
Cey¦lon¦ese
  plural Cey¦lon¦ese
Cé¦zanne, Paul
  (French painter)
cha (use char)
Chab¦lis
  plural Chab¦lis
Chab¦rier, Al¦exis
  Em¦man¦uel
  (French
  composer)
Chab¦rol, Claude
  (French film
  director)
cha-cha
  cha-chas
  cha-chaed or cha-
    cha'd
  cha-chaing
cha-cha-cha
  cha-cha-chas
  cha-cha-chaed or
    cha-cha-cha'd
  cha-cha-chaing
Chaco (plain, S.
  America)
cha¦conne +s
Chad (country;
  name)
Chad, Lake (in
  central Africa)
cha¦dar +s (use
  chador)
Chad¦ian +s
Chad¦ic
cha¦dor +s
Chad¦wick, James
  (English physicist)
chae¦tog¦nath +s
chaeto¦pod +s
chafe
  chafes
  chafed
  chaf¦ing
chafer +s
chaff +s +ed +ing
chaff-cutter +s
chaf¦fer +s +ed
  +ing
chaf¦fer¦er +s
chaf¦finch
  chaf¦finches
chaffi¦ness
chaffy
chaf¦ing dish
  chaf¦ing dishes

Cha¦gall, Marc
  (Russian-born
  painter)
Cha¦gas' dis¦ease
Cha¦gas's dis¦ease
  (use Chagas'
  disease)
Cha¦gos
  Archi¦pel¦ago (in
  Indian Ocean)
chag¦rin
Chain, Er¦nest
  (British
  biochemist)
chain +s +ed +ing
chain armor Am.
chain ar¦mour Br.
chain gang +s
chain gear +s
chain¦less
chain let¦ter +s
chain link +s
  adjective and noun
chain mail
chain re¦ac¦tion +s
chain¦saw +s
chain-smoke
  chain-smokes
  chain-smoked
  chain-smoking
chain-smoker +s
chain stitch
chain store +s
chain-wale +s
chain wheel +s
chair +s +ed +ing
chair-bed +s
chair-borne
chair-car +s
chair¦lady
  chair¦ladies
chair¦lift +s
chair¦man
  chair¦men
chair¦man¦ship +s
chair¦per¦son +s
chair¦woman
  chair¦women
chaise +s
chaise longue
  chaise longues or
  chaises longues
chaise lounge +s
Chaka (use Shaka)
chakra +s
cha¦laza
  cha¦lazae
Chal¦ce¦don
  (ancient city, Asia
  Minor)
Chal¦ce¦don¦ian +s
chal¦ce¦don¦ic

chal¦ced¦ony
chal¦ced¦onies
Chal¦cis (town,
  Euboea, Greece)
chal¦co¦lith¦ic
chal¦co¦pyr¦ite
Chal¦dea (part of
  Babylonia)
Chal¦dean +s
Chal¦dee +s
  (language; native
  of Chaldea)
cha¦let +s
Cha¦lia¦pin,
  Fyo¦dor
  Ivan¦ovich
  (Russian singer)
chal¦ice +s (goblet.
  △ challis)
chalk +s +ed +ing
chalk¦board +s
chalkie +s
chalki¦ness
chalk pit +s
chalk-stone
chalk-stripe +s
chalk-striped
chalky
  chalk¦ier
  chalki¦est
chal¦lah
  chal¦lahs or
  chal¦lot
chal¦lenge
  chal¦lenges
  chal¦lenged
  chal¦len¦ging
chal¦lenge¦able
chal¦len¦ger +s
Chal¦len¦ger Deep
  (in N. Pacific)
chal¦len¦ging¦ly
chal¦lis (cloth.
  △ chalice)
cha¦lyb¦eate
chamae¦phyte +s
cham¦ber +s
cham¦bered
Cham¦ber¦lain,
  Jo¦seph (British
  statesman)
Cham¦ber¦lain,
  Nev¦ille (British
  prime minister)
Cham¦ber¦lain,
  Owen (American
  physicist)
cham¦ber¦lain +s
cham¦ber¦lain¦ship
cham¦ber¦maid +s
cham¦ber music
cham¦ber pot +s

**Cham|bers,
Wil|liam**
(Scottish
architect)
Cham|ber|tin +s
(wine)
Cham|béry (town,
France)
cham|bray +s
(cloth)
cham|bré (brought
to room
temperature)
cha|meleon +s
cha|mele|on|ic
cham|fer +s +ed
+ing
cham|ois
plural **cham|ois**
chamo|mile (use
camomile)
Cham|onix (ski
resort, France)
champ +s +ed
+ing
Cham|pagne (area,
France)
cham|pagne +s
(wine)
**Champagne-
Ardenne**
(administrative
region, France)
cham|paign +s
(open country)
cham|pen|oise (in
'méthode
champenoise')
cham|pers
cham|per|tous
cham|perty
cham|per|ties
cham|pion +s +ed
+ing
**Cham|pion of
Eng|land**
cham|pion|ship +s
Cham|plain, Lake
(in N. America)
**Cham|plain,
Sam|uel de**
(French explorer
and statesman)
champ|levé
**Cham|pol|lion,
Jean-François**
(French
Egyptologist)
Champs Élysées
(street, Paris)
chance
chances

chance (*cont.*)
chanced
chan|cing
chan|cel +s
chan|cel|lery
chan|cel|ler|ies
chan|cel|lor +s
chan|cel|lor|ship
+s
chance-medley +s
(Law)
chan|cer +s
Chan|cery (Lord
Chancellor's
court)
chan|cery
chan|cer|ies
Chan Chan (ruined
city, Peru)
Chan-chiang
(= Zhanjiang)
chan|cily
chan|ci|ness
chan|cre +s
chan|croid
chancy
chan|cier
chan|ci|est
chan|de|lier +s
Chan|di|garh
(territory and city,
India)
**Chand|ler,
Ray|mond**
(American writer)
chand|ler +s
chand|lery
chand|ler|ies
**Chan|dra|sekhar,
Su|brah-
man|yan** (Indian-
born American
astronomer)
Cha|nel, Coco
(French couturière
and perfumer)
Chan|gan (former
name of **Xian**)
Chang-chiakow
(= Zhangjiakou)
Chang|chun (city,
China)
change
changes
changed
chan|ging
change|abil|ity
change|able
change|able|ness
change|ably
change|ful

change|ful|ness
change|less
change|less|ly
change|less|ness
change|ling +s
change|over +s
chan|ger +s
change-ringer +s
change-ringing
chan|ging room +s
Chang|sha (city,
China)
Cha|nia (port,
Crete)
chan|nel
chan|nels
chan|nelled *Br.*
chan|neled *Am.*
chan|nel|ling *Br.*
chan|nel|ing *Am.*
chan|nel|ise *Br.*
(use channelize)
chan|nel|ises
chan|nel|ised
chan|nel|is|ing
chan|nel|ize
chan|nel|izes
chan|nel|ized
chan|nel|iz|ing
chan|son +s
chan|son de geste
chan|sons de geste
chant +s +ed +ing
chant|er +s
chan|ter|elle +s
chant|eur +s *male*
chant|euse +s
female
chan|ti|cleer +s
Chan|tilly (lace;
cream)
chan|try
chan|tries
chanty (use
shanty)
chan|ties
Cha|nuk|kah (use
Hanukkah)
Cha|nute, Oc|tave
(Franco-American
aviation pioneer)
chaol|ogy
Chao Phraya
(river, Thailand)
Chaos *Greek
Mythology*
chaos (confusion)
cha|ot|ic
cha|ot|ic|al|ly
chap
chaps

chap (*cont.*)
chapped
chap|ping
chapa|rajos
chap|ar|ral +s
cha|patti +s
chap|book +s
chape +s
chapeau-bras
chapeaux-bras
chapel +s
chap|el|ry
chap|el|ries
chap|eron +s +ed
+ing (use
chaperone)
chap|er|on|age
chap|er|one
chap|er|ones
chap|er|oned
chap|er|on|ing
chap-fallen
chap|lain +s
chap|lain|cy
chap|lain|cies
chap|let +s
chap|let|ed
Chap|lin, Char|lie
(British actor)
**Chap|man,
George** (English
writer)
chap|man
chap|men
chap|pal +s
Chap|pa|quid|dick
(island, USA)
Chap|pell, Greg
(Australian
cricketer)
chap|pie +s
(person)
chappy (chapped)
chaps
(= chaparajos)
chap|stick +s
chap|ter +s
char
chars
charred
char|ring
(burn;
charwoman; tea)
char
plural char
(fish)
chara|banc +s
chara|cin +s
char|ac|ter +s
char|ac|ter|ful
char|ac|ter|ful|ly

char¦ac¦ter¦
isa¦tion *Br.* +s
(use
characterization)
char¦ac¦ter¦ise *Br.*
(use characterize)
char¦ac¦ter¦ises
char¦ac¦ter¦ised
char¦ac¦ter¦is¦ing
char¦ac¦ter¦is¦tic
+s
char¦ac¦ter¦is¦tic¦
al¦ly
char¦ac¦ter¦
iza¦tion +s
char¦ac¦ter¦ize
char¦ac¦ter¦izes
char¦ac¦ter¦ized
char¦ac¦ter¦iz¦ing
char¦ac¦ter¦less
char¦ac¦ter¦ology
cha¦rade +s
charas
char¦broil +s +ed
+ing
char¦coal +s
Char¦cot, Jean-
Martin (French
neurologist)
char¦cu¦terie
chard +s
(vegetable.
△ charred)
Char¦don¦nay +s
(grape; wine)
Char¦ente (river,
France)
charge
charges
charged
char¦ging
charge¦able
charge card +s
charge-coupled
chargé d'af¦faires
chargés
d'af¦faires
charge¦hand +s
charge nurse +s
char¦ger +s
charge sheet +s
chari¦ly
chari¦ness
char¦iot +s
char¦iot¦eer +s
cha¦risma
cha¦ris¦mata
cha¦ris¦mat¦ic +s
cha¦ris¦mat¦ic¦
al¦ly

Cha¦risse, Cyd
(American
actress)
char¦it¦able
char¦it¦able¦ness
char¦it¦ably
Char¦ity (name)
char¦ity
char¦ities
(help for needy)
cha¦ri¦vari +s
char¦lady
char¦ladies
char¦la¦tan +s
char¦la¦tan¦ism
char¦la¦tan¦ry
Charle¦magne
(ruler of Franks)
Char¦lene
Charle¦roi (city,
Belgium)
Charles (British,
French, Spanish
and Swedish
kings)
Charles, Prince
(Prince of Wales)
Charles' Law
Chemistry
Charles Mar¦tel
(Frankish ruler)
Charles's Law (use
Charles' Law)
Charles's Wain
(constellation)
Charles¦ton (cities,
USA)
charles¦ton +s
(dance)
char¦ley horse
Char¦lie (name)
char¦lie +s (fool)
char¦lock
Char¦lotte (city,
USA; name)
char¦lotte +s
(dessert)
Char¦lotte Ama¦lie
(capital of the US
Virgin Islands)
Char¦lotte Dun¦das
(steamship)
char¦lotte russe
Char¦lotte¦town
(city, Canada)
Charl¦ton, Bobby
and Jack (English
footballers)
charm +s +ed +ing
Char¦maine
charm brace¦let
+s

charm¦er +s
charm¦euse
Char¦mian
charm¦ing
charm¦ing¦ly
charm¦less
charm¦less¦ly
charm¦less¦ness
char¦nel +s
char¦nel house +s
Charo¦lais
plural Charo¦lais
Char¦ol¦lais (use
Charolais)
plural Char¦ol¦lais
Cha¦ron (*Greek
Mythology*; moon
of Pluto)
char¦poy +s
charr (use char)
plural charr
chart +s +ed +ing
chart¦bust¦er +s
char¦ter +s +ed
+ing
char¦ter¦er +s
char¦ter mem¦ber
+s
char¦ter party
char¦ter par¦ties
Chart¦ism
Chart¦ist +s
Char¦tres (city,
France)
char¦treuse +s
chart-topper +s
chart-topping
char¦woman
char¦women
chary
chari¦er
chari¦est
Cha¦ryb¦dis *Greek
Legend*
chase
chases
chased
chas¦ing
chaser +s
Cha¦sid (use
Hasid)
Cha¦sid¦im
Cha¦sid¦ism (use
Hasidism)
chasm +s
chas¦mic
chassé
chas¦sés
chas¦séd
chas¦sé¦ing
(step)
chasse +s (liqueur)

chas¦seur +s
chas¦sis
plural chas¦sis
chaste (pure etc.
△ chased)
chaste¦ly
chas¦ten +s +ed
+ing
chas¦ten¦er +s
chaste¦ness
chaste-tree +s
chas¦tise
chas¦tises
chas¦tised
chas¦tis¦ing
chas¦tise¦ment +s
chas¦tiser +s
Chas¦tity (name)
chas¦tity (being
chaste; simplicity)
chas¦uble +s
chat
chats
chat¦ted
chat¦ting
cha¦teau
cha¦teaux
Cha¦teau¦bri¦and,
François-René
(French writer and
diplomat)
cha¦teau¦bri¦and
+s (steak)
chat¦elaine +s
Chat¦ham (town,
England)
Chat¦ham Is¦lands
(in SW Pacific)
chat¦line +s
chat show +s
chat¦tel +s
chat¦ter +s +ed
+ing
chat¦ter¦box
chat¦ter¦boxes
chat¦ter¦er +s
Chat¦ter¦ton,
Thomas (English
poet)
chat¦tery
chat¦ti¦ly
chat¦ti¦ness
chatty
chat¦tier
chat¦ti¦est
chat-up +s *adjective
and noun*
Chat¦win, Bruce
(Australian writer)
Chau¦cer,
Geof¦frey
(English writer)

Chau¦cer¦ian +s
chaud-froid +s
chauf¦feur +s +ed
+ing (*male driver*;
verb drive.
△ shofar)
chauf¦feuse +s
female
Chau¦liac, Guy de
(French physician)
chaul¦moo¦gra +s
chau¦tau¦qua +s
chau¦vin¦ism +s
chau¦vin¦ist +s
chau¦vin¦is¦tic
chau¦vin¦is¦tic¦
al¦ly
Cha¦vin
cheap +er +est
(inexpensive.
△ cheep)
cheap¦en +s +ed
+ing
cheapie +s
cheap¦ish
cheap¦jack +s
cheap¦ly
cheap¦ness
cheapo
Cheap¦side (street,
London)
cheap¦skate +s
cheat +s +ed +ing
cheat¦er +s (person
who cheats.
△ cheetah)
cheat¦ing¦ly
Cheb¦ok¦sary (city,
Russia)
Che¦chen
plural Che¦chen *or*
Che¦chens
Chech¦nya
(republic, Russia)
check +s +ed +ing
(verify; stop, slow;
act of verifying,
stopping or
slowing; pattern;
Chess. △ cheque)
check *Am.* +s
(*Banking. Br.*
cheque)
check¦able
check¦book *Am.* +s
(*Br.* chequebook)
check¦er +s
(person or thing
that checks;
cashier.
△ chequer)

check¦er *Am.* +s
+ed +ing (pattern.
Br. chequer)
check¦er¦berry
check¦er¦berries
check¦er¦board
Am. +s (*Br.*
chequerboard)
check¦er¦man
check¦er¦men
check¦ers (game)
check-in +s *noun*
and attributive
check¦ing
ac¦count +s
check¦list +s
check¦mate
check¦mates
check¦mated
check¦mat¦ing
check¦out +s
check¦point +s
check-rein +s
check¦room +s
check sum +s
check-up +s *noun*
check valve +s
check¦weigh¦man
check¦weigh¦men
Ched¦dar (village,
England; cheese)
cheek +s +ed +ing
cheek¦bone +s
cheek¦ily
cheeki¦ness
cheeky
cheek¦ier
cheeki¦est
cheep +s +ed +ing
(bird's cry.
△ cheap)
cheer +s +ed +ing
cheer¦ful
cheer¦ful¦ly
cheer¦ful¦ness
cheer¦ily
cheeri¦ness
cheerio +s
cheer¦lead¦er +s
cheer¦less
cheer¦less¦ly
cheer¦less¦ness
cheer¦ly
cheery
cheer¦ier
cheeri¦est
cheese
cheeses
cheesed
chees¦ing
cheese¦board +s
cheese¦bur¦ger +s

cheese¦cake +s
cheese¦cloth +s
cheese-cutter +s
cheesed
cheesed-off
attributive
cheese-fly
cheese-flies
cheese-head +s
cheese¦maker +s
cheese¦mak¦ing
cheese-mite +s
cheese¦mon¦ger +s
cheese-paring +s
cheese plant +s
cheese-skipper +s
cheese straw +s
cheese¦wood +s
cheesi¦ness
cheesy
chees¦ier
cheesi¦est
chee¦tah +s
(animal.
△ cheater)
chef +s
chef-d'œuvre
chefs-d'œuvre
Che¦foo (former
name of Yantai)
Cheka (Soviet
organization)
Chek¦hov, Anton
(Russian writer)
Chek¦hov¦ian
Che¦kiang
(= Zhejiang)
chela
che¦lae
(claw)
chela +s (Buddhist
novice; pupil)
che¦late
che¦lates
che¦lated
che¦lat¦ing
che¦la¦tion
chel¦icera
chel¦icerae
chel¦icer¦ate +s
Chel¦lean
Chelms¦ford (city,
England)
che¦lo¦nian +s
Chel¦sea (district,
London)
Chel¦sea ware
Chel¦ten¦ham
(town, England)
Chel¦ya¦binsk
(city, Russia)
chem¦ical +s

chem¦ical¦ly
chemi¦lu¦min¦
es¦cence
chemi¦lu¦min¦
es¦cent
che¦min de fer
che¦mins de fer
(gambling game)
che¦mise +s
chemi¦sorp¦tion
chem¦ist +s
chem¦is¦try
chem¦is¦tries
Chem¦nitz (city,
Germany)
chemo
(= chemotherapy)
chemo¦recep¦tor
+s
chemo¦syn¦thesis
chemo¦tac¦tic
chemo¦taxis
chemo¦ther¦ap¦ist
+s
chemo¦ther¦apy
chem¦ur¦gic
chem¦urgy
Che¦nab (river,
India and Punjab)
Chen-chiang
(= Zhenjiang)
Cheng¦chow
(= Zhengzhou)
Chengdu (city,
China)
che¦nille +s
cheong¦sam +s
Cheops (pharaoh)
cheque *Br.* +s (*Am.*
check. *Banking.*
△ check)
cheque¦book *Br.*
+s (*Am.*
checkbook)
cheque card *Br.* +s
chequer *Br.* +s +ed
+ing (*Am.*
checker. pattern.
△ checker)
chequer¦board *Br.*
+s (*Am.*
checkerboard)
che¦quered
Che¦quers (home
of British prime
minister)
che¦quers *Br.* (in
'Chinese
chequers'.
△ checkers. *Am.*
checkers)
Cher (river, France)

Cher (American singer and actress)

Cher|bourg (port, France)

Cher|en|kov, Pavel (Soviet physicist; use Cerenkov)

Cher|en|kov ra¦di|ation (use Cerenkov radiation)

Cher¦epo|vets (city, Russia)

Che|rida

cher|ish
cher|ishes
cher|ished
cher|ish|ing

cher|ish|able

Cher|kassy (port, Ukraine)

Cher|kessk (city, Russia)

Cher|nenko, Kon|stan|tin (Soviet president)

Cher¦ni|gov (port, Ukraine)

Cher|niv|tsi (city, Ukraine)

Cher¦no|byl (city, Ukraine)

Cher¦no|reche (former name of Dzerzhinsk)

Cher|nov|tsy (Russian name for Chernivtsi)

cher¦no|zem

Chero|kee +s

che|root +s

Cherry (name)

cherry
cher|ries
(fruit)

cherry laurel
plural **cherry laurel**

cherry-pick
cherry-picks
cherry-picked
cherry-picking

cherry pick¦er +s

cherry pie +s

cherry plum +s

cherry red +s noun and adjective

cherry-red attributive

cherry to¦mato
cherry to¦ma|toes

cherry tree +s

cher¦ry|wood +s

Cher|son|ese (ancient name for Thracian or Gallipoli peninsula)

cher¦son|ese (other peninsula)

chert +s

cherty

cherub
cher|ubs or
cher|ubim

cher¦ub¦ic

cher¦ub¦ic|al¦ly

Cheru|bini, Luigi (Italian composer)

cher|vil

Cher|well, Lord (German-born British physicist)

Cheryl

Chesa|peake Bay (in USA)

Chesh|ire (county, England; cheese; cat)

Chesil Beach (in England)

chess

chess|board +s

ches|sel +s

chess|man
chess|men

chess piece +s

chess play¦er +s

chest +s

Ches|ter (city, England)

Ches¦ter|field (town, England)

ches¦ter|field +s (sofa)

Ches¦ter|ton, G. K. (English writer)

chest|ily

chesti|ness

chest|nut +s

chest voice +s

chesty
chest|ier
chesti|est

Ches|van (use Hesvan)

chet|nik +s

Chetu|mal (port, Mexico)

che|val glass
che|val glasses

Che|va¦lier, Mau|rice (French singer and actor)

cheva|lier +s

che|vet +s

Chev|iot +s (sheep)

chev|iot (wool)

Chev|iot Hills (in England)

Chev|iots (= Cheviot Hills)

chèvre +s (cheese)

chev|ron +s

chev¦ro|tain +s

chev¦ro|tin +s (use chevrotain)

chevy
chev|ies
chev|ied
chevy|ing

chew +s +ed +ing

chew|able

chew|er +s

chewi|ness

chew|ing gum

chewy
chew|ier
chewi|est

Chey|enne (city, USA)

Chey|enne
plural **Chey|enne**
(American Indian)

Cheyne–Stokes (respiration)

chez

chi +s (Greek letter)

chi¦ack +s +ed +ing

Chi|ang Kai-shek (Chinese leader)

Chi|ang|mai (city, Thailand)

Chi|anti +s (region, Italy; wine)

Chi|apas (state, Mexico)

chiaro|scuro +s

chi|asma
chi|as¦mata
chi|as¦mus
chi|asmi

chi|as¦tic

Chiba (city, Japan)

Chib|cha
plural **Chib|cha**

Chib|chan

chi|bouk +s

chi|bouque +s (use chibouk)

chic
chic-er
chic-est
(stylish)

Chi|cago (city, USA)

Chi|cago¦an +s

chi|cane
chi|canes
chi|caned
chi|can¦ing

chi|can¦ery
chi|can|er¦ies

Chi|cano +s

Chi|chén Itzá (in Mexico)

Chi|ches|ter (city, England)

Chi|ches|ter, Fran|cis (English yachtsman)

chi|chi

Chi|chi|mec
plural **Chi|chi|mec**

chick +s (young bird)

chicka|dee +s

chick|en +s +ed +ing

chicken-and-egg adjective

chick|en feed

chicken-hearted

chick|en|pox

chick|en wire

chick|ling +s

chick|pea +s

chick|weed +s

chi|cle (chewing-gum ingredient)

chic¦ly (stylishly)

chic|ness

chic|ory
chic|or¦ies

chide
chides
chided or chid
chid¦ing
chided or
chid|den

chider +s

chid|ing¦ly

chief +s

chief|dom +s

chief¦ly

Chief of Staff
Chiefs of Staff

chief|tain +s

chief|tain¦cy
chief|tain|cies

chief|tain|ship +s

chiff|chaff +s

chif|fon +s
chif¦fon|ier +s
chig|ger +s
chi|gnon +s
chi¦goe +s
Chi¦hli, Gulf of
 (alternative name
 for Bo Hai)
Chi|hua|hua (state
 and city, Mexico)
chi|hua|hua +s
 (dog)
chil|blain +s
chil|blained
chil̦d
 chil|dren
child|bear¦ing
child|bed
child|birth
child|care
child-centered Am.
child-centred Br.
Childe (in 'Childe
 Harold' etc.)
Chil¦der|mas
Chil|ders, Er|skine
 (Irish nationalist)
child|hood +s
child|ish
child|ish¦ly
child¦ish|ness
child|less
child|less¦ly
child|less|ness
child|like
child|mind¦er +s
child|proof
child-rearing
chil|dren
child's play
Chile (in S.
 America)
chile +s (food. use
 chili Am. chilli Br.
 △ chilly)
Chil|ean +s
chili +s Am. (food.
 Br. chilli. △ chilly)
chili|ad +s
chili|asm
chili|ast +s
chili|as¦tic
chill +s +ed +ing
chill¦er +s
chilli Br.
 chil|lies or
 chil|lis
 (food. Am. chili
 △ chilly)
chilli con carne
chil¦li|ness
chill|ing¦ly

chill|ness
chill|some
chilly
 chill|ier
 chilli|est
 (cold. △ chili,
 chilli)
Chil¦pan|cingo
 (city, Mexico)
Chil|tern Hills
 (England)
Chil|tern
 Hun|dreds
Chil|terns
 (= Chiltern Hills)
chi|maera +s (use
 chimera)
Chim¦bo|razo
 (mountain,
 Ecuador)
chime
chimes
chimed
chim¦ing
chimer +s
chi|mera +s
 (monster)
chi|mere +s (robe)
chi|mer¦ic
chi¦mer|ic¦al
chi¦mer|ic¦al¦ly
chimi|changa +s
chim|ney +s
chim|ney breast
 +s
chim|ney piece +s
chim|ney pot +s
chim|ney stack +s
chim|ney sweep
 +s
chimp +s
chim¦pan|zee +s
Chimu
 plural Chimu
Chin (Hills, in
 Burma)
Chin (Chinese
 dynasty; = Jin)
Ch'in (Chinese
 dynasty; = Qin)
chin +s (part of
 face)
China (country)
china +s (ceramic
 ware)
china|graph +s
China|man
 China|men
 (offensive when
 used of a person)
China|town +s
china|ware

chinch
 chinches
chin|cher¦in|chee
 +s
chin|chilla +s
chin-chin
Chin|dit +s
Chin|dwin (river,
 Burma)
chine
 chines
 chined
 chin¦ing
 (backbone; ridge;
 ravine; on ship)
chiné (mottled)
Chi|nese
 plural Chi|nese
Ching (in 'I Ching')
Ch'ing (Chinese
 dynasty; = Qing)
Chin Hills (in
 Burma)
Chink +s (offensive
 Chinese)
chink +s +ed +ing
 (crack; ringing
 sound)
Chin|kiang
 (= Zhenjiang)
Chinky
 Chink|ies
 (offensive)
chin|less
chino +s
chi¦nois|erie
Chi|nook
 plural Chi|nook
 (American Indian)
chi|nook +s (wind;
 salmon)
chin|strap +s
chintz
 chintzes
chintz|ily
chintzi|ness
chintzy
 chintz|ier
 chintzi|est
chin-up +s noun
chin|wag
 chin|wags
 chin|wagged
 chin|wag|ging
 chin|wags
chi¦ono|doxa +s
Chios (Greek
 island)
chip
 chips

chip (cont.)
 chipped
 chip|ping
chip|board +s
chip|munk +s
chipo|lata +s
Chip¦pen|dale,
 Thomas (English
 cabinet-maker;
 style of furniture)
chip|per
chip|pie +s (use
 chippy)
chip¦pi|ness
chip|ping +s
chippy
 chip|pies
Chips (carpenter)
chip shot +s
Chirac, Jacques
 (French
 statesman)
chiral
chir¦al|ity
chi-rho
Chi¦rico, Gior|gio
 de (Italian
 painter)
chir|og¦raphy
chiro|mancy
Chiron (Greek
 Mythology;
 asteroid)
chir|opo¦dist +s
chir|opody
chiro|prac¦tic
chiro|prac¦tor +s
chir|op¦teran +s
chir|op¦ter|ous
chirp +s +ed +ing
chirp¦er +s
chirp|ily
chirpi|ness
chirpy
 chirp|ier
 chirpi|est
chirr +s +ed +ing
chir|rup
 chir|rups
 chir|ruped
 chir|rup|ing
 chir|rupy
chisel
 chis|els
 chis|elled Br.
 chis|eled Am.
 chis|el|ling Br.
 chis|el¦ing Am.
 chis|el¦er Am. +s
 chis|el|ler Br. +s
Chiși|nău (capital
 of Moldova)

chi-square (test)
Chis|wick (in London)
chit +s
chi|tal
chit-chat
  chit-chat
  chit-chatted
  chit-chatting
chi|tin
chi|tin|ous
chi|ton +s
Chit|ta|gong (city, Bangladesh)
chit|ter|ling +s
chitty
  chit|ties
chiv
  chivs
  chivved
  chiv|ving
chiv|al|ric
chiv|al|rous
chiv|al|rous|ly
chiv|alry
  chiv|al|ries
chive +s
chivvy
  chiv|vies
  chiv|vied
  chivvy|ing
Chka|lov (former name of Orenburg)
chla|mydia
  chla|mydiae
chla|myd|ial
chlamy|do|mo|nas
Chloe
chlor|acne
chlor|al
chlor|am|pheni|col
chlor|ate +s
chlor|ella +s
chlor|ic
chlor|ide +s
chlor|in|ate
  chlor|in|ates
  chlor|in|ated
  chlor|in|at|ing
chlor|in|ation
chlor|in|ator +s
chlor|ine +s
Chloris
chlor|ite +s
chlor|it|ic
chloro|fluoro|car|bon +s
chloro|form +s +ed +ing

Chloro|my|cetin *Propr.*
chloro|phyll
chloro|phyl|lous
chloro|plast +s
chloro|quine
chlor|osis
  chlor|oses
chlor|ot|ic
chlor|ous
chlor|pro|maz|ine
choc +s (chocolate. △chock)
choc-a-bloc (use chock-a-block)
choca|hol|ic +s (use chocoholic)
choccy
  choc|cies
chocho +s
choc ice +s
chock +s +ed +ing (wedge. △choc)
chock-a-block
chocker
chock-full
chock|stone +s
choco|hol|ic +s
choc|olate +s
choc|olate box
  choc|olate boxes *noun*
chocolate-box *attributive*
choc|olate brown +s *noun and adjective*
chocolate-brown *attributive*
choc|olatey
Choc|taw
  plural Choc|taw *or* Choc|taws
choice
  choices
  choicer
  choicest
choice|ly
choice|ness
choir +s (singers; part of church. △quire)
choir|boy +s
choir|girl +s
choir|man
  choir|men
choir|mas|ter +s
choir stall +s
choke
  chokes
  choked
  chok|ing

choke|berry
  choke|berries
choke chain +s
choke-cherry
  choke-cherries
choke-damp
choker +s
chokey +s (use choky)
choki|ly
choki|ness
choko +s
choky
  chokies
  choki|er
  choki|est (prison; causing choking)
chol|an|gi|og|raphy
chole|cal|cif|erol
chole|cyst|og|raphy
choler (anger; bile. △collar)
chol|era
chol|er|aic
chol|er|ic
chol|er|ic|al|ly
chol|es|terol
choli +s (bodice. △coaly, coley)
cho|li|amb +s
cho|li|am|bic
cho|line +s
cholla +s
chomp +s +ed +ing
Chom|skian +s
Chom|sky, Noam (American linguist)
chon|drite +s
chon|dro|cra|nium +s
Chong|jin (port, North Korea)
Chong|qing (city, China)
choo-choo +s
chook +s
chookie +s
choose
  chooses
  chose
  choos|ing
  chosen
chooser +s
choos|ily
choosi|ness

choosy
  choosi|er
  choosi|est
chop
  chops
  chopped
  chop|ping
chop-chop
Cho|pin, Fréd|éric (Polish composer and pianist)
chop|per +s
chop|pily
chop|pi|ness
chop|ping block +s
choppy
  chop|pier
  chop|pi|est
chop|stick +s
chop suey +s
choral (of a choir or chorus)
chor|ale +s (hymn tune; choir. △corral)
chor|al|ly
chord +s (in music or mathematics. △cord)
chord|al (of a chord. △caudal)
Chord|ata
chord|ate +s (animal. △caudate, cordate)
chord|ing (playing etc. of chords. △cording)
chore +s
cho|rea
choreo|graph +s +ed +ing
chore|og|raph|er +s
choreo|graph|ic
choreo|graph|ic|al
choreo|graph|ic|al|ly
chore|og|raphy
chore|olo|gist +s
chore|ol|ogy
chori|am|bic
chori|am|bus
  chori|ambi
chor|ic
chor|ine +s
chor|ion +s
chori|on|ic
chor|is|ter +s
chor|og|raph|er +s

choro|graph|ic
choro|graph|ic|
    al|ly
chor|og|raphy
chor|oid +s
choro|logic|al
choro|logic|al|ly
chor|olo|gist +s
chor|ology
chor|tle
  chor|tles
  chor|tled
  chort|ling
chorus
  chor|uses
  chor|used
  chor|us|ing
chorus girl +s
chorus-master +s
chose
chosen
Chou (= Zhou)
Chou En-lai
  (= Zhou
  Enlai)
chough +s (crow.
  △ chuff)
choux (pastry; bun.
  △ shoe)
chow +s (food;
  dog. △ ciao)
chow-chow +s
chow|der +s
chow|ki|dar +s
chow mein
chre|ma|tis|tic
chre|ma|tis|tics
chres|tom|athy
  chres|tom|athies
Chré|tien de
  Troyes (French
  poet)
Chris
chrism (oil)
chrisom +s (robe)
chrisom-cloth +s
Chris|sie
Christ (title)
Christa *also* Krista
Christa|bel
Christa|delph|ian
  +s
Christ|church
  (city, New
  Zealand)
chris|ten +s +ed
  +ing
Chris|ten|dom
chris|ten|er +s
chris|ten|ing +s
Christ|hood

Chris|tian +s
  (follower of Christ;
  name)
Chris|tian,
  Fletch|er (*Bounty*
  mutineer)
Chris|ti|ana
Chris|ti|ania
  (former name of
  Oslo)
Chris|tian|isa|tion
  Br. (use
  Christianization)
Chris|tian|ise *Br.*
  (use Christianize)
  Chris|tian|ises
  Chris|tian|ised
  Chris|tian|is|ing
Chris|tian|ity
Chris|tian|iza|tion
Chris|tian|ize
  Chris|tian|izes
  Chris|tian|ized
  Chris|tian|iz|ing
Chris|tian|ly
Chris|tian name
  +s
Chris|tian Sci|ence
Chris|tian
  Sci|en|tist +s
Chris|tie +s *Skiing*
Chris|tie, Aga|tha
  (English writer)
Chris|tie, Lin|ford
  (Jamaican-born
  British sprinter)
Chris|tina
Chris|tine
Christ|in|gle +s
Christ|like
Christ|ly
Christ|mas
  Christ|mases
Christ|mas Is|land
  (in Indian Ocean;
  also former name
  of Kiritimati)
Christ|massy
Christ|mas tide
Christ|mas time
Christ|ol|atry
Christ|ology
Christ|oph|any
Chris|to|pher
  (legendary saint;
  name)
Christ's Hos|pital
  (school, England)
Christy
  Chris|ties

Christy (*cont.*)
  (*Skiing*; use
  Christie)
chroma
chro|mate +s
chro|mat|ic
chro|mat|ic|al|ly
chro|mati|cism
chro|ma|ti|city
chro|ma|tid +s
chro|ma|tin
chro|ma|tism
chro|mato|gram
  +s
chro|mato|graph
  +s
chro|ma|to|
      graph|ic
chro|ma|to|
      graph|ic|al|ly
chro|ma|tog|raphy
chro|ma|top|sia
chrome
  chromes
  chromed
  chrom|ing
chrome lea|ther
  +s
chrome-moly
chrome steel
chro|mic
chro|min|ance
chro|mite +s
chro|mium
chromium-plate
  chromium-plates
  chromium-plated
  chromium-
    plating
  noun and verb
chromo +s
chromo|
      dy|nam|ics
chromo|litho|
      graph +s
chromo|
  lith|og|raph|er
  +s
chromo|litho|
      graph|ic
chromo|
  lith|og|raphy
chromo|somal
chromo|some +s
chromo|sphere +s
chromo|spheric
chron|ic
chron|ic|al|ly
chron|icity
chron|icle
  chron|icles

chron|icle (*cont.*)
  chron|icled
  chron|ic|ling
chron|ic|ler +s
chrono|gram +s
chrono|gram|
      mat|ic
chrono|graph +s
chrono|graph|ic
chrono|logic|al
chrono|logic|al|ly
chrono|logic|al|ly
chrono|logisa|
  tion *Br.* (use
  chronologization)
chron|olo|gise *Br.*
  (use
  chronologize)
  chron|olo|gises
  chron|olo|gised
  chron|olo|gis|ing
chron|olo|gist +s
chro|nolo|giza|
      tion
chron|olo|gize
  chron|olo|gizes
  chron|olo|gized
  chron|olo|giz|ing
chron|ology
  chron|olo|gies
chron|om|eter +s
chrono|met|ric
chrono|met|ric|al
chrono|met|ric|
      al|ly
chron|om|etry
chrono|scope +s
chrys|alid +s
chrys|alis
  chrys|al|ises *or*
  chrys|al|ides
chrys|anth +s
  (= chrys-
  anthemum)
chrys|an|the|mum
  +s
chrys|ele|phant|
      ine
chryso|beryl +s
chryso|lite +s
chryso|prase +s
Chrys|os|tom,
  John (early saint)
chryso|tile
Chrys|tal *also*
  Crys|tal
chthon|ian
chthon|ic
chub
  plural chub *or*
  chubs
  (fish)

Chubb +s (lock)
Propr.
chub|bily
chub|bi|ness
chubby
  chub|bier
  chub|bi|est
Chubu (region, Japan)
chuck +s +ed +ing
chucker-out +s
chuckle
  chuckles
  chuckled
  chuck|ling
chuckle|head +s
chuckle|head|ed
chuck|ler +s
chuck|wagon +s
chud|dar +s (use chador)
chuff +s +ed +ing (make a puffing sound; delighted. △ chough)
chug
  chugs
  chugged
  chug|ging
Chu|goku (region, Japan)
chu|kar +s (partridge)
Chuk|chi Sea (part of Arctic Ocean)
chukka +s (in polo)
chukka boot +s
chuk|ker +s (use chukka)
chum
  chums
  chummed
  chum|ming
chum|mily
chum|mi|ness
chummy
  chum|mier
  chum|mi|est
chump +s
chun|der +s +ed +ing
Chung|king (= Chongqing)
Chung-shan (= Zhongshan)
chunk +s +ed +ing
chunk|ily
chun|ki|ness
chunky
  chunk|ies
  chunk|ier
  chunki|est

Chun|nel (= Channel Tunnel)
chun|ter +s +ed +ing
chu|patty (use chapatti)
  chu|pat|ties
Chu|qui|saca (former name of Sucre)
Church (body of Christians)
church
  churches
  churched
  church|ing (building; service; bring to church)
church|goer +s
church|going
Church|ill, Caryl (English writer)
Church|ill, Win|ston (British prime minister)
Church|ill|ian
churchi|ness
church|man
  church|men
church|man|ship
Church|ward, George (English railway engineer)
church|war|den +s
church|woman
  church|women
churchy
  church|ier
  churchi|est
church|yard +s
chur|inga +s
churl +s
churl|ish
churl|ish|ly
churl|ish|ness
churn +s +ed +ing
churr +s +ed +ing (use chirr)
chur|ras|caria +s
chur|rasco +s
Chur|ri|guer|esque
chute +s (sloping channel or slide. △ shoot)
chut|ist +s
chut|ney +s
chutz|pah
Chu|vashia (republic, Russia)

chy|ack +s +ed +ing (use chiack)
chyle
chyl|ous
chyme
chym|ous
chy|pre +s
cia|batta
  cia|bat|tas or cia|batte
ciao (hallo; goodbye. △ chow)
ci|bor|ium
  ci|boria
ci|cada
  ci|ca|das or ci|ca|dae
cica|trice +s
cica|tri|cial
cica|trisa|tion *Br.* (use cicatrization)
cica|trise *Br.* (use cicatrize)
  cica|trises
  cica|trised
  cica|tris|ing
cica|trix
  cica|tri|ces
cica|triza|tion
cica|trize
  cica|trizes
  cica|trized
  cica|triz|ing
Ci|cely (name)
ci|cely
  ci|cel|lies (plant)
Ci|cero (Roman statesman and writer)
ci|cer|one
  ci|cer|oni
Ci|cero|nian
cich|lid +s
Cid, El (Spanish warrior)
cider +s
cider press
  cider presses
ci-devant
cig +s (= cigarette)
ci|gala +s
cigar +s
cig|aret +s (use cigarette)
cig|ar|ette +s
cig|ar|ette end +s
cig|ar|illo +s

ciggy
  cig|gies (= cigarette)
cilia (plural of cilium △ sillier)
cil|iary
cili|ate
cili|ated
cili|ation
cil|ice +s
Cil|icia (ancient name of part of Asia Minor)
Cil|ician +s
cil|ium
  cilia
cill +s (use sill)
cim|ba|lom +s
Cim|mer|ian +s
cinch
  cinches
  cinched
  cinch|ing
cin|chona +s
cin|chon|ic
cin|chon|ine
Cin|cin|nati (city, USA)
cinc|ture
  cinc|tures
  cinc|tured
  cinc|tur|ing
cin|der +s
Cin|der|ella +s (in fairy story; neglected person)
cin|dery
Cindy *also* **Sindy**
cine|aste +s
cine-camera +s
cin|ema +s
cinema-goer +s
cinema-going
Cinema|Scope *Propr.*
cine|ma|theque +s
cine|mat|ic
cine|mat|ic|al|ly
cine|mato|graph +s
cine|ma|tog|raph|er +s
cine|mato|graph|ic
cine|mato|graph|ic|al|ly
cine|ma|tog|raphy
cinéma-vérité
cine|phile +s
cin|er|aria +s (plant)

cin|er|arium +s
(place for cinerary
urns)
cin|er|ary
cin|er|eous
ciné-vérité
Cin|gal|ese
plural Cin|gal|ese
cin|gu|lum
cin|gula
cin|na|bar +s
cin|na|mon
cinq +s (use
cinque)
cinque +s (5 on dice.
△ sink)
cin|que|cen|tist +s
cin|que|cento
cinque|foil +s
Cinque Ports (in
England)
Cin|tra (use Sintra)
cion Am. +s (use
scion)
ci|pher +s +ed
+ing
cipo|lin
circa
cir|ca|dian
Cir|cas|sian +s
Circe Greek Legend
Cir|ce|an
cir|cin|ate
cir citer
cir|cle
cir|cles
cir|cled
circ|ling
circ|ler +s
circ|let +s
cir|clip +s
circs
(= circumstances.
△ cirques)
cir|cuit +s +ed
+ing
circuit-breaker +s
cir|cu|it|ous
cir|cu|it|ous|ly
cir|cu|it|ous|ness
cir|cuit|ry
cir|cuit|ries
cir|cu|lar +s
cir|cu|lar|isa|tion
Br. (use
circularization)
cir|cu|lar|ise Br.
(use circularize)
cir|cu|lar|ises
cir|cu|lar|ised
cir|cu|lar|is|ing
cir|cu|lar|ity
cir|cu|lar|ities

cir|cu|lar|iza|tion
cir|cu|lar|ize
cir|cu|lar|izes
cir|cu|lar|ized
cir|cu|lar|iz|ing
cir|cu|lar|ly
cir|cu|late
cir|cu|lates
cir|cu|lated
cir|cu|lat|ing
cir|cu|la|tion +s
cir|cu|la|tive
cir|cu|la|tor +s
cir|cu|la|tory
cir|cum|am|bi|
ence
cir|cum|am|bi|
ency
cir|cum|am|bi|ent
cir|cum|am|bu|
late
cir|cum|am|bu|
lates
cir|cum|am|bu|
lated
cir|cum|am|bu|
lat|ing
cir|cum|am|bu|
la|tion +s
cir|cum|am|bu|
la|tory
cir|cum|circle +s
cir|cum|cise
cir|cum|cises
cir|cum|cised
cir|cum|cis|ing
cir|cum|ci|sion +s
cir|cum|fer|ence
+s
cir|cum|fer|en|tial
cir|cum|fer|en|
tial|ly
cir|cum|flex
cir|cum|flexes
cir|cum|flu|ence
cir|cum|flu|ent
cir|cum|fuse
cir|cum|fuses
cir|cum|fused
cir|cum|fus|ing
cir|cum|ja|cent
cir|cum|lit|toral
cir|cum|lo|cu|tion
+s
cir|cum|lo|cu|
tion|al
cir|cum|lo|cu|
tion|ary
cir|cum|lo|cu|tion|
ist +s
cir|cum|lo|cu|tory
cir|cum|lunar

cir|cum|navi|gate
cir|cum|navi|
gates
cir|cum|navi|
gated
cir|cum|navi|
gat|ing
cir|cum|navi|
ga|tion +s
cir|cum|navi|
ga|tor +s
cir|cum|po|lar
cir|cum|scrib|able
cir|cum|scribe
cir|cum|scribes
cir|cum|scribed
cir|cum|scrib|ing
cir|cum|scriber +s
cir|cum|scrip|tion
+s
cir|cum|solar
cir|cum|spect
cir|cum|spec|tion
cir|cum|spect|ly
cir|cum|stance +s
cir|cum|stanced
cir|cum|stan|tial
+s
cir|cum|stan|ti|al|
ity
cir|cum|
stan|ti|al|ly
cir|cum|ter|res|
trial
cir|cum|val|late
cir|cum|val|lates
cir|cum|val|lated
cir|cum|
val|lat|ing
cir|cum|vent +s
+ed +ing
cir|cum|ven|tion
+s
cir|cum|vo|lu|tion
+s
cir|cus
cir|cuses
(travelling show;
junction in town;
Roman arena; etc.
△ cercus)
ciré
Ciren|ces|ter
(town, England)
cire per|due
cirque +s (hollow.
△ circs)
cir|rho|sis
cir|rho|ses
(of liver.
△ sorosis)
cir|rhot|ic

cirri
cirri|ped +s
cirro|cumu|lus
cir|rose
cirro|stra|tus
cir|rous (of cirrus.
△ scirrhous)
cir|rus
cirri
(cloud. △ scirrhus)
cis|alpine
cis|at|lan|tic
cisco
cis|coes
Cis|kei (former
homeland, South
Africa)
cis|lu|nar
Cis|neros,
Fran|cisco de
(Spanish
statesman)
cis|pad|ane
cis|pont|ine
cissy (use sissy)
cis|sies
cist +s (coffin;
burial chamber;
box for sacred
vessels. △ cyst)
Cis|ter|cian +s
cis|tern +s
cis|tus
plural cis|tus
cit|able
cita|del +s
cit|ation +s
cite
cites
cited
cit|ing
(quote. △ sight,
site)
CITES (Convention
on International
Trade in
Endangered
Species)
cit|ies
citi|fied
cit|ify
citi|fies
citi|fied
citi|fy|ing
citi|zen +s
citi|zen|hood +s
citi|zen|ly
citi|zen|ry
Citi|zens' Ad|vice
Bur|eau
Citi|zens' Ad|vice
Bur|eaux

citi|zen's ar|rest +s

citi|zens' band

Citi|zen's Char|ter

citi|zen|ship +s

Cit|lal|té|petl (mountain, Mexico)

cit|ole +s

cit|rate +s

cit|ric

cit|rin (substance in fruit)

cit|rine +s (stone)

cit|ron +s

cit|ron|ella

cit|rous *adjective*

cit|rus

  cit|ruses *noun*

cit|tern +s

City, the (in London)

city

  cit|ies

city cen|ter *Am.* +s

city centre *Br.* +s

city dwell|er +s

city|fied (use citified)

city|scape +s

city slick|er +s

city state +s

city|ward

city|wards

Ciu|dad Bolí|var (city, Venezuela)

Ciu|dad Tru|jillo (former name of Santo Domingo)

Ciu|dad Vic|toria (city, Mexico)

civet +s

civet-cat +s

civic

civ|ic|al|ly

civ|ics

civil

ci|vil|ian +s

ci|vil|ian|isa|tion *Br.* (use civilianization)

ci|vil|ian|ise *Br.* (use civilianize)

ci|vil|ian|ises

ci|vil|ian|ised

ci|vil|ian|is|ing

ci|vil|ian|iza|tion

ci|vil|ian|ize

ci|vil|ian|izes

ci|vil|ian|ized

ci|vil|ian|iz|ing

civ|il|is|able *Br.* (use civilizable)

civ|il|isa|tion *Br.* +s (use civilization)

civ|il|ise *Br.* (use civilize)

civ|il|ises

civ|il|ised

civ|il|is|ing

civ|il|iser *Br.* +s (use civilizer)

ci|vil|ity

  ci|vil|ities

civ|il|iz|able

civ|il|iza|tion +s

civ|il|ize

civ|il|izes

civ|il|ized

civ|il|iz|ing

civ|il|izer +s

Civil List

civ|il|ly

civvy

  civ|vies

Civvy Street

clack +s +ed +ing (sound; chatter. △ claque)

clack|er +s

Clac|ton|ian

clad

  clads

  clad|ded *or* clad

  clad|ding

clad|ding +s

clade +s

clad|ism

cla|dis|tic

cla|dis|tics

clad|ode +s

clado|gram +s

claim +s +ed +ing

claim|able

claim|ant +s (person making a claim. △ clamant)

claim|er +s

Clair *also* Claire, Clare

Clair, René (French film director)

clair|au|di|ence

clair|au|di|ent +s

Claire *also* Clair, Clare

clair|voy|ance

clair|voy|ant +s

clair|voy|ant|ly

clam

  clams

clam (*cont.*)

  clammed

  clam|ming

cla|mant (insistent. △ claimant)

cla|mant|ly

clam|ber +s +ed +ing

clam|mily

clam|mi|ness

clammy

  clam|mier

  clam|mi|est

clamor *Am.* +s +ed +ing (*Br.* clamour)

clam|or|ous

clam|or|ous|ly

clam|or|ous|ness

clam|our *Br.* +s +ed +ing (*Am.* clamor)

clamp +s +ed +ing

clamp|down +s

clam|shell +s

clan +s

clan|des|tine

clan|des|tine|ly

clan|des|tin|ity

clang +s +ed +ing

clang|er +s (mistake. △ clangor, clangour)

clangor *Am.* (*Br.* clangour. clanging; uproar. △ clanger)

clang|or|ous

clang|or|ous|ly

clang|our *Br.* (*Am.* clangor. clanging; uproar. △ clanger)

clank +s +ed +ing

clank|ing|ly

clan|nish

clan|nish|ly

clan|nish|ness

clan|ship +s

clans|man

  clans|men (member of clan. △ Klansman)

clans|woman

  clans|women

clap

  claps

  clapped

  clap|ping

clap|board

clapped out *adjective*

clapped-out *attributive*

clap|per +s

clap|per|board +s

Clap|ton, Eric (English guitarist)

clap|trap

claque +s (hired applauders. △ clack)

cla|queur +s

Clara

clara|bella +s

Clare, John (English poet)

Clare *also* Clair, Claire (name)

Clare (county, Republic of Ireland)

Clar|ence (name)

clar|ence +s (carriage)

Clar|en|ceux *Heraldry*

Clar|en|don, Earl of (English statesman and historian)

Clare of As|sisi (Italian saint)

claret +s

Clar|ice

clari|fi|ca|tion +s

clari|fi|ca|tory

clari|fier +s

clari|fy

  clari|fies

  clari|fied

  clari|fy|ing

clari|net +s

clari|net|tist +s

clar|ion +s

clar|ion call +s

Clar|issa

clar|ity

  clar|ities

Clark

Clark, Wil|liam (American army officer)

Clarke, Ar|thur C. (English writer of science fiction)

Clarke, Mar|cus (Anglo-Australian writer)

clar|kia +s

Clar|rie

clary

  clar|ies

clash
 clashes
 clashed
 clash|ing
clash|er +s
clasp +s +ed +ing
clasp|er +s
clasp-knife
 clasp-knives
class
 classes
 classed
 class|ing
class|able
class-conscious
class-
 conscious|ness
clas|sic +s
clas|sic|al
clas|sic|al|ism
clas|sic|al|ist +s
clas|sic|al|ity
clas|sic|al|ly
clas|si|cise Br. (use
 classicize)
 clas|si|cises
 clas|si|cised
 clas|si|cis|ing
clas|si|cism +s
clas|si|cist +s
clas|si|cize
 clas|si|cizes
 clas|si|cized
 clas|si|ciz|ing
clas|si|cus (in
 'locus classicus')
clas|si|fi|able
clas|si|fi|ca|tion +s
clas|si|fi|ca|tory
clas|si|fied +s
clas|si|fier +s
clas|sify
 clas|si|fies
 clas|si|fied
 clas|si|fy|ing
class|ily
classi|ness
class|ism
class|ist +s
class|less
class|less|ness
class-list +s
class|mate +s
class|room +s
classy
 class|ier
 classi|est
clas|tic
clath|rate +s
clat|ter +s +ed
 +ing
Claud also Claude

Claude also Claud
Claude Lor|rain
 (French painter)
Claud|ette
Clau|dia
clau|di|ca|tion
Claud|ine
Claud|ius (Roman
 emperor)
claus|al
claus|al|ly
clause +s
Clause|witz, Karl
 von (Prussian
 soldier)
Claus|ius, Ru|dolf
 (German
 physicist)
claus|tral
claus|tro|phobe +s
claus|tro|pho|bia
claus|tro|pho|bic
 +s
claus|tro|pho|bic|
 al|ly
cla|vate
clave +s
clavi|cem|balo +s
clavi|chord +s
cla|vicu|lar
cla|vier +s
clavi|form
claw +s +ed +ing
claw|back +s
claw|er +s
claw ham|mer +s
claw|less
claw-mark +s
Clay, Cas|sius
 (real name of
 Muhammad Ali)
clay +s
clayey
clay|ish
clay|like
clay|more +s
clay-pan +s
clay pi|geon +s
Clay|ton's
 (illusory)
clean +s +ed +ing
 +er +est
clean|able
clean-cut
clean|er +s
clean|ish
clean|lily
clean|li|ness
clean-living

clean|ly
clean|lier
clean|li|est
clean|ness
clean-out +s noun
cleanse
 cleanses
 cleansed
 cleans|ing
cleans|er +s
clean-shaven
clean|skin +s
clean-up +s noun
clear +s +ed +ing
 +er +est
clear|able
clear|ance +s
clear|cole
 clear|coles
 clear|coled
 clear|col|ing
clear-cut
clear|er +s
clear-headed
clear|ing +s
clear|ing bank +s
clear|ing house +s
clear|ly
clear|ness
clear-out +s noun
clear-sighted
clear|story Am.
 clear|stor|ies
 (Br. clerestory)
clear-thinking
clear-up +s noun
 and attributive
clear|way +s
clear|wing +s
cleat +s
cleav|able
cleav|age +s
cleave
 cleaves
 clove or cleft or
 cleaved
 cleav|ing
 clo|ven or cleft
 (split)
cleave
 cleaves
 cleaved or clave
 cleav|ing
 (adhere)
cleav|er +s
 (chopper)
cleav|ers (plant)
Cleese, John
 (English actor)
clef +s
cleft +s (split.
 △ klepht)

cleg +s
Cleis|the|nes
 (Athenian
 statesman)
cleis|to|gam|ic
cleis|to|gam|ic|
 al|ly
Clem
cle|ma|tis
 plural cle|ma|tis
Clem|ence
Cle|men|ceau,
 Georges (French
 statesman)
Clem|ency (name)
clem|ency (mercy)
Clem|ens, Sam|uel
 (real name of
 Mark Twain)
Clem|ent (name)
clem|ent (mild)
Clem|en|tine
 (name)
clem|en|tine +s
 (fruit)
Clem|ent of
 Alex|an|dria
 (Greek saint)
Clem|ent of Rome
 (pope and saint)
Clem|mie
clench
 clenches
 clenched
 clench|ing
Cleo also Clio
Cleo|patra
 (Egyptian queen)
clep|sydra +s
clere|story Br.
 clere|stor|ies
 (Am. clearstory)
clergy
 cler|gies
cler|gy|man
 cler|gy|men
clergy|woman
 clergy|women
cler|ic +s
cler|ic|al +s
cler|ic|al|ism
cler|ic|al|ist +s
cler|ic|al|ity
cler|ic|al|ly
cleri|hew +s
cler|isy
 cleri|sies
clerk +s +ed +ing
clerk|dom +s
clerk|ess
 clerk|esses
clerk|ish

clerk¦ly
clerk¦ship +s
Clermont-Ferrand
(city, France)
Cleve¦land
(county, England;
city, USA)
Cleve¦land,
  Grover
  (American
  president)
clever +er +est
clever-clever
clever Dick +s
clev¦er¦ly
clev¦er¦ness
Cleves, Anne of
(wife of Henry
VIII of England)
clevis
  clev¦ises
clew +s +ed +ing
  (Nautical. △clou,
  clue)
cli¦an¦thus
  plural cli¦an¦thus
cli¦ché +s
cli¦chéd
cliché-ridden
click +s +ed +ing
  (sound. △clique)
click-clack +s +ed
  +ing
click¦er +s
clickety-click
cli¦ent +s
cli¦en¦tele +s
client-server
  adjective
client¦ship +s
Clif¦den
  non¦par¦eil +s
Cliff (name)
cliff +s (rock face)
cliff¦hang¦er +s
cliff¦hang¦ing
cliffi¦ness
cliff¦like
Clif¦ford
cliff¦side +s
cliff¦top +s
cliffy
  cliff¦ier
  cliffi¦est
cli¦mac¦ter¦ic +s
cli¦mac¦tic
cli¦mac¦tic¦al¦ly
cli¦mate +s
cli¦mat¦ic
cli¦mat¦ic¦al
cli¦mat¦ic¦al¦ly
cli¦ma¦to¦logic¦al

cli¦mat¦olo¦gist +s
cli¦mat¦ology
cli¦max
  cli¦maxes
  cli¦maxed
  cli¦max¦ing
climb +s +ed +ing
  (mount. △clime)
climb¦able
climb¦down +s
climb¦er +s
climb¦ing frame
  +s
climb¦ing iron +s
clime +s (region;
  climate. △climb)
cli¦nal
clinch
  clinches
  clinched
  clinch¦ing
clinch¦er +s
clincher-built
cline +s
  (continuum.
  △Klein)
cling
  clings
  clung
  cling¦ing
cling¦er +s
cling film +s
clingi¦ness
cling¦ing¦ly
cling¦stone +s
clingy
  cling¦ier
  cling¦iest
clin¦ic +s
clin¦ic¦al
clin¦ic¦al¦ly
clin¦ician +s
clink +s +ed +ing
clink¦er +s
clinker-built
clink¦stone +s
clin¦om¦eter +s
Clint (name)
clint +s Geology
Clin¦ton, Bill
  (American
  president)
Clio also **Cleo**
  (name)
Clio Greek and
  Roman Mythology
clio¦met¦rics
clip
  clips
  clipped
  clip¦ping
clip¦board +s

clip-clop
  clip-clops
  clip-clopped
  clip-clopping
clip joint +s
clip-on +s adjective
  and noun
clip¦pable
clip¦per +s
clip¦pie +s
clip¦ping +s
clique +s
  (exclusive group.
  △click)
cliquey
  cliqui¦er
  cliqui¦est
cliqu¦ish
cliqu¦ish¦ness
cliqu¦ism
cliquy (use
  cliquey)
clit¦ic
cliti¦cisa¦tion Br.
  (use cliticization)
cliti¦ciza¦tion
clit¦or¦al
clit¦ori¦dec¦tomy
  clit¦ori¦
    dec¦tomies
clit¦oris
  clit¦orises
Clive
Clive, Rob¦ert
  (British general)
cliv¦ers (use
  cleavers)
clo¦aca
  clo¦acae
clo¦acal
cloak +s +ed +ing
cloak-and-dagger
cloak¦room +s
clob¦ber +s +ed
  +ing
cloche +s
clock +s +ed +ing
clock¦maker +s
clock¦mak¦ing
clock radio +s
clock tower +s
clock-watch
  clock-watches
  clock-watched
  clock-watching
clock-watcher +s
clock¦wise
clock¦work
clod +s
Clo¦dagh
clod¦dish
clod¦dish¦ly

clod¦dish¦ness
cloddy
clod¦hop¦per +s
clod¦hop¦ping
clod¦poll +s
clog
  clogs
  clogged
  clog¦ging
clog dance +s noun
clog-dance
  clog-dances
  clog-danced
  clog-dancing
  verb
cloggy
  clog¦gier
  clog¦gi¦est
clois¦onné
clois¦ter +s +ed
  +ing
clois¦tral
clomp +s +ed +ing
clo¦nal
clone
  clones
  cloned
  clon¦ing
clon¦ic
clonk +s +ed +ing
Clon¦mel (town,
  Republic of
  Ireland)
clo¦nus
clop
  clops
  clopped
  clop¦ping
clo¦qué
clos¦able
close
  closes
  closed
  clos¦ing
  (shut. △cloze)
close
  closer
  clos¦est
  (near; stuffy; road;
  etc.)
close-coupled
close-cropped
closed-circuit
closed-door
  adjective
closed-end
closed-ended
closed-in
close-down +s
  noun
closed shop
close-fisted

close-fitting
close-grained
close-hauled
close-in *adjective*
close-knit
close¦ly
close-mouthed
close¦ness
close-out +s *noun*
close-quarter
  attributive
close quar¦ters
  noun
close-range
  adjective
close-run
close sea¦son
close-set
close shave
close-shaven
closet +s +ed +ing
close-up +s
  adjective and noun
close-woven
clos¦ing time +s
clos¦ish
clos¦trid¦ial
clos¦ure +s
clot
  clots
  clot¦ted
  clot¦ting
cloth +s
cloth cap +s
cloth-cap *attributive*
clothe
  clothes
  clothed
  cloth¦ing
cloth-eared
clothes
clothes horse +s
clothes line +s
clothes-moth +s
clothes-peg +s
clothes-pin +s
clo¦thier +s
cloth¦ing
Clotho *Greek*
  Mythology
clot¦ted cream
clo¦ture +s
clou +s (central
  point or idea.
  △ clew, clue)
cloud +s +ed +ing
cloud base
cloud¦berry
  cloud¦berries
cloud¦burst +s
cloud-castle +s
cloud cham¦ber +s

cloud cover
cloud-cuckoo-
  land
cloud-hopping
cloud¦ily
cloudi¦ness
cloud-land
cloud¦less
cloud¦less¦ly
cloud¦let +s
cloud¦scape +s
cloudy
  cloud¦ier
  cloudi¦est
Clou¦et (Flemish
  family of painters)
Clough, Ar¦thur
  Hugh (English
  poet)
clough +s
clout +s +ed +ing
clove +s
clove hitch
  clove hitches
clo¦ven
cloven-footed
cloven-hoofed
Clo¦ver (name)
clo¦ver +s (plant)
clo¦ver¦leaf +s
  (shape;
  intersection)
clo¦ver leaf
  clo¦ver leaves
  (leaf)
Clo¦vis *Archaeology*
clown +s +ed +ing
clown¦ery
clown¦ish
clown¦ish¦ly
clown¦ish¦ness
cloy +s +ed +ing
cloy¦ing¦ly
cloze +s (test.
  △ close)
club
  clubs
  clubbed
  club¦bing
club¦babil¦ity
club¦bable
club¦bable¦ness
club¦bably
club¦ber +s
clubby
  club¦bier
  club¦bi¦est
club class
club-foot
  club-feet
club-footed
club¦house +s

club¦land
club¦man
  club¦men
club¦mate +s
club¦moss
  club¦mosses
club¦root
club sand¦wich
  club sand¦wiches
cluck +s +ed +ing
cluck¦ily
clucki¦ness
clucky
  cluck¦ier
  clucki¦est
clue
  clues
  clued
  clue¦ing
  (piece of evidence
  etc. △ clew, clou)
clue¦less
clue¦less¦ly
clue¦less¦ness
Cluj–Napoca (city,
  Romania)
clump +s +ed +ing
clumpy
  clump¦ier
  clumpi¦est
clum¦si¦ly
clum¦si¦ness
clumsy
  clum¦sier
  clum¦si¦est
clung
Clu¦niac +s
clunk +s +ed +ing
clunk¦er +s
clunky
  clunk¦ier
  clunki¦est
Cluny (town,
  France)
clus¦ter +s +ed
  +ing
clus¦ter bomb +s
clutch
  clutches
  clutched
  clutch¦ing
clutch bag +s
Clu¦tha (river, New
  Zealand)
clut¦ter +s +ed
  +ing
Clwyd (county,
  Wales)
Clyde (river,
  Scotland; name)
Clydes¦dale +s
cly¦peal

cly¦pe¦ate
clyp¦eus
  clypei
clys¦ter +s +ed
  +ing
Cly¦tem¦nes¦tra
  Greek Legend
Cnut (Danish king
  of England)
Co. (= company)
co-accused
  plural co-accused
co¦acer¦vate +s
co¦acer¦va¦tion
coach
  coaches
  coached
  coach¦ing
coach¦build¦er +s
coach-built
coach house +s
coach¦load +s
coach¦man
  coach¦men
coach¦wood
coach¦work
co¦ad¦ju¦tor +s
co¦agul¦able
co¦agu¦lant +s
co¦agu¦late
  co¦agu¦lates
  co¦agu¦lated
  co¦agu¦lat¦ing
co¦agu¦la¦tion
co¦agu¦la¦tive
co¦agu¦la¦tor
co¦agu¦la¦tory
co¦agu¦lum
  co¦ag¦ula
Coa¦huila (state,
  Mexico)
coal +s (rock, fuel.
  △ cole kohl)
coal-bed +s
coal black *noun*
  and adjective
coal-black
  attributive
coal-burning
coal dust
coal¦er +s (ship.
  △ cola)
co¦alesce
  co¦alesces
  co¦alesced
  co¦ales¦cing
co¦ales¦cence
co¦ales¦cent
coal¦face +s
coal¦field +s
coal-fired

coal|fish
  plural coal|fish
coal gas
coal-hole +s
coal|house +s
co|ali|tion +s
co|ali|tion|ist +s
coal|man
  coal|men
coal mine +s
coal miner +s
coal min|ing
coal|mouse
  coal|mice
coal oil
Coal|port (town,
  England; china)
coal-sack +s
coal scut|tle +s
coal-seam +s
coal tar
coal tit +s
coaly (like coal.
  △ coley, choli)
coam|ing +s
co|arc|tate
co|arc|ta|tion +s
coarse
  coars|er
  coars|est
  (rough etc.
  △ corse, course)
coarse fish|ing
coarse|ly
coars|en +s +ed
  +ing
coarse|ness
coars|ish
coast +s +ed +ing
coast|al
coast|er +s
coast|guard +s
coast|land +s
coast|line +s
coast-to-coast
coast|wise
coat +s +ed +ing
  (garment; layer; to
  cover. △ cote)
coat dress
  coat dresses
coatee +s
coat-hanger +s
coat hook +s
coati +s
co|ati|mundi +s
coat|ing +s
coat|less
coat of arms
  coats of arms
coat|room +s

Coats Land
  (region,
  Antarctica)
coat-stand +s
coat-tail +s
co-author +s +ed
  +ing
coax
  coaxes
  coaxed
  coax|ing
coax|er +s
co|axial
co|axial|ly
coax|ing|ly
cob +s (lump of
  coal etc.; loaf;
  corn cob;
  hazelnut; horse;
  swan. △ kob)
co|balt +s
co|balt blue +s
  noun and adjective
cobalt-blue
  attributive
co|balt|ic
co|balt|ous
cob|ber +s
Cob|bett, Wil|liam
  (English political
  reformer)
cob|ble
  cob|bles
  cob|bled
  cob|bling
cob|bler +s
cobble|stone +s
Cob|den, Rich|ard
  (British political
  reformer)
Cob|den|ism
COBE (satellite)
co-belliger|ence
co-belliger|ency
co-belliger|ent +s
coble +s
cob|nut +s
COBOL *Computing*
cobra +s
cob|web +s
cob|webbed
cob|webby
coca +s (plant.
  △ coker)
Coca-Cola +s
  Propr.
co|caine
co|cain|ism
coc|cal
coc|ci|di|osis
  coc|ci|di|oses
coc|coid

coc|cus
  cocci
coc|cy|geal
coc|cyx
  coc|cy|ges *or*
  coc|cyxes
Cocha|bamba
  (city, Bolivia)
co-chairman
  co-chairmen
Co|chin (port,
  India)
co|chin +s (fowl)
Cochin-China
  (former name of
  part of Vietnam)
cochin-china +s
  (= cochin)
coch|in|eal
coch|lea
  coch|leae
coch|lear
Coch|ran, Charles
  (American
  theatrical
  producer)
Coch|ran,
  Jacque|line
  (American
  aviator)
cock +s +ed +ing
cocka|bully
  cocka|bul|lies
cock|ade +s
cock|aded
cock-a-doodle-
  doo +s
cock-a-hoop
cock-a-leekie
cocka|lorum
cock and bull
  adjective and noun
cocka|tiel +s
cocka|too +s
cocka|trice +s
cock|boat +s
cock|chafer +s
Cock|croft, John
  (English physicist)
cock|crow
cock|er +s
  (spaniel)
cock|erel +s
Cock|er|ell,
  Chris|to|pher
  (English engineer,
  inventor of the
  hovercraft)
cock|er spaniel +s
cock-eyed
cock|fight +s
cock|fight|ing

cock-horse +s
cock|ily
cocki|ness
cockle
  cockles
  cockled
  cock|ling
cockle|bur +s
cockle|shell +s
cock loft +s
cock|ney +s
cock|ney|ism
cock-of-the-rock
  +s
cock-of-the-walk
  cocks-of-the-
  walk
cock-of-the-wood
  +s
cock|pit +s
cock|roach
  cock|roaches
cocks|comb +s
cocks|foot
cock|shy
cock spar|row +s
cock|sure
cock|sure|ly
cock|sure|ness
cock|tail +s
cock-up +s *noun*
cocky
  cock|ies
  cock|ier
  cocki|est
cocky-leeky (use
  cock-a-leekie)
coco +s (palm tree
  bearing coconuts)
cocoa +s (powder
  or drink from
  cacao beans)
co|coa|nut +s (use
  coconut)
coco-de-mer
  plural coco-de-
  mer palms *or*
  coco-de-mer
  trees
Cocom
  (= Coordinating
  Committee on
  Multilateral Export
  Controls)
co-conspira|tor +s
co|co|nut +s
co|coon +s +ed
  +ing
co|coon|ery
Cocos Is|lands (in
  Indian Ocean)
co|cotte +s

Coc|teau, Jean
(French dramatist)
cod
  plural cod
  (fish)
cod
  cods
  cod|ded
  cod|ding
  (hoax)
coda +s
  (concluding part.
  △ coder)
cod|dle
  cod|dles
  cod|dled
  cod|dling
cod|dler +s
code
  codes
  coded
  cod|ing
code book +s
code-breaker +s
code-breaking
co-defend|ant +s
co|deine
code name +s
code-named
code num|ber +s
co|depend|ency
co|depend|ent +s
coder +s (encoder.
  △ coda)
co-determin|ation
code word +s
codex
  co|di|ces *or*
  codexes
cod|fish
  plural cod|fish
cod|ger +s
co|di|ces
co|di|cil +s
co|di|cil|lary
co|di|co|logic|al
co|di|co|logic|al|ly
co|di|col|ogy
co|difi|ca|tion +s
co|di|fier +s
co|dify
  co|di|fies
  co|di|fied
  co|di|fy|ing
co-director +s
cod|ling +s
codlings-and-
  cream
cod liver oil
co|do|main
codon +s
cod|piece +s

co-driver +s
cods|wal|lop
Cody, Wil|liam
  (Buffalo Bill)
Coe, Se|bas|tian
  (English runner)
coe|cil|ian +s (use
  caecilian)
coed +s
co-editor +s
co-education
co-education|al
co-education|al|ly
co|ef|fi|cient +s
coela|canth +s
coel|en|ter|ate +s
coel|iac *Br.* (*Am.*
  celiac)
coelom *Br.*
  coel|oms *or*
  coel|omata
  (*Am.* celom)
coel|om|ate *Br.*
  (*Am.* celomate)
coelo|stat +s
coeno|bite *Br.* +s
  (*Am.* cenobite)
coeno|bit|ic *Br.*
  (*Am.* cenobitic)
coeno|bit|ic|al *Br.*
  (*Am.* cenobitical)
co|en|zyme +s
co-equal +s
co-equality
co-equally
co|erce
  co|erces
  co|erced
  co|er|cing
co|ercer +s
co|er|cible
co|er|cion +s
co|er|cive
co|er|cive|ly
co|er|cive|ness
co|er|civ|ity
co|essen|tial
co|eter|nal
co|eter|nal|ly
Coet|zee, J. M.
  (South African
  novelist)
Coeur de Lion,
  Rich|ard (English
  king)
co|eval
co|ev|al|ity
co|ev|al|ly
co|ex|ist
co|ex|ist|ence
co|ex|ist|ent
co|ex|ten|sive

cof|fee +s
cof|fee bar +s
cof|fee bean +s
cof|fee break +s
cof|fee cup +s
cof|fee es|sence
cof|fee grind|er +s
cof|fee house +s
coffee-maker +s
cof|fee mill +s
cof|fee morn|ing
  +s
cof|fee pot +s
cof|fee shop +s
cof|fee spoon +s
cof|fee table +s
  noun
coffee-table
  adjective
cof|fer +s (box.
  △ cougher)
coffer-dam +s
cof|fered
cof|fin +s +ed +ing
coffin-bone +s
cof|fin cor|ner +s
coffin-joint +s
coffin-nail +s
cof|fle +s
co-founder +s
cog +s
co|gency
co|gent
co|gent|ly
cogged
cogit|able
cogi|tate
  cogi|tates
  cogi|tated
  cogi|tat|ing
cogi|ta|tion +s
cogi|ta|tive
cogi|ta|tor +s
co|*gito*
Co|gnac (town,
  France)
co|gnac +s
  (brandy)
cog|nate +s
cog|nate|ly
cog|nate|ness
cog|nat|ic
cog|nis|able *Br.*
  (use cognizable)
cog|nis|ably *Br.*
  (use cognizably)
cog|ni|sance *Br.*
  (use cognizance)
cog|ni|sant *Br.* (use
  cognizant)
cog|nise *Br.* (use
  cognize)

cog|nise (*cont.*)
  cog|nises
  cog|nised
  cog|nis|ing
cog|ni|tion +s
cog|ni|tion|al
cog|ni|tive
cog|ni|tive|ly
cog|ni|tiv|ism
cog|ni|tiv|ist +s
cog|niz|able
cog|niz|ably
cog|niz|ance
cog|ni|zant
cog|nize
  cog|nizes
  cog|nized
  cog|niz|ing
cog|no|men +s
co|gnos|cente
  co|gnos|centi
cog|wheel +s
co|habit +s +ed
  +ing
co|hab|it|ant +s
co|hab|it|ation
co|hab|it|ee +s
co|hab|it|er +s
Cohen, Leon|ard
  (Canadian singer
  and writer)
co|here
  co|heres
  co|hered
  co|her|ing
co|her|ence +s
co|her|ency
co|her|ent
co|her|ent|ly
co|herer +s
co|he|sion +s
co|he|sive
co|he|sive|ly
co|he|sive|ness
Cohn, Fer|di|nand
  (German botanist)
coho +s
cohoe +s (use
  coho)
co|hort +s
COHSE
  (= Confederation
  of Health Service
  Employees)
co|hune
coif +s
coif|feur +s *male*
coif|feuse +s
  female
coif|fure
  coif|fures

coif|fure (cont.)
coif|fured
coif|fur|ing

coign +s
(favourable
position. △ coin,
quoin)

coil +s +ed +ing

Co|im|ba|tore (city,
India)

Co|im|bra (city,
Portugal)

coin +s +ed +ing
(money. △ coign,
quoin)

coin|age

coin box
coin boxes

co|in|cide
co|in|cides
co|in|cided
co|in|cid|ing

co|in|ci|dence +s

co|in|ci|dent

co|in|ci|den|tal

co|in|ci|den|tal|ly

co|in|ci|dent|ly

coin|er +s

coin-op +s

Coin|treau
+s Propr.

coir

co|it|al

co|ition

co|itus

co|itus
inter|rup|tus

Coke +s (drink)
Propr.

coke
cokes
coked
cok|ing
(form of coal;
cocaine)

coker +s (person
who cokes coal.
△ coca)

col +s

cola +s (tree; drink.
△ coaler)

col|an|der +s

co-latitude +s

Col|bert,
Claud|ette
(French actress)

Col|bert, Jean
(French
statesman)

col|can|non (Irish
dish)

Col|ches|ter (town,
England)

col|chi|cine +s

col|chi|cum (plant)

Col|chis (ancient
region, SW Asia)

cold +s +er +est

cold-blooded

cold-blooded|ly

cold-blooded|ness

cold call +s +ed
+ing

cold cream +s

cold-eyed

cold frame +s

cold-hearted

cold-hearted|ly

cold-hearted|ness

cold|ish

Cold|itz (town and
prison, Germany)

cold|ly

cold|ness

cold room +s

cold-short

cold shoul|der
noun

cold-shoulder +s
+ed +ing verb

cold sore +s

cold store +s

cold war

cold-work
cold-works
cold-worked
cold-working
verb

Cole (name)

cole +s (cabbage.
△ coal, kohl)

co-leader +s

cole|mouse (use
coalmouse)
cole|mice

Cole|op|tera

cole|op|teran +s

cole|op|ter|ist +s

cole|op|ter|ous

cole|op|tile +s

Cole|raine (town,
Northern Ireland)

Cole|ridge,
Sam|uel Tay|lor
(English poet and
critic)

cole|seed

cole|slaw

cole tit +s (use
coal tit)

Col|lette (French
novelist)

Col|lette also
Col|lette

co|leus
plural co|leus or
co|leuses

coley +s (fish.
△ coaly, choli)

colic +s

col|icky

Col|ima (state and
city, Mexico)

Colin

coli|seum +s
(stadium. △ the
Colosseum)

col|itis

Coll (Scottish
island)

col|lab|or|ate
col|lab|or|ates
col|lab|or|ated
col|lab|or|at|ing

col|lab|or|ation +s

col|lab|ora|tion|ist
+s

col|lab|ora|tive

col|lab|ora|tive|ly

col|lab|or|ator +s

col|lage +s

col|la|gen +s

col|lagist +s

col|lap|sar +s

col|lapse
col|lapses
col|lapsed
col|laps|ing

col|laps|ibil|ity

col|laps|ible

col|lar +s +ed +ing
(on garment;
accost. △ choler)

collar-beam +s

col|lar|bone +s

col|lar|less

col|lard +s
(cabbage.
△ collared)

col|lar|ette +s

col|lar|less

col|late
col|lates
col|lated
col|lat|ing

col|lat|eral +s

col|lat|eral|ise Br.
(use collateralize)
col|lat|eral|ises
col|lat|eral|ised
col|lat|eral|is|ing

col|lat|eral|ity

col|lat|eral|ize
col|lat|eral|izes

col|lat|eral|ize
(cont.)
col|lat|eral|ized
col|lat|eral|iz|ing

col|lat|eral|ly

col|la|tion +s

col|la|tor +s

col|league +s

col|lect +s +ed
+ing

col|lect|abil|ity

col|lect|able +s

col|lec|ta|nea

col|lect|ed|ly

col|lect|ible +s
(use collectable)

col|lec|tion +s

col|lect|ive +s

col|lect|ive|ly

col|lect|ive|ness

col|lect|iv|isa|tion
Br. (use
collectivization)

col|lect|iv|ise Br.
(use collectivize)
col|lect|iv|ises
col|lect|iv|ised
col|lect|iv|is|ing

col|lect|iv|ism

col|lect|iv|ist +s

col|lect|iv|is|tic

col|lect|iv|ity
col|lect|iv|ities

col|lect|iv|iza|tion

col|lect|iv|ize
col|lect|iv|izes
col|lect|iv|ized
col|lect|iv|iz|ing

col|lect|or +s

col|lect|or's item
+s

Col|leen (name)

col|leen +s (Irish
girl)

col|lege +s

col|leger +s

col|le|gial

col|le|gi|al|ity

col|le|gian +s

col|le|gi|ate +s

col|le|gi|ate|ly

col|len|chyma

Colles' frac|ture
+s

col|let +s

Col|lette also
Col|lette

col|lide
col|lides
col|lided
col|lid|ing

col|lider +s

col|lie +s
col|lier +s
col|liery
　col|lier|ies
col|li|gate
　col|li|gates
　col|li|gated
　col|li|gat|ing
col|li|ga|tion +s
col|li|mate
　col|li|mates
　col|li|mated
　col|li|mat|ing
col|li|ma|tion +s
col|li|ma|tor +s
col|lin|ear
col|lin|ear|ity
col|lin|ear|ly
Col|lins
　Col|linses
　(drink; in 'Tom
　Collins')
Col|lins, Joan
　(English actress)
Col|lins, Mi|chael
　(Irish
　revolutionary)
Col|lins, Wil|kie
　(English novelist)
col|li|sion +s
col|li|sion|al
col|lo|cate
　col|lo|cates
　col|lo|cated
　col|lo|cat|ing
col|lo|ca|tion +s
col|locu|tor +s
col|lo|dion +s
col|lo|graph +s
col|logue
　col|logues
　col|logued
　col|loguing
col|loid +s
col|loid|al
col|lop +s
col|lo|quial
col|lo|qui|al|ism
　+s
col|lo|qui|al|ly
col|lo|quium
　col|lo|qui|ums or
　col|lo|quia
col|lo|quy
　col|lo|quies
col|lo|type +s
col|lude
　col|ludes
　col|luded
　col|lud|ing
col|luder +s
col|lu|sion +s

col|lu|sive
col|lu|sive|ly
col|lyrium
　col|lyria
colly|wob|bles
colo|bus
　colo|buses
colo|cynth +s
Col|logne (city,
　Germany)
co|logne +s
Co|lom|bia
Co|lom|bian +s
Col|ombo (capital
　of Sri Lanka)
Colón (port,
　Panama)
colon +s
　(punctuation;
　intestine)
colón
　col|lo|nes
　(Costa Rican and
　Salvadorean
　currency)
col|onel +s (officer.
　△ kernel)
Col|onel Blimp +s
col|on|el|cy
　col|on|el|cies
co|lo|nial +s
co|lo|ni|al|ism
co|lo|ni|al|ist +s
co|lo|ni|al|ly
co|lon|ic
col|on|isa|tion Br.
　(use colonization)
col|on|ise Br. (use
　colonize)
　col|on|ises
　col|on|ised
　col|on|is|ing
col|on|iser Br. +s
　(use colonizer)
col|on|ist +s
col|on|iza|tion
col|on|ize
　col|on|izes
　col|on|ized
　col|on|iz|ing
col|on|izer +s
col|on|nade +s
col|on|naded
col|ony
　col|onies
colo|phon +s
col|oph|ony
colo|quin|tida +s
　(use colocynth)
color Am. +s +ed
　+ing (Br. colour)

col|or|able Am. (Br.
　colourable)
col|or|ably Am. (Br.
　colourably)
Col|or|ado (state
　and river, USA;
　beetle)
col|or|ant Am. +s
　(Br. colourant)
col|or|ation +s
col|ora|tura +s
color-blind Am.
　(Br. colour-blind)
color-blindness
　Am. (Br. colour-
　blindness)
color code Am. +s
　(noun. Br. colour
　code)
color-code Am.
　color-codes
　color-coded
　color-coding
　(verb. Br. colour-
　code)
Col|ored Am. +s
　(often offensive
　person. Br.
　Coloured)
col|ored Am. +s
　(having colour;
　clothes. Br.
　coloured)
color fast Am. (Br.
　colour fast)
color fast|ness Am.
　(Br. colour
　fastness)
color-field Am.
　attributive (Br.
　colour-field)
col|or|ful Am. (Br.
　colourful)
col|or|ful|ly Am.
　(Br. colourfully)
col|or|ful|ness Am.
　(Br.
　colourfulness)
col|or|if|ic
col|or|im|eter +s
　(for measuring
　colour intensity.
　△ calorimeter)
col|ori|met|ric
col|or|im|etry
col|or|ing Am. +s
　(Br. colouring)
col|or|ist Am. +s
　(Br. colourist)
col|or|ize Am.
　col|or|izes
　col|or|ized

col|or|ize (cont.)
　col|or|iz|ing
　(Br. colourise)
col|or|less Am. (Br.
　colourless)
col|or|less|ly Am.
　(Br. colourlessly)
color scheme Am.
　+s (Br. colour
　scheme)
color wash Am.
　color washes
　(noun. Br. colour
　wash)
color-wash Am.
　color-washes
　color-washed
　color-washing
　(verb. Br. colour-
　wash)
col|or|way Am. +s
　(Br. colourway)
col|ory Am. (Br.
　coloury)
col|os|sal
col|os|sal|ly
Col|os|seum, the
　(in Rome)
col|os|seum +s
　(other stadium.
　use coliseum)
Col|os|sians Bible
col|os|sus
　col|ossi or
　col|os|suses
Col|os|sus of
　Rhodes (statue)
col|os|tomy
　col|os|tomies
col|os|trum
col|ot|omy
　col|ot|omies
col|our Br. +s +ed
　+ing (Am. color)
col|our|able Br.
　(Am. colorable)
col|our|ably Br.
　(Am. colorably)
col|our|ant Br. +s
　(Am. colorant)
col|our|ation +s
　(use coloration)
colour-blind Br.
　(Am. color-blind)
colour-blindness
　Br. (Am. color-
　blindness)
col|our code Br. +s
　(noun. Am. color
　code)
colour-code Br.
　colour-codes

colour-code (*cont.*)
  colour-coded
  colour-coding
  (*Am.* color-code)
Col|oured *Br.* +s
  (*often offensive*
  person. *Am.*
  Colored)
col|oured *Br.* +s
  (having colour;
  clothes. *Am.*
  colored)
col¦our fast *Br.*
  (*Am.* color fast)
col¦our fast|ness
  Br. (*Am.* color
  fastness)
colour-field *Br.*
  attributive (*Am.*
  color-field)
col¦our|ful *Br.* (*Am.*
  colorful)
col¦our|ful¦ly *Br.*
  (*Am.* colorfully)
col¦our|ful|ness *Br.*
  (*Am.*
  colorfulness)
col¦our|ing *Br.* +s
  (*Am.* coloring)
col¦our|ise *Br.* (use
  colourize)
col¦our|ises
col¦our|ised
col¦our|is¦ing
  (*Am.* colorize)
col¦our|ist *Br.* +s
  (*Am.* colorist)
col¦our|less *Br.*
  (*Am.* colorless)
col¦our|less¦ly *Br.*
  (*Am.* colorlessly)
col¦our scheme *Br.*
  +s (*Am.* color
  scheme)
colour-sergeant
  Br. +s
col¦our wash *Br.*
  col¦our washes
  (*noun. Am.* color
  wash)
colour-wash *Br.*
  colour-washes
  colour-washed
  colour-washing
  (*verb. Am.* color-
  wash)
col¦our|way *Br.* +s
  (*Am.* colorway)
col¦oury *Br.* (*Am.*
  colory)
col|por¦teur +s
col|po|scope +s

col|pos¦copy
  col|pos¦copies
col|pot¦omy
  col|pot¦omies
Colt +s (gun) *Propr.*
colt +s (young male
  horse)
col¦ter *Am.* +s (*Br.*
  coulter)
colt|hood +s
colt|ish
colt|ish¦ly
colt|ish|ness
Col|trane, John
  (American jazz
  musician)
colts|foot +s
colu|brid +s
colu|brine
co|lugo +s
Col|umba (Irish
  saint)
col|um|bar|ium
  col¦um|baria *or*
  col¦um|bar|iums
Col|um|bia (river,
  city, and
  university, USA)
Col|um|bia,
  Dis|trict of (in
  USA)
Col|um|bine
  (pantomime
  character)
col|um|bine +s
col|um|bite
col|um|bium
Col|um|bus (city,
  USA)
Col|um|bus,
  Chris|to|pher
  (Italian explorer)
col|umn +s
col|um|nar
col|um|nated
col|umned
column-inch
  column-inches
col|um|nist +s
col¦ure +s
colza
coma
  comae
  (gas round
  comet's tail; tuft
  on seed)
coma +s
  (unconsciousness)
Coma Bere|ni|ces
  (constellation)

Com|an|che
  plural Com|an|che
  or Com|an|ches
Coma|neci, Nadia
  (Romanian
  gymnast)
co|ma|tose
comb +s +ed +ing
com|bat
  com|bats
  com|bat¦ed *or*
  com|bat|ted
  com|bat|ing *or*
  com|bat|ting
com|bat|ant +s
com|bat|ive
com|bat|ive¦ly
com|bat|ive|ness
combe +s (use
  coomb. valley.
  △ cwm, khoum)
comb|er +s
combi +s
com|bin|able
com|bin|ation +s
com|bin|ation|al
com|bina|tive
com|bina|tor|ial
com|bin|atory
com|bine
  com|bines
  com|bined
  com|bin|ing
com|bine
  har|vest¦er +s
comb|ings
comb-jelly
  comb-jellies
combo +s
combs
  (= combinations)
com|bust +s +ed
  +ing
com|bust|ibil|ity
com|bust|ible +s
com|bust|ibly
com|bus¦tion
com|bus|tive
come
  comes
  came
  come
  com|ing
  (move towards
  speaker etc.
  △ cum)
come-at-able
come|back +s *noun*
Com|econ
  (= Council for
  Mutual Economic
  Assistance)

com|edian +s
com|edic
Com|édie
  Fran|çaise
  (French national
  theatre)
com|edi|enne +s
com|ed|ist +s
com|edo
  com|edo|nes
come|down +s
  noun
com|edy
  com|ed|ies
come-hither
  adjective
come|li|ness
come|ly
  come|lier
  come|li|est
come-on +s *noun*
comer +s
com|est|ible +s
comet +s
com|et|ary
come-uppance
com|fily
com|fi|ness
com|fit +s (sweet)
com|fort +s +ed
  +ing (ease;
  console)
com|fort|able
com|fort|able|ness
com|fort|ably
com|fort¦er +s
com|fort|ing|ly
com|fort|less
com|frey +s
comfy
  com|fier
  com|fi|est
comic +s
com|ic|al
com|ic|al|ity
com|ic|al|ly
comic book +s
comic strip +s
com|ing +s
Com|ino (island,
  Malta)
COMINT
  (= communica-
  tions intelligence)
Com|in|tern
  (communist
  organization)
comi|tadji +s
com|ity
  com|ities
comma +s

com|mand +s +ed
+ing
com|mand|ant +s
Commandant-in-
  Chief
Commandants-in-
  Chief
com|mand|ant|
          ship +s
com|man|deer +s
+ed +ing
com|mand|er +s
commander-in-
  chief
commanders-in-
  chief
com|mand|er|ship
+s
com|mand|ing|ly
com|mand|ment
+s
com|mando +s
comme ci, comme
  ça
com|media
  dell'arte
comme il faut
com|mem|or|ate
com|mem|or|ates
com|mem|or|ated
com|mem|or|
          at|ing
com|mem|or|ation
+s
com|mem|ora|tive
com|mem|or|ator
+s
com|mence
com|mences
com|menced
com|men|cing
com|mence|ment
+s
com|mend +s +ed
+ing
com|mend|able
com|mend|ably
com|men|da|tion
+s
com|men|da|tory
com|mens|al +s
com|mens|al|ism
com|mens|al|ity
com|men|sur|
          abil|ity
com|men|sur|able
com|men|sur|ably
com|men|sur|ate
com|men|sur|
          ate|ly
com|ment +s +ed
+ing

com|men|tary
com|men|tar|ies
com|men|tate
com|men|tates
com|men|tated
com|men|tat|ing
com|men|ta|tor +s
com|ment|er +s
com|merce
com|mer|cial +s
com|mer|cial|
  isa|tion Br. (use
  commercializa-
  tion)
com|mer|cial|ise
  Br. (use
  commercialize)
com|mer|cial|ises
com|mer|cial|ised
com|mer|cial|
          is|ing
com|mer|cial|ism
com|mer|ci|al|ity
com|mer|cial|
          iza|tion
com|mer|cial|ize
com|mer|cial|izes
com|mer|cial|ized
com|mer|cial|
          iz|ing
com|mer|cial|ly
com|mère +s
Com|mie +s
  (= Communist.
  △ commis)
com|min|ation +s
com|min|atory
com|min|gle
com|min|gles
com|min|gled
com|min|gling
com|min|ute
com|min|utes
com|min|uted
com|min|ut|ing
com|minu|tion +s
com|mis
  plural com|mis
  (waiter; chef.
  △ Commie)
com|mis|er|ate
com|mis|er|ates
com|mis|er|ated
com|mis|er|at|ing
com|mis|er|ation
+s
com|mis|era|tive
com|mis|er|ator
+s
com|mis|sar +s
com|mis|sar|ial
com|mis|sar|iat +s

com|mis|sary
com|mis|sar|ies
com|mis|sary|ship
+s
com|mis|sion +s
com|mis|sion
  agent +s
com|mis|sion|aire
+s
com|mis|sion|er
+s
com|mis|sural
com|mis|sure +s
com|mit
com|mits
com|mit|ted
com|mit|ting
com|mit|ment +s
com|mit|table
com|mit|tal +s
com|mit|tee +s
com|mit|tee man
com|mit|tee men
com|mit|tee
  woman
com|mit|tee
  women
com|mit|ter +s
com|mix
com|mixes
com|mixed
com|mix|ing
com|mix|ture +s
Commo +s
com|mode +s
com|modi|fi|
          ca|tion
com|mod|ify
com|modi|fies
com|modi|fied
com|modi|fy|ing
com|modi|ous
com|modi|ous|ly
com|modi|ous|
          ness
com|mod|ity
com|mod|ities
com|mo|dore +s
Commodore-in-
  Chief
Commodores-in-
  Chief
com|mon
com|mons
com|mon|er
com|mon|est
com|mon|able
com|mon|age
com|mon|al|ity
com|mon|al|ities
com|mon|alty
com|mon|al|ties

com|mon|er +s
com|mon|hold
com|mon|hold|er
+s
com|mon law noun
common-law
  attributive
com|mon|ly
com|mon|ness
com|mon|place +s
com|mon|place
  book +s
com|mon|place|
          ness
com|mon room +s
Com|mons, the
  (House of
  Commons)
com|mons (daily
  fare; in 'short
  commons')
com|mon sense
com|mon|
      sen|sic|al
com|mon weal
com|mon|wealth
+s
com|mo|tion +s
com|mu|nal
com|mu|nal|
  isa|tion Br. (use
  communal-
  ization)
com|mu|nal|ise Br.
  (use
  communalize)
com|mu|nal|ises
com|mu|nal|ised
com|mu|nal|
          is|ing
com|mu|nal|ism
com|mu|nal|ist +s
com|mu|nal|is|tic
com|mu|nal|is|tic|
          al|ly
com|mu|nal|ity
com|mu|nal|ities
com|mu|nal|
          iza|tion
com|mu|nal|ize
com|mu|nal|izes
com|mu|nal|ized
com|mu|nal|
          iz|ing
com|mu|nal|ly
com|mu|nard +s
com|mune
com|munes
com|muned
com|mun|ing
com|mu|nic|
          abil|ity

com|mu|nic|able
com|mu|nic|ably
com|mu|ni|cant +s
com|mu|ni|cate
  com|mu|ni|cates
  com|mu|ni|cated
  com|mu|ni|
            cat|ing
com|mu|ni|ca|tion
  +s
com|mu|ni|
        ca|tion|al
com|mu|ni|ca|tion
  sat|el|lite +s
com|mu|ni|ca|tive
com|mu|ni|
        ca|tive|ly
com|mu|ni|ca|tor
  +s
com|mu|ni|ca|tory
Com|mu|nion
  (Eucharist)
com|mu|nion +s
  (sharing)
com|mu|ni|qué +s
com|mun|isa|tion
  Br. (use
  communization)
com|mun|ise *Br.*
  (use communize)
  com|mun|ises
  com|mun|ised
  com|mun|is|ing
Com|mun|ism
  (system; society)
com|mun|ism
  (political theory)
Com|mun|ism
  Peak (mountain,
  Tadjikistan)
Com|mun|ist +s
  (member of party)
com|mun|ist +s
  (supporter of
  social system)
com|mun|is|tic
com|mun|is|tic|
        al|ly
com|mu|ni|tar|ian
  +s
com|mu|nity
  com|mu|nities
com|mun|iza|tion
com|mun|ize
  com|mun|izes
  com|mun|ized
  com|mun|iz|ing
com|mut|abil|ity
com|mut|able
com|mu|tate
  com|mu|tates

com|mu|tate
  (*cont.*)
  com|mu|tated
  com|mu|tat|ing
com|mu|ta|tion +s
com|mu|ta|tive
com|mu|ta|tor +s
com|mute
  com|mutes
  com|muted
  com|mut|ing
com|muter +s
Como, Lake (in
  Italy)
Como|doro
  Riva|davia (port,
  Argentina)
Com|orin, Cape (in
  India)
Com|oros (islands,
  Indian Ocean)
co|mose
comp +s +ed +ing
com|pact +s +ed
  +ing
com|pact disc +s
com|pact disk +s
  (use compact
  disc)
com|pac|tion
com|pact|ly
com|pact|ness
com|pact|or +s
com|padre +s
com|pa|ges
  plural com|pa|ges
com|pand +s +ed
  +ing
com|pand|er +s
com|pand|or +s
  (use compander)
com|pan|ion +s
com|pan|ion|able
com|pan|ion|able|
        ness
com|pan|ion|ably
com|pan|ion|ate
com|pan|ion hatch
  com|pan|ion
  hatches
com|pan|ion
  hatch|way +s
companion-in-
  arms
  companions-in-
  arms
com|pan|ion|ship
com|pan|ion|way
  +s
com|pany
  com|panies
com|par|abil|ity

com|par|able
com|par|able|ness
com|par|ably
com|para|tist +s
com|para|tive +s
com|para|tive|ly
com|para|tor +s
com|pare
  com|pares
  com|pared
  com|par|ing
  (liken. △ compère)
com|pari|son +s
com|part|ment +s
  +ed +ing
com|part|men|tal
com|part|men|tal|
  isa|tion *Br.* (use
  compartmental-
  ization)
com|part|men|tal|
  ise *Br.* (use
  compartmental-
  ize)
com|part|men|tal|
        ises
com|part|men|tal|
        ised
com|part|men|tal|
        is|ing
com|part|men|tal|
        iza|tion
com|part|men|tal|
        ize
com|part|men|tal|
        izes
com|part|men|tal|
        ized
com|part|men|tal|
        iz|ing
com|part|
      men|tal|ly
com|part|men|
      ta|tion
com|pass
  com|passes
  com|passed
  com|pass|ing
com|pass|able
com|pas|sion
com|pas|sion|ate
com|pas|sion|
      ate|ly
com|pati|bil|ity
  com|pati|bil|ities
com|pat|ible +s
com|pat|ibly
com|pat|riot +s
com|pat|ri|ot|ic
com|peer +s
com|pel
  com|pels

com|pel (*cont.*)
  com|pelled
  com|pel|ling
com|pel|lable
com|pel|ling|ly
com|pen|di|ous
com|pen|di|ous|ly
com|pen|dium
  com|pen|diums *or*
  com|pen|dia
com|pen|sate
  com|pen|sates
  com|pen|sated
  com|pen|sat|ing
com|pen|sa|tion
  +s
com|pen|sa|tion|al
com|pen|sa|tive
com|pen|sa|tor +s
com|pen|sa|tory
com|père
  com|pères
  com|pèred
  com|pèr|ing
  (MC. △ compare)
com|pete
  com|petes
  com|peted
  com|pet|ing
com|pe|tence +s
com|pe|tency
  com|pe|ten|cies
com|pe|tent
com|pe|tent|ly
com|pe|ti|tion +s
com|peti|tive
com|peti|tive|ly
com|peti|tive|ness
com|peti|tor +s
com|pil|ation +s
com|pile
  com|piles
  com|piled
  com|pil|ing
com|piler +s
com|pla|cence (self-
  satisfaction.
  △ complaisance)
com|pla|cency
com|pla|cent (self-
  satisfied.
  △ complaisant)
com|pla|cent|ly
com|plain +s +ed
  +ing
com|plain|ant +s
com|plain|er +s
com|plain|ing|ly
com|plaint +s
com|plai|sance
  (acquiescence.
  △ complacence)

com|plai|sant
(acquiescent.
△ complacent)
com|pleat (*archaic*
= complete)
com|ple|ment+s
+ed +ing
(something that
completes; full
number of people;
Grammar;
Biochemistry;
Mathematics;
Geometry; go well
with.
△ compliment)
com|ple|men|tal
com|ple|
men|tar|ily (in a
complementary
way. △ com-
plimentarily)
com|ple|men|tari|
ness
com|ple|
men|tar|ity
com|ple|
men|tar|ities
com|ple|men|tary
(that
complements;
Geometry. △ com-
plimentary)
com|plete
com|pletes
com|pleted
com|plet|ing
com|plete|ly
com|plete|ness
com|ple|tion+s
com|plet|ist+s
com|plex
com|plexes
com|plex|ation
com|plex|ion+s
com|plex|ioned
com|plex|ion|less
com|plex|ity
com|plex|ities
com|plex|ly
com|pli|ance
com|pli|ancy
com|pli|ant
com|pli|ant|ly
com|pli|cacy
com|pli|cacies
com|pli|cate
com|pli|cates
com|pli|cated
com|pli|cat|ing
com|pli|cated|ly
com|pli|cated|ness

com|pli|ca|tion+s
com|pli|cit
com|pli|city
com|pli|ment+s
+ed +ing (praise;
greetings.
△ complement)
com|pli|
men|tar|ily (in a
complimentary
way. △ com-
plementarily)
com|pli|men|tary
com|pli|
men|tar|ies
(expressing praise;
free. △ com-
plementary)
com|pli|ments slip
+s
com|pline+s
com|ply
com|plies
com|plied
com|ply|ing
compo+s
com|pon|ent+s
com|pon|en|tial
com|port+s +ed
+ing
com|port|ment
com|pos
com|pose
com|poses
com|posed
com|pos|ing
com|posed|ly
com|poser+s
com|pos|ite
com|pos|ites
com|pos|ited
com|pos|it|ing
com|pos|ite|ly
com|pos|ite|ness
com|pos|ition+s
com|pos|ition|al
com|pos|ition|
al|ly
com|posi|tor+s
com|pos men|tis
com|pos|sible
com|post+s +ed
+ing
com|pound|able
com|pound|er+s
com|pra|dor+s
com|pra|dore+s
(use comprador)

com|pre|hend+s
+ed +ing
com|pre|hen|
si|bil|ity
com|pre|hen|sible
com|pre|hen|sibly
com|pre|hen|sion
+s
com|pre|hen|sive
+s
com|pre|hen|
sive|ly
com|pre|hen|sive|
ness
com|press
com|presses
com|pressed
com|press|ing
com|press|ibil|ity
com|pres|sible
com|pres|sion+s
com|pres|sive
com|pres|sor+s
com|pris|able
com|prise
com|prises
com|prised
com|pris|ing
com|prom|ise
com|prom|ises
com|prom|ised
com|prom|is|ing
com|prom|iser+s
com|prom|
is|ing|ly
compte rendu
comptes rendus
Comp|tom|eter+s
Propr.
Comp|ton, Ar|thur
Holly (American
physicist)
Compton-Burnett,
Ivy (English
novelist)
comp|trol|ler+s
com|pul|sion+s
com|pul|sive
com|pul|sive|ly
com|pul|sive|ness
com|pul|sor|ily
com|pul|sori|ness
com|pul|sory
com|punc|tion+s
com|punc|tious
com|punc|tious|ly
com|pur|ga|tion
+s
com|pur|ga|tor+s
com|pur|ga|tory
com|put|abil|ity
com|put|able
com|put|ably

com|pu|ta|tion+s
com|pu|ta|tion|al
com|pu|ta|tion|
al|ly
com|pute
com|putes
com|puted
com|put|ing
com|puter+s
computer-aided
computer-
assist|ed
com|puter|ate
computer-based
computer-
controlled
computer-
generated
com|pu|ter|
isa|tion *Br.* (use
computerization)
com|pu|ter|ise *Br.*
(use
computerize)
com|pu|ter|ises
com|pu|ter|ised
com|pu|ter|is|ing
com|pu|ter|
iza|tion
com|pu|ter|ize
com|pu|ter|izes
com|pu|ter|ized
com|pu|ter|iz|ing
computer-literate
com|rade+s
comrade-in-arms
comrades-in-
arms
com|rade|ly
com|rade|ship
Com|sat+s
Comte, Au|guste
(French
philosopher)
Comt|ism
Comt|ist+s
con
cons
conned
con|ning
(trick; against; a
convict; to study)
con *Br.*
cons
conned
con|ning
(steer ship. *Am.*
conn)
con|acre
Con|akry (capital
of Guinea)
con amore

Conan
Conan Doyle,
  Ar|thur (Scottish
  novelist)
con|ation +s
cona|tive
con brio
con|cat|en|ate
  con|cat|en|ates
  con|cat|en|ated
  con|cat|en|at|ing
con|cat|en|ation
  +s
con|cave
con|cave|ly
con|cav|ity
  con|cav|ities
con|ceal +s +ed
  +ing
con|ceal|er +s
con|ceal|ment +s
con|cede
  con|cedes
  con|ceded
  con|ced|ing
con|ceder +s
con|ceit +s
con|ceit|ed
con|ceit|ed|ly
con|ceit|ed|ness
con|ceiv|abil|ity
con|ceiv|able
con|ceiv|ably
con|ceive
  con|ceives
  con|ceived
  con|ceiv|ing
con|cele|brant +s
con|cele|brate
  con|cele|brates
  con|cele|brated
  con|cele|brat|ing
con|cele|bra|tion
  +s
con|cen|ter Am. +s
  +ed +ing (Br.
  concentre)
con|cen|trate
  con|cen|trates
  con|cen|trated
  con|cen|trat|ing
con|cen|trated|ly
con|cen|tra|tion +s
con|cen|tra|tion
  camp +s
con|cen|tra|tive
con|cen|tra|tor +s
con|centre Br.
  con|centres
  con|centred
  con|cen|tring
  (Am. concenter)

con|cen|tric
con|cen|tric|al|ly
con|cen|tri|city
Con|cep|ción (city,
  Chile)
con|cept +s
con|cep|tion +s
con|cep|tion|al
con|cep|tion|al|ly
con|cep|tive
con|cep|tual
con|cep|tu|al|
  isa|tion Br. +s
  (use conceptual-
  ization)
con|cep|tu|al|ise
  Br. (use
  conceptualize)
  con|cep|tu|al|ises
  con|cep|tu|al|ised
  con|cep|tu|al|
    is|ing
con|cep|tu|al|ism
con|cep|tu|al|ist
  +s
con|cep|tu|al|
    iza|tion +s
con|cep|tu|al|ize
  con|cep|tu|al|izes
  con|cep|tu|al|ized
  con|cep|tu|al|
    iz|ing
con|cep|tu|al|ly
con|cep|tus
  con|cep|tuses
con|cern +s +ed
  +ing
con|cern|ed|ly
con|cern|ed|ness
con|cern|ing
con|cern|ment +s
con|cert +s +ed
  +ing
con|cer|tante
  con|cer|tanti
concert-goer +s
concert hall +s
con|cer|tina
  con|cer|tinas
  con|cer|tinaed
  con|cer|tina|ing
con|cer|tino +s
con|cert mas|ter
  +s
con|certo
  con|cer|tos or
  con|certi
con|certo grosso
  con|certi grossi
con|ces|sion +s
con|ces|sion|aire
  +s

con|ces|sion|ary
con|ces|sive +s
conch
  conchs or
  conches
  (shell; domed
  roof. △ conk)
con|cha
  conchae
  (hollow of ear.
  △ conker,
  conquer)
con|chie +s
con|choid|al
con|cho|logic|al
con|cho|logic|al|ly
conch|olo|gist +s
conch|ology
con|chy (use
  conchie)
  con|chies
con|ci|erge +s
con|cili|ar
con|cili|ate
  con|cili|ates
  con|cili|ated
  con|cili|at|ing
con|cili|ation +s
con|cilia|tive
con|cili|ator +s
con|cili|atori|ness
con|cili|atory
con|cin|nity
con|cin|nous
con|cise
con|cise|ly
con|cise|ness
con|ci|sion +s
con|clave +s
con|clude
  con|cludes
  con|cluded
  con|clud|ing
con|clu|sion +s
con|clu|sive
con|clu|sive|ly
con|clu|sive|ness
con|coct +s +ed
  +ing
con|coct|er +s
con|coc|tion +s
con|coct|or +s
  (use concocter)
con|comi|tance
con|comi|tancy
con|comi|tant +s
con|comi|tant|ly
Con|cord (towns,
  USA.
  △ Concorde)
con|cord +s
  (agreement)

con|cord|ance
  con|cord|ances
  con|cord|anced
  con|cord|an|cing
con|cord|ant +s
con|cord|ant|ly
con|cordat +s
Con|corde +s
  (aircraft.
  △ Concord)
con|course +s
con|cres|cence
con|cres|cent
con|crete
  con|cretes
  con|creted
  con|cret|ing
con|crete|ly
con|crete mixer
  +s
con|crete|ness
con|cre|tion +s
con|cre|tion|ary
con|cre|tisa|tion
  Br. +s (use
  concretization)
con|cret|ise Br.
  (use concretize)
  con|cret|ises
  con|cret|ised
  con|cret|is|ing
con|cre|tiza|tion
  +s
concret|ize
  con|cret|izes
  con|cret|ized
  con|cret|iz|ing
con|cu|bin|age
con|cu|bin|ary
con|cu|bine +s
con|cu|pis|cence
con|cu|pis|cent
con|cur
  con|curs
  con|curred
  con|cur|ring
con|cur|rence +s
con|cur|rent
con|cur|rent|ly
con|cuss
  con|cusses
  con|cussed
  con|cuss|ing
con|cus|sion +s
con|demn +s +ed
  +ing
con|dem|nable
con|dem|na|tion
  +s
con|dem|na|tory
con|dens|able
con|den|sate +s

con|den|sa|tion +s
con|den|sa|tion
   trail
con|dense
  con|denses
  con|densed
  con|dens|ing
con|dens|er +s
con|dens|ery
  con|dens|er|ies
con|des|cend +s
  +ed +ing
con|des|cend|
        ing|ly
con|des|cen|sion
  +s
con|dign
con|dign|ly
con|di|ment +s
con|di|tion +s +ed
  +ing
con|di|tion|al +s
con|di|tion|al|ity
con|di|tion|al|ly
con|di|tion|er +s
condo +s
con|do|la|tory
con|dole
  con|doles
  con|doled
  con|dol|ing
con|dol|ence +s
con|dom +s
con|do|min|ium +s
con|don|ation
con|done
  con|dones
  con|doned
  con|don|ing
con|doner +s
con|dor +s
con|dot|tiere
  con|dot|tieri
con|duce
  con|duces
  con|duced
  con|du|cing
con|du|cive
con|du|cive|ness
con|duct +s +ed
  +ing
con|duct|ance +s
con|ducti|bil|ity
con|duct|ible
con|duc|tion
con|duct|ive
con|duct|ive|ly
con|duct|iv|ity
  con|duct|iv|ities
con|duct|or +s
con|duct|or|ship
  +s

con|duc|tress
  con|duc|tresses
con|duc|tus
  con|ducti
con|duit +s
con|dylar
con|dyle +s
con|dyl|oid
cone
  cones
  coned
  con|ing
cone-shell +s
coney +s (rabbit;
  use cony)
Coney Is|land
  (resort, USA)
con|fab
  con|fabs
  con|fabbed
  con|fab|bing
con|fabu|late
  con|fabu|lates
  con|fabu|lated
  con|fabu|lat|ing
con|fabu|la|tion +s
con|fabu|la|tory
con|fect +s +ed
  +ing
con|fec|tion +s
con|fec|tion|ary
  (*adjective.*
   △ confectionery)
con|fec|tion|er +s
con|fec|tion|er's
  cus|tard
con|fec|tion|er's
  sugar
con|fec|tion|ery
  con|fec|tion|er|ies
  (*noun.*
   △ confectionary)
Con|fed|er|acy,
  the *US History*
con|fed|er|acy
  con|fed|er|acies
Con|fed|er|ate +s
  US History
con|fed|er|ate
  con|fed|er|ates
  con|fed|er|ated
  con|fed|er|at|ing
con|fed|er|ation
  +s
con|fer
  con|fers
  con|ferred
  con|fer|ring
con|fer|ee +s
con|fer|ence +s
con|fer|en|cing
con|fer|en|tial

con|fer|ment +s
con|fer|rable
con|fer|ral +s
con|fess
  con|fesses
  con|fessed
  con|fess|ing
con|fes|sant +s
con|fess|ed|ly
con|fes|sion +s
con|fes|sion|al +s
con|fes|sion|ary
con|fes|sor +s
con|fetti
con|fi|dant +s *male*
  (trusted person.
   △ confident)
con|fi|dante +s
  female (trusted
  person.
   △ confident)
con|fide
  con|fides
  con|fided
  con|fid|ing
con|fi|dence +s
con|fi|dent (self-
  assured.
   △ confidant,
  confidante)
con|fi|den|tial
con|fi|den|ti|al|ity
con|fi|den|ti|al|
        ities
con|fi|den|tial|ly
con|fi|dent|ly
con|fid|ing|ly
con|fig|ur|ation +s
con|fig|ur|ation|al
con|fig|ure
  con|fig|ures
  con|fig|ured
  con|fig|ur|ing
con|fine
  con|fines
  con|fined
  con|fin|ing
con|fine|ment +s
con|firm +s +ed
  +ing
con|firm|and +s
con|firm|ation +s
  (verification;
  religious rite.
   △ conformation)
con|firma|tive
con|firma|tory
con|fis|cable
con|fis|cate
  con|fis|cates
  con|fis|cated
  con|fis|cat|ing

con|fis|ca|tion +s
con|fis|ca|tor +s
con|fis|ca|tory
con|flag|ra|tion +s
con|flate
  con|flates
  con|flated
  con|flat|ing
con|fla|tion +s
con|flict +s +ed
  +ing
con|flic|tion
con|flict|ual
con|flu|ence +s
con|flu|ent
con|flux
  con|fluxes
con|form +s +ed
  +ing
con|form|abil|ity
con|form|able
con|form|ably
con|form|al
con|form|al|ly
con|form|ance
con|form|ation +s
  (shape;
  adjustment.
   △ confirmation)
con|form|er +s
con|form|ism
con|form|ist +s
con|form|ity
con|found +s +ed
  +ing
con|found|ed|ly
con|fra|tern|ity
  con|fra|tern|ities
con|frère +s
con|front +s +ed
  +ing
con|fron|ta|tion +s
con|fron|ta|tion|al
Con|fu|cian +s
Con|fu|cian|ism
Con|fu|cian|ist +s
Con|fu|cius
  (Chinese
  philosopher)
con|fus|abil|ity
con|fus|able +s
con|fuse
  con|fuses
  con|fused
  con|fus|ing
con|fused|ly
con|fus|ing|ly
con|fu|sion +s
con|fut|ation +s
con|fute
  con|futes

con|fute (*cont.*)
  con|futed
  con|fut|ing
conga +s +ed +ing
  (dance. ⚠ conger)
congé +s
con|geal +s +ed
  +ing
con|geal|able
con|geal|ment
con|gel|ation +s
con|gener +s
con|gen|eric
con|gen|er|ous
con|gen|ial
con|geni|al|ity
con|geni|al|ly
con|geni|tal
con|geni|tal|ly
con|ger +s (eel.
  ⚠ conga)
con|ger|ies
  plural con|ger|ies
con|gest +s +ed
  +ing
con|ges|tion +s
con|gest|ive
con|glom|er|ate
  con|glom|er|ates
  con|glom|er|ated
  con|glom|er|
    at|ing
con|glom|er|ation
  +s
Congo (river and
  country, Africa.
  ⚠ Kongo)
Con|go|lese
  plural Con|go|lese
con|gou
con|grats (= con-
  gratulations)
con|gratu|lant +s
con|gratu|late
  con|gratu|lates
  con|gratu|lated
  con|gratu|lat|ing
con|gratu|la|tion
  +s
con|gratu|la|tive
con|gratu|la|tor +s
con|gratu|la|tory
con|gre|gant +s
con|gre|gate
  con|gre|gates
  con|gre|gated
  con|gre|gat|ing
con|gre|ga|tion +s
Con|gre|ga|tion|al
  (of Congregational-
  ism)

con|gre|ga|tion|al
  (generally)
Con|gre|ga|tion|al|
  ise *Br.* (use
  Congregational-
  ize)
Con|gre|ga|tion|al|
  ises
Con|gre|ga|tion|al|
  ised
Con|gre|ga|tion|al|
  is|ing
Con|gre|ga|tion|al|
  ism
Con|gre|ga|tion|al|
  ist +s
Con|gre|ga|tion|al|
  ize
Con|gre|ga|tion|al|
  izes
Con|gre|ga|tion|al|
  ized
Con|gre|ga|tion|al|
  iz|ing
Con|gress
  (legislative body)
con|gress
  con|gresses
  (meeting)
con|gres|sion|al
con|gress|man
  con|gress|men
con|gress|woman
  con|gress|women
Con|greve,
  Wil|liam (English
  dramatist)
con|gru|ence +s
con|gru|ency
  con|gru|en|cies
con|gru|ent
con|gru|ent|ly
con|gru|ity
  con|gru|ities
con|gru|ous
con|gru|ous|ly
conic +s
con|ic|al
con|ic|al|ly
con|ics
co|nid|ium
  co|nidia
con|ifer +s
con|ifer|ous
coni|form
coni|ine
con|jec|tur|able
con|jec|tur|ably
con|jec|tural
con|jec|tur|al|ly
con|jec|ture
  con|jec|tures

con|jec|ture (*cont.*)
  con|jec|tured
  con|jec|tur|ing
con|join +s +ed
  +ing
con|joint
con|joint|ly
con|ju|gal +s
con|ju|gal|ity
con|ju|gal|ly
con|ju|gate
  con|ju|gates
  con|ju|gated
  con|ju|gat|ing
con|ju|gate|ly
con|ju|ga|tion +s
con|ju|ga|tion|al
con|junct +s
con|junc|tion +s
con|junc|tion|al
con|junc|tion|al|ly
con|junc|tiva +s
con|junc|tival
con|junct|ive +s
con|junct|ive|ly
con|junc|tiv|itis
con|junc|ture +s
con|jur|ation +s
con|jure
  con|jures
  con|jured
  con|jur|ing
con|juror +s
conk +s +ed +ing
  (nose; head;
  punch; in 'conk
  out'. ⚠ conch)
conk|er +s (fruit of
  horse chestnut.
  ⚠ concha,
  conquer)
con|man
  con|men
con moto
conn *Am.*
  conns
  conned
  con|ning
  (*Br.* con. steer
  ship. ⚠ con)
Con|nacht
  (province,
  Republic of
  Ireland)
con|nate
con|nat|ural
con|nat|ural|ly
Con|naught (use
  Connacht)
con|nect +s +ed
  +ing
con|nect|able

con|nect|ed|ly
con|nect|ed|ness
con|nect|er +s
  (person.
  ⚠ connector)
con|nect|ible (use
  connectable)
Con|necti|cut
  (state, USA)
con|nect|ing rod
  +s
con|nec|tion +s
con|nec|tion|al
con|nec|tion|ism
con|nec|tion|ist +s
con|nect|ive +s
con|nect|iv|ity
con|nect|or +s
  (device; thing that
  connects.
  ⚠ connecter)
Con|ne|mara
  (region, Republic
  of Ireland)
Con|nery, Sean
  (Scottish actor)
con|nex|ion *Br.* +s
  (use connection)
Con|nie
con|ning tower +s
con|niv|ance
con|nive
  con|nives
  con|nived
  con|niv|ing
con|niver +s
con|nois|seur +s
con|nois|seur|ship
Con|nolly,
  Maur|een ('Little
  Mo', American
  tennis player)
Con|nors, Jimmy
  (American tennis
  player)
con|no|ta|tion +s
con|no|ta|tive
con|note
  con|notes
  con|noted
  con|not|ing
con|nu|bial +s
con|nu|bi|al|ity
con|nu|bi|al|ly
con|oid +s
con|oid|al
con|quer +s +ed
  +ing (defeat,
  overcome.
  ⚠ concha,
  conker)
con|quer|able

con|queror+s
con|quest+s
con|quis|ta|dor
  con|quis|ta|dores
  or
  con|quis|ta|dors
Con|rad(name)
Con|rad, Jo|seph
  (Polish-born
  British novelist)
Con|ran, Ter|ence
  (English designer
  and businessman)
con-rod+s
con|san|guin|eous
con|san|guin|ity
con|science+s
con|science|less
conscience-
  stricken
conscience-struck
con|scien|tious
con|scien|tious|ly
con|scien|tious|
         ness
con|scious
con|scious|ly
con|scious|ness
consciousness-
  raising
con|scribe
  con|scribes
  con|scribed
  con|scrib|ing
con|script+s +ed
  +ing
con|scrip|tion
con|se|crate
  con|se|crates
  con|se|crated
  con|se|crat|ing
con|se|cra|tion+s
con|se|cra|tor+s
con|se|cra|tory
con|se|cu|tion+s
con|secu|tive
con|secu|tive|ly
con|secu|tive|ness
con|sen|sual
con|sen|su|al|ly
con|sen|sus
con|sent+s +ed
  +ing
con|sent|an|eous
con|sen|tient
con|se|quence+s
con|se|quent+s
con|se|quen|tial
con|se|quen|tial|
        ism
con|se|quen|tial|
        ist+s

con|se|quen|ti|al|
        ity
con|se|quen|tial|ly
con|se|quent|ly
con|ser|vancy
con|ser|van|cies
con|ser|va|tion+s
con|ser|va|tion|al
con|ser|va|tion|ist
  +s
Con|ser|va|tism
  Politics
con|ser|va|tism
Con|ser|va|tive+s
  Politics
con|ser|va|tive+s
con|ser|va|tive|ly
con|ser|va|tive|
        ness
con|ser|va|toire+s
con|ser|va|tor+s
con|ser|va|tor|ium
  +s
con|ser|va|tory
con|ser|va|tor|ies
con|serve
  con|serves
  con|served
  con|serv|ing
con|sider+s +ed
  +ing
con|sid|er|able
con|sid|er|ably
con|sid|er|ate
con|sid|er|ate|ly
con|sid|er|ation+s
con|sign+s +ed
  +ing
con|sign|ee+s
con|sign|ment+s
con|signor+s
con|sist+s +ed
  +ing
con|sist|ence+s
con|sist|ency
con|sist|en|cies
con|sist|ent
con|sist|ent|ly
con|sis|tor|ial
con|sis|tory
con|sis|tor|ies
con|so|ci|ate
  con|so|ci|ates
  con|so|ci|ated
  con|so|ci|at|ing
con|so|ci|ation+s
con|sol|able
con|sola|tion+s
con|sola|tory
con|sole
  con|soles
  con|soled

con|sole(*cont.*)
  con|sol|ing
  (comfort;
  instrument panel;
  dresser)
con|soler+s
con|soli|date
  con|soli|dates
  con|soli|dated
  con|soli|dat|ing
con|soli|da|tion+s
con|soli|da|tor+s
con|soli|da|tory
con|sol|ing|ly
con|sols
con|sommé+s
con|son|ance
con|son|ant+s
con|son|ant|al
con|son|ant|ly
con sor|dino
con|sort+s +ed
  +ing
con|sor|tium
  con|sor|tia *or*
  con|sor|tiums
con|spe|cif|ic
con|spec|tus
  con|spec|tuses
con|spicu|ous
con|spicu|ous|ly
con|spicu|ous|
        ness
con|spir|acy
  con|spir|acies
con|spir|ator+s
con|spira|tor|ial
con|spira|tori|al|ly
con|spire
  con|spires
  con|spired
  con|spir|ing
Con|stable, John
  (English painter)
con|stable+s
con|stabu|lary
  con|stabu|lar|ies
Con|stance(name)
Con|stance, Lake
  (in SE Germany)
con|stancy
  con|stan|cies
Con|stant(name)
con|stant+s
  (unchanging; thing
  that never varies)
Con|stanţa(port,
  Romania)
con|stantan
Con|stan|tine
  (Roman emperor)

Con|stan|tine(city,
  Algeria)
Con|stan|tin|ople
  (former name of
  Istanbul)
con|stant|ly
Con|stanza(use
  Constanţa)
con|sta|ta|tion+s
con|stel|late
  con|stel|lates
  con|stel|lated
  con|stel|lat|ing
con|stel|la|tion+s
con|ster|nate
  con|ster|nates
  con|ster|nated
  con|ster|nat|ing
con|ster|na|tion
con|sti|pate
  con|sti|pates
  con|sti|pated
  con|sti|pat|ing
con|sti|pa|tion
con|stitu|ency
  con|stitu|en|cies
con|stitu|ent+s
con|sti|tute
  con|sti|tutes
  con|sti|tuted
  con|sti|tut|ing
con|sti|tu|tion+s
con|sti|tu|tion|al
  +s
con|sti|tu|tion|al|
  ise*Br.* (use
  constitutionalize)
con|sti|tu|tion|al|
        ises
con|sti|tu|tion|al|
        ised
con|sti|tu|tion|al|
        is|ing
con|sti|tu|tion|al|
        ism
con|sti|tu|tion|al|
        ist+s
con|sti|tu|tion|
        al|ity
con|sti|tu|tion|al|
        ize
con|sti|tu|tion|al|
        izes
con|sti|tu|tion|al|
        ized
con|sti|tu|tion|al|
        iz|ing
con|sti|tu|tion|
        al|ly
con|sti|tu|tive
con|sti|tu|tive|ly
con|sti|tu|tor+s

con|strain +s +ed
+ing
con|strain|ed|ly
con|straint +s
con|strict +s +ed
+ing
con|stric|tion +s
con|strict|ive
con|strict|or +s
con|stru|able
con|stru|al +s
con|struct +s +ed
+ing
con|struc|tion +s
con|struc|tion|al
con|struc|tion|
al|ly
con|struc|tion|ism
con|struc|tion|ist
+s
con|struct|ive
con|struct|ive|ly
con|struct|ive|
ness
con|struct|iv|ism
con|struct|iv|ist +s
con|struct|or +s
con|strue
con|strues
con|strued
con|stru|ing
con|sub|stan|tial
con|sub|stan|ti|al|
ity
con|sub|stan|ti|ate
con|sub|stan|ti|
ates
con|sub|stan|ti|
ated
con|sub|stan|ti|
at|ing
con|sub|stan|ti|
ation
con|sue|tude
con|sue|tud|in|ary
con|sul +s
con|su|lar
con|sul|ate +s
con|sul|ship +s
con|sult +s +ed
+ing
con|sult|ancy
con|sult|an|cies
con|sult|ant +s
con|sult|ation +s
con|sulta|tive
con|sult|ee +s
con|sult|ing room
+s
con|sum|able +s
con|sume
con|sumes

con|sume (cont.)
con|sumed
con|sum|ing
con|sumer +s
con|sumer
dur|able +s
con|sumer|ism
con|sumer|ist +s
con|sum|ing|ly
con|sum|mate
con|sum|mates
con|sum|mated
con|sum|mat|ing
con|sum|mate|ly
con|sum|ma|tion
+s
con|sum|ma|tive
con|sum|ma|tor +s
con|sump|tion +s
con|sump|tive +s
con|sump|tive|ly
con|tact +s +ed
+ing
con|tact|able
con|tact lens
con|tact lenses
con|ta|gion +s
con|ta|gious
con|ta|gious|ly
con|ta|gious|ness
con|tain +s +ed
+ing
con|tain|able
con|tain|er +s
container-grown
con|tain|er|
isa|tion Br. (use
containerization)
con|tain|er|ise Br.
(use containerize)
con|tain|er|ises
con|tain|er|ised
con|tain|er|is|ing
con|tain|er|
iza|tion
con|tain|er|ize
con|tain|er|izes
con|tain|er|ized
con|tain|er|iz|ing
con|tain|ment
con|tam|in|ant +s
con|tam|in|ate
con|tam|in|ates
con|tam|in|ated
con|tam|in|at|ing
con|tam|in|ation
+s
con|tam|in|ator +s
con|tango +s
Conté (pencil etc.)
conte +s (story)

con|temn +s +ed
+ing
con|tem|ner +s
con|tem|plate
con|tem|plates
con|tem|plated
con|tem|plat|ing
con|tem|pla|tion
+s
con|tem|pla|tive
+s
con|tem|
pla|tive|ly
con|tem|pla|tor +s
con|tem|por
an|eity
con|tem|por
an|eous
con|tem|por
an|eous|ly
con|tem|por
an|eous|ness
con|tem|por|ar|ily
con|tem|por|ari
ness
con|tem|por|ary
con|
tem|por|ar|ies
con|tem|por|ise Br.
(use
contempórize)
con|tem|por|ises
con|tem|por|ised
con|tem|por|
is|ing
con|tem|por|ize
con|tem|por|izes
con|tem|por|ized
con|tem|por|
iz|ing
con|tempt +s
con|tempt|ibil|ity
con|tempt|ible
con|tempt|ibly
con|temp|tu|ous
con|temp|tu|
ous|ly
con|temp|tu|ous|
ness
con|tend +s +ed
+ing
con|tend|er +s
con|tent +s +ed
+ing
con|tent|ed|ly
con|tent|ed|ness
con|ten|tion +s
con|ten|tious
con|ten|tious|ly
con|ten|tious|ness
con|tent|ment
con|ter|min|ous

con|ter|min|ous|ly
con|tessa +s
con|test +s +ed
+ing
con|test|able
con|test|ant +s
con|test|ation
con|test|er +s
con|text +s
context-
depend|ent
context-specif|ic
con|text|ual
con|text|ual|
isa|tion Br. +s
(use contextual-
ization)
con|text|ual|ise Br.
(use
contextualize)
con|text|ual|ises
con|text|ual|ised
con|text|ual|
is|ing
con|text|ual|ism
con|text|ual|ist +s
con|text|ual|ity
con|text|ual|
iza|tion +s
con|text|ual|ize
con|text|ual|izes
con|text|ual|ized
con|text|ual|
iz|ing
con|text|ual|ly
con|tigu|ity
con|tigu|ous
con|tigu|ous|ly
con|tigu|ous|ness
con|tin|ence
Con|tin|ent
(European
mainland)
con|tin|ent +s
Con|tin|en|tal +s
(European)
con|tin|en|tal
con|tin|en|tal|ly
con|tin|ent|ly
con|tin|gency
con|tin|gen|cies
con|tin|gent +s
con|tin|gent|ly
con|tinu|able
con|tinu|al
con|tinu|al|ly
con|tinu|ance +s
con|tinu|ant +s
con|tinu|ation +s
con|tinu|ative
con|tinu|ator +s

con|tinue
  con|tinues
  con|tinued
  con|tinu|ing
con|tinu|er +s
con|tinu|ity
  con|tinu|ities
con|tinuo +s
con|tinu|ous
con|tinu|ous|ly
con|tinu|ous|ness
con|tinuum
  con|tinua
con|tort +s +ed
  +ing
con|tor|tion +s
con|tor|tion|ist +s
con|tour +s +ed
  +ing
con|tra +s
  (revolutionary)
con|*tra* preposition
con|tra|band
con|tra|band|ist
  +s
con|tra|bass
  con|tra|basses
con|tra|bas|soon
  +s
con|tra|cep|tion
con|tra|cep|tive +s
con|tract +s +ed
  +ing
con|tract|able (of a
  disease, able to be
  contracted.
  ⚠ contractible)
contracted-out
  adjective
con|tract|ible (able
  to be shrunk etc.
  ⚠ contractable)
con|tract|ile
con|tract|il|ity
con|trac|tion +s
con|tract|ive
con|tract|or +s
con|tract|ual
con|trac|tu|al|ly
con|tra|dict +s
  +ed +ing
con|tra|dict|able
con|tra|dic|tion +s
con|tra|dic|tious
con|tra|dict|or +s
con|tra|dic|tor|ily
con|tra|dict|ori|
            ness
con|tra|dict|ory
con|tra|
      dis|tinc|tion +s

con|tra|dis|tin|
            guish
con|tra|dis|tin|
            guishes
con|tra|dis|tin|
            guished
con|tra|
  dis|tin|guish|ing
con|tra|flow +s
con|trail +s
con|tra|indi|cate
  con|tra|indi|cates
  con|tra|indi|cated
  con|tra|indi|
            cat|ing
con|tra|indi|
      ca|tion +s
con|tralto +s
con|tra|pos|ition
  +s
con|tra|posi|tive
  +s
con|trap|tion +s
con|tra|pun|tal
con|tra|pun|tal|ly
con|tra|pun|tist +s
con|trar|iety
  con|trar|ieties
con|trar|ily
con|trari|ness
con|trari|wise
con|trary
  con|trar|ies
con|trast +s +ed
  +ing
con|trast|ing|ly
con|trast|ive +s
con|trasty
contra-
  suggest|ible
con|trate
con|tra|vene
  con|tra|venes
  con|tra|vened
  con|tra|ven|ing
con|tra|vener +s
con|tra|ven|tion
  +s
con|tre|temps
  plural
  con|tre|temps
con|trib|ute
  con|trib|utes
  con|trib|uted
  con|trib|ut|ing
con|tri|bu|tion +s
con|tribu|tive
con|tribu|tor +s
con|tribu|tory
con-trick +s
con|trite
con|trite|ly

con|tri|tion
con|triv|able
con|triv|ance +s
con|trive
  con|trives
  con|trived
  con|triv|ing
con|triver +s
con|trol
  con|trols
  con|trolled
  con|trol|ling
con|trol|labil|ity
con|trol|lable
con|trol|lably
con|trol|ler +s
con|trol|ler|ship
  +s
con|tro|ver|sial
con|tro|ver|sial|
            ism
con|tro|ver|sial|ist
  +s
con|tro|ver|sial|ly
con|tro|versy
  con|tro|ver|sies
con|tro|vert +s
  +ed +ing
con|tro|vert|ible
con|tu|ma|cious
con|tu|ma|cious|ly
con|tu|macy
con|tu|me|li|ous
con|tu|me|li|ous|ly
con|tumely
con|tuse
  con|tuses
  con|tused
  con|tus|ing
con|tu|sion +s
con|un|drum +s
con|ur|ba|tion +s
con|ure +s
con|va|lesce
  con|va|lesces
  con|va|lesced
  con|va|les|cing
con|va|les|cence
  +s
con|va|les|cent +s
con|vec|tion +s
con|vec|tion|al
con|vect|ive
con|vect|or +s
con|ven|able
con|*ven*|*ance* +s
con|vene
  con|venes
  con|vened
  con|ven|ing
con|vener +s
con|veni|ence +s

con|veni|ent
con|veni|ent|ly
con|venor +s (use
  convener)
con|vent +s
con|ven|ticle +s
con|ven|tion +s
con|ven|tion|al
con|ven|tion|al|ise
  Br. (use
  conventionalize)
  con|ven|tion|al|
            ises
  con|ven|tion|al|
            ised
  con|ven|tion|al|
            is|ing
con|ven|tion|al|
            ism
con|ven|tion|al|ist
  +s
con|ven|tion|al|ity
  con|ven|tion|
            al|ities
con|ven|tion|al|ize
  con|ven|tion|al|
            izes
  con|ven|tion|al|
            ized
  con|ven|tion|al|
            iz|ing
con|ven|tion|al|ly
con|ven|tion|eer
  +s
con|ven|tual +s
con|verge
  con|verges
  con|verged
  con|ver|ging
con|ver|gence +s
con|ver|gency
con|ver|gent
con|ver|sance
con|ver|sancy
con|ver|sant
con|ver|sa|tion +s
con|ver|sa|tion|al
con|ver|sa|tion|al|
            ist +s
con|ver|sa|tion|
            al|ly
con|ver|sa|tion|ist
  +s
conversation-
  stopper +s
con|*ver*|*saz*|*ione*
  con|*ver*|*saz*|*ioni* or
  con|*ver*|*saz*|*iones*
con|verse
  con|verses
  con|versed
  con|vers|ing

con|verse|ly
con|ver|ser +s
con|ver|sion +s
con|vert +s +ed +ing
con|vert|er +s
con|vert|ibil|ity
con|vert|ible +s
con|vert|ibly
con|ver|tor +s (use converter)
con|vex
con|vex|ity
  con|vex|ities
con|vex|ly
con|vey +s +ed +ing
con|vey|able
con|vey|ance +s
con|vey|an|cer +s
con|vey|an|cing
con|vey|er +s (use conveyor)
con|vey|or +s
con|vey|or belt +s
con|vict +s +ed +ing
con|vic|tion +s
con|vict|ive
con|vince
  con|vinces
  con|vinced
  con|vin|cing
con|vince|ment
con|vin|cer +s
con|vin|cible
con|vin|cibly
con|vin|cing|ly
con|viv|ial
con|vivi|al|ity
con|vivi|al|ly
con|vo|ca|tion +s
con|vo|ca|tion|al
con|voke
  con|vokes
  con|voked
  con|vok|ing
con|vo|luted
con|vo|luted|ly
con|vo|lu|tion +s
con|vo|lu|tion|al
con|volve
  con|volves
  con|volved
  con|volv|ing
con|vol|vu|lus
  con|vol|vu|luses
  or con|vol|vuli
con|voy +s +ed +ing
con|vul|sant +s

con|vulse
  con|vulses
  con|vulsed
  con|vuls|ing
con|vul|sion +s
con|vul|sion|ary
con|vul|sive
con|vul|sive|ly
cony
  conies
coo +s +ed +ing (sound of dove. △ coup)
co-occur
  co-occurs
  co-occurred
  co-occurring
co-occurrence +s
Cooder, Ry (American musician and composer)
cooee
  coo|ees
  coo|eed
  cooee|ing
cool|ing|ly
Cook, James (English explorer)
Cook, Thomas (English tourist agent)
Cook, Mount (in New Zealand)
cook +s +ed +ing
cook|abil|ity
cook|able
cook|book +s
cook-chill
Cooke, Wil|liam Fother|gill (English inventor)
cook|er +s
cook|ery
  cook|er|ies
cook|ery book +s
cook|house +s
cookie +s
cook|ing pot +s
Cook Is|lands (in SW Pacific)
cook|out +s
cook|shop +s
Cook|son, Cath|er|ine (English novelist)
Cook Strait (off New Zealand)
cook|ware
cool +s +ed +ing
coola|bah +s
cool|ant +s

cool bag +s
cool box
  cool boxes
cool|er +s
Cool|gar|die safe +s
cool-headed
cool-headed|ness
coo|li|bah +s (use coolabah)
Cool|idge, Cal|vin (American president)
coolie +s (labourer. △ coolly)
cooling-off noun and attributive
cool|ish
cool|ly (coldly. △ coolie)
cool|ness
coolth
cooly (use coolie)
coomb +s (valley. △ cwm, khoum)
coon +s (offensive when used of a person)
coon-can
coon|skin +s
coop +s +ed +ing (cage. △ coupe)
co-op +s (cooperative enterprise)
Coop|er, Gary (American actor. △ Cowper)
Coop|er, James Feni|more (American novelist. △ Cowper)
coop|er +s +ed +ing
coop|er|age
co|oper|ant
co|oper|ate
  co|oper|ates
  co|oper|ated
  co|oper|at|ing
co|oper|ation
co|opera|tive +s
co|opera|tive|ly
co|opera|tive|ness
co|oper|ator +s
co-opt +s +ed +ing
co-optation +s
co-option +s
co-optive
co|ord|in|ate
  co|ord|in|ates

co|ord|in|ate (cont.)
  co|ord|in|ated
  co|ord|in|at|ing
co|ord|in|ate|ly
co|ord|in|ation +s
co|ord|ina|tive
co|ord|in|ator +s
coot +s
cootie +s
co-own +s +ed +ing
co-owner +s
co-ownership
cop
  cops
  copped
  cop|ping (police officer; catch; receive; spindle of thread; also in phrases. △ Kop, kop)
Copa|ca|bana Beach (resort, Brazil)
copa|cet|ic
co|paiba
copal
Copán (ancient Mayan city)
co-partner +s
co-partner|ship
cope
  copes
  coped
  cop|ing
co|peck +s
Cop|en|hagen (capital of Denmark)
co|pe|pod +s
coper +s
Co|per|ni|can +s
Co|per|ni|cus, Nico|laus (Polish astronomer)
cope|stone +s
copi|able
copier +s
co-pilot +s
cop|ing +s
cop|ing saw +s
cop|ing stone +s
co|pi|ous
co|pi|ous|ly
co|pi|ous|ness
co|pita +s
co|pla|nar
co|pla|nar|ity

Cop|land, Aaron (American composer)
Cop|ley, John Single|ton (American painter)
co|poly|mer +s
co|poly|mer| isa|tion Br. (use copolymerization)
co|poly|mer|ise Br. (use copolymerize)
co|poly|mer|ises
co|poly|mer|ised
co|poly|mer|is|ing
co|poly|mer| iza|tion
co|poly|mer|ize
co|poly|mer|izes
co|poly|mer|ized
co|poly|mer| iz|ing
cop-out +s noun
cop|per +s
Cop|per Age
cop|peras
Cop|per|belt (province, Zambia)
cop|per belt (area of central Africa)
copper-bit +s
copper-bottomed
cop|per|head +s
cop|per|plate +s
cop|per|smith +s
cop|pery
cop|pice
cop|pices
cop|piced
cop|picing
Cop|pola, Fran|cis Ford (American film director and writer)
copra
co-precipi|ta|tion
co-present +s +ed +ing
co-present|er +s
co|pro|ces|sor +s
co-produce
co-produces
co-produced
co-producing
co-producer +s
co-produc|tion +s
cop|ro|lite
cop|rol|ogy

cop|ropha|gous
copro|philia
copro|phil|iac +s
cop|rosma +s
copse
copses
copsed
cops|ing
copse|wood
cop shop +s
copsy
Copt +s
Cop|tic +s
cop|ula +s noun
copu|lar adjective
copu|late
copu|lates
copu|lated
copu|lat|ing
copu|la|tion +s
copu|la|tive +s
copu|la|tive|ly
copu|la|tory
copy
cop|ies
cop|ied
copy|ing (imitate; imitation; single specimen; matter for printing; etc. △ kopi, koppie)
copy|book +s
copy|cat +s
copy|desk +s
copy-edit +s +ed +ing
copy ed|itor +s
copy|hold +s
copy|hold|er +s
copy|ist +s
copy|read
copy|reads
copy|read
copy|read|ing
copy|read|er +s
copy|right +s +ed +ing (legal right. △ copywriting)
copy-typist +s
copy|writer +s
copy|writ|ing (writing. △ copyrighting)
coq au vin
co|quet|ry
co|quet|ries
co|quette
co|quettes
co|quet|ted
co|quet|ting
co|quet|tish

co|quet|tish|ly
co|quet|tish|ness
co|quina
co|quito +s
cor (interjection. △ caw, core, corps)
Cora
cor|acle +s
cor|acoid +s
Coral (name)
coral +s (in sea)
Cora|lie
cor|all|ine +s
cor|all|ite +s
cor|all|oid +s
coral-root +s (plant)
Coral Sea (part of SW Pacific)
coral snake +s
coram pop|ulo
cor an|glais
cors an|glais
cor|bel
cor|bels
cor|belled Br.
cor|beled Am.
cor|bel|ling Br.
cor|bel|ing Am.
corbel-table +s
cor|bie +s
corbie-step +s
Corby (town, England)
Cor|co|vado (mountain, Brazil)
Cor|cyra (former name of Corfu)
cord +s +ed +ing (twine etc.; vocal membrane. △ chord)
cord|age
cord|ate (heart-shaped. △ caudate, chordate)
Cor|day, Char|lotte (French revolutionary)
Cor|delia (name)
Cor|del|ier +s (Franciscan monk)
cor|dial +s (polite; drink)
cor|di|ale (in 'entente cordiale')
cor|di|al|ity
cor|di|al|ly

cor|dil|lera +s
cord|ite
cord|less
cord|like
Cor|doba (cities, Argentina and Spain)
cor|doba +s (Nicaraguan currency)
cor|don +s +ed +ing
cor|don bleu
cor|dons bleus
cor|don sani|taire
cor|dons sani|taires
Cor|dova (= Cordoba)
cor|do|van +s
cor|du|roy +s
cord|wain|er +s
cord|wood +s
CORE (= Congress of Racial Equality)
core
cores
cored
cor|ing (centre. △ caw, cor, corps)
co-referen|tial
co|rela|tion +s (use correlation)
co-religion|ist +s
cor|ella +s
Cor|elli, Arc|angelo (Italian composer)
Cor|elli, Marie (English writer)
core|op|sis
core|op|ses
corer +s
co-respond|ent +s (in divorce. △ correspondent)
corf
corves
Corfu (Greek island)
corgi +s
cori|aceous
cori|an|der
Corin (man's name)
Cor|inna
Cor|inne (woman's name)
Cor|inth (city, Greece)
Cor|inth, Gulf of (off Greece)

Cor|inth|ian +s
Corio|lanus
(Roman general)
Cori|olis ef|fect
cor|ium
Cork (city and
county, Republic
of Ireland)
cork +s +ed +ing
(bark; stopper.
△ calk, caulk)
cork|age
cork|er +s
(excellent person
or thing.△ calker,
caulker)
cork|like
cork oak +s
cork|screw +s +ed
+ing
cork-tipped
cork|wood +s
corky
cork|ier
corki|est
corm +s
Cor|mac
cor|mor|ant +s
corn +s
corn|brash
corn|bread
corn chand|ler +s
corn cob +s
corn-cob pipe +s
corn|cockle +s
corn|crake +s
corn dolly
corn dol|lies
cor|nea +s
cor|neal
corned beef
Cor|neille, Pierre
(French dramatist)
cor|nel +s
Cor|ne|lia
cor|ne|lian +s
Cor|ne|lius
corn|eous (horny)
cor|ner +s +ed
+ing
cor|ner|back +s
cor|ner shop +s
cor|ner|stone +s
cor|ner|ways
cor|ner|wise
cor|net +s (brass
instrument; wafer;
cavalry officer.
△ cornett)
cor|net|cy
cor|net|cies

cor|net|ist +s (use
cornettist)
cor|nett +s
(cornetto)
cor|net|tist +s
cor|netto
cor|netti
(wind instrument)
corn-factor +s
corn-fed
corn|field +s
corn|flake +s
corn|flour (maize
flour)
corn|flower +s
(plant)
cor|nice
cor|nices
cor|niced
cor|nicing
cor|niche +s
corn|ily
corni|ness
Corn|ish
Cor|nish|man
Cor|nish|men
Cor|nish|woman
Cor|nish|women
corn on the cob
corn|rows
corn salad
corn|starch
corn|stone
cor|nu|co|pia +s
cor|nu|co|pian
Corn|wall (county,
England)
corny
corn|ier
corni|est
cor|olla +s
cor|ol|lary
cor|ol|lar|ies
Coro|man|del
Coast (in India)
cor|ona +s (cigar)
cor|ona
co|ro|nae
(halo)
Cor|ona Bor|ealis
coro|nach +s
cor|ona|graph +s
cor|on|al +s
cor|on|ary
cor|on|ar|ies
cor|on|ation +s
cor|on|er +s
cor|on|er|ship +s
cor|onet +s
cor|on|et|ed

Corot, Jean-
Baptiste
Cam|ille (French
painter)
cor|ozo +s
corozo-nut +s
Corp. (= Corporal)
cor|pora
cor|poral +s
cor|por|al|ity
cor|por|al|ities
cor|por|al|ly
cor|por|ate +s
cor|por|ate|ly
cor|por|at|ic
cor|por|ation +s
cor|por|at|ism
cor|por|at|ist
cor|pora|tive
cor|pora|tiv|ism
cor|pora|tiv|ist
cor|por|eal
cor|por|eal|ity
cor|por|eal|ly
cor|por|eity
cor|po|sant +s
corps
    plural corps
    (body of troops
    etc. △ caw, cor,
    core)
corps de bal|let
    plural corps de
    bal|let
corps d'élite
    plural corps d'élite
corps
    dip|lo|ma|tique +s
corpse +s (dead
body)
corpse-candle +s
cor|pu|lence
cor|pu|lency
cor|pu|lent
cor|pus
    cor|pora or
    cor|puses
    (collection of
    texts; anatomical
    structure)
cor|pus cal|lo|sum
    cor|pora cal|losa
Cor|pus Christi
(Christian festival;
city, USA)
cor|puscle +s
cor|pus|cu|lar
cor|pus de|licti
cor|pus lu|teum
    cor|pora lutea
cor|ral
    cor|rals

cor|ral (cont.)
    cor|ralled
    cor|ral|ling
    (animal pen.
    △ chorale)
cor|ra|sion
cor|rect +s +ed
    +ing
cor|rec|tion +s
cor|rec|tion|al
cor|rec|ti|tude
cor|rect|ive +s
cor|rect|ive|ly
cor|rect|ly
cor|rect|ness
cor|rect|or +s
Cor|reg|gio,
    An|tonio Al|legri
    da (Italian
    painter)
cor|rel|ate
cor|rel|ates
cor|rel|ated
cor|rel|at|ing
cor|rel|ation +s
cor|rel|ation|al
cor|rela|tive +s
cor|rela|tive|ly
cor|rela|tiv|ity
cor|res|pond +s
    +ed +ing
cor|res|pond|ence
    +s
cor|res|pond|ent
    +s (letter-writer.
    △ co-respondent)
cor|res|pond|
        ent|ly
cor|res|pond|
        ing|ly
cor|rida +s
cor|ri|dor +s
cor|rie +s
cor|ri|gen|dum
    cor|ri|genda
cor|ri|gible
cor|ri|gibly
cor|rob|or|ate
    cor|rob|or|ates
    cor|rob|or|ated
    cor|rob|or|at|ing
cor|rob|or|ation +s
cor|rob|ora|tive
cor|rob|ora|tor +s
cor|rob|ora|tory
cor|rob|oree +s
cor|rode
    cor|rodes
    cor|roded
    cor|rod|ing
cor|rod|ible
cor|ro|sion

cor¦ro¦sive +s
cor¦ro¦sive¦ly
cor¦ro¦sive¦ness
cor¦ru¦gate
  cor¦ru¦gates
  cor¦ru¦gated
  cor¦ru¦gat¦ing
cor¦ru¦ga¦tion +s
cor¦ru¦ga¦tor +s
cor¦rupt +s +ed
  +ing
cor¦rupt¦er +s
cor¦rupt¦ibil¦ity
cor¦rupt¦ible
cor¦rup¦tion +s
cor¦rup¦tive
cor¦rupt¦ly
cor¦rupt¦ness
cor¦sac +s
cor¦sage +s
cor¦sair +s
cor¦sak +s (use
  corsac)
corse +s (*archaic*
  corpse. △ coarse,
  course)
corse∥let +s (use
  corselette,
  corslet)
corse∥lette +s
  (woman's
  foundation
  garment.
  △ corslet)
cor¦set +s +ed
  +ing
cor¦set¦ière +s
cor¦set¦ry
Cor¦sica (island,
  Mediterranean)
Cor¦sican +s
cors∥let +s (close-
  fitting garment;
  armour.
  △ corselette)
Cort, Henry
  (English
  ironmaster)
cor¦tège +s
Cor¦tes (Spanish
  legislative
  assembly)
Cor¦tés,
  Her¦nando
  (Spanish
  conqueror of
  Mexico)
cor¦tex
  cor¦ti¦ces
Cor¦tez,
  Her¦nando (use
  Cortés)

Corti (organ of)
cor¦tical
cor¦ti¦cate
cor¦ti¦cated
cor¦ti¦co¦ster¦oid
  +s
cor¦ti¦co¦troph¦ic
cor¦ti¦co¦troph¦in
cor¦ti¦co¦trop¦ic
cor¦ti¦co¦trop¦in
cor¦ti¦sol
cor¦ti¦sone +s
cor¦un¦dum +s
Cor¦unna (port,
  Spain)
cor¦us¦cate
  cor¦us¦cates
  cor¦us¦cated
  cor¦us¦cat¦ing
cor¦us¦ca¦tion +s
cor¦vée
corves
cor¦vette +s
cor¦vid +s
cor¦vine
cory¦ban¦tic
cor¦ymb +s
cor¦ymb¦ose
cory¦phaeus
  cory¦phaei
cory¦phée +s
cor¦yza
Cos (Greek island,
  Aegean Sea)
cos
  plural cos
  (lettuce)
cos (= cosine;
  because)
'cos (= because;
  use cos)
Cosa Nos¦tra
  (criminal
  organization)
cosec (= cosecant)
co¦se¦cant +s
co¦seis¦mal +s
coset +s
cosh
  coshes
  coshed
  cosh¦ing
cosh¦er +s
co-signatory
  co-signator¦ies
cosi¦ly
Cos¦ima
Cos¦imo de'
  Med¦ici
  (Florentine
  statesman and
  banker)

co¦sine +s
cosi¦ness
cos¦met¦ic +s
cos¦met¦ic¦al¦ly
cos¦met¦ician +s
cos¦met¦ology
cos¦mic
cos¦mic¦al
cos¦mic¦al¦ly
Cosmo
cosmo¦gon¦ic
cosmo¦gon¦ic¦al
cos¦mog¦on¦ist +s
cos¦mog¦ony
cos¦mog¦raph¦er
  +s
cosmo¦graph¦ic
cosmo¦graph¦ic¦al
cos¦mog¦raphy
cosmo¦logic¦al
cos¦molo¦gist +s
cos¦mol¦ogy
cosmo¦naut +s
cosmop¦olis
cosmo¦pol¦itan +s
cosmo¦pol¦it¦an¦
  ise *Br.* (use
  cosmopolitanize)
  cosmo¦pol¦it¦an¦
    ises
  cosmo¦pol¦it¦an¦
    ised
  cosmo¦pol¦it¦an¦
    is¦ing
cosmo¦pol¦it¦an¦
  ism
cosmo¦pol¦it¦an¦
  ize
  cosmo¦pol¦it¦an¦
    izes
  cosmo¦pol¦it¦an¦
    ized
  cosmo¦pol¦it¦an¦
    iz¦ing
cos¦mopo¦lite +s
cos¦mos (universe;
  system of ideas;
  experience.)
cos¦mos
  plural cos¦mos
  (plant)
COSPAR
  (= Committee on
  Space Research)
co-sponsor +s +ed
  +ing
Cos¦sack +s
cos¦set +s +ed
  +ing
cos¦sie +s

Cos¦syra (Roman
  name for
  Pantelleria)
cost
  costs
  cost
  cost¦ing
  (have as a price)
cost +s +ed +ing
  (estimate price of)
Costa, Lúcio
  (Brazilian
  architect)
Costa Blanca
  (region, Spain)
Costa Brava
  (region, Spain)
cost ac¦count¦ing
Costa del Sol
  (region, Spain)
Costa-Gavras,
  Con¦stan¦tin
  (Greek film
  director)
cos¦tal
co-star
  co-stars
  co-starred
  co-starring
cos¦tard +s
Costa Rica
Costa Rican +s
cos¦tate
cost-benefit +s
cost-conscious
cost-cutting
cost-effective
cost-effect¦ive¦ly
cost-
  effect¦ive¦ness
cost-efficient
coster +s
cos¦ter¦mon¦ger +s
cost¦ing +s
cos¦tive
cos¦tive¦ly
cos¦tive¦ness
cost¦li¦ness
cost¦ly
  cost¦lier
  cost¦li¦est
cost¦mary
Cost¦ner, Kevin
  (American actor)
cost of liv¦ing
cost-plus
cos¦tume
  cos¦tumes
  cos¦tumed
  cos¦tum¦ing
cos¦tu¦mier +s

cosy *Br.*
  cosies
  cosied
  cosy|ing
  cosi|er
  cosi|est
  (*Am.* cozy)
cot
  cots
  cot|ted
  cot|ting
co|tan|gent +s
cot-case +s
cot death +s
cote +s (shelter.
  ⚠ coat)
Côte d'Azur
  (region, France)
co|terie +s
co|ter|min|ous
co|ter|min|ous|ly
coth (= hyperbolic
  cotangent)
co-tidal
co|til|lion +s
co|tinga +s
Cot|man, John
  Sell (English
  artist)
co|to|neas|ter +s
Coto|nou (city,
  Benin)
Coto|paxi
  (volcano,
  Ecuador)
co-trustee +s
Cots|wold Hills (in
  England)
Cots|wolds
  (= Cotswold
  Hills)
cotta +s (surplice.
  ⚠ cottar, cotter)
cot|tage +s
cot|tager +s
cot|tagey
cot|ta|ging
cot|tar +s (farm
  labourer. ⚠ cotta,
  cotter)
Cott|bus (city,
  Germany)
cot|ter +s (bolt;
  pin. ⚠ cotta,
  cotter)
cot|tier +s
cot|ton +s +ed
  +ing
cot|ton cake
cot|ton candy
cot|ton gin +s
cot|ton grass

cotton-picking
cot|ton|tail +s
cot|ton waste
cot|ton|wood +s
cot|ton wool
cot|tony
coty|le|don +s
coty|le|don|ary
coty|le|don|ous
cou|cal +s
couch
  couches
  couched
  couch|ing
couch|ant
couch|ette +s
couch grass
couch po|tato
  couch po|ta|toes
coudé +s
Coué, Emile
  (French
  psychologist)
Coué|ism
cou|gar +s
cough +s +ed +ing
cough|er +s
  (person who
  coughs. ⚠ coffer)
could
couldn't (= could
  not)
cou|lée +s
cou|lis
  plural cou|lis
cou|lisse +s
coul|oir +s
Cou|lomb, Charles-
  Augustin de
  (French physicist
  and engineer)
cou|lomb +s (unit)
cou|lo|met|ric
cou|lom|etry
coul|ter *Br.* +s (*Am.*
  colter)
cou|ma|rin
cou|ma|rone
coun|cil +s
  (assembly.
  ⚠ counsel)
coun|cil cham|ber
  +s
coun|cil house +s
coun|cil|lor *Br.* +s
  (member of
  council.
  ⚠ counsellor)
coun|cil|lor|ship
  +s
coun|cil|man
  coun|cil|men

coun|cil of war
  coun|cils of war
coun|cil|or *Am.* +s
  (member of
  council.
  ⚠ counselor)
coun|cil|woman
  coun|cil|women
coun|sel
  coun|sels
  coun|selled *Br.*
  coun|seled *Am.*
  coun|sel|ling *Br.*
  coun|sel|ing *Am.*
  (advice; barrister;
  advise. ⚠ council)
coun|sel|lor *Br.* +s
  (adviser; in 'Privy
  Counsellor'.
  ⚠ councillor)
Coun|sel|lor of
  State
  Coun|sel|lors of
  State
coun|sel|or *Am.* +s
  (adviser.
  ⚠ councilor)
count +s +ed +ing
count|able
count|back
count|down +s
  noun
coun|ten|ance
  coun|ten|ances
  coun|ten|anced
  coun|ten|an|cing
coun|ter +s +ed
  +ing
coun|ter|act +s
  +ed +ing
coun|ter|action +s
coun|ter|active
counter-attack +s
  +ed +ing
counter-
  attrac|tion +s
coun|ter|bal|ance
  coun|ter|
        bal|ances
  coun|ter|
        bal|anced
  coun|ter|
        bal|an|cing
coun|ter|blast +s
coun|ter|change
  coun|ter|changes
  coun|ter|changed
  coun|ter|
        chan|ging
coun|ter|charge
  coun|ter|charges
  coun|ter|charged

coun|ter|charge
  (*cont.*)
  coun|ter|
        char|ging
coun|ter|check +s
  +ed +ing
counter-claim +s
  +ed +ing
counter-clockwise
counter-cultural
counter-culture +s
counter-
  demonstra|tion
  +s
counter-
  demonstra|tor
  +s
counter-
  espion|age
counter-example
  +s
coun|ter|feit +s
  +ed +ing
coun|ter|feit|er +s
coun|ter|foil +s
counter-
  inflation|ary
counter-
  insurgency
  attributive
counter-
  intelli|gence
counter-intuitive
coun|ter|ir|ri|tant
  +s
coun|ter|ir|ri|
        ta|tion
coun|ter|mand +s
  +ed +ing
coun|ter|march
  coun|ter|marches
  coun|ter|marched
  coun|ter|march|
        ing
coun|ter|meas|ure
  +s
coun|ter|mine
  coun|ter|mines
  coun|ter|mined
  coun|ter|min|ing
coun|ter|move
  coun|ter|moves
  coun|ter|moved
  coun|ter|mov|ing
counter|move|
        ment +s
counter-offensive
  +s
coun|ter|pane +s
coun|ter|part +s
coun|ter|plot
  coun|ter|plots

coun¦ter¦plot
(*cont.*)
coun¦ter¦plot¦ted
coun¦ter¦plot¦ting
coun¦ter¦point +s
+ed +ing
coun¦ter¦poise
coun¦ter¦poises
coun¦ter¦poised
coun¦ter¦pois¦ing
counter-
product¦ive
counter-proposal
+s
coun¦ter¦punch
coun¦ter¦punches
coun¦ter¦punched
coun¦ter¦punch¦
ing
coun¦ter¦punch¦er
+s
Counter-
Reform¦ation
History
counter-
reform¦ation +s
counter-
revolu¦tion +s
counter-
revolu¦tion¦ary
counter-
revolu¦tion¦ar¦ies
coun¦ter¦scarp +s
coun¦ter¦shaft +s
coun¦ter¦sign +s
+ed +ing
counter-signature
+s
coun¦ter¦sink
coun¦ter¦sinks
coun¦ter¦sunk
coun¦ter¦sink¦ing
coun¦ter¦stroke +s
counter-tenor +s
counter-
transfer¦ence
coun¦ter¦vail
coun¦ter¦vails
coun¦ter¦vailed
coun¦ter¦vail¦ing
coun¦ter¦value +s
coun¦ter¦weight +s
count¦ess
count¦esses
count¦ing house
+s
count¦less
Count Pala¦tine
Counts Pala¦tine
coun¦tri¦fied
coun¦try
coun¦tries

coun¦try and
west¦ern
coun¦try club +s
coun¦try¦fied (use
countrified)
coun¦try house +s
coun¦try¦man
coun¦try¦men
coun¦try music
coun¦try¦side
country-wide
coun¦try¦woman
coun¦try¦women
count¦ship +s
county
coun¦ties
County Pala¦tine
Coun¦ties
Pala¦tine
county-wide
coup +s (notable
move. △ coo)
coup de foudre
coups de foudre
coup de grâce
coups de grâce
coup de main
coups de main
coup d'état
coups d'état
coup d'œil
coups d'œil
coupe +s (dish.
△ coop)
coupe *Am.* +s (car.
△ coop)
coupé *Br.* +s (car)
Coupe¦rin,
Fran¦çois (French
composer)
couple
couples
coupled
coup¦ling
coup¦ler +s
coup¦let +s
coup¦ling +s
cou¦pon +s
cour¦age
cour¦age¦ous
cour¦age¦ous¦ly
cour¦age¦ous¦ness
cour¦ante +s
Cour¦bet,
Gus¦tave (French
painter)
cour¦gette +s
cour¦ier +s
cour¦lan +s
Cour¦règes, André
(French couturier)

course
courses
coursed
cours¦ing
(direction etc.;
flow; hunt.
△ coarse, corse)
course¦book +s
cour¦ser +s (person
or animal that
hunts; fast-running
horse or bird.
△ coarser)
course¦work
court +s +ed +ing
(court of law;
enclosed space;
tennis court etc.
△ caught)
Cour¦tauld,
Sam¦uel (English
industrialist)
court bouil¦lon
court card +s
cour¦te¦ous
cour¦te¦ous¦ly
cour¦te¦ous¦ness
cour¦tesan +s
cour¦tesy
cour¦tesies
court¦house +s
court¦ier +s
court¦li¦ness
court¦ly
court¦lier
court¦li¦est
court mar¦tial
courts mar¦tial
noun
court-martial
court-martials
court-martialled
Br.
court-martialed
Am.
court-martial¦ling
Br.
court-martial¦ing
Am.
verb
Court¦ney
Court of St
James's (British
royal court)
Cour¦trai (French
name for Kortrijk)
court¦room +s
court¦ship +s
court¦yard +s
cous¦cous
(semolina dish.

cous¦cous (*cont.*)
△ cuscus, khus-
khus)
cousin +s (relation.
△ cozen)
cousin ger¦man
cousins ger¦man
cous¦in¦hood
cous¦in¦ly
cous¦in¦ship
Cous¦teau,
Jacques-Yves
(French
oceanographer)
couth
cou¦ture
cou¦tur¦ier +s *male*
cou¦turi¦ère +s
female
cou¦vade
cou¦vert +s
cou¦ver¦ture +s
co¦va¦lence
co¦va¦lency
co¦va¦lent +s
co¦va¦lent¦ly
cove
coves
coved
cov¦ing
coven +s
cov¦en¦ant +s +ed
+ing
cov¦en¦ant¦al
Cov¦en¦ant¦er +s
Scottish history
cov¦en¦ant¦er +s
(person who
covenants; use
covenantor)
cov¦en¦ant¦or +s
(person who
covenants)
Cov¦ent Gar¦den
(district, London)
Cov¦en¦try (city,
England)
cover +s +ed +ing
cov¦er¦able
cov¦er¦age +s
cov¦er¦all +s
Cov¦er¦dale, Miles
(translator of the
Bible into English)
cover drive +s
cov¦er¦er +s
cov¦er¦ing +s
cov¦er¦let +s
cover point +s
cov¦ert +s
cov¦ert¦ly
cov¦ert¦ness

cov¦er¦ture +s
cover-up +s *noun*
covet
  covets
  cov¦eted
  cov¦et¦ing
cov¦et¦able
cov¦et¦ous
cov¦et¦ous¦ly
cov¦et¦ous¦ness
covey +s
covin +s
cov¦ing +s
cow +s +ed +ing
cowa¦bunga
cow¦age
Cow¦ard, Noël
  (English writer,
  actor, and
  composer)
cow¦ard +s
cow¦ard¦ice
cow¦ard¦li¦ness
cow¦ard¦ly
cow¦ardy
cow¦bane
cow¦bell +s
cow¦berry
  cow¦berries
cow¦bird +s
cow¦boy +s
cow¦catch¦er +s
cower +s +ed +ing
Cowes (town,
  England)
cow¦fish
  plural cow¦fish
cow¦girl +s
cow¦hage (use
  cowage)
cow¦hand +s
cow-heel +s
cow¦herd +s
cow¦hide +s
cow-house +s
cowl +s
cowled
cow-lick +s
cowl¦ing
cow¦man
  cow¦men
co-worker +s
cow-parsley
cow-pat +s
cow¦pea +s
Cow¦per, Wil¦liam
  (English poet.
  △ Cooper)
cow¦poke +s
cow¦pox
cow¦punch¦er +s

cow¦rie +s (shell.
  △ kauri)
co-write
  co-writes
  co-wrote
  co-writing
  co-written
co-writer +s
cow¦shed +s
cow¦slip +s
cow-tree +s
cow-wheat +s
Cox
  Coxes
  (apple)
cox
  coxes
  coxed
  cox¦ing
  (coxswain)
coxa
  coxae
coxal
cox¦comb +s
  (dandy.
  △ cockscomb)
cox¦comb¦ry
  cox¦comb¦ries
cox¦less
Cox's Bazar (port,
  Bangladesh)
Cox's or¦ange
  pip¦pin +s
cox¦swain +s
cox¦swain¦ship
coy +er +est
coyly
coy¦ness
coy¦ote +s
coypu +s
coz (*archaic* cousin)
cozen +s +ed +ing
  (cheat. △ cousin)
coz¦en¦age
Cozu¦mel (island,
  Caribbean)
cozy *Am.*
  cozies
  cozied
  cozy¦ing
  cozi¦er
  cozi¦est
  (*Br.* cosy)
coz¦zie +s
Crab, the
  (constellation;
  sign of zodiac)
crab
  crabs
  crabbed
  crab¦bing
crab apple +s

Crabbe, George
  (English poet)
crab¦bed¦ly
crab¦bed¦ness
crab¦bily
crab¦bi¦ness
crabby
crab¦bier
crab¦bi¦est
crab¦grass
  crab¦grasses
crab¦like
crab¦meat
Crab Neb¦ula
crab pot +s
crab¦wise
crack +s +ed +ing
crack-brained
crack¦down +s
crack¦er +s
cracker-barrel
  adjective
crack¦er¦jack +s
crack¦ers
cracki¦ness
crack¦ing
crack-jaw
crackle
  crackles
  crackled
  crack¦ling
crack¦ly
crack¦nel +s
crack¦pot +s
cracks¦man
  cracks¦men
crack-up +s *noun*
crack-willow
cracky
Cra¦cow (city,
  Poland)
cra¦dle
  cra¦dles
  cra¦dled
  crad¦ling
cradle-snatcher
  +s
cradle-song +s
craft +s +ed +ing
  (skill; trade;
  vessel; to make.
  △ kraft)
craft-brother
  craft-brothers *or*
  craft-brethren
craft guild +s
craft¦ily
craft¦i¦ness
crafts¦man
  crafts¦men
crafts¦man¦ship

crafts¦person
crafts¦people
crafts¦woman
  crafts¦women
craft¦work
craft¦work¦er +s
crafty
  craft¦ier
  crafti¦est
crag +s
crag¦gily
crag¦gi¦ness
craggy
  crag¦gier
  crag¦gi¦est
crags¦man
  crags¦men
crags¦woman
  crags¦women
Craig
Cra¦iova (city,
  Romania)
crake +s
cram
  crams
  crammed
  cram¦ming
crambo
cram-full
cram¦mer +s
cramp +s +ed +ing
cramp-iron +s
cram¦pon +s
cran +s
Cra¦nach, Lucas
  (German painter)
cran¦age
cran¦berry
  cran¦berries
Crane, Ste¦phen
  (American writer)
crane
  cranes
  craned
  cran¦ing
crane-fly
  crane-flies
cranes¦bill +s
  (plant)
crane's-bill +s (use
  cranesbill)
cra¦nial
cra¦ni¦ate +s
cra¦nio¦logic¦al
cra¦ni¦olo¦gist +s
cra¦ni¦ology
cra¦nio¦met¦ric
cra¦ni¦om¦etry
cra¦ni¦ot¦omy
  cra¦ni¦oto¦mies

cra|nium
  cra|ni|ums or
  cra|nia
crank +s +ed +ing
crank|case +s
crank|ily
cranki|ness
crank|pin +s
crank|shaft +s
cranky
  crank|ier
  cranki|est
Cran|mer,
  Thomas (English
  archbishop)
cran|nied
cran|nog +s
cranny
  cran|nies
crap
  craps
  crapped
  crap|ping
  (coarse slang)
crape +s (black
  crêpe fabric.
  △ crêpe)
crape fern +s
crape hair
crappy
  crap|pier
  crap|pi|est
  (coarse slang)
craps (gambling
  game)
crapu|lence
crapu|lent
crapu|lous
crapy (like crape.
  △ crêpey)
craque|lure
crash
  crashes
  crashed
  crash|ing
crash bar|rier +s
crash-dive
  crash-dives
  crash-dived
  crash-diving
crash-halt +s
crash hel|met +s
crash-land +s +ed
  +ing verb
crash land|ing +s
  noun
crash pad +s
crash-stop +s
crash-tackle +s
cra|sis
  cra|ses
crass +er +est

cras|si|tude
crass|ly
crass|ness
Cras|sus, Mar|cus
  Li|cin|ius (Roman
  politician)
catch
  cratches
crate
  crates
  crated
  crat|ing
crate|ful +s
crater +s +ed +ing
cra|ter|ous
cra|ton +s
cra|vat +s
cra|vat|ted
crave
  craves
  craved
  crav|ing
cra|ven
cra|ven|ly
cra|ven|ness
craver +s
crav|ing +s
craw +s (Zoology.
  △ crore)
craw|fish
  plural craw|fish
Craw|ford, Joan
  (American
  actress)
Craw|ford, Os|bert
  (British
  archaeologist)
crawl +s +ed +ing
crawl|er +s
crawl|ing|ly
crawl space +s
crawly
cray +s
cray|fish
  plural cray|fish
crayon +s +ed
  +ing
craze
  crazes
  crazed
  craz|ing
crazi|ly
cra|zi|ness
crazy
  cra|zier
  crazi|est
Crazy Horse
  (Sioux chief)
crazy pav|ing +s
creak +s +ed +ing
  (noise. △ creek)
creak|ily

creaki|ness
creak|ing|ly
creaky
  creak|ier
  creaki|est
cream +s +ed +ing
cream-colored Am.
cream-coloured
  Br.
cream|er +s
cream|ery
  cream|er|ies
cream|ily
creami|ness
cream-laid
cream|ware
creamy
  cream|ier
  creami|est
crease
  creases
  creased
  creas|ing
  (fold; line. △ kris)
cre|at|able
cre|ate
  cre|ates
  cre|ated
  cre|at|ing
cre|at|ine
cre|ation +s
cre|ation|ism
cre|ation|ist +s
cre|ative
cre|ative|ly
cre|ative|ness
cre|ativ|ity
cre|ator +s
cre|atrix
  cre|at|ri|ces
crea|ture +s
crea|ture|ly
crèche +s
Crécy (battle,
  France)
cred
cre|dal
cre|dence +s
cre|den|tial +s
cre|denza +s
cred|ibil|ity
cred|ible
cred|ibly
credit +s +ed +ing
cred|it|abil|ity
cred|it|able
cred|it|ably
cred|it|or +s
credit|worthi|ness
credit|worthy
Credo +s (Apostles'
  or Nicene Creed)

credo +s
cre|du|lity
credu|lous
credu|lous|ly
credu|lous|ness
Cree
  plural Cree or
  Crees
creed +s
creed|al (use
  credal)
Creek
  plural Creek
  (American Indian)
creek +s (river.
  △ creak)
creel +s
creep
  creeps
  crept
  creep|ing
creep|er +s
creep|ily
creepi|ness
creep|ing Jenny
  creep|ing
  Jen|nies
creepy
  creep|ier
  creepi|est
creepy-crawly
  creepy-crawlies
creese +s (dagger;
  use kris)
cre|mate
  cre|mates
  cre|mated
  cre|mat|ing
cre|ma|tion +s
cre|ma|tor +s
crema|tor|ium
  crema|toria or
  crema|tor|iums
crema|tory
  crema|tor|ies
crème brû|lée
  crèmes brû|lées
crème cara|mel
  crèmes cara|mels
crème de cas|sis
crème de la crème
crème de menthe
crème fraiche
Cre|mona (city,
  Italy)
cren|ate
cren|ated
cren|ation +s
crena|ture
crenel +s
cren|el|late
  cren|el|lates

cren|el|late (*cont.*)
  cren|el|lated
  cren|el|lat|ing
cren|el|lation +s
cren|elle +s
Cre|ole +s
cre|ol|isa|tion *Br.*
  (use creolization)
cre|ol|ise *Br.* (use
  creolize)
  cre|ol|ises
  cre|ol|ised
  cre|ol|is|ing
cre|ol|iza|tion
cre|ol|ize
  cre|ol|izes
  cre|ol|ized
  cre|ol|iz|ing
creo|sote
  creo|sotes
  creo|soted
  creo|sot|ing
crêpe +s (fabric;
  pancake; rubber;
  paper. △ crape)
crêpe de Chine
crêpe Su|zette
  crêpes Su|zette
crêpey (like crêpe.
  △ crapy)
crepi|tant
crepi|tate
  crepi|tates
  crepi|tated
  crepi|tat|ing
crepi|ta|tion +s
crepi|tus
crept
cre|pus|cu|lar
crêpy (use crêpey.
  like crêpe.
  △ crapy)
cres|cendo +s
Cres|cent, the
  (Islamic world)
cres|cent +s
  (shape)
cres|cent|ic
cre|sol +s
cress
  cresses
cres|set +s
Cres|sida
  (legendary Greek
  woman)
Cres|sida
crest +s +ed +ing
Cresta Run (in
  Switzerland)
crest|fall|en
crest|less
cre|syl

Cret|aceous
  (period)
cret|aceous
  (chalky)
Cre|tan +s
Crete (Greek
  island)
cre|tic +s
cre|tin +s
cret|in|ise *Br.* (use
  cretinize)
  cret|in|ises
  cret|in|ised
  cret|in|is|ing
cret|in|ism
cret|in|ize
  cret|in|izes
  cret|in|ized
  cret|in|iz|ing
cret|in|ous
cre|tonne +s
Creutzfeldt–Jakob
  dis|ease
cre|vasse +s
crev|ice +s
crew +s +ed +ing
  (ship's company
  etc.; past tense of
  crow. △ *cru*)
crew-cut +s
Crewe (town,
  England)
crewel +s (yarn.
  △ cruel)
crewel work
crew|man
  crew|men
crew neck +s
crib
  cribs
  cribbed
  crib|bing
crib|bage
crib|bage board
  +s
crib|ber +s
crib-biting
crib death +s
cribo +s
crib|ri|form
crib|work
Crichton, James
  ('the Admirable',
  Scottish
  adventurer)
Crick, Fran|cis
  (British
  biophysicist)
crick +s +ed +ing
cricket +s +ed
  +ing
cricket bag +s

cricket bat +s
crick|et|er +s
cri|coid +s
cri de cœur
  cris de cœur
cried
crier +s
cri|key
crim +s
crime
  crimes
  crimed
  crim|ing
Cri|mea (peninsula,
  Ukraine)
Cri|mean +s
crime fight|er +s
crime-fighting
crime pas|sion|nel
  crimes
  pas|sion|nels
crime sheet +s
crime wave +s
crime writer +s
crim|inal +s
crim|in|al|isa|tion
  Br. (use
  criminalization)
crim|in|al|ise *Br.*
  (use criminalize)
  crim|in|al|ises
  crim|in|al|ised
  crim|in|al|is|ing
crim|in|al|is|tic
crim|in|al|is|tics
crim|in|al|ity
crim|in|al|iza|tion
crim|in|al|ize
  crim|in|al|izes
  crim|in|al|ized
  crim|in|al|iz|ing
crim|in|al|ly
crim|in|ate
  crim|in|ates
  crim|in|ated
  crim|in|at|ing
crim|in|ation +s
crim|ina|tive
crim|in|atory
crim|ino|logic|al
crim|in|olo|gist +s
crim|in|ology
crimp +s +ed +ing
crimp|er +s
crimp|ily
crimpi|ness
crimp|lene *Propr.*
crimpy
crim|son +s +ed
  +ing
cringe
  cringes

cringe (*cont.*)
  cringed
  crin|ging
crin|ger +s
crin|gle +s
crin|kle
  crin|kles
  crin|kled
  crink|ling
crinkle-cut
crin|kly
  crink|lier
  crink|li|est
crin|oid +s
crin|oid|al
crin|ol|ine +s
cri|ollo +s
cripes
Crip|pen, Doc|tor
  (American-born
  British murderer)
crip|ple
  crip|ples
  crip|pled
  crip|pling
cripple|dom
cripple|hood
crip|pler +s
crip|pling|ly
cris
  crises
  (use kris. dagger.
  △ crease)
cri|sis
  cri|ses
cri|sis
  man|age|ment
crisp +s +ed +ing
  +er +est
crisp|ate
crisp|bread +s
crisp|er +s
Cris|pian
Cris|pin
crispi|ness
crisp|ly
crisp|ness
crispy
  crisp|ier
  crispi|est
criss-cross
  criss-crosses
  criss-crossed
  criss-crossing
crista
  cris|tae
cris|tate
cris|to|bal|ite
crit +s
cri|ter|ial
cri|ter|ion
  cri|teria

crit|ic +s
crit|ic|al
crit|ic|al|ity
  crit|ic|al|ities
crit|ic|al|ly
crit|ic|al|ness
criti|cas|ter +s
criti|cis|able *Br.*
  (use **criticizable**)
criti|cise *Br.* (use
  criticize)
  criti|cises
  criti|cised
  criti|cis|ing
criti|ciser *Br.* +s
  (use **criticizer**)
criti|cism +s
criti|ciz|able
criti|cize
  criti|cizes
  criti|cized
  criti|ciz|ing
criti|cizer +s
cri|tique
  cri|tiques
  cri|tiqued
  cri|tiquing
crit|ter +s
croak +s +ed +ing
croak|er +s
croak|ily
croaki|ness
croaky
  croak|ier
  croak|iest
Croat +s
Cro|atia
Cro|atian +s
croc +s (crocodile.
  △ crock)
Croce, Bene|detto
  (Italian
  philosopher)
cro|ce|ate
cro|chet +s +ed
  +ing
cro|chet|er +s
croci (plural of
  crocus)
cro|cido|lite
crock +s +ed +ing
  (pot; worn-out
  person or thing;
  collapse. △ croc)
crock|ery
crocket +s
  Architecture
Crock|ett, Davy
  (American
  frontiersman)
Crock|ford (clerical
  directory)

croco|dile +s
croco|dil|ian +s
cro|cus
  cro|cuses *or* croci
Croe|sus (Lydian
  king)
croft +s +ed +ing
croft|er +s
Crohn's dis|ease
  (△ crone)
crois|sant +s
Cro-Magnon
Crom|arty
  (shipping area off
  Scotland; in 'Ross
  and Cromarty')
Crom|arty Firth
  (inlet, Scotland)
crom|bec +s
Crome, John
  (English artist)
crom|lech +s
Cromp|ton,
  Rich|mal (English
  writer)
Cromp|ton,
  Sam|uel (English
  inventor)
Crom|well, Oli|ver
  (English general
  and statesman)
Crom|well,
  Thomas (English
  statesman)
crone +s (old
  woman.
  △ Crohn's
  disease)
Cro|nen|berg,
  David (Canadian
  film director)
Cro|nin, A. J.
  (Scottish writer)
cronk
Cro|nus *Greek*
  Mythology
crony
  cro|nies
cro|ny|ism
crook +s +ed +ing
  (hooked staff; to
  bend; criminal;
  unwell; etc.)
crook|back +s
crook-backed
crooked +er +est
  (slanting;
  deformed;
  dishonest)
crook|ed|ly
crook|ed|ness
crook|ery

Crookes, Wil|liam
  (English physicist
  and chemist)
croon +s +ed +ing
  (hum or sing.
  △ kroon)
croon|er +s
crop
  crops
  cropped
  crop|ping
crop dust|ing
crop-eared
crop-full
crop-over
crop|per +s
cro|quet +s +ed
  +ing (game)
cro|quette +s (roll
  or ball of food
  etc.)
crore +s (ten
  million. △ craw)
Crosby, Bing
  (American singer
  and actor)
cro|sier +s
cross
  crosses
  crossed
  cross|ing
  cross|er
  cross|est
  (two intersecting
  lines; traverse;
  angry; etc.
  △ crosse)
cross|bar +s
cross-beam +s
cross-bedding
cross-bench
  cross-benches
cross-bencher +s
cross|bill +s
cross|bones
cross-border
  adjective
cross|bow +s
cross|bow|man
  cross|bow|men
cross-breed
  cross-breeds
  cross-bred
  cross-breeding
cross-Channel
cross-check +s
  +ed +ing
cross-country
  cross-countries
cross-cultural
cross-current +s
cross-curricu|lar

cross-cut
  cross-cuts
  cross-cut
  cross-cutting
cross-dating
cross-dress
  cross-dresses
  cross-dressed
  cross-dressing
cross-dresser +s
crosse +s (lacrosse
  stick. △ cross)
cross-
  examin|ation +s
cross-examine
  cross-examines
  cross-examined
  cross-examin|ing
cross-examiner +s
cross-eyed
cross-fade
  cross-fades
  cross-faded
  cross-fading
cross-
  fertil|isa|tion *Br.*
  (use cross-
  fertilization)
cross-fertilise *Br.*
  (use cross-
  fertilize)
  cross-fertilises
  cross-fertilised
  cross-fertilising
cross-
  fertil|iza|tion
cross-fertilize
  cross-fertilizes
  cross-fertilized
  cross-fertilizing
cross|field
cross|fire
cross-grain +s
cross-grained
cross-hair +s
cross-hatch
  cross-hatches
  cross-hatched
  cross-hatching
cross-head +s
cross-heading +s
cross-holding +s
cross|ing +s
cross|ing point +s
cross-keys
cross-legged
cross-link +s +ed
  +ing
cross-linkage +s
cross|ly
cross|match
  cross|matches

cross|match (cont.)
  cross|matched
  cross|match|ing
cross|ness
cross|over +s noun
cross|patch
  cross|patches
cross|piece +s
cross-ply
cross-pollin|ate
  cross-pollin|ates
  cross-pollin|ated
  cross-
    pollin|at|ing
cross-pollin|ation
cross purposes
cross-question +s
  +ed +ing
cross-refer
  cross-refers
  cross-referred
  cross-referring
cross-reference
  cross-references
  cross-referenced
  cross-
    referen|cing
cross-rhythm +s
cross|road +s
cross-ruff +s +ed
  +ing
cross-section +s
  +ed +ing
cross-section|al
cross-spar +s
cross-species
  adjective
cross stitch noun
cross-stitch
  cross-stitches
  cross-stitched
  cross-stitch|ing
  verb
cross-subsidise Br.
  (use cross-
  subsidize)
  cross-subsidises
  cross-subsidised
  cross-subsidis|ing
cross-subsidize
  cross-subsidizes
  cross-subsidized
  cross-
    subsidiz|ing
cross-subsidy
  cross-subsidies
cross-tabula|tion
  +s
cross|talk
cross|trees
cross-voting
cross|walk +s

cross|ways
cross|wind +s
cross-wire
  cross-wires
  cross-wired
  cross-wiring
cross|wise
cross|word +s
cros|tini
crotch
  crotches
crot|chet +s
crot|cheti|ness
crot|chety
cro|ton +s
crouch
  crouches
  crouched
  crouch|ing
croup
croup|ier +s
croupy
crou|ton +s
crow
  crows
  crowed or crew
  crow|ing
crow|bar +s
crow|berry
  crow|berries
crow-bill +s
crowd +s +ed +ing
crowd|ed|ness
crowd-pleaser +s
crowd-pleasing
crowd-puller +s
crowd-pulling
crow|foot +s
  (plant. △ crow's-
  foot)
Crown (the)
  (the monarch)
crown +s +ed +ing
  (for head; top;
  etc.)
Crown prince +s
Crown prin|cess
  Crown prin|cesses
crown roast +s
crow's-foot
  crow's-feet
  (wrinkle.
  △ crowfoot)
crow's-nest +s
crow step +s
crow-stepped
crow-toe +s
Cro|zet Is|lands (in
  Indian Ocean)
croz|ier +s (use
  crosier)

cru +s (vineyard;
  wine. △ crew)
cru|ces (plural of
  crux)
cru|cial
cru|ci|al|ity
cru|cial|ly
cru|cian +s
cru|ci|ate
cru|cible +s
cru|ci|fer +s
cru|cif|er|ous
cru|ci|fier +s
cru|ci|fix
  cru|ci|fixes
cru|ci|fix|ion +s
cru|ci|form
cru|cify
  cru|ci|fies
  cru|ci|fied
  cru|ci|fy|ing
cruck +s
crud
cruddy
  crud|dier
  crud|di|est
crude
  cruder
  cru|dest
crude|ly
crude|ness
cru|di|tés
cru|dity
  cru|dities
  (crude remarks or
  actions)
cruel
  cruel|ler
  cruel|lest
  (causing pain.
  △ crewel)
cruel|ly
cruel|ness
cruelty
  cruel|ties
cruelty-free
cruet +s
cruet-stand +s
Crufts (dog show)
**Cruik|shank,
  George** (English
  artist)
cruise
  cruises
  cruised
  cruis|ing
  (sea journey;
  travel at moderate
  speed. △ cruse)
cruise con|trol
cruise mis|sile +s

cruiser +s
cruis|er|weight +s
cruise|way +s
crul|ler +s
crumb +s +ed +ing
crum|ble
  crum|bles
  crum|bled
  crum|bling
crum|bli|ness
crum|bly
  crum|blier
  crum|bli|est
crumby
  crumb|ier
  crumbi|est
  (like crumbs.
  △ crummy)
crum|horn +s
crum|mily
crum|mi|ness
crummy
  crum|mier
  crum|mi|est
  (inferior.
  △ crumby)
crump +s +ed
  +ing
crum|pet +s
crum|ple
  crum|ples
  crum|pled
  crum|pling
crum|ply
  crum|plier
  crum|pli|est
crunch
  crunches
  crunched
  crunch|ing
crunch|er +s
crunch|ily
crunchi|ness
crunchy
  crunch|ier
  crunchi|est
crup|per +s
crural
cru|sade
  cru|sades
  cru|saded
  cru|sad|ing
cru|sader +s
cruse +s (jar.
  △ cruise)
crush
  crushes
  crushed
  crush|ing
crush|able
crush bar|rier +s

crush|er +s
crush|ing|ly
crust +s +ed +ing
Crust|acea
crust|acean +s
crust|ace|ology
crust|aceous
crust|al
crust|ily
crusti|ness
crust|ose
crusty
  crust|ies
  crust|ier
  crusti|est
crutch
  crutches
Crutched Friars
crux
  cruxes or cru|ces
Crux (Aus|tralis)
  (constellation)
Cruyff, Johan
  (Dutch footballer)
cru|zado +s
cru|zeiro +s
cry
  cries
  cried
  cry|ing
  (shout; weep.
  ⚠ krai)
cry-baby
  cry-babies
cryer +s (use crier)
cryo|bio|logic|al
cryo|biolo|gist +s
cryo|biol|ogy
cryo|gen +s
cryo|gen|ic
cryo|gen|ics
cryo|lite
cry|on|ic
cry|on|ics
cryo|pro|tect|ant
  +s
cryo|pump +s
cryo|stat +s
cryo|sur|gery
crypt +s
crypt|analy|sis
crypt|ana|lyst +s
crypt|ana|lyt|ic
crypt|ana|lyt|ic|al
cryp|tic +s
cryp|tic|al|ly
crypto +s
crypto|crys|tal|
        line
crypto-fascist +s
crypto|gam +s
crypto|gam|ic

crypt|og|am|ous
crypto|gram +s
crypt|og|raph|er
  +s
crypto|graph|ic
crypto|graph|ic|
      al|ly
crypt|og|raphy
crypt|olo|gist +s
crypt|ology
crypto|meria +s
crypto|
     spor|idi|osis
crypto|
     spor|id|ium
crypto|spor|idia
crypto|zoic
crypto|zo|ology
Crys|tal also
  Chrys|tal
  (name)
crys|tal +s
  (mineral)
crys|tal ball +s
crys|tal clear
crystal-clear
  attributive
crystal-gazing
crys|tal|line
crys|tal|lin|ity
crys|tal|lis|able Br.
  (use
  crystallizable)
crys|tal|lisa|tion
  Br. (use
  crystallization)
crys|tal|lise Br.
  (use crystallize)
crys|tal|lises
crys|tal|lised
crys|tal|lis|ing
crys|tal|lite +s
crys|tal|liz|able
crys|tal|liza|tion
crys|tal|lize
crys|tal|lizes
crys|tal|lized
crys|tal|liz|ing
crys|tal|
    log|raph|er +s
crys|tal|lo|
      graph|ic
crys|tal|log|raphy
crys|tal|loid +s
Crys|tal Pal|ace
  (in London)
csar|das
  plural csar|das
cten|oid
cteno|phore +s
Ctesi|phon
  (ancient city, Iraq)

cub
  cubs
  cubbed
  cub|bing
Cuba
Cuban +s
Cu|bango
  (= Okavango)
cubby
  cub|bies
cub|by|hole +s
cube
  cubes
  cubed
  cu|bing
cubeb +s
cuber +s
cube root +s
cub|hood
cubic
cu|bic|al (cube-
  shaped)
cu|bic|al|ly
cu|bicle +s (small
  room)
cu|bi|form
cu|bism
cu|bist +s
cubit +s
cu|bit|al
cu|boid +s
cu|boid|al
Cub Scout +s
cucking-stool +s
cuck|old +s +ed
  +ing
cuck|old|ry
cuckoo +s
cuckoo clock +s
cuckoo flower +s
cuckoo pint +s
cuckoo spit
cu|cum|ber +s
cu|cur|bit +s
cu|cur|bit|aceous
cud
  cuds
  cud|ded
  cud|ding
cud|bear
cud|dle
  cud|dles
  cud|dled
  cud|dling
cuddle|some
cud|dly
  cud|dlier
  cud|dli|est
cuddy
  cud|dies
cudgel
  cudgels

cudgel (cont.)
  cudg|elled Br.
  cudg|eled Am.
  cudgel|ling Br.
  cudgel|ing Am.
Cud|lipp, Hugh
  (British journalist)
cud|weed +s
cue
  cues
  cued
  cue|ing or cuing
  (signal; hint; in
  billiards etc.
  ⚠ queue)
cue ball +s
cue-bid +s
cue|ist +s
Cuenca (city,
  Ecuador)
Cuer|na|vaca
  (town, Mexico)
cuesta +s
cuff +s +ed +ing
cuff link +s
Cufic (use Kufic)
Cui|abá (city and
  port, Brazil)
cui bono?
Cuil|lin Hills
  (mountain range,
  Skye)
Cuil|lins (= Cuillin
  Hills)
cuir|ass
  cuir|asses
cuir|ass|ier +s
cuish
  cuishes
cuis|ine +s
cuisse +s
Cukor, George
  (American film
  director)
Cul|bert|son, Ely
  (American bridge
  player)
cul|chie +s
Cul|dee +s
cul-de-sac
  culs-de-sac or cul-
  de-sacs
Culi|acán Ros|ales
  (city, Mexico)
cul|in|ar|ily
cu|lin|ary
cull +s +ed +ing
cull|er +s
cul|let
Cul|loden
  (battlefield,
  Scotland)

culm +s
cul¦mif¦er¦ous
cul¦min¦ant
cul¦min¦ate
  cul¦min¦ates
  cul¦min¦ated
  cul¦min¦at¦ing
cul¦min¦ation +s
cul¦lotte *attributive*
cul¦lottes
culpa
culp¦abil¦ity
culp¦able
culp¦ably
Cul¦peper,
  Nich¦olas
  (English herbalist)
cul¦prit +s
cul¦shie +s
cult +s
cult¦ic
cult¦ism
cult¦ist +s
cul¦tiv¦able
cul¦ti¦var +s
cul¦ti¦vat¦able
cul¦ti¦vate
  cul¦ti¦vates
  cul¦ti¦vated
  cul¦ti¦vat¦ing
cul¦ti¦va¦tion +s
cul¦ti¦va¦tor +s
cul¦tural
cul¦tur¦al¦ism
cul¦tur¦al¦ist +s
cul¦tur¦al¦ly
cul¦ture
  cul¦tures
  cul¦tured
  cul¦tur¦ing
culture-bound
cul¦tus
  plural cul¦tus
cul¦verin +s
cul¦vert +s
cum (combined
  with. △ come)
cum¦ber +s +ed
  +ing
Cum¦ber¦land
  (former county,
  England; sauce,
  sausage)
Cum¦ber¦land,
  Duke of (English
  prince)
Cum¦ber¦nauld
  (town, Scotland)
cum¦ber¦some
cum¦ber¦some¦ly
cum¦ber¦some¦
       ness

cum¦bia +s
Cum¦bria (county,
  England)
Cum¦brian +s
cum¦brous
cum¦brous¦ly
cum¦brous¦ness
cum grano salis
cumin
cum¦mer¦bund +s
cum¦min (use
  cumin)
cum¦mings, e. e.
  (American writer)
cum¦quat +s (use
  kumquat)
cu¦mu¦late
  cu¦mu¦lates
  cu¦mu¦lated
  cu¦mu¦lat¦ing
cu¦mu¦la¦tion +s
cu¦mu¦la¦tive
cu¦mu¦la¦tive¦ly
cu¦mu¦la¦tive¦ness
cu¦mu¦lo¦nim¦bus
  plural
  cu¦mu¦lo¦
  nim¦buses *or*
  cu¦mu¦lo¦nimbi
cu¦mu¦lous
  adjective
cu¦mu¦lus
  cu¦muli
  noun
Cu¦nard, Sam¦uel
  (British-Canadian
  shipowner)
cu¦ne¦ate
cu¦nei¦form
Cu¦nene (river,
  Angola)
cun¦je¦voi +s
cun¦ni¦lin¦gus
cun¦ning
Cun¦ning¦ham,
  Merce (American
  dancer and
  choreographer)
cun¦ning¦ly
cun¦ning¦ness
Cu¦no¦be¦li¦nus
  (Latin name for
  Cymbeline)
cunt +s (*coarse
  slang*)
cup
  cups
  cupped
  cup¦ping
Cupar (town,
  Scotland)
cup¦bear¦er +s

cup¦board +s
cup¦cake +s
cupel
  cu¦pels
  cu¦pelled *Br.*
  cu¦peled *Am.*
  cu¦pel¦ling *Br.*
  cu¦pel¦ing *Am.*
cu¦pel¦la¦tion
Cup Final +s
cup¦ful +s
Cupid *Roman
  Mythology*
cu¦pid¦ity
Cupid's bow +s
cu¦pola +s
cu¦po¦laed
cupola-furnace +s
cuppa +s
cup¦per +s (use
  cuppa)
cu¦pram¦mo¦nium
cu¦preous
cu¦pric
cu¦prif¦er¦ous
cu¦prite
cupro-nickel
cu¦prous
cup-tie +s
cu¦pule +s
cur +s
cur¦abil¦ity
cur¦able
Cura¦çao (island,
  Netherlands
  Antilles)
cura¦çao +s (drink.
  △ curassow)
cura¦çoa +s (use
  curaçao)
cur¦acy
  cur¦acies
cur¦are +s
cur¦ar¦ine
cur¦ar¦ise *Br.* (use
  curarize)
  cur¦ar¦ises
  cur¦ar¦ised
  cur¦ar¦is¦ing
cur¦ar¦ize
  cur¦ar¦izes
  cur¦ar¦ized
  cur¦ar¦iz¦ing
cur¦as¦sow +s
  (bird. △ curaçao)
cur¦ate
  cur¦ates
  cur¦ated
  cur¦at¦ing
curate-in-charge
  curates-in-charge
cur¦ate's egg

cur¦ation
cura¦tive
cur¦ator +s
cura¦tor¦ial
cur¦ator¦ship +s
curb +s +ed +ing
  (restrain. △ kerb)
curb roof +s
cur¦cuma +s
curd +s
cur¦dle
  cur¦dles
  cur¦dled
  curd¦ling
curd¦ler +s
curdy
cure
  cures
  cured
  cur¦ing
  (remedy;
  preserve)
curé +s (priest)
cure-all +s
curer
cur¦et¦tage
cur¦ette
  cur¦ettes
  cur¦et¦ted
  cur¦et¦ting
cur¦few +s
Curia (papal court)
Cur¦ial
Curie, Marie and
  Pierre (physicists)
curie +s (unit)
curio +s
curi¦osa
curi¦os¦ity
  curi¦os¦ities
curi¦ous +er
curi¦ous¦ly
curi¦ous¦ness
Curi¦tiba (city,
  Brazil)
cur¦ium
curl +s +ed +ing
curl¦er +s
cur¦lew
  plural cur¦lew *or*
  cur¦lews
cur¦li¦cue +s
curli¦ness
curl¦ing iron +s
curl¦ing pins
curl¦ing tongs
curly
  curl¦ier
  curli¦est
cur¦mudg¦eon +s
cur¦mudg¦eon¦ly

cur|rach +s
(coracle)
Cur|ragh, the
(plain, Republic of
Ireland)
cur|ragh +s (use
currach)
cur|ra|jong +s (use
kurrajong)
cur|rant +s (dried
fruit. △ current)
cur|ra|wong +s
cur|rency
cur|ren|cies
cur|rent +s
(present; tide;
electricity.
△ currant)
cur|rent ac|count
+s
cur|rent|ly
cur|rent|ness
cur|ricle +s
cur|ricu|lar
adjective
cur|ricu|lum
cur|ric|ula *or*
cur|ricu|lums
noun
cur|ricu|lum vitae
cur|ric|ula vitae
cur|rier +s
cur|rish
cur|rish|ly
cur|rish|ness
curry
cur|ries
cur|ried
curry|ing
curry-comb +s
+ed +ing
curry pow|der +s
curse
curses
cursed
or curst *archaic*
curs|ing
curs|ed|ly
curs|ed|ness
curser +s (person
who curses.
△ cursor)
cur|sillo +s
cur|sive
cur|sive|ly
cur|sor +s
(*Computing*;
Mathematics.
△ curser)
cur|sor|ial
cur|sor|ily
cur|sori|ness

curs|ory
curst (*archaic*
= cursed)
Curt (name)
curt +er +est
(brusque; short)
cur|tail +s +ed
+ing
cur|tail|ment +s
cur|tain +s +ed
+ing
cur|tain call +s
cur|tain fire +s
curtain-raiser +s
cur|tain wall +s
cur|tana +s
cur|til|age +s
Cur|tin, John
(Australian prime
minister)
Cur|tis, Tony
(American actor)
Cur|tiss, Glenn
Ham|mond
(American
aviation pioneer)
curt|ly
curt|ness
curt|sey (use
curtsy) +s +ed
+ing
curtsy
curt|sies
curt|sied
curt|sy|ing
cur|ule
curv|aceous
curva|ture +s
curve
curves
curved
curv|ing
cur|vet
cur|vets
cur|vet|ted
cur|vet|ting
curvi|fo|li|ate
curvi|form
curvi|lin|ear
curvi|lin|ear|ly
curvi|ness
curvi|ros|tral
curvy
cur|vier
cur|vi|est
cus|cus
cus|cuses
(animal.
△ couscous, khus-
khus)
cusec +s
Cush *Bible*

Cush (part of
ancient Nubia.
△ Hindu Kush)
cush
cushes
(= cushion)
cushat +s
cush-cush
cush-cushes
cushi|ness
Cush|ing, Har|vey
Wil|liams
(American
surgeon)
Cush|ing's
dis|ease
Cush|ing's
syn|drome
cush|ion +s +ed
+ing
cush|iony
Cush|it|ic
cushy
cush|ier
cushi|est
cusp +s
cus|pate
cusped
cus|pid +s
cus|pid|al
cus|pid|ate
cus|pi|dor +s
cuss
cusses
cussed
cuss|ing
cuss|ed|ly
cuss|ed|ness
cuss word +s
cus|tard +s
cus|tard apple +s
cus|tard pie +s
cus|tardy (like
custard.
△ custody)
Cus|ter, George
Arm|strong
(American cavalry
general)
cus|to|dial
cus|to|dian +s
cus|to|dian|ship
cus|tody
(imprisonment
etc. △ custardy)
cus|tom +s
cus|tom|ar|ily
cus|tom|ari|ness
cus|tom|ary
cus|tom|ar|ies
custom-built
custom-designed

cus|tom|er +s
cus|tom house +s
cus|tom|ise *Br.*
(use customize)
cus|tom|ises
cus|tom|ised
cus|tom|is|ing
cus|tom|ize
cus|tom|izes
cus|tom|ized
cus|tom|iz|ing
custom-made
Cus|toms
(Government
department)
customs house +s
cut
cut|ting
cut-and-come-
again *adjective*
cut and dried
cut-and-dried
attributive
cut-and-paste
cut and thrust
noun
cut-and-thrust
attributive
cu|ta|ne|ous
cut|away +s *noun*
and adjective
cut|back +s *noun*
cut-down *adjective*
cute
cuter
cutest
cute|ly
cute|ness
cutesy
cut glass *noun*
cut-glass *adjective*
Cuth|bert (English
saint; name)
cut|icle +s
cu|ticu|lar
cutie +s
cut-in +s *noun*
cutis
cut|lass
cut|lasses
cut|ler +s
cut|lery
cut|let +s
cut-line +s
cut-off +s *adjective*
and noun
cut-out +s *adjective*
and noun
cut-price
cut|purse +s

cut-rate
cut¦ter +s
cut-throat +s
cut¦ting +s
cut¦ting edge +s
cut¦ting¦ly
cut¦tle +s
cuttle-bone +s
cuttle¦fish
  plural cuttle¦fish
cutty
  cut¦ties
Cutty Sark (tea
  clipper)
cutty-stool +s
cut-up +s *adjective
  and noun*
cut¦water +s
cut¦worm +s
cuvée +s
cu¦vette +s
Cu¦vier, Georges
  (French naturalist)
Cuzco (city, Peru)
cwm +s (valley.
  △ coomb,
  khoum)
Cwm¦bran (town,
  Wales)
Cy
cyan
cy¦ana¦mide +s
cy¦an¦ate +s
cy¦an¦ic
cy¦an¦ide
cy¦ano¦bac¦terium
  cy¦ano¦bac¦teria
cy¦ano¦co¦bal¦
    amin +s
cy¦ano¦gen +s
cy¦ano¦gen¦ic
cy¦an¦osis
  cy¦an¦oses
cy¦an¦ot¦ic
Cy¦bele *Mythology*
cy¦ber¦nate
  cy¦ber¦nates
  cy¦ber¦nated
  cy¦ber¦nat¦ing
cy¦ber¦na¦tion
cy¦ber¦net¦ic
cy¦ber¦net¦ician +s
cy¦ber¦neti¦cist +s
cy¦ber¦net¦ics
cy¦ber¦punk +s
cyber¦space
cy¦borg +s
cycad +s
Cyc¦la¦des (islands,
  Aegean)
Cyc¦lad¦ic
cyc¦la¦mate +s

cyc¦la¦men +s
cycle
  cycles
  cycled
  cyc¦ling
cycle track +s
cycle-way +s
cyc¦lic
cyc¦lic¦al
cyc¦lic¦al¦ly
cyc¦list +s
cyclo¦alk¦ane +s
cyclo-cross
cyclo¦dex¦trin +s
cyclo¦graph +s
cyclo¦hex¦ane +s
cyclo¦hexyl
cyc¦loid +s
cyc¦loid¦al
cyc¦lom¦eter +s
cyc¦lone +s
cyc¦lon¦ic
cyc¦lon¦ic¦al¦ly
cyclo¦pae¦dia +s
  (use cyclopedia)
cyclo¦pae¦dic (use
  cyclopedic)
cyclo¦paraf¦fin +s
Cyc¦lo¦pean
cyclo¦pedia +s
cyclo¦pedic
cyclo¦pro¦pane
cyclo¦propyl
Cyc¦lops
  plural Cyc¦lops *or*
  Cyc¦lopses *or*
  Cyc¦lo¦pes
  (one-eyed giant)
cyc¦lops
  plural cyc¦lops *or*
  cyc¦lo¦pes
  (crustacean)
cyclo¦rama +s
cyclo¦ram¦ic
cyclo¦sporin
cyclo¦stome +s
cyclo¦style
  cyclo¦styl¦ing
cyclo¦thy¦mia
cyclo¦thy¦mic
cyclo¦tron +s
cyder +s (use
  cider)
cyg¦net +s (young
  swan. △ signet)
Cyg¦nus
  (constellation)
cy¦lin¦der +s
cy¦lin¦dric¦al
cy¦lin¦dric¦al¦ly
cyma +s

cym¦bal +s
  (percussion
  instrument.
  △ symbol)
cym¦bal¦ist +s
  (cymbal player.
  △ symbolist)
cym¦balo +s
Cym¦bel¦ine
  (ancient British
  king)
cym¦bid¦ium +s
cym¦bi¦form
cyme +s
cym¦ose
Cym¦ric
Cymru (Welsh
  name for Wales)
Cyne¦wulf (Anglo-
  Saxon poet)
cyn¦ghan¦edd
Cynic +s (member
  of Greek sect)
cynic +s (doubter)
cyn¦ic¦al
cyn¦ic¦al¦ly
cyni¦cism
cyno¦ceph¦alus
  cyno¦ceph¦ali
cyno¦sure +s
Cyn¦thia
cy¦pher +s (use
  cipher)
cy pres *Law*
cy¦press
  cy¦presses
  (tree)
Cyp¦rian +s (of
  Cyprus)
Cyp¦rian
  (Carthaginian
  saint)
cyp¦rin¦oid +s (like
  carp)
Cyp¦riot +s
cyp¦ri¦pe¦dium +s
Cy¦prus (island,
  Mediterranean)
cyp¦sela
  cyp¦selae
Cyr¦ano de
  Ber¦gerac
  (French soldier
  and writer)
Cyre¦na¦ic +s
Cyre¦na¦ica
  (region, Libya)
Cyr¦ene (region,
  Libya)
Cyril (Greek saint;
  name)
Cyr¦il¦lic +s

Cyril of
  Alex¦an¦dria
  (saint)
Cyrus (name)
Cyrus the Great
  (Persian king)
Cyrus the
  Young¦er
  (Persian
  commander)
cyst +s (*Medicine.*
  △ cist)
cyst¦eine
cys¦tic
cyst¦ine +s
  (*Biochemistry.*
  △ Sistine)
cyst¦itis
cysto¦scope +s
cysto¦scop¦ic
cyst¦os¦copy
  cyst¦os¦copies
cyst¦ot¦omy
  cyst¦oto¦mies
cyti¦dine
cyto¦chrome +s
cyto¦gen¦et¦ic
cyto¦gen¦et¦ic¦al
cyto¦gen¦et¦ic¦al¦ly
cyto¦gen¦eti¦cist
  +s
cyto¦gen¦et¦ics
cyto¦logic¦al
cyto¦logic¦al¦ly
cy¦tolo¦gist +s
cy¦tology
cyto¦megalo¦virus
  cyto¦megalo¦
    viruses
cyto¦plasm
cyto¦plas¦mic
cyto¦sine
cyto¦skel¦eton +s
cyto¦toxic
czar +s (use tsar)
czar¦das (use
  csardas)
czar¦evich (use
  tsarevich)
  czar¦eviches
czar¦evna +s (use
  tsarevna)
czar¦ina +s (use
  tsarina)
czar¦ism (use
  tsarism)
czar¦ist +s (use
  tsarist)
Czech +s
Czecho¦slo¦vak +s
Czecho¦slo¦vakia

Czecho|slo|vak|
ian

Dd

Czerny, Karl
(Austrian
composer and
musician)
Częs|to|chowa
(city, Poland)

'd (= had; would)
dab
dabs
dabbed
dab|bing
dab|ber +s
dab|ble
dab|bles
dab|bled
dab|bling
dab|bler +s
dab|bling +s
dab|chick +s
dab hand +s
da capo
Dacca (use Dhaka)
dace
plural dace
(fish. △ dais)
dacha +s
Dachau
(concentration
camp, Germany)
dachs|hund +s
Dacia (ancient E.
European country)
Da|cian +s
da|cite +s
dac|oit +s
dac|tyl +s
dac|tyl|ic +s
dad +s
Dada
Dada|ism
Dada|ist +s
Dada|is|tic
daddy
dad|dies
daddy-long-legs
plural daddy-long-
legs
dado +s
Dadra and Nagar
Ha|veli (territory,
India)
Dae|da|lian +s
Dae|da|lus Greek
Mythology
dae|mon +s (use
demon)
dae|mon|ic (use
demonic)
dae|mono|logic|al
(use
demonological)
daff +s
daf|fily
daf|fi|ness

daf|fo|dil +s
daffy
daf|fier
daf|fi|est
daft +er +est
daft|ly
daft|ness
Daf|ydd
dag
dags
dagged
dag|ging
da Gama, Vasco
(Portuguese
explorer)
Dag|estan
(republic, Russia)
dagga +s (plant;
hemp)
dag|ger +s
(weapon)
dagger|board +s
daggy
dag|gier
dag|gi|est
Dag|mar
dago +s (offensive)
Dagon Bible
Da|guerre, Louis
(French inventor)
da|guerre|otype
+s
dah +s
Dahl, Roald
(British writer)
Dah|lia (name)
dah|lia +s (flower)
Da|ho|mey (former
name of Benin)
Dai (man's name.
△ Di)
Dáil (Éire|ann)
(Irish parliament)
daily
dai|lies
Daim|ler,
Gott|lieb
(German
engineer)
dai|mon +s (use
demon)
dai|mon|ic (use
demonic)
dain|tily
dain|ti|ness
dainty
dain|ties
dain|tier
dain|ti|est
dai|quiri +s
Dai|ren (former
name of Dalian)

dairy
dair|ies
dairy-free
dairy|ing
dairy|maid +s
dairy|man
dairy|men
dais
daises
(platform. △ dace)
Daisy (name)
daisy
dai|sies
(flower)
daisy chain +s
daisy-cutter +s
daisy wheel +s
Dakar (capital of
Senegal)
Dak|ota, North
and South (states,
USA)
dal +s (use dhal)
Dalai Lama
da|lasi
plural da|lasi or
da|lasis
Dal|croze (see
Jaques-
Dalcroze)
Dale, Henry
Hall|lett (English
physiologist and
pharmacologist)
Dale (name)
dale +s (valley)
dalek +s
dales|folk
dales|man
dales|men
dales|woman
dales|women
Daley (name)
Dal|housie,
Mar|quis of
(British colonial
administrator)
Dali, Sal|va|dor
(Spanish painter)
Da|lian (port,
China)
Dalit +s
Dal|la|pic|cola,
Luigi (Italian
composer)
Dal|las (city, USA)
dal|li|ance +s
dal|lier +s
dally
dal|lies
dal|lied
dally|ing

Dal|ma|tia (region, Croatia)
Dal|ma|tian +s
dal|mat|ic
Dal|ri|ada (ancient kingdom, Scotland)
dal segno
Dal|ton, John (English chemist)
dal|ton +s (unit)
Dal|ton|ise Br. (use Daltonize)
Dal|ton|ises
Dal|ton|ised
Dal|ton|is|ing
dal|ton|ism
Dal|ton|ize
Dal|ton|izes
Dal|ton|ized
Dal|ton|iz|ing
dam
dams
dammed
dam|ming (barrier; mother; block up; etc. △ damn)
dam|age
dam|ages
dam|aged
dam|aging
dam|age|able
dam|aging|ly
Daman and Diu (territory, India)
Da|mara
plural Da|mara or Da|ma|ras
Dam|ara|land (region, Namibia)
Dam|aris
dam|as|cene
dam|as|cenes
dam|as|cened
dam|as|cen|ing
Da|mas|cus (capital of Syria)
dam|ask +s +ed +ing
Dama|vand (mountain, Iran)
Dam|buster +s
Dame (title)
dame +s (woman)
dame school +s
dam|fool +s (noun; use damn fool)
dam|fool (attributive; use damn-fool)
Da|mian

Dami|etta (E. Nile delta and port, Egypt)
dam|mar +s
dam|mit
damn +s +ed +ing (condemn. △ dam)
dam|nable
dam|nably
dam|na|tion +s
dam|na|tory
damned +est
damn fool +s noun
damn-fool adjective
dam|ni|fi|ca|tion
dam|nify
dam|ni|fies
dam|ni|fied
dam|ni|fy|ing
damn|ing|ly
dam|num
damna
Damo|cles (legendary figure; in 'sword of Damocles')
Damon (legendary Syracusan; name)
damp +s +ed +ing +er +est
damp course +s
damp|en +s +ed +ing
damp|en|er +s
damp|er +s
Damp|ier, Wil|liam (English explorer)
damping-off noun and adjective
damp|ish
damp|ly
damp|ness
damp-proof +s +ed +ing
dam|sel +s
dam|sel|fish
plural dam|sel|fish
dam|sel|fly
dam|sel|flies
dam|son +s
Dan (Bible; name)
dan +s (in judo; buoy)
Dana, James Dwight (American mineralogist)
Dana, Rich|ard Henry (American writer)

Danae Greek Mythology
Dan|aids Greek Mythology
Dana|kil
plural Dana|kil or Dana|kils
Dana|kil De|pres|sion (region, NE Africa)
Da Nang (city, Vietnam)
dance
dances
danced
dan|cing
dance|able
dance band +s
dance floor +s
dance hall +s
dan|cer +s
dance|wear
dan|cing girl +s
dan|delion +s
dan|der +s
dan|dify
dan|di|fies
dan|di|fied
dan|di|fy|ing
dan|dle
dan|dles
dan|dled
dand|ling
Dan|dong (port, China)
dan|druff
dandy
dan|dies
dan|dier
dan|di|est
dandy brush
dandy brushes
dandy|ish
dandy|ism
Dane +s
Dane|geld
Dane|law
dane|weed
dane|wort
dan|ger +s
dan|ger man
dan|ger men
dan|ger|ous
dan|ger|ous|ly
dan|ger|ous|ness
dan|gle
dan|gles
dan|gled
dan|gling
dan|gler +s
dan|gly

Dan|iel (Bible; man's name)
Dan|iela
Dan|iell cell +s
Dan|ielle (woman's name)
Dan|ish
Dan|ishes
dank +er +est
dank|ly
dank|ness
Dank|worth, John (British jazz musician)
d'An|nun|zio, Gab|ri|ele (Italian poet)
Danny
Dano-Norwegian
danse ma|cabre
danses ma|cabres
dan|seur +s male
dan|seuse +s female
Dante (Ali|ghieri) (Italian poet)
Dan|te|an
Dant|esque
dan|tho|nia
Dan|ton, Georges Jacques (French revolutionary)
Dan|ube (river, Europe)
Dan|ub|ian +s
Dan|zig (German name for Gdańsk)
Dão (river and region, Portugal)
dap
daps
dapped
dap|ping
Daphne (Greek Mythology; name)
daphne +s (shrub)
daph|nia
plural daph|nia
Daph|nis Greek Mythology
Da Ponte, Lor|enzo (Italian librettist and poet)
dap|per
dap|per|ly
dap|per|ness
dap|ple
dap|ples
dap|pled
dap|pling
dap|ple gray Am. +s

dap|ple grey *Br.* +s
Dap|sang
  (alternative name
  for K2)
dap|sone
Da|qing (city,
  China)
dar|bies (handcuffs)
Darby (name.
  △ Derby)
Darby and Joan
Darby and Joan
  Club +s
Darcy
Dard +s
Dar|da|nelles, the
  (strait between
  Europe and
  Asiatic Turkey)
Dard|ic
dare
  dares
  dared
  dar|ing
dare|devil +s
dare|devil|ry
Dar|ell *also*
  Dar|rell, Dar|ryl,
  Daryl
Daren *also* Dar|ren
daren't (= dare
  not)
darer +s
dare say (in 'I dare
  say')
Dar es Sa|laam
  (city, Tanzania)
Dar|fur (region,
  Sudan)
darg +s
Dari
Dar|ien (province,
  Panama)
Dar|ien, Gulf of
  (part of
  Caribbean)
dar|ing
daring-do (use
  derring-do)
dar|ing|ly
dari|ole +s
Dar|ius (Persian
  king; name)
Dar|jee|ling (town,
  India; tea)
dark +s +er +est
dark|en +s +ed
  +ing
dark|en|er +s
dark-eyed
dark-haired

Dar|khan (city,
  Mongolia)
darkie +s (*offensive*)
dark|ish
dark|ling
dark|ly
dark|ness
  dark|nesses
dark|room +s
dark-skinned
dark|some
darky (use darkie)
  dark|ies
  (*offensive*)
Dar|lene
Dar|ling, Grace
  (English heroine)
dar|ling +s
Dar|ling River (in
  Australia)
Dar|ling|ton (town,
  England)
Darm|stadt (town,
  Germany)
darn +s +ed +ing
darned|est
dar|nel +s
darn|er +s
darn|ing nee|dle
  +s
darn|ing wool
Darn|ley, Lord
  (husband of Mary
  Queen of Scots)
Dar|rell *also*
  Dar|ell, Dar|ryl,
  Daryl
Dar|ren *also* Daren
Dar|ryl *also* Dar|ell,
  Dar|rell, Daryl
Dart, Ray|mond
  Ar|thur
  (Australian-born
  South African
  anthropologist)
dart +s +ed +ing
dart|board +s
dart|er +s
Dart|moor (region,
  England)
Dart|mouth (port
  and naval college,
  England)
Dar|win (city,
  Australia)
Dar|win, Charles
  (English
  naturalist)
Dar|win|ian +s
Dar|win|ism
Dar|win|ist +s
Dar|win's finches

Daryl *also* Dar|ell,
  Dar|rell, Dar|ryl
dash
  dashes
  dashed
  dash|ing
dash|board +s
dash|iki +s
dash|ing|ly
dash|ing|ness
dash|pot +s
das|sie +s
das|tard +s
das|tard|li|ness
das|tard|ly
dasy|ure +s
data
data bank +s
data|base +s
dat|able
Data|Glove +s
data pro|cess|ing
data pro|ces|sor
  +s
date
  dates
  dated
  dat|ing
date|less
Date Line
  (on world)
date line +s
  (in newspapers)
date palm +s
date rape
date-stamp +s +ed
  +ing
dat|ival
dat|ival|ly
dat|ive +s
Da|tong (city,
  China)
datum
  data
da|tura +s
daub +s +ed +ing
  (smear)
daube +s (stew)
daub|er +s
Dau|bigny,
  Charles-
  François (French
  painter)
daub|ster +s
dauby
Dau|det,
  Al|phonse
  (French novelist)
daugh|ter +s
daugh|ter|hood
daughter-in-law
  daughters-in-law
daugh|ter|ly

Daryl *also* Dar|ell,
  Dar|rell, Dar|ryl
dau|mier, Hon|oré
  (French artist)
daunt +s +ed +ing
daunt|ing|ly
daunt|less
daunt|less|ly
daunt|less|ness
dau|phin +s
Dau|phiné (former
  province, France)
Davao (port,
  Philippines)
Dave
Daven|port +s
Davey *also* Davie,
  Davy
David *Bible*
David (Scottish
  kings)
David (patron saint
  of Wales)
David, Eliza|beth
  (English cookery
  writer)
David, Jacques-
  Louis (French
  painter)
Davie *also* Davey,
  Davy
Davies, Peter
  Max|well
  (English
  composer)
Davies,
  Rob|ert|son
  (Canadian writer)
Davies, W. H.
  (English poet)
da Vinci,
  Leo|nardo
  (Italian painter
  and designer)
Davis (breathing
  apparatus)
Davis, Bette
  (American
  actress)
Davis, Joe and
  Fred (English
  snooker players)
Davis, Miles
  (American jazz
  musician)
Davis, Steve
  (English snooker
  player)
Davis Cup
Davis|son,
  Clin|ton Jo|seph
  (American
  physicist)

Davis Strait
(between
Greenland and
Baffin Island)
davit +s
Davos (resort,
Switzerland)
Davy also **Davey**,
Davie
(name)
Davy
Davies
(lamp)
Davy, Hum|phry
(English chemist)
**Davy Jones's
locker**
daw +s (jackdaw.
△dor, door)
daw|dle
daw|dles
daw|dled
dawd|ling
dawd|ler +s
**Daw|kins,
Rich|ard** (English
biologist)
Dawn (name)
dawn +s +ed +ing
(daybreak)
dawn|ing +s
Day, Doris
(American
actress)
day +s
Dayak +s (use
Dyak)
Dayan, Moshe
(Israeli politician
and general)
day|bed +s
day|book +s
day-boy +s
day|break
day-by-day
adjective
day care
day centre +s
day|dream +s +ed
+ing
day|dream|er +s
day-girl +s
Day-Glo *Propr.*
day|less
Day-Lewis, Cecil
(English writer)
**Day-Lewis,
Dan|iel** (English
actor)
day|light +s
day lily
day lil|ies

day-long
day nur|sery
day nur|ser|ies
day-old *attributive*
day-owl +s
day|pack +s
day re|lease
day re|turn +s
day room +s
day|sack +s
day school +s
day|side
day|time +s
day-to-day
adjective
Day|ton (city, USA)
day trip +s
day trip|per +s
day|work
daze
dazes
dazed
daz|ing
dazed|ly
daz|zle
daz|zles
daz|zled
daz|zling
dazzle|ment +s
daz|zler +s
daz|zling|ly
D-Day
de|ac|ces|sion +s
+ed +ing
dea|con +s
dea|con|ate +s
dea|con|ess
dea|con|esses
dea|con|ship +s
de|acti|vate
de|acti|vates
de|acti|vated
de|acti|vat|ing
de|acti|va|tion
de|acti|va|tor +s
dead +er +est
dead-and-alive
dead-ball *adjective*
dead|beat +s
dead|bolt +s
dead|en +s +ed
+ing
dead end +s *noun*
dead-end *adjective*
dead|en|er +s
dead|eye +s
dead|fall +s
dead-head +s +ed
+ing *noun and*
verb
dead heat +s *noun*

dead-heat +s +ed
+ing *verb*
dead let|ter +s
dead|light +s
dead|line +s
dead|li|ness
dead|lock +s +ed
+ing
dead|ly
dead|lier
dead|li|est
dead march
dead marches
dead|ness
dead-nettle +s
dead on
dead|pan
dead|pans
dead|panned
dead|pan|ning
dead reck|on|ing
Dead Sea (in Near
East)
dead|stock
dead weight +s
de-aerate
de-aerates
de-aerated
de-aerating
de-aeration
deaf +er +est
(unable to hear.
△def)
deaf aid +s
deaf-blind *adjective*
deaf|en +s +ed
+ing
deaf|en|ing|ly
deaf|ly
deaf mute +s
deaf|ness
deal
deals
dealt
deal|ing
deal|er +s
deal|er|ship +s
deal|ing +s
dealt
de|am|bu|la|tion
de|am|bu|la|tory
de|am|bu|
la|tor|ies
Dean (name)
**Dean,
Chris|to|pher**
(English ice-
skater)
Dean, James
(American actor)

dean +s (head of
faculty; doyen.
△dene)
dean|ery
dean|er|ies
(dean's house;
group of parishes.
△denary)
De|anna
dear +s +er +est
(beloved;
expensive.
△deer)
dearie +s
Dear John
attributive
dear|ly
dear|ness
dearth +s
deasil (clockwise.
△diesel)
death +s
death|bed +s
death blow +s
death camp +s
death-defying
death knell
death|less
death|less|ness
death|like
death|li|ness
death|ly
death|lier
death|li|est
death mask +s
death rate +s
death rat|tle +s
death roll +s
death row +s
death toll +s
death trap +s
Death Val|ley
(desert basin,
USA)
death war|rant +s
**death-watch
bee|tle** +s
death wish
death wishes
de|at|trib|ute
de|at|trib|utes
de|at|trib|uted
de|at|trib|ut|ing
de|at|tri|bu|tion +s
deb +s
de|bacle +s
debag
de|bags
de|bagged
de|bag|ging
debar
de|bars

debar (cont.)
de|barred
de|bar|ring
de|bark +s +ed
+ing
de|bark|ation
de|bar|ment +s
de|base
de|bases
de|based
de|bas|ing
de|base|ment +s
de|baser +s
de|bat|able
de|bat|ably
de|bate
de|bates
de|bated
de|bat|ing
de|bater +s
de|bauch
de|bauches
de|bauched
de|bauch|ing
de|bauch|ee +s
de|bauch|er +s
de|bauch|ery
Deb|bie
de|beak +s +ed
+ing
de Beau|voir,
Sim|one (French
writer)
de|ben|ture +s
de|bili|tate
de|bili|tates
de|bili|tated
de|bili|tat|ing
de|bili|tat|ing|ly
de|bili|ta|tion
de|bili|ta|tive
de|bil|ity
de|bil|ities
debit +s +ed +ing
deb|on|air
deb|on|air|ly
Deb|orah (Bible;
name)
de|bouch
de|bouches
de|bouched
de|bouch|ing
de|bouch|ment
Deb|re|cen (city,
Hungary)
De|brett (peerage
book)
de|bride|ment
de|brief +s +ed
+ing
de|brief|ing +s

deb|ris
de Brog|lie, Louis
(French physicist;
wavelength)
debt +s
debt|or +s
debug
de|bugs
de|bugged
de|bug|ging
de|bug|ger +s
de|bunk +s +ed
+ing
de|bunk|er +s
debus
de|busses
de|bussed
de|bus|sing
De|bussy, Claude
(French
composer)
debut +s +ed +ing
debu|tant +s male
debu|tante +s
female
Debye, Peter
(Dutch-born
American
chemical
physicist)
dec|adal
dec|ade +s
deca|dence
deca|dent +s
deca|dent|ism
deca|dent|ly
de|cad|ic
decaf Propr.
de|caf|fein|ate
de|caf|fein|ates
de|caf|fein|ated
de|caf|fein|at|ing
deca|gon +s
dec|agon|al
dec|agyn|ous
deca|he|dral
deca|he|dron
deca|he|dra or
deca|he|drons
decal +s
de|cal|ci|fi|ca|tion
de|cal|ci|fier +s
de|cal|cify
de|cal|ci|fies
de|cal|ci|fied
de|cal|ci|fy|ing
de|cal|co|mania
+s
deca|liter Am. +s
deca|litre Br. +s
Deca|logue
De|cam|eron

deca|meter Am. +s
deca|metre Br. +s
de|camp +s +ed
+ing
de|camp|ment
de|can|al
de|can|drous
de|cani
de|cant +s +ed
+ing
de|cant|er +s
de|capi|tate
de|capi|tates
de|capi|tated
de|capi|tat|ing
de|capi|ta|tion +s
de|capi|ta|tor +s
deca|pod +s
deca|pod|an
de|car|bon|isa|tion
Br. (use
decarbonization)
de|car|bon|ise Br.
(use decarbonize)
de|car|bon|ises
de|car|bon|ised
de|car|bon|is|ing
de|car|bon|iza|tion
de|car|bon|ize
de|car|bon|izes
de|car|bon|ized
de|car|bon|iz|ing
deca|style +s
de|casu|al|isa|tion
Br. (use
decasualization)
de|casu|al|ise Br.
(use decasualize)
de|casu|al|ises
de|casu|al|ised
de|casu|al|is|ing
de|casu|al|iza|tion
de|casu|al|ize
de|casu|al|izes
de|casu|al|ized
de|casu|al|iz|ing
deca|syl|lab|ic
deca|syl|lable +s
dec|ath|lete +s
dec|ath|lon +s
decay +s +ed +ing
decay|able
Dec|can (plateau,
India)
de|cease
de|ceases
de|ceased
de|ceas|ing
de|ce|dent +s
de|ceit +s
de|ceit|ful
de|ceit|ful|ly

de|ceit|ful|ness
de|ceiv|able
de|ceive
de|ceives
de|ceived
de|ceiv|ing
de|ceiver +s
de|cel|er|ate
de|cel|er|ates
de|cel|er|ated
de|cel|er|at|ing
de|cel|er|ation +s
de|cel|er|ator +s
de|cel|er|om|eter
+s
De|cem|ber +s
De|cem|brist +s
de|cency
de|cen|cies
de|cen|nial
de|cen|ni|al|ly
de|cen|nium
de|cen|nia
de|cent
de|cen|ter Am. +s
+ed +ing (Br.
decentre)
de|cent|ly
de|cen|tral|
isa|tion Br. (use
decentralization)
de|cen|tral|ise Br.
(use decentralize)
de|cen|tral|ises
de|cen|tral|ised
de|cen|tral|is|ing
de|cen|tral|ist +s
de|cen|tral|
iza|tion
de|cen|tral|ize
de|cen|tral|izes
de|cen|tral|ized
de|cen|tral|iz|ing
de|centre Br.
de|centres
de|centred
de|cen|tring
(Am. decenter)
de|cep|tion +s
de|cep|tive
de|cep|tive|ly
de|cep|tive|ness
de|cere|brate
de|chlor|in|ate
de|chlor|in|ates
de|chlor|in|ated
de|chlor|in|at|ing
de|chlor|in|ation
+s
De|cian
deci|bel +s
de|cid|able

de|cide
de|cides
de|cided
de|cid|ing
de|cided|ly
de|cided|ness
de|cider +s
de|cidu|ous
de|cidu|ous|ness
deci|gram +s
deci|gramme *Br.*
+s
decile +s
deci|liter *Am.* +s
deci|litre *Br.* +s
deci|mal +s
deci|mal|isa|tion
Br. (use
decimalization)
deci|mal|ise *Br.*
(use decimalize)
deci|mal|ises
deci|mal|ised
deci|mal|is|ing
deci|mal|iza|tion
deci|mal|ize
deci|mal|izes
deci|mal|ized
deci|mal|iz|ing
deci|mal|ly
deci|mate
deci|mates
deci|mated
deci|mat|ing
deci|ma|tion
deci|ma|tor +s
deci|meter *Am.* +s
deci|metre *Br.* +s
de|cipher +s +ed
+ing
de|cipher|able
de|cipher|ment
de|ci|sion +s
de|ci|sion maker
+s
decision-making
de|cisive
de|cisive|ly
de|cisive|ness
Dec|ius, Gaius
Mes|sius
Quin|tus (Roman
emperor)
deck +s +ed +ing
deck|chair +s
deck|hand +s
deckle +s
deckled
deckle edge +s
deckle-edged
de|claim +s +ed
+ing

de|claim|er +s
dec|lam|ation +s
de|clama|tory
Dec|lan
de|clar|able
de|clar|ant +s
dec|lar|ation +s
de|clara|tive +s
de|clara|tive|ly
de|clara|tive|ness
de|clara|tory
de|clare
de|clares
de|clared
de|clar|ing
de|clared|ly
de|clarer +s
de|class
de|classes
de|classed
de|class|ing
dé|classé *male*
dé|clas|sée *female*
de|clas|si|fi|ca|tion
+s
de|clas|sify
de|clas|si|fies
de|clas|si|fied
de|clas|si|fy|ing
de-claw +s +ed
+ing
de|clen|sion +s
de|clen|sion|al
de|clin|able
dec|lin|ation +s
dec|lin|ation|al
de|cline
de|clines
de|clined
de|clin|ing
de|cliner +s
dec|lin|om|eter +s
de|cliv|itous
de|cliv|ity
de|cliv|ities
de|clutch
de|clutches
de|clutched
de|clutch|ing
deco (= art deco.
△ dekko)
de|coct +s +ed
+ing
de|coc|tion +s
de|cod|able
de|code
de|codes
de|coded
de|cod|ing
de|coder +s
de|coke
de|cokes

de|coke (*cont.*)
de|coked
de|cok|ing
de|col|late
de|col|lates
de|col|lated
de|col|lat|ing
de|col|la|tion +s
dé|col|le|tage +s
dé|col|leté
dé|col|letée (use
décolleté)
de|col|on|isa|tion
Br. (use
decolonization)
de|col|on|ise *Br.*
(use decolonize)
de|col|on|ises
de|col|on|ised
de|col|on|is|ing
de|col|on|iza|tion
de|col|on|ize
de|col|on|izes
de|col|on|ized
de|col|on|iz|ing
de|col|or|isa|tion
Br. (use
decolorization)
de|col|or|ise *Br.*
(use decolorize)
de|col|or|ises
de|col|or|ised
de|col|or|is|ing
de|col|or|iza|tion
de|col|or|ize
de|col|or|izes
de|col|or|ized
de|col|or|iz|ing
de|com|mis|sion
+s +ed +ing
de|com|mun|isa|
tion *Br.* (use
decommuniza-
tion)
de|com|mun|ise
Br. (use
decommunize)
de|com|mun|ises
de|com|mun|ised
de|com|
mun|is|ing
de|com|mun|iza|
tion
de|com|mun|ize
de|com|mun|izes
de|com|mun|ized
de|com|
mun|iz|ing
de|com|pos|able
de|com|pose
de|com|poses

de|com|pose
(*cont.*)
de|com|posed
de|com|pos|ing
de|com|poser +s
de|com|pos|ition
+s
de|com|pound +s
+ed +ing
de|com|press
de|com|presses
de|com|pressed
de|com|press|ing
de|com|pres|sion
de|com|pres|sor
+s
de|con|gest|ant +s
de|con|se|crate
de|con|se|crates
de|con|se|crated
de|con|se|crat|ing
de|con|se|cra|tion
+s
de|con|struct +s
+ed +ing
de|con|struc|tion
+s
de|con|struc|tion|
ism
de|con|struc|tion|
ist +s
de|con|struct|ive
de|con|tam|in|ate
de|con|tam|in|
ates
de|con|tam|in|
ated
de|con|tam|in|
at|ing
de|con|tam|in|
ation
de|con|text|ual|ise
Br. (use
decontextualize)
de|con|text|ual|
ises
de|con|text|ual|
ised
de|con|text|ual|
is|ing
de|con|text|ual|ize
de|con|text|ual|
izes
de|con|text|ual|
ized
de|con|text|ual|
iz|ing
de|con|trol
de|con|trols
de|con|trolled
de|con|trol|ling
decor +s

dec¦or¦ate
  dec¦or¦ates
  dec¦or¦ated
  dec¦or¦at¦ing
dec¦or¦ation +s
dec¦ora¦tive
dec¦ora¦tive¦ly
dec¦ora¦tive¦ness
dec¦or¦ator +s
dec¦or¦ous
dec¦or¦ous¦ly
dec¦or¦ous¦ness
de¦cor¦ti¦cate
  de¦cor¦ti¦cates
  de¦cor¦ti¦cated
  de¦cor¦ti¦cat¦ing
de¦cor¦ti¦ca¦tion +s
de¦corum
dé¦coup¦age
de¦couple
  de¦couples
  de¦coupled
  de¦coup¦ling
decoy +s +ed +ing
de¦crease
  de¦creases
  de¦creased
  de¦creas¦ing
de¦creas¦ing¦ly
de¦cree
  de¦crees
  de¦creed
  de¦cree¦ing
de¦cree ab¦so¦lute
  de¦crees
  ab¦so¦lute
de¦cree nisi
  de¦crees nisi
dec¦re¦ment +s
de¦crepit
de¦crepi¦tate
  de¦crepi¦tates
  de¦crepi¦tated
  de¦crepi¦tat¦ing
de¦crepi¦ta¦tion
de¦crepi¦tude
de¦cres¦cendo +s
de¦cres¦cent
de¦cretal +s
de¦crial +s
de¦crier +s
de¦crim¦in¦al¦
  isa¦tion *Br.* (use
  decriminaliza-
  tion)
de¦crim¦in¦al¦ise
  Br. (use
  decriminalize)
  de¦crim¦in¦al¦ises
  de¦crim¦in¦al¦ised
  de¦crim¦in¦al¦
    is¦ing

de¦crim¦in¦al¦
    iza¦tion
de¦crim¦in¦al¦ize
  de¦crim¦in¦al¦izes
  de¦crim¦in¦al¦ized
  de¦crim¦in¦al¦
    iz¦ing
decry
  de¦cries
  de¦cried
  de¦cry¦ing
de¦crypt +s +ed
  +ing
de¦cryp¦tion
de¦cum¦bent
dec¦uple
  dec¦uples
  dec¦upled
  decu¦pling
decu¦plet +s
de¦cur¦va¦ture +s
de¦curve
  de¦curves
  de¦curved
  de¦curv¦ing
de¦cus¦sate
  de¦cus¦sates
  de¦cus¦sated
  de¦cus¦sat¦ing
de¦cus¦sa¦tion
de¦dans
  plural de¦dans
Dede¦kind,
  Rich¦ard
  (German
  mathematician)
dedi¦cate
  dedi¦cates
  dedi¦cated
  dedi¦cat¦ing
dedi¦cated¦ly
dedi¦catee +s
dedi¦ca¦tion +s
dedi¦ca¦tive
dedi¦ca¦tor +s
dedi¦ca¦tory
de¦duce
  de¦duces
  de¦duced
  de¦du¦cing
de¦du¦cible
de¦duct +s +ed
  +ing
de¦duct¦ibil¦ity
de¦duct¦ible +s
de¦duc¦tion +s
de¦duct¦ive
de¦duct¦ive¦ly
de Duve,
  Chris¦tian René
  (Belgian
  biochemist)

Dee (river,
  Scotland; river,
  Wales and
  England)
dee +s
deed +s
deed-box
  deed-boxes
deed poll
dee¦jay +s
deem +s +ed +ing
  (judge. △ deme)
de-emphasise *Br.*
  (use de-
  emphasize)
  de-emphasises
  de-emphasised
  de-emphasis¦ing
de-emphasize
  de-emphasizes
  de-emphasized
  de-emphasiz¦ing
deem¦ster +s
deep +s +er +est
deep-down
  attributive
deep-drawn
deep¦en +s +ed
  +ing
deep fat *attributive*
deep-freeze
  deep-freezes
  deep-froze
  deep-freezing
  deep-frozen
deep-fry
  deep-fries
  deep-fried
  deep-frying
deep¦ing +s
deep-laid
deep¦ly
deep-mined
deep-mouthed
deep¦ness
deep-rooted
deep-sea *attributive*
deep-seated
deep-throat¦ed
deep-water
  attributive
deer
  plural deer
  (animal. △ dear)
deer for¦est +s
deer¦hound +s
deer-lick +s
deer mouse
  deer mice
deer¦skin +s
deer¦stalk¦er +s
deer stalk¦ing

de-escalate
  de-escalates
  de-escalated
  de-escalat¦ing
de-escalation +s
Dee¦side (regions,
  Scotland and
  Wales)
def (excellent.
  △ deaf)
de¦face
  de¦faces
  de¦faced
  de¦facing
de¦face¦able
de¦face¦ment +s
de¦facer +s
de facto
de¦fal¦cate
  de¦fal¦cates
  de¦fal¦cated
  de¦fal¦cat¦ing
de¦fal¦ca¦tion +s
de¦fal¦ca¦tor +s
de Falla, Ma¦nuel
  (Spanish
  composer)
def¦am¦ation +s
de¦fama¦tory
de¦fame
  de¦fames
  de¦famed
  de¦fam¦ing
de¦famer +s
defat
  de¦fats
  de¦fat¦ted
  de¦fat¦ting
de¦fault +s +ed
  +ing
de¦fault¦er +s
de¦feas¦ance
de¦feas¦ibil¦ity
de¦feas¦ible
de¦feas¦ibly
de¦feat +s +ed
  +ing
de¦feat¦ism
de¦feat¦ist +s
defe¦cate
  defe¦cates
  defe¦cated
  defe¦cat¦ing
defe¦ca¦tion
defe¦ca¦tor +s
de¦fect +s +ed
  +ing
de¦fec¦tion +s
de¦fect¦ive +s
de¦fect¦ive¦ly
de¦fect¦ive¦ness
de¦fect¦or +s

de|fence*Br.* +s
(*Am.* defense)
de|fence|less*Br.*
(*Am.* defenseless)
de|fence|less|ly*Br.*
(*Am.*
defenselessly)
de|fence|less|ness
Br. (*Am.*
defenselessness)
de|fence|man
de|fence|men
(*Am.*
defenseman)
de|fend+s +ed
+ing
de|fend|able
de|fend|ant+s
de|fend|er+s
de|fen|es|trate
de|fen|es|trates
de|fen|es|trated
de|fen|es|trat|ing
de|fen|es|tra|tion
+s
de|fense*Am.* +s
(*Br.* defence)
de|fense|less*Am.*
(*Br.* defenceless)
de|fense|less|ly
Am. (*Br.*
defencelessly)
de|fense|less|ness
Am. (*Br.*
defencelessness)
de|fense|man*Am.*
de|fense|men
(*Br.* defenceman)
de|fens|ibil|ity
de|fens|ible
de|fens|ibly
de|fen|sive
de|fen|sive|ly
de|fen|sive|ness
defer
de|fers
de|ferred
de|fer|ring
def|er|ence
def|er|ens (in
'vas deferens')
def|er|en|tial
def|er|en|tial|ly
de|fer|ment+s
de|fer|rable
de|fer|ral+s
de|fer|rer+s
de|fi|ance
de|fi|ant
de|fi|ant|ly
de|fib|ril|la|tion
de|fib|ril|la|tor+s

dc|fi|ciency
de|fi|cien|cies
de|fi|cient
de|fi|cient|ly
def|icit+s
de|fier+s
def|il|ade
def|il|ades
def|il|aded
def|il|ad|ing
de|file
de|files
de|filed
de|fil|ing
de|file|ment
de|filer+s
de|fin|able
de|fin|ably
de|fine
de|fines
de|fined
de|fin|ing
de|finer+s
def|in|ite+s
def|in|ite|ly
def|in|ite|ness
def|in|ition+s
def|in|ition|al
def|in|ition|al|ly
de|fini|tive+s
de|fini|tive|ly
def|la|grate
def|la|grates
def|la|grated
def|la|grat|ing
def|la|gra|tion
def|la|gra|tor+s
de|flate
de|flates
de|flated
de|flat|ing
de|fla|tion+s
de|fla|tion|ary
de|fla|tion|ist+s
de|fla|tor+s
de|flect+s +ed
+ing
de|flec|tion+s
de|flec|tor+s
de|flex|ion+s (use
deflection)
de|flor|ation
de|flower+s +ed
+ing
de|fo|cus
de|fo|cuses *or*
de|fo|cus|ses
de|focused *or*
de|fo|cussed
de|fo|cus|ing *or*
de|fo|cus|sing

Defoe, Dan|iel
(English writer)
de|foli|ant+s
de|foli|ate
de|foli|ates
de|foli|ated
de|foli|at|ing
de|foli|ation
de|foli|ator+s
De For|est, Lee
(American
physicist)
de|for|est+s +ed
+ing
de|for|est|ation
de|form+s +ed
+ing
de|form|able
de|form|ation+s
de|form|ation|al
de|form|ity
de|form|ities
de|fraud+s +ed
+ing
de|fraud|er+s
de|fray+s +ed
+ing
de|fray|able
de|fray|al
de|fray|ment
de|frock+s +ed
+ing
de|frost+s +ed
+ing
de|frost|er+s
deft+er +est
deft|ly
deft|ness
de|funct
de|funct|ness
de|fuse
de|fuses
de|fused
de|fus|ing
defy
de|fies
de|fied
defy|ing
dé|gagé *male*
dé|gagée *female*
Degas, Edgar
(French artist)
degas
de|gasses
de|gassed
de|gas|sing
de Gaulle, Charles
(French
statesman)
de|gauss
de|gausses

de|gauss(*cont.*)
de|gaussed
de|gauss|ing
de|gauss|er+s
de|gen|er|acy
de|gen|er|ate
de|gen|er|ates
de|gen|er|ated
de|gen|er|at|ing
de|gen|er|ate|ly
de|gen|er|ation
de|gen|era|tive
de|grad|abil|ity
de|grad|able
deg|rad|ation+s
de|grada|tive
de|grade
de|grades
de|graded
de|grad|ing
de|grad|er+s
de|grad|ing|ly
de|granu|late
de|granu|lates
de|granu|lated
de|granu|lat|ing
de|granu|la|tion
de|grease
de|greases
de|greased
de|greas|ing
de|greaser+s
de|gree+s
de|gree|less
de|gres|sive
de haut en bas
**de Hav|il|land,
Geof|frey**
(English aircraft
designer)
de|hire
de|hires
de|hired
de|hir|ing
de|hisce
de|hisces
de|hisced
de|his|cing
de|his|cence
de|his|cent
de|his|tori|cise*Br.*
(use
dehistoricize)
de|his|tori|cises
de|his|tori|cised
de|his|tori|cis|ing
de|his|tori|cize
de|his|tori|cizes
de|his|tori|cized
de|his|tori|ciz|ing
de Hooch, Pieter
(Dutch painter)

de Hoogh, Pieter (use de Hooch)

de¦horn +s +ed +ing

de¦hu¦man¦isa¦tion *Br.* (use dehumanization)

de¦hu¦man¦ise *Br.* (use dehumanize)
  de¦hu¦man¦ises
  de¦hu¦man¦ised
  de¦hu¦man¦is¦ing

de¦hu¦man¦iza¦tion

de¦hu¦man¦ize
  de¦hu¦man¦izes
  de¦hu¦man¦ized
  de¦hu¦man¦iz¦ing

de¦hu¦midi¦fi¦ca¦tion

de¦hu¦midi¦fier +s

de¦hu¦mid¦ify
  de¦hu¦midi¦fies
  de¦hu¦midi¦fied
  de¦hu¦midi¦fy¦ing

de¦hy¦drate
  de¦hy¦drates
  de¦hy¦drated
  de¦hy¦drat¦ing

de¦hy¦dra¦tion

de¦hy¦dra¦tor +s

de¦hydro¦gen¦ate
  de¦hydro¦gen¦ates
  de¦hydro¦gen¦ated
  de¦hydro¦gen¦at¦ing

de¦hydro¦gen¦ation

Deia¦nira *Greek Mythology*

de-ice
  de-ices
  de-iced
  de-icing

de-icer +s

dei¦cide

deic¦tic +s

dei¦fi¦ca¦tion

dei¦form

deify
  dei¦fies
  dei¦fied
  dei¦fy¦ing

Deigh¦ton, Len (English writer)

deign +s +ed +ing

Dei gra¦tia

Dei¦mos (*Greek Mythology*; moon of Mars)

de-industrial¦isa¦tion *Br.* (use de-industrialization)

de-industrial¦iza¦tion

dei¦nony¦chus
  dei¦nony¦chuses

dei¦no¦there +s

de¦insti¦tu¦tion¦al¦isa¦tion *Br.* (use deinstitutionaliza-tion)

de¦insti¦tu¦tion¦al¦ise *Br.* (use deinstitutional-ize)
  de¦insti¦tu¦tion¦al¦ises
  de¦insti¦tu¦tion¦al¦ised
  de¦insti¦tu¦tion¦al¦is¦ing

de¦insti¦tu¦tion¦al¦iza¦tion

de¦insti¦tu¦tion¦al¦ize
  de¦insti¦tu¦tion¦al¦izes
  de¦insti¦tu¦tion¦al¦ized
  de¦insti¦tu¦tion¦al¦iz¦ing

de¦ion¦isa¦tion *Br.* (use deionization)

de¦ion¦ise *Br.* (use deionize)
  de¦ion¦ises
  de¦ion¦ised
  de¦ion¦is¦ing

de¦ion¦iser *Br.* +s (use deionizer)

de¦ion¦iza¦tion

de¦ion¦ize
  de¦ion¦izes
  de¦ion¦ized
  de¦ion¦iz¦ing

de¦ion¦izer +s

deip¦noso¦phist +s

Deir¦dre (*Irish Mythology*; name)

deism

deist +s

de¦is¦tic

de¦is¦tic¦al

deity
  de¦ities

déjà vu

de¦ject +s +ed +ing

de¦ject¦ed¦ly

de¦jec¦tion

de jure

Dek¦ker, Thomas (English dramatist)

dekko +s (look. △ deco)

de Klerk, F. W. (South African statesman)

de Koon¦ing, Wil¦lem (Dutch-born American painter)

de la Beche, Henry (English geologist)

De¦la¦croix, Eu¦gène (French painter)

de¦laine

de la Mare, Wal¦ter (English writer)

De¦la¦roche, Paul (French painter)

de¦late
  de¦lates
  de¦lated
  de¦lat¦ing

de¦la¦tion

de¦la¦tor +s

De¦lau¦nay, Rob¦ert (French painter)

Delaunay-Terk, Sonia (Russian-born painter and textile designer)

Dela¦ware (state, USA)

Dela¦ware
  plural Dela¦ware or Dela¦wares (American Indian)

delay +s +ed +ing

delayed-action
  attributive

de¦lay¦er +s

del cre¦dere

dele
  deles
  deled
  dele¦ing

de¦lect¦abil¦ity

de¦lect¦able

de¦lect¦ably

de¦lect¦ation

del¦eg¦able

dele¦gacy
  dele¦ga¦cies

dele¦gate
  dele¦gates

dele¦gate (*cont.*)
  dele¦gated
  dele¦gat¦ing

dele¦ga¦tion +s

dele¦ga¦tor +s

de Len¦clos, Ninon (French courtesan)

de¦lete
  de¦letes
  de¦leted
  de¦let¦ing

dele¦teri¦ous

dele¦teri¦ous¦ly

de¦le¦tion +s

Del¦font, Ber¦nard (Lord Delfont, Russian-born British impresario)

Delft (city, the Netherlands)

delft (china)

delft¦ware

Delhi (capital of India)

deli +s (= delicatessen)

Delia

Delian +s

de¦lib¦er¦ate
  de¦lib¦er¦ates
  de¦lib¦er¦ated
  de¦lib¦er¦at¦ing

de¦lib¦er¦ate¦ly

de¦lib¦er¦ate¦ness

de¦lib¦er¦ation +s

de¦lib¦era¦tive

de¦lib¦era¦tive¦ly

de¦lib¦era¦tive¦ness

de¦lib¦era¦tor +s

De¦libes, Léo (French composer)

deli¦cacy
  deli¦ca¦cies

deli¦cate

deli¦cate¦ly

deli¦cate¦ness

deli¦ca¦tes¦sen +s

de¦li¦cious

de¦li¦cious¦ly

de¦li¦cious¦ness

de¦lict +s

de¦light +s +ed +ing

de¦light¦ed¦ly

de¦light¦ful

de¦light¦ful¦ly

de¦light¦ful¦ness

De¦li¦lah *Bible*

de|limit +s +ed
+ing
de|limi|tate
de|limi|tates
de|limi|tated
de|limi|tat|ing
de|limi|ta|tion +s
de|lim|it|er +s
de|lin|eate
de|lin|eates
de|lin|eated
de|lin|eat|ing
de|lin|ea|tion +s
de|lin|ea|tor +s
de|lin|quency
de|lin|quen|cies
de|lin|quent +s
de|lin|quent|ly
deli|quesce
deli|quesces
deli|quesced
deli|ques|cing
deli|ques|cence
deli|ques|cent
de|li|ri|ous
de|li|ri|ous|ly
de|lir|ium +s
de|lir|ium
tre|mens
De|lius, Fred|erick
(English
composer)
de|liver +s +ed
+ing
de|liver|able +s
de|liv|er|ance +s
de|liv|er|er +s
de|liv|ery
de|liv|er|ies
dell +s
Della
Della Crus|can +s
della Fran|cesca,
Piero (Italian
painter)
della Quer|cia,
Ja|copo (Italian
sculptor)
della Rob|bia,
Luca (Florentine
sculptor)
de|lo|cal|isa|tion
Br. (use
delocalization)
de|lo|cal|ise Br.
(use delocalize)
de|lo|cal|ises
de|lo|cal|ised
de|lo|cal|is|ing
de|lo|cal|iza|tion
de|lo|cal|ize
de|lo|cal|izes

de|lo|cal|ize (cont.)
de|lo|cal|ized
de|lo|cal|iz|ing
Del|lores also
Do|lores
De|lors, Jacques
(French
statesman)
Delos (Greek
island)
de|louse
de|louses
de|loused
de|lous|ing
Del|phi (city and
site, ancient
Greece)
Del|phian +s
Del|phic
Del|phine
del|phin|ium +s
del|phin|oid +s
del Sarto, An|drea
(Italian painter)
delta +s
del|ta|ic
del|ti|olo|gist +s
del|ti|ology
del|toid +s
de|lude
de|ludes
de|luded
de|lud|ing
de|luder +s
del|uge
del|uges
del|uged
del|uging
de|lu|sion +s
de|lu|sion|al
de|lu|sive
de|lu|sive|ly
de|lu|sive|ness
de|lu|sory
de|lus|ter Am.+s
+ed +ing
de|lustre Br.
de|lustres
de|lustred
de|lus|tring
de luxe
delve
delves
delved
delv|ing
delver +s
delv|ing +s
de|mag|net|
isa|tion Br. (use
demagnetization)
de|mag|net|ise Br.
(use

de|mag|net|ise
(cont.)
demagnetize)
de|mag|net|ises
de|mag|net|ised
de|mag|net|is|ing
de|mag|net|iser Br.
+s (use
demagnetizer)
de|mag|net|
iza|tion
de|mag|net|ize
de|mag|net|izes
de|mag|net|ized
de|mag|net|iz|ing
de|mag|net|izer +s
dema|gog|ic
dema|gogue +s
dema|goguery
dema|gogy
de|mand +s +ed
+ing
de|mand|able
de|mand|ant +s
de|mand|er +s
de|mand|ing|ly
demand-led
adjective
de|mant|oid +s
de|mar|cate
de|mar|cates
de|mar|cated
de|mar|cat|ing
de|mar|ca|tion +s
de|mar|ca|tor +s
dé|marche +s
de|materi|al|
isa|tion Br. (use
dematerializa-
tion)
de|materi|al|ise Br.
(use
dematerialize)
de|materi|al|ises
de|materi|al|ised
de|materi|al|
is|ing
de|materi|al|
iza|tion
de|materi|al|ize
de|materi|al|izes
de|materi|al|ized
de|materi|al|
iz|ing
de Mau|pas|sant,
Guy (French
writer)
Dema|vend (use
Damavand)
deme +s (political
division, Greece;
Biology. ⚠ deem)

de|mean +s +ed
+ing
de|meanor Am. +s
de|mean|our Br. +s
de' Med|ici
(Florentine family)
de' Med|ici,
Cath|er|ine
(French queen)
de' Med|ici,
Cos|imo
(Florentine
statesman and
banker)
de' Med|ici,
Gio|vanni (Pope
Leo X)
de' Med|ici,
Lor|enzo
(Florentine
statesman and
scholar)
de' Med|ici, Maria
(Italian name for
Marie de
Médicis)
de Mé|di|cis,
Marie (French
queen)
De|melza
de|ment +s
de|men|ted
de|men|ted|ly
de|men|ted|ness
dé|menti +s
de|men|tia
de|men|tia
prae|cox
Dem|er|ara (river,
Guyana)
dem|er|ara (sugar)
de|merge
de|merges
de|merged
de|mer|ging
de|mer|ger +s
de|merit +s
de|meri|tori|ous
de|mer|sal
de|mesne +s
Dem|eter Greek
Mythology
demi|god +s
demi|god|dess
demi|god|desses
demi|john +s
de|mili|tar|isa|tion
Br. (use
demilitarization)
de|mili|tar|ise Br.
(use demilitarize)
de|mili|tar|ises

de|mili|tar|ise
(cont.)
de|mili|tar|ised
de|mili|tar|is|ing
de|mili|tar|iza|tion
de|mili|tar|ize
de|mili|tar|izes
de|mili|tar|ized
de|mili|tar|iz|ing
de Mille, Cecil B.
(American film
producer and
director)
demi-mondaine +s
demi-monde
de|min|er|al|
    isa|tion *Br.* (use
    demineralization)
de|min|er|al|ise *Br.*
(use
demineralize)
de|min|er|al|ises
de|min|er|al|ised
de|min|er|al|
        is|ing
de|min|er|al|
            iza|tion
de|min|er|al|ize
de|min|er|al|izes
de|min|er|al|ized
de|min|er|al|
            iz|ing
demi-pension
demi|rep +s
de|mise
de|mises
de|mised
de|mis|ing
demi|semi|quaver
+s
de|mis|sion
de|mist +s +ed
+ing
de|mist|er +s
demit
de|mits
de|mit|ted
de|mit|ting
demi|tasse +s
demi|urge +s
demi|ur|gic
demi-vierge +s
Demme,
Jona|than
(American film
director)
demo +s
demob
de|mobs
de|mobbed
de|mob|bing

de|mo|bil|isa|tion
Br. (use
demobilization)
de|mo|bil|ise *Br.*
(use demobilize)
de|mo|bil|ises
de|mo|bil|ised
de|mo|bil|is|ing
de|mo|bil|iza|tion
de|mo|bil|ize
de|mo|bil|izes
de|mo|bil|ized
de|mo|bil|iz|ing
dem|oc|racy
dem|oc|ra|cies
Demo|crat +s
(supporter of US
Democratic Party)
demo|crat +s
Demo|crat|ic (of
US political party)
demo|crat|ic
demo|crat|ic|al|ly
dem|oc|ra|tisa|
tion *Br.* (use
democratization)
dem|oc|ra|tise *Br.*
(use democratize)
dem|oc|ra|tises
dem|oc|ra|tised
dem|oc|ra|tis|ing
dem|oc|ra|tism
dem|oc|ra|
        tiza|tion
dem|oc|ra|tize
dem|oc|ra|tizes
dem|oc|ra|tized
dem|oc|ra|tiz|ing
Dem|oc|ri|tus
(Greek
philosopher)
démodé
de|modu|late
de|modu|lates
de|modu|lated
de|modu|lat|ing
de|modu|la|tion
de|modu|la|tor +s
dem|og|raph|er +s
demo|graph|ic
demo|graph|ical
demo|graph|ic|
            al|ly
demo|graph|ics
dem|og|raphy
de|mois|elle +s
de|mol|ish
de|mol|ishes
de|mol|ished
de|mol|ish|ing
de|mol|ish|er +s
demo|li|tion +s

demo|li|tion|ist +s
demon +s
de|mon|et|isa|tion
Br. (use
demonetization)
de|mon|et|ise *Br.*
(use demonetize)
de|mon|et|ises
de|mon|et|ised
de|mon|et|is|ing
de|mon|et|iza|tion
de|mon|et|ize
de|mon|et|izes
de|mon|et|ized
de|mon|et|iz|ing
de|mon|iac
de|mon|iac|al
de|mon|iac|al|ly
de|mon|ic
de|mon|isa|tion *Br.*
(use
demonization)
de|mon|ise *Br.* (use
demonize)
de|mon|ises
de|mon|ised
de|mon|is|ing
de|mon|ism
de|mon|iza|tion
de|mon|ize
de|mon|izes
de|mon|ized
de|mon|iz|ing
de|mon|olatry
de|mono|logic|al
de|mono|lo|gist +s
de|mon|ology
de|mon|op|ol|ise
Br. (use
demonopolize)
de|mon|op|ol|ises
de|mon|op|ol|
            ised
de|mon|op|ol|
            is|ing
de|mon|op|ol|ize
de|mon|op|ol|izes
de|mon|op|ol|
            ized
de|mon|op|ol|
            iz|ing
dem|on|stra|bil|ity
dem|on|strable
dem|on|strably
dem|on|strate
dem|on|strates
dem|on|strated
dem|on|strat|ing
dem|on|stra|tion
+s
de|mon|
        stra|tion|al

de|mon|stra|tive
de|mon|
        stra|tive|ly
de|mon|stra|tive|
            ness
dem|on|stra|tor +s
de Mont|fort,
Simon (English
soldier)
de|mor|al|isa|tion
Br. (use
demoralization)
de|mor|al|ise *Br.*
(use demoralize)
de|mor|al|ises
de|mor|al|ised
de|mor|al|is|ing
de|moral|is|ing|ly
Br. (use
demoralizingly)
de|mor|al|iza|tion
de|mor|al|ize
de|mor|al|izes
de|mor|al|ized
de|mor|al|iz|ing
de|moral|iz|ing|ly
De|mos|thenes
(Athenian orator)
de|mote
de|motes
de|moted
de|mot|ing
de|mot|ic
de|mo|tion +s
de|mo|tiv|ate
de|mo|tiv|ates
de|mo|tiv|ated
de|mo|tiv|at|ing
de|mo|tiv|ation
de|mount +s +ed
+ing
de|mount|able
Demp|sey, Jack
(American boxer)
de|mul|cent +s
demur
de|murs
de|murred
de|mur|ring
de|mure
de|murer
de|mur|est
de|mure|ly
de|mure|ness
de|mur|rable
de|mur|rage +s
de|mur|ral +s
de|mur|rer +s
demy (paper size)
de|mys|ti|fi|ca|tion
de|mys|tify
de|mys|ti|fies

de|mys|tify (*cont.*)
de|mys|ti|fied
de|mys|ti|fy|ing
de|myth|olo|gise
Br. (use
demythologize)
de|myth|olo|gises
de|myth|
olo|gised
de|myth|
olo|gis|ing
de|myth|olo|gize
de|myth|olo|gizes
de|myth|
olo|gized
de|myth|
olo|giz|ing
den +s
den|ar|ius
den|arii
den|ary (decimal.
△ deanery)
de|nation|al|
isa|tion Br. (use
denationalization)
de|nation|al|ise Br.
(use
denationalize)
de|nation|al|ises
de|nation|al|ised
de|nation|al|
is|ing
de|nation|al|
iza|tion
de|nation|al|ize
de|nation|al|izes
de|nation|al|ized
de|nation|al|
iz|ing
de|natur|al|
isa|tion Br. (use
denaturalization)
de|natur|al|ise Br.
(use
denaturalize)
de|natur|al|ises
de|natur|al|ised
de|natur|al|is|ing
de|natur|al|
iza|tion
de|natur|al|ize
de|natur|al|izes
de|natur|al|ized
de|natur|al|iz|ing
de|natur|ant +s
de|natur|ation
de|nature
de|natures
de|natured
de|natur|ing
de|nazi|fi|ca|tion

de|nazify
de|nazi|fies
de|nazi|fied
de|nazi|fy|ing
Den|bigh|shire
(former county,
Wales)
Dench, Judi
(English actress)
den|drite +s
den|drit|ic
den|drit|ic|al|ly
den|dro|
chrono|logic|al
den|dro|
chron|olo|gist +s
den|dro|
chron|ology
den|dro|gram +s
den|droid
den|dro|logic|al
den|drolo|gist +s
den|drol|ogy
dene +s (sandhill;
vale. △ dean)
Deneb (star)
dene-hole +s
de|nest +s +ed
+ing
de-net
de-nets
de-netted
de-netting
De|neuve,
Cath|érine
(French actress)
dengue
Deng Xiao|ping
(Chinese
statesman)
Den Haag
(Dutch name for
The Hague)
deni|abil|ity
deni|able
de|nial +s
de|nier +s (person
who denies)
den|ier
plural den|ier
(unit)
deni|grate
deni|grates
deni|grated
deni|grat|ing
deni|gra|tion
deni|gra|tor +s
deni|gra|tory
denim +s
De Niro, Rob|ert
(American actor)

Denis, Maur|ice
(French painter)
Denis also Den|nis,
Denys
Denis (Italian-born
patron saint of
France)
Den|ise
de|nitri|fi|ca|tion
de|nitrify
de|nitri|fies
de|nitri|fied
de|nitri|fy|ing
deni|zen +s
deni|zen|ship
Den|mark
Den|mark Strait
(shipping area, N.
Atlantic)
Den|nis also Denis,
Denys
de|nom|in|ate
de|nom|in|ates
de|nom|in|ated
de|nom|in|at|ing
de|nom|in|ation
+s
de|nom|in|ation|al
de|nom|in|ation|al|
ism
de|nom|in|ation|al|
ist +s
de|nom|ina|tive
de|nom|in|ator +s
de nos jours
de|nota|tion +s
de|nota|tive
de|note
de|notes
de|noted
de|not|ing
de|noue|ment +s
de|nounce
de|nounces
de|nounced
de|noun|cing
de|nounce|ment
+s
de|noun|cer +s
de nou|veau
de novo
Den|pa|sar (city,
Bali)
dense
dens|er
dens|est
dense|ly
dense|ness
densi|tom|eter +s
dens|ity
dens|ities
dent +s +ed +ing

den|tal
den|tal|ise Br. (use
dentalize)
den|tal|ises
den|tal|ised
den|tal|is|ing
den|ta|lium
den|ta|lia
den|tal|ize
den|tal|izes
den|tal|ized
den|tal|iz|ing
den|tate
den|ticle +s
den|ticu|late
den|ti|frice +s
den|til +s
Architecture
denti|lin|gual
den|tinal
den|tine +s
den|tist +s
den|tis|try
den|ti|tion
den|ture +s
den|tur|ist +s
de|nuclear|isa|tion
Br. (use
denuclearization)
de|nuclear|ise Br.
(use
denuclearize)
de|nuclear|ises
de|nuclear|ised
de|nuclear|is|ing
de|nuclear|
iza|tion
de|nuclear|ize
de|nuclear|izes
de|nuclear|ized
de|nuclear|iz|ing
de|nuda|tion
de|nuda|tive
de|nude
de|nudes
de|nuded
de|nud|ing
de|numer|abil|ity
de|numer|able
de|numer|ably
de|nun|ci|ate
de|nun|ci|ates
de|nun|ci|ated
de|nun|ci|at|ing
de|nun|ci|ation +s
de|nun|cia|tive
de|nun|ci|ator +s
de|nun|ci|atory
Den|ver (city, USA)
deny
de|nies

deny (cont.)
de¦nied
deny¦ing
Denys (saint; use
'Denis)
Denys also **Denis**,
Den¦nis
(name)
Den¦zil
deoch an doris
deo¦dar +s
de¦odor¦ant +s
de¦odor¦isa¦tion
Br. (use
Jeodorization)
de¦odor¦ise Br. (use
deodorize)
de¦odor¦ises
de¦odor¦ised
de¦odor¦is¦ing
de¦odor¦iser Br. +s
(use deodorizer)
de¦odor¦iza¦tion
de¦odor¦ize
de¦odor¦izes
de¦odor¦ized
de¦odor¦iz¦ing
de¦odor¦izer +s
Deo gra¦tias
de¦ontic
de¦onto¦logic¦al
de¦ontolo¦gist +s
de¦ontol¦ogy
Deo vol¦ente
de¦oxy¦gen¦ate
de¦oxy¦gen¦ates
de¦oxy¦gen¦ated
de¦oxy¦gen¦at¦ing
de¦oxy¦gen¦ation
de¦oxy¦ribo¦
nucle¦ic
de¦oxy¦ri¦bose
De¦par¦dieu,
Gér¦ard (French
actor)
de¦part +s +ed
+ing
de¦part¦ment +s
de¦part¦men¦tal
de¦part¦men¦tal¦
isa¦tion Br. (use
departmentaliza-
tion)
de¦part¦men¦tal¦
ise Br. (use
departmentalize)
de¦part¦men¦tal¦
ises
de¦part¦men¦tal¦
ised
de¦part¦men¦tal¦
is¦ing

de¦part¦men¦tal¦
ism
de¦part¦men¦tal¦
iza¦tion
de¦part¦men¦tal¦
ize
de¦part¦men¦tal¦
izes
de¦part¦men¦tal¦
ized
de¦part¦men¦tal¦
iz¦ing
de¦part¦men¦tal¦ly
de¦part¦ure +s
de¦pas¦tur¦age
de¦pas¦ture
de¦pas¦tures
de¦pas¦tured
de¦pas¦tur¦ing
dé¦paysé male
dé¦pay¦sée female
de¦pend +s +ed
+ing
de¦pend¦abil¦ity
de¦pend¦able
de¦pend¦able¦ness
de¦pend¦ably
de¦pend¦ant Br. +s
noun (Am.
dependent)
de¦pend¦ence
de¦pend¦ency
de¦pend¦en¦cies
de¦pend¦ent
adjective
de¦pend¦ent Am.
+s noun (Br.
dependant)
de¦pend¦ent¦ly
de¦pend¦ing
de¦per¦son¦al¦
isa¦tion Br. (use
depersonaliza-
tion)
de¦per¦son¦al¦ise
Br. (use
depersonalize)
de¦per¦son¦al¦ises
de¦per¦son¦al¦ised
de¦per¦son¦al¦
is¦ing
de¦per¦son¦al¦
iza¦tion
de¦per¦son¦al¦ize
de¦per¦son¦al¦izes
de¦per¦son¦al¦ized
de¦per¦son¦al¦
iz¦ing
de¦pict +s +ed
+ing
de¦pict¦er +s
de¦pic¦tion +s

de¦pict¦ive
de¦pict¦or +s (use
depicter)
dep¦il¦ate
dep¦il¦ates
dep¦il¦ated
dep¦il¦at¦ing
dep¦il¦ation +s
de¦pila¦tory
de¦pila¦tor¦ies
de Pisan,
Chris¦tine (Italian-
born writer)
de Pizan,
Chris¦tine (use de
Pisan)
de¦plane
de¦planes
de¦planed
de¦plan¦ing
de¦plete
de¦pletes
de¦pleted
de¦plet¦ing
de¦ple¦tion +s
de¦plor¦able
de¦plor¦ably
de¦plore
de¦plores
de¦plored
de¦plor¦ing
de¦plor¦ing¦ly
de¦ploy +s +ed
+ing
de¦ploy¦ment +s
de¦plume
de¦plumes
de¦plumed
de¦plum¦ing
de¦polar¦isa¦tion
Br. (use
depolarization)
de¦polar¦ise Br.
(use depolarize)
de¦polar¦ises
de¦polar¦ised
de¦polar¦is¦ing
de¦polar¦iza¦tion
de¦polar¦ize
de¦polar¦izes
de¦polar¦ized
de¦polar¦iz¦ing
de¦pol¦iti¦cisa¦tion
Br. (use
depoliticization)
de¦pol¦iti¦cise Br.
(use depoliticize)
de¦pol¦iti¦cises
de¦pol¦iti¦cised
de¦pol¦iti¦cis¦ing
de¦pol¦iti¦ciza¦tion
de¦pol¦iti¦cize
de¦pol¦iti¦cizes

de¦pol¦iti¦cize
(cont.)
de¦pol¦iti¦cized
de¦pol¦iti¦ciz¦ing
de¦poly¦mer¦
isa¦tion Br. (use
depolymeriza-
tion)
de¦poly¦mer¦ise Br.
(use
depolymerize)
de¦poly¦mer¦ises
de¦poly¦mer¦ised
de¦poly¦mer¦is¦ing
de¦poly¦mer¦
iza¦tion
de¦poly¦mer¦ize
de¦poly¦mer¦izes
de¦poly¦mer¦ized
de¦poly¦mer¦
iz¦ing
de¦pon¦ent +s
de¦popu¦late
de¦popu¦lates
de¦popu¦lated
de¦popu¦lat¦ing
de¦popu¦la¦tion
de¦port +s +ed
+ing
de¦port¦able
de¦port¦ation +s
de¦port¦ee +s
de¦port¦ment +s
de¦pose
de¦poses
de¦posed
de¦pos¦ing
de¦posit +s +ed
+ing
de¦pos¦it¦ary
de¦pos¦it¦ar¦ies
(person.
△ depository)
de¦pos¦ition +s
de¦pos¦ition¦al
de¦pos¦it¦or +s
de¦posi¦tory
de¦posi¦tor¦ies
(storehouse.
△ depositary)
depot +s
dep¦rav¦ation +s
(perversion,
corruption.
△ deprivation)
de¦prave
de¦praves
de¦praved
de¦prav¦ing
de¦prav¦ity
de¦prav¦ities

dep|re|cate
  dep|re|cates
  dep|re|cated
  dep|re|cat|ing
  (disapprove of)
dep|re|cat|ing|ly
dep|re|ca|tion +s
dep|re|ca|tive
dep|re|ca|tor +s
dep|re|ca|tory
de|pre|ci|ate
  de|pre|ci|ates
  de|pre|ci|ated
  de|pre|ci|at|ing
  (lower in value;
  belittle)
de|pre|ci|at|ing|ly
de|pre|ci|ation +s
de|pre|ci|atory
dep|re|da|tion +s
dep|re|da|tor +s
dep|re|da|tory
de|press
  de|presses
  de|pressed
  de|press|ing
de|pres|sant +s
de|press|ible
de|press|ing|ly
de|pres|sion +s
de|pres|sive +s
de|pres|sor +s
  (muscle)
de|pres|sur|isa|
  tion Br. (use
  depressurization)
de|pres|sur|ise Br.
  (use
  depressurize)
de|pres|sur|ises
de|pres|sur|ised
de|pres|sur|is|ing
de|pres|sur|iza|
         tion
de|pres|sur|ize
  de|pres|sur|izes
  de|pres|sur|ized
  de|pres|sur|iz|ing
De|prez, Jos|quin
  (use des Prez)
de|priv|able
de|prival
de|priv|ation +s
  (hardship, loss.
  △ depravation)
de|prive
  de|prives
  de|prived
  de|priv|ing
de pro|fun|dis
depth +s
depth bomb +s

depth charge +s
depth|less
dep|ur|ate
  dep|ur|ates
  dep|ur|ated
  dep|ur|at|ing
dep|ur|ation
de|pura|tive +s
de|pura|tor +s
depu|ta|tion +s
de|pute
  de|putes
  de|puted
  de|put|ing
depu|tise Br. (use
  deputize)
  depu|tises
  depu|tised
  depu|tis|ing
depu|tize
  depu|tizes
  depu|tized
  depu|tiz|ing
dep|uty
  dep|uties
dep|uty|ship +s
De Quin|cey,
  Thomas (English
  writer)
de|racin|ate
  de|racin|ates
  de|racin|ated
  de|racin|at|ing
de|racin|ation
de|rail +s +ed +ing
de|rail|leur +s
de|rail|ment +s
De|rain, André
  (French artist)
de|range
  de|ranges
  de|ranged
  de|ran|ging
de|range|ment +s
de|rate
  de|rates
  de|rated
  de|rat|ing
de|ration +s +ed
  +ing
Der|bent (city,
  Dagestan)
Derby
  Der|bies
  (city, England;
  horse race.
  △ Darby)
derby
  der|bies
  (shoe. △ darbies)
Derby Day

Derby|shire
  (county, England)
de|rec|og|nise Br.
  (use derecognize)
  de|rec|og|nises
  de|rec|og|nised
  de|rec|og|nis|ing
de|rec|og|ni|tion
de|rec|og|nize
  de|rec|og|nizes
  de|rec|og|nized
  de|rec|og|niz|ing
de|regis|ter +s +ed
  +ing
de|regis|tra|tion
  +s
de règle
de|regu|late
  de|regu|lates
  de|regu|lated
  de|regu|lat|ing
de|regu|la|tion
Derek *also* Der|rick
dere|lict +s
dere|lic|tion
de|re|qui|si|tion
de|res|trict +s +ed
  +ing
de|res|tric|tion +s
de|ride
  de|rides
  de|rided
  de|rid|ing
de|rider +s
de|rid|ing|ly
de-rig
  de-rigs
  de-rigged
  de-rigging
de ri|gueur
de|ris|ible
de|ri|sion
de|ri|sive
de|ri|sive|ly
de|ri|sive|ness
de|ri|sory
de|riv|able
der|iv|ation +s
der|iv|ation|al
de|riva|tive +s
de|riva|tive|ly
de|rive
  de|rives
  de|rived
  de|riv|ing
derm
derma
der|mal
derma|titis
der|ma|to|glyph|ic
der|ma|to|glyph|ic|
         al|ly

der|ma|to|
         glyph|ics
der|ma|to|logic|al
der|ma|to|logic|
         al|ly
derma|tolo|gist +s
derma|tol|ogy
der|mic
der|mis
Der|mot
der|nier cri
dero|gate
  dero|gates
  dero|gated
  dero|gat|ing
dero|ga|tion
de|roga|tive
de|roga|tor|ily
de|roga|tory
Der|rick *also* Derek
  (name)
der|rick +s (crane)
Der|rida, Jacques
  (French
  philospher and
  critic)
Der|rid|ean
der|rière +s
derring-do
der|rin|ger +s
der|ris
  plural der|ris
Derry
  (= Londonderry,
  town; name)
derry (in 'have a
  derry on
  someone')
derv (fuel oil)
der|vish
  der|vishes
de|sal|in|ate
  de|sal|in|ates
  de|sal|in|ated
  de|sal|in|at|ing
de|sal|in|ation
de|sal|in|isa|tion
  Br. (use
  desalinization)
de|sal|in|ise Br.
  (use desalinize)
  de|sal|in|ises
  de|sal|in|ised
  de|sal|in|is|ing
de|sal|in|iza|tion
de|sal|in|ize
  de|sal|in|izes
  de|sal|in|ized
  de|sal|in|iz|ing
de|salt +s +ed
  +ing
des|apare|cido +s

de|scale
  de|scales
  de|scaled
  de|scal|ing
des|cant +s +ed
  +ing
Des|cartes, René
  (French
  philosopher and
  mathematician)
des|cend +s +ed
  +ing
des|cend|ant +s
  noun
des|cend|ent
  adjective
des|cend|er +s
des|cend|ible
des|cent +s (act of
  descending.
  △ dissent)
de|scram|ble
  de|scram|bles
  de|scram|bled
  de|scram|bling
de|scram|bler +s
de|scrib|able
de|scribe
  de|scribes
  de|scribed
  de|scrib|ing
de|scriber +s
de|scrip|tion +s
de|scrip|tive
de|scrip|tive|ly
de|scrip|tive|ness
de|scrip|tor +s
des|cry
  des|cries
  des|cried
  des|cry|ing
Des|de|mona
dese|crate
  dese|crates
  dese|crated
  dese|crat|ing
dese|cra|tion +s
dese|cra|tor +s
de|seed +s +ed
  +ing
de|seed|er +s
de|seg|re|gate
  de|seg|re|gates
  de|seg|re|gated
  de|seg|re|gat|ing
de|seg|re|ga|tion
de|select +s +ed
  +ing
de|selec|tion
de|sen|si|tisa|tion
  Br. (use
  desensitization)

de|sen|si|tise *Br.*
  (use **desensitize**)
  de|sen|si|tises
  de|sen|si|tised
  de|sen|si|tis|ing
de|sen|si|tiser *Br.*
  +s (use
  desensitizer)
de|sen|si|tiza|tion
de|sen|si|tize
  de|sen|si|tizes
  de|sen|si|tized
  de|sen|si|tiz|ing
de|sen|si|tizer +s
des|ert +s +ed
  +ing (barren
  region; abandon;
  recompense.
  △ dessert)
de|sert|er +s
desert|ifi|ca|tion
de|ser|tion +s
desert rat +s
de|serve
  de|serves
  de|served
  de|serv|ing
de|served|ly
de|served|ness
de|serv|er +s
de|serv|ing|ly
de|serv|ing|ness
desex
  de|sexes
  de|sexed
  de|sex|ing
de|sexu|al|isa|tion
  Br. (use
  desexualization)
de|sexu|al|ise *Br.*
  (use **desexualize**)
  de|sexu|al|ises
  de|sexu|al|ised
  de|sexu|al|is|ing
de|sexu|al|iza|tion
de|sexu|al|ize
  de|sexu|al|izes
  de|sexu|al|ized
  de|sexu|al|iz|ing
dés|ha|billé
De Sica, Vit|torio
  (Italian film
  director and actor)
des|ic|cant +s
des|ic|cate
  des|ic|cates
  des|ic|cated
  des|ic|cat|ing
des|ic|ca|tion
des|ic|ca|tive
des|ic|ca|tor +s

de|sid|er|ate
  de|sid|er|ates
  de|sid|er|ated
  de|sid|er|at|ing
de|sid|era|tive
de|sid|er|atum
  de|sid|er|ata
de|sign +s +ed
  +ing
des|ig|nate
  des|ig|nates
  des|ig|nated
  des|ig|nat|ing
des|ig|na|tion +s
des|ig|na|tor +s
de|sign|ed|ly
de|sign|er +s
de|sign|ing|ly
de|sir|abil|ity
de|sir|able +s
de|sir|able|ness
de|sir|ably
de|sire
  de|sires
  de|sired
  de|sir|ing
De|sir|ée
de|sir|ous
de|sist +s +ed +ing
desk +s
desk-bound
de|skill +s +ed
  +ing
desk|top +s
des|man +s
des|mid +s
Des Moines (city,
  USA)
Des|mond
deso|late
  deso|lates
  deso|lated
  deso|lat|ing
deso|late|ly
deso|late|ness
deso|la|tion +s
deso|la|tor +s
de|sorb +s +ed
  +ing
de|sorb|ent +s
de|sorp|tion +s
des|pair +s +ed
  +ing
des|pair|ing|ly
des|patch (use
  dispatch)
  des|patches
  des|patched
  des|patch|ing
des|patch box
  des|patch boxes

des|patch box
  (*cont.*)
  (use dispatch
  box)
des|patch|er +s
  (use dispatcher)
des|patch rider
  des|patch riders
  (use dispatch
  rider)
des|per|ado
  des|per|adoes
des|per|ate
des|per|ate|ly
des|per|ate|ness
des|per|ation
de|spic|able
de|spic|ably
de Spin|oza,
  Bar|uch (Dutch
  philosopher)
des|pise
  des|pises
  des|pised
  des|pis|ing
des|piser +s
des|pite
des|pite|ful
de|spoil +s +ed
  +ing
de|spoil|er +s
de|spoil|ment
de|spoli|ation
des|pond
des|pond|ence
des|pond|ency
des|pond|ent
des|pond|ent|ly
des|pot +s
des|pot|ic
des|pot|ic|al|ly
des|pot|ism
des Prés, Jos|quin
  (use des Prez)
des Prez, Jos|quin
  (Flemish
  composer)
des|quam|ate
  des|quam|ates
  des|quam|ated
  des|quam|at|ing
des|quam|ation
des|quama|tive
des|quama|tory
des res
  plural des res
Des|sau (city,
  Germany)
des|sert +s (sweet
  course. △ desert)
des|sert|spoon +s

des¦sert¦spoon¦ful
+s
de¦sta¦bil¦isa¦tion
Br. (use
destabilization)
de¦sta¦bil¦ise Br.
(use destabilize)
de¦sta¦bil¦ises
de¦sta¦bil¦ised
de¦sta¦bil¦is¦ing
de¦sta¦bil¦iza¦tion
de¦sta¦bil¦ize
de¦sta¦bil¦izes
de¦sta¦bil¦ized
de¦sta¦bil¦iz¦ing
de-stalin¦isa¦tion
Br. (use de-
stalinization)
de-stalin¦iza¦tion
De Stijl (Dutch art
movement)
des¦tin¦ation +s
des¦tine
des¦tines
des¦tined
des¦tin¦ing
des¦tiny
des¦tinies
des¦ti¦tute +s
des¦ti¦tu¦tion
de¦stock +s +ed
+ing
dest¦rier +s
des¦troy +s +ed
+ing
des¦troy¦able
des¦troy¦er +s
de¦struct +s +ed
+ing
de¦struct¦ibil¦ity
de¦struct¦ible
de¦struc¦tion +s
de¦struc¦tive
de¦struc¦tive¦ly
de¦struc¦tive¦ness
de¦struc¦tor +s
de¦sue¦tude
de¦sul¦fur¦iza¦tion
Am.
de¦sul¦fur¦ize Am.
de¦sul¦fur¦izes
de¦sul¦fur¦ized
de¦sul¦fur¦iz¦ing
de¦sul¦phur¦
isa¦tion Br. (use
desulphurization)
de¦sul¦phur¦ise Br.
(use
desulphurize)
de¦sul¦phur¦ises
de¦sul¦phur¦ised
de¦sul¦phur¦is¦ing

de¦sul¦phur¦
iza¦tion Br.
de¦sul¦phur¦ize Br.
de¦sul¦phur¦izes
de¦sul¦phur¦ized
de¦sul¦phur¦iz¦ing
des¦ul¦tor¦ily
des¦ul¦tori¦ness
des¦ul¦tory
de¦tach
de¦taches
de¦tached
de¦tach¦ing
de¦tach¦able
de¦tach¦ed¦ly
de¦tach¦ment
de¦tail +s +ed +ing
de¦tain +s +ed
+ing
de¦tain¦ee +s
de¦tain¦er +s
de¦tain¦ment
de¦tect +s +ed
+ing
de¦tect¦able
de¦tect¦ably
de¦tec¦tion +s
de¦tect¦ive +s
de¦tect¦or +s
de¦tent +s
(mechanical
catch)
dé¦tente +s
de¦ten¦tion +s
deter
de¦ters
de¦terred
de¦ter¦ring
de¦ter¦gent +s
de¦teri¦or¦ate
de¦teri¦or¦ates
de¦teri¦or¦ated
de¦teri¦or¦at¦ing
de¦teri¦or¦ation +s
de¦teri¦ora¦tive
de¦ter¦ment
de¦ter¦min¦able
de¦ter¦min¦acy
de¦ter¦min¦ant +s
de¦ter¦min¦ate
de¦ter¦min¦ate¦ly
de¦ter¦min¦ate¦
ness
de¦ter¦min¦ation
+s
de¦ter¦mina¦tive
de¦ter¦mina¦tive¦ly
de¦ter¦mine
de¦ter¦mines
de¦ter¦mined
de¦ter¦min¦ing
de¦ter¦mined¦ly

de¦ter¦mined¦ness
de¦ter¦miner +s
de¦ter¦min¦ism
de¦ter¦min¦ist +s
de¦ter¦min¦is¦tic
de¦ter¦min¦is¦tic¦
al¦ly
de¦ter¦rence
de¦ter¦rent +s
de¦test +s +ed
+ing
de¦test¦able
de¦test¦ably
de¦test¦ation
de¦test¦er +s
de¦throne
de¦thrones
de¦throned
de¦thron¦ing
de¦throne¦ment
det¦on¦ate
det¦on¦ates
det¦on¦ated
det¦on¦at¦ing
det¦on¦ation +s
det¦ona¦tive
det¦on¦ator +s
de¦tour +s +ed
+ing
detox
de¦toxes
de¦toxed
de¦tox¦ing
de¦toxi¦cate
de¦toxi¦cates
de¦toxi¦cated
de¦toxi¦cat¦ing
de¦toxi¦ca¦tion
de¦toxi¦fi¦ca¦tion
de¦tox¦ify
de¦toxi¦fies
de¦toxi¦fied
de¦toxi¦fy¦ing
de¦tract +s +ed
+ing
de¦trac¦tion +s
de¦tract¦ive
de¦tract¦or +s
de¦train +s +ed
+ing
de¦train¦ment
de¦trib¦al¦isa¦tion
Br. (use
detribalization)
de¦trib¦al¦ise Br.
(use detribalize)
de¦trib¦al¦ises
de¦trib¦al¦ised
de¦trib¦al¦is¦ing
de¦trib¦al¦iza¦tion
de¦trib¦al¦ize
de¦trib¦al¦izes

de¦trib¦al¦ize
(cont.)
de¦trib¦al¦ized
de¦trib¦al¦iz¦ing
det¦ri¦ment
det¦ri¦men¦tal
det¦ri¦men¦tal¦ly
de¦trital
de¦trited
de¦tri¦tion
de¦tritus
De¦troit (city, USA)
de trop
de Troyes,
Chré¦tien (French
poet)
Det¦tol Propr.
de¦tumes¦cence
de¦tune
de¦tunes
de¦tuned
de¦tun¦ing
Deu¦cal¦ion Greek
Mythology
deuce +s
deuced
deuced¦ly
deus ex mach¦ina
deu¦ter¦ag¦on¦ist
+s
deu¦ter¦ate
deu¦ter¦ates
deu¦ter¦ated
deu¦ter¦at¦ing
deu¦ter¦ation
deu¦ter¦ium
deu¦tero¦
canon¦ic¦al
Deutero-Isaiah
(Old Testament
author)
deu¦teron +s
Deu¦tero¦nom¦ic
Deu¦tero¦nom¦ical
Deu¦ter¦on¦om¦ist
+s
Deu¦ter¦on¦omy
Deutsch¦mark +s
deut¦zia +s
Dev, Kapil (Indian
cricketer)
deva +s (divine
being)
de Val¦era, Eamon
(Irish statesman)
de Val¦ois,
Nin¦ette (Irish
dancer and
choreographer)
de¦valu¦ation +s
de¦value
de¦values

de|value (*cont.*)
de|valued
de|valu|ing
Deva|nag|ari
dev|as|tate
dev|as|tates
dev|as|tated
dev|as|tat|ing
dev|as|tat|ing|ly
dev|as|ta|tion +s
dev|as|ta|tor +s
de|vein +s +ed
+ing
de|velop +s +ed
+ing
de|vel|op|able
de|vel|op|er +s
de|vel|op|ment +s
de|vel|op|men|tal
de|vel|op|
men|tal|ly
Devi *Hinduism*
de|vi|ance
de|vi|ancy
de|vi|an|cies
de|vi|ant +s
de|vi|ate
de|vi|ates
de|vi|ated
de|vi|at|ing
de|vi|ation +s
de|vi|ation|al
de|vi|ation|ism
de|vi|ation|ist +s
de|vi|ator +s
de|vi|atory
de|vice +s
devil
dev|ils
dev|illed *Br.*
dev|iled *Am.*
dev|il|ling *Br.*
dev|il|ing *Am.*
devil|dom
devil|fish
plural devil|fish *or*
devil|fishes
devil|ish
devil|ish|ly
devil|ish|ness
devil|ism
devil-may-care
devil|ment +s
dev|il|ry
dev|il|ries
devil's ad|vo|cate
+s
devil's bit +s
devil's coach-
horse +s
devil's darn|ing
nee|dle +s

Devil's Island (off
coast of French
Guiana)
devils-on-
horseback
de|vi|ous
de|vi|ous|ly
de|vi|ous|ness
de|vis|able
(able to be devised.
△divisible)
de|vise
de|vises
de|vised
de|vis|ing
de|visee +s
de|viser +s
(inventor.
△devisor,
divisor)
de|visor +s (person
leaving property
to another.
△deviser,
divisor)
de|vi|tal|isa|tion
Br. (use
devitalization)
de|vi|tal|ise *Br.*
(use devitalize)
de|vi|tal|ises
de|vi|tal|ised
de|vi|tal|is|ing
de|vi|tal|iza|tion
de|vi|tal|ize
de|vi|tal|izes
de|vi|tal|ized
de|vi|tal|iz|ing
de|vit|ri|fi|ca|tion
de|vit|rify
de|vit|ri|fies
de|vit|ri|fied
de|vit|ri|fy|ing
de|void
de|voir +s
de|vo|lute
de|vo|lutes
de|vo|luted
de|vo|lut|ing
de|vo|lu|tion +s
de|vo|lu|tion|ary
de|vo|lu|tion|ist +s
de|volve
de|volves
de|volved
de|volv|ing
de|volve|ment +s
Devon (county,
England)
Dev|on|ian +s
Dev|on|shire
(= Devon)

dé|vot +s *male*
de|vote
de|votes
de|voted
de|vot|ing
dé|vote +s *female*
de|voted|ly
de|voted|ness
de|votee +s
de|vote|ment
de|vo|tion +s
de|vo|tion|al
de|vour +s +ed
+ing
de|vour|er +s
de|vour|ing|ly
de|vout
de|vout|ly
de|vout|ness
Devoy, Susan
(New Zealand
squash player)
de Vries, Hugo
(Dutch plant
physiologist)
dew +s +ed +ing
(moisture. △due)
dewan +s
Dewar, James
(Scottish physicist
and chemist)
dewar +s (flask)
de|water +s +ed
+ing
dew|berry
dew|berries
dew|claw +s
dew|drop +s
Dewey (library
system)
Dewey, John
(American
philosopher)
Dewey, Maur|ice
(American
librarian)
dew|fall +s
Dewi (name; for
Welsh saint, use
David)
dew|ily
dewi|ness
dew|lap +s
de|worm +s +ed
+ing
dew point +s
dew-pond +s
Dews|bury (town,
England)
dewy
dewy-eyed
Dexe|drine *Propr.*
Dex|ter (name)

dex|ter +s
(*Heraldry* on the
right; cattle)
dex|ter|ity
dex|ter|ous
dex|ter|ous|ly
dex|ter|ous|ness
dex|tral
dex|tral|ity
dex|tral|ly
dex|tran +s
dex|trin
dex|tro|rota|tion
dex|tro|rota|tory
dex|trorse
dex|trose
dex|trous (use
dexterous)
dex|trous|ly (use
dexterously)
dex|trous|ness
(use
dexterousness)
Dhaka (capital of
Bangladesh)
dhal +s
Dhan|bad (city,
India)
dharma
Dharuk
Dhau|la|giri
(mountain,
Himalayas)
dhobi +s (washer-
man. △dobe)
dhobi itch
dhobi's itch
Dho|far (province,
Oman)
dhole
plural dhole *or*
dholes
(dog. △dole)
dhoti +s
dhow +s
dhurra +s (use
durra)
Di (woman's name)
dia|base +s
dia|betes
dia|bet|ic +s
diab|lerie
dia|bol|ic
dia|bol|ical
dia|bol|ical|ly
di|ab|ol|ise *Br.* (use
diabolize)
di|ab|ol|ises
di|ab|ol|ised
di|ab|ol|is|ing
di|ab|ol|ism
di|ab|ol|ist +s

di|ab|ol|ize
di|ab|ol|izes
di|ab|ol|ized
di|ab|ol|iz|ing
dia|chron|ic
dia|chron|ic|al|ly
di|achron|ism
dia|chron|is|tic
di|achron|ous
di|achrony
di|ac|onal
di|ac|on|ate +s
dia|crit|ic +s
dia|crit|ic|al
di|adel|phous
dia|dem +s
dia|demed
Dia|dochi
(Macedonian
generals)
di|aer|esis Br.
di|aer|eses
(Am. dieresis)
dia|gen|esis
Di|ag|hi|lev,
Ser|gei
Pav|lo|vich
(Russian ballet
impresario)
diag|nos|able
diag|nose
diag|noses
diag|nosed
diag|nos|ing
diag|no|sis
diag|no|ses
diag|nos|tic +s
diag|nos|tic|al|ly
diag|nos|ti|cian +s
diag|nos|tics
di|ag|onal +s
di|ag|onal|ly
dia|gram
dia|grams
dia|grammed Br.
dia|gramed Am.
dia|gram|ming Br.
dia|gram|ing Am.
dia|gram|mat|ic
dia|gram|mat|ic|
    al|ly
dia|gram|ma|tise
Br. (use
diagrammatize)
dia|gram|ma|tises
dia|gram|
    ma|tised
dia|gram|
    ma|tis|ing
dia|gram|ma|tize
dia|gram|ma|tizes

dia|gram|ma|tize
(cont.)
dia|gram|
    ma|tized
dia|gram|
    ma|tiz|ing
dia|grid +s
dia|kin|esis
dial
dials
dialled Br.
dialed Am.
dial|ling Br.
dial|ing Am.
dia|lect +s
dia|lect|al
dia|lect|ic +s
dia|lect|ic|al
dia|lect|ic|al|ly
dia|lect|ician +s
dia|lect|ics
dia|lect|olo|gist +s
dia|lect|ology
dial|er Am. +s
dial|ler Br. +s
dia|log Am. +s
dia|logic
dialo|gist +s
dia|logue Br. +s
dia|lyse Br.
dia|lyses
dia|lysed
dia|lys|ing
dia|ly|sis
dia|ly|ses
dia|lyt|ic
dia|lyze Am.
dia|lyzes
dia|lyzed
dia|lyz|ing
dia|mag|net|ic +s
dia|mag|net|ic|
    al|ly
dia|mag|net|ism
dia|mantê
dia|man|tifer|ous
dia|mant|ine
diam|eter +s
diam|etral
dia|met|ric
dia|met|ric|al
dia|met|ric|al|ly
dia|mond +s
dia|mond|back +s
diamond-bird +s
dia|mond|ifer|ous
Diana (Roman
Mythology;
Princess of Wales)
di|an|drous
Diane also Di|anne
Dia|net|ics

di|an|thus
    plural di|an|thus
    or di|an|thuses
dia|pa|son +s
dia|pause +s
di|aper +s +ed
    +ing (nappy;
    pattern)
di|aph|an|ous
di|aph|an|ous|ly
dia|phor|esis
dia|phor|et|ic +s
dia|phragm +s
dia|phrag|mat|ic
dia|pir +s Geology
dia|posi|tive +s
di|arch|al
di|arch|ic
di|archy
di|arch|ies
diar|ise Br. (use
    diarize)
diar|ises
diar|ised
diar|is|ing
diar|ist +s
diar|is|tic
diar|ize
diar|izes
diar|ized
diar|iz|ing
diar|rhea Am.
diar|rhe|al Am.
diar|rhe|ic Am.
diar|rhoea Br.
diar|rhoe|al Br.
diar|rhoe|ic Br.
diary
diar|ies
Dias,
    Bar|tolo|meu
    (Portuguese
    explorer)
dia|scope +s
Dias|pora (of Jews)
dias|pora +s
    (generally)
dia|stase +s
dia|stasic
dia|stat|ic
dia|stema +s
dia|stole +s
dia|stol|ic
dia|ther|mancy
dia|ther|man|ous
dia|ther|mic
dia|ther|mous
dia|thermy
di|ath|esis
di|ath|eses
dia|tom +s
dia|tom|aceous

dia|atom|ic
di|atom|ite
dia|ton|ic +s
dia|tribe +s
Diaz,
    Bar|tolo|meu
    (use Dias)
Diaz, Por|firio
    (Mexican
    president)
di|aze|pam +s
diazo
di|azo|type +s
dib
dibs
dibbed
dib|bing
di|basic
dib|ber +s
dib|ble
dib|bles
dib|bled
dib|bling
dibs
dice
    plural dice
    (noun; also plural
    of die)
dice
dices
diced
di|cing
    verb
dicer +s
dicey
dici|er
dici|est
di|cho|tom|ic
di|chot|om|ise Br.
    (use dichotomize)
di|chot|om|ises
di|chot|om|ised
di|chot|om|is|ing
di|chot|om|ize
di|chot|om|izes
di|chot|om|ized
di|chot|om|iz|ing
di|chot|om|ous
di|chot|omy
di|choto|mies
di|chro|ic
di|chro|ism
di|chro|mat|ic
di|chro|ma|tism
Dick (name)
dick +s (detective
    etc.)
dicken
Dick|ens, Charles
    (English writer)
dick|ens (in 'what
    the dickens?' etc.)

Dick|ens|ian +s
Dick|ens|ian|ly
dicker +s +ed +ing
dick|er|er +s
dick|head +s
(*coarse slang*)
Dickie *also* Dicky
Dick|in|son, Emily
(American poet)
Dicky *also* Dickie
(name)
dicky
dick|ies
dick|ier
dick|iest
(shirt-front; seat;
unsound)
dicky bird +s
dicot +s
di|coty|ledon +s
di|coty|ledon|ous
di|crot|ic
dicta
Dic|ta|phone *Propr.*
dic|tate
dic|tates
dic|tated
dic|tat|ing
dic|ta|tion +s
dic|ta|tor +s
dic|ta|tor|ial
dic|ta|tori|al|ly
dic|ta|tor|ship +s
dic|tion +s
dic|tion|ary
dic|tion|ar|ies
Dicto|graph *Propr.*
dic|tum
dicta *or* dic|tums
dicty
did
di|dac|tic
di|dac|tic|al|ly
di|dac|ti|cism
dida|kai +s (use
didicoi)
did|di|coy +s (use
didicoi)
did|dle
did|dles
did|dled
did|dling
did|dler +s
diddly-squat
did|dums
Di|derot, Denis
(French
philosopher)
didg|eri|doo +s
didi|coi +s
didn't

Dido (queen of
Carthage)
dido
didos *or* di|does
(antic)
didst
Did|yma
(sanctuary of
Apollo)
di|dym|ium
die
dice
(numbered cube.
△dye)
die
dies
died
dying
(cease living.
△dye)
die-away *adjective*
die-back *noun*
die-cast
die-casting
di|ecious *Am.* (*Br.*
dioecious)
dief|fen|bachia +s
Diego Gar|cia
(island, Indian
Ocean)
die|hard +s
Die|kirch (town,
Luxembourg)
diel|drin
di|elec|tric
di|elec|tric|al|ly
Dien Bien Phu
(siege, Vietnam)
diene +s (organic
compound)
Dieppe (port,
France)
di|er|esis *Am.*
di|er|eses
(*Br.* diaeresis)
diesel +s (fuel.
△deasil)
diesel-electric
diesel|ise *Br.* (use
dieselize)
diesel|ises
diesel|ised
diesel|is|ing
diesel|ize
diesel|izes
diesel|ized
diesel|iz|ing
diesel-powered
die-sinker +s
Dies irae
dies non
die-stamping

di|es|trus *Am.* (*Br.*
dioestrus)
diet +s +ed +ing
diet|ary
diet|ar|ies
diet|er +s
diet|et|ic
diet|et|ic|al|ly
diet|et|ics
di|ethyl
di|ethyl|amide
diet|ician +s (use
dietitian)
diet|itian +s
Diet|rich,
Mar|lene
(German-born
American actress
and singer)
dif|fer +s +ed +ing
dif|fer|ence +s
dif|fer|ent
dif|fer|en|tia
dif|fer|en|tiae
dif|fer|en|tial +s
dif|fer|en|tial|ly
dif|fer|en|ti|ate
dif|fer|en|ti|ates
dif|fer|en|ti|ated
dif|fer|en|ti|at|ing
dif|fer|en|ti|ation
+s
dif|fer|en|ti|ator
+s
dif|fer|ent|ly
dif|fer|ent|ly
abled
dif|fer|ent|ness
dif|fi|cult
dif|fi|cult|ly
dif|fi|cult|ness
dif|fi|culty
dif|fi|cul|ties
dif|fi|dence
dif|fi|dent
dif|fi|dent|ly
dif|fract +s +ed
+ing
dif|frac|tion +s
dif|fract|ive
dif|fract|ive|ly
dif|fract|om|eter
+s
dif|fuse
dif|fuses
dif|fused
dif|fus|ing
dif|fuse|ly
dif|fuse|ness
dif|fuser +s
dif|fus|ible
dif|fu|sion +s

dif|fu|sion|ist +s
dif|fu|sive
dig
digs
dug
dig|ging
Di|gam|bara +s
dig|am|ist +s
di|gamma +s
dig|am|ous
dig|amy
di|gas|tric
di|gest +s +ed
+ing
di|gest|er +s
di|gest|ibil|ity
di|gest|ible
di|ges|tion +s
di|gest|ive +s
di|gest|ive|ly
Dig|ger +s (English
dissenter)
dig|ger +s (person
who digs;
machine;
Australian; New
Zealander)
dig|ging +s
dight
digit +s
digit|al +s
digi|talin
digi|talis
digit|al|ise *Br.* (use
digitalize)
digit|al|ises
digit|al|ised
digit|al|is|ing
digit|al|ize
digit|al|izes
digit|al|ized
digit|al|iz|ing
digit|al|ly
digi|tate
digi|tate|ly
digi|ta|tion
digi|ti|grade +s
digit|isa|tion *Br.*
(use digitization)
digit|ise *Br.* (use
digitize)
digit|ises
digit|ised
digit|is|ing
digit|iza|tion
digit|ize
digit|izes
digit|ized
digit|iz|ing
dig|ni|fied|ly
dig|nify
dig|ni|fies

dig|nify (*cont.*)
 dig|ni|fied
 dig|ni|fy|ing
dig|ni|tary
 dig|ni|tar|ies
dig|nity
 dig|nities
di|graph +s
di|graph|ic
di|gress
 di|gresses
 di|gressed
 di|gress|ing
di|gress|er +s
di|gres|sion +s
di|gres|sive
di|gres|sive|ly
di|gres|sive|ness
di|he|dral +s
di|hy|brid +s
di|hy|dric
Dijon (city, France;
 mustard)
dik-dik +s
dike +s (use dyke)
dik|tat +s
di|lapi|date
 di|lapi|dates
 di|lapi|dated
 di|lapi|dat|ing
di|lapi|da|tion +s
di|lat|able
dila|ta|tion
di|late
 di|lates
 di|lated
 di|lat|ing
dila|tion
dila|tor +s
dila|tor|ily
dila|tori|ness
dila|tory
dildo +s
di|lemma +s
dil|et|tante
 dil|et|tanti *or*
 dil|et|tan|tes
dil|et|tant|ish
dil|et|tant|ism
Dili (seaport,
 Timor)
dili|gence +s
dili|gent
dili|gent|ly
dill +s
dill pickle +s
dill-water
dilly
 dil|lies
dilly|bag +s
dilly-dally
 dilly-dallies

dilly-dally (*cont.*)
 dilly-dallied
 dilly-dallying
di|lo|pho|saur +s
di|lopho|saurus
 di|lopho|
         saur|uses
di|lu|ent +s
di|lute
 di|lutes
 di|luted
 di|lut|ing
di|lutee +s
di|luter +s
di|lu|tion +s
di|lu|vial
di|lu|vi|al|ist +s
di|lu|vium
 di|lu|via
Dilys
dim
 dims
 dimmed
 dim|ming
 dim|mer
 dim|mest
Di|Maggio, Joe
 (American
 baseball player)
Dim|bleby,
 Rich|ard, David,
 and Jona|than
 (English
 broadcasters)
dime +s
di|men|sion +s
di|men|sion|al
di|men|sion|al|ity
di|men|sion|al|ly
di|men|sion|less
dimer +s
di|mer|ic
di|mer|isa|tion *Br.*
 (use
 dimerization)
di|mer|ise *Br.* (use
 dimerize)
 di|mer|ises
 di|mer|ised
 di|mer|is|ing
di|mer|iza|tion
di|mer|ize
 di|mer|izes
 di|mer|ized
 di|mer|iz|ing
di|mer|ous
dim|eter +s
di|methyl|
  sulf|ox|ide *Am.*
di|methyl|
  sulph|ox|ide *Br.*
di|met|ro|don +s

di|midi|ate
di|min|ish
 di|min|ishes
 di|min|ished
 di|min|ish|ing
di|min|ish|able
di|minu|endo +s
dim|in|ution
di|minu|tival
di|minu|tive +s
di|minu|tive|ly
di|minu|tive|ness
di|mis|sory
dim|ity
 dim|ities
dimly
dim|mer +s
dim|mish
dim|ness
di|morph|ic
di|morph|ism
di|morph|ous
dimple
 dimples
 dimpled
 dim|pling
dim|ply
 dim|plier
 dim|pli|est
dim sum
 plural dim sum
dil|wit +s
dim-witted
DIN (technical
 standard)
din
 dins
 dinned
 din|ning
 (noise; instill)
Dinah
dinar +s
Din|aric Alps (in S.
 Europe)
din-din
din-dins
dine
 dines
 dined
 din|ing
 (eat dinner.
 △ dyne)
diner +s
din|ero +s
diner-out
 diners-out
din|ette +s
ding +s +ed +ing
Ding an sich
ding|bat +s
ding-dong +s
dinge
 dinges

dinge (*cont.*)
 dinged
 dinge|ing
dinghy
 din|ghies
 (small boat.
 △ dingy)
din|gily
din|gi|ness
din|gle +s
dingo
 din|goes *or*
 din|gos
Ding|wall (town,
 Scotland)
dingy
 din|gier
 din|gi|est
 (dull. △ dinghy)
din|ing car +s
din|ing chair +s
din|ing hall +s
din|ing room +s
din|ing table +s
dink +s +ed +ing
Dinka
 plural Dinka *or*
 Din|kas
din|kum
dinky
 dink|ier
 dink|iest
din|ner +s
din|ner dance +s
din|ner jacket +s
din|ner party
 din|ner par|ties
din|ner ser|vice +s
din|ner table +s
din|ner time
dino|fla|gel|late +s
dino|saur +s
dino|saur|ian
dino|there +s (use
 deinothere)
dint +s +ed +ing
di|nucleo|tide +s
dio|cesan +s
dio|cese +s
Dio|cle|tian
 (Roman emperor)
diode +s
di|oe|cious *Br.* (*Am.*
 diecious)
di|oes|trus *Br.* (*Am.*
 diestrus)
Dioge|nes (Greek
 philosopher)
diol +s *Chemistry*
Dione (*Greek
 Mythology*; moon
 of Saturn)

Dio|nys|iac
Dio|nys|ian
Dio|nys|ius (I and
II, Syracusan
rulers)
Dio|nys|ius
Ex|ig|uus
(Scythian monk
and chronologer)
Dio|nys|ius of
Hali|car|nas|sus
(Greek historian
and writer)
Dio|nys|ius the
Are|opa|gite
(Greek saint)
Dio|nysus *Greek
Mythology*
Dio|phan|tine
Dio|phan|tus
(Greek
mathematician)
di|opter *Am.* +s
di|optre *Br.* +s
di|op|tric
di|op|trics
Dior, Chris|tian
(French couturier)
dio|rama +s
dio|ram|ic
di|or|ite +s
di|or|it|ic
Dio|scuri (*Greek
and Roman
Mythology*,
= Castor and
Pollux)
di|oxan
di|oxane
di|ox|ide +s
di|oxin +s
DIP (*Computing*
= dual in-line
package)
dip
  dips
  dipped
  dip|ping
  (plunge etc.)
Dip. Ed.
  (= Diploma in
  Education)
di|pep|tide +s
di|phos|phate +s
diph|theria
diph|ther|ial
diph|ther|ic
diph|ther|it|ic
diph|ther|oid
diph|thong +s
diph|thong|al

diph|thong|
  isa|tion *Br.* (use
  diphthongiza-
  tion)
diph|thong|ise *Br.*
  (use
  diphthongize)
diph|thong|ises
diph|thong|ised
diph|thong|is|ing
diph|thong|
      iza|tion
diph|thong|ize
diph|thong|izes
diph|thong|ized
diph|thong|iz|ing
diplo|coc|cus
diplo|cocci
dip|lod|ocus
dip|lod|ocuses
dip|loid +s
dip|loidy
dip|loma +s
dip|lo|macy
dip|lo|maed
dip|lo|mat +s
  (official; tactful
  person)
dip|lo|mate +s
  (holder of
  diploma)
dip|lo|mat|ic
dip|lo|mat|ic|al|ly
dip|lo|ma|tise *Br.*
  (use diplomatize)
dip|lo|ma|tises
dip|lo|ma|tised
dip|lo|ma|tis|ing
dip|lo|ma|tist +s
dip|lo|ma|tize
dip|lo|ma|tizes
dip|lo|ma|tized
dip|lo|ma|tiz|ing
dip|lont +s
dip|lo|pia
dip|lo|tene +s
di|polar
di|pole +s
dip|per +s
dippy
  dip|pier
  dip|pi|est
dip|shit +s (*coarse
  slang*)
dipso +s
dipso|mania
dipso|maniac +s
dip|stick +s
dip switch
  dip switches
Dip|tera
dip|teral

dip|teran +s
dip|ter|ist +s
dip|ter|ous
dip|tych +s
Dirac, Paul
  (English physicist)
dire
  direr
  dir|est
dir|ect +s +ed +ing
dir|ect dial
  (telephone)
dir|ect dial|ing
  Am.
dir|ect dial|ling *Br.*
direct-grant
  attributive
dir|ec|tion +s
dir|ec|tion|al
dir|ec|tion|al|ity
dir|ec|tion|al|ly
direction-finder
  +s
direction-finding
dir|ec|tion|less
dir|ect|ive +s
dir|ect|ly
dir|ect mail
dir|ect mail|ing
dir|ect|ness
Dir|ect|oire
dir|ect|or +s
dir|ect|or|ate +s
director-general
  +s
dir|ect|or|ial
dir|ect|or|ship +s
Dir|ec|tory *History*
dir|ec|tory
  dir|ec|tor|ies
dir|ec|tress
  dir|ec|tresses
dir|ec|trix
  dir|ec|tri|ces
dire|ful
dire|ful|ly
dire|ly
dire|ness
dirge +s
dirge|ful
dir|ham +s
diri|gible +s
diri|gisme
diri|giste
diri|ment
dirk +s
dirndl +s
dirt
dirt cheap
dirt|ily
dirti|ness

dirt track +s
dirt-tracker +s
dirty
  dirt|ies
  dirt|ied
  dirty|ing
  dirt|ier
  dirti|est
dis
  disses
  dissed
  dis|sing
dis|abil|ity
  dis|abil|ities
dis|able
  dis|ables
  dis|abled
  dis|ab|ling
dis|able|ment
dis|ablist
dis|abuse
  dis|abuses
  dis|abused
  dis|abus|ing
di|sac|char|ide +s
dis|ac|cord +s +ed
  +ing
dis|ad|van|tage
dis|ad|van|tages
dis|ad|van|taged
dis|ad|van|ta|ging
dis|ad|van|
      ta|geous
dis|ad|van|
      ta|geous|ly
dis|af|fect|ed
dis|af|fect|ed|ly
dis|af|fec|tion
dis|af|fili|ate
dis|af|fili|ates
dis|af|fili|ated
dis|af|fili|at|ing
dis|af|fili|ation
dis|af|firm +s
  +ed +ing
dis|af|firm|ation
dis|af|for|est +s
  +ed +ing
dis|af|for|est|ation
dis|ag|gre|gate
dis|ag|gre|gates
dis|ag|gre|gated
dis|ag|gre|gat|ing
dis|ag|gre|ga|tion
dis|agree
  dis|agrees
  dis|agreed
  dis|agree|ing
dis|agree|able
dis|agree|able|
            ness

dis|agree|ably
dis|agree|ment +s
dis|allow +s +ed
  +ing
dis|allow|ance +s
dis|am|bigu|ate
  dis|am|bigu|ates
  dis|am|bigu|ated
  dis|am|bigu|
        at|ing
dis|am|bigu|ation
  +s
dis|amen|ity
  dis|amen|ities
dis|annul
  dis|annuls
  dis|annulled
  dis|annul|ling
dis|annul|ment
dis|ap|pear +s +ed
  +ing
dis|ap|pear|ance
  +s
dis|ap|point +s
  +ed +ing
dis|ap|point|ed|ly
dis|ap|point|ing|ly
dis|ap|point|ment
  +s
dis|ap|pro|ba|tion
dis|ap|proba|tive
dis|ap|pro|ba|tory
dis|ap|proval +s
dis|ap|prove
  dis|ap|proves
  dis|ap|proved
  dis|ap|prov|ing
dis|ap|prover +s
dis|ap|prov|ing|ly
dis|arm +s +ed
  +ing
dis|arma|ment
dis|arm|er +s
dis|arm|ing
dis|arm|ing|ly
dis|ar|range
  dis|ar|ranges
  dis|ar|ranged
  dis|ar|ran|ging
dis|ar|range|ment
dis|array
dis|ar|ticu|late
  dis|ar|ticu|lates
  dis|ar|ticu|lated
  dis|ar|ticu|lat|ing
dis|ar|ticu|la|tion
dis|as|sem|ble
  dis|as|sem|bles
  dis|as|sem|bled
  dis|as|sem|bling
dis|as|sem|bler +s
dis|as|sem|bly

dis|as|so|ci|ate
  dis|as|so|ci|ates
  dis|as|so|ci|ated
  dis|as|so|ci|at|ing
dis|as|so|ci|ation
dis|as|ter +s
dis|as|trous
dis|as|trous|ly
dis|avow +s +ed
  +ing
dis|avowal +s
dis|band +s +ed
  +ing
dis|band|ment
dis|bar
  dis|bars
  dis|barred
  dis|bar|ring
dis|bar|ment
dis|be|lief
dis|be|lieve
  dis|be|lieves
  dis|be|lieved
  dis|be|liev|ing
dis|be|liever +s
dis|be|liev|ing|ly
dis|bene|fit +s
dis|bound
dis|bud
  dis|buds
  dis|bud|ded
  dis|bud|ding
dis|bur|den +s +ed
  +ing
dis|bur|sal
dis|burse
  dis|burses
  dis|bursed
  dis|burs|ing
dis|burse|ment +s
dis|bur|ser +s
disc *Br.* +s (senses
  other than
  Computing. Am. disk.
  ⚠ disk)
dis|calced
dis|card +s +ed
  +ing
dis|card|able
dis|car|nate
dis|cern +s +ed
  +ing
dis|cern|er +s
dis|cern|ible
dis|cern|ibly
dis|cern|ing|ly
dis|cern|ment +s
dis|cerp|ti|bil|ity
dis|cerp|tible
dis|cerp|tion +s
dis|charge
  dis|charges

dis|charge (*cont.*)
  dis|charged
  dis|char|ging
dis|charge|able
dis|char|ger +s
dis|ciple +s
dis|ciple|ship +s
dis|cip|lin|able
dis|cip|linal
dis|cip|lin|ar|ian +s
dis|cip|lin|ary
dis|cip|line
  dis|cip|lines
  dis|cip|lined
  dis|cip|lin|ing
dis|cipu|lar
disc jockey +s
dis|claim +s +ed
  +ing
dis|claim|er +s
dis|close
  dis|closes
  dis|closed
  dis|clos|ing
dis|closer +s
dis|clos|ure +s
disco +s *noun*
disco
  dis|coes
  dis|coed
  dis|coing
  verb
disc|ob|olus
  disc|ob|oli
disc|og|raph|er +s
disc|og|raphy
  disc|og|raph|ies
dis|coid
dis|color *Am.* +s
  +ed +ing
dis|col|or|ation
dis|col|our *Br.* +s
  +ed +ing
dis|com|bobu|late
  dis|com|bobu|
         lates
  dis|com|bobu|
         lated
  dis|com|bobu|
         lat|ing
dis|comfit +s +ed
  +ing (baffle;
  thwart.
  ⚠ discomfort)
dis|com|fit|ure
dis|com|fort +s
  +ed +ing (unease;
  make uneasy.
  ⚠ discomfit)
dis|com|mode
  dis|com|modes
  dis|com|moded
  dis|com|mod|ing

dis|com|mo|di|ous
dis|com|pose
  dis|com|poses
  dis|com|posed
  dis|com|pos|ing
dis|com|pos|ure
dis|con|cert +s
  +ed +ing
dis|con|cert|ed|ly
dis|con|cert|ing
dis|con|cert|ing|ly
dis|con|cer|tion
dis|con|cert|ment
dis|con|firm +s
  +ed +ing
dis|con|firm|ation
dis|con|form|ity
  dis|con|form|ities
dis|con|nect +s
  +ed +ing
dis|con|nect|ed|ly
dis|con|nect|ed|
          ness
dis|con|nec|tion
  +s
dis|con|so|late
dis|con|so|late|ly
dis|con|so|late|
          ness
dis|con|sol|ation
dis|con|tent +s
  +ed +ing
dis|con|tent|ly
dis|con|tent|ment
  +s
dis|con|tent|ness
dis|con|tinu|ance
dis|con|tinu|ation
dis|con|tinue
  dis|con|tinues
  dis|con|tinued
  dis|con|tinu|ing
dis|con|tinu|ity
  dis|con|tinu|ities
dis|con|tinu|ous
dis|con|tinu|ous|ly
dis|cord +s +ed
  +ing
dis|cord|ance
dis|cord|ancy
  dis|cord|an|cies
dis|cord|ant
dis|cord|ant|ly
disco|theque +s
dis|count +s +ed
  +ing
dis|count|able
dis|coun|ten|ance
dis|coun|ten|
          ances
dis|coun|ten|
          anced

dis|coun|ten|ance
(cont.)
dis|coun|te|nan|
cing
dis|counter +s
dis|cour|age
dis|cour|ages
dis|cour|aged
dis|cour|aging
dis|cour|age|ment
+s
dis|cour|aging|ly
dis|course
dis|courses
Jis|coursed
dis|cours|ing
dis|cour|teous
dis|cour|teous|ly
dis|cour|teous|
ness
dis|cour|tesy
dis|cour|tesies
dis|cover +s +ed
+ing
dis|cov|er|able
dis|cov|er|er +s
dis|cov|ery
dis|cov|er|ies
dis|credit +s +ed
+ing
dis|cred|it|able
dis|cred|it|ably
dis|creet
(circumspect;
tactful.
△discrete)
dis|creet|ly
dis|creet|ness
dis|crep|ancy
dis|crep|an|cies
dis|crep|ant
dis|crete (separate.
△discreet)
dis|crete|ly
dis|crete|ness
dis|cre|tion
dis|cre|tion|ary
dis|crim|in|ant
dis|crim|in|ate
dis|crim|in|ates
dis|crim|in|ated
dis|crim|in|at|ing
dis|crim|in|ate|ly
dis|crim|in|
at|ing|ly
dis|crim|in|ation
+s
dis|crim|ina|tive
dis|crim|in|ator +s
dis|crim|in|atory
dis|cur|sive
dis|cur|sive|ly

dis|cur|sive|ness
dis|cus
dis|cuses
(disc)
dis|cuss
dis|cusses
dis|cussed
dis|cuss|ing
(debate)
dis|cuss|able
dis|cuss|ant +s
dis|cuss|er +s
dis|cuss|ible
dis|cus|sion +s
dis|dain +s +ed
+ing
dis|dain|ful
dis|dain|ful|ly
dis|dain|ful|ness
dis|ease +s
dis|eased
dis|econ|omy
dis|em|bark +s
+ed +ing
dis|em|bark|ation
dis|em|bar|rass
dis|em|bar|rasses
dis|em|bar|rassed
dis|em|bar|rass|
ing
dis|em|bar|rass|
ment
dis|em|bodi|ment
dis|embody
dis|em|bod|ies
dis|em|bod|ied
dis|em|body|ing
dis|em|bogue
dis|em|bogues
dis|em|bogued
dis|em|boguing
dis|em|bowel
dis|em|bowels
dis|em|bow|elled
Br.
dis|em|bow|eled
Am.
dis|em|bowel|ling
Br.
dis|em|bowel|ing
Am.
dis|em|bowel|
ment
dis|em|broil +s
+ed +ing
dis|em|power +s
+ed +ing
dis|en|chant +s
+ed +ing
dis|en|chant|ing|ly
dis|en|chant|ment
+s

dis|en|cum|ber +s
+ed +ing
dis|en|dow +s +ed
+ing
dis|en|dow|ment
dis|en|fran|chise
dis|en|fran|chises
dis|en|fran|chised
dis|
en|fran|chis|ing
dis|en|fran|chise|
ment
dis|en|gage
dis|en|gages
dis|en|gaged
dis|en|gaging
dis|en|gage|ment
dis|en|tail +s +ed
+ing
dis|en|tangle
dis|en|tan|gles
dis|en|tan|gled
dis|en|tan|gling
dis|en|tangle|ment
dis|en|thral Br.
dis|en|thrals
dis|en|thralled
dis|en|thral|ling
dis|en|thrall Am.+s
+ed +ing
dis|en|thrall|ment
Am.
dis|en|thral|ment
Br.
dis|en|title
dis|en|titles
dis|en|titled
dis|en|tit|ling
dis|en|title|ment
dis|en|tomb +s
+ed +ing
dis|en|tomb|ment
dis|equi|lib|rium
dis|es|tab|lish
dis|es|tab|lishes
dis|es|tab|lished
dis|es|tab|lish|ing
dis|es|tab|lish|
ment
dis|es|teem +s +ed
+ing
dis|eur +s male
dis|euse +s female
dis|favor Am. +s
+ed +ing
dis|favour Br. +s
+ed +ing
dis|fig|ure
dis|fig|ures
dis|fig|ured
dis|fig|ur|ing
dis|fig|ure|ment +s

dis|for|est +s +ed
+ing
dis|for|est|ation
dis|fran|chise
dis|fran|chises
dis|fran|chised
dis|fran|chis|ing
dis|fran|chise|
ment +s
dis|frock +s +ed
+ing
dis|gorge
dis|gorges
dis|gorged
dis|gor|ging
dis|gorge|ment +s
dis|grace
dis|graces
dis|graced
dis|gra|cing
dis|grace|ful
dis|grace|ful|ly
dis|grun|tled
dis|gruntle|ment
dis|guise
dis|guises
dis|guised
dis|guis|ing
dis|guise|ment
dis|gust +s +ed
+ing
dis|gust|ed|ly
dis|gust|ful
dis|gust|ing|ly
dis|gust|ing|ness
dish
dishes
dished
dish|ing
dis|ha|bille
dis|habitu|ation
dis|har|mo|ni|ous
dis|har|mo|ni|
ous|ly
dis|har|mon|ise Br.
(use
disharmonize)
dis|har|mon|ises
dis|har|mon|ised
dis|har|mon|is|ing
dis|har|mon|ize
dis|har|mon|izes
dis|har|mon|ized
dis|har|mon|
iz|ing
dis|har|mony
dis|har|monies
dish|cloth +s
dis|heart|en +s
+ed +ing
dis|heart|en|ing|ly
dis|heart|en|ment

dish|evel
  dish|evels
  dish'ev|elled *Br.*
  dish'ev|eled *Am.*
  dish'ev|el|ling *Br.*
  dish'ev|el|ing *Am.*
dish'ev|el|ment
dish|ful +s
dish|like
dis|hon'est
dis|hon'est|ly
dis|hon'esty
  dis|hon'est|ies
dis|honor *Am.* +s
  +ed +ing
dis|hon'or|able
  Am.
dis|hon'or|able|
          ness *Am.*
dis|hon'or|ably
  Am.
dis|hon'our *Br.* +s
  +ed +ing
dis|hon'our|able
  Br.
dis|hon'our|able|
          ness *Br.*
dis|hon'our|ably
  Br.
dish|rag +s
dish|wash'er +s
dish|water
dishy
  dish|ier
  dishi|est
dis|il|lu'sion +s
  +ed +ing
dis|il|lu'sion|ise
  ·*Br.* (use
  disillusionize)
  dis|il|lu'sion|ises
  dis|il|lu'sion|ised
  dis|il|lu'sion|
            is|ing
dis|il|lu'sion|ize
  dis|il|lu'sion|izes
  dis|il|lu'sion|ized
  dis|il|lu'sion|
            iz|ing
dis|il|lu'sion|ment
  +s
dis|in'cen|tive +s
dis|in'clin|ation
dis|in'cline
  dis|in'clines
  dis|in'clined
  dis|in'clin'ing
dis|in'cor'por|ate
  dis|in'cor'por|
            ates
  dis|in'cor'por|
            ated

dis|in'cor'por|ate
  (*cont.*)
  dis|in'cor'por|
          at'ing
dis|in'fect +s +ed
  +ing
dis|in'fect|ant +s
dis|in'fec'tion
dis|in'fest +s +ed
  +ing
dis|in'fest|ation
dis|in'fla'tion
dis|in'fla'tion|ary
dis|in'for'ma'tion
dis|in'genu|ous
dis|in'genu|ous|ly
dis|in'genu|ous|
            ness
dis|in'herit +s +ed
  +ing
dis|in'herit|ance
dis|in'te|grate
  dis|in'te|grates
  dis|in'te|grated
  dis|in'te|grat'ing
dis|in'te|gra'tion
dis|in'te|gra'tive
dis|in'te|gra'tor +s
dis|in'ter
  dis|in'ters
  dis|in'terred
  dis|in'ter|ring
dis|in'ter|est
dis|in'ter|est'ed
dis|in'ter|est|ed|ly
dis|in'ter|est|ed|
            ness
dis|in'ter|ment +s
dis|in'vest +s +ed
  +ing
dis|in'vest|ment
dis|jecta mem'|bra
dis|join +s +ed
  +ing
dis|joint +s +ed
  +ing
dis|joint|ed|ly
dis|joint|ed|ness
dis|junct +s
dis|junc'tion +s
dis|junct'ive
dis|junct'ive|ly
dis|junc'ture +s
disk *Am.* +s (*Br.*
  disc)
disk +s *Computing*
disk drive
disk|ette +s
disk|less
Disko (island,
  Greenland)
dis|lik'able

dis|like
  dis|likes
  dis|liked
  dis|lik'ing
dis|like|able (use
  dislikable)
dis|locate
  dis|locates
  dis|located
  dis|locat'ing
dis|loca'tion +s
dis|lodge
  dis|lodges
  dis|lodged
  dis|lodg'ing
dis|lodge|ment
dis|loyal
dis|loy'al|ist +s
dis|loy'al|ly
dis|loy'alty
  dis|loy'al'ties
dis|mal
dis|mal'ly
dis|mal|ness
dis|man'tle
  dis|man'tles
  dis|man'tled
  dis|mant'ling
dis|mantle|ment
dis|mant'ler +s
dis|mast +s +ed
  +ing
dis|may +s +ed
  +ing
dis|mem'ber +s
  +ed +ing
dis|mem'ber|ment
  +s
dis|miss
  dis|misses
  dis|missed
  dis|miss'ing
dis|miss'able (use
  dismissible)
dis|missal +s
dis|miss'ible
dis|mis'sion
dis|mis'sive
dis|mis'sive'ly
dis|mis'sive|ness
dis|mount +s +ed
  +ing
Dis'ney, Walt
  (cartoon
  producer)
Dis'ney|esque
dis|obedi'ence
dis|obedi'ent
dis|obedi'ent|ly
dis|obey +s +ed
  +ing
dis|obey'er +s

dis|oblige
  dis|obliges
  dis|obliged
  dis|obli'ging
dis|order +s +ed
  +ing
dis|or'der|li|ness
dis|or'der|ly
dis|or'gan|isa'tion
  Br. (use
  disorganization)
dis|or'gan|ise *Br.*
  (use disorganize)
  dis|or'gan|ises
  dis|or'gan|ised
  dis|or'gan|is'ing
dis|or'gan|iza'tion
dis|or'gan|ize
  dis|or'gan|izes
  dis|or'gan|ized
  dis|or'gan|iz'ing
dis|orient +s +ed
  +ing
dis|own +s +ed
  +ing
dis|own'er +s
dis|par'age
  dis|par'ages
  dis|par'aged
  dis|para'ging
dis|par'age|ment
  +s
dis|para'ging'ly
dis|par'ate
dis|par'ate'ly
dis|par'ate|ness
dis|par'ity
  dis|par'ities
dis|pas'sion|ate
dis|pas'sion|ate'ly
dis|pas'sion|ate|
            ness
dis|patch
  dis|patches
  dis|patched
  dis|patch|ing
dis|patch box
  dis|patch boxes
dis|patch'er +s
dis|patch rider +s
dis|pel
  dis|pels
  dis|pelled
  dis|pel'ling
dis|pel'ler +s
dis|pens|abil'ity
dis|pens|able

dis¦pens¦ary
  dis¦pens¦ar¦ies
dis¦pen¦sa¦tion +s
dis¦pen¦sa¦tion¦al
dis¦pen¦sa¦tory
dis¦pense
  dis¦penses
  dis¦pensed
  dis¦pens¦ing
dis¦pen¦ser +s
dis¦pers¦able (use
  dispersible)
dis¦per¦sal +s
dis¦pers¦ant +s
dis¦perse
  dis¦perses
  dis¦persed
  dis¦per¦sing
dis¦perser +s
dis¦pers¦ible
dis¦per¦sion +s
dis¦per¦sive
dis¦pirit +s +ed
  +ing
dis¦pir¦it¦ed¦ly
dis¦pir¦it¦ed¦ness
dis¦pir¦it¦ing
dis¦pir¦it¦ing¦ly
dis¦place
  dis¦places
  dis¦placed
  dis¦placing
dis¦place¦ment +s
dis¦play +s +ed
  +ing
dis¦play¦er +s
dis¦please
  dis¦pleases
  dis¦pleased
  dis¦pleas¦ing
dis¦pleas¦ing¦ly
dis¦pleas¦ure
  dis¦pleas¦ures
  dis¦pleas¦ured
  dis¦pleas¦ur¦ing
dis¦port +s +ed
  +ing
dis¦pos¦abil¦ity
dis¦pos¦able +s
dis¦posal +s
dis¦pose
  dis¦poses
  dis¦posed
  dis¦pos¦ing
dis¦poser +s
dis¦pos¦ition +s
dis¦pos¦sess
  dis¦pos¦sesses
  dis¦pos¦sessed
  dis¦pos¦sess¦ing
dis¦pos¦ses¦sion +s

dis¦praise
  dis¦praises
  dis¦praised
  dis¦prais¦ing
dis¦proof +s
dis¦pro¦por¦tion +s
dis¦pro¦por¦tion¦al
dis¦pro¦por¦tion¦
    al¦ly
dis¦pro¦por¦tion¦
    ate
dis¦pro¦por¦tion¦
    ate¦ly
dis¦pro¦por¦tion¦
    ate¦ness
dis¦prov¦able
dis¦prove
  dis¦proves
  dis¦proved
  dis¦prov¦ing
Dis¦pur (city, India)
dis¦put¦able
dis¦put¦ably
dis¦pu¦tant +s
dis¦pu¦ta¦tion +s
dis¦pu¦ta¦tious
dis¦pu¦ta¦tious¦ly
dis¦pu¦ta¦tious¦
    ness
dis¦pute
  dis¦putes
  dis¦puted
  dis¦put¦ing
dis¦puter +s
dis¦quali¦fi¦ca¦tion
  +s
dis¦qual¦ify
  dis¦quali¦fies
  dis¦quali¦fied
  dis¦quali¦fy¦ing
dis¦quiet +s +ed
  +ing
dis¦quiet¦ing¦ly
dis¦quiet¦ude
dis¦quisi¦tion +s
dis¦quisi¦tion¦al
Dis¦raeli,
  Ben¦ja¦min
  (British prime
  minister)
dis¦rate
  dis¦rates
  dis¦rated
  dis¦rat¦ing
dis¦re¦gard +s +ed
  +ing
dis¦re¦gard¦ful
dis¦re¦gard¦ful¦ly
dis¦rel¦ish
  dis¦rel¦ishes
  dis¦rel¦ished
  dis¦rel¦ish¦ing

dis¦re¦mem¦ber +s
  +ed +ing
dis¦re¦pair
dis¦rep¦ut¦able
dis¦rep¦ut¦able¦
    ness
dis¦rep¦ut¦ably
dis¦re¦pute
dis¦res¦pect
dis¦res¦pect¦ful
dis¦res¦pect¦ful¦ly
dis¦robe
  dis¦robes
  dis¦robed
  dis¦rob¦ing
dis¦rupt +s +ed
  +ing
dis¦rupt¦er +s
dis¦rup¦tion +s
dis¦rup¦tive
dis¦rup¦tive¦ly
dis¦rup¦tive¦ness
diss (use dis)
  disses
  dissed
  diss¦ing
dis¦sat¦is¦fac¦tion
  +s
dis¦sat¦is¦fac¦tory
dis¦sat¦is¦fied¦ly
dis¦sat¦isfy
  dis¦sat¦is¦fies
  dis¦sat¦is¦fied
  dis¦sat¦is¦fy¦ing
dis¦sect +s +ed
  +ing
dis¦sec¦tion +s
dis¦sect¦or +s
dis¦sem¦blance
dis¦sem¦ble
  dis¦sem¦bles
  dis¦sem¦bled
  dis¦sem¦bling
dis¦sem¦bler +s
dis¦sem¦bling¦ly
dis¦sem¦in¦ate
  dis¦sem¦in¦ates
  dis¦sem¦in¦ated
  dis¦sem¦in¦at¦ing
dis¦sem¦in¦ation
dis¦sem¦in¦ator +s
dis¦sen¦sion +s
dis¦sent +s +ed
  +ing (disagree;
  disagreement.
  ⚠ descent)
Dis¦sent¦er +s
  (Nonconformist)
dis¦sent¦er +s
  (generally)
dis¦sen¦tient +s
dis¦sent¦ing¦ly

dis¦ser¦ta¦tion +s
dis¦ser¦ta¦tion¦al
dis¦serve
  dis¦serves
  dis¦served
  dis¦serv¦ing
dis¦ser¦vice +s
dis¦sever +s +ed
  +ing
dis¦sev¦er¦ance
dis¦sev¦er¦ment
dis¦si¦dence
dis¦si¦dent +s
dis¦simi¦lar
dis¦simi¦lar¦ity
  dis¦simi¦lar¦ities
dis¦simi¦lar¦ly
dis¦simi¦late
  dis¦simi¦lates
  dis¦simi¦lated
  dis¦simi¦lat¦ing
dis¦simi¦la¦tion +s
dis¦simi¦la¦tory
dis¦sim¦ili¦tude
dis¦simu¦late
  dis¦simu¦lates
  dis¦simu¦lated
  dis¦simu¦lat¦ing
dis¦simu¦la¦tion
dis¦simu¦la¦tor +s
dis¦si¦pate
  dis¦si¦pates
  dis¦si¦pated
  dis¦si¦pat¦ing
dis¦si¦pater +s
  (use dissipator)
dis¦si¦pa¦tion +s
dis¦si¦pa¦tive
dis¦si¦pa¦tor +s
dis¦so¦ci¦ate
  dis¦so¦ci¦ates
  dis¦so¦ci¦ated
  dis¦so¦ci¦at¦ing
dis¦so¦ci¦ation +s
dis¦so¦cia¦tive
dis¦solu¦bil¦ity
dis¦sol¦uble
dis¦sol¦ubly
dis¦sol¦ute
dis¦sol¦ute¦ly
dis¦sol¦ute¦ness
dis¦sol¦ution +s
dis¦sol¦ution¦ary
dis¦solv¦able
dis¦solve
  dis¦solves
  dis¦solved
  dis¦solv¦ing
dis¦solv¦ent +s
dis¦son¦ance +s
dis¦son¦ant
dis¦son¦ant¦ly

dis|suade
  dis|suades
  dis|suaded
  dis|suad|ing
dis|suader+s
dis|sua|sion
dis|sua|sive
dis|syl|lable+s
  (use disyllable)
dis|sym|met|rical
dis|sym|metry
  dis|sym|metries
dis|taff+s
dis|tal
dis|tal|ly
dis|tance
  dis|tances
  dis|tanced
  dis|tan|cing
dis|tance learn|ing
dis|tance post+s
dis|tant
dis|tant|ly
dis|taste
dis|taste|ful
dis|taste|ful|ly
dis|taste|ful|ness
dis|tem|per+s +ed
  +ing
dis|tend+s +ed
  +ing
dis|ten|si|bil|ity
dis|ten|sible
dis|ten|sion +s
dis|tich +s
dis|tich|ous
dis|til Br.
  dis|tils
  dis|tilled
  dis|til|ling
dis|till Am. +s +ed
  +ing
dis|til|late +s
dis|til|la|tion +s
dis|til|la|tory
dis|til|ler +s
dis|til|lery
  dis|til|ler|ies
dis|tinct
dis|tinc|tion +s
dis|tinct|ive
dis|tinct|ive|ly
dis|tinct|ive|ness
dis|tinct|ly
dis|tinct|ness
dis|tin|gué male
dis|tin|guée female
dis|tin|guish
  dis|tin|guishes
  dis|tin|guished
  dis|tin|guish|ing
dis|tin|guish|able

dis|tin|guish|ably
dis|tort+s +ed
  +ing
dis|tort|ed|ly
dis|tort|ed|ness
dis|tort|er+s
dis|tor|tion+s
dis|tor|tion|al
dis|tor|tion|less
dis|tract+s +ed
  +ing
dis|tract|ed|ly
dis|trac|tion+s
dis|tract|or+s
dis|train+s +ed
  +ing
dis|train|ee+s
dis|train|er+s
dis|train|ment
dis|train|or+s
  (use distrainer)
dis|traint
dis|trait *male*
dis|traite *female*
dis|traught
dis|tress
  dis|tresses
  dis|tressed
  dis|tress|ing
dis|tress|ful
dis|tress|ful|ly
dis|tress|ing|ly
dis|trib|ut|able
dis|tribu|tary
  dis|tribu|tar|ies
dis|trib|ute
  dis|trib|utes
  dis|trib|uted
  dis|trib|ut|ing
dis|tri|bu|tion+s
dis|tri|bu|tion|al
dis|tribu|tive
dis|tribu|tive|ly
dis|tribu|tor +s
dis|trict +s
dis|trust +s +ed
  +ing
dis|trust|er +s
dis|trust|ful
dis|trust|ful|ly
dis|turb +s +ed
  +ing
dis|turb|ance+s
dis|turb|er +s
dis|turb|ing|ly
di|sul|fide Am. +s
di|sul|phide Br. +s
dis|union
dis|unite
  dis|unites
  dis|united
  dis|unit|ing

dis|unity
  dis|unities
dis|use
  dis|uses
  dis|used
  dis|us|ing
dis|util|ity
di|syl|lab|ic
di|syl|lable+s
dit+s
ditch
  ditches
  ditched
  ditch|ing
ditch|er+s
ditch|water
di|theism
di|theist+s
dither+s +ed +ing
dith|er|er+s
dith|ery
dithy|ramb+s
dithy|ramb|ic
ditsy (use ditzy)
  dit|sier
  ditsi|est
dit|tany
  dit|tanies
ditto +s *noun*
ditto
  dit|toes
  dit|toed
  ditto|ing
  verb
dit|to|graph|ic
dit|tog|raphy
  dit|tog|raph|ies
ditto marks
ditty
  dit|ties
ditty-bag+s
ditty-box
  ditty-boxes
ditzy
  ditz|ier
  ditzi|est
Diu (island, India)
di|ur|esis
  di|ur|eses
di|ur|et|ic+s
di|ur|nal
di|ur|nal|ly
diva +s
di|val|gate
  di|val|gates
  di|val|gated
  di|val|gat|ing
di|val|ga|tion+s
di|va|lency
di|va|lent
divan +s

di|vari|cate
di|vari|cates
di|vari|cated
di|vari|cat|ing
di|vari|ca|tion
dive
  dives
  dived
  dove *Am.*
  div|ing
dive-bomb+s +ed
  +ing
dive-bomber+s
diver+s
di|verge
  di|verges
  di|verged
  di|ver|ging
di|ver|gence+s
di|ver|gency
  di|ver|gen|cies
di|ver|gent
di|ver|gent|ly
divers (sundry)
di|verse
di|verse|ly
di|ver|si|fi|able
di|ver|si|fi|ca|tion
  +s
di|ver|sify
  di|ver|si|fies
  di|ver|si|fied
  di|ver|si|fy|ing
di|ver|sion +s
di|ver|sion|al
di|ver|sion|ary
di|ver|sion|ist+s
di|ver|sity
  di|ver|sities
di|vert+s +ed
  +ing
di|ver|ticu|lar
di|ver|ticu|litis
di|ver|ticu|losis
di|ver|ticu|lum
  di|ver|tic|ula
di|ver|ti|mento
  di|ver|ti|menti *or*
  di|ver|ti|men|tos
di|vert|ing|ly
di|ver|tisse|ment
  +s
Dives (rich man)
di|vest +s +ed
  +ing
di|vesti|ture
di|vest|ment +s
di|vest|ure
divi +s (use divvy)
div|ide
  div|ides

div|ide (*cont.*)
div|ided
div|id|ing
divi|dend +s
dividend-
stripping
div|ider +s
divi-divi +s
div|in|ation +s
div|in|atory
div|ine
div|ines
div|ined
div|in|ing
div|iner
div|inest
div|ine|ly
div|ine|ness
div|iner +s
div|ing bell +s
div|ing board +s
div|ing suit +s
div|in|ing rod +s
div|in|ise *Br.* (use
divinize)
div|in|ises
div|in|ised
div|in|is|ing
div|in|ity
div|in|ities
div|in|ize
div|in|izes
div|in|ized
div|in|iz|ing
div|isi|bil|ity
div|is|ible (capable
of being divided.
△devisable)
div|ision +s
div|ision|al
div|ision|al|
isa|tion (use
divisionalization)
div|ision|al|ise
(use
divisionalize)
div|ision|al|ises
div|ision|al|ised
div|ision|al|is|ing
div|ision|al|
iza|tion
div|ision|al|ize
div|ision|al|izes
div|ision|al|ized
div|ision|al|iz|ing
div|ision|al|ly
div|ision|ary
div|ision|ism
div|isive
div|isive|ly
div|isive|ness

div|isor +s
(number.
△deviser,
devisor)
di|vorce
di|vorces
di|vorced
di|vor|cing
di|vorcé *Am.* +s
male
di|vor|cee *Br.* +s
di|vorcée *Am.* +s
female
di|vorce|ment
divot +s
di|vul|ga|tion
di|vulge
di|vulges
di|vulged
di|vul|ging
di|vulge|ment
di|vul|gence
divvy
div|vies
div|vied
divvy|ing
Di|wali
Dixie (southern
states of USA)
dixie +s (cooking
pot)
Dixie|land
Di|yar|ba|kir (city
and province,
Turkey)
diz|zily
diz|zi|ness
dizzy
diz|zies
diz|zied
dizzy|ing
diz|zier
diz|zi|est
Dja|karta (capital
of Indonesia)
djel|laba +s
djel|la|bah +s (use
djellaba)
Djerba (island,
Tunisia)
djibba +s
(Muslim's coat;
use jibba .
△gibber, jibber)
djib|bah +s
(Muslim's coat;
use jibba .
△gibber, jibber)
Dji|bouti
Dji|bou|tian +s
djinn
plural djinn *or*

djinn (*cont.*)
djinns
(= jinnee. △gin)
D-layer
D.Litt. (= Doctor of
Literature)
D.Mus. (= Doctor
of Music)
DNase
Dnie|per (river,
Russia, Belarus,
and Ukraine)
Dnies|ter (river,
Ukraine and
Moldova)
Dni|pro|
dzer|zhinsk (city,
Ukraine)
Dni|pro|petrovsk
(city, Ukraine)
D-notice +s
do
does
did
doing
done
verb
do
dos *or* do's
noun
do (*Music*; use doh .
△doe, dough)
do|able
dob
dobs
dobbed
dob|bing
dob|bin +s
dobe (adobe.
△dhobi)
Do|bell, Wil|liam
(Australian
painter)
Do|ber|man
(pin|scher) *Am.* +s
Do|ber|mann
(pin|scher) *Br.* +s
Do|brich (city,
Bulgaria)
Do|bruja (region,
Romania and
Bulgaria)
dob|son|fly
dob|son|flies
doc +s (doctor.
△dock)
Do|cetae
Do|cet|ism
Do|cet|ist +s
doch an dorris
(use deoch an
doris)
do|cile
do|cile|ly

do|cil|ity
dock +s +ed +ing
(for ships etc.; join
spacecraft; in law
court; weed; cut
short. △doc)
dock|age
dock|er +s
docket +s +ed
+ing
dock-glass
dock-glasses
dock|land +s
dock leaf
dock leaves
dock|side +s
dock-tailed
dock work|er +s
dock|yard +s
Doc Mar|ten
adjective Propr.
Doc Mar|tens
(= Dr Martens)
doc|tor +s +ed
+ing
doc|tor|al
doc|tor|ate +s
doctor-blade +s
doc|tor|hood
doc|tor|ial
doc|tor|ly
Doc|tor Mar|tens
(use Dr Martens)
doctor-patient
attributive
doc|tor|ship +s
doc|trin|aire +s
doc|trin|air|ism
doc|tri|nal
doc|tri|nal|ly
doc|trin|ar|ian +s
doc|trine +s
doc|trin|ism
doc|trin|ist +s
docu|drama +s
docu|ment +s +ed
+ing
docu|men|tal
docu|men|tal|ist
+s
docu|men|tar|ian
+s
docu|men|tar|ily
docu|men|tar|ist
+s
docu|men|tary
docu|men|tar|ies
docu|men|ta|tion
dod|der +s +ed
+ing
dod|der|er +s
dodder-grass
dod|deri|ness

dod|dery
dod|dle +s
do|deca|gon +s
do|deca|he|dral
do|deca|he|dra *or*
do|deca|he|drons
Do|decan|ese
(Greek islands)
do|deca|phon|ic
dodge
dodges
dodged
dodg|ing
Dodge City (city,
USA)
dodgem +s
dodger +s
Dodg|son, Charles
('Lewis Carroll',
English writer)
dodgy
dodgi|er
dodgi|est
dodo +s
Do|doma (capital
of Tanzania)
doe +s (deer.
△ doh, dough)
doe-eyed
doek +s
doer +s
does (plural of doe;
in 'he does' etc.)
doe|skin +s
doesn't (= does
not)
doest
doeth
doff +s +ed +ing
dog
dogs
dogged
dog|ging
dog|berry
dog|berries
dog bis|cuit +s
dog box
dog boxes
dog cart +s
dog-clutch
dog-clutches
dog col|lar +s
dog daisy
dog dai|sies
dog days
doge +s
dog-eared
dog-eat-dog
dog-end +s
dog|face +s
dog-fall +s

dog|fight +s
dog|fight|er +s
dog|fight|ing
dog|fish
plural dog|fish *or*
dog|fishes
dog food
dog|ged
dog|ged|ly
dog|ged|ness
Dog|ger (shipping
area, North Sea)
dog|ger +s (boat;
Geology)
Dog|ger Bank (in
North Sea)
dog|gerel
Dog|gett's Coat
and Badge
dog|gie +s (use
doggy)
dog|gi|ness
dog|gish
dog|gish|ly
dog|gish|ness
doggo
dog|gone
doggy
dog|gies
doggy bag +s
doggy-paddle
doggy-paddles
doggy-paddled
doggy-paddling
dog hand|ler +s
dog-handling
dog|house +s
dogie +s
dog-leg
dog-legs
dog-legged
dog-legging
dog|like
dogma +s
dog|man
dog|men
dog|mat|ic
dog|mat|ic|al|ly
dog|mat|ics
dog|ma|tise *Br.*
(use dogmatize)
dog|ma|tises
dog|ma|tised
dog|ma|tis|ing
dog|ma|tism
dog|ma|tist +s
dog|ma|tize
dog|ma|tizes
dog|ma|tized
dog|ma|tiz|ing
do-good +s *noun
and adjective*
do-gooder +s

do-goodery
do-goodism
dog-paddle
dog-paddles
dog-paddled
dog-paddling
dog ra|cing
dog rose +s
dogs|body
dogs|bodies
dog|shore +s
dog|skin
dog sled +s
dog's meat
dog's mer|cury
(plant)
dog's-tail +s
dog-star
dog's tooth
dog tag
dog-tail +s
dog-tired
dog-tooth
dog trials
dog|trot
dog-violet +s
dog|watch
dog|wood +s
doh (*Music.* △ doe,
dough)
Doha (capital of
Qatar)
doily
doi|lies
doing +s
Dois|neau,
Rob|ert (French
photographer)
doit +s
do-it-yourself
dojo +s
Dolby *Propr.*
dolce far ni|ente
Dolce|latte
dolce vita
dol|drums
dole
doles
doled
dol|ing
(benefit; woe.
△ dhole)
dole-bludger +s
dole|ful
dole|ful|ly
dole|ful|ness
doler|ite
doli|cho|ceph|al|ic
doli|cho|
ceph|al|ous
doli|cho|ceph|aly
Dolin, Anton
(British dancer

Dolin (*cont.*)
and
choreographer)
do|lina +s
do|line +s
Doll, Rich|ard
(English
physician)
doll +s +ed +ing
dol|lar +s
dol|lar|isa|tion
(use
dollarization)
dol|lar|iza|tion
Doll|fuss,
Engel|bert
(Austrian
statesman)
doll|house +s
dol|lop +s +ed
+ing
doll's house +s
Dolly (name)
dolly
dol|lies
dol|lied
dolly|ing
(doll; dress up
smartly)
dolly-bird +s
dolly mix|ture +s
Dolly Var|den +s
dolma
dol|mas *or*
dol|ma|des
dol|man +s
(sleeve)
dol|men +s (tomb)
dolo|mite (mineral
or rock)
Dolo|mite
Moun|tains (in
Italy)
Dolo|mites
(= Dolomite
Mountains)
dolo|mit|ic
dolor *Am.*
Dol|ores *also*
Del|ores
dol|or|ous
dol|or|ous|ly
dol|our *Br.*
dol|phin +s
dol|phin|arium
dol|phin|ariums
or dol|phin|aria
dolt +s
dolt|ish
dolt|ish|ly
dolt|ish|ness
Dom (title)

do|main +s (realm)
do|maine +s
  (vineyard)
do|man|ial
dome
  domes
  domed
  dom|ing
dome|like
Domes|day (Book)
  (1086 English
  record.
  ⚠ doomsday)
do|mes|tic +s
do|mes|tic|able
do|mes|tic|al|ly
do|mes|ti|cate
  do|mes|ti|cates
  do|mes|ti|cated
  do|mes|ti|cat|ing
do|mes|ti|ca|tion
do|mes|ti|city
  do|mes|ti|ci|ties
domi|cile
  domi|ciles
  domi|ciled
  domi|cil|ing
domi|cil|iary
dom|in|ance
dom|in|ant +s
dom|in|ant|ly
dom|in|ate
  dom|in|ates
  dom|in|ated
  dom|in|at|ing
dom|in|ation +s
dom|in|ator +s
dom|in|atrix
  dom|in|atrixes or
  dom|in|atri|ces
  female
dom|in|eer +s +ed
  +ing
dom|in|eer|ing|ly
Dom|ingo,
  Pla|cido (Spanish
  tenor)
Dom|inic (Spanish
  saint; name)
Do|min|ica (island,
  West Indies)
do|min|ical
Do|min|ic|an +s
dom|inie +s
do|min|ion +s
Dom|in|ique
Dom|ino, Fats
  (American
  musician)
dom|ino
  dom|inoes

Dom|itian (Roman
  emperor)
Don (rivers, Russia,
  Scotland, and
  Yorkshire; name)
Don +s (Spanish
  male title)
don
  dons
  donned
  don|ning
  (university
  teacher; put on)
dona +s (woman.
  ⚠ doner, donor)
donah +s (woman;
  use dona.
  ⚠ doner, donor)
Don|ald
Don|ald Duck
  (cartoon
  character)
do|nate
  do|nates
  do|nated
  do|nat|ing
Dona|tello
  (Florentine
  sculptor)
do|na|tion +s
Donat|ism
Donat|ist +s
do|na|tive +s
do|na|tor +s
Do|na|tus (Roman
  grammarian)
Don|bas (Ukrainian
  name for the
  Donets Basin)
Don|bass (Russian
  name for the
  Donets Basin)
Don|cas|ter (town,
  England)
done (past
  participle of do.
  ⚠ dun)
donee +s
  (recipient)
Don|egal (county,
  Republic of
  Ireland)
doner (kebab.
  ⚠ dona, donna,
  donor)
Don|ets (river, E.
  Europe)
Don|ets Basin
  (region, Ukraine)
Don|etsk (city,
  Ukraine)
dong +s +ed +ing

donga +s
don|gle +s
Doni|zetti,
  Gae|tano (Italian
  composer)
don|jon +s (castle
  keep. ⚠ dungeon)
Don Juan
  (legendary
  Spanish libertine)
don|key +s
don|key cart +s
don|key jacket +s
don|key's years
don|key work
Don|kin, Bryan
  (English engineer)
Donna (name;
  Italian, Spanish, or
  Portuguese female
  title)
donna +s (Italian,
  Spanish, or
  Portuguese lady;
  in 'prima donna'.
  ⚠ doner)
Donne, John
  (English poet and
  divine. ⚠ Dunne)
donné +s (use
  donnée)
don|née +s
don|nish
don|nish|ly
don|nish|ness
Donny|brook +s
donor +s (giver.
  ⚠ dona, doner)
Dono|van
Don Quix|ote
  (fictional hero)
don't +s (= do not)
donut +s (use
  doughnut)
doo|dad +s
doo|dah +s
doo|dle
  doo|dles
  doo|dled
  dood|ling
doodle|bug +s
dood|ler +s
dood|ling +s
doodly-squat
doo|hickey +s
doo|jig|ger +s
Doo|lit|tle, Hilda
  (American poet)
doom +s +ed +ing
  (fate. ⚠ doum)
doom-laden
doom|say|er +s

dooms|day (Last
  Judgement.
  ⚠ Domesday)
doom|ster +s
doom|watch
doom|watch|er +s
Doona +s
door +s (of house
  etc. ⚠ daw, dor)
door|bell +s
door|case +s
do-or-die attributive
doored
door frame +s
door handle +s
door head +s
door jamb +s
door|keeper +s
door|knob +s
door|knock +s
door knock|er +s
door|man
  door|men
door|mat +s
door|nail +s
Door|nik (Flemish
  name for
  Tournai)
door plate +s
door|post +s
Doors, the
  (American rock
  group)
door|step
  door|steps
  door|stepped
  door|step|ping
door|stop +s
door-to-door
door|way +s
door|yard +s
doozy
  doo|zies
dop +s
dopa (amino acid.
  ⚠ doper)
dopa|mine
dop|ant +s
dope
  dopes
  doped
  dop|ing
doper +s (person
  who gives or takes
  drugs. ⚠ dopa)
dopey
dopi|er
dopi|est
dop|ily
dopi|ness
dop|pel|gän|ger +s
Dop|per +s

Dop|pler (effect)
dopy (use **dopey**)
  dopi|er
  dopi|est
dor +s (beetle.
  △ **daw, door**)
Dora
Dor|ado
  (constellation)
dor|ado +s (fish)
Dor|cas
Dor|ches|ter (town,
  England)
Dor|dogne
  (department,
  France)
Dor|drecht (city,
  the Netherlands)
Doré, Gus|tave
  (French
  illustrator)
Dor|een
Dor|ian +s (ancient
  Hellenic people;
  name)
Dor|ian mode
Doric +s
Dor|inda
Doris
dork +s
dorm +s
dor|mancy
dor|mant
dormer +s
dor|mi|tion
dor|mi|tory
  dor|mi|tor|ies
Dor|mo|bile +s
  Propr.
dor|mouse
  dor|mice
dormy
do|ron|icum +s
Doro|thea
Doro|thy
dorp +s
dor|sal
dor|sal|ly
Dor|set (county,
  England)
dor|sum
  dorsa
Dort (alternative
  name for
  Dordrecht)
Dort|mund (city,
  Germany)
dory
  dor|ies
dory|phore +s
DOS *Computing*
dos-à-dos

dos|age +s
dose
  doses
  dosed
  dos|ing
do-se-do +s
dosh
do-si-do +s (use do-
  se-do)
dos|im|eter +s
dosi|met|ric
dos|im|etry
Dos Passos, John
  (American writer)
doss
  dosses
  dossed
  doss|ing
dos|sal
doss|er +s
doss-house +s
dos|sier +s
dost (in 'thou dost'.
  △ **dust**)
Dos|to|ev|sky,
  Fyodor (Russian
  novelist)
dot
  dots
  dot|ted
  dot|ting
dot|age
dot|ard +s
dote
  dotes
  doted
  dot|ing
doter +s
doth
dot|ing|ly
dot mat|rix
dot mat|rix
  print|er +s
dot|ter +s
dot|terel
dot|tily
dot|ti|ness
dot|tle +s
dotty
  dot|tier
  dot|ti|est
Dou|ala (city,
  Cameroon)
dou|ane +s
Douay Bible
double
  doubles
  doubled
  doub|ling
double act +s
double-acting
double-banking

double-barreled
  Am.
double-barrelled
  Br.
double bass
  double basses
double bill +s
double-blind
double bluff +s
double-book +s
  +ed +ing
double-breast|ed
double-check +s
  +ed +ing
double-chinned
double-cross
  double-crosses
  double-crossed
  double-crossing
double-crosser +s
double-dealer +s
double-dealing
double-decker +s
double-declutch
  **double-
  declutches**
  **double-
  declutched**
  **double-
  declutch|ing**
double Dutch
double-dyed
double-edged
double en|ten|dre
  +s
double-faced
double fault +s
  noun
double-fault +s
  +ed +ing *verb*
double-fronted
double-ganger +s
double-glazed
double glaz|ing
**double
  Glouces|ter**
double-headed
double head|er +s
double-jointed
double knit|ting
double-length
  adjective
double-lock +s
  +ed +ing
double-minded
double|ness
double-park +s
  +ed +ing
double quick
doub|ler +s
double-sided
double|speak

double stop +s
double-stopping
doub|let +s
double take +s
double-talk
double-thick
double|think
double time
double-tonguing
double whammy
  **double
  wham|mies**
doub|loon +s
doub|lure +s
doubly
doubt +s +ed +ing
doubt|able
doubt|er +s
doubt|ful
doubt|ful|ly
doubt|ful|ness
doubt|ing|ly
doubt|less
doubt|less|ly
douce
dou|ceur +s
douche
  douches
  douched
  douch|ing
Doug
dough +s (mixture
  for bread etc.
  △ **doe, doh**)
dough|boy +s
doughi|ness
dough|nut +s
dough|nut|ting
dought|ily
doughti|ness
doughty
  dought|ier
  doughti|est
doughy
  dough|ier
  doughi|est
Doug|las (capital of
  the Isle of Man;
  name)
Doug|las, Kirk and
  Mi|chael
  (American actors)
Doug|las fir +s
Douglas-Home,
  Alec (Lord Home,
  British prime
  minister)
doum +s (palm.
  △ **doom**)
doum-palm +s
dour
dour|ly

dour|ness
Douro (river, Spain and Portugal)
dou¦rou|couli +s
douse
  douses
  doused
  dous|ing
  (drench; extinguish, △ dowse)
dove +s (bird)
dove (Am. past tense of dive)
dove|cote +s
dove gray Am. +s
  noun and adjective
dove-gray Am.
  attributive
dove grey Br. +s
  noun and adjective
dove-grey Br.
  attributive
dove¦kie +s
dove|like
Dover (port, England; city, USA; shipping area)
dove's-foot +s
dove|tail +s +ed +ing
dove tree +s
dow|ager +s
dow¦dily
dow¦di|ness
dowdy
  dow|dier
  dow¦di|est
dowel
  dowels
  dow|elled Br.
  dow|eled Am.
  dowel|ling Br.
  dowel|ing Am.
dower +s +ed +ing
dower|less
dow|itcher +s
Dow–Jones index
Down (county, Northern Ireland)
down +s +ed +ing
down and out
  adjective
down-and-out +s
  noun and attributive
down at heel
  adjective
down-at-heel
  attributive
down|beat +s
down|cast

down|comer +s
down draft Am. +s
down draught Br. +s
down¦er +s
down|fall +s
down|field
down|fold +s
down|grade
  down|grades
  down|graded
  down|grad¦ing
down|haul +s
down|heart¦ed
down|heart¦ed¦ly
down|heart¦ed|ness
down|hill +s
down|hill¦er +s
down-home
down¦ily
downi|ness
Down|ing Street
  (in London)
down in the mouth
down|land +s
down|light¦er +s
down|load +s +ed +ing
down|mar¦ket
down|most
down pay|ment +s
down|pipe +s
down|play +s +ed +ing
down|pour +s
down|rate
  down|rates
  down|rated
  down|rat¦ing
down|right
down|right|ness
down|river
Downs, the (hill region, England)
down|scale
  down|scales
  down|scaled
  down|scal¦ing
down|shaft +s +ed +ing
down|shift +s +ed +ing
down|side +s
down|size
  down|sizes
  down|sized
  down|siz¦ing
Down|son, Er¦nest (English poet)
down|spout +s

Down's syn|drome
down|stage
down|stairs
down|state
down|stream
down|stroke +s
down|swing +s
down|throw
  down|throws
  down|threw
  down|throw|ing
  down|thrown
down time
down-to-earth
down|town +s
down|trod¦den
down|turn +s +ed +ing
down under
down|ward
down|ward¦ly
down|wards
down|warp +s
down|wind
downy
  down|ier
  downi|est
dowry
  dow|ries
dowse
  dowses
  dowsed
  dows|ing
  (search for water. △ douse)
dowser +s
Dow|sing (light vessel, North Sea)
dows|ing rod +s
doxo|logic¦al
dox|ology
  dox|ologies
doxy
  doxies
doyen +s male
doy|enne +s female
Doyle, Ar¦thur Conan (Scottish novelist)
doy¦ley +s (use doily)
D'Oyly Carte, Rich¦ard (English impresario)
doze
  dozes
  dozed
  doz¦ing
dozen +s
doz¦enth
dozer +s
dozi¦ly

dozi|ness
dozy
  dozi¦er
  dozi|est
D.Phil. (= Doctor of Philosophy)
drab
  drab|ber
  drab|best
Drab¦ble, Mar|ga¦ret (English novelist)
drab¦ble
  drab|bles
  drab|bled
  drab|bling
drab¦ly
drab|ness
dra|caena +s
drachm +s (unit. △ DRAM, dram)
drachma +s
drack
Draco (Athenian legislator; constellation)
drac|one +s
dra|co|nian
dra|con¦ic
Drac|ula, Count (vampire)
draff
draft +s +ed +ing (preliminary writing or drawing; money order; Military. △ draught)
draft Am. +s (current of air; act of drinking; drawing in; depth of water. Br. draught)
draft dodger +s
draft dodg¦ing
draft¦ee +s
draft¦er +s
draft horse Am. +s (Br. draught horse)
draft¦ily Am. (Br. draughtily)
drafti|ness Am. (Br. draughtiness)
draft-proof Am. +s +ed +ing (Br. draught-proof)
drafts|man Am. drafts|men (Br. draughtsman)

drafts|man|ship
   Am. (*Br.* draughts-
   manship)
drafts|woman *Am.*
   drafts|women
   (*Br.*
   draughtswoman)
drafty *Am.*
   draft|ier
   drafti|est
   (*Br.* draughty)
drag
   drags
   dragged
   drag|ging
drag-anchor +s
dra|gée +s
drag|gle
   drag|gles
   drag|gled
   drag|gling
draggle-tailed
draggy
   drag|gier
   drag|gi|est
drag-hound +s
drag|line +s
drag|net +s
drago|man
   drago|mans *or*
   drago|men
dragon +s
drag|onet +s
dragon|fish
   plural dragon|fish
   or dragon|fishes
dragon|fly
   dragon|flies
dragon|ish
drag|on|nade
   drag|on|nades
   drag|on|naded
   drag|on|nad|ing
dragon's blood
dragon's teeth
dragon tree +s
drag|oon +s +ed
   +ing
drag|ster +s
drail +s
drain +s +ed +ing
drain|age +s
drain|board +s
drain|cock +s
drain|er +s
drain|ing board +s
drain|pipe +s
Drake, Fran|cis
   (English explorer)
drake +s

Drak|ens|berg
   Moun|tains (in
   southern Africa)
Drake Pas|sage
   (off S. America)
Dra|lon *Propr.*
DRAM (= dynamic
   random access
   memory.
   ⚠ drachm)
dram +s (drink.
   ⚠ drachm)
drama +s
drama|doc +s
drama-
   documen|tary
   drama-
   documen|tar|ies
dra|mat|ic
dra|mat|ic|al|ly
dra|mat|ics
drama|tisa|tion *Br.*
   +s (use
   dramatization)
drama|tise *Br.* (use
   dramatize)
   drama|tises
   drama|tised
   drama|tis|ing
drama|tis
   per|sonae
drama|tist +s
drama|tiza|tion +s
drama|tize
   drama|tizes
   drama|tized
   drama|tiz|ing
drama|turge +s
drama|tur|gic
drama|tur|gic|al
drama|turgy
   drama|tur|gies
Dram|buie *Propr.*
Dram|men (port,
   Norway)
drank
drape
   drapes
   draped
   drap|ing
draper +s
dra|pery
   dra|per|ies
dras|tic
dras|tic|al|ly
drat
drat|ted
draught *Br.* +s +ed
   +ing (current of
   air; act of
   drinking; drawing
   in; depth of water.

draught (*cont.*)
   In other senses
   use draft. *Am.*
   draft)
draught|board +s
draught horse *Br.*
   +s (*Am.* draft
   horse)
draught|ily *Br.*
   (*Am.* draftily)
draughti|ness *Br.*
   (*Am.* draftiness)
draught-proof *Br.*
   +s +ed +ing
   (*Am.* draft-proof)
draughts (game)
draughts|man *Br.*
   draughts|men
   (*Am.* draftsman)
draughts|man|
   ship *Br.* (*Am.*
   draftsmanship)
draughts|woman
   Br.
   draughts|women
   (*Am.*
   draftswoman)
draughty *Br.*
   draught|ier
   draughti|est
   (*Am.* drafty)
Dra|vid|ian +s
draw
   draws
   drew
   draw|ing
   drawn
draw|back +s
draw|bridge +s
draw|cord +s
draw|down +s
draw|ee +s
drawer +s
drawer|ful +s
draw|ing +s
draw|ing board +s
draw|ing paper
draw|ing pin +s
draw|ing room +s
drawl +s +ed +ing
drawl|er +s
drawn
drawn-out
   attributive
drawn work
draw-sheet +s
draw|string +s
draw-well +s
dray +s (cart.
   ⚠ drey)
dray horse +s
dray|man
   dray|men

dread +s +ed +ing
dread|ful
dread|ful|ly
dread|ful|ness
dread|locked
dread|locks
dread|nought +s
dream
   dreams
   dreamed *or*
   dreamt
   dream|ing
dream|boat +s
dream|er +s
dream|ful
dream|ily
dreami|ness
dream|land +s
dream|less
dream|like
dream|scape +s
dream|time
dream-world +s
dreamy
   dream|ier
   dreami|est
drear +er +est
drear|ily
dreari|ness
dreary
   drear|ier
   dreari|est
dreck
dredge
   dredges
   dredged
   dredg|ing
dredger +s
dree
   drees
   dreed
   dree|ing
dreg +s
dreggy
Drei|ser,
   Theo|dore
   (American
   novelist)
drench
   drenches
   drenched
   drench|ing
Drenthe (province,
   the Netherlands)
Dres|den (city,
   Germany)
dress
   dresses
   dressed
   dress|ing
dress|age
dress circle +s

dress|er +s
dressi|ness
dress|ing +s
dress|ing case +s
dress|ing down
noun
dress|ing gown +s
dress|ing room +s
dress|ing sta|tion
+s
dress|ing table +s
dress|ing up noun
dress|maker +s
dress|mak|ing
dress shield +s
dress shirt +s
dressy
dress|ier
dressi|est
Drew (name)
drew (past tense of
draw)
drey +s (squirrel's
nest. △ dray)
Drey|fus, Al|fred
(French army
officer)
drib|ble
drib|bles
drib|bled
drib|bling
drib|bler +s
drib|bly
drib|let +s
dribs and drabs
dried
dried-out adjective
dried-up adjective
drier (comparative
of dry. △ dryer)
dri|est
drift +s +ed +ing
drift|age
drift|er +s
drift-ice
drift-net +s
drift-netter +s
drift-netting
drift|wood
drill +s +ed +ing
drill|er +s
drill ser|geant +s
drily
drink
drinks
drank
drink|ing
drunk
drink|able
drink-drive
attributive
drink-driver +s

drink-driving
drink|er +s
drinking-song +s
drinking-up time
drink|ing water
drip
drips
dripped
drip|ping
drip-dry
drip-dries
drip-dried
drip-drying
drip-feed
drip-feeds
drip-fed
drip-feeding
drip-mat +s
drip-moulding
drip|pily
drip|pi|ness
drippy
drip|pier
drip|pi|est
drip|stone +s
driv|able
drive
drives
drove
driv|ing
driven
drive|able (use
drivable)
drive-by adjective
drive-in +s
adjective and noun
drivel
driv|els
driv|elled Br.
driv|eled Am.
driv|el|ling Br.
driv|el|ing Am.
driv|el|er Am. +s
driv|el|ler Br. +s
driven
drive-on adjective
drive-on/drive-off
adjective
driver +s
driver|less
driver's li|cense
Am. +s (Br.
driving licence)
drive|shaft +s
drive-through +s
adjective and noun
drive-thru Am. +s
adjective and noun
(Br. drive-
through)
drive-time
drive|way +s

driv|ing licence Br.
+s (Am. driver's
license)
driv|ing range +s
driv|ing test +s
driv|ing wheel +s
driz|zle
driz|zles
driz|zled
driz|zling
driz|zly
Dr Mar|tens Propr.
Dro|gheda (port,
Republic of
Ireland)
drogue +s
droit +s
droit de sei|gneur
droll +er +est
droll|ery
droll|er|ies
droll|ness
drolly
drome +s
drom|ed|ary
drom|ed|ar|ies
drom|ond +s
drone
drones
droned
dron|ing
drongo +s
droob +s
drool +s +ed +ing
droop +s +ed +ing
(sag. △ drupe)
droop|ily
droopi|ness
droop-snoot +s
droopy
droop|ier
droopi|est
drop
drops
dropped
drop|ping
drop cur|tain +s
drop-dead adjective
drop-forge
drop-forges
drop-forged
drop-forging
drop goal +s
drop ham|mer +s
drop|head +s
drop-in +s noun
and adjective
drop kick +s
drop-leaf
drop-leaves
drop|let +s
drop-off +s

drop-out +s noun
drop|per +s
drop|ping +s
drop scene +s
drop scone +s
drop shot +s
drop|si|cal
dropsy
drop|sies
drop test +s noun
drop-test +s +ed
+ing verb
drop|wort +s
droshky
drosh|kies
Dros|oph|ila
(genus)
dros|oph|ila +s
(fly)
dross
drossy
dros|sier
drossi|est
Drott|ning|holm
(town, Sweden)
drought +s
droughty
drouth
Drouzhba (resort,
Bulgaria)
drove
droves
droved
drov|ing
drover +s
drove road +s
drown +s +ed
+ing
drown|ing +s
drowse
drowses
drowsed
drows|ing
drows|ily
drow|si|ness
drowsy
drows|ier
drowsi|est
drub
drubs
drubbed
drub|bing
drudge
drudges
drudged
drudg|ing
drudg|ery
drudg|er|ies
drug
drugs
drugged
drug|ging

drug-crazed
drug deal|er +s
drug deal|ing
drug|get +s
drug|gie +s (use
  druggy)
drug|gist +s
druggy
  drug|gies
drug ped|dler +s
drug push|er +s
drug smug|gler +s
drug smug|gling
drug|store +s
drug traf|fick|er
  +s
drug traf|fick|ing
Druid +s
Druid|ess
  Druid|esses
Dru|id|ic
Dru|id|ic|al
Dru|id|ism
drum
  drums
  drummed
  drum|ming
drum|beat +s
drum|fire
drum fish
  plural drum fish or
  drum fishes
drum|head +s
drum kit +s
drum|lin +s
drum|lin|oid
drum|mer +s
drum|stick +s
drunk +s +er +est
drunk|ard +s
drunk|en adjective
drunk|en|ly
drunk|en|ness
drup|aceous
drupe +s (fruit.
  △ droop)
drupel +s
drupe|let +s
Drury Lane (in
  London)
Druse +s (Muslim;
  use Druze)
druse +s (cavity)
Dru|silla
druther +s
Druzba (use
  Drouzhba)
Druze +s (Muslim.
  △ druse)
dry
  dries
  dried

dry (cont.)
  dry|ing
  drier
  dri|est
dryad +s
dry cell +s
dry-clean +s +ed
  +ing
dry-cleaner +s
dry cure
  dry cures
  dry cured
  dry cur|ing
Dry|den, John
  (English writer)
dry dock +s
dryer +s (device.
  △ drier)
dry-eyed
dry fly
  dry flies
dry-fly
  dry-flies
  dry-flied
  dry-flying
  verb and attributive
dry|ish
dry|land +s (land
  with low rainfall)
dry land (not sea)
dryly (use drily)
dry|ness
dry-nurse +s
dryo|pith|ecine
Dryo|pith|ecus
dry plate +s
dry-point +s
dry-salt +s +ed
  +ing
dry-salter +s
Drys|dale, Rus|sell
  (Australian
  painter)
dry-shod
dry|stone
dry|suit +s
dry|wall
dual
  duals
  dualled Br.
  dualed Am.
  dual|ling Br.
  dual|ing Am.
  (double. △ duel)
dual|ise Br. (use
  dualize)
  dual|ises
  dual|ised
  dual|is|ing
dual|ism +s
dual|ist +s

dual|is|tic
dual|is|tic|al|ly
dual|ity
  dual|ities
dual|ize
  dual|izes
  dual|ized
  dual|iz|ing
dual|ly
dual-purpose
Duane also Dwane
dub
  dubs
  dubbed
  dub|bing
Dubai (state and
  city, UAE)
dub|bin +s +ed
  +ing
Dub|ček,
  Alex|an|der
  (Czech statesman)
du|bi|ety
du|bi|ous
du|bi|ous|ly
du|bi|ous|ness
du|bi|ta|tion
du|bi|ta|tive
du|bi|ta|tive|ly
Dub|lin (capital and
  county of the
  Republic of
  Ireland)
Dub|lin Bay
  prawn +s
Dub|lin|er +s
Du Bois, W. E. B.
  (American writer
  and political
  activist)
Du|bon|net Propr.
Du|brov|nik (port,
  Croatia)
ducal
ducat +s
Duc|cio di
  Buon|in|segna
  (Sienese painter)
Duce, Il (Mussolini)
Du|champ,
  Mar|cel (French
  artist)
Du|chenne
  (muscular
  dystrophy)
duch|ess
  duch|esses
  (noblewoman)
du|chesse +s
  (furniture; lace;
  potatoes)
duchy
  duch|ies

duck +s +ed +ing
duck|bill +s
duck-billed
  platy|pus
duck-billed
  platy|puses
duck|board +s
duck|er +s
duck-hawk +s
duckie +s (use
  ducky)
ducking-stool +s
duck|ling +s
duck's arse Br.
duck's ass Am.
duck|weed +s
ducky
  duck|ies
duct +s +ed +ing
duc|tile
duc|til|ity
duct|less
dud +s
dude +s
dudgeon
dudish
Dud|ley (name)
Dud|ley, Rob|ert
  (Earl of Leicester,
  courtier of
  Elizabeth I)
due +s (owed.
  △ dew)
duel
  duels
  duelled Br.
  dueled Am.
  duel|ling Br.
  duel|ing Am.
  (fight. △ dual)
duel|er Am. +s
duel|ist Am. +s
duel|ler Br. +s
duel|list Br. +s
du|ende +s
du|enna +s
Duero (Spanish
  name for the
  Douro)
duet
  duets
  duet|ted
  duet|ting
duet|tist +s
Dufay, Guil|laume
  (Franco-Flemish
  composer and
  singer)
duff
  duffs
  duffed
  duff|ing

duf¦fel
duf¦fel bag +s
duf¦fel coat +s
duf¦fer +s
duf¦fle (use duffel)
Dufy, Raoul
 (French artist)
dug +s
du¦gong
 plural du¦gong or
 du¦gongs
dug¦out +s
duiker +s
Duis|burg (city,
 Germany)
Dukas, Paul
 (French
 composer)
duke +s
duke|dom +s
Du¦kho|bor +s
dul¦cet
Dul¦cie
dul¦ci|fi|ca¦tion
dul¦cify
 dul¦ci|fies
 dul¦ci|fied
 dul¦ci¦fy|ing
dul¦ci¦mer +s
dul¦ci|tone
dulia
dull +s +ed +ing
 +er +est
dull|ard +s
Dulles, John
 Foster (American
 statesman)
dull|ish
dull|ness
dull-witted
dully
dulse
duly
duma +s (Russian
 council)
Dumas,
 Alex|andre (père
 and fils, French
 writers)
Du Maur|ier,
 Daphne (English
 writer)
Du Maur|ier,
 George (French-
 born illustrator
 and writer)
dumb +er +est
Dum|bar¦ton
 (town, Scotland)
dumb-bell +s
dumb|found +s
 +ed +ing

dumb|head +s
dumb-iron +s
dumb¦ly
dumb|ness
dumbo +s
dumb|show +s
dumb|struck
dum¦dum +s
dum|found +s +ed
 +ing (use
 dumbfound)
Dum|fries (town,
 Scotland)
Dum|fries and
 Gallo|way
 (region, Scotland)
Dum¦fries|shire
 (former county,
 Scotland)
dummy
 dum|mies
 dum|mied
 dummy|ing
dump +s +ed +ing
dump¦er +s
dump¦er truck +s
dump|ily
dumpi|ness
dump|ling +s
dump truck +s
dumpy
 dump|ier
 dumpi|est
dun
 duns
 dunned
 dun|ning
 (colour; creditor;
 pester; etc.
 △ done)
Dun¦bar, Wil|liam
 (Scottish poet)
Dun¦bar¦ton|shire
 (former county,
 Scotland)
dun-bird +s
Dun¦can (name)
Dun¦can, Isa|dora
 (American dancer)
dunce +s
dunce's cap +s
Dun|dalk (town,
 Republic of
 Ireland)
Dun|dee (city,
 Scotland)
dun¦der|head +s
dun¦der|head¦ed
dun-diver +s
dune +s
Dun|edin (city,
 New Zealand)

Dun|ferm|line
 (city, Scotland)
dung +s +ed +ing
dun|garee +s
Dun¦gar|van
 (town, Republic of
 Ireland)
dung-beetle +s
dun|geon +s
 (underground
 prison. △ donjon)
dung-fly
 dung-flies
dung|hill +s
dung-worm +s
dunk +s +ed +ing
Dun|kirk (port,
 France)
Dun Lao¦ghaire
 (port, Republic of
 Ireland)
dun|lin +s
Dun|lop, John
 Boyd (Scottish
 inventor)
Dun¦mow flitch
dun|nage
Dunne, John
 Wil|liam (English
 philosopher.
 △ Donne)
Dun|net Head (in
 Scotland)
dunno +s (= don't
 know)
dun|nock +s
dunny
 dun|nies
Duns Scotus,
 John (Scottish
 theologian)
Dun|stable, John
 (English
 composer)
Dun|stan (Anglo-
 Saxon saint;
 name)
duo +s
duo|deci|mal
duo|deci¦mal|ly
duo|decimo +s
duo|denal
duo|de¦nary
duo|den|itis
duo|de¦num +s
duo¦log Am. +s
duo|logue +s
duomo +s
du|op|oly
 du|op|olies
duo|tone +s
dup|able

dupe
dupes
duped
dup¦ing
duper +s
dupery
du¦pion +s
duple
du¦plet +s
du¦plex
du|plexes
du|plic|able
du¦pli|cate
 du|pli|cates
 du|pli|cated
 du|pli|cat|ing
du|pli|ca¦tion +s
du|pli|ca¦tor +s
du|pli|ci|tous
du|pli¦city
 du|pli|ci¦ties
duppy
 dup|pies
du Pré,
 Jacque|line
 (English cellist)
dura +s (use durra)
dur|abil|ity
dur|able +s
dur|able|ness
dur¦ably
Dur|alu|min (alloy)
 Propr.
dura mater +s
dur|amen
dur|ance
Dur|ango (state
 and city, Mexico)
Duras,
 Mar|guer|ite
 (French writer)
dur|ation +s
dur|ation|al
dura|tive
Dur¦ban (city,
 South Africa)
dur¦bar +s
durch|kom¦pon|
 iert
Dürer, Al|brecht
 (German artist)
dur|ess
Durex
 plural Durex
 Propr.
Durey, Louis
 (French
 composer)
Durga Hinduism
Dur¦ham (city,
 England)
dur¦ian +s

duri|crust +s
dur|ing
Durk|heim, Émile
(French
philosopher)
Durk|heim|ian
dur|mast +s
durn
durned
durra +s
Dur|rell,
Law|rence
(English writer)
Dur|rës (port,
Albania)
durst
durum
durzi +s
Du|shanbe (capital
of Tadjikistan)
dusk +s
dusk|ily
duski|ness
dusk-to-dawn
dusky
dusk|ies
dusk|ier
duski|est
Düs|sel|dorf (city,
Germany)
dust +s +ed +ing
(particles. △ dost)
dust bag +s
dust-bath +s
dust|bin +s
dust bowl +s
dust|cart +s
dust cover +s
dust devil +s
dust|er +s
dust|ily
Dus|tin
dusti|ness
dust|ing pow|der
dust jacket +s
dust|less
dust|man
dust|men
dust|pan +s
dust sheet +s
dust-shot
dust storm +s
dust-trap +s
dust-up +s noun
dust-wrapper +s
dusty
dust|ier
dusti|est
Dutch (of the
Netherlands etc.;
in 'go Dutch')

dutch
dutches
(= duchess)
Dutch|man
Dutch|men
Dutch|man's
breeches
Dutch|man's pipe
Dutch|woman
Dutch|women
du|teous
du|teous|ly
du|teous|ness
duti|able
duti|ful
duti|ful|ly
duti|ful|ness
duty
du|ties
duty-bound
duty-free +s
duty of|ficer +s
duty-paid
du|um|vir +s
du|um|vir|ate
Du|val|ier, Papa
Doc (Haitian
statesman)
duvet +s
Du Vig|neaud,
Vin|cent
(American
biochemist)
dux
duxes
duyker +s (use
duiker)
Dvořák, An|tonin
(Czech composer)
dwale
Dwane also Duane
dwarf
dwarfs or
dwarves
noun
dwarf +s +ed +ing
verb
dwarf|ish
dwarf|ism
dweeb +s
dwell
dwells
dwelled or dwelt
dwell|ing
dwell|er +s
dwell|ing +s
dwell|ing house
+s
dwell|ing place +s
Dwight
dwin|dle
dwin|dles

dwin|dle (cont.)
dwin|dled
dwin|dling
dyad +s
dyad|ic
Dyak +s
dy|archy (use
diarchy)
dy|arch|ies
dyb|buk
dyb|buk|im or
dyb|buks
dye
dyes
dyed
dye|ing
(colour, stain.
△ die)
dye|able
dyed-in-the-wool
dye-line +s
dyer +s
dyer's broom
dyer's green|weed
dyer's oak +s
(tree)
dye|stuff +s
Dyfed (county,
Wales)
dying (present
participle of die.
△ dyeing)
dyke
dykes
dyked
dyk|ing
Dylan (name)
Dylan, Bob
(American singer
and songwriter)
Dymphna
dy|nam|ic
dy|nam|ic|al
dy|nam|ic|al|ly
dy|nami|cist
dy|nam|ics
dyna|misa|tion Br.
(use
dynamization)
dyna|mise Br. (use
dynamize)
dyna|mises
dyna|mised
dyna|mis|ing
dyna|mism
dyna|mist +s
dyna|mite
dyna|mites
dyna|mited
dyna|mit|ing
dyna|miter +s
dyna|miza|tion

dyna|mize
dyna|mizes
dyna|mized
dyna|miz|ing
dy|namo +s
dyna|mom|eter +s
dyn|ast +s
dyn|as|tic
dyn|as|tic|al|ly
dyn|asty
dyn|as|ties
dyna|tron +s
dyne +s (unit.
△ dine)
dys|en|ter|ic
dys|en|tery
dys|func|tion +s
+ed +ing
dys|func|tion|al
dys|gen|ic
dys|graphia
dys|graph|ic
dys|lec|tic +s
dys|lexia
dys|lex|ic +s
dys|lo|gis|tic
dys|lo|gis|tic|al|ly
dys|men|or|rhea
Am.
dys|men|or|rhoea
Br.
dys|pep|sia
dys|pep|tic
dys|pha|sia
dys|phasic
dys|phem|ism +s
dys|phoria
dys|phoric
dys|pla|sia
dys|plas|tic
dys|pnea Am.
dys|pneic Am.
dys|pnoea Br.
dys|pnoeic Br.
dys|pro|sium
dys|to|cia
dys|to|pia +s
dys|to|pian +s
dys|troph|ic
dys|trophy
dys|uria
Dzaou|dzi (town,
Mayotte)
Dzau|dzhi|kau
(former name of
Vladikavkaz)
Dzer|zhinsk (city,
Russia)
Dzer|zhin|sky,
Fe|liks
Ed|mund|ovich
(Russian leader)

dzho (use dzo)
plural dzho *or*
dzhos
dzo
plural dzo *or* dzos
Dzong¦kha

Ee

each
Ead¦wig (English
king)
eager (keen.
△ eagre)
eager¦ly
eagerly-awaited
eager|ness
eagle
eagles
eagled
eag¦ling
eagle eye +s
eagle-eyed
eag¦let +s
eagre +s (wave.
△ eager)
Ea¦kins, Thomas
(American artist)
Eal¦ing (borough,
London; film
studios)
Eamon *also*
Ea¦monn
Ea¦monn *also*
Eamon
ear +s
ear|ache +s
ear|bash
ear|bashes
ear|bashed
ear|bash|ing
ear|bash¦er +s
ear drops
ear|drum +s
eared
ear¦ful +s
Ear|hart, Am¦elia
(American
aviator)
ear|hole +s
ear¦ing +s (rope.
△ earring)
earl +s
earl|dom +s
ear|less
Earl Grey (tea)
earli|ness
Earl Mar|shal
ear lobe +s
Earl Pal¦at|ine
Earls Pal¦at|ine
early
earl¦ies
earl¦ier
earli|est
ear|mark +s +ed
+ing

ear|muff +s
earn +s +ed +ing
(gain. △ ern, erne,
urn)
earn¦er +s
earn¦est
earn¦est¦ly
earn¦est|ness
earn|ings
earnings-related
EAROM
(= electrically
alterable read-only
memory)
Earp, Wyatt
(American
frontiersman)
ear|phone +s
ear|piece +s
ear-piercing
ear|plug +s
ear|ring +s
(jewellery.
△ earing)
ear|shot
ear-splitting
ear-stopple +s
earth +s +ed +ing
earth|bound
earth closet +s
earth¦en
earth¦en|ware
earth-hog +s
earth|ily
earthi|ness
earth|li|ness
earth|ling +s
earth¦ly
earth mother +s
earth mover +s
earth-moving
earth-nut +s
earth-pig +s
earth|quake +s
earth-shaking
earth-shatter¦ing
earth-
shatter¦ing¦ly
earth|shine
earth|star +s
earth|ward
earth|wards
earth|work +s
earth|worm +s
earthy
earth|ier
earthi|est
ear-trumpet +s
ear-tuft +s
ear¦wax
ear¦wig
ear|wigs

ear¦wig (*cont.*)
ear|wigged
ear|wig|ging
ease
eases
eased
eas|ing
ease|ful
easel +s
ease|ment +s
easer +s
eas|ily
easi|ness
East, the (part of
country etc.; E.
Europe; E. Asia)
east +s (point;
direction)
east|about
East An¦glia
(region, England)
east|bound
East|bourne (town,
England)
East Ender +s
Easter +s
Easter Is¦land (in
SE Pacific)
east|er¦ly
east|er¦lies
east|ern
east|ern¦er +s
east|ern|most
East¦er|tide
East India|man +s
east|ing +s
East|man, George
(American
inventor)
east-north-east
east-south-east
east|ward
east|ward¦ly
east|wards
East-West
attributive
East|wood, Clint
(American actor
and director)
easy
eas¦ier
easi|est
easy chair +s
easy|going
easy-peasy
easy-to-follow
attributive
easy-to-use
attributive
eat
eats
ate

eat (*cont.*)
eat|ing
eaten
eat|able +s
eater +s (person or
animal that eats.
△ eta)
eat|ery
eat|er|ies
eat|ing apple +s
eat|ing house +s
eat|ing place +s
eau de Co|logne
+s
eau-de-Nil
eau de toi|lette +s
eau-de-vie +s
eau su|crée
eave +s (under
roof. △ eve)
eaves|drop
eaves|drops
eaves|dropped
eaves|drop|ping
eaves|drop|per +s
ebb +s +ed +ing
Eben|ezer
Ebla (city, ancient
Syria)
E-boat +s
eb|on|ite
ebony
Ebor|acum (Roman
name for York)
Ebro (river, Spain)
ebul|li|ence
ebul|li|ency
ebul|li|ent
ebul|li|ent|ly
ebul|li|tion
ecad +s
écarté
Ecce Homo
ec|cen|tric +s
ec|cen|tric|al|ly
ec|cen|tri|city
ec|cen|tri|ci|ties
ec|chym|osis
ec|chym|oses
Ec|cles, John
(Australian
physiologist)
Ec|cles cake +s
ec|cle|sial
Ec|cle|si|as|tes
Bible
ec|cle|si|as|tic +s
ec|cle|si|as|tic|al
ec|cle|si|as|tic|
al|ly
ec|cle|si|as|ti|cism

Ec|cle|si|as|ti|cus
Bible
ec|cle|sio|logic|al
ec|cle|si|olo|gist
+s
ec|cle|si|ology
ec|crine
ec|dy|sis
ec|dy|ses
ech|elon +s
eche|veria +s
ech|idna +s
ech|in|ite +s
ech|ino|derm +s
ech|in|oid +s
ech|inus
ech|inuses
Echo *Greek
Mythology*
echo
echoes
echoed
echo|ing
echo|car|dio|gram
+s
echo|car|dio|graph
+s
echo|car|di|
og|raph|er +s
echo|car|di|
og|raphy
echo cham|ber +s
echo|en|ceph|alo|
gram +s
echo|en|ceph|al|
og|raphy
echo|er +s
echoey
echo|gram +s
echo|graph +s
echo|ic
echo|ic|al|ly
echo|ism
echo|la|lia
echo|less
echo|locate
echo|locates
echo|located
echo|locat|ing
echo|loca|tion
echo sound|er +s
echo-sounding
echo|virus
echt
éclair +s
éclair|cisse|ment
eclamp|sia
eclamp|tic
éclat
eclec|tic +s
eclec|tic|al|ly

eclec|ti|cism
eclipse
eclipses
eclipsed
eclips|ing
eclip|ser +s
eclip|tic +s
eclip|tic|al|ly
ec|logue +s
eclo|sion
eclo|sions
Eco, Um|berto
(Italian novelist)
eco|cide
eco|cli|mate +s
eco-friend|ly
eco-label +s
eco-labeling *Am.*
eco-labelling *Br.*
eco|logic|al
eco|logic|al|ly
ecolo|gist +s
ecol|ogy
ecol|ogies
econo|met|ric
econo|met|ric|al
econo|met|ric|
al|ly
econo|met|ri|cian
+s
econo|met|rics
econo|met|rist +s
eco|nom|ic
eco|nom|ic|al
eco|nom|ic|al|ly
eco|nom|ics
econo|misa|tion
Br. (use
economization)
econo|mise *Br.*
(use economize)
econo|mises
econo|mised
econo|mis|ing
econo|miser *Br.* +s
(use economizer)
econo|mist +s
econo|miza|tion
econo|mize
econo|mizes
econo|mized
econo|miz|ing
econo|mizer +s
econ|omy
econ|omies
econ|omy class
eco|sphere +s
écos|saise +s
eco|sys|tem +s
eco-terror|ism
eco-terror|ist +s

eco|tour|ism
eco|tour|ist +s
eco|type +s
ecru +s
ec|sta|sise *Br.* (use
ecstasize)
ec|sta|sises
ec|sta|sised
ec|sta|sis|ing
ec|sta|size
ec|sta|sizes
ec|sta|sized
ec|sta|siz|ing
ec|stasy
ec|sta|sies
ec|stat|ic
ec|stat|ic|al|ly
ecto|blast +s
ecto|blast|ic
ecto|derm +s
ecto|der|mal
ecto|gen|esis
ecto|gen|et|ic
ecto|gen|et|ic|al|ly
ecto|gen|ic
ecto|gen|ic|al|ly
ecto|morph +s
ecto|morph|ic
ecto|morphy
ecto|para|site +s
ec|top|ic
ecto|plasm
ecto|plas|mic
ecto|zoon
ecu
plural ecu *or* ecus
(= European
currency unit)
écu +s (French
coin)
Ecua|dor
Ecua|dor|ean +s
ecu|men|ic|al +s
ecu|men|ic|al|ism
ecu|men|ic|al|ly
ecu|meni|cism
ecu|men|icity
ecu|men|ism
ec|zema (inflamma-
tion. △ excimer)
ec|zema|tous
Ed (name)
eda|cious
eda|city
Edam (town, the
Netherlands;
cheese)
ed|aph|ic
Edda
Eddie
Ed|ding|ton,
Ar|thur Stan|ley

Ed¦ding¦ton (*cont.*)
(English
astronomer and
physicist)
eddo
ed¦does
Eddy, Mary Baker
(American
founder of the
Christian Science
movement)
eddy
ed¦dies
ed¦died
eddy¦ing
Eddy¦stone Rocks
(in English
Channel)
edel¦weiss
plural edel¦weiss
edema *Am.*
ede¦mas *or*
ede¦mata
(*Br.* oedema)
edema¦tous *Am.*
(*Br.* oedematous)
Eden, An¦thony
(British prime
minister)
Eden, Gar¦den of
Bible
edent¦ate +s
Edgar (English
king; name)
edge
edges
edged
edging
Edge¦hill
(battlefield,
England)
edge¦less
edger +s
edge-tool +s
edge¦ways
edge¦wise
**Edge¦worth,
Maria** (Anglo-
Irish novelist)
edgi¦ly
edgi¦ness
edging +s
edg¦ing shears
edgy
edgi¦er
edgi¦est
edh +s
edi¦bil¦ity
ed¦ible +s
edict +s
edict¦al
Edie

edi¦fi¦ca¦tion
edi¦fice +s
edify
edi¦fies
edi¦fied
edify¦ing
edify¦ing¦ly
Ed¦in¦burgh
(capital of
Scotland)
Edi¦son, Thomas
(American
inventor)
edit +s +ed +ing
Edith
edi¦tion +s (version
of book etc.
△ addition)
edi¦tio prin¦ceps
*edi¦ti¦ones
prin¦cipes*
edi¦tor +s
edi¦tor¦ial +s
edi¦tori¦al¦ise *Br.*
(use editorialize)
edi¦tori¦al¦ises
edi¦tori¦al¦ised
edi¦tori¦al¦is¦ing
edi¦tori¦al¦ist +s
edi¦tori¦al¦ize
edi¦tori¦al¦izes
edi¦tori¦al¦ized
edi¦tori¦al¦iz¦ing
edi¦tori¦al¦ly
editor-in-chief
editors-in-chief
edit¦or¦ship +s
edit¦ress
edit¦resses
Ed¦mond *also*
Ed¦mund
Ed¦mon¦ton (city,
Canada)
Ed¦mund *also*
Ed¦mond
(name)
Ed¦mund (English
kings and saint)
Ed¦mund Iron¦side
(English king)
**Ed¦mund the
Mar¦tyr** (East
Anglian king and
saint)
Edna
Edom (ancient
region, Middle
East)
Edom¦ite +s
educ¦abil¦ity
educ¦able
edu¦cat¦able

edu¦cate
edu¦cates
edu¦cated
edu¦cat¦ing
edu¦ca¦tion +s
edu¦ca¦tion¦al
edu¦ca¦tion¦al¦ist
+s
edu¦ca¦tion¦al¦ly
edu¦ca¦tion¦ist +s
edu¦ca¦tive
edu¦ca¦tor +s
educe
educes
educed
edu¦cing
edu¦cible
educ¦tion
educ¦tive
edul¦cor¦ate
edul¦cor¦ates
edul¦cor¦ated
edul¦cor¦at¦ing
edul¦cor¦ation
edu¦tain¦ment
Ed¦ward (English
and British kings;
Prince; name)
Ed¦ward, Lake (in
E. Africa)
Ed¦ward¦ian +s
Ed¦ward¦iana
Ed¦wards, Gar¦eth
(Welsh rugby
player)
**Ed¦ward the
Con¦fes¦sor**
(English king and
saint)
**Ed¦ward the
Mar¦tyr** (English
king and saint)
Edwin
Ed¦wina
Edwy (English
king)
eegit +s (use eejit)
eejit +s
eel +s
Eelam (proposed
homeland, Sri
Lanka)
eel¦grass
eel¦grasses
eel-like
eel¦pout +s
eel¦worm +s
eely
e'en (= even)
e'er (= ever. △ air,
ere, heir)

eerie
eer¦ier
eeri¦est
(weird. △ eyrie)
eer¦ily
eeri¦ness
eff +s +ed +ing
ef¦face
ef¦faces
ef¦faced
ef¦facing
ef¦face¦able
ef¦face¦ment
ef¦fect +s +ed +ing
(result; bring
about. △ affect)
ef¦fect¦ive (having
an effect; efficient.
△ affective)
ef¦fect¦ive¦ly (in an
effective way.
△ affectively)
ef¦fect¦ive¦ness
ef¦fect¦iv¦ity
(degree of being
effective.
△ affectivity)
ef¦fect¦or +s
ef¦fec¦tual
ef¦fec¦tu¦al¦ity
ef¦fec¦tu¦al¦ly
ef¦fec¦tual¦ness
ef¦fec¦tu¦ate
ef¦fec¦tu¦ates
ef¦fec¦tu¦ated
ef¦fec¦tu¦at¦ing
ef¦fec¦tu¦ation
ef¦fem¦in¦acy
ef¦fem¦in¦ate
ef¦fem¦in¦ate¦ly
ef¦fendi +s
ef¦fer¦ence
ef¦fer¦ent
ef¦fer¦vesce
ef¦fer¦vesces
ef¦fer¦vesced
ef¦fer¦ves¦cing
ef¦fer¦ves¦cence
ef¦fer¦ves¦cency
ef¦fer¦ves¦cent
ef¦fete
ef¦fete¦ness
ef¦fi¦ca¦cious
ef¦fi¦ca¦cious¦ly
ef¦fi¦ca¦cious¦ness
ef¦fi¦cacy
ef¦fi¦ciency
ef¦fi¦cien¦cies
ef¦fi¦cient
ef¦fi¦cient¦ly
ef¦figy
ef¦fi¦gies

ef¦fleur¦age
 ef¦fleur¦ages
 ef¦fleur¦aged
 ef¦fleur¦aging
ef¦flor¦esce
 ef¦flor¦esces
 ef¦flor¦esced
 ef¦flor¦es¦cing
 ef¦flor¦es¦cence +s
 ef¦flor¦es¦cent
ef¦flu¦ence
ef¦flu¦ent +s
ef¦flu¦vium
 ef¦flu¦via
ef¦flux
 ef¦fluxes
 ef¦flux¦ion +s
ef¦fort +s
ef¦fort¦ful
 ef¦fort¦ful¦ly
ef¦fort¦less
 ef¦fort¦less¦ly
 ef¦fort¦less¦ness
ef¦front¦ery
ef¦ful¦gence
ef¦ful¦gent
 ef¦ful¦gent¦ly
ef¦fuse
 ef¦fuses
 ef¦fused
 ef¦fus¦ing
ef¦fu¦sion +s
ef¦fu¦sive
 ef¦fu¦sive¦ly
 ef¦fu¦sive¦ness
Efik
 plural Efik
eft +s
Efta (= European
 Free Trade
 Association)
EFTPOS
 (= electronic
 funds transfer at
 point of sale)
egad
egali¦tar¦ian +s
egali¦tar¦ian¦ism
Egas Moniz,
 An¦tonio
 (Portuguese
 neurologist)
Eg¦bert (king of
 Wessex)
Eger (town,
 Hungary)
egg +s +ed +ing
eggar +s (use
 egger)
egg-beater +s
egg¦cup +s
egg cus¦tard

egger +s
egg-flip +s
egg¦head +s
eggi¦ness
egg-laying
 attributive
egg¦less
egg-nog +s
egg¦plant +s
egg-shaped
egg¦shell +s
egg-spoon +s
egg-timer +s
egg-tooth
 egg-teeth
egg white +s
eggy
 eggi¦er
 eggi¦est
egg yolk +s
eg¦lan¦tine +s
Eg¦mont, Mount
 (in New Zealand)
ego +s
ego¦cen¦tric +s
ego¦cen¦tric¦al¦ly
ego¦cen¦tri¦city
ego¦cen¦trism
ego-ideal
ego¦ism
ego¦ist +s
ego¦is¦tic
ego¦is¦tic¦al
ego¦is¦tic¦al¦ly
ego¦mania
ego¦maniac +s
ego¦mani¦ac¦al
egot¦ise *Br.* (use
 egotize)
 egot¦ises
 egot¦ised
 egot¦is¦ing
egot¦ism
egot¦ist +s
egot¦is¦tic
egot¦is¦tic¦al
egot¦is¦tic¦al¦ly
egot¦ize
 egot¦izes
 egot¦ized
 egot¦iz¦ing
ego trip +s
egre¦gious
egre¦gious¦ly
egre¦gious¦ness
egress
 egresses
egres¦sion
egret +s
Egypt
Egypt¦ian +s

Egyp¦tian¦isa¦tion
 Br. (use
 Egyptianization)
Egyp¦tian¦ise *Br.*
 (use Egyptianize)
 Egyp¦tian¦ises
 Egyp¦tian¦ised
 Egyp¦tian¦is¦ing
Egyp¦tian¦iza¦tion
Egyp¦tian¦ize
 Egyp¦tian¦izes
 Egyp¦tian¦ized
 Egyp¦tian¦iz¦ing
Egypt¦olo¦gist +s
Egypt¦ology
eh (*interjection*.
 △ aye)
Ehr¦en¦burg, Ilya
 Gri¦gori¦evich
 (Russian writer)
Ehr¦lich, Paul
 (German scientist)
Eich¦mann, Karl
 Adolf (German
 Nazi
 administrator)
Eid (Muslim
 festival)
eider +s
ei¦der¦down +s
 (quilt)
eider-down (down
 of eider)
eider duck +s
ei¦det¦ic
ei¦det¦ic¦al¦ly
ei¦do¦lon
 ei¦do¦lons *or*
 ei¦dola
Eif¦fel, Alex¦andre
 Gus¦tave (French
 engineer)
Eif¦fel Tower (in
 Paris)
eigen¦fre¦quency
eigen¦
 fre¦quen¦cies
eigen¦func¦tion +s
eigen¦value +s
Eiger (mountain,
 Switzerland)
Eigg (Scottish
 island)
eight +s (number.
 △ ait, ate)
eight¦een +s
eight¦eenmo +s
eight¦eenth +s
eight¦fold
eighth +s
eighth¦ly
eight¦ieth +s

eight-iron +s
eight¦some +s
eight-track
 attributive
8vo (= octavo)
eighty
 eight¦ies
eighty-first, eighty-
 second, etc.
eighty¦fold
eighty-one, eighty-
 two, etc.
Eijk¦man,
 Chris¦tiaan
 (Dutch physician)
Eilat (town, Israel)
Ei¦leen
Eind¦hoven (city,
 the Netherlands)
ein¦korn
Ein¦stein, Al¦bert
 (German
 physicist)
ein¦stein¦ium
Eint¦hoven,
 Wil¦lem (Dutch
 physiologist)
Eire (former name
 of Republic of
 Ireland)
eir¦en¦ic (use
 irenic)
eir¦en¦ic¦al (use
 irenical)
eir¦eni¦con +s
Ei¦sen¦hower,
 Dwight ('Ike')
 (American
 president)
Ei¦sen¦stadt (city,
 Austria)
Ei¦sen¦stein,
 Ser¦gei
 Mikh¦ail¦ovich
 (Russian film
 director)
ei¦stedd¦fod
 plural
 ei¦stedd¦fods *or*
 ei¦stedd¦fodau
ei¦stedd¦fod¦ic
ei¦ther
either/or
eius¦dem gen¦eris
ejacu¦late
 ejacu¦lates
 ejacu¦lated
 ejacu¦lat¦ing
ejacu¦la¦tion +s
ejacu¦la¦tor +s
ejacu¦la¦tory
eject +s +ed +ing
ejecta (lava etc.
 △ ejector)

ejec|tion +s
eject|ive
eject|ment
eject|or +s (device.
△ ejecta)
Ekat|er|in|burg
(use
Yekaterinburg)
Ekat|er|ino|dar
(use
Yekaterinodar;
former name of
Krasnodar)
Ekat|er|ino|slav
(use
Yekaterinoslav;
former name of
Dnipropetrovsk)
eke
ekes
eked
eking
ekka +s
Ekman, Vagn
Wal|frid (Swedish
oceanographer)
El Aaiún (Arabic
name for
La'youn)
elab|or|ate
elab|or|ates
elab|or|ated
elab|or|at|ing
elab|or|ate|ly
elab|or|ate|ness
elab|or|ation +s
elab|ora|tive
elab|or|ator +s
Ela|gab|alus
(Roman emperor)
Elaine
El Ala|mein
(battlefield, N.
Africa)
Elam (ancient
kingdom, Middle
East)
Elam|ite +s
élan
eland +s
elapse
elapses
elapsed
elap|sing
elasmo|branch +s
elasmo|saurus
elasmo|saur|uses
elas|tane
elas|tic +s
elas|tic|al|ly
elas|ti|cated

elas|ti|cise Br. (use
elasticize)
elas|ti|cises
elas|ti|cised
elas|ti|cis|ing
elas|ti|city
elas|ti|ci|ties
elas|ti|cize
elas|ti|cizes
elas|ti|cized
elas|ti|ciz|ing
elas|tin +s
elasto|mer +s
elasto|mer|ic
Elasto|plast +s
Propr.
Elat (use Eilat)
elate
elates
elated
elat|ing
elated|ly
elated|ness
elater +s
ela|tion +s
E-layer
Elba (Italian island)
El|ba|san (city,
Romania)
Elbe (river,
Germany)
El|bert, Mount (in
USA)
elbow +s +ed +ing
elbow grease
elbow room
El|brus (mountain,
Russia)
El|burz
Moun|tains (in
Iran)
Elche (town, Spain)
El Cid (Spanish
warrior)
eld
elder +s
elder|berry
elder|berries
elder brother
elder breth|ren
(Trinity House)
elder|flower +s
elder|li|ness
eld|er|ly
elder|ship
eld|est
El Djem (town,
Tunisia)
El Dor|ado
(fictitious country)

el|dor|ado +s (any
imaginary rich
place)
el|dritch
Elea|nor also
Eli|nor
Elea|nor Cross
Elea|nor Crosses
Elea|nor of
Aqui|taine
(English queen)
Elea|nor of
Cas|tile (English
queen)
Ele|at|ic +s
ele|cam|pane +s
elect +s +ed +ing
elect|able
elec|tion +s
elec|tion|eer +s
+ed +ing
elect|ive +s
elect|ive|ly
Elect|or +s
(German prince)
elect|or +s (citizen)
elect|or|al
elect|or|al|ly
elect|or|ate +s
elect|or|ship +s
Elec|tra Greek
Mythology
Elect|ress
Elect|resses
(wife of Elector)
elec|tret +s
elec|tric +s
elec|tric|al +s
elec|tric|al|ly
elec|tric blue +s
noun and adjective
electric-blue
attributive
elec|tri|cian +s
elec|tri|city
elec|tri|fi|ca|tion
elec|tri|fier +s
elec|trify
elec|tri|fies
elec|tri|fied
elec|tri|fy|ing
elec|tro +s
electro-acoustic
elec|tro|biol|ogy
elec|tro|car|dio|
gram +s
elec|tro|car|dio|
graph +s
elec|tro|car|dio|
graph|ic
elec|tro|car|di|
og|raphy

elec|tro|chem|ical
elec|tro|
chem|ical|ly
elec|tro|chem|ist
+s
elec|tro|
chem|is|try
elec|tro|
con|vul|sive
elec|tro|cute
elec|tro|cutes
elec|tro|cuted
elec|tro|cut|ing
elec|tro|cu|tion +s
elec|trode +s
elec|tro|di|aly|sis
elec|tro|dynam|ic
elec|tro|dynam|ics
elec|tro|
enceph|alo|gram
+s
elec|tro|
enceph|alo|
graph +s
elec|tro|en|ceph|al|
og|raphy
elec|tro|lumin|
es|cence
elec|tro|lumin|
es|cent
elec|tro|lyse Br.
elec|tro|lyses
elec|tro|lysed
elec|tro|lys|ing
elec|tro|lyser Br.
+s
elec|troly|sis
elec|troly|ses
elec|tro|lyte +s
elec|tro|lyt|ic
elec|tro|lyt|ic|al
elec|tro|lyt|ic|al|ly
elec|tro|lyze Am.
elec|tro|lyzes
elec|tro|lyzed
elec|tro|lyz|ing
elec|tro|lyzer Am.
+s
elec|tro|mag|net
+s
elec|tro|mag|net|ic
elec|tro|mag|net|ic|
al|ly
elec|tro|mag|net|
ism
elec|tro|
mech|an|ic|al
elec|trom|eter +s
elec|trom|et|ric
elec|trom|etry
elec|tro|mo|tive
elec|tron +s

elec|tro|nega|tive
elec|tron|ic
elec|tron|ic|al|ly
elec|tron|ics
elec|tron|volt +s
elec|tro|phile +s
elec|tro|phil|ic
elec|tro|phon|ic
elec|tro|phor|esis
elec|tro|phor|et|ic
elec|troph|orus
elec|tro|
   physio|logic|al
elec|tro|
   physi|ology
elec|tro|plate
elec|tro|plates
elec|tro|plated
elec|tro|plat|ing
elec|tro|plater +s
elec|tro|plexy
elec|tro|por|ation
elec|tro|posi|tive
elec|tro|scope +s
elec|tro|scop|ic
electro-shock
elec|tro|stat|ic
elec|tro|stat|ics
elec|tro|tech|nic
elec|tro|tech|nic|al
elec|tro|tech|nics
elec|tro|tech|
   nol|ogy
elec|tro|thera|
   peut|ic
elec|tro|thera|
   peut|ic|al
elec|tro|ther|ap|ist
   +s
elec|tro|ther|apy
elec|tro|ther|mal
elec|tro|type
elec|tro|types
elec|tro|typed
elec|tro|typ|ing
elec|tro|typer +s
elec|tro|va|lence
elec|tro|va|lency
elec|tro|va|lent
elec|tro|weak
elec|trum
elec|tu|ary
   elec|tu|ar|ies
ele|emo|syn|ary
ele|gance
ele|gant
ele|gant|ly
ele|giac
ele|giac|al|ly
ele|giacs
ele|gise *Br.* (use
   elegize)

ele|gise (*cont.*)
   ele|gises
   ele|gised
   ele|gis|ing
ele|gist +s
ele|gize
   ele|gizes
   ele|gized
   ele|giz|ing
elegy
   ele|gies
elem|ent +s
elem|en|tal +s
elem|en|tal|ism
elem|en|tar|ily
elem|en|tari|ness
elem|en|tary
   elem|en|tar|ies
elemi +s
elen|chus
elen|chi
elenc|tic
Eleo|nora
ele|phant +s
elephant-bird +s
ele|phant|ia|sis
ele|phant|ine
ele|phant|oid
Eleu|sin|ian
ele|vate
   ele|vates
   ele|vated
   ele|vat|ing
ele|va|tion +s
ele|va|tion|al
ele|va|tor +s
ele|va|tory
eleven +s
eleven|fold
eleven-plus
elev|enses
elev|enth +s
ele|von +s
elf
   elves
elfin
elf|ish
elf-lock +s
Elgar, Ed|ward
   (English
   composer)
Elgin, Earl of
   (British colonial
   statesman)
Elgin Mar|bles
El Giza (full name
   of Giza)
Elgon, Mount (in
   E. Africa)
El Greco (Cretan-
   born Spanish
   painter)

Eli (*Bible*; name)
Elia (pseudonym of
   Charles Lamb)
Elias
elicit +s +ed +ing
   (draw out.
   △ illicit)
elicit|ation +s
elicit|or +s
elide
   elides
   elided
   elid|ing
eli|gi|bil|ity
eli|gible
eli|gibly
Eli|jah (*Bible*;
   name)
elim|in|able
elim|in|ate
   elim|in|ates
   elim|in|ated
   elim|in|at|ing
elim|in|ation +s
elim|in|ator +s
elim|in|atory
ELINT (covert
   electronic
   intelligence-
   gathering)
Eliot *also* El|liot,
   El|liott
Eliot, George
   (English novelist)
Eliot, T. S. (Anglo-
   American poet,
   dramatist, and
   critic)
Elisa|beth *also*
   Eliza|beth
Elisa|beth|ville
   (former name of
   Lubumbashi)
Eli|sha *Bible*
eli|sion +s
El|ista (city, Russia)
elite +s
elit|ism
elit|ist +s
elixir +s
Eliza
Eliza|beth *also*
   Elisa|beth (name)
Eliza|beth (English
   and British
   queens; Queen
   Mother)
Eliza|bethan +s
Eliza|vet|pol
   (former name of
   Gäncä)

elk
   plural elk *or* elks
elk-hound +s
ell +s
Ella
Ellen
Elles|mere Is|land
   (in Canadian
   Arctic)
Elles|mere Port
   (port, England)
El|lice Is|lands
   (former name of
   Tuvalu. △ Ellis
   Island)
Ellie
El|ling|ton, Duke
   (American jazz
   musician)
El|liot *also* Eliot,
   El|liott
El|liott *also* Eliot,
   El|liot
el|lipse +s
el|lip|sis
   el|lip|ses
el|lips|oid +s
el|lips|oid|al
el|lip|tic
el|lip|tic|al
el|lip|tic|al|ly
el|lip|ti|city
Ellis Is|land (in
   New York Bay,
   USA. △ Ellice
   Islands)
Ells|worth,
   Lin|coln
   (American
   explorer)
Ells|worth Land
   (region,
   Antarctica)
elm +s
Elmer
elm|wood
elmy
El Niño +s (ocean
   current; climatic
   changes)
elo|cu|tion
elo|cu|tion|ary
elo|cu|tion|ist +s
Elo|him *Bible*
Elo|hist +s
elong|ate
   elong|ates
   elong|ated
   elong|at|ing
elonga|tion +s
elope
   elopes

elope (cont.)
  eloped
  elop|ing
elope|ment +s
eloper +s
elo|quence
elo|quent
elo|quent|ly
El Paso (city, USA)
Elsa
El Sal|va|dor
Elsan +s Propr.
else
else|where
Elsie
El|si|nore (port,
  Denmark)
Ell|speth
Elton
elu|ant +s (use
  eluent)
Éluard, Paul
  (French poet)
elu|ate +s
elu|ci|date
  elu|ci|dates
  elu|ci|dated
  elu|ci|dat|ing
elu|ci|da|tion +s
elu|ci|da|tive
elu|ci|da|tor +s
elu|ci|da|tory
elude
  eludes
  eluded
  elud|ing
  (avoid; escape.
  △ allude, illude)
elu|ent +s
Elul (Jewish month)
elu|sive (difficult to
  catch; avoiding
  the point.
  △ allusive,
  illusive)
elu|sive|ly (in an
  elusive way.
  △ allusively,
  illusively)
elu|sive|ness
  (elusive nature.
  △ allusiveness,
  illusiveness)
elu|sory (evasive.
  △ illusory)
elute
  elutes
  eluted
  elut|ing
elu|tion
elu|tri|ate
  elu|tri|ates

elu|tri|ate (cont.)
  elu|tri|ated
  elu|tri|at|ing
elu|tri|ation
elver +s
elves
El|vira
Elvis
elv|ish
Ely (city, England)
Ely, Isle of (former
  county, England)
Ely|sée Pal|ace (in
  Paris)
Elys|ian
Elys|ium Greek
  Mythology
ely|tron
ely|tra
El|ze|vir (family of
  Dutch printers)
em +s (printing
  measure)
'em (= them)
ema|ci|ate
  ema|ci|ates
  ema|ci|ated
  ema|ci|at|ing
ema|ci|ation
e-mail +s +ed +ing
ema|lan|geni
  (plural of
  lilangeni)
em|an|ate
  em|an|ates
  em|an|ated
  em|an|at|ing
em|an|ation +s
em|ana|tive
eman|ci|pate
  eman|ci|pates
  eman|ci|pated
  eman|ci|pat|ing
eman|ci|pa|tion
eman|ci|pa|tion|ist
  +s
eman|ci|pa|tor +s
eman|ci|pa|tory
Eman|uel also
  Em|man|uel
emas|cu|late
  emas|cu|lates
  emas|cu|lated
  emas|cu|lat|ing
emas|cu|la|tion
emas|cu|la|tor +s
emas|cu|la|tory
em|balm +s +ed
  +ing
em|balm|er +s
em|balm|ment

em|bank +s +ed
  +ing
em|bank|ment +s
em|bargo
  em|bar|goes
  em|bar|goed
  em|bargo|ing
em|bark +s +ed
  +ing
em|bark|ation +s
em|bar|ras de
  choix
em|bar|ras de
  ri|chesse
em|bar|ras de
  ri|chesses (use
  embarras de
  richesse)
em|bar|rass
  em|bar|rasses
  em|bar|rassed
  em|bar|rass|ing
  em|bar|rassed|ly
  em|bar|rass|ing|ly
em|bar|rass|ment
  +s
em|bassy
  em|bassies
em|bat|tle
  em|bat|tles
  em|bat|tled
  em|bat|tling
embay +s +ed
  +ing
em|bay|ment +s
embed
  em|beds
  em|bed|ded
  em|bed|ding
em|bed|ment +s
em|bel|lish
  em|bel|lishes
  em|bel|lished
  em|bel|lish|ing
em|bel|lish|er +s
em|bel|lish|ment
  +s
ember +s
Ember days
ember-goose
  ember-geese
em|bez|zle
  em|bez|zles
  em|bez|zled
  em|bez|zling
em|bezzle|ment
  +s
em|bez|zler +s
em|bit|ter +s +ed
  +ing
em|bit|ter|ment

em|bla|zon +s +ed
  +ing
em|bla|zon|ment
  +s
em|bla|zon|ry
em|blem +s
em|blem|at|ic
em|blem|at|ic|al
em|blem|at|ic|
      al|ly
em|blem|at|ise Br.
  (use
  emblematize)
  em|blem|at|ises
  em|blem|at|ised
  em|blem|at|is|ing
em|blem|at|ize
  em|blem|at|izes
  em|blem|at|ized
  em|blem|at|iz|ing
em|ble|ments
em|bodi|ment +s
em|body
  em|bodies
  em|bodied
  em|body|ing
em|bold|en +s +ed
  +ing
em|bol|ism +s
em|bol|is|mic
em|bolus
  em|boli
em|bon|point
em|bosom +s +ed
  +ing
em|boss
  em|bosses
  em|bossed
  em|boss|ing
em|boss|er +s
em|boss|ment +s
em|bouch|ure +s
em|bowel
  em|bowels
  em|bow|elled Br.
  em|bow|eled Am.
  em|bowel|ling Br.
  em|bowel|ing Am.
em|bower +s +ed
  +ing
em|brace
  em|braces
  em|braced
  em|bra|cing
em|brace|able
em|brace|ment +s
em|bracer +s
em|branch|ment
  +s
em|bran|gle
  em|bran|gles

em|bran|gle (*cont.*)
em|bran|gled
em|bran|gling
em|brangle|ment
em|bras|ure +s
em|bras|ured
em|brit|tle
em|brit|tles
em|brit|tled
em|brit|tling
em|brittle|ment
em|bro|ca|tion +s
em|broi|der +s
  +ed +ing
em|broi|der|er +s
em|broi|dery
  em|broi|der|ies
em|broil +s +ed
  +ing
em|broil|ment +s
em|brown +s +ed
  +ing
em|bryo +s
em|bryo|gen|esis
em|bry|oid
em|bryo|logic
em|bryo|logic|al
em|bryo|logic|
  al|ly
em|bry|olo|gist +s
em|bry|ology
em|bry|on|al
em|bry|on|ic
em|bry|on|ic|al|ly
embus
  em|bus|ses *or*
  em|buses
  em|bussed *or*
  em|bused
  em|buss|ing *or*
  em|bus|ing
emcee
  em|cees
  em|ceed
  em|cee|ing
em dash
  em dashes
emend +s +ed
  +ing (remove
  errors. △amend)
emend|ation +s
emend|ator +s
emen|da|tory
em|er|ald +s
em|er|ald|ine
emerge
  emerges
  emerged
  emer|ging
emer|gence
emer|gency
  emer|gen|cies

emer|gent
emeri|tus
emerse
emersed
emer|sion
Emer|son, Ralph
  Waldo (American
  writer and
  philosopher)
emery
emery board +s
emery cloth
emery paper
emery wheel +s
Emesa (ancient
  city, Syria)
emet|ic +s
emi|grant +s
emi|grate
  emi|grates
  emi|grated
  emi|grat|ing
emi|gra|tion +s
emi|gra|tory
émi|gré +s
Emi Koussi
  (mountain, Chad)
Emilia-Romagna
  (region, Italy)
Emily
emi|nence +s
émi|nence grise
  émi|nences grises
emi|nent
emi|nent|ly
emir +s (title of
  some Muslim
  rulers; Arab
  prince,
  commander, etc.
  △amir)
emir|ate +s
  (position or
  territory of an
  emir. △amirate)
emis|sary
  emis|sar|ies
emis|sion +s
emis|sive
emis|siv|ity
emit
  emits
  emit|ted
  emit|ting
  (give off. △omit)
emit|ter +s
Emlyn
Emma (name)
Em|man|uel *also*
  Eman|uel
Em|me|line

Em|men|tal (Swiss
  valley; cheese)
Em|men|thal (use
  Emmental)
emmer (wheat)
emmet +s
Emmy
  Em|mies
  (television award;
  name)
emol|li|ence
emol|li|ent +s
emolu|ment +s
Emona (Roman
  name for
  Ljubljana)
emote
  emotes
  emoted
  emot|ing
emoter +s
emoti|con +s
emo|tion +s
emo|tion|al
emo|tion|al|ise *Br.*
  (use
  emotionalize)
  emo|tion|al|ises
  emo|tion|al|ised
  emo|tion|al|is|ing
emo|tion|al|ism
emo|tion|al|ist +s
emo|tion|al|ity
emo|tion|al|ize
  emo|tion|al|izes
  emo|tion|al|ized
  emo|tion|al|iz|ing
emo|tion|al|ly
emo|tion|less
emo|tive
emo|tive|ly
emo|tive|ness
emo|tiv|ity
em|panel
  em|panels
  em|pan|elled *Br.*
  em|pan|eled *Am.*
  em|pan|el|ling *Br.*
  em|pan|el|ling *Am.*
em|panel|ment
em|path|et|ic
em|path|et|ic|al|ly
em|path|ic
em|path|ic|al|ly
em|pa|thise *Br.*
  (use empathize)
  em|pa|thises
  em|pa|thised
  em|pa|this|ing
em|pa|thist +s
em|pa|thize
  em|pa|thizes

em|pa|thize (*cont.*)
  em|pa|thized
  em|pa|thiz|ing
em|pathy
  em|pathies
Em|pedo|cles
  (Greek
  philosopher)
em|pen|nage +s
em|peror +s
em|per|or|ship +s
em|phasis
  em|phases
em|pha|sise *Br.*
  (use emphasize)
  em|pha|sises
  em|pha|sised
  em|pha|sis|ing
em|pha|size
  em|pha|sizes
  em|pha|sized
  em|pha|siz|ing
em|phat|ic
em|phat|ic|al|ly
em|phy|se|ma
Em|pire (style)
em|pire +s
em|pire build|er
  +s
em|pire build|ing
em|pir|ic
em|pir|ic|al
em|pir|ic|al|ly
em|piri|cism
em|piri|cist +s
em|place|ment +s
em|plane
  em|planes
  em|planed
  em|plan|ing
em|ploy +s +ed
  +ing
em|ploy|abil|ity
em|ploy|able
em|ploy|ee +s
em|ploy|er +s
em|ploy|ment +s
em|pol|der +s +ed
  +ing (use
  impolder)
em|por|ium
  em|poria *or*
  em|por|iums
em|power +s +ed
  +ing
em|power|ment
em|press
  em|presses
Emp|son, Wil|liam
  (English poet and
  critic)
emp|ti|ly

emp|ti|ness
empty
  emp|ties
  emp|tied
  empty|ing
  emp|tier
  emp|ti|est
empty-handed
empty-headed
empty-nester +s
em|pur|ple
  em|pur|ples
  em|pur|pled
  em|purp|ling
em|py|ema
em|pyr|eal
em|pyr|ean +s
em rule +s
Emrys
emu +s (bird)
emu|late
  emu|lates
  emu|lated
  emu|lat|ing
emu|la|tion +s
emu|la|tive
emu|la|tor +s
emu|lous
emu|lous|ly
emul|si|fi|able
emul|si|fi|ca|tion
emul|si|fier +s
emul|sify
  emul|si|fies
  emul|si|fied
  emul|si|fy|ing
emul|sion +s +ed
  +ing
emul|sion|ise Br.
  (use emulsionize)
  emul|sion|ises
  emul|sion|ised
  emul|sion|is|ing
emul|sion|ize
  emul|sion|izes
  emul|sion|ized
  emul|sion|iz|ing
emul|sive
en +s (printing
  measure)
Ena
en|able
  en|ables
  en|abled
  en|ab|ling
en|able|ment
en|abler +s
enact +s +ed +ing
en|act|able
en|action
en|act|ive
en|act|ment +s

en|act|or +s
en|act|ory
en|amel
  en|amels
  en|am|elled Br.
  en|am|eled Am.
  en|am|el|ling Br.
  en|am|el|ing Am.
en|amel|ler +s
en|amel|ling
en|amel|ware
en|amel|work
en|amor Am. +s
  +ed +ing
en|am|our Br. +s
  +ed +ing
en|an|thema
en|an|the|mas or
  en|an|the|mata
en|an|tio|mer +s
en|an|tio|mer|ic
en|an|tio|morph
  +s
en|an|tio|morph|ic
en|an|tio|morph|
        ism
en|an|tio|morph|
        ous
en|arth|ro|sis
  en|arth|ro|ses
en bloc
en brosse
en cabo|chon
en|cae|nia +s
en|cage
  en|cages
  en|caged
  en|caging
en|camp +s +ed
  +ing
en|camp|ment +s
en|cap|su|late
  en|cap|su|lates
  en|cap|su|lated
  en|cap|su|lat|ing
en|cap|su|la|tion
  +s
en|case
  en|cases
  en|cased
  en|cas|ing
en|case|ment +s
en|cash
  en|cashes
  en|cashed
  en|cash|ing
en|cash|able
en|cash|ment +s
en|caus|tic +s
en|ceinte +s

En|cela|dus (Greek
  Mythology; moon
  of Saturn)
en|ceph|al|ic
en|ceph|alin +s
  (use enkephalin)
en|ceph|al|it|ic
en|ceph|al|itis
en|ceph|al|itis
  leth|ar|gica
en|ceph|alo|gram
  +s
en|ceph|alo|graph
  +s
en|ceph|alo|
      my|eli|tis
en|cepha|lon
en|ceph|al|
      op|athy
en|chain +s +ed
  +ing
en|chain|ment
en|chant +s +ed
  +ing
en|chant|ed|ly
en|chant|er +s
en|chant|ing|ly
en|chant|ment +s
en|chant|ress
  en|chant|resses
en|chase
  en|chases
  en|chased
  en|chas|ing
en|chil|ada +s
en|chir|id|ion
  en|chir|id|ions or
  en|chir|idia
en|cipher +s +ed
  +ing
en|cipher|ment
en|cir|cle
  en|cir|cles
  en|cir|cled
  en|circ|ling
en|circle|ment
en clair
en|clasp +s +ed
  +ing
en|clave +s
en|clit|ic +s
en|clit|ic|al|ly
en|close
  en|closes
  en|closed
  en|clos|ing
en|clos|ure +s
en|code
  en|codes
  en|coded
  en|cod|ing
en|coder +s

en|comi|ast +s
en|comi|as|tic
en|co|mium
  en|co|miums or
  en|co|mia
en|com|pass
  en|com|passes
  en|com|passed
  en|com|pass|ing
en|com|pass|ment
en|core
  en|cores
  en|cored
  en|cor|ing
en|coun|ter +s +ed
  +ing
en|cour|age
  en|cour|ages
  en|cour|aged
  en|cour|aging
en|cour|age|ment
  +s
en|cour|ager +s
en|cour|aging|ly
en|crin|ite +s
en|croach
  en|croaches
  en|croached
  en|croach|ing
en|croach|er +s
en|croach|ment +s
en|crust +s +ed
  +ing
en|crust|ation +s
  (use incrustation)
en|crust|ment
en|crypt +s +ed
  +ing
en|cryp|tion
en|cum|ber +s +ed
  +ing
en|cum|ber|ment
en|cum|brance +s
en|cyc|lic
en|cyc|lic|al +s
en|cyclo|pae|dia
  +s (use
  encyclopedia)
en|cyclo|pae|dic
  (use
  encyclopedic)
en|cyclo|pae|dism
  (use
  encyclopedism)
en|cyclo|pae|dist
  +s (use
  encyclopedist)
en|cyc|lo|pe|dia +s
  (also
  encyclopaedia)

en|cyclo|pe|dic
(also
encyclopaedic)
en|cyclo|ped|ism
(also
encyclopaedism)
en|cyclo|ped|ist
+s (also
encyclopaedist)
en|cyst +s +ed
+ing
en|cyst|ation
en|cyst|ment
end +s +ed +ing
en|dan|ger +s +ed
+ing
en|dan|ger|ment
end-around +s
en dash
en dashes
en|dear +s +ed
+ing
en|dear|ing|ly
en|dear|ment +s
en|deavor *Am.* +s
+ed +ing
en|deav|our *Br.* +s
+ed +ing
en|dem|ic
en|dem|ic|al|ly
en|dem|icity
en|dem|ism
ender +s
End|erby Land
(region,
Antarctica)
en|der|mic
en|der|mic|al|ly
En|ders, John
Frank|lin
(American
virologist)
end|game +s
end|ing +s
en|dive +s
end|less
end|less|ly
end|less|ness
end|most
end|note +s
endo|card|it|ic
endo|card|itis
endo|car|dium
endo|carp +s
endo|carp|ic
endo|crine
endo|crino|logic|al
endo|crin|olo|gist
+s
endo|crin|ology
endo|derm +s
endo|der|mal

endo|der|mic
end-of-season
attributive
end-of-term
attributive
end-of-year
attributive
en|dog|am|ous
en|dog|amy
endo|gen +s
en|dog|en|esis
en|dogen|ous
en|dogeny
endo|lymph
endo|met|rial
endo|met|ri|osis
endo|met|ri|tis
endo|met|rium
endo|morph +s
endo|morph|ic
endo|morphy
endo|para|site +s
endo|plasm
endo|plas|mic
re|ticu|lum
en|dor|phin +s
en|dors|able
en|dorse
en|dorses
en|dorsed
en|dors|ing
en|dor|see +s
en|dorse|ment +s
en|dor|ser +s
endo|scope +s
endo|scop|ic
endo|scop|ic|al|ly
en|dos|co|pist +s
en|dos|copy
endo|skel|eton +s
endo|sperm
endo|spore +s
endo|the|lial
endo|the|lium
endo|the|lia
endo|ther|mic
endo|thermy
endo|toxin +s
endow +s +ed
+ing
en|dow|er +s
en|dow|ment +s
end|paper +s
end-play +s
end point +s
end prod|uct +s
end re|sult +s
end-stopped
endue
en|dues
en|dued
en|du|ing

en|dur|abil|ity
en|dur|able
en|dur|ance
en|dure
en|dures
en|dured
en|dur|ing
en|dur|ing|ly
en|duro +s
end-user +s
end|ways
end|wise
En|dym|ion *Greek
Mythology*
enema +s
enemy
en|emies
en|er|get|ic
en|er|get|ic|al|ly
en|er|get|ics
ener|gise *Br.* (use
energize)
ener|gises
ener|gised
ener|gis|ing
en|er|giser *Br.* +s
(use energizer)
ener|gize
ener|gizes
ener|gized
ener|giz|ing
en|er|gizer +s
en|er|gu|men +s
en|ergy
en|er|gies
energy-efficiency
energy-efficient
ener|vate
ener|vates
ener|vated
ener|vat|ing
en|er|va|tion
En|ewe|tak (use
Eniwetok)
en fam|ille
en|fant gâté
en|fants gâtés
en|fant ter|rible
en|fants ter|ribles
en|fee|ble
en|fee|bles
en|fee|bled
en|feeb|ling
en|feeble|ment
en|feoff +s +ed
+ing
en|feoff|ment
en fête
en|fet|ter +s +ed
+ing
en|fil|ade
en|fil|ades

en|fil|ade (*cont.*)
en|fil|aded
en|fil|ad|ing
en|fold +s +ed
+ing (envelop.
△ infold)
en|force
en|forces
en|forced
en|for|cing
en|force|abil|ity
en|force|able
en|force|ably
en|forced|ly
en|force|ment
en|for|cer +s
en|fran|chise
en|fran|chises
en|fran|chised
en|fran|chis|ing
en|fran|chise|ment
en|gage
en|gages
en|gaged
en|gaging
en|gagé
en|gage|ment +s
en|gager +s
en|ga|ging|ly
en|ga|ging|ness
en|gar|land +s +ed
+ing
En|gels, Fried|rich
(German political
philosopher)
en|gen|der +s +ed
+ing
en|gine
en|gines
en|gined
en|gin|ing
en|gine driver +s
en|gin|eer +s +ed
+ing
en|gin|eer|ing
en|gin|eer|ship
en|gine house +s
en|gine|less
en|gine room +s
en|gin|ery
en|gird +s +ed
+ing
en|gir|dle
en|gir|dles
en|gir|dled
en|gir|dling
Eng|land
Eng|lish
Eng|lishes
Eng|lish|man
Eng|lish|men
Eng|lish|ness

Eng|lish|woman
Eng|lish|women
en|gorge
  en|gorges
  en|gorged
  en|gor|ging
en|gorge|ment
en|graft +s +ed
  +ing
en|graft|ment
en|grail +s +ed
  +ing
en|grain +s +ed
  +ing (use ingrain)
en|gram +s
en|gram|mat|ic
en|grave
  en|graves
  en|graved
  en|grav|ing
en|graver +s
en|grav|ing +s
en|gross
  en|grosses
  en|grossed
  en|gross|ing
en|gross|ment
en|gulf +s +ed
  +ing
en|gulf|ment
en|hance
  en|hances
  en|hanced
  en|han|cing
en|hance|ment +s
en|hancer +s
en|har|mon|ic
en|har|mon|ic|
  al|ly
Enid
en|igma +s
en|ig|mat|ic
en|ig|mat|ic|al
en|ig|mat|ic|al|ly
en|igma|tise Br.
  (use enigmatize)
  en|igma|tises
  en|igma|tised
  en|igma|tis|ing
en|igma|tize
  en|igma|tizes
  en|igma|tized
  en|igma|tiz|ing
En|iwe|tok (island,
  N. Pacific)
en|jamb|ment +s
en|join +s +ed
  +ing
en|join|ment
enjoy +s +ed +ing
en|joy|abil|ity
en|joy|able

en|joy|able|ness
en|joy|ably
en|joy|er +s
en|joy|ment +s
en|keph|alin +s
en|kin|dle
  en|kin|dles
  en|kin|dled
  en|kind|ling
en|lace
  en|laces
  en|laced
  en|lacing
en|lace|ment
en|large
  en|larges
  en|larged
  en|lar|ging
en|large|able
en|large|ment +s
en|lar|ger +s
en|light|en +s +ed
  +ing
en|light|en|er +s
en|light|en|ment
  +s
en|list +s +ed +ing
en|list|er +s
en|list|ment
en|liven +s +ed
  +ing
en|liven|er +s
en|liven|ment
en masse
en|mesh
  en|meshes
  en|meshed
  en|mesh|ing
en|mesh|ment
en|mity
  en|mities
en|nead +s
Ennis (town,
  Republic of
  Ireland)
En|nis|kil|len
  (town, Northern
  Ireland)
En|nius, Quin|tus
  (Roman writer)
en|noble
  en|nobles
  en|nobled
  en|nob|ling
en|noble|ment
ennui +s
Enoch (Bible;
  name)
eno|logic|al Am.
  (Br. oenological)
en|olo|gist Am. +s
  (Br. oenologist)

en|ol|ogy Am. (Br.
  oenology)
eno|phile Am. +s
  (Br. oenophile)
en|oph|il|ist Am.
  +s (Br.
  oenophilist)
enor|mity
  enor|mities
enor|mous
enor|mous|ly
enor|mous|ness
eno|sis
enough
enounce
  enounces
  enounced
  enoun|cing
enounce|ment
en pas|sant
en pen|sion
en|plane
  en|planes
  en|planed
  en|plan|ing
en|print +s
en|quire Br.
  en|quires
  en|quired
  en|quir|ing
  (ask. △ inquire.
  Am. inquire)
en|quir|er Br. +s
  (person asking for
  information.
  △ inquirer. Am.
  inquirer)
en|quir|ing|ly Br.
  (Am. inquiringly)
en|quiry Br.
  en|quir|ies
  (request for
  information.
  △ inquiry. Am.
  inquiry)
en|rage
  en|rages
  en|raged
  en|raging
en|rage|ment
en rap|port
en|rap|ture
  en|rap|tures
  en|rap|tured
  en|rap|tur|ing
en|rich
  en|riches
  en|riched
  en|rich|ing
en|rich|ment +s
en|robe
  en|robes

en|robe (cont.)
  en|robed
  en|rob|ing
enrol Br.
  en|rols
  en|rolled
  en|rol|ling
en|roll Am. +s +ed
  +ing
en|rol|lee +s
en|rol|ler +s
en|roll|ment Am.
  +s
en|rol|ment Br. +s
en route
en rule +s
ENSA
  (= Entertainments
  National Service
  Association)
En|schede (city, the
  Netherlands)
en|sconce
  en|sconces
  en|sconced
  en|scon|cing
en|sem|ble +s
en|shrine
  en|shrines
  en|shrined
  en|shrin|ing
en|shrine|ment
en|shroud +s +ed
  +ing
en|si|form
en|sign +s
en|signcy
en|sil|age
  en|sil|ages
  en|sil|aged
  en|sil|aging
en|sile
  en|siles
  en|siled
  en|sil|ing
en|slave
  en|slaves
  en|slaved
  en|slav|ing
en|slave|ment
en|slaver +s
en|snare
  en|snares
  en|snared
  en|snar|ing
en|snare|ment
Ensor, James
  (Belgian artist)
ensue
  en|sues
  en|sued
  en|su|ing

en suite
en|sure
  en|sures
  en|sured
  en|sur|ing
  (make sure.
  △ insure)
en|surer +s (person
  who makes sure.
  △ insurer)
en|swathe
  en|swathes
  en|swathed
  en|swath|ing
en|swathe|ment
en|tab|la|ture +s
en|table|ment
en|tail +s +ed +ing
en|tail|ment +s
en|tan|gle
  en|tan|gles
  en|tan|gled
  en|tan|gling
en|tangle|ment +s
en|tasis
  en|tases
En|tebbe (town,
  Uganda)
en|tel|echy
en|tel|lus
  en|tel|luses
en|tendre +s (in
  'double entendre'
  etc.)
en|tente +s
en|tente cor|di|ale
enter +s +ed +ing
en|ter|able
en|ter|er +s
en|ter|ic
en|ter|itis
en|ter|os|tomy
  en|ter|os|tomies
en|ter|ot|omy
  en|ter|oto|mies
en|tero|virus
  en|tero|viruses
en|ter|prise +s
en|ter|priser +s
en|ter|pris|ing
en|ter|pris|ing|ly
en|ter|tain +s +ed
  +ing
en|ter|tain|er +s
en|ter|tain|ing|ly
en|ter|tain|ment
  +s
en|thalpy
en|thral Br.
  en|thrals
  en|thralled
  en|thral|ling

en|thrall Am. +s
  +ed +ing
en|thrall|ment Am.
en|thral|ment Br.
en|throne
  en|thrones
  en|throned
  en|thron|ing
en|throne|ment
en|thuse
  en|thuses
  en|thused
  en|thus|ing
en|thu|si|asm +s
en|thu|si|ast +s
en|thu|si|as|tic
en|thu|si|as|tic|
         al|ly
en|thy|meme +s
en|tice
  en|tices
  en|ticed
  en|ticing
en|tice|ment +s
en|ticer +s
en|ticing|ly
en|tire
en|tire|ly
en|tir|ety
  en|tir|eties
en|ti|ta|tive
en|title
  en|titles
  en|titled
  en|tit|ling
en|title|ment +s
en|tity
  en|tities
en|tomb +s +ed
  +ing
en|tomb|ment +s
en|tom|ic
en|to|mo|logic|al
en|to|molo|gist +s
en|to|mol|ogy
en|to|mopha|gous
en|to|moph|ill|ous
en|to|para|site +s
en|to|phyte +s
en|tou|rage +s
en|tr'acte +s
en|trails
en|train +s +ed
  +ing (put on a
  train; carry along)
en|train
  (enthusiasm)
en|train|ment
en|tram|mel
  en|tram|mels
  en|tram|melled Br.
  en|tram|meled Am.

en|tram|mel (cont.)
  en|tram|mel|ling Br.
  en|tram|mel|ing
  Am.
en|trance
  en|trances
  en|tranced
  en|tran|cing
en|trance hall +s
en|trance|ment
en|tran|cing|ly
en|trant +s
en|trap
  en|traps
  en|trapped
  en|trap|ping
en|trap|ment +s
en|trap|per +s
en|treat +s +ed
  +ing
en|treat|ing|ly
en|treaty
  en|treaties
entre|chat +s
en|tre|côte +s
en|trée +s
entre|mets
  plural entre|mets
en|trench
  en|trenches
  en|trenched
  en|trench|ing
en|trench|ment +s
entre nous
entre|pôt +s
entre|pre|neur +s
entre|pre|neur|ial
entre|pre|neur|ial|
        ism
entre|pre|neur|
        ial|ly
entre|pre|neur|
        ship
entre|sol +s
en|trism
en|trist +s
en|trop|ic
en|trop|ic|al|ly
en|tropy
en|trust +s +ed
  +ing
en|trust|ment
entry
  en|tries
entry|ism
entry|ist +s
entry|phone +s
  Propr.
en|twine
  en|twines

en|twine (cont.)
  en|twined
  en|twin|ing
en|twine|ment
enu|cle|ate
  enu|cle|ates
  enu|cle|ated
  enu|cle|at|ing
enu|cle|ation
E-number +s
enu|mer|able
  (countable.
  △ innumerable)
enu|mer|ate
  enu|mer|ates
  enu|mer|ated
  enu|mer|at|ing
  (mention; count.
  △ innumerate)
enu|mer|ation +s
enu|mera|tive
enu|mer|ator +s
enun|ci|ate
  enun|ci|ates
  enun|ci|ated
  enun|ci|at|ing
enun|ci|ation
enun|cia|tive
enun|ci|ator +s
enure
  en|ures
  en|ured
  en|ur|ing
  (Law take effect.
  △ inure)
en|ur|esis
en|ur|et|ic +s
en|velop +s +ed
  +ing
en|vel|ope +s
en|velop|ment +s
en|venom +s +ed
  +ing
Enver Pasha
  (Turkish leader)
en|vi|able
en|vi|ably
en|vi|er +s
en|vi|ous
en|vi|ous|ly
en|viron +s +ed
  +ing
en|vir|on|ment +s
en|vir|on|men|tal
en|vir|on|men|tal|
        ism
en|vir|on|men|tal|
        ist +s
en|vir|on|
        men|tal|ly

en|vir|on|
    men|tal|ly
    friend|ly
environment-
    friend|ly
en|vir|ons
en|vis|age
    en|vis|ages
    en|vis|aged
    en|vis|aging
en|vis|age|ment
en|vi|sion +s +ed
    +ing
envoi +s
    (concluding stanza
    or passage)
envoy +s
    (messenger,
    representative)
en|voy|ship +s
envy
    en|vies
    en|vied
    envy|ing
en|weave (use
    inweave)
    en|weaves
    en|wove
    en|weav|ing
    en|woven
en|wind
    en|winds
    en|wound
    en|wind|ing
en|wrap
    en|wraps
    en|wrapped
    en|wrap|ping
en|wreathe
    en|wreathes
    en|wreathed
    en|wreath|ing
Enzed
    Enzeds
En|zed|der +s
en|zo|ot|ic
en|zym|at|ic
en|zyme +s
en|zym|ic
en|zym|ology
Eo|cene
EOKA (Greek-
    Cypriot
    organization)
eo|lian Am. (Br.
    aeolian)
Eolic Am. (Br.
    Aeolic)
eo|lith +s
eo|lith|ic
eon +s (use aeon)

Eos (Greek
    goddess. △ Ios)
eosin
eo|sino|phil +s
epact +s
ep|arch +s
ep|archy
    ep|arch|ies
ep|aulet Am. +s
ep|aul|ette Br. +s
épée +s
épée|ist +s
epeiro|gen|esis
epeiro|gen|ic
epeir|ogeny
epen|thesis
    epen|theses
epen|thet|ic
ep|ergne +s
ep|exe|gesis
    ep|exe|geses
ep|exe|get|ic
ep|exe|get|ic|al
ep|exe|get|ic|al|ly
eph|ebe +s
eph|ebic
eph|edra +s
ephe|drine
ephem|era
    ephem|eras or
    ephem|erae
    (insect; also plural
    of ephemeron)
ephem|eral +s
ephem|eral|ity
ephem|eral|ly
ephem|eral|ness
ephem|eris
    ephem|er|ides
ephem|er|ist +s
ephem|eron
    ephem|era
    (printed item;
    short-lived thing)
ephem|eron +s
    (insect)
Ephe|sian +s
Eph|esus (city,
    ancient Greece)
ephod +s
ephor
    eph|ors or eph|ori
eph|or|ate +s
eph|or|ship +s
Eph|raim
epi|blast +s
epic +s
epic|al
ep|ic|al|ly
epi|carp +s
epi|ce|dian
epi|ce|dium
    epi|ce|dia

epi|cene +s
epi|cen|ter Am. +s
epi|cen|tral
epi|centre Br. +s
epi|clesis
    epi|cleses
epi|con|tin|en|tal
epi|cotyl +s
Epic|te|tus (Greek
    philosopher)
epi|cure +s
Epi|cur|ean +s (of
    Epicurus)
epi|cur|ean +s
    (devoted to
    enjoyment)
Epi|cur|ean|ism
epi|cur|ism
Epi|curus (Greek
    philosopher)
epi|cycle +s
epi|cyc|lic
epi|cyc|loid +s
epi|cyc|loid|al
Epi|daurus (city,
    ancient Greece)
epi|deic|tic
epi|dem|ic +s
epi|dem|ic|al
epi|dem|ic|al|ly
epi|demi|ologic|al
epi|demi|olo|gist
    +s
epi|demi|ology
epi|der|mal
epi|der|mic
epi|der|mis
epi|derm|oid
epi|dia|scope +s
epi|didy|mis
    epi|didy|mides
epi|dural +s
epi|fauna
epi|faun|al
epi|gas|tric
epi|gas|trium
    epi|gas|tria
epi|geal
epi|gene
epi|gen|esis
epi|gen|et|ic
epi|glot|tal
epi|glot|tic
epi|glot|tis
    epi|glot|tises
epi|gone
    epi|gones or
    epi|goni
epi|gram +s
epi|gram|mat|ic
epi|gram|mat|ic|
                al|ly

epi|gram|ma|tise
    Br. (use
    epigrammatize)
epi|gram|ma|tises
epi|gram|
                ma|tised
epi|gram|
                ma|tis|ing
epi|gram|ma|tist
    +s
epi|gram|ma|tize
epi|gram|ma|tizes
epi|gram|
                ma|tized
epi|gram|
                ma|tiz|ing
epi|graph +s
epi|graph|ic
epi|graph|ic|al
epi|graph|ic|al|ly
epig|raph|ist +s
epig|raphy
epil|late
    epil|lates
    epil|lated
    epil|lat|ing
epil|lation
epi|lepsy
epi|lep|tic +s
epi|lim|nion
    epi|lim|nia
epi|log +s (use
    epilogue)
epi|log|ist +s
epi|logue +s
epi|mer +s
epi|mer|ic
epi|mer|ise Br. (use
    epimerize)
epi|mer|ises
epi|mer|ised
epi|mer|is|ing
epi|mer|ism
epi|mer|ize
epi|mer|izes
epi|mer|ized
epi|mer|iz|ing
epi|nasty
epi|neph|rine
epi|phan|ic
Epiph|any
    Christianity
epiph|any
    epiph|anies
    (generally)
epi|phe|nom|en|al
epi|phe|nom|enon
    epi|phe|nom|ena
epiphy|sis
    epiphy|ses
epi|phyt|al
epi|phyte +s

epi|phyt|ic
Epi|rus (coastal region, NW Greece)
epis|cop|acy
epis|cop|acies
Epis|cop|al (Church)
epis|cop|al (of a bishop)
Epis|co|pa|lian +s (of the Episcopal Church)
epis|co|pa|lian +s (advocating church government by bishops)
epis|co|pa|lian|ism
epis|co|pal|ism
epis|co|pal|ly
epis|co|pate +s
epi|scope +s
epi|sem|at|ic
episi|ot|omy
episi|oto|mies
epi|sode +s
epi|sod|ic
epi|sod|ic|al|ly
epi|staxis
epi|staxes
epi|stem|ic
epi|stem|ic|al|ly
epi|stemo|logic|al
epi|stemo|log|ic|al|ly
epis|te|molo|gist +s
epis|te|mol|ogy
epis|te|mol|ogies
epis|tle +s
epis|tol|ary
epis|tol|er +s
epis|trophe +s
epi|style +s
epi|taph +s
epi|tax|ial
epi|taxy
epi|tha|la|mial
epi|tha|lam|ic
epi|tha|la|mium
epi|tha|la|miums or epi|tha|la|mia
epi|the|lial
epi|the|lium
epi|the|lia
epi|thet +s
epi|thet|ic
epi|thet|ic|al
epi|thet|ic|al|ly
epit|ome +s

epit|om|isa|tion Br. (use epitomization)
epit|om|ise Br. (use epitomize)
epit|om|ises
epit|om|ised
epit|om|is|ing
epit|om|ist +s
epit|om|iza|tion
epit|om|ize
epit|om|izes
epit|om|ized
epit|om|iz|ing
epi|zoon
epi|zoa
epi|zo|ot|ic
epoch +s
epoch|al
epoch-making
epode +s
ep|onym +s
eponym|ous
EPOS (= electronic point-of-sale)
ep|ox|ide +s
epoxy
epox|ies
EPROM (= erasable programmable read-only memory)
ep|si|lon +s
Epsom (town, England; salts)
Ep|stein, Jacob (American-born British sculptor)
Epstein–Barr (virus)
epyl|lion
epyl|lia
equa|bil|ity
equ|able
equ|ably
equal
equals
equalled Br.
equaled Am.
equal|ling Br.
equal|ing Am.
equal|isa|tion Br. (use equalization)
equal|ise Br. (use equalize)
equal|ises
equal|ised
equal|is|ing
equal|iser Br. +s (use equalizer)
equali|tar|ian +s
equali|tar|ian|ism

equal|ity
equal|ities
equal|iza|tion
equal|ize
equal|izes
equal|ized
equal|iz|ing
equal|izer +s
equal|ly
equa|nim|ity
equani|mous
equat|able
equat|ably
equate
equates
equated
equat|ing
equa|tion +s
equa|tion|al
equa|tor +s
equa|tor|ial
equa|tori|al|ly
equerry
equer|ries
eques|trian +s
eques|tri|an|ism
eques|tri|enne +s female
equi|angu|lar
equi|dis|tant
equi|dis|tant|ly
equi|lat|eral
equili|brate
equili|brates
equili|brated
equili|brat|ing
equili|bra|tion
equili|bra|tor +s
equili|brist +s
equi|lib|rium
equi|lib|ria or equi|lib|riums
equine
equi|noc|tial +s
equi|nox
equi|noxes
equip
equips
equipped
equip|ping
equip|age +s
equi|par|ti|tion
equip|ment +s
equi|poise
equi|poises
equi|poised
equi|pois|ing
equi|pol|lence
equi|pol|lency
equi|pol|lent +s
equi|pon|der|ant

equi|pon|der|ate
equi|pon|der|ates
equi|pon|der|ated
equi|pon|der| at|ing
equi|poten|tial
equip|per +s
equi|prob|abil|ity
equi|prob|able
equi|setum
equi|seta or equi|setums
equit|able
equit|able|ness
equit|ably
equi|ta|tion
equity
equi|ties
equiva|lence +s
equiva|lency
equiva|len|cies
equiva|lent +s
equiva|lent|ly
equivo|cacy
equivo|cal
equivo|cal|ity
equivo|cal|ly
equivo|cal|ness
equivo|cate
equivo|cates
equivo|cated
equivo|cat|ing
equivo|ca|tion +s
equivo|ca|tor +s
equivo|ca|tory
equi|voke +s (use equivoque)
equi|voque +s
Equu|leus (constellation)
er +s (hesitation. △ err)
era +s
erad|ic|able
eradi|cate
eradi|cates
eradi|cated
eradi|cat|ing
eradi|ca|tion
eradi|ca|tor +s
eras|able
erase
erases
erased
eras|ing
eraser +s
Eras|mus, Desi|der|ius (Dutch humanist)
Eras|tian +s
Eras|tian|ism

Eras|tus, Thomas
(Swiss physician
and writer)

eras|ure +s

Erato *Greek and
Roman Mythology*

Era|tos|thenes
(Hellenistic
scholar)

er|bium

ere (before. △ air,
e'er, heir)

Ere|bus *Greek
Mythology*

Ere|bus, Mount
(volcano,
Antarctica)

Erech (biblical
name for Uruk)

Erech|theum (in
Athens)

erect +s +ed +ing

erect|able

erect|ile

erec|tion +s

erect|ly

erect|ness

erect|or +s

E-region +s

er|em|ite +s

er|em|it|ic

er|em|it|ic|al

er|em|it|ism

ereth|ism

Er|furt (city,
Germany)

erg +s (unit of
energy)

erg
  areg
  (sand dunes)

erga|tive +s

ergo

ergo|cal|cif|erol +s

ergo|nom|ic

ergo|nom|ic|al|ly

ergo|nom|ics

er|gono|mist +s

er|gos|terol +s

ergot +s

er|got|ism

Eric

Erica (name)

erica +s (heather)

eri|ca|ceous

Eric|son, Leif (use
Ericsson)

Erics|son, John
(Swedish
engineer)

Erics|son, Leif
(Norse explorer)

Eric the Red
(Norse explorer)

Eri|danus
(constellation)

Erie, Lake (in N.
America)

erig|eron +s

Eriks|son, Leif
(use Ericsson)

Erin (= Ireland;
name)

Erinys
  Erinyes
  Greek Mythology

eris|tic +s

eris|tic|al|ly

Eri|trea (province,
Ethiopia)

Eri|trean +s

erk +s (naval
rating;
aircraftman;
disliked person.
△ irk)

**Er|lang, Agner
Krarup** (Danish
mathematician)

Er|langer, Jo|seph
(American
physiologist)

erl-king +s

er|mine
  plural er|mine *or*
  er|mines

er|mined

Er|min|trude

ern *Am.* +s (*Br.*
erne. eagle.
△ earn, urn)

erne *Br.* +s (*Am.*
ern. eagle. △ earn,
urn)

Er|nest

Er|nest|ine

Ernie (= electronic
random number
indicating
equipment)

Ernst, Max
(German-born
artist)

erode

erodes

eroded

erod|ing

erod|ible

er|ogen|ous

Eros (*Greek
Mythology*;
asteroid; statue,
London)

ero|sion +s

ero|sion|al

ero|sive

erot|ic

erot|ica

erot|ic|al|ly

eroti|cise *Br.* (use
eroticize)

eroti|cises

eroti|cised

eroti|cis|ing

eroti|cism

eroti|cize

eroti|cizes

eroti|cized

eroti|ciz|ing

erot|ism

eroto|gen|ic

erot|ogen|ous

erot|ology

eroto|mania

eroto|maniac +s

err +s +ed +ing (be
mistaken. △ er)

er|rancy

er|rand +s

er|rand boy +s

er|rand girl +s

er|rant

er|rant|ry
  er|rant|ries

er|rat|ic +s

er|rat|ic|al|ly

er|rati|cism

er|ratum
  er|rata

Er Rif (= Rif
Mountains)

Errol *also* Er|roll

er|ro|ne|ous

er|ro|ne|ous|ly

er|ro|ne|ous|ness

error +s

error|less

er|satz

Erse

erst

erst|while

Erté (Russian-born
designer)

Erte|bølle
  Archaeology

eru|bes|cent

eruc|ta|tion +s

eru|dite

eru|dite|ly

eru|di|tion

erupt +s +ed +ing
(break out
suddenly; eject
lava. △ irrupt)

erup|tion +s
(breakout;

erup|tion (*cont.*)
ejection of lava.
△ irruption)

erup|tive

erup|tiv|ity

eryngo +s

ery|sip|elas

ery|thema

ery|themal

ery|them|at|ic

eryth|rism

eryth|ro|blast +s

eryth|ro|cyte +s

eryth|ro|cyt|ic

eryth|roid

Erz|ge|birge
(mountains,
Central Europe)

Erzu|rum (city,
Turkey)

Esaki, Leo
(Japanese
physicist)

Esau *Bible*

Es|bjerg (port,
Denmark)

es|ca|drille +s

es|cal|ade +s

es|cal|ate

es|cal|ates

es|cal|ated

es|cal|at|ing

es|cal|ation +s

es|cal|ator +s

es|cal|lo|nia +s

es|cal|lop +s
  Heraldry

es|cal|ope +s
(meat)

es|cap|able

es|cap|ade +s

es|cape

es|capes

es|caped

es|cap|ing

es|capee +s

es|cape hatch
  es|cape hatches

es|cape|ment +s

escape-proof

es|caper +s

es|cap|ism

es|cap|ist +s

es|cap|olo|gist +s

es|cap|ology

es|car|got +s

es|carp +s

es|carp|ment +s

eschato|logic|al

eschat|olo|gist +s

eschat|ology
  eschat|ol|ogies

es|cheat +s +ed +ing
es|chew +s +ed +ing
es|chew|al
esch|scholt|zia +s
Es|cof|fier, Georges-Auguste (French chef)
Es|cor|ial, El (in Madrid)
es|cort +s +ed +ing
es|cribe
  es|cribes
  es|cribed
  es|crib|ing
es|cri|toire +s
es|crow +s +ed +ing
es|cudo +s
es|cu|lent
es|cut|cheon +s
es|cut|cheoned
Es|dras
Es|fa|han (use Isfahan)
eskar +s (use esker)
esker +s
Es|kimo +s (may cause offence; prefer Inuit)
Esky
  Eskies
Es|mer|alda
Es|mond
ESOL (= English for speakers of other languages)
esopha|geal Am. (Br. oesophageal)
esopha|gus Am.
  esoph|agi (Br. oesophagus)
eso|ter|ic
eso|ter|ic|al
eso|ter|ic|al|ly
eso|teri|cism
eso|teri|cist +s
es|pa|drille +s
es|pal|ier +s
es|parto +s
es|pe|cial
es|pe|cial|ly
Es|per|ant|ist +s
Es|per|anto
es|pial +s
es|pi|on|age
Es|pir|ito Santo (state, Brazil)

es|plan|ade +s
es|pousal
es|pouse
  es|pouses
  es|poused
  es|pous|ing
es|pouser +s
es|pres|sivo
es|presso +s
es|prit
es|prit de corps
es|prit de l'es|cal|ier
espy
  espies
  espied
  espy|ing
Es|qui|mau (use Eskimo, but may cause offence; prefer Inuit)
  Es|qui|maux
Es|qui|pu|las (town, Guatemala)
es|quire +s
essay +s +ed +ing
es|say|ist +s
Essen (city, Germany)
es|sence +s
Es|sene +s
es|sen|tial +s
es|sen|tial|ism
es|sen|tial|ist +s
es|sen|ti|al|ity
es|sen|tial|ly
es|sen|tial|ness
Esse|quibo (river, Guyana)
Essex (county, England)
es|tab|lish
  es|tab|lishes
  es|tab|lished
  es|tab|lish|ing
es|tab|lish|er +s
es|tab|lish|ment +s
es|tab|lish|ment|arian +s
es|tab|lish|ment|arian|ism
es|tam|inet +s
es|tate +s
es|tate agent +s
es|tate car +s
es|teem +s +ed +ing
Es|telle
ester +s (chemical compound)

es|teri|fy
  es|teri|fies
  es|teri|fied
  es|teri|fy|ing
Es|ther (Bible; name)
es|thete Am. +s (Br. aesthete)
es|thet|ic Am. (Br. aesthetic)
es|thet|ic|al|ly Am. (Br. aesthetically)
es|thet|ician Am. +s (Br. aesthetician)
es|theti|cism Am. (Br. aestheticism)
es|thet|ics Am. (Br. aesthetics)
es|tim|able
es|tim|ably
es|ti|mate
  es|ti|mates
  es|ti|mated
  es|ti|mat|ing
es|ti|ma|tion +s
es|tima|tive
es|ti|ma|tor +s
es|tival Am. (Br. aestival)
es|tiv|ate Am.
  es|tiv|ates
  es|tiv|ated
  es|tiv|at|ing (Br. aestivate)
es|tiv|ation Am. (Br. aestivation)
Es|tonia
Es|to|nian +s
estop
  es|tops
  es|topped
  es|top|ping
es|top|page
es|top|pel
Esto|ril (resort, Portugal)
est|overs
es|trade +s
es|tral Am. (Br. oestral)
es|trange
  es|tranges
  es|tranged
  es|tran|ging
es|trange|ment +s
es|treat +s +ed +ing
Es|tre|ma|dura (region, Portugal)
es|tro|gen Am. +s (Br. oestrogen)

es|tro|gen|ic Am. (Br. oestrogenic)
es|trous Am. adjective (Br. oestrous)
es|trum Am. (Br. oestrum)
es|trus Am. noun (Br. oestrus)
es|tu|ar|ine
es|tu|ary
  es|tu|ar|ies
esuri|ence
esuri|ency
esuri|ent
esuri|ent|ly
Esz|ter|gom (town, Hungary)
ETA (Basque separatist movement)
eta +s (Greek letter. △ eater)
et|aerio +s
eta|lon +s
et cet|era
et|cet|eras
etch
  etches
  etched
  etch|ing
etch|ant +s
etch|er +s
etch|ing +s
eter|nal
eter|nal|ise Br. (use eternalize)
  eter|nal|ises
  eter|nal|ised
  eter|nal|is|ing
eter|nal|ity
eter|nal|ize
  eter|nal|izes
  eter|nal|ized
  eter|nal|iz|ing
eter|nal|ly
eter|nal|ness
eter|nise Br. (use eternize)
  eter|nises
  eter|nised
  eter|nis|ing
eter|nity
  eter|nities
eter|nize
  eter|nizes
  eter|nized
  eter|niz|ing
Et|es|ian
eth +s
Ethan
etha|nal

eth|ane
eth|ane|diol
eth|ano|ate +s
eth|an|oic
etha|nol
Ethel
Ethel|red the
  Un|ready
  (English king)
eth|ene
ether +s
ether|eal
ethere|al|ity
ether|eal|ly
eth|er|ial (use
  ethereal)
etheri|al|ity (use
  ethereality)
eth|eri|al|ly (use
  ethereally)
eth|er|ic
eth|er|isa|tion Br.
  (use etherization)
eth|er|ise Br. (use
  etherize)
  eth|er|ises
  eth|er|ised
  eth|er|is|ing
eth|er|iza|tion
eth|er|ize
  eth|er|izes
  eth|er|ized
  eth|er|iz|ing
Ether|net
ethic +s
eth|ic|al
eth|ic|al|ity
eth|ic|al|ly
ethi|cise Br. (use
  ethicize)
  ethi|cises
  ethi|cised
  ethi|cis|ing
ethi|cist +s
ethi|cize
  ethi|cizes
  ethi|cized
  ethi|ciz|ing
eth|ics
Ethi|opia
Ethi|op|ian +s
Ethi|op|ic +s
eth|moid
eth|moid|al
Ethna
eth|narch +s
eth|narchy
  eth|narch|ies
eth|nic +s
eth|nic|al
eth|nic|al|ly
eth|ni|city

ethno|archaeo|
  logic|al Br.
ethno|archae|
  olo|gist Br. +s
ethno|archae|
  ology Br.
ethno|archeo|
  logic|al Am.
ethno|arche|
  olo|gist Am. +s
ethno|arche|ology
  Am.
ethno|bot|any
ethno|cen|tric
ethno|cen|tric|
  al|ly
ethno|cen|tri|city
ethno|cen|trism
eth|nog|raph|er +s
ethno|graph|ic
ethno|graph|ic|al
ethno|graph|ic|
  al|ly
eth|nog|raphy
  eth|nog|raph|ies
ethno|logic
ethno|logic|al
ethno|logic|al|ly
eth|nolo|gist +s
eth|nol|ogy
ethno|meth|odo|
  logic|al
ethno|meth|od|
  olo|gist +s
ethno|method|
  ology
ethno|music|
  olo|gist +s
ethno|music|ology
etho|gram +s
etho|logic|al
etho|logic|al|ly
eth|olo|gist +s
eth|ol|ogy
ethos
eth|oxy|ethane
ethyl
ethyl|ene
ethyl|en|ic
eth|yne
eti|ol|ate
  eti|ol|ates
  eti|ol|ated
  eti|ol|at|ing
eti|ola|tion
etio|logic Am. (Br.
  aetiologic)
etio|logic|al Am.
  (Br. aetiological)
etio|logic|al|ly Am.
  (Br.
  aetiologically)

eti|ology Am. (Br.
  aetiology)
eti|quette +s
Etna (volcano,
  Sicily)
Eton (college,
  England; collar;
  fives; jacket; wall
  game)
Eton|ian +s
Etosha Pan
  (depression,
  Namibia)
étrier +s
Etru|ria (ancient
  state, Italy)
Etrus|can +s
Etrus|col|ogy
étude +s
étui +s
etymo|logic
etymo|logic|al
etymo|logic|al|ly
ety|molo|gise Br.
  (use etymologize)
  ety|molo|gises
  ety|molo|gised
  ety|molo|gis|ing
ety|molo|gist +s
ety|molo|gize
  ety|molo|gizes
  ety|molo|gized
  ety|molo|giz|ing
ety|mol|ogy
  ety|molo|gies
ety|mon
  etyma or
  ety|mons
Euan also Ewan
Eu|boea (Greek
  island)
eu|ca|lypt +s
eu|ca|lyp|tus
  eu|ca|lyp|tuses or
  eu|ca|lypti
eu|cary|ote (use
  eukaryote)
eu|cary|ot|ic (use
  eukaryotic)
eu|charis
  plural eu|charis
Eu|char|ist +s
Eu|char|is|tic
Eu|char|is|tic|al
eu|chre
  eu|chres
  eu|chred
  eu|chring
Eu|clid (Greek
  mathematician)
Eu|clid|ean

eu|dae|mon|ic (use
  eudemonic)
eu|dae|mon|ism
  (use
  eudemonism)
eu|dae|mon|ist +s
  (use eudemonist)
eu|dae|mon|is|tic
  (use
  eudemonistic)
eu|de|mon|ic
eu|de|mon|ism
eu|de|mon|ist +s
eu|de|mon|is|tic
eudi|om|eter +s
eudio|met|ric
eudio|met|ric|al
eudi|om|etry
Eu|dora
Eu|gene
Eu|genia
eu|gen|ic
eu|gen|ic|al|ly
eu|gen|icist +s
eu|gen|ics
Eugé|nie (French
  empress)
eu|gen|ist +s
eu|glena
eu|hem|er|ism
eu|kary|ote +s
eu|kary|ot|ic
Euler, Leon|hard
  (Swiss-born
  mathematician)
Euler, Ulf Svante
  von (Swedish
  physiologist)
Euler-Chelpin,
  Hans van
  (German-born
  Swedish
  biochemist)
eu|lo|gise Br. (use
  eulogize)
  eu|lo|gises
  eu|lo|gised
  eu|lo|gis|ing
eu|lo|gist +s
eu|lo|gis|tic
eu|lo|gis|tic|al|ly
eu|lo|gium +s
eu|lo|gize
  eu|lo|gizes
  eu|lo|gized
  eu|lo|giz|ing
eu|logy
  eu|logies
Eu|men|ides Greek
  Mythology
Eu|nice
eu|nuch +s

eu|nuch|oid
eu|ony|mus
  plural eu|ony|mus
eu|pep|tic
Eu|phe|mia
eu|phem|ise *Br.*
  (use **euphemize**)
eu|phem|ises
eu|phem|ised
eu|phem|is|ing
eu|phem|ism +s
eu|phem|ist +s
eu|phem|is|tic
eu|phem|is|tic|
        al|ly
eu|phem|ize
eu|phem|izes
eu|phem|ized
eu|phem|iz|ing
eu|phon|ic
eu|pho|ni|ous
eu|pho|ni|ous|ly
eu|phon|ise *Br.*
  (use **euphonize**)
eu|phon|ises
eu|phon|ised
eu|phon|is|ing
eu|pho|nium +s
eu|phon|ize
eu|phon|izes
eu|phon|ized
eu|phon|iz|ing
eu|phony
eu|phonies
eu|phor|bia +s
eu|phoria
eu|phori|ant +s
eu|phor|ic
eu|phor|ic|al|ly
eu|phrasy
eu|phrasies
Eu|phra|tes (river,
  SW Asia)
eu|phu|ism
eu|phu|ist +s
eu|phu|is|tic
eu|phu|is|tic|al|ly
Eur|asian +s
Eur|atom
eur|eka
eu|rhyth|mic *Br.*
  (*Am.* eurythmic)
eu|rhyth|mics *Br.*
  (*Am.* eurythmics)
eu|rhythmy *Br.*
  (*Am.* eurythmy)
Eu|ripi|des (Greek
  dramatist)
Euro +s (European;
  Eurodollar)
euro +s (animal)
Euro|bond +s

Euro|cen|tric
Euro|cen|trism
Euro|cheque *Br.* +s
Euro|
  com|mun|ism
Euro|com|mun|ist
 . +s
Euro|crat +s
Euro-currency
Euro|dol|lar +s
Euro-election +s
Euro|mar|ket +s
Euro-MP +s
Eur|opa (*Greek
  Mythology*; moon
  of Jupiter)
Euro|par|lia|ment
Euro|par|lia|men|
      tar|ian +s
Euro|par|lia|men|
      tary
Eur|ope
Euro|pean +s
Euro|pean|isa|tion
  Br. (use
  Europeanization)
Euro|pean|ise *Br.*
  (use
  Europeanize)
Euro|pean|ises
Euro|pean|ised
Euro|pean|is|ing
Euro|pean|ism
Euro|pean|iza|tion
Euro|pean|ize
Euro|pean|izes
Euro|pean|ized
Euro|pean|iz|ing
Euro|phile +s
euro|pium
Euro|poort (port,
  the Netherlands)
Euro-rebel +s
Euro-sceptic +s
Euro-sceptic|al
Euro|tun|nel
Euro|vision
Eury|dice *Greek
  Mythology*
eu|ryth|mic *Am.*
  (*Br.* eurhythmic)
eu|ryth|mics *Am.*
  (*Br.* eurhythmics)
eu|rythmy *Am.* (*Br.*
  eurhythmy)
Euse|bius (early
  bishop)
Eus|tace
Eus|ta|chian (tube)
eu|stasy
eu|stat|ic

Eus|ton (railway
  station, London)
eu|tec|tic +s
Eu|terpe *Greek and
  Roman Mythology*
eu|tha|nasia
eu|ther|ian +s.
eu|troph|ic
eu|trophi|cate
  eu|trophi|cates
  eu|trophi|cated
  eu|trophi|cat|ing
  eu|trophi|ca|tion
eu|trophy
Eva
evacu|ant +s
evacu|ate
  evacu|ates
  evacu|ated
  evacu|at|ing
evacu|ation +s
evacu|ative
evacu|ator +s
evac|uee +s
evad|able
evade
  evades
  evaded
  evad|ing
evader +s
Evadne
eva|gin|ate
  eva|gin|ates
  eva|gin|ated
  eva|gin|at|ing
eva|gin|ation
evalu|ate
  evalu|ates
  evalu|ated
  evalu|at|ing
evalu|ation +s
evalu|ative
evalu|ator +s
Evan
evan|esce
  evan|esces
  evan|esced
  evan|es|cing
evan|es|cence
evan|es|cent
evan|es|cent|ly
evan|gel +s
evan|gel|ic
evan|gel|ic|al +s
evan|gel|ic|al|ism
evan|gel|ic|al|ly
Evan|gel|ine
evan|gel|isa|tion
  Br. (use
  evangelization)
evan|gel|ise *Br.*
  (use **evangelize**)

evan|gel|ise (*cont.*)
  evan|gel|ises
  evan|gel|ised
  evan|gel|is|ing
evan|gel|iser *Br.*
  +s (use
  evangelizer)
evan|gel|ism
evan|gel|ist +s
evan|gel|is|tic
evan|gel|iza|tion
evan|gel|ize
  evan|gel|izes
  evan|gel|ized
  evan|gel|iz|ing
evan|gel|izer +s
Evans, Ar|thur
  (British
  archaeologist)
Evans, Edith
  (English actress)
Evans-Pritch|ard,
  Ed|ward (English
  anthropologist)
evap|or|able
evap|or|ate
  evap|or|ates
  evap|or|ated
  evap|or|at|ing
evap|or|ation
evap|ora|tive
evap|or|ator +s
evap|or|ite +s
eva|sion +s
eva|sive
eva|sive|ly
eva|sive|ness
Eve (*Bible*; name)
eve +s (time before
  something)
evec|tion
Eve|lyn (name)
Eve|lyn, John
  (English writer)
even +s +ed +ing
  +er +est
even-handed
even-handed|ly
even-handed|ness
even|ing +s *noun*
even|ing dress
  even|ing dresses
  (single garment;
  formal outfit)
even|ly
even-money
  attributive
even|ness
even|song +s
even Ste|phen
even Ste|phens

even Ste|ven (use
  even Stephen)
even Ste|vens (use
  even Stephens)
event +s +ed +ing
even-tempered
event|er +s
event|ful
event|ful|ly
event|ful|ness
even|tide
event|less
event|less|ly
even|tual
even|tu|al|ity
  even|tu|al|ities
even|tu|al|ly
even|tu|ate
  even|tu|ates
  even|tu|ated
  even|tu|at|ing
even|tu|ation
ever
ever-changing
Ever|est, Mount
  (in Himalayas)
Ever|glades, the
  (area, USA)
ever|green +s
ever|last|ing
ever|last|ing|ly
ever|last|ing|ness
ever|more
ever-present
ever|sion
Evert, Chris
  (American tennis
  player)
evert +s +ed +ing
  (turn inside out)
every
every|body
every|day
  (ordinary)
every day (each
  day)
Every|man
every|one (every
  person,
  everybody)
every one (each
  one)
every|thing
every way
every|where
Every|woman
Ev|ette also Yv|ette
evict +s +ed +ing
evic|tion +s
evict|or +s
evi|dence
  evi|dences

evi|dence (cont.)
  evi|denced
  evi|den|cing
evi|dent
evi|den|tial
evi|den|tial|ly
evi|den|tiary
evi|dent|ly
evil +s
evil|doer +s
evil|doing
evil|ly
evil-minded
evil|ness
evince
  evinces
  evinced
  evin|cing
evin|cible
evin|cive
evis|cer|ate
  evis|cer|ates
  evis|cer|ated
  evis|cer|at|ing
evis|cer|ation
evo|ca|tion +s
evoca|tive
evoca|tive|ly
evoca|tive|ness
evoca|tory
evoke
  evokes
  evoked
  evok|ing
evoker +s
evo|lute
  evo|lutes
  evo|luted
  evo|lut|ing
evo|lu|tion +s
evo|lu|tion|al
evo|lu|tion|al|ly
evo|lu|tion|ar|ily
evo|lu|tion|ary
evo|lu|tion|ism
evo|lu|tion|ist +s
evo|lu|tion|is|tic
evo|lu|tive
evolv|able
evolve
  evolves
  evolved
  evolv|ing
evolve|ment
Evonne also
  Yvonne
evul|sion
ev|zone +s
Ewan also Euan
Ewart
ewe +s (sheep.
  △ yew, you)

ewe-necked
ewer +s
ex
  exes
ex|acer|bate
  ex|acer|bates
  ex|acer|bated
  ex|acer|bat|ing
ex|acer|ba|tion
exact +s +ed +ing
exact|able
exact|ing|ly
exact|ing|ness
exac|tion +s
exac|ti|tude
exact|ly
exact|ness
exact|or +s
ex|ag|ger|ate
  ex|ag|ger|ates
  ex|ag|ger|ated
  ex|ag|ger|at|ing
  ex|ag|ger|ated|ly
  ex|ag|ger|at|ing|ly
ex|ag|ger|ation +s
ex|ag|gera|tive
ex|ag|ger|ator +s
exalt +s +ed +ing
exalt|ation +s
ex|alt|ed|ly
exalt|ed|ness
ex|alt|er +s
exam +s
exa|meter Am. +s
exa|metre Br. +s
exam|in|able
exam|in|ation +s
exam|in|ation|al
exam|ine
  exam|ines
  exam|ined
  exam|in|ing
exam|inee +s
exam|in|er +s
ex|ample +s
ex|ani|mate
ex ante
exan|thema
  exan|the|mas or
  exan|the|mata
ex|arch +s
ex|arch|ate +s
ex|as|per|ate
  ex|as|per|ates
  ex|as|per|ated
  ex|as|per|at|ing
  ex|as|per|ated|ly
  ex|as|per|at|ing|ly
ex|as|per|ation
Ex|cali|bur
ex cath|edra

ex|cav|ate
  ex|cav|ates
  ex|cav|ated
  ex|cav|at|ing
ex|cav|ation +s
ex|cav|ator +s
ex|ceed +s +ed
  +ing (go beyond;
  be greater than.
  △ accede)
ex|ceed|ing|ly
excel
  ex|cels
  ex|celled
  ex|cel|ling
ex|cel|lence +s
Ex|cel|lency
Ex|cel|len|cies
  (in titles)
ex|cel|lency
  ex|cel|len|cies
ex|cel|lent
ex|cel|lent|ly
ex|cel|sior
ex|cen|tric (use
  eccentric)
ex|cept +s +ed
  +ing (leave out;
  not including.
  △ accept)
ex|cep|tion +s
ex|cep|tion|able
ex|cep|tion|ably
ex|cep|tion|al +s
ex|cep|tion|al|ity
ex|cep|tion|al|ly
ex|cerpt +s +ed
  +ing
ex|cerpt|ible
ex|cerp|tion
ex|cess
  ex|cesses
ex|ces|sive
ex|ces|sive|ly
ex|ces|sive|ness
ex|change
  ex|changes
  ex|changed
  ex|chan|ging
ex|change|abil|ity
ex|change|able
ex|chan|ger +s
ex|change rate +s
exchange-rate
  mech|an|ism +s
ex|chequer +s
ex|cimer +s
  (chemical
  compound.
  △ eczema)
ex|cis|able

ex|cise·
 ex|cises
 ex|cised
 ex|cis|ing
ex|cise|man
 ex|cise|men
ex|ci|sion +s
ex|cit|abil|ity
ex|cit|able
ex|cit|ably
ex|cit|ant +s
ex|ci|ta|tion +s
ex|ci|ta|tive
ex|ci|ta|tory
ex|cite
 ex|cites
 ex|cited
 ex|cit|ing
ex|cited|ly
ex|cited|ness
ex|cite|ment +s
ex|citer +s
ex|cit|ing|ly
ex|cit|ing|ness
ex|citon +s
ex|claim +s +ed
 +ing
ex|clam|ation +s
ex|clama|tory
ex|clave +s
ex|clos|ure +s
ex|clud|able
ex|clude
 ex|cludes
 ex|cluded
 ex|clud|ing
ex|cluder +s
ex|clu|sion +s
ex|clu|sion|ary
ex|clu|sion|ist +s
ex|clu|sive +s
ex|clu|sive|ly
ex|clu|sive|ness
ex|clu|siv|ity
ex|cogit|able
ex|cogi|tate
 ex|cogi|tates
 ex|cogi|tated
 ex|cogi|tat|ing
ex|cogi|ta|tion
ex|cogi|ta|tive
ex|com|mu|ni|cate
 ex|com|mu|ni|
  cates
 ex|com|mu|ni|
  cated
 ex|com|mu|ni|
  cat|ing
ex|com|mu|ni|
 ca|tion +s
ex|com|mu|ni|
 ca|tive

ex|com|mu|ni|
 ca|tor +s
ex|com|mu|ni|
 ca|tory
ex-con +s
ex|cori|ate
 ex|cori|ates
 ex|cori|ated
 ex|cori|at|ing
ex|cori|ation +s
ex|cre|ment +s
ex|cre|men|tal
ex|cres|cence
ex|cres|cent
ex|cres|cen|tial
ex|creta (body
 waste.
 △ excreter)
ex|crete
 ex|cretes
 ex|creted
 ex|cret|ing
ex|creter +s
 (person or thing
 that excretes.
 △ excreta)
ex|cre|tion +s
ex|cre|tive
ex|cre|tory
ex|cru|ci|ate
 ex|cru|ci|ates
 ex|cru|ci|ated
 ex|cru|ci|at|ing
 ex|cru|ci|at|ing|ly
ex|cru|ci|ation
ex|cul|pate
 ex|cul|pates
 ex|cul|pated
 ex|cul|pat|ing
ex|cul|pa|tion +s
ex|cul|pa|tory
ex|cur|sion +s
ex|cur|sion|al
ex|cur|sion|ary
ex|cur|sion|ist
ex|cur|sive
ex|cur|sive|ly
ex|cur|sive|ness
ex|cur|sus
 plural ex|cur|sus
 or ex|cur|suses
ex|cus|able
ex|cus|ably
ex|cusa|tory
ex|cuse
 ex|cuses
 ex|cused
 ex|cus|ing
ex|cuse me
 (apology)
excuse-me +s
 (dance)

ex-directory
ex div. (= ex
 dividend)
ex divi|dend
Exe (river, England)
exeat +s
exec +s
exe|crable
exe|crably
exe|crate
 exe|crates
 exe|crated
 exe|crat|ing
exe|cra|tion +s
exe|cra|tive
exe|cra|tory
exe|cut|able
ex|ecu|tant +s
exe|cute
 exe|cutes
 exe|cuted
 exe|cut|ing
exe|cu|tion +s
exe|cu|tion|ary
exe|cu|tion|er +s
ex|ecu|tive +s
ex|ecu|tive|ly
ex|ecu|tor +s (of a
 will)
exe|cu|tor +s (of a
 plan etc.)
ex|ecu|tor|ial
ex|ecu|tor|ship +s
ex|ecu|tory
ex|ecu|trix
 ex|ecu|tri|ces
 female
exe|gesis
 exe|geses
exe|gete +s
exe|get|ic
exe|get|ic|al
exe|ge|tist +s
ex|em|plar +s
ex|em|plar|ily
ex|em|plari|ness
ex|em|plary
ex|em|pli|fi|ca|tion
 +s
ex|em|plify
 ex|em|pli|fies
 ex|em|pli|fied
 ex|em|pli|fy|ing
ex|em|plum
 ex|em|pla
ex|empt +s +ed
 +ing
ex|emp|tion +s
exe|qua|tur +s
exe|quies
ex|er|cis|able

ex|er|cise
 ex|er|cises
 ex|er|cised
 ex|er|cis|ing
 (mental or
 physical activity;
 engage in this.
 △ exorcize)
ex|er|cise book +s
ex|er|ciser +s
ex|ergual
ex|ergue +s
exert +s +ed +ing
 (exercise.
 △ exsert)
ex|er|tion +s
Exe|ter (city,
 England)
exe|unt
ex|fil|trate
 ex|fil|trates
 ex|fil|trated
 ex|fil|trat|ing
ex|fil|tra|tion
ex|foli|ate
 ex|foli|ates
 ex|foli|ated
 ex|foli|at|ing
ex|foli|ation
ex|folia|tive
ex gra|tia
ex|hal|able
ex|hal|ation +s
ex|hale
 ex|hales
 ex|haled
 ex|hal|ing
ex|haust +s +ed
 +ing
ex|haust|er +s
ex|haust|ibil|ity
ex|haust|ible
ex|haust|ibly
ex|haus|tion
ex|haust|ive
ex|haust|ive|ly
ex|haust|ive|ness
ex|haust pipe +s
ex|hibit +s +ed
 +ing
ex|hib|ition +s
ex|hib|ition|er +s
ex|hib|ition|ism
ex|hib|ition|ist +s
ex|hib|ition|is|tic
ex|hib|ition|is|tic|
 al|ly
ex|hib|it|or +s
ex|hibi|tory
ex|hil|ar|ant +s
ex|hil|ar|ate
 ex|hil|ar|ates

ex|hil|ar|ate (*cont.*)
  ex|hil|ar|ated
  ex|hil|ar|at|ing
  ex|hil|ar|at|ing|ly
  ex|hil|ar|ation +s
  ex|hil|ara|tive
ex|hort +s +ed
  +ing
ex|hort|ation +s
ex|hor|ta|tive
ex|hor|ta|tory
ex|hort|er +s
ex|hum|ation +s
ex|hume
  ex|humes
  ex|humed
  ex|hum|ing
ex hy|poth|esi
exi|gence
exi|gency
  exi|gen|cies
exi|gent
exi|gible
exi|gu|ity
exi|igu|ous
exi|igu|ous|ly
exi|igu|ous|ness
exile
  exiles
  exiled
  ex|il|ing
exil|ic
exist +s +ed +ing
ex|ist|ence +s
ex|ist|ent
ex|ist|en|tial
ex|ist|en|tial|ism
ex|ist|en|tial|ist +s
ex|ist|en|tial|ly
exit +s +ed +ing
ex-libris
  plural ex-libris
  (label)
Ex|moor (area,
  England)
ex ni|hilo
exo|biolo|gist +s
exo|biol|ogy
Exo|cet +s
exo|crine
exo|derm +s
Exo|dus *Bible*
exo|dus
  exo|duses
  (departure)
ex of|fi|cio
ex|og|am|ous
ex|og|amy
exo|gen +s
ex|ogen|ous
ex|ogen|ous|ly

exon +s
  (commander of
  Yeomen of the
  Guard)
ex|on|er|ate
  ex|on|er|ates
  ex|on|er|ated
  ex|on|er|at|ing
  ex|on|er|ation
ex|on|era|tive
ex|oph|thal|mia
ex|oph|thal|mic
ex|oph|thal|mos
ex|oph|thal|mus
  (use
  exophthalmos)
exo|plasm
ex|or|bi|tance
ex|or|bi|tant
ex|or|bi|tant|ly
ex|or|cisa|tion *Br.*
  (use exorcization)
ex|or|cise *Br.* (use
  exorcize)
  ex|or|cises
  ex|or|cised
  ex|or|cis|ing
  (drive away evil
  spirits.
  ⚠ exercise)
ex|or|cism +s
ex|or|cist +s
ex|or|ciza|tion
ex|or|cize
  ex|or|cizes
  ex|or|cized
  ex|or|ciz|ing
  (drive away evil
  spirit. ⚠ exercise)
ex|or|dial
ex|or|di|al|ly
ex|or|dium
  ex|or|dia *or*
  ex|or|diums
exo|skel|etal
exo|skel|eton +s
exo|sphere +s
exo|ter|ic
exo|ter|ic|al
exo|ter|ic|al|ly
exo|teri|cism
exo|ther|mal
exo|ther|mal|ly
exo|ther|mic
exo|ther|mic|al|ly
exot|ic +s
exot|ica
exot|ic|al|ly
exoti|cism
exo|toxin +s
ex|pand +s +ed
  +ing

ex|pand|able
ex|pand|er +s
ex|panse +s
ex|pan|si|bil|ity
ex|pan|sible
ex|pan|sile
ex|pan|sion +s
ex|pan|sion|ary
ex|pan|sion|ism
ex|pan|sion|ist +s
ex|pan|sion|is|tic
ex|pan|sive
ex|pan|sive|ly
ex|pan|sive|ness
ex|pan|siv|ity
ex parte
expat +s
ex|pati|ate
  ex|pati|ates
  ex|pati|ated
  ex|pati|at|ing
ex|pati|ation +s
ex|pati|atory
ex|patri|ate
  ex|patri|ates
  ex|patri|ated
  ex|patri|at|ing
ex|patri|ation
ex|pect +s +ed
  +ing
ex|pect|able
ex|pect|ancy
  ex|pect|an|cies
ex|pect|ant
ex|pect|ant|ly
ex|pect|ation +s
ex|pec|tor|ant +s
ex|pec|tor|ate
  ex|pec|tor|ates
  ex|pec|tor|ated
  ex|pec|tor|at|ing
ex|pec|tor|ation
ex|pec|tor|ator +s
ex|pe|di|ence
ex|pe|di|ency
ex|pe|di|ent +s
ex|pe|di|ent|ly
ex|ped|ite
  ex|ped|ites
  ex|ped|ited
  ex|ped|it|ing
ex|ped|iter +s
ex|ped|ition +s
ex|ped|ition|ary
ex|ped|ition|ist +s
ex|ped|itious
ex|ped|itious|ly
ex|ped|itious|ness
expel
  ex|pels
  ex|pelled
  ex|pel|ling

ex|pel|lable
ex|pel|lee +s
ex|pel|lent +s
ex|pel|ler +s
ex|pend +s +ed
  +ing
ex|pend|abil|ity
ex|pend|able
ex|pend|ably
ex|pend|iture +s
ex|pense +s
ex|pen|sive
ex|pen|sive|ly
ex|pen|sive|ness
ex|peri|ence
  ex|peri|ences
  ex|peri|enced
  ex|peri|en|cing
ex|peri|ence|able
ex|peri|en|tial
ex|peri|en|tial|ism
ex|peri|en|tial|ist
  +s
ex|peri|en|tial|ly
ex|peri|ment +s
  +ed +ing
ex|peri|men|tal
ex|peri|men|tal|ise
  Br. (use
  experimentalize)
  ex|peri|men|tal|
      ises
  ex|peri|men|tal|
      ised
  ex|peri|men|tal|
      is|ing
ex|peri|men|tal|
      ism
ex|peri|men|tal|ist
  +s
ex|peri|men|tal|
      ize
  ex|peri|men|tal|
      izes
  ex|peri|men|tal|
      ized
  ex|peri|men|tal|
      iz|ing
ex|peri|men|tal|ly
ex|peri|men|
      ta|tion
ex|peri|ment|er +s
ex|pert +s
ex|pert|ise *noun*
ex|pert|ise *Br.* (use
  expertize)
  ex|pert|ises
  ex|pert|ised
  ex|pert|is|ing
  verb
ex|pert|ize
  ex|pert|izes

ex|pert|ize (cont.)
  ex|pert|ized
  ex|pert|iz|ing
  verb
ex|pert|ly
ex|pert|ness
ex|pi|able
ex|pi|ate
  ex|pi|ates
  ex|pi|ated
  ex|pi|at|ing
ex|pi|ation
ex|pi|ator +s
ex|pi|atory
ex|pir|ation +s
ex|pira|tory
ex|pire
  ex|pires
  ex|pired
  ex|pir|ing
ex|piry
ex|plain +s +ed
  +ing
ex|plain|able
ex|plain|er +s
ex|plan|ation +s
ex|plana|tor|ily
ex|plana|tory
ex|plant +s +ed
  +ing
ex|plant|ation
ex|ple|tive +s
ex|plic|able
ex|pli|cate
  ex|pli|cates
  ex|pli|cated
  ex|pli|cat|ing
ex|pli|ca|tion +s
ex|pli|ca|tive
ex|pli|ca|tor +s
ex|pli|ca|tory
ex|pli|cit
ex|pli|cit|ly
ex|pli|cit|ness
ex|plode
  ex|plodes
  ex|ploded
  ex|plod|ing
ex|ploder +s
ex|ploit +s +ed
  +ing
ex|ploit|able
ex|ploit|ation +s
ex|ploit|ative
ex|ploit|er +s
ex|ploit|ive
ex|plor|ation +s
ex|plor|ation|al
ex|plora|tive
ex|plora|tory
ex|plore
  ex|plores

ex|plore (cont.)
  ex|plored
  ex|plor|ing
ex|plorer +s
ex|plo|sion +s
ex|plo|sive +s
ex|plo|sive|ly
ex|plo|sive|ness
Expo +s
ex|po|nent +s
ex|po|nen|tial
ex|po|nen|tial|ly
ex|port +s +ed
  +ing
ex|port|abil|ity
ex|port|able
ex|port|ation
ex|port|er +s
ex|pose
  ex|poses
  ex|posed
  ex|pos|ing
ex|posé +s
ex|poser +s
ex|pos|ition +s
ex|pos|ition|al
ex|posi|tive
ex|posi|tor +s
ex|posi|tory
ex post
ex post facto
ex|pos|tu|late
  ex|pos|tu|lates
  ex|pos|tu|lated
  ex|pos|tu|lat|ing
ex|pos|tu|la|tion
  +s
ex|pos|tu|la|tory
ex|pos|ure +s
ex|pound +s +ed
  +ing
ex|pound|er +s
ex|press
  ex|presses
  ex|pressed
  ex|press|ing
ex|press|er +s
ex|press|ible
ex|pres|sion +s
ex|pres|sion|al
ex|pres|sion|ism
ex|pres|sion|ist +s
ex|pres|sion|is|tic
ex|pres|sion|is|tic|
  al|ly
ex|pres|sion|less
ex|pres|sion|
  less|ly
ex|pres|sion|less|
  ness
expression-mark
  +s

ex|pres|sive
ex|pres|sive|ly
ex|pres|sive|ness
ex|pres|siv|ity
ex|press|ly
ex|presso +s
ex|press|way +s
ex|pro|pri|ate
  ex|pro|pri|ates
  ex|pro|pri|ated
  ex|pro|pri|at|ing
ex|pro|pri|ation +s
ex|pro|pri|ator +s
ex|pul|sion +s
ex|pul|sive
ex|punc|tion
ex|punge
  ex|punges
  ex|punged
  ex|pun|ging
ex|punger +s
ex|pur|gate
  ex|pur|gates
  ex|pur|gated
  ex|pur|gat|ing
ex|pur|ga|tion
ex|pur|ga|tor +s
ex|pur|ga|tor|ial
ex|pur|ga|tory
ex|quis|ite
ex|quis|ite|ly
ex|quis|ite|ness
ex|san|guin|ate
  ex|san|guin|ates
  ex|san|guin|ated
  ex|san|guin|at|ing
ex|san|guin|ation
ex|scind +s +ed
  +ing
ex|sert +s +ed
  +ing (*Biology* put
  forth. △ exert)
ex-service
ex-serviceman
  ex-servicemen
ex-servicewoman
  ex-servicewomen
ex|sic|cate
  ex|sic|cates
  ex|sic|cated
  ex|sic|cat|ing
ex si|len|tio
ex|tant
ex|tem|por|an|eous
ex|tem|por|
  an|eous|ly
ex|tem|por|an|eous|
  ness
ex|tem|por|ar|ily
ex|tem|por|ari|
  ness
ex|tem|por|ary

ex|tem|pore
ex|tem|por|isa|
  tion *Br.* +s (use
  extemporization)
ex|tem|por|ise *Br.*
  (use
  extemporize)
ex|tem|por|ises
ex|tem|por|ised
ex|tem|por|is|ing
ex|tem|por|iza|
  tion +s
ex|tem|por|ize
ex|tem|por|izes
ex|tem|por|ized
ex|tem|por|iz|ing
ex|tend +s +ed
  +ing
ex|tend|abil|ity
ex|tend|able
extended-play
  attributive
ex|tend|er +s
ex|tend|ibil|ity
  (use
  extendability)
ex|tend|ible (use
  extendable)
ex|ten|si|bil|ity
ex|ten|sible
ex|ten|sile
ex|ten|sion +s
ex|ten|sion|al
ex|ten|sive
ex|ten|sive|ly
ex|ten|sive|ness
ex|tens|om|eter +s
ex|ten|sor +s
ex|tent +s
ex|tenu|ate
  ex|tenu|ates
  ex|tenu|ated
  ex|tenu|at|ing
ex|tenu|at|ing|ly
ex|tenu|ation +s
ex|tenu|atory
ex|ter|ior +s
ex|ter|ior|ise *Br.*
  (use exteriorize)
ex|ter|ior|ises
ex|ter|ior|ised
ex|ter|ior|is|ing
ex|ter|ior|ity
ex|ter|ior|ize
ex|ter|ior|izes
ex|ter|ior|ized
ex|ter|ior|iz|ing
ex|ter|ior|ly
ex|ter|min|ate
  ex|ter|min|ates
  ex|ter|min|ated
  ex|ter|min|at|ing

ex|ter|min|ation
+s
ex|ter|min|ator +s
ex|ter|min|atory
ex|ter|nal +s
ex|ter|nal|isa|tion
Br. (use
externalization)
ex|ter|nal|ise *Br.*
(use externalize)
ex|ter|nal|ises
ex|ter|nal|ised
ex|ter|nal|is|ing
ex|ter|nal|ity
ex|ter|nal|ities
ex|ter|nal|iza|tion
ex|ter|nal|ize
ex|ter|nal|izes
ex|ter|nal|ized
ex|ter|nal|iz|ing
ex|ter|nal|ly
ex|tero|cep|tive
ex|ter|ri|tor|ial
ex|ter|ri|tori|al|ity
ex|tinct
ex|tinc|tion +s
ex|tinct|ive
ex|tin|guish
ex|tin|guishes
ex|tin|guished
ex|tin|guish|ing
ex|tin|guish|able
ex|tin|guish|er +s
ex|tin|guish|ment
ex|tir|pate
ex|tir|pates
ex|tir|pated
ex|tir|pat|ing
ex|tir|pa|tion
ex|tir|pa|tor +s
extol
ex|tols
ex|tolled
ex|tol|ling
ex|tol|ler +s
ex|tol|ment
ex|tort +s +ed
+ing
ex|tort|er +s
ex|tor|tion +s
ex|tor|tion|ate
ex|tor|tion|ate|ly
ex|tor|tion|er +s
ex|tor|tion|ist +s
ex|tort|ive
extra +s
extra|cel|lu|lar
extra|cra|nial
ex|tract +s +ed
+ing
ex|tract|abil|ity
ex|tract|able

ex|trac|tion +s
ex|tract|ive
ex|tract|or +s
extra-curricu|lar
extra|dit|able
extra|dite
extra|dites
extra|dited
extra|dit|ing
extra|di|tion +s
ex|tra|dos
ex|tra|doses
extra|gal|ac|tic
extra|judi|cial
extra|judi|cial|ly
extra|lin|guis|tic
extra|mar|it|al
extra|mar|it|al|ly
extra|mun|dane
extra|mural
extra|mural|ly
ex|tra|ne|ous
ex|tra|ne|ous|ly
ex|tra|ne|ous|ness
extra|or|din|ar|ily
extra|or|din|ari|
    ness
extra|or|din|ary
extra|or|din|ar|ies
extra|phys|ic|al
ex|trapo|late
ex|trapo|lates
ex|trapo|lated
ex|trapo|lat|ing
ex|trapo|la|tion +s
ex|trapo|la|tive
ex|trapo|la|tor +s
extra|sens|ory
extra|ter|res|trial
+s
extra|ter|ri|tor|ial
extra|ter|ri|tori|
    al|ity
ex|trava|gance +s
ex|trava|gancy
ex|trava|gan|cies
ex|trava|gant
ex|trava|gant|ly
ex|trava|ganza +s
ex|trava|sate
ex|trava|sates
ex|trava|sated
ex|trava|sat|ing
ex|trava|sa|tion
extra|vehicu|lar
extra|ver|sion (use
extroversion)
extra|vert +s (use
extrovert)
extra|vert|ed (use
extroverted)

ex|trema (plural of
extremum)
Ex|tre|ma|dura
(region, Spain)
ex|tremal
ex|treme
ex|tremes
ex|trem|est
ex|treme|ly
ex|treme|ness
ex|tremis (in *'in
extremis'*)
ex|trem|ism
ex|trem|ist +s
ex|trem|ity
ex|trem|ities
ex|tremum
ex|trem|ums *or*
ex|trema
ex|tric|able
ex|tri|cate
ex|tri|cates
ex|tri|cated
ex|tri|cat|ing
ex|tri|ca|tion +s
ex|trin|sic
ex|trin|sic|al|ly
ex|tro|ver|sion
ex|tro|vert +s
ex|tro|vert|ed
ex|trude
ex|trudes
ex|truded
ex|trud|ing
ex|tru|sile
ex|tru|sion +s
ex|tru|sive
ex|uber|ance
ex|uber|ant
ex|uber|ant|ly
ex|uber|ate
ex|uber|ates
ex|uber|ated
ex|uber|at|ing
ex|ud|ate +s
ex|ud|ation +s
ex|uda|tive
exude
ex|udes
ex|uded
ex|ud|ing
exult +s +ed +ing
ex|ult|ancy
ex|ult|ant
ex|ult|ant|ly
ex|ult|ation +s
ex|ult|ing|ly
Exuma Cays
(island group,
Bahamas)
exurb +s
ex|urban

ex|ur|ban|ite +s
ex|ur|bia
ex|uviae
ex|uvial
ex|uvi|ate
ex|uvi|ates
ex|uvi|ated
ex|uvi|at|ing
ex|uvi|ation
ex-voto +s
eyas
eyases
eye
eyes
eyed
eye|ing *or* eying
(organ of sight.
△ aye, I)
eye|ball +s +ed
+ing
eye|bath +s
eye|black
eye bolt +s
eye|bright
eye|brow +s
eye-catching
eye con|tact
eye|ful +s
eye|glass
eye|glasses
eye|hole +s
eye|lash
eye|lashes
eye|less
eye|let +s
eye level
eye-level *attributive*
eye|lid +s
eye|liner +s
eye-opener +s
eye-opening
eye|patch
eye|patches
eye|piece +s
eye-rhyme +s
eye-shade +s
eye|shadow +s
eye|shot
eye|sight
eye socket +s
eye|sore +s
eye-spot +s
eye-stalk +s
eye strain
Eye|tie +s
(*offensive*)
eye-tooth
eye-teeth
eye|wash
eye|wit|ness
eye|wit|nesses
eye-worm +s

eyot +s (use ait.
⚠ ate, eight)
eyra +s
Eyre, Ed¦ward
John (Australian
explorer and
statesman)
Eyre, Lake (in
Australia)
eyrie +s (nest.
⚠ eerie)
Ey|senck, Hans
(German-born
British
psychologist)
Eze|kiel (Bible;
name)
Ezra (Bible; name)

Ff

fa (Music; use fah.
⚠ far)
fab
Fab|ergé, Peter
Carl (Russian
jeweller)
Fabia
Fa¦bian +s
(member of
Fabian Society;
name)
Fa¦bian|ism
Fa¦bian|ist +s
Fa¦bius (Roman
general and
statesman)
fable
  fables
  fabled
  fab¦ling
fa¦bler +s
fab¦liau
  fab¦li|aux
Fab¦lon Propr.
Fab¦ri|ano,
  Gen¦tile da
  (Italian painter)
fab¦ric +s
fab¦ri|cate
  fab¦ri|cates
  fab¦ri|cated
  fab¦ri|cat¦ing
fab¦ri|ca¦tion +s
fab¦ri|ca¦tor +s
Fab¦ri|cius, bursa
  of
fabu|list +s
fabu|los¦ity
fabu|lous
fabu|lous¦ly
fabu|lous|ness
fa¦çade +s
face
  faces
  faced
  fa¦cing
face-ache +s
face card +s
face|cloth +s
face cream +s
face flannel +s
face|less
face|less¦ly
face|less|ness
face|lift +s
face|lift¦ed
face mask +s
face-off +s noun

face pack +s
face paint
face-painter +s
face-painting
face|plate +s
face pow¦der +s
facer +s
face-saver +s
face-saving
facet +s
fa¦cet¦ed
fa¦cetiae
fa¦cetious
fa¦cetious¦ly
fa¦cetious|ness
face to face
  adverbial
face-to-face +s
  attributive and
  noun
fa¦cet|ted (use
  faceted)
face value
face|work¦er +s
facia +s (use
  fascia)
fa¦cial +s (of a face.
  ⚠ fascial)
fa¦cial¦ly
fa¦cies
  plural fa¦cies
fa¦cile
fa¦cile¦ly
fa¦cile|ness
fa¦cili|tate
  fa¦cili|tates
  fa¦cili|tated
  fa¦cili|tat¦ing
fa¦cili|ta¦tion
fa¦cili|ta¦tive
fa¦cili|ta¦tor +s
fa¦cil|ity
  fa¦cil|ities
fa¦cing +s
fac|sim|ile +3
fact +s
fact-finding
fac|tice
fac|tion +s
fac|tion|al
fac|tion|al|ise Br.
  (use factionalize)
  fac|tion|al|ises
  fac|tion|al|ised
  fac|tion|al|is|ing
fac|tion|al|ism
fac|tion|al|ize
  fac|tion|al|izes
  fac|tion|al|ized
  fac|tion|al|iz|ing
fac|tion|al¦ly
fac|tious

fac|tious¦ly
fac|tious|ness
fac|ti¦tious
fac|ti¦tious¦ly
fac|ti¦tious|ness
fac|ti|tive +s
facto (in 'de facto')
fac|toid +s
fac|tor +s +ed +ing
fac|tor|able
fac|tor|age +s
fac|tor eight (use
  factor VIII)
fac|tor VIII (blood
  protein)
fac|tor|ial +s
fac|tori|al¦ly
fac|tor|isa¦tion Br.
  (use
  factorization)
fac|tor|ise Br. (use
  factorize)
  fac|tor|ises
  fac|tor|ised
  fac|tor|is|ing
fac|tor|iza¦tion
fac|tor|ize
  fac|tor|izes
  fac|tor|ized
  fac|tor|iz|ing
fac|tory
  fac|tor|ies
fac|tory farm +s
fac|tory farm|ing
factory-made
fac|to¦tum +s
fact sheet +s
fac|tual
fact|ual|ism
fact|ual|ist +s
factu|al|ity
fact|ual¦ly
fact|ual|ness
fac|tum
  fac|tums or facta
fac|ture
fac¦ula
  facu|lae
  noun
facu|lar adjective
facu|lous
fac|ul|ta|tive
fac|ul|ta|tive¦ly
fac|ulty
  fac|ul|ties
FA Cup (football)
fad +s
fad|dily
fad|di|ness
fad|dish
fad|dish¦ly
fad|dish|ness

fad|dism
fad|dist +s
faddy
  fad|dier
  fad|di|est
fade
  fades
  faded
  fad|ing
fade-in +s *noun*
fade|less
fade-out +s *noun*
fader +s
fadge +s
fado +s
fae|cal *Br.* (*Am.* fecal)
fae|ces *Br.* (*Am.* feces)
Fa|enza (town, Italy)
fae|rie (*archaic* Fairyland; visionary. △ fairy)
Faeroe Is|lands (in N. Atlantic)
Faer|oes (shipping area, N. Atlantic; also = Faeroe Islands)
Faero|ese
  plural Faero|ese
faery (*archaic*; use faerie)
faff +s +ed +ing
fag
  fags
  fagged
  fag|ging
Faga|togo (city, Samoa)
fag end +s
fag|got +s (*offensive* homosexual; food)
fag|got *Br.* +s +ed +ing (bundle; embroider. *Am.* fagot)
fag|goty
Fagin (character in Dickens)
fagot *Am.* +s +ed +ing (bundle; embroider. *Br.* faggot △ faggot)
fah (*Music.* △ far)
Fahr|en|heit, Gab|riel Dan|iel (German physicist)

Fahr|en|heit (temperature scale)
fai|ence
fail +s +ed +ing
fail|ing +s
fail-safe
fail|ure +s
fain (gladly. △ fane, feign)
fai|né|ancy
fai|né|ant +s
faint +s +ed +ing +er +est (lose consciousness; pale, dim. △ feint)
faint-hearted
faint-hearted|ly
faint-hearted|ness
faint|ing fit +s
faint|ly
faint|ness
fair +s +er +est (just; light-coloured. △ fare, fayre)
Fair|banks, Doug|las (Senior and Junior, American actors)
Fair|fax, Thomas (Lord Fairfax, English Parliamentary general)
fair|ground +s
fair-haired
fair|ing +s (streamlining. △ faring)
fair|ish
Fair Isle (in North Sea; knitwear; shipping area, NE Atlantic)
fair|lead +s
fair|ly
fair-minded
fair-minded|ly
fair-minded|ness
fair|ness
fair-spoken
fair|water
fair|way +s
fair-weather friend +s.
fairy
  fair|ies (imaginary being; *offensive* homosexual. △ faerie, faery)

fairy cake +s
fairy cycle +s
fairy god|mother +s
fairy|land
fairy lights
fairy-like
fairy ring +s
fairy story
  fairy stor|ies
fairy tale +s *noun*
fairy-tale *attributive*
Fai|sal (Iraqi kings)
Fai|sal|abad (city, Pakistan)
fait ac|com|pli
  faits ac|com|plis
Faith (name)
faith +s (belief; trust)
faith|ful
faith|ful|ly
faith|ful|ness
faith heal|er +s
faith heal|ing
faith|less
faith|less|ly
faith|less|ness
fa|jita +s
fake
  fakes
  faked
  fak|ing
faker +s (person who fakes)
fak|ery
  fak|er|ies
fakir +s (holy man)
fala|fel +s (use felafel)
Fa|lange (Spanish political group. △ Phalange)
Fa|lan|gism
Fa|lan|gist +s
Fa|lasha
  plural Fa|lasha
fal|bala
fal|cate
fal|chion +s
fal|ci|form
fal|con +s
fal|con|er +s
fal|con|et +s
fal|con|ry
fal|deral +s
Faldo, Nick (British golfer)
fald|stool +s
Fa|ler|nian
Falk|land Is|lands (in S. Atlantic)

Falk|lands (= Falkland Islands)
fall
  falls
  fell
  fall|ing
  fall|en
Falla, Ma|nuel de (Spanish composer)
fal|la|cious
fal|la|cious|ly
fal|la|cious|ness
fal|lacy
  fal|la|cies
fall-back +s *noun and adjective*
fall|en
fall|en|ness
fall|er +s
fall|fish
  plural fall|fish
fall guy +s
fal|li|bil|ity
fall|ible
fall|ibly
falling-out
  fallings-out
fall-off +s *noun*
Fal|lo|pian
fall|out +s
fal|low
fal|low|ness
fall-pipe +s
false
false|hood +s
false|ly
false|ness
false posi|tive +s
fal|setto +s
false|work
fal|sies
fal|si|fi|abil|ity
fal|si|fi|able
fal|si|fi|ca|tion +s
fals|ify
  fal|si|fies
  fal|si|fied
  fal|si|fy|ing
fal|sity
  fal|sities
Fal|staff (in Shakespeare)
Fal|staff|ian
Fal|ster (Danish island)
fal|ter +s +ed +ing (waver. △ faulter)
fal|ter|er +s
fal|ter|ing|ly

Fama|gusta (port,
Cyprus)
fame
famed
fa|mil|ial
fa|mil|iar +s
fa|mil|iar|isa|tion
Br. (use
familiarization)
fa|mil|iar|ise Br.
(use familiarize)
fa|mil|iar|ises
fa|mil|iar|ised
fa|mil|iar|is|ing
fa|mil|iar|ity
fa|mil|iar|ities
fa|mil|iar|iza|tion
fa|mil|iar|ize
fa|mil|iar|izes
fa|mil|iar|ized
fa|mil|iar|iz|ing
fa|mil|iar|ly
fa| *mille* (in 'en
famille')
fa| *mille jaune*
fa| *mille noire*
fa| *mille rose*
fa| *mille verte*
fam|ily
fam|ilies
family-owned
attributive
fam|ily plan|ning
family-run
attributive
fam|ily tree +s
fam|ine +s
fam|ish
fam|ishes
fam|ished
fam|ish|ing
fam|ous
fam|ous|ly
fam|ous|ness
famu|lus
fam|uli
Fan
plural Fan *or* Fans
(people; language)
fan
fans
fanned
fan|ning
(make air
circulate; device
for doing this etc.)
fan|at|ic +s
fan|at|ic|al
fan|at|ic|al|ly
fan|ati|cise Br. (use
fanaticize)
fan|ati|cises

fan|ati|cise (cont.)
fan|ati|cised
fan|ati|cis|ing
fan|ati|cism
fan|ati|cize
fan|ati|cizes
fan|ati|cized
fan|ati|ciz|ing
fan belt +s
fan|ci|able
fan|cier +s
fan|ci|ful
fan|ci|ful|ly
fan|ci|ful|ness
fan|cily
fan|ci|ness
fan club +s
fancy
fan|cies
fan|cied
fancy|ing
fan|cier
fan|ci|est
fancy dress
fancy-free
fancy-work
fan|dan|gle +s
fan|dango
fan|dan|goes
fan|dom
fane +s (temple.
△ fain, feign)
fan|fare +s
fan|faro|nade +s
Fang (use Fan)
fang +s
fanged
Fan|gio, Juan
Ma|nuel
(Argentinian
racing driver)
fang|less
fan-jet +s
fan|light +s
fan|like
fan mail
fan|ner +s
fanny
fan|nies
(*coarse slang*)
Fanny Adams
fanny pack +s
fan|tail +s
fan|tailed
fan-tan
fan|ta|sia +s
fan|ta|sise Br. (use
fantasize)
fan|ta|sises
fan|ta|sised
fan|ta|sis|ing
fan|ta|sist +s

fan|ta|size
fan|ta|sizes
fan|ta|sized
fan|ta|siz|ing
fan|tas|mat|ic
fan|tast +s
fan|tas|tic
fan|tas|tic|al
fan|tas|tic|al|ity
fan|tas|tic|al|ly
fan|tas|ti|cate
fan|tas|ti|cates
fan|tas|ti|cated
fan|tas|ti|cat|ing
fan|tas|ti|ca|tion
fan|tas|ti|cism
fan|tasy
fan|ta|sies
fan|ta|sied
fan|tasy|ing
Fante (use Fanti)
plural Fante *or*
Fantes
Fanti
plural Fanti *or*
Fantis
fan|tod +s
fan|zine +s
fa|quir +s (use
fakir)
far
fur|ther *or* far|ther
fur|thest *or*
far|thest
(distant. △ fa, fah)
farad +s
fara|daic
Fara|day,
Mi|chael (English
scientist)
fara|day +s (unit)
fa|rad|ic
far|an|dole +s
far|away *adjective*
farce +s
far|ceur +s
far|ci|cal
far|ci|cal|ity
far|ci|cal|ly
farcy (illness.
△ Farsi)
fard|ed
fare
fares
fared
far|ing
(get on; payment
for travel; food.
△ fair, fayre)
Far East|ern
fare stage +s

Fare|well, Cape (in
Greenland and
New Zealand)
fare|well +s
far-fetched
far-fetched|ness
far-flung
far gone
Fa|rida|bad (city,
India)
far|ina +s
far|in|aceous
farl +s
farm +s +ed +ing
farm|able
farm|er +s
farm|hand +s
farm|house +s
farm|land +s
farm|stead +s
farm work
farm|work|er +s
farm|yard +s
Farn|borough
(town, England)
Farne Is|lands (off
NE England)
Far|nese (Italian
ducal family)
far|ness
Faro (port,
Portugal)
faro (game)
Faro|ese (use
Faeroese)
plural Faro|ese
far-off *attributive*
fa|rouche
Far|ouk (Egyptian
king)
far-out *attributive*
Far|quhar, George
(Irish writer)
far|ra|gin|ous
far|rago +s
far-reaching
Far|rell, J. G.
(English novelist)
Far|rell, James T.
(American
novelist)
far|rier +s
far|ri|ery
far|row +s +ed
+ing
far|ruca +s
far-seeing
Farsi (language.
△ farcy)
far-sighted
far-sighted|ly
far-sighted|ness

fart +s +ed +ing
  (*coarse slang*)
far|ther
  (comparative of
  far. ⚠ father)
far|thest
far|thing +s
far|thin|gale +s
fart|lek
Far|vel, Kap
  (Danish name for
  Cape Farewell in
  Greenland)
fas|ces
fa,scia +s
fa|scial (of a fascia.
  ⚠ facial)
fa|sci|ate
fa|sci|ated
fa|scia|tion
fas|cicle +s
fas|cicled
fas|ci|cu|lar
fas|ci|cu|late
fas|ci|cu|la|tion
fas|ci|cule +s
fas|cic|ulus
  fas|cic|uli
fas|ci|itis
fas|cin|ate
  fas|cin|ates
  fas|cin|ated
  fas|cin|at|ing
fas|cin|at|ing|ly
fas|cin|ation +s
fas|cin|ator +s
fas|cine +s
Fas|cism
Fas|cist +s
Fas|cis|tic
fash|ion +s +ed
  +ing
fash|ion|abil|ity
fash|ion|able
fash|ion|able|ness
fash|ion|ably
fash|ion|er +s
Fass|bin|der,
  Rai|ner Wer|ner
  (German film
  director)
fast +s +ed +ing
  +er +est
fast|back +s
fast breed|er +s
fas|ten +s +ed
  +ing
fas|ten|er +s
fas|ten|ing +s
fast|er +s
fast food
fast-growing

fas|tidi|ous
fas|tidi|ous|ly
fas|tidi|ous|ness
fas|tigi|ate
fast|ing +s
fast-moving
fast|ness
  fast|nesses
Fast|net (island, N.
  Atlantic; shipping
  area, Celtic Sea)
fast-talk +s +ed
  +ing
fast-wind
  fast-winds
  fast-wound
  fast-winding
fat
  fats
  fat|ted
  fat|ting
  fat|ter
  fat|test
Fatah, Al
  (Palestinian
  organization)
fatal +s
fa|tal|ism
fa|tal|ist +s
fa|tal|is|tic
fa|tal|is|tic|al|ly
fa|tal|ity
  fa|tal|ities
fa|tal|ly
fa|tal|ness
Fata Morgana
fate
  fates
  fated
  fat|ing
  (doom; destiny.
  ⚠ fête)
fate|ful
fate|ful|ly
fate|ful|ness
Fates, the *Greek*
  Mythology
fat-free
fat-head
fat-headed
fat-headed|ness
father +s +ed +ing
  (male parent.
  ⚠ farther)
Father Christ|mas
  Father
  Christ|mases
father fig|ure +s
father|hood
father-in-law
  fathers-in-law
father|land +s

father|less
father|less|ness
father|like
father|li|ness
father|ly
Father's Day
father|ship
fathom +s +ed
  +ing
fathom|able
Fath|om|eter +s
fathom|less
fa|tidi|cal
fa|tigu|abil|ity
fa|tigu|able
fa|tigue
  fa|tigues
  fa|tigued
  fa|tiguing
fa|tigue|less
Fat|iha
Fat|ihah (use
  Fatiha)
Fat|ima (daughter
  of Muhammad)
Fát|ima (village,
  Portugal)
Fati|mid +s
Fati|mite +s
fat|ism (use
  fattism)
fat|ist +s (use
  fattist)
fat|less
fat|ling +s
fatly
fat|ness
fatso
  fat|soes
  (*offensive*)
fat|stock
fat|ten +s +ed
  +ing
fat|tily
fat|ti|ness
fat|tish
fat|tism
fat|tist +s
fatty
  fat|ties
  fat|tier
  fat|ti|est
fa|tu|ity
fatu|ous
fatu|ous|ly
fatu|ous|ness
fatwa +s
fau|bourg +s
fau|ces
fau|cet +s
fau|cial
Faulk|ner,
  Wil|liam

Faulk|ner (*cont.*)
  (American
  novelist)
fault +s +ed +ing
fault|er +s
  (accuser. ⚠ falter)
fault-finder +s
fault-finding
fault|ily
faulti|ness
fault|less
fault|less|ly
fault|less|ness
faulty
  fault|ier
  faulti|est
faun +s (deity.
  ⚠ fawn)
fauna
  fau|nas *or* fau|nae
  (animals. ⚠ fawner)
fau|nal
faun|ist +s
faun|is|tic
faun|is|tic|al
Faunt|leroy,
  (Lit|tle) Lord
  (boy hero of
  novel)
Fau|nus *Roman*
  Mythology
Fauré, Gab|riel
  (French
  composer)
Faust (astronomer
  and necromancer)
Faust|ian
faute de mieux
fau|teuil +s
fauve +s
fauv|ism
fauv|ist +s
faux (false. ⚠ foe)
faux pas
  plural faux pas
fave +s
fa|vela +s
favor *Am.* +s +ed
  +ing (*Br.* favour)
fa|vor|able *Am.* (*Br.*
  favourable)
fa|vor|able|ness
  Am. (*Br.*
  favourableness)
fa|vor|ably *Am.* (*Br.*
  favourably)
fa|vor|er *Am.* +s
  (*Br.* favourer)
fa|vor|ite *Am.* +s
  (*Br.* favourite)
fa|vor|it|ism *Am.*
  (*Br.* favouritism)

fa¦vour *Br.* +s +ed
+ing (*Am.* favor)
fa¦vour|able *Br.*
(*Am.* favorable)
fa¦vour|able|ness
Br. (*Am.*
favorableness)
fa¦vour|ably *Br.*
(*Am.* favorably)
fa¦vour|er *Br.* +s
(*Am.* favorer)
fa¦vour|ite *Br.* +s
(*Am.* favorite)
fa¦vour|it|ism *Br.*
(*Am.* favoritism)
Fawkes, Guy
(English arsonist)
fawn +s +ed +ing
(deer; brown;
behave servilely.
△ faun)
fawn¦er +s
(person who fawns.
△ fauna)
fawn|ing¦ly
fax
faxes
faxed
fax¦ing
Fay *also* **Faye**
(name)
fay +s (*literary* fairy.
△ fey)
Faye *also* **Fay**
(name)
fayre +s (*pseudo-
archaic* fête, sale;
food. △ fair, fare)
faze
fazes
fazed
faz¦ing
(disconcert.
△ phase)
fealty
feal|ties
fear +s +ed +ing
fear|ful
fear|ful¦ly
fear|ful|ness
fear|less
fear|less¦ly
fear|less|ness
fear|some
fear|some¦ly
fear|some|ness
feasi|bil|ity
feas|ible
feas|ibly
feast +s +ed +ing
feast day +s
feast¦er +s

feat +s
(achievement.
△ feet)
fea¦ther +s +ed
+ing
fea¦ther bed +s
noun
feather-bed
feather-beds
feather-bedded
feather-bedding
verb
feather-brain +s
feather-brained
fea¦ther edge +s
feather-edged
fea¦ther|head +s
fea¦theri|ness
fea¦ther|less
feather-light
fea¦ther stitch
noun
fea¦ther|weight +s
fea¦thery
fea|ture
fea|tures
fea|tured
fea|tur|ing
feature-length
adjective
fea|ture|less
feb¦ri|fugal
feb¦ri|fuge +s
fe|brile
fe|bril|ity
Feb¦ru|ary
Feb¦ru|ar|ies
fecal *Am.* (*Br.*
faecal)
feces *Am.* (*Br.*
faeces)
**Fech|ner, Gus¦tav
Theo|dor**
(German poet,
physicist, and
psychologist)
feck|less
feck|less¦ly
feck|less|ness
fecu|lence
fecu|lent
fec¦und
fe¦cund|abil|ity
fe¦cund|ate
fe¦cund|ates
fe¦cund|ated
fe¦cund|at|ing
fe¦cund|ation
fe¦cund|ity
Fed (Federal
Reserve Board)

fed +s (past tense
and past participle
of feed; FBI
agent)
fed|eral +s
fed|er|al|isa|tion
Br. (use
federalization)
fed|er|al|ise *Br.*
(use federalize)
fed|er|al|ises
fed|er|al|ised
fed|er|al|is|ing
fed|er|al|ism
fed|er|al|ist +s
fed|er|al|iza|tion
fed|er|al|ize
fed|er|al|izes
fed|er|al|ized
fed|er|al|iz|ing
fed|er|al¦ly
fed|er|ate
fed|er|ates
fed|er|ated
fed|er|at|ing
fed|er|ation +s
fed|er|ation|ist +s
fed|er|ative
fe|dora +s
fed up
fed-up *attributive*
fed-upness
fee
fees
fee'd
fee|ing
fee¦ble
fee¦bler
feeb|lest
feeble-minded
feeble-minded¦ly
feeble-
minded¦ness
feeble|ness
fee|blish
feebly
feed
feeds
fed
feed|ing
feed|able
feed-and-
expansion tank
+s
feed|back *noun*
feed¦er +s
feed|ing bot¦tle +s
feed|stock
feed|stuff +s
feel
feels

feel (*cont.*)
felt
feel|ing
feel¦er +s
feel-good *adjective*
feel|ing +s
feel|ing|less
feel|ing¦ly
fee-paying
feet (plural of foot.
△ feat)
feign +s +ed +ing
(pretend. △ fain,
fane)
fei¦joa +s
feint +s +ed +ing
(sham attack;
pretend; of ruled
lines. △ faint)
feis
feis|eanna
feist|ily
feisti|ness
feisty
feist|ier
feisti|est
fela|fel +s
felch|ing
feld|spar +s
feld|spath¦ic
feld|spath|oid +s
feli|cif¦ic
fe|lici|tate
fe|lici|tates
fe|lici|tated
fe|lici|tat|ing
fe|lici|ta¦tion +s
fe|lici|tous
fe|lici|tous¦ly
fe|lici|tous|ness
Fe|li¦city (name)
fe|li¦city
fe|li¦ci¦ties
(happiness)
fe|line +s
fe|lin|ity
Felix
Felix|stowe (port,
England)
fell +s +ed +ing
fel¦lah
fel|la¦hin
(Egyptian peasant.
△ feller)
fel¦lah +s (= fellow.
△ feller)
fel|late
fel|lates
fel|lated
fel|lat|ing
fel|la|tio
fel|la¦tor +s

fell¦er +s (person
who fells; also
= fellow. △ fellah)
Fel¦lini, Fe¦de¦rico
(Italian film
director)
fell¦mon¦ger +s
fel¦loe +s (wheel
rim)
fel¦low +s (man;
person)
fel¦low
  country¦man
  fel¦low
  country¦men
fel¦low feel¦ing
fel¦low¦ship +s
fellow-travel¦er
  Am. +s
fellow-travel¦ler
  Br. +s
fell walk¦er +s
fell walk¦ing
felly
  fel¦lies
felon +s
fe¦loni¦ous
fe¦loni¦ous¦ly
fel¦on¦ry
fel¦ony
  fel¦on¦ies
fell¦spar +s (use
feldspar)
fell¦spath¦ic (use
feldspathic)
fell¦spath¦oid +s
  (use feldspathoid)
felt +s +ed +ing
felt tip +s
felt-tipped
felty
fel¦ucca +s
fel¦wort +s
fe¦male +s
fe¦male¦ness
feme +s
feme co¦vert
  femes co¦vert
feme sole
  femes sole
fem¦inal
femi¦nal¦ity
femi¦neity
femi¦nine
femi¦nine¦ly
femi¦nine¦ness
femi¦nin¦ity
  femi¦nin¦ities
femi¦nisa¦tion *Br.*
  (use
  feminization)

femi¦nise *Br.* (use
  feminize)
femi¦nises
femi¦nised
femi¦nis¦ing
femi¦nism
femi¦nist +s
fe¦min¦ity
femi¦niza¦tion
femi¦nize
  femi¦nizes
  femi¦nized
  femi¦niz¦ing
femme +s
femme fa¦tale
  femmes fa¦tales
fem¦oral
femto¦meter *Am.*
  +s
femto¦metre *Br.* +s
femur
  fem¦ora *or*
  fe¦murs
fen +s (marsh)
fen
  plural fen
  (Chinese currency)
fen-berry
  fen-berries
fence
  fences
  fenced
  fen¦cing
fence¦less
fence post +s
fen¦cer +s
fen¦cible
fen¦cing +s
fend +s +ed +ing
Fen¦der, Leo
  (American guitar-
  maker)
fend¦er +s
Fen¦ella
fen¦es¦tella +s
fen¦es¦tra
  fen¦es¦trae
fen¦es¦trate
fen¦es¦trated
fen¦es¦tra¦tion
fen-fire
feng shui
Fe¦nian +s
Fe¦nian¦ism
fen¦land +s
fen¦man
  fen¦men
fen¦nec +s
fen¦nel (plant.
  △ phenyl)
Fenno¦scan¦dia
  (NW Europe)

fenny
fenu¦greek
feof¦fee +s
feoff¦ment +s
feof¦for +s
feral
fer de lance
  fers de lance
Fer¦di¦nand
  (Spanish king)
Fer¦gal
Fer¦gus
fer¦ial
Fer¦man¦agh
  (county, Northern
  Ireland)
Fer¦mat, Pierre de
  (French
  mathematician)
fer¦mata +s
fer¦ment +s +ed
  +ing
fer¦ment¦able
fer¦men¦ta¦tion +s
fer¦men¦ta¦tive
fer¦ment¦er +s
Fermi, En¦rico
  (Italian-born
  physicist)
fermi +s (unit)
fer¦mion +s
fer¦mium
fern
  plural fern *or* ferns
Fer¦nando Póo
  (former name of
  Bioko)
fern¦ery
  fern¦er¦ies
fern¦less
ferny
fer¦ocious
fer¦ocious¦ly
fer¦ocious¦ness
fer¦ocity
Fer¦ranti,
  Se¦bas¦tian Ziani
  de (English
  electrical
  engineer)
Fer¦rara (city and
  province, Italy)
Fer¦rari, Enzo
  (Italian racing-car
  designer and
  manufacturer)
fer¦rate +s
fer¦rel +s (use
  ferrule)
fer¦ret +s +ed +ing
fer¦ret¦er +s
fer¦rety

fer¦ri¦age +s
fer¦ric
Fer¦rier, Kath¦leen
  (English contralto)
ferri¦mag¦net¦ic
ferri¦mag¦net¦ism
Fer¦ris wheel +s
fer¦rite +s
fer¦rit¦ic
ferro¦con¦crete
ferro¦elec¦tric
ferro¦elec¦tri¦city
ferro¦mag¦net¦ic
ferro¦mag¦net¦ism
fer¦rous
fer¦ru¦gin¦ous
fer¦rule +s (metal
  cap. △ ferule)
ferry
  fer¦ries
  fer¦ried
  ferry¦ing
ferry boat +s
ferry¦man
  ferry¦men
fer¦tile
fer¦til¦is¦able *Br.*
  (use fertilizable)
fer¦til¦isa¦tion *Br.*
  +s (use
  fertilization)
fer¦til¦ise *Br.* (use
  fertilize)
fer¦til¦ises
fer¦til¦ised
fer¦til¦is¦ing
fer¦til¦iser *Br.* +s
  (use fertilizer)
fer¦til¦ity
fer¦til¦iz¦able
fer¦til¦iza¦tion +s
fer¦til¦ize
  fer¦til¦izes
  fer¦til¦ized
  fer¦til¦iz¦ing
fer¦til¦izer +s
fer¦ula +s
fer¦ule
  fer¦ules
  fer¦uled
  fer¦ul¦ing
  (cane. △ ferrule)
fer¦vency
fer¦vent
fer¦vent¦ly
fer¦vid
fer¦vid¦ly
fer¦vor *Am.*
fer¦vour *Br.*
Fès (use Fez)
Fes¦cen¦nine
fes¦cue +s

fess
fesses
fesse +s (use fess)
Fes|sen|den,
  Regi|nald
  Aub|rey
  (Canadian-born
  American
  physicist)
fes|tal
fes|tal|ly
fes|ter +s +ed +ing
fes|ti|val +s
fes|tive
fes|tive|ly
fes|tive|ness
fes|tiv|ity
  fes|tiv|ities
fes|toon +s +ed
  +ing
fes|toon|ery
Fest|schrift
  Fest|schrift|en or
  Fest|schrifts
feta (cheese. △ fetter)
fetal Am. (Br.
  foetal)
fetch
  fetches
  fetched
  fetch|ing
fetch|er +s
fetch|ing|ly
fête
  fêtes
  fêted
  fêt|ing
  (fair; festival;
  honour or
  entertain lavishly.
  △ fate)
fête cham|pêtre
  fêtes cham|pêtres
fête gal|ante
  fêtes gal|antes
feti|cidal Am. (Br.
  foeticidal)
feti|cide Am. (Br.
  foeticide)
fetid
fetid|ly
fetid|ness
fet|ish
  fet|ishes
fet|ish|ise Br. (use
  fetishize)
  fet|ish|ises
  fet|ish|ised
  fet|ish|is|ing
fet|ish|ism
fet|ish|ist +s
fet|ish|is|tic

fet|ish|ize
  fet|ish|izes
  fet|ish|ized
  fet|ish|iz|ing
fet|lock +s
fetor
fetta (cheese; use feta)
fet|ter +s +ed +ing
  (shackle)
fet|ter|lock +s
fet|tle
  fet|tles
  fet|tled
  fet|tling
fet|tler +s
fet|tuc|cine
fet|tu|cine (use
  fettuccine)
fetus Am.
  fetuses
  (Br. foetus)
feu +s +ed +ing
feud +s +ed +ing
feu|dal
feu|dal|isa|tion Br.
  (use
  feudalization)
feu|dal|ise Br. (use
  feudalize)
  feu|dal|ises
  feu|dal|ised
  feu|dal|is|ing
feu|dal|ism
feu|dal|ist +s
feu|dal|is|tic
feu|dal|ity
feu|dal|iza|tion
feu|dal|ize
  feu|dal|izes
  feu|dal|ized
  feu|dal|iz|ing
feu|dal|ly
feud|atory
  feud|ator|ies
feu de joie
  feux de joie
feud|ist +s
feuille|ton +s
fever +s +ed +ing
fever|few
fe|ver|ish
fe|ver|ish|ly
fe|ver|ish|ness
fe|ver|ous
few +er +est (not
  many. △ phew)
few|ness
fey (strange etc.
  △ fay)
Fey|deau, Georges
  (French
  playwright)

feyly
fey|ness
Feyn|man,
  Rich|ard
  (American
  physicist)
Feyn|man
  dia|gram +s
Fez (city, Morocco)
fez
  fezzes
  (hat)
fezzed
Ffes|tin|iog
  Rail|way (in
  Wales)
fi|acre +s
fi|ancé +s male
fi|an|cée +s female
fian|chetto
  fian|chet|toes
  fian|chet|toed
  fian|chetto|ing
Fianna Fáil (Irish
  political party)
fi|asco +s
fiat +s
fib
  fibs
  fibbed
  fib|bing
fib|ber +s
fiber Am. +s (Br.
  fibre)
fiber|board Am. +s
  (Br. fibreboard)
fibered Am. (Br.
  fibred)
fiber|fill Am. (Br.
  fibrefill)
fiber|glass Am. (Br.
  fibreglass)
fiber|less Am. (Br.
  fibreless)
fiber-optic Am.
  adjective (Br. fibre-
  optic)
fiber op|tics Am.
  noun (Br. fibre
  optics)
Fi|bo|nacci,
  Leo|nardo
  (Italian
  mathematician)
fibre Br. +s (Am.
  fiber)
fibre|board Br. +s
  (Am. fiberboard)
fibred Br. (Am.
  fibered)
fibre|fill Br. (Am.
  fiberfill)

fibre|glass Br. (Am.
  fiberglass)
fibre|less Br. (Am.
  fiberless)
fibre-optic Br.
  adjective (Am.
  fiber-optic)
fibre op|tics Br.
  noun (Am. fiber
  optics)
fib|ri|form
fi|bril +s
fi|bril|lar
fi|bril|lary
fib|ril|late
  fib|ril|lates
  fib|ril|lated
  fib|ril|lat|ing
fib|ril|la|tion +s
fi|brin
fi|brino|gen
fi|brin|oid
fibro +s
fibro|blast +s
fibro-cement
fi|broid +s
fi|broin
fi|broma
  fi|bro|mas or
  fi|bro|mata
fi|bro|sis
  fi|bro|ses
fi|bro|sit|ic
fi|bro|si|tis
fi|brot|ic
fi|brous
fi|brous|ly
fi|brous|ness
fib|ula
  fibu|lae or fibu|las
  noun
fibu|lar
  adjective
fiche
  plural fiche or
  fiches
Fichte, Jo|hann
  Gott|lieb
  (German
  philosopher)
fichu +s
fickle
fickle|ness
fickly
fic|tile
fic|tion +s
fic|tion|al
fic|tion|al|isa|tion
  Br. +s (use
  fictionalization)
fic|tion|al|ise Br.
  (use fictionalize)
  fic|tion|al|ises

fic|tion|al|ise
(*cont.*)
  fic|tion|al|ised
  fic|tion|al|is|ing
fic|tion|al|ity
fic|tion|al|iza|tion
+s
fic|tion|al|ize
  fic|tion|al|izes
  fic|tion|al|ized
  fic|tion|al|iz|ing
fic|tion|al|ly
fic|tion|ist +s
fic|ti|tious
fic|ti|tious|ly
fic|ti|tious|ness
fic|tive
fic|tive|ly
fic|tive|ness
ficus
  plural ficus *or*
  fi|cuses
fid +s
fid|dle
  fid|dles
  fid|dled
  fid|dling
fiddle-back +s
fiddle-de-dee
fiddle-faddle
  fiddle-faddles
  fiddle-faddled
  fiddle-faddling
fiddle-head +s
fid|dler +s
Fid|dler's Green
(sailor's Elysium)
fiddle|stick +s
fid|dly
  fid|dlier
  fid|dli|est
Fidei De|fen|sor
fide|ism
fide|ist +s
fide|is|tic
fi|del|ity
  fi|del|ities
fidget +s +ed +ing
fidgeti|ness
fidgety
Fido (fog dispersal
device; dog's
name)
fi|du|cial
fi|du|ci|al|ly
fi|du|ciary
  fi|du|ciar|ies
fidus Acha|tes
fie (*interjection*.
  △ phi)
fief +s
fief|dom +s

Field, John (Irish
composer and
pianist)
field +s +ed +ing
field-book +s
field-cornet
field day +s
field-effect
  tran|sis|tor +s
field|er +s
field|fare +s
field glasses
Field|ing, Henry
(English writer)
field mar|shal +s
field mouse
  field mice
field note +s
Fields, Gracie
(English singer)
Fields, W. C.
(American
comedian)
fields|man
  fields|men
field|stone +s
field|work
field|worker +s
fiend +s
fiend|ish
fiend|ish|ly
fiend|ish|ness
fiend|like
fierce
  fier|cer
  fier|cest
fierce|ly
fierce|ness
fieri fa|cias
fier|ily
fieri|ness
fiery
  fier|ier
  fieri|est
fi|esta +s
FIFA ('International
Football
Federation')
Fife (region,
Scotland)
fife (musical
instrument)
  fifes
  fifed
  fif|ing
fifer +s
fife-rail +s
FIFO (= first in, first
out)
fif|teen +s
fif|teenth +s
fifth +s

fifth col|umn
fifth col|umn|ist
+s
fifth-genera|tion
fifth|ly
Fifth-monarchy-
man
  Fifth-monarchy-
men
fif|ti|eth +s
fifty
  fif|ties
fifty-fifty
fifty-first, fifty-
second, etc.
fifty|fold
fifty-one, fifty-
two, etc.
fig
  figs
  figged
  fig|ging
fight
  fights
  fought
  fight|ing
fight|back +s *noun*
fight|er +s
fighter-bomber +s
fighting-top +s
fig leaf
  fig leaves
fig|ment +s
fig tree +s
fi|gura +s
fig|ural
fig|ur|ant +s male
fig|ur|ante +s
  (French, *female*)
fig|ur|ante
  fig|ur|anti
  (Italian, *male and
  female*)
fig|ur|ation +s
fig|ura|tive
fig|ura|tive|ly
fig|ura|tive|ness
fig|ure
  fig|ures
  fig|ured
  fig|ur|ing
fig|ure|head +s
fig|ure|less
fig|ure of eight
  fig|ures of eight
  noun
figure-of-eight
  attributive
fig|ure skat|er +s
fig|ure skat|ing
fig|ur|ine +s
fig|wort +s

Fiji
Fiji|an +s
fila|gree +s (use
filigree)
fila|greed (use
filigreed)
fila|ment +s
fila|men|tary
fila|ment|ed
fila|ment|ous
fil|aria
  fil|ariae
fil|ar|ial
fil|ar|ia|sis
fila|ture +s
fil|bert +s
filch
  filches
  filched
  filch|ing
filch|er +s
file
  files
  filed
  fil|ing
  (folder; line; tool.
  △ phial)
file|fish
  plural file|fish
filer +s (person or
thing that files.
  △ phyla)
file serv|er +s
filet +s (net.
  △ fillet)
filet mi|gnon +s
fil|ial
fili|al|ly
fili|ation +s
fili|beg +s
fili|bus|ter +s +ed
+ing
fili|bus|ter|er +s
fili|gree +s
fili|greed
fil|ing +s
fil|ing cabi|net +s
Filio|que
Fi|li|pina +s *female*
Fi|li|pino +s *male*
fill +s +ed +ing
fille de joie
  filles de joie
fill|er +s
fil|let +s +ed +ing
  (meat; strip; band.
  △ filet)
fil|let|er +s
fill|ing +s
fill|ing sta|tion +s
fil|lip +s +ed +ing
fil|lis

fil|lis|ter +s
Fill|more, Mil|lard
(American
president)
fill-up +s *noun*
filly
  fil|lies
film +s +ed +ing
film-goer +s
film-going
film|ic
film|ily
filmi|ness
film-maker +s
film-making
film noir
  films noirs
film|og|raphy
film|set
  film|sets
  film|set
  film|set|ting
  Printing
film set +s *Film-
making*
film|set|ter +s
film star +s
film|strip +s
filmy
  film|ier
  filmi|est
filo
Filo|fax
  Filo|faxes
  Propr.
filo|plume +s
fi|lo|selle
fils
fil|ter +s +ed +ing
  (remove
  impurities; device
  for doing this.
  △ philter, philtre)
fil|ter|able
filter-bed +s
filter-feeder +s
filter-feeding
filter-paper +s
fil|ter tip +s
filter-tipped
filth
filth|ily
filthi|ness
filthy
  filth|ier
  filthi|est
fil|trable
fil|trate
  fil|trates
  fil|trated
  fil|trat|ing
fil|tra|tion
fim|bri|ate

fim|bri|ated
fin
  fins
  finned
  fin|ning
  (part of fish etc.
  △ Finn)
fin|able
fin|agle
  fin|agles
  fin|agled
  fin|agl|ing
fin|agler +s
final +s
fi|nale +s
fi|nal|isa|tion *Br.*
  (use finalization)
fi|nal|ise *Br.* (use
  finalize)
  fi|nal|ises
  fi|nal|ised
  fi|nal|is|ing
fi|nal|ism
fi|nal|ist +s
fi|nal|is|tic
fi|nal|ity
  fi|nal|ities
fi|nal|iza|tion
fi|nal|ize
  fi|nal|izes
  fi|nal|ized
  fi|nal|iz|ing
fi|nal|ly
fi|nance
  fi|nances
  fi|nanced
  fi|nan|cing
fi|nan|cial +s
fi|nan|cial|ly
fi|nan|cier +s
fin-back +s
Fin|bar
finch
  finches
find
  finds
  found
  find|ing
  (discover.
  △ fined)
find|able
find|er +s
fin de siècle
Find|horn
  (community,
  Scotland)
find|ing +s
find-spot +s
fine
  fines
  fined
  fin|ing

fine (*cont.*)
  finer
  fin|est
fine arts
fine-draw
  fine-draws
  fine-drew
  fine-drawing
  fine-drawn
Fine Gael (Irish
  political party)
fine-grained
fine|ly
fine|ness
fine print
fin|ery
  fin|eries
fines herbes
fine-spun
fi|nesse
  fi|nesses
  fi|nessed
  fi|ness|ing
fine-tooth comb
  +s
fine-tune
  fine-tunes
  fine-tuned
  fine-tuning
Fingal (character in
  poem)
Fingal's Cave (in
  Hebrides)
fin|ger +s +ed +ing
fin|ger|board +s
fin|ger bone +s
fin|ger bowl +s
finger-dry
  finger-dries
  finger-dried
  finger-drying
fin|ger|ing +s
fin|ger|less
finger-licking
fin|ger|ling
fin|ger|mark +s
fin|ger|nail +s
finger-paint +s
  +ed +ing
fin|ger|pick +s +ed
  +ing
finger-plate +s
finger-post +s
fin|ger|print +s
  +ed +ing
finger-stall +s
fin|ger|tip +s
fin|ial +s
fini|cal
fini|cal|ity
fini|cal|ly
fini|cal|ness

fin|icki|ness
fin|ick|ing
fin|icky
finis
fin|ish
  fin|ishes
  fin|ished
  fin|ish|ing
  (end. △ Finnish)
fin|ish|er +s
fin|ish|ing school
  +s
Fin|is|terre
  (shipping area off
  Spain)
Fin|is|terre, Cape
  (in Spain)
fi|nite
fi|nite|ly
fi|nite|ness
fi|nit|ism
fi|nit|ist +s
fini|tude
fink +s +ed +ing
Fin|land
Fin|land|isa|tion
  Br. (use
  Finlandization)
Fin|land|ise *Br.*
  (use Finlandize)
  Fin|land|ises
  Fin|land|ised
  Fin|land|is|ing
Fin|land|iza|tion
Fin|land|ize
  Fin|land|izes
  Fin|land|ized
  Fin|land|iz|ing
fin|less
Finn +s (person
  from Finland;
  name. △ fin)
fin|nan had|dock
  plural fin|nan
  had|dock
finned
Fin|ne|gans Wake
  (novel)
fin|ner +s
fin|nesko
  plural fin|nesko
Finn|ic
Finn|ish (of
  Finland. △ finish)
Finn Mac|Cool
  Irish Mythology
Finno-Ugrian
Finno-Ugric
finny
fino +s
Fiona
fiord +s (use fjord)

fi¦ori¦tura
  fi¦ori¦ture
fip¦ple +s
fip¦ple flute +s
fir +s (tree. △ fur)
fir cone +s
fire
  fires
  fired
  fir¦ing
fire alarm +s
fire¦arm +s
fire¦back +s
fire¦ball +s
fire-balloon +s
fire-bird +s
fire blight
fire¦bomb +s +ed
  +ing
fire¦box
  fire¦boxes
fire¦brand +s
fire¦break +s
fire-breath¦ing
fire¦brick +s
fire bri¦gade +s
fire¦bug +s
fire¦clay
fire-control
fire¦crack¦er +s
fire¦crest +s
fire¦damp
fire¦dog +s
fire-drake +s
fire drill +s
fire-eater +s
fire en¦gine +s
fire es¦cape +s
fire ex¦tin¦guish¦er
  +s
fire¦fight +s
fire¦fight¦er +s
fire-fighting
fire¦fly
  fire¦flies
fire¦guard +s
fire hose +s
fire¦house +s
fire-irons
fire¦less
fire¦light
fire¦light¦er +s
fire¦lock +s
fire¦man
  fire¦men
fire-office +s
fire-opal +s
fire¦place +s
fire¦plug +s
fire¦power
fire prac¦tice +s
fire¦proof

firer +s
fire-raiser +s
fire-raising
fire-resist¦ant
fire screen +s
fire¦ship +s
fire¦side +s
fire-step +s
fire-stone
fire¦storm +s
fire¦thorn +s
fire-tongs
fire trap +s
fire-walker +s
fire-walking
fire-watcher +s
fire-watching
fire¦water
fire¦weed +s
fire¦woman
  fire¦women
fire¦wood
fire¦work +s
fir¦ing +s
fir¦ing line +s
fir¦ing party
  fir¦ing par¦ties
fir¦ing squad +s
firing-step +s
fir¦kin +s
firm +s +ed +ing
  +er +est
firma¦ment +s
firma¦men¦tal
fir¦man +s
firm¦ly
firm¦ness
firm¦ware
firry (of fir trees.
  △ furry)
first +s
first aid noun
first-aid attributive
first aider +s
first-born +s
first-class adjective
  and adverb
first-day cover +s
first-degree
  adjective
first-foot +s +ed
  +ing
first-fruit +s
first-hand adjective
  and adverb
first¦ling +s
first¦ly
first name +s
first-nighter +s
first-past-the-post
  attributive
first-rate adjective

first-strike
  attributive
first-time attributive
firth +s
Firth of Forth
  (estuary,
  Scotland)
Firth of Tay
  (estuary,
  Scotland)
fir tree +s
fisc +s (in ancient
  Rome. △ fisk)
fis¦cal +s
fis¦cal¦ity
fis¦cal¦ly
Fisch¦er, Bobby
  (American chess
  player)
**Fisch¦er, Emil
  Her¦mann**
  (German chemist)
Fisch¦er, Hans
  (German chemist)
**Fischer-Dieskau,
  Diet¦rich**
  (German baritone)
Fish, the also the
  Fishes
  (constellation;
  sign of zodiac)
fish
  plural fish or
  fishes
  noun
fish
  fishes
  fished
  fish¦ing
  verb
fish¦able
fish and chips
fish-bolt +s
fish¦bowl +s
fish cake +s
Fish¦er (shipping
  area, North Sea)
Fish¦er, Geof¦frey
  (English
  archbishop, died
  1972)
**Fish¦er, Ron¦ald
  Ayl¦mer** (English
  statistician)
Fish¦er, St John
  (English
  churchman, died
  1535)
fish¦er +s (person
  who fishes.
  △ fissure)
fish¦er¦folk

fish¦er¦man
  fish¦er¦men
fish¦er¦woman
  fish¦er¦women
fish¦ery
  fish¦er¦ies
fish-eye +s (lens)
fish farm +s
fish fin¦ger +s
fish-glue
fish-hawk +s
fish-hook +s
fish¦ily
fishi¦ness
fish¦ing boat +s
fishing-fly
  fishing-flies
fish¦ing ground +s
fish¦ing line +s
fish¦ing net +s
fish¦ing rod +s
fish¦ing tackle
fish¦ing ves¦sel +s
fish ket¦tle +s
fish-knife
  fish-knives
fish¦like
fish¦meal
fish¦mon¦ger +s
fish¦net +s
fish-plate +s
fish pond +s
fish¦pot +s
fish slice +s
fish¦tail +s +ed
  +ing
fish¦wife
  fish¦wives
fishy
  fish¦ier
  fishi¦est
fisk +s (in
  Scotland. △ fisc)
fis¦sile
fis¦sil¦ity
fis¦sion +s +ed
  +ing
fis¦sion¦able
fis¦si¦par¦ity
fis¦si¦par¦ous
fis¦si¦par¦ous¦ly
fis¦si¦par¦ous¦ness
fis¦sure
  fis¦sures
  fis¦sured
  fis¦sur¦ing
  (crack. △ fisher)
fist +s +ed +ing
fist fight +s
fist¦ful +s
fist¦ic
fist¦ic¦al
fisti¦cuffs

fis|tula +s

fis|tu|lar

fis|tu|lous

fit

   fits

   fit|ted

   fit|ting

   fit|ter

   fit|test

fitch

   fitches

fit|chew +s

fit|ful

fit|ful|ly

fit|ful|ness

fitly

fit|ment +s

fit|ness

   fit|nesses

fit|ter +s

fit|ting +s

fit|ting|ly

fit|ting|ness

fit|ting shop +s

Fit|ti|paldi,

   Emer|son

   (Brazilian racing

   driver)

fit-up +s noun

Fitz|Gerald,

   George Fran|cis

   (Irish physicist)

Fitz|ger|ald,

   Ed|ward (English

   scholar and poet)

Fitz|ger|ald, Ella

   (American jazz

   singer)

Fitz|ger|ald, Scott

   and Zelda

   (American

   writers)

Fitz|Gerald

   con|trac|tion

FitzGerald–Lorentz

   con|trac|tion

Fitz|wil|liam

   Mu|seum (in

   Cambridge,

   England)

Fiume (Italian

   name for Rijeka)

five +s

five-a-side +s

five-corner +s

five-eighth +s

five-finger

   exer|cise +s

five|fold

five-iron +s

five o'clock

   shadow +s

five|pence +s

five|penny

   five|pen|nies

fiver +s

five-star *attributive*

five|stones

five-year plan +s

fix

   fixes

   fixed

   fix|ing

fix|able

fix|ate

   fix|ates

   fix|ated

   fix|at|ing

fix|ation +s

fixa|tive +s

fixed-doh

fix|ed|ly

fix|ed|ness

fixer +s

fix|ing +s

fix|ity

   fix|ities

fix|ture +s

fiz|gig +s

fizz

   fizzes

   fizzed

   fizz|ing

   (effervesce; hiss.

   △ phiz)

fizz|er +s

fizz|ily

fizzi|ness

fiz|zle

   fiz|zles

   fiz|zled

   fiz|zling

fizzy

   fizz|ier

   fizzi|est

fjord +s

flab

flab|ber|gast +s

   +ed +ing

flab|bi|ly

flab|bi|ness

flabby

   flab|bier

   flab|bi|est

flac|cid

flac|cid|ity

flac|cid|ly

flack +s (publicity

   agent. △ flak)

flag

   flags

   flagged

   flag|ging

flag-boat +s

flag-captain +s

Flag Day (14 June

   in USA)

flag day +s (money-

   raising day)

fla|gel|lant +s

fla|gel|lar

fla|gel|late

   fla|gel|lates

   fla|gel|lated

   fla|gel|lat|ing

fla|gel|la|tion +s

fla|gel|la|tor +s

fla|gel|la|tory

fla|gel|li|form

fla|gel|lum

   fla|gella

fla|geo|let +s

flag-feather +s

flag|ger +s

fla|gi|tious

fla|gi|tious|ly

fla|gi|tious|ness

flag-lieuten|ant +s

flag-list +s

flag|man

   flag|men

flag-officer +s

flagon +s

flag|pole +s

fla|grancy

flag-rank +s

fla|grant

fla|grante (in 'in

   flagrante delicto')

fla|grant|ly

flag|ship +s

flag|staff +s

flag-station +s

flag|stone +s

flag|stoned

flag-wagging

flag-waver +s

flag-waving

flail +s +ed +ing

flair +s (instinct;

   talent. △ flare)

flak (anti-aircraft

   fire; criticism.

   △ flack)

flake

   flakes

   flaked

   flak|ing

flaki|ly

flaki|ness

flak jacket +s

flaky

   flaki|er

   flaki|est

flambé +s +ed

   +ing

flam|beau

   flam|beaus or

   flam|beaux

Flam|bor|ough

   Head

   (promontory,

   England)

flam|boy|ance

flam|boy|ancy

flam|boy|ant

flam|boy|ant|ly

flame

   flames

   flamed

   flam|ing

flame gun +s

flame|less

flame|like

fla|men

   fla|mens or

   fla|mi|nes

fla|menco +s

flame|out +s

flame|proof

flame-thrower +s

flame tree +s

fla|mingo +s

flam|ma|bil|ity

flam|mable

Flam|steed, John

   (English

   astronomer)

flamy

   flami|er

   flami|est

flan +s

flanch

   flanches

   flanched

   flanch|ing

Flan|ders (former

   principality, NW

   Europe)

flân|erie

flân|eur +s

flange

   flanges

   flanged

   flan|ging

flange|less

flank +s +ed +ing

flank|er +s

flan|nel

   flan|nels

   flan|nelled *Br.*

   flan|neled *Am.*

   flan|nel|ling *Br.*

   flan|nel|ing *Am.*

flan|nel|board +s

flan|nel|ette

flan|nel|graph +s

flan|nel|ly

flannel-mouth +s
flap
  flaps
  flapped
  flap|ping
flap|doo|dle
flap|jack +s
flap|per +s
flappy
  flap|pier
  flap|pi|est
flare
  flares
  flared
  flar|ing
  (widen; widening;
  flame. △ flair)
flare-path +s
flare-up +s noun
flash
  flashes
  flashed
  flash|ing
flash|back +s
flash-board +s
flash|bulb +s
flash burn +s
flash|card +s
flash-cube +s
flash|er +s
flash flood +s
flash|gun +s
flash|ily
flashi|ness
flash|ing +s
flash|ing point +s
flash lamp +s
flash|light +s
flash-over +s noun
flash|point +s
flashy
  flash|ier
  flashi|est
flask +s
flat
  flats
  flat|ted
  flat|ting
  flat|ter
  flat|test
flat-bottomed
flat|car +s
flat-chested
flat|fish
  plural flat|fish
flat|foot
  flat|feet
flat-footed
flat-footed|ly
flat-footed|ness
flat-four
flat-head +s

flat iron +s
flat|let +s
flat|ly
flat|mate +s
flat|ness
flat out
flat-pack +s +ed
  +ing
flat race +s
flat ra|cing
flat rate +s
flat|ten +s +ed
  +ing
flat|ten|er +s
flat|ter +s +ed
  +ing
flat|ter|er +s
flat|ter|ing|ly
flat|tery
  flat|ter|ies
flat|tie +s
flat|tish
flat-top +s
flatu|lence
flatu|lency
flatu|lent
flatu|lent|ly
fla|tus
flat|ware
flat|worm +s
Flau|bert,
  Gus|tave (French
  novelist)
flaunch
  flaunches
  flaunched
  flaunch|ing
flaunt +s +ed +ing
flaunt|er +s
flaunty
flaut|ist +s
fla|ves|cent
Fla|via
Fla|vian +s
fla|vin (yellow dye)
fla|vine (antiseptic)
fla|vone +s
flavo|pro|tein +s
fla|vor Am. +s +ed
  +ing (Br. flavour)
fla|vor|ful Am. (Br.
  flavourful)
fla|vor|ing Am. +s
  (Br. flavouring)
fla|vor|less Am.
  (Br. flavourless)
fla|vor|ous Am.
fla|vor|some Am.
  (Br. flavoursome)
fla|vour Br. +s +ed
  +ing (Am. flavor)

fla|vour|ful Br.
  (Am. flavorful)
fla|vour|ing Br. +s
  (Am. flavoring)
fla|vour|less Br.
  (Am. flavorless)
fla|vour|some Br.
  (Am. flavorsome)
flaw +s +ed +ing
  (imperfection;
  squall. △ floor)
flaw|less
flaw|less|ly
flaw|less|ness
flax
  flaxes
flax|en
flax-lily
  flax-lilies
Flax|man, John
  (English sculptor)
flax|seed
flay +s +ed +ing
F-layer
flay|er +s
flea +s (insect.
  △ flee)
flea|bag +s
flea|bane
flea bite +s
flea-bitten
flea-bug +s
flea-circus
  flea-circuses
flea col|lar +s
flea mar|ket +s
flea|pit +s
flea|wort
flèche +s
fleck +s +ed +ing
Fleck|er, James
  Elroy (English
  poet)
flec|tion +s (use
  flexion)
flec|tion|al (use
  flexional)
flec|tion|less (use
  flexionless)
fled
fledge
  fledges
  fledged
  fledg|ing
fledge|ling +s (use
  fledgling)
fledg|ling +s
flee
  flees
  fled
  flee|ing
  (run away. △ flea)

fleece
  fleeces
  fleeced
  flee|cing
fleece|able
fleece-picker +s
flee|cily
fleeci|ness
fleecy
  flee|cier
  flee|ci|est
fleer +s +ed +ing
fleet +s +ed +ing
  +er +est
fleet-footed
fleet|ing
fleet|ing|ly
fleet|ly
fleet|ness
Fleet Street (in
  London)
Flem|ing +s
  (member of
  Flemish-speaking
  people)
Flem|ing,
  Alex|an|der
  (Scottish doctor
  and scientist)
Flem|ing, Ian
  (English writer)
Flem|ing, John
  Am|brose
  (English engineer)
Flem|ish
flense
  flenses
  flensed
  flen|sing
flesh
  fleshes
  fleshed
  flesh|ing
flesh color Am.
flesh-colored Am.
flesh col|our Br.
flesh-coloured Br.
flesh|er +s
flesh-fly
  flesh-flies
fleshi|ness
flesh|ings
flesh|less
flesh|li|ness
flesh|ly
flesh|pots
flesh wound +s
fleshy
  flesh|ier
  fleshi|est

Fletch¦er, John
(English
dramatist)
fletch¦er +s
Fleur
fleur-de-lis
　plural fleur-de-lis
fleur-de-lys (use
　fleur-de-lis)
　plural fleur-de-lys
fleuret +s
fleuron +s
fleury
Flevo¦land
　(province, the
　Netherlands)
flew (past tense of
　fly. △ flu, flue)
flews (lips of
　bloodhound)
flex
　flexes
　flexed
　flex¦ing
flexi¦bil¦ity
flex¦ible
flex¦ibly
flex¦ile
flex¦il¦ity
flex¦ion +s
flex¦ion¦al
flex¦ion¦less
flexi¦time
flexo¦graph¦ic
flex¦og¦raphy
flex¦or +s
flexu¦os¦ity
flexu¦ous
flexu¦ous¦ly
flex¦ural
flex¦ure +s
flib¦ber¦ti¦gib¦bet
　+s
flick +s +ed +ing
flicker +s +ed +ing
flick¦er¦ing +s
flick knife
　flick knives
flier +s (use flyer)
flight +s +ed +ing
　(act or manner of
　flying; retreat;
　shoot wildfowl etc.
　△ flyting)
flight bag +s
flight con¦trol
flight deck +s
flight fea¦ther +s
flight¦ily
flighti¦ness
flight¦less

flight lieu¦ten¦ant
　+s
flight of¦ficer +s
flight path +s
flight plan +s
flight re¦cord¦er +s
flight ser¦geant +s
flight-test +s +ed
　+ing
flighty
　flight¦ier
　flighti¦est
flim¦flam
　flim¦flams
　flim¦flammed
　flim¦flam¦ming
flim¦flam¦mer +s
flim¦flam¦mery
flim¦sily
flim¦si¦ness
flimsy
　flim¦sies
　flim¦sier
　flim¦si¦est
finch
　finches
　finched
　finch¦ing
finch¦er +s
finch¦ing¦ly
Flin¦ders,
　Mat¦thew
　(English explorer)
flin¦ders
Flin¦ders Is¦land
　(off Australia)
fling
　flings
　flung
　fling¦ing
fling¦er +s
flint +s
flint¦ily
flinti¦ness
flint¦lock +s
Flint¦shire (former
　county, Wales)
flinty
　flint¦ier
　flinti¦est
flip
　flips
　flipped
　flip¦ping
flip chart +s
flip-flop
　flip-flops
　flip-flopped
　flip-flopping
flip¦pancy
flip¦pant
flip¦pant¦ly

flip¦per +s
flip side +s
flirt +s +ed +ing
flir¦ta¦tion +s
flir¦ta¦tious
flir¦ta¦tious¦ly
flir¦ta¦tious¦ness
flirty
　flirt¦ier
　flirti¦est
flit
　flits
　flit¦ted
　flit¦ting
flitch
　flitches
flitch beam +s
flit¦ter +s +ed +ing
flitter-mouse
　flitter-mice
fliv¦ver +s
flix¦weed
Flo (name)
float +s +ed +ing
float¦abil¦ity
float¦able
float¦age
float¦ation +s (use
　flotation)
float-board +s
floatel +s
float¦er +s
float¦ing¦ly
float¦plane +s
float-stone
floaty
floc +s (mass of
　fine particles.
　△ flock)
floc¦cu¦late
　floc¦cu¦lates
　floc¦cu¦lated
　floc¦cu¦lat¦ing
floc¦cu¦la¦tion +s
floc¦cule +s
floc¦cu¦lence
floc¦cu¦lent
floc¦cu¦lus
　floc¦culi
floc¦cus
　flocci
flock +s +ed +ing
　(group of birds or
　animals; go in a
　crowd; wallpaper.
　△ floc)
flock paper +s
flocky
　flock¦ier
　flocki¦est

Flod¦den (Field)
　(battle site,
　England)
floe +s (mass of ice.
　△ flow)
Flo¦ella
flog
　flogs
　flogged
　flog¦ging
flog¦ger +s
flong
Flood, the *Bible*
flood +s +ed +ing
flood¦gate +s
flood¦ing +s
flood¦light
　flood¦lights
　flood¦lit
　flood¦light¦ing
flood plain +s
flood tide +s
flood water +s
floor +s +ed +ing
　(of room; storey;
　knock down.
　△ flaw)
floor¦board +s
floor¦cloth +s
floor cover¦ing +s
floor¦ing +s
floor lamp +s
floor lead¦er +s
floor-length
floor¦less
floor man¦ager +s
floor plan +s
floor pol¦ish
　floor pol¦ishes
floor show +s
floor¦walk¦er +s
floo¦zie +s
floozy (use floozie)
　floo¦zies
flop
　flops
　flopped
　flop¦ping
flop¦house +s
flop¦pily
flop¦pi¦ness
floppy
　flop¦pies
　flop¦pier
　flop¦pi¦est
flop¦tic¦al *Propr.*
Flora (*Roman
　Mythology*; name)
flora
　floras *or* florae
floral
flor¦al¦ly

flor|eat
Flor|ence (city,
Italy; name)
Flor|en|tine +s
Flores (island,
Indonesia)
flor|es|cence
floret +s
Florey, How|ard
Wal|ter
(Australian
pathologist)
Flor|ian|ópo|lis
(city, Brazil)
flori|ate
flori|ates
flori|ated
flori|at|ing
flori|bunda +s
flori|cul|tural
flori|cul|ture
flori|cul|tur|ist +s
florid
Flor|ida (state,
USA)
Flor|id|ian +s
flor|id|ity
flor|id|ly
flor|id|ness
flor|ifer|ous
flori|le|gium
flori|legia
florin +s
Florio, John
(English scholar)
flor|ist +s
flor|is|tic
flor|is|tic|al|ly
flor|is|tics
flor|is|try
flor|uit
flory
flos|cu|lar
flos|cu|lous
floss
flosses
flossed
floss|ing
flossy
floss|ier
flossi|est
flo|ta|tion +s
flo|tilla +s
flot|sam
flounce
flounces
flounced
floun|cing
floun|der +s +ed
+ing
floun|der|er +s

flour +s +ed +ing
(grain meal.
△**flower**)
flouri|ness (state of
being floury.
△**floweriness**)
flour|ish
flour|ishes
flour|ished
flour|ish|ing
flour|ish|er +s
flour|ishy
floury
flour|ier
flouri|est
(like flour.
△**flowery**)
flout +s +ed +ing
flow +s +ed +ing
(move along etc.
△**floe**)
flow chart +s
flower +s +ed +ing
(plant. △**flour**)
flower bed +s
flower|er +s
flow|eret +s
flower girl +s
flower head +s
flow|eri|ness (state
of being flowery.
△**flouriness**)
flower|ing +s
flower|less
flower|like
flower|pot +s
flower show +s
flowery
flower|ier
floweri|est
(having flowers;
ornate. △**floury**)
flow|ing|ly
flow|meter +s
flown
flow-on +s noun
flow|sheet +s
flow|stone +s
Floyd
flu +s (illness.
△**flew**, **flue**)
flub
flubs
flubbed
flub|bing
fluc|tu|ate
fluc|tu|ates
fluc|tu|ated
fluc|tu|at|ing
fluc|tu|ation +s
flue +s (smoke
duct. △**flew**, **flu**)

flue-cure
flue-cures
flue-cured
flue-curing
flu|ence
flu|ency
flu|ent
flu|ent|ly
flue pipe +s
fluff +s +ed +ing
fluf|fily
fluf|fi|ness
fluffy
fluff|ier
fluffi|est
flu|gel|horn +s
fluid +s
fluid drachm Br.
+s (Am. fluidram)
flu|id|ic
flu|id|ics
flu|id|ify
flu|idi|fies
flu|idi|fied
flu|idi|fy|ing
flu|idi|sa|tion Br.
(use fluidization)
flu|id|ise Br. (use
fluidize)
flu|id|ises
flu|id|ised
flu|id|is|ing
flu|id|ity
flu|id|iza|tion
flu|id|ize
flu|id|izes
flu|id|ized
flu|id|iz|ing
flu|id|ly
flu|id|ness
flu|id|ounce Am.
+s
fluid ounce Br. +s
flui|dram Am. +s
(Br. fluid drachm)
fluke
flukes
fluked
fluk|ing
fluki|ly
fluki|ness
fluky
fluki|er
fluki|est
flume
flumes
flumed
flum|ing
flum|mery
flum|mer|ies
flum|mox
flum|moxes

flum|mox (cont.)
flum|moxed
flum|mox|ing
flump +s +ed +ing
flung
flunk +s +ed +ing
flun|key +s
flun|key|ism
flunky (use
flunkey)
flun|kies
fluor|esce
fluor|esces
fluor|esced
fluor|es|cing
fluor|es|cein
fluor|es|cence
fluor|es|cent
fluorid|ate
fluorid|ates
fluorid|ated
fluorid|at|ing
fluorid|ation
fluor|ide +s
fluor|id|isa|tion Br.
(use
fluoridization)
fluor|id|iza|tion
fluorin|ate
fluorin|ates
fluorin|ated
fluorin|at|ing
fluorin|ation
fluor|ine
fluor|ite +s
fluoro|car|bon +s
fluoro|scope +s
fluor|osis
fluor|spar +s
flurry
flur|ries
flur|ried
flurry|ing
flush
flushes
flushed
flush|ing
flush|er +s
Flush|ing (English
name for
Vlissingen)
flush|ness
flus|ter +s +ed
+ing
flute
flutes
fluted
flut|ing
flute|like
flut|ist +s
flut|ter +s +ed
+ing

flut|ter|er +s
flut|tery
fluty
  fluti|er
  fluti|est
flu|vial
flu|via|tile
flu|vio|gla|cial
flu|vi|om|eter +s
flux
  fluxes
  fluxed
  flux|ing
flux|ion +s
flux|ion|al
flux|ion|ary
fly
  flies
  flew
  fly|ing
  flown
  (insect; move
  through air; flap;
  scenery; part of
  clockwork)
fly
  flys *or* flies
  (carriage)
fly +er +est
  (clever)
fly|able
fly|away *attributive*
fly-blow
fly|blown
fly but|ton +s
fly-by +s *noun*
fly-by-night +s
fly-by-wire
fly|catch|er +s
fly-drive
flyer +s
fly-fish
  fly-fishes
  fly-fished
  fly-fishing
fly-half
  fly-halves
fly|ing boat +s
fly|ing fish
  plural fly|ing fish
fly|leaf
  fly|leaves
fly|ness
Flynn, Errol
  (American actor)
fly|over +s *noun*
fly-paper +s
fly-past +s *noun*
fly-pitcher +s
fly-pitching
fly-post +s +ed
  +ing

fly|sheet +s
flyt|ing +s
  (contention.
  △ flighting)
fly-tip
  fly-tips
  fly-tipped
  fly-tipping
fly-tipper +s
fly|trap +s
fly|way +s
fly|weight +s
fly|wheel +s
f-number +s
Fo, Dario (Italian
  playwright)
foal +s +ed +ing
foam +s +ed +ing
foam|less
foam rub|ber
foamy
  foam|ier
  foami|est
fob
  fobs
  fobbed
  fob|bing
fo|cac|cia
focal
fo|cal|isa|tion *Br.*
  (use focalization)
fo|cal|ise *Br.* (use
  focalize)
  fo|cal|ises
  fo|cal|ised
  fo|cal|is|ing
fo|cal|iza|tion
fo|cal|ize
  fo|cal|izes
  fo|cal|ized
  fo|cal|iz|ing
Foch, Fer|di|nand
  (French general)
fo'c'sle +s
  (= forecastle)
focus
  fo|cuses *or* foci
  noun
focus
  fo|cuses *or*
  fo|cusses
  fo|cused *or*
  fo|cussed
  fo|cus|ing *or*
  fo|cus|sing
  verb
fo|cus|er +s
fod|der +s +ed
  +ing
foe +s (enemy.
  △ faux)
foehn +s (use föhn)

foe|man
  foe|men
foe|tal *Br.* (*Am.*
  fetal)
foeti|cidal *Br.* (*Am.*
  feticidal)
foeti|cide *Br.* (*Am.*
  feticide)
foe|tid (use fetid)
foe|tus *Br.*
  foe|tuses
  (*Am.* fetus)
fog
  fogs
  fogged
  fog|ging
fog bank +s
fog|bound
fog-bow +s
fogey +s
fogey|dom
fogey|ish
Fo|ggia (town,
  Italy)
fog|gily
fog|gi|ness
foggy
  fog|gier
  fog|gi|est
fog|horn +s
fog lamp +s
fog|light +s
fog sig|nal +s
fogy (use fogey)
  fo|gies
fogy|dom (use
  fogeydom)
fogy|ish (use
  fogeyish)
föhn +s
foi|ble +s
foie gras
foil +s +ed +ing
foil|ist +s
foist +s +ed +ing
Fo|kine, Mi|chel
  (Russian-born
  choreographer)
Fok|ker, An|thony
  Her|man Ger|ard
  (Dutch-born
  American aircraft
  designer)
fola|cin
fold +s +ed +ing
fold|able
fold|away *adjective*
fold|back +s
  attributive and
  noun
fold|boat +s
fold|er +s

fol|de|rol +s
fold-out *adjective*
fold-up *adjective*
fo|li|aceous
fo|li|age
fo|liar
fo|li|ate
  fo|li|ates
  fo|li|ated
  fo|li|at|ing
fo|li|ation
folic
Folies-Bergère
folio +s
fo|li|ole +s
fo|li|ose
fo|liot +s
folk
  plural folk *or* folks
folk dance +s
folk dan|cer +s
folk dan|cing
Folke|stone (port,
  England)
folk hero
  folk heroes
folkie +s (person.
  △ folky)
folki|ness
folk|ish
folk|lore
folk|lor|ic
folk|lor|ist +s
folk|lor|is|tic
folk music
folk rock
folk|si|ness
folk sing|er +s
folk song +s
folksy
  folks|ier
  folksi|est
folk tale +s
folk|ways
folk|weave
folk wis|dom
folky
  folk|ier
  folki|est
  (*adjective*.
  △ folkie)
fol|licle +s
fol|licu|lar
fol|licu|late
fol|licu|lated
fol|low +s +ed
  +ing
fol|low|er +s
fol|low|ing +s
follow-on +s *noun*
follow-through
  noun

follow-up+s *noun*

folly
fol|lies
Fol|som
(archaeological
site, USA)
Fom|al|haut(star)
fo|ment+s +ed
+ing
fo|men|ta|tion
fo|ment|er+s
Fon
plural Fon or Fons
fond+er +est
Fonda, Henry,
Jane, Peter, and
Bridget
(American actors)
fon|dant+s
fon|dle
fon|dles
fon|dled
fond|ling
fond|ler+s
fond|ly
fond|ness
fon|due+s
font+s
Fon|taine|bleau
(town and palace,
France)
fon|tal
fon|ta|nel *Am.* +s
fon|ta|nelle *Br.* +s
Fon|teyn, Mar|got
(British ballet
dancer)
Foo|chow
(= Fuzhou)
food+s
food chain+s
foodie+s
food poi|son|ing
food pro|ces|sor
+s
food|stuff+s
fool+s +ed +ing
fool|ery
fool|er|ies
fool|har|dily
fool|hardi|ness
fool|hardy
fool|ish
fool|ish|ly
fool|ish|ness
fool|proof
fools|cap
fool's er|rand+s
fool's gold
fool's mate
fool's para|dise
fool's pars|ley

foot
feet
noun
foot+s +ed +ing
verb
foot|age
foot-and-mouth
(disease)
foot|ball+s +ed
+ing
foot|ball|er+s
foot|bath+s
foot|bed+s
foot|board+s
foot|brake+s
foot|bridge+s
foot|er+s
foot|fall+s
foot-fault+s +ed
+ing
foot|hill+s
foot|hold+s
footie(use footy)
foot|ing+s
foo|tle
foo|tles
foo|tled
foot|ling
foot|less
foot|lights
foot|loose
foot|man
foot|men
foot|mark+s
foot|note+s
foot|pad+s
foot|path+s
foot pedal+s
foot|plate+s
foot-pound+s
foot-pound-
second
foot|print+s
foot|rest+s
foot-rot
foot-rule+s
Foot|sie *Stock
Exchange*
foot|sie(amorous
play with feet)
footsie-footsie
foot|slog
foot|slogs
foot|slogged
foot|slog|ging
foot|slog|ger+s
foot sol|dier+s
foot|sore
foot|stalk+s
foot|step+s
foot|stool+s
foot|strap+s

foot|sure
foot-tapping
foot|way+s
foot|wear
foot|well+s
foot|work
footy
foo yong+s
fop+s
fop|pery
fop|per|ies
fop|pish
fop|pish|ly
fop|pish|ness
for (preposition and
conjunction.
△ fore four)
for|age
for|ages
for|aged
for|aging
for|age cap+s
for|ager+s
fora|men
for|am|ina
for|am|in|ate
for|am|in|ates
for|am|in|ated
for|am|in|at|ing
fora|mini|fer+s
for|am|in|if|er|an
+s
for|am|in|ifer|ous
for|as|much
foray+s +ed +ing
for|bade
for|bear
for|bears
for|bore
for|bear|ing
for|borne
(refrain; abstain.
△ forebear)
for|bear|ance
for|bear|ing|ly
for|bid
for|bids
for|bade
for|bid|ding
for|bid|den
for|bid|dance
for|bid|ding|ly
for|bore
for|borne
for|bye
force
forces
forced
for|cing
force|able
(able to be forced.
△ forcible)

force-feed
force-feeds
force-fed
force-feeding
force field+s
force|ful
force|ful|ly
force|ful|ness
force-land+s +ed
+ing
force ma|jeure
force|meat
for|ceps
plural for|ceps
force-pump+s
for|cer+s
for|cible
(involving force.
△ forceable)
for|cible|ness
for|cibly
Ford, Ford Madox
(English writer)
Ford, Ger|ald
(American
president)
Ford, Har|ri|son
(American actor)
Ford, Henry
(American car
maker)
Ford, John
(American film
director)
ford+s +ed +ing
ford|able
fore+s (front etc.
△ for. four)
fore-and-aft
attributive
fore|arm+s +ed
+ing
fore|bear+s
(ancestor.
△ forbear)
fore|bode
fore|bodes
fore|boded
fore|bod|ing
fore|bod|ing+s
fore|bod|ing|ly
fore|brain+s
fore|cast
fore|casts
fore|cast *or*
fore|cast|ed
fore|cast|ing
fore|cast|er+s
fore|castle+s
fore|close
fore|closes
fore|closed
fore|clos|ing

fore|clos|ure +s
fore|con|scious
fore|court +s
fore|deck +s
for|edge +s (use
  fore-edge)
fore|doom +s +ed
  +ing
fore-edge +s
fore-end +s
fore|father +s
fore|feel
  fore|feels
  fore|felt
  fore|feel|ing
fore|fin|ger +s
fore|foot
  fore|feet
fore|front
fore|gather +s +ed
  +ing
fore|go
  fore|goes
  fore|went
  fore|going
  fore|gone
  (precede; in 'the
  foregoing' and
  'foregone
  conclusion'.
  △ forgo)
fore|go|er +s
fore|ground +s
  +ed +ing
fore|hand +s
fore|head +s
fore|hock +s
fore|hold +s
for|eign
for|eign|er +s
for|eign|ness
fore|judge
  fore|judges
  fore|judged
  fore|judg|ing
fore|know
  fore|knows
  fore|knew
  fore|know|ing
  fore|known
fore|know|ledge
fore|lady
  fore|ladies
fore|land +s
fore|leg +s
fore|limb +s
fore|lock +s
fore|man
  fore|men
fore|mast +s
fore|most
fore|mother +s

fore|name +s
fore|noon +s
fo|ren|sic
fo|ren|sic|al|ly
fo|ren|sics
fore|or|dain +s
  +ed +ing
fore|or|din|ation
fore|part +s
fore|paw +s
fore|peak +s
fore|play
fore|quar|ter +s
fore|run
  fore|runs
  fore|ran
  fore|run|ning
  fore|run
fore|run|ner +s
fore|sail +s
fore|see
  fore|sees
  fore|saw
  fore|see|ing
  fore|seen
fore|see|abil|ity
fore|see|able
fore|see|ably
fore|seer +s
fore|shadow +s
  +ed +ing
fore|sheets
fore|shock +s
fore|shore +s
fore|short|en +s
  +ed +ing
fore|show
  fore|shows
  fore|showed
  fore|show|ing
  fore|shown
fore|sight
fore|sight|ed
fore|sight|ed|ly
fore|sight|ed|ness
fore|skin +s
for|est +s +ed +ing
fore|stall +s +ed
  +ing
fore|stall|er +s
fore|stal|ment
for|est|ation
fore|stay +s
for|est dwell|er +s
forest-dwelling
  attributive
For|est|er, C. S.
  (English novelist)
for|est|er +s
for|est land +s
for|est|ry
for|est tree +s

fore|taste
  fore|tastes
  fore|tas|ted
  fore|tast|ing
fore|tell
  fore|tells
  fore|told
  fore|tell|ing
fore|tell|er +s
fore|thought
fore|to|ken +s +ed
  +ing
fore|told
fore|top +s
fore-topgal|lant
  +s
fore-topgal|lant-
  mast +s
fore-topgal|lant-
  sail +s
fore-topmast +s
fore-topsail +s
for|ever
  (continually)
for ever (for
  always)
for|ever|more *Am.*
for ever|more *Br.*
fore|warn +s +ed
  +ing
fore|warn|er +s
fore|went
fore|wing +s
fore|woman
  fore|women
fore|word +s
fore|yard +s
For|far (town,
  Scotland)
For|far|shire
  (former name of
  Angus, Scotland)
for|feit +s +ed
  +ing
for|feit|able
for|feit|er +s
for|feit|ure
for|fend +s +ed
  +ing
for|gather +s +ed
  +ing (use
  foregather)
for|gave
forge
  forges
  forged
  for|ging
forge|able
for|ger +s
for|gery
  for|ger|ies

for|get
  for|gets
  for|got
  for|get|ting
  for|got|ten
for|get|ful
for|get|ful|ly
for|get|ful|ness
forget-me-not +s
for|get|table
for|get|ter +s
for|giv|able
for|giv|ably
for|give
  for|gives
  for|gave
  for|giv|ing
  for|given
for|give|ness
for|giver +s
for|giv|ing|ly
forgo
  for|goes
  for|went
  for|go|ing
  for|gone
  (go without.
  △ forego)
for|got
for|got|ten
for|int +s
fork +s +ed +ing
Fork|beard,
  Sweyn (king of
  Denmark and
  England)
fork-lift +s
for|lorn
for|lorn|ly
for|lorn|ness
form +s +ed +ing
  (all senses except
  Br. Printing.
  △ forme)
for|mal +s
for|mal|de|hyde
for|ma|lin
for|mal|isa|tion *Br.*
  (use
  formalization)
for|mal|ise *Br.* (use
  formalize)
  for|mal|ises
  for|mal|ised
  for|mal|is|ing
for|mal|ism +s
for|mal|ist +s
for|mal|is|tic
for|mal|ity
  for|mal|ities
for|mal|iza|tion

for¦mal¦ize
for¦mal¦izes
for¦mal¦ized
for¦mal¦iz¦ing
for¦mal¦ly
(officially.
△ formerly)
for¦mal¦ness
form¦ant +s
for¦mat
for¦mats
for¦mat¦ted
for¦mat¦ting
for¦mate
for¦ma¦tion +s
for¦ma¦tion¦al
for¦ma¦tive
for¦ma¦tive¦ly
Formby, George
(English
comedian)
forme Br. +s (Am.
form. Printing.
△ form.)
For¦men¦tera
(Spanish island)
for¦mer +s
for¦mer¦ly
(previously.
△ formally)
for¦mic
For¦mica Propr.
for¦mi¦ca¦tion
for¦mid¦able
for¦mid¦able¦ness
for¦mid¦ably
form¦less
form¦less¦ly
form¦less¦ness
For¦mosa (former
name of Taiwan)
for¦mula
for¦mu¦las or
for¦mu¦lae
for¦mu¦la¦ic
for¦mu¦lar¦ise Br.
(use formularize)
for¦mu¦lar¦ises
for¦mu¦lar¦ised
for¦mu¦lar¦is¦ing
for¦mu¦lar¦ize
for¦mu¦lar¦izes
for¦mu¦lar¦ized
for¦mu¦lar¦iz¦ing
for¦mu¦lary
for¦mu¦lar¦ies
for¦mu¦late
for¦mu¦lates
for¦mu¦lated
for¦mu¦lat¦ing
for¦mu¦la¦tion +s
for¦mu¦la¦tor +s

for¦mu¦lise Br.
(use formulize)
for¦mu¦lises
for¦mu¦lised
for¦mu¦lis¦ing
for¦mu¦lism
for¦mu¦list +s
for¦mu¦lis¦tic
for¦mu¦lize
for¦mu¦lizes
for¦mu¦lized
for¦mu¦liz¦ing
form¦work
for¦ni¦cate
for¦ni¦cates
for¦ni¦cated
for¦ni¦cat¦ing
for¦ni¦ca¦tion +s
for¦ni¦ca¦tor +s
for¦rad¦er
(= forwarder)
For¦rest, John
(Australian
statesman)
for¦sake
for¦sakes
for¦sook
for¦sak¦ing
for¦saken
for¦saken¦ness
for¦saker +s
for¦sooth
For¦ster, E. M.
(English novelist.
△ Vorster)
for¦swear
for¦swears
for¦swore
for¦swear¦ing
for¦sworn
For¦syth,
Fred¦erick
(English writer)
for¦sythia +s
fort +s (fortified
building.
△ fought)
For¦ta¦leza (port,
Brazil)
Fort-de-France
(capital of
Martinique)
forte +s (strong
point; Music loudly)
forte¦piano +s
(musical
instrument)
forte piano (Music
loud then soft)
Forth (river,
Scotland; shipping
area off Scotland)

forth (forward.
△ fourth)
forth¦com¦ing
forth¦com¦ing¦ness
forth¦right
forth¦right¦ly
forth¦right¦ness
forth¦with
For¦ties (part of
North Sea
between Scotland
and S. Norway;
shipping area off
Scotland)
for¦ti¦eth +s
for¦ti¦fi¦able
for¦ti¦fi¦ca¦tion +s
for¦ti¦fier +s
for¦tify
for¦ti¦fies
for¦ti¦fied
for¦ti¦fy¦ing
for¦tis¦simo
for¦tis¦simos or
for¦tis¦simi
for¦ti¦tude
Fort Knox (gold
depository, USA)
Fort Lamy (former
name of
N'Djamena)
fort¦night +s
fort¦night¦ly
fort¦night¦lies
For¦tran
fort¦ress
fort¦resses
for¦tuit¦ism
for¦tuit¦ist +s
for¦tuit¦ous
for¦tuit¦ous¦ly
for¦tuit¦ous¦ness
for¦tu¦ity
for¦tu¦ities
for¦tu¦nate +s
for¦tu¦nate¦ly
for¦tune +s
for¦tune cookie +s
for¦tune hunt¦er
+s
fortune-teller +s
fortune-telling
Fort Wil¦liam
(town, Scotland)
Fort Worth (city,
USA)
forty
for¦ties
forty-first, forty-
second, etc.
Forty-five, the
(1745 rebellion)

forty-five +s
(gramophone
record)
forty¦fold
forty-niner +s
forty-one, forty-
two, etc.
forum
forums or fora
for¦ward +s +ed
+ing
for¦ward¦er +s
forward-looking
for¦ward¦ly
for¦ward¦ness
for¦wards
for¦went
Fos¦bury, Dick
(American high-
jumper)
fossa
fos¦sae
fosse +s
Fosse Way
(ancient road,
England)
fos¦sick +s +ed
+ing
fos¦sick¦er +s
fos¦sil +s
fos¦sil-fuel
fos¦sil¦ifer¦ous
fos¦sil¦isa¦tion Br.
(use fossilization)
fos¦sil¦ise Br. (use
fossilize)
fos¦sil¦ises
fos¦sil¦ised
fos¦sil¦is¦ing
fos¦sil¦iza¦tion
fos¦sil¦ize
fos¦sil¦izes
fos¦sil¦ized
fos¦sil¦iz¦ing
fos¦sor¦ial
Fos¦ter, Jodie
(American
actress)
Fos¦ter, Ste¦phen
(American
composer)
fos¦ter +s +ed +ing
fos¦ter¦age
foster-brother +s
foster-child
foster-children
foster-daughter +s
fos¦ter¦er +s
foster-father +s
fos¦ter¦ling +s
foster-mother +s
foster-parent +s

foster-sister+s
foster-son+s
Fou|cault, Jean
  Ber|nard Léon
  (French physicist)
Fou|cault, Mi|chel
  (French
  philosopher)
fou|etté+s
fought (past tense
  and past participle
  of fight △ fort)
Fou-hsin (= Fuxin)
foul+s +ed +ing
  +er +est (dirty;
  unpleasant;
  tangle; etc.
  △ fowl)
fou|lard+s
foul|ly
foul-mouthed
foul|ness
foul-up+s noun
fou|mart+s
found+s +ed +ing
foun|da|tion+s
foun|da|tion|al
foun|da|tion|er+s
foun|da|tion stone
  +s
found|er+s
  (person who
  founds)
foun|der+s +ed
  +ing (sink; fail;
  horse disorder)
found|er mem|ber
  +s
found|er|ship
found|ling+s
found|ress
  found|resses
foun|dry
  foun|dries
fount+s
foun|tain+s
foun|tained
foun|tain|head+s
foun|tain pen+s
four+s (number.
  △ for, fore)
four|chette+s
four-eyes
  plural four-eyes
four-flush
  four-flushes
  four-flushed
  four-flushing
four-flusher+s
four|fold
Fourier, Jean
  Bap|tiste

Fourier (cont.)
  Jo|seph (French
  mathematician)
Fourier an|aly|sis
Fourier|ism
Fourier ser|ies
four-in-hand+s
four-iron+s
four-leaf clo|ver
  +s
four-leaved
  clo|ver+s
four-letter word
  +s
four o'clock+s
  (plant)
four|pence+s
four|penny
  four|pen|nies
four-poster+s
four|score
four|some+s
four-square
four-stroke+s
four|teen+s
four|teenth+s
fourth+s (in
  number. △ forth)
fourth|ly
4to (= quarto)
four-wheel drive
fovea
  fo|veae
fo|veal
fo|ve|ate
fo|ve|ola
  fo|ve|olae
fo|ve|ol|ate
fowl
  plural fowl or
  fowls
  (bird. △ foul)
Fowl|er, H. W.
  (English
  lexicographer)
fowl|er+s
Fowles, John
  (English novelist)
fowl|ing
fowl pest
fowl-run+s
Fox, George
  (English preacher
  and founder of
  Quakers)
fox
  foxes
  foxed
  fox|ing
Foxe, John
  (English author of

Foxe (cont.)
  The Book of
  Martyrs)
fox|glove+s
fox|hole+s
fox|hound+s
fox hunt+s noun
fox-hunt+s +ed
  +ing verb
Fox|hunt|er
  (horse)
fox-hunter+s
fox|ily
foxi|ness
fox|like
fox|tail+s
Fox Tal|bot,
  Wil|liam Henry
  (English
  photography
  pioneer)
fox ter|rier+s
fox|trot
  fox|trots
  fox|trot|ted
  fox|trot|ting
foxy
  fox|ier
  foxi|est
foyer+s
Fra (Italian monk;
  see also under
  name)
frab|jous
frab|jous|ly
fra|cas
  plural fra|cas
frac|tal+s
frac|tion+s
frac|tion|al
frac|tion|al|ise Br.
  (use
  fractionalize)
frac|tion|al|ises
frac|tion|al|ised
frac|tion|al|is|ing
frac|tion|al|ize
frac|tion|al|izes
frac|tion|al|ized
frac|tion|al|iz|ing
frac|tion|al|ly
frac|tion|ary
frac|tion|ate
frac|tion|ates
frac|tion|ated
frac|tion|at|ing
frac|tion|ation
frac|tion|ise Br.
  (use fractionize)
frac|tion|ises
frac|tion|ised
frac|tion|is|ing

frac|tion|ize
frac|tion|izes
frac|tion|ized
frac|tion|iz|ing
frac|tious
frac|tious|ly
frac|tious|ness
frac|ture
  frac|tures
  frac|tured
  frac|tur|ing
frae|nu|lum Br.
  frae|nula
  (Am. frenulum)
frae|num Br.
  fraena
  (Am. frenum)
fra|gile
fra|gile|ly
fra|gil|ity
frag|ment+s +ed
  +ing
frag|men|tal
frag|men|tar|ily
frag|men|tary
frag|men|ta|tion
frag|ment|ise Br.
  (use fragmentize)
frag|ment|ises
frag|ment|ised
frag|ment|is|ing
frag|ment|ize
frag|ment|izes
frag|ment|ized
frag|ment|iz|ing
Fra|go|nard, Jean-
  Honoré (French
  painter)
fra|grance+s
fra|granced
fra|grancy
fra|grant
fra|grant|ly
frail+s +er +est
frail|ly
frail|ness
frailty
  frail|ties
Frak|tur
framable
fram|be|sia Am.
fram|boe|sia Br.
frame
  frames
  framed
  fram|ing
frame house+s
frame|less
framer+s
frame-saw+s
frame-up+s noun
frame|work+s

Fran
franc +s (French,
  Swiss, etc.
  currency. △ frank)
France (country)
France, Ana|tole
  (French writer)
Fran|ces (woman's
  name. △ Francis)
Fran|cesca
Franche-Comté
  (region, France)
fran|chise
  fran|chises
  fran|chised
  fran|chis|ing
fran|chisee +s
fran|chiser +s
Fran|cine
Fran|cis (man's
  name. △ Frances)
Fran|cis, Dick
  (British writer)
Fran|cis|can +s
Fran|cis of As|sisi
  (Italian saint)
Fran|cis of Sales
  (French saint)
Fran|cis Xa|vier
  (Spanish
  missionary)
fran|cium
Franck, César
  (Belgian
  composer)
Franck, James
  (German-born
  American
  physicist)
Franco, Fran|cisco
  (Spanish general
  and statesman)
Franco-German
fran|co|lin +s
Franco|mania
Fran|conia
  (medieval duchy,
  Germany)
Franco|phile +s
Franco|phobe +s
Franco|pho|bia
franco|phone +s
Franco-Prussian
fran|gible
fran|gi|pane +s
  (almond paste;
  cake)
fran|gi|pani +s
  (perfume tree)
fran|glais

Frank +s
  (Germanic tribe;
  name)
Frank, Anne
  (German Jewish
  diarist)
frank +s +ed +ing
  +er +est (stamp
  or mark for
  posting. △ franc)
frank|able
Fran|ken|stein, Dr
  (scientist in novel)
frank|er +s
Frank|fort (city,
  USA)
Frank|furt in full
  Frank|furt am
  Main
  (city, western
  Germany)
Frank|furt in full
  Frank|furt an der
  Oder
  (city, eastern
  Germany)
frank|furt|er +s
frank|in|cense
Frank|ish
Frank|lin, Aretha
  (American singer)
Frank|lin,
  Ben|ja|min
  (American
  statesman and
  scientist)
Frank|lin,
  Rosa|lind
  (English scientist)
frank|lin +s
frank|ly
frank|ness
fran|tic
fran|tic|al|ly
fran|tic|ness
Franz Josef
  (emperor of
  Austria and king
  of Hungary)
Franz Josef Land
  (island group,
  Arctic Ocean)
frap
  fraps
  frapped
  frap|ping
frappé +s
Fras|cati (region,
  Italy)
fras|cati +s (wine)
Fra|ser (river,
  Canada)

Fra|ser, Dawn
  (Australian
  swimmer.
  △ Frazer)
frass
frat
  frats
  frat|ted
  frat|ting
fra|ter|nal +s
fra|ter|nal|ism
fra|ter|nal|ly
frat|er|nisa|tion
  Br. (use
  fraternization)
frat|er|nise Br. (use
  fraternize)
  frat|er|nises
  frat|er|nised
  frat|er|nis|ing
fra|ter|nity
  fra|ter|nities
frat|er|niza|tion
frat|er|nize
  frat|er|nizes
  frat|er|nized
  frat|er|niz|ing
frat|ri|cidal
frat|ri|cide +s
Frau
  Frauen
  (German woman.
  △ frow)
fraud +s
fraud|ster +s
fraudu|lence
fraudu|lent
fraudu|lent|ly
fraught
Fräu|lein +s
Fraun|hof|er,
  Jo|seph von
  (German optician;
  lines)
fraxi|nella +s
fray +s +ed +ing
Fray Ben|tos (port,
  Uruguay)
Fra|zer, James
  George (Scottish
  anthropologist.
  △ Fraser)
fra|zil (ice crystals
  in stream)
fraz|zle
  fraz|zles
  fraz|zled
  fraz|zling
  (exhaustion; to
  exhaust)
freak +s +ed +ing
freak|ily

freaki|ness
freak|ish
freak|ish|ly
freak|ish|ness
freak-out +s noun
freak show +s
freaky
  freaki|er
  freaki|est
freckle
  freckles
  freckled
  freck|ling
freckle-faced
freckly
Fred
Fred|die also
  Freddy
Freddy also
  Fred|die
Fred|erick
Fred|erick
  Bar|ba|rossa
  (Frederick I,
  German king and
  Holy Roman
  emperor)
Fred|erick the
  Great (Frederick
  II, Prussian king)
Fred|erick
  Wil|liam (Elector
  of Brandenburg)
Fred|eric|ton (city,
  Canada)
free
  frees
  freed
  free|ing
  freer
  freest
free and easy
free|base
  free|bases
  free|based
  free|bas|ing
free|bie +s
free|board +s
free|boot +s +ed
  +ing
free|boot|er +s
free|born
freed|man
  freed|men
free|dom +s
free|dom fight|er
  +s
free fall noun
free-fall
  free-falls
  free-fell

free-fall (*cont.*)
free-falling
attributive and verb
Free|fone *Propr.*
free-for-all +s
free-form *attributive*
free|hand
(drawing)
free hand (freedom
to act)
free-handed
free-handed|ly
free-handed|ness
free|hold +s
free|hold|er +s
free-kick +s
free|lance
free|lances
free|lanced
free|lan|cing
free-liver +s
free-living
free|load +s +ed
+ing
free|load|er +s
free|ly
free|man
free|men
free mar|ket +s
noun
free-market
attributive
free|mar|tin +s
Free|mason +s
Free|mason|ry
(of Freemasons)
free|mason|ry
free|mason|ries
(generally)
free|ness
Free|phone (use
Freefone)
Free|post
freer
free-range
free sheet +s
free|sia +s
free-spoken
freest
free-standing
free|stone +s
free|style
free|styler +s
free|think|er +s
free|think|ing
Free|town (capital
of Sierra Leone)
free trade *noun*
free-trade
attributive
free|ware
free|way +s

free|wheel +s +ed
+ing (cog
assembly; coast)
free wheel +s
(wheel)
freez|able
freeze
freezes
froze
freez|ing
fro|zen
(turn to ice.
△ frieze)
freeze-dry
freeze-dries
freeze-dried
freeze-drying
freeze-frame +s
freezer +s
freeze-up +s *noun*
freezing-mixture
+s
freez|ing point +s
Frege, Gott|lob
(German
philosopher and
mathematician)
Frei|burg (city,
Germany)
freight +s +ed
+ing
freight|age +s
freight|er +s
Freight|liner +s
Propr.
Fre|limo (political
party,
Mozambique)
Fre|man|tle (city,
Australia)
**Fré|mont, John
Charles**
(American
explorer and
statesman)
French
French Can|adian
+s *noun*
French-Canadian
adjective
French fried
(potatoes)
French fries
French horn +s
French|ifi|ca|tion
French|ify
Frenchi|fies
Frenchi|fied
Frenchi|fy|ing
French let|ter +s
French|man
French|men

French|ness
French pol|ish
French pol|ishes
French pol|ished
French
pol|ish|ing
French-speaking
French toast
French win|dow
+s
French|woman
French|women
Frenchy
French|ies
fre|net|ic
fre|net|ic|al|ly
frenu|lum *Am.*
fren|ula
(*Br.* fraenulum)
fre|num *Am.*
frena
(*Br.* fraenum)
fren|zied|ly
frenzy
fren|zies
fren|zied
frenzy|ing
freon +s *Propr.*
fre|quency
fre|quen|cies
fre|quent +s +ed
+ing
fre|quen|ta|tion
fre|quen|ta|tive
fre|quent|er +s
fre|quent|ly
fresco
fres|cos *or*
fres|coes
fres|coed
fresco secco
fresh +er +est
fresh|en +s +ed
+ing
fresh|er +s
freshet +s
fresh-faced
fresh|ly
fresh|man
fresh|men
fresh|ness
fresh|water
adjective
fresh|woman
fresh|women
**Fres|nel,
Au|gus|tin Jean**
(French physicist)
fres|nel +s
Fresno (city, USA)

fret
frets
fret|ted
fret|ting
fret|board +s
fret|ful
fret|ful|ly
fret|ful|ness
fret|less
fret|saw +s
fret|work
Freud, Lu|cian
(German-born
British painter)
Freud, Sig|mund
(Austrian
psychotherapist)
Freud|ian +s
Freud|ian|ism
Frey *Scandinavian
Mythology*
Freya
(*Scandinavian
Mythology*; name)
**Frey|berg,
Ber|nard Cyril**
(New Zealand
general)
Freyr (*Scandinavian
Mythology*,
= Frey)
fri|abil|ity
fri|able
fri|able|ness
friar +s (*Religion.*
△ fryer)
fri|ar|ly
friar's bal|sam
fri|ary
fri|ar|ies
frib|ble
frib|bles
frib|bled
frib|bling
Fri|bourg (town
and canton,
Switzerland)
fri|can|deau
fri|can|deaux
noun
fri|can|deau +s
+ed +ing
verb
fric|as|see
fric|as|sees
fric|as|seed
fric|as|see|ing
frica|tive +s
fric|tion +s
fric|tion|al
fric|tion ball +s

fric¦tion|less
Fri¦day +s
fridge +s
fridge-freezer +s
Frie|dan, Betty
(American
feminist and
writer)
Fried|man,
Mil¦ton
(American
economist)
Fried|rich,
Cas¦par David
(German painter)
friend +s +ed +ing
friend|less
friend|lily
friend|li|ness
friend¦ly
friend|lies
friend|lier
friend¦li|est
Friend¦ly Is¦lands
(= Tonga)
Friend¦ly So¦ci|ety
Friend¦ly
So¦ci|eties
friend|ship +s
frier +s (use fryer.
△ friar)
Frie|sian +s (cattle.
△ Frisian)
Fries|land
(province, the
Netherlands)
frieze +s
(decoration; cloth.
△ freeze)
frig
frigs
frigged
frig|ging
(coarse slang)
frig|ate +s
frig|ate bird +s
Frigga Scandinavian
Mythology
fright +s +ed +ing
fright¦en +s +ed
+ing
fright|en¦er +s
fright|en|ing¦ly
fright|ful
fright|ful¦ly
fright|ful|ness
fri¦gid
fri¦gid|arium
fri¦gid|ariums or
fri¦gid|aria
fri¦gid|ity
fri¦gid¦ly

fri¦gid|ness
fri¦jo¦les
frill +s +ed +ing
frill|ery
frill|er¦ies
fril¦li|ness
frill|ing +s
frilly
frill|ies
frill|ier
frill|iest
fringe
fringes
fringed
frin¦ging
fringe|less
fringy
Frink, Elisa|beth
(English sculptor
and artist)
frip|pery
frip|per¦ies
frip|pet +s
fris|bee +s Propr.
Frisch, Karl von
(Austrian
zoologist)
Frisch, Max (Swiss
writer)
Frisch, Otto
(Austrian-born
British physicist)
Frisch, Rag¦nar
(Norwegian
economist)
frisé +s (fabric)
fri¦sée +s (lettuce)
Frisia (ancient
region of NW
Europe)
Fris|ian +s (of
Friesland; person;
language.
△ Friesian)
Fris|ian Is¦lands
(off NW Europe)
frisk +s +ed +ing
frisk|er +s
fris|ket +s
frisk|ily
friski|ness
frisky
frisk|ier
friski|est
fris|son +s
frit
frits
frit|ted
frit|ting
frit-fly
frit-flies

Frith, Wil|liam
Pow¦ell (British
painter)
frith +s
fri¦til|lary
fri¦til|lar¦ies
frit|tata
frit|ter +s +ed
+ing
fritto misto
fritz (in 'on the
fritz')
Friuli-Venezia
Giu¦lia (region,
Italy)
frivol
friv|ols
friv|olled Br.
friv|oled Am.
friv|ol|ling Br.
friv|ol|ing Am.
fri¦vol|ity
fri¦vol|ities
frivo|lous
frivo|lous|ly
frivo|lous|ness
frizz
frizzes
frizzed
friz¦zing
friz|zi|ness
friz¦zle
friz¦zles
friz¦zled
friz¦zling
friz|zly
frizzy
frizz|ier
friz¦zi|est
fro (in 'to and fro'.
△ froe)
Fro|bi¦sher,
Mar¦tin (English
explorer)
frock +s +ed +ing
frock coat +s
froe +s (tool. △ fro)
Froe|bel,
Fried|rich
(German
educationist)
Froe|bel|ian +s
Froe|bel|ism
Frog +s (offensive
French person)
frog +s (animal;
coat-fastening;
etc.)
frog|bit +s (plant)
frog|fish
plural frog|fish or
frog|fishes

frogged
frog|ging +s
Froggy
Frog|gies
(offensive French
person)
froggy (like a frog;
offensive French)
frog|hop¦per +s
frog|man
frog|men
frog|march
frog|marches
frog|marched
frog|march|ing
frog|mouth +s
frog|spawn
froid|eur
fro|ing +s (in 'toing
and froing')
frolic
frolics
frol|icked
frol|ick|ing
frol|ick|er +s
frol|ic|some
frol|ic|some¦ly
frol|ic|some|ness
from
from|age blanc
from|age frais
frond +s
frond|age
Fronde
frond|eur +s
frond|ose
front +s +ed +ing
front|age +s
front|ager +s
front|al
front|al¦ly
front bench
front benches
front|bench¦er +s
front door +s
fron|tier +s
fron|tier|less
fron|tiers|man
fron|tiers|men
fron|tiers|woman
fron|tiers|women
fron|tis|piece +s
front|less
front|let +s
front line +s noun
front-line attributive
front|man
front|men
fronto|gen¦esis
fron|to|genet¦ic
fron|ton +s
front|ward

front|wards
front-wheel drive
frore
Frost, Rob|ert
  (American poet)
frost +s +ed +ing
frost|bite
frost-bitten
frost-free
frost|ily
frosti|ness
frost|ing +s
frost|less
frost-work
frosty
  frost|ier
  frosti|est
froth +s +ed +ing
froth-blower +s
froth|ily
frothi|ness
frothy
  froth|ier
  frothi|est
frot|tage
frou-frou +s
frow +s
  (Dutchwoman;
  housewife.
  △ Frau)
fro|ward
fro|ward|ly
fro|ward|ness
frown +s +ed +ing
frown|er +s
frown|ing|ly
frowst +s +ed +ing
frowst|er +s
frow|sti|ness
frow|sty
  frow|stier
  frow|sti|est
frow|zi|ness
frowzy
  frow|zier
  frow|zi|est
froze
frozen
fro|zen|ly
fruc|tif|er|ous
fruc|ti|fi|ca|tion +s
fruc|tify
  fruc|ti|fies
  fruc|ti|fied
  fruc|ti|fy|ing
fruc|tose
fruc|tu|ous
fru|gal
fru|gal|ity
fru|gal|ly
fru|gal|ness
fru|giv|or|ous

fruit +s +ed +ing
fruit|age
fruit|ar|ian +s
fruit|bat +s
fruit-body
  fruit-bodies
fruit|cake +s
  (person)
fruit cake +s
  (food)
fruit|er +s
fruit|er|er +s
fruit fly
  fruit flies
fruit|ful
fruit|ful|ly
fruit|ful|ness
fruit|ily
fruiti|ness
fru|ition
fruit juice +s
fruit|less
fruit|less|ly
fruit|less|ness
fruit|let +s
fruit tree +s
fruit|wood +s
fruity
  fruit|ier
  fruiti|est
fru|menty
frump +s
frump|ily
frumpi|ness
frump|ish
frump|ish|ly
frumpy
  frump|ier
  frumpi|est
Frunze (city,
  Kirghizia)
frus|trate
  frus|trates
  frus|trated
  frus|trat|ing
frus|trated|ly
frus|trater +s
frus|trat|ing|ly
frus|tra|tion +s
frust|ule +s
frus|tum
  frusta or
  frus|tums
fru|tes|cent
fru|tex
  fru|ti|ces
fru|ti|cose
Fry, Chris|to|pher
  (English writer)
Fry, Eliza|beth
  (English reformer)

fry
  fries
  fried
  fry|ing
Frye, North|rop
  (Canadian literary
  critic)
fryer +s (person
  who fries; device
  for frying. △ friar)
fry|ing pan +s
fry|pan +s
fry-up +s *noun*
Fuad (Egyptian
  kings)
fubsy
  fub|sier
  fub|si|est
Fuchs, Klaus
  (German-born
  British physicist)
fuch|sia +s
fuchs|ine
fuck +s +ed +ing
  (*coarse slang*)
fuck all (*coarse
  slang*)
fuck|er +s (*coarse
  slang*)
fuck-up +s *noun*
  (*coarse slang*)
fu|coid
fucus
  fuci
fud|dle
  fud|dles
  fud|dled
  fud|dling
fuddy-duddy
  fuddy-duddies
fudge
  fudges
  fudged
  fudg|ing
fudge|able
fueh|rer +s (use
  führer)
fuel
  fuels
  fuelled *Br.*
  fueled *Am.*
  fuel|ling *Br.*
  fuel|ing *Am.*
fuel-inject|ed
fuel in|jec|tion
fuel rod +s
Fuen|tes, Car|los
  (Mexican writer)
fug
  fugs
  fugged
  fug|ging

fu|ga|cious
fu|ga|cious|ly
fu|ga|cious|ness
fu|ga|city
fugal
fu|gal|ly
Fu|gard, Athol
  (South African
  playwright)
fuggy
  fug|gier
  fug|gi|est
fu|gi|tive +s
fu|gi|tive|ly
fu|gi|tive|ness
fugle
  fugles
  fugled
  fug|ling
fugle|man
  fugle|men
fugue
  fugues
  fugued
  fu|guing
fu|guist +s
Füh|rer (Hitler)
füh|rer +s (leader)
Fu|jai|rah (state
  and city, UAE)
Fuji, Mount
  (volcano, Japan)
Fu|jian (province,
  China)
Fu|ji|yama
  (Japanese name
  for Mount Fuji)
Fu|kien (= Fujian)
Fu|ku|oka (city,
  Japan)
Fu|lani
  plural Fu|lani or
  Fu|la|nis
Ful|bright,
  Wil|liam
  (American
  senator; education
  awards)
ful|crum
  ful|cra or
  ful|crums
ful|fil *Br.*
  ful|fils
  ful|filled
  ful|fil|ling
ful|fill *Am.*
  +s +ed +ing
ful|fill|able
ful|fill|er +s
ful|fill|ment *Am.*
  +s
ful|fil|ment *Br.* +s

ful|gent
ful|gur|ation +s
ful|gur|ite
fu|li|gin|ous
full +s +ed +ing
  +er +est
full-back +s
full-blooded
full-blooded|ly
full-blooded|ness
full-blown
full-bodied
full-bottomed
full-color _Am._
  attributive
full-colour _Br._
  attributive
full-cream
full dress (formal
  clothes)
full-dress
  (important)
full dress uni|form
Ful|ler,
  Buck|min|ster
  (American
  designer)
Ful|ler, Thomas
  (English cleric and
  historian)
full|er +s
full|er|ene +s
full|er's earth
full face _adverbial_
full-face _adjective_
full-fashioned
full-fledged
full-frontal
full-grown
full-hearted
full-hearted|ly
full-hearted|ness
full house
full-length _adjective_
full-mouthed
full|ness
full-page _adjective_
full-scale
full-size _adjective_
full-sized (use full-
  size)
full-time _adjective_
full-timer +s
fully
full-year _attributive_
fully-fashioned
fully-fledged
  attributive
fully grown
ful|mar +s
ful|min|ant

ful|min|ate
ful|min|ates
ful|min|ated
ful|min|at|ing
ful|min|ation +s
ful|min|atory
ful|min|ic
ful|ness (use
  fullness)
ful|some
ful|some|ly
ful|some|ness
Ful|ton, Rob|ert
  (American
  engineer)
ful|ves|cent
ful|vous
fu|ma|role +s
fu|ma|rol|ic
fum|ble
fum|bles
fum|bled
fum|bling
fum|bler +s
fum|bling|ly
fume
fumes
fumed
fum|ing
fume|less
fu|mi|gant +s
fu|mi|gate
fu|mi|gates
fu|mi|gated
fu|mi|gat|ing
fu|mi|ga|tion +s
fu|mi|ga|tor +s
fum|ing|ly
fu|mi|tory
fu|mi|tor|ies
fumy
fumi|er
fumi|est
fun
Fu|na|futi (capital
  of Tuvalu)
fu|nam|bu|list +s
fun|board +s
Fun|chal (capital of
  Madeira)
func|tion +s +ed
  +ing
func|tion|al
func|tion|al|ism
func|tion|al|ist +s
func|tion|al|ity
func|tion|al|ities
func|tion|al|ly
func|tion|ary
func|tion|ar|ies
func|tion|less
fund +s +ed +ing

fun|da|ment +s
fun|da|men|tal +s
fun|da|men|tal|
  ism +s
fun|da|men|tal|ist
  +s
fun|da|men|tal|ity
fun|da|men|tal|
  ities
fun|da|men|tal|ly
fund|hold|er +s
fund|hold|ing
fund-raiser +s
fund-raising
fun|dus
fundi
Fundy, Bay of (on
  E coast of
  Canada)
fu|neb|rial
fu|neral +s
fu|ner|ary
fu|ner|eal
fu|ner|eal|ly
fun|fair +s
fun|gal
fungi
fun|gi|bil|ity
fun|gible
fun|gi|cidal
fun|gi|cide +s
fun|gi|form
fun|gi|stat|ic
fun|gi|stat|ic|al|ly
fun|giv|or|ous
fun|goid
fun|gous _adjective_
fun|gus
  fungi _or_ fun|guses
  noun
fu|nicu|lar +s
Funk, Casi|mir
  (Polish-born
  American
  biochemist)
funk +s +ed +ing
fun|kia +s
funk|ily
funki|ness
funky
funk|ier
funki|est
fun-lover +s
fun-loving
fun|nel
fun|nels
fun|nelled _Br._
fun|neled _Am._
fun|nel|ling _Br._
fun|nel|ing _Am._
funnel-like
fun|nily

fun|ni|ness
fun|ni|os|ity
fun|ni|os|ities
funny
fun|nies
fun|nier
fun|ni|est
funny bone +s
funny-face _jocular_
funny-ha-ha
funny man
  funny men
  (clown)
funny-peculiar
fun run +s
fun|ster +s
fur
  furs
  furred
  fur|ring
  (animal hair;
  coating. △ fir)
fur|below +s
fur|bish
  fur|bishes
  fur|bished
  fur|bish|ing
fur|bish|er +s
fur|cate
  fur|cates
  fur|cated
  fur|cat|ing
fur|ca|tion
fur|cula +s
fur|fur|aceous
Fur|ies, the _Greek_
  Mythology
furi|ous
furi|ous|ly
furi|ous|ness
furl +s +ed +ing
furl|able
fur|less
fur|long +s
fur|lough +s
fur|mety
  (= frumenty)
fur|nace
  fur|naces
  fur|naced
  fur|na|cing
Fur|neaux
  Is|lands (off
  Australia)
fur|nish
  fur|nishes
  fur|nished
  fur|nish|ing
fur|nish|er +s
fur|nish|ing +s
fur|ni|ture
furor _Am._
fur|ore _Br._

furphy
  fur|phies
fur|rier +s (fur-
  dealer; more
  furry)
fur|riery
fur|ri|ness
fur|row +s +ed
  +ing
fur|row|less
furrow-slice +s
fur|rowy
furry
  fur|rier
  fur|ri|est
  (covered with fur.
  △ firry)
fur seal +s
fur|ther +s +ed
  +ing
fur|ther|ance
fur|ther|er +s
fur|ther|more
fur|ther|most
fur|thest
fur|tive
fur|tive|ly
fur|tive|ness
Furt|wän|gler,
  Wil|helm
  (German
  conductor)
fur|uncle +s
fu|run|cu|lar
fu|run|cu|lo|sis
fu|run|cu|lous
Fury
  Fur|ies
  (Greek
  Mythology)
fury
  fur|ies
  (anger)
furze
furzy
fus|cous
fuse
  fuses
  fused
  fus|ing
fuse box
  fuse boxes
fusee Br. +s (Am.
  fuzee)
fusel (oil. △ fusil)
fu|sel|age +s
fuse|less
Fu|shun (city,
  China)
fusi|bil|ity
fus|ible
fu|si|form

fusil +s (musket.
  △ fusel)
fu|si|lier +s
fu|sil|lade
  fu|sil|lades
  fu|sil|laded
  fu|sil|lad|ing
fu|silli
fu|sion +s
fu|sion|al
fu|sion|ist +s
fuss
  fusses
  fussed
  fuss|ing
fuss|er +s
fuss|ily
fussi|ness
fuss|pot +s
fussy
  fuss|ier
  fussi|est
fus|ta|nella +s
fus|tian
fus|tic
fus|ti|gate
  fus|ti|gates
  fus|ti|gated
  fus|ti|gat|ing
fus|ti|ga|tion
fus|tily
fusti|ness
fusty
  fus|tier
  fus|ti|est
fu|thorc
fu|tile
fu|tile|ly
fu|tili|tar|ian
fu|til|ity
  fu|til|ities
futon +s
fut|tock +s
fu|ture +s
fu|ture|less
fu|tur|ism
fu|tur|ist +s
fu|tur|is|tic
fu|tur|is|tic|al|ly
fu|tur|ity
fu|tur|olo|gist +s
fu|tur|ology
Fuxin (city, China)
fuze +s (use fuse)
fuzee Am. +s (Br.
  fusee)
Fu|zhou (city,
  China)
fuzz
  fuzzes
  fuzzed
  fuzz|ing

fuzz-ball +s
fuzz|box
  fuzz|boxes
fuzz|ily
fuzzi|ness
fuzzy
  fuzz|ies
  fuzz|ier
  fuzzi|est
fuzzy-wuzzy
  fuzzy-wuzzies
  (*offensive*)
F-word +s
fyl|fot +s
fyrd +s
fytte +s (use fit)

Gg

gab
  gabs
  gabbed
  gab|bing
gab|ar|dine +s
  (cloth; garment,
  esp. raincoat.
  △ gaberdine)
gab|ber +s
gab|ble
  gab|bles
  gab|bled
  gab|bling
gab|bler +s
gab|bro +s
gab|bro|ic
gab|broid
gabby
  gab|bier
  gab|bi|est
gab|elle +s
gab|er|dine +s
  (former long,
  loose upper
  garment.
  △ gabardine)
Gabès (port,
  Tunisia)
ga|bion +s
ga|bion|ade +s
ga|bion|age
Gable, Clark
  (American actor)
gable +s
gabled
gable end +s
gab|let +s
Gabo, Naum
  (Russian-born
  American
  sculptor)
Gabon
Gab|on|ese
  plural Gab|on|ese
Gabor, Den|nis
  (Hungarian-born
  British electrical
  engineer)
Gab|or|one (capital
  of Botswana)
Gab|riel (*Bible*;
  Islam; man's
  name)
Gab|ri|elle
  (woman's name)
Gad (Hebrew
  patriarch)

gad
  gads
  gad¦ded
  gad¦ding
  (go about idly etc.;
  in 'by gad')
gad¦about +s
Gad¦ar¦ene
Gad¦dafi,
  Mu'am¦mer
  Mu¦ham¦mad al
  (Libyan president)
gad¦fly
  gad¦flies
gadget +s
gadget¦eer +s
gadget¦ry
gadgety
Gad¦hel¦ic
gad¦oid +s
gado¦lin¦ite
gado¦lin¦ium
gad¦roon +s
gad¦rooned
Gads¦den
  Pur¦chase (area,
  USA)
gad¦wall
  plural gad¦wall *or*
  gad¦walls
gad¦zooks
Gaea (use Gaia)
Gael +s
Gael¦dom
Gael¦ic (Celtic.
  △ Gallic)
Gael¦tacht +s
Gae¦nor *also*
  Gay¦nor
gaff +s +ed +ing
  (spear; spar; in
  'blow the gaff')
gaffe +s (blunder)
gaf¦fer +s
Gafsa (town,
  Tunisia)
gag
  gags
  gagged
  gag¦ging
gaga
Ga¦garin, Yuri
  (Russian
  cosmonaut)
gag-bit +s
gage *Am.*
  gages
  gaged
  ga¦ging
  (measure. *Br.*
  gauge)

gage
  gages
  gaged
  ga¦ging
  (pledge;
  greengage;
  position relative to
  wind. △ gauge)
gage¦able *Am.* (*Br.*
  gaugeable)
gager *Am.* +s (*Br.*
  gauger)
gag¦gle
  gag¦gles
  gag¦gled
  gag¦gling
gag man
  gag men
gag¦ster +s
Gaia (*Greek
  Mythology*; theory
  of earth. △ Gaya)
Gaian +s
gai¦ety
  gai¦eties
gai¦jin
  plural gai¦jin
Gail *also* Gale,
  Gayle
gail¦lar¦dia +s
gaily
gain +s +ed +ing
gain¦able
gain¦er +s
gain¦ful
gain¦ful¦ly
gain¦ful¦ness
gain¦ings
gain¦say
  gain¦says
  gain¦said
  gain¦say¦ing
  gain¦say¦er +s
Gains¦bor¦ough,
  Thomas (English
  painter)
'gainst (= against)
gait +s (manner of
  walking. △ gate)
gai¦ter +s (legging.
  △ geta)
gai¦tered
Gait¦skell, Hugh
  (British politician)
gal +s (girl; unit of
  acceleration)
gala +s
gal¦ac¦ta¦gogue +s
gal¦ac¦tic
gal¦act¦ose
gal¦ago +s
galah +s

Gala¦had
  (Arthurian knight)
gal¦an¦gal +s
gal¦an¦tine +s
gal¦anty show +s
Gal¦apa¦gos
  Is¦lands (in E.
  Pacific)
Gal¦atea *Greek
  Mythology*
Gal¦aţi (city,
  Romania)
Gal¦atia (ancient
  region, Asia
  Minor)
Gal¦atian +s
Gal¦axy, the (ours)
gal¦axy
  gal¦ax¦ies
Galba (Roman
  emperor)
gal¦ba¦num
Gal¦braith, John
  Ken¦neth
  (Canadian-born
  American
  economist)
Gale *also* Gail,
  Gayle
  (name)
gale +s
galea
  ga¦leae *or* ga¦leas
gal¦eate
gal¦eated
Galen (Greek
  physician)
ga¦lena
gal¦en¦ic
gal¦en¦ic¦al
gal¦ette +s
galia melon +s
Gal¦ibi
  plural Gal¦ibi *or*
  Gal¦ibis
Gal¦icia
Gal¦ician +s
Gali¦lean +s
Gali¦lee (region,
  ancient Palestine)
Gali¦lee, Lake (in
  Israel)
gali¦lee +s (church
  porch)
Gali¦leo (American
  space probe)
Gali¦leo Gali¦lei
  (Italian
  astronomer)
gali¦ma¦tias
gal¦in¦gale +s

gal¦iot +s (use
  galliot)
gali¦pot (resin.
  △ gallipot)
gall +s +ed +ing
Galla
  plural Galla *or*
  Gallas
gal¦lant +s +ed
  +ing
gal¦lant¦ly
gal¦lant¦ry
  gal¦lant¦ries
gall blad¦der +s
Galle (port, Sri
  Lanka)
gal¦leon +s
gal¦le¦ria +s
gal¦ler¦ied
gal¦lery
  gal¦ler¦ies
gal¦lery¦ite +s
gal¦ley +s
gal¦ley proof +s
gal¦ley slave +s
gall-fly
  gall-flies
gal¦li¦am¦bic +s
Gal¦lia
  Nar¦bon¦en¦sis
  (province,
  Transalpine Gaul)
gal¦li¦ard +s
Gal¦lic (Gaulish
  French. △ Gaelic)
gal¦lic (acid)
Gal¦lican +s
Gal¦lican¦ism
gal¦lice
Gal¦li¦cise *Br.* (use
  Gallicize)
Gal¦li¦cises
Gal¦li¦cised
Gal¦li¦cis¦ing
Gal¦li¦cism +s
Gal¦li¦cize
  Gal¦li¦cizes
  Gal¦li¦cized
  Gal¦li¦ciz¦ing
Gal¦li¦formes
gal¦li¦gas¦kins
gal¦li¦maufry
  gal¦li¦mauf¦ries
gal¦li¦mi¦mus
  plural
  gal¦li¦mi¦mus *or*
  gal¦li¦mi¦mus¦es
gal¦lin¦aceous
gall¦ing¦ly
gal¦li¦nule +s
gal¦liot +s

Gal|lip|oli
(peninsula,
Turkey)
gal|li|pot +s (small
pot. △ galipot)
gal|lium
gal|li|vant +s +ed
+ing
gal|li|wasp +s
gall|nut +s
Gallo|mania
Gallo|maniac +s
gal|lon +s
gal|lon|age +s
gal|loon +s
gal|lop
gal|lops
gal|loped
gal|lop|ing
(horse's pace.
△ galop)
gal|lop|er +s
Gallo|phile +s
Gallo|phobe +s
Gallo|pho|bia
Gallo-Roman +s
Gal|lo|way (area,
Scotland)
gal|lo|way +s
(cattle)
gal|lows
gall|stone +s
Gal|lup poll +s
gal|lus
gal|lus|es
gall wasp +s
Gal|ois, Éva|riste
(French
mathematician;
theory)
gal|oot +s
galop +s +ed +ing
(dance. △ gallop)
gal|ore
gal|osh
gal|oshes
gal|pon
Gals|worthy, John
(English novelist
and dramatist)
Gal|tieri,
Leo|poldo
For|tu|nato
(Argentinian
president)
Gal|ton, Fran|cis
(English scientist)
gal|umph +s +ed
+ing
Gal|vani, Luigi
(Italian anatomist)
gal|van|ic

gal|van|ic|al|ly
gal|van|isa|tion +s
(use
galvanization)
gal|van|ise Br. (use
galvanize)
gal|van|ises
gal|van|ised
gal|van|is|ing
gal|van|is|er Br. +s
(use galvanizer)
gal|van|ism
gal|van|ist +s
gal|van|iza|tion +s
gal|van|ize
gal|van|izes
gal|van|ized
gal|van|iz|ing
gal|van|iz|er +s
gal|van|om|eter +s
gal|vano|met|ric
Gal|ves|ton (port,
USA)
galvo +s
Gal|way (county,
Republic of
Ireland)
Gama, Vasco da
(Portuguese
explorer)
gamba +s
gam|bade +s
gam|bado
gam|ba|dos or
gam|ba|does
Gam|bia (in W.
Africa. △ Gambier
Islands)
Gam|bian +s
Gambia River (in
W. Africa)
gam|bier +s
Gam|bier Is|lands
(in French
Polynesia.
△ Gambia)
gam|bit +s
gam|ble
gam|bles
gam|bled
gam|bling
(bet. △ gambol)
gam|bler +s
gam|boge
gam|bol
gam|bols
gam|bolled Br.
gam|boled Am.
gam|bol|ling Br.
gam|bol|ing Am.
(frolic. △ gamble)
gam|brel +s

game
games
gamed
gam|ing
gamer
gamest
game bird +s
game|book +s
Game Boy +s
Propr.
game|cock +s
game fish|ing
game|fowl
plural game|fowl
or game|fowls
game|keep|er +s
game|keep|ing
gam|elan +s
game|ly
game|ness
game plan +s
gamer +s
game show +s
games|man
games|men
games|man|ship
game|some
game|some|ly
game|some|ness
games|play|er +s
game|ster +s
gam|et|an|gium
gam|et|an|gia
gam|ete +s
game the|ory
gam|et|ic
gam|eto|cyte +s
gam|eto|gen|esis
gam|eto|phyte +s
gam|eto|phyt|ic
game-warden +s
gami|ly
gamin +s male
gam|ine +s female
gami|ness
gaming-house +s
gaming-table +s
gamma +s (Greek
letter. △ gammer)
gam|ma|dion +s
gam|mer +s (old
woman.
△ gamma)
gam|mon +s +ed
+ing
gammy
gam|mier
gam|mi|est
Gamow, George
(Russian-born
American
physicist)

gamp +s
gamut +s
gamy
gami|er
gami|est
Ga|na|pati
Hinduism
Gäncä (city,
Azerbaijan)
Gance, Abel
(French film
director)
Gan|der (town and
airport, Canada)
gan|der +s +ed
+ing (male goose;
look)
Gan|dhi, In|dira
(Indian prime
minister)
Gan|dhi,
Ma|hatma
(Indian statesman)
Gan|dhi, Rajiv
(Indian prime
minister)
Gan|dhi|nagar
(city, India)
Gan|esha Hinduism
gang +s +ed +ing
(band, group; in
'gang up'.
△ gangue)
gang-bang +s +ed
+ing
gang|board +s
gang|er +s
Gan|ges (river,
India)
Gan|get|ic
gang|land
gan|gle
gan|gles
gan|gled
gan|gling
gan|gliar
gan|gli|form
gan|glion
gan|glia
gan|gli|on|ated
gan|gli|on|ic
gan|gly
gan|glier
gan|gli|est
gang|plank +s
gang rape +s noun
gang-rape
gang-rapes
gang-raped
gang-raping
verb

gan|grene
  gan|grenes
  gan|grened
  gan|gren|ing
  gan|gren|ous
gang|sta (music)
gang|ster +s
  (criminal)
gang|ster|ism
Gang|tok (city,
  India)
gangue (earth.
  △ gang)
gang|way +s
gan|is|ter
ganja
gan|net +s
gan|net|ry
  gan|net|ries
gan|oid +s
Gansu (province,
  China)
gant|let *Am.* +s
gan|try
  gan|tries
Gany|mede (*Greek
  Mythology*; moon
  of Jupiter)
gaol *Br.* +s +ed
  +ing (use jail)
gaol|er *Br.* +s (use
  jailer)
gap +s
gape
  gapes
  gaped
  gap|ing
gaper +s
gape|worm +s
gap|ing|ly
gapped
gappy
  gap|pier
  gap|pi|est
gap-toothed
gar +s (fish)
gar|age
  gar|ages
  gar|aged
  gar|aging
garam ma|sala
garb +s +ed +ing
gar|bage
gar|ble
  gar|bles
  gar|bled
  garb|ling
garb|ler +s
Garbo, Greta
  (Swedish actress)
gar|board +s
garb|olo|gist +s

garb|ology
Gar|cía Lorca,
  Fe|de|rico
  (Spanish poet and
  dramatist)
Gar|cía Már|quez,
  Gab|riel
  (Colombian
  novelist)
gar|çon +s
Garda
  Gar|dai
  (Irish police)
Garda, Lake (in
  Italy)
Gar|den, the (of
  Epicurus)
gar|den +s +ed
  +ing
gar|den|er +s
gardener-bird +s
gar|den|esque
gar|denia +s
Gard|ner, Erle
  Stan|ley
  (American
  novelist)
Gar|eth
Gar|field, James
  (American
  president)
gar|fish
  plural gar|fish
gar|ganey +s
gar|gan|tuan
gar|get
gar|gle
  gar|gles
  gar|gled
  garg|ling
gar|goyle +s
gar|goyl|ism
Ga|ri|baldi,
  Giu|seppe (Italian
  military leader)
ga|ri|baldi +s
  (blouse; biscuit;
  fish)
gar|ish
gar|ish|ly
gar|ish|ness
Gar|land, Judy
  (American singer
  and actress)
gar|land +s
  (wreath; wreathe)
gar|lic
gar|licky
gar|ment +s
gar|ment|ed
Garmo, Mount
  (former name of

Garmo (*cont.*)
  Communism
  Peak)
gar|ner +s +ed
  +ing
gar|net +s
gar|nish
  gar|nishes
  gar|nished
  gar|nish|ing
gar|nish|ee
  gar|nish|ees
  gar|nish|eed
  gar|nish|ee|ing
  gar|nish|ing +s
gar|nish|ment +s
gar|ni|ture +s
Ga|ronne (river,
  France)
gar|otte *Br.* (use
  garrotte)
  garottes
  gar|ot|ted
  gar|ot|ting
  (*Am.* garrote)
Ga|roua (river port,
  Cameroon)
gar|pike
  plural gar|pike *or*
  gar|pikes
Gar|ret (name)
gar|ret +s (attic)
gar|ret|eer +s
Gar|rick, David
  (English actor)
gar|rison +s +ed
  +ing
gar|rotte *Br.*
  gar|rottes
  gar|rott|ed
  gar|rott|ing
  (*Am.* garrote)
gar|rot|ter +s
gar|ru|lity
gar|rul|ous
gar|rul|ous|ly
gar|rul|ous|ness
Garry *also* Gary
gar|rya +s
gar|ter +s +ed +ing
Garth (name)
garth +s (open
  space in cloisters)
Ga|ruda *Hinduism*
Gar|vey, Mar|cus
  (Jamaican
  political activist)
Gary *also* Garry
gas
  gases
  gassed
  gas|sing

gas|bag +s
Gas|con +s (native
  of Gascony)
gas|con +s
  (braggart)
gas|con|ade +s
Gas|cony (former
  region, France)
gas-cooled
gas|eous
gas|eous|ness
gas field +s
gas fire +s
gas-fired
gash
  gashes
  gashed
  gash|ing
gas|hold|er +s
gasifi|ca|tion
gas|ify
  gasifies
  gasi|fied
  gasi|fy|ing
Gas|kell, Mrs
  Eliza|beth
  (English novelist)
gas|ket +s
gas|kin +s
gas|light +s
gas|lit
gas|man
  gas|men
gas mask +s
gaso|hol
gas|olene +s (use
  gasoline)
gas|oline +s
gas|om|eter +s
gasp +s +ed +ing
gasp|er +s
gas|per|eau
  gas|per|eaus *or*
  gas|per|eaux
gas-permeable
Gas|pra (asteroid)
gas-proof
gas ring +s
Gas|sendi, Pierre
  (French
  astronomer and
  philosopher)
Gas|ser, Her|bert
  Spen|cer
  (American
  physiologist)
gas|ser +s
gas|si|ness
gas sta|tion +s
gassy
  gas|sier
  gas|si|est

Gast|ar|bei|ter
  plural
  Gast|ar|bei|ter or
  Gast|ar|bei|ters
gas|tero|pod +s
  (use gastropod)
gast|haus
  gast|häuser
gast|hof
  gast|hofs or
  gast|höfe
gas-tight
gas|trec|tomy
  gas|trec|tomies
gas|tric
gas|tri|tis
gas|tro|en|ter|ic
gas|tro|en|ter|itis
gas|tro|entero|
      logic|al
gas|tro|enter|
     olo|gist +s
gas|tro|enter|
      ology
gas|tro|intest|inal
gas|tro|lith +s
gas|tro|nome +s
gas|tro|nom|ic
gas|tro|nom|ic|al
gas|tro|nom|ic|
      al|ly
gas|tron|omy
gas|tro|pod +s
gas|trop|odous
gas|tro|scope +s
gas|trula
  gas|tru|lae
gas|works
gat +s (gun.
  △ ghat)
gate
  gates
  gated
  gat|ing
  (barrier etc.;
  confine. △ gait)
gat|eau
  gat|eaux or
  gat|eaus
gate|crash
  gate|crashes
  gate|crashed
  gate|crash|ing
gate|crash|er +s
gate|fold +s
gate|house +s
gate|keep|er +s
gate|leg +s
gate|legged
gate|man
  gate|men
gate money

gate|post +s
Gates, Bill
  (American
  computer
  entrepreneur)
Gates|head (town,
  England)
gate valve +s
gate|way +s
gather +s +ed +ing
gath|er|er +s
gath|er|ing +s
Gat|ling +s
GATT (= General
  Agreement on
  Tariffs and Trade)
Gat|wick (airport,
  England)
gauche
gauche|ly
gauche|ness
gauch|erie +s
gau|cho +s
gaud +s
Gaudí, An|tonio
  (Spanish architect)
Gaudier-Brzeska,
  Henri (French
  sculptor)
gaud|ily
gaudi|ness
gaudy
  gau|dies
  gaud|ier
  gaudi|est
gauge *Br.*
  gauges
  gauged
  gauging
  (measure. *Am.*
  gage. △ gage)
gauge|able *Br.* (*Am.*
  gageable)
gauger *Br.* +s (*Am.*
  gager)
Gau|guin, Paul
  (French painter)
Gau|hati (city,
  India)
Gaul (ancient
  region, Europe)
gau|leiter +s
Gaul|ish
Gaulle, Charles de
  (French
  statesman)
Gaull|ism
Gaull|ist +s
Gaull|oise +s *Propr.*
gault
gaul|theria +s

Gaunt, John of
  (son of Edward III
  of England)
gaunt +er +est
gaunt|let +s
gaunt|ly
gaunt|ness
gaun|try
  gaun|tries
gaur +s
Gauss, Karl
  Fried|rich
  (German
  mathematician
  and physicist)
gauss
  plural gauss or
  gausses
Gauss|ian
Gau|tama (family
  name of Buddha)
gauze +s
gauz|ily
gauzi|ness
gauzy
  gauz|ier
  gauzi|est
Gav|as|kar, Sunil
  (Indian cricketer)
gave
gavel
  gavels
  gav|elled *Br.*
  gav|eled *Am.*
  gav|el|ling *Br.*
  gav|el|ing *Am.*
ga|vial +s
Gavin
ga|votte +s
Ga|wain (Arthurian
  knight)
Gawd (= God in
  exclamations)
gawk +s +ed +ing
gawk|ily
gawki|ness
gawk|ish
gawky
  gawk|ier
  gawki|est
gawp +s +ed +ing
gawp|er +s
Gay, John (English
  poet and
  dramatist)
Gay *also* Gaye
  (name)
gay +s +er +est
  (cheerful;
  homosexual)
Gaya (city, India.
  △ Gaia)

gayal +s
Gaye *also* Gay
gay|ety *Am.* (use
  gaiety)
Gayle *also* Gail
Gay-Lussac,
  Jo|seph Louis
  (French chemist
  and physicist)
gay|ness
Gay|nor *also*
  Gae|nor
gaz|ania +s
Ga|zan|kulu
  (former homeland,
  South Africa)
gazar +s
Gaza Strip (coastal
  territory, SE
  Mediterranean)
gaze
  gazes
  gazed
  gaz|ing
gaz|ebo +s
gaz|elle +s
gazer +s
gaz|ette
  gaz|ettes
  gaz|et|ted
  gaz|et|ting
gaz|et|teer +s
Gazi|an|tep (city,
  Turkey)
gaz|pa|cho +s
gaz|ump +s +ed
  +ing
gaz|ump|er +s
  noun
gaz|un|der +s +ed
  +ing verb
Gdańsk (port,
  Poland)
Gdy|nia (port,
  Poland)
Ge (*Greek
  Mythology,*
  = Gaia)
gean +s (cherry)
gear +s +ed +ing
gear|box
  gear|boxes
gear change +s
gear|ing
gear lever +s
gear|stick +s
gear|wheel +s
Geber (Arab
  chemist)
gecko
  geckos or
  geckoes

gee
 gees
 geed
 gee¦ing
gee-gee +s
geek +s
Gee¦long (port, Australia)
geese
gee-string +s (use G-string)
Ge'ez (language)
gee¦zer +s (person. △ geyser)
Ge¦henna (hell)
Geh¦rig, Lou (American baseball player)
Gei¦ger, Hans Wil¦helm (German nuclear physicist)
Gei¦ger count¦er +s
Gei¦kie, Archi¦bald (Scottish geologist)
gei¦sha
 plural **gei¦sha** *or* **gei¦shas**
Geiss¦ler tube +s
Gejiu (city, China)
Geju (use Gejiu)
gel
 gels
 gelled
 gel¦ling
 (semi-solid; form jel. △ jell)
gel¦ada
 plural **gel¦ada** *or* **gel¦adas**
gel¦atin +s (in technical use)
gel¦atine +s (generally)
gel¦at¦in¦isa¦tion *Br.* (use gelatinization)
gel¦at¦in¦ise *Br.* (use gelatinize)
 gel¦at¦in¦ises
 gel¦at¦in¦ised
 gel¦at¦in¦is¦ing
gel¦at¦in¦iza¦tion
gel¦at¦in¦ize
 gel¦at¦in¦izes
 gel¦at¦in¦ized
 gel¦at¦in¦iz¦ing
gel¦at¦in¦ous
gel¦at¦in¦ous¦ly

gel¦ation
gel¦ato
 gel¦ati *or* gel¦atis *or* gel¦atos
geld +s +ed +ing
Gel¦der¦land (province, the Netherlands)
geld¦ing +s
gelid
gel¦ig¦nite
Gell-Mann, Mur¦ray (American physicist)
gelly (= gelignite. △ jelly)
gel¦se¦mium
Gel¦sen¦kir¦chen (city, Germany)
gem
 gems
 gemmed
 gem¦ming
Gem¦ara *Judaism*
Gem¦ayel, Pierre (Lebanese political leader)
gem¦in¦al
gem¦in¦al¦ly
gemin¦ate
 gemin¦ates
 gemin¦ated
 gemin¦at¦ing
gemin¦ation
Gem¦ini (constellation; sign of zodiac)
Gemi¦nian +s
Gem¦in¦ids (meteor shower)
gem¦like
Gemma *also* **Jemma** (name)
gemma
 gem¦mae (cellular body)
gem¦ma¦tion
gem¦mif¦er¦ous
gem¦mip¦ar¦ous
gem¦molo¦gist +s
gem¦mol¦ogy
gem¦mule +s
gemmy (having gems. △ jemmy)
gems¦bok +s
gem¦stone +s
ge¦müt¦lich
gen
 gens

gen (*cont.*)
 genned
 gen¦ning
genco +s
gen¦darme +s
gen¦darm¦erie +s
gen¦der +s
gen¦dered
Gene (man's name. △ Jean)
gene +s (*Biology*. △ jean, jeans)
ge¦nea¦logic¦al
ge¦nea¦logic¦al¦ly
ge¦neal¦ogise *Br.* (use genealogize)
 ge¦neal¦ogises
 ge¦neal¦ogised
 ge¦neal¦ogis¦ing
ge¦neal¦ogist +s
ge¦neal¦ogize
 ge¦neal¦ogizes
 ge¦neal¦ogized
 ge¦neal¦ogiz¦ing
ge¦neal¦ogy
 ge¦neal¦ogies
gen¦era
gen¦er¦able
gen¦eral +s
gen¦er¦al¦is¦abil¦ity *Br.* (use generalizability)
gen¦er¦al¦is¦able *Br.* (use generalizable)
gen¦er¦al¦isa¦tion *Br.* +s (use generalization)
gen¦er¦al¦ise *Br.* (use generalize)
 gen¦er¦al¦ises
 gen¦er¦al¦ised
 gen¦er¦al¦is¦ing
gen¦er¦al¦iser *Br.* +s (use generalizer)
gen¦er¦al¦is¦simo +s
gen¦er¦al¦ist +s
gen¦er¦al¦ity
 gen¦er¦al¦ities
gen¦er¦al¦iz¦abil¦ity
gen¦er¦al¦iz¦able
gen¦er¦al¦iza¦tion
gen¦er¦al¦ize
 gen¦er¦al¦izes
 gen¦er¦al¦ized
 gen¦er¦al¦iz¦ing
gen¦er¦al¦izer *Am.* +s

gen¦er¦al¦ly
gen¦er¦al¦ness
general-purpose *adjective*
gen¦eral
 sec¦re¦tary
gen¦eral
 sec¦re¦tar¦ies
gen¦er¦al¦ship +s
gen¦er¦ate
 gen¦er¦ates
 gen¦er¦ated
 gen¦er¦at¦ing
gen¦er¦ation +s
gen¦er¦ation¦al
gen¦era¦tive
gen¦er¦ator +s
gen¦er¦ic
gen¦er¦ic¦al¦ly
gen¦er¦os¦ity
 gen¦er¦os¦ities
gen¦er¦ous
gen¦er¦ous¦ly
gen¦er¦ous¦ness
Gen¦esis *Bible*
gen¦esis
Genet, Jean (French writer)
genet +s (catlike mammal. △ jennet)
gen¦et¦ic
gen¦et¦ic¦al¦ly
gen¦eti¦cist +s
gen¦et¦ics
Gen¦ette *also* **Jan¦ette,** **Jean¦ette,** **Jean¦nette** (name)
ge¦nette +s (catlike mammal; use genet. △ jennet)
Gen¦eva (city, Switzerland)
gen¦eva (gin)
gen¦ever +s
Gene¦vieve
Gen¦ghis Khan (founder of Mongol empire)
gen¦ial
geni¦al¦ity
geni¦al¦ly
genic
genie
 genii *or* gen¦ies
genii (plural of genie and genius)
gen¦ista +s
geni¦tal +s
geni¦talia

geni|tival
geni|tival¦ly
geni|tive +s
genito-urinary
ge|nius
  ge|niuses
  (exceptional
  ability; person
  with this)
ge|nius
  ge|niuses *or* genii
  (spirit; influence)
ge|ni|zah +s
Genoa (port, Italy;
  cake)
genoa +s (sail)
geno|cidal
geno|cide +s
Geno|ese
  plural Geno|ese
gen|ome +s
geno|type +s
geno|typ|ic
genre +s
gens
  gen¦tes
Gent (Flemish
  name for Ghent)
gent +s
gen|teel
gen|teel|ism
gen|teel¦ly
gen|teel|ness
gen|tes
gen|tian +s
Gen|tile +s (non-
  Jewish; non-Jew)
gen|tile +s
  (indicating
  nationality; such a
  word)
Gen|tile da
  Fab|ri|ano
  (Italian painter)
gen|til|ity
  gen|til|ities
Gen|ting
  High|lands (hill
  resort, Malaysia)
gen|tle
  gen|tles
  gen|tled
  gent|ling
  gent|ler
  gent|lest
gentle|folk
gentle|man
  gentle|men
gentleman-at-
  arms
  gentlemen-at-
  arms

gentle|man
  farm¦er +s
gentle|man|li|ness
gentle|man¦ly
gentle|man's
  agree|ment +s
gentle|men's
  agree|ment +s
  (use gentleman's
  agreement)
gentle|ness
gentle|woman
  gentle|women
gen¦tly
gen¦too +s
gen¦tri|fi|ca|tion
gen¦tri|fier +s
gen¦tri¦fy
  gen¦tri|fies
  gen¦tri|fied
  gen¦tri|fy|ing
gen¦try
Gents, the (men's
  lavatory)
genu|flect +s +ed
  +ing
genu|flec¦tion +s
genu|flect¦or +s
genu|flect¦ory
genu|flex¦ion *Br.*
  +s (use
  genuflection)
genu|ine
genu|ine¦ly
genu|ine|ness
genus
  gen¦era
geo|bot|an¦ist +s
geo|bot¦any
geo|cen¦tric
geo|cen¦tric|al¦ly
geo|chem|ical
geo|chem|ist +s
geo|chem|is¦try
geo|chrono|
        logic|al
Geo|chrono|olo|gist
  +s
geo|chron|ology
geode +s
geo|des|ic
geo|des|ist +s
geo|desy
geo|det|ic (use
  geodesic)
geo¦dic
Geoff *also* Jeff
Geof|frey *also*
  Jef|frey
Geof|frey of
  Mon|mouth
  (British chronicler)

geog|raph¦er +s
geo|graph|ic
geo|graph|ic|al
geo|graph|ic|al¦ly
geog|raphy
  geog|raph¦ies
geoid +s
geo|logic
geo|logic|al
geo|logic|al¦ly
geolo|gise *Br.* (use
  geologize)
  geolo|gises
  geolo|gised
  geolo|gis¦ing
geolo|gist +s
geolo|gize
  geolo|gizes
  geolo|gized
  geolo|giz¦ing
geol|ogy
geo|mag|net¦ic
geo|mag|net¦ic|
        al¦ly
geo|mag|net¦ism
geo|mancy
geo|man¦tic
geom|eter +s
geo|met¦ric
geo|met¦ric|al
geo|met¦ric|al¦ly
geom|etri|cian +s
geo|met¦rid +s
  (moth)
geom|etrise *Br.*
  (use geometrize)
  geom|etrises
  geom|etrised
  geom|etris¦ing
geom|etrize
  geom|etrizes
  geom|etrized
  geom|etriz¦ing
geom|etry
  geom|etries
geo|mor|pho|
        logic|al
geo|morph|
     olo|gist +s
geo|morph|ology
ge|oph¦agy
geo|phone +s
geo|phys|ic|al
geo|phys|ic|al¦ly
geo|physi¦cist +s
geo|phys|ics
geo|pol|it¦ical
geo|pol|it¦ic|al¦ly
geo|pol|it¦ician +s
geo|pol|it¦ics
Geor|die +s

George (British
  kings)
George (patron
  saint of England)
George (automatic
  pilot)
George Cross
  George Crosses
George|town
  (capital of
  Guyana)
George Town
  (capital of the
  Cayman Islands)
George Town
  (port, Malaysia)
Geor|gette (name)
geor|gette +s
  (fabric)
Geor|gia (country,
  SE Europe; state,
  USA; name)
Geor|gian +s
Geor|giana
Geor|gie
Geor|gina
geo|science +s
geo|sci|en¦tist +s
geo|sphere +s
geo|sta|tion|ary
geo|stroph¦ic
geo|syn|chron|ous
geo|tech|nic|al
geo|ther¦mal
geo|ther¦mal|ly
geo|trop¦ic
geo|trop|ism
Gera (city,
  Germany)
Ger|aint
Ger|ald
Ger|ald|ine
Ger|ald|ton (port,
  Australia)
ge|ra|nium +s
Ger|ard *also*
  Ger|rard
ger|bera +s
ger|bil +s
ger|enuk
  plural ger|enuk *or*
  ger|enuks
ger|fal|con +s (use
  gyrfalcon)
geri +s
geri|at¦ric +s
geria|tri|cian +s
geri|at¦rics
geria|trist +s
Gé|ri|cault,
  Théo|dore
  (French painter)

germ +s
Ger|maine
Ger|man +s (from
  Germany)
ger|man (having
  same parents.
  △ germen,
  germon)
Ger|man Bight
  (shipping area,
  North Sea)
ger|man|der +s
ger|mane
ger|mane|ly
ger|mane|ness
Ger|man|ic (having
  German
  characteristics
  etc.; language)
ger|man|ic
  (*Chemistry* of
  germanium)
Ger|mani|cism +s
Ger|man|isa|tion
  Br. (use
  Germanization)
Ger|man|ise *Br.*
  (use Germanize)
Ger|man|ises
Ger|man|ised
Ger|man|is|ing
Ger|man|iser *Br.*
  +s (use
  Germanizer)
Ger|man|ism +s
Ger|man|ist +s
ger|ma|nium
Ger|man|iza|tion
Ger|man|ize
Ger|man|izes
Ger|man|ized
Ger|man|iz|ing
Ger|man|izer +s
Ger|man mea|sles
Ger|man shepherd
  +s
Ger|man sil|ver
Ger|many
  Ger|manies
germ cell +s
ger|men +s
  (*Botany.*
  △ German,
  german, germon)
ger|mi|cidal
ger|mi|cide +s
ger|min|al
ger|min|al|ly
ger|min|ant
ger|min|ate
  ger|min|ates

ger|min|ate (*cont.*)
  ger|min|ated
  ger|min|at|ing
ger|min|ation
ger|mina|tive
ger|min|ator +s
Ger|mis|ton (town,
  South Africa)
ger|mon
  plural ger|mon *or*
  ger|mons
  (fish. △ German,
  german, germen)
germy
  germ|ier
  germi|est
Ger|on|imo
  (Apache chief)
ger|on|toc|racy
  ger|on|toc|ra|cies
ger|on|to|logic|al
ger|on|tolo|gist +s
ger|on|tol|ogy
Ger|rard *also*
  Ger|ard
Gerry *also* Jerry
ger|ry|man|der +s
  +ed +ing
ger|ry|man|der|er
  +s
Gersh|win,
  George
  (American
  composer and
  pianist)
Ger|trude
ger|und +s
ger|und|ial
ger|und|ival
ger|und|ive +s
Ger|vaise *also*
  Ger|vase
Ger|vase *also*
  Ger|vaise
gesso
  ges|soes
ges|ta|gen +s
ges|ta|gen|ic
ge|stalt +s
ge|stalt|ism
ge|stalt|ist +s
Ge|stapo (Nazi
  German secret
  police)
ges|tate
  ges|tates
  ges|tated
  ges|tat|ing
ges|ta|tion
ges|ta|tor|ial
ges|ticu|late
  ges|ticu|lates

ges|ticu|late (*cont.*)
  ges|ticu|lated
  ges|ticu|lat|ing
ges|ticu|la|tion +s
ges|ticu|la|tive
ges|ticu|la|tor +s
ges|ticu|la|tory
ges|tural
ges|ture
  ges|tures
  ges|tured
  ges|tur|ing
ges|tur|er +s
ge|sund|heit
get
  gets
  got
  get|ting
  got *or*
  got|ten *Am.*
geta (Japanese
  shoes. △ gaiter)
get-at-able
get|away +s
Geth|sem|ane,
  Gar|den of (in
  Jerusalem)
get-out +s *noun*
  and adjective
get-rich-quick
get|table
get|ter +s
get-together +s
Getty, J. Paul
  (American
  industrialist)
Gettys|burg (town,
  USA)
get-up +s *noun*
get-up-and-go
geum +s
gew|gaw +s
Ge|würz|tram|iner
  +s
gey|ser +s (hot
  spring; water
  heater. △ geezer)
Ghana
Ghan|aian +s
ghar|ial +s
gharry
  ghar|ries
ghast|lily
ghast|li|ness
ghastly
  ghast|lier
  ghast|li|est
ghat +s (flight of
  river-steps etc.
  △ gat)

Ghats, East|ern
  and West|ern
  (mountains, India)
ghaut +s (use ghat)
Ghazi +s
Ghazia|bad (city,
  India)
Ghaz|na|vid +s
ghee
Gheg
  plural Gheg *or*
  Ghegs
Ghent (city,
  Belgium)
ghe|rao +s
gher|kin +s
ghetto +s *noun*
ghetto
  ghet|toes
  ghet|toed
  ghetto|ing
  verb
ghetto blast|er +s
ghetto|ise *Br.* (use
  ghettoize)
ghetto|ises
ghetto|ised
ghetto|is|ing
ghetto|ize
ghetto|izes
ghetto|ized
ghetto|iz|ing
ghi (use ghee)
Ghib|el|line +s
  (Italian history)
Ghib|el|lin|ism
Ghi|berti,
  Lor|enzo
  (Florentine
  sculptor)
ghil|lie +s (use
  gillie)
Ghir|lan|daio
  (Italian painter)
ghost +s +ed +ing
ghost|bust|er +s
ghost|bust|ing
  noun
ghost|like
ghost|li|ness
ghost|ly
  ghost|lier
  ghost|li|est
ghost story
  ghost stor|ies
ghost town +s
ghost word +s
ghost-write
  ghost-writes
  ghost-wrote
  ghost-writing
  ghost-written

ghost-writer +s
ghoul +s
ghoul|ish
ghoul|ish|ly
ghoul|ish|ness
Ghul|ghu|leh
(ancient city,
Afghanistan)
ghyll +s (use gill)
Gia|co|metti,
Al|berto (Swiss
sculptor and
painter)
giant +s
giant|ess
giant|esses
giant|ism
giant-killer +s
giant-killing
giant-like
Giant's
Cause|way
(rocks, Northern
Ireland)
gia|our +s (*offensive*)
Giap, Vo Ngu|yen
(Vietnamese
defence minister)
giar|dia|sis
Gib (= Gibraltar)
gib +s (bolt, wedge,
etc. △jib)
gib|ber +s +ed
+ing (speak
incoherently;
boulder. △jibba,
jibber)
gib|ber|el|lin
gib|ber|ish
gib|bet +s +ed
+ing
Gib|bon, Ed|ward
(English historian)
gib|bon +s
Gib|bons,
Grin|ling (English
sculptor)
gib|bos|ity
gib|bous
gib|bous|ly
gib|bous|ness
Gibbs, James
(Scottish
architect)
Gibbs, Jo|siah
Wil|lard
(American
physical chemist)
gibe
gibes
gibed
gib|ing

gibe (*cont.*)
(taunt. △jibe,
gybe)
giber +s
gib|lets
Gib|ral|tar
Gib|ral|tar|ian +s
Gib|son, Al|thea
(American tennis
player)
Gib|son Des|ert (in
Australia)
Gib|son girl +s
gid|di|ly
gid|di|ness
giddy
gid|dies
gid|died
giddy|ing
gid|dier
gid|di|est
giddy-up
Gide, André
(French writer)
Gid|eon (*Bible*
Israelite leader;
name)
Gid|eon bible +s
gie
gies
gied
gie|ing
gien
Giel|gud, John
(English actor)
GIFT (= gamete
intrafallopian
transfer)
gift +s +ed +ing
gift|ed|ly
gift|ed|ness
gift-horse +s
gift token +s
gift|ware
gift|wrap +s *noun*
gift-wrap
gift-wraps
gift-wrapped
gift-wrapping
verb
Gifu (city, Japan)
gig
gigs
gigged
gig|ging
giga|byte +s
giga|flop +s
giga|meter *Am.* +s
giga|metre *Br.* +s
gi|gant|esque
gi|gan|tic
gi|gan|tic|al|ly

gi|gant|ism
Gi|gan|to|pith|ecus
giga|watt +s
gig|gle
gig|gles
gig|gled
gig|gling
gig|gler +s
gig|gli|ness
gig|gly
gig|glier
gig|gli|est
Gigli, Ben|ia|mino
(Italian singer)
GIGO (= garbage
in, garbage out)
gig|olo +s
gigot +s (meat;
sleeve)
gigue +s
Gijón (port, Spain)
Gila mon|ster +s
Gil|bert,
Hum|phrey
(English explorer)
Gil|bert, Wil|liam
(English scientist)
Gil|bert, W. S.
(English librettist)
Gil|bert
Gil|bert and
El|lice Is|lands
(in Pacific Ocean)
Gil|bert|ian
Gil|bert Is|lands
(now part of
Kiribati)
gild +s +ed +ing
(cover with gold.
△guild)
gild|er +s (person
who gilds.
△guilder)
Giles *also* Gyles
gilet +s
gil|gai +s
Gil|ga|mesh
(legendary
Sumerian king)
Gil|git (town and
district, Pakistani
Kashmir)
Gill, Eric (English
sculptor etc.)
Gill *also* Jill
(name)
gill +s +s +ed +ing
gil|la|roo
plural gil|la|roo or
gil|la|roos
gill cover +s
gilled

Gil|les|pie, Dizzy
(American jazz
trumpeter)
Gil|lian *also* Jil|lian
gil|lie +s
Gil|ling|ham
(town, England)
gil|lion
plural gil|lion or
gil|lions
gill-net +s
Gilly *also* Jilly
gilly|flower +s
gilt +s (past tense
and past participle
of gild; gold layer;
government
security. △guilt)
gilt-edged
gilt|wood
gim|bal
gim|bals
gim|balled
gim|bal|ling
gim|crack +s
gim|crack|ery
gim|cracky
gim|let +s
gim|mick +s
gim|mick|ry
gim|micky
gimp +s (lame
person or leg.
△guimp, gymp)
gin
gins
ginned
gin|ning
Gina
ging +s
gin|ger +s +ed
+ing
gin|ger|bread +s
gin|ger|li|ness
gin|ger|ly
gin|gery
ging|ham +s
gin|gili
gin|giva
gin|gi|vae
gin|gival
gin|gi|vitis
gingko (use
ginkgo)
ging|kos or
ging|koes
gin|gly|mus
gin|glymi
gink +s
ginkgo
gink|gos or
gink|goes

gin|ner +s

Ginny

gi|nor|mous

Gins|berg, Allen (American poet)

gin|seng

Gio|conda, La

Gio|litti, Gio|vanni (Italian statesman)

Gior|gione (Italian painter)

Giotto (European space probe)

G¹otto di Bon|done (Italian painter)

Gio|vanni de' Med|ici (Pope Leo X)

gippy (tummy)

gipsy (use gypsy) gip|sies

gir|affe +s

gir|an|dole +s

gira|sol +s

gira|sole +s (use girasol)

gird girds gird|ed or girt gird|ing (encircle; fasten)

gird +s +ed +ing (jeer)

gird|er +s

gir|dle gir|dles gir|dled gird|ling

girl +s

girl Fri|day +s

girl|friend +s

Girl Guide +s (former name for a Guide)

girl|hood +s

girlie +s (noun; also in 'girlie magazine')

girl|ish

girl|ish|ly

girl|ish|ness

Girl Scout +s

girly (girlish)

girn +s +ed +ing (use gurn)

girn|er +s (use gurner)

giro +s (credit transfer. △ gyro)

giro giroes giroed

giro (cont.) giro|ing (pay by giro. △ gyro)

Gir|onde (estuary, France)

Gir|on|din +s

Gir|ond|ist +s

girt +s +ed +ing

girth +s +ed +ing

Gis|borne (port, New Zealand)

Giscard d'Estaing, Val|éry (French statesman)

Gis|elle

Gish, Lil|lian (American actress)

gismo +s

Gis|sing, George (English writer)

gist +s

git +s

gîte +s

Gi|tega (town, Burundi)

git|tern +s

give gives gave giv|ing given

give|able

give-away +s noun and adjective

given +s

giver +s

Giza, El (city, Egypt)

gizmo +s (use gismo)

giz|zard +s

gla|bella gla|bel|lae

gla|bel|lar

glab|rous

glacé

gla|cial

gla|ci|al|ly

gla|ci|ated

gla|ci|ation +s

gla|cier +s

gla|cio|logic|al

gla|ci|olo|gist +s

gla|ci|ology

gla|cis plural gla|cis

glad glads glad|ded glad|ding

glad (cont.) glad|der glad|dest

glad|den +s +ed +ing (make glad. △ gladden)

glad|den|er +s

glad|die +s

glad|don +s (flower. △ gladden)

glade +s

glad hand noun

glad-hand +s +ed +ing verb

glad-hander +s

gladi|ator +s

gladia|tor|ial

gladi|olus gladi|oli or gladi|olus|es

glad|ly

glad|ness

glad|some

Glad|stone, Wil|liam Ewart (British prime minister)

Glad|stone bag +s

Gladys

Gla|go|lit|ic

glair (white of egg. △ glare)

glaire (use glair. △ glare)

glair|eous

glairy

glaive +s

glam glams glammed glam|ming

glamor Am. (use glamour)

Gla|mor|gan (former county, Wakes)

glam|or|isa|tion Br. (use glamorization)

glam|or|ise Br. (use glamorize)

glam|or|ises glam|or|ised glam|or|is|ing

glam|or|iza|tion

glam|or|ize glam|or|izes glam|or|ized glam|or|iz|ing

glam|or|ous

glam|or|ous|ly

glam|our

glam|our|isa|tion (use glamorization)

glam|our|ise (use glamorize)

glam|our|iza|tion (use glamorization)

glam|our|ize (use glamorize)

glam|our|ous (use glamorous)

glam|our|ous|ly (use glamorously)

glance glances glanced glan|cing

glan|cing|ly

gland +s

glan|dered

glan|der|ous

glan|ders

glan|du|lar

gland|ule +s

glans glan|des

glare glares glared glar|ing (look angrily or fixedly. △ glair, glaire)

glar|ing|ly

glar|ing|ness

glary

Glas|gow (city, Scotland)

glas|nost

Glass, Philip (American composer)

glass glasses glassed glass|ing

glass-blower +s

glass-blowing

glass cloth (fabric made of glass)

glass-cloth +s (for drying glasses; abrasive)

glass cut|ter +s

glass fibre

glass|ful +s

glass-gall

glass|house +s

glassie +s *noun*
(use glassy)
glass|ily
glass|ine
glassi|ness
glass|less
glass|like
glass|maker +s
glass-making
glass|paper
glass snake +s
(snakelike lizard.
⚠ grass snake)
glass|ware
glass wool
glass|work (glass
objects)
glass|works
(factory)
glass|wort +s
glassy
glass|ies
glass|ier
glassi|est
Glas|ton|bury
(town, England)
Glas|we|gian +s
Glau|ber's salt
Glau|ber's salts
(use Glauber's
salt)
glau|coma
glau|comat|ous
glau|cous
glaze
glazes
glazed
glaz|ing
glazer +s
glaz|ier +s
glaz|iery
Glaz|unov,
Alex|an|der
(Russian
composer)
glazy
gleam +s +ed +ing
gleam|ing|ly
gleamy
glean +s +ed +ing
glean|er +s
glean|ings
glebe +s
glee +s
glee|ful
glee|ful|ly
glee|ful|ness
glee|some
gleet
Gleich|schal|tung
Glen *also* Glenn
glen +s

Glen|coe (glen,
Scotland)
Glenda
Glen|dower,
Owen (Welsh
prince)
Glen|eagles (valley
and golf course,
Scotland)
glen|garry
glen|gar|ries
Glen More (valley,
Scotland)
Glenn *also* Glen
glen|oid cav|ity
glen|oid cav|ities
Glen|rothes (town,
Scotland)
Glenys
gley +s
glia +s
glial
glib
glib|ber
glib|best
glib|ly
glib|ness
glide
glides
glided
glid|ing
glider +s
glid|ing|ly
glim +s
glim|mer +s +ed
+ing
glim|mer|ing +s
glim|mer|ing|ly
glimpse
glimpses
glimpsed
glimps|ing
Glinka, Mikh|ail
Ivan|ovich
(Russian
composer)
glint +s +ed +ing
glis|sade
glis|sades
glis|saded
glis|sad|ing
glis|sando
glis|sandi *or*
glis|san|dos
glissé +s
glis|ten +s +ed
+ing
glis|ter +s +ed
+ing
glitch
glitches

glit|ter +s +ed
+ing
glit|ter|ati
glit|ter|ing|ly
Glit|ter|tind
(mountain,
Norway)
glit|tery
glitz
glitz|ily
glitzi|ness
glitzy
glitz|ier
glitzi|est
Gli|wice (city,
Poland)
gloam|ing *noun*
gloat +s +ed +ing
gloat|er +s
gloat|ing|ly
glob +s
global
glob|al|isa|tion *Br.*
(use
globalization)
glob|al|ise *Br.* (use
globalize)
glob|al|ises
glob|al|ised
glob|al|is|ing
glob|al|iza|tion
glob|al|ize
glob|al|izes
glob|al|ized
glob|al|iz|ing
glob|al|ly
globe
globes
globed
glob|ing
globe-fish
plural globe-fish
or globe-fishes
globe|flower +s
globe|like
globe-trotter +s
Globe|trot|ters (in
'the Harlem
Globetrotters')
globe-trotting
glo|bi|ger|ina
glo|bi|ger|inas *or*
glo|bi|ger|inae
glob|oid +s
glob|ose
globu|lar
globu|lar|ity
globu|lar|ly
glob|ule +s
globu|lin
globu|lous
glock|en|spiel +s

glom
gloms
glommed
glom|ming
glom|er|ate
glom|eru|lar
glom|eru|le +s
glom|eru|lus
glom|eruli
gloom +s +ed +ing
(darkness; be
gloomy etc.
⚠ glume)
gloom|ily
gloomi|ness
gloomy
gloom|ier
gloomi|est
gloop
gloopy
glop +s
Gloria (name;
doxology)
gloria +s
(doxology)
Glori|ana
(Elizabeth I)
glori|fi|ca|tion
glori|fier +s
glori|fy
glori|fies
glori|fied
glori|fy|ing
glori|ole +s
glori|ous
glori|ous|ly
glori|ous|ness
glory
glor|ies
glor|ied
glory|ing
glory-box
glory-boxes
glory-hole +s
glory-of-the-snow
gloss
glosses
glossed
gloss|ing
glossal
gloss|ar|ial
gloss|ar|ist +s
gloss|ary
gloss|ar|ies
gloss|ator +s
gloss|eme +s
gloss|er +s
gloss|ily
glossi|ness
gloss|itis
glos|sog|raph|er
+s

glos¦so¦lalia
glosso¦
    phar¦yn¦geal
glossy
  gloss¦ies
  gloss¦ier
  glossi¦est
glot¦tal
glot¦tal¦isa¦tion *Br.*
  (use
  glottalization)
glot¦tal¦ise *Br.* (use
  glottalize)
  glot¦tal¦ises
  glot¦tal¦ised
  glot¦tal¦is¦ing
glot¦tal¦iza¦tion
glot¦tal¦ize
  glot¦tal¦izes
  glot¦tal¦ized
  glot¦tal¦iz¦ing
glot¦tis
  glot¦tises
Glouces¦ter (city,
  England)
Glouces¦ter¦shire
  (county, England)
glove
  gloves
  gloved
  glov¦ing
glove¦box
  glove¦boxes
glow +s +ed +ing
glow¦er +s
glow-worm +s
glox¦inia +s
gloze
  glozes
  glozed
  gloz¦ing
glu¦ca¦gon
Gluck, Chris¦toph
  Wil¦li¦bald von
  (German
  composer)
glu¦cose
glu¦co¦side
glu¦co¦sid¦ic
glue
  glues
  glued
  glu¦ing *or* glue¦ing
glue ear
glue-like
glue-pot +s
gluer +s
glue-sniffer +s
glue-sniffing
gluey
  glu¦ier
  glui¦est

gluey¦ness
glug
  glugs
  glugged
  glug¦ging
glüh¦wein +s
glum
  glum¦mer
  glum¦mest
glu¦ma¦ceous
glume +s (*Botany.*
  △ gloom)
glum¦ly
glum¦ness
glu¦mose
gluon +s
glut
  gluts
  glut¦ted
  glut¦ting
glu¦tam¦ate +s
glu¦tam¦ic
glu¦tam¦ine
glu¦teal +s
glu¦ten +s
glu¦teus
  glu¦tei
glu¦tin¦ous
glu¦tin¦ous¦ly
glu¦tin¦ous¦ness
glut¦ton +s
glut¦ton¦ise *Br.*
  (use gluttonize)
  glut¦ton¦ises
  glut¦ton¦ised
  glut¦ton¦is¦ing
glut¦ton¦ize
  glut¦ton¦izes
  glut¦ton¦ized
  glut¦ton¦iz¦ing
glut¦ton¦ous
glut¦ton¦ous¦ly
glut¦tony
gly¦cer¦ide +s
gly¦cerin *Am.*
gly¦cer¦ine *Br.*
gly¦cerol
gly¦cine
glyco¦gen
glyco¦gen¦esis
glyco¦gen¦ic
gly¦col +s
gly¦col¦ic
gly¦col¦lic (use
  glycolic)
gly¦coly¦sis
glyco¦pro¦tein +s
glyco¦side +s
glyco¦sid¦ic
glyco¦suria
glyco¦sur¦ic

Glyn *also* Glynn
Glynde¦bourne
  (opera festival,
  England)
Glynis *also*
  Glyn¦nis
Glynn *also* Glyn
Glyn¦nis *also*
  Glynis
glyph +s
glyph¦ic
glyp¦tal +s
glyp¦tic
glyp¦to¦dont +s
glyp¦tog¦raphy
G-man
  G-men
gnamma +s
gnarl +s
gnarled
gnarly
  gnarl¦ier
  gnarli¦est
gnash
  gnashes
  gnashed
  gnash¦ing
gnash¦er +s
gnat +s
gnath¦ic
gnaw
  gnaws
  gnawed
  gnaw¦ing
  gnawed *or* gnawn
  (bite. △ nor)
gnaw¦ing¦ly
gneiss
  gneisses
gneiss¦ic
gneiss¦oid
gneiss¦ose
gnoc¦chi
gnome +s
gno¦mic
gnom¦ic¦al¦ly
gnom¦ish
gnomon +s
gnom¦on¦ic
gno¦sis
  gno¦ses
Gnos¦tic +s (early
  Christian heretic)
gnos¦tic (of
  knowledge)
gnos¦ti¦cise *Br.*
  (use gnosticize)
  gnos¦ti¦cises
  gnos¦ti¦cised
  gnos¦ti¦cis¦ing
Gnos¦ti¦cism

gnos¦ti¦cize
  gnos¦ti¦cizes
  gnos¦ti¦cized
  gnos¦ti¦ciz¦ing
gnu
  plural gnu *or* gnus
go
  goes
  went
  going
  gone
Goa (state, India)
goa
  plural goa *or* goas
  (gazelle. △ goer)
goad +s +ed +ing
go-ahead *noun and*
  adjective
goak +s
goal +s
goal¦ball
goalie +s
goal¦keep¦er +s
goal¦keep¦ing
goal kick +s
goal-kicker +s
goal-kicking
goal¦less
goal line +s
goal¦mind¦er +s
goal¦mouth +s
goal¦post +s
goal¦scorer +s
goal¦scor¦ing *noun*
  and attributive
goal¦tend¦er +s
goal¦tend¦ing
Goan +s
Goan¦ese
  plural Goan¦ese
go¦anna +s
goat +s
goat-antelope +s
goatee +s
goat-god
goat¦herd +s
goat¦ish
goat¦ling +s
goat moth +s
goats¦beard *Am.*
  +s
goat's-beard +s
goat¦skin +s
goat¦suck¦er +s
goaty
  goat¦ier
  goati¦est
gob
  gobs
  gobbed
  gob¦bing
go¦bang

Göb|bels, Jo|seph
(use Goebbels)
gob|bet +s
Gobbi, Tito (Italian
baritone)
gob|ble
  gob|bles
  gob|bled
  gob|bling
gobble|de|gook
gobble|dy|gook
  (use
  gobbledegook)
gob|bler +s
gobby
  gob|bies
Gobe|lins (French
tapestry factory)
gobe|mouche +s
go-between +s
  noun
Gobi Des|ert
  (Mongolia and
  China)
**Gobi|neau,
Jo|seph Ar|thur de**
  (French
  anthropologist)
gob|let +s
gob|lin +s
gob|smacked
gob|smack|ing
gob|stop|per +s
goby
  go|bies
  (fish)
go-by (*noun* snub)
go-cart +s (hand-
  cart. △ go-kart)
God (chiefly in
  Christianity and
  Judaism)
god +s (other
  superhuman
  being)
God|ard, Jean-Luc
  (French film
  director)
Go|da|vari (river,
  India)
God-awful
god|child
  god|chil|dren
god|dam
god|damn (use
  goddam)
god|damned
**God|dard, Rob|ert
Hutch|ings**
  (American
  physicist)

god-daughter +s
god|dess
  god|desses
Gödel, Kurt
  (Austrian
  mathematician)
godet +s
go|de|tia +s
go-devil +s
god|father +s
God-fearing
god|for|saken
God|frey
God-given
God|havn (town,
  Greenland)
god|head +s
god|hood +s
God|iva, Lady
  (English
  noblewoman)
god|less
god|less|ness
god|like
god|li|ness
godly
god|man
god|mother +s
go|down +s
god|par|ent +s
god|send +s
god|ship +s
god|son +s
God|speed
Godt|håb (former
  name of Nuuk)
Godu|nov, Boris
  (Russian tsar)
god|ward
god|wards
God|win, Wil|liam
  (English
  philosopher)
**Godwin-Austen,
Mount** (= K2)
god|wit +s
God|wot|tery
**Goeb|bels,
Jo|seph** (German
  Nazi leader)
goer +s
  (person or thing
  that goes. △ goa)
**Goer|ing,
Her|mann**
  (German Nazi
  leader)
**Goes, Hugo van
der** (Flemish
  painter)
goes (in 'she goes'
  etc.; plural of go)
goest

goeth
**Goethe, Jo|hann
Wolf|gang von**
  (German
  polymath)
Goe|thean +s
Goe|thian +s (use
  Goethean)
gofer +s (person
  who runs errands.
  △ gopher)
gof|fer +s +ed
  +ing (to crimp;
  crimping iron.
  △ gofer, gopher)
Gog and Magog
  Bible
go-getter +s
gog|gle
  gog|gles
  gog|gled
  gog|gling
goggle-box
  goggle-boxes
goggle-dive +s
goggle-eyed
gog|let +s
go-go
Gogol, Ni|ko|lai
  (Russian writer)
Goi|ânia (city,
  Brazil)
Goiás (state, Brazil)
Goi|del +s
Goi|del|ic
going +s
going away *noun*
going-away
  attributive
going on (for)
  (approaching)
going-over
  goings-over
goings-on
goi|ter *Am.* +s
goitre *Br.* +s
goitred
goi|trous
go-kart +s (racing
  car. △ go-cart)
**Go|khale, Gopal
Krishna** (Indian
  political leader)
Golan Heights (in
  Syria and Israel)
Gol|conda +s
gold +s
gold-beater +s
gold-beater's skin
  +s
gold bloc +s (bloc
  of countries)

gold block|ing
  (stamping with
  gold leaf)
gold|brick +s +ed
  +ing *verb*
gold brick +s *noun*
Gold Coast (former
  name of Ghana;
  resort region,
  Australia)
gold|crest +s
gold-digger +s
gold dust
gold|en
golden-ager +s
golden-eye +s
Gold|en Hind
  (Francis Drake's
  ship)
Gold|en Horde (of
  Mongols and
  Tartars)
Gold|en Horn
  (harbour, Istanbul)
gold|en|ly
gold|en|ness
gold|en|rod +s
gold|field +s
gold|finch
  gold|finches
gold|fish
  plural **gold|fish** *or*
  gold|fishes
goldi|locks
  plural **goldi|locks**
Gold|ing, Wil|liam
  (English novelist)
gold leaf
Gold|man, Emma
  (Lithuanian-born
  American political
  activist)
**Gold|mark, Peter
Carl** (Hungarian-
  born American
  inventor)
gold mine +s
gold plate *noun*
gold-plate
  gold-plates
  gold-plated
  gold-plating
  verb
gold rush
  gold rushes
**Gold|schmidt,
Vic|tor Mor|itz**
  (Swiss-born
  Norwegian
  chemist)

Gold|smith, Oli|ver (Irish writer)
gold|smith +s
Gold|wyn, Sam|uel (Polish-born American film director)
golem +s
golf +s +ed +ing
golf bag +s
golf ball +s
golf cart +s
golf club +s (implement; premises; association)
golf course +s
golf|er +s
golf links
Golgi, Cam|illo (Italian histologist; body, apparatus)
Gol|gotha (site of crucifixion of Jesus)
Gol|iath *Bible*
Gol|iath bee|tle +s
Gol|iath frog +s
Gol|lancz, Vic|tor (British publisher)
gol|li|wog +s
gol|lop +s +ed +ing
golly
gol|lies
gol|osh (use galosh)
gol|oshes
gom|been
Gomel (Russian name for Homel)
Gom|or|rah (town, ancient Palestine)
gonad +s
gon|adal
gon|ado|troph|ic
gon|ado|troph|in +s
gon|ado|trop|ic
Gon|court, Ed|mond de and Jules de (French writers)
gon|dola +s
gon|do|lier +s
Gon|dwana (ancient continent)
gone

goner +s (doomed person etc. ⚠ gonna)
gon|fa|lon +s
gon|fa|lon|ier +s
gong +s +ed +ing
gon|gooz|ler +s
goni|om|eter +s
go|nio|met|ric
go|nio|met|ric|al
goni|om|etry
gonk +s
gonna (*slang* = going to. ⚠ goner)
gono|coc|cal
gono|coc|cus
gono|cocci
gon|or|rhea *Am.*
gon|or|rhe|al *Am.*
gon|or|rhoea *Br.*
gon|or|rhoe|al *Br.*
gonzo
goo +s
good
goods
bet|ter
best
good|by +s *Am.* (use goodbye)
good|bye +s
good-for-nothing +s
good-hearted
good-humored *Am.*
good-humored|ly *Am.*
good-humoured *Br.*
good-humoured|ly *Br.*
goodie +s (use goody)
good|ish
Good King Henry (plant)
good|li|ness
good-looker
good-looking
good luck *noun*
good-luck *attributive*
good|ly
Good|man, Benny (American jazz musician)
good-natured
good-natured|ly
good|ness

good|night +s (parting wish)
goodo (*Australian & New Zealand good*)
good-oh *interjection*
good-sized
good-tempered
good-tempered|ly
good-time *attributive*
good-timer +s
good|wife
good|wives
good|will (kindly feeling; reputation of business)
good will (intention and hope that good will result)
Good|win Sands (off England)
Good|wood (racecourse, England)
goody
good|ies
goody-goody
goody-goodies
gooey
goo|ier
gooi|est
gooey|ness
goof +s +ed +ing
go-off
goof|ily
goofi|ness
goofy
goof|ier
goof|iest
goog +s
googly
goog|lies
goo|gol
goo|gol|plex
gook +s (*offensive*)
goolie +s
goom|bah +s
goon +s
goop +s
goopi|ness
goopy
goop|ier
goopi|est
goos|an|der
plural goos|an|der *or* goos|an|ders
goose
geese (bird)

goose +s (tailor's iron)
goose
gooses
goosed
goos|ing *verb*
goose|berry
goose|berries
goose bumps
goose egg +s
goose-flesh
goose|foot
goose|feet (thing in shape of goose's foot)
goose|foot +s (plant)
goose|gog +s
goose|grass
goose|grasses
goose|herd +s
goose-like
goose-pimpled
goose pim|ples
goose-skin
goose-step
goose-steps
goose-stepped
goose-stepping
Goos|sens, Eu|gene, Leon, Marie, and Sid|onie (English musicians)
gopak +s
go|pher +s (tree; rodent; tortoise. ⚠ gofer, goffer)
go|pher snake +s
go|pher wood
Gor|ak|pur (city, India)
goral +s
Gor|ba|chev, Mikh|ail (Soviet president)
Gor|bals, the (district, Glasgow)
gor|bli|mey +s
gor|cock +s
Gor|dian knot +s
Gor|di|mer, Nad|ine (South African writer)
Gor|dium (ancient city, Turkey)
gordo +s
Gor|don (name; setter; Riots)

Gor¦don, Charles George (British general)

gore
gores
gored
gor¦ing

Gó¦recki, Hen¦ryk (Polish composer)

Gör¦eme (valley, Turkey)

Gore-Tex *Propr.*

gorge
gorges
gorged
gor¦ging

gor¦geous¦ly
gor¦geous¦ness
gor¦ger +s
gor¦get +s

Gor¦gio +s

gor¦gon +s

gor¦go¦nia
gor¦go¦nias *or*
gor¦go¦niae

gor¦go¦nian +s

gor¦gon¦ise *Br.* (use gorgonize)
gor¦gon¦ises
gor¦gon¦ised
gor¦gon¦is¦ing

gor¦gon¦ize
gor¦gon¦izes
gor¦gon¦ized
gor¦gon¦iz¦ing

Gor¦gon¦zola +s (cheese)

gor¦illa +s (ape.
△ guerrilla)

gor¦ily

gori¦ness

Gör¦ing, Her¦mann (use Goering)

Gorky (former name of Nizhni Novgorod)

Gorky, Ar¦shile (Turkish-born American painter)

Gorky, Maxim (Russian writer)

Gor¦lovka (city, Ukraine)

gor¦mand¦ise *Br.* (eat voraciously; use gormandize.
△ gourmandise)
gor¦mand¦ises
gor¦mand¦ised
gor¦mand¦is¦ing

gor¦mand¦iser *Br.* +s (use gormandizer)

gor¦mand¦ize
gor¦mand¦izes
gor¦mand¦ized
gor¦mand¦iz¦ing
(eat voraciously.
△ gourmandise)

gor¦mand¦izer +s

gorm¦less
gorm¦less¦ly
gorm¦less¦ness

Gorno-Altai (republic, Russia)

Gorno-Altaisk (city, Russia)

gorse +s

Gor¦sedd

gorsy
gor¦sier
gor¦si¦est

gory
gor¦ier
gori¦est

gosh

gos¦hawk +s

gos¦ling +s

go-slow +s *noun*

Gos¦pel +s *Bible*

gos¦pel +s (Christ's teaching; truth; principle; singing)

gos¦pel¦er *Am.* +s

gos¦pel¦ler +s

gos¦samer +s

gos¦sa¦mered

gos¦sa¦mery

gos¦sip +s +ed +ing

gos¦sip¦er +s

gos¦sip¦mon¦ger +s

gos¦sipy

gos¦soon +s

got

Gö¦te¦borg (Swedish name for Gothenburg)

Goth +s (Germanic tribe)

goth +s (rock music; performer)

Gotha (city, Germany)

Gotham (village, England; nickname for New York City)

Goth¦am¦ite +s

Goth¦en¦burg (port, Sweden)

Goth¦ic

Goth¦ic¦al¦ly

Gothi¦cise *Br.* (use Gothicize)
Gothi¦cises
Gothi¦cised
Gothi¦cis¦ing

Gothi¦cism +s

Gothi¦cize
Gothi¦cizes
Gothi¦cized
Gothi¦ciz¦ing

Got¦land (island, Sweden)

go-to-meeting

gotta (= got to)

got¦ten

Göt¦ter¦däm¦mer¦ung

Göt¦tingen (town, Germany)

gou¦ache +s

Gouda (town, the Netherlands; also the cheese orig. made there)

gouge
gouges
gouged
gou¦ging

gou¦ger +s

Gough Is¦land (in S. Atlantic)

gou¦jons

gou¦lash
gou¦lashes

Gould, Glenn (Canadian pianist)

Gould, Ste¦phen Jay (American palaeontologist)

Gou¦nod, Charles (French composer)

gou¦rami
plural gou¦rami *or* gou¦ramis

gourd +s (plant; fruit)

gourde +s (Haitian currency)

gourd¦ful +s

gour¦mand +s (glutton)

gour¦mand¦ise (gluttony.
△ gormandize)

gour¦mand¦ism

gour¦met +s (connoisseur)

gout +s

gout-fly
gout-flies

gout¦ily

gouti¦ness

gout¦weed +s

gouty

gov¦ern +s +ed +ing

gov¦ern¦abil¦ity

gov¦ern¦able
gov¦ern¦able¦ness

gov¦ern¦ance

gov¦ern¦ess
gov¦ern¦esses

gov¦ern¦essy

gov¦ern¦ment +s

gov¦ern¦men¦tal
gov¦ern¦men¦tal¦ly

gov¦ern¦or +s

gov¦er¦nor¦ate +s

Governor-General +s

gov¦er¦nor¦ship +s

gowan +s

gowk +s

gown +s +ed +ing

gowns¦man
gowns¦men

Gowon, Ya¦kubu (Nigerian statesman)

goy
goyim *or* goys (*offensive*)

Goya (Spanish painter)

goy¦isch (use goyish)

goy¦ish

Gozo (Maltese island)

Graaf¦ian

grab
grabs
grabbed
grab¦bing

grab bag +s

grab¦ber +s

grab¦ble
grab¦bles
grab¦bled
grab¦bling

grabby
grab¦bier
grab¦bi¦est

gra¦ben
plural gra¦ben *or* gra¦bens

grab han¦dle +s

grab rail +s

Grac¦chus (Roman tribune)

Grace, W. G. (English cricketer)

Grace (name)

grace
  graces
  graced
  gra¦cing
  (attractiveness;
  thanksgiving; add
  grace to)
grace and fa¦vour
  (home etc.)
grace¦ful
grace¦ful¦ly
grace¦ful¦ness
grace¦less
grace¦less¦ly
grace¦less¦ness
grace note+s
Graces *Greek*
  Mythology
Gra¦cias a Dios,
  Cape (in Central
  America)
Gra¦cie
gra¦cile
gra¦cil¦ity
graci¦os¦ity
gra¦cious
gra¦cious¦ly
gra¦cious¦ness
grackle+s
grad+s
grad¦ate
  grad¦ates
  grad¦ated
  grad¦at¦ing
grad¦ation+s
grad¦ation¦al
grad¦ation¦al¦ly
Grade, Lew (Lord
  Grade, Russian-
  born British
  television
  producer)
grade
  grades
  graded
  grad¦ing
grader+s
Grad¦grind+s
gra¦di¦ent+s
gra¦din+s (use
  gradine)
gra¦dine+s
grad¦ing+s
grad¦ual+s
grad¦ual¦ism
grad¦ual¦ist+s
grad¦ual¦is¦tic
grad¦ual¦ly
grad¦ual¦ness
gradu¦and+s
gradu¦ate
  gradu¦ates

gradu¦ate (*cont.*)
  gradu¦ated
  gradu¦at¦ing
gradu¦ation+s
gradu¦ator+s
Grae¦cise *Br.* (use
  Graecize)
  Grae¦cises
  Grae¦cised
  Grae¦cis¦ing
Grae¦cism+s
Grae¦cize
  Grae¦cizes
  Grae¦cized
  Grae¦ciz¦ing
Graeco¦mania
Graeco¦maniac+s
Graeco¦phile+s
Graeco-Roman
Graf, Steffi
  (German tennis
  player)
graf¦fi¦tied
graf¦fi¦tist+s
graf¦fito
graf¦fiti
graft+s+ed+ing
graft¦er+s
graft¦ing clay+s
graft¦ing wax
  graft¦ing waxes
Graf¦ton, Duke of
  (British prime
  minister)
Gra¦ham, Billy
  (American
  evangelical
  preacher)
Gra¦ham, Mar¦tha
  (American dancer)
Gra¦ham, Thomas
  (Scottish physical
  chemist)
Gra¦ham
Gra¦hame,
  Ken¦neth
  (Scottish writer)
Gra¦ham Land
  (part of
  Antarctica)
Grail (Holy Grail, in
  medieval legend)
grain+s+ed+ing
grain¦er+s
Grain¦ger, Percy
  (Australian-born
  American
  composer)
graini¦ness
grain lea¦ther
grain¦less
grain-side

grainy
  grain¦ier
  graini¦est
gral¦la¦tor¦ial
gram+s
gram-atom+s
gram-equiva¦lent
  +s
gram-force
  grams-force
gra¦min¦aceous
gram¦in¦eous
grami¦niv¦or¦ous
gram¦ma¦logue+s
gram¦mar+s
gram¦mar¦ian+s
gram¦mar¦less
gram¦mat¦ical
gram¦mat¦ical¦ity
gram¦mat¦ical¦ly
gram¦mat¦ical¦
      ness
gram¦mati¦cise *Br.*
  (use
  grammaticize)
  gram¦mati¦cises
  gram¦mati¦cised
  gram¦mati¦cis¦ing
gram¦mati¦cize
  gram¦mati¦cizes
  gram¦mati¦cized
  gram¦mati¦ciz¦ing
gramme+s (use
  gram)
gram-molecule+s
Gram-negative
gramo¦phone+s
gramo¦phon¦ic
Gram¦pian (region,
  Scotland)
Gram¦pians
  (mountains,
  Scotland)
Gram-positive
gram¦pus
  gram¦puses
Gram¦sci,
  An¦tonio (Italian
  political theorist)
Gram stain
gran+s
Gran¦ada (cities,
  Spain and
  Nicaragua)
grana¦dilla+s (use
  grenadilla)
gran¦ary
  gran¦ar¦ies
Gran Can¦aria
  (capital of the
  Canary Islands)

Gran Chaco (plain,
  S. America)
grand+s+er+est
  (*adjective*; piano)
grand
  plural grand
  (thousand)
gran¦dad+s
gran¦dam+s
  archaic
gran¦dame+s (use
  grandam *archaic*)
grand-aunt+s
grand¦child
  grand¦chil¦dren
grand¦dad+s (use
  grandad)
grand-daddy
  grand-daddies
grand¦daugh¦ter
  +s
Grande Co¦more
  (island off
  Madagascar)
grande dame+s
gran¦dee+s
grand¦eur
grand¦father+s
grand¦father¦ly
Grand Gui¦gnol+s
gran¦di¦flora
grand¦ilo¦quence
grand¦ilo¦quent
grand¦ilo¦quent¦ly
gran¦di¦ose
gran¦di¦ose¦ly
gran¦di¦os¦ity
Gran¦di¦son¦ian
grand¦ly
grand¦ma+s
grand mal
grand¦mama+s
Grand Mas¦ter+s
  (of knighthood,
  Freemasons, etc.)
grand¦mas¦ter+s
  Chess
grand¦mother+s
grand¦mother¦ly
grand-nephew+s
grand¦ness
grand-niece+s
grand¦pa+s
grand¦papa+s
grand¦pappy
  grand¦pap¦pies
grand¦par¦ent+s
Grand Prix
  Grands Prix
grand siècle
grand¦sire+s
grand¦son+s

grand|stand +s
grand-uncle +s
grange +s
gran|ifer|ous
grani|form
gran|ita
  gran|ite
  (crushed ice drink)
gran|ite +s (rock)
gran|ite|ware
gran|it|ic
gran|it|oid
grani|vore +s
gran|iv|or|ous
gran|ma +s (use
  grandma)
granny
  gran|nies
Granny Smith +s
grano|di|or|ite
grano|lith|ic
gran|pa +s (use
  grandpa)
Grant (name)
Grant, Cary
  (English-born
  American actor)
Grant, Ulys|ses
  Simp|son
  (American
  president)
grant +s +ed +ing
grant|able
grant aid noun
grant-aid +s +ed
  +ing verb
grant|ee +s
grant|er +s
  (generally.
  △ grantor)
Gran|tha (Indian
  alphabet)
Granth (Sahib)
  (= Adi Granth)
grant-in-aid
  grants-in-aid
grant-maintained
grant|or +s (Law.
  △ granter)
gran tur|ismo +s
granu|lar
granu|lar|ity
granu|lar|ly
granu|late
  granu|lates
  granu|lated
  granu|lat|ing
granu|la|tion +s
granu|la|tor +s
gran|ule +s
gran|ulo|cyte +s
gra|nu|lo|cyt|ic
gra|nu|lo|met|ric

Granville-Barker,
  Har|ley (English
  dramatist)
grape +s
grape|fruit
  plural grape|fruit
gra|pery
  gra|per|ies
grape|seed oil
grape|shot
grape-sugar
grape|vine +s
grapey
  grapi|er
  grapi|est
graph +s +ed +ing
graph|em|at|ic
graph|eme +s
graph|em|ic
graph|em|ic|al|ly
graph|em|ics
graph|ic +s
graphi|cacy
graph|ic|al
graph|ic|al|ly
graph|ic|ness
graph|ics
graph|ite +s
graph|it|ic
graph|it|ise Br.
  (use graphitize)
  graph|it|ises
  graph|it|ised
  graph|it|is|ing
graph|it|ize
  graph|it|izes
  graph|it|ized
  graph|it|iz|ing
grapho|logic|al
graph|olo|gist +s
graph|ology
grap|nel +s
grappa +s
Grap|pelli,
  Ste|phane
  (French jazz
  violinist)
grap|ple
  grap|ples
  grap|pled
  grap|pling
grap|pler +s
grap|pling hook
  +s
grap|pling iron +s
grap|to|lite +s
grapy (use grapey)
Gras|mere (village
  and lake, England)
grasp +s +ed +ing
grasp|able
grasp|er +s

grasp|ing|ly
grasp|ing|ness
Grass, Gün|ther
  (German writer)
grass
  grasses
  grassed
  grass|ing
grass box
  grass boxes
grass|cloth +s
Grasse (town,
  France)
grass|hop|per +s
grassi|ness
grass|land +s
grass|less
grass|like
grass of
  Par|nas|sus
grass-root
  attributive
grass roots noun
grass-roots
  attributive
grass snake +s
  (non-venomous
  snake. △ glass
  snake)
grass-wrack +s
grassy
  grass|ier
  grassi|est
grate
  grates
  grated
  grat|ing
  (grind etc.; in
  fireplace. △ great)
grate|ful
grate|ful|ly
grate|ful|ness
grater +s (used for
  grating cheese etc.
  △ greater)
grat|icule +s
grat|ifi|ca|tion +s
grati|fier +s
grat|ify
  grati|fies
  grati|fied
  grati|fy|ing
grati|fy|ing|ly
gra|tin +s
grat|iné +s noun
  and masculine
  adjective
grat|inéed
grat|inée feminine
  adjective
grat|ing +s
grat|ing|ly

gra|tis
grati|tude
gra|tuit|ous
gra|tuit|ous|ly
gra|tuit|ous|ness
gra|tu|ity
  gra|tu|ities
gratu|la|tory
graunch
  graunches
  graunched
  graunch|ing
grav|ad|lax (use
  gravlax)
gra|va|men
gra|va|mens or
gra|va|mina
grave
  graves
  graved
  grav|ing
  graved or gra|ven
  graver
  grav|est
grave-clothes
grave|dig|ger +s
gravel
  gravels
  grav|elled Br.
  grav|eled Am.
  grav|el|ling Br.
  grav|el|ing Am.
gravel-blind
grave|less
grav|el|ly (of or
  like gravel; deep
  voiced etc.)
grave|ly (seriously)
graven
grave|ness
graver +s
Graves, Rob|ert
  (English writer)
Graves
  plural Graves
  (wine)
Graves' dis|ease
grave|side
grave|stone +s
Gra|vet|tian
grave|ward
grave|yard +s
gravid
grav|im|eter +s
gravi|met|ric
grav|im|etry
grav|itas
gravi|tate
  gravi|tates
  gravi|tated
  gravi|tat|ing
gravi|ta|tion

gravi|ta|tion|al
gravi|ta|tion|al|ly
gravi|ton +s
grav|ity
  grav|ities
gravity-fed
grav|ity feed
grav|lax
grav|ure
gravy
  gra|vies
gravy boat +s
gravy train
Gray, Asa
  (American
  botanist)
Gray, Thomas
  (English poet)
gray *Am.* +s +ed
  +ing +er +est
  (colour. *Br.* grey)
gray +s (unit.
  △ grey)
gray|beard *Am.* +s
  (*Br.* greybeard)
gray|ling
  plural gray|ling *or*
  gray|lings
gray|ly *Am.Br.*
  greyly
gray|ness *Am.* (*Br.*
  greyness)
gray|wacke *Am.* +s
  (*Br.* greywacke)
Graz (city, Austria)
graze
  grazes
  grazed
  graz|ing
grazer +s
gra|zier +s
gra|ziery
  gra|zier|ies
grease
  greases
  greased
  greas|ing
grease gun +s
grease|less
grease|paint +s
grease|proof
greaser +s
grease|wood +s
greas|ily
greasi|ness
greasy
  greas|ier
  greasi|est
great +s +er +est
  (big, important,
  etc.; outstanding

great (*cont.*)
  person or thing.
  △ grate, grater)
great-aunt +s
Great Bar|rier
  Reef (off
  Australian coast)
Great Bear Lake
  (in Canada)
Great Brit|ain
great|coat +s
great-grand|child
  great-
  grand|chil|dren
great-
  grand|daughter
  +s
great-grand|father
  +s
great-
  grand|mother +s
great-
  grand|par|ent +s
great-grand|son
  +s
great-hearted
great-
  hearted|ness
Great Lakes (in N.
  America)
great|ly
great-nephew +s
great|ness
great-niece +s
Greats (classics and
  philosophy at
  Oxford University)
great-uncle +s
greave +s (armour.
  △ grieve)
grebe +s
grebo +s
Gre|cian +s
Gre|cise *Br.* (use
  Graecize)
  Gre|cises
  Gre|cised
  Gre|cis|ing
Gre|cism +s
Gre|cize
  Gre|cizes
  Gre|cized
  Gre|ciz|ing
Greco, El (Cretan-
  born Spanish
  painter)
Greece
greed
greed|ily
greedi|ness

greedy
  greed|ier
  greedi|est
greedy-guts
  plural greedy-guts
gree|gree +s
Greek +s
Greek|ness
green +s +ed +ing
  +er +est
Green|away, Kate
  (English artist)
green|back +s
Green Beret +s
green|bot|tle +s
Greene, Gra|ham
  (English novelist)
green|ery
  green|er|ies
green-eyed
green fee +s
green|feed
green|field
  attributive
green|finch
  green|finches
green-fingered
green fin|gers
green|fly
  plural green|fly *or*
  green|flies
green|gage +s
green|gro|cer +s
green|gro|cery
  green|gro|cer|ies
green|head +s
green|heart +s
green|hide +s
green|horn +s
green|house +s
greenie +s
green|ing +s
green|ish
green|keep|er +s
green|keep|ing
Green|land
Green|land|er +s
green|let +s
green|ly
green|mail
green|mail|er +s
green|ness
Green|ock (port,
  Scotland)
Green|peace
green|sand +s
green|shank
  plural
  green|shank *or*
  green|shanks
green|sick
green|sick|ness

greens|keep|er +s
green-stick
  (fracture)
green|stone +s
green|stuff +s
green|sward +s
green|weed +s
Green|wich
  (borough,
  London)
Green|wich Mean
  Time
Green|wich
  me|rid|ian
Green|wich
  Vil|lage (district,
  New York City)
green|wood +s
greeny
green|yard +s
Greer, Ger|maine
  (Australian writer)
Greer *also* Grier
greet +s +ed +ing
greet|er +s
greet|ing +s
gref|fier +s
Greg
gre|gari|ous
gre|gari|ous|ly
gre|gari|ous|ness
Gregor
Gre|gor|ian
Greg|ory (saint;
  popes; name)
Greg|ory of
  Nazi|an|zus
  (early saint)
Greg|ory of Nyssa
  (early saint)
Greg|ory of Tours
  (early saint)
Greg|ory pow|der
grem|ial +s
grem|lin +s
Gren|ada (in West
  Indies)
gren|ade +s
Gren|adian +s
grena|dier +s
  (soldier; fish)
Grena|dier Guards
  (British regiment)
Grena|diers
  (= Grenadier
  Guards)
grena|dilla +s
grena|dine +s
Grena|dine
  Is|lands (in West
  Indies)
Gren|del

Gre|noble (city, France)

Gren|ville, George (British prime minister)

Grepo +s

Gres|ham, Thomas (English financier)

Gres|ham's law

Gres|ley, Nigel (British railway engineer)

gres|sor|ial

Greta

Gretel (in 'Hansel and Gretel')

Gretna Green (village, Scotland)

Gretzky, Wayne (Canadian ice-hockey player)

Greuze, Jean-Baptiste (French painter)

grew (past tense of grow. △ grue)

Grey, Lord (British prime minister)

Grey, George (British prime minister of New Zealand)

Grey, Lady Jane (English queen)

grey Br. +s +ed +ing +er +est (Am. gray. colour. △ gray)

grey-back +s

grey|beard Br. +s (Am. graybeard)

Grey Friar +s (Franciscan friar)

Grey|friars (in names of roads, schools, etc.)

grey|hen +s

grey|hound +s

grey|ish

grey|lag
plural grey|lag or grey|lags

grey|ly Br. (Am. grayly)

Grey|mouth (city, New Zealand)

grey|ness Br. (Am. grayness)

grey|wacke Br. +s (Am. graywacke)

grid +s

grid|ded

grid|dle

grid|dles

grid|dled

grid|dling

grid|iron +s

grid|lock

grid|locked

grief +s

grief-stricken

Grieg, Ed|vard (Norwegian composer)

Grier also Greer

Grier|son, John (Scottish film director)

griev|ance +s

grieve

grieves

grieved

griev|ing (mourn. △ greave)

griev|er +s

griev|ous

griev|ous|ly

griev|ous|ness

grif|fin +s (fabulous creature. △ griffon)

Grif|fith, Ar|thur (Irish president)

Grif|fith, D. W. (American film director)

Grif|fith

grif|fon +s (vulture; dog. △ griffin)

grift +s +ed +ing

grift|er +s

grig +s

Gri|gnard re|agent +s

grike +s

grill +s +ed +ing (cooking apparatus; food. △ grille)

grill|ade +s

grill|age +s

grille +s (grating. △ grill)

grill|er +s

grill|ing +s

grilse
plural grilse

grim

grim|mer

grim|mest

grim|ace

grim|aces

grim|ace (cont.)

grim|aced

grim|acing

grim|acer +s

Gri|maldi, Fran|cesco Maria (Italian physicist)

Gri|maldi, Jo|seph (English clown)

gri|mal|kin +s

grime

grimes

grimed

grim|ing

grim-faced

grimi|ly

grimi|ness

grim|ly

Grimm, Jacob and Wil|helm (German philologists)

Grimm's law

grim|ness

Grim|ond, Jo (British Liberal politician)

Grimsby (port, England)

grimy

grimi|er

grimi|est

grin

grins

grinned

grin|ning

grind

grinds

ground

grind|ing

grind|er +s

grind|ing|ly

grind|stone +s

gringo +s

grin|ner +s

grin|ning|ly

grip

grips

gripped

grip|ping

gripe

gripes

griped

grip|ing

griper +s

gripe water Propr.

grip|ing|ly

grippe (influenza)

grip|per +s

grip|ping|ly

grippy

grip|pier

grip|pi|est

Gris, Juan (Spanish painter)

gris|aille +s

Gri|selda

griseo|ful|vin

gris|ette +s

gris|kin +s

gris|li|ness

grisly

gris|lier

gris|li|est (horrible. △ gristly, grizzly)

grison +s

Gris|ons (canton, Switzerland)

gris|sini

grist

gris|tle

gris|tly (containing gristle. △ grisly, grizzly)

grit

grits

grit|ted

grit|ting

grit|stone +s

grit|ter +s

grit|tily

grit|ti|ness

gritty

grit|tier

grit|ti|est

Gri|vas, George Theo|dorou (Greek-Cypriot patriot)

griz|zle

griz|zles

griz|zled

griz|zling

griz|zler +s

griz|zly

griz|zlies

griz|zlier

griz|zli|est (bear; grey; complaining. △ grisly, gristly)

groan +s +ed +ing (moan. △ grown)

groan|er +s

groan|ing|ly

groat +s (coin)

groats (grain)

gro|cer +s

gro|cery

gro|cer|ies

grockle +s

Grodno (city, Belarus)

grog
  grogs
  grogged
  grog|ging
  grog|gily
  grog|gi|ness
  groggy
  grog|gier
  grog|gi|est
  grog|ram +s
groin +s +ed +ing
  Anatomy;
  Architecture
groin *Am.* +s (on seashore. *Br.* groyne)
grom|met +s
grom|well +s
Gro|myko, An|drei (Soviet president)
Gron|ing|en (city and province, the Netherlands)
groom +s +ed +ing
grooms|man
  grooms|men
groove
  grooves
  grooved
  groov|ing
  groov|ily
  groovi|ness
  groovy
  groov|ier
  groovi|est
grope
  gropes
  groped
  grop|ing
  grop|ing|ly
Gro|pius, Wal|ter (German-born American architect)
gros|beak +s
gro|schen
  plural gro|schen
  or gro|schens
gros|grain +s
gros point
gross
  grosses
  grossed
  gross|ing
  gross|er
  gross|est
  verb and adjective

gross
  plural gross
  (*noun* = 144)
Grosse|teste, Rob|ert (English churchman)
Gross|glock|ner (mountain, Austria)
gross|ly
gross|ness
Grosz, George (German-born American painter)
grot +s
gro|tesque +s
gro|tesque|ly
gro|tesque|ness
gro|tesque|rie +s
Gro|tius, Hugo (Dutch jurist)
grotti|ness
grotto
  grot|toes *or* grottos
grotty
  grot|tier
  grot|ti|est
grouch
  grouches
  grouched
  grouch|ing
  grouch|ily
  grouchi|ness
  grouchy
  grouch|ier
  grouchi|est
ground +s +ed +ing
ground|age
ground ash
  ground ashes
ground|bait +s
ground cover
ground crew +s
ground|er +s
ground floor *noun*
ground-floor *attributive*
ground|hog +s
ground|ing +s
ground|less
ground|less|ly
ground|less|ness
ground|ling +s
ground|nut +s
ground plan +s
ground rule +s
ground|sel +s
ground|sheet +s
grounds|keep|er +s

grounds|man
  grounds|men
ground squir|rel +s
ground staff
ground stroke +s
ground|swell
ground|water +s
ground|work +s
group +s +ed +ing
group|age
group cap|tain +s
group|er +s
groupie +s
group|ing +s
group|think
group|ware
group work
grouse
  grouses
  groused
  grous|ing
grouser +s
grout +s +ed +ing
grout|er +s
Grove, George (English musicologist)
grove +s
grovel
  grovels
  grov|elled *Br.*
  grov|eled *Am.*
  grov|el|ling *Br.*
  grov|el|ing *Am.*
  grov|el|er +s *Am.*
  grov|el|ing|ly *Am.*
  grov|el|ler +s *Br.*
  grov|el|ling|ly *Br.*
grovy
grow
  grows
  grew
  grow|ing
  grown
grow|able
grow|bag +s
grow|er +s
grow|ing bag +s
grow|ing pains
growl +s +ed +ing
growl|er +s
growl|ing|ly
Grow|more
grown (past participle of grow.
  △ groan)
grown-up +s
  adjective and noun
growth +s

growth in|dus|try
growth in|dus|tries
groyne *Br.* +s (*Am.* groin. on seashore. △ groin)
Grozny (capital of the Chechen Republic)
grub
  grubs
  grubbed
  grub|bing
  grub|ber +s
  grub|bily
  grubbi|ness
  grubby
  grub|bier
  grub|bi|est
grub-screw +s
grub|stake
  grub|stakes
  grub|staked
  grub|stak|ing
  grub|staker +s
Grub Street (writers)
grudge
  grudges
  grudged
  grudg|ing
  grudger +s
  grudg|ing|ly
  grudg|ing|ness
grue
  grues
  grued
  gru|ing
  (ice; feel horror.
  △ grew)
gruel +s
gruel|ling *Am.*
gruel|ling|ly *Am.*
gruel|ling *Br.*
gruel|ling|ly *Br.*
grue|some
grue|some|ly
grue|some|ness
gruff +er +est
gruff|ly
gruff|ness
grum|ble
  grum|bles
  grum|bled
  grum|bling
grum|bler +s
grum|bling +s
grum|bling|ly
grum|bly
grum|met +s (use grommet)
grum|ous

grump +s
grump|ily
grumpi|ness
grump|ish
grump|ish|ly
grumpy
  grump|ier
  grumpi|est
Grundy
  Grun|dies
Grundy|ism
Grüne|wald,
  Mathias (German
  painter)
grunge
grungy
  grun|gier
  grun|gi|est
grun|ion
  plural grun|ion *or*
  grun|ions
grunt +s +ed +ing
grunt|er +s
Gruy|ère +s
  (district,
  Switzerland;
  cheese)
gryke +s (use
  grike)
gryphon +s (use
  griffin)
grys|bok
  plural grys|bok *or*
  grys|boks
Gryt|viken
  (settlement, South
  Georgia)
Gstaad (ski resort,
  Switzerland)
G-string +s
G-suit +s
gua|ca|mole
gua|charo +s
Gua|da|la|jara
  (cities, Spain and
  Mexico)
Gua|dal|ca|nal
  (island, Solomon
  Islands)
Gua|dal|qui|vir
  (river, Spain)
Gua|de|loupe
  (group of islands,
  Lesser Antilles)
Gua|de|loup|ian
  +s
Gua|di|ana (river,
  Spain and
  Portugal)
guaiac +s
guai|acum +s

Guam (in Mariana
  Islands)
guan +s
gua|naco +s
Gua|na|juato (state
  and city, Mexico)
Guang|dong
  (province, China)
Guangxi Zhu|ang
  (region, China)
Guang|zhou (city,
  China)
guan|ine
guano +s *noun*
guano
  gua|noes
  gua|noed
  guano|ing
  verb
Guan|tánamo Bay
  (on Cuba)
Guar|ani
  plural Guar|ani *or*
  Guar|anis
  (S. American
  Indian; language)
guar|ani +s
  (Paraguayan
  currency)
guar|an|tee
  guar|an|tees
  guar|an|teed
  guar|an|tee|ing
guar|an|tor +s
guar|anty
  guar|an|ties
  (undertaking of
  liability)
guard +s +ed +ing
guard|ant *Heraldry*
guard|ed|ly
guarded|ness
guard|ee +s
guard|er +s
guard|house +s
Guardi,
  Fran|cesco
  (Italian painter)
guard|ian +s
guard|ian angel
  +s
guard|ian|ship +s
guard|less
guard rail +s
guard ring +s
guard|room +s
guards|man
  guards|men
guard's van +s
Guar|neri,
  Giu|seppe (Italian
  violin-maker)

Guar|ner|ius
Gua|te|mala (in
  Central America)
Gua|te|mal|an +s
guava +s
Guaya|quil (city,
  Ecuador)
guay|ule +s
gub|bins
gu|ber|na|tor|ial
gudgeon
  plural gudgeon
  (fish)
gudgeon +s
  (person; pivot,
  pin, etc.)
gudgeon pin +s
Gud|run *Norse*
  Legend
guel|der rose +s
Guelph +s
Guelph|ic
Guelph|ism
gue|non +s
guer|don +s +ed
  +ing
Gue|ricke, Otto
  von (German
  engineer)
guer|illa +s (use
  guerrilla)
Guer|nica (town,
  Spain)
Guern|sey +s
  (Channel Island;
  cattle)
guern|sey +s
  (garment)
Guer|rero (state,
  Mexico)
guer|rilla +s
  (fighter. △ gorilla)
guess
  guesses
  guessed
  guess|ing
guess|able
guess|er +s
guess-rope +s (use
  guest-rope)
guess|ti|mate
  guess|ti|mates
  guess|ti|mated
  guess|ti|mat|ing
guess|work
guest +s +ed +ing
  (invited person.
  △ guessed)
guest house +s
gues|ti|mate
  gues|ti|mates
  gues|ti|mated

gues|ti|mate (*cont.*)
  gues|ti|mat|ing
  (use guesstimate)
guest night +s
guest room +s
guest-rope +s
guest|ship
Gue|vara, Che
  (Argentinian
  revolutionary)
guff
guf|faw +s +ed
  +ing
Gug|gen|heim,
  Meyer (Swiss-
  born American
  industrialist)
gug|gle
  gug|gles
  gug|gled
  gug|gling
Gui|ana +s (region,
  S. America; also in
  'French Guiana'
  etc. △ Guyana)
Gui|ana
  High|lands
  (plateau, S.
  America)
guid|able
guid|ance
Guide +s (member
  of Guides
  Association)
guide
  guides
  guided
  guid|ing
  (leader, book, etc.;
  to lead)
guide|book +s
guide dog +s
Guide Guider +s
guide|line +s
guide|post +s
Guider +s (leader
  in Guides)
guide rope +s
guide|way +s
gui|don +s
Gui|enne (use
  Guyenne)
Gui|gnol (puppet
  character)
Gui|gnol|esque
guild +s
  (association.
  △ gild)
guil|der +s (Dutch
  currency.
  △ gilder)

Guild|ford (town, England)

Guild|hall, the (in London)

guild|hall +s

guilds|man
  guilds|men

guilds|woman
  guilds|women

guile +s

guile|ful

guile|ful|ly

guile|ful|ness

guile|less

guile|less|ly

guile|less|ness

Gui|lin (city, China)

guil|le|mot +s

guil|loche +s

guil|lo|tine
  guil|lo|tines
  guil|lo|tined
  guil|lo|tin|ing
  guil|lo|tin|er +s

guilt +s
  (culpability.
  △ gilt)

guilt com|plex
  guilt com|plexes

guilt|ily

guilti|ness

guilt|less

guilt|less|ly

guilt|less|ness

guilty
  guilt|ier
  guilti|est

guimp +s (use gimp)

Guinea (in W. Africa)

Guinea, Gulf of (off W. Africa)

guinea +s (money)

Guinea-Bissau (in W. Africa)

guinea fowl
  plural guinea fowl
  or guinea fowls

guinea hen +s

guinea pig +s

Guinea worm +s

Guin|evere
  Arthurian Legend

Guin|ness, Alec (English actor)

gui|pure

guise +s

gui|tar +s

gui|tar|ist +s

gui|tar play|er +s

guiver

Gui|yang (city, China)

Gui|zhou (province, China)

Gu|ja|rat (state, India)

Gu|ja|rati +s

Gu|je|rat (use Gujarat)

Gu|je|rati +s (use Gujarati)

Guj|ran|wala (city, Pakistan)

Guj|rat (city, Pakistan)

Gulag +s

Gul|barga (city, India)

Gul|ben|kian, Cal|ouste (Turkish-born British oil magnate)

gulch
  gulches

gul|den
  plural gul|den or gul|dens

gules

gulf +s +ed +ing

Gulf Stream

gulf|weed

gull +s +ed +ing

Gul|lah +s

gull|ery
  gull|er|ies

gul|let +s

gul|ley +s +ed +ing (use gully)

gul|li|bil|ity

gul|lible

gul|libly

gull-wing attributive

gully
  gul|lies
  gul|lied
  gully|ing

gully-hole +s

gulp +s +ed +ing

gulp|er +s

gulp|ing|ly

gulpy

gum
  gums
  gummed
  gum|ming

gum arab|ic

gum ben|ja|min

Gumbo (patois)

gumbo +s (okra; soup)

gum|boil +s

gum|boot +s

gum|drop +s

gumma
  gum|mas or
  gum|mata

gum|ma|tous

gum|mily

gum|mi|ness

gummy
  gum|mies
  gum|mier
  gum|mi|est

gump|tion

gum resin +s

gum|shield +s

gum|shoe +s

gum tree +s

gun
  guns
  gunned
  gun|ning

gun bar|rel +s

gun|boat +s

gun car|riage +s

gun cot|ton

gun crew +s

gun dog +s

gundy

gun|fight +s

gun|fight|er +s

gun|fire

gunge
  gunges
  gunged
  gun|ging

gung-ho

gungy

gunk

gun|less

gun|lock +s

gun|maker +s

gun|man
  gun|men

gun|metal

Gunn, Thom (English poet)

gun|nel +s (fish. △ gunwale)

gun|ner +s

gun|nera +s

gun|nery

gunny
  gun|nies

gun|play

gun|point

gun|pow|der +s

gun|power

gun|room +s

gun-runner +s

gun-running

gun|sel +s

gun|ship +s

gun|shot +s

gun-shy

gun|sight +s

gun-site +s

gun|sling|er +s

gun|sling|ing

gun|smith +s

gun|stock +s

gun|ter (sail)

Gun|ter's chain +s

gun-toting

Gun|tur (city, India)

gun|wale +s (of ship. △ gunnel)

gun|yah +s

Guo|min|dang (= Kuomintang)

guppy
  gup|pies

Gupta

Gup|tan

Gur|djieff, George Ivan|ovich (Russian spiritual leader)

gurd|wara +s

gur|gi|ta|tion

gur|gle
  gur|gles
  gur|gled
  gurg|ling

gurg|ler +s

gur|jun +s

Gur|kha +s

gurn +s +ed +ing

gur|nard
  plural gur|nard or
  gur|nards

gurn|er +s

gur|net
  plural gur|net or
  gur|nets

Gur|ney, Ivor (English poet and composer)

guru +s

Gus (name)

gush
  gushes
  gushed
  gush|ing

gush|er +s

gush|ily

gushi|ness

gush|ing|ly

gushy

gus|set +s

gus|set|ed

gussy
  gus|sies

gussy(*cont.*)
gus|sied
gussy|ing
gust+s +ed +ing
gus|ta|tion
gus|ta|tive
gus|ta|tory
Gus|tavus
Adol|phus
(Swedish king)
gust|ily
gusti|ness
gusto
gus|toes
gusty
gust|ier
gusti|est
gut
guts
gut|ted
gut|ting
Guten|berg,
Jo|han|nes
(German printer)
Guth|rie, Woody
(American folk
singer-songwriter)
Gu|tiér|rez,
Gus|tavo
(Peruvian
theologian)
gut|less
gut|less|ly
gut|less|ness
gut-rot
gut|ser+s (use
gutzer)
guts|ily
gutsi|ness
gutsy
guts|ier
gutsi|est
gutta-percha
gut|tate
gut|ter +s +ed
+ing
gut|ter press
gut|ter|snipe +s
gut|tle
gut|tles
gut|tled
gut|tling
gut|tur|al +s
gut|tur|al|ise *Br.*
(use gutturalize)
gut|tur|al|ises
gut|tur|al|ised
gut|tur|al|is|ing
gut|tur|al|ism
gut|tur|al|ize
gut|tur|al|izes

gut|tur|al|ize
(*cont.*)
gut|tur|al|ized
gut|tur|al|iz|ing
gut|tur|al|ly
gut|zer+s
guv
Guy (name)
guy+s +ed +ing
(man; ridicule)
Guy|ana (country,
S. America.
△ Guiana)
Guy|an|ese
plural Guy|an|ese
Guy|enne (region,
France)
guz|zle
guz|zles
guz|zled
guz|zling
guz|zler+s
Gwa|llior (city,
India)
Gwen
Gwenda
Gwen|do|len *also*
Gwen|do|line
Gwen|do|line *also*
Gwen|do|len
Gwent (county,
Wales)
Gwen|yth *also*
Gwyn|eth
Gwyn|edd (county,
Wales)
Gwyn|eth *also*
Gwen|yth
Gwynn, Nell
(English comedy
actress; mistress
of Charles II)
Gyan|dzhe
(Russian name for
Gäncä)
gybe *Br.*
gybes
gybed
gyb|ing
(*Am.* jibe. *Sailing.*
△ jibe, gibe)
Gyles *also* Giles
gym +s
gym|khana +s
gym|na|sial
gym|na|sium
gym|na|siums *or*
gym|na|sia
gym|nast +s
gym|nas|tic
gym|nas|tic|al|ly
gym|nas|tics

gym|noso|phist+s
gym|noso|phy
gym|no|sperm +s
gym|no|sperm|ous
gymp+s (use
gimp)
gym|slip+s
gym tunic +s
gy|nae|ceum+s
(women's
apartments.
△ gynoecium)
gy|nae|coc|racy
Br.
gy|nae|coc|ra|cies
(*Am.*
gynecocracy)
gy|nae|co|logic|al
Br. (*Am.*
gynecological)
gy|nae|co|logic|
al|ly *Br.* (*Am.*
gynecologically)
gy|nae|colo|gist
Br. +s (*Am.*
gynecologist)
gy|nae|col|ogy *Br.*
(*Am.* gynecology)
gy|nae|co|mas|tia
Br. (*Am.*
gynecomastia)
gy|nan|dro|morph
+s
gy|nan|dro|
morph|ic
gy|nan|dro|morph|
ism
gy|nan|drous
gyne|coc|racy *Am.*
gyne|coc|ra|cies
(*Br.*
gynaecocracy)
gyne|co|logic *Am.*
(*Br.*
gynaecologic)
gyne|co|logic|al
Am. (*Br.*
gynaecological)
gyne|co|logic|al|ly
Am. (*Br.*
gynaecologically)
gyne|colo|gist *Am.*
+s (*Br.*
gynaecologist)
gyne|cology *Am.*
(*Br.* gynaecology)
gyne|co|mas|tia
Am. (*Br.*
gynaecomastia)
gyn|oc|racy
gyn|oc|ra|cies

gy|noe|cium
gy|noe|cia
(part of flower.
△ gynaeceum)
gyno|pho|bia
gyp
gyps
gypped
gyp|ping
gyppy (use gippy)
gyp|seous
gyp|sif|er|ous
gypso|phila+s
gyp|sum
gypsy
gyp|sies
Gypsy|dom
Gypsy|fied
Gypsy|hood
Gypsy|ish
gypsy moth+s
gyr|ate
gyr|ates
gyr|ated
gyr|at|ing
gyr|ation+s
gyr|ator+s
gyr|atory
gyre
gyres
gyred
gyr|ing
gyr|fal|con+s
gyri
gyro+s
(gyroscope;
gyrocompass.
△ giro)
gyro|com|pass
gyro|com|passes
gyro|graph+s
gyro|mag|net|ic
gyro|pilot+s
gyro|plane+s
gyro|scope+s
gyro|scop|ic
gyro|sta|bil|iser
Br. +s (use
gyrostabilizer)
gyro|sta|bil|izer
+s
gyrus
gyri
gyt|tja
Gyumri (city,
Armenia)
gyver (use guiver)

Hh

ha
  ha's
  ha'd
  ha'ing
Haag, Den (Dutch
  name for **The
  Hague**)
haar +s (fog)
Haar|lem (city, the
  Netherlands.
  ⚠ Harlem)
Hab¦ak¦kuk *Bible*
haba|nera +s
hab|dabs
hab¦eas cor¦pus
**Haber–Bosch
  pro|cess**
hab¦er|dash¦er +s
hab¦er|dash¦ery
  hab¦er|dash¦er¦ies
hab¦er|geon +s
ha¦bili|ment +s
ha¦bili|tate
  ha¦bili|tates
  ha¦bili|tated
  ha¦bili|tat¦ing
ha¦bili|ta¦tion
habit +s
hab¦it|abil|ity
hab¦it|able
hab¦it|able|ness
hab¦it|ably
hab¦it|ant +s
habi|tat +s
habi|ta¦tion +s
hab¦it|ed
habit-forming
ha¦bit|ual
ha¦bit|ual¦ly
ha¦bit|ual|ness
ha¦bitu|ate
  ha¦bitu|ates
  ha¦bitu|ated
  ha¦bitu|at¦ing
ha¦bitu|ation
habi|tude +s
ha¦bi|tué +s
Habs|burg +s (use
  Hapsburg)
habu|tai
háček +s
hach|ure
  hach|ures
  hach|ured
  hach|ur|ing
ha¦ci|enda +s
hack +s +ed +ing

hack|berry
  hack|berries
hack¦er +s
hack|ery
  hack|er¦ies
hack|ette +s
hackle
  hackles
  hackled
  hack|ling
hackly
hack|ma¦tack +s
Hack|ney (in
  London)
hack|ney +s
  (carriage)
hack|neyed
hack|saw +s +ed
  +ing
had
had¦die +s
had|dock
  plural had|dock
hade
  hades
  haded
  had¦ing
  (incline)
Ha¦dean
Hades *Greek
  Mythology*
Hadhra|maut
  (coastal region,
  Yemen)
Had¦ith
hadj (use haj)
hadji (use haji)
Had¦lee, Rich|ard
  (New Zealand
  cricketer)
hadn't (= had not)
Ha¦drian (Roman
  emperor)
Ha¦drian's Wall (in
  N. England)
had¦ron +s
had|ron¦ic
had¦ro|saur +s
hadst
haec|ce¦ity
  haec|ce¦ities
**Haeckel, Ernst
  Hein|rich**
  (German biologist
  and philosopher)
haem *Br.* +s (*Am.*
  heme)
haem|al *Br.* (*Am.*
  hemal)
haem|at¦ic *Br.* (*Am.*
  hematic)

haem|atin *Br.* (*Am.*
  hematin)
haem|atite *Br.* (*Am.*
  hematite)
haem¦ato|cele *Br.*
  +s (*Am.*
  hematocele)
haem¦ato|crit *Br.*
  +s (*Am.*
  hematocrit)
haem¦ato|logic *Br.*
  (*Am.*
  hematologic)
haem¦ato|logic¦al
  Br. (*Am.*
  hematological)
haema|tolo¦gist *Br.*
  +s (*Am.*
  hematologist)
haema|tol¦ogy *Br.*
  (*Am.* hematology)
haem|atoma *Br.* +s
  (*Am.* hematoma)
haema|topha¦gous
  Br. (*Am.*
  hematophagous)
haem|aturia *Br.*
  (*Am.* hematuria)
haemo|coel *Br.* +s
  (*Am.* hemocoel)
haemo|cya¦nin *Br.*
  (*Am.*
  hemocyanin)
haemo|di¦aly¦sis
  Br.
  haemo|di¦aly¦ses
  (*Am.*
  hemodialysis)
haemo|globin *Br.*
  +s (*Am.*
  hemoglobin)
haemo|lymph *Br.*
  (*Am.* hemolymph)
haem|oly¦sis *Br.*
  haem|oly¦ses
  (*Am.* hemolysis)
haemo|lyt¦ic *Br.*
  (*Am.* hemolytic)
haemo|philia *Br.*
  (*Am.* hemophilia)
haemo|phil¦iac *Br.*
  +s (*Am.*
  hemophiliac)
haemo|phil¦ic *Br.*
  (*Am.* hemophilic)
haem|or|rhage *Br.*
  haem|or|rhages
  haem|or|rhaged
  haem|or|rha¦ging
  (*Am.*
  hemorrhage)

haem|or|rhagic *Br.*
  (*Am.*
  hemorrhagic)
haem|or|rhoid *Br.*
  +s (*Am.*
  hemorrhoid)
haem|or|rhoid¦al
  Br. (*Am.*
  hemorrhoidal)
haemo|stasis *Br.*
  haemo|stases
  (*Am.* hemostasis)
haemo|stat¦ic *Br.*
  (*Am.* hemostatic)
haere mai
hafiz
haf|nium
haft +s +ed +ing
hag +s
Hagar *Bible*
Hagen (city,
  Germany)
hag|fish
  plural hag|fish *or*
  hag|fishes
Hag|ga|dah
  Hag|ga|doth
Hag|gad¦ic
Hag|gai *Bible*
Hag|gard, Rider
  (English writer)
hag|gard +s
hag|gard¦ly
hag|gard|ness
hag|gis
  hag|gises
hag|gish
hag|gle
  hag|gles
  hag|gled
  hag|gling
hag|gler +s
Hagia So¦phia
  (= St Sophia)
hagi|oc¦racy
  hagi|oc¦racies
Hagi|og|rapha
  (part of Hebrew
  Bible)
hagi|og|raph¦er +s
  (writer)
hagio|graph¦ic
hagio|graph¦ic¦al
hagi|og|raphy
  hagi|og|raph¦ies
hagi|ol|ater +s
hagi|ol|atry
hagio|logic¦al
hagi|olo¦gist +s
hagi|ology
hagio|scop¦ic
hag-ridden

Hague, The (city, the Netherlands)

hah *interjection* (use ha)

ha ha (laughter)

ha-ha +s (ditch)

Hahn, Otto (German chemist)

hahn¦ium

haick +s (use haik)

Haida
plural **Haida** *or* **Haidas**

Haifa (port, Israel)

Haig, Doug¦las (Earl Haig, British field marshal)

haik +s (Arab garment. △ hake)

Hai¦kou (capital of Hainan)

haiku
plural **haiku**

hail +s +ed +ing (frozen rain; greet. △ hale)

hail¦er +s

Haile Sel¦as¦sie (Ethiopian emperor)

Hai¦ley *also* **Hay¦ley**

hail-fellow-well-met

Hail Mary
Hail Mar¦ies

hail¦stone +s

hail¦storm +s

Hail¦wood, Mike (English racing motorcyclist)

haily

Hai¦nan (Chinese island)

Hain¦aut (province, Belgium)

Hai¦phong (port, Vietnam)

hair +s (on head etc. △ hare)

hair¦breadth
attributive

hair¦brush
hair¦brushes

hair¦care

hair¦cloth

hair¦cut +s

hair¦do +s

hair¦dress¦er +s

hair¦dress¦ing

hair¦drier +s (use hairdryer)

hair¦dryer +s

haired

hair-grass
hair-grasses

hair¦grip +s

hair¦ily

hair¦ness

hair¦less

hair¦less¦ness

hair¦like

hair¦line +s

hair¦net +s

hair¦piece +s

hair¦pin +s

hair-raising

hair's breadth +s

hair shirt +s

hair-shirt *attributive*

hair¦slide +s

hair-splitter +s

hair-splitting

hair¦spray +s

hair¦spring +s

hair¦streak +s

hair¦style +s

hair¦styl¦ing

hair¦styl¦ist +s

hair-trigger +s

hairy
hair¦ier
hairi¦est

Haiti (in Caribbean)

Hai¦tian +s

haj (pilgrimage)

haji +s (pilgrim)

hajj (use haj)

hajji +s (use haji)

haka +s

hake
plural **hake** *or* **hakes**
(fish. △ haik)

ha¦ken¦kreuz
ha¦ken¦kreuze

hakim +s

Hakka +s

Hak¦luyt, Rich¦ard (English geographer and historian)

Hako¦date (port, Japan)

Hal

Ha¦la¦cha

Ha¦la¦ch¦ic

Ha¦la¦fian

Ha¦la¦kah (use Halacha)

halal
halals
hal¦alled
halal¦ling

hal¦ation

hal¦berd +s

hal¦berd¦ier +s

hal¦cyon +s

Hal¦dane, John Bur¦don San¦der¦son (Scottish biologist)

Hale, George El¦lery (American astronomer)

hale
hales
haled
hal¦ing (healthy; drag. △ hail)

hale¦ness

haler
plural **haler** *or* **hal¦eru** (Bohemian, Moravian, and Slovak currency)

Hales¦owen (town, England)

Haley, Bill (American rock and roll singer)

half
halves

half a crown

half a dozen

half a litre

half-and-half

half an hour

half an inch

half-back +s

half-baked

half-beak
plural **half-beak** *or* **half-beaks**

half-binding

half-blood +s

half-blooded

half-blue +s

half board *noun*

half-board
attributive

half-boot +s

half-bottle +s

half-breed +s (offensive)

half-brother +s

half-caste +s (offensive)

half-century
half-centur¦ies

half-crown +s

half-cut

half-deck +s

half-dozen +s

half-duplex

half-hardy
half-hardies

half-hearted

half-hearted¦ly

half-hearted¦ness

half hitch
half hitches

half holi¦day +s

half-hose

half-hour +s

half-hourly

half-hunter +s

half-inch
half-inches
half-inched
half-inching (unit; steal)

half-integral

half-landing +s

half-lap

half-length +s

half-life
half-lives

half-light

half-litre +s

half-marathon +s

half-mast

half meas¦ures

half-moon +s

half nel¦son +s

half note +s

half pay

half¦penny
half¦pen¦nies *or* **half¦pence**

half¦penny¦worth

half-pie

half-plate +s

half-price

half-relief +s

half-seas-over

half share +s

half-sister +s

half-size

half-sole +s

half-sovereign +s

half-starved

half-step +s

half-term +s

half-timbered

half-timber¦ing

half-time

half-title +s

half-tone +s

half-track +s

half-truth +s

half-volley +s

half¦way

half¦wit +s

half-witted

half-witted¦ly

half-witted|ness
half year +s *noun*
half-year *attributive*
half-yearly
hali|but
   plural hali|but
Hali|car|nas|sus
   (ancient Greek
   city, Asia Minor)
hal|ide +s
hali|eut|ic
Hali|fax (city,
   Canada; town,
   England)
hali|otis
   plural hali|otis
hal|ite +s
hali|tosis
Hall, Charles
   Mar|tin
   (American
   industrial chemist)
Hall, Rad|clyffe
   (English writer)
hall +s (room.
   △ haul)
hal|lal (use halal)
Halle (city,
   Germany)
Hallé, Charles
   (German-born
   conductor)
hal|le|lu|jah +s
Hal|ler, Al|brecht
   von (Swiss
   physiologist)
Hal|ley, Ed|mond
   (English
   astronomer)
Hal|ley's Comet
hal|liard +s (use
   halyard)
hall|mark +s +ed
   +ing
hallo (use hello)
   hal|loes
   hal|loed
   hallo|ing
hal|loo +s +ed
   +ing
hal|low +s +ed
   +ing
Hal|low|e'en
Hal|lowes, Odette
   (French secret
   agent)
hall|stand +s
Hall|statt (village,
   Austria;
   Archaeology)
hal|lu|ces
hal|lu|cin|ant +s

hal|lu|cin|ate
hal|lu|cin|ates
hal|lu|cin|ated
hal|lu|cin|at|ing
hal|lu|cin|ation +s
hal|lu|cin|ator +s
hal|lu|cin|atory
hal|lu|cino|gen +s
hal|lu|cino|gen|ic
hal|lux
hal|lu|ces
hall|way +s
halm +s (use
   haulm)
halma
Hal|ma|hera
   (island, Moluccas)
halo
   ha|loes *or* halos
   noun
halo
   ha|loes
   ha|loed
   ha|lo|ing
   verb
halo|car|bon +s
halo|gen +s
halo|gen|ated
halo|gen|ation
halo|gen|ic
halon +s
halo|peri|dol
halo|phyte +s
halo|thane
Hals, Frans (Dutch
   painter)
halt +s +ed +ing
hal|ter +s
halter-break
   halter-breaks
   halter-broke
   halter-breaking
   halter-broken
hal|tere +s
halter-neck +s
   noun and
   attributive
halt|ing|ly
halva +s
halve
   halves
   halved
   halv|ing
   verb
   halves (plural of
   half)
hal|yard +s
Ham *Bible*
ham
   hams
   hammed
   ham|ming

ham (*cont.*)
   (meat; actor; radio
   operator)
Hama (city, Syria)
Ham|ada, Shoji
   (Japanese potter)
hama|dryad +s
   (nymph; snake)
hama|dryas
   hama|dry|ases
   (baboon)
Hamah (use
   Hama)
Hama|matsu (city,
   Japan)
hama|melis
   plural hama|melis
ha|mar|tia
Hamas (Palestinian
   Islamic
   fundamentalist
   movement)
hamba
ham|bone +s
Ham|burg (city,
   Germany)
ham|burg|er +s
   (food)
Ham|elin (English
   name for Hameln)
Ham|eln (town,
   Germany)
hames
ham-fisted
ham-fisted|ly
ham-fisted|ness
ham-handed
ham-handed|ly
ham-handed|ness
Ham|hung (city,
   North Korea)
Ham|il|car
   (Carthaginian
   general)
Ham|il|ton (town,
   Scotland, port,
   Canada; city, New
   Zealand; capital of
   Bermuda)
Ham|il|ton,
   Charles (New
   Zealand inventor
   and racing driver)
Ham|il|ton, Emma
   (mistress of Lord
   Nelson)
Ham|il|ton,
   Wil|liam Rowan
   (Irish
   mathematician
   and physicist)
Ha|mish

Ham|ite +s
Ham|it|ic +s
Hamito-Semitic
Ham|let (Danish
   prince)
ham|let +s (village)
Hamm (city,
   Germany)
ham|mer +s +ed
   +ing
ham|mer and
   tongs (vigorously)
ham|mer|beam +s
ham|mer drill +s
ham|mer|er +s
Ham|mer|fest
   (port, Norway)
ham|mer|head +s
   (shark; bird)
ham|mer head +s
   (head of hammer)
ham|mer|ing +s
ham|mer|less
ham|mer|lock +s
ham|mer|man
   ham|mer|men
Ham|mer|stein,
   Oscar (American
   librettist)
hammer-toe +s
Ham|mett,
   Dash|iell
   (American
   detective-story
   writer)
ham|mock +s
Ham|mond, Joan
   (Australian
   soprano)
Ham|mu|rabi
   (Babylonian king)
hammy
   ham|mier
   ham|mi|est
Ham|nett,
   Kath|ar|ine
   (English fashion
   designer)
ham|per +s +ed
   +ing
Hamp|shire
   (county, England)
Hamp|stead
   (district, London)
Hamp|ton (city,
   USA)
Hamp|ton Court
   (palace, London)
Hamp|ton Roads
   (estuary, USA)
ham|sin +s (use
   khamsin)

ham|ster +s
ham|string
  ham|strings
  ham|stringed *or*
  ham|strung
  ham|string|ing
Ham|sun, Knut
  (Norwegian
  novelist)
ham|ulus
  ham|uli
Han (Chinese
  dynasty)
Han|cock, Tony
  (English
  comedian)
hand +s +ed +ing
hand-axe +s
hand|bag
  hand|bags
  hand|bagged
  hand|bag|ging
hand|ball +s
hand|basin +s
hand|bell +s
hand|bill +s
hand|book +s
hand|brake +s
hand-built
hand|cart +s
hand|clap +s
hand|clap|ping
hand|craft +s +ed
  +ing
hand cream +s
hand|cuff +s +ed
  +ing
hand|ed|ness
Han|del, George
  Fred|erick
  (German-born
  composer)
hand-eye
  co|ordin|ation
hand|ful +s
hand|glass
  hand|glasses
hand gren|ade +s
hand|grip +s
hand|gun +s
hand-held +s
hand|hold +s
hand-holding
hand-hot
handi|cap
  handi|caps
  handi|capped
  handi|cap|ping
han|di|cap|per +s
han|di|craft +s
hand|ily
handi|ness

hand in glove
hand in hand
  adverbial
hand-in-hand
  attributive
han|di|work
hand|ker|chief
  hand|ker|chiefs *or*
  hand|ker|chieves
hand-knit +s *noun*
  and attributive
hand-knitted
hand-knitting
han|dle
  han|dles
  han|dled
  hand|ling
handle|abil|ity
handle|able
handle|bar +s
hand|ler +s
hand|less
Hand|ley Page,
  Fred|erick
  (English aircraft
  designer)
hand|line
  hand|lines
  hand|lined
  hand|lin|ing
hand|list +s
hand|made (made
  by hand)
hand|maid +s
  (servant)
hand|maiden +s
hand-me-down +s
hand-off +s *noun*
hand|out +s
hand|over +s
hand-painted
hand-pick +s +ed
  +ing
hand|pump +s
hand|rail +s
hand|saw +s
hand|sel
  hand|sels
  hand|selled *Br.*
  hand|seled *Am.*
  hand|sel|ling *Br.*
  hand|sel|ing *Am.*
hand|set +s
hand|shake +s
hands off
  (warning)
hands-off *adjective*
hand|some
  hand|somer
  hand|som|est
  (good-looking.
  ⚠ hansom)

hand|some|ly
hand|some|ness
hands-on *adjective*
hand|spike +s
hand|spring +s
hand|stand +s
hand-to-hand
hand-to-mouth
  attributive
hand tool +s
hand|work
hand|worked
hand|writ|ing +s
hand|writ|ten
handy
  hand|ier
  handi|est
handy|man
  handy|men
hang
  hangs
  hung
  hang|ing
  (suspend)
hang +s +ed +ing
  (execute)
hangar +s (shed.
  ⚠ hanger)
hang|ar|age
Hang|chow
  (= Hangzhou)
hang|dog
hanger +s (coat-
  hanger etc.; wood
  on side of hill.
  ⚠ hangar)
hanger-on
  hangers-on
hang-glide
  hang-glides
  hang-glided
  hang-gliding
hang-glider +s
hang|ing +s *noun*
hang|man
  hang|men
hang|nail +s
hang-out +s *noun*
hang|over +s
Hang Seng index
hang-up +s *noun*
Hang|zhou (city,
  China)
hank +s
han|ker +s +ed
  +ing
han|ker|er +s
han|kie +s (use
  hanky)
hanky
  han|kies
hanky-panky

Han|nah
Han|ni|bal
  (Carthaginian
  general)
Han|nover
  (German name for
  Hanover)
Hanoi (capital of
  Vietnam)
Han|over (city,
  Germany)
Han|over|ian +s
Hansa (guild;
  Hanseatic league)
Han|sard (British
  parliament)
Hanse (use Hansa)
Han|se|at|ic
Han|sel (and
  Gretel)
han|sel (gift; use
  handsel)
  han|sels
  han|selled *Br.*
  han|seled *Am.*
  han|sel|ling *Br.*
  han|sel|ing *Am.*
Han|sen's dis|ease
han|som +s (cab.
  ⚠ handsome)
Hants
  (= Hampshire)
Ha|nuk|kah
  (Jewish festival)
Ha|nu|man (Hindu
  mythological
  creature)
ha|nu|man +s
  (monkey)
Haora (use
  Howrah)
hap
  haps
  happed
  hap|ping
hapax
  leg|om|enon
hapax leg|om|ena
ha'|penny
  ha'|pennies *or*
  ha'|pence
hap|haz|ard
hap|haz|ard|ly
hap|haz|ard|ness
hap|less
hap|less|ly
hap|less|ness
hap|log|raphy
hap|loid +s
hap|lol|ogy
ha'p'|orth (= half-
  pennyworth)

hap|pen +s +ed +ing
hap|pen|ing +s
hap|pen|stance +s
happi +s (Japanese coat. △ happy)
happi-coat +s
hap|pily
hap|pi|ness
   hap|pi|nesses
happy
   hap|pier
   hap|pi|est (feeling pleasure. △ happi)
happy-go-lucky
Haps|burg +s (central European dynasty; member of this)
hap|tic
hara-kiri
har|angue
   har|angues
   har|angued
   har|anguing
har|anguer +s
Har|appa (ancient city, Pakistan)
Har|are (capital of Zimbabwe)
har|ass
   har|asses
   har|assed
   har|ass|ing
har|ass|er +s
har|ass|ing|ly
har|ass|ment +s
Har|bin (city, China)
har|bin|ger +s +ed +ing
har|bor Am. +s +ed +ing
har|bor|age Am.
har|bor|less Am.
har|bor|mas|ter Am. +s
har|bour Br. +s +ed +ing
har|bour|age Br.
har|bour|less Br.
har|bour mas|ter Br.
hard +s +er +est
hard and fast
hard|back +s
hard|bake
hard-baked
hard|ball +s +ed +ing
hard|bit|ten

hard|board +s
hard-boiled
hard|core (rubble; music)
hard core +s (nucleus)
hard-core adjective
hard|cover +s
hard disk +s
hard-done-by
hard-earned
hard|en +s +ed +ing
hard|en|er +s
hard hat +s
hard-headed
hard-headed|ly
hard-headed|ness
hard|heads
   plural hard|heads (plant)
hard-hearted
hard-hearted|ly
hard-hearted|ness
hard hit adjective
hard-hit attributive
hard-hitting
Har|die, Keir (Scottish politician. △ Hardy)
hardi|hood
har|dily
hardi|ness
Hard|ing, War|ren (American president)
hard|ish
hard|line attributive
hard line noun (unyielding adherence to policy)
hard|liner +s
hard lines (bad luck)
hard|ly
hard|ness
hard-nosed
hard of hear|ing
hard-on +s (coarse slang)
hard|pan
hard-paste adjective
hard-pressed
hard|shell adjective
hard|ship +s
hard|stand|ing
hard tack
hard-top +s (car; roof)

hard up adjective
hard-up attributive
Har|dwar (city, India)
hard|ware
hard-wearing
hard-wired
hard|wood +s
hard-working
Hardy, Oli|ver (American comedian. △ Hardie)
Hardy, Thomas (English writer. △ Hardie)
hardy
   har|dier
   har|di|est
Hare, Wil|liam (Irish body-snatcher)
hare
   hares
   hared
   har|ing (animal. △ hair)
hare|bell +s
hare-brained
Hare|foot, Har|old (English king)
Hare Krishna +s (chant; sect; member of sect)
hare|lip +s (offensive; to avoid offence, use cleft lip)
hare|lipped (offensive)
harem +s
hare's-ear +s
hare's-foot +s
hare|wood
Har|geisa (city, Somalia)
Har|geysa (use Hargeisa)
Har|greaves, James (English inventor)
hari|cot +s
Hari|jan +s
hark +s +ed +ing
hark|en +s +ed +ing (use hearken)
harl
harle (use harl)
Har|lech (village, Wales)

Har|lem (district, New York City; Globetrotters; Renaissance. △ Haarlem)
Har|le|quin (in pantomine)
har|le|quin (duck etc.)
har|le|quin|ade +s
Har|ley Street (in London)
har|lot +s
har|lot|ry
Har|low (town, England)
harm +s +ed +ing
har|mat|tan
harm|ful
harm|ful|ly
harm|ful|ness
harm|less
harm|less|ly
harm|less|ness
har|mon|ic +s
har|mon|ica +s
har|mon|ic|al|ly
har|mo|ni|ous
har|mo|ni|ous|ly
har|mo|ni|ous|ness
har|mon|isa|tion Br. (use harmonization)
har|mon|ise Br. (use harmonize)
   har|mon|ises
   har|mon|ised
   har|mon|is|ing
har|mon|ist +s
har|mon|is|tic
har|mo|nium +s
har|mon|iza|tion
har|mon|ize
   har|mon|izes
   har|mon|ized
   har|mon|iz|ing
har|mony
   har|monies
Harms|worth, Al|fred Charles Wil|liam (Lord Northcliffe)
har|ness
   har|nesses
   har|nessed
   har|ness|ing
har|ness|er +s
Har|old (English kings)

Haroun-al-
  Raschid (use
  Harun ar-Rashid)
harp +s +ed +ing
har|per +s
Har|pers Ferry
  (town, USA)
harp|ist +s
Har|poc|ra|tes
  Greek Mythology
har|poon +s +ed
  +ing
har|poon|er +s
har|poon gun +s
harp seal +s
harp|si|chord +s
harp|si|chord|ist
  +s
harpy
  har|pies
har|que|bus
  har|que|buses
har|que|bus|ier +s
har|ri|dan +s
har|rier +s
Har|riet
Har|ris (Scottish
  island; tweed)
Har|ris|burg (town,
  USA)
Har|ri|son,
  Ben|ja|min
  (American
  president)
Har|ri|son, Rex
  (English actor)
Har|ri|son,
  Wil|liam Henry
  (American
  president)
Har|rod, Charles
  Henry (English
  grocer)
Har|ro|vian +s
Har|row (school,
  England)
har|row +s +ed
  +ing (tool etc.)
har|row|er +s
har|row|ing|ly
har|rumph +s +ed
  +ing
Harry (name)
harry
  har|ries
  har|ried
  harry|ing
  (ravage; worry)
harsh +er +est
harsh|en +s +ed
  +ing
harsh|ly

harsh|ness
hars|let +s
hart +s (deer.
  △ heart)
har|tal
Harte, Bret
  (American writer)
har|te|beest
  plural har|te|beest
  or har|te|beests
Hart|ford (city,
  USA. △ Hertford)
Hart|le|pool (port,
  England)
Hart|ley, L. P.
  (English novelist)
Hart|nell,
  Nor|man (English
  couturier)
harts|horn
hart's tongue +s
harum-scarum +s
Harun ar-Rashid
  (caliph of
  Baghdad)
haru|spex
  haru|spi|ces
haru|spicy
Har|vard
  (university, USA;
  classification)
har|vest +s +ed
  +ing
har|vest|able
har|vest|er +s
har|vest|man
  har|vest|men
Har|vey
Har|vey, Wil|liam
  (English
  physician)
Har|wich (port,
  England)
Ha|ry|ana (state,
  India)
Harz Moun|tains
  (in Germany)
has
has-been +s
Has|dru|bal (two
  Carthaginian
  generals)
Hašek, Jaro|slav
  (Czech writer)
hash
  hashes
  hashed
  hash|ing
Hash|em|ite +s
hash|ish
Hasid
  Has|id|im

Ha|sid|ic
Has|id|ism
has|let +s
Has|mon|ean
hasn't (= has not)
hasp +s +ed +ing
Has|selt (city,
  Belgium)
has|sle
  has|sles
  has|sled
  has|sling
has|sock +s
hast (in 'thou hast')
hast|ate
haste
  hastes
  hasted
  hast|ing
  (hurry)
has|ten +s +ed
  +ing
hasti|ly
hasti|ness
Hast|ings (town
  and battle site,
  England)
Hast|ings,
  War|ren
  (governor-general
  of India)
hasty
  hasti|er
  hasti|est
hat
  hats
  hat|ted
  hat|ting
hat|able (deserving
  to be hated)
hat|band +s
hat|box
  hat|boxes
hatch
  hatches
  hatched
  hatch|ing
hatch|back +s
hatch|ery
  hatch|er|ies
hatchet +s
hatchet-faced
hatchet job +s
hatchet man
  hatchet men
hatch|ing +s
hatch|ling +s
hatch|ment +s
hatch|way +s
hate
  hates

hate (*cont.*)
  hated
  hat|ing
hate|ful
hate|ful|ly
hate|ful|ness
hater +s
hat|ful +s
hath
Hath|away, Anne
  (wife of
  Shakespeare)
hatha yoga
Hathor *Egyptian
  Mythology*
hat|less
hat|peg +s
hat|pin +s
hat|red +s
Hat|shep|sut
  (Egyptian queen)
hat|stand +s
hat|ter +s
Hat|tie
hat-trick +s
Hat|tusa (ancient
  city, Turkey)
hau|berk +s
haught|ily
haughti|ness
haughty
  haught|ier
  haught|iest
haul +s +ed +ing
  (pull in. △ hall)
haul|age
haul|er +s
haul|ier +s
haulm +s
haunch
  haunches
haunt +s +ed +ing
haunt|er +s
haunt|ing|ly
Haupt|mann,
  Ger|hart (German
  dramatist)
Hausa
  plural Hausa *or*
  Hau|sas
haus|frau
  haus|fraus *or*
  haus|frau|en
haut|boy +s
haute cou|ture
haute cuis|ine
haute école
Haute-Normandie
  (region, France)
haut|eur
haut monde
haut-relief +s

Hav¦ana +s (capital of Cuba; cigar)
Hav¦ant (town, England)
have
has
had
hav¦ing
have-a-go *attributive*
Havel, Vác¦lav (Czech writer and president)
have¦lock +s
ha¦ven +s
have-not +s
haven't (= have not)
haver +s +ed +ing
hav¦er¦sack +s
hav¦er¦sin (abbreviation of haversine)
hav¦er¦sine +s
hav¦il¦dar +s
havoc
havocs
hav¦ocked
hav¦ock¦ing
haw +s +ed +ing (hawthorn; eyelid; in 'hum and haw'. △ hoar, whore)
Ha¦waii (state and island, USA)
Ha¦wai¦ian +s
haw¦finch
haw¦finches
hawk +s +ed +ing
hawk¦bit +s
Hawke, Bob (Australian prime minister)
Hawke Bay (bay, New Zealand)
hawk¦er +s
Hawke's Bay (region, New Zealand)
hawk-eyed
Hawk¦ing, Ste¦phen (English theoretical physicist)
Haw¦kins, Cole¦man (American jazz saxophonist)
Haw¦kins, John (English sailor)
hawk¦ish
hawk¦ish¦ness

hawk¦like
hawk¦moth +s
hawk-nosed
Hawks, How¦ard (American film director)
hawks¦bill +s
Hawks¦moor, Nich¦olas (English architect)
hawk¦weed +s
Haw¦kyns, John (use Hawkins)
Ha¦worth, Wal¦ter Nor¦man (English organic chemist)
hawse +s
hawse-hole +s
hawse-pipe +s
haw¦ser +s
haw¦thorn +s
Haw¦thorne, Na¦than¦iel (American writer)
hay +s +ed +ing (dried grass; dance. △ heigh-hey)
hay¦box
hay¦boxes
hay¦cock +s
Haydn, Jo¦seph (Austrian composer)
Hayek, Fried¦rich Au¦gust von (Austrian-born economist)
Hayes, Ruth¦er¦ford (American president)
hay fever
hay¦field +s
hay-fork +s
Hay¦ley *also* Hai¦ley
hay¦loft +s
hay¦maker +s
hay¦mak¦ing
hay¦mow
hay¦rick +s
hay¦seed +s
hay¦stack +s
hay¦ward +s
hay¦wire
Hay¦worth, Rita (American actress)
haz¦ard +s +ed +ing
haz¦ard¦ous

haz¦ard¦ous¦ly
haz¦ard¦ous¦ness
haze
hazes
hazed
haz¦ing
Hazel (name)
hazel +s (tree)
hazel-grouse *plural* hazel-grouse
hazel¦nut +s
haz¦ily
hazi¦ness
Haz¦litt, Wil¦liam (British essayist)
hazy
hazi¦er
hazi¦est
H-block +s
H-bomb +s
he +s
Head, Edith (American costume designer)
head +s +ed +ing
head¦ache +s
head¦achy
head¦age
head¦band +s
head¦bang¦er +s
head¦bang¦ing
head¦board +s
head-butt +s +ed +ing
head case +s
head-cloth +s
head¦count +s
head¦dress
head¦dresses
head¦er +s
head¦fast +s
head first
head¦gear
head height
head¦hunt +s +ed +ing
head¦hunt¦er +s
head¦ily
headi¦ness
head¦ing +s
head¦lamp +s
head¦land +s
head¦less
head lice
head¦light +s
head¦line
head¦lines
head¦lined
head¦lin¦ing
head¦liner +s
head¦lock +s

head¦long
head louse
head lice
head¦man
head¦men
head¦mas¦ter +s
head¦mas¦ter¦ly
head¦mis¦tress
head¦mis¦tresses
head¦most
head¦note +s
head of state
heads of state
head-on
head¦phone +s
head¦piece +s
head¦quar¦ter +s +ed +ing
head¦rest +s
head¦room
head¦sail +s
head¦scarf
head¦scarves
head¦set +s
head¦ship +s
head¦shrink¦er +s
heads¦man
heads¦men
head¦spring +s
head¦square +s
head¦stall +s
head start
head¦stock +s
head¦stone +s
head¦strong
head¦strong¦ly
head¦strong¦ness
head teach¦er +s
head-to-head
head-up *adjective*
head voice
head¦ward
head¦water +s
head¦way
head¦wind +s
head¦word +s
head¦work
heady
head¦ier
head¦iest
heal +s +ed +ing (cure. △ heel, hele, he'll)
heal¦able
heal-all +s
heald +s
heal¦er +s
health
health¦ful
health¦ful¦ly
health¦ful¦ness
health¦ily

healthi|ness
healthy
  health|ier
  healthi|est
Hea|ney, Sea|mus
  (Irish poet)
heap +s +ed +ing
hear
  hears
  heard
  hear|ing
  (listen to. △ here)
hear|able
heard (past tense
  and past participle
  of hear. △ herd)
Heard and
  Mc|Donald
  Is|lands (in
  Indian Ocean)
hear|er +s
hear|ing +s
hear|ing aid +s
heark|en +s +ed
  +ing
hear|say
hearse +s
Hearst, Wil|liam
  Ran|dolph
  (American
  newspaper
  publisher)
heart +s (body
  organ. △ hart)
heart|ache +s
heart|beat +s
heart|break
heart|break|er +s
heart|break|ing
heart|broken
heart|burn
heart|en +s +ed
  +ing
heart|en|ing|ly
heart|felt
hearth +s
hearth|rug +s
hearth|stone +s
heart|ily
hearti|ness
heart|land +s
heart|less
heart|less|ly
heart|less|ness
heart-lung
  ma|chine +s
heart-rending
heart-rending|ly
heart's-blood
heart-searching
hearts|ease
heart|sick

heart|sick|ness
heart|sore
heart|strings
heart-throb +s
heart to heart
  adverb
heart-to-heart +s
  adjective and noun
heart-warming
heart|wood
hearty
  heart|ier
  hearti|est
heat +s +ed +ing
heat|er +s
heat-exchan|ger
  +s
Heath, Ed|ward
  (British prime
  minister)
heath +s
heath-bell +s
hea|then +s
hea|then|dom
hea|then|ish
hea|then|ism
hea|then|ry
Hea|ther (name)
hea|ther +s (shrub)
hea|thery
heath|land +s
heath|less
heath|like
Heath Rob|in|son
  adjective
Heath Rob|in|son,
  W. (English
  cartoonist)
Heath|row (airport,
  London)
heathy
heat lamp +s
heat|proof
heat-resist|ant
heat-seeking
heat|stroke
heat-treat +s +ed
  +ing
heat treat|ment
heat|wave +s
heave
  heaves
  heaved
  or **hove** *Nautical*
  heav|ing
heave-ho
heaven +s
heav|en|li|ness
heav|en|ly
heaven-sent
heav|en|ward
heav|en|wards

heaver +s
heavier-than-air
  attributive
heav|ily
heavi|ness
Heavi|side, Oli|ver
  (English physicist)
Heavi|side layer
heavy
  heav|ies
  heav|ied
  heavy|ing
  heav|ier
  heavi|est
heavy-duty
heavy-footed
heavy-handed
heavy-handed|ly
heavy-
  handed|ness
heavy-hearted
heavy|ish
heavy-lidded
heavy-set
heavy|weight +s
heb|dom|adal
Hebe (*Greek*
  Mythology;
  asteroid)
hebe +s (shrub)
Hebei (province,
  China)
hebe|tude
Heb|raic
Heb|ra|ic|al|ly
Heb|ra|ise *Br.* (use
  Hebraize)
  Heb|ra|ises
  Heb|ra|ised
  Heb|ra|is|ing
Heb|ra|ism +s
Heb|ra|ist +s
Heb|ra|is|tic
Heb|ra|ize
  Heb|ra|izes
  Heb|ra|ized
  Heb|ra|iz|ing
Heb|rew +s
Heb|ri|dean +s
Heb|ri|des
  (shipping area off
  Scotland)
Heb|ri|des, the
  (islands off
  Scotland)
Heb|ron (city, West
  Bank)
Heb|ros (ancient
  Greek name for
  the Maritsa)
Hec|ate *Greek*
  Mythology

heca|tomb +s
heck
heck|el|phone +s
heckle
  heckles
  heckled
  heck|ling
heck|ler +s
hec|tar|age
hec|tare +s
hec|tic
hec|tic|al|ly
hecto|gram +s
hecto|graph +s
hecto|liter *Am.* +s
hecto|litre *Br.* +s
hecto|meter *Am.*
  +s
hecto|metre *Br.* +s
Hec|tor (*Greek*
  Mythology; name)
hec|tor +s +ed
  +ing (bully)
hec|tor|ing|ly
Hec|uba *Greek*
  Mythology
he'd (= he had; he
  would. △ **heed**)
hed|dle +s
hedge
  hedges
  hedged
  hedg|ing
hedge|hog +s
hedge|hoggy
hedge-hop
  hedge-hops
  hedge-hopped
  hedge-hopping
hedger +s
hedge|row +s
hedge spar|row +s
hedge trim|mer +s
he|don|ic
he|don|ism
he|don|ist +s
he|don|is|tic
heebie-jeebies,
  the
heed +s +ed +ing
  (take notice of.
  △ **he'd**)
heed|ful
heed|ful|ly
heed|ful|ness
heed|less
heed|less|ly
heed|less|ness
hee-haw +s +ed
  +ing
heel +s +ed +ing
  (part of foot or

heel (*cont.*)
shoe; kick with
heel; replace heel
on shoe. △ heal,
hele, he'll)
heel|ball
heel|less
heel|tap +s
Hefei (city, China)
heft +s +ed +ing
heft|ily
hefti|ness
hefty
heft|ier
hefti|est
Hegel, Georg
Wil|helm
Fried|rich
(German
philosopher)
He|gel|ian +s
He|gel|ian|ism
hege|mon|ic
he|gem|ony
he|gem|onies
Heg|ira
(Muhammad's
departure from
Mecca to Medina)
heg|ira +s
(generally)
Hei|deg|ger,
Mar|tin (German
philosopher)
Hei|del|berg (city,
Germany)
Heidi
heifer +s
heigh (*interjection*
expressing
encouragement or
enquiry. △ hay,
hey)
heigh-ho
height +s
(highness.
△ hight)
height|en +s +ed
+ing
Heil|bronn (city,
Germany)
Hei|long (Chinese
name for **Amur**)
Hei|long|jiang
(province, China)
Hei|lung|kiang
(= Heilongjiang)
Heine, Hein|rich
(German poet)
hein|ous
hein|ous|ly
hein|ous|ness

Heinz, Henry
John (American
food
manufacturer)
heir +s (inheritor.
△ air, e're, ere)
heir ap|par|ent
heirs ap|par|ent
heir-at-law
heirs-at-law
heir|dom
heir|ess
heir|esses
heir|less
(without an heir.
△ airless)
heir|loom +s
heir pre|sump|tive
heirs
pre|sump|tive
heir|ship (being an
heir. △ airship)
Hei|sen|berg, Karl
(German
physicist;
uncertainty
principle)
heist +s +ed +ing
hei-tiki +s
Hejaz (region,
Saudi Arabia)
Hej|ira (use
Hegira)
hej|ira +s (use
hegira)
Hekla (volcano,
Iceland)
HeLa (cells)
held
Hel|den|tenor +s
hele
heles
heled
hel|ing
(put plant in
ground. △ heal,
heel, he'll)
Helen (daughter of
Zeus and Leda;
name. △ Hellen)
Hel|ena (town,
USA; name)
Hel|ena (Roman
empress and
saint)
hel|en|ium +s
Helga
he|li|acal
he|li|an|the|mum
+s
he|li|an|thus
plural
he|li|an|thus

hel|ic|al
hel|ic|al|ly
heli|ces
heli|chry|sum +s
he|li|city
heli|coid +s
Heli|con, Mount
(in Greece)
heli|con +s (tuba)
heli|cop|ter +s +ed
+ing
Heli|go|land
(German island)
he|lio|cen|tric
he|lio|cen|tric|
al|ly
He|lio|ga|balus
(Roman emperor)
he|lio|gram +s
he|lio|graph +s
+ed +ing
heli|og|raphy
he|lio|gra|vure
he|lio|lith|ic
he|li|om|eter +s
He|li|opo|lis
(ancient city,
Egypt)
Hel|ios Greek
Mythology
he|lio|stat +s
he|lio|stat|ic
he|lio|ther|apy
he|lio|trope +s
he|lio|trop|ic
he|lio|trop|ism
he|lio|type +s
heli|pad +s
heli|port +s
heli-skiing
he|lium
helix
heli|ces
hell (abode of the
dead; etc.)
he'll (= he shall; he
will. △ heel, hill)
hell|acious
hell|acious|ly
Hel|lad|ic +s
hell|bend|er +s
hell-bent
hell-cat +s
hel|le|bore +s
hel|le|bor|ine +s
Hel|len (son or
brother of
Deucalion.
△ Helen)
Hel|lene +s
Hel|len|ic

Hel|len|isa|tion Br.
(use
Hellenization)
Hel|len|ise Br. (use
Hellenize)
Hel|len|ises
Hel|len|ised
Hel|len|is|ing
Hel|len|ism
Hel|len|ist +s
Hel|len|is|tic
Hel|len|iza|tion
Hel|len|ize
Hel|len|izes
Hel|len|ized
Hel|len|iz|ing
Hel|ler, Jo|seph
(American
novelist)
Hel|les|pont, the
(ancient name for
the Dardanelles)
hell|fire
hell|gram|mite +s
hell-hole +s
hell-hound +s
hell|lion +s
hell|ish
hell|ish|ly
hell|ish|ness
hell-like
Hell|man, Lil|lian
(American
dramatist)
hello +s *noun*
hello
hel|loes
hel|loed
hel|lo|ing
verb
hell|raiser +s
hell|rais|ing
Hell's Angel +s
Hell's Can|yon (in
USA)
hell|luva (= 'hell of
a')
hell|ward
helm +s +ed +ing
Hel|mand (river,
Afghanistan)
hel|met +s +ed
+ing
Helm|holtz,
Her|mann
Lud|wig
Fer|di|nand von
(German
physiologist and
physicist)
hel|minth +s
hel|minth|ia|sis

hel¦minth¦ic
hel¦minth¦oid
hel¦minth¦olo¦gist
+s
hel¦minth¦ology
Hel¦mont,
Jo¦an¦nes
Bap¦tista van
(Belgian chemist)
helms¦man
helms¦men
Hélo¦ïse (French
abbess and lover
of Peter Abelard)
Helot (serf in
ancient Sparta)
helot (serf
generally)
hel¦ot¦ism
hel¦ot¦ry
help +s +ed +ing
help¦er +s
help¦ful
help¦ful¦ly
help¦ful¦ness
help¦ing +s
help¦less
help¦less¦ly
help¦less¦ness
help¦line +s
Help¦mann,
Rob¦ert
(Australian ballet
dancer and
choreographer)
help¦mate +s
help¦meet +s
Hel¦sing¦borg
(port, Sweden)
Hel¦sing¦fors
(Swedish name for
Helsinki)
Hel¦sing¦ør (Danish
name for
Elsinore)
Hel¦sinki (capital of
Finland)
helter-skelter +s
helve +s
Hel¦ve¦tian +s
hem
hems
hemmed
hem¦ming
hemal *Am.* (*Br.*
haemal)
he-man
he-men
hem¦at¦ic *Am.* (*Br.*
haematic)
hema¦tin *Am.* (*Br.*
haematin)

hema¦tite *Am.* (*Br.*
haematite)
hema¦to¦cele *Am.*
+s (*Br.*
haematocele)
hema¦to¦crit *Am.*
+s (*Br.*
haematocrit)
hema¦to¦logic *Am.*
(*Br.*
haematologic)
hema¦to¦logic¦al
Am. (*Br.*
haematological)
hema¦tolo¦gist *Am.*
+s (*Br.*
haematologist)
hema¦tol¦ogy *Am.*
(*Br.*
haematology)
hema¦toma *Am.* +s
(*Br.* haematoma)
hema¦topha¦gous
Am. (*Br.* haema-
tophagous)
hema¦turia *Am.*
(*Br.* haematuria)
heme *Am.* +s (*Br.*
haem)
Hemel
Hemp¦stead
(town, England)
hem¦ero¦cal¦lis
plural
hem¦ero¦cal¦lis
hemi¦an¦opia (use
hemianopsia)
hemi¦an¦op¦sia
hemi¦cel¦lu¦lose +s
hemi¦chord¦ate +s
hemi¦cycle +s
hemi¦demi¦semi¦
quaver +s
hemi¦he¦dral
Hem¦ing¦way,
Er¦nest
(American
novelist)
hemi¦ple¦gia
hemi¦ple¦gic +s
hemi¦sphere +s
hemi¦spher¦ic
hemi¦spher¦ic¦al
hemi¦stich +s
Hem¦kund, Lake
(in India)
hem¦line +s
hem¦lock +s
hemo¦coel *Am.* +s
(*Br.* haemocoel)

hemo¦cya¦nin *Am.*
(*Br.*
haemocyanin)
hemo¦di¦aly¦sis
Am. (*Br.*
haemodialysis)
hemo¦globin *Am.*
(*Br.*
haemoglobin)
hemo¦lymph *Am.*
(*Br.*
haemolymph)
hem¦oly¦sis *Am.*
(*Br.* haemolysis)
hemo¦lyt¦ic *Am.*
(*Br.* haemolytic)
hemo¦philia *Am.*
(*Br.* haemophilia)
hemo¦phil¦iac *Am.*
(*Br.*
haemophiliac)
hemo¦phil¦ic *Am.*
(*Br.* haemophilic)
hem¦or¦rhage *Am.*
hem¦or¦rhages
hem¦or¦rhaged
hem¦or¦rha¦ging
(*Br.*
haemorrhage)
hem¦or¦rhagic *Am.*
(*Br.*
haemorrhagic)
hem¦or¦rhoid *Am.*
+s (*Br.*
haemorrhoid)
hem¦or¦rhoid¦al
Am. (*Br.*
haemorrhoidal)
hemo¦stasis *Am.*
hemo¦stases
(*Br.* haemostasis)
hemo¦stat¦ic *Am.*
(*Br.* haemostatic)
hemp +s
hemp¦en
hemp-nettle +s
hem¦stitch
hem¦stitches
hem¦stitched
hem¦stitch¦ing
hen +s
Henan (province,
China)
hen and chick¦ens
plural hen and
chick¦ens
(plant)
hen¦bane
hence
hence¦forth
hence¦for¦ward

hench¦man
hench¦men
hen-coop +s
hen¦deca¦gon +s
hen¦deca¦
syl¦lab¦ic
hen¦deca¦syl¦lable
+s
hen¦dia¦dys
Hen¦drix, Jimi
(American rock
musician)
hen¦equen
henge +s
Hen¦gist (Jutish
leader)
hen har¦rier +s
hen house +s
Henley-on-
Thames (town,
England)
Hen¦ley (Royal
Re¦gatta)
henna
hen¦naed
heno¦the¦ism
hen-party
hen-parties
hen¦peck +s +ed
+ing
Henri, Rob¦ert
(American
painter)
Henri¦etta
Henri¦etta Maria
(French queen
consort)
hen-roost +s
hen-run +s
Henry (English and
French kings)
Henry ('the
Fowler', Henry I
of the Germans)
Henry ('the
Navigator',
Portuguese
prince)
henry
hen¦ries *or* henrys
(unit)
Henry's law
Henze, Hans
Wer¦ner (German
composer)
he¦or¦tolo¦gist +s
he¦or¦tol¦ogy
hep (fruit; stylish;
use hip)
hep¦arin
hep¦ar¦in¦ise *Br.*
(use heparinize)

hep|ar|in|ise (*cont.*)
 hep|ar|in|ises
 hep|ar|in|ised
 hep|ar|in|is|ing
hep|ar|in|ize
 hep|ar|in|izes
 hep|ar|in|ized
 hep|ar|in|iz|ing
hep|at|ic
hep|at|ica
hepa|titis
hep|ato|meg|aly
Hep|burn, Aud|rey
 (British actress)
Hep|burn,
 Kath|ar|ine
 (American
 actress)
hep|cat +s
Heph|aes|tus *Greek
 Mythology*
Heph|zi|bah
Hepple|white
hepta|chord +s
hep|tad +s
hepta|glot +s
hepta|gon +s
hept|agon|al
hepta|he|dral
hepta|he|dron
 hepta|he|dra *or*
 hepta|he|drons
hept|am|eter +s
hept|ane +s
hept|arch|ic
hept|arch|ic|al
hept|archy
 hept|arch|ies
hepta|syl|lab|ic
Hepta|teuch *Bible*
hept|ath|lete +s
hept|ath|lon +s
hepta|va|lent
Hep|worth,
 Bar|bara (English
 sculptor)
her
Hera *Greek
 Mythology*
Hera|cles (Greek
 form of Hercules)
Hera|cli|tus (Greek
 philosopher)
Hera|klion (capital
 of Crete)
her|ald +s +ed
 +ing
her|al|dic
her|al|dic|al|ly
her|ald|ist +s
her|ald|ry
Her|alds' Col|lege

Herat (city,
 Afghanistan)
herb +s
herb|aceous
herb|age
herb|al +s
herb|al|ism
herb|al|ist +s
herb|arium
 herb|aria
herb ben|net
herb Chris|to|pher
Her|bert
Her|bert, A. P.
 (English humorist)
Her|bert, George
 (English poet)
herb Ger|ard
herbi|cidal
herbi|cide +s
herb|ifer|ous
herbi|vore +s
herb|iv|or|ous
herb|less
herb|like
herb Paris
herb Rob|ert
herb tea +s
herb to|bacco
herby
 herb|ier
 herbi|est
Her|ce|gov|ina
 (use
 Herzegovina)
Her|ce|gov|in|ian
 +s (use
 Herzegovinian)
Her|cu|la|neum
 (ancient Roman
 town)
Her|cu|lean
Her|cu|les (*Greek
 and Roman
 Mythology;*
 constellation)
Her|cu|les bee|tle
 +s
Her|cyn|ian
herd +s +ed +ing
 (group of animals.
 △ heard)
herd book +s
herd|er +s
herds|man
 herds|men
Herd|wick +s
 (sheep)
here (this place.
 △ hear)
here|about
here|abouts

here|after
here|at
here|by
her|ed|it|able
her|ed|ita|ment +s
her|edi|tar|ily
her|edi|tari|ness
her|edi|tary
her|ed|ity
Here|ford +s (city,
 England; cattle)
Here|ford|shire
 (former county,
 England)
here|in
here|in|after
here|in|before
here|of
Her|ero
 plural Her|ero *or*
 Her|eros
her|esi|arch +s
her|esi|ology
her|esy
 her|esies
her|et|ic +s
her|et|ic|al
her|et|ic|al|ly
here|to
here|to|fore
here|under
here|unto
here|upon
Here|ward the
 Wake (Anglo-
 Saxon rebel
 leader)
here|with
her|iot +s
her|it|abil|ity
her|it|able
her|it|ably
heri|tage +s
heri|tor +s
herl (fibre. △ hurl)
Herm (Channel
 Island)
herm +s (pillar)
Her|man
herm|aph|ro|dite
 +s
herm|aph|ro|dit|ic
herm|aph|ro|
 dit|ic|al
herm|aph|ro|dit|
 ism
Herm|aph|ro|ditus
 Greek Mythology
her|men|eut|ic
her|men|eut|ic|al
her|men|eut|ic|
 al|ly

her|men|eut|ics
Her|mes *Greek
 Mythology*
Her|mes
 Tris|me|gis|tus
 Mythology
her|met|ic (airtight.
 △ hermitic)
her|met|ic|al|ly
her|met|ism
Her|mia
Her|mione
her|mit +s
Her|mit|age, the
 (art museum,
 Russia)
her|mit|age +s
her|mit crab +s
Her|mit|ian
her|mit|ic (of a
 hermit.
 △ hermetic)
Hermo|sillo (city,
 Mexico)
her|nia
 her|nias *or*
 her|niae
her|nial
her|ni|ary
her|ni|ated
Her|ning (city,
 Denmark)
Hero *Greek
 Mythology*
hero
 her|oes
Herod Agrippa
 (two rulers of
 ancient Palestine)
Herod Anti|pas
 (ruler of ancient
 Palestine)
Her|od|otus (Greek
 historian)
Herod the Great
 (ruler of ancient
 Palestine)
hero|ic
hero|ic|al|ly
heroi-comic
heroi-comical
hero|ics
her|oin (drug)
hero|ine +s
 (person)
hero|ise *Br.* (use
 heroize)
hero|ises
hero|ised
hero|is|ing
hero|ism

hero|ize
  hero|izes
  hero|ized
  hero|iz|ing
heron +s
her|on|ry
  her|on|ries
hero-worship
  hero-worships
  hero-
    worshipped *Br.*
  hero-
    worshiped *Am.*
  hero-
    worship|ping *Br.*
  hero-
    worship|ing *Am.*
her|pes
her|pes sim|plex
her|pes|virus
  her|pes|viruses
  her|pes zos|ter
her|pet|ic
her|peto|logic|al
her|pe|tolo|gist +s
her|pe|tol|ogy
herp|tile +s
Herr
  Herren
Herren|volk
Her|rick, Rob|ert
  (English poet)
her|ring
  plural her|ring or
  her|rings
her|ring|bone
  her|ring|bones
  her|ring|boned
  her|ring|bon|ing
her|ring gull +s
Her|riot, James
  (English writer
  and veterinary
  surgeon)
Herrn|huter +s
hers
Her|schel, John
  and Wil|liam
  (British
  astronomers)
her|self
Hert|ford (town,
  England.
  △ Hartford)
Hert|ford|shire
  (county, England)
Herts.
  (= Hertfordshire)
Hertz, Hein|rich
  Ru|dolf (German
  physicist)

hertz
  plural hertz
  (unit)
Hertz|ian
Hertzsprung–
  Russel dia|gram
Herut
Her|ze|gov|ina
  (region, Bosnia–
  Herzegovina)
Her|ze|gov|in|ian
  +s
Herzl, Theo|dor
  (Hungarian-born
  writer and Zionist
  leader)
he's (= he has; he
  is)
Hesh|van (use
  Hesvan)
Hes|iod (Greek
  poet)
hesi|tance
hesi|tancy
  hesi|tan|cies
hesi|tant
hesi|tant|ly
hesi|tate
  hesi|tates
  hesi|tated
  hesi|tat|ing
hesi|tat|er +s
hesi|tat|ing|ly
hesi|ta|tion +s
hesi|ta|tive
Hes|per|ian
Hes|peri|des, the
  Greek Mythology
hes|per|idium
hes|per|idia
Hes|perus (planet
  Venus)
Hess, Myra
  (English pianist)
Hess, Vic|tor
  Franz (Austrian-
  born American
  physicist)
Hess, (Wal|ther
  Rich|ard)
  Ru|dolf (German
  Nazi politician)
Hesse (state,
  Germany)
Hesse, Her|mann
  (German-born
  Swiss novelist)
Hes|sen (German
  name for Hesse)
Hes|sian +s (of
  Hesse; person;
  boot; fly)

hes|sian +s (coarse
  cloth)
hest
Hes|ter
Hes|van (Jewish
  month)
het|aera
  het|aeras or
  het|aerae
het|aer|ism
het|aira
  het|airas or
  het|airai
het|air|ism
het|ero +s
het|ero|
    chro|mat|ic
het|ero|clite +s
het|ero|cyc|lic
het|ero|dox
het|ero|doxy
  het|ero|dox|ies
het|ero|dyne
  het|ero|dynes
  het|ero|dyned
  het|ero|dyn|ing
heter|og|am|ous
heter|og|amy
het|ero|gen|eity
het|ero|ge|neous
het|ero|
    ge|neous|ly
het|ero|ge|neous|
    ness
het|ero|gen|esis
het|ero|gen|et|ic
heter|ogen|ous
  (use
  heterogeneous)
heter|ogen|ous|ly
  (use
  heterogeneously)
heter|ogeny
heter|og|on|ous
heter|og|ony
het|ero|graft +s
heter|ol|ogous
heter|ology
heter|om|er|ous
het|ero|morph|ic
het|ero|morph|ism
heter|on|om|ous
heter|on|omy
het|ero|path|ic
het|er|ophony
  het|ero|phonies
het|ero|phyl|lous
het|ero|phylly
het|ero|plast|ic
het|ero|ploid
het|ero|polar
het|ero|sex|ism

het|ero|sex|ist
het|ero|sex|ual +s
het|ero|sexu|al|ity
het|ero|sexu|al|ly
heter|osis
  heter|oses
het|ero|taxy
het|ero|
    trans|plant +s
het|ero|troph|ic
het|ero|zy|gote +s
het|ero|zy|got|ic
het|ero|zy|gous
het|man
  het|men
het up
heu|chera +s
heur|is|tic +s
heur|is|tic|al|ly
hevea +s
Hev|esy, George
  Charles de
  (Hungarian-born
  radiochemist)
hew
  hews
  hewed
  hew|ing
  hewn or hewed
  (chop. △ hue)
hewer +s
hex
  hexes
  hexed
  hex|ing
hexa|chord +s
hexad +s
hexa|deci|mal
hexa|deci|mal|ly
hexa|gon +s
hex|agon|al
hex|agon|al|ly
hexa|gram +s
hexa|he|dral
hexa|he|dron
  hexa|he|dra or
  hexa|he|drons
hex|am|eron
hex|am|eter +s
hexa|met|ric
hex|am|etrist +s
hex|ane
hex|apla
hex|aple +s
hexa|pod +s
hexa|pody
  hexa|podies
hexa|style +s
hexa|syl|lab|ic
Hexa|teuch
hexa|va|lent
hex|ode +s

hex|ose +s
hey (*interjection*
  calling attention or
  expressing
  surprise etc.
  △ hay, heigh)
hey|day +s
Heyer, Geor|gette
  (English writer)
Heyer|dahl, Thor
  (Norwegian
  anthropologist)
Heyhoe-Flint,
  Ra|chael (English
  cricketer)
hey presto!
Hez|bol|lah
  (radical Shiite
  Muslim group)
H-hour
hi (*interjection*.
  △ high)
hia|tal
hia|tus
  hia|tuses
Hia|watha
  (legendary
  American Indian)
Hib (bacterium)
hi|ber|nate
  hi|ber|nates
  hi|ber|nated
  hi|ber|na|ting
hi|ber|na|tion
hi|ber|na|tor +s
Hi|ber|nian +s
Hi|ber|ni|cism +s
hi|bis|cus
  plural hi|bis|cus *or*
  hi|bis|cuses
hic
hic|cough +s +ed
  +ing (use hiccup)
hic|coughy (use
  hiccupy)
hic|cup +s +ed
  +ing
hic|cupy
hic jacet +s
hick +s
hickey +s
hick|ory
  hick|or|ies
Hicks, John
  Rich|ard (English
  economist)
hid
Hid|algo (state,
  Mexico)
hid|algo +s
  (Spanish
  gentleman)

hid|den
hid|den|ness
hide
  hides
  hid
  hid|ing
  hid|den
  (conceal; place)
hide
  hides
  hided
  hid|ing
  (leather; flog)
hide-and-seek
hide|away +s
hide|bound
hid|eos|ity
  hid|eos|ities
hid|eous
hid|eous|ly
hid|eous|ness
hide|out +s
hider +s
hidey-hole +s
hid|ing place +s
hid|rosis
hid|rot|ic
hie
  hies
  hied
  hie|ing *or* hying
hier|arch +s
hier|arch|al
hier|arch|ic
hier|arch|ic|al
hier|arch|ic|al|ly
hier|arch|ise *Br.*
  (use hierarchize)
  hier|arch|ises
  hier|arch|ised
  hier|arch|is|ing
hier|arch|ism
hier|arch|ize
  hier|arch|izes
  hier|arch|ized
  hier|arch|iz|ing
hier|archy
  hier|arch|ies
hier|at|ic
hier|at|ic|al|ly
hier|oc|racy
  hier|oc|ra|cies
hiero|glyph +s
hiero|glyph|ic +s
hiero|glyph|ic|al
hiero|glyph|ic|
  al|ly
hiero|gram +s
hiero|graph +s
hier|ol|atry
hier|ology
hiero|phant +s

hiero|phant|ic
hi-fi +s
hig|gle
  hig|gles
  hig|gled
  hig|gling
higgledy-piggledy
high +s +er +est
  (tall etc. △ hi)
high and mighty
high|ball +s
high|bind|er +s
high-born
high|boy +s
high|brow +s
high chair +s
High Church *noun*
  and adjective
High Church|man
  High Church|men
high-class *adjective*
High|er +s
  (Scottish exam)
high|er
  (comparative of
  high. △ hire, hiya)
higher-up +s
high ex|plo|sive
  +s
high|fa|lu|tin
high fi|del|ity
high-five
  high-fives
  high-fived
  high-fiving
high-flier +s (use
  high-flyer)
high-flown
high-flyer +s
high-flying
high-grade
high-handed
high-handed|ly
high-handed|ness
high hat +s *noun*
high-hat
  high-hats
  high-hatted
  high-hatting
  adjective and verb
high-heeled
high jinks
high jump
high-jumper +s
high-key
high-kicking
High|land (fling,
  games, etc.)
high|land +s (high
  land)
High|land|er +s (in
  Scotland)

high|land|er +s
  (generally)
High|land|man
  High|land|men
High|lands, the
  (mountains,
  Scotland)
high-level *adjective*
high life
high|light +s +ed
  +ing
high|light|er +s
high-lows (boots)
high|ly
high|ly strung
  adjective
highly-strung
  attributive
High Mass
  High Masses
high-minded
high-minded|ly
high-minded|ness
high-muck-a-
  muck +s
high|ness
  high|nesses
high-octane
high-pitched
high-powered
high-quality
high-ranking
high relief +s
high-rise +s
high-risk
high school +s
high-security
high-sounding
high-speed
  attributive
high-spirit|ed
high-
  spirit|ed|ness
high-stepper +s
high-stepping
  adjective
High Stew|ard +s
high street *noun*
high-street
  attributive
high-strung
hight (called.
  △ height)
high|tail +s +ed
  +ing
high tech *noun*
high-tech *attributive*
high tech|nol|ogy
  noun
high-technol|ogy
  attributive
high-tensile
high-toned

high-up +s *noun*
high water mark +s
high|way +s
high|way|man
  high|way|men
high wire +s
hi|jack +s +ed +ing
hi|jack|er +s
Hijaz (use Hejaz)
Hijra (use Hegira)
hijra +s (use hegira)
hike
  hikes
  hiked
  hik|ing
hiker +s
hila (plural of hilum)
hil|ari|ous
hil|ari|ous|ly
hil|ari|ous|ness
hil|ar|ity
Hil|ary (French saint; term)
Hil|ary *also* Hil|lary (name)
Hil|bert, David (German mathematician)
Hilda *also* Hylda
Hil|de|gard of Bin|gen (German saint)
Hil|des|heim (city, Germany)
Hill, Benny (English comedian)
Hill, Oc|ta|via (English housing reformer)
Hill, Row|land (British founder of penny post)
hill +s +ed +ing (raised land. △ heal, hele, he'll)
Hil|lary, Ed|mund (New Zealand mountaineer)
Hil|lary *also* Hil|ary
hill-billy
  hill-billies
hill climb +s
hill fort +s
hil|li|ness

hill|man
  hill|men
hill|lock +s
hill|locky
Hills|bor|ough (football stadium disaster, England)
hill|side +s
hill sta|tion +s
hill|top +s
hill|walk|er +s
hill|walk|ing
hilly
  hill|ier
  hilli|est
hilt +s +ed +ing
hilum
  hila
Hil|ver|sum (town, the Netherlands)
him (objective case of he. △ hymn)
Hi|ma|chal Pra|desh (state, India)
Hima|layan +s
Hima|layas, the (mountain range, S. Asia)
hi|mat|ion
Himm|ler, Hein|rich (German Nazi leader)
Hims (= Homs)
him|self
Hin|ault, Ber|nard (French racing cyclist)
Hi|na|yana (Buddhism)
hind +s
hind|brain +s
Hin|de|mith, Paul (German composer)
Hin|den|burg, Paul von (German president)
Hin|den|burg (German name for Zabrze)
Hin|den|burg Line (German fortification in First World War)
hin|der +s +ed +ing
Hindi
hind leg +s
hind|limb +s

hind|most
Hin|doo +s (use Hindu)
hind|quar|ters
hin|drance +s
hind|sight +s
Hindu +s
Hin|du|ise *Br.* (use Hinduize)
Hin|du|ises
Hin|du|ised
Hin|du|is|ing
Hin|du|ism
Hin|du|ize
Hin|du|izes
Hin|du|ized
Hin|du|iz|ing
Hindu Kush (mountain range, Pakistan and Afghanistan)
Hin|du|stan
Hin|du|stani +s
hind|wing +s
hinge
  hinges
  hinged
  hinge|ing *or* hin|ging
hinge|less
hinge-like
hinge|wise
hinny
  hin|nies
Hin|shel|wood, Cyril Nor|man (English physical chemist)
hint +s +ed +ing
hin|ter|land +s
hip
  hips
  hip|per
  hip|pest
hip bath +s
hip bone +s
hip flask +s
hip hop
hip joint +s
hip-length
hip|less
hip|ness
Hip|par|chus (Greek astronomer and geographer)
Hip|par|cos (space satellite)
hip|pe|as|trum +s
hipped
hip|per +s

hip|pie +s (person. △ hippy)
hippo +s
hippo|cam|pus
  hippo|campi
hippo|cen|taur +s
hip pocket +s
hippo|cras
Hip|poc|ra|tes (Greek physician)
Hippo|crat|ic oath
Hippo|crene (natural spring, Greece)
hippo|drome +s
hippo|griff +s
hippo|gryph +s (use hippogriff)
Hip|poly|tus *Greek Mythology*
hip|poph|agy
hippo|phile +s
hippo|pho|bia
hippo|pot|amus
  hippo| pot|amuses *or* hippo|pot|ami
Hippo Re|gius (ancient Roman city)
hippy
  hip|pier
  hip|pi|est (large-hipped. △ hippie)
hip roof +s
hip|ster +s
hip|ster|ism
hira|gana
Hiram
hir|cine
hire
  hires
  hired
  hir|ing (borrow for a fee. △ higher, hiya)
hire|able
hire car +s
hire|ling +s
hire pur|chase *noun*
hire-purchase *attributive*
hirer +s
Hiro|hito (Japanese emperor)
H-iron +s
Hiro|shima (city, Japan)
hir|sute

hir|sute|ness
hir|sut|ism
hi|run|dine +s
his
His|pan|ic +s
His|pani|cise *Br.*
(use Hispanicize)
His|pani|cises
His|pani|cised
His|pani|cis|ing
His|pani|cist +s
His|pani|cize
His|pani|cizes
His|pani|cized
His|pani|ciz|ing
His|pani|ola
(island, West
Indies)
His|pan|ist +s
his|pid
hiss
hisses
hissed
hiss|ing
hist
his|ta|mine
his|ta|min|ic
his|ti|dine
histo|chem|ical
histo|chem|is|try
histo|gen|esis
histo|gen|et|ic
histo|gen|ic
hist|ogeny
histo|gram +s
histo|logic|al
hist|olo|gist +s
hist|ology
hist|oly|sis
histo|lyt|ic
his|tone +s
histo|patho|
logic|al
histo|path|olo|gist
+s
histo|path|ology
his|tor|ian +s
his|tori|ated
his|tor|ic
his|tor|ic|al
his|tor|ic|al|ly
his|tori|cism
his|tori|cist +s
his|tor|icity
his|tori|ograph|er
+s
his|torio|graph|ic
his|torio|
graph|ic|al
his|tori|og|raphy
his|tory
his|tor|ies

his|tri|on|ic
his|tri|on|ic|al|ly
his|tri|oni|cism
his|tri|on|ics
his|tri|on|ism
hit
hits
hit
hit|ting
hit-and-miss
hit-and-run
attributive
hitch
hitches
hitched
hitch|ing
Hitch|cock,
Al|fred (English
film director)
Hitch|ens, Ivon
(English painter)
hitch|er +s
hitch-hike
hitch-hikes
hitch-hiked
hitch-hiking
hitch-hiker +s
hi-tech *noun and
adjective*
hither
hith|er|to
hith|er|ward
Hit|ler, Adolf
(Austrian-born
German Nazi
leader)
Hit|ler|ism
Hit|ler|ite +s
hit list +s
hit man
hit men
hit-or-miss
hit-out *noun*
hit|ter +s
Hit|tite +s
hive
hives
hived
hiv|ing
hiya (greeting.
△ higher, hire)
Hiz|bol|lah
(Lebanese militia)
h'm
hmm (use h'm)
ho (*interjection.*
△ hoe)
hoar (grey with
age; hoar-frost;
hoariness. △ haw,
whore)

hoard +s +ed +ing
(store. △ horde)
hoard|er +s
hoard|ing +s
hoar frost
hoar|hound (use
horehound)
hoar|ily
hoari|ness
hoarse
hoars|er
hoars|est
(of voice.
△ horse)
hoarse|ly
hoars|en +s +ed
+ing
hoarse|ness
hoar|stone +s
hoary
hoar|ier
hoari|est
hoat|zin +s
hoax
hoaxes
hoaxed
hoax|ing
hoax|er +s
hob +s
Ho|bart (capital of
Tasmania)
Hob|bema,
Mein|dert (Dutch
painter)
Hobbes, Thomas
(English
philosopher)
hob|bit +s
hob|bit|ry
hob|ble
hob|bles
hob|bled
hob|bling
hobble|de|hoy +s
hob|bler +s
Hobbs, Jack
(English cricketer)
hobby
hob|bies
hobby-horse +s
hob|by|ist +s
hob|day +s +ed
+ing
hob|gob|lin +s
hob|nail +s
hob|nailed
hob|nob
hob|nobs
hob|nobbed
hob|nob|bing
hobo
ho|boes *or* hobos

Hob|son's choice
Ho Chi Minh
(North
Vietnamese
president)
Ho Chi Minh City
(official name of
Saigon)
hock +s +ed +ing
(leg joint; wine;
pawn. △ hough)
hockey (field game.
△ oche)
hock|ey|ist +s
Hock|ney, David
(English painter)
Hock|tide
hocus
ho|cus|ses *or*
ho|cuses
ho|cussed *or*
ho|cused
ho|cus|sing *or*
ho|cus|ing
hocus-pocus
hocus-pocusses
or hocus-pocuses
hocus-pocussed
or hocus-pocused
hocus-pocussing
or hocus-
pocusing
hod +s
hod|den
hod|die +s
Ho|deida (port,
Yemen)
Hodge +s
(farmworker)
hodge|podge +s
(use hotchpotch)
Hodg|kin,
Doro|thy (British
chemist)
Hodg|kin's
dis|ease
ho|di|ernal
hod|man
hod|men
hodo|graph +s
hod|om|eter +s
(use odometer)
Hoe, Rich|ard
March (American
inventor and
industrialist)
hoe
hoes
hoed
hoe|ing
(tool. △ ho)
hoe|cake +s

hoe|down +s
Hoek van
  Hol|land (Dutch
  name for the
  Hook of Holland)
hoer +s
Hofei (= Hefei)
Hoff|man, Dus|tin
  Lee (American
  actor)
Hoff|mann, Ernst
  Theo|dor
  Ama|deus
  (German writer)
Hof|manns|thal,
  Hugo von
  (Austrian
  dramatist)
hog
  hogs
  hogged
  hog|ging
hogan +s
Ho|garth, Wil|liam
  (English artist)
hog|back +s
Hogg, James
  (Scottish poet)
hogg +s (use hog)
Hog|gar
  Moun|tains (in
  Algeria)
hog|ger +s
hog|gery
  hog|ger|ies
hog|get +s
hog|gin
hog|gish
hog|gish|ly
hog|gish|ness
hog|like
hog|ma|nay +s
hog's back +s
hogs|head +s
hog-tie
  hog-ties
  hog-tied
  hog-tying
hog|wash
hog|weed +s
Hohen|stau|fen
  (German dynastic
  family)
Hohen|zol|lern
  (German dynastic
  family)
Hoh|hot (capital of
  Inner Mongolia)
ho-ho
ho-hum
hoick +s +ed +ing
hoi pol|loi

hoist +s +ed +ing
hoist|er +s
hoity-toity
hokey
  hoki|er
  hoki|est
  (melodramatic.
  △ hoki)
hokey-cokey
  (dance)
hokey|ness
hokey-pokey
hoki
  plural hoki
  (fish. △ hokey)
hoki|ly
Hok|kaido (island,
  Japan)
hokku
  plural hokku
hokum
Hoku|sai,
  Kat|su|shika
  (Japanese artist)
hoky
  hoki|er
  hoki|est
  (use hokey.
  melodramatic.
  △ hoki)
Hol|arc|tic
Hol|bein, Hans
  (German painter)
hold
  holds
  held
  hold|ing
hold|able
hold|all +s
hold|back +s noun
hold|er +s
Höl|der|lin,
  Jo|hann
  Chris|toph
  Fried|rich
  (German poet)
hold|fast +s
hold|ing +s
hold|out +s
hold-over +s noun
hold-up +s noun
hole
  holes
  holed
  hol|ing
  (empty space.
  △ whole)
hole-and-corner
hole-in-one
  holes-in-one
hole-proof
holey (full of holes.
  △ holy, wholly)

Holi (Hindu festival.
  △ holy, wholly)
holi|but
  plural holi|but
Holi|day, Bil|lie
  (American jazz
  singer)
holi|day +s +ed
  +ing (vacation)
holi|day|maker +s
holier-than-thou
holi|ly
holi|ness
Hol|in|shed,
  Raph|ael (English
  chronicler)
hol|ism
hol|ist +s
hol|is|tic
hol|is|tic|al|ly
holla
  hol|las
  hol|laed or
  holla'd
  holla|ing
  (interjection calling
  attention; to shout.
  △ holler)
Hol|land (the
  Netherlands;
  region, the
  Netherlands;
  former region,
  England)
hol|land (linen)
hol|land|aise
  sauce
Hol|land|er +s
Hol|lands (gin)
hol|ler +s +ed
  +ing (a shout; to
  shout. △ holla)
Hol|ler|ith,
  Her|man
  (American
  computer
  scientist)
hollo +s (noun
  shout)
hollo
  hol|loes
  hol|loed
  hollo|ing
  (verb shout)
hol|low +s +ed
  +ing (empty)
hollow-cheeked
hollow-eyed
hollow-hearted
hol|low|ly
hol|low|ness
hol|low|ware

Holly, Buddy
  (American rock
  and roll musician)
Holly (name)
holly
  hol|lies
  (shrub)
hol|ly|hock +s
Hol|ly|wood
  (centre of
  American film
  industry, Los
  Angeles)
holm +s (islet; oak
  tree. △ hom,
  home)
holme +s (islet; use
  holm)
Holmes, Ar|thur
  (English geologist)
Holmes, Oli|ver
  Wen|dell
  (American
  physician and
  writer)
Holmes, Sher|lock
  (fictional
  detective)
Holmes|ian
hol|mium
holm-oak +s
Holo|caust, the
  (Nazi mass
  murder of Jews)
holo|caust +s
Holo|cene
holo|en|zyme +s
Holo|fer|nes Bible
holo|gram +s
holo|graph +s
holo|graph|ic
holo|graph|ic|al|ly
hol|og|raphy
holo|he|dral
holo|met|abol|ous
holo|phote +s
holo|phyte +s
holo|phyt|ic
holo|thur|ian +s
holo|type +s
hols (= holidays)
Holst, Gus|tav
  (English
  composer)
Hol|stein (former
  duchy, NW
  Europe)
hol|ster +s
holt +s
holus-bolus
holy
  holies
  holi|er

holy (cont.)
holi|est
(sacred. ⚠ holey,
  Holi, wholly)
holy day +s
  (religious festival)
Holy|head (port,
  Wales)
holy Joe +s
Holy|oake, Keith
  (New Zealand
  prime minister)
Holy Rood Day
Holy See (the
  papacy)
holy|stone
holy|stones
holy|stoned
holy|ston|ing
hom (plant; juice.
  ⚠ holm, home)
homa (= hom)
hom|age +s
hom|bre +s
Hom|burg +s
Home, Lord in full
  Lord Home of the
  Hir|sel of
  Cold|stream
  (British prime
  minister.
  ⚠ Hume)
home
  homes
  homed
  hom|ing
  (residence;
  provide with a
  home; be guided.
  ⚠ hom, holm)
home-bird +s
home|body
  home|bodies
home|boy +s
home-brew +s
home-brewed
home|buy|er +s
home|com|ing +s
home cook|ing
Home Coun|ties
  (in SE England)
home-felt
home from home
home-grown
home help +s
Homel (city,
  Belarus)
home|land +s
home|less
home|less|ness

home life
  home lives
home|like
home|li|ness
home loan +s
home|ly
home-made
home|maker +s
home-making
home movie +s
homeo|box
  homeo|boxes
homeo|path Am.
  +s (Br.
  homoeopath)
homeo|path|ic Am.
  (Br.
  homoeopathic)
homeo|path|ic|
  al|ly Am. (Br.
  homoeopathic-
  ally)
hom|eop|ath|ist
  Am. +s (Br.
  homoeopathist)
hom|eop|athy Am.
  (Br.
  homoeopathy)
homeo|stasis Am.
  homeo|stases
  (Br.
  homoeostasis)
homeo|stat|ic Am.
  (Br.
  homoeostatic)
homeo|therm Am.
  +s (Br.
  homoeotherm)
homeo|ther|mal
  Am. (Br.
  homoeothermal)
homeo|ther|mic
  Am. (Br.
  homoeothermic)
homeo|thermy
  Am. (Br.
  homoeothermy)
home|owner +s
home own|er|ship
Homer (Greek epic
  poet)
homer +s (pigeon;
  home run)
Hom|er|ic
home run +s
home shop|ping
home|sick
home|sick|ness
home|spun
home|stead +s
home|stead|er +s
home|stead|ing

home|style
home town +s
home|ward
homeward-bound
home|wards
home|work
home|work|er +s
homey
  homi|er
  homi|est
homey|ness
homi|cidal
homi|cidal|ly
homi|cide +s
homi|let|ic
homi|let|ics
ho|mil|iary
ho|mil|iar|ies
hom|il|ist +s
hom|ily
  hom|ilies
hom|inid +s
hom|in|oid +s
hom|iny
homo +s
  (homosexual)
Homo (genus)
homo|cen|tric
hom|oeo|box (use
  homeobox)
  hom|oeo|boxes
hom|oeo|path Br.
  +s (Am.
  homeopath)
hom|oeo|path|ic
  Br. (Am.
  homeopathic)
hom|oeo|path|ic|
  al|ly Br. (Am.
  homeopathically)
hom|oe|op|ath|ist
  Br. +s (Am.
  homeopathist)
hom|oe|op|athy
  Br. (Am.
  homeopathy)
hom|oeo|stasis Br.
  hom|oeo|stases
  (Am.
  homeostasis)
hom|oeo|stat|ic Br.
  (Am.
  homeostatic)
hom|oeo|therm Br.
  +s (Am.
  homeotherm)
hom|oeo|therm|al
  Br. (Am.
  homeothermal)
hom|oeo|therm|ic
  Br. (Am.
  homeothermic)

hom|oeo|thermy
  Br. (Am.
  homeothermy)
homo|erot|ic
homo|gam|et|ic
hom|og|am|ous
hom|og|amy
hom|ogen|ate +s
homo|gen|eity
homo|ge|neous (of
  same kind;
  uniform.
  ⚠ homogenous)
homo|ge|neous|ly
homo|ge|neous|
  ness
homo|gen|et|ic
hom|ogen|isa|tion
  Br. (use
  homogenization)
hom|ogen|ise Br.
  (use homogenize)
  hom|ogen|ises
  hom|ogen|ised
  hom|ogen|is|ing
hom|ogen|iser Br.
  +s (use
  homogenizer)
hom|ogen|iza|tion
hom|ogen|ize
  hom|ogen|izes
  hom|ogen|ized
  hom|ogen|iz|ing
hom|ogen|izer
homo|gen|ous
  (Biology having
  common descent.
  ⚠ homogeneous)
hom|ogeny
homo|graft +s
homo|graph +s
hom|oio|therm +s
  (use homeotherm
  Am.,
  homoeotherm
  Br.)
hom|oio|ther|mal
  (use
  homeothermal
  Am.,
  homoeothermal
  Br.)
hom|oio|ther|mic
  (use
  homeothermic
  Am.,
  homoeothermic
  Br.)
hom|oio|thermy
  (use
  homeothermy
  Am.,

hom|oio|thermy
(*cont.*)
  homoeothermy
  Br.)
homoi|ous|ian +s
homo|log *Am.* +s
  (*Br.* homologue)
hom|olo|gate
  hom|olo|gates
  hom|olo|gated
  hom|olo|gat|ing
hom|olo|ga|tion
homo|logic|al
hom|olo|gise *Br.*
  (use homologize)
  hom|olo|gises
  hom|olo|gised
  hom|olo|gis|ing
hom|olo|gize
  hom|olo|gizes
  hom|olo|gized
  hom|olo|giz|ing
hom|olo|gous
homo|logue *Br.* +s
  (*Am.* homolog)
hom|ology
  hom|olo|gies
homo|morph +s
homo|morph|ic
homo|morph|ic|
    al|ly
homo|morph|ism
  +s
homo|morph|ous
homo|morphy
homo|nym +s
homo|nym|ic
hom|onym|ous
homo|ous|ian +s
homo|phobe +s
homo|pho|bia
homo|pho|bic
homo|phone +s
homo|phon|ic
homo|phon|ic|
    al|ly
hom|oph|onous
hom|oph|ony
homo|plas|tic
homo|polar
Homo sa|pi|ens
homo|sex|ual +s
homo|sexu|al|ity
homo|sexu|al|ly
homo|trans|plant
  +s
hom|ous|ian +s
  (use homoousian)
homo|zy|gote +s
homo|zy|gous
Homs (city, Syria)
hom|un|cule +s
  (use homunculus)

hom|un|cu|lus
hom|un|culi
homy (use homey)
Hon. (= Honorary;
  Honourable)
hon (= honey.
  ⚠ Hun)
Honan (= Henan;
  former name of
  Luoyang)
hon|cho +s *noun*
hon|cho
  hon|choes
  hon|choed
  hon|cho|ing
  verb
Honda, Soi|chiro
  (Japanese car
  maker)
Hon|duran +s
Hon|duras (in
  Central America)
hone
  hones
  honed
  hon|ing
Hon|ecker, Erich
  (East German
  head of state)
Hon|eg|ger,
  Ar|thur (French
  composer)
hon|est
hon|est Injun
hon|est|ly
honest-to-God
honest-to-
  goodness
hon|esty
honey +s
honey badger +s
honey bee +s
honey|bun +s
honey|bunch
  honey|bunches
honey buz|zard +s
honey|comb +s
  +ed +ing
honey|creep|er +s
honey|dew +s
honey|eater +s
hon|eyed
honey-fungus
honey|guide +s
honey|moon +s
  +ed +ing
honey|moon|er +s
honey pot +s
honey sac +s
honey|suckle +s
honey-sweet
Hong Kong

Ho|ni|ara (capital
  of the Solomon
  Islands)
hon|ied (use
  honeyed)
Honi|ton (town,
  England; lace)
honk +s +ed +ing
honky
  hon|kies
  (*offensive*)
honky-tonk +s
hon|nête homme
hon|nêtes hommes
Hono|lulu (capital
  of Hawaii)
Honor (name)
honor *Am.* +s +ed
  +ing (glory;
  respect. *Br.*
  honour)
Hon|or|able *Am.*
  (in titles. *Br.*
  Honourable)
hon|or|able *Am.*
  (worthy of honour.
  Br. honourable)
hon|or|able|ness
  Am. (*Br.*
  honourableness)
hon|or|ably *Am.*
  (*Br.* honourably)
hon|or|and +s
hon|or|arium
  hon|or|ariums or
  hon|or|aria
hon|or|ary
hon|or|if|ic +s
hon|or|if|ic|al|ly
hon oris causa
hon|our *Br.* +s +ed
  +ing (*Am.* honor)
Hon|our|able *Br.*
  (in titles. *Am.*
  Honorable)
hon|our|able *Br.*
  (worthy of honour.
  Am. honorable)
hon|our|able|ness
  Br. (*Am.*
  honorableness)
hon|our|ably *Br.*
  (*Am.* honorably)
honour-trick +s
Hon. Sec.
  (= Honorary
  Secretary)
Hon|shu (island,
  Japan)
Hooch, Pieter de
  (Dutch painter)
hooch

Hood, Thomas
  (English poet)
hood +s +ed +ing
hoodie +s
hood|less
hood|like
hood|lum +s
hood-mould +s
hood-moulding +s
hoo|doo +s +ed
  +ing
hood|wink +s +ed
  +ing
hooey
hoof
  hooves or hoofs
  noun
hoof +s +ed +ing
  verb
hoof|er +s
Hoogh, Pieter de
  (use Hooch)
Hoo|ghly (river,
  India)
hoo-ha +s
hoo-hah +s (use
  hoo-ha)
hook +s +ed +ing
hoo|kah +s
Hooke, Rob|ert
  (English scientist)
Hook|er, Jo|seph
  Dal|ton (English
  botanist)
hook|er +s
Hooke's law
hookey
hook|less
hook|let +s
hook|like
hook-nose +s
hook-nosed
Hook of Hol|land
  (port, the
  Netherlands)
hook-up +s *noun*
hook|worm +s
hooky (use
  hookey)
hoo|li|gan +s
hooli|gan|ism
hoon +s +ed +ing
hoop +s +ed +ing
  (ring; arch.
  ⚠ whoop)
hoop-iron
hoopla +s
hoo|poe +s
hoo|ray +s
Hoo|ray Henry
  Hoo|ray Hen|ries
hoo|roo +s

hoose|gow +s
Hoo|sier +s
hoot +s +ed +ing
hootch (use hooch)
hoote|nanny
hoote|nan|nies
hoot|er +s
hoots *interjection*
Hoo|ver, Her|bert
Clark (American
president)
Hoo|ver, J. Edgar
(American FBI
director)
Hoo|ver +s
(vacuum cleaner)
Propr.
hoo|ver +s +ed
+ing *verb*
Hoo|ver|ville +s
(shanty town,
USA)
hooves
hop
hops
hopped
hop|ping
hop-bind +s
hop-bine +s
Hope, Bob (British-
born American
comedian)
Hope (name)
hope
hopes
hoped
hop|ing
(wish)
hope|ful +s
hope|ful|ly
hope|ful|ness
Hopeh (former
name of Hebei)
hope|less
hope|less|ly
hope|less|ness
hoper +s
hop|head +s
Hopi
plural Hopi *or*
Hopis
Hop|kins,
An|thony (Welsh
actor)
Hop|kins,
Fred|er|ick
(English
biochemist)
Hop|kins, Ger|ard
Man|ley (English
poet)
hop|lite +s

hop-o'-my-thumb
+s
Hop|per, Ed|ward
(American
painter)
hop|per +s
hop|ping mad
hop|ple
hop|ples
hop|pled
hop|pling
hop|sack
hop|scotch
hop, skip, and
jump
hop, step, and
jump
Hor|ace (Roman
poet; name)
hor|ary
Hor|atia
Hor|atian
Hor|atio
horde +s (group;
gang. △ hoard)
hore|hound +s
hori|zon +s
hori|zon|tal
hori|zon|tal|ity
hori|zon|tal|ly
hori|zon|tal|ness
Hork|heimer, Max
(German
philosopher)
hor|mo|nal
hor|mo|nal|ly
hor|mone +s
Hor|muz (island
and strait, Persian
Gulf)
Horn, Cape (in S.
America)
horn +s +ed +ing
horn|beam +s
horn|bill +s
horn|blende +s
horn|book +s
horn|er +s
hor|net +s
horn|fels
horni|ness
horn|ist +s
horn|less
horn|like
Horn of Af|rica
(peninsula in NE
Africa)
horn|pipe +s
horn play|er +s
horn-rimmed
horn|stone

horn|swog|gle
horn|swog|gles
horn|swog|gled
horn|swog|gling
Hor|nung, Er|nest
Wil|liam (English
novelist)
horn|wort +s
horny
horn|ier
horni|est
horo|loge +s
hor|ol|oger +s
horo|logic
horo|logic|al
hor|olo|gist +s
hor|ol|ogy
horo|scope +s
horo|scop|ic
horo|scop|ic|al
hor|os|copy
Horow|henua
(region, New
Zealand)
Horo|witz,
Vlad|imir
(Russian-born
pianist)
hor|ren|dous
hor|ren|dous|ly
hor|ren|dous|ness
hor|rent
hor|rible
hor|rible|ness
hor|ribly
hor|rid
hor|rid|ly
hor|rid|ness
hor|rif|ic
hor|rif|ic|al|ly
hor|ri|fi|ca|tion
hor|ri|fied|ly
hor|rify
hor|ri|fies
hor|ri|fied
hor|ri|fy|ing
hor|ri|fy|ing|ly
hor|ri|pi|la|tion
hor|ror +s
horror-stricken
horror-struck
Horsa (Jutish
leader)
hors con|cours
hors de com|bat
hors d'oeuvre +s
horse
horses
horsed
hors|ing
(animal.
△ hoarse)

horse-and-buggy
attributive
horse|back
horse|bean +s
horse-block +s
horse|box
horse|boxes
horse brass
horse brasses
horse|break|er +s
horse breed|er +s
horse chest|nut +s
horse-cloth +s
horse-coper +s
horse-doctor +s
horse-drawn
horse|flesh
horse|fly
horse|flies
Horse Guards
(cavalry brigade;
its headquarters)
horse|hair
Horse|head
Neb|ula
horse|leech
horse|leeches
horse|less
horse|like
horse mack|erel
plural horse
mack|erel *or*
horse mack|erels
horse|man
horse|men
horse|man|ship
horse mush|room
+s
Hor|sens (port,
Denmark)
horse opera +s
horse-pistol +s
horse|play
horse-pond +s
horse|power
plural
horse|power
horse race +s
horse ra|cing
horse|rad|ish
horse sense
horse|shoe +s
horse|shoe crab
+s
horse's neck +s
(drink)
horse-soldier +s
horse|tail +s
horse-trading
horse|whip
horse|whips

horse|whip (cont.)
horse|whipped
horse|whip|ping
horse|woman
  horse|women
horsey (use horsy)
hors|ily
horsi|ness
horst +s
Horst Wes|sel
  Song
horsy
  hors|ier
  horsi|est
Horta, Vic|tor
  (Belgian architect)
hor|ta|tion +s
hor|ta|tive
hor|ta|tory
Hor|tense
hor|ten|sia +s
horti|cul|tural
horti|cul|tur|al|ist
  +s
horti|cul|ture
horti|cul|tur|ist +s
hor|tus sic|cus
  horti sicci
Horus *Egyptian*
  Mythology
hos|anna +s
hose
  hoses
  hosed
  hos|ing
Hosea *Bible*
hose|pipe +s
ho|sier +s
ho|siery
hos|pice +s
hos|pit|able
hos|pit|ably
hos|pital +s
hos|pi|tal|er *Am.*
  +s (*Br.*
  hospitaller)
hos|pi|tal|isa|tion
  Br. +s (use
  hospitalization)
hos|pi|tal|ise *Br.*
  (use hospitalize)
  hos|pi|tal|ises
  hos|pi|tal|ised
  hos|pi|tal|is|ing
hos|pi|tal|ism
hos|pi|tal|ity
hos|pi|tal|iza|tion
  +s
hos|pi|tal|ize
  hos|pi|tal|izes
  hos|pi|tal|ized
  hos|pi|tal|iz|ing

hos|pi|tal|ler *Br.* +s
  (*Am.* hospitaler)
hos|pital ship +s
hos|pital train +s
host +s +ed +ing
hosta +s
hos|tage +s
hos|tage|ship
hos|tel +s
hos|tel|er *Am.* +s
  (*Br.* hosteller)
hos|tel|ing *Am.* (*Br.*
  hostelling)
hos|tel|ler *Br.* +s
  (*Am.* hosteler)
hos|tel|ling *Br.*
  (*Am.* hosteling)
hos|tel|ry
  hos|tel|ries
host|ess
  host|esses
hos|tile +s
hos|tile|ly
hos|til|ity
  hos|til|ities
host|ler +s
  (mechanic.
  △ ostler)
hot
  hots
  hot|ted
  hot|ting
  hot|ter
  hot|test
hot-air bal|loon +s
hot|bed +s
hot-blooded
Hotch|kiss gun +s
hotch|pot
hotch|potch
hot cross bun +s
hot-desking
hot|dog
  hot|dogs
  hot|dogged
  hot|dog|ging
  verb
hot dog +s *noun*
hot|dog|ger +s
hotel +s
ho|tel|ier +s
hotel-keeper +s
hot|foot +s +ed
  +ing *adverb, verb,*
  and adjective
hot gos|pel|er *Am.*
  +s
hot gos|pel|ler *Br.*
  +s
hot|head +s
hot-headed
hot-headed|ly
hot-headed|ness

hot|house
hot|houses
hot|housed
hot|hous|ing
hot|line +s
hotly
hot|ness
hot pants
hot|plate +s
hot|pot +s
hot-press
  hot-presses
  hot-pressed
  hot-pressing
hot rod
hot-rodder +s
hot-rodding
hot seat +s
hot shoe +s
  Photography
hot-short
hot|shot +s
hot spot +s
Hot|spur, Harry
  (Sir Henry Percy)
hot|spur +s
hot-tempered
Hot|ten|tot
  plural Hot|ten|tot
  or Hot|ten|tots
hot|ter +s
hot|tie +s
hot|tish
hotty (use hottie)
  hot|ties
hot-water bag +s
hot-water bot|tle
  +s
hot-wire
  hot-wires
  hot-wired
  hot-wiring
Hou|dini, Harry
  (Hungarian-born
  American
  escapologist)
hough +s +ed +ing
  (cut of beef; to
  hamstring.
  △ hock.)
hough|er +s
houm|mos (use
  hummus.
  △ humus)
hound +s +ed +ing
hound|er +s
hound|ish
hound's-tongue
  +s
hounds|tooth +s
hour +s (unit of
  time. △ our)

hour|glass
  hour|glasses
hour hand +s
houri +s
hour-long
hour|ly
house
  houses
  housed
  hous|ing
house agent +s
house ar|rest
house|boat +s
house|bound
house|boy +s
house|break|er +s
house|break|ing
house-broken
house|build|er +s
house|build|ing
house|buy|er +s
house-buying
house|carl +s
house|carle +s
  (use housecarl)
house|coat +s
house|craft
house-dog +s
house-father +s
house-flag +s
house|fly
  house|flies
house|ful +s
house|group +s
house guest +s
house|hold +s
house|hold|er +s
house-hunt +s +ed
  +ing
house-hunter +s
house-husband +s
house|keep
  house|keeps
  house|kept
house|keep|ing
house|keep|er +s
house|leek +s
house|less
house lights
house|maid +s
house|maid's
  knee
house|man
  house|men
house mar|tin +s
house|mas|ter +s
house|mis|tress
  house|mis|tresses
house-mother +s
house owner +s
house-parent +s

house party
  house par|ties
house plant +s
house-proud
house|room
house-sit
  house-sits
  house-sat
  house-sitting
house|sit|ter +s
house spar|row +s
house style +s
house-to-house
house|top +s
house-train +s
  +ed +ing
house-warming
house|wife
  house|wives
house|wife|li|ness
house|wife|ly
house|wif|ery
house|work
housey-housey
hous|ing +s
Hous|man, A. E.
  (English poet)
Hous|ton (city,
  Texas)
hout|ing
  plural hout|ing
Hove (seaside
  resort, England)
hove (past tense
  and past participle
  of **heave**)
hovel +s
hover +s +ed +ing
hov|er|craft
  plural hov|er|craft
hov|er|er +s
hov|er|fly
  hov|er|flies
hov|er|port +s
hov|er|train +s
how +s
How|ard (name)
**How|ard,
  Cath|er|ine** (wife
  of Henry VIII of
  England)
How|ard, John
  (English prison
  reformer)
how|beit
how|dah +s
how-do-you-do +s
  (awkward
  situation)
howdy
  how|dies

how-d'ye-do +s
  (use **how-do-you-
  do**)
Howe, Elias
  (American
  inventor)
how|e'er
  (= however)
How|erd, Fran|kie
  (English
  comedian)
how|ever
how|itz|er +s
howl +s +ed +ing
howl|er +s
How|rah (city,
  India)
how|so|e'er
  (= howsoever)
how|so|ever
how|zat *Cricket*
Hoxha, Enver
  (Albanian prime
  minister)
hoy +s +ed +ing
hoya +s
hoy|den +s
hoy|den|ish
Hoyle, Fred
  (English
  astrophysicist)
Hradec Králové
  (town, Czech
  Republic)
Hrodno (city,
  Belarus)
Hsia-men
  (= Xiamen)
Hsian (= Xian)
Hsi|ning (= Xining)
Hsu-chou
  (= Xuzhou)
Huai|nan (city,
  China)
Hual|laga (river,
  Peru)
Huambo (city,
  Angola)
Huang Hai
  (Chinese name for
  the Yellow Sea)
Huang He
  (= Huang Ho)
Huang Ho (Chinese
  name for the
  Yellow River)
Huas|ca|rán
  (extinct volcano,
  Peru)
hub +s
**Hub|ble, Edwin
  Pow|ell**

Hub|ble (*cont.*)
  (American
  astronomer;
  classification;
  telescope)
hubble-bubble +s
**Hub|ble's
  constant**
hub|bub
hubby
  hub|bies
hub|cap +s
Hubei (province,
  China)
Hu|bert
Hubli (city, India)
hu|bris
hu|bris|tic
hucka|back
huckle +s
huckle-back +s
huckle|berry
  huckle|berries
huck|ster +s +ed
  +ing
huck|ster|ism
huck|stery
Hud|ders|field
  (town, England)
hud|dle
  hud|dles
  hud|dled
  hud|dling
Hu|di|bras|tic
Hud|son, Henry
  (English explorer)
Hud|son Bay
  (inland sea,
  Canada)
Hud|son River (in
  N. America)
**Hud|son's Bay
  Com|pany**
Hué (city, Vietnam)
hue +s (colour.
  ⚠ hew)
hue|less
huff +s +ed +ing
huff|ily
huffi|ness
huff|ish
huffy
  huff|ier
  huffi|est
hug
  hugs
  hugged
  hug|ging
huge
  huger
  hug|est
huge|ly

huge|ness
hug|gable
hug|ger +s
hugger-mugger
**Hug|gins,
  Wil|liam** (British
  astronomer)
Hugh *also* Huw
Hughes, How|ard
  (American
  industrialist)
Hughes, Ted
  (English poet)
Hughie
Hugli (= Hooghly)
Hugo
Hugo, Vic|tor
  (French writer)
Hu|gue|not +s
huh
Huhe|hot
  (= Hohhot)
hula +s
hula hoop +s
hula-hula +s
hula skirt +s
hulk +s
hulk|ing
Hull (official name
  Kingston-upon-
  Hull; city,
  England)
hull +s +ed +ing
hul|la|ba|loo +s
hullo (use hello)
  hul|loes
  hul|loed
  hullo|ing
hum
  hums
  hummed
  hum|ming
human +s
hu|mane
hu|mane|ly
hu|mane|ness
hu|man|isa|tion
  Br. (use
  humanization)
hu|man|ise *Br.* (use
  humanize)
  hu|man|ises
  hu|man|ised
  hu|man|is|ing
hu|man|ism
hu|man|ist +s
hu|man|is|tic
hu|man|is|tic|al|ly
hu|mani|tar|ian +s
**hu|mani|tar|ian|
           ism**

hu¦man¦ity
  hu¦man¦ities
hu¦man¦iza¦tion
hu¦man¦ize
  hu¦man¦izes
  hu¦man¦ized
  hu¦man¦iz¦ing
hu¦man¦kind
hu¦man¦ly
hu¦man¦ness
hu¦man¦oid +s
Hum¦ber (estuary
  and shipping area,
  England)
Hum¦ber¦side
  (county, England)
hum¦ble
  hum¦bles
  hum¦bled
  hum¦bling
  hum¦bler
  hum¦blest
humble-bee +s
hum¦ble¦ness
hum¦bly
Hum¦boldt,
  Fried¦rich
  (German explorer)
hum¦bug
  hum¦bugs
  hum¦bugged
  hum¦bug¦ging
hum¦bug¦gery
hum¦ding¦er +s
hum¦drum
Hume, David
  (Scottish
  philosopher.
  △ Home)
hu¦mec¦tant +s
hu¦meral
hu¦merus
  hu¦meri
  (bone.
  △ humorous)
humic
humid
hu¦midi¦fi¦ca¦tion
hu¦midi¦fier +s
hu¦mid¦ify
  hu¦midi¦fies
  hu¦midi¦fied
  hu¦midi¦fy¦ing
hu¦mid¦ity
  hu¦mid¦ities
hu¦mid¦ly
hu¦midor +s
hu¦mifi¦ca¦tion
hum¦ify
  humi¦fies
  humi¦fied
  humi¦fy¦ing

hu¦mili¦ate
  hu¦mili¦ates
  hu¦mili¦ated
  hu¦mili¦at¦ing
hu¦mili¦at¦ing¦ly
hu¦mili¦ation +s
hu¦mili¦ator +s
hu¦mil¦ity
  hu¦mil¦ities
hum¦mable
hum¦mer +s
hum¦ming¦bird +s
humming-top +s
hum¦mock +s
hum¦mocky
hum¦mus (chick
  pea spread.
  △ humous,
  humus)
hu¦mon¦gous
humor Am. +s +ed
  +ing
hu¦moral
hu¦mor¦esque +s
hu¦mor¦ist +s
hu¦mor¦is¦tic
hu¦mor¦less Am.
hu¦mor¦less¦ly Am.
hu¦mor¦less¦ness
  Am.
hu¦mor¦ous
  (amusing.
  △ humerus)
hu¦mor¦ous¦ly
hu¦mor¦ous¦ness
hu¦mour Br. +s
  +ed +ing
hu¦mour¦less Br.
hu¦mour¦less¦ly Br.
hu¦mour¦less¦ness
  Br.
hum¦ous (of
  humus.
  △ hummus,
  humus)
hump +s +ed +ing
hump¦back +s
hump¦back bridge
  +s
hump¦backed
hump bridge +s
Hum¦per¦dinck,
  Engel¦bert
  (German
  composer)
humph
Hum¦phrey also
  Hum¦phry
Hum¦phries, Barry
  (Australian
  comedian)

Hum¦phry also
  Hum¦phrey
hump¦less
humpty
  hump¦ties
Humpty-Dumpty
  (nursery-rhyme
  character)
humpty-dumpty
  humpty-
  dumpties
  (person; thing)
humpy
  hump¦ies
  hump¦ier
  humpi¦est
hu¦mun¦gous (use
  humongous)
humus (soil
  constituent.
  △ hummus,
  humous)
hu¦mus¦ify
  hu¦musi¦fies
  hu¦musi¦fied
  hu¦musi¦fy¦ing
Hun +s (Asiatic
  tribe. △ hon)
Hunan (province,
  China)
hunch
  hunches
  hunched
  hunch¦ing
hunch¦back +s
hunch¦backed
hun¦dred
  plural hun¦dred or
  hun¦dreds
hun¦dred¦fold
hun¦dredth +s
hun¦dred¦weight
  plural
  hun¦dred¦weight
  or
  hun¦dred¦weights
hung
Hun¦gar¦ian +s
Hun¦gary
hun¦ger +s +ed
  +ing
hun¦ger march
  hun¦ger marches
hun¦ger march¦er
  +s
hun¦ger strike +s
hun¦ger striker +s
hung-over adjective
hun¦grily
hun¦gri¦ness

hun¦gry
  hun¦grier
  hun¦gri¦est
hunk +s
hun¦ker +s +ed
  +ing
hunky
  hun¦kies
hunky-dory
Hun¦nish
Hunt, Wil¦liam
  Hol¦man (English
  painter)
hunt +s +ed +ing
hunt¦away +s
Hunt¦er, John
  (Scottish
  anatomist)
hunt¦er +s
hunter-gather¦er
  +s
hunter-killer
hunt¦er's moon
hunt¦ing crop +s
hunt¦ing dog +s
Hun¦ting¦don
  (town, England)
Hun¦ting¦don,
  Count¦ess of
  (English religious
  leader)
Hun¦ting¦don¦
  shire (former
  English county)
hunt¦ing ground
  +s
hunt¦ing horn +s
hunt¦ing pink
Hun¦ting¦ton (city,
  West Virginia,
  USA)
Hun¦ting¦ton
  Beach (city,
  California, USA)
Hun¦ting¦ton's
  chorea
hunt¦ress
  hunt¦resses
hunts¦man
  hunts¦men
Hunts¦ville (city,
  USA)
Hupeh (= Hubei)
hur¦dle
  hur¦dles
  hur¦dled
  hurd¦ling
hurd¦ler +s
hurdy-gurdy
  hurdy-gurdies
hurl +s +ed +ing
  (throw. △ herl)

Hur|ler's
syn|drome
hur|ley
hurly-burly
Huron
plural Huron *or*
Hurons
(American Indian)
Huron, Lake (in N.
America)
hur|rah +s +ed
+ing
hur|ray +s (use
hooray)
Hurri
plural Hurri *or*
Hur|ris
Hur|rian
hur|ri|cane +s
hurricane-bird +s
hur|ri|cane deck
+s
hur|ri|cane lamp
+s
hur|ried|ly
hur|ried|ness
hur|roo +s
hurry
hur|ries
hur|ried
hurry|ing
hurry-scurry
hurst +s
Hur|ston, Zora
Neale (American
novelist)
hurt
hurts
hurt
hurt|ing
hurt|ful
hurt|ful|ly
hurt|ful|ness
hur|tle
hur|tles
hur|tled
hurt|ling
hurt|less
Hus|ain (use
Hussein)
Husák, Gus|táv
(Czechoslovak
statesman)
hus|band +s +ed
+ing
hus|band|er +s
hus|band|hood
hus|band|less
hus|band|like
hus|band|ly

hus|band|man
hus|band|men
hus|band|ry
hus|band|ship
hush
hushes
hushed
hush|ing
hush|aby
hush|abye (use
hushaby)
hush-hush
husk +s +ed +ing
husk|ily
huski|ness
husky
husk|ies
husk|ier
huski|est
Huss, John
(Bohemian
religious reformer)
huss
plural huss
hus|sar +s
Hus|sein
(Jordanian king,
1953–)
Hus|sein,
Ab|dul|lah ibn
(Jordanian king,
1946–51)
Hus|sein,
Sad|dam (Iraqi
president)
Hus|serl, Ed|mund
(German
philosopher)
Huss|ite +s
Huss|it|ism
hussy
hus|sies
hust|ings
hus|tle
hus|tles
hus|tled
hust|ling
hust|ler +s
Hus|ton, John
(American-born
film director)
hut
huts
hut|ted
hut|ting
hutch
hutches
hut|like
hut|ment +s
Hut|ter|ite +s

Hut|ton, James
(Scottish
geologist)
Hut|ton, Len
(English cricketer)
Hutu
plural Hutu *or*
Ba|hutu
Huw *also* Hugh
Hux|ley, Al|dous
(English writer)
Hux|ley, Ju|lian
(English biologist)
Hux|ley, Thomas
(English biologist)
Huy|gens,
Chris|tiaan
(Dutch physicist;
eyepiece)
huzzy
huz|zies
Hwange (town,
Zimbabwe)
hwyl (fervour)
Hya|cinth (name)
hya|cinth +s
(flower)
hya|cinth|ine
Hya|cin|thus *Greek
Mythology*
Hya|des (star
cluster)
hy|aena +s (use
hyena)
hya|lin *noun*
hya|line *adjective*
hya|lite
hya|loid
hyal|uron|ic
hy|brid +s
hy|brid|is|able *Br.*
(use hybridizable)
hy|brid|isa|tion *Br.*
(use
hybridization)
hy|brid|ise *Br.* (use
hybridize)
hy|brid|ises
hy|brid|ised
hy|brid|is|ing
hy|brid|ism
hy|brid|ity
hy|brid|iz|able
hy|brid|iza|tion
hy|brid|ize
hy|brid|izes
hy|brid|ized
hy|brid|iz|ing
hyda|tid +s
hyda|tidi|form
Hyde, Ed|ward
(Earl of

Hyde (*cont.*)
Clarendon,
English statesman
and historian)
Hyde (in 'Jekyll and
Hyde')
Hyde Park (in
London)
Hy|dera|bad
(cities, India and
Pakistan; former
state, India)
Hydra (*Greek
Mythology*;
constellation)
hydra +s
hy|dran|gea +s
hy|drant +s
hy|drat|able
hy|drate
hy|drates
hy|drated
hy|drat|ing
hy|dra|tion
hy|dra|tor +s
hy|draul|ic
hy|draul|ic|al|ly
hy|draul|icity
hy|draul|ics
hy|dra|zine +s
hy|dric
hy|dride +s
hy|dri|od|ic
hydro +s
hydro|bro|mic
hydro|car|bon +s
hydro|cele +s
hydro|ceph|al|ic
hydro|cepha|lus
hydro|chlor|ic
hydro|chlor|ide +s
hydro|cor|ti|sone
hydro|cyan|ic
hydro|dynam|ic
hydro|dynam|ic|al
hydro|
dy|nami|cist +s
hydro|dynam|ics
hydro|elec|tric
hydro|elec|tri|city
hydro|fined
hydro|fin|ing
hydro|fluor|ic
hydro|foil +s
hydro|gel +s
hydro|gen
hy|dro|gen|ase +s
hy|dro|gen|ate
hy|dro|gen|ates
hy|dro|gen|ated
hy|dro|gen|at|ing
hy|dro|gen|ation

hydro|gen bond
+s
hydrogen-bonded
hy|dro|gen|ous
hydro|geo|logic|al
hydro|geolo|gist
+s
hydro|geol|ogy
hy|drog|raph|er +s
hydro|graph|ic
hydro|graph|ic|al
hydro|graph|ic|
al¦ly
hy|drog|raphy
hy|droid +s
hydro|lase +s
hydro|logic
hydro|logic|al
hydro|logic|al|ly
hy|drolo|gist +s
hy|drol|ogy
hydro|lyse *Br.*
hydro|lyses
hydro|lysed
hydro|lys¦ing
hy|droly|sis
hy|droly¦ses
hydro|lyt¦ic
hydro|lyze *Am.*
hydro|lyzes
hydro|lyzed
hydro|lyz¦ing
hydro|mag¦net¦ic
hydro|mag¦net¦ics
hydro|mania
hydro|mechan¦ics
hydro|mel
hy|drom|eter +s
hydro|met¦ric
hy|drom|et¦ry
hy|dro|nium ion
+s
hydro|path¦ic
hy|drop|ath¦ist +s
hy|drop|athy
hydro|phane +s
hydro|phil
hydro|phile
hydro|phil¦ic
hydro|pho¦bia
hydro|pho¦bic
hydro|phone +s
hydro|phyte +s
hy|drop¦ic
hydro|plane
hydro|planes
hydro|planed
hydro|plan¦ing
hydro|pneu¦mat¦ic
hydro|pon¦ic
hydro|pon¦ic|al¦ly
hydro|pon¦ics

hydro|quin¦one
hydro|sphere
hydro|stat¦ic
hydro|stat¦ic|al
hydro|stat¦ic|al¦ly
hydro|stat¦ics
hydro|ther|apic
hydro|ther|apist
+s
hydro|ther|apy
hydro|ther|mal
hydro|ther|mal¦ly
hydro|thorax
hydro|trop¦ism
hy|drous
hy|drox¦ide +s
hy|drox|onium ion
+s
hy|droxyl +s
hydro|zoan +s
hyena +s
Hy¦geia
hy|geian
hy|giene
hy|gien¦ic
hy|gien¦ic|al¦ly
hy|gien¦ics
hy|gien¦ist +s
hy|grol¦ogy
hy|grom|eter +s
hygro|met¦ric
hy|grom|etry
hy|grophil¦ous
hygro|phyte +s
hygro|phyt¦ic
hygro|scope +s
hygro|scop¦ic
hygro|scop¦ic|al¦ly
hying
Hyk¦sos
Hylda *also* Hilda
hylic
hylo|morph¦ism
hylo|the¦ism
hylo|zo¦ism
hylo|zo¦ist +s
Hymen (cry used at
ancient Greek
weddings)
hymen +s
(membrane)
hy|men|al (of
hymen)
hy|men|eal (of
marriage)
hy|men|ium
hy|menia
Hy¦men|op¦tera
hy|men|op¦teran
+s
hy|men|op¦ter|ous

hymn +s +ed +ing
(song. △ him)
hym|nal +s
hym|nary
hym|nar¦ies
hymn book +s
hym¦nic
hym|nist +s
hym|nod|ist +s
hym|nody
hym|nod¦ies
hymn|og|raph|er
+s
hymn|og|raphy
hymn|olo¦gist +s
hymn|ology
hyoid +s
hyos|cine
hyos|cya¦mine
hyp|aes|the¦sia *Br.*
(*Am.*
hypoesthesia.
abnormally low
sensitivity.
△ hyper-
aesthesia)
hyp|aes|thet¦ic *Br.*
(*Am.*
hypoesthetic.
having
hypaesthesia.
△ hyperaesthetic)
hyp|aeth¦ral
hyp|al¦lage +s
Hyp|atia (Greek
philosopher and
mathematician)
hype
hypes
hyped
hyp¦ing
hyper
hyper|active
hyper|activ¦ity
hyper|aemia *Br.*
(*Am.* hyperemia)
hyper|aem¦ic *Br.*
(*Am.* hyperemic)
hyper|aes|the¦sia
Br. (*Am.*
hyperesthesia.
abnormally high
sensitivity.
△ hypaesthesia)
hyper|aes|thet¦ic
Br. (*Am.*
hyperesthetic.
having
hyperaesthesia.
△ hypaesthetic)
hyper|bar¦ic
hyper|ba¦ton

hyper|bola
hyper|bolas *or*
hyper|bolae
(curve)
hyper|bole +s
(exaggeration)
hyper|bol¦ic (of
hyperbola)
hyper|bol¦ic|al (of
hyperbole)
hyper|bol¦ic|al¦ly
(using hyperbole)
hyper|bol|ism (use
of hyperbole)
hyper|bol|ist (user
of hyperbole)
hyper|bol|oid +s
hyper|bol|oid|al
Hyper|bor¦ean +s
Greek Mythology
hyper|bor¦ean +s
(person; of
extreme north)
Hyper¦Card *Propr.*
hyper|cata|lec¦tic
hyper|
cho¦les¦ter¦ol|
aemia *Br.*
hyper|
cho¦les¦ter¦ol|
emia *Am.*
hyper|con¦scious
hyper|crit¦ic|al
(over-critical.
△ hypocritical)
hyper|crit¦ic|al¦ly
(over-critically.
△ hypocritically)
hyper|criti¦cism
hyper|cube +s
hyper|du¦lia
hyper|emia *Am.*
(*Br.* hyperaemia)
hyper|em¦ic *Am.*
(*Br.* hyperaemic)
hyper|es|the¦sia
Am. (*Br.*
hyperaesthesia.
abnormally high
sensitivity.
△ hypoesthesia)
hyper|es|thet¦ic
Am. (*Br.*
hyperaesthetic.
having
hyperesthesia.
△ hypoesthetic)
hyper|focal
hyper|gamy
hyper|gly¦caemia
Br. (excess of

hyper|gly|caemia
(cont.)
glucose. ⚠ hypo-
glycaemia)
hyper|gly|caem|ic
Br. (of
hyperglycaemia.
⚠ hypo-
glycaemic)
hyper|gly|cemia
Am. (excess of
glucose.
⚠ hypoglycemia)
hyper|gly|cem|ic
Am. (of
hyperglycemia.
⚠ hypoglycemic)
hy|per|gol|ic
hy|peri|cum +s
hyper|in|fla|tion
Hy|perion (Greek
Mythology; moon
of Saturn)
hyper|kin|esia
hyper|kin|esis
hyper|kin|et|ic
hyper|lip|id|aemia
Br.
hyper|lip|id|
aem|ic Br.
hyper|lip|id|emia
Am.
hyper|lip|id|em|ic
Am.
hyper|mar|ket +s
hyper|media
hyper|met|ric
hyper|met|ric|al
hyper|me|tro|pia
hyper|me|trop|ic
hyper|nym +s
(more general
term.
⚠ hyponym)
hyp|eron +s
hyper|on|ic
hyper|opia
hyper|op|ic
hyper|phys|ic|al
hyper|phys|ic|al|ly
hyper|pla|sia
hyper|sen|si|tive
hyper|sen|si|tive|
ness
hyper|sen|si|tiv|ity
hyper|son|ic
hyper|son|ic|al|ly
hyper|space
hyper|sthene
hyper|ten|sion
(abnormally high

hyper|ten|sion
(cont.)
blood pressure.
⚠ hypotension)
hyper|ten|sive
(having
abnormally high
blood pressure.
⚠ hypotensive)
hyper|text +s
hyper|ther|mia
(abnormally high
temperature.
⚠ hypothermia)
hyper|ther|mic
hyper|thy|roid (of
hyperthyroidism.
⚠ hypothyroid)
hyper|thy|roid|ic
hyper|thy|roid|ism
(excessive thyroid
activity. ⚠ hypo-
thyroidism)
hyper|tonia
hyper|ton|ic
hyper|ton|icity
hyper|troph|ic
hyper|tro|phied
hyper|trophy
hyper|tro|phies
hyper|ven|ti|late
hyper|ven|ti|lates
hyper|ven|ti|lated
hyper|ven|ti|
lat|ing
(breathe
abnormally
rapidly.
⚠ hypoventilate)
hyper|ven|ti|
la|tion
(abnormally rapid
breathing. ⚠ hypo-
ventilation)
hyp|es|the|sia Am.
(use
hypoesthesia. Br.
hypaesthesia)
hyp|es|thetic Am.
(use
hypoesthetic. Br.
hypaesthetic)
hyp|eth|ral (use
hypaethral)
hypha
hy|phae
hy|phal
Hy|pha|sis (ancient
Greek name for
the Beas)
hy|phen +s +ed
+ing

hy|phen|ate
hy|phen|ates
hy|phen|ated
hy|phen|at|ing
hy|phen|ation
hypno|gen|esis
hyp|nolo|gist +s
hyp|nol|ogy
hypno|pae|dia Br.
hypno|pe|dia Am.
Hyp|nos Greek
Mythology
hyp|no|sis
hyp|no|ses
hypno|ther|ap|ist
+s
hypno|ther|apy
hyp|not|ic
hyp|not|ic|al|ly
hyp|no|tis|able Br.
(use
hypnotizable)
hyp|no|tise Br. (use
hypnotize)
hyp|no|tises
hyp|no|tised
hyp|no|tis|ing
hyp|no|tism
hyp|no|tist +s
hyp|no|tiz|able
hyp|no|tize
hyp|no|tizes
hyp|no|tized
hyp|no|tiz|ing
hypo +s
hypo|aes|the|sia
Br. (use
hypaesthesia.
Am.
hypoesthesia.
abnormally high
sensitivity.
⚠ hyper-
aesthesia)
hypo|aes|thet|ic
Br. (use
hypaesthetic. Am.
hypoesthetic.
having
hypaesthesia.
⚠ hyperaesthetic)
hypo-allergen|ic
hypo|blast +s
hypo|caust +s
hypo|chlor|ite +s
hypo|chlor|ous
hypo|chon|dria
hypo|chon|driac
+s
hypo|cor|is|tic
hypo|cotyl +s
hypo|oc|risy
hyp|ocri|sies

hypo|crite +s
hypo|crit|ical
(of hypocrisy.
⚠ hypercritical)
hypo|crit|ic|al|ly
(with hypocrisy.
⚠ hypercritically)
hypo|cyc|loid +s
hypo|cyc|loid|al
hypo|derma
hypo|der|mata
hypo|der|mal
hypo|der|mic +s
hypo|der|mic|al|ly
hypo|es|the|sia
Am. (Br.
hypaesthesia.
abnormally low
sensitivity.
⚠ hyperesthesia)
hypo|es|thet|ic
Am. (Br.
hypaesthetic.
having
hypoesthesia.
⚠ hyperesthetic)
hypo|gas|tric
hypo|gas|trium
hypo|gas|tria
hypo|geal
hypo|gene
hypo|geum
hypo|gea
hypo|gly|caemia
Br. (glucose
deficiency.
⚠ hyper-
glycaemia)
hypo|gly|caem|ic
Br. (of
hypoglycaemia.
⚠ hyper-
glycaemic)
hypo|gly|cemia
Am. (glucose
deficiency.
⚠ hyper-
glycemia)
hypo|gly|cem|ic
Am. (of
hypoglycemia.
⚠ hyperglycemic)
hy|poid +s
hypo|lim|nion
hypo|lim|nia
hypo|mania
hypo|maniac +s
hypo|man|ic +s
hypo|nas|tic
hypo|nasty
hypo|nym +s
(more specific

hypo|nym (*cont.*)
   term.
   △ **hypernym**)
hyp|onym|ous
hyp|onymy
hypo|phys|eal
hypo|phys|ial (use
   hypophyseal)
hyp|ophy|sis
   hyp|ophy|ses
hy|pos|tasis
   hy|pos|tases
hy|pos|ta|sise *Br.*
   (use hypostasize)
   hy|pos|ta|sises
   hy|pos|ta|sised
   hy|pos|ta|sis|ing
hy|pos|ta|size
   hy|pos|ta|sizes
   hy|pos|ta|sized
   hy|pos|ta|siz|ing
hypo|stat|ic
hypo|stat|ic|al (use
   hypostatic)
hypo|stat|ic|al|ly
hy|pos|ta|tise *Br.*
   (use hypostatize)
   hy|pos|ta|tises
   hy|pos|ta|tised
   hy|pos|ta|tis|ing
hy|pos|ta|tize
   hy|pos|ta|tizes
   hy|pos|ta|tized
   hy|pos|ta|tiz|ing
hypo|style
hypo|sul|fite *Am.*
   +s
hypo|sul|phite *Br.*
   +s
hypo|tac|tic
hypo|taxis
hypo|ten|sion
   (abnormally low
   blood pressure.
   △ **hypertension**)
hypo|ten|sive
   (having
   abnormally low
   blood pressure.
   △ **hypertensive**)
hypot|en|use +s
hypo|thal|am|ic
hypo|thal|amus
   hypo|thal|ami
hypo|thec
hy|pothe|cary
   hy|pothe|car|ies
hy|pothe|cate
   hy|pothe|cates
   hy|pothe|cated
   hy|pothe|cat|ing
hy|pothe|ca|tion

hy|pothe|ca|tor +s
hypo|ther|mia
   (abnormally low
   temperature.
   △ **hyperthermia**)
hy|poth|esis
   hy|poth|eses
hy|pothe|sise *Br.*
   (use hypothesize)
   hy|pothe|sises
   hy|pothe|sised
   hy|pothe|sis|ing
hy|pothe|siser *Br.*
   +s (use
   hypothesizer)
hy|pothe|sist +s
hy|pothe|size
   hy|pothe|sizes
   hy|pothe|sized
   hy|pothe|siz|ing
hy|pothe|sizer +s
hypo|thet|ic|al
hypo|thet|ic|al|ly
hypo|thy|roid (of
   hypothyroidism.
   △ **hyperthyroid**)
hypo|thy|roid|ic
   (suffering from
   hypothyroidism.
   △ **hyperthyroid-
   ic**)
hypo|thy|roid|ism
   (subnormal
   thyroid activity.
   △ **hyperthyroid-
   ism**)
hypo|ven|ti|late
   hypo|ven|ti|lates
   hypo|ven|ti|lated
   hypo|ven|ti|
              lat|ing
   (breathe
   abnormally
   slowly.
   △ **hyperventilate**)
hypo|ven|ti|la|tion
   (abnormally slow
   breathing.
   △ **hyperventila-
   tion**)
hyp|ox|aemia *Br.*
hyp|ox|emia *Am.*
hyp|oxia
hyp|ox|ic
hypsi|lopho|don
   +s
hypso|graph|ic
hypso|graph|ic|al
hyp|sog|raphy
hyp|som|eter +s
hypso|met|ric

hyrax
   hyr|axes *or*
   hyr|aces
hyson
hys|sop
hys|ter|ec|tom|ise
   Br. (use
   hysterectomize)
hys|ter|
         ec|tom|ises
hys|ter|
         ec|tom|ised
hys|ter|
         ec|tom|is|ing
hys|ter|ec|tom|ize
hys|ter|
         ec|tom|izes
hys|ter|
         ec|tom|ized
hys|ter|
         ec|tom|iz|ing
hys|ter|ec|tomy
   hys|ter|ec|to|mies
hys|ter|esis
   hys|ter|eses
hys|teria +s
hys|ter|ic +s
hys|ter|ic|al
hys|ter|ic|al|ly
hys|teron pro|ton

Ii

I (myself. △ **aye**,
   eye)
Iain *also* Ian
iamb +s
iam|bic +s
iam|bus
   iam|buses *or*
   iambi
Ian *also* Iain
Iap|etus (*Greek
   Mythology*; moon
   of Saturn)
Iași (city, Romania)
IATA
   (= International
   Air Transport
   Association)
iat|ro|gen|ic
Iba|dan (city,
   Nigeria)
Iban
   plural Iban
**Ibá|ñez, Vi|cente
   Blasco** (Spanish
   novelist)
**Ibar|ruri Gomez,
   Dol|ores** ('La
   Pasionaria',
   Spanish
   Communist
   politician)
I-beam +s
Iberia (ancient
   name for Spain
   and Portugal)
Iber|ian
Ibero-American
   +s
ibex
   ibexes
ibid.
ibis
   ibises
Ibiza (Spanish
   island and city)
Ibn Ba|tuta (Arab
   explorer)
**ibn Hus|sein,
   Ab|dul|lah**
   (Jordanian king,
   1946–51)
Ibo
   plural Ibo *or* Ibos
Ibsen, Hen|rik
   (Norwegian
   dramatist)
ibu|profen

Ica¦rus *Greek Mythology*
ice
  ices
  iced
  icing
ice age +s
ice axe +s
ice-bag +s
ice¦berg +s
ice¦blink +s
ice¦block +s (lolly)
ice block +s (block of ice)
ice blue +s *noun and adjective*
ice-blue *attributive*
ice-boat +s
ice-bound
ice¦box
  ice¦boxes
ice-breaker +s
ice bucket +s
ice cap +s
ice-cold
ice cream +s
ice cube +s
ice dan¦cing
iced lolly
  iced lol¦lies
ice¦fall +s
ice field +s
ice fish
  plural ice fish *or* ice fishes
ice floe +s
ice hockey
ice house +s
Ice¦land
Ice¦land¦er +s
Ice¦land¦ic
Ice¦land spar +s
ice lolly
  ice lol¦lies
ice¦man
  ice¦men
Iceni
ice pack +s
ice pick +s
ice plant +s
ice rink +s
ice sheet +s
ice shelf
  ice shelves
ice-skate
  ice-skates
  ice-skated
  ice-skating
ice-skater +s
ice sta¦tion +s
ice storm +s
ice water

Icha¦bod *Bible*
I Ching
ich¦neu¦mon +s
ich¦nog¦raphy
  ich¦nog¦raph¦ies
ichor +s
ich¦or¦ous
ich¦thy¦og¦raph¦er +s
ich¦thy¦og¦raphy
ich¦thy¦oid +s
ich¦thy¦ol¦atry
ich¦thyo¦lite +s
ich¦thyo¦logic¦al
ich¦thy¦olo¦gist +s
ich¦thy¦ol¦ogy
ich¦thy¦opha¦gous
ich¦thy¦oph¦agy
ich¦thyo¦saur +s
ich¦thyo¦saurus
  ich¦thyo¦sauri
ich¦thy¦osis
ich¦thy¦ot¦ic
I-chun (= Yichun)
icicle +s
icily
ici¦ness
icing +s
icing sugar +s
Ick¦nield Way (ancient track, England)
icky
icon +s
icon¦ic
icon¦icity
icono¦clasm
icono¦clast +s
icono¦clas¦tic
icono¦clas¦tic¦al¦ly
icon¦og¦raph¦er +s
icono¦graph¦ic
icono¦graph¦ic¦al
icono¦graph¦ic¦al¦ly
icon¦og¦raphy
  icon¦og¦raph¦ies
icon¦ol¦ater +s
icon¦ol¦atry
icon¦ology
  icon¦olo¦gies
icon¦om¦eter +s
icon¦om¦etry
icon¦osta¦sis
  icon¦osta¦ses
ico¦sa¦he¦dral
ico¦sa¦he¦dron
  ico¦sa¦he¦dra *or* ico¦sa¦he¦drons
ico¦si¦do¦deca¦he¦dron
ico¦si¦do¦deca¦

ico¦si¦do¦deca¦he¦dron (*cont.*)
  he¦dra *or*
ico¦si¦do¦deca¦he¦drons
ic¦ter¦ic
ic¦terus
Ic¦ti¦nus (Greek architect)
ictus
  plural ictus *or* ic¦tuses
icy
  icier
  ici¦est
Id (use Eid)
I'd (= I had; I should; I would. △ ide)
id +s *Psychology*
Ida (name; asteroid)
Ida, Mount (in Crete)
Idaho (state, USA)
ID card +s
ide +s (fish. △ ides, I'd)
idea +s
ideal +s
idea¦less
ideal¦isa¦tion *Br.* +s (use idealization)
ideal¦ise *Br.* (use idealize)
  ideal¦ises
  ideal¦ised
  ideal¦is¦ing
ideal¦iser *Br.* +s (use idealizer)
ideal¦ism
ideal¦ist +s
ideal¦is¦tic
ideal¦is¦tic¦al¦ly
ideal¦ity
  ideal¦ities
ideal¦iza¦tion +s
ideal¦ize
  ideal¦izes
  ideal¦ized
  ideal¦iz¦ing
ideal¦izer +s
ideal¦ly
ide¦ate
  ide¦ates
  ide¦ated
  ideat¦ing
idea¦tion +s
idea¦tion¦al
idea¦tion¦al¦ly

idée fixe
  idées fixes
idée reçue
  idées reçues
idem
iden¦tic
iden¦ti¦cal
iden¦ti¦cal¦ly
iden¦ti¦cal¦ness
iden¦ti¦fi¦able
iden¦ti¦fi¦ably
iden¦ti¦fi¦ca¦tion +s
iden¦ti¦fier +s
iden¦tify
  iden¦ti¦fies
  iden¦ti¦fied
  iden¦ti¦fy¦ing
iden¦ti¦kit +s *Propr.*
iden¦tity
  iden¦tities
iden¦tity card +s
ideo¦gram +s
ideo¦graph +s
ideo¦graph¦ic
ideo¦graph¦ic¦al
ideo¦logic¦al
ideo¦logic¦al¦ly
ideolo¦gist +s
ideo¦logue +s
ideol¦ogy
  ideolo¦gies
ides
idi¦ocy
  idi¦ocies
idio¦lect +s
idiom +s
idiom¦at¦ic
idiom¦at¦ic¦al¦ly
idio¦path¦ic
idi¦op¦athy
  idi¦op¦athies
idio¦syn¦crasy
  idio¦syn¦cra¦sies
idio¦syn¦crat¦ic
idio¦syn¦crat¦ic¦al¦ly
idiot +s
idi¦ot¦ic
idi¦ot¦ic¦al¦ly
idiot sav¦ant
  plural idiot sav¦ants *or* idiots sav¦ants
idle
  idles
  idled
  id¦ling
  (lazy; be inactive. △ idol)
idle¦ness
idler +s
idly

Ido (language)
idol +s (object of
  worship. △ idle)
idol|ater +s
idol|atress
  idol|atresses
idol|atrous
idol|atry
  idol|atries
idol|isa|tion Br.
  (use idolization)
idol|ise Br. (use
  idolize)
  idol|ises
  idol|ised
  idol|is|ing
idol|iser Br. +s (use
  idolizer)
idol|iza|tion
idol|ize
  idol|izes
  idol|ized
  idol|iz|ing
idol|izer +s
ido|lum
  idola
Idome|neus Greek
  Mythology
idyll +s
idyl|lic
idyl|lic|al|ly
idyl|lise Br. (use
  idyllize)
  idyl|lises
  idyl|lised
  idyl|lis|ing
idyl|list +s
idyl|lize
  idyl|lizes
  idyl|lized
  idyl|liz|ing
if +s
iff Logic;
  Mathematics
iffy
  if|fier
  if|fi|est
Ifni (former Spanish
  province,
  Morocco)
Ifor also **Ivor**
Igbo
  plural **Igbo** or
  Igbos
Igle|sias, Julio
  (Spanish singer)
igloo +s
Ig|na|tius Loy|ola
  (Spanish saint)
ig|ne|ous
ig|nim|brite
ignis fat|uus
  ignes fatui

ig|nit|abil|ity
ig|nit|able
ig|nite
  ig|nites
  ig|nited
  ig|nit|ing
ig|niter +s
ig|ni|tion +s
ig|ni|tron +s
ig|no|bil|ity
ig|noble
  ig|nobler
  ig|nob|lest
ig|nobly
ig|no|mini|ous
ig|no|mini|ous|ly
**ig|no|mini|ous|
                ness**
ig|no|miny
  ig|no|minies
ig|nor|amus
  ig|nor|amuses
ig|nor|ance
ig|nor|ant
ig|nor|ant|ly
ig|nore
  ig|nores
  ig|nored
  ig|nor|ing
ig|norer +s
*ig|no|tum per
  ig|no|tius*
Iguaçu (river,
  Brazil)
igu|ana +s
iguano|don +s
IJs|sel (river, the
  Netherlands)
IJs|sel|meer (lake,
  the Netherlands)
ike|bana
Ikh|na|ton (use
  Akhenaten)
ikky (use icky)
ikon +s (use icon)
ilang-ilang (use
  ylang-ylang)
ILEA (= Inner
  London Education
  Authority)
ilea (plural of
  ileum)
ileac (of the ileum.
  △ iliac)
ileal
Île-de-France
  (region, France)
ile|itis
ile|os|tomy
  ile|os|tomies
Il|esha (city,
  Nigeria)

ileum
ilea
  (part of small
  intestine. △ ilium)
ileus
ilex
  ilexes
ilia (plural of ilium)
iliac (of the lower
  body or ilium.
  △ ileac)
Iliad (Greek epic
  poem)
Ilium (ancient
  Greek city)
ilium
  ilia
  (pelvic bone.
  △ ileum)
ilk +s
I'll (I shall; I will.
  △ aisle, isle)
ill +s (sick;
  sickness)
ill-advised
ill-advised|ly
ill-affect|ed
ill-assort|ed
il|la|tion +s
il|la|tive
il|la|tive|ly
ill-behaved
ill blood
ill-bred
ill breed|ing
ill-conceived
ill-consid|ered
ill-defined
ill-disposed
il|legal
il|legal|ity
  il|legal|ities
il|legal|ly
il|legi|bil|ity
il|legible
il|legibly
il|legit|im|acy
il|legit|im|ate
  il|legit|im|ates
  il|legit|im|ated
  il|legit|im|at|ing
il|legit|im|ate|ly
il|legit|im|ation
il|legit|im|ise Br.
  (use illegitimize)
  il|legit|im|ises
  il|legit|im|ised
  il|legit|im|is|ing
il|legit|im|ize
  il|legit|im|izes
  il|legit|im|ized
  il|legit|im|iz|ing

ill-equipped
ill-fated
ill-favored Am.
ill-favoured Br.
ill feel|ing
ill-fitting
ill-founded
ill-gotten
ill-humored Am.
ill-humoured Br.
il|lib|eral
il|lib|er|al|ity
  il|lib|er|al|ities
il|li|ber|al|ly
Il|lich, Ivan
  (Austrian-born
  American
  educationalist)
il|licit (unlawful.
  △ elicit)
il|licit|ly
il|licit|ness
il|lim|it|abil|ity
il|lim|it|able
il|lim|it|able|ness
il|lim|it|ably
ill-informed
Il|li|nois (state,
  USA)
il|liquid
il|liquid|ity
il|lit|er|acy
il|lit|er|ate +s
il|lit|er|ate|ly
il|lit|er|ate|ness
ill-judged
ill-mannered
ill-matched
ill nature +s
ill-natured
ill-natured|ly
ill|ness
  ill|nesses
il|logic|al
il|logic|al|ity
  il|logic|al|ities
il|logic|al|ly
ill-omened
ill-prepared
ill-starred
ill-suited
ill tem|per +s
ill-tempered
ill-timed
ill-treat +s +ed
  +ing
ill-treatment +s
il|lude
  il|ludes
  il|luded
  il|lud|ing
  (deceive.
  △ allude, elude)

il¦lume
  ill¦lumes
  ill¦lumed
  ill¦lum¦ing
il¦lu¦min¦ance +s
il¦lu¦min¦ant +s
il¦lu¦min¦ate
  il¦lu¦min¦ates
  il¦lu¦min¦ated
  il¦lu¦min¦at¦ing
il¦lu¦min¦ati
il¦lu¦min¦at¦ing¦ly
il¦lu¦min¦ation +s
il¦lu¦mina¦tive
il¦lu¦min¦ator +s
il¦lu¦mine
  il¦lu¦mines
  il¦lu¦mined
  il¦lu¦min¦ing
il¦lu¦min¦ism
il¦lu¦min¦ist +s
ill use *noun*
ill-use
  ill-uses
  ill-used
  ill-using
  verb
il¦lu¦sion +s (false
  perception.
  △ allusion)
il¦lu¦sion¦al
il¦lu¦sion¦ism
il¦lu¦sion¦ist +s
il¦lu¦sion¦is¦tic
il¦lu¦sive
  (deceptive.
  △ allusive,
  elusive)
il¦lu¦sive¦ly (in an
  illusive way.
  △ allusively,
  elusively)
il¦lu¦sive¦ness
  (illusive nature.
  △ allusiveness,
  elusiveness)
il¦lu¦sor¦ily
il¦lu¦sori¦ness
il¦lu¦sory
  (deceptive.
  △ elusory)
il¦lus¦trate
  il¦lus¦trates
  il¦lus¦trated
  il¦lus¦trat¦ing
il¦lus¦tra¦tion +s
il¦lus¦tra¦tion¦al
il¦lus¦tra¦tive
il¦lus¦tra¦tive¦ly
il¦lus¦tra¦tor +s
il¦lus¦tri¦ous
il¦lus¦tri¦ous¦ly

il¦lus¦tri¦ous¦ness
ill will
Il¦lyria (ancient
  region, S. Europe)
Il¦lyr¦ian +s
il¦ly¦whack¦er +s
il¦men¦ite +s
Ilo¦ilo (port,
  Philippines)
Ilona
Ilorin (city, Nigeria)
I'm (= I am)
image
  im¦ages
  im¦aged
  im¦aging
im¦age¦able
im¦age¦less
image-maker +s
im¦agery
  im¦ager¦ies
im¦agin¦able
im¦agin¦ably
im¦agi¦nal
im¦agin¦ar¦ily
im¦agin¦ary
im¦agin¦ation +s
im¦agina¦tive
im¦agina¦tive¦ly
im¦agina¦tive¦ness
im¦agine
  im¦agines
  im¦agined
  im¦agin¦ing
im¦aginer +s
im¦agines (plural of
  imago)
im¦agin¦ing +s
im¦agism
im¦agist +s
im¦agis¦tic
imago
  im¦agos *or*
  im¦agi¦nes
imam +s
imam¦ate +s
IMAX
  Cinematography
im¦bal¦ance +s
im¦be¦cile +s
im¦be¦cile¦ly
im¦be¦cil¦ic
im¦be¦cil¦ity
  im¦be¦cil¦ities
imbed (use embed)
  im¦beds
  im¦bed¦ded
  im¦bed¦ding
im¦bibe
  im¦bibes
  im¦bibed
  im¦bib¦ing

im¦biber +s
im¦bi¦bi¦tion +s
im¦bri¦cate
  im¦bri¦cates
  im¦bri¦cated
  im¦bri¦cat¦ing
im¦bri¦ca¦tion +s
im¦bro¦glio +s
Im¦bros (island,
  Turkey)
im¦brue
  im¦brues
  im¦brued
  im¦bru¦ing
im¦brute
  im¦brutes
  im¦bruted
  im¦brut¦ing
imbue
  im¦bues
  im¦bued
  im¦bu¦ing
Im¦ho¦tep (ancient
  Egyptian architect
  and scholar)
imide +s
imine +s
im¦it¦able
imi¦tate
  imi¦tates
  imi¦tated
  imi¦tat¦ing
imi¦ta¦tion +s
imi¦ta¦tive
imi¦ta¦tive¦ly
imi¦ta¦tive¦ness
imi¦ta¦tor +s
im¦macu¦lacy
im¦macu¦late
im¦macu¦late¦ly
im¦macu¦late¦ness
im¦ma¦nence
  (inherency.
  △ imminence)
im¦ma¦nency
  (inherency.
  △ imminency)
im¦ma¦nent
  (inherent.
  △ imminent)
im¦ma¦nent¦ism
im¦ma¦nent¦ist +s
Im¦man¦uel (*Bible.*
  △ Emanuel,
  Emmanuel)
im¦ma¦ter¦ial
im¦ma¦teri¦al¦ise
  Br. (use
  immaterialize)
  im¦ma¦teri¦al¦ises
  im¦ma¦teri¦al¦ised

im¦ma¦teri¦al¦ise
  (*cont.*)
  im¦ma¦teri¦al¦
    is¦ing
im¦ma¦teri¦al¦ism
im¦ma¦teri¦al¦ist
  +s
im¦ma¦teri¦al¦ity
im¦ma¦teri¦al¦ize
  im¦ma¦teri¦al¦izes
  im¦ma¦teri¦al¦ized
  im¦ma¦teri¦al¦
    iz¦ing
im¦ma¦teri¦al¦ly
im¦ma¦ture
im¦ma¦ture¦ly
im¦ma¦tur¦ity
im¦meas¦ur¦
    abil¦ity
im¦meas¦ur¦able
im¦meas¦ur¦able¦
    ness
im¦meas¦ur¦ably
im¦me¦di¦acy
im¦me¦di¦ate
im¦me¦di¦ate¦ly
im¦me¦di¦ate¦ness
im¦med¦ic¦able
im¦med¦ic¦ably
im¦me¦mor¦ial
im¦me¦mori¦al¦ly
im¦mense
im¦mense¦ly
im¦mense¦ness
im¦mens¦ity
  im¦mens¦ities
im¦merse
  im¦merses
  im¦mersed
  im¦mers¦ing
im¦mer¦sion +s
im¦mi¦grant +s
im¦mi¦grate
  im¦mi¦grates
  im¦mi¦grated
  im¦mi¦grat¦ing
im¦mi¦gra¦tion +s
im¦mi¦gra¦tory
im¦mi¦nence
  (impending
  nature.
  △ immanence)
im¦mi¦nency
  (impending
  nature.
  △ immanancy)
im¦mi¦nent
  (impending.
  △ immanent)
im¦mi¦nent¦ly
Im¦ming¦ham
  (port, England)

im¦mis¦ci¦bil¦ity
im¦mis¦cible
im¦mis¦cibly
im¦mit¦ig¦able
im¦mit¦ig¦ably
im¦mit¦tance +s
im¦mix¦ture +s
im¦mo¦bile
im¦mo¦bil¦isa¦tion
  Br. +s (use
  immobilization)
im¦mo¦bil¦ise *Br.*
  (use immobilize)
im¦mo¦bil¦ises
im¦mo¦bil¦ised
im¦mo¦bil¦is¦ing
im¦mo¦bil¦iser *Br.*
  +s (use
  immobilizer)
im¦mo¦bil¦ism
im¦mo¦bil¦ity
  im¦mo¦bil¦ities
im¦mo¦bil¦iza¦tion
  +s
im¦mo¦bil¦ize
im¦mo¦bil¦izes
im¦mo¦bil¦ized
im¦mo¦bil¦iz¦ing
im¦mo¦bil¦izer +s
im¦mod¦er¦ate
im¦mod¦er¦ate¦ly
im¦mod¦er¦ate¦
        ness
im¦mod¦er¦ation
im¦mod¦est
im¦mod¦est¦ly
im¦mod¦esty
  im¦mod¦est¦ies
im¦mol¦ate
  im¦mol¦ates
  im¦mol¦ated
  im¦mol¦at¦ing
im¦mol¦ation +s
im¦mol¦ator +s
im¦moral
im¦mor¦al¦ity
  im¦mor¦al¦ities
im¦mor¦al¦ly
im¦mor¦tal +s
im¦mor¦tal¦isa¦tion
  Br. +s (use
  immortalization)
im¦mor¦tal¦ise *Br.*
  (use immortalize)
  im¦mor¦tal¦ises
  im¦mor¦tal¦ised
  im¦mor¦tal¦is¦ing
im¦mor¦tal¦ity
  im¦mor¦tal¦ities
im¦mor¦tal¦
    iza¦tion +s

im¦mor¦tal¦ize
  im¦mor¦tal¦izes
  im¦mor¦tal¦ized
  im¦mor¦tal¦iz¦ing
im¦mor¦tal¦ly
im¦mor¦telle +s
  (flower)
im¦mov¦abil¦ity
im¦mov¦able
im¦mov¦able¦ness
im¦mov¦ably
im¦move¦able (use
  immovable)
im¦move¦able¦ness
  (use
  immovableness)
im¦move¦ably (use
  immovably)
im¦mune
im¦mun¦isa¦tion
  Br. +s (use
  immunization)
im¦mun¦ise *Br.* (use
  immunize)
  im¦mun¦ises
  im¦mun¦ised
  im¦mun¦is¦ing
im¦mun¦iser *Br.* +s
  (use immunizer)
im¦mun¦ity
  im¦mun¦ities
im¦mun¦iza¦tion
  +s
im¦mun¦ize
  im¦mun¦izes
  im¦mun¦ized
  im¦mun¦iz¦ing
im¦mun¦izer +s
im¦muno¦assay +s
im¦muno¦
    chem¦is¦try
im¦muno¦
    com¦pe¦tence
im¦muno¦
    com¦pe¦tent
im¦muno¦
    com¦prom¦ised
im¦muno¦
    defi¦ciency
im¦mu¦no¦
    defi¦cien¦cies
im¦muno¦
    defi¦cient
im¦muno¦
    depressed
im¦muno¦
    depres¦sion
im¦muno¦gen¦ic
im¦muno¦globu¦lin
  +s
im¦muno¦logic
im¦muno¦logic¦al

im¦muno¦logic¦
        al¦ly
im¦mun¦olo¦gist +s
im¦mun¦ology
im¦muno¦sup¦pres¦
       sant +s
im¦muno¦
    sup¦pressed
im¦muno¦
    sup¦pres¦sion
im¦muno¦
    sup¦pres¦sive +s
im¦muno¦ther¦apy
im¦muno¦
    ther¦apies
im¦mure
  im¦mures
  im¦mured
  im¦mur¦ing
im¦mure¦ment +s
im¦mut¦abil¦ity
  im¦mut¦abil¦ities
im¦mut¦able
im¦mut¦ably
Imo¦gen
imp +s +ed +ing
im¦pact +s +ed
  +ing
im¦pac¦tion +s
im¦pair +s +ed
  +ing
im¦pair¦ment +s
im¦pala
  plural im¦pala
im¦pale
  im¦pales
  im¦paled
  im¦pal¦ing
im¦pale¦ment +s
im¦palp¦abil¦ity
im¦palp¦able
im¦palp¦ably
im¦panel (use
  empanel)
  im¦panels
  im¦pan¦elled *Br.*
  im¦pan¦eled *Am.*
  im¦panel¦ling *Br.*
  im¦panel¦ing *Am.*
im¦pari¦syl¦lab¦ic
im¦park +s +ed
  +ing
im¦part +s +ed
  +ing
im¦part¦able
im¦par¦ta¦tion +s
im¦par¦tial
im¦par¦ti¦al¦ity
im¦par¦tial¦ly
im¦part¦ible
im¦part¦ment +s

im¦pass¦abil¦ity (of
  road etc.
  △ impassibility)
im¦pass¦able
  (impossible to
  travel over.
  △ impassible)
im¦pass¦able¦ness
  (of road etc.
  △ impassible-
  ness)
im¦pass¦ably (in an
  impassable way.
  △ impassibly)
im¦passe +s
im¦passi¦bil¦ity
  (impassivity.
  △ impassability)
im¦pass¦ible
  (impassive.
  △ impassable)
im¦pass¦ible¦ness
  (impassivity.
  △ impassable-
  ness)
im¦pass¦ibly
  (impassively.
  △ impassably)
im¦pas¦sion +s
  +ed +ing
im¦pas¦sioned
im¦pas¦sive
im¦pas¦sive¦ly
im¦pas¦sive¦ness
im¦pas¦siv¦ity
im¦pasto +s
im¦pa¦tience (lack
  of patience)
im¦pa¦tiens (plant)
im¦pa¦tient
im¦pa¦tient¦ly
im¦peach
  im¦peaches
  im¦peached
  im¦peach¦ing
im¦peach¦able
im¦peach¦ment +s
im¦pec¦cabil¦ity
im¦pec¦cable
im¦pec¦cably
im¦pec¦cancy
im¦pec¦cant
im¦pe¦cu¦ni¦os¦ity
im¦pe¦cu¦ni¦ous
im¦pe¦cu¦ni¦ous¦
        ness
im¦ped¦ance +s
im¦pede
  im¦pedes
  im¦peded
  im¦ped¦ing
im¦pedi¦ment +s

im|pedi|menta
im|pedi|men|tal
impel
  im|pels
  im|pelled
  im|pel|ling
im|pel|lent +s
im|pel|ler +s
im|pend +s +ed
  +ing
im|pend|ence
im|pend|ency
im|pend|ent +s
im|pene|tra|bil|ity
im|pene|trable
im|pene|trable|
                 ness
im|pene|trably
im|pene|trate
  im|pene|trates
  im|pene|trated
  im|pene|trat|ing
im|peni|tence
im|peni|tency
im|peni|tent
im|peni|tent|ly
im|pera|tival
im|pera|tive +s
im|pera|tive|ly
im|pera|tive|ness
im|per|ator +s
im|pera|tor|ial
im|per|cepti|bil|ity
im|per|cept|ible
im|per|cept|ibly
im|per|cipi|ence
im|per|cipi|ent
im|per|fect +s
im|per|fec|tion +s
im|per|fect|ive +s
im|per|fect|ly
im|per|for|ate
im|per|ial +s
im|peri|al|ise Br.
  (use imperialize)
  im|peri|al|ises
  im|peri|al|ised
  im|peri|al|is|ing
im|peri|al|ism
im|peri|al|ist +s
im|peri|al|is|tic
im|peri|al|is|tic|
                 al|ly
im|peri|al|ize
  im|peri|al|izes
  im|peri|al|ized
  im|peri|al|iz|ing
im|peri|al|ly
im|peril
  im|perils
  im|perilled Br.
  im|periled Am.

im|peril (cont.)
  im|peril|ling Br.
  im|peril|ing Am.
im|peri|ous
im|peri|ous|ly
im|peri|ous|ness
im|per|ish|abil|ity
im|per|ish|able
im|per|ish|able|
                 ness
im|per|ish|ably
im|per|ium
im|per|man|ence
im|per|man|ency
im|per|man|en|
                 cies
im|per|man|ent
im|per|man|ent|ly
im|per|me|abil|ity
im|per|me|able
im|per|mis|si|
                 bil|ity
im|per|mis|sible
im|per|script|ible
im|per|son|al
im|per|son|al|ity
im|per|son|al|ly
im|per|son|ate
  im|per|son|ates
  im|per|son|ated
  im|per|son|at|ing
im|per|son|ation
                 +s
im|per|son|ator +s
im|per|tin|ence +s
im|per|tin|ent
im|per|tin|ent|ly
im|per|turb|
                 abil|ity
im|per|turb|able
im|per|turb|able|
                 ness
im|per|turb|ably
im|per|vi|ous
im|per|vi|ous|ly
im|per|vi|ous|ness
im|pe|ti|gin|ous
im|pe|tigo +s
im|pe|trate
  im|pe|trates
  im|pe|trated
  im|pe|trat|ing
im|pe|tra|tion +s
im|pe|tra|tory
im|petu|os|ity
  im|petu|os|ities
im|petu|ous
im|petu|ous|ly
im|petu|ous|ness
im|petus
  im|petuses

Im|phal (city,
  India)
impi +s
im|pi|ety
  im|pi|eties
im|pinge
  im|pinges
  im|pinged
  im|pin|ging
im|pinge|ment +s
im|pin|ger +s
im|pious
im|pious|ly
im|pious|ness
imp|ish
imp|ish|ly
imp|ish|ness
im|plac|abil|ity
im|plac|able
im|plac|ably
im|plant +s +ed
  +ing
im|plant|ation +s
im|plaus|ibil|ity
im|plaus|ible
im|plaus|ibly
im|plead +s +ed
  +ing
im|ple|ment +s
  +ed +ing
im|ple|men|ta|tion
  +s
im|ple|ment|er +s
im|pli|cate
  im|pli|cates
  im|pli|cated
  im|pli|cat|ing
im|pli|ca|tion +s
im|pli|ca|tive
im|pli|ca|tive|ly
im|pli|cit
im|pli|cit|ly
im|pli|cit|ness
im|plied|ly
im|plode
  im|plodes
  im|ploded
  im|plod|ing
im|plore
  im|plores
  im|plored
  im|plor|ing
im|plor|ing|ly
im|plo|sion +s
im|plo|sive +s
imply
  im|plies
  im|plied
  im|ply|ing
im|pol|der +s +ed
  +ing
im|pol|icy

im|pol|ite
im|pol|ite|ly
im|pol|ite|ness
im|pol|it|ic
im|pol|it|ic|ly
im|pon|der|abil|ity
im|pon|der|
                 abil|ities
im|pon|der|able +s
im|pon|der|ably
im|pon|ent +s
im|port +s +ed
  +ing
im|port|able
im|port|ance
im|port|ant
im|port|ant|ly
im|port|ation +s
im|port|er +s
im|por|tun|ate
im|por|tun|ate|ly
im|por|tune
  im|por|tunes
  im|por|tuned
  im|por|tun|ing
im|por|tun|ity
  im|por|tun|ities
im|pose
  im|poses
  im|posed
  im|pos|ing
im|pos|ing|ly
im|pos|ing|ness
im|pos|ition +s
im|pos|si|bil|ity
  im|pos|si|bil|ities
im|pos|sible
im|pos|sibly
im|post +s
im|pos|ter +s (use
  impostor)
im|pos|tor +s
im|pos|tor|ous
im|pos|trous
im|pos|ture +s
im|po|tence
im|po|tency
im|po|tent
im|po|tent|ly
im|pound +s +ed
  +ing
im|pound|able
im|pound|er +s
im|pound|ment +s
im|pov|er|ish
  im|pov|er|ishes
  im|pov|er|ished
  im|pov|er|ish|ing
im|pov|er|ish|
                 ment +s

im|prac|tic|abil|ity
  im|prac|tic|
          abil|ities
im|prac|tic|able
im|prac|tic|able|
          ness
im|prac|tic|ably
im|prac|ti|cal
im|prac|ti|cal|ity
  im|prac|ti|
          cal|ities
im|prac|tic|al|ly
im|pre|cate
  im|pre|cates
  im|pre|cated
  im|pre|cat|ing
im|pre|ca|tion +s
im|pre|ca|tory
im|pre|cise
im|pre|cise|ly
im|pre|cise|ness
im|pre|ci|sion +s
im|preg|na|bil|ity
im|preg|nable
im|preg|nably
im|preg|nat|able
im|preg|nate
  im|preg|nates
  im|preg|nated
  im|preg|nat|ing
im|preg|na|tion +s
im|pres|ario +s
im|pre|script|ible
im|press
  im|presses
  im|pressed
  im|press|ing
im|press|ible
im|pres|sion
im|pres|sion|
         abil|ity
im|pres|sion|able
im|pres|sion|ably
im|pres|sion|al
Im|pres|sion|ism
Im|pres|sion|ist +s
  (painter etc.)
im|pres|sion|ist +s
  (entertainer)
im|pres|sion|is|tic
im|pres|sion|is|tic|
         al|ly
im|pres|sive
im|pres|sive|ly
im|pres|sive|ness
im|press|ment
im|prest +s
im|pri|ma|tur +s
im|pri|ma|tura +s
im|print +s +ed
  +ing

im|prison +s +ed
  +ing
im|pris|on|ment
  +s
impro +s
im|prob|abil|ity
  im|prob|abil|ities
im|prob|able
im|prob|ably
im|prob|ity
  im|prob|ities
im|promptu +s
im|proper
im|prop|er|ly
im|pro|pri|ate
  im|pro|pri|ates
  im|pro|pri|ated
  im|pro|pri|at|ing
im|pro|pri|ation
  +s
im|pro|pri|ator +s
im|pro|pri|ety
  im|pro|pri|eties
im|prov +s
im|prov|abil|ity
  im|prov|abil|ities
im|prov|able
im|prove
  im|proves
  im|proved
  im|prov|ing
im|prove|ment +s
im|prover +s
im|provi|dence +s
im|provi|dent
im|provi|dent|ly
im|pro|visa|tion
  +s
im|pro|visa|tion|al
im|pro|visa|tor|ial
im|pro|visa|tory
im|pro|vise
  im|pro|vises
  im|pro|vised
  im|pro|vis|ing
im|pro|viser +s
im|pru|dence +s
im|pru|dent
im|pru|dent|ly
im|pu|dence +s
im|pu|dent
im|pu|dent|ly
im|pu|di|city
im|pugn +s +ed
  +ing
im|pugn|able
im|pugn|ment +s
im|pu|is|sance
im|pu|is|sant
im|pulse +s
im|pul|sion +s
im|pul|sive

im|pul|sive|ly
im|pul|sive|ness
im|pun|ity
  im|pun|ities
im|pure
im|pure|ly
im|pure|ness
im|pur|ity
  im|pur|ities
im|put|able
im|put|ation +s
im|pu|ta|tive
im|pute
  im|putes
  im|puted
  im|put|ing
Imroz (Turkish
  name for Imbros)
imshi
in (*preposition* inside
  etc. △ inn)
Ina (name)
in|abil|ity
  in|abil|ities
in ab|sen|tia
in|access|ibil|ity
in|access|ible
in|access|ible|ness
in|access|ibly
in|accur|acy
  in|ac|cur|acies
in|accur|ate
in|accur|ate|ly
in|action
in|acti|vate
  in|acti|vates
  in|acti|vated
  in|acti|vat|ing
in|acti|va|tion
in|active
in|active|ly
in|activ|ity
in|ad|equacy
  in|ad|equa|cies
in|ad|equate
in|ad|equate|ly
in|ad|mis|si|bil|ity
  in|ad|mis|si|
         bil|ities
in|ad|mis|sible
in|ad|mis|sibly
in|ad|ver|tence
in|ad|ver|tency
  in|ad|ver|ten|cies
in|ad|vert|ent
in|ad|vert|ent|ly
in|ad|vis|abil|ity
in|ad|vis|able
in|ali|en|abil|ity
in|ali|en|able
in|ali|en|ably
in|alter|abil|ity

in|alter|able
in|alter|ably
in|am|or|ata +s
  female
in|am|or|ato +s
  male
inane
in|ane|ly
in|ane|ness
in|anga +s
in|ani|mate
in|ani|mate|ly
in|ani|ma|tion
in|an|ition
in|an|ity
  in|an|ities
in|appell|able
in|appe|tence
in|appe|tency
in|appe|tent
in|applic|abil|ity
in|applic|able
in|applic|ably
in|appo|site
in|appo|site|ly
in|appo|site|ness
in|appre|ciable
in|appre|ciably
in|appre|ci|ation
in|appre|cia|tive
in|appre|hen|sible
in|appro|pri|ate
in|appro|pri|ate|ly
in|appro|pri|ate|
         ness
inapt
in|apti|tude +s
in|apt|ly
in|apt|ness
in|arch
  in|arches
  in|arched
  in|arch|ing
in|argu|able
in|argu|ably
in|articu|lacy
in|articu|late
in|articu|late|ly
in|articu|late|ness
in|art|is|tic
in|art|is|tic|al|ly
in|as|much
in|atten|tion
in|atten|tive
in|atten|tive|ly
in|atten|tive|ness
in|audi|bil|ity
in|aud|ible
in|aud|ibly
in|aug|ural
in|aug|ur|ate
  in|aug|ur|ates

in|aug|ur|ate
(*cont.*)
in|aug|ur|ated
in|aug|ur|at|ing
in|aug|ur|ation +s
in|aug|ur|ator +s
in|aug|ur|atory
in|aus|pi|cious
in|aus|pi|cious|ly
in|aus|pi|cious|
      ness
in|authen|tic
in|authen|ti|city
in-between
attributive
in|board
in|born
in|breathe
in|breathes
in|breathed
in|breath|ing
in|breed
in|breeds
in|bred
in|breed|ing
in|built
Inc.
(= Incorporated)
Inca
plural Inca *or*
Incas
Inca|ic
in|cal|cul|abil|ity
in|cal|cul|able
in|cal|cul|ably
in cam|era
Incan
in|can|desce
in|can|desces
in|can|desced
in|can|des|cing
in|can|des|cence
in|can|des|cent
in|can|des|cent|ly
in|can|ta|tion +s
in|can|ta|tion|al
in|can|ta|tory
in|cap|abil|ity
in|cap|abil|ities
in|cap|able
in|cap|ably
in|cap|aci|tant +s
in|cap|aci|tate
in|cap|aci|tates
in|cap|aci|tated
in|cap|aci|tat|ing
in|cap|aci|ta|tion
   +s
in|cap|acity
in|cap|aci|ties
in-car

in|car|cer|ate
in|car|cer|ates
in|car|cer|ated
in|car|cer|at|ing
in|car|cer|ation +s
in|car|cer|ator +s
in|car|na|dine
in|car|na|dines
in|car|na|dined
in|car|na|din|ing
in|car|nate
in|car|nates
in|car|nated
in|car|nat|ing
in|car|na|tion +s
in|case (use
   encase)
in|cases
in|cased
in|cas|ing
in|cau|tion +s
in|cau|tious
in|cau|tious|ly
in|cau|tious|ness
in|cen|di|ar|ism
in|cen|di|ary
in|cen|di|ar|ies
in|cen|sa|tion +s
in|cense
in|censes
in|censed
in|cens|ing
in|cens|ory
in|cens|or|ies
in|cen|tive +s
in|cept +s +ed
   +ing
in|cep|tion +s
in|cep|tive
in|cept|or +s
in|cer|ti|tude +s
in|ces|sancy
in|ces|sant
in|ces|sant|ly
in|ces|sant|ness
in|cest
in|ces|tu|ous
in|ces|tu|ous|ly
in|ces|tu|ous|ness
inch
inches
inched
inch|ing
Inch|cape Rock
   (off E. Scotland)
inch|meal
in|cho|ate
in|cho|ates
in|cho|ated
in|cho|at|ing
in|cho|ate|ly
in|cho|ate|ness

in|cho|ation +s
in|cho|ative
In|chon (port,
   Korea)
inch|worm +s
in|ci|dence +s
in|ci|dent +s
in|ci|den|tal +s
in|ci|den|tal|ly
in|cin|er|ate
in|cin|er|ates
in|cin|er|ated
in|cin|er|at|ing
in|cin|er|ation +s
in|cin|er|ator +s
in|cipi|ence
in|cipi|ency
in|cipi|en|cies
in|cipi|ent
in|cipi|ent|ly
in|cipit +s
in|cise
in|cises
in|cised
in|cis|ing
in|ci|sion +s
in|ci|sive
in|ci|sive|ly
in|ci|sive|ness
in|ci|sor +s
in|cit|ation +s
in|cite
in|cites
in|cited
in|cit|ing
(stir up. △ insight)
in|cite|ment +s
in|citer +s
in|civil|ity
in|civil|ities
in|civ|ism
in|clem|ency
in|clem|en|cies
in|clem|ent
in|clem|ent|ly
in|clin|able
in|clin|ation +s
in|cline
in|clines
in|clined
in|clin|ing
in|cliner +s
in|clin|om|eter +s
in|close (use
   enclose)
in|closes
in|closed
in|clos|ing
in|clos|ure +s (use
   enclosure)
in|clud|able

in|clude
in|cludes
in|cluded
in|clud|ing
in|clud|ible (use
   includable)
in|clu|sion +s
in|clu|sive
in|clu|sive|ly
in|clu|sive|ness
incog (= incognito)
in|cog|ni|sance *Br.*
   (use
   incognizance)
in|cog|ni|sant *Br.*
   (use incognizant)
in|cog|nito +s
in|cog|ni|zance
in|cog|ni|zant
in|co|her|ence
in|co|her|ency
in|co|her|en|cies
in|co|her|ent
in|co|her|ent|ly
in|com|bust|
      ibil|ity
in|com|bust|ible
in|come +s
in|comer +s
in|come tax
in|come taxes
in|come tax
   re|turn +s
in|com|ing +s
in|com|men|sur|
      abil|ity
in|com|men|sur|
      able +s
in|com|men|sur|
      ably
in|com|men|sur|
      ate
in|com|men|sur|
      ate|ly
in|com|men|sur|
      ate|ness
in|com|mode
in|com|modes
in|com|moded
in|com|mod|ing
in|com|mo|di|ous
in|com|mo|di|
      ous|ly
in|com|mo|di|ous|
      ness
in|com|mu|nic|
      abil|ity
in|com|mu|nic|
      able
in|com|mu|nic|
      able|ness

in|com|mu|nic|
ably
in|com|mu|ni|cado
in|com|mu|ni|
ca|tive
in|com|mu|ni|
ca|tive|ly
in|com|mu|ni|
ca|tive|ness
in|com|mut|able
in|com|mut|ably
in|com|par|abil|ity
in|com|par|able
in|com|par|able|
ness
in|com|par|ably
in|com|pati|bil|ity
in|com|pat|ible
in|com|pat|ible|
ness
in|com|pat|ibly
in|com|pe|tence
in|com|pe|tency
in|com|pe|tent +s
in|com|pe|tent|ly
in|com|plete
in|com|plete|ly
in|com|plete|ness
in|com|pre|hen|
si|bil|ity
in|com|pre|
hen|sible
in|com|pre|
hen|sible|ness
in|com|pre|
hen|sibly
in|com|pre|
hen|sion
in|com|press|
ibil|ity
in|com|press|ible
in|con|ceiv|abil|ity
in|con|ceiv|able
in|con|ceiv|able|
ness
in|con|ceiv|ably
in|con|clu|sive
in|con|clu|sive|ly
in|con|clu|sive|
ness
in|con|dens|able
in|con|dite
in|con|gru|ity
in|con|gru|ities
in|con|gru|ous
in|con|gru|ous|ly
in|con|gru|ous|
ness
in|con|secu|tive
in|con|secu|tive|ly
in|con|secu|tive|
ness

in|con|se|quence
in|con|se|quent
in|con|se|quen|tial
in|con|se|
quen|ti|al|ity
in|con|se|
quen|ti|al|ities
in|con|se|
quen|tial|ly
in|con|se|quen|tial|
ness
in|con|se|quent|ly
in|con|sid|er|able
in|con|sid|er|able|
ness
in|con|sid|er|ably
in|con|sid|er|ate
in|con|sid|er|ate|ly
in|con|sid|er|ate|
ness
in|con|sid|er|ation
in|con|sist|ency
in|con|sist|en|cies
in|con|sist|ent
in|con|sist|ent|ly
in|con|sol|abil|ity
in|con|sol|able
in|con|sol|able|
ness
in|con|sol|ably
in|con|son|ance
in|con|son|ant
in|con|son|ant|ly
in|con|spicu|ous
in|con|spicu|
ous|ly
in|con|spicu|ous|
ness
in|con|stancy
in|con|stan|cies
in|con|stant
in|con|stant|ly
in|con|test|abil|ity
in|con|test|able
in|con|test|ably
in|con|tin|ence
in|con|tin|ent
in|con|tin|ent|ly
in|con|tro|vert|
ibil|ity
in|con|tro|vert|ible
in|con|tro|vert|
ibly
in|con|veni|ence
in|con|veni|ences
in|con|veni|enced
in|con|veni|
en|cing
in|con|veni|ent
in|con|veni|ent|ly
in|con|vert|ibil|ity
in|con|vert|ible

in|con|vert|ibly
in|co|ord|in|ation
in|corp|or|ate
in|corp|or|ates
in|corp|or|ated
in|corp|or|at|ing
in|corp|or|ation +s
in|corp|or|ator +s
in|cor|por|eal
in|cor|por|eal|ity
in|cor|por|eal|ly
in|cor|por|eity
in|cor|rect
in|cor|rect|ly
in|cor|rect|ness
in|cor|ri|gi|bil|ity
in|cor|ri|gible
in|cor|ri|gible|ness
in|cor|ri|gibly
in|cor|rupt|ibil|ity
in|cor|rupt|ible
in|cor|rupt|ibly
in|cor|rup|tion
in|crass|ate
in|crass|ates
in|crass|ated
in|crass|at|ing
in|creas|able
in|crease
in|creases
in|creased
in|creas|ing
in|creaser +s
in|creas|ing|ly
in|credi|bil|ity
in|cred|ible
in|cred|ible|ness
in|cred|ibly
in|credu|lity
in|credu|lous
in|credu|lous|ly
in|credu|lous|ness
in|cre|ment +s
in|cre|men|tal
in|cre|men|tal|ly
in|crim|in|ate
in|crim|in|ates
in|crim|in|ated
in|crim|in|at|ing
in|crim|in|at|ing|ly
in|crim|in|ation +s
in|crim|in|atory
in|crust +s +ed
+ing (use
encrust)
in|crust|ation +s
in|cu|bate
in|cu|bates
in|cu|bated
in|cu|bat|ing
in|cu|ba|tion +s
in|cu|ba|tion|al

in|cu|ba|tive
in|cu|ba|tor +s
in|cu|ba|tory
in|cu|bus
in|cu|buses or
in|cubi
in|cu|des
in|cul|cate
in|cul|cates
in|cul|cated
in|cul|cat|ing
in|cul|ca|tion +s
in|cul|ca|tor +s
in|cul|pate
in|cul|pates
in|cul|pated
in|cul|pat|ing
in|cul|pa|tion +s
in|cul|pa|tive
in|cul|pa|tory
in|cum|bency
in|cum|ben|cies
in|cum|bent +s
in|cun|able +s
in|cu|nabu|lum
in|cu|nab|ula
incur
in|curs
in|curred
in|cur|ring
in|cur|abil|ity
in|cur|able +s (not
curable)
in|cur|able|ness
in|cur|ably
in|curi|os|ity
in|curi|ous
in|curi|ous|ly
in|curi|ous|ness
in|cur|rable (able
to happen)
in|cur|sion +s
in|cur|sive
in|curv|ation +s
in|curve
in|curves
in|curved
in|curv|ing
incus
in|cu|des
in|cuse
in|cuses
in|cused
in|cus|ing
in|daba +s
In|de|bele (plural of
Ndebele)
in|debt|ed
in|debt|ed|ness
in|decency
in|decen|cies
in|decent

in|decent|ly
in|de|cipher|able
in|deci|sion +s
in|deci|sive
in|deci|sive|ly
in|deci|sive|ness
in|declin|able
in|dec|or|ous
in|dec|or|ous|ly
in|dec|or|ous|ness
in|decorum
in|deed (*adverb* really and
 interjection really;
 admittedly; etc.)
in deed (in 'in deed
 but not in word')
in|defat|ig|abil|ity
in|defat|ig|able
in|defat|ig|ably
in|defeasi|bil|ity
in|defeas|ible
in|defeas|ibly
in|defect|ible
in|defens|ibil|ity
in|defens|ible
in|defens|ibly
in|defin|able
in|defin|ably
in|def|in|ite
in|def|in|ite|ly
in|def|in|ite|ness
in|dehis|cence
in|dehis|cent
in|deli|bil|ity
in|del|ible
in|del|ibly
in|deli|cacy
 in|deli|ca|cies
in|deli|cate
in|deli|cate|ly
in|dem|ni|fi|
 ca|tion +s
in|dem|ni|fier +s
in|dem|nify
 in|dem|ni|fies
 in|dem|ni|fied
 in|dem|ni|fy|ing
in|dem|nity
 in|dem|nities
in|dem|on|strable
in|dene +s
in|dent +s +ed
 +ing
in|den|ta|tion +s
in|dent|er +s
 (device)
in|den|tion +s
in|dent|or +s
 (person)
in|den|ture
 in|den|tures
 in|den|tured
 in|den|tur|ing

in|den|ture|ship
 +s
in|de|pend|ence
in|de|pend|ency
 in|de|pend|en|
 cies
in|de|pend|ent +s
in|de|pend|ent|ly
in-depth *attributive*
in|des|crib|abil|ity
in|des|crib|able
in|des|crib|ably
in|des|truct|
 ibil|ity
in|des|truct|ible
in|des|truct|ibly
in|de|ter|min|able
in|de|ter|min|ably
in|de|ter|min|acy
in|de|ter|min|ate
in|de|ter|min|
 ate|ly
in|de|ter|min|ate|
 ness
in|de|ter|min|ation
in|de|ter|min|ism
in|de|ter|min|ist
 +s
in|de|ter|min|is|tic
index
 in|dexes
 (list)
index
 in|dices *or*
 in|dexes
 (number)
index
 in|dexes
 in|dexed
 in|dex|ing
 verb
in|dex|ation +s
in|dex|er +s
in|dex|ible
in|dex|ic|al
in|dex|less
Index Libr|orum
 Pro|hib|it|orum
index-linked
index-linking
India
India|man
 India|men
In|dian +s
In|di|ana (state,
 USA)
In|dian|apo|lis
 (city, USA)
In|dian rope-trick
 +s
India rub|ber +s
Indic

in|di|cate
 in|di|cates
 in|di|cated
 in|di|cat|ing
in|di|ca|tion +s
in|di|ca|tive +s
in|di|ca|tive|ly
in|di|ca|tor +s
in|di|ca|tory
in|dices (plural of
 index)
in|di|cia
in|di|cial
in|di|cium
 in|di|cia
in|dict +s +ed +ing
 (accuse. △ indite)
in|dict|able
in|dict|ee +s
in|dict|er +s
in|dic|tion +s
in|dict|ment +s
indie +s
 (independent pop
 group etc. △ Indy)
In|dies (in S. Asia;
 also in 'East
 Indies', 'West
 Indies')
in|dif|fer|ence
in|dif|fer|ent
in|dif|fer|ent|ism
in|dif|fer|ent|ist +s
in|dif|fer|ent|ly
in|di|gence
in|di|gen|isa|tion
 Br. (use
 indigenization)
in|di|gen|ise *Br.*
 (use indigenize)
 in|di|gen|ises
 in|di|gen|ised
 in|di|gen|is|ing
in|di|gen|iza|tion
in|di|gen|ize
 in|di|gen|izes
 in|di|gen|ized
 in|di|gen|iz|ing
in|di|gen|ous
in|di|gen|ous|ly
in|di|gen|ous|ness
in|di|gent
in|di|gest|ed
in|di|gest|ibil|ity
in|di|gest|ible
in|di|gest|ibly
in|di|ges|tion
in|di|gest|ive
In|di|girka (river,
 Siberia)
in|dig|nant
in|dig|nant|ly

in|dig|na|tion
in|dig|nity
 in|dig|nities
in|digo +s
in|dig|ot|ic
In|dira Gan|dhi
 Canal (in India)
in|dir|ect
in|dir|ec|tion
in|dir|ect|ly
in|dir|ect|ness
in|dis|cern|ibil|ity
in|dis|cern|ible
in|dis|cern|ibly
in|dis|cip|line
in|dis|creet (not
 discreet;
 injudicious.
 △ indiscrete)
in|dis|creet|ly
in|dis|creet|ness
in|dis|crete (not
 divided into
 distinct parts.
 △ indiscreet)
in|dis|cre|tion +s
in|dis|crim|in|ate
in|dis|crim|in|
 ate|ly
in|dis|crim|in|ate|
 ness
in|dis|crim|in|
 ation
in|dis|crim|
 ina|tive
in|dis|pens|abil|ity
in|dis|pens|able
in|dis|pens|able|
 ness
in|dis|pens|ably
in|dis|pose
 in|dis|poses
 in|dis|posed
 in|dis|pos|ing
in|dis|pos|ition +s
in|dis|put|abil|ity
in|dis|put|able
in|dis|put|able|
 ness
in|dis|put|ably
in|dis|solu|bil|ist
 +s
in|dis|solu|bil|ity
in|dis|sol|uble
in|dis|sol|ubly
in|dis|tinct
in|dis|tinct|ive
in|dis|tinct|ive|ly
in|dis|tinct|ive|
 ness
in|dis|tinct|ly
in|dis|tinct|ness

in|dis|tin|guish|
    able
in|dis|tin|guish|
    able|ness
in|dis|tin|guish|
    ably
in|dite
 in|dites
 in|dited
 in|dit|ing
 (put into words.
 △ indict)
in|dium
in|divert|ible
in|divert|ibly
in|di|vid|ual +s
in|di|vidu|al|isa|
 tion Br. +s (use
 individualization)
in|di|vidu|al|ise Br.
 (use
 individualize)
 in|di|vidu|al|ises
 in|di|vidu|al|ised
 in|di|vidu|al|is|ing
in|di|vidu|al|ism
 +s
in|di|vidu|al|ist +s
in|di|vidu|al|is|tic
in|di|vidu|al|is|tic|
    al|ly
in|di|vidu|al|ity
 in|di|vidu|al|ities
in|di|vidu|al|
   iza|tion +s
in|di|vidu|al|ize
 in|di|vidu|al|izes
 in|di|vidu|al|ized
 in|di|vidu|al|
   iz|ing
in|di|vidu|al|ly
in|di|vidu|ate
 in|di|vidu|ates
 in|di|vidu|ated
 in|di|vidu|at|ing
in|di|vidu|ation +s
in|di|vis|ibil|ity
in|di|vis|ible
in|di|vis|ibly
Indo-Aryan +s
Indo-China
Indo-Chinese
 plural Indo-Chinese
in|docile
in|docil|ity
in|doc|trin|ate
 in|doc|trin|ates
 in|doc|trin|ated
 in|doc|trin|at|ing
in|doc|trin|ation
 +s
in|doc|trin|ator +s
Indo-European +s

Indo-German|ic
Indo-Iranian
in|dole +s
in|dole|acet|ic
in|do|lence +s
in|do|lent
in|do|lent|ly
Ind|olo|gist +s
Ind|ology
in|dom|it|abil|ity
in|dom|it|able
in|dom|it|able|
    ness
in|dom|it|ably
Indo|nesia
Indo|nes|ian +s
in|door
in|doors
Indo-Pacific
In|dore (city, India)
in|dorse (use
 endorse)
 in|dorses
 in|dorsed
 in|dors|ing
in|dorse|ment +s
 (use
 endorsement)
Indra *Hinduism*
in|draft Am. +s
in|draught Br. +s
in|drawn
indri +s
in|dub|it|able
in|dub|it|ably
in|duce
 in|duces
 in|duced
 in|du|cing
in|duce|ment +s
in|ducer +s
in|du|cible
in|duct +s +ed
 +ing
in|duct|ance +s
in|duct|ee +s
in|duc|tion +s
in|duct|ive
in|duct|ive|ly
in|duct|ive|ness
in|duct|or +s
indue (use endue)
 in|dues
 in|dued
 in|du|ing
in|dulge
 in|dulges
 in|dulged
 in|dul|ging
in|dul|gence +s
in|dul|genced
in|dul|gent

in|dul|gent|ly
in|dul|ger +s
in|dult +s
in|du|men|tum
 in|du|menta
in|duna +s
in|dur|ate
 in|dur|ates
 in|dur|ated
 in|dur|at|ing
in|dur|ation +s
in|dura|tive
Indus (river, Asia)
in|du|sial
in|du|sium
 in|du|sia
in|dus|trial +s
in|dus|tri|al|isa|
 tion Br. (use
 industrialization)
in|dus|tri|al|ise Br.
 (use industrialize)
 in|dus|tri|al|ises
 in|dus|tri|al|ised
 in|dus|tri|al|is|ing
in|dus|tri|al|ism
in|dus|tri|al|ist +s
in|dus|tri|al|iza|
    tion
in|dus|tri|al|ize
 in|dus|tri|al|izes
 in|dus|tri|al|ized
 in|dus|tri|al|iz|ing
in|dus|tri|al|ly
industrial-
 strength *adjective*
in|dus|tri|ous
in|dus|tri|ous|ly
in|dus|tri|ous|ness
in|dus|try
 in|dus|tries
in|dwell
 in|dwells
 in|dwelt
 in|dwell|ing
in|dwell|er +s
Indy
 (= Indianapolis.
 △ indie)
Indy|car +s
Ine (king of
 Wessex)
in|ebri|ate
 in|ebri|ates
 in|ebri|ated
 in|ebri|at|ing
in|ebri|ation
in|ebri|ety
in|edi|bil|ity
in|ed|ible
in|edit|ed
in|educ|abil|ity

in|educ|able
in|effa|bil|ity
in|effable
in|effably
in|ef|face|abil|ity
in|ef|face|able
in|ef|face|ably
in|ef|fect|ive
in|ef|fect|ive|ly
in|ef|fect|ive|ness
in|ef|fec|tual
in|ef|fec|tu|al|ity
in|ef|fec|tu|al|
    ities
in|ef|fec|tu|al|ly
in|ef|fec|tu|al|ness
in|ef|fi|ca|cious
in|ef|fi|ca|cious|ly
in|ef|fi|ca|cious|
    ness
in|ef|fi|cacy
in|ef|fi|ca|cies
in|ef|fi|ciency
in|ef|fi|cien|cies
in|ef|fi|cient
in|ef|fi|cient|ly
in|egali|tar|ian +s
in|elas|tic
in|elas|tic|al|ly
in|elas|ti|city
in|ele|gance
in|ele|gant
in|ele|gant|ly
in|eli|gi|bil|ity
in|eli|gible
in|eli|gibly
in|eluct|abil|ity
in|eluct|able
in|eluct|ably
inept
in|epti|tude
in|ept|ly
in|ept|ness
in|equable
in|equal|ity
 in|equal|ities
in|equit|able
in|equit|ably
in|equity
 in|equi|ties
in|erad|ic|able
in|erad|ic|ably
in|err|abil|ity
in|err|able
in|err|ably
in|err|ancy
in|err|ant
inert
in|er|tia
in|er|tial
in|er|tia|less
in|er|tia reel +s

in|er|tia sell|ing
in|ert|ly
in|ert|ness
in|escap|abil|ity
in|escap|able
in|escap|ably
in|es|cutch|eon
in|es|sen|tial +s
in|estim|able
in|estim|ably
in|ev|it|abil|ity
  in|ev|it|abil|ities
in|ev|it|able
in|ev|it|able|ness
in,ev|it|ably
in|exact
in|exacti|tude +s
in|exact|ly
in|exact|ness
in|ex|cus|able
in|ex|cus|ably
in|ex|haust|ibil|ity
in|ex|haust|ible
in|ex|haust|ibly
in|ex|or|abil|ity
in|ex|or|able
in|ex|or|ably
in|ex|pedi|ency
in|ex|pedi|ent
in|ex|pen|sive
in|ex|pen|sive|ly
in|ex|pen|sive|
           ness
in|ex|peri|ence
in|ex|peri|enced
in|ex|pert
in|ex|pert|ly
in|ex|pert|ness
in|ex|pi|able
in|ex|pi|ably
in|ex|plic|abil|ity
in|ex|plic|able
in|ex|plic|ably
in|ex|pli|cit
in|ex|pli|cit|ly
in|ex|pli|cit|ness
in|ex|press|ible
in|ex|press|ibly
in|ex|pres|sive
in|ex|pres|sive|ly
in|ex|pres|sive|
           ness
in|ex|pugn|able
in|ex|pun|gible
in ex|tenso
in|ex|tin|guish|
           able
in ex|tre|mis
in|ex|tric|abil|ity
in|ex|tric|able
in|ex|tric|ably
in fact

in|fal|li|bil|ity
in|fal|lible
in|fal|libly
in|fam|ous
in|fam|ous|ly
in|famy
  in|famies
in|fancy
  in|fan|cies
in|fant +s
in|fanta +s *female*
in|fante +s *male*
in|fanti|cidal
in|fanti|cide +s
in|fant|ile
in|fant|il|ism
in|fant|il|ity
  in|fant|il|ities
in|fant|ine
in|fan|try
  in|fan|tries
in|fan|try|man
  in|fan|try|men
in|farct +s
in|farc|tion +s
in|fatu|ate
  in|fatu|ates
  in|fatu|ated
  in|fatu|at|ing
in|fatu|ation +s
in|fauna
in|faun|al
in|feasi|bil|ity
in|feas|ible
in|fect +s +ed +ing
in|fec|tion +s
in|fec|tious
in|fec|tious|ly
in|fec|tious|ness
in|fect|ive
in|fect|ive|ness
in|fect|or +s
in|fe|li|ci|tous
in|fe|li|ci|tous|ly
in|feli|city
  in|feli|ci|ties
infer
  in|fers
  in|ferred
  in|fer|ring
in|fer|able
in|fer|ence +s
in|fer|en|tial
in|fer|en|tial|ly
in|fer|ior +s
in|fer|ior|ity
in|fer|ior|ly
in|fer|nal
in|fer|nal|ly
in|ferno +s
in|fer|tile
in|fer|til|ity

in|fest +s +ed +ing
in|fest|ation +s
in|fibu|late
  in|fibu|lates
  in|fibu|lated
  in|fibu|lat|ing
in|fibu|la|tion +s
in|fi|del +s
in|fi|del|ity
  in|fi|del|ities
in|field +s
in|field|er +s
in|fight|er +s
in|fight|ing
in|fill +s +ed +ing
in|fil|trate
  in|fil|trates
  in|fil|trated
  in|fil|trat|ing
in|fil|tra|tion +s
in|fil|tra|tor +s
in|fin|ite +s
in|fin|ite|ly
in|fin|ite|ness
in|fini|tesi|mal +s
in|fini|tesi|mal|ly
in|fini|tival
in|fini|tival|ly
in|fini|tive +s
in|fini|tude +s
in|fin|ity
  in|fin|ities
in|firm
in|firm|ary
  in|firm|ar|ies
in|firm|ity
  in|firm|ities
in|firm|ly
infix
  in|fixes
  in|fixed
  in|fix|ing
in|fix|ation +s
in fla|grante
  de|licto
in|flame
  in|flames
  in|flamed
  in|flam|ing
in|flamer +s
in|flam|ma|bil|ity
in|flam|mable +s
in|flam|mable|
           ness
in|flam|mably
in|flam|ma|tion +s
in|flam|ma|tory
in|flat|able +s
in|flate
  in|flates
  in|flated
  in|flat|ing

in|flated|ly
in|flated|ness
in|flater +s (use
  inflator)
in|fla|tion +s
in|fla|tion|ary
in|fla|tion|ism
in|fla|tion|ist +s
in|fla|tor +s
in|flect +s +ed
  +ing
in|flec|tion +s
in|flec|tion|al
in|flec|tion|al|ly
in|flec|tion|less
in|flect|ive
in|flex|ibil|ity
  in|flex|ibil|ities
in|flex|ible
in|flex|ibly
in|flex|ion +s (use
  inflection)
in|flex|ion|al (use
  inflectional)
in|flex|ion|al|ly
  (use
  inflectionally)
in|flex|ion|less
  (use
  inflectionless)
in|flict +s +ed +ing
in|flict|able
in|flict|er +s
in|flic|tion +s
in|flict|or +s (use
  inflicter)
in-flight *attributive*
in|flor|es|cence +s
in|flow +s
in|flow|ing +s
in|flu|ence
  in|flu|ences
  in|flu|enced
  in|flu|en|cing
in|flu|ence|able
in|flu|en|cer +s
in|flu|ent +s
in|flu|en|tial
in|flu|en|tial|ly
in|flu|enza +s
in|flu|en|zal
in|flux
  in|fluxes
info (= information)
info|bit +s
in|fold +s +ed +ing
  (fold in. △ enfold)
info|mania
info|mer|cial +s
info|pren|eur +s
in|form +s +ed
  +ing
in|for|mal

in|for|mal|ity
in|for|mal|ities
in|for|mal|ly
in|form|ant +s
in|form|at|ics
in|for|ma|tion +s
in|for|ma|tion|al
in|for|ma|tion|
  al|ly
in|forma|tive
in|forma|tive|ly
in|forma|tive|ness
in|forma|tory
in|form|ed|ly
in|form|ed|ness
in|form|er +s
infor|mer|cial +s
  (use infomercial)
info|sphere +s
info|tain|ment
info|tech
infra (below)
in|fra|class
  in|fra|classes
in|fract +s +ed
  +ing
in|frac|tion +s
in|fract|or +s
in|fra|dian
infra dig
in|fra|lap|sar|ian
  +s
in|fran|gi|bil|ity
in|fran|gible
in|fran|gible|ness
in|fran|gibly
in|fra|red (*Am.* and
  in scientific *Br.*
  use)
infra-red (in
  general *Br.* use)
in|fra|renal
in|fra|son|ic
in|fra|son|ic|al|ly
in|fra|sound
in|fra|struc|tural
in|fra|struc|ture +s
in|fre|quency
in|fre|quent
in|fre|quent|ly
in|fringe
  in|fringes
  in|fringed
  in|frin|ging
in|fringe|ment +s
in|frin|ger +s
in|fruct|es|cence
  +s
in|fula
  in|fu|lae
in|fun|dibu|lar

in|furi|ate
  in|furi|ates
  in|furi|ated
  in|furi|at|ing
in|furi|at|ing|ly
in|furi|ation +s
in|fus|able (able to
  be infused.
  △ infusible)
in|fuse
  in|fuses
  in|fused
  in|fus|ing
in|fuser +s
in|fus|ibil|ity
in|fus|ible (not
  fusible or
  meltable.
  △ infusable)
in|fu|sion +s
in|fu|sive
in|fus|oria
in|fus|or|ial
in|gather +s +ed
  +ing
in|gem|in|ate
  in|gem|in|ates
  in|gem|in|ated
  in|gem|in|at|ing
Ingen|housz, Jan
  (Dutch scientist)
in|geni|ous (clever)
in|geni|ous|ly
  (cleverly)
in|geni|ous|ness
  (cleverness)
in|génue +s
in|genu|ity
  (cleverness)
in|genu|ous
  (innocent)
in|genu|ous|ly
  (innocently)
in|genu|ous|ness
  (innocence)
in|gest +s +ed
  +ing
in|ges|tion +s
in|gest|ive
ingle|nook +s
in|glori|ous
in|glori|ous|ly
in|glori|ous|ness
in-goal area +s
in|going
ingot +s
in|graft +s +ed
  +ing (use engraft)
in|grain +s +ed
  +ing
in|grain|ed|ly
in|grate +s

in|grati|ate
  in|grati|ates
  in|grati|ated
  in|grati|at|ing
in|grati|at|ing|ly
in|grati|ation +s
in|grati|tude +s
in|grav|es|cence
  +s
in|grav|es|cent
in|gre|di|ent +s
Ingres, Jean
  Au|guste
  Dom|in|ique
  (French painter)
in|gress
  in|gresses
in|gres|sion +s
In|grid
in-group +s
in|grow|ing
in|grown
in|growth +s
in|guin|al
in|guin|al|ly
in|gulf +s +ed +ing
  (use engulf)
in|gur|gi|tate
  in|gur|gi|tates
  in|gur|gi|tated
  in|gur|gi|tat|ing
in|gur|gi|ta|tion +s
in|habit +s +ed
  +ing
in|hab|it|abil|ity
in|hab|it|able
in|hab|it|ance +s
in|hab|it|ancy
  in|hab|it|an|cies
in|hab|it|ant +s
in|hab|it|ation +s
in|hal|ant +s
in|hal|ation +s
in|hale
  in|hales
  in|haled
  in|hal|ing
in|haler +s
in|har|mon|ic
in|har|mo|ni|ous
in|har|mo|ni|
  ous|ly
in|here
  in|heres
  in|hered
  in|her|ing
in|her|ence +s
in|her|ent
in|her|ent|ly
in|herit +s +ed
  +ing
in|her|it|abil|ity

in|her|it|able
in|her|it|ance +s
in|heri|tor +s
in|heri|tress
  in|heri|tresses
in|heri|trix
  in|heri|trices
  female
in|he|sion +s
in|hibit +s +ed
  +ing
in|hib|ition +s
in|hibi|tive
in|hibi|tor +s
in|hibi|tory
in|homo|gen|eity
in|homo|gen|eous
in|hos|pit|able
in|hos|pit|able|
    ness
in|hos|pit|ably
in|hos|pi|tal|ity
in-house
in|human
in|hu|mane
in|hu|mane|ly
in|human|ity
  in|human|ities
in|human|ly
in|hum|ation +s
in|hume
  in|humes
  in|humed
  in|hum|ing
Inigo
in|imi|cal
in|imi|cal|ly
in|im|it|abil|ity
in|im|it|able
in|im|it|able|ness
in|im|it|ably
ini|qui|tous
ini|qui|tous|ly
ini|qui|tous|ness
ini|quity
  ini|qui|ties
ini|tial
  ini|tials
  ini|tialled *Br.*
  ini|tialed *Am.*
  ini|tial|ling *Br.*
  ini|tial|ing *Am.*
ini|tial|isa|tion *Br.*
  +s (use
  initialization)
ini|tial|ise *Br.* (use
  initialize)
  ini|tial|ises
  ini|tial|ised
  ini|tial|is|ing
ini|tial|ism +s
ini|tial|iza|tion +s

ini|tial|ize
  ini|tial|izes
  ini|tial|ized
  ini|tial|iz|ing
ini|tial|ly
ini|ti|ate
  ini|ti|ates
  ini|ti|ated
  ini|ti|at|ing
ini|ti|ation +s
ini|tia|tive +s
ini|ti|ator +s
ini|ti|atory
in|ject +s +ed +ing
in|ject|able +s
in|jec|tion +s
injection-moulded
in|jec|tion
  mould|ing +s
in|ject|or +s
in-joke +s
in|ju|di|cious
in|ju|di|cious|ly
in|ju|di|cious|ness
Injun +s *offensive*
in|junct +s +ed
  +ing
in|junc|tion +s
in|junct|ive
in|jure
  in|jures
  in|jured
  in|jur|ing
in|jurer +s
in|juri|ous
in|juri|ous|ly
in|juri|ous|ness
in|jury
  in|jur|ies
in|jury time
in|just|ice +s
ink +s +ed +ing
In|ka|tha (Zulu
  organization)
ink-blot test +s
ink-cap +s
inker +s
ink|horn +s
inki|ness
ink-jet print|er +s
ink|ling +s
ink-pad +s
ink|stand +s
ink|well +s
inky
  ink|ier
  inki|est
in|laid
in|land
in|land|er +s
in|land|ish

In|land Sea (off
  Japan)
in|land sea +s
  (generally)
in-law +s
inlay
  in|lays
  in|laid
  in|lay|ing
in|lay|er +s
inlet +s
in|lier +s
in-line
in loco par|en|tis
inly
in|ly|ing
In|mar|sat
in|mate +s
in med|ias res
in me|mor|iam +s
in|most
inn +s (pub. △ in)
in|nards
in|nate
in|nate|ly
in|nate|ness
inner +s
inner-city
  attributive
inner-direct|ed
in|ner|ly
in|ner|most
in|ner|ness
inner-spring
  attributive
in|nerv|ate
  in|nerv|ates
  in|nerv|ated
  in|nerv|at|ing
  (supply with nerves.
  △ innovate)
in|nerv|ation +s
  (supply of nerves.
  △ innovation)
in|ning +s *Baseball*
in|nings
  plural in|nings *or*
  in|ningses
  (*Cricket*; period of
  office etc.)
inn|keep|er +s
in|no|cence
in|no|cency
in|no|cent +s
in|no|cent|ly
In|no|cents' Day
in|nocu|ity
in|nocu|ous
in|nocu|ous|ly
in|nocu|ous|ness
in|nom|in|ate

in|nov|ate
  in|nov|ates
  in|nov|ated
  in|nov|at|ing
  (bring in
  something new.
  △ innervate)
in|nov|ation +s
  (new thing.
  △ innervation)
in|nov|ation|al
in|nova|tive
in|nova|tive|ly
in|nova|tive|ness
in|nov|ator +s
in|nov|atory
Inns|bruck (city,
  Austria)
in|nu|endo
  in|nu|en|does *or*
  in|nu|en|dos
In|nuit (use Inuit)
  plural In|nuit *or*
  In|nuits
in|nu|mer|abil|ity
in|nu|mer|able (too
  many to count.
  △ enumerable)
in|nu|mer|ably
in|nu|mer|acy
in|nu|mer|ate (not
  numerate.
  △ enumerate)
in|nu|tri|tion
in|nu|tri|tious
in|ob|serv|ance +s
in|ocul|able
in|ocu|late
  in|ocu|lates
  in|ocu|lated
  in|ocu|lat|ing
in|ocu|la|tion +s
in|ocu|la|tive
in|ocu|la|tor +s
in|ocu|lum
  in|oc|ula
in|odor|ous
in-off +s
in|offen|sive
in|offen|sive|ly
in|offen|sive|ness
in|offi|cious
in|op|er|abil|ity
in|op|er|able
in|op|er|ably
in|op|era|tive
in|op|por|tune
in|op|por|tune|ly
in|op|por|tune|
          ness
in|or|din|ate
in|or|din|ate|ly

in|or|gan|ic
in|or|gan|ic|al|ly
in|oscu|late
  in|oscu|lates
  in|oscu|lated
  in|oscu|lat|ing
in|oscu|la|tion +s
in-patient +s
in pro|pria
  per|sona
input
  in|puts
  input *or*
  in|put|ted
  in|put|ting
input-output
in|put|ter +s
in|quest +s
in|qui|et|ude
in|quil|ine +s
in|quil|in|ous
in|quire
  in|quires
  in|quired
  in|quir|ing
  (investigate; (*Am.*
  only) ask; *Br.*
  enquire)
in|quirer +s
  (investigator; (*Am.*
  only) person
  asking for
  information; *Br.*
  enquirer)
in|quir|ing|ly *Am.*
  (*Br.* enquiringly)
in|quiry
  in|quir|ies
  (investigation;
  (*Am.* only) request
  for information;
  Br. enquiry)
in|qui|si|tion +s
in|qui|si|tion|al
in|quisi|tive
in|quisi|tive|ly
in|quisi|tive|ness
in|quisi|tor +s
Inquisitor-General
  +s (head of
  Spanish
  Inquisition)
in|quisi|tor|ial
in|quisi|tori|al|ly
in|quor|ate
in re
in|road +s
in|rush
  in|rushes
in|rush|ing +s
in|salu|bri|ous

in|salu|brity
in|sane
in|sane|ly
in|sane|ness
in|sani|tary
in|san|ity
  in|san|ities
in|sati|abil|ity
in|sati|able
in|sati|ably
in|sati|ate
in|scape +s
in|scrib|able
in|scribe
  in|scribes
  in|scribed
  in|scrib|ing
in|scriber +s
in|scrip|tion +s
in|scrip|tion|al
in|scrip|tive
in|scrut|abil|ity
in|scrut|able
in|scrut|able|ness
in|scrut|ably
in|sect +s
in|sect|arium +s
in|sect|ary
  in|sect|ar|ies
in|secti|cidal
in|secti|cide +s
in|sect|ile
In|sect|iv|ora
in|sect|ivore +s
in|sect|iv|or|ous
in|sect|ology
in|se|cure
in|se|cure|ly
in|se|cur|ity
  in|se|cur|ities
in|sel|berg +s
in|sem|in|ate
  in|sem|in|ates
  in|sem|in|ated
  in|sem|in|at|ing
in|sem|in|ation +s
in|sem|in|ator +s
in|sens|ate
in|sens|ate|ly
in|sens|ibil|ity
in|sens|ible
in|sens|ibly
in|sensi|tive
in|sensi|tive|ly
in|sensi|tive|ness
in|sensi|tiv|ity
  in|sensi|tiv|ities
in|sen|tience
in|sen|tient
in|sep|ar|abil|ity
in|sep|ar|able
in|sep|ar|ably

in|sert +s +ed +ing
in|sert|able
in|sert|er +s
in|ser|tion +s
in-service
  attributive
INSET (= in-service
education and
training)
inset
  in|sets
  inset *or* in|set|ted
  in|set|ting
  (insert)
in|set|ter +s
in|shal|lah
in|shore
in|side +s
in|side for|ward
  +s
in|side left +s
in|side out
inside-out
  attributive
in|sider +s
in|sider deal|ing
  +s
in|side right +s
in|sider trad|ing
in|sidi|ous
in|sidi|ous|ly
in|sidi|ous|ness
in|sight +s (keen
understanding.
△ incite)
in|sight|ful
in|sight|ful|ly
in|sig|nia
in|sig|nifi|cance +s
in|sig|nifi|cancy
in|sig|nifi|cant
in|sig|nifi|cant|ly
in|sin|cere
in|sin|cere|ly
in|sin|cer|ity
  in|sin|cer|ities
in|sinu|ate
  in|sinu|ates
  in|sinu|ated
  in|sinu|at|ing
in|sinu|at|ing|ly
in|sinu|ation +s
in|sinu|ative
in|sinu|ator +s
in|sinu|atory
in|sipid
in|sip|id|ity
  in|sip|id|ities
in|sip|id|ly
in|sip|id|ness
in|sist +s +ed +ing
in|sist|ence +s

in|sist|ency
in|sist|ent
in|sist|ent|ly
in|sist|er +s
in|sist|ing|ly
in situ
in|so|bri|ety
in|so|far
in|so|la|tion
  (exposure to sun.
  △ insulation)
in|sole +s
in|so|lence
in|so|lent
in|so|lent|ly
in|solu|bil|ise *Br.*
  (use insolubilize)
  in|solu|bil|ises
  in|solu|bil|ised
  in|solu|bil|is|ing
in|solu|bil|ity
in|solu|bil|ize
  in|solu|bil|izes
  in|solu|bil|ized
  in|solu|bil|iz|ing
in|sol|uble
in|sol|uble|ness
in|sol|ubly
in|solv|able
in|solv|ency
  in|solv|en|cies
in|solv|ent +s
in|som|nia
in|som|niac +s
in|so|much
in|sou|ci|ance
in|sou|ci|ant
in|sou|ci|ant|ly
in|span
  in|spans
  in|spanned
  in|span|ning
in|spect +s +ed
  +ing
in|spec|tion +s
in|spect|or +s
in|spect|or|ate +s
in|spect|or
  gen|eral +s
in|spect|or|ial
in|spect|or|ship +s
in|spir|ation +s
in|spir|ation|al
in|spir|ation|ism
in|spir|ation|ist +s
in|spira|tor +s
in|spira|tory
in|spire
  in|spires
  in|spired
  in|spir|ing
in|spired|ly

in|spirer +s
in|spir|ing
in|spir|ing|ly
in|spirit +s +ed
  +ing
in|spir|it|ing|ly
in|spis|sate
  in|spis|sates
  in|spis|sated
  in|spis|sat|ing
in|spis|sa|tion +s
in|spis|sa|tor +s
in spite of
in|stabil|ity
  in|stabil|ities
in|stal (use install)
  in|stals
  in|stalled
  in|stall|ing
in|stall +s +ed
  +ing
in|stal|lant +s
in|stal|la|tion +s
in|stall|er +s
in|stall|ment *Am.*
  +s
in|stal|ment *Br.* +s
in|stance
  in|stances
  in|stanced
  in|stan|cing
in|stancy
in|stant +s
in|stant|an|eity
in|stant|an|eous
in|stant|an|eous|ly
in|stant|an|eous|
    ness
in|stan|ter *adverb*
in|stan|ti|ate
  in|stan|ti|ates
  in|stan|ti|ated
  in|stan|ti|at|ing
in|stan|ti|ation +s
in|stant|ly
in|star +s
in|state
  in|states
  in|stated
  in|stat|ing
in statu pu|pil|lari
in|staur|ation +s
in|staur|ator +s
in|stead
in|step +s
in|sti|gate
  in|sti|gates
  in|sti|gated
  in|sti|gat|ing
in|sti|ga|tion +s
in|sti|ga|tive
in|sti|ga|tor +s

in|stil *Br.*
  in|stils
  in|stilled
  in|stil|ling
in|still *Am.* +s +ed
  +ing
in|stil|la|tion +s
in|stil|ler +s
in|still|ment *Am.*
  +s
in|stil|ment *Br.* +s
in|stinct +s
in|stinct|ive
in|stinct|ive|ly
in|stinct|ual
in|stinc|tu|al|ly
in|sti|tute
  in|sti|tutes
  in|sti|tuted
  in|sti|tut|ing
in|sti|tu|tion +s
in|sti|tu|tion|al
in|sti|tu|tion|al|
  isa|tion *Br.* (use
  institutional-
  ization)
in|sti|tu|tion|al|ise
  Br. (use
  institutionalize)
in|sti|tu|tion|al|
       ises
in|sti|tu|tion|al|
       ised
in|sti|tu|tion|al|
      is|ing
in|sti|tu|tion|al|
       ism
in|sti|tu|tion|al|
      iza|tion
in|sti|tu|tion|al|ize
in|sti|tu|tion|al|
       izes
in|sti|tu|tion|al|
       ized
in|sti|tu|tion|al|
      iz|ing
in|sti|tu|tion|al|ly
in-store *attributive*
INSTRAW
  (= International
  Research and
  Training Institute
  for the
  Advancement of
  Women)
in|struct +s +ed
  +ing
in|struc|tion +s
in|struc|tion|al
in|struct|ive
in|struct|ive|ly
in|struct|ive|ness

in|struct|or +s
in|struct|or|ship
  +s
in|struc|tress
  in|struc|tresses
in|stru|ment +s
  +ed +ing
in|stru|men|tal +s
in|stru|men|tal|ist
  +s
in|stru|men|tal|ity
in|stru|men|tal|ly
in|stru|men|ta|tion
  +s
in|sub|or|din|ate
in|sub|or|din|
      ate|ly
in|sub|or|din|ation
  +s
in|sub|stan|tial
in|sub|stan|ti|al|
         ity
in|sub|stan|ti|al|
        ities
in|sub|stan|tial|ly
in|suf|fer|able
in|suf|fer|able|
        ness
in|suf|fer|ably
in|suf|fi|ciency
  in|suf|fi|cien|cies
in|suf|fi|cient
in|suf|fi|cient|ly
in|suf|flate
  in|suf|flates
  in|suf|flated
  in|suf|flat|ing
in|suf|fla|tion +s
in|suf|fla|tor +s
in|su|lar
in|su|lar|ism
in|su|lar|ity
in|su|lar|ly
in|su|late
  in|su|lates
  in|su|lated
  in|su|lat|ing
in|su|lat|ing tape
  +s
in|su|la|tion +s
  (separation.
  ⚠ insolation)
in|su|la|tor +s
in|su|lin +s
in|sult +s +ed +ing
in|sult|er +s
in|sult|ing|ly
in|su|per|abil|ity
  in|su|per|abil|ities
in|su|per|able
in|su|per|ably
in|sup|port|able

in|sup|port|able|
        ness
in|sup|port|ably
in|sur|abil|ity
in|sur|able
in|sur|ance +s
in|sur|ant +s
in|sure
  in|sures
  in|sured
  in|sur|ing
  (secure payment
  against damage,
  theft, etc.
  ⚠ ensure)
in|sured +s
in|surer +s (person
  who insures.
  ⚠ ensurer)
in|sur|gence +s
in|sur|gency
  in|sur|gen|cies
in|sur|gent +s
in|sur|mount|able
in|sur|mount|ably
in|sur|rec|tion +s
in|sur|rec|tion|al
in|sur|rec|tion|ary
in|sur|rec|tion|ism
in|sur|rec|tion|ist
  +s
in|sus|cep|ti|bil|ity
in|sus|cep|tible
in-swinger +s
in|tact
in|tact|ness
in|tagli|ated
in|taglio +s *noun*
in|taglio
  in|taglioes
  in|taglioed
  in|taglio|ing
  verb
in|take +s
in|tan|gi|bil|ity
in|tan|gible +s
in|tan|gibly
in|tar|sia +s
in|te|ger +s
in|te|gra|bil|ity
in|te|grable
in|te|gral +s
in|te|gral|ity
  in|te|gral|ities
in|te|gral|ly
in|te|grand +s
in|te|grant
in|te|grate
  in|te|grates
  in|te|grated
  in|te|grat|ing
in|te|gra|tion +s

in|te|gra|tion|ist
  +s
in|te|gra|tive
in|te|gra|tor +s
in|teg|rity
in|tegu|ment +s
in|tegu|men|tal
in|tegu|ment|ary
in|tel|lect +s
in|tel|lec|tion +s
in|tel|lect|ive
in|tel|lec|tual +s
in|tel|lec|tual|ise
  Br. (use
  intellectualize)
in|tel|lec|tual|ises
in|tel|lec|tual|ised
in|tel|lec|tual|
      is|ing
in|tel|lec|tual|ism
in|tel|lec|tual|ist
  +s
in|tel|lec|tu|al|ity
in|tel|lec|tual|ize
in|tel|lec|tual|izes
in|tel|lec|tual|
       ized
in|tel|lec|tual|
      iz|ing
in|tel|lec|tual|ly
in|tel|li|gence +s
in|tel|li|gent
in|tel|li|gen|tial
in|tel|li|gent|ly
in|tel|li|gent|sia +s
in|tel|li|gi|bil|ity
in|tel|li|gible
in|tel|li|gibly
In|tel|post
In|tel|sat
in|tem|per|ance
in|tem|per|ate
in|tem|per|ate|ly
in|tem|per|ate|
        ness
in|tend +s +ed
  +ing
in|tend|ancy
  in|tend|an|cies
in|tend|ant +s
in|tend|ed +s
in|tend|ed|ly
in|tend|ment +s
in|tense
  in|tenser
  in|tens|est
in|tense|ly
in|tense|ness
in|tensi|fi|ca|tion
  +s
in|ten|si|fier +s

in¦ten¦sify
  in¦ten¦si¦fies
  in¦ten¦si¦fied
  in¦ten¦si¦fy¦ing
in¦ten¦sion +s
  (intensity; *Logic*.
  △ intention)
in¦ten¦sion¦al
  (*Philosophy*.
  △ intentional)
in¦ten¦sion¦al¦ity
  (*Philosophy*.
  △ intentionality)
in¦ten¦sion¦al¦ly
  (*Philosophy*.
  △ intentionally)
in¦ten¦sity
  in¦ten¦sities
in¦ten¦sive
in¦ten¦sive¦ly
in¦ten¦sive¦ness
in¦tent +s
in¦ten¦tion +s
  (purpose.
  △ intension)
in¦ten¦tion¦al
  (deliberately.
  △ intensional)
in¦ten¦tion¦al¦ity
  (deliberateness.
  △ intensionality)
in¦ten¦tion¦al¦ly
  (deliberately.
  △ intensionally)
in¦ten¦tioned
in¦tent¦ly
in¦tent¦ness
inter
  in¦ters
  in¦terred
  in¦ter¦ring
inter|act +s +ed
  +ing
inter|act|ant +s
inter|action +s
inter|action¦al
inter|active
inter|active¦ly
inter alia
inter-allied
inter|ar¦ticu¦lar
inter|atom¦ic
inter|bank
inter|bed
  inter|beds
  inter|bed¦ded
  inter|bed¦ding
inter|blend +s +ed
  +ing
inter|breed
  inter|breeds

inter|breed (*cont.*)
  inter|bred
  inter|breed|ing
inter|cal¦ary
inter|cal¦ate
  inter|cal¦ates
  inter|cal¦ated
  inter|cal¦at¦ing
inter|cal¦ation +s
inter|cede
  inter|cedes
  inter|ceded
  inter|ced¦ing
inter|ceder +s
inter|cel¦lu¦lar
inter|cen¦sal
inter|cept +s +ed
  +ing
inter|cep¦tion +s
inter|cep¦tive
inter|cept¦or +s
inter|ces¦sion +s
inter|ces¦sion¦al
inter|ces¦sor +s
inter|ces¦sor¦ial
inter|ces¦sory
inter|change
  inter|changes
  inter|changed
  inter|chan¦ging
inter|change|
      abil¦ity
inter|change|able
inter|change|able|
      ness
inter|change|ably
Inter|City
  Propr.
inter|city
  inter|cities
inter-class
inter|col¦le¦gi¦ate
inter|co¦lo¦nial
inter|com +s
inter|com¦mu¦ni¦
      cate
  inter|com¦mu¦ni¦
      cates
  inter|com¦mu¦ni¦
      cated
  inter|com¦mu¦ni¦
      cat¦ing
inter|com¦mu¦ni¦
      ca¦tion
inter|com¦mu¦ni¦
      ca¦tive
inter|com¦mu¦nion
inter|com¦mu¦nity
inter|con¦nect +s
  +ed +ing
inter|con¦nec¦tion
  +s

inter|con¦tin¦en¦tal
inter|con¦tin¦
      en¦tal¦ly
inter|con¦ver¦sion
  +s
inter|con¦vert +s
  +ed +ing
inter|con¦vert|ible
inter|cool +s +ed
  +ing
inter|cool¦er +s
inter|cor¦rel¦ate
  inter|cor¦rel¦ates
  inter|cor¦rel¦ated
  inter|cor¦rel¦
      at¦ing
inter|cor¦rel¦ation
  +s
inter|cos¦tal
inter|cos¦tal¦ly
inter|county
inter|course
inter|crop
  inter|crops
  inter|cropped
  inter|crop|ping
inter|cross
  inter|crosses
  inter|crossed
  inter|cross¦ing
inter|crural
inter|cur¦rence
inter|cur¦rent
inter|cut
  inter|cuts
  inter|cut
  inter|cut¦ting
inter|de¦nom¦in¦
      ation¦al
inter|de¦nom¦in¦
      ation¦al¦ly
inter|de¦part|
      men¦tal
inter|de¦part|
      men¦tal¦ly
inter|de¦pend +s
  +ed +ing
inter|de¦pend¦ence
inter|
      de¦pend¦ency
  inter|de¦pend¦en|
      cies
inter|de¦pend¦ent
inter|dict +s +ed
  +ing
inter|dic¦tion +s
inter|dict¦ory
inter|digit¦al
inter|digit¦al¦ly
inter|digi¦tate
  inter|digi¦tates

inter|digi¦tate
  (*cont.*)
  inter|digi¦tated
  inter|digi¦tat¦ing
inter|dis¦cip¦lin|
      ary
inter|est +s +ed
  +ing
inter|est|ed¦ly
inter|est|ed|ness
inter|est|ing¦ly
inter|est|ing|ness
inter|face
  inter|faces
  inter|faced
  inter|facing
inter|facial
inter|facial¦ly
inter|facing +s
inter|faith
inter|femor¦al
inter|fere
  inter|feres
  inter|fered
  inter|fer¦ing
inter|fer¦ence +s
inter|fer¦en|tial
inter|ferer +s
inter|fer¦ing¦ly
inter|fer|om¦eter
  +s
inter|fero|met¦ric
inter|fero|met¦ric|
      al¦ly
inter|fer|om¦etry
inter|feron +s
inter|fib¦ril|lar
inter|file
  inter|files
  inter|filed
  inter|fil¦ing
inter|flow +s +ed
  +ing
inter|flu¦ent
inter|fuse
  inter|fuses
  inter|fused
  inter|fus¦ing
inter|fusion +s
inter|gal¦act¦ic
inter|gal¦act¦ic|
      al¦ly
inter|gla¦cial +s
inter|gov¦ern|
      men¦tal
inter|gov¦ern|
      men¦tal¦ly
inter|grad|ation
  +s
inter|grade
  inter|grades

inter|grade (*cont.*)
inter|graded
inter|grad|ing
inter|growth +s
in|terim +s
in|ter|ior +s
in|ter|ior|ise *Br.*
  (use interiorize)
in|ter|ior|ises
in|ter|ior|ised
in|ter|ior|is|ing
in|ter|ior|ize
in|ter|ior|izes
in|ter|ior|ized
in|ter|ior|iz|ing
in|ter|ior|ly
interior-sprung
inter|ject +s +ed
  +ing
inter|jec|tion +s
inter|jec|tion|al
inter|jec|tion|ary
inter|ject|ory
inter|knit
inter|knits
inter|knit|ted *or*
inter|knit
inter|knit|ting
inter|lace
inter|laces
inter|laced
inter|lacing
inter|lace|ment +s
In|ter|laken (town,
  Switzerland)
inter|lan|guage +s
inter|lap
inter|laps
inter|lapped
inter|lap|ping
inter|lard +s +ed
  +ing
inter|leaf
inter|leaves
inter|leave
inter|leaves
inter|leaved
inter|leav|ing
inter|leu|kin +s
inter|lib|rary
inter|line
inter|lines
inter|lined
inter|lin|ing
inter|lin|ear
inter|lin|ea|tion +s
inter|lin|ing +s
inter|link +s +ed
  +ing
inter|lobu|lar
inter|lock +s +ed
  +ing

inter|lock|er +s
inter|locu|tion +s
inter|locu|tor +s
inter|locu|tory
inter|locu|trix
inter|locu|trixes
  female
inter|lope
inter|lopes
inter|loped
inter|lop|ing
inter|loper +s
inter|lude +s
inter|mar|riage +s
inter|marry
inter|mar|ries
inter|mar|ried
inter|marry|ing
inter|medi|acy
inter|medi|ary
inter|medi|ar|ies
inter|medi|ate
inter|medi|ates
inter|medi|ated
inter|medi|at|ing
inter|medi|ate|ly
inter|medi|ate|
  ness
inter|medi|ation
  +s
inter|medi|ator +s
inter|medium
inter|media
in|ter|ment +s
inter|mesh
inter|meshes
inter|meshed
inter|mesh|ing
inter|mezzo
inter|mezzi *or*
inter|mezzos
in|ter|min|able
in|ter|min|able|
  ness
in|ter|min|ably
inter|min|gle
inter|min|gles
inter|min|gled
inter|min|gling
inter|mis|sion +s
inter|mit
inter|mits
inter|mit|ted
inter|mit|ting
inter|mit|tence +s
inter|mit|tency
inter|mit|tent
inter|mit|tent|ly
inter|mix
inter|mixes
inter|mixed
inter|mix|ing

inter|mix|able
inter|mix|ture +s
inter|modal
inter|mo|lecu|lar
in|tern +s +ed
  +ing
in|tern|al
internal-
  combus|tion
  attributive
in|tern|al|isa|tion
  Br. (use
  internalization)
in|tern|al|ise *Br.*
  (use internalize)
in|tern|al|ises
in|tern|al|ised
in|tern|al|is|ing
in|tern|al|ity
in|tern|al|iza|tion
in|tern|al|ize
in|tern|al|izes
in|tern|al|ized
in|tern|al|iz|ing
in|tern|al|ly
inter|nation|al +s
Inter|nation|ale,
  the (song;
  organization)
inter|nation|al|
  isa|tion *Br.* (use
  international-
  ization)
inter|nation|al|ise
  Br. (use
  internationalize)
inter|nation|al|
    ises
inter|nation|al|
    ised
inter|nation|al|
    is|ing
inter|nation|al|ism
inter|nation|al|ist
  +s
inter|nation|al|ity
inter|nation|al|
    iza|tion
inter|nation|al|ize
inter|nation|al|
    izes
inter|nation|al|
    ized
inter|nation|al|
    iz|ing
inter|nation|al|ly
in|terne +s (use
  intern)
inter|necine
in|tern|ee +s

Inter|net
  (computer
  network)
in|tern|ist +s
in|tern|ment +s
inter|node +s
in|tern|ship +s
inter|nuclear
inter|nun|cial
inter|nun|cio +s
inter|ocean|ic
in|tero|cep|tive
inter|oper|abil|ity
inter|oper|able
inter|oscu|late
inter|oscu|lates
inter|oscu|lated
inter|oscu|lat|ing
inter|osse|ous
inter|page
inter|pages
inter|paged
inter|paging
inter|pari|et|al
inter|pari|et|al|ly
in|ter|pel|late
in|ter|pel|lates
in|ter|pel|lated
in|ter|pel|lat|ing
  (question minister.
  △ interpolate)
in|ter|pel|la|tion
  +s (action of
  interpellating.
  △ interpolation)
in|ter|pel|la|tor +s
  (person who
  interpellates.
  △ interpolator)
inter|pene|trate
inter|pene|trates
inter|pene|trated
inter|
  pene|trat|ing
inter|pene|tra|tion
  +s
inter|pene|tra|tive
inter|per|son|al
inter|per|son|al|ly
inter|phase
inter|plait +s +ed
  +ing
inter|plan|et|ary
inter|play +s
inter|plead +s +ed
  +ing
inter|plead|er +s
Inter|pol
in|ter|pol|ate
in|ter|pol|ates
in|ter|pol|ated
in|ter|pol|at|ing

in|ter|pol|ate
(cont.)
(insert; interject.
△interpellate)
in|ter|pol|ation +s
(insertion;
interjection.
△interpellation)
in|ter|pola|tive
in|ter|pol|ator +s
(person who
interpolates.
△interpellator)
inter|posal +s
inter|pose
inter|poses
inter|posed
inter|pos|ing
inter|pos|ition +s
in|ter|pret +s +ed
+ing
in|ter|pret|abil|ity
in|ter|pret|able
in|ter|pret|ation
+s
in|ter|pret|ation|al
in|ter|pret|ative
in|ter|pret|er +s
in|ter|pret|ive
in|ter|pret|ive|ly
inter|pro|vin|cial
inter|racial
inter|racial|ly
inter|reg|num
inter|reg|nums or
inter|regna
inter|relate
inter|relates
inter|related
inter|relat|ing
inter|rela|tion +s
inter|rela|tion|ship
+s
in|ter|ro|gate
in|ter|ro|gates
in|ter|ro|gated
in|ter|ro|gat|ing
in|ter|ro|ga|tion +s
in|ter|ro|ga|tion|al
inter|roga|tive +s
inter|roga|tive|ly
in|ter|ro|ga|tor +s
inter|roga|tory
inter|rupt +s +ed
+ing
inter|rupt|er +s
inter|rupt|ible
inter|rup|tion +s
inter|rup|tive
inter|rupt|or +s
inter|rup|tory

inter|sect +s +ed
+ing
inter|sec|tion +s
inter|sec|tion|al
inter|sep|tal
inter|sex
inter|sexes
inter|sex|ual
inter|sexu|al|ity
inter|sexu|al|ly
inter|space
inter|spaces
inter|spaced
inter|spacing
inter|spe|cif|ic
inter|sperse
inter|sperses
inter|spersed
inter|spers|ing
inter|sper|sion +s
inter|spinal
inter|spin|ous
inter|sta|dial +s
inter|state +s
inter|stel|lar
in|ter|stice +s
inter|sti|tial
inter|sti|tial|ly
inter|text|ual|ity
inter|text|ual|ities
inter|tidal
inter|tribal
inter|trigo +s
inter|twine
inter|twines
inter|twined
inter|twin|ing
inter|twine|ment
+s
inter|twist +s +ed
+ing
inter|val +s
inter|val|lic
inter|vene
inter|venes
inter|vened
inter|ven|ing
inter|vener +s
inter|ve|ni|ent
inter|venor +s
(use intervener)
inter|ven|tion +s
inter|ven|tion|ism
inter|ven|tion|ist
+s
inter|ver|te|bral
inter|view +s +ed
+ing
inter|view|ee +s
inter|view|er +s
inter vivos
inter-war

inter|weave
inter|weaves
inter|wove
inter|weav|ing
inter|woven
inter|wind
inter|winds
inter|wound
inter|wind|ing
inter|work +s +ed
+ing
in|tes|tacy
in|tes|ta|cies
in|tes|tate +s
in|tes|tinal
in|tes|tine +s
in|thrall Am. +s
+ed +ing (use
enthrall. Br.
enthral)
inti
plural inti
in|ti|fada
in|tim|acy
in|tim|acies
in|tim|ate
in|tim|ates
in|tim|ated
in|tim|at|ing
in|tim|ate|ly
in|tim|ater +s
in|tim|ation +s
in|timi|date
in|timi|dates
in|timi|dated
in|timi|dat|ing
in|timi|dat|ing|ly
in|timi|da|tion +s
in|timi|da|tor +s
in|timi|da|tory
in|tinc|tion +s
in|tit|ule
in|tit|ules
in|tit|uled
in|tit|ul|ing
into
in|toler|able
in|toler|able|ness
in|toler|ably
in|toler|ance
in|toler|ant
in|toler|ant|ly
in|ton|ate
in|ton|ates
in|ton|ated
in|ton|at|ing
in|ton|ation +s
in|ton|ation|al
in|tone
in|tones
in|toned
in|ton|ing

in|toner +s
in toto
in|toxi|cant +s
in|toxi|cate
in|toxi|cates
in|toxi|cated
in|toxi|cat|ing
in|toxi|cat|ing|ly
in|toxi|ca|tion +s
intra|cel|lu|lar
intra|cra|nial
intra|cra|ni|al|ly
in|tract|abil|ity
in|tract|able
in|tract|able|ness
in|tract|ably
in|tra|dos
in|tra|doses
intra|mo|lecu|lar
intra|mural
intra|mur|al|ly
intra|mus|cu|lar
intra|nation|al
in|transi|gence
in|transi|gency
in|transi|gent +s
in|transi|gent|ly
in|transi|tive +s
in|transi|tive|ly
in|transi|tiv|ity
intra|pre|neur +s
intra|pre|neur|ial
intra|uter|ine
intra|ven|ous
intra|ven|ous|ly
in-tray +s
in|trepid
in|trep|id|ity
in|trep|id|ly
in|tri|cacy
in|tri|ca|cies
in|tri|cate
in|tri|cate|ly
in|tri|gant +s male
in|tri|gante +s
female
in|trigue
in|trigues
in|trigued
in|tri|guing
in|tri|guer +s
in|tri|guing|ly
in|trin|sic
in|trin|sic|al|ly
intro +s
intro|duce
intro|duces
intro|duced
intro|du|cing
intro|ducer +s
intro|du|cible
intro|duc|tion +s

intro|duc|tory
intro|flex|ion +s
intro|gres|sion +s
in|troit +s
intro|jec|tion +s
intro|mis|sion +s
intro|mit
  intro|mits
  intro|mit|ted
  intro|mit|ting
intro|mit|tent
intro|spect +s +ed +ing
intro|spec|tion +s
intro|spect|ive
intro|spect|ive|ly
intro|spect|ive|
                ness
intro|sus|cep|tion +s
intro|ver|sible
intro|ver|sion +s
intro|ver|sive
intro|vert +s +ed +ing
intro|vert|ive
in|trude
  in|trudes
  in|truded
  in|trud|ing
in|truder +s
in|trud|ing|ly
in|tru|sion +s
in|tru|sion|ist +s
in|tru|sive
in|tru|sive|ly
in|tru|sive|ness
in|trust +s +ed +ing (use entrust)
in|trust|ment (use entrustment)
in|tub|ate
  in|tub|ates
  in|tub|ated
  in|tub|at|ing
in|tub|ation +s
in|tuit +s +ed +ing
in|tuit|able
in|tu|ition +s
in|tu|ition|al
in|tu|ition|al|ism
in|tu|ition|al|ist +s
in|tu|ition|ism
in|tu|ition|ist +s
in|tui|tive
in|tui|tive|ly
in|tui|tive|ness
in|tui|tiv|ism
in|tui|tiv|ist +s
in|tu|mesce
  in|tu|mesces

in|tu|mesce (cont.)
  in|tu|mesced
  in|tu|mes|cing
in|tu|mes|cence +s
in|tu|mes|cent
in|tus|sus|cep|tion +s
in|twine (use entwine)
  in|twines
  in|twined
  in|twin|ing
in|twine|ment (use entwinement)
Inuit
  plural Inuit or In|uits
Inuk
  plural Inuk or Inuks
Inuk|ti|tut
in|unc|tion +s
in|un|date
  in|un|dates
  in|un|dated
  in|un|dat|ing
in|un|da|tion +s
Inu|piaq
  plural Inu|piaq or Inu|piaqs
Inu|piat (use Inupiaq)
  plural Inu|piat or Inu|piats
Inu|pik (use Inupiaq)
  plural Inu|pik or Inu|piks
inure
  in|ures
  in|ured
  in|ur|ing
  (accustom to something unpleasant. ⚠ enure)
in|ure|ment +s
in utero
in vacuo
in|vade
  in|vades
  in|vaded
  in|vad|ing
in|vader +s
in|va|gin|ate
  in|va|gin|ates
  in|va|gin|ated
  in|va|gin|at|ing
in|va|gin|ation +s
in|valid +s +ed +ing

in|vali|date
  in|vali|dates
  in|vali|dated
  in|vali|dat|ing
in|vali|da|tion +s
in|val|id|ism
in|val|id|ity
  in|val|id|ities
in|val|id|ly
in|valu|able
in|valu|able|ness
in|valu|ably
Invar Propr.
in|vari|abil|ity
  in|vari|abil|ities
in|vari|able
in|vari|able|ness
in|vari|ably
in|vari|ance +s
in|vari|ant +s
in|va|sion +s
in|va|sive
in|vec|tive +s
in|veigh +s +ed +ing
in|vei|gle
  in|vei|gles
  in|vei|gled
  in|veig|ling
in|veigle|ment +s
in|vent +s +ed +ing
in|vent|able
in|ven|tion +s
in|vent|ive
in|vent|ive|ly
in|vent|ive|ness
in|vent|or +s
in|ven|tory
  in|ven|tor|ies
  in|ven|tor|ied
  in|ven|tory|ing
in|vent|ress
  in|vent|resses
In|ver|car|gill (city, New Zealand)
In|ver|ness (city, Scotland)
Inverness-shire (former county, Scotland)
in|verse +s
in|verse|ly
in|verse square law
in|ver|sion +s
in|ver|sive
in|vert +s +ed +ing
in|vert|ase
in|ver|te|brate +s
in|vert|er +s

in|vert|ibil|ity
in|vert|ible
in|vest +s +ed +ing
in|vest|able
in|vest|ible (use investable)
in|ves|ti|gate
  in|ves|ti|gates
  in|ves|ti|gated
  in|ves|ti|gat|ing
in|ves|ti|ga|tion +s
in|ves|ti|ga|tion|al
in|ves|ti|ga|tive
in|ves|ti|ga|tor +s
in|ves|ti|ga|tory
in|ves|ti|ture +s
in|vest|ment +s
in|vest|or +s
in|vet|er|acy
  in|vet|er|acies
in|vet|er|ate
in|vet|er|ate|ly
in|vidi|ous
in|vidi|ous|ly
in|vidi|ous|ness
in|vigi|late
  in|vigi|lates
  in|vigi|lated
  in|vigi|lat|ing
in|vigi|la|tion +s
in|vigi|la|tor +s
in|vig|or|ate
  in|vig|or|ates
  in|vig|or|ated
  in|vig|or|at|ing
in|vig|or|at|ing|ly
in|vig|or|ation +s
in|vig|ora|tive
in|vig|or|ator +s
in|vin|ci|bil|ity
in|vin|cible +s
in|vin|cible|ness
in|vin|cibly
in|viol|abil|ity
in|viol|able
in|viol|ably
in|viol|acy
in|viol|ate
in|viol|ate|ly
in|viol|ate|ness
in|visi|bil|ity
in|vis|ible +s
in|vis|ible|ness
in|vis|ibly
in|vi|ta|tion +s
in|vi|ta|tion|al +s
in|vi|ta|tory
in|vite
  in|vites
  in|vited
  in|vit|ing

in|vitee +s
in|viter +s
in|vit|ing|ly
in|vit|ing|ness
in vitro adverbial
  and attributive
in vivo
in|voc|able
in|vo|ca|tion +s
in|vo|ca|tory
in|voice
  in|voices
  in|voiced
  in|voi|cing
in|voke
  in|vokes
  in|voked
  in|vok|ing
in|voker +s
in|vo|luc|ral
in|vo|lucre +s
in|vol|un|tar|ily
in|vol|un|tari|ness
in|vol|un|tary
in|vo|lute +s
in|vo|luted
in|vo|lu|tion +s
in|vo|lu|tion|al
in|volve
  in|volves
  in|volved
  in|volv|ing
in|volve|ment +s
in|vul|ner|abil|ity
in|vul|ner|able
in|vul|ner|ably
in|ward
inward-looking
in|ward|ly
in|ward|ness
in|wards
in|weave
  in|weaves
  in|wove
  in|weav|ing
  in|woven
in|wrap (use
  enwrap)
  in|wraps
  in|wrapped
  in|wrap|ping
in|wreathe (use
  enwreathe)
  in|wreathes
  in|wreathed
  in|wreath|ing
in|wrought
in-your-face
  adjective
Io (*Greek Mythology*;
  moon of Jupiter)
iod|ate +s

iodic
iod|ide +s
iod|in|ate
  iod|in|ates
  iod|in|ated
  iod|in|at|ing
iod|in|ation
iod|ine
iod|in|ise *Br.* (use
  iodinize)
  iod|in|ises
  iod|in|ised
  iod|in|is|ing
iod|in|ize
  iod|in|izes
  iod|in|ized
  iod|in|iz|ing
iod|isa|tion *Br.*
  (use iodization)
iod|ise *Br.* (use
  iodize)
  iod|ises
  iod|ised
  iod|is|ing
iod|ism +s
iod|iza|tion
iod|ize
  iod|izes
  iod|ized
  iod|iz|ing
iodo|form
ion +s (charged
  molecule etc.
  △ iron)
Iona (Scottish
  island; name)
Ion|esco, Eu|gene
  (Romanian-born
  French dramatist)
Ionia (ancient
  region, Asia
  Minor)
Ion|ian +s
Ion|ian Is|lands
  (off W. Greece)
Ion|ian mode
  Music
Ion|ian Sea (part of
  Mediterranean)
Ionic +s
  (architectural
  order; Greek
  dialect)
ionic (of ions)
ion|ic|al|ly
ion|is|able *Br.* (use
  ionizable)
ion|isa|tion *Br.*
  (use ionization)
ion|ise *Br.* (use
  ionize)
  ion|ises

ion|ise (*cont.*)
  ion|ised
  ion|is|ing
ion|iser *Br.* +s (use
  ionizer)
ion|ium
ion|iz|able
ion|iza|tion
ion|ize
  ion|izes
  ion|ized
  ion|iz|ing
ion|izer +s
iono|sphere
iono|spher|ic
Ios (Greek island.
  △ Eos)
iota +s
Iowa (state, USA)
Iowa City (in USA)
Ipati|eff, Vlad|imir
  Ni|ko|lai|ev|ich
  (Russian-born
  American
  chemist)
ipe|cac +s
ipe|cacu|anha +s
Iphi|ge|nia *Greek
  Mythology*
Ipoh (city,
  Malaysia)
ipo|moea +s
ipse dixit
ip|si|lat|eral
ip|sis|sima verba
ipso facto
Ips|wich (town,
  England)
Iqbal,
  Mu|ham|mad
  (Indian poet and
  philosopher)
Iqui|tos (port,
  Peru)
Ira
irade +s
Iran
Iran-Contra
  attributive
Iran|gate (US
  political scandal)
Iran|ian +s
Iraq
Iraqi +s
IRAS (= Infrared
  Astronomical
  Satellite)
iras|ci|bil|ity
iras|cible
iras|cibly
irate
ir|ate|ly

ir|ate|ness
ire (anger. △ ayah)
ire|ful
Ire|land
Ire|naeus (Greek
  saint)
Irene
iren|ic
iren|ic|al
iren|icon +s (use
  eirenicon)
Irgun (Zionist
  organization)
Irian Jaya
  (province,
  Indonesia)
iri|da|ceous
iri|des|cence +s
iri|des|cent
iri|des|cent|ly
irid|ium
iri|dolo|gist +s
iri|dol|ogy
Iris (*Greek
  Mythology*; name)
iris
  irises
  (flower)
Irish
Ir|ish|man
  Ir|ish|men
Ir|ish|ness
Ir|ish|woman
  Ir|ish|women
ir|itis
irk +s +ed +ing
  (irritate. △ erk)
irk|some
irk|some|ly
irk|some|ness
Ir|kutsk (city,
  Siberia)
Irma
iroko +s
iron +s +ed +ing
  (metal; tool;
  laundry
  implement; etc.
  △ ion)
Iron Age
iron|bark +s
iron-bound
iron|clad +s
iron|er +s
iron|ic
iron|ic|al
iron|ic|al|ly
iron|ing board +s
iron|ise *Br.* (use
  ironize)
  iron|ises

iron|ise (*cont.*)
iron|ised
iron|is|ing
iron|ist +s
iron|ize
iron|izes
iron|ized
iron|iz|ing
iron|less
iron-like
iron|mas|ter +s
iron-mold *Am.* +s
iron|mon|ger +s
iron|mon|gery
iron|mon|ger|ies
iron-mould *Br.* +s
iron-on *adjective*
Iron|side (Edmund II)
Iron|sides
(Cromwell's cavalry)
iron|stone +s
iron|ware
iron|work
iron|works
irony
iron|ies
(like iron; expression)
Iro|quoian +s
Iro|quois
plural Iro|quois
ir|radi|ance +s
ir|radi|ant
ir|radi|ate
ir|radi|ates
ir|radi|ated
ir|radi|at|ing
ir|radi|ation +s
ir|radia|tive
ir|ration|al
ir|ration|al|ise *Br.*
(use irrationalize)
ir|ration|al|ises
ir|ration|al|ised
ir|ration|al|is|ing
ir|ration|al|ity
ir|ration|al|ities
ir|ration|al|ize
ir|ration|al|izes
ir|ration|al|ized
ir|ration|al|iz|ing
ir|ration|al|ly
Ir|ra|waddy (river, Burma)
ir|re|claim|able
ir|re|claim|ably
ir|re|con|cil|
abil|ity
ir|re|con|cil|able

ir|re|con|cil|able|
ness
ir|re|con|cil|ably
ir|re|cov|er|able
ir|re|cov|er|ably
ir|re|cus|able
ir|re|deem|abil|ity
ir|re|deem|able
ir|re|deem|ably
ir|re|den|tism
Ir|re|den|tist +s
(Italian nationalist)
ir|re|den|tist +s
(generally)
ir|re|du|ci|bil|ity
ir|re|du|cible
ir|re|du|cibly
ir|ref|rag|able
ir|ref|rag|ably
ir|re|fran|gible
ir|re|fut|abil|ity
ir|re|fut|able
ir|re|fut|ably
ir|re|gard|less
ir|regu|lar +s
ir|regu|lar|ity
ir|regu|lar|ities
ir|regu|lar|ly
ir|rela|tive
ir|rela|tive|ly
ir|rele|vance +s
ir|rele|vancy
ir|rele|van|cies
ir|rele|vant
ir|rele|vant|ly
ir|re|li|gion
ir|re|li|gion|ist +s
ir|re|li|gious
ir|re|li|gious|ly
ir|re|li|gious|ness
ir|re|me|di|able
ir|re|me|di|ably
ir|re|mis|sible
ir|re|mis|sibly
ir|re|mov|abil|ity
ir|re|mov|
abil|ities
ir|re|mov|able
ir|re|mov|ably
ir|rep|ar|abil|ity
ir|rep|ar|able
ir|rep|ar|able|ness
ir|rep|ar|ably
ir|re|place|able
ir|re|place|ably
ir|re|press|ibil|ity
ir|re|press|ible
ir|re|press|ible|
ness
ir|re|press|ibly

ir|re|proach|
abil|ity
ir|re|proach|able
ir|re|proach|able|
ness
ir|re|proach|ably
ir|re|sist|ibil|ity
ir|re|sist|ible
ir|re|sist|ible|ness
ir|re|sist|ibly
ir|reso|lute
ir|reso|lute|ly
ir|reso|lute|ness
ir|reso|lu|tion +s
ir|re|solv|able
ir|re|spect|ive
ir|re|spect|ive|ly
ir|re|spon|si|bil|ity
ir|re|spon|sible
ir|re|spon|sibly
ir|re|spon|sive
ir|re|spon|sive|ly
ir|re|spon|sive|
ness
ir|re|ten|tive
ir|re|triev|abil|ity
ir|re|triev|able
ir|re|triev|ably
ir|rev|er|ence
ir|rev|er|ent
ir|rev|er|en|tial
ir|rev|er|ent|ly
ir|re|ver|si|bil|ity
ir|re|vers|ible
ir|re|vers|ibly
ir|rev|oc|abil|ity
ir|rev|oc|able
ir|rev|oc|ably
ir|rig|able
ir|ri|gate
ir|ri|gates
ir|ri|gated
ir|ri|gat|ing
ir|ri|ga|tion +s
ir|ri|ga|tive
ir|ri|ga|tor +s
ir|rit|abil|ity
ir|rit|able
ir|rit|ably
ir|ri|tancy
ir|ri|tant +s
ir|ri|tate
ir|ri|tates
ir|ri|tated
ir|ri|tat|ing
ir|ri|tated|ly
ir|ri|tat|ing|ly
ir|ri|ta|tion +s
ir|ri|ta|tive
ir|ri|ta|tor +s

ir|rupt +s +ed +ing
(enter forcibly.
△ erupt)
ir|rup|tion +s
(forcible entry.
△ eruption)
Ir|tysh (river, central Asia)
Irv|ing (name)
Irv|ing, Henry
(English actor-manager)
Irv|ing, Wash|ing|ton
(American writer)
Irv|ing|ite +s
(member of Catholic Apostolic Church)
is
Isaac (*Bible*; name)
Isa|bel *also*
Isa|belle, Iso|bel
Isa|bella (Castilian queen; English queen consort)
Isa|belle *also*
Isa|bel, Iso|bel
isa|bel|line
Isa|dora
isa|gogic
isa|gogics
Isaiah (*Bible*; name)
isa|tin +s
is|chae|mia *Br.*
is|chae|mic *Br.*
is|che|mia *Am.*
is|che|mic *Am.*
Is|chia (Italian island)
is|chi|ad|ic
is|chial
is|chi|at|ic
is|chium
is|chia
Ise (city, Japan)
is|en|trop|ic
Is|eult (legendary beloved of Tristram)
Is|fa|han (city, Iran)
Ish|er|wood, Chris|to|pher
(English writer)
Ishi|guro, Kazuo
(Japanese-born British novelist)
Ish|mael *Bible*
Ish|mael|ite +s

Ish|tar *Babylonian
and Assyrian
Mythology*
Isi|dore (Greek
mathematician
and engineer;
name)
Isi|dore of Sev|ille
(Spanish saint)
is|in|glass
Isis *Egyptian
Mythology*
Is|ken|de|run (port,
Turkey)
Isla
Islam
Is|lama|bad
(capital of
Pakistan)
Is|lam|ic
Is|lam|isa|tion *Br.*
(use Islamization)
Is|lam|ise *Br.* (use
Islamize)
Is|lam|ises
Is|lam|ised
Is|lam|is|ing
Is|lam|ism
Is|lam|ist +s
Is|lam|ite +s
Is|lam|it|ic
Is|lam|iza|tion
Is|lam|ize
Is|lam|izes
Is|lam|ized
Is|lam|iz|ing
Is|land (Icelandic
name for **Iceland**)
is|land +s (land
surrounded by
water; etc.)
is|land|er +s
island-hop
island-hops
island-hopped
island-hopping
Islay (Scottish
island)
isle +s (island.
△ aisle, I'll)
Isle of Man (in
Irish Sea)
Isle of Wight
(English island)
islet +s
**is|lets of
Lang|er|hans**
ism +s
Is|maili +s
isn't (= is not)
iso|bar +s
iso|bar|ic

Iso|bel *also* Isa|bel,
Isa|belle
iso|cheim +s
iso|chro|mat|ic
isoch|ron|ous
isoch|ron|ous|ly
iso|clinal
iso|clin|ic
isoc|racy
iso|cra|cies
Isoc|ra|tes
(Athenian orator)
iso|crat|ic
iso|cyan|ate +s
iso|cyan|ic
iso|cyc|lic
iso|dy|nam|ic
iso|elec|tric
iso|en|zyme +s
isog|amy
iso|geo|therm +s
iso|geo|ther|mal
iso|gloss
iso|glosses
iso|gon|ic
iso|hel +s
iso|hyet +s
iso|kin|et|ic
isol|able
isol|at|able
isol|ate
isol|ates
isol|ated
isol|at|ing
isol|ation +s
isol|ation|ism
isol|ation|ist +s
isola|tive
isol|ator +s
Is|olde
iso|leu|cine +s
iso|mer +s
iso|mer|ic
isom|er|ise *Br.* (use
isomerize)
isom|er|ises
isom|er|ised
isom|er|is|ing
isom|er|ism
isom|er|ize
isom|er|izes
isom|er|ized
isom|er|iz|ing
isom|er|ous
iso|met|ric
iso|met|ric|al|ly
iso|met|rics
isom|etry
iso|morph +s
iso|morph|ic
iso|morph|ism
iso|morph|ous

ison|omy
iso|phote +s
iso|pod +s
isos|celes
iso|seis|mal
iso|seis|mic
isos|tasy
iso|stat|ic
iso|there +s
iso|therm +s
iso|ther|mal
iso|ther|mal|ly
iso|ton|ic
iso|ton|ic|al|ly
iso|ton|icity
iso|tope +s
iso|top|ic
iso|top|ic|al|ly
isot|opy
iso|trop|ic
iso|trop|ic|al|ly
isot|ropy
Is|pa|han (use
Isfahan)
I-spy
Is|rael
Is|raeli +s
Is|rael|ite +s
Is|ra|fel (Muslim
angel)
Issa +s
Is|sa|char *Bible*
Is|si|gonis, Alec
(British engineer
and car designer)
is|su|able
is|su|ance
is|su|ant *Heraldry*
issue
issues
is|sued
is|su|ing
is|sue|less
is|suer +s
Is|tan|bul (port,
Turkey)
Isth|mian (of the
Isthmus of
Corinth)
isth|mian (of an
isthmus)
isth|mus
isth|muses *or*
isthmi
istle +s
Is|tria (peninsula in
Adriatic Sea)
Is|trian +s
it
Itaipu (dam, Brazil)
Ital|ian +s

Ital|ian|ate
Ital|ic (of Italy)
ital|ic +s (sloping
type)
itali|cisa|tion *Br.*
+s (use
italicization)
itali|cise *Br.* (use
italicize)
itali|cises
itali|cised
itali|cis|ing
itali|ciza|tion +s
itali|cize
itali|cizes
itali|cized
itali|ciz|ing
Ital|iot +s
Italy
Ita|nagar (city,
India)
ITAR-Tass
(Russian news
agency)
itch
itches
itched
itch|ing
itchi|ness
itch|ing pow|der
+s
itch-mite +s
itchy
itch|ier
itchi|est
it'd (= it had; it
would)
item +s
item|isa|tion *Br.*
(use itemization)
item|ise *Br.* (use
itemize)
item|ises
item|ised
item|is|ing
item|iser *Br.* +s
(use itemizer)
item|iza|tion
item|ize
item|izes
item|ized
item|iz|ing
item|izer +s
it|er|ance +s
it|er|ancy
it|er|ate
it|er|ates
it|er|ated
it|er|at|ing
it|er|ation +s
it|era|tive
it|era|tive|ly

Ith¦aca (Greek
island)
ithy|phal¦lic
it|in¦er|acy
it|in¦er|ancy
it|in¦er|ant +s
it|in¦er|ary
  it|in¦er|ar¦ies
it|in¦er|ate
  it|in¦er|ates
  it|in¦er|ated
  it|in¦er|at¦ing
itin|er|ation +s
it'll (= it will; it
  shall)
Ito, Prince
  Hiro|bumi
  (Japanese
  statesman)
its (of it)
it's (= it is)
it¦self
itsy-bitsy
itty-bitty
IUPAC
  (= International
  Union of Pure and
  Applied
  Chemistry)
Ivan also Ivon
  (name)
Ivan (rulers of
  Russia)
I've (= I have)
Ives, Charles
  (American
  composer)
ivied
Ivon also Ivan
Ivor also Ifor
ivor|ied
Ivory, James
  (American film
  director)
ivory
  iv¦or|ies
Ivory Coast
  (country, W.
  Africa)
ivory-nut +s
Ivy (name)
ivy
  ivies
  (plant)
Iwo Jima (island,
  NW Pacific)
ixia +s
Ixion Greek
  Mythology
Iyyar (Jewish
  month)
izard +s

Izh¦evsk (city,
  Russia)
Izmir (port, W.
  Turkey)
Izmit (city, NW
  Turkey)
Iznik (town,
  Turkey)
Iz¦ves¦tia (Russian
  newspaper)

Jj

jab
  jabs
  jabbed
  jab|bing
Jab¦al|pur (city,
  India)
jab¦ber +s +ed
  +ing
jab¦ber|wock +s
jab¦ber|wocky
  jab¦ber|wockies
jab¦iru +s
jabo|randi +s
jabot +s
jaca|mar +s
jac¦ana +s
jaca|randa +s
ja¦cinth +s
Jack (name)
jack +s +ed +ing
  (lifting device;
  card; flag; ball;
  etc.)
jackal +s
jacka|napes
  plural jacka|napes
jack|aroo +s
jack|ass
  jack|asses
jack|boot +s
jack|boot¦ed
Jack-by-the-
  hedge
jack|daw +s
jack|eroo +s (use
  jackaroo)
jacket +s +ed +ing
jack|fish
  plural jack|fish
Jack Frost
jack|fruit
  plural jack|fruit
jack|ham¦mer +s
Jackie also Jacqui,
  Jacky
jack-in-office
  jacks-in-office
jack-in-the-box
  jack-in-the-boxes
Jack-in-the-pulpit
jack|knife
  jack|knives
  noun
jack|knife
  jack|knifes
  jack|knifed
  jack|knif¦ing
  verb

jack of all trades
  jacks of all trades
jack-o'-lantern +s
jack plane +s
jack plug +s
jack|pot +s
jack|rab¦bit +s
Jack Rus|sell +s
  (terrier)
jack snipe
  plural jack snipe
jack socket +s
Jack|son, An¦drew
  (American
  president)
Jack|son, Glenda
  (English actress
  and politician)
Jack|son, Jesse
  (American
  politician and
  clergyman)
Jack|son,
  Mi¦chael
  (American singer)
Jack|son,
  Stone|wall
  (American
  general)
Jack|son|ville
  (city, USA)
jack|staff +s
jack|stone +s
jack|straw +s
Jack tar +s
Jack the lad
Jack the Rip¦per
  (English
  murderer)
Jacky also Jackie,
  Jacqui
  (name)
Jacky
  Jack|ies
  (offensive Australian
  Aborigine)
Jacob (Bible; name)
Jaco|bean +s
Ja¦cobi, Karl
  Gus¦tav Jacob
  (German
  mathematician)
Jaco|bin +s
  (extreme radical;
  friar)
jaco|bin +s
  (pigeon)
Jaco|bin¦ic
Jaco|bin|ic¦al
Jaco|bin|ism
Jac¦ob|ite +s
Jaco|bit|ic¦al
Jaco|bit|ism

Ja¦cobs, W. W.
(English writer)
Jacob's lad¦der +s
Jacob's staff +s
jaco|net +s
Ja¦copo della
  Quer¦cia (Italian
  sculptor)
jac¦quard +s
Jacque|line also
  Jacque|lyn
Jacque|lyn also
  Jacque|line
Jac¦quetta
Jac¦qui also Jackie,
  Jacky
jacti|ta¦tion +s
ja|cuzzi +s Propr.
Jade (name)
jade +s (stone;
  horse; woman)
jaded
jaded¦ly
jaded|ness
jade|ite +s
j'adoube
jae¦ger +s
Jaffa +s (city,
  Israel; orange)
Jaffna (district and
  city, Sri Lanka)
jag
  jags
  jagged
  jag|ging
Jag|an|na¦tha
  Hinduism
jag|ged¦ly
jag|ged|ness
Jag¦ger, Mick
  (English singer)
jag¦ger +s (thing
  that jags; ship)
jaggy
  jag|gier
  jag|gi|est
Jago
jag¦uar +s
jag¦uar|undi +s
Jah¦veh (use
  Yahweh)
jai alai
jail +s +ed +ing
jail|bait
jail|bird +s
jail|break +s
jail¦er +s
jail|house +s
Jain +s (adherent
  of Jainism.
  △ Jane, Jayne)
Jain|ism

Jain|ist +s
Jai¦pur (city, India)
Ja|karta (use
  Djakarta)
Jake (name)
jake (all right)
Ja¦kob|son,
  Roman (Russian-
  born American
  linguist)
Jal|ala|bad (city,
  Afghanistan)
Jalal ad-Din ar-
  Rumi (founder of
  whirling
  dervishes)
Jal|an|dhar (use
  Jullundur)
jalap
Jal¦apa
  (En¦ri|quez) (city,
  Mexico)
jala|peño +s
Jal|isco (state,
  Mexico)
jal¦opy
  jal|op¦ies
jal|ou|sie +s
jam
  jams
  jammed
  jam|ming
  (squeeze; block;
  food; etc. △ jamb)
Ja|maica
Ja|mai¦can +s
jamb +s (part of
  door frame.
  △ jam)
jam|ba|laya
jam|be¦roo +s
jam|bo|ree +s
James (Scottish
  and English kings)
James, C. L. R.
  (Trinidadian
  writer)
James, Henry
  (American writer)
James, Jesse
  (American outlaw)
James, P. D.
  (English writer)
James, Wil|liam
  (American
  philosopher)
James Bay (in
  Canada)
Jame|son Raid (in
  South Africa)
James|town
  (former

James|town (cont.)
  settlement, USA;
  capital of St
  Helena)
Jamie
jam jar +s
jam¦mer +s
Jammu (city, India)
Jammu and
  Kash|mir (state,
  India)
jammy
  jam|mier
  jam|mi|est
Jam|nagar (city,
  India)
jam-packed
jam pot +s
Jam¦shed|pur
  (city, India)
Jam|shid
  (legendary Persian
  king)
Jan
Janá¦ček, Leoš
  (Czech composer)
Jan¦cis
Jane also Jayne
  (name. △ Jain)
jane +s (woman)
JANET (= Joint
  Academic
  Network)
Janet (name)
Jan|ette also
  Gen|ette,
  Jean|ette,
  Jean|nette
Janey also Janie
jan|gle
  jan|gles
  jan|gled
  jan|gling
Jang|lish (use
  Japlish)
Jan|ice also Janis
Jan|ine
Janis also Jan|ice
jan|is|sary (use
  janizary)
jan|is|sar¦ies
jani|tor +s
jani|tor|ial
jani|zary
  jani|zar|ies
jank|ers
Jan Mayen (island,
  Arctic Ocean)
Jan|sen,
  Cor|ne¦lius
  (Dutch
  theologian)

Jan¦sen|ism
Jan¦sen|ist +s
Jan|sens,
  Cor|ne¦lius
  (Dutch painter;
  use Johnson)
Janu|ary
  Janu|ar¦ies
Janus (Roman
  Mythology; moon
  of Saturn)
Jap +s offensive
Japan
japan
  ja¦pans
  ja|panned
  ja|pan|ning
Jap|an|ese
  plural Jap|an|ese
jape
  japes
  japed
  jap|ing
jap¦ery
  jap¦er|ies
Ja|pheth Bible
Ja|phet¦ic
Jap|lish
ja|pon|ica +s
Jaques-Dalcroze,
  Émile (Swiss
  music teacher)
jar
  jars
  jarred
  jar|ring
jar¦di|nière +s
jar¦ful +s
jar¦gon +s
  (language; stone)
jar¦gon|elle +s
jar¦gon|ise Br. (use
  jargonize)
jar¦gon|ises
jar¦gon|ised
jar¦gon|is¦ing
jar¦gon|is¦tic
jar¦gon|ize
jar¦gon|izes
jar¦gon|ized
jar¦gon|iz¦ing
jar¦goon +s
jarl +s
jar¦rah +s
Jar¦row (town,
  England)
Jarry, Al¦fred
  (French dramatist)
Jaru|zel¦ski,
  Woj|ciech (Polish
  general and
  statesman)

Jas¦min *also*
Jas¦mine
(name)
jas¦min +s (plant;
use jasmine)
Jas¦mine *also*
Jas¦min
(name)
jas¦mine +s (plant)
Jason (*Greek
Mythology*; name)
jaspé
Jas¦per (name)
jas¦per +s (stone)
Jassy (German
name for Iaşi)
Jat +s
Jat¦aka +s
jato +s (= jet-
assisted take-off)
jaun¦dice
jaun¦dices
jaun¦diced
jaun¦dicing
jaunt +s +ed +ing
jaunt¦ily
jaunti¦ness
jaunt¦ing car +s
jaunty
jaunt¦ier
jaunti¦est
Java (island,
Indonesia)
Java Man
Javan +s
Ja¦van¦ese
plural Ja¦van¦ese
jav¦elin +s
Jav¦elle water
jaw +s +ed +ing
jaw¦bone +s
jaw-breaker +s
jaw-jaw +s +ed
+ing
jaw¦line +s
Jay (name)
jay +s (bird)
Jayne *also* Jane
(name. △ Jain)
jay¦walk +s +ed
+ing
jay¦walk¦er +s
jazz
jazzes
jazzed
jazz¦ing
Jazz Age
(American 1920s)
jazz¦er +s
jazz¦ily
jazzi¦ness

jazz¦man
jazz¦men
jazzy
jazz¦ier
jazzi¦est
J-cloth +s *Propr.*
jeal¦ous
jeal¦ous¦ly
jeal¦ousy
jeal¦ousies
Jean (woman's
name. △ Gene)
jean (cloth. △ gene)
Jean¦ette *also*
Gen¦ette,
Jan¦ette,
Jean¦nette
Jeanie *also*
Jean¦nie
Jean¦ne¦ret,
Charles
Édou¦ard (= Le
Corbusier)
Jean¦nette *also*
Gen¦ette,
Jan¦ette,
Jean¦ette
Jean¦nie *also*
Jeanie
Jean Paul (German
novelist)
Jeans, James
Hop¦wood
(English physicist)
jeans (trousers.
△ genes)
Jed¦burgh (town,
Scotland)
Jed¦dah (= Jiddah)
jeep +s *Propr.*
jee¦pers
jeer +s +ed +ing
jeer¦ing¦ly
Jeeves, Regi¦nald
(in P. G.
Wodehouse
novels)
Jeez *interjection*
Jeff *also* Geoff
Jef¦feries,
Rich¦ard (English
writer)
Jef¦fer¦son,
Thomas
(American
president)
Jef¦fer¦son City
(town, USA)
Jef¦frey *also*
Geof¦frey
Jef¦freys, George
(Welsh judge)

jehad (use jihad)
Je¦hosha¦phat
Je¦ho¦vah
Je¦ho¦vah's
Wit¦ness
Je¦ho¦vah's
Wit¦nesses
Je¦hov¦ist +s
Jehu *Bible*
je¦june
je¦june¦ly
je¦june¦ness
je¦junum +s
Je¦kyll, Ger¦trude
(British gardener)
Jek¦yll and Hyde
jell +s +ed +ing
(set as jelly. △ gel)
jel¦laba +s (use
djellaba)
Jel¦li¦coe, Earl
(British admiral)
jel¦li¦fi¦ca¦tion
jel¦lify
jel¦li¦fies
jel¦li¦fied
jel¦li¦fy¦ing
Jell-O +s *Propr.*
jello +s
jelly
jel¦lies
jel¦lied
jelly¦ing
(confection; set as
jelly. △ gelly)
jelly baby
jelly babies
jelly bean +s
jel¦ly¦fish
plural jel¦ly¦fish *or*
jel¦ly¦fishes
jelly-like
Jem
Jem¦ima
Jemma *also*
Gemma
jemmy
jem¦mies
jem¦mied
jemmy¦ing
(crowbar; force
open. △ gemmy)
Jena (town,
Germany)
je ne sais quoi
Jeni¦fer *also*
Jen¦ni¦fer
Jen¦kins's Ear,
War of (Anglo-
Spanish war)
Jenna

Jen¦ner, Ed¦ward
(English
physician)
jen¦net +s (horse.
△ genet)
Jen¦ni¦fer *also*
Jeni¦fer
Jenny *also* Jen¦nie
(name)
jenny
jen¦nies
(spinning-jenny;
female donkey;
crane)
jenny-wren +s
jeon
plural jeon
(South Korean
currency)
jeop¦ard¦ise *Br.*
(use jeopardize)
jeop¦ard¦ises
jeop¦ard¦ised
jeop¦ard¦is¦ing
jeop¦ard¦ize
jeop¦ard¦izes
jeop¦ard¦ized
jeop¦ard¦iz¦ing
jeop¦ardy
Jeph¦thah *Bible*
je¦quir¦ity
je¦quir¦ities
Jerba (use Djerba)
jer¦bil +s (use
gerbil)
jer¦boa +s
jere¦miad +s
Jere¦miah +s
(*Bible*; pessimistic
person)
Jer¦emy
Jerez (de la
Fron¦tera) (town,
Spain)
Jeri¦cho (town,
Israel)
jerk +s +ed +ing
jerk¦er +s
jerk¦ily
jer¦kin +s
jerki¦ness
jerky
jerk¦ier
jerki¦est
jero¦boam +s
Je¦rome
Je¦rome
(Dalmatian-born
saint)
Je¦rome, Je¦rome
K. (English writer)

Jerry
Jer|ries
(*offensive* German;
name)
jerry
jer|ries
(chamber pot)
jerry-builder+s
jerry-building
jerry-built
jer|ry|can+s
jer|ry|man|der+s
+ed +ing (use
gerrymander)
Jer|sey+s
(Channel Island;
cattle)
jer|sey+s
(garment)
Jer|sey City (in
USA)
Je|ru|sa|lem
(capital of Israel;
artichoke)
Jer|vis, John (Earl
St Vincent, British
admiral)
Jes|per|sen, Otto
(Danish
philologist)
Jess (name)
jess
jesses
jessed
jess|ing
(strap on a hawk's
leg)
jes|sa|min+s
(= jasmine)
jes|sa|mine+s
(= jasmine)
Jesse (*Bible*; name.
△ Jessie)
Jesse win|dow+s
Jes|sica
Jes|sie (name
△ Jesse)
jest+s +ed +ing
jest|er+s
jest|ful
Jesu
Jes|uit+s
Jesu|it|ic|al
Jesu|it|ic|al|ly
Jesus (Christ)
JET (= Joint
European Torus)
jet
jets
jet|ted
jet|ting

jet (*cont.*)
(stream; engine;
stone)
jet black *noun and
adjective*
jet-black *attributive*
jeté+s
Jet|foil *Am.* +s
Propr.
jet|foil *Br.* +s
Jethro
jet lag
jet-lagged
jet-propelled
jet|sam
jet set
jet-setter+s
jet-setting
jet ski+s *noun
Propr.*
jet-ski+s +ed +ing
verb
jet stream+s
jet|ti|son+s +ed
+ing
jet|ton+s
jetty
jet|ties
jeu d'es|prit
jeux d'es|prit
jeunesse dorée
Jew+s
jewel
jewels
jew|elled *Br.*
jew|eled *Am.*
jew|el|ling *Br.*
jew|el|ing *Am.*
jew|el|er *Am.* +s
jewel-fish
plural jewel-fish *or*
jewel-fishes
jew|el|ler *Br.* +s
jew|el|ler's rouge
jew|el|lery *Br.* (*Am.*
jewelry)
jewel-like
jew|el|ly
jew|el|ry *Am.* (*Br.*
jewellery)
Jew|ess
Jew|esses
jew|fish
plural jew|fish *or*
jew|fishes
Jew|ish
Jew|ish|ly
Jew|ish|ness
Jewry (Jews.
△ jury)
Jew's ear+s
(fungus)

jew's harp+s
jez|ail+s
Jez|ebel+s (*Bible*;
shameless
woman)
Jhansi (city, India)
Jhe|lum (river, S.
Asia)
Jiang Jie Shi (=
Chiang Kai-shek)
Jiangsu (province,
China)
Jiangxi (province,
China)
jib
jibs
jibbed
jib|bing
(sail; crane arm;
to baulk. △ gib)
jibba+s (Muslim's
coat. △ gibber,
jibber)
jib|bah+s (use
jibba)
jib|ber+s (person
who jibs.
△ gibber, jibba)
jib-boom+s
jibe (taunt; use
gibe △ gybe)
jibes
jibed
jib|ing
jibe *Am.*
jibes
jibed
jib|ing
(*Sailing. Br.* gybe
△ gibe)
jibe
jibes
jibed
jib|ing
(agree. △ gibe,
gybe)
jib sheet+s
Jib|uti (use
Djibouti)
JICTAR (= Joint
Industry
Committee for
Television
Advertising and
Research)
Jid|dah (city, Saudi
Arabia)
jiff+s
jiffy
jif|fies
Jiffy bag+s *Propr.*

jig
jigs
jigged
jig|ging
jig|ger+s +ed +ing
jiggery-pokery
jig|gle
jig|gles
jig|gled
jig|gling
jig|gly
jig|saw+s
jig|saw puz|zle+s
jihad+s
Jilin (province,
China)
Jill (name)
jill+s (use gill)
jill|aroo+s
jill|eroo+s (use
jillaroo)
Jil|lian *also* Gil|lian
jilt+s +ed +ing
Jim
Jim Crow+s
(*offensive when
used of a person*)
Jim Crow|ism
**Ji|mé|nez de
Cis|neros**
(Spanish
inquisitor)
jim-jams
Jimmu (legendary
Japanese
emperor)
Jimmy (name)
jimmy
jim|mies
jim|mied
jimmy|ing
(jemmy)
jim|my|grant+s
Jimmy Wood|ser
+s
jim|son
jim|son weed+s
Jin (Chinese
dynasty)
Jina+s *Jainism*
Jinan (city, China)
jin|gle
jin|gles
jin|gled
jin|gling
jin|gly
jin|glier
jin|gli|est
jingo
jin|goes
jin|go|ism
jin|go|ist+s

jin¦go¦is¦tic
jink +s +ed +ing
jink¦er +s
jinn
    plural jinn or jinns
    (= jinnee. ⚠ gin)
Jin¦nah,
    Mu¦ham¦mad Ali
    (Indian, then
    Pakistani,
    statesman)
jin¦nee
    plural jin¦nee or
    jin¦nees
jinx
    jinxes
    jinxed
    jinx¦ing
ji¦pil¦japa +s (plant;
    hat)
jit¦ter +s +ed +ing
jit¦ter¦bug
    jit¦ter¦bugs
    jit¦ter¦bugged
    jit¦ter¦bug¦ging
jit¦teri¦ness
jit¦tery
jiu-jitsu (use ju-
    jitsu)
jive
    jives
    jived
    jiv¦ing
jiver +s
jizz
Jo also Joe
    (man's name)
Jo (woman's name)
jo
    joes
    (sweetheart)
Joa¦chim (saint;
    father of the Virgin
    Mary)
Joa¦chim, Jo¦seph
    (Hungarian
    violinist)
Joa¦chim
Joan
Joan, Pope
    (legendary female
    pope)
Jo¦anna
Jo¦anne
Joan of Arc
    (French saint)
João Pes¦soa (city,
    Brazil)
Job Bible
job
    jobs

job (cont.)
    jobbed
    job¦bing
job¦ber +s
job¦bery
job¦bie +s
job¦centre +s
job-control
    lan¦guage +s
job-hunt +s +ed
    +ing
job¦less
job¦less¦ness
job lot +s
Job's com¦fort¦er
    +s
job-share +s
job-sharer +s
job-sharing
job¦sheet +s
Job's tears
jobs¦worth +s
Joburg
    (= Johannesburg)
job¦work
Jo¦casta Greek
    Mythology
Joce¦lyn also
    Josce¦line
Jock +s (name;
    Scotsman)
jock +s (jockey)
jockey +s +ed
    +ing
jockey¦dom
jockey¦ship
jock¦strap +s
joc¦ose
joc¦ose¦ly
joc¦ose¦ness
joc¦os¦ity
    joc¦os¦ities
jocu¦lar
jocu¦lar¦ity
jocu¦lar¦ly
joc¦und
joc¦und¦ity
joc¦und¦ly
Jodh¦pur (city,
    India)
jodh¦purs
    (garment)
Jodie also Jody
Jod¦rell Bank (site
    of radio telescope,
    England)
Jody also Jodie
Joe also Jo
    (man's name)
Joe Bloggs
Joe Blow
Joel Bible

joey +s
Joffre, Jo¦seph
    (French marshal)
jog
    jogs
    jogged
    jog¦ging
jog¦ger +s
jog¦gle
    jog¦gles
    jog¦gled
    jog¦gling
Jog¦ja¦karta (=
    Yogyakarta)
jog-shuttle
    attributive
jog¦trot
    jog¦trots
    jog¦trot¦ted
    jog¦trot¦ting
Jo¦hanna
Jo¦han¦nes¦burg
    (city, South
    Africa)
John also Jon
    (name)
John (English and
    Portuguese kings)
John (Apostle and
    saint)
John, Aug¦us¦tus
    (British painter)
John, Barry
    (Welsh rugby
    player)
John, Don
    (Spanish general)
John, Elton
    (English singer
    and songwriter)
John, Gwen
    (British painter)
john +s (lavatory)
Johna¦than also
    Jona¦than,
    Jona¦thon
    (name.
    ⚠ Jonathan)
John Bull (typical
    Englishman)
John Chrys¦ostom
    (early saint)
John Doe +s
John Dory
    John Dories
John Hop +s
John Lack¦land
    (English king)
Johnny (name)
johnny
    john¦nies
    (fellow)

johnny-come-
    lately +s
John of Gaunt
    (son of Edward III
    of England)
John o'Groats
    (village, Scotland)
Johns, Jas¦per
    (American artist)
John Sob¦ieski
    (Polish king)
John¦son, Amy
    (English aviator)
John¦son,
    An¦drew
    (American
    president)
John¦son,
    Cor¦ne¦lius
    (English-born
    Dutch painter)
John¦son, Jack
    (American boxer)
John¦son, Lyn¦don
    Baines (American
    president)
John¦son, Sam¦uel
    ('Dr Johnson',
    English writer and
    lexicographer)
John¦son¦ian
Johor (state,
    Malaysia)
Johor Ba¦haru
    (city, Malaysia)
Jo¦hore (use
    Johor)
joie de vivre
join +s +ed +ing
join¦able
join¦der
join¦er +s
join¦ery
joint +s +ed +ing
joint¦ed¦ly
joint¦ed¦ness
joint¦er +s
joint¦less
joint¦ly
joint¦ress
    joint¦resses
joint-stock
    attributive
join¦ture
    join¦tures
    join¦tured
    join¦tur¦ing
joist +s +ed +ing
jo¦joba +s
joke
    jokes

joke (*cont.*)
  joked
  jok|ing
joker +s
joke|smith +s
jokey
  joki|er
  joki|est
joki|ly
joki|ness
jok|ing|ly
joky (use jokey)
  jok|ier
  jok|iest
Jo|lene
jolie laide
  jolies laides
Jol|iot, Jean-
  Frédéric (French
  nuclear physicist)
jol|li|fi|ca|tion +s
jol|lify
  jol|li|fies
  jol|li|fied
  jol|li|fy|ing
jol|lily
jol|li|ness
jol|lity
  jol|lities
jollo +s
jolly
  jol|lies
  jol|lied
  jolly|ing
  jol|lier
  jol|li|est
Jolly Roger +s
Jol|son, Al
  (American singer
  and actor)
jolt +s +ed +ing
jolty
  jolt|ier
  jolti|est
Jo|lyon
Jomon
Jon *also* John
Jonah +s (*Bible*;
  bringer of bad
  luck)
Jona|than +s
  (*Bible*; apple)
Jona|than *also*
  Johna|than,
  Jona|thon
  (name)
Jona|thon *also*
  Johna|than,
  Jona|than
  (name)

Jones, Dan|iel
  (British
  phonetician)
Jones, Inigo
  (English architect)
Jones, John Paul
  (American
  admiral)
Jones, Bobby
  (American golfer)
Joneses, the
Jong, Erica
  (American writer)
jon|gleur +s
Jön|kö|ping (city,
  Sweden)
jon|quil +s
Jon|son, Ben
  (English
  dramatist)
Jop|lin, Scott
  (American
  musician)
Joppa (biblical
  name for Jaffa)
Jor|daens, Jacob
  (Flemish painter)
Jor|dan (country;
  river; name)
Jor|dan|ian +s
jorum +s
Jor|vik (Viking
  name for York)
Josce|line *also*
  Joce|lyn
Jo|seph (*Bible*;
  name)
Jo|seph (husband
  of the Virgin
  Mary; saint)
Jo|seph|ine
  (French empress;
  name)
Jo|seph of
  Ari|ma|thea
Jo|se|phus,
  Fla|vius (Jewish
  historian and
  general)
Josh (name)
josh
  joshes
  joshed
  josh|ing
  (joke; tease)
josh|er +s
Joshua *Bible*
Joshua tree +s
Jos|iah
Josie

Jos|quin des Prez
  (Flemish
  composer)
joss
  josses
joss|er +s
joss stick +s
jos|tle
  jos|tles
  jos|tled
  jost|ling
jot
  jots
  jot|ted
  jot|ting
jot|ter +s
Jotun
  (Scandinavian
  mythological
  giant)
Jotun|heim
  (mountain range,
  Norway)
Joule, James
  (English physicist)
joule +s (unit)
Joule–Thomson
  ef|fect
jounce
  jounces
  jounced
  joun|cing
jour|nal +s
jour|nal|ese
jour|nal|ise *Br.*
  (use journalize)
  jour|nal|ises
  jour|nal|ised
  jour|nal|is|ing
jour|nal|ism
jour|nal|ist +s
jour|nal|is|tic
jour|nal|is|tic|al|ly
jour|nal|ize
  jour|nal|izes
  jour|nal|ized
  jour|nal|iz|ing
jour|ney +s +ed
  +ing
jour|ney|er +s
jour|ney|man
  jour|ney|men
journo +s
joust +s +ed +ing
joust|er +s
Jove (*Roman
  Mythology*; in 'by
  Jove')
jo|vial
jovi|al|ity
jo|vial|ly

Jo|vian
jowar
jowl +s
jowly
Joy (name)
joy +s +ed +ing
  (great pleasure;
  rejoice)
Joyce (name)
Joyce, James
  (Irish writer)
Joy|cean
joy|ful
joy|ful|ly
joy|ful|ness
joy|less
joy|less|ly
joy|ous
joy|ous|ly
joy|ous|ness
joy|ride
  joy|rides
  joy|rode
  joy|rid|ing
  joy|rid|den
joy|rider +s
joy|stick +s
Juan Car|los
  (Spanish king)
Juan Fer|nan|dez
  Is|lands (off
  Chile)
Juá|rez, Ben|ito
  Pablo (Mexican
  president)
Juba (city, Sudan)
Jubba (river, E.
  Africa)
jube +s
ju|bi|lance
ju|bi|lant
ju|bi|lant|ly
ju|bi|late
  ju|bi|lates
  ju|bi|lated
  ju|bi|lat|ing
ju|bi|la|tion
ju|bi|lee +s
Ju|daea *Br.*
  (ancient region, S.
  Palestine. *Am.*
  Judea)
Ju|daean *Br.* +s
  (*Am.* Judean)
Judaeo-Christian
  Br. (*Am.* Judeo-
  Christian)
Judah (Hebrew
  patriarch; tribe;
  kingdom)
Ju|da|ic

Ju|da|ism
Ju|da|ist +s
Ju|da|iza|tion
Ju|da|ize
  Ju|da|izes
  Ju|da|ized
  Ju|da|iz|ing
Judas
  Ju|dases
  (traitor)
judas
  ju|dases
  (peep-hole)
Judas Is|car|iot
  (Apostle)
Judas
  Mac|ca|baeus
  (Jewish leader)
Judas tree +s
jud|der +s +ed
  +ing
Jude (Apostle and
  saint)
Judea *Am.* (ancient
  region, Palestine.
  Br. Judaea)
Ju|dean *Am.* +s
  (*Br.* Judaean)
Judeo-Christian
  Am. (*Br.* Judaeo-
  Christian)
judge
  judges
  judged
  judg|ing
Judge Ad|vo|cate
  Gen|eral +s
judge|like
judge|mat|ic
judge|mat|ic|al
judge|mat|ic|al|ly
judge|ment +s
judge|men|tal
judge|men|tal|ly
judgement-seat +s
judge|ship +s
judge's mar|shal
  +s
Judges' Rules
judg|ment +s (use
  judgement)
judg|men|tal (use
  judgemental)
judg|men|tal|ly
  (use
  judgementally)
judgment-seat +s
  (use judgement-
  seat)
Judi *also* Judy
ju|di|ca|ture +s
ju|di|cial

ju|di|cial|ly
ju|di|ciary
  ju|di|ciar|ies
ju|di|cious
ju|di|cious|ly
ju|di|cious|ness
Ju|dith (*Apocrypha*;
  name)
judo
judo|ist +s
ju|doka
  plural ju|doka *or*
  ju|dokas
Judy *also* Judi
  (name)
Judy
  Ju|dies
  (*slang* woman)
jug
  jugs
  jugged
  jug|ging
Ju|gend|stil
jug|ful +s
Jug|ger|naut +s
  (institution; idea;
  etc.)
jug|ger|naut +s
  (vehicle)
jug|gins
jug|gle
  jug|gles
  jug|gled
  jug|gling
jug|gler +s
jug|glery
  jug|gler|ies
Jugo|slav +s (use
  Yugoslav)
Jugo|slavia (use
  Yugoslavia)
Jugo|slav|ian +s
  (use Yugoslavian)
jugu|lar +s
jugu|late
  jugu|lates
  jugu|lated
  jugu|lat|ing
Ju|gur|tha
  (Numidian ruler)
juice
  juices
  juiced
  juicing
juice|less
juicer +s
juici|ly
juici|ness
juicy
  juici|er
  juici|est
ju-jitsu

ju-ju +s
ju|jube +s
ju-jutsu (use ju-
  jitsu)
juke|box
  juke|boxes
julep +s
Julia
Ju|lian (Roman
  emperor; name)
Ju|lian (of Julius
  Caesar)
Ju|lian Alps
  (mountain range,
  Italy and Slovenia)
Ju|lian cal|en|dar
Ju|lian of
  Nor|wich
  (English mystic)
Julie
ju|li|enne
  ju|li|ennes
  ju|li|enned
  ju|li|en|ning
Ju|liet
Ju|liet cap +s
Ju|lius
Ju|lius Cae|sar
  (Roman
  statesman)
Jul|lun|dur (city,
  India)
July +s
jum|ble
  jum|bles
  jum|bled
  jum|bling
jum|bly
  jum|blier
  jum|bli|est
jumbo +s
jumbo|ise *Br.* (use
  jumboize)
  jumbo|ises
  jumbo|ised
  jumbo|is|ing
jumbo|ize
  jumbo|izes
  jumbo|ized
  jumbo|iz|ing
jum|buck +s
Jumna (river,
  India)
jump +s +ed +ing
jump|able
jumped-up
  adjective
jump|er +s
jump|ily
jumpi|ness
jump|ing jack +s

jumping-off place
  +s
jumping-off point
  +s
jump jet +s
jump lead +s
jump-off +s *noun*
jump rope +s
jump seat +s
jump-start +s +ed
  +ing
jump|suit +s
jumpy
  jump|ier
  jumpi|est
jun
  plural jun
  (North Korean
  currency)
junco
  jun|cos *or*
  jun|coes
junc|tion +s
junc|ture +s
June +s (name;
  month)
Ju|neau (port,
  USA)
June bug +s
Jung, Carl
  Gus|tav (Swiss
  psychologist)
Jung|frau
  (mountain,
  Switzerland)
Jung|ian +s
jun|gle +s
jun|gled
jun|gly
  jun|glier
  jun|gli|est
jun|ior +s
jun|ior|ate +s
jun|ior|ity
ju|ni|per +s
junk +s +ed +ing
junk bond +s
jun|ker +s
jun|ker|dom
jun|ket +s +ed
  +ing
junk food +s
junkie +s
junk mail
junk shop +s
junk|yard +s
Juno (*Roman
  Mythology*;
  asteroid; D-Day
  beach)
Ju|no|esque
junta +s

Ju¦pi¦ter (*Roman Mythology*; planet)

Jura (mountain range, France and Switzerland; Scottish island)

jural

Jur¦as¦sic

jurat +s

jur¦id¦ic¦al

jur¦id¦ic¦al¦ly

juried

jur¦is¦con¦sult +s

jur¦is¦dic¦tion +s

jur¦is¦dic¦tion¦al

jur¦is¦pru¦dence

jur¦is¦pru¦dent

jur¦is¦pru¦den¦tial

jur¦ist +s

jur¦is¦tic

jur¦is¦tic¦al

juror +s

jury

  jur¦ies

  (in court.
  ⚠ Jewry)

jury box

  jury boxes

jury¦man

  jury¦men

jury-mast +s

jury-rigged

jury¦woman

  jury¦women

Jus¦sieu, An¦toine (French botanist)

jus¦sive

just

just¦ice +s

just¦ice¦ship

jus¦ti¦ciable

jus¦ti¦ciar

jus¦ti¦ciary

  jus¦ti¦ciar¦ies

jus¦ti¦fi¦abil¦ity

jus¦ti¦fi¦able

jus¦ti¦fi¦able¦ness

jus¦ti¦fi¦ably

jus¦ti¦fi¦ca¦tion +s

jus¦ti¦fi¦ca¦tory

jus¦ti¦fier +s

jus¦tify·

  jus¦ti¦fies

  jus¦ti¦fied

  jus¦ti¦fy¦ing

Jus¦tin *also*

  Jus¦tine
  (name)

Jus¦tin (early saint)

Jus¦tine *also*

  Jus¦tin

Jus¦tin¦ian (Roman emperor)

just-in-time
  attributive

just¦ly

just¦ness

jut

  juts

  jut¦ted

  jut¦ting

Jute +s (German tribe)

jute +s (fibre)

Jut¦ish

Jut¦land
  (peninsula, NW
  Europe)

Juv¦enal (Roman satirist)

ju¦ven¦es¦cence

ju¦ven¦es¦cent

ju¦ven¦ile +s

ju¦ven¦ile¦ly

ju¦ven¦ilia

ju¦ven¦il¦ity

juxta¦pose

  juxta¦poses

  juxta¦posed

  juxta¦pos¦ing

juxta¦pos¦ition +s

juxta¦pos¦ition¦al

Jy¦väs¦kylä (city, Finland)

Kk

ka +s (spirit. ⚠ car, carr)

Kaaba (in Mecca)

ka¦baddi

Kaba¦lega (national park, Uganda)

Kaba¦lega Falls (in Uganda)

Kabarda-Balkar

Kabardino-
Balkaria
  (republic, Russia)

Kab¦bala (*Judaism*; use Kabbalah)

kab¦bala (mystic interpretation; use cabbala)

Kab¦ba¦lah *Judaism*

Kab¦bal¦ism
  Judaism

kab¦bal¦ism
  (generally; use cabbalism)

Kab¦bal¦ist +s
  Judaism

kab¦bal¦ist +s
  (generally; use cabbalist)

Kab¦bal¦is¦tic
  Judaism

kab¦bal¦is¦tic
  (generally; use cabbalistic)

ka¦buki

Kabul (capital of Afghanistan)

Kabwe (town, Zambia)

Ka¦byle +s

ka¦china +s
  (dancer; doll)

ka¦dai¦tcha +s (use kurdaitcha)

Kádár, János
  (Hungarian prime
  minister)

Kad¦dish (Jewish prayer.
  ⚠ caddish)

kadi +s (use cadi)

Ka¦di¦köy (Turkish name for Chalcedon)

Kaf¦fir +s (people; language; *offensive* black person.
  ⚠ Kafir)

kaf¦fi¦yeh +s (use keffiyeh)

Kafir +s (native of Nuristan. ⚠ Kaffir)

Kafka, Franz
  (Czech-born
  novelist)

Kaf¦ka¦esque

kaf¦tan +s

Kago|shima (city, Japan)

kai (food)

Kai¦feng (city, China)

kail +s (use kale)

kail¦yard +s (use kaleyard)

kain¦ite

Kair¦ouan (city, Tunisia)

Kai¦ser, Georg
  (German
  dramatist)

kai¦ser +s

kai¦ser|ship +s

Kai¦sers¦lau¦tern
  (city, Germany)

kai¦zen

kaka +s

ka¦kapo +s

kake|mono +s

Ka¦laal¦lit Nu¦naat
  (Inuit name for
  Greenland)

kala-azar

Kala|hari (desert, Africa)

kal¦an¦choe +s

Ka¦lash¦ni¦kov +s

kale +s

kal¦eido|scope +s

kal¦eido|scop¦ic

kal¦eido|scop¦ic¦al

kal¦ends (use calends)

Kale|vala

kale|yard +s

Kal|goor¦lie (town, Australia)

Kali *Hinduism*

kali +s (plant)

Kali|dasa (Indian poet and dramatist)

Kali¦man¦tan
  (region,
  Indonesia)

Ka¦li¦nin, Mikh¦ail
  Ivan¦ovich
  (Soviet statesman)

Ka¦li¦nin (former name of Tver)

Ka¦li¦nin¦grad
(port, Russia)
Ka¦lisz (city,
Poland)
Kal¦mar (city,
Sweden)
Kal¦mar Sound
(off Sweden)
kal¦mia +s
Kal¦muck
plural Kal¦muck or
Kal¦mucks
Kal¦mykia
(republic, Russia)
K..lmykia-Khalmg
Tangch (official
name of
Kalmykia)
ka¦long +s
kalpa Hinduism;
Buddhism
Kal¦uga (city,
Russia)
Kal¦yan (city,
India)
Kama (Hindu god.
⚠ calmer, karma)
Kama Sutra
Kam¦chatka
(peninsula,
Russia)
kame +s (glacial
deposit. ⚠ came)
Ka¦men¦skoe
(former name of
Dniprodzer-
zhinsk)
Kamensk-Uralsky
(city, Russia)
Ka¦mer¦lingh
Onnes, Heike
(Dutch physicist)
Kamet (mountain,
Himalayas)
kami¦kaze +s
Kam¦ila¦roi
plural Kam¦ila¦roi
Kam¦pala (capital
of Uganda)
kam¦pong +s
Kam¦pong Cham
(port, Cambodia)
Kam¦pong Som
(port, Cambodia)
Kam¦pu¦chea
(Khmer name for
Cambodia)
Kam¦pu¦chean +s
kana +s
kan¦aka +s
Kan¦ar¦ese
plural Kan¦ar¦ese

Kan¦awa, Kiri Te
(New Zealand
soprano)
kan¦ban
Kan¦chen¦junga
(mountain,
Himalayas)
Kan¦da¦har (city,
Afghanistan)
Kan¦din¦sky,
Was¦sily (Russian
artist)
Kandy (town, Sri
Lanka)
Kan¦dy¦an +s
kanga +s
Kan¦gar (city,
Malaysia)
kan¦ga¦roo +s
kan¦ga¦roo rat +s
Kang¦chen¦junga
(use
Kanchenjunga)
Ka¦Ngwane
(former homeland,
South Africa)
kanji
Kan¦nada
(language.
⚠ Canada)
Kano (city, Nigeria)
kan¦oon +s
Kan¦pur (city,
India)
Kan¦sas (state,
USA)
Kan¦sas City (two
cities, USA)
Kansu (= Gansu)
Kant, Im¦man¦uel
(German
philosopher)
Kant¦ian +s
Kanto (region,
Japan)
KANU (= Kenya
African National
Union)
Kao¦hsiung (port,
Taiwan)
kao¦lin
kao¦lin¦ic
kao¦lin¦ise Br. (use
kaolinize)
kao¦lin¦ises
kao¦lin¦ised
kao¦lin¦is¦ing
kao¦lin¦ite
kao¦lin¦ize
kao¦lin¦izes
kao¦lin¦ized
kao¦lin¦iz¦ing

kaon +s
Kapa¦chira Falls
(in Malawi)
ka¦pell¦meis¦ter
plural
ka¦pell¦meis¦ter
Kap Far¦vel
(Danish name for
Cape Farewell)
Kapil Dev (Indian
cricketer)
kapok
Ka¦poor, Raj
(Indian actor and
film-maker)
Ka¦posi's
sar¦coma
kappa +s
kaput
kara¦bin¦er +s
(in mountaineering.
⚠ carabineer)
Karachai-
Cherkess
Karachai-
Cherkes¦sia
(republic, Russia)
Ka¦ra¦chi (city,
Pakistan)
Kara¦džić, Vuk
Stef¦an¦ović
(Serbian writer
and linguist)
Kara¦futo
(Japanese name
for Sakhalin)
Kara¦ganda
(Russian name for
Qaraghandy)
Kara¦ite +s
Karaj (city, Iran)
Kara¦jan, Her¦bert
von (Austrian
conductor)
Kara¦koram
(mountain range,
Himalayas)
Kara¦korum
(ruined city,
Mongolia)
kara¦kul +s (sheep.
⚠ caracal)
Kara Kum (desert,
central Asia)
Kara¦kumy
(Russian name for
the Kara Kum)
kara¦oke
Kara Sea (part of
Arctic Ocean)

karat Am. +s (Br.
carat measure of
purity of gold.
⚠ carat, caret,
carrot)
kar¦ate
Kar¦bala (city, Iraq)
Ka¦re¦lia (region,
Russia and
Finland)
Ka¦re¦lian +s
Karen also Karin
(name)
Karen +s (people;
language)
Karen State (state,
Burma)
kar¦ezza
Ka¦riba (town,
Zimbabwe)
Ka¦riba, Lake (in
Zimbabwe)
Karin also Karen
Karl also Carl
Karl-Marx-Stadt
(former name of
Chemnitz)
Kar¦loff, Boris
(English-born
American actor)
Kar¦lovy Vary
(town, Czech
Republic)
Karls¦bad (German
name for Karlovy
Vary)
Karls¦ruhe (port,
Germany)
karma +s (Hindu
and Buddhist
doctrine.
⚠ calmer, Kama)
kar¦mic
Kar¦nak (village,
Egypt. ⚠ Carnac)
Kar¦na¦taka (state,
India)
Karoo (plateau,
South Africa)
Kar¦pov, Ana¦toli
(Russian chess
player)
karri +s (tree.
⚠ carry)
Kar¦roo (use
Karoo)
Kars (city, Turkey)
karst +s (Geology.
⚠ cast, caste)
kart +s (motor-
racing vehicle.

kart (*cont.*)
△ cart, carte,
khat, quart)
kart|ing
karyo|kin|esis
karyo|type +s
kas|bah +s
Kash|mir (region,
Indian
subcontinent.
△ cashmere)
Kash|miri +s
Kas|parov, Gary
(Russian chess
player)
Kas'sel (city,
Germany)
Kas|site +s
Kasur (city,
Pakistan)
ka|ta|bat|ic
ka|tab|ol|ism (use
catabolism)
kata|kana +s
Kat|anga (former
name of Shaba)
kata|ther|
mom|eter +s
Kate
Kath *also* Cath
kath|ar|evousa
Kath|ar|ine *also*
Cath|ar|ine,
Cath|er|ine,
Cath|ryn,
Kath|er|ine,
Kath|ryn
Kath|er|ine *also*
Cath|ar|ine,
Cath|er|ine,
Cath|ryn,
Kath|ar|ine,
Kath|ryn
Kathia|war
(peninsula, India)
Kathie *also* Cathie,
Cathy, Kathy
Kath|leen *also*
Cath|leen
Kath|mandu
(capital of Nepal)
kath|ode +s (use
cathode)
Kath|ryn *also*
Cath|ar|ine,
Cath|er|ine,
Cath|ryn,
Kath|ar|ine,
Kath|er|ine
Kathy *also* Cathie,
Cathy, Kathie
Katia *also* Katya

Katie *also* Katy
Kat|mandu (use
Kathmandu)
Kato|wice (city,
Poland)
Kat|te|gat (channel
between Sweden
and Denmark)
Katy *also* Katie
Katya *also* Katia
ka|ty|did +s
Kauai (island,
Hawaii)
Kauff|mann,
An|gel|ica (Swiss
artist)
Kau|nas (city,
Lithuania)
Ka|unda, Ken|neth
(Zambian
statesman)
kauri +s (tree.
△ cowrie)
kava +s (shrub;
drink made from
it. △ carver, *cava*)
Ka|válla (port,
Greece)
Kav|eri
(= Cauvery)
Kawa|bata,
Yasu|nari
(Japanese
novelist)
kawa|kawa +s
Kawa|saki (city,
Japan)
Kaw|thoo|lay
(former name of
Karen State, Burma)
Kaw|thu|lei
(former name of
Karen State, Burma)
Kay *also* Kaye
(name)
kayak +s +ed +ing
Kaye, Danny
(American actor
and comedian)
Kaye *also* Kay
(name)
kayo
kayoes
kayoed
kayo|ing
verb
kayo +s *noun*
Kay|seri (city,
Turkey)
Kaz|akh
Kaz|akhs *or*
Kaz|akhi

Kaz|akh|stan
Kazan (capital of
Tatarstan, Russia)
Kazan, Elia
(Turkish-born
American film and
stage director)
kazoo +s
kbyte +s
(= kilobyte)
kea +s (bird.
△ keyer)
Kean, Ed|mund
(English actor.
△ Keene)
Keat|ing, Paul
(Australian prime
minister)
Kea|ton, Bus|ter
(American actor
and director)
Keats, John
(English poet)
Keats|ian +s
kebab +s
Keble, John
(English
churchman)
Keb|ne|kaise
(mountain,
Sweden)
keck +s +ed +ing
ked +s
Kedah (state,
Malaysia)
kedge
kedges
kedged
kedg|ing
kedg|eree +s
keek +s +ed +ing
keel +s +ed +ing
keel|boat +s
Keeley
keel|haul +s +ed
+ing
Keel|ing Is|lands
(alternative name
for the Cocos
Islands)
keel|less
keel|son +s
keen +s +ed +ing
+er +est
Keene, Charles
Sam|uel (English
caricaturist.
△ Kean)
keen|ly
keen|ness
keep
keeps

keep (*cont.*)
kept
keep|ing
keep|able
keep|er +s
keep-fit *noun and
adjective*
keep|net +s
keep|sake +s
kees|hond +s
kef +s
Ke|fal|linía (Greek
name for
Cephalonia)
kef|fi|yeh +s
Kef|la|vik (port,
Iceland)
keg +s
keis|ter +s
Keith
Kek|ulé,
Fried|rich
Au|gust (German
chemist)
Ke|lan|tan (state,
Malaysia)
kelim +s (use
kilim)
Kel|ler, Helen
Adams
(American writer
and social
reformer)
Kel|logg, Will
Keith (American
food
manufacturer)
Kel|logg Pact
Kells, Book of
Kelly, Gene
(American dancer
and actor)
Kelly, Grace
(American
actress)
Kelly, Ned
(Australian
bushranger)
Kelly, Petra
(German political
leader)
Kelly
ke|loid +s
kelp +s
kel|pie +s
kel|son +s (use
keelson)
kelt (fish. △ Celt,
celt)
kel|ter
Kel|vin, Wil|liam
Thom|son (Lord

Kel|vin (*cont.*)
Kelvin, British
physicist)
Kel|vin (name)
kel|vin +s (unit)
Kemal Pasha
(alternative name
of Atatürk)
Kem|ble, Fanny
(English actress)
**Kem|ble, John
Philip, Ste|phen,
and Charles**
(English actors)
Kem|er|ovo (city,
Russia)
kemp
**Kem|pis, Thomas
à** (German
theologian)
kempt
kempy
Ken (name)
ken
kens
kenned *or* kent
ken|ning
(knowledge;
know)
Ken|dal (town,
England)
**Ken|dall, Ed|ward
Cal|vin**
(American
biochemist)
kendo
**Ken|eally,
Thomas**
(Australian
novelist)
Ken|elm
**Ken|nedy,
Ed|ward**
('Teddy')
(American
Democratic
politician)
**Ken|nedy, John
Fitz|ger|ald**
(American
President)
Ken|nedy, Rob|ert
('Bobby')
(American
Democratic
statesman)
ken|nel
ken|nels
ken|nelled *Br.*
ken|neled *Am.*
ken|nel|ling *Br.*
ken|nel|ing *Am.*

**Ken|nelly, Ar|thur
Edwin** (American
electrical
engineer)
Ken|neth (Scottish
kings; name)
ken|ning +s
ken|osis
ken|ot|ic
keno|tron
Ken|sing|ton (in
London)
ken|speckle
Kent (county,
England)
Kent, Wil|liam
(English architect,
designer and
painter)
kent (past tense
and past participle
of ken)
Kent|ish
kent|ledge
Ken|tucky (state,
USA)
Kenya
Kenya, Mount
Ken|yan +s
Ken|yatta, Jomo
(Kenyan
statesman)
kepi +s
**Kep|ler,
Jo|han|nes**
(German
astronomer and
mathematician)
Kep|ler|ian
kept
Ker|ala (state,
India)
Ker|al|ite +s
kera|tin
kera|tin|isa|tion
Br. (use
keratinization)
kera|tin|ise *Br.* (use
keratinize)
kera|tin|ises
kera|tin|ised
kera|tin|is|ing
kera|tin|iza|tion
kera|tin|ize
kera|tin|izes
kera|tin|ized
kera|tin|iz|ing
kera|titis
kera|tose
kera|tot|omy
kerb +s (pavement
edge. △ curb)

kerb-crawler +s
kerb-crawling
kerb|side
kerb|stone +s
Kerch (city,
Ukraine)
ker|chief +s
ker|chiefed
kerf +s +ed +ing
ker|fuf|fle +s
**Ker|gue|len
Is|lands** (in
Indian Ocean)
Kerk|rade (town,
the Netherlands)
**Ker|madec
Is|lands** (in SW
Pacific)
ker|mes
plural ker|mes
(oak)
ker|mes (insects)
ker|mis (carnival;
fair)
Kern, Je|rome
(American
composer)
kern +s +ed +ing
(Irish soldier;
Printing)
ker|nel +s (centre
of nut. △ colonel)
kero (= kerosene)
kero|sene
kero|sine (use
kerosene)
Ker|ouac, Jack
(American
novelist)
Kerry
Ker|ries
(county, Republic
of Ireland; cattle;
name)
Kerry blue +s
ker|sey +s
ker|sey|mere +s
ker|ygma
ker|yg|mata
ker|yg|mat|ic
Kesey, Ken
(American
novelist)
kes|ki|dee +s (use
kiskadee)
Kes|te|ven (area in
Lincolnshire,
England)
kes|trel +s
Kes|wick (town,
England)
keta|mine

ketch
ketches
ketchup +s
keto|acid|osis
ke|tone +s
ke|ton|ic
ke|to|nuria
ke|to|sis
ke|tot|ic
**Ket|ter|ing,
Charles
Frank|lin**
(American
engineer)
ket|tle +s
kettle|drum +s
kettle|drum|mer
+s
kettle|ful +s
Kevin
Kev|lar *Propr.*
Kew Gar|dens (in
London)
kew|pie +s
key +s +ed +ing
(for lock. △ quay)
key|board +s +ed
+ing
key|board|er +s
key|board|ist +s
key|board play|er
+s
keyer +s
(electronic device.
△ kea)
key|hold|er +s
key|hole +s
Key Largo (island,
USA)
key|less
**Keynes, John
May|nard**
(English
economist)
Keynes|ian +s
Keynes|ian|ism
key|note +s
key|pad +s
key|punch
key|punches
key|punch|er +s
key|ring +s
Keys, House of
(Isle of Man)
Key|stone
(American film
company)
key|stone +s
(stone; principle)
Key|stone Kops
key|stroke +s
key|way +s

Key West (city, USA)
key|word +s
Kezia also **Ke|ziah**
Ke|ziah also **Kezia**
Kha|ba|rovsk (city and territory, Russia)
khad|dar +s
Kha|kas|sia (republic, Russia)
khaki +s
kha|lasi +s
Khal|kis (Greek name for **Chalcis**)
Khama, Ser|etse (Botswanan statesman)
Kham|bat, Gulf of
kham|sin +s
Khan, Imran (Pakistani cricketer)
Khan, Ja|han|gir (Pakistani squash player)
khan +s (ruler; caravanserai)
khan|ate +s
Kharg Is|land (in Persian Gulf)
Khar|kiv (city, Ukraine)
Khar|kov (Russian name for **Kharkiv**)
Khar|toum (capital of Sudan)
khat +s (shrub. ⚠ cart, carte, kart, quart)
Khay|litsa (township, South Africa)
Khe|dival
Khe|dive +s
Khe|div|ial
Kher|son (port, Ukraine)
Khi|tai (= Cathay)
Khmer +s
Khmer Rouge
Khoi|khoi plural **Khoi|khoi**
Khoi|san
Kho|meini, Aya|tol|lah (Iranian Shiite Muslim leader)
Khon|su Egyptian Mythology
Khor|ram|shahr (port, Iran)

khoum +s (Mauritanian currency. ⚠ **coomb, cwm**)
Khrush|chev, Ni|kita (Soviet statesman)
Khufu (Egyptian name for **Cheops**)
Khulna (city, Bangladesh)
Khun|jerab Pass (in Himalayas)
khus-khus (aromatic root. ⚠ **couscous, cuscus**)
Khy|ber Pass (between Pakistan and Afghanistan)
kiang +s
Ki|angsi (= Jiangxi)
Ki|angsu (= Jiangsu)
kib|ble
kib|bles
kib|bled
kib|bling
kib|butz
kib|butz|im
kib|butz|nik +s
kibe +s
kib|itka +s
kib|itz
kib|itzes
kib|itzed
kib|itz|ing
kib|itz|er +s
kib|lah
ki|bosh
ki|boshes
ki|boshed
ki|bosh|ing
kick +s +ed +ing
kick|able
kick-ass adjective (coarse slang)
kick|back +s
kick|ball +s
kick-boxer +s
kick-boxing
kick-down +s noun
kick|er +s
kick-off +s noun
kick-pleat +s
kick|shaw +s
kick|sort|er +s
kick|stand +s
kick-start +s +ed +ing
kick-turn +s

kid
kids
kid|ded
kid|ding
Kidd, Wil|liam (British pirate)
kid|der +s
Kid|der|min|ster (town, England; carpet)
kid|die +s
kid|ding|ly
kid|dle +s
kiddo +s
kiddy
kid|dies
kid-glove attributive
kid|nap
kid|naps
kid|napped Br.
kid|naped Am.
kid|nap|ping Br.
kid|nap|ing Am.
kid|nap|er Am. +s
kid|nap|ing Am. +s
kid|nap|per Br. +s
kid|nap|ping Br. +s
kid|ney +s
kidney-shaped
kid|ology
kid|skin +s
kid|vid +s
kie|kie +s
Kiel (port, Germany)
Kiel Canal (in Germany)
Kielce (city, Poland)
Kiel|der Water (reservoir, England)
kier +s (vat. ⚠ **Kir**)
Kieran also **Kieron**
Kier|ke|gaard, Søren (Danish philosopher)
Kieron also **Kieran**
kies|el|guhr
Kiev (capital of Ukraine)
kif +s
Ki|gali (capital of Rwanda)
kike +s (offensive)
Ki|kongo
Ki|kuyu plural **Ki|kuyu** or **Ki|ku|yus**
Kila|uea (volcano, Hawaii)

Kil|dare (county, Republic of Ireland)
kil|der|kin +s
kilim +s
Kili|man|jaro (in Tanzania)
Kil|kenny (town and county, Republic of Ireland; cats)
kill +s +ed +ing
Kil|lar|ney (town and county, Republic of Ireland)
kill|deer +s (bird)
kill|er +s
kil|lick +s
kil|li|fish plural **kil|li|fish** or **kil|li|fishes**
kill|ing +s
kill|ing bot|tle +s
kill|ing|ly
kill|joy +s
Kil|mar|nock (town, Scotland)
kiln +s +ed +ing
kiln-dry
kiln-dries
kiln-dried
kiln-drying
kilo +s
kilo|base +s
kilo|byte +s
kilo|cal|orie +s
kilo|cycle +s
kilo|gram +s
kilo|gramme Br. +s
kilo|hertz plural **kilo|hertz**
kilo|joule +s
kilo|liter Am. +s
kilo|litre Br. +s
kilo|meter Am. +s
kilo|metre Br. +s
kilo|met|ric
kilo|ton +s
kilo|tonne +s (use kiloton)
kilo|volt +s
kilo|watt +s
kilowatt-hour +s
Kil|roy (mythical person)
kilt +s
kilt|ed
kilt|er +s
kil|tie +s
Kim

Kim¦ber¦ley (city, South Africa)

Kim¦ber¦ley also **Kim¦berly** (name)

kim¦ber¦lite

Kim¦berly also **Kim¦ber¦ley** (name)

Kim Il Sung (Korean statesman)

ki¦mono +s

ki¦mo|noed

kin

kina *plural* **kina** (currency of Papua New Guinea. △**keener**)

Kina|balu (mountain, Malaysia)

kin¦aes¦the¦sia *Br.* (*Am.* **kinesthesia**)

kin¦aes|thet¦ic *Br.* (*Am.* **kinesthetic**)

kin¦aes|thet¦ic|al¦ly *Br.* (*Am.* **kinesthetically**)

Kin¦car¦dine|shire (former county, Scotland)

Kin¦chin|junga (use **Kanchenjunga**)

kin¦cob

kind +s +er +est

kinda (= kind of. △**kinder**)

kin¦der +s (= kindergarten)

kin¦der|gar¦ten +s

Kin¦der Scout (mountain, England)

kind-hearted

kind-hearted¦ly

kind-hearted¦ness

kin¦dle kin¦dles kin¦dled kind¦ling

kind|ler +s

kind¦lily

kind¦li|ness

kind¦ling +s

kind¦ly kind¦lier kind¦li|est

kind|ness kind|nesses

kin|dred

kine

kin¦emat¦ic

kin¦emat¦ic|al

kin¦emat¦ic|al¦ly

kin¦emat¦ics

kin¦emato|graph +s

kin¦es|ics

kin¦esi|ology

kin¦esis

kin¦es|the¦sia *Am.* (*Br.* **kinaesthesia**)

kin¦es|thet¦ic *Am.* (*Br.* **kinaesthetic**)

kin¦es|thet¦ic|al¦ly *Am.* (*Br.* **kinaesthetically**)

kin¦et¦ic

kin¦et¦ic|al¦ly

kin¦et¦ics

kin¦etin +s

kin¦folk

King, B. B. (American blues musician)

King, Bil¦lie Jean (American tennis player)

King, Mar¦tin Lu¦ther (American civil rights leader and churchman)

King, Wil¦liam Lyon Mac¦ken¦zie (Canadian statesman)

king +s +ed +ing

king|bird +s

king|bolt +s

king cobra +s

king crab +s

king|craft

king|cup +s

king|dom +s

king|domed

king|fish *plural* **king|fish** or **king|fishes**

king|fish¦er +s

king|hood +s

King Kong

king|less

king|let +s

king|like

king|li|ness

king|ling +s

King Log (in Roman fable)

king¦ly

king|maker +s

king|pin +s

king post +s

Kings Can¦yon Na¦tion|al Park (in USA)

Kings Cross (railway station, London)

king|ship +s

king-size

king-sized

Kings|ley, Charles (English writer)

Kings|ton (capital of Jamaica; port, Canada)

Kingston-upon-Hull (city, Humberside, England)

Kingston-upon-Thames (town, Surrey, England)

King Stork (in Roman fable)

Kings|town (capital of St Vincent)

kinin +s

kink +s

kin¦ka|jou +s

Kinki (region, Japan)

kink|ily

kinki|ness

kinky kink|ier kinki|est

kin|less

kino +s

Kin|ross (town, Scotland)

Kinross-shire (former county, Scotland)

Kin¦sey, Al¦fred Charles (American zoologist and sex researcher)

kins|folk

Kin|shasa (capital of Zaire)

kin|ship +s

kins|man kins|men

kins|woman kins|women

Kin|tyre (peninsula, Scotland)

kiosk +s

kip kips kipped kip|ping (sleep; animal hide)

kip *plural* **kip** or **kips** (Laotian currency)

Kip|ling, Rud|yard (English writer)

kip|per +s +ed +ing

kip¦sie +s

kipsy (use **kipsie**) kip|sies

Kir +s (drink. △**kier**) *Propr.*

kirby grip +s

Kirch|ner, Ernst Lud|wig (German painter)

Kir|ghiz (use **Kyrgyz**)

Kir|ghizia (alternative name for **Kyrgyzstan**)

Kir|giz (use **Kyrgyz**)

Kir|gizia (use **Kirghizia**)

Kiri|bati (island group, SW Pacific)

Kirin (= **Jilin**)

Kiri|ti|mati (atoll, SW Pacific)

Kirk (name)

kirk +s (church)

Kirk|caldy (town, Scotland)

Kirk|cud|bright (town, Scotland)

Kirk|cud|bright|shire (former county, Scotland)

kirk|man kirk|men

Kirk-session +s

Kir|kuk (city, Iraq)

Kirk|wall (town, Orkneys)

Kirov (former name of Vyatka; Ballet)

Ki|rova|bad (former name of Gyandzhe)

kirsch kirsches

kirsch|was¦ser +s

Kir|sten

Kir|stie *also* Kirsty
kir|tle +s
Kir|una (town, Sweden)
Kir|undi (language)
Ki|san|gani (city, Zaire)
Kishi|nev (Russian name for Chişinău)
kis|ka|dee +s
Kis|lev (Jewish month)
Kis|lew (use Kislev)
kis|met
kiss
  kisses
  kissed
  kiss|ing
kiss|able
kiss and tell
kiss-curl +s
kiss|er +s
Kis|sin|ger, Henry (American diplomat)
kiss|ing gate +s
kiss-me-quick
  attributive
kiss-off +s *noun*
kiss of life
kisso|gram +s
kissy
kist +s (coffin; burial chamber; use cist)
Ki|swa|hili
Kit (name)
kit
  kits
  kit|ted
  kit|ting
  (equipment etc.)
Kita|kyu|shu (city, Japan)
kit|bag +s
kit-cat +s (portrait)
Kit-Cat Club (political club)
kit|chen +s
Kit|chener (city, Canada)
Kit|chener, Ho|ra|tio Her|bert (British soldier and statesman; bun)
kit|chen|ette +s
kitchen-sink
  attributive
kit|chen|ware

kite
  kites
  kited
  kit|ing
kite-flying
Kite|mark +s
kit-fox
  kit-foxes
kith
kith and kin
kitsch
kitschi|ness
kitschy
  kitsch|ier
  kitschi|est
kit|ten +s +ed +ing
kit|ten|ish
kit|ten|ish|ly
kit|ten|ish|ness
kit|ti|wake +s
kit|tle
Kitty (name)
kitty
  kit|ties
  (common fund; cat)
kitty-cornered
Kitty Hawk (town, USA)
Kitwe (city, Zambia)
Kitz|bühel (winter-sports resort, Austria)
Kitz|inger, Sheila (English childbirth educator)
Kivu, Lake (in central Africa)
Kiwi +s (New Zealander)
kiwi +s (bird)
kiwi fruit
  plural kiwi fruit *or* kiwi fruits
Kla|gen|furt (city, Austria)
Klai|peda (port, Lithuania)
Klans|man
Klans|men (= Ku Klux Klansman. △ clansman)
Klap|roth, Mar|tin Hein|rich (German chemist)
Klaus|en|burg (German name for Cluj–Napoca)
klaxon +s *Propr.*

Klee, Paul (Swiss painter)
Klee|nex
  plural Klee|nex *or* Klee|nexes *Propr.*
Klein (bottle. △ cline)
Klein, Cal|vin (American couturier)
Klein, Mel|anie (Austrian-born psychoanalyst)
Klem|perer, Otto (German-born conductor and composer)
klepht +s (in Greek history. △ cleft)
klep|to|mania
klep|to|maniac +s
Klerk, F. W. de (South African statesman)
Klerks|dorp (city, South Africa)
klieg +s
Klimt, Gus|tav (Austrian painter)
klip|spring|er +s
Klon|dike (river and district, Canada)
klong +s
kloof +s
Klos|ters (ski resort, Switzerland)
kludge +s
klutz
  klutzes
klutzy
  klutz|ier
  klutzi|est
klys|tron +s
K-meson +s
knack +s
knacker +s +ed +ing
knack|ery
  knack|er|ies
knag +s (knot in wood. △ nag)
knaggy
  knag|gier
  knag|gi|est
knap
  knaps
  knapped
  knap|ping

knap (*cont.*) (break stones. △ nap, nappe)
knap|per +s (stone breaker. △ nappa, napper)
knap|sack +s
knap|weed +s
knar +s
knave +s (rogue. △ nave)
knav|ery
  knav|er|ies
knav|ish
knav|ish|ly
knav|ish|ness
kna|wel +s
knead +s +ed +ing (work dough. △ need)
knead|able
knead|er +s
knee
  knees
  kneed
  knee|ing
knee-bend +s
knee-breeches
knee|cap
  knee|caps
  knee|capped
  knee|cap|ping
knee|cap|ping +s
knee-deep
knee-high
knee|hole +s
knee-jerk +s
knee joint +s
kneel
  kneels
  kneeled *or* knelt
  kneel|ing
knee-length
kneel|er +s
knee-pad +s
knee-pan +s
knees-up +s
knee-trembler +s
knell +s +ed +ing
Knel|ler, God|frey (German-born painter)
knelt
Knes|set (Israeli parliament)
knew (past tense of know. △ new, nu)
knicker *attributive* (of knickers. △ nicker)
Knick|er|bocker +s (New Yorker)

Knick|er|bocker
  Glory
  Knick|er|bocker
    Glor|ies
knick|er|bock|ers
  (breeches)
knick|ers
knick-knack +s
knick-knackery
knick-knackish
knife
  knives
  noun
knife
  knifes
  knifed
  knif|ing
  verb
knife blade +s
knife-board +s
knife-edge +s
knife-grinder +s
knife han|dle +s
knife|like
knife ma|chine +s
knife-pleat +s
knife|point
knifer +s
knife rest +s
knife-throwing
knight +s +ed +ing
  (person. △ night,
  nite)
knight|age +s
knight|hood +s
Knight
  Hos|pit|al|ler
  Knights
  Hos|pit|al|lers
knight|like
knight|li|ness
knight|ly (of a
  knight. △ nightly)
Knights|bridge
  (district, London)
knight-service
Knight Temp|lar
  Knights
  Temp|lars
kni|pho|fia +s
knish
  knishes
knit
  knits
  knit|ted
  knit|ting
  (make with yarn
  and needles.
  △ nit)
knit|ter +s
knit|ting ma|chine
  +s

knit|ting nee|dle
  +s
knit|wear
knives
knob
  knobs
  knobbed
  knob|bing
  (rounded
  protuberance etc.
  △ nob)
knob|bi|ness
knob|ble +s (small
  knob. △ nobble)
knob|bly
  knob|blier
  knob|bli|est
knobby
  knob|bier
  knob|bi|est
knob|ker|rie +s
knob|like
knob|stick +s
knock +s +ed +ing
  (strike, rap.
  △ nock)
knock|about +s
knock-back +s
  noun
knock-down +s
  noun and adjective
knock|er +s
knocker-up
  knockers-up
knock|ing shop +s
knock-kneed
knock knees
knock-off +s
knock-on +s
  adjective and noun
knock|out +s
knock-up +s *noun
  and adjective*
knoll +s +ed +ing
knop +s
knop|kierie +s
  (*South African*
  = knobkerrie)
Knos|sos (ancient
  city, Crete)
knot
  knots
  knot|ted
  knot|ting
  (bow, reef knot,
  etc.; unit of speed;
  in timber; tangle;
  tie; bird. △ not)
knot-garden +s
knot|grass
  knot|grasses
knot-hole +s

knot|less
knot|ter +s
knot|tily
knot|ti|ness
knot|ting +s
knotty
  knot|tier
  knot|ti|est
knot|weed +s
knot|work
knout +s +ed +ing
  (scourge. △ nowt)
know
  knows
  knew
  know|ing
  known
  (be aware of.
  △ no, Noh)
know|able
know-all +s
know|er +s
know-how
  (expertise.
  △ nohow)
know|ing|ly
know|ing|ness
know-it-all +s
know|ledg|abil|ity
  (use knowledge-
  ability)
know|ledg|able
  (use knowledge-
  able)
know|ledg|able|
  ness (use
  knowledgeable-
  ness)
know|ledg|ably
  (use
  knowledgeably)
know|ledge +s
know|ledge|
       abil|ity
know|ledge|able
know|ledge|able|
       ness
know|ledge|ably
known (past
  participle of
  know. △ none)
know-nothing +s
Knox, John
  (Scottish
  Protestant
  reformer)
Knox, Ron|ald
  (English
  theologian)
Knox|ville (city,
  USA)

knuckle
  knuckles
  knuckled
  knuck|ling
knuckle-bone +s
knuckle|dust|er +s
knuckle|head +s
knuckly
knur +s
knurl +s
knurled
knurr +s (use knur)
Knut (use Cnut)
koa +s
koala +s
koan +s
kob
  plural kob
  (antelope. △ cob)
Kobe (port, Japan)
ko|bold *Germanic
  Mythology*
Koch, Rob|ert
  (German
  bacteriologist)
Kö|chel (number)
KO'd (= knocked
  out)
Ko|dály, Zol|tán
  (Hungarian
  composer)
Ko|diak +s
koel +s
Koest|ler, Ar|thur
  (Hungarian-born
  writer)
kofta +s
Ko|hima (city,
  India)
Koh-i-noor
  (diamond)
Kohl, Hel|mut
  (German
  statesman)
kohl (powder.
  △ coal, cole)
kohl|rabi
  kohl|rabies
koi
  plural koi
Koil (former city,
  India)
koine +s
Ko|koschka,
  Oskar (Austrian
  artist)
kola +s (use cola)
Kola Pen|in|sula
  (Russia)
Kol|ha|pur (city,
  India)

kol|in|sky
  kol|in|skies
Kol|khis (Greek
  name for Colchis)
kol|khoz
  plural kol|khozy
Ko|lyma (river,
  Siberia)
Komi (republic,
  Russia)
komi|tadji +s (use
  comitadji)
Ko|modo (island,
  Indonesia;
  dragon)
Kom|pong Cham
  (port, Cambodia)
Kom|pong Som
  (port, Cambodia)
Kom|somol +s
Kom|so|molsk
  (city, Russia)
Kongo
  plural Kongo *or*
  Kon|gos
  (people; language.
  △ Congo)
Kö|nig|grätz
  (German name for
  Hradec Králové)
Kö|nigs|berg
  (German name for
  Kaliningrad)
Kon-Tiki
Konya (city,
  Turkey)
koo|doo +s (use
  kudu)
kook +s
kooka|burra +s
kook|ily
kooki|ness
kooky
  kook|ier
  kooki|est
Koon|ing, Wil|lem
  de (Dutch-born
  American painter)
Kop +s (*Football.*
  △ cop)
kop +s (hill. △ cop)
kopek +s (use
  copeck)
kopi (gypsum.
  △ copy)
kopje +s (use
  koppie. △ copy)
kop|pie +s (small
  hill. △ copy)
kor|adji +s
Koran +s
Kor|an|ic
Kor|but, Olga
  (Soviet gymnast)

Korda,
  Alex|an|der
  (Hungarian-born
  film producer and
  director)
Kor|do|fan (region,
  Sudan)
Korea
Kor|ean +s
korf|ball
korma +s
Kort|rijk (city,
  Belgium)
kor|una +s
  (Bohemian,
  Moravian, or
  Slovak currency)
Korup (national
  park, Cameroon)
Kos (Greek name
  for Cos)
Kos|ciusko,
  Thad|deus
  (Polish soldier)
Kos|ciusko,
  Mount (in
  Australia)
ko|sher
Ko|šice (city,
  Slovakia)
Kos|ovo (province,
  Serbia)
Kos|suth, Lajos
  (Hungarian
  statesman and
  patriot)
Kost|roma (city,
  Russia)
Ko|sy|gin, Alex|sei
  (Soviet statesman)
Kota (city, India)
Kota Ba|haru (city,
  Kelantan)
Kota Kina|balu
  (city, Borneo)
Kotka (port,
  Finland)
koto +s
kotow +s +ed +ing
Kotze|bue,
  Au|gust von
  (German
  dramatist)
kou|miss
kou|prey +s
kour|bash
  kour|bashes
Kou|rou (town,
  French Guiana)
kow|hai +s

Kow|loon
  (peninsula, Hong
  Kong)
kow|tow +s +ed
  +ing
Kra, Isth|mus of
  (in Thailand)
kraal +s
Krafft-Ebing,
  Rich|ard von
  (German
  physician and
  psychologist)
kraft (paper.
  △ craft)
Kra|gu|jevac (city,
  Serbia)
krai +s (Russian
  administrative
  territory. △ cry)
krait +s
Kraka|toa
  (volcanic island,
  Indonesia)
kra|ken +s
Kra|ków (Polish
  name for Cracow)
krans
  kranses
Kras|no|dar
  (territory, Russia;
  its capital)
Kras|no|yarsk
  (territory, Russia;
  its capital)
Kraut +s (*offensive*)
Krebs, Hans Adolf
  (German-born
  British biochemist;
  cycle)
Kre|feld (town,
  Germany)
Kreis|ler, Fritz
  (Austrian-born
  violinist and
  composer)
Krem|en|chuk
  (city, Ukraine)
Krem|lin (Russian
  government)
krem|lin +s
  (Russian citadel)
Krem|lin|olo|gist
  +s
Krem|lin|ology
krieg|spiel +s
Kriem|hild
  *Germanic
  Mythology*
krill
  plural krill
krim|mer +s

kris
  krises
Krishna *Hinduism*
Krishna|ism
Krish|na|murti,
  Jiddu (Indian
  spiritual leader)
Krishna River (in
  India)
Krista *also* Christa
Kris|tall|nacht
Kris|ti|ania (former
  name of Oslo)
Kris|tian|sand
  (port, Norway)
Kri|voy Rog
  (Russian name for
  Kryvy Rih)
krom|esky
  krom|eskies
krona
kro|nor
  (Swedish
  currency)
krona
kro|nur
  (Icelandic
  currency)
krone
kro|ner
  (Danish or
  Norwegian
  currency)
Kro|nos (use
  Cronus)
Kron|stadt
  (German name for
  Brașov)
Kroo (use Kru)
  plural Kroo
kroon +s (Estonian
  currency.
  △ croon)
Kro|pot|kin, Peter
  (Russian
  anarchist)
Kru
  plural Kru
  (people; language)
Kru Coast (in
  Liberia)
Kru|ger, Paul
  (South African
  soldier and
  statesman)
Kru|ger Na|tion|al
  Park (in South
  Africa)
kru|ger|rand +s
krumm|horn +s

Krupp, Al¦fred
(German arms
manufacturer)
kryp¦ton
Kryvy Rih(city,
Ukraine)
Kshat¦riya+s
K/T bound¦ary
K2(mountain,
Himalayas)
Kuala Lum¦pur
(capital of
Malaysia)
**Kuala
Ter¦eng¦ganu**
(use **Kuala
Trengganu**)
Kuala Treng¦ganu
(town, Malaysia)
Kuan¦tan(city,
Malaysia)
Kuan Yin *Chinese
Buddhism*
Kub¦lai Khan
(Mongol emperor)
Ku¦brick, Stan¦ley
(American film
director)
Ku¦ching(city,
Sarawak)
kudos
kudu
 plural **kudus** or
 kudu
kudzu+s
Kufic
Kui¦by¦shev
(former name of
Samara)
Ku Klux Klan
**Ku Klux
Klans¦man**
 Ku Klux
 Klans¦men
kukri+s
kulak+s
kulan+s
Kul¦tur
Kul¦tur¦kampf
Kum(use **Qom**)
Kuma¦moto(city,
Japan)
ku¦mara+s
Ku¦masi(city,
Ghana)
Ku¦mayri(Russian
name for **Gyumri**)
kumis(use
koumiss)
ku¦miss(use
koumiss)
küm¦mel+s

kum¦quat+s
Kun¦dera, Milan
(Czech novelist)
Kung
 plural **Kung**
kung fu
Kung Fu-tzu
(Chinese name of
Confucius)
Kun¦lun Shan
(mountains,
China)
Kun¦ming(city,
China)
Kuo¦min¦tang
Kuo¦pio(province,
Finland)
kur¦bash(use
kourbash)
 kur¦bashes
kur¦cha¦tov¦ium
 Chemistry
Kurd+s
kur¦dai¦tcha+s
Kurd¦ish
Kur¦di¦stan(region,
E. Europe and W.
Asia)
Kure(city, Japan)
Kur¦gan(city,
Russia)
**Kuria Muria
Is¦lands**(in
Arabian Sea)
Kur¦ile Is¦lands(in
NW Pacific)
Kuro¦sawa, Akira
(Japanese film
director)
kur¦ra¦jong+s
kur¦saal+s
Kursk(city, Russia)
kurta+s
kur¦tha+s (use
kurta)
kur¦tosis
kuru
Kuşa¦dasi(town,
Turkey)
Kuta¦isi(city,
Georgia)
Kutch, Gulf of
(inlet, India)
Kutch, Rann of
(salt marsh, India
and Pakistan)
Ku¦wait
Ku¦wait City
(capital of Kuwait)
Ku¦waiti+s
Kuz¦bass
(alternative name

Kuz¦bass(*cont.*)
for the **Kuznets
Basin**)
Kuz¦nets Basin
(region, Russia)
kvass
kvetch
 kvetches
 kvetched
 kvetch¦ing
kvetch¦er+s
Kwa
 plural **Kwa**
KWAC(= keyword
and context)
kwa¦cha+s
Kwa¦Nde¦bele
(former homeland,
South Africa)
Kwang¦chow
(= **Guangzhou**)
Kwangju(city,
South Korea)
Kwangsi Chuang
(= **Guangxi
Zhuang**)
Kwang¦tung
(= **Guangdong**)
kwanza
 plural **kwanza** or
 kwan¦zas
kwashi¦or¦kor
Kwa¦Zulu(former
homeland, South
Africa)
Kwa¦Zulu/Natal
(province, South
Africa)
Kwei¦chow
(= **Guizhou**)
Kwei¦lin(= **Guilin**)
Kwei¦yang
(= **Guiyang**)
Kwesui(former
name of **Hohhot**)
KWIC(= keyword
in context)
KWOC(= keyword
out of context)
kyan¦ise *Br.* (use
kyanize)
 kyan¦ises
 kyan¦ised
 kyan¦is¦ing
kyan¦ite
kyan¦it¦ic
kyan¦ize *Am.*
 kyan¦izes
 kyan¦ized
 kyan¦iz¦ing

kyat
 plural **kyat** or
 kyats
ky¦bosh(use
kibosh)
Kyd, Thomas
(English
dramatist)
kyle+s
Kylie(name)
kylie+s
(boomerang)
kylin+s
kyloe+s
kymo¦graph+s
kymo¦graph¦ic
Kyoto(city, Japan)
ky¦phosis
 ky¦phoses
ky¦phot¦ic
**Kyp¦ri¦anou,
Spy¦ros**(Cypriot
statesman)
Kyr¦enia(port,
Cyprus)
Kyr¦gyz
 plural **Kyr¦gyz**
Kyr¦gyz¦stan
(country, central
Asia)
Kyrie+s
Kyu¦shu(island,
Japan)
Kyzyl(city, Russia)
Kyzyl Kum(desert,
central Asia)

Ll

Labor Party *Am.*,
Austral.
　Labor Par|ties
labor-saving *Am.*
la|bour *Br.* +s +ed
　+ing
la|bour|er *Br.* +s
labour-intensive
　Br.
la|bour|ism *Br.*
La|bour|ite *Br.* +s
La|bour Party *Br.*
　La|bour Par|ties
labour-saving *Br.*
labra
Lab|ra|dor +s
　(region, Canada,
　dog)
lab|ra|dor|ite
lab|ret +s
lab|rum
　labra
La Bru|yère, Jean
de (French
　moralist)
La|buan (island,
　Malaysia)
la|bur|num +s
laby|rinth +s
laby|rin|thian
laby|rin|thine
lac +s (resin; insect.
　△ lack, lakh)
Lacan, Jacques
　(French
　psychoanalyst and
　philosopher)
La|can|ian +s
Lac|ca|dive
Is|lands (now
　part of the
　Lakshadweep
　Islands)
lac|co|lith +s
lace
　laces
　laced
　la|cing
lace-glass
　lace-glasses
La Ceiba (port,
　Honduras)
lace|maker +s
lace|mak|ing
lace-pillow +s
la|cer|able
la|cer|ate
　la|cer|ates
　la|cer|ated
　la|cer|at|ing
la|cer|ation +s
la|cer|tian +s

la (*Music*; use lah)
laa|ger +s +ed
　+ing
　(encampment.
　△ lager)
Laa|youne (use
　La'youn)
lab +s
　(= laboratory)
Laban, Ru|dolf
von (Hungarian
　dance
　theoretician)
la|ba|rum +s
lab|da|num
labe|fac|tion +s
label
　la|bels
　la|belled *Br.*
　la|beled *Am.*
　la|bel|ling *Br.*
　la|bel|ing *Am.*
la|bel|ler +s
la|bel|lum
　la|bella
labia
la|bial
la|bial|ise *Br.* (use
　labialize)
　la|bial|ises
　la|bial|ised
　la|bial|is|ing
la|bial|ism +s
la|bial|ize
　la|bial|izes
　la|bial|ized
　la|bial|iz|ing
la|bi|al|ly
labia ma|jora
labia mi|nora
la|bi|ate +s
la|bile
la|bil|ity
la|bio|den|tal
la|bio|velar
la|bium
　labia
labor *Am.* +s +ed
　+ing
la|bora|tory
　la|bora|tor|ies
la|bor|er *Am.* +s
labor-intensive
　Am.
la|bori|ous
la|bori|ous|ly
la|bori|ous|ness
La|bor|ite *Am.* +s

la|cer|til|ian +s
la|cer|tine
lace-up +s *adjective
　and noun*
lace|wing +s
lace|wood
lace|work
lacey (use lacy)
la|ches
La|che|sis *Greek
　Mythology*
Lach|lan (river,
　Australia; name)
lach|ryma Christi
lach|ry|mal +s (in
　Anatomy, use
　lacrimal)
lach|ry|ma|tion (in
　Medicine, use
　lacrimation)
lach|ry|ma|tor +s
lach|ry|ma|tory
　lach|ry|ma|tor|ies
lach|ry|mose
lach|ry|mose|ly
laci|ly
laci|ness
la|cing +s
la|cini|ate
　la|cini|ated
la|cini|ation +s
lack +s +ed +ing
　(want. △ lac,
　lakh)
lacka|dai|si|cal
lacka|dai|si|cal|ly
lacka|dai|si|cal|
　ness
lacker +s +ed +ing
　(use lacquer)
lackey +s
Lack|land (King
　John of England)
lack|land +s
lack|lus|ter *Am.*
lack|lustre *Br.*
La|clos, Pierre
Cho|der|los de
　(French novelist)
La|co|nia
　(department,
　Greece)
La|co|nian +s
la|con|ic
la|con|ic|al|ly
la|coni|cism +s
lac|on|ism
La Co|ruña (port,
　Spain)
lac|quer +s +ed
　+ing
lac|quer|er +s

lac|quer tree +s
lac|quer|ware
lac|quey +s (use
　lackey)
lac|ri|mal +s
　(*Anatomy*;
　generally, use
　lachrymal)
lac|ri|ma|tion
　(*Medicine*;
　generally, use
　lachrymation)
lac|ri|ma|tor +s
　(use lachrymator)
la|crosse
lac|ry|mal +s (use
　lachrymal or, in
　Anatomy,
　lacrimal)
lac|ry|ma|tion (use
　lachrymation or,
　in *Medicine*,
　lacrimation)
lac|tase +s
lac|tate
　lac|tates
　lac|tated
　lac|tat|ing
lac|ta|tion
lac|teal +s
lac|tes|cence +s
lac|tes|cent
lac|tic
lac|tif|er|ous
lacto|ba|cil|lus
　lacto|ba|cilli
lac|tom|eter +s
lac|tone +s
lacto|pro|tein +s
lac|tose
la|cuna
　la|cu|nae *or*
　la|cu|nas
la|cu|nal
la|cu|nar
la|cu|nary
la|cu|nose
la|cus|trine
lacy
　laci|er
　laci|est
lad +s
La|dakh (in India)
lada|num (plant
　resin.
　△ laudanum)
lad|der +s +ed
　+ing
ladder-back +s
lad|der stitch
　lad|der stitches
lad|die +s

lad|dish
lad|dish|ness
lade
  lades
  laded
  lad|ing
  (load. ⚠ laid)
la-di-da +s
la|dies
la|dies' chain +s
la|dies' fin|gers
  (okra.
  ⚠ ladyfinger,
  lady's finger)
La|dies' Gal|lery
  (in the House of
  Commons)
la|dies' man
  la|dies' men
la|dies' night +s
la|dies' room +s
la|dify (use ladyfy)
  la|di|fies
  la|di|fied
  la|di|fy|ing
Ladin
lad|ing +s
La|dino +s (dialect;
  person)
la|dino +s (plant)
La|dis|laus
  (Hungarian king
  and saint)
ladle
  ladles
  ladled
  lad|ling
ladle|ful +s
ladler +s
La|doga, Lake (in
  Russia)
lady
  la|dies
lady|bird +s
lady|bug +s
Lady chapel +s
Lady Day +s
lady-fern +s
lady|fin|ger Am. +s
  (cake. ⚠ ladies'
  fingers, lady's
  finger)
lady|fy
  lady|fies
  lady|fied
  lady|fy|ing
lady|hood
lady-in-waiting
  ladies-in-waiting
lady|kill|er +s
lady|like
lady-love +s

lady's bed|straw
lady's
  com|pan|ion +s
lady's fin|ger +s
  (vetch. ⚠ ladies'
  fingers,
  ladyfinger)
lady|ship +s
lady's maid +s
lady's man (use
  ladies' man)
lady's man|tle +s
Lady|smith (town,
  Natal)
lady-smock +s
  (use lady's
  smock)
lady's slip|per +s
lady's smock +s
lady's tresses
Lae (port, Papua
  New Guinea)
Lae|ti|tia also
  Le|ti|tia
laevo|dopa
laevo|rota|tory
laevo|tar|tar|ic
lae|vu|lose
La|fay|ette,
  Mar|quis de
  (French soldier
  and statesman)
La Fon|taine, Jean
  de (French poet)
lag
  lags
  lagged
  lag|ging
lagan +s
lager +s (beer.
  ⚠ laager)
La|ger|kvist, Pär
  (Swedish novelist
  and dramatist)
La|ger|löf, Selma
  (Swedish writer)
lager lout +s
la|ger|phone +s
lag|gard +s
lag|gard|ly
lag|gard|ness
lag|ger +s
lag|ging +s
lago|morph +s
la|goon +s
la|goon|al
Lagos (city,
  Nigeria)
La|grange,
  Jo|seph Louis,
  Comte de

La|grange (cont.)
  (French
  mathematician)
La|gran|gian point
  +s
lah Music
lahar +s
La|hore (city,
  Pakistan)
laic +s
la|ical
la|ic|al|ly
lai|cisa|tion Br.
  (use laicization)
lai|cise Br. (use
  laicize)
lai|cises
lai|cised
lai|cis|ing
lai|city
lai|ciza|tion
lai|cize
lai|cizes
lai|cized
lai|ciz|ing
laid (past tense and
  past participle of
  lay; paper.
  ⚠ lade)
laid-back
lain (past participle
  of lie. ⚠ lane)
Laing, R. D.
  (Scottish
  psychoanalyst)
lair +s +ed +ing
  (animal's den.
  ⚠ layer)
lair|age +s
laird +s
laird|ship +s
lairy
laissez-aller
laissez-faire
laissez-passer
laity
  la|ities
Laius Greek
  Mythology
lake +s
Lake Dis|trict (in
  England)
lake-dweller +s
lake-dwelling +s
Lake|land (= Lake
  District etc.)
lake|less
lake|let +s
lake|side +s
lakh +s (hundred
  thousand. ⚠ lac,
  lack)

La|ko|nia (use
  Laconia)
Lak|shad|weep
  Is|lands (in India)
Lak|shmi Hinduism
La|lage
Lal|lan
Lal|lans
Lalla Rookh
lal|la|tion
lally|gag
  lally|gags
  lally|gagged
  lally|gag|ging
Lalo, Édouard
  (French
  composer)
La Lou|vière (city,
  Belgium)
lam
  lams
  lammed
  lam|ming
  (thrust. ⚠ lamb)
lama +s (monk.
  ⚠ llama)
Lama|ism
Lama|ist
La|marck, Jean
  Bap|tiste de
  (French botanist
  and zoologist)
La|marck|ian +s
La|marck|ism
La|mar|tine,
  Al|phonse de
  (French poet)
la|ma|sery
  la|ma|ser|ies
Lamb, Charles
  (English essayist
  and critic)
lamb +s +ed +ing
  (young sheep.
  ⚠ lam)
lam|bada +s
lam|bast +s +ed
  +ing
  (use lambaste)
lam|baste
  lam|bastes
  lam|basted
  lam|bast|ing
lambda +s
lam|bency
lam|bent
lam|bent|ly
lamb|er +s
Lam|bert,
  Con|stant
  (English
  composer)

lam|bert +s
Lam|beth
 (borough,
 London)
Lam|beth Pal|ace
lamb|hood
lamb|kin +s
lamb|like
lam|bre|quin +s
lamb's ears (plant)
lamb|skin +s
lamb's let|tuce
lamb's-tails
lambs|wool +s
lame
 lames
 lamed
 lam|ing
 lamer
 lam|est
lamé
lame|brain +s
la|mella
 la|mel|lae
la|mel|lar
la|mel|late
la|mel|li|branch +s
la|mel|li|corn +s
la|mel|li|form
la|mel|lose
lame|ly
lame|ness
lam|ent +s +ed
 +ing
lam|ent|able
lam|ent|ably
lam|en|ta|tion +s
Lam|en|ta|tions
 Bible
lam|ent|er +s
lam|ent|ing|ly
lam|ina
 lam|inae
lam|inar
lamin|ate
 lamin|ates
 lamin|ated
 lamin|at|ing
lamin|ation +s
lamin|ator +s
lam|ing|ton +s
lamin|itis
lamin|ose
lam|ish
Lam|mas
lam|mer|geier +s
lam|mer|geyer +s
 (use
 lammergeier)
lamp +s +ed +ing

lamp|black
lamp-chimney +s
lam|pern +s
lamp hold|er +s
lamp|less
lamp|light
lamp|light|er +s
lamp|lit
lam|poon +s +ed
 +ing
lam|poon|er +s
lam|poon|ery
lam|poon|ist +s
lamp-post +s
lam|prey +s
lamp|shade +s
LAN (= local area
 network)
Lana
Lan|ark|shire
 (former county,
 Scotland)
Lan|ca|shire
Lan|cas|ter (city,
 England)
Lan|cas|trian +s
Lance (name)
lance
 lances
 lanced
 lan|cing
 (weapon; pipe;
 pierce; cut open.
 △ launce)
lance
 bom|bard|ier +s
lance cor|poral +s
lance-jack +s
lance|let +s
Lance|lot
 (Arthurian knight;
 name)
lan|ceo|late
lan|cer +s
lance-sergeant +s
lance-snake +s
lan|cet +s
lan|cet|ed
lance|wood +s
Lan|chow
 (= Lanzhou)
lan|cin|ate
 lan|cin|ates
 lan|cin|ated
 lan|cin|at|ing
Lancs.
 (= Lancashire)
land +s +ed +ing
 (solid part of
 earth; come to
 shore etc.)

Land
 Län|der
 (province)
land agency
 land agen|cies
land agent +s
Lan|dau, Lev
 (Russian physicist)
lan|dau +s
 (carriage)
lan|dau|let +s
land bank +s
land-based
land bridge +s
land crab +s
land|er +s (person
 or thing that
 lands)
Län|der (plural of
 Land)
Landes
 (department,
 France)
land|fall +s
land|fill +s
land force +s
land|form +s
land girl +s
land-grabber +s
land|grave +s *male*
land|gravi|ate +s
land|gra|vine +s
 female
land|hold|er +s
land|hold|ing +s
land|ing +s
land|ing craft
 plural land|ing
 craft
land|ing gear +s
land|ing net +s
land|ing place +s
land|ing stage +s
land|ing strip +s
land|lady
 land|ladies
land-law +s
länd|ler +s
land|less
land|line +s
land|locked
land|loper +s
land|lord +s
land|lub|ber +s
land|mark +s
land mass
 land masses
land|mine +s
land|oc|ra|cy
 land|oc|ra|cies
lando|crat +s

land-office
 busi|ness
Lan|dor, Wal|ter
 Sav|age (English
 writer)
land|owner +s
land|owner|ship
land|owning
land|rail +s
Land|sat
land|scape
 land|scapes
 land|scaped
 land|scap|ing
land|scape
 gar|den|er +s
land|scape
 gar|den|ing
landscape-marble
land|scape
 paint|er +s
land|scap|ist +s
Land|seer, Edwin
 (English painter)
Land's End (in
 England)
Lands|hut (city,
 Germany)
land|side
land|slide +s
land|slip +s
Lands|mål
lands|man
 lands|men
Land|steiner, Karl
 (Austrian
 physician)
land tax
 land taxes
land-tie +s
land|ward
land|wards
land-wind +s
lane +s (track etc.
 △ lain)
Lang, Fritz
 (Austrian-born
 film director)
Lang|land,
 Wil|liam (English
 poet)
lang|lauf
lang|lauf|er +s
Lang|ley, Sam|uel
 Pier|point
 (American
 astronomer and
 aviation pioneer)
Lang|muir, Ir|ving
 (American
 chemist)

Lango
  plural **Lango**
lan|gouste+s
lan|gous|tine+s
lang syne
Lang|ton,
  Ste|phen(English
  churchman)
Lang|try, Lil|lie
  (British actress)
lan|guage+s
langue
langue de chat
  langues de chat
Langue|doc
  (former province,
  France)
langue d'oc
Languedoc-
  Roussil|lon
  (region, France)
langue d'oïl
lan|guid
lan|guid|ly
lan|guid|ness
lan|guish
  lan|guishes
  lan|guished
  lan|guish|ing
lan|guish|er+s
lan|guish|ing|ly
lan|guish|ment
lan|guor (idleness.
  △ **langur**)
lan|guor|ous
lan|guor|ous|ly
lan|gur+s
  (monkey.
  △ **languor**)
lani|ary
  lani|ar|ies
lan|ifer|ous
lan|iger|ous
lank
lank|ily
lanki|ness
lank|ly
lank|ness
lanky
  lank|ier
  lank|iest
lan|ner+s
lan|neret+s
lano|lin
Lan|sing (city,
  USA)
lans|que|net+s
lan|tana+s
Lan|tau (island,
  Hong Kong)
lan|tern+s

lantern-fish
  plural **lantern-fish**
  or **lantern-fishes**
lantern-fly
  lantern-flies
lantern-jawed
lan|tern jaws
lan|tern slide+s
lantern-wheel+s
lan|tha|nide+s
lan|tha|num
la|nugo
lan|yard+s
Lan|zar|ote (one of
  the Canary
  Islands)
Lan|zhou (city,
  China)
Laoc|oon *Greek*
  Mythology
Lao|di|cean+s
Laoighis (use
  Laois)
Laois (county,
  Republic of
  Ireland)
Laos (in SE Asia)
Lao|tian+s
Lao-tzu (legendary
  founder of
  Taoism)
Laoze (use **Lao-**
  tzu)
lap
  laps
  lapped
  lap|ping
La Palma (one of
  the Canary
  Islands. △ **Las**
  Palmas, **Palma**)
lap|aro|scope+s
lapar|os|copy
  lapar|os|cop|ies
lapar|ot|omy
  lapar|oto|mies
La Paz (capital of
  Bolivia)
lap|dog+s
lapel+s
la|pelled
lap|ful+s
lapi|cide+s
lapi|dary
  lapi|dar|ies
lapi|date
  lapi|dat|ing
lapi|da|tion
la|pilli
lapis laz|uli
La|pita

Lap|ith+s *Greek*
  Mythology
lap joint+s
La|place, Mar|quis
  de(French
  mathematician
  and physicist)
Lap|land(region,
  N. Europe)
Lap|land|er+s
Lapp+s
lap|pet+s
lap|pet|ed
Lapp|ish
lap|sang
  sou|chong
lapse
  lapses
  lapsed
  laps|ing
lapser+s
lap|stone+s
lap-strake+s
lap|sus ca|lami
lap|sus lin|guae
Lap|tev Sea(part
  of Arctic Ocean)
lap|top+s
La|pu|tan+s
lap-weld+s +ed
  +ing
lap|wing+s
Lara (first name)
Lara, Brian(West
  Indian cricketer)
Lara|mie(city,
  USA)
lar|board+s
lar|cen|er+s
lar|cen|ist+s
lar|cen|ous
lar|ceny
  lar|cenies
larch
  larches
larch-lap
larch|wood+s
lard+s +ed +ing
lar|der+s
larding-needle+s
larding-pin+s
lar|don+s
lar|doon+s
lardy
lardy-cake+s
lardy-dardy
lares
large
  larger
  largest
large|ly
large-minded

lar|gen+s +ed
  +ing
large|ness
large-scale
lar|gess(use
  largesse)
lar|gesse
lar|ghet|to+s
lar|gish
largo+s
lari
  plural **lari** or **laris**
lar|iat+s
La|ris|sa(city,
  Greece)
lark+s +ed +ing
Lar|kin, Philip
  (English poet and
  novelist)
lar|ki|ness
lark|spur+s
larky
larn+s +ed +ing
La
  Roche|fou|cauld,
  Fran|çois de
  Mar|sil|lac, Duc
  de(French
  moralist)
La Ro|chelle(port,
  France)
La|rousse, Pierre
  (French
  lexicographer and
  encyclopedist)
lar|ri|kin+s
lar|rup+s +ed
  +ing
Larry
larva
  lar|vae
  (form of insect.
  △ **lava**)
lar|val
lar|vi|cide+s
la|ryn|geal
la|ryn|ges
la|ryn|gic
laryn|git|ic
laryn|gi|tis
laryn|gol|ogy
la|ryn|go|scope+s
laryn|got|omy
  laryn|goto|mies
lar|ynx
  la|ryn|ges
la|sagne+s
La Salle, Rob|ert
  Ca|va|lier
  (French explorer)
La Scala (opera
  house, Italy)

Las¦car +s
Las¦caux (in
  France)
  Archaeology
las¦civi¦ous
las¦civi¦ous¦ly
las¦civi¦ous¦ness
lase
  lases
  lased
  las¦ing
laser +s
laser¦disc +s
Laser¦Vision *Propr.*
lash
  lashes
  lashed
  lash¦ing
lash¦er +s
lash¦ing +s
lash¦ing¦ly
lash¦kar +s
lash¦less
lash-up +s *adjective
  and noun*
Las Pal¦mas
  (capital of the
  Canary Islands.
  △ La Palma)
La Spe¦zia (port,
  Italy)
lass
  lasses
Lassa fever
las¦sie +s
las¦si¦tude
lasso
  las¦sos *or* las¦soes
  noun
lasso
  las¦soes
  las¦soed
  lasso¦ing
  verb
las¦so¦er +s
Las¦sus, Or¦lande
  de (Flemish
  composer)
last +s +ed +ing
last-ditch *attributive*
last¦ing¦ly
last¦ing¦ness
last¦ly
last-minute
  adjective
Las Vegas (city,
  USA)
lat. (= latitude)
La¦ta¦kia (port,
  Syria)
latch
  latches

latch (*cont.*)
  latched
  latch¦ing
latchet +s
latch¦key +s
late
  later
  lat¦est
late¦comer +s
la¦teen +s
late¦ish (use latish)
late la¦ment¦ed
late¦ly
laten +s +ed +ing
la¦tency
  la¦ten¦cies
La Tène
late¦ness
la¦tent
la¦tent¦ly
lat¦eral +s
lat¦eral¦ly
Lat¦eran (in Rome;
  Council; Palace;
  Treaty)
lat¦ere (in 'legate a
  latere')
lat¦er¦ite +s
lat¦er¦it¦ic
latex
  la¦texes *or*
  la¦ti¦ces
lath +s +ed +ing
  (thin strip)
lathe +s (machine)
la¦ther +s +ed
  +ing
la¦thery
lathi +s
lathy
la¦ti¦ces
la¦ti¦fun¦dium
  la¦ti¦fun¦dia
Lati¦mer, Hugh
  (English martyr)
Latin +s
La¦tina +s
Lat¦in¦ate
Lat¦in¦isa¦tion *Br.*
  (use Latinization)
Lat¦in¦ise *Br.* (use
  Latinize)
  Lat¦in¦ises
  Lat¦in¦ised
  Lat¦in¦is¦ing
Lat¦in¦iser *Br.* +s
  (use Latinizer)
Lat¦in¦ism +s
Lat¦in¦ist +s
Lat¦in¦iza¦tion
Lat¦in¦ize
  Lat¦in¦izes

Lat¦in¦ize (*cont.*)
  Lat¦in¦ized
  Lat¦in¦iz¦ing
Lat¦in¦izer +s
La¦tino +s
lat¦ish
lati¦tude +s
lati¦tu¦din¦al
lati¦tu¦din¦al¦ly
lati¦tu¦din¦ar¦ian
  +s
lati¦tu¦din¦ar¦ian¦
              ism
La¦tium (ancient
  region, Italy)
La¦tona *Roman
  Mythology*
la¦tria +s
la¦trine +s
lat¦ten +s
lat¦ter
latter-day
Latter-day Saints
lat¦ter¦ly
lat¦tice +s
lat¦ticed
lattice-work
lat¦ticing
Lat¦via
Lat¦vian +s
Laud, Wil¦liam
  (English
  churchman)
laud +s +ed +ing
  (praise. △ lord)
Lauda, Niki
  (Austrian motor-
  racing driver)
laud¦abil¦ity
laud¦able
laud¦ably
laud¦anum (drug.
  △ ladanum)
laud¦ation +s
laud¦ative
laud¦atory
lauds (prayers.
  △ lords)
laugh +s +ed +ing
laugh¦able
laugh¦ably
laugh¦er +s
laughing gas
laugh¦ing¦ly
laughing stock +s
laugh¦ter
Laugh¦ton,
  Charles (English-
  born American
  actor)
launce +s (fish.
  △ lance)

Launce¦lot
  (Arthurian knight;
  use Lancelot)
Laun¦ces¦ton (city,
  Tasmania; town,
  Cornwall)
launch
  launches
  launched
  launch¦ing
launch¦er +s
launch pad +s
laun¦der +s +ed
  +ing
laun¦der¦er +s
laun¦der¦ette +s
laun¦dress
  laun¦dresses
laun¦drette +s (use
  launderette)
laun¦dro¦mat +s
laun¦dry
  laun¦dries
laun¦dry¦man
  laun¦dry¦men
Laura
Laur¦asia (ancient
  continent)
laure¦ate +s
laure¦ate¦ship +s
Laurel (name)
laurel
  laurels
  laur¦elled *Br.*
  laur¦eled *Am.*
  laurel¦ling *Br.*
  laurel¦ing *Am.*
  (plant)
Laurel and Hardy
  in full Stan Laurel
  and Oli¦ver Hardy
  (American
  comedians)
Lau¦ren
Laur¦ence *also*
  Law¦rence
Laur¦en¦tian
Plat¦eau (in
  Canada)
Lau¦rie
Laur¦ier, Wil¦frid
  (Canadian prime
  minister)
lau¦rus¦ti¦nus
  lau¦rus¦ti¦nuses
Lau¦sanne (town,
  Switzerland)
LAUTRO (= Life
  Assurance and
  Unit Trust
  Regulatory
  Organization)

lav (= lavatory)
lava +s (volcanic material. △ larva, laver)
la|vabo +s
lav|age
lav|ation
lava|tor|ial
lav|atory
  lav|ator|ies
lave
  laves
  laved
  lav|ing
Lav|en|der (name)
lav|en|der +s (plant)
lavender-water +s
Laver, Rod (Australian tennis player)
laver +s (seaweed; bread; washing-vessel. △ lava, larva)
lav|er|ock +s
Lav|in|ia
lav|ish
  lav|ishes
  lav|ished
  lav|ish|ing
lav|ish|ly
lav|ish|ness
La|vois|ier, An|toine Laur|ent (French scientist)
lavvy
  lav|vies (= lavatory)
Law, Bonar (Canadian-born British prime minister)
law +s (rule. △ lore)
law-abiding
law-abiding|ness
law|break|er +s
law|break|ing
law court +s
law|ful
law|ful|ly
law|ful|ness
law|giv|er +s
lawks
law|less
law|less|ly
law|less|ness
law|maker +s
law-making

law|man
  law|men
lawn +s +ed +ing (grass. △ lorn)
lawn|mow|er +s
lawn ten|nis
lawny
Law|rence also Laur|ence
Law|rence (Roman saint)
Law|rence, D. H. (English writer and painter)
Law|rence, Er|nest Or|lando (American physicist)
Law|rence, Thomas (English painter)
Law|rence, T. E. (English soldier and writer)
law|ren|cium
law|suit +s
law term +s
law|yer +s
law|yer|ly
lax +er +est
laxa|tive +s
lax|ity
  lax|ities
laxly
lax|ness
lay
  lays
  laid
  lay|ing (place; produce egg; not ordained; not professional; poem; song; past tense of lie. △ lei, ley)
lay|about +s
Laya|mon (English poet and priest)
lay-by +s noun
layer +s (person or thing that lays. △ lair)
layer +s +ed +ing (thickness; arrange in layers. △ lair)
layer-out
  layers-out
lay|ette +s
laying-out noun and adjective

lay|man
  lay|men
lay-off +s noun
La'youn (capital of Western Sahara)
lay|out +s
lay|over +s
lay|per|son +s
lay|shaft +s
lay|stall +s
lay|woman
  lay|women
lazar +s
laza|ret +s
laza|retto +s
Laz|ar|ist +s
laze
  lazes
  lazed
  laz|ing
lazi|ly
lazi|ness
Lazio (region, Italy)
laz|uli
lazy
  lazi|er
  lazi|est
lazy|bones
  plural lazy|bones
l-dopa (= levodopa)
L-driver +s
lea (meadow. △ lee, ley)
Leach, Ber|nard (British potter)
leach
  leaches
  leached
  leach|ing (percolate. △ leech)
leach|er +s
Lea|cock, Ste|phen (Canadian humorist and economist)
lead +s +ed +ing (metal. △ led)
lead
  leads
  led
  lead|ing (guide. △ lied, lead = metal)
lead|able
lead|en
lead|en|ly
lead|en|ness
lead|er +s
lead|er board +s

lead|er|ene +s
lead|er|less
lead|er|ship +s
lead-free
lead-in +s noun
lead|ing +s
leading-rein +s
lead|less
lead-off +s noun
lead poi|son|ing
lead time +s
lead|work
lead|wort +s
leaf
  leaves (on tree; paper; etc. △ lief)
leaf +s +ed +ing verb
leaf|age
leaf-beetle +s
leaf|cut|ter +s
leaf green +s noun and adjective
leaf-green attributive
leaf|hop|per +s
leafi|ness
leaf|less
leaf|less|ness
leaf|let +s +ed +ing
leaf|like
leaf miner +s
leaf mon|key +s
leaf mould +s
leaf-stalk +s
leafy
  leafi|er
  leafi|est
league
  leagues
  leagued
  lea|guing
lea|guer +s
Leah
leak +s +ed +ing (escape of liquid etc. △ leek)
leak|age +s
leak|er +s
Lea|key, Louis (British archaeologist and anthropologist)
leaki|ness
leak|proof
leaky
  leaki|er
  leaki|est
leal

Leam¦ing¦ton Spa
  official name **Royal
  Leam¦ing¦ton Spa**
  (town, England)
Lean, David
  (English film
  director)
lean
  leans
  leaned *or* leant
  lean¦ing
lean-burn
Le¦an¦der *Greek
  Mythology*
lean¦ing +s
lean¦ly
Le¦anne
lean¦ness
leant (past tense
  and past participle
  of lean. △ lent)
lean-to +s
leap
  leaps
  leaped *or* leapt
  leap¦ing
leap¦er +s
leap¦frog
  leap¦frogs
  leap¦frogged
  leap¦frog¦ging
leap year +s
Lear, Ed¦ward
  (English artist and
  poet)
Lear
  (Shakespearean
  character)
learn
  learns
  learned *or* learnt
  learn¦ing
learn¦abil¦ity
learn¦able
learn¦ed
  (knowledgeable)
learn¦ed¦ly
learn¦ed¦ness
learn¦er +s
leas¦able
lease
  leases
  leased
  leas¦ing
lease¦back +s
lease¦hold +s
lease¦hold¦er +s
Lease-Lend
leas¦er +s
leash
  leashes

leash (*cont.*)
  leashed
  leash¦ing
least
least¦ways
least¦wise
leat +s
  (watercourse.
  △ leet, lied)
lea¦ther +s +ed
  +ing
lea¦ther¦back +s
leather-bound
lea¦ther¦cloth +s
lea¦ther¦ette
lea¦theri¦ness
lea¦ther¦jacket +s
lea¦thern
lea¦ther¦neck +s
lea¦ther¦oid
lea¦ther¦wear
lea¦thery
leave
  leaves
  left
  leav¦ing
leaved
leaven +s +ed
  +ing
leav¦er +s
leave-taking +s
leav¦ings
Lea¦vis, F. R.
  (English literary
  critic)
Leba¦nese
  plural **Leba¦nese**
Leba¦non
**Leba¦non
  Moun¦tains**
Le¦bens¦raum
Le¦blanc, Nico¦las
  (French surgeon
  and chemist)
Le¦bowa (former
  homeland, South
  Africa)
Le¦brun, Charles
  (French painter,
  designer, and
  decorator)
Le Carré, John
  (English novelist)
lech
  leches
  leched
  lech¦ing
lech¦er +s
lech¦er¦ous
lech¦er¦ous¦ly
lech¦er¦ous¦ness
lech¦ery

leci¦thin
**Le¦clan¦ché,
  Georges** (French
  chemist; cell)
**Le¦conte de Lisle,
  Charles-Marie-
  René** (French
  poet)
Le Cor¦bu¦sier
  (French architect)
lec¦tern +s
lec¦tin +s
lec¦tion +s
lec¦tion¦ary
lec¦tion¦ar¦ies
lec¦tor +s (in
  'lecturer' sense,
  male)
lec¦trice +s *female*
lec¦ture
  lec¦tures
  lec¦tured
  lec¦tur¦ing
lec¦tur¦er +s
lec¦tur¦er¦ship +s
lec¦ture¦ship +s
lecy¦thus
lecy¦thi
led (past tense and
  past participle of
  lead = guide.
  △ lead = metal)
Leda *Greek
  Mythology*
leder¦hosen
ledge +s
ledged
ledger +s
ledger line +s (use
  leger line)
ledger-tackle
ledgy
Led Zep¦pe¦lin
  (British rock
  group)
Lee (name)
Lee, Bruce
  (American actor)
Lee, Gypsy Rose
  (American
  striptease artist)
**Lee, Rob¦ert
  Ed¦ward**
  (American soldier)
lee (shelter. △ lea,
  ley)
lee-board +s
leech
  leeches
  (worm; healer; on
  sail. △ leach)
leech¦craft

Leeds (city,
  England)
leek +s (vegetable.
  △ leak)
leer +s +ed +ing
  (look slyly. △ lehr)
leeri¦ness
leer¦ing¦ly
leery
  leer¦ier
  leeri¦est
lees
lee shore +s
lee side +s
leet +s (court.
  △ leat, lied)
Leeu¦war¦den
  (town, the
  Netherlands)
**Leeu¦wen¦hoek,
  An¦toni van**
  (Dutch naturalist)
lee¦ward +s
Lee¦ward Is¦lands
  (in the Caribbean)
lee¦ward¦ly
lee¦way
**Le Fanu, Jo¦seph
  Sheri¦dan** (Irish
  novelist)
Left *Politics*
left +s (opposite of
  'right'; past tense
  and past participle
  of leave)
left-back +s
Left Bank (district,
  Paris)
left bank +s
left-footed
left hand +s
left-hand *attributive*
left-handed
left-handed¦ly
left-handed¦ness
left-hander +s
leftie +s (use lefty)
left¦ish
left¦ism
left¦ist +s
left lug¦gage
left¦most
left¦over +s
left¦ward
left¦wards
left wing +s *noun*
left-wing *adjective*
left-winger +s
lefty
  left¦ies
leg
  legs

leg (*cont.*)
legged
leg¦ging
leg¦acy
leg¦acies
legacy-hunter +s
legal
legal aid
le¦gal¦ese
le¦gal¦isa¦tion *Br.*
(use legalization)
le¦gal¦ise *Br.* (use
legalize)
le¦gal¦ises
le¦gal¦ised
le¦gal¦is¦ing
le¦gal¦ism +s
le¦gal¦ist +s
le¦gal¦is¦tic
le¦gal¦is¦tic¦al¦ly
le¦gal¦ity
le¦gal¦ities
le¦gal¦iza¦tion
le¦gal¦ize
le¦gal¦izes
le¦gal¦ized
le¦gal¦iz¦ing
le¦gal¦ly
leg¦ate +s
leg¦ate a lat¦ere
leg¦ates a lat¦ere
lega¦tee +s
leg¦ate¦ship +s
lega¦tine
le¦ga¦tion +s
le¦gato +s
lega¦tor +s
leg-break +s
leg-bye +s
leg-cutter +s
le¦gend +s
le¦gend¦ar¦ily
le¦gend¦ary
(remarkable; of or
connected with
legends)
le¦gend¦ry (legends
collectively)
Léger, Fer¦nand
(French painter)
leger +s
le¦ger¦de¦main
leger line +s
leg¦ger +s
leg¦gi¦ness
leg¦ging +s
leg-guard +s
leggy
leg¦gier
leg¦gi¦est

**Leg¦hari, Far¦ooq
Ahmed** (Pakistani
president)
Leg¦horn +s
(English name for
Livorno; domestic
fowl)
leg¦horn +s (straw;
hat)
le¦gi¦bil¦ity
le¦gible
le¦gibly
le¦gion +s
le¦gion¦aire +s (use
legionnaire)
le¦gion¦ary
le¦gion¦ar¦ies
le¦gioned
le¦gion¦ella
le¦gion¦naire +s
le¦gion¦naires'
dis¦ease
leg-iron +s
le¦gis¦late
le¦gis¦lates
le¦gis¦lated
le¦gis¦lat¦ing
le¦gis¦la¦tion
le¦gis¦la¦tive
le¦gis¦la¦tive¦ly
le¦gis¦la¦tor +s
le¦gis¦la¦ture +s
legit +s
(= legitimate)
le¦git¦im¦acy
le¦git¦im¦ate
le¦git¦im¦ates
le¦git¦im¦ated
le¦git¦im¦at¦ing
le¦git¦im¦ate¦ly
le¦git¦im¦ation
le¦git¦ima¦tisa¦tion
Br. (use
legitimatization)
le¦git¦ima¦tise *Br.*
(use legitimatize)
le¦git¦ima¦tises
le¦git¦ima¦tised
le¦git¦ima¦tis¦ing
le¦git¦ima¦tiza¦tion
le¦git¦ima¦tize
le¦git¦ima¦tizes
le¦git¦ima¦tized
le¦git¦ima¦tiz¦ing
le¦git¦im¦isa¦tion
Br. (use
legitimization)
le¦git¦im¦ise *Br.*
(use legitimize)
le¦git¦im¦ises

le¦git¦im¦ise (*cont.*)
le¦git¦im¦ised
le¦git¦im¦is¦ing
le¦git¦im¦ism
le¦git¦im¦ist +s
le¦git¦im¦iza¦tion
le¦git¦im¦ize
le¦git¦im¦izes
le¦git¦im¦ized
le¦git¦im¦iz¦ing
leg¦less
leg¦man
leg¦men
Lego *Propr.*
leg-of-mutton
attributive
leg-pull +s
leg-pulling
leg-rest +s
leg¦room
leg-show +s
leg slip +s
leg spin +s
leg-spinner +s
leg stump +s
leg the¦ory
leg trap +s
leg¦ume +s
leg¦um¦in¦ous
leg-up
leg warm¦er +s
leg¦work
Leh (town, India)
Lehár, Franz
(Hungarian
composer)
Le Havre (port,
France)
lehr +s (furnace.
△leer)
lei +s (garland;
wine-vessel.
△lay, ley)
lei (plural of leu.
△lay, ley)
**Leib¦niz,
Gott¦fried
Wil¦helm**
(German
philosopher)
Leib¦niz¦ian +s
Leices¦ter (city,
England; cheese)
Leices¦ter¦shire
(county, England)
**Leich¦hardt,
Fried¦rich
Wil¦helm
Lud¦wig** (German-
born explorer)
Lei¦den (city, the
Netherlands)

Leif Erics¦son
(Norse explorer)
Leigh, Viv¦ien
(British actress)
**Leigh¦ton,
Fred¦eric** (English
painter and
sculptor)
Leila
Lein¦ster (province,
Republic of
Ireland)
Leip¦zig (city,
Germany)
leish¦man¦ia¦sis
leis¦ter +s +ed
+ing
leis¦ure
leis¦ured
leis¦ure¦less
leis¦ure¦li¦ness
leis¦ure¦ly
leis¦ure¦wear
leit¦motif +s
leit¦motiv +s
Lei¦trim (county,
Republic of
Ireland)
Leix (use Laois)
lek +s
Lely, Peter (Dutch-
born painter)
LEM (= lunar
excursion module)
leman +s (lover.
△lemon)
Le Mans (town,
France)
lemma
lem¦mas *or*
lem¦mata
lemme
lem¦ming +s
Lem¦mon, Jack
(American actor)
Lem¦nos (island,
Greece)
lemon +s (fruit.
△leman)
lem¦on¦ade +s
lemon-squeezer
+s
lem¦ony
lem¦pira +s
lemur +s
lem¦ur¦ine
lem¦ur¦oid
Len
Lena (river, Siberia;
name)

Len|clos, Ninon de (French wit and beauty)
lend
lends
lent
lend|ing
lend|able
lend|er +s
lend|ing lib|rary
lend|ing
lib|rar|ies
Lendl, Ivan (Czech-born American tennis player)
Lend-Lease
length +s
length|en +s +ed +ing
length|en|er +s
length|ily
lengthi|ness
length|man
length|men
length|ways
length|wise
lengthy
length|ier
lengthi|est
le|ni|ence
le|ni|ency
le|ni|ent
le|ni|ent|ly
Lenin, Vlad|imir Ilich (Soviet statesman)
Len|in|akan (city, Armenia)
Len|in|grad (former name of St Petersburg)
Len|in|ism
Len|in|ist +s
Len|in|ite +s
len|ition +s
leni|tive +s
len|ity
len|ities
Len|non, John (English rock musician)
Len|nox
Lenny
leno +s
Le|nora
Le Nôtre, André (French landscape gardener)
lens
lenses
lensed
lens|less

lens|man
lens|men
Lent (period before Easter)
lent (past tense and past participle of lend. △ leant)
Lent|en (of or to do with Lent)
len|ti|cel +s
len|ticu|lar
len|tigo
len|ti|gi|nes
len|til +s
len|tisk +s
lento
len|toid
Leo (constellation; sign of zodiac; popes and Byzantine emperors)
León (cities, Spain, Mexico and Nicaragua)
Leona
Leon|ard
Leo|nardo da Vinci (Italian painter and designer)
leone +s
Leo|nids (meteor shower)
Léo|nie
Leo|nine (of Pope Leo)
leo|nine (of lions)
Leo|nine City (Vatican, Italy)
Leo|nora
leop|ard +s
leop|ard|ess
leop|ard|esses
leop|ard's bane
Leo|pold (Belgian king; name)
Léo|pold|ville (former name of Kinshasa)
leo|tard +s
Le|pan|to (naval battle off Greece)
Le|pan|to, Gulf of (alternative name for the Gulf of Corinth)
leper +s
Le|pi|dop|tera
le|pi|dop|teran +s
le|pi|dop|ter|ist +s
le|pi|dop|ter|ous

Lepi|dus, Mar|cus Aem|il|ius (Roman statesman and triumvir)
lep|or|ine
lep|re|chaun +s
lep|ro|sarium
lep|ro|saria
lep|rosy
lep|rous
lepta
Lep|tis Magna (ancient port, Libya)
lepto|ceph|al|ic
lepto|ceph|al|ous
lepto|dac|tyl +s
lep|ton lepta (coin)
lep|ton +s (particle)
lep|ton|ic
lepto|spir|osis
lepto|tene +s
Lepus (constellation)
Ler|mon|tov, Mikh|ail (Russian novelist and poet)
Leroy
Ler|wick (capital of the Shetland Islands)
Les (name)
Le|sage, Alain-René (French novelist and playwright)
Les|bian +s (of Lesbos)
les|bian +s (homosexual woman)
les|bian|ism
Les|bos (island, Greece)
lèse-majesté
lese-majesty
le|sion +s
Les|ley (chiefly woman's name)
Les|lie (chiefly man's name)
Le|so|tho (in southern Africa)
less
les|see +s
les|see|ship +s
less|en +s +ed +ing (diminish. △ lesson)

Les|seps, Fer|di|nand Marie, Vi|comte de (French diplomat)
less|er (not so great. △ lessor)
lesser-known
Les|sing, Doris (English novelist and short-story writer)
Les|sing, Gott|hold Eph|raim (German dramatist and critic)
Les Six (French composers)
les|son +s (period of tuition; assignment etc. △ lessen)
les|sor +s (person who lets property by lease. △ lessor)
lest
Les|ter
let
lets
let
let|ting
letch (use lech)
letches
letched
letch|ing
let-down +s *noun and adjective*
le|thal
le|thal|ity
le|thal|ly
leth|ar|gic
leth|ar|gic|al|ly
leth|argy
leth|ar|gies
Lethe *Greek Mythology*
Le|the|an
Le|ti|cia (port, Colombia)
Le|ti|tia *also* **Lae|ti|tia**
Leto *Greek Mythology*
let-off +s *noun*
let-out +s *noun and adjective*
let's (= let us)
Lett +s *archaic* = Latvian
let|ter +s +ed +ing

let¦ter bomb +s
let¦ter box
  let¦ter boxes
letter-card +s
letter-carrier +s
let¦ter¦er +s
let¦ter¦head +s
letter-heading +s
let¦ter¦ing
let¦ter¦less
letter-perfect
let¦ter¦press
  let¦ter¦presses
letter-quality
letter-writer +s
Let¦tic
Let¦tice (name)
let¦ting +s
Lett¦ish (*archaic*
  = Latvian)
let¦tuce +s
let-up +s *noun*
Letze¦burg¦esch
  (= Luxemburg-
  ish)
leu
  lei
  (Romanian
  currency)
leu¦cine +s
leuco¦blast *Br.* +s
  (*Am.* leukoblast)
leuco¦cyte *Br.* +s
  (*Am.* leukocyte)
leuco¦cyt¦ic *Br.*
  (*Am.* leukocytic)
leu¦coma +s
leu¦cor¦rhea *Am.*
leu¦cor¦rhoea *Br.*
leuco¦tome +s
leu¦cot¦omy
  leu¦coto¦mies
leu¦kae¦mia *Br.* +s
leu¦kaem¦ic *Br.*
leu¦ke¦mia *Am.* +s
leu¦kem¦ic *Am.*
leuko¦blast *Am.* +s
  (*Br.* leucoblast)
leuko¦cyte *Am.* +s
  (*Br.* leucocyte)
leuko¦cytic *Am.*
  (*Br.* leucocytic)
Leu¦ven (town,
  Belgium)
lev
  plural lev *or* levs
leva
  plural leva *or*
  levas
  (Bulgarian
  currency; = lev)
Le¦val¦lois

Le¦val¦lois¦ean +s
Le¦vant (E.
  Mediterranean)
le¦vant +s +ed
  +ing (abscond)
Le¦vant¦er +s
  (native or
  inhabitant of the
  Levant)
le¦vant¦er +s
  (breeze; person
  who levants)
Lev¦an¦tine +s (of
  the Levant)
le¦vator +s
levee +s
  (reception;
  embankment.
  ⚠ levy)
level
  levels
  lev¦elled *Br.*
  lev¦eled *Am.*
  lev¦el¦ling *Br.*
  lev¦el¦ing *Am.*
level cros¦sing +s
lev¦el¦er *Am.* +s
level-headed
level-headed¦ly
level-headed¦ness
Lev¦el¦ler +s
  (dissenter)
lev¦el¦ler *Br.* +s
levelling-screw +s
lev¦el¦ly
lev¦el¦ness
lever +s +ed +ing
le¦ver¦age
le¦ver¦ages
le¦ver¦aged
le¦ver¦aging
lev¦eret +s
Le¦ver¦hulme,
  Lord (William
  Lever, English
  industrialist)
Le¦ver¦ku¦sen (city,
  Germany)
Le Ver¦rier,
  Ur¦bain (French
  mathematician)
Levi *Bible*
Levi, Peter
  (English poet,
  scholar, and
  writer)
Levi, Primo (Italian
  writer and
  chemist)
levi¦able
le¦via¦than +s

levi¦gate
  levi¦gates
  levi¦gated
  levi¦gat¦ing
levi¦ga¦tion +s
levin +s
levi¦ir¦ate
le¦vir¦at¦ic
le¦vir¦at¦ic¦al
Levis (jeans) *Propr.*
Lévi-Strauss,
  Claude (French
  social
  anthropologist)
levi¦tate
  levi¦tates
  levi¦tated
  levi¦tat¦ing
levi¦ta¦tion +s
levi¦ta¦tor +s
Le¦vite +s
Le¦vit¦ic¦al
Le¦vit¦icus *Bible*
lev¦ity
levo¦dopa
levo¦rota¦tory *Am.*
le¦vu¦lose *Am.*
levy
  lev¦ies
  lev¦ied
  levy¦ing
  (tax; impose.
  ⚠ levee)
lewd +er +est
lewd¦ly
lewd¦ness
Lewes (town,
  England)
Lewis (island,
  Scotland; name)
Lewis, Carl
  (American athlete)
Lewis, C. S.
  (English scholar
  and writer)
Lewis,
  Meri¦wether
  (American
  explorer)
Lewis, Percy
  Wynd¦ham
  (British novelist
  and painter)
Lewis, Sin¦clair
  (American
  novelist)
lewis
  lewises
  (lifting device)
Lewis gun +s
Lew¦isham (suburb
  of London)

lew¦is¦ite
lex do¦mi¦ci¦lii
lex¦eme +s
lex fori
lex¦ic¦al
lex¦ic¦al¦ly
lexi¦cog¦raph¦er +s
lex¦ico¦graph¦ic
lex¦ico¦graph¦ic¦al
lex¦ico¦graph¦ic¦
  al¦ly
lexi¦cog¦raphy
lex¦ico¦logic¦al
lex¦ico¦logic¦al¦ly
lexi¦colo¦gist +s
lexi¦col¦ogy
lexi¦con +s
lex¦ig¦raphy
Lex¦ing¦ton (town,
  USA)
lexis
lex loci
lex tali¦onis
ley +s (field
  temporarily under
  grass; line of
  ancient track.
  ⚠ lay, lea, lei, lee)
Ley¦den (town; use
  Leiden)
Ley¦den, Lucas
  van (Dutch
  painter)
Ley¦den jar +s
ley farm¦ing
ley line +s
Leyte (island,
  Philippines)
Lhasa (capital of
  Tibet)
li¦abil¦ity
  li¦abil¦ities
li¦able
li¦aise
  li¦aises
  li¦aised
  li¦ais¦ing
li¦aison +s
Liam
liana +s
Liane (name)
liane +s (plant)
Liao
Liao¦dong
  Pen¦in¦sula (in
  China)
Liao¦ning (in
  China)
liar +s (person who
  tells a lie. ⚠ lyre)
Lias (Jurassic
  strata)

lias (blue limestone)
li|as|sic
lib (= liberation)
li|ba|tion +s
lib|ber +s
Libby
Lib Dem +s
(= Liberal Democrat)
libel
li|bels
li|belled *Br.*
li|beled *Am.*
li|bel|ling *Br.*
li|bel|ing *Am.*
li|bel|ant *Am.* +s
li|bel|ee *Am.* +s
li|bel|er *Am.* +s
li|bel|ist *Am.* +s
li|bel|lant *Br.* +s
li|bel|lee *Br.* +s
li|bel|ler *Br.* +s
li|bel|list *Br.* +s
li|bel|lous *Br.*
li|bel|lous|ly *Br.*
li|bel|ous *Am.*
li|bel|ous|ly *Am.*
liber +s
Li|ber|ace
(American pianist and entertainer)
Lib|eral +s *Politics*
lib|eral +s
Lib|eral Demo|crat +s *Politics*
lib|er|al|isa|tion *Br.* (use liberalization)
lib|er|al|ise *Br.* (use liberalize)
lib|er|al|ises
lib|er|al|ised
lib|er|al|is|ing
lib|er|al|iser *Br.* +s (use liberalizer)
lib|er|al|ism
lib|er|al|ist +s
lib|er|al|is|tic
lib|er|al|ity
lib|er|al|ities
lib|er|al|iza|tion
lib|er|al|ize
lib|er|al|izes
lib|er|al|ized
lib|er|al|iz|ing
lib|er|al|izer +s
lib|er|al|ly
lib|er|al|ness
lib|er|ate
lib|er|ates

lib|er|ate (*cont.*)
lib|er|ated
lib|er|at|ing
lib|er|ation +s
lib|er|ation|ist +s
lib|er|ator +s
Li|beria (in W. Africa)
Li|ber|ian +s
li|bero +s
lib|er|tar|ian +s
lib|er|tar|ian|ism
lib|er|tin|age
lib|er|tine +s
lib|er|tin|ism
lib|erty
lib|er|ties
Lib|erty Bell
lib|erty bod|ice +s
lib|erty hall
li|bid|in|al
li|bid|in|al|ly
li|bid|in|ous
li|bid|in|ous|ly
li|bid|in|ous|ness
li|bido +s
lib|itum (in 'ad libitum')
Lib-Lab (= Liberal and Labour)
Li Bo (alternative name for Li Po)
LIBOR (= London Inter-Bank Offered Rate)
Libra (constellation; sign of zodiac)
Libran +s
li|brar|ian +s
li|brar|ian|ship +s
li|brary
li|brar|ies
li|brary edi|tion +s
li|brate
li|brates
li|brated
li|brat|ing
li|bra|tion +s
li|bra|tory
li|bret|tist +s
li|bretto
li|bretti *or*
li|bret|tos
Libre|ville (capital of Gabon)
Lib|rium *Propr.*
Libya (in Africa)
Libyan +s
lice
li|cence *Br.* +s *noun*

li|cence (*verb*; use license)
li|cences
li|cenced
li|cen|cing
li|cens|able
li|cense
li|censes
li|censed
li|cens|ing *verb*
li|cense *Am.* +s *noun*
li|cen|see +s
li|cen|ser +s (use licensor)
li|cen|sor +s
li|cen|ti|ate +s
li|cen|tious
li|cen|tious|ly
li|cen|tious|ness
li|chee +s (use lychee)
li|chen +s
li|chened
li|chen|ology
li|chen|ous
Lich|field (town, England)
lich-gate +s
Lich|ten|stein, Roy (American painter and sculptor)
licit
licit|ly
lick +s +ed +ing
lick|er +s
lick|er|ish (lecherous. △ liquorish)
lickety-split
lick|ing +s
lick|spit|tle +s
lic|orice +s
lic|tor +s
lid +s
lid|ded
Lid|dell, Eric (British athlete)
Lid|dell Hart, Basil Henry (British military historian)
Li|dingö (island, Baltic Sea)
lid|less
lido +s
lido|caine
Lido (di Mala|mocco) (island off Venice)

Lie, Tryg|ve Halv|dan (Norwegian politician)
lie
lies
lay
lying
lain
(be horizontal. △ lye)
lie
lies
lied
lying
(tell untruths. △ lye)
Lieb|frau|milch +s
Lie|big, Jus|tus von (German chemist)
Liech|ten|stein
Liech|ten|stein|er +s
lied
lieder
(German song. △ lead, leader, leat, leet)
lie de|tect|or +s
lie-down +s
lief (gladly. △ leaf)
Liège (city and province, Belgium)
liege +s
liege|man
liege|men
lie-in +s *noun*
lien +s
li|erne +s
lieu +s (in 'in lieu of)'. △ loo)
lieu|ten|ancy
lieu|ten|an|cies
lieu|ten|ant +s
lieu|ten|ant col|onel +s
lieu|ten|ant com|mand|er +s
lieu|ten|ant gen|eral +s
lieutenant-governor +s
life
lives
life-and-death *attributive*
life|belt +s
life|blood +s
life|boat +s

life|boat|man
  life|boat|men
life|buoy +s
life cycle +s
life ex|pect|ancy
  life
    ex|pect|an|cies
life-force +s
life form +s
life-giving
life|guard +s (on
  beach etc.)
Life Guards
  (British regiment)
life his|tory
  life his|tor|ies
life jacket +s
life|less
life|less|ly
life|less|ness
life|like
life|like|ness
life|line +s
life|long
life-preserver +s
lifer +s
life-raft +s
life-saver +s
life size *noun*
life-size *adjective*
life-sized
life|span +s
life|style +s
life-support
  attributive
life's work
life-threaten|ing
life|time +s
life-work
Liffe (= London
  International
  Financial Futures
  Exchange)
Lif|fey (river,
  Republic of
  Ireland)
Lif|ford (town,
  Republic of
  Ireland)
LIFO (= last in, first
  out)
lift +s +ed +ing
lift|able
lift|er +s
lift-off +s *noun*
lig
  ligs
  ligged
  lig|ging
liga|ment +s
liga|men|tal
liga|men|tary

liga|ment|ous
lig|and +s
li|gate
  li|gates
  li|gated
  li|gat|ing
li|ga|tion +s
liga|ture
  liga|tures
  liga|tured
  liga|tur|ing
liger +s
Lig|eti, György
  (Hungarian
  composer)
lig|ger +s
light
  lights
  lit *or* light|ed
  light|ing
  light|er
  light|est
  (visible radiation;
  illuminate; bright;
  not heavy; (*lights*)
  lungs. △ lite)
light bulb +s
light-emitting
light|en +s +ed
  +ing
light|en|ing +s (in
  pregnancy.
  △ lightning)
light|er +s
light|er|age
light|er|man
  light|er|men
lighter-than-air
  attributive
light|fast
light-fingered
light|foot +s
light-footed
light-footed|ly
light-gun +s
light-headed
light-headed|ly
light-headed|ness
light-hearted
light-hearted|ly
light-hearted|ness
light|house +s
light|ing +s
lighting-up time
  +s
light|ish
light|less
light|ly
light meter +s
light|ness

light|ning (electric
  discharge.
  △ lightening)
light|ning
  con|duct|or +s
light|ning strike
  +s
light-o'-love
light-pen +s
light|proof
lights (lungs)
light|ship +s
light show +s
light|some
light|some|ly
light|some|ness
light|ves|sel +s
light|weight +s
light|wood +s
light year +s
lign-aloe +s
lig|neous
lig|nif|er|ous
ligni|form
lig|nify
  lig|ni|fies
  lig|ni|fied
  lig|ni|fy|ing
lig|nin
lig|nite +s
lig|nit|ic
lig|no|caine
lig|num vitae
lig|roin
ligu|late
lig|ule +s
Li|guria (region,
  Italy)
Li|gur|ian +s
Li|gur|ian Sea (in
  Mediterranean)
li|gus|trum +s
lik|abil|ity (use
  likeability)
lik|able (use
  likeable)
lik|able|ness (use
  likeableness)
lik|ably (use
  likeably)
like
  likes
  liked
  lik|ing
like|abil|ity
like|able
like|able|ness
like|ably
like|li|hood +s
like|li|ness

like|ly
  like|lier
  like|li|est
like-minded
like-minded|ly
like-minded|ness
liken +s +ed +ing
like|ness
  like|nesses
like|wise
lik|ing +s
Likud (Israeli
  political coalition)
li|kuta
  ma|kuta
lilac +s
li|lan|geni
  ema|lan|geni
lili|aceous
Lil|ian *also* Lil|lian
lil|ied
Li|lien|thal, Otto
  (German aviator)
Lil|ith (*Jewish
  Mythology*; name)
Lille (city, France)
Lil|lee, Den|nis
  (Australian
  cricketer)
Lil|lian *also* Lil|ian
Lil|li|bur|lero
lil|li|pu|tian +s
Lilo +s Propr.
Li|longwe (capital
  of Malawi)
lilt +s +ed +ing
Lily (name)
lily
  lil|ies
  (flower)
lily-livered
lily of the val|ley
  lil|ies of the
  val|ley
lily pad +s
lily-trotter +s
lily white +s *noun
  and adjective*
lily-white
  attributive
Lima (capital of
  Peru)
lima bean +s
Lim|as|sol (port,
  Cyprus)
limb +s (arm, leg,
  etc.; *Astronomy*;
  Botany. △ limn)
limbed
lim|ber +s +ed
  +ing
lim|ber|ness

lim|bic
limb|less
limbo +s
Lim|burg
  (province,
  Belgium and the
  Netherlands)
Lim|burg|er +s
lime
  limes
  limed
  lim|ing
lime|ade +s
lime green +s *noun*
  and adjective
lime-green
  attributive
lime|kiln +s
lime|less
lime|light
limen +s
lime|pit +s
Lim|er|ick (county
  and town,
  Republic of
  Ireland)
lim|er|ick +s
  (verse)
lime|stone +s
lime tree +s
lime|wash
  lime|washes
lime-wort +s
Limey +s (*offensive*
  Briton. △ limy)
limey *Br.*
  limi|er
  limi|est
  (containing lime.
  Am. limy)
limi|nal
limi|nal|ity
limit +s +ed +ing
limit|able
limit|ary
limi|ta|tion +s
limi|ta|tive
limit|ed|ly
limit|ed|ness
limit|er +s
limit|less
limit|less|ly
limit|less|ness
limn +s +ed +ing
  (paint. △ limb)
lim|ner +s
lim|no|logic|al
lim|nolo|gist +s
lim|nol|ogy
Lim|nos (Greek
  name for **Lemnos**)
limo +s

Li|moges (city,
  France)
Limón (port, Costa
  Rica)
Li|mou|sin (region,
  France)
lim|ou|sine +s
limp +s +ed +ing
  +er +est
lim|pet +s
lim|pid
lim|pid|ity
lim|pid|ly
lim|pid|ness
limp|ing|ly
limp|kin +s
limp|ly
limp|ness
Lim|popo (river,
  Africa)
limp|wort +s
limp-wristed
lim|ulus
  lim|uli
limy *Am.*
  limi|er
  limi|est
  (*Br.* limey.
  containing lime.
  △ Limey)
Lin|acre, Thomas
  (English physician
  and scholar)
lin|age +s (number
  of lines.
  △ lineage)
Lin Biao (Chinese
  statesman)
linch|pin +s
Lin|coln (cities,
  Canada and
  England)
Lin|coln,
  Abra|ham
  (American
  president)
Lin|coln|shire (in
  England)
Lin|coln's Inn
Lin|crusta *Propr.*
Lincs.
  (= Lincolnshire)
linc|tus
  linc|tuses
Lind, James
  (Scottish
  physician)
Lind, Jenny
  (Swedish soprano)
Linda *also* **Lynda**
lin|dane

Lind|bergh,
  Charles
  Au|gus|tus
  (American
  aviator)
Linde|mann,
  Fred|erick
  Alex|an|der
  (Lord Cherwell,
  German-born
  British physicist)
Lin|den (name)
lin|den +s (tree)
Lin|dis|farne
  (island, England)
Lind|say, Lio|nel
  and **Nor|man**
  (Australian artists)
Lind|say *also*
  Lind|sey, Lyn|sey
Lind|sey *also*
  Lind|say, Lyn|sey
Lin|dum Col|onia
  (Roman name for
  Lincoln, England)
Lindy
line
  lines
  lined
  lin|ing
lin|eage +s
  (ancestry.
  △ linage)
lin|eal
lin|eal|ly
lin|ea|ment +s
lin|ear
Lin|ear A
Lin|ear B
lin|ear|ise *Br.* (use
  linearize)
  lin|ear|ises
  lin|ear|ised
  lin|ear|is|ing
lin|ear|ity
lin|ear|ize
  lin|ear|izes
  lin|ear|ized
  lin|ear|iz|ing
lin|ear|ly
lin|ea|tion +s
line|back|er +s
line draw|ing +s
line|feed
Line Is|lands (in
  SW Pacific)
line|man
  line|men
linen +s
linen bas|ket +s
lin|en|fold
line-out +s *noun*

line print|er +s
liner +s
line|side
lines|man
  lines|men
line-up +s *noun*
Lin|ford
ling +s
linga +s (phallus.
  △ linger)
Lin|gala
lin|gam +s
lin|ger +s +ed +ing
  (be slow to leave.
  △ linga)
lin|ger|er +s
lin|ge|rie
lin|ger|ing|ly
lingo
  lin|gos *or* lin|goes
lin|gua franca +s
lin|gual
lin|gual|ise *Br.* (use
  lingualize)
  lin|gual|ises
  lin|gual|ised
  lin|gual|is|ing
lin|gual|ize
  lin|gual|izes
  lin|gual|ized
  lin|gual|iz|ing
lin|gual|ly
lin|gui|form
lin|guine
lin|guist +s
lin|guis|tic
lin|guis|tic|al|ly
lin|guis|ti|cian +s
lin|guis|tics
lin|guo|den|tal
lingy
lini|ment +s
lin|ing +s
link +s +ed +ing
link|age +s
link|man
  link|men
Lin|köp|ing (town,
  Sweden)
links (golf course.
  △ lynx)
link up
  links up
  linked up
  link|ing up
link-up +s *noun*
Lin|lith|gow (town,
  Scotland)
linn +s
Lin|naean +s
Lin|naeus,
  Caro|lus

Lin|naeus (*cont.*)
(Swedish
naturalist)
lin|net +s
lino +s
lino|cut +s
lino|cut|ting +s
lino|leic
lino|len|ic
li|no|leum +s
li|no|leumed
Lino|type *Propr.*
Lin Piao (= Lin
Biao)
lin|sang +s
lin|seed +s
linsey-woolsey +s
lin|stock +s
lint +s
lin|tel +s
lin|teled *Am.*
lin|telled *Br.*
lint|er +s
lint-free
linty
Linus
liny
lini|er
lini|est
Linz (city, Austria)
Lion, the
(constellation;
sign of zodiac)
lion +s
Lio|nel
lion|ess
lion|esses
Lion-Heart,
Rich|ard the
(English king)
lion-heart +s
lion-hearted
lion|hood
lion|isa|tion *Br.*
(use lionization)
lion|ise *Br.* (use
lionize)
lion|ises
lion|ised
lion|is|ing
lion|iser *Br.* +s (use
lionizer)
lion|iza|tion
lion|ize
lion|izes
lion|ized
lion|iz|ing
lion|izer +s
lion-like
Lions (British
Rugby Union
team)

lion-tamer +s
lip
lips
lipped
lip|ping
Li|pari Is|lands (off
Italy)
lip|ase +s
Lip|etsk (city,
Russia)
lipid +s
lip|id|osis
lip|id|oses
Lip|iz|za|ner +s
lip|less
lip|like
Li Po (Chinese
poet)
lip|og|raphy
lip|oid
lipo|pro|tein +s
lipo|some +s
lipo|suc|tion
Lippi, Fil|ip|pino
and Fra Fi|lippo
(Italian painters)
Lip|pi|za|ner +s
(use Lipizzaner)
Lipp|mann,
Gab|riel Jonas
(French physicist)
lippy
lip|pier
lip|pi|est
lip-read
lip-reads
lip-read
lip-reading
lip-reader +s
lip|salve +s
lip-service
lip|stick +s
lip-sync +s +ed
+ing
lip-syncer +s
lip-synch +s +ed
+ing (use lip-
sync)
lip-syncher +s (use
lip-syncer)
li|quate
li|quates
li|quated
li|quat|ing
li|qua|tion
li|que|fa|cient
li|que|fac|tion
li|que|fac|tive
li|que|fi|able
li|que|fier +s
li|quefy
li|que|fies

li|quefy (*cont.*)
li|que|fied
li|que|fy|ing
li|ques|cent
li|queur +s
li|quid +s
li|quid|am|bar +s
li|quid|ate
li|quid|ates
li|quid|ated
li|quid|at|ing
li|quid|ation +s
li|quid|ator +s
li|quid crys|tal +s
li|quid crys|tal
dis|play +s
li|quid|ise *Br.* (use
liquidize)
li|quid|ises
li|quid|ised
li|quid|is|ing
li|quid|iser *Br.* +s
(use liquidizer)
li|quid|ity
li|quid|ities
li|quid|ize
li|quid|izes
li|quid|ized
li|quid|iz|ing
li|quid|izer +s
li|quid|ly
li|quid|ness
li|qui|dus
li|qui|duses
li|quify (use
liquefy)
li|qui|fies
li|qui|fied
li|qui|fy|ing
li|quor +s
li|quor|ice +s
li|quor|ish (fond of
liquor.
△ lickerish)
li|quor|ish|ly
li|quor|ish|ness
lira
lire
Lisa *also* Liza
Lis|bon (capital of
Portugal)
Lis|burn (town,
Northern Ireland)
Lis|doon|varna
(town, Republic of
Ireland)
li|sente (plural of
sente)
lisle +s
lisp +s +ed +ing
lisp|er +s
lisp|ing|ly

lis|som
lis|some (use
lissom)
lis|som|ly
lis|som|ness
list +s +ed +ing
list|able
lis|ten +s +ed +ing
lis|ten|abil|ity
lis|ten|able
lis|ten|er +s
lis|ten|ing post +s
Lis|ter, Jo|seph
(English surgeon)
list|er +s
lis|teria +s
lis|teri|osis
list|ing +s
list|less
list|less|ly
list|less|ness
list price +s
Liszt, Franz
(Hungarian
composer and
pianist)
lit
Li T'ai Po
(alternative name
for Li Po)
lit|any
lit|anies
lit|chi +s (use
lychee)
lit crit (= literary
criticism)
lite (low-calorie;
over-simplified.
△ light)
liter *Am.* +s
lit|er|acy
lit|erae
hu|ma|ni|ores
lit|eral +s (to the
letter; misprint.
△ littoral)
lit|er|al|ise *Br.* (use
literalize)
lit|er|al|ises
lit|er|al|ised
lit|er|al|is|ing
lit|er|al|ism
lit|er|al|ist +s
lit|er|al|is|tic
lit|er|al|ity
lit|er|al|ize
lit|er|al|izes
lit|er|al|ized
lit|er|al|iz|ing
lit|er|al|ly
literal-minded
lit|er|al|ness

lit¦er¦ar¦ily
lit¦er¦ari¦ness
lit¦er¦ary
lit¦er¦ate +s
lit¦er¦ate¦ly
lit¦er¦ati
lit¦er¦atim
lit¦er¦ation
lit¦er¦ator +s
lit¦era¦ture +s
lith¦arge
lithe
lithe¦ly
lithe¦ness
lithe¦some
lithia
lith¦ic
lith¦ium
litho +s +ed +ing
litho¦graph +s +ed +ing
lith¦og¦raph¦er +s
litho¦graph¦ic
litho¦graph¦ic¦al¦ly
lith¦og¦raphy
litho¦logic¦al
lith¦olo¦gist +s
lith¦ology
litho¦phyte +s
litho¦pone
litho¦sphere
litho¦spher¦ic
lith¦ot¦om¦ist +s
lith¦ot¦om¦ize
  lith¦ot¦om¦izes
  lith¦ot¦om¦ized
  lith¦ot¦om¦iz¦ing
lith¦ot¦omy
  lith¦oto¦mies
litho¦tripsy
litho¦trip¦ter +s
litho¦trip¦tic
lith¦ot¦rity
  lith¦ot¦rities
Lithu¦ania
Lithu¦anian +s
lit¦ig¦able
liti¦gant +s
liti¦gate
  liti¦gates
  liti¦gated
  liti¦gat¦ing
liti¦ga¦tion
liti¦ga¦tor +s
li¦ti¦gious
li¦ti¦gious¦ly
li¦ti¦gious¦ness
lit¦mus
lit¦mus test +s
li¦to¦tes
litre +s
litre¦age +s

Litt.D. (= Doctor of Letters)
lit¦ter +s +ed +ing
lit¦tér¦ateur +s
lit¦ter¦bug +s
lit¦ter lout +s
lit¦tery
lit¦tle
  lit¦tler
  lit¦tlest
Lit¦tle Big¦horn (battle site, USA)
Lit¦tle Eng¦land¦er +s
lit¦tle known
little-known *attributive*
little¦ness
Lit¦tle Rus¦sian +s (= Ukrainian)
Little¦wood, Joan (English theatre director)
lit¦toral +s (shore. △ literal)
Littré, Émile (French philosopher and lexicographer)
li¦tur¦gic¦al
li¦tur¦gic¦al¦ly
li¦tur¦gics
li¦tur¦gi¦ology
lit¦ur¦gist +s
lit¦urgy
  lit¦ur¦gies
Liu¦chow (= Liuzhou)
Liu¦zhou (city, China)
liv¦abil¦ity (use liveability)
liv¦able (use liveable)
liv¦able¦ness (use liveableness)
live
  lives
  lived
  liv¦ing
  verb
live *adjective*
live¦abil¦ity
live¦able
live¦able¦ness
lived-in *adjective*
live-in +s *adjective and noun*
live¦li¦hood +s
live¦lily
live¦li¦ness
live¦long +s

live¦ly
live¦lier
live¦li¦est
liven +s +ed +ing
liver +s
liver color *Am.*
liver col¦our *Br.*
liv¦er¦ied
liv¦er¦ish
liv¦er¦ish¦ly
liv¦er¦ish¦ness
liv¦er¦less
Liv¦er¦pool (city, England)
Liv¦er¦pud¦lian +s
liv¦er¦wort +s
liv¦ery
  liv¦er¦ies
liv¦ery¦man
  liv¦ery¦men
lives (plural of life)
live¦stock
live¦ware
live wire +s
Livia
livid
liv¦id¦ity
liv¦id¦ly
liv¦id¦ness
liv¦ing +s
liv¦ing room +s
Liv¦ing¦stone (former name of Maramba)
Liv¦ing¦stone, David (Scottish missionary and explorer)
Li¦vo¦nia
Li¦vorno (port, Italy)
Livy (Roman historian)
lix¦ivi¦ate
  lix¦ivi¦ates
  lix¦ivi¦ated
  lix¦ivi¦at¦ing
lix¦ivi¦ation
Liz
Liza *also* **Lisa**
liz¦ard +s
Liz¦zie *also* **Lizzy**
Lizzy *also* **Liz¦zie**
Ljub¦ljana (capital of Slovenia)
llama +s (animal. △ lama)
Llan¦drin¦dod Wells (town, Wales)
Llan¦dudno (town, Wales)

lla¦nero +s
Llan¦gollen (town, Wales)
llano +s
Lle¦we¦lyn (Welsh prince)
Llosa, Mario Var¦gas (Peruvian writer)
Lloyd, Marie (English music-hall singer)
Lloyd George, David (British prime minister)
Lloyd's *Insurance*
Lloyd's List
Lloyd's Regis¦ter
Lloyd Web¦ber, An¦drew (English composer)
Llu¦llai¦llaco (mountain, Argentina; volcano, Chile)
lo (*interjection.* △ low)
loa *plural* **loa** *or* **loas** (voodoo god. △ lower)
loach
  loaches
load +s +ed +ing (burden; to carry. △ lode)
load-bearing
load-draught +s
load¦er +s
load¦ing +s
load line +s
load¦star +s (use lodestar)
load¦stone +s (use lodestone)
loaf +s +ed +ing (to idle)
loaf
  loaves (bread)
loaf¦er +s (idler)
loaf¦er +s (shoe) *Propr.*
loam +s
loami¦ness
loamy
  loami¦er
  loami¦est
loan +s +ed +ing (lend; something lent. △ lone)
loan¦able

loan|ee +s
loan|er +s (lender.
  △ loner)
loan|hold|er +s
loan shark +s
loan-transla|tion
  +s
loan|word +s
loath (reluctant)
loathe
  loathes
  loathed
  loath|ing
  (despise)
loath|er +s
loath|some
loath|some|ly
loath|some|ness
loaves
lob
  lobs
  lobbed
  lob|bing
Lo|ba|chev|ski,
  Ni|ko|lai
  Ivan|ovich
  (Russian
  mathematician)
lobar
lo|bate
lob|ation
lobby
  lob|bies
  lob|bied
  lobby|ing
lob|by|er +s
lobby|ism
lobby|ist +s
lobe +s
lob|ec|tomy
  lob|ec|to|mies
lobed
lobe|less
lo|belia +s
Lo|bito (port,
  Angola)
lob|lolly
  lob|lol|lies
lob|ot|om|ise Br.
  (use lobotomize)
lob|ot|om|ises
lob|ot|om|ised
lob|ot|om|is|ing
lob|ot|om|ize
  lob|ot|om|izes
  lob|ot|om|ized
  lob|ot|om|iz|ing
lob|ot|omy
  lo|boto|mies
lob|scouse
lob|ster +s +ed
  +ing

lob|ster pot +s
lob|ster
  ther|mi|dor
  Cookery
lobu|lar
lobu|late
lob|ule +s
lob|worm +s
local +s
lo|cale +s
lo|cal|is|able Br.
  (use localizable)
lo|cal|isa|tion Br.
  (use localization)
lo|cal|ise Br. (use
  localize)
lo|cal|ises
lo|cal|ised
lo|cal|is|ing
lo|cal|ism
lo|cal|ity
  lo|cal|ities
lo|cal|iz|able
lo|cal|iza|tion
lo|cal|ize
  lo|cal|izes
  lo|cal|ized
  lo|cal|iz|ing
lo|cal|ly
lo|cal|ness
Lo|carno (town,
  Switzerland)
lo|cat|able
lo|cate
  lo|cates
  lo|cated
  lo|cat|ing
lo|ca|tion +s
lo|ca|tion|al
loca|tive +s
lo|ca|tor +s
loc. cit. (= loco
  citato)
loch +s (Scottish
  lake. △ lough)
lochan +s
Loch|gilp|head
  (town, Scotland)
lo|chia +s
lo|chial
Loch Lo|mond
  (lake, Scotland)
Loch Maree (lake,
  Scotland)
Loch Ness (lake,
  Scotland)
loch|side
loci
loci clas|sici
lock +s +ed +ing
lock|able
lock|age +s

Locke, John
  (English
  philosopher)
Locke, Jo|seph
  (English railway
  designer)
lock|er +s
Lock|er|bie (town,
  Scotland)
lock|er room +s
locket +s
lock|fast
lock|jaw
lock-keeper +s
lock-knit
lock|less
lock|nut +s
lock|out +s
locks|man
  locks|men
lock|smith +s
lock-up +s adjective
  and noun
Lock|yer, Jo|seph
  Nor|man (English
  astronomer)
loco +s
loco|mo|tion
loco|mo|tive +s
loco|motor
loco|mo|tory
loco-weed +s
locu|lar
locu|lus
  loc|uli
locum +s
locum ten|ency
  locum ten|en|cies
locum ten|ens
  locum ten|en|tes
locus
  loci
locus clas|si|cus
  loci clas|sici
locus standi Law
lo|cust +s
locust-bird +s
locust-eater +s
lo|cu|tion +s
locu|tory
  locu|tor|ies
lode +s (vein of
  metal ore. △ load)
loden +s
lode|star +s
lode|stone +s
Lodge, Oli|ver
  Jo|seph (English
  physicist)
lodge
  lodges

lodge (cont.)
  lodged
  lodg|ing
lodge|ment +s
lodg|er +s
lodg|ing +s
lodg|ing house +s
lo|di|cule +s
Łódź (city, Poland)
loess
loes|sial
Loewi, Otto
  (German-born
  American
  physiologist)
Lo|fo|ten Is|lands
  (in Norwegian
  Sea)
loft +s +ed +ing
loft|er +s
loft|ily
lofti|ness
lofty
  loft|ier
  lofti|est
log
  logs
  logged
  log|ging
Logan, Mount (in
  Canada)
logan +s
lo|gan|berry
  lo|gan|berries
logan-stone +s
loga|oed|ic
loga|rithm +s
loga|rith|mic
loga|rith|mic|al|ly
log|book +s
loge +s
log.
  (= natural
  logarithm)
log|ger +s
log|ger|head +s
log|gia +s (open-
  sided gallery.
  △ logia)
logia (plural of
  logion. △ loggia)
logic +s
lo|gic|al
logic|al|ity
logic|al|ly
lo|gi|cian +s
log|ion
  logia
lo|gis|tic
lo|gis|tic|al
lo|gis|tic|al|ly
lo|gis|tics

log|jam +s
log-line +s
logo +s
logo|gram +s
logo|graph|ic
log|om|achy
  log|om|achies
log|or|rhea *Am.*
log|or|rhe|ic *Am.*
log|or|rhoea *Br.*
log|or|rhoe|ic *Br.*
Logos (word of
  God)
logo|type +s
log|roll +s +ed
  +ing
log|roll|er +s
Lo|groño (town,
  Spain)
log|wood
Lo|hen|grin
  (legendary figure)
loin +s
loin|cloth +s
Loire (river,
  France)
Lois
loi|ter +s +ed +ing
loi|ter|er +s
Loki *Scandinavian*
  Mythology
Lola
Lola Mon|tez
  (mistress of
  Ludwig I of
  Bavaria)
Lo|lita
loll +s +ed +ing
Lol|land (island,
  Baltic Sea)
lol|la|pa|looza +s
Lol|lard +s
Lol|lard|ism
Lol|lardy
loll|er +s
lol|li|pop +s
lol|lop +s +ed +ing
lolly
  lol|lies
Lom|bard +s
Lom|bard|ic
Lom|bard Street
  (in London)
Lom|bardy (region,
  Italy)
Lom|bok (island,
  Indonesia)
Lomé (capital of
  Togo;
  Convention)
lo|ment +s
lo|ment|aceous

lo|men|tum
  lo|menta
Lo|mond, Loch
  (lake, Scotland)
Lon|don (capital of
  the United
  Kingdom; city,
  Canada)
Lon|don, Jack
  (American
  novelist)
Lon|don|derry
  (city, Northern
  Ireland)
Lon|don|er +s
lone (solitary.
  △ loan)
lone|li|ness
lone|ly
  lone|lier
  lone|li|est
loner +s (solitary
  person. △ loaner)
lone|some
lone|some|ly
lone|some|ness
long +s +ed +ing
  +er +est (not
  short; have a
  longing)
long. (= longitude)
long-ago *adjective*
long-awaited
Long Beach (city,
  USA)
long|board +s
long|boat +s
long|bow +s
long-case (clock)
long-chain
  attributive
long-dated
long-day *adjective*
long-dead
  attributive
long-delayed
long-distance
  adjective
long-drawn
long-drawn-out
longe
  longes
  longed
  longe|ing
lon|geron +s
long-established
  attributive
lon|gev|ity
long-faced
Long|fel|low,
  Henry

Long|fel|low
  (*cont.*)
  Wads|worth
  (American poet)
Long|ford (county,
  Republic of
  Ireland)
long|hair +s
long|hand +s
long-haul *adjective*
long-headed
long-headed|ness
long hop +s
long|horn +s
long|house +s
lon|gi|corn +s
long|ing +s
long|ing|ly
Lon|gi|nus (Greek
  writer)
long|ish
Long Is|land (in
  USA)
lon|gi|tude +s
lon|gi|tu|din|al
lon|gi|tu|din|al|ly
long johns
long jump
long-jumper +s
long-lasting
long-legged
long-life *adjective*
long-lived
long-lost
long off *Cricket*
long on *Cricket*
Long Par|lia|ment
  (1640–1653,
  England)
long-player +s
long-playing
long-range
  adjective
long-running
Long|shan (ancient
  Chinese
  civilization)
long|ship +s
long|shore
long|shore|man
  long|shore|men
long shot +s
long-sighted
long-sighted|ly
long-sighted|ness
long-sleeved
long|spur +s
long-standing
  adjective
long-stay *adjective*
long|stop
long-suffer|ing

long-suffering|ly
long-term *adjective*
long-time *adjective*
lon|gueur +s
long|ways
long-winded
long-winded|ly
long-winded|ness
long|wise
lo|ni|cera +s
Lons|dale (belt)
loo +s (lavatory;
  card game. △ lieu)
loof +s +ed +ing
loo|fah +s
look +s +ed +ing
look|alike +s
look|er +s
looker-on
  lookers-on
look-in +s *noun*
looking-glass
  looking-glasses
look|out +s
look-see +s *noun*
loom +s +ed +ing
loon +s
loo|ni|ness
loony
  loon|ies
  loon|ier
  loon|iest
loony-bin +s
  (*offensive*)
loop +s +ed +ing
loop|er +s
loop|hole
  loop|holes
  loop|holed
  loop|hol|ing
loopi|ness
loop line +s
loop-the-loop +s
  noun
loopy
  loop|ier
  loopi|est
loose
  looses
  loosed
  loos|ing
  loos|er
  loos|est
  (release; untie; not
  tight. △ lose, luce)
loose box
  loose boxes
loose-leaf *adjective*
loose-limbed
loose|ly
loose|ly twist|ed
loose|ly woven

loos¦en +s +ed
+ing
loos¦en¦er +s
loose|ness
loose|strife +s
(plant)
loos¦ish
loot +s +ed +ing
(booty. △lute)
loot¦er +s
lop
lops
lopped
lop¦ping
lope
lopes
loped
lop¦ing
lop-eared
lop-ears
lopho|branch +s
lopho|dont +s
lopho|phore +s
Lop Nor (area,
China)
lopo|lith +s
lop¦per +s
loppy
lop¦pier
lop¦pi¦est
lop|sided
lop|sided¦ly
lop|sided|ness
lo|qua¦cious
lo|qua¦cious¦ly
lo|qua¦cious|ness
lo|qua¦city
lo|quat +s
lo¦qui¦tur
lor interjection
loran +s
Lorca, Fe¦de¦rico
Gar¦cía (Spanish
poet and
dramatist)
lorch
lorches
lor¦cha +s
Lord (God)
lord +s +ed +ing
(noble; in 'lord it'.
△laud, lauds)
lord|less
lord|like
lord¦li|ness
lord|ling +s
lord¦ly
lord¦lier
lord¦li|est
lor|do¦sis
lor|do¦ses

lor|do¦tic
Lord's (cricket
ground, London)
Lord's Day
lord|ship +s
Lord's Prayer
Lord's Sup¦per
Lordy interjection
lore +s (traditions;
Zoology. △law)
Lore|lei +s
Loren, So¦phia
(Italian actress)
Lor|entz, Hen¦drik
An¦toon (Dutch
physicist)
Lor¦enz, Kon¦rad
(Austrian
zoologist)
Lor¦enzo de'
Med¦ici
(Florentine
statesman and
scholar)
Lor¦eto (town,
Italy; name)
Lor|etta
lor|gnette +s
lor|gnon +s
lori|cate +s
Lori|ent (port,
France)
lori|keet +s
loris
plural loris
lorn (abandoned.
△lawn)
Lorna
Lor|rain, Claude
(French painter)
Lor|raine (name)
Lor|raine (region,
France)
lorry
lor¦ries
lorry|load +s
lory
lor¦ies
los¦able
Los Ala¦mos (town,
USA)
Los Angel¦eno +s
Los An¦geles (city,
USA)
lose
loses
lost
los¦ing
(cease to have.
△loose)
loser +s

loss
losses
loss ad|just¦er +s
loss-leader +s
loss-maker +s
loss-making
lost
Lot Bible
Lot (river, France)
lot
lots
lot¦ted
lot¦ting
loth (use loath)
Lo|thario +s
Lo|thian (region,
Scotland)
Lo|thians, the
(former counties,
Scotland)
Loti, Pierre
(French novelist)
loti
ma¦loti
(Lesotho
currency)
lo|tion +s
lotsa (= lots of)
lotta (= lot of)
lot|tery
lot|ter¦ies
Lot¦tie
Lotto, Lor|enzo
(Italian painter)
lotto (game)
lotus
lo|tuses
lotus-eater +s
lotus-land +s
Lotus Sutra
Buddhism
Lou
Lou¦ang|
phra¦bang
(alternative name
for Luang
Prabang)
louche
loud +er +est
loud¦en +s +ed
+ing
loud hail¦er +s
loud|ish
loud¦ly
loud|mouth +s
loud-mouthed
loud|ness
loud|speak¦er +s
Lou|ella
Lou Geh¦rig's
disease

lough +s (Irish lake.
△loch)
Lough|bor¦ough
(town, England)
Louie
Louis (French and
Hungarian kings;
name)
Louis, Joe
(American boxer)
louis
plural louis
(= louis d'or)
Lou¦isa
louis d'or
plural louis d'or
(coin)
Lou¦ise
Lou¦isi|ana (state,
USA)
Louis-Napoleon
(Napoleon III of
France)
Louis Phil¦ippe
(French king)
Louis|ville (city,
USA)
lounge
lounges
lounged
loun¦ging
loun¦ger +s
loupe +s
louping-ill
lour +s +ed +ing
Lourdes (town,
France)
Lou|renço
Mar¦ques (former
name of Maputo)
lour|ing¦ly
loury
louse
louses
loused
lous|ing
verb
louse
lice
noun
louse|wort +s
lous|ily
lousi|ness
lousy
lous|ier
lousi|est
lout +s
Louth (county,
Republic of
Ireland; town,
Lincolnshire)
lout|ish

lout|ish|ly
lout|ish|ness
Lou|vain (French name for Leuven)
lou¦ver +s (use louvre)
Louvre (in Paris)
louvre +s
louvre-board +s
louvred
lov|abil|ity
lov¦able
lov¦able|ness
lov¦ably
lov¦age +s
lo¦vat +s
love
  loves
  loved
  lov¦ing
love|able
love af|fair +s
love-apple +s
love|bird +s
love|bite +s
love child
  love chil|dren
love feast +s
love game +s Sport
love-in-a-mist
Love|lace, Count|ess of (English mathematician)
Love|lace, Rich|ard (English poet)
love|less
love|less¦ly
love|less|ness
love let¦ter +s
love-lies-bleeding (plant)
love life
  love lives
love|lily
love|li|ness
Lov¦ell, Ber|nard (English physicist and astronomer)
Love|lock, James (British scientist)
love|lock +s
love|lorn
love¦ly
  love|lies
  love|lier
  love|li|est
love|mak¦ing
love match
  love matches
love nest +s

lover +s
lover|less
lover|like
love seat +s
love|sick
love|sick|ness
love|some
love song +s
love story
  love stor|ies
love|worthy
lovey +s (sweetheart. △ luvvy)
lovey-dovey
lov¦ing cup +s
lov¦ing kind|ness
lov¦ing¦ly
lov¦ing|ness
low +s +ed +ing +er +est (not high; moo. △ lo)
low-born
low¦boy +s
low-bred
low|brow
low|browed
low-calorie
Low Church noun and adjective
low-class adjective
Low Coun|tries (= The Netherlands, Belgium, and Luxembourg)
low-cut
low-density adjective
low-down +s noun and attributive
Low¦ell, Amy Law|rence (American poet)
Low¦ell, James Rus|sell (American poet and critic)
Low¦ell, Per|ci|val (American astronomer)
Low¦ell, Rob|ert Traill Spence (American poet)
lower +s +ed +ing (comparative of low; let down; make lower. △ loa, lour)
lower case noun
lower-case attributive

lower-class adjective
Lower Hutt (city, New Zealand)
lower-middle-class adjective
lower|most
Low¦es|toft (port, England)
low-fat
low-flying
low gear +s
low-grade
low-growing
low-income
low¦ish
low-key
low|land +s
low|land¦er +s
low-level adjective
low|life
  plural low|lifes or low|lives (member of the underworld)
low life (degenerate living; criminal existence)
low-life (to do with low life)
low|light +s (dull feature; dark tint)
low light (dim light)
low-light (in or needing little light)
low|lily
low|li|ness
low-loader +s
lowly
  low|lier
  low|li|est
low-lying
low-minded
low-minded¦ness
low|ness
low-paid
low-pitched
low-price adjective
low-priced
low-profile adjective
low-rise adjective
Lowry, Law|rence Ste|phen (English artist)
Lowry, Mal|colm (English novelist)
low-spirit¦ed
low-spirit¦ed|ness
low spi¦rits

low water mark +s
lox (liquid oxygen; smoked salmon)
loxo|drome +s
loxo|drom¦ic
loyal
loyal|ism
loyal|ist +s
loy|al¦ly
loy|alty
  loy|al|ties
Loy|alty Is|lands (in SW Pacific)
loz|enge +s
loz|enged
loz|engy
L-plate +s
Lua|laba (river, Zaire)
Lu|anda (capital of Angola)
Luang Pra|bang (town, Laos)
lub¦ber +s
lub¦ber|like
lub¦ber line +s
lub¦ber¦ly
Lub|bock (city, USA)
Lü¦beck (port, Germany)
Lu|bianka (use Lubyanka)
Lub¦lin (city, Poland)
lubra +s (may cause offence)
lu|bri¦cant +s
lu|bri¦cate
  lu¦bri|cates
  lu¦bri|cated
  lu¦bri|cat¦ing
lu|bri|ca¦tion +s
lu|bri|ca¦tive
lu|bri|ca¦tor +s
lu|bri¦cious
lu|bri¦city
lu|bri¦cous
Lu|bum|bashi (city, Zaire)
Lu|byanka, the (KGB headquarters etc., Moscow)
Lucan (of St Luke)
Lucan (Roman poet)
Lu|ca¦nia (ancient region, Italy)
lu|carne +s

Lucas, George (American film director)

Lucas van Ley¦den (Dutch painter)

Lucca (city, Italy)

luce
plural **luce**
(fish. △ **loose**)

lu¦cency

lu¦cent

lu¦cent¦ly

Lu¦cerne (town, Switzerland)

Lu¦cerne, Lake (in Switzerland)

lu¦cerne +s (plant)

Lucia

Lu¦cian (Greek writer)

lucid

lu¦cid¦ity

lu¦cid¦ly

lu¦cid¦ness

Lu¦ci¦fer (Satan)

lu¦ci¦fer +s (match)

Lu¦cille

Lu¦cinda

luck +s +ed +ing

luck¦ily

lucki¦ness

luck¦less

luck¦less¦ly

luck¦less¦ness

Luck¦now (city, India)

lucky
luck¦ier
lucki¦est

lu¦cra¦tive

lu¦cra¦tive¦ly

lu¦cra¦tive¦ness

lucre

Lu¦cre¦tia *Roman Legend*

Lu¦cre¦tius (Roman poet)

lucu¦brate
lucu¦brates
lucu¦brated
lucu¦brat¦ing

lucu¦bra¦tion

lucu¦bra¦tor +s

Lu¦cul¦lan

Lucy

lud (in 'm'lud')

Luda (city, China)

Lud¦dism

Lud¦dite +s

Lud¦dit¦ism

Lu¦den¦dorff, Erich (German general)

Lud¦hiana (city, India)

ludi¦crous

ludi¦crous¦ly

ludi¦crous¦ness

Ludo (= Ludovic)

ludo (game)

Lu¦do¦vic

Lud¦wig (Bavarian kings)

Lud¦wigs¦hafen (city, Germany)

lues (**ven¦erea**)

lu¦et¦ic

luff +s +ed +ing

luffa +s

Luft¦waffe

lug
lugs
lugged
lug¦ging

Lu¦gano (town, Italy)

Lu¦gansk (Russian name for Luhansk)

Lug¦du¦num (Roman name for Lyons)

luge
luges
luged
lu¦ging

Luger +s (gun)

lug¦gable +s

lug¦gage

lug¦gage van +s

lug¦ger +s

lug¦hole +s

Lu¦gosi, Bela (Hungarian-born American actor)

lug¦sail +s

lu¦gu¦bri¦ous

lu¦gu¦bri¦ous¦ly

lu¦gu¦bri¦ous¦ness

lug¦worm +s

Lu¦hansk (city, Ukraine)

Lu¦kács, György (Hungarian Marxist philosopher)

Luke (evangelist and saint)

luke¦warm

luke¦warm¦ly

luke¦warm¦ness

lull +s +ed +ing

lul¦laby
lul¦la¦bies
lul¦la¦bied
lul¦la¦by¦ing

Lully, Jean-Baptiste (Italian-born French composer)

lulu +s

lum¦bago

lum¦bar (relating to the lower back)

lum¦ber +s +ed +ing (useless objects; timber; move awkwardly; encumber)

lum¦ber¦er +s

lum¦ber¦jack +s

lumber-jacket +s

lum¦ber¦man
lum¦ber¦men

lumber-room +s

lum¦ber¦some

lum¦bri¦cal (muscle)

lumen
plural **lumen**
Physics

lumen
lu¦mina
Anatomy

Lu¦mière, Au¦guste and Louis (French inventors and pioneers of cinema)

lu¦min¦aire +s

Lu¦min¦al (drug) *Propr.*

lu¦min¦al (of a lumen)

lu¦mi¦nance +s

lu¦mi¦nary
lu¦mi¦nar¦ies

lu¦mi¦nes¦cence

lu¦mi¦nes¦cent

lu¦mi¦nif¦er¦ous

lu¦mi¦nos¦ity
lu¦mi¦nos¦ities

lu¦mi¦nous

lu¦mi¦nous¦ly

lu¦mi¦nous¦ness

lumme *interjection*

lum¦mox
lum¦moxes

lump +s +ed +ing

lump¦ec¦tomy
lump¦ec¦to¦mies

lump¦en

lump¦en¦pro¦le¦tar¦iat

lump¦er +s

lump¦fish
plural **lump¦fish** *or* **lump¦fishes**

lump¦ily

lumpi¦ness

lump¦ish

lump¦ish¦ly

lump¦ish¦ness

lump¦suck¦er +s

lump sum +s *noun*

lump-sum *attributive*

lumpy
lump¦ier
lumpi¦est

Luna (Soviet moon probes)

lu¦nacy
lu¦na¦cies

luna moth +s

lunar

lun¦ate

lu¦na¦tic +s

lun¦ation +s

lunch
lunches
lunched
lunch¦ing

lunch box
lunch boxes

lunch break +s

lunch¦eon +s

lunch¦eon¦ette +s

lunch¦er +s

lunch hour +s

lunch¦time +s

Lund (city, Sweden)

Lundy (island or shipping area off SW England)

lune +s

lu¦nette +s

lung +s

lunge
lunges
lunged
lun¦ging
(thrust etc.)

lunge
lunges
lunged
lunge¦ing
(horse's rein)

lung¦fish
plural **lung¦fish** *or* **lung¦fishes**

lung¦ful +s

lungi +s

lung|less
lung-power
lung|worm +s
lung|wort +s
luni|solar
lun|ula
  lunu|lae
Luo
  plural Luo *or* Luos
Luo|yang (city,
  China)
Lu|per|calia
lupi|form
lupin +s (flower)
lu|pine +s (flower;
  use lupin)
lu|pine (like a wolf)
lu|poid
lu|pous *adjective*
lupus (vul|garis)
  noun
lur +s
lurch
  lurches
  lurched
  lurch|ing
lurch|er +s
lure
  lures
  lured
  lur|ing
  (entice;
  enticement)
lure +s (trumpet;
  use lur)
lurex *Propr.*
lurgy
  lur|gies
lurid
lur|id|ly
lur|id|ness
lur|ing|ly
lurk +s +ed +ing
lurk|er +s
Lu|saka (capital of
  Zambia)
lus|cious
lus|cious|ly
lus|cious|ness
lush
  lushes
  lushed
  lush|ing
  lush|er
  lush|est
lush|ly
lush|ness
Lu|shun (port,
  China)
Lu|si|ta|nia
  (ancient province,
  SW Europe)

Lu|si|ta|nia
  (Cunard liner)
lust +s +ed +ing
lust|er *Am.* +s +ed
  +ing (*Br.* lustre)
lust|er|less *Am.*
  (*Br.* lustreless)
lust|er|ware *Am.*
  (*Br.* lustreware)
lust|ful
lust|ful|ly
lust|ful|ness
lust|ily
lusti|ness
lus|tra
lus|tral
lus|trate
  lus|trates
  lus|trated
  lus|trat|ing
lus|tra|tion +s
lustre *Br.*
  lustres
  lustred
  lus|tring
  (*Am.* luster)
lustre|less *Br.* (*Am.*
  lusterless)
lustre|ware *Br.*
  (*Am.* lusterware)
lus|trous
lus|trous|ly
lus|trous|ness
lus|trum
  lus|tra *or*
  lus|trums
lusty
  lust|ier
  lusti|est
lusus
lu|tan|ist +s (use
  lutenist)
lute
  lutes
  luted
  lut|ing
  (musical
  instrument;
  sealant. △ loot)
lut|ecium (use
  lutetium)
lu|tein +s
lu|tein|iz|ing
  (hormone)
lu|ten|ist +s
luteo|ful|vous
lu|teous
lute|string +s
Lu|te|tia (Roman
  name for Paris)
lu|te|tium
Lu|ther (name)

Lu|ther, Mar|tin
  (German
  Protestant
  theologian)
Lu|ther|an +s
Lu|ther|an Church
Lu|ther|an|ise *Br.*
  (use Lutheranize)
Lu|ther|an|ises
Lu|ther|an|ised
Lu|ther|an|is|ing
Lu|ther|an|ism
Lu|ther|an|ize
Lu|ther|an|izes
Lu|ther|an|ized
Lu|ther|an|iz|ing
lu|thier +s
Lu|thuli, Al|bert
  John (South
  African political
  leader)
Lu|tine Bell
lut|ing +s
Luton (town,
  England)
Lu|to|sław|ski,
  Wi|told (Polish
  composer)
Lu|tuli, Al|bert
  John (use
  Luthuli)
Lut|yens, Edwin
  (English architect)
Lut|yens,
  Eliza|beth
  (English
  composer)
lutz
  lutzes
luv|vie +s (use
  luvvy)
luvvy
  luv|vies
  (effusive actor or
  actress. △ lovey)
lux
  plural lux
  (unit of
  illumination)
lux|ate
  lux|ates
  lux|ated
  lux|at|ing
lux|ation +s
luxe +s (luxury; in
  'de luxe')
Lux|em|bourg
Lux|em|bourg|er
  +s
Lux|em|burg,
  Rosa (Polish-born
  German

Lux|em|burg
  (*cont.*)
  revolutionary
  leader)
Lux|em|burg|ish
Luxor (city, Egypt)
lux|uri|ance
lux|uri|ant
lux|uri|ant|ly
lux|uri|ate
lux|uri|ates
lux|uri|ated
lux|uri|at|ing
lux|uri|ous
lux|uri|ous|ly
lux|uri|ous|ness
lux|ury
  lux|ur|ies
Luzon (island,
  Philippines)
Lviv (city, Ukraine)
Lvov (Russian
  name for Lviv)
lwei +s
Ly|all|pur (former
  name of
  Faisalabad)
ly|can|thrope +s
ly|can|thropy
lycée +s
Ly|ceum *Philosophy*
ly|ceum +s (lecture
  hall etc.)
ly|chee +s
lych-gate +s
lych|nis
  lych|nises
Lycia (ancient
  region, Asia
  Minor)
Ly|cian +s
ly|co|pod +s
ly|co|po|dium
Lycra *Propr.*
Ly|cur|gus (reputed
  founder of Sparta)
Lyd|gate, John
  (English poet)
Lydia (ancient
  name for part of
  Asia Minor; name)
Lyd|ian +s
lye +s (alkaline
  liquid. △ lie)
Lyell, Charles
  (Scottish
  geologist)
lying
lying-in-state *noun*
ly|ing|ly
lyke wake +s

Lyly, John (English poet and dramatist)
Lyme dis|ease
lyme-grass
  lyme-grasses
Lyme Regis (town, England)
lymph
lymph|aden|
     op|athy
lymph|at|ic
lympho|cyte +s
lympho|cyt|ic
lymph|oid
lymph|oma
  lymph|omas or
  lymph|omata
lymph|ous
Lyn also **Lynn**, Lynne
lyn|cean
lynch
  lynches
  lynched
  lynch|ing
lynch|er +s
lynchet +s
lynch|ing +s
lynch|pin +s (use linchpin)
Lynda also **Linda**
Lyn|ette
Lynn also **Lyn**, Lynne (name)
Lynn, Vera (English singer)
Lynne also **Lyn**, Lynn (name)
Lyn|sey also Lind|say, Lind|sey
lynx
  lynxes
  (animal. ⚠ **links**)
lynx-eyed
lynx|like
Lyon (French name for **Lyons**)
Ly|on|nais (of Lyons)
Lyons (city, France)
lyo|phil|ic
ly|oph|il|ise Br. (use **lyophilize**)
  ly|oph|il|ises
  ly|oph|il|ised
  ly|oph|il|is|ing

ly|oph|il|ize
  ly|oph|il|izes
  ly|oph|il|ized
  ly|oph|il|iz|ing
lyo|pho|bic
Lyra (constellation)
lyr|ate
lyre +s (musical instrument. ⚠ **liar**)
lyre-bird +s
lyre-flower +s
lyric +s
lyr|ic|al
lyr|ic|al|ly
lyri|cism
lyri|cist +s
lyr|ist +s
Ly|san|der (Spartan general and statesman)
lyse
  lyses
  lysed
  lys|ing
Ly|senko, Trofim Den|iso|vich (Soviet biologist and geneticist)
lys|er|gic
lysin +s (blood protein)
ly|sine (amino acid)
Ly|sip|pus (Greek sculptor)
lysis
  lyses
Lysol Propr.
lyso|some +s
lyso|zyme +s
lytic
lytta
  lyt|tae
Lyt|ton, Lord (title of Edward Bulwer-Lytton)

Mm

m' (= my)
ma (= mother. ⚠ **mar**)
ma'am (= madam. ⚠ **marm**)
Maas (Flemish and Dutch name for the **Meuse**)
Maas|tricht (city, the Netherlands)
Maat Egyptian Mythology
Mabel
Mabi|no|gion Celtic Mythology
Ma|buse, Jan (Flemish painter)
Mac +s (Scotsman; form of address)
mac +s (= mackintosh)
ma|cabre
ma|caco +s
mac|adam +s
maca|da|mia +s
mac|ad|am|ise Br. (use macadamize)
  mac|ad|am|ises
  mac|ad|am|ised
  mac|ad|am|is|ing
mac|ad|am|ize
  mac|ad|am|izes
  mac|ad|am|ized
  mac|ad|am|iz|ing
Mac|Alpin, Ken|neth (Scottish king)
Maca|nese
  plural Maca|nese
Macao (Portuguese dependency, China)
Ma|capá (town, Brazil)
ma|caque +s
Maca|ro|nesia (region of island groups, NE Atlantic)
Maca|ro|nes|ian
maca|roni +s (pasta; penguin)
maca|roni
  maca|ro|nies (dandy)
maca|ron|ic +s
maca|roon +s

Mac|Arthur, Doug|las (American general)
Ma|cas|sar (former name of Ujung Padang)
Ma|cas|sar|ese (use **Makasarese**) plural Ma|cas|sar|ese
Ma|cas|sar oil +s
Macau (Portuguese name for **Macao**)
Mac|aulay, Rose (English writer)
Mac|aulay, Thomas Bab|ing|ton (Lord Macaulay, English historian)
macaw +s
Mac|beth (Scottish king)
Mac|ca|baeus, Judas (Jewish leader)
Mac|ca|bean
Mac|ca|bee +s
Mac|Diarmid, Hugh (Scottish poet)
Mac|Donald, Flora (Scottish Jacobite heroine)
Mac|Donald, Ram|say (British prime minister)
Mac|don|ald, John (Scottish-born Canadian prime minister)
Mac|Donnell Ranges (mountains, Australia)
Mace (chemical)
mace +s (club; spice)
mace-bearer +s
ma|cé|doine +s
Ma|ce|don (= Macedonia)
Ma|ce|do|nia (ancient country, SE Europe)
Ma|ce|do|nian +s
Ma|ceió (port, Brazil)
macer +s
ma|cer|ate
  ma|cer|ates

ma¦cer¦ate (cont.)
ma¦cer¦ated
ma¦cer¦at¦ing
ma¦cer¦ation +s
ma¦cer¦ator +s
Mac¦gil¦li¦cuddy's
Reeks (hills,
Republic of
Ireland)
Mach, Ernst
(Austrian
physicist)
Mach 1 etc.
ma¦chete +s
Ma¦chia¦velli,
Nic¦colò di
Ber¦nardo dei
(Florentine
statesman)
ma¦chia¦vel¦lian
ma¦chia¦vel¦lian¦
ism
ma¦chico¦late
ma¦chico¦lates
ma¦chico¦lated
ma¦chico¦lat¦ing
ma¦chico¦la¦tion
+s
ma¦chin¦abil¦ity
ma¦chin¦able
ma¦chin¦ate
ma¦chin¦ates
ma¦chin¦ated
ma¦chin¦at¦ing
ma¦chin¦ation +s
ma¦chin¦ator +s
ma¦chine
ma¦chines
ma¦chined
ma¦chin¦ing
machine-gun
machine-guns
machine-gunned
machine-gunning
machine-gunner
+s
machine-minder
+s
ma¦chine pis¦tol
+s
machine-readable
ma¦chin¦ery
ma¦chin¦er¦ies
ma¦chine tool +s
machine-tooled
machine-
washable
ma¦chin¦ist +s
mach¦ismo
Mach¦meter +s
Mach num¦ber +s
macho +s

Mach's prin¦ciple
Macht¦poli¦tik
Machu Pic¦chu
(Inca town, Peru)
Ma¦cias Nguema
(former name of
Bioko)
mac¦in¦tosh (use
mackintosh)
mac¦in¦toshes
mack +s (use mac)
Mac¦kay (port,
Australia)
Mac¦ken¦zie,
Alex¦an¦der
(Scottish explorer)
Mac¦ken¦zie,
Comp¦ton
(English writer)
Mac¦ken¦zie,
Wil¦liam Lyon
(Canadian
revolutionary)
Mac¦ken¦zie River
(in Canada)
mack¦erel
plural mack¦erel
or mack¦erels
mack¦erel shark
+s
mack¦erel sky
mack¦erel skies
Mack¦in¦tosh,
Charles Ren¦nie
(Scottish architect
and designer)
mack¦in¦tosh
mack¦in¦toshes
mackle +s (printing
blemish)
macle +s (twin
crystal; spot in a
mineral)
Mac¦lean, Ali¦stair
(Scottish writer)
Mac¦lean, Don¦ald
(British Soviet
spy)
Mac¦leod, John
James Rick¦ard
(Scottish
physiologist)
Mac¦mil¦lan,
Har¦old (British
prime minister)
Mac¦Neice, Louis
(British poet)
Mâcon +s (city,
France; wine)
Mac¦qua¦rie,
Lach¦lan
(Scottish-born

Mac¦qua¦rie (cont.)
Australian colonial
administrator)
Mac¦quarie River
(in Australia)
mac¦ramé
macro +s
macro¦bi¦ot¦ic
macro¦bi¦ot¦ics
macro¦carpa +s
macro¦ceph¦alic
macro¦ceph¦al¦ous
macro¦ceph¦aly
macro¦cosm +s
macro¦cos¦mic
macro¦cos¦mic¦
al¦ly
macro¦eco¦nom¦ic
macro¦
eco¦nom¦ics
macro¦evo¦lu¦tion
macro¦evo¦lu¦tion¦
ary
macro-instruction
+s
macro¦lepi¦
dop¦tera
macro¦mol¦ecu¦lar
macro¦mol¦ecule
+s
mac¦ron +s
macro¦nu¦tri¦ent
+s
macro¦phage +s
macro¦
photog¦raphy
macro¦pod +s
macro¦scop¦ic
macro¦scop¦ic¦
al¦ly
mac¦ula
macu¦lae
mac¦ula lutea
macu¦lae lu¦teae
macu¦lar
macu¦la¦tion +s
mad
mads
mad¦ded
mad¦ding
mad¦der
mad¦dest
Mada¦gas¦can +s
Mada¦gas¦car
(island, Indian
Ocean)
madam +s (English
form of address;
conceited girl;
brothel-keeper)
Ma¦dame
Mes¦dames

Ma¦dame (cont.)
(French-speaking
woman)
mad¦cap +s
mad cow dis¦ease
mad¦den +s +ed
+ing
mad¦den¦ing¦ly
mad¦der +s
Mad¦die *also*
Maddy
Maddy *also*
Mad¦die
made (past tense
and past participle
of make. △ maid)
Ma¦deira (island,
Atlantic Ocean)
Ma¦deira (river,
Brazil)
Ma¦deira +s (wine)
Ma¦deir¦an +s
Mad¦elaine *also*
Mad¦eleine,
Mad¦eline
Mad¦eleine *also*
Mad¦elaine,
Mad¦eline
(name)
mad¦eleine +s
(cake)
Mad¦eline *also*
Mad¦elaine,
Mad¦eleine
Ma¦de¦mois¦elle
Mes¦de¦mois¦elles
made-to-measure
attributive
made-up *attributive*
mad¦house +s
Madhya Pra¦desh
(state, India)
Madi¦son (city,
USA)
Madi¦son, James
(American
president)
madly
mad¦man
mad¦men
mad¦ness
mad¦nesses
Ma¦donna, the
(Virgin Mary)
Ma¦donna
(American singer)
ma¦donna +s
(picture; statue;
etc.)
ma¦donna lily
ma¦donna lil¦ies

Ma¦dras (port, India)

ma¦dras (striped cotton)

mad¦re|pore +s

mad¦re|por¦ic

Ma¦drid (capital of Spain)

mad¦ri¦gal +s

mad¦ri¦gal|esque

mad¦ri¦gal|ian

mad¦ri¦gal|ist +s

ma|drona +s

ma|droño +s

Ma¦dura (island, Indonesia)

Madu|rai (city, India)

Madur|ese

  plural Madur|ese

mad|woman

  mad|women

Mae *also* May

Mae|an¦der (ancient name for the Menderes)

Mae|ce¦nas, Gaius (Roman writer)

mael|strom +s

mae|nad +s

mae|nad¦ic

maes|toso +s *Music*

maes|tro

  maes|tri *or* maes|tros

Mae|ter|linck, Maur|ice (Belgian writer)

Maeve

Mae West +s (American actress; life jacket)

Mafe|king (town, South Africa)

MAFF (= Ministry of Agriculture, Fisheries, and Food)

maf|fick +s +ed +ing

Mafia (in Sicily, USA, etc.)

mafia +s (similar group)

Mafi|keng (use Mafeking)

Mafi|oso

  Mafi|osi (member of Mafia)

mafi|oso

  mafi|osi (member of Mafia)

mag +s (= magazine)

Mag|adha (ancient kingdom, India)

Mag¦adi, Lake (in Kenya)

Mag¦ahi

maga|logue +s

maga|zine +s

mag|da|len +s

Mag|da|lena (river, Colombia; name)

Magd|alen Col|lege (at Oxford University)

Mag|da|lene (in 'Mary Magdalene')

Magd¦alene Col|lege (at Cambridge University)

Mag|da|len¦ian

Mag|de|burg (city, Germany)

mage +s

Ma¦gel|lan, Fer¦di|nand (Portuguese explorer)

Ma¦gel|lan, Strait of (off S. America)

Mag|el|lan¦ic clouds (galaxies)

ma|genta +s

Mag¦gie

Mag|giore, Lake (Italy and Switzerland)

mag|got +s

mag|goty

Magh|rib (region, Africa)

Magi (the 'wise men')

magi (plural of magus)

ma¦gian

ma¦gian|ism

magic

  magics

  ma¦gicked

  ma¦gick|ing

magic¦al

magic|al¦ly

ma|gi¦cian +s

ma¦gilp (use megilp)

Magi|not Line (French fortification)

magis|ter¦ial

magis|teri|al¦ly

magis|ter¦ium

magis|tracy

  magis|tra¦cies

magis|tral

magis|trate +s

magis|trate|ship +s

magis|tra¦ture +s

Mag¦le|mo¦sian

mag¦lev +s

magma

  magmas *or* mag|mata

mag¦mat¦ic

Magna Carta (political charter)

Magna Grae¦cia (group of ancient Greek cities, Italy)

mag|na|nim¦ity

mag|nani|mous

mag|nani|mous|ly

mag|nate +s

mag|nes¦ian

mag|ne¦sia +s

mag|ne¦site +s

mag|ne¦sium

mag|net +s

mag|net¦ic

mag|net¦ic|al¦ly

mag|net¦ics

mag|net¦is|able *Br.* (use magnetizable)

mag¦net|isa¦tion *Br.* +s (use magnetization)

mag|net|ise *Br.* (use magnetize)

  mag|net|ises

  mag|net|ised

  mag|net|is¦ing

mag¦net|iser *Br.* +s (use magnetizer)

mag|net|ism

mag|net|ite

mag|net¦iz|able

mag|net|iza¦tion +s

mag|net|ize

  mag|net|izes

  mag|net|ized

  mag|net|iz¦ing

mag|net|izer +s

mag|neto +s

magneto-electric

magneto-electri¦city

mag|neto|graph +s

mag|neto|hydro|dynam¦ic

mag|neto|hydro|dynam¦ics

mag|net|om|eter +s

mag|net|om|etry

mag|neto|mo¦tive

mag|ne¦ton +s

mag|neto|sphere +s

mag|neto|stric¦tion +s

mag|ne¦tron +s

mag|ni¦fi¦able

Mag|nifi|cat (canticle)

mag|nifi|cat +s (song of praise)

mag|ni¦fi|ca¦tion +s

mag|nifi|cence

mag|nifi|cent

mag|nifi|cent¦ly

mag|nif|ico

  mag|nif|icoes

mag|ni¦fier +s

mag|nify

  mag|ni|fies

  mag|ni|fied

  mag|ni|fy|ing

  mag|ni|fy|ing glass

  mag|ni|fy|ing glasses

mag|nilo|quence

mag|nilo|quent

mag|nilo|quent¦ly

Mag|nito|gorsk (city, Russia)

mag|ni|tude +s

mag|no|lia +s

mag|nox

  mag|noxes

mag|num +s

mag|num opus

  mag|num opuses *or* magna opera

Mag|nus

Magog (in 'Gog and Magog')

mag|pie +s

Ma|gritte, René (Belgian painter)

mags|man

  mags|men

ma|guey +s

magus

  magi

Mag¦yar +s

Maha|bad (city, Iran)

Maha|bhar|ata
(Hindu Sanskrit
epic poem)
maha|leb +s
maha|raja +s *male*
maha|ra|jah +s
(use maharaja)
maha|ra|nee +s
female
maha|rani +s (use
maharanee)
Maha|rash|tra
(state, India)
Maha|rash|trian
+s
maha|rishi +s
ma|hatma +s
Maha|weli (river,
Sri Lanka)
Maha|yana
Buddhism
Mahdi +s *Islam*
Mahd|ism
Mahd|ist +s
Mah|fouz, Na|guib
(Egyptian writer)
Ma|hi|lyow (city,
Belarus)
mah-jong
Mah|ler, Gus|tav
(Austrian
composer)
mahl|stick +s
ma|hog|any
ma|hog|anies
Mahón (capital of
Minorca)
ma|ho|nia +s
Ma|hore
(alternative name
for Mayotte)
ma|hout +s
Mah|ratta +s (use
Maratha)
Mah|ratti (use
Marathi)
mah|seer +s
Maia *Greek and
Roman Mythology*
maid +s (servant;
girl. △ made)
mai|dan +s (open
space)
maid|en +s (girl)
maid|en|hair
Maid|en|head
(town, England)
maid|en|head +s
(virginity)
maid|en|hood +s
maid|en|ish
maid|en|like

maid|en|ly
maid|en name +s
maid|en over +s
maid|ish
maid|ser|vant +s
Maid|stone (town,
England)
mai|eu|tic
maigre
Mai|gret (fictional
detective)
Mai|kop (city,
Russia)
mail +s +ed +ing
(post. △ male)
mail|able
mail|bag +s
mail|boat +s
mail|box
mail|boxes
mail car|rier +s
mail coach
mail coaches
mail drop +s
Mail|er, Nor|man
(American writer)
mail|er +s
mail|ing +s
mail|ing list +s
mail|lot +s
mail|man
mail|men
mail order +s *noun*
mail-order
attributive
mail|shot +s
mail train +s
maim +s +ed +ing
Mai|moni|des
(Spanish-born
Jewish
philosopher)
Main (river,
Germany)
main +s (principal;
pipe; cable; ocean.
△ mane)
main brace +s
main-course
attributive
main|crop
attributive
Maine (state, USA)
main|frame +s
Main|land (islands,
Orkney and
Shetland)
main|land +s
main|land|er +s
main|line
main|lines
main|lined

main|line (*cont.*)
main|lin|ing
(inject drugs
intravenously)
main line +s
(railway line;
principal vein)
main|liner +s
main|ly
main|mast +s
main|plane +s
main|sail +s
main|sheet +s
main|spring +s
main|stay +s
main|stream +s
main street +s
main|tain +s +ed
+ing
main|tain|abil|ity
main|tain|able
main|tain|er +s
(generally)
main|tain|or +s
Law
main|ten|ance +s
**Main|te|non,
Mar|quise de**
(wife of Louis XIV
of France)
main|top +s
main|top|mast +s
main yard +s
Mainz (city,
Germany)
mai|ol|ica (use
majolica)
Mai|sie
mai|son|ette +s
Mai|thili
maître d'hôtel
maîtres d'hôtel
maize +s (cereal.
△ maze)
ma|jes|tic
ma|jes|tic|al|ly
maj|esty
maj|es|ties
Maj|lis
ma|jol|ica +s
Major, John
(British prime
minister)
major +s +ed +ing
major axis
major axes
Ma|jorca (Spanish
island)
Ma|jor|can +s
major-domo +s
ma|jor|ette +s
major gen|eral +s

Ma|jor|ism
ma|jor|ity
ma|jor|ities
ma|jor|ship +s
maj|us|cu|lar
maj|us|cule +s
mak|able
Ma|ka|rios III
(Greek Cypriot
archbishop and
president)
Ma|ka|sa|rese
plural
Ma|ka|sa|rese
Ma|kas|sar (former
name of Ujung
Padang)
Ma|kas|sar Strait
(between Borneo
and Sulawesi)
make
makes
made
mak|ing
make-belief
make-believe
make-over +s
maker +s
make-ready
make|shift +s
make-up +s *noun*
make|weight +s
**Mak|ga|dik|gadi
Pans** (region,
Botswana)
Makh|ach|kala
(port, Russia)
mak|ing +s
mako +s
Mak|su|tov
(telescope)
ma|kuta (plural of
likuta)
**Mala|bar
Chris|tians**
Mala|bar Coast
(region, India)
Ma|labo (capital of
Equatorial Guinea)
mal|ab|sorp|tion
+s
Ma|lacca (former
name of Melaka)
Ma|lacca, Strait of
(between Malaysia
and Sumatra)
ma|lacca (cane)
Mal|achi *Bible*
mal|ach|ite +s
mala|col|ogy
mala|con

mala|cos|tra|can +s

mal|adap|ta|tion +s

mal|adap|tive

mal|adjust|ed

mal|adjust|ment +s

mal|admin|is|ter +s +ed +ing

mal|admin|is|tra|tion +s

mal|adroit

mal|adroit|ly

mal|adroit|ness

mal|ady
  mal|ad|ies

mala fide

Mal|aga (port, Spain; wine)

Mala|gasy
  Mala|gas|ies

mala|gueña +s

mal|aise +s

Mala|mud, Ber|nard (American writer)

mala|mute +s

mal|an|ders (use mallenders)

mala|pert +s

mala|prop +s

mala|prop|ism +s

mal|apro|pos

malar +s

Mäla|ren (lake, Sweden)

mal|aria +s

mal|ar|ial

mal|ar|ian

mal|ari|ous

ma|lar|key

mala|thion

Ma|lawi

Ma|la|wian +s

Malay +s

Ma|laya (former country, SE Asia)

Ma|lay|alam

Ma|lay|an +s

Malayo-Chinese
  plural Malayo-Chinese

Malayo-Polynes|ian +s

Ma|lay|sia

Ma|lay|sian +s

Mal|colm (Scottish kings; name)

Mal|colm X (American political activist)

mal|con|tent +s

mal de mer

mal|dis|trib|uted

mal|dis|tri|bu|tion

Mal|dives (islands, Indian Ocean)

Mal|div|ian +s

Male (capital of the Maldives)

male +s (masculine. △ mail)

mal|edic|tion +s

mal|edic|tive

mal|edic|tory

mal|efac|tion +s

mal|efac|tor +s

ma|lef|ic

ma|lefi|cence

ma|lefi|cent

Male|gaon (city, India)

ma|leic

mal|emute +s (use malamute)

male|ness

ma|levo|lence

ma|levo|lent

ma|levo|lent|ly

mal|fea|sance

mal|fea|sant +s

mal|for|ma|tion +s

mal|formed

mal|func|tion +s +ed +ing

Mal|herbe, Fran|çois de (French poet)

Mali (country)

mali +s (gardener)

Mali|an +s

Mal|ibu (resort, USA)

malic

mal|ice

ma|li|cious

ma|li|cious|ly

ma|li|cious|ness

ma|lign +s +ed +ing (malignant; slander. △ moline)

ma|lig|nancy
  ma|lig|nan|cies

ma|lig|nant

ma|lig|nant|ly

ma|lign|er +s

ma|lig|nity
  ma|lig|nities

ma|lign|ly

Malin (shipping area off Ireland)

Ma|lines (French name for Mechelen)

ma|lin|ger +s +ed +ing

ma|lin|ger|er +s

Malin Head (on Irish coast; weather station off Ireland)

Ma|li|now|ski, Bron|isław Kas|par (Polish anthropologist)

mal|ism

mall +s (walk; shopping centre. △ maul)

mal|lard
  plural mal|lard *or* mal|lards

Mal|lar|mé, Sté|phane (French poet)

mal|le|abil|ity

mal|le|able

mal|le|ably

mal|lee +s

mal|lee bird +s

mal|lee fowl
  plural mal|lee fowl

mal|lee hen +s

mal|lei (plural of malleus)

mal|le|muck +s

mal|len|ders

mal|le|olus
  mal|le|oli

mal|let +s

mal|leus
  mal|lei

Mal|lorca (Spanish name for Majorca)

Mal|lor|can +s (use Majorcan)

mal|low +s

malm +s (rock, brick. △ ma'am)

Malmö (port, Sweden)

malm|sey +s

mal|nour|ished

mal|nour|ish|ment

mal|nu|tri|tion

mal|occlu|sion

mal|odor|ous

Mal|ory, Thomas (English writer)

ma|loti (plural of loti)

Mal|pi|ghi, Mar|cello (Italian microscopist)

Mal|pig|hian

Mal|pla|quet (battle site, France)

mal|prac|tice +s

malt +s +ed +ing

Malta

Mal|tese
  plural Mal|tese

mal|tha +s

malt|house +s

Mal|thus, Thomas Rob|ert (English economist)

Mal|thu|sian +s

malti|ness

malt|ing +s

mal|tose

mal|treat +s +ed +ing

mal|treat|er +s

mal|treat|ment +s

malt|ster +s

malty
  malt|ier
  malti|est

Ma|luku (Indonesian name for the Moluccas)

mal|va|ceous

Mal|vern Hills (in W. England)

Mal|verns (= Malvern Hills)

mal|ver|sa|tion

Mal|vi|nas, Islas (Argentinian name for the Falkland Islands)

mal|voisie +s

mam +s

mama +s

mamba +s

mambo +s

mam|elon +s

Mam|eluke +s

Mamet, David (American dramatist)

Mamie

ma|milla *Br.*

ma|mil|las *or* ma|mil|lae (*Am.* mammilla)

mam|il|lary (use mammillary)

mam|il|late (use mammillate)

mamma
mam¦mae
(breast)
mamma +s
(mother)
mam¦mal +s
Mam¦ma¦lia
mam¦ma¦lian +s
mam¦mal¦ifer¦ous
mam¦mal¦ogy
mam¦mary
mam¦mar¦ies
mam¦mary gland
+s
mam¦mee +s (tree.
△ mammy)
mam¦mi¦form
mam¦milla Am.
mam¦mil¦las or
mam¦mil¦lae
(Br. mamilla)
mam¦mil¦lary
mam¦mil¦late
mam¦mo¦gram +s
mam¦mog¦raphy
Mam¦mon
Mam¦mon¦ish
Mam¦mon¦ism
Mam¦mon¦ist +s
Mam¦mon¦ite +s
mam¦moth +s
mammy
mam¦mies
(mother.
△ mammee)
Ma¦mou¦tzu
(capital of
Mayotte)
Man, Isle of (in
Irish Sea)
man
men
noun
man
mans
manned
man¦ning
verb
mana
man¦acle
man¦acles
man¦acled
man¦ac¦ling
man¦age
man¦ages
man¦aged
man¦aging
man¦age¦abil¦ity
man¦age¦able
man¦age¦able¦ness
man¦age¦ably
man¦age¦ment +s

man¦ager +s
man¦ager¦ess
man¦ager¦esses
man¦ager¦ial
man¦ageri¦al¦ly
man¦ager¦ship +s
Ma¦na¦gua (capital
of Nicaragua)
man¦akin +s (bird.
△ manikin,
mannequin,
mannikin)
Ma¦nama (capital
of Bahrain)
ma¦¦ñana +s
Mana Pools
(national park,
Zimbabwe)
Ma¦nas¦seh *Bible*
Ma¦nas¦ses,
Prayer of
man-at-arms
men-at-arms
mana¦tee +s
Ma¦naus (city,
Brazil)
Mana¦watu (river,
New Zealand)
Man¦ches¦ter (city,
England)
man¦chi¦neel +s
Man¦chu +s
Man¦chu¦ria
(region, China)
Man¦chu¦rian +s
man¦ciple +s
Man¦cu¦nian +s
Man¦dae¦an +s
man¦dala +s
Man¦da¦lay (port,
Burma)
man¦da¦mus
Man¦da¦rin
(language)
man¦da¦rin +s
(official; orange)
man¦da¦rin¦ate +s
man¦da¦rine +s
(use mandarin)
man¦da¦tary
man¦da¦tar¦ies
(person who
receives a
mandate.
△ mandatory)
man¦date
man¦dates
man¦dated
man¦dat¦ing
man¦da¦tor +s
man¦da¦tor¦ily

man¦da¦tory
man¦da¦tor¦ies
(compulsory.
△ mandatary)
man-day +s
Mande
plural **Mande** or
Mandes
Man¦dela, Nel¦son
(South African
president)
Man¦del¦brot
Mathematics
Man¦del¦stam,
Osip (Russian
poet)
Man¦de¦ville,
John (English
nobleman)
man¦dible +s
man¦dibu¦lar
man¦dibu¦late
man¦dola +s (large
mandolin.
△ mandorla)
man¦do¦lin +s
(musical
instrument)
man¦do¦line +s
(vegetable-slicer)
man¦do¦lin¦ist +s
man¦dorla +s
(almond-shape.
△ mandola)
man¦drag¦ora +s
man¦drake +s
man¦drel +s (shaft;
rod)
man¦drill +s
(baboon)
man¦du¦cate
man¦du¦cates
man¦du¦cated
man¦du¦cat¦ing
man¦du¦ca¦tion
man¦du¦ca¦tory
mane +s (hair on
horse, lion, etc.
△ main)
man-eater +s
man-eating
maned
ma¦nège +s
mane¦less
Manes (Persian
founder of
Manichaeism)
manes (deified
souls; ghost)
Manet, Édouard
(French painter)

Ma¦netho
(Egyptian priest)
man¦eu¦ver Am. +s
+ed +ing (Br.
manoeuvre)
man¦eu¦ver¦
abil¦ity Am. (Br.
manoeuvrability)
man¦eu¦ver¦able
Am. (Br.
manoeuvrable)
man¦eu¦ver¦er Am.
+s (Br.
manoeuvrer)
man¦eu¦ver¦ing
Am. +s (Br.
manoeuvring)
Man¦fred
man¦ful
man¦ful¦ly
man¦ful¦ness
man¦ga¦bey +s
man¦ga¦nate +s
man¦ga¦nese
man¦gan¦ic
man¦gan¦ous
mange +s
man¦gel +s (beet.
△ mangle)
mangel-wurzel +s
man¦ger +s
mange¦tout
plural mange¦tout
or mange¦touts
man¦gily
man¦gi¦ness
man¦gle
man¦gles
man¦gled
man¦gling
(laundry machine;
mutilate.
△ mangel)
man¦gler +s
mango
man¦goes
man¦gold +s
mangold-wurzel
+s
man¦gonel +s
man¦go¦steen +s
man¦grove +s
mangy
man¦gier
man¦gi¦est
man¦handle
man¦han¦dles
man¦han¦dled
man¦hand¦ling
Man¦hat¦tan
(island, New York
City)

man|hat|tan +s
(cocktail)
man|hole +s
man|hood +s
man-hour +s
man|hunt +s
mania +s
ma|niac +s
ma|ni|acal
ma|ni|ac|al|ly
manic +s
Ma|nica|land
(province,
Zimbabwe)
man|ic|al|ly
manic
de|pres|sion
manic-depres|sive
+s
Mani|chae|an +s
Mani|chae|ism
Mani|che|an +s
(use Manichaean)
Mani|chee +s
Mani|che|ism (use
Manichaeism)
mani|cure
mani|cures
mani|cured
mani|cur|ing
mani|cur|ist +s
mani|fest +s +ed
+ing
mani|fest|ation +s
mani|fest|ative
mani|fest|ly
mani|festo +s
mani|fold +s
(various;
branching pipe.
△ manyfold)
mani|fold|ly
mani|fold|ness
mani|kin +s (little
man. △ manakin,
mannequin)
Ma|nila (capital of
the Philippines)
ma|nila +s (fibre;
paper. △ manilla)
ma|nilla +s
(bracelet.
△ manila)
ma|nille +s
man|ioc +s
man|iple +s
ma|nipu|la|bil|ity
ma|nipu|lable
ma|nipu|lat|able
ma|nipu|late
ma|nipu|lates

ma|nipu|late
(cont.)
ma|nipu|lated
ma|nipu|lat|ing
ma|nipu|la|tion +s
ma|nipu|la|tive
ma|nipu|la|tive|ly
ma|nipu|la|tive|
ness
ma|nipu|la|tor +s
ma|nipu|la|tory
Mani|pur (state,
India)
Mani|puri +s
Mani|toba
(province,
Canada)
mani|tou +s
man|kind
manky
mank|ier
manki|est
man|less
Man|ley, Mi|chael
Nor|man
(Jamaican prime
minister)
man|like
man|li|ness
manly
man|lier
man|li|est
man-made
Mann, Thomas
(German writer)
manna (food.
△ manner)
manna-ash
manna-ashes
(tree)
Man|nar (island
and town, Sri
Lanka)
Man|nar, Gulf of
(between India
and Sri Lanka)
manned
man|ne|quin +s
(dressmaker's
model.
△ manakin,
manikin)
man|ner +s (way;
behaviour.
△ manna)
man|nered
man|ner|ism +s
man|ner|ist +s
man|ner|is|tic
man|ner|is|tic|al
man|ner|is|tic|
al|ly

man|ner|less
man|ner|li|ness
man|ner|ly
Mann|heim (city,
Germany)
man|ni|kin +s
(little man; use
manikin.
△ manakin,
mannequin)
man|nish
man|nish|ly
man|nish|ness
Mano (river, W.
Africa)
man|oeuv|ra|
bil|ity Br. (Am.
maneuverability)
man|oeuv|rable
Br. (Am.
maneuverable)
man|oeuvre Br.
man|oeuvres
man|oeuvred
man|oeuv|ring
(Am. maneuver)
man|oeuv|rer Br.
+s (Am.
maneuverer)
man|oeuv|ring Br.
+s (Am.
maneuvering)
man-of-war
men-of-war
man|om|eter +s
mano|met|ric
ma non troppo
manor +s
manor house +s
man|orial
man|power
man|qué
Man Ray
(American
photographer)
Mans, Le (town,
France; its motor-
racing circuit)
man|sard +s
Man|sart,
Fran|çois (French
architect)
manse +s
Man|sell, Nigel
(English motor-
racing driver)
man|ser|vant
men|ser|vants or
man|ser|vants
Mans|field,
Kath|er|ine (New
Zealand writer)

man|sion +s
Man|sion House
(official residence
of Lord Mayor,
London)
man|sion house
+s (house of lord
mayor or landed
proprietor)
man-size
man-sized
man|slaugh|ter +s
+ed +ing
Man|son, Pat|rick
(Scottish
physician)
man|sue|tude
manta +s
Man|tegna,
An|drea (Italian
painter)
man|tel +s
(mantelpiece.
△ mantle)
man|tel|et +s
man|tel|piece +s
man|tel|shelf
man|tel|shelves
man|tic
man|tid +s
man|tilla +s
man|tis
plural man|tis or
man|tises
man|tissa +s
man|tle
man|tles
man|tled
mant|ling
(cloak. △ mantel)
mant|let +s
mant|ling +s
Heraldry
man|tra +s
man|trap +s
man|tua +s
Manu Hindu
Mythology
man|ual +s
manu|al|ly
manu|fac|tory
manu|fac|tor|ies
manu|fac|tur|
abil|ity
manu|fac|tur|able
manu|fac|ture
manu|fac|tures
manu|fac|tured
manu|fac|tur|ing
manu|fac|tur|er +s
ma|nuka +s

manu|mis|sion +s
manu|mit
  manu|mits
  manu|mit|ted
  manu|mit|ting
ma|nure
  ma|nures
  ma|nured
  ma|nur|ing
ma|nur|ial
manu|script +s
Manu|tius, Aldus
  (Italian printer)
Manx
Manx|man
  Manx|men
Manx|woman
  Manx|women
many
many|fold (by
  many times.
  △ manifold)
many|plies
  plural many|plies
many-sided
many-sidedness
many-splendored
  Am.
many-
  splendoured *Br.*
man|za|nilla +s
man|za|nita +s
Man|zoni,
  Ales|san|dro
  (Italian writer)
Mao|ism
Mao|ist +s
Maori
  plural Maori *or*
  Maoris
  (New Zealand
  people and
  language. △ Mari)
Maori|land
Mao Tse-tung (=
  Mao Zedong)
Mao Ze|dong
  (Chinese head of
  state)
map
  maps
  mapped
  map|ping
maple +s
map|less
map-maker +s
map-making
map|pable
Mappa Mundi
map|per +s
map-read
  map-reads

map-read (*cont.*)
  map-read
  map-reading
map-reader +s
Ma|puto (capital of
  Mozambique)
ma|quette +s
ma|quil|lage
Ma|quis (French
  resistance
  movement)
mar
  mars
  marred
  mar|ring
  (spoil. △ ma)
mara|bou +s
  (stork; feather)
mara|bout +s
  (Muslim hermit or
  monk; shrine)
ma|raca +s
Mara|caibo (city
  and port,
  Venezuela)
Mara|caibo, Lake
  (in Venezuela)
Mara|dona, Diego
  (Argentinian
  footballer)
Ma|ramba (city,
  Zambia)
Mara|nhão (state,
  Brazil)
Mara|ñón (river,
  Peru)
mar|as|chino +s
mar|as|mic
mar|as|mus
Marat, Jean Paul
  (French
  revolutionary)
Ma|ra|tha +s
Ma|ra|thi
  (language)
mara|thon +s
mara|thon|er +s
ma|raud +s +ed
  +ing
ma|raud|er +s
mara|vedi +s
Mar|bella (resort,
  Spain)
mar|ble
  mar|bles
  mar|bled
  marb|ling
marb|ling +s
marbly
Mar|burg (city,
  Germany; German

Mar|burg (*cont.*)
  name for
  Maribor)
Marc *also* Mark
  (name)
marc +s (brandy.
  △ mark, marque)
Marc|an (of or
  relating to St.
  Mark)
mar|cas|ite +s
mar|cato (Music)
Mar|ceau, Mar|cel
  (French mime
  artist)
Mar|cel (name)
mar|cel
  mar|cels
  mar|celled
  marcel|ling
  (wave in hair)
Mar|cella
mar|ces|cence +s
mar|ces|cent
March
  Marches
  (month)
march
  marches
  marched
  march|ing
Marche (region,
  Italy)
march|er +s
Marches, the
  (English name for
  Marche; region,
  English-Welsh
  border)
March hare +s
march|ing order
  +s
mar|chion|ess
  mar|chion|esses
march|pane
march past *noun*
Mar|cia
Mar|ci|ano, Rocky
  (American boxer)
Mar|coni,
  Gugli|elmo
  (Italian electrical
  engineer)
Marco Polo (Italian
  traveller)
Mar|cus
Mar|cus Aur|elius
  (Roman emperor)
Mar|cuse,
  Her|bert (German-
  born American
  philosopher)

Mar del Plata
  (town, Argentina)
Mardi Gras
Mar|duk
  Babylonian
  Mythology
mardy
Mare, Wal|ter de
  la (English writer)
mare +s (female
  horse. △ mayor)
mare
  maria *or* mares
  (sea; flat area on
  the moon or Mars)
ma|remma
  ma|remme
Ma|rengo (battle
  site, Italy)
mare's nest +s
mare's tail +s
Mar|ga|ret
  (Scottish queen
  and saint; British
  princess)
mar|gar|ine +s
Mar|ga|rita (port,
  Venezuela)
mar|gay +s
marge +s (margin;
  edge; margarine)
Mar|gery *also*
  Mar|jorie
mar|gin +s +ed
  +ing
mar|gin|al +s
mar|gi|na|lia
mar|gin|al|isa|tion
  Br. +s (use
  marginalization)
mar|gin|al|ise *Br.*
  (use marginalize)
  mar|gin|al|ises
  mar|gin|al|ised
  mar|gin|al|is|ing
mar|gin|al|ity
  mar|gin|al|ities
mar|gin|al|iza|tion
  +s
mar|gin|al|ize
  mar|gin|al|izes
  mar|gin|al|ized
  mar|gin|al|iz|ing
mar|gin|al|ly
mar|gin|ate
  mar|gin|ates
  mar|gin|ated
  mar|gin|at|ing
mar|gin|ation +s
Margo *also* Mar|got
Mar|got *also* Margo
mar|grav|ate +s

mar|grave +s *male*
mar|grav|ine +s
female
Mar|guer|ite
(name)
mar|guer|ite +s
(flower)
Mari (ancient city,
Syria)
Mari (language of
European Russia.
△ Maori)
Maria (name)
maria (plural of
mare)
Maria de' Med|ici
(Italian name of
Marie de
Médicis)
*mari| age de
con|ve|nance
mari| ages de
con|ve|nance*
Mar|ian (of the
Virgin Mary)
Mar|ian *also*
Mar|ion
(name)
Mari|ana Is|lands
(in W. Pacific)
Mari|anas
(= Mariana
Islands)
Mari|ana Trench
(in W. Pacific)
Mari|anne
Maria Ther|esa
(Habsburg queen)
Mari|bor (city,
Slovenia)
Marie
Marie An|toin|ette
(French queen)
Marie Byrd Land
(region,
Antarctica)
Marie de Mé|di|cis
(French queen)
Mari El (republic,
Russia)
Mari|gold (name)
mari|gold +s
(flower)
ma|ri|huana (use
marijuana)
ma|ri|juana
Mari|lyn
ma|rimba +s
Mar|ina (name)
mar|ina +s
(harbour for

mar|ina (*cont.*)
pleasure boats
etc.)
mar|in|ade
mar|in|ades
mar|in|aded
mar|in|ad|ing
marin|ate
marin|ates
marin|ated
marin|at|ing
marin|ation +s
mar|ine +s
Mari|ner
(American space
probes)
mari|ner +s
Mari|netti,
Fi|lippo (Italian
writer)
Mari|ol|atry
Mari|ology
Mar|ion *also*
Mar|ian
mar|io|nette +s
Mar|isa
Mar|ist +s
mari|tal
mari|tal|ly
mari|time
Mari|times
(= Maritime
Provinces)
Ma|ritsa (river,
Bulgaria and
Greece)
Ma|riu|pol (port,
Russia)
Mar|ius, Gaius
(Roman general)
mar|joram +s
Mar|jorie *also*
Mar|gery
Mark *also* Marc
(name)
Mark (Apostle and
saint)
mark +s +ed +ing
(sign etc. △ marc,
marque)
Mark An|tony
(Roman general)
mark|down +s
mark|ed|ly
mark|ed|ness
mark|er +s
mar|ket +s +ed
+ing
mar|ket|abil|ity
mar|ket|able
mar|ket|eer +s
mar|ket|er +s

mar|ket|ing +s
mar|ket maker +s
mar|ket place +s
mark|hor +s
mark|ing +s
mark|ing ink +s
markka +s
Mar|kova, Ali|cia
(English dancer)
Marks, Simon
(Lord Marks,
English
businessman)
marks|man
marks|men
marks|man|ship
marks|woman
marks|women
mark-up +s *noun*
marl +s +ed +ing
Marl|bor|ough
(town and school,
England; region,
New Zealand)
Marl|bor|ough,
Duke of (British
general)
Marl|bur|ian +s
Mar|lene
Mar|ley, Bob
(Jamaican
musician)
mar|lin +s (fish)
mar|line +s (thin
rope)
marline-spike +s
(use marlinspike)
mar|lin|spike +s
mar|lite +s
Mar|lon
Mar|lowe,
Chris|to|pher
(English
dramatist)
marly
Mar|ma|duke
mar|ma|lade +s
Mar|mara, Sea of
(off Turkey)
Mar|mite (yeast
extract) *Propr.*
mar|mite +s
(cooking pot)
mar|mo|lite +s
mar|mor|eal
mar|mor|eal|ly
mar|mo|set +s
mar|mot +s
Marne (river,
France)
maro|cain +s
Maro|nite +s

ma|roon +s +ed
+ing
mar|plot +s
marque +s (make
of car; licence.
△ marc, mark)
mar|quee +s
Mar|que|sas
Is|lands (in S.
Pacific)
mar|quess
mar|quesses
(British nobleman.
△ marquis)
mar|quess|ate +s
mar|quet|ry
Mar|quette,
Jacques (French
missionary)
Már|quez,
Gab|riel Gar|cía
(Colombian
novelist)
mar|quis
mar|quises
(non-British
nobleman.
△ marquess)
mar|quis|ate +s
mar|quise +s (wife
or widow of
marquis; female
marquis)
mar|qui|sette +s
Mar|ra|kesh (town,
Morocco)
mar|ram +s
Mar|rano +s
mar|riage +s
mar|riage|abil|ity
mar|riage|able
mar|ried +s
mar|ron glacé
mar|rons glacés
mar|row +s
mar|row|bone +s
mar|row|fat
marry
mar|ries
mar|ried
marry|ing
Mar|ryat, Cap|tain
(English novelist)
Mars (*Roman
Mythology*; planet)
Mar|sala (town,
Sicily; wine.
△ masala)
Mar|seil|laise
(French national
anthem)

Mar|seille (French name for Marseilles)
Mar|seilles (port, France)
Marsh, Ngaio (New Zealand writer of detective fiction)
marsh
  marshes
Mar|sha
mar|shal
  mar|shals
  mar|shalled *Br.*
  mar|shaled *Am.*
  mar|shal|ling *Br.*
  mar|shal|ing *Am.*
Mar|shall, George C. (American general and statesman)
Mar|shall Is|lands (in NW Pacific)
Mar|shall Plan
mar|shal|ship +s
marshi|ness
marsh|land +s
marsh|mal|low +s
marshy
  marsh|ier
  marshi|est
Mars|ton Moor (battle site, England)
mar|su|pial +s
Mar|syas *Greek Mythology*
mart +s
Mar|ta|ban, Gulf of (on the coast of Burma)
mar|ta|gon +s
Mar|tel, Charles (Frankish ruler)
Mar|tello +s (tower)
mar|ten +s (weasel-like mammal. △ martin)
Mar|tens, Doc (= Dr Martens)
Mar|tens, Dr *Propr.*
mar|tens|ite
Mar|tha (*Bible*; name)
Mar|tha's Vine|yard (island, USA)
Mar|tial (Spanish-born Roman poet)
mar|tial

mar|tial|ise *Br.* (use martialize)
  mar|tial|ises
  mar|tial|ised
  mar|tial|is|ing
mar|tial|ize
  mar|tial|izes
  mar|tial|ized
  mar|tial|iz|ing
mar|tial|ly
Mar|tian +s
Mar|tin *also* **Mar|tyn** (name)
Mar|tin (French saint)
mar|tin +s (bird. △ marten)
Mar|tina
Mar|tine
mar|tinet +s
mar|tin|gale +s
Mar|tini (vermouth) *Propr.*
Mar|tini +s (cocktail)
Mar|tini, Sim|one (Italian painter)
Mar|ti|nique (island, Lesser Antilles)
Mar|tin|mas
mart|let +s
mar|tyr +s +ed +ing
mar|tyr|dom +s
mar|tyr|isa|tion *Br.* +s (use martyrization)
mar|tyr|ise *Br.* (use martyrize)
  mar|tyr|ises
  mar|tyr|ised
  mar|tyr|is|ing
mar|tyr|iza|tion +s
mar|tyr|ize
  mar|tyr|izes
  mar|tyr|ized
  mar|tyr|iz|ing
mar|tyr|ology
  mar|tyr|olo|gist +s
  mar|tyr|ol|ogies
mar|tyry
  mar|tyr|ies
Mar|uts *Hinduism*
mar|vel
  mar|vels
  mar|velled *Br.*
  mar|veled *Am.*

mar|vel (*cont.*)
  mar|vel|ling *Br.*
  mar|vel|ing *Am.*
mar|vel|er *Am.* +s
Mar|vell, An|drew (English poet)
mar|vel|ler *Br.* +s
mar|vel|lous *Br.*
mar|vel|lous|ly *Br.*
mar|vel|lous|ness *Br.*
mar|vel|ous *Am.*
mar|vel|ous|ly *Am.*
mar|vel|ous|ness *Am.*
Mar|vin
Marx, Karl (German political philosopher)
Marx Broth|ers, Chico, Harpo, Groucho, and **Zeppo** (family of American comedians)
Marx|ian +s
Marx|ism
Marxism-Leninism
Marx|ist +s
Marxist-Leninist +s
Mary (name)
Mary (Blessed Virgin Mary)
Mary (English queens)
Mary|bor|ough (town, Australia)
Mary Ce|leste (ship)
Mary|land (state, USA)
Mary Mag|da|lene *Bible*
Mary, Queen of Scots
Mary Rose (ship)
Mary Stu|art (Mary, Queen of Scots)
mar|zi|pan
  mar|zi|pans
  mar|zi|panned
  mar|zi|pan|ning
Ma|sac|cio (Italian painter)
Ma|sada (fortress, Near East)
Masai
  plural Masai or Mas|ais

ma|sala +s (spice; dish. △ Marsala)
Mas|aryk, Tomáš (Czech statesman)
Mas|bate (island, Philippines)
Mas|cagni, Pietro (Italian composer)
mas|cara +s
Mas|car|ene Is|lands (in Indian Ocean)
Mas|car|enes (= Mascarene Islands)
mas|car|pone
mas|cle +s
mas|con +s
mas|cot +s
mas|cu|line +s
mas|cu|line|ly
mas|cu|line|ness
mas|cu|lin|isa|tion *Br.* (use masculinization)
mas|cu|lin|ise *Br.* (use masculinize)
  mas|cu|lin|ises
  mas|cu|lin|ised
  mas|cu|lin|is|ing
mas|cu|lin|ist +s
mas|cu|lin|ity
  mas|cu|lin|ities
mas|cu|lin|iza|tion
mas|cu|lin|ize
  mas|cu|lin|izes
  mas|cu|lin|ized
  mas|cu|lin|iz|ing
mas|cu|list +s
Mase|field, John (English poet)
maser +s (electronic device. △ mazer)
Mas|eru (capital of Lesotho)
mash
  mashes
  mashed
  mash|ing
mash|er +s
Mash|had (city, Iran)
mashie +s
Ma|shona
  plural Ma|shona or Ma|sho|nas
Ma|shona|land (province, Rhodesia)

mask

mask +s +ed +ing
(cover.
⚠ masque)
mask|er +s
mask|ing tape +s
mas|kin|onge +s
maso|chism
maso|chist +s
maso|chis|tic
maso|chis|tic|al|ly
Mason +s
(= Freemason)
mason +s +ed
+ing
Mason–Dixon
Line (boundary
line between
Pennsylvania and
Maryland)
Ma|son|ic
Ma|son|ry
(= Freemasonry)
ma|son|ry
Ma|sorah
Mas|or|ete +s
Mas|or|et|ic
masque +s
(dramatic
entertainment.
⚠ mask)
mas|quer +s
mas|quer|ade
mas|quer|ades
mas|quer|aded
mas|quer|ad|ing
mas|quer|ader +s
Mass
Masses
(Eucharist)
mass
masses
massed
mass|ing
(quantity of matter
etc.)
Mas|sa|chu|setts
(state, USA)
mas|sacre
mas|sacres
mas|sacred
mas|sac|ring
mas|sage
mas|sages
mas|saged
mas|sa|ging
mas|sager +s
mas|sa|sauga +s
Mas|sawa (port,
Ethiopia)
massé +s Billiards
mas|seter +s
mas|seur +s male

mas|seuse +s
female
mas|si|cot
mas|sif +s
Mas|sif Cen|tral
(plateau, France)
Mas|sine,
Léo|nide (Russian-
born dancer)
Mas|sin|ger,
Philip (English
dramatist)
mas|sive
mas|sive|ly
mas|sive|ness
mass|less
mass mar|ket +s
noun
mass-market +s
+ed +ing
attributive and verb
Mas|son, André
(French painter)
Mas|so|rah (use
Masorah)
Mas|sor|ete (use
Masorete)
mass-produce
mass-produces
mass-produced
mass-producing
mass pro|duc|tion
mast +s +ed +ing
mas|taba +s
mast|ec|tomy
mast|ec|to|mies
mas|ter +s +ed
+ing
master-at-arms
masters-at-arms
mas|ter build|er
+s
mas|ter|class
mas|ter|classes
mas|ter|dom
mas|ter|ful
mas|ter|ful|ly
mas|ter|ful|ness
mas|ter|hood +s
mas|ter key +s
mas|ter|less
mas|ter|li|ness
mas|ter|ly
mas|ter mari|ner
+s
mas|ter mason +s
mas|ter|mind +s
+ed +ing
Mas|ter of the
Rolls
Mas|ters of the
Rolls

mas|ter|piece +s
mas|ter plan +s
mas|ter|ship +s
mas|ter|sing|er +s
mas|ter stroke +s
mas|ter switch
mas|ter switches
mas|ter|work +s
mas|tery
mas|ter|ies
mast foot
mast feet
mast|head +s +ed
+ing
mas|tic +s
mas|ti|cate
mas|ti|cates
mas|ti|cated
mas|ti|cat|ing
mas|ti|ca|tion
mas|ti|ca|tor +s
mas|ti|ca|tory
mas|tiff +s
mas|titis
mas|to|don +s
mas|to|don|tic
mas|toid +s
mas|toid|itis
mas|tur|bate
mas|tur|bates
mas|tur|bated
mas|tur|bat|ing
mas|tur|ba|tion
mas|tur|ba|tor +s
mas|tur|ba|tory
Ma|suria (region,
Poland)
Ma|sur|ian Lakes
(alternative name
for Masuria)
mat
mats
mat|ted
mat|ting
(on floor;
entangle; matrix.
⚠ matt, matte)
Mata|bele
plural Mata|bele
Mata|bele|land
(province,
Rhodesia)
mata|dor +s
Mata Hari (Dutch
spy)
match
matches
matched
match|ing
match|able
match|board +s

match|box
match|boxes
matchet +s
match|less
match|less|ly
match|lock +s
match|maker +s
match|mak|ing +s
match|play +s
match point +s
match|stick +s
match|wood
mate
mates
mated
mat|ing
maté (herbal tea)
mate|less
mate|lot +s (sailor)
mate|lote (fish
stew)
mater +s
mater|fami|lias
ma|ter|ial +s
ma|teri|al|isa|tion
Br. +s (use
materialization)
ma|teri|al|ise Br.
(use materialize)
ma|teri|al|ises
ma|teri|al|ised
ma|teri|al|is|ing
ma|teri|al|ism
ma|teri|al|ist +s
ma|teri|al|is|tic
ma|teri|al|is|tic|
al|ly
ma|teri|al|ity
ma|teri|al|iza|tion
+s
ma|teri|al|ize
ma|teri|al|izes
ma|teri|al|ized
ma|teri|al|iz|ing
ma|teri|al|ly
ma|teria med|ica
ma|tér|iel
ma|ter|nal
ma|ter|nal|ism
ma|ter|nal|is|tic
ma|ter|nal|ly
ma|ter|nity
ma|ter|nities
mate|ship +s
matey
mateys
mati|er
mati|est
ma|tey|ness
math
(= mathematics)

math|emat|ic|al
math|emat|ic|al|ly
math|em|at|ician
+s
math|emat|ics
Mathew *also*
Mat|thew
Ma|thias *also*
Mat|thias
Ma|thilda *also*
Ma|tilda
maths
(= mathematics)
ma|tico +s
Ma|tilda *also*
Ma|thilda
(name)
Ma|tilda (English
queen)
Ma|tilda +s
(bundle)
mati|ly
mat|inée +s
mati|ness (use
mateyness)
mat|ins
Ma|tisse, Henri
(French painter)
Mat|lock (town,
England)
Mat|mata (town,
Tunisia)
Mato Grosso
(plateau and state,
Brazil)
Mato Grosso do
Sul (state, Brazil)
mat|rass
mat|rasses
(glass vessel.
△ mattress)
ma|tri|arch +s
ma|tri|arch|al
ma|tri|archy
ma|tri|arch|ies
ma|tric
(= matriculation)
matri|ces
matri|cidal
matri|cide +s
ma|tric|ulate
ma|tric|ulates
ma|tric|ulated
ma|tric|ulat|ing
ma|tricu|la|tion +s
ma|tricu|la|tory
matri|lin|eal
matri|lin|eal|ly
matri|local
matri|mo|nial
matri|mo|ni|al|ly

matri|mony
matri|monies
mat|rix
matri|ces *or*
mat|rixes
ma|tron +s
ma|tron|al
ma|tron|hood +s
ma|tron|ly
Mat|su|yama (city,
Japan)
Matt (name)
matt +s +ed +ing
(dull. △ mat,
matte)
mat|ta|more +s
matte (smelting
product; mask.
△ mat, matt)
mat|ter +s +ed
+ing
Mat|ter|horn
(mountain, Swiss-
Italian border)
matter-of-fact
adjective
matter-of-factly
matter-of-factness
mat|tery
Mat|thew *also*
Mathew
(name)
Mat|thew (Apostle
and saint)
Mat|thew Paris
(English
chronicler)
Mat|thews,
Stan|ley (English
footballer)
Mat|thias *also*
Ma|thias
(name)
Mat|thias (Apostle
and saint)
mat|ting +s
mat|tins (use
matins)
mat|tock +s
mat|toid +s
mat|tress
mat|tresses
(on bed.
△ matrass)
mat|ur|ate
mat|ur|ates
mat|ur|ated
mat|ur|at|ing
mat|ur|ation +s
mat|ur|ation|al
ma|tur|ative

ma|ture
ma|tures
ma|tured
ma|tur|ing
ma|turer
ma|tur|est
ma|ture|ly
ma|ture|ness
ma|tur|ity
ma|tur|ities
ma|tu|tinal
maty (use matey)
mat|ier
mat|iest
matzo
matzos *or*
mat|zoth
Maud *also* Maude
(name)
maud +s (plaid;
rug)
Maude *also* Maud
maud|lin
Maugham,
Som|er|set
(English writer)
Maui (island,
Hawaii)
maul +s +ed +ing
(hammer;
mutilate. △ mall)
maul|er +s
maul|stick +s
Mau Mau (African
secret society)
Mauna Kea
(extinct volcano,
Hawaii)
Mauna Loa
(volcano, Hawaii)
maun|der +s +ed
+ing
maun|der|ing +s
Maundy
Maundy money
Maundy
Thurs|day +s
Mau|pas|sant,
Guy de (French
writer)
Maura
Maur|een
Maure|tania
(ancient name for
part of Morocco
and Algeria.
△ Mauritania)
Maure|ta|nian +s
Maur|iac,
Fran|çois (French
writer)

Maur|ice *also*
Mor|ris
Maur|ist +s
Mauri|ta|nia
(modern country,
W. Africa.
△ Mauretania)
Mauri|ta|nian +s
Maur|itian +s
Maur|itius (island,
Indian Ocean)
Maury, Mat|thew
Fon|taine
(American
oceanographer)
Mau|rya
mau|so|leum
mau|so|leums *or*
mau|so|lea
mauve +s
mauv|ish
maven +s
mav|er|ick +s
Mavis (name)
mavis
mavises
(bird)
maw +s (stomach;
throat. △ mor,
moor, more)
mawk|ish
mawk|ish|ly
mawk|ish|ness
Maw|lana
(alternative name
for Jalal ad-Din
ar-Rumi)
Max (name)
max
maxes
maxed
max|ing
maxi +s
max|illa
max|il|lae
max|il|lary
Maxim, Hiram
Ste|vens
(American
engineer)
maxim +s
(principle)
max|ima
max|imal
max|imal|ist +s
max|imal|ly
Maxim gun +s
Max|imil|ian
(emperor of
Mexico; name)

maxi|misa|tion *Br.*
+s (use
maximization)
maxi|mise *Br.* (use
maximize)
maxi|mises
maxi|mised
maxi|mis|ing
maxi|miser *Br.* +s
(use maximizer)
maxi|miza|tion +s
maxi|mize
maxi|mizes
maxi|mized
maxi|miz|ing
maxi|mizer +s
max|imum
plural max|ima *or*
max|imums
Max|ine
Max|well, James
Clerk (Scottish
physicist)
Max|well, Rob|ert
(Czech-born
British publisher)
max|well +s (unit)
May +s (name;
month)
may +s (hawthorn)
may *auxiliary verb*
Maya
plural Maya *or*
Mayas
(Central American
people; language;
name)
maya +s *Hinduism;
Buddhism*
Maya|kov|sky,
Vlad|imir (Soviet
poet)
Mayan +s
may-apple +s
maybe +s
(perhaps)
may be *verb*
May-bug +s
May Day +s (1st
May)
may|day +s (radio
distress signal)
Mayer, Louis B.
(Russian-born
American film
executive)
may|est
May|fair +s (fair
held in May;
district, London)
may|flower +s
(flower)

May|flower
(Pilgrim Fathers'
ship)
may|fly
may|flies
may|hap
may|hem +s
may|ing +s
May|nooth (village,
Republic of
Ireland)
mayn't (= may not)
Mayo (county,
Republic of
Ireland)
may|on|naise +s
mayor +s (council
official. △ mare)
may|or|al
may|or|alty
may|or|al|ties
may|or|ess
may|or|esses
may|or|ship +s
May|otte (island,
Indian Ocean)
may|pole +s
May queen +s
mayst
may|weed +s
maz|ard +s
Mazar-e-Sharif
(city, Afghanistan)
Maza|rin, Jules
(Italian-born
French statesman)
Maza|rin Bible
maza|rine +s
Maz|at|lán (port,
Mexico)
Maz|da|ism
maze
mazes
mazed
maz|ing
(labyrinth.
△ maize)
mazer +s (bowl.
△ maser)
mazi|ly
mazi|ness
ma|zuma
ma|zurka +s
mazy
mazi|er
mazi|est
maz|zard +s (use
mazard)
Maz|zini,
Giu|seppe (Italian
political leader)

Mba|bane (capital
of Swaziland)
Mc|Carthy,
Jo|seph R.
(American
politician)
Mc|Carthy, Mary
(American writer)
Mc|Carthy|ism
Mc|Cartney, Paul
(English pop and
rock singer)
McCoy +s
Mc|Enroe, John
(American tennis
player)
Mc|Gona|gall,
Wil|liam
(Scottish writer)
Mc|Kinley,
Wil|liam
(American
president)
Mc|Kinley, Mount
(in Alaska)
Mc|Luhan,
Mar|shall
(Canadian
communications
scholar)
Mc|Naugh|ten
rules
me (objective case
of I; *Music*)
mea culpa
Mead, Mar|ga|ret
(American
anthropologist)
mead +s (drink,
meadow. △ meed)
meadow +s
meadow|land
meadow|lark +s
meadow|sweet +s
mead|owy
mea|ger *Am.*
mea|ger|ly *Am.*
mea|ger|ness *Am.*
meagre *Br.*
meagre|ly *Br.*
meagre|ness *Br.*
meal +s
meal-beetle +s
mealie +s (maize.
△ mealy)
meali|ness
meals on wheels
meal|time +s
meal|worm +s
mealy
meali|er
meali|est

mealy (*cont.*)
(powdery; pale.
△ mielie)
mealy bug +s
mealy-mouthed
mean
means
meant
mean|ing
mean|er
mean|est
(intend; signify;
not generous;
unkind; inferior;
average. △ mien,
mesne)
Me|ander (river,
Turkey; use
Meander)
me|ander +s +ed
+ing
me|ander|ing +s
me|an|drine
meanie +s
mean|ing +s
mean|ing|ful
mean|ing|ful|ly
mean|ing|ful|ness
mean|ing|less
mean|ing|less|ly
mean|ing|less|ness
mean|ing|ly
mean|ly
mean|ness
mean-spirit|ed
means test +s
noun
means-test +s +ed
+ing *verb*
meant
mean|time
(meanwhile;
intervening
period)
mean time +s
(time based on the
mean sun; but
Greenwich Mean
Time)
mean|while
meany (use
meanie)
meanies
mea|sles
measly
meas|lier
meas|li|est
meas|ur|abil|ity
meas|ur|able
meas|ur|ably
meas|ure
meas|ures

meas|ure (*cont.*)
meas|ured
meas|ur|ing
meas|ured|ly
meas|ure|less
meas|ure|less|ly
meas|ure|ment +s
meat +s (flesh.
⚠ meet, mete)
meat-axe +s
meat|ball +s
meat-fly
meat-flies
Meath (county,
Republic of
Ireland)
meat|ily
meati|ness
meat|less
meat loaf
meat loaves
meat safe +s
me|atus
plural me|atus or
me|atuses
meaty
meat|ier
meati|est
Mecca (city, Saudi
Arabia)
Mec|cano *Propr.*
mech|an|ic +s
mech|an|ic|al +s
mech|an|ic|al|ism
mech|an|ic|al|ly
mech|an|ic|al|ness
mech|an|ician +s
mech|an|ics
mech|an|isa|tion
Br. (use
mechanization)
mech|an|ise Br.
(use mechanize)
mech|an|ises
mech|an|ised
mech|an|is|ing
mech|an|iser Br.
+s (use
mechanizer)
mech|an|ism +s
mech|an|ist +s
mech|an|is|tic
mech|an|is|tic|
al|ly
mech|an|iza|tion
mech|an|ize
mech|an|izes
mech|an|ized
mech|an|iz|ing
mech|an|izer +s
mech|ano|
recep|tor +s

mecha|tron|ics
Me|che|len (city,
Belgium)
Mech|lin +s
Meck|len|burg
(former state,
Germany)
Mecklenburg-
West
Pom|er|ania
(state, Germany)
meco|nium +s
mecu +s
Med
(= Mediterranean)
medal +s (award.
⚠ meddle)
med|aled Am.
med|al|ist Am. +s
med|alled Br.
med|al|lic
med|al|lion +s
med|al|list Br. +s
Medan (city,
Indonesia)
Meda|war, Peter
(English
immunologist)
med|dle
med|dles
med|dled
med|dling
(interfere.
⚠ medal)
med|dler +s
(busybody.
⚠ medlar)
meddle|some
meddle|some|ly
meddle|some|ness
Mede +s
Medea Greek
Mythology
Me|de|llin (city,
Colombia)
Media (country of
the Medes)
media
med|iae
Phonetics
media (plural of
medium;
newspapers,
television, etc.)
medi|aeval (use
medieval)
med|ial
medi|al|ly
Me|dian +s (of
Media)
me|dian +s
Anatomy;

me|dian (*cont.*)
Geometry;
Mathematics
me|dian|ly
me|di|ant +s
me|di|as|tin|al
me|di|as|tinum
me|di|as|tina
me|di|ate
me|di|ates
me|di|ated
me|di|at|ing
me|di|ate|ly
me|di|ation +s
me|dia|tisa|tion
Br. +s (use
mediatization)
me|dia|tise Br. (use
mediatize)
me|dia|tises
me|dia|tised
me|dia|tis|ing
me|dia|tiza|tion +s
me|dia|tize
me|dia|tizes
me|dia|tized
me|dia|tiz|ing
me|di|ator +s
me|di|ator|ial
me|di|atory
me|di|atrix
me|di|atri|ces
female
medic +s (doctor.
⚠ medick)
med|ic|able
Me|dic|aid
med|ic|al +s
med|ic|al|ly
med|ic|ament +s
Medi|care
medi|cate
medi|cates
medi|cated
medi|cat|ing
medi|ca|tion +s
med|ica|tive
Me|di|cean
Med|ici also
Médi|cis
(Florentine family;
see also under first
name)
me|di|cin|al
me|di|cin|al|ly
medi|cine +s
Medi|cine Hat
(town, Canada)
medi|cine man
medi|cine men
Méd|icis also
Med|ici

Méd|icis (*cont.*)
(Florentine family;
see also under first
name)
med|ick +s (plant.
⚠ medic)
med|ico +s
medi|eval
medi|eval|ise Br.
(use medievalize)
medi|eval|ises
medi|eval|ised
medi|eval|is|ing
medi|eval|ism
medi|eval|ist +s
medi|eval|ize
medi|eval|izes
medi|eval|ized
medi|eval|iz|ing
medi|eval|ly
Me|dina (city,
Saudi Arabia)
me|dina +s (district
of N African town)
me|di|ocre
me|di|oc|rity
me|di|oc|rities
medi|tate
medi|tates
medi|tated
medi|tat|ing
medi|ta|tion +s
medi|ta|tive
medi|ta|tive|ly
medi|ta|tive|ness
medi|ta|tor +s
Medi|ter|ra|nean
+s
me|dium +s
(spiritualist)
me|dium
media or
me|diums
(other senses)
me|dium|ism
me|dium|is|tic
medium-range
me|dium|ship +s
medium-sized
med|lar +s (tree.
⚠ meddler)
med|ley +s
Medoc +s (wine)
Médoc (region,
France)
me|dulla +s
me|dul|lary
Me|dusa Greek
Mythology
me|dusa
me|du|sae or

me|dusa (*cont.*)
me|dusas
(jellyfish)
me|du|san
meed +s (reward.
△ mead)
meek +er +est
meek|ly
meek|ness
meer|kat +s
meer|schaum +s
Mee|rut (city,
India)
meet
meets
met
meet|ing
(encounter.
△ meat, mete)
meet|er +s (person
who meets.
△ meter, metre)
meet|ing +s
meet|ing house +s
meet|ly
meet|ness
Meg
mega
mega|buck +s
mega|byte +s
mega|ceph|al|ic
mega|cycle +s
mega|death +s
Me|gaera *Greek
Mythology*
mega|flop +s
mega|hertz
plural mega|hertz
mega|lith +s
mega|lith|ic
meg|alo|mania +s
meg|alo|maniac
+s
meg|alo|
        mani|ac|al
meg|alo|man|ic
meg|alop|olis
meg|alop|olises
meg|alo|pol|itan
meg|alo|saur +s
meg|alo|saurus
meg|alo|saur|uses
Megan
mega|phone +s
mega|pod +s (use
megapode)
mega|pode +s
meg|aron +s
mega|scop|ic
mega|spore +s
mega|star +s
mega|store +s

mega|ther|ium
mega|theria
mega|ton +s
mega|tonne +s
(use megaton)
mega|volt +s
mega|watt +s
Meg|ger +s *Propr.*
Meg|ha|laya (state,
India)
Me|giddo (ancient
city, Israel)
meg|ilp +s
meg|ohm +s
meg|rim +s
Meiji Tenno
(Japanese
emperor)
mei|osis
mei|oses
(cell division;
litotes. △ miosis)
mei|ot|ic (to do
with meiosis.
△ miotic)
mei|otic|al|ly
Meir, Golda
(Israeli prime
minister)
Meis|sen (city,
Germany;
porcelain
produced there)
Meis|ter|singer
plural
Meis|ter|singer
Meit|ner, Lise
(Austrian-born
Swiss physicist)
Me|kele (city,
Ethiopia)
Mek|nès (city,
Morocco)
Me|kong (river, SE
Asia)
Mel
Me|laka (state and
port, Malaysia)
mela|mine +s
mel|an|cho|lia +s
mel|an|chol|ic
mel|an|chol|ic|
        al|ly
mel|an|choly
mel|an|chol|ies
Mel|anch|thon,
Phil|ipp (German
Protestant
reformer)
Mela|nesia (island
group, SW Pacific)
Mela|nes|ian +s

mé|lange +s
Mel|anie
mel|anin +s
mel|an|ism +s
mela|noma +s
mela|nosis
mela|noses
mela|not|ic
Melba, Nel|lie
(Australian
soprano; sauce;
toast)
Mel|bourne (city,
Australia)
Mel|bourne, Lord
(British prime
minister)
Mel|chior (one of
the Magi)
Mel|chite +s
Mel|chiz|edek
Bible
meld +s +ed +ing
Me|le|ager (Greek
hero; Greek poet)
melee *Am.* +s
mêlée *Br.* +s
melic
Me|lilla (Spanish
enclave, Morocco)
meli|lot +s
Me|linda
meli|or|ate
meli|or|ates
meli|or|ated
meli|or|at|ing
meli|or|ation +s
meli|ora|tive
meli|or|ism
meli|or|ist +s
me|lisma
me|lis|mata *or*
me|lis|mas
mel|is|mat|ic
Me|lissa
mel|lif|er|ous
mel|lif|lu|ence
mel|lif|lu|ent
mel|lif|lu|ous
mel|lif|lu|ous|ly
mel|lif|lu|ous|ness
Mel|lon, An|drew
Wil|liam
(American
financier)
mel|low +s +ed
+ing
mel|low|ly
mel|low|ness
me|lo|deon +s
me|lod|ic
me|lod|ic|al|ly

me|lo|di|ous
me|lo|di|ous|ly
me|lo|di|ous|ness
melo|dise *Br.* (use
melodize)
melo|dises
melo|dised
melo|dis|ing
melo|diser *Br.* +s
(use melodizer)
melo|dist +s
melo|dize
melo|dizes
melo|dized
melo|diz|ing
melo|dizer +s
melo|dra|ma +s
melo|dra|mat|ic
melo|dra|mat|ic|
        al|ly
melo|dra|mat|ics
melo|drama|tise
Br. (use
melodramatize)
melo|drama|tises
melo|drama|tised
melo|drama|
        tis|ing
melo|drama|tist
+s
melo|drama|tize
melo|drama|tizes
melo|drama|tized
melo|drama|
        tiz|ing
Mel|ody (name)
mel|ody
mel|od|ies
(tune)
melon +s
Melos (Greek
island)
Mel|pom|ene *Greek
and Roman
Mythology*
melt +s +ed +ing
melt|able
melt|down +s
melt|er +s
melt|ing|ly
melt|ing point +s
melt|ing pot +s
mel|ton +s (cloth)
Mel|ton
Mow|bray (town,
England)
melt water +s
Mel|ville,
Her|man
(American writer)
Mel|vin *also*
Mel|vyn

mem¦ber +s
mem¦bered
mem¦ber¦less
mem¦ber¦ship +s
mem¦ber state +s
mem¦bran¦aceous
mem¦brane +s
mem¦bran¦eous
mem¦bran¦ous
mem¦brum virile
Memel (German
  name for
  Klaipeda; former
  district, East
  Prussia; lower part
  of River Neman)
me¦mento
  me¦men¦toes *or*
  me¦mentos
me¦mento mori
Mem¦non *Greek*
  Mythology
memo +s
mem¦oir +s
mem¦oir¦ist +s
mem¦ora¦bilia
mem¦or¦abil¦ity
mem¦or¦able
mem¦or¦able¦ness
mem¦or¦ably
memo¦ran¦dum
  memo¦randa *or*
  memo¦ran¦dums
me¦mor¦ial +s
Me¦mor¦ial Day
  Am. +s
me¦mor¦ial¦ise *Br.*
  (use memorialize)
  me¦mor¦ial¦ises
  me¦mor¦ial¦ised
  me¦mor¦ial¦is¦ing
me¦mor¦ial¦ize
  me¦mor¦ial¦izes
  me¦mor¦ial¦ized
  me¦mor¦ial¦iz¦ing
me¦moria
  tech¦nica +s
mem¦or¦is¦able *Br.*
  (use
  memorizable)
mem¦or¦isa¦tion
  Br. (use
  memorization)
mem¦or¦ise *Br.* (use
  memorize)
  mem¦or¦ises
  mem¦or¦ised
  mem¦or¦is¦ing
mem¦or¦iser *Br.* +s
  (use memorizer)
mem¦or¦iz¦able

mem¦or¦iza¦tion
mem¦or¦ize
  mem¦or¦izes
  mem¦or¦ized
  mem¦or¦iz¦ing
mem¦or¦izer +s
mem¦ory
  mem¦or¦ies
mem¦ory bank +s
Mem¦phis (ancient
  city, Egypt; port,
  USA)
mem¦sahib +s
men (plural of
  man)
men¦ace
  men¦aces
  men¦aced
  men¦acing
men¦acer +s
men¦acing¦ly
mé¦nage +s
mé¦nage à trois
  mé¦nages à trois
men¦agerie +s
Menai Strait
  (channel between
  Anglesey and
  Wales)
Me¦nan¦der (Greek
  writer)
mena¦quin¦one +s
me¦nar¦che +s
Men¦cius (Chinese
  philosopher)
Men¦cken, Henry
  Louis (American
  journalist)
mend +s +ed +ing
mend¦able
men¦da¦cious
men¦da¦cious¦ly
men¦da¦cious¦ness
men¦da¦city
  men¦da¦ci¦ties
Men¦del, Gre¦gor
  Jo¦hann
  (Moravian monk
  and geneticist)
Men¦de¦leev,
  Dmi¦tri
  Ivan¦ovich
  (Russian chemist)
men¦del¦evium
Men¦del¦ian
Men¦del¦ism
Men¦dels¦sohn,
  Felix (German
  composer)
mend¦er +s
Men¦deres (river,
  Turkey)

men¦di¦cancy
men¦di¦cant +s
men¦di¦city
Men¦dip Hills (in
  England)
Men¦dips
  (= Mendip Hills)
Men¦doza,
  An¦tonio de (1st
  viceroy of Mexico)
Men¦doza (city and
  province,
  Argentina)
Mene¦laus *Greek*
  Mythology
Menes (pharaoh)
men¦folk
Meng-tzu (Chinese
  name of Mencius)
Mengzi (alternative
  Chinese name of
  Mencius)
men¦haden +s
men¦hir +s
me¦nial +s
me¦ni¦al¦ly
men¦in¦geal
men¦in¦git¦ic
men¦in¦gi¦tis
men¦in¦go¦cele +s
men¦in¦go¦coc¦cus
  men¦in¦go¦cocci
men¦inx
  men¦in¦ges
me¦nis¦coid
me¦nis¦cus
  me¦nisci
Men¦non¦ite +s
men¦ol¦ogy
  men¦olo¦gies
Men¦om¦ini
  plural Men¦om¦ini
meno¦pausal
meno¦pause +s
me¦norah +s
Men¦orca (Spanish
  name for
  Minorca)
Men¦or¦can +s (use
  Minorcan)
men¦or¦rha¦gia
men¦or¦rhea *Am.*
men¦or¦rhoea *Br.*
Mensa
men¦ses
Men¦she¦vik +s
mens rea
men¦strual
men¦stru¦ate
  men¦stru¦ates
  men¦stru¦ated
  men¦stru¦at¦ing

men¦stru¦ation +s
men¦stru¦ous
men¦struum
  men¦strua
men¦sur¦able
men¦sural
men¦sur¦ation +s
mens¦wear
men¦tal
men¦tal¦ism
men¦tal¦ist +s
men¦tal¦is¦tic
men¦tal¦ity
  men¦tal¦ities
men¦tal¦ly
men¦ta¦tion +s
men¦thol +s
men¦thol¦ated
men¦tion +s +ed
  +ing
men¦tion¦able
men¦tor +s
menu +s
menu-driven
Men¦uhin, Ye¦hudi
  (American-born
  British violinist)
Men¦zies, Rob¦ert
  (Australian prime
  minister)
meow +s +ed +ing
  (use miaow)
mepa¦crine
me¦peri¦dine
Meph¦is¦to¦
  phe¦lean
Meph¦is¦toph¦eles
  (German legend)
Meph¦is¦to¦
  phe¦lian (use
  Mephisto-
  phelean)
meph¦it¦ic
meph¦itis
  meph¦itises
me¦ranti +s
mer¦can¦tile
mer¦can¦til¦ism
mer¦can¦til¦ist +s
mer¦cap¦tan
Mer¦ca¦tor,
  Ger¦ar¦dus
  (Flemish-born
  geographer;
  projection)
Mer¦cedes
mer¦cen¦ari¦ness
mer¦cen¦ary
  mer¦cen¦ar¦ies
mer¦cer +s
mer¦cer¦ise *Br.* (use
  mercerize)

mer|cer|ise (*cont.*)
mer|cer|ises
mer|cer|ised
mer|cer|is|ing
mer|cer|ize
mer|cer|izes
mer|cer|ized
mer|cer|iz|ing
mer|cery
mer|cer|ies
mer|chan|dis|able
mer|chan|dise
mer|chan|dises
mer|chan|dised
mer|chan|dis|ing
mer|chan|diser +s
Mer|chant, Is|mail
(Indian film
producer)
mer|chant +s
mer|chant|able
Mer|chant
Ad|ven|turers
(English trading
guild)
mer|chant|man
mer|chant|men
Mer|cia (ancient
kingdom, central
England)
Mer|cian +s
mer|ci|ful
mer|ci|ful|ly
mer|ci|ful|ness
mer|ci|less
mer|ci|less|ly
mer|ci|less|ness
Merckx, Eddy
(Belgian racing
cyclist)
Mer|cur|ial (of the
planet Mercury)
mer|cur|ial
(volatile;
containing
mercury)
mer|curi|al|ism
mer|curi|al|ity
mer|curi|al|ly
mer|cur|ic
mer|cur|ous
Mer|cury (*Roman
Mythology*; planet)
mer|cury (metal)
Mercy (name)
mercy
mer|cies
(clemency)
mere
meres
mer|est

Mere|dith (name)
Mere|dith, George
(English writer)
mere|ly
mer|en|gue +s
mere|tri|cious
mere|tri|cious|ly
mere|tri|cious|
        ness
mer|gan|ser +s
merge
merges
merged
mer|ging
mer|gence +s
mer|ger +s
Mé|rida (cities,
Spain and Mexico)
me|rid|ian +s
me|rid|ion|al
Me|riel
mer|ingue +s
me|rino +s
Meri|on|eth|shire
(former county,
Wales)
meri|stem +s
meri|stem|at|ic
merit +s +ed +ing
mer|it|oc|racy
mer|it|oc|ra|cies
mer|ito|crat|ic
meri|tori|ous
meri|tori|ous|ly
meri|tori|ous|ness
Merle (name)
merle +s
(blackbird)
Mer|lin *Arthurian
Legend*
Mer|lin *also*
Mer|lyn
(name)
mer|lin +s (falcon)
mer|lon +s
(parapet)
Mer|lot +s
Mer|lyn *also*
Mer|lin
mer|maid +s
mer|maid's purse
+s
mer|man
mer|men
mero|blast +s
Meroe (ancient
city, Sudan)
mero|he|dral
me|ron|ymy
Mero|vin|gian +s
mer|rily
mer|ri|ment

mer|ri|ness
merry
mer|rier
mer|ri|est
merry an|drew +s
merry-go-round
+s
merry|maker +s
merry|mak|ing
merry thought +s
Mersa Ma|truh
(town, Egypt)
Mer|sey (river,
England)
Mer|sey|side
(metropolitan
county, England)
Mer|sin (port,
Turkey)
Mer|thyr Tyd|fil
(town, Wales)
Mer|vin *also*
Mer|vyn
Mer|vyn *also*
Mer|vin
Meryl
mesa +s
més|al|li|ance +s
mes|cal +s
mes|cal but|tons
mes|ca|lin (use
mescaline)
mes|ca|line
Mes|dames (plural
of Madame)
Mes|de|moi|selles
(plural of
Mademoiselle)
mes|em|bry|
    an|the|mum +s
mes|en|ceph|alon
+s
mes|en|ter|ic
mes|en|ter|itis
mes|en|tery
mes|en|ter|ies
mesh
meshes
meshed
mesh|ing
Me|shed
(alternative name
for Mashhad)
me|sial
me|si|al|ly
mesic
Mes|mer, Franz
Anton (Austrian
physician)
mes|mer|ic
mes|mer|ic|al|ly

mes|mer|isa|tion
Br. (use
mesmerization)
mes|mer|ise *Br.*
(use mesmerize)
mes|mer|ises
mes|mer|ised
mes|mer|is|ing
mes|mer|iser *Br.*
+s (use
mesmerizer)
mes|mer|is|ing|ly
Br. (use
mesmerizingly)
mes|mer|ism
mes|mer|ist +s
mes|mer|iza|tion
mes|mer|ize
mes|mer|izes
mes|mer|ized
mes|mer|iz|ing
mes|mer|izer +s
mes|mer|iz|ing|ly
mesne +s (*Law*
intermediate.
△ mean, mien)
Meso-America
(Central America)
Meso-American
+s
meso|blast +s
meso|carp +s
meso|ceph|al|ic
meso|derm +s
meso|gas|ter +s
meso|lith|ic
meso|morph +s
meso|morph|ic
meso|morphy
meson +s
mes|on|ic
meso|pause +s
meso|phyll +s
meso|phyte +s
Meso|po|ta|mia
(region, Iraq)
Meso|po|ta|mian
+s
meso|sphere +s
meso|tron +s
Meso|zo|ic
mes|quit +s (use
mesquite)
mes|quite +s
(shrub)
mess
messes
messed
mess|ing
mes|sage
mes|sages

mes|sage (cont.)
mes|saged
mes|sa|ging
Mes|sa|lina,
Val|eria (Roman
empress)
Mes|sei|gneurs
mes|sen|ger +s
Mes|ser|schmitt,
Willy (German
aircraft designer)
Mes|siaen,
Oli|vier (French
composer)
Mes|siah +s
Mes|siah|ship +s
Mes|si|an|ic
Mes|si|an|ism
Mes|sieurs
mess|ily
Mes|sina (city,
Sicily)
messi|ness
mess jack|et +s
mess kit +s
mess|mate +s
Messrs
(= Messieurs)
mess tin +s
mes|suage +s
messy
mess|ier
messi|est
mes|tiza +s *female*
mes|tizo +s *male*
met (past tense and
past participle of
meet;
= meteorological,
metropolitan)
meta|bi|sul|phite
+s
meta|bol|ic
meta|bol|ic|al|ly
me|tab|ol|is|able
Br. (use
metabolizable)
me|tab|ol|ise *Br.*
(use metabolize)
me|tab|ol|ises
me|tab|ol|ised
me|tab|ol|is|ing
me|tab|ol|ism +s
me|tab|ol|iz|able
me|tab|ol|ize
me|tab|ol|izes
me|tab|ol|ized
me|tab|ol|iz|ing
meta|car|pal +s
meta|car|pus
meta|carpi

meta|cen|ter *Am.*
+s
meta|centre +s
me|tage +s
meta|gen|esis
meta|gen|eses
meta|ge|net|ic
metal
metals
met|alled *Br.*
met|aled *Am.*
met|al|ling *Br.*
met|al|ing *Am.*
(iron; copper; etc.
△ metol, mettle)
meta|lan|guage +s
meta|lin|guis|tic
meta|lin|guis|tics
met|al|ize *Am.* (use
metallize)
met|al|izes
met|al|ized
met|al|iz|ing
me|tal|lic
me|tal|lic|al|ly
metal|lif|er|ous
met|al|line
met|al|lisa|tion *Br.*
(use
metallization)
met|al|lise *Br.* (use
metallize)
met|al|lises
met|al|lised
met|al|lis|ing
met|al|liza|tion
met|al|lize
met|al|lizes
met|al|lized
met|al|liz|ing
met|al|lo|graph|ic
met|al|lo|
graph|ic|al
met|al|lo|graph|ic|
al|ly
met|al|log|raphy
met|al|loid +s
met|al|lo|phone +s
met|al|lur|gic
met|al|lur|gic|al
met|al|lur|gic|al|ly
met|al|lur|gist +s
met|al|lurgy
metal|work
met|al|work|er +s
met|al|work|ing
meta|mer +s
meta|mere +s
meta|mer|ic
me|tam|er|ism
meta|morph|ic

meta|morph|ism
meta|morph|ose
meta|morph|oses
meta|morph|osed
meta|
morph|os|ing
meta|mor|phosis
meta|mor|phoses
meta|phase +s
meta|phor +s
meta|phor|ic
meta|phor|ic|al
meta|phor|ic|al|ly
meta|phrase
meta|phrases
meta|phrased
meta|phras|ing
meta|phras|tic
meta|phys|ic +s
meta|phys|ic|al
meta|phys|ic|al|ly
meta|phys|ician
+s
meta|physi|cise
Br. (use
metaphysicize)
meta|physi|cises
meta|physi|cised
meta|physi|
cis|ing
meta|physi|cize
meta|physi|cizes
meta|physi|cized
meta|physi|
ciz|ing
meta|phys|ics
meta|pla|sia +s
meta|plasm +s
meta|plas|tic
meta|pol|itics
meta|psy|cho|
logic|al
meta|psych|ology
meta|sta|bil|ity
meta|sta|ble
me|tas|ta|sis
me|tas|ta|ses
me|tas|ta|sise *Br.*
(use metastasize)
me|tas|ta|sises
me|tas|ta|sised
me|tas|ta|sis|ing
me|tas|ta|size
me|tas|ta|sizes
me|tas|ta|sized
me|tas|ta|siz|ing
meta|stat|ic
meta|tar|sal +s
meta|tar|sus
meta|tarsi
meta|ther|ian +s

me|tath|esis
me|tath|eses
meta|thet|ic
meta|thet|ic|al
meta|zoan +s
mete
metes
meted
met|ing
(apportion;
boundary.
△ meat. meet)
met|em|psy|chosis
met|
em|psy|choses
met|em|psy|chos|
ist +s
me|teor +s
Met|eora (region,
Greece)
me|teor|ic
me|teoric|al|ly
me|teor|ite +s
me|teor|it|ic
me|teoro|graph +s
me|teor|oid +s
me|teor|oid|al
me|teoro|logic|al
me|teoro|logic|
al|ly
me|teor|olo|gist +s
me|teor|ology
meter +s +ed +ing
(measuring
device; to
measure.
△ meeter, metre)
meter *Am.* +s (unit;
rhythm. *Br.* metre.
△ meeter)
meter|age *Am.* +s
(*Br.* metreage)
metha|done
meth|am|pheta|
mine +s
metha|nal
me|thane
metha|no|ate +s
metha|no|ic
metha|nol
methe|drine *Propr.*
me|thinks
me|thought
me|thio|nine
metho +s
method +s
method act|ing
method actor +s
mé|thode
cham|pen|oise
meth|od|ic
meth|od|ic|al

meth|od|ic|al|ly
meth|od|ise *Br.*
  (use methodize)
meth|od|ises
meth|od|ised
meth|od|is|ing
meth|od|iser *Br.*
  +s (use
  methodizer)
Meth|od|ism
Meth|od|ist +s
  (religious
  denomination)
meth|od|ist +s
  (methodical
  person)
Meth|od|is|tic
Meth|od|is|tic|al
Me|tho|dius (Greek
  saint)
meth|od|ize
  meth|od|izes
  meth|od|ized
  meth|od|iz|ing
meth|od|izer +s
meth|odo|logic|al
meth|odo|logic|
  al|ly
meth|od|olo|gist
  +s
meth|od|olo|ology
  meth|od|olo|gies
me|thought
meths
  (= methylated
  spirits)
Me|thu|selah +s
  (*Bible*; very old
  person or thing)
me|thu|selah +s
  (wine bottle)
me|thyl +s
meth|yl|ate
  meth|yl|ates
  meth|yl|ated
  meth|yl|at|ing
meth|yl|a|tion
meth|yl|ene
me|thyl|ic
metic +s
meti|cal +s
me|ticu|lous
me|ticu|lous|ly
me|ticu|lous|ness
mé|tier +s
metif +s
Metis
  plural Metis
metol +s
  (photographic
  developer.
  △ metal, mettle)

Me|ton|ic
meto|nym +s
meto|nym|ic
meto|nym|ic|al
meto|nym|ic|al|ly
me|ton|ymy
  me|ton|ymies
met|ope +s
metre *Br.* +s
  (metric unit;
  poetic rhythm.
  Am. meter.
  △ meeter, meter)
metre|age *Br.* +s
  (*Am.* meterage)
metre-kilogram-
  second +s
met|ric +s
met|ric|al
met|ric|al|ly
met|ri|cate
  met|ri|cates
  met|ri|cated
  met|ri|cat|ing
met|ri|ca|tion
met|ri|cian +s
met|ri|cise *Br.* (use
  metricize)
  met|ri|cises
  met|ri|cised
  met|ri|cis|ing
met|ri|cize
  met|ri|cizes
  met|ri|cized
  met|ri|ciz|ing
met|ric ton +s
met|rist +s
me|tri|tis
metro +s
met|ro|logic
met|ro|logic|al
me|trol|ogy
met|ro|nome +s
met|ro|nom|ic
met|ro|nym|ic +s
me|trop|olis
  plural
  me|trop|olises *or*
  me|trop|oles
met|ro|pol|itan +s
met|ro|pol|it|an|
  ate +s
met|ro|pol|it|an|
    ism
me|tror|rha|gia
Met|ter|nich,
  Kle|mens
  (Austrian prince
  and statesman)
met|tle +s
  (courage, spirit.
  △ metal, metol)

met|tled
mettle|some
Metz (city, France)
meu +s (plant.
  △ mew, mu)
meu|nière
Meuse (river, NW
  Europe)
mew +s +ed +ing
  (cat's cry; gull;
  cage for hawks.
  △ meu, mu)
mewl +s +ed +ing
  (whimper.
  △ mule)
mews (stabling.
  △ muse)
Mexi|cali (city,
  Mexico)
Mex|ican +s
Mex|ico
Mex|ico City
  (capital of
  Mexico)
Meyer|beer,
  Gia|como
  (German
  composer)
Meyer|hof, Otto
  Fritz (German-
  born American
  biochemist)
me|zer|eon +s
me|zu|zah
me|zu|zoth
mez|za|nine +s
mezza voce
mezzo +s
mezzo forte
Mez|zo|giorno (in
  Italy)
mezzo piano
mezzo-relievo +s
mezzo-rilievo +s
  (use mezzo-
  relievo)
mezzo-soprano +s
mezzo|tint +s +ed
  +ing
mezzo|tint|er +s
mho +s (unit.
  △ mo, mow)
mi (*Music*; use me)
Mia
Miami (city, USA)
miaow +s +ed
  +ing
mi|asma
  mi|as|mata *or*
  mi|asmas
mi|as|mal
mi|as|mat|ic

mi|as|mic
mi|as|mic|al|ly
miaul +s +ed +ing
mica +s (mineral)
mi|ca|ceous
Micah *Bible*
mica-schist
Mi|caw|ber +s
Mi|caw|ber|ish
Mi|caw|ber|ism
mice
mi|celle +s
Mi|chael
  (archangel and
  saint; name)
Mi|chaela
Mich|ael|mas
  Mich|ael|mases
Mi|chel|an|gelo
  (Buon|ar|roti)
  (Italian artist)
Mich|èle *also*
  Mich|elle
Miche|lin, André
  and Édu|ard
  (French tyre
  manufacturers)
Mich|elle *also*
  Mich|èle
Mi|chel|ozzo
  (Italian architect)
Mich|el|son,
  Al|bert
  Abra|ham
  (American
  physicist)
Mich|igan (state,
  USA)
Mich|igan, Lake
  (in N. America)
Mi|cho|acán (state,
  Mexico)
mick +s (*offensive*)
mick|erie +s (use
  mickery)
mick|ery
  mick|er|ies
Mickey *also* Micky
  (name)
mickey (in 'take the
  mickey')
Mickey Finn +s
Mickey Mouse
  (cartoon
  character)
mickey-taking
mickle +s
Mick the Mil|ler
  (racing
  greyhound)
Micky *also* Mickey
  (name)

micky (in 'take the
micky'; use
mickey)
Mic¦mac
plural **Mic¦mac** *or*
Mic¦macs
micro +s
micro|analy¦sis
micro|analy¦ses
mi¦crobe +s
mi¦cro¦bial
mi¦cro¦bic
micro|bio¦logic¦al
micro|bio¦logic¦
al¦ly
micro|biolo¦gist +s
micro|biol¦ogy
micro|burst +s
micro|ceph¦al¦ic
micro|ceph¦alous
micro|ceph¦aly
micro|chip +s
micro|cir¦cuit +s
micro|cir¦cuit¦ry
micro|cli¦mate +s
micro|cli¦mat¦ic
micro|cli¦mat¦ic¦
al¦ly
micro|cline +s
micro|code +s
micro|com¦puter
+s
micro|copy
micro|copies
micro|copied
micro|copy¦ing
micro|cosm +s
micro|cos¦mic
micro|cos¦mic¦
al¦ly
micro|crys¦tal|line
micro|dot +s
micro|eco¦nom¦ic
micro|eco¦nom¦ics
micro|elec¦tron¦ics
micro|evo¦lu¦tion
micro|evo¦lu¦tion¦
ary
micro|fiche
plural micro|fiche
or micro|fiches
micro|film +s +ed
+ing
micro|floppy
micro|flop¦pies
micro|form +s
micro|gram +s
micro|graph +s
micro|grav¦ity
micro|groove +s
micro|in¦struc¦tion
+s

micro|
lepi¦dop¦tera
micro|light +s
micro|lith +s
micro|lith¦ic
micro|mesh
micro|meshes
mi¦crom|eter +s
(gauge)
micro|meter *Am.*
+s (unit)
micro|metre *Br.* +s
(unit)
mi¦crom|etry
micro|mini¦atur|
isa|tion *Br.* +s
(use micro-
miniaturization)
micro|mini¦atur|
iza|tion +s
mi¦cron +s
Micro|nesia (area
of W. Pacific;
Federated States
of Micronesia)
Micro|nes¦ian +s
micro|nu¦trient +s
micro-organ|ism
+s
micro|phone +s
micro|phon¦ic
micro|photo¦graph
+s
micro|phyte +s
micro|pro¦ces¦sor
+s
micro|pro¦gram +s
micro|pyle +s
micro|scope +s
micro|scop¦ic
micro|scop¦ic¦al
micro|scop¦ic¦al¦ly
mi¦cro|scop¦ist +s
mi¦cro|scopy
micro|sec¦ond +s
micro|seism +s
Micro|soft *Propr.*
micro|some +s
micro|spore +s
micro|struc¦ture
+s
micro|sur¦gery
micro|sur¦gi¦cal
micro|switch
micro|switches
micro|tech¦nique
+s
micro|tome +s
micro|tone +s
micro|tu¦bule +s
micro|wave
micro|waves

micro|wave (*cont.*)
micro|waved
micro|wav¦ing
micro|wave|able
mic¦rurgy
mic¦tur|ition
mid (= amid)
Midas *Greek
Mythology*
mid|brain +s
mid|day +s
mid|den +s
mid¦dle
mid¦dles
mid¦dled
mid¦dling
mid¦dle age (time
of life)
middle-aged
Mid¦dle Ages
(period of
European history)
**middle-age
spread**
middle|brow +s
middle-class
adjective
Mid¦dle East|ern
middle|man
middle|men
**middle-of-the-
road** *attributive*
Middles|brough
(town, England)
Middle|sex (former
county, England)
middle-sized
**Middle|ton,
Thomas** (English
dramatist)
middle|weight +s
mid|dling +s
mid|dling¦ly
middy
mid¦dies
Mid|east
mid|field +s
mid|field¦er +s
Mid|gard
*Scandinavian
Mythology*
midge +s
midget +s
Mid Gla|mor¦gan
(county, Wales)
mid|gut +s
MIDI +s (= musical
instrument digital
interface)
Midi (region,
France)
midi +s (dress etc.)

midi|bus
midi|buses
midi|nette +s
Midi-Pyrénées
(region, France)
mid|iron +s
Mid|land
(*attributive* of the
Midlands)
mid|land +s
mid|land¦er +s
Mid|lands, the
(inland counties of
central England)
mid-life
mid|line +s
Mid|lothian
(former county,
Scotland)
mid|most
mid|night +s
mid|night blue +s
noun and adjective
midnight-blue
attributive
mid-off +s *Cricket*
mid-on +s *Cricket*
Mid|rash
Mid|rash¦im
mid|rib +s
mid|riff +s
mid|ship +s
mid|ship|man
mid¦ship|men
mid|ships *adverb*
midst
mid|stream
mid|sum¦mer +s
Mid|sum¦mer Day
+s
**Mid|sum¦mer's
Day** +s
mid|town
mid|way
Mid¦way Is¦lands
(in Pacific Ocean)
mid|week
Mid|west
mid|wicket +s
mid|wife
mid|wives
mid|wif¦ery
mid|win¦ter +s
mie¦lie +s (use
mealie. △ mealy)
mien +s (look;
bearing. △ mean,
mesne)
**Mies van der
Rohe, Lud¦wig**
(German-born
architect)

mife|pris|tone

miff +s +ed +ing

miffy

might (*auxiliary verb*; strength. △ mite)

might|est

might-have-been +s

might|ily

mighti|ness

mightn't (= might not)

mighty

might|ier

mighti|est

mign|on|ette +s

mi|graine +s

mi|grain|ous

mi|grant +s

mi|grate

mi|grates

mi|grated

mi|grat|ing

mi|gra|tion +s

mi|gra|tion|al

mi|gra|tor +s

mi|gra|tory

Mi|hail|ović, Drag|oljub (Draža) (Yugoslav soldier)

mih|rab +s

mi|kado +s

Mike (name)

mike

mikes

miked

mik|ing (microphone; shirk)

Mi|ko|nos (Greek name for Mykonos)

mil

plural mil *or* mils (thousandth of an inch. △ mill)

mi|lady

mi|la|dies

mil|age +s (use mileage)

Milan (city, Italy)

Mil|an|ese

plural Mil|an|ese

milch

milch cow +s

mild +er +est

mild|en +s +ed +ing

mil|dew +s +ed +ing

mil|dewy

mild|ish

mild|ly

mild-mannered

mild|ness

Mil|dred

mild steel +s *noun and attributive*

mile +s (unit. △ myall)

mile|age +s

mile|post +s

miler +s

Miles *also* Myles

Mi|le|sian +s

mile|stone +s

Mi|le|tus (ancient Greek city in Asia Minor)

mill|foil +s

Mil|haud, Da|rius (French composer)

mill|iary

mi|lieu

mi|lieux *or* mi|lieus

mili|tancy

mili|tan|cies

Mili|tant (British political organization)

mili|tant +s (combative; person)

mili|tant|ly

mili|taria

mili|tar|ily

mili|tari|ness

mili|tar|isa|tion *Br.* (use militarization)

mili|tar|ise *Br.* (use militarize)

mili|tar|ises

mili|tar|ised

mili|tar|is|ing

mili|tar|ism

mili|tar|ist +s

mili|tar|is|tic

mili|tar|is|tic|al|ly

mili|tar|iza|tion

mili|tar|ize

mili|tar|izes

mili|tar|ized

mili|tar|iz|ing

mili|tary

mili|tar|ies

mili|tate

mili|tates

mili|tated

mili|tat|ing

mili|tia +s

mili|tia|man

mili|tia|men

milk +s +ed +ing

milk|er +s

milk float +s

milki|ness

milk-leg +s

milk-loaf

milk-loaves

milk|maid +s

milk|man

milk|men

Milk of Mag|nesia Propr.

milk shake +s

milk|sop +s

milk tooth

milk teeth

milk-vetch

milk-vetches

milk|weed +s

milk white +s *noun and adjective*

milk-white *attributive*

milk|wort +s

milky

milk|ier

milki|est

Milky Way Astronomy

Mill, John Stu|art (English philosopher)

mill +s +ed +ing (building or apparatus for grinding. △ mil)

mill|able

Mil|lais, John Everett (English painter)

mill|board +s

mill-dam +s

Mille, Cecil B. de (American film producer and director)

mille|feuille +s

mil|len|ar|ian +s

mil|len|ar|ian|ism

mil|len|ar|ian|ist +s

mil|len|ary

mil|len|ar|ies

mil|len|nial

mil|len|nial|ist +s

mil|len|nium

mil|len|niums *or* mil|len|nia

mille|pede +s (use millipede)

mille|pore +s

Mil|ler, Ar|thur (American playwright)

Mil|ler, Glenn (American jazz musician)

mill|er +s

mill|er's thumb +s (fish)

mil|lesi|mal

mil|lesi|mal|ly

mil|let +s

millet-grass

millet-grasses

mill|hand +s

milli|am|meter +s

milli|amp +s

milli|am|pere +s

mil|liard +s

milli|bar +s

Mil|li|cent

Mil|lie

milli|gram +s

milli|gramme +s (use milligram)

Mil|li|kan, Rob|ert An|drews (American physicist)

milli|liter *Am.* +s

milli|litre *Br.* +s

milli|meter *Am.* +s

milli|metre *Br.* +s

mill|iner +s

mill|in|ery

mil|lion +s

mil|lion|aire +s

mil|lion|air|ess

mil|lion|air|esses

mil|lion|fold

mil|lionth +s

milli|pede +s

milli|sec|ond +s

milli|volt +s

mill owner +s

mill|pond +s

mill-race +s

mill-rind +s

Mills, John (English actor)

Mills bomb +s (grenade)

mill|stone +s

mill|stream +s

mill-wheel +s

mill|work|er +s

mill|wright +s

Milne, A. A. (English writer)

Milo
mil|om|eter +s
mi|lord +s
Milos (island,
Cyclades)
milt +s
milt|er +s
Mil|ton, John
(English poet)
Mil|ton|ian +s
Mil|ton|ic
Mil|ton Keynes
(town, England)
Mil|wau|kee (city,
USA)
Mimas (*Greek
Mythology*; moon
of Saturn)
mim|bar +s
mime
mimes
mimed
mim|ing
mim|eo|graph +s
+ed +ing
mimer +s
mi|mesis
mi|meses
mi|met|ic
mi|met|ic|al|ly
Mimi
mimic
mim|ics
mim|icked
mim|ick|ing
mim|ick|er +s
mim|ic|ry
miminy-piminy
mi|mosa +s
mimu|lus
mimu|luses
Min (Chinese
dialect)
min +s (= minute)
mina +s (bird; use
mynah. △ miner,
minor)
min|acious
min|acity
min|aci|ties
Min|aean +s
min|aret +s
min|aret|ed
Minas Ge|rais
(state, Brazil)
min|atory
min|bar +s
mince
minces
minced
min|cing
(grind up; walk;

mince (*cont.*)
minced meat.
△ mints)
minced meat
(meat)
mince|meat +s
(mixture of
currants, apples,
etc.)
mince pie +s
min|cer +s
Minch, the
Minches
(channel off
Scotland)
min|cing|ly
mind +s +ed +ing
(intellect; lood
after; etc.
△ mined)
Min|da|nao (island,
Philippines)
mind-bending
mind-blowing
mind-boggling
mind-boggling|ly
mind|er +s
mind|ful
mind|ful|ly
mind|ful|ness
mind|less
mind|less|ly
mind|less|ness
mind-numbing
Min|doro (island,
Philippines)
mind-read
mind-reads
mind-read
mind-reading
mind-reader +s
mind|set +s
mine
mines
mined
min|ing
mine-detect|or +s
mine|field +s
mine hunt|er +s
mine|lay|er +s
miner +s
(mineworker.
△ minor, myna,
mynah)
min|eral +s
min|er|al|isa|tion
Br. (use
mineralization)
min|er|al|ise *Br.*
(use mineralize)
min|er|al|ises

min|er|al|ise (*cont.*)
min|er|al|ised
min|er|al|is|ing
min|er|al|iza|tion
min|er|al|ize
min|er|al|izes
min|er|al|ized
min|er|al|iz|ing
min|er|al|ogic|al
min|er|al|ogist +s
min|er|al|ogy
Min|erva *Roman
Mythology*
mine shaft +s
min|es|trone +s
mine|sweeper +s
min|ever +s (use
miniver)
mine|work|er +s
Ming
min|gily
min|gle
min|gles
min|gled
min|gling
min|gler +s
Min|gus, Charles
(American jazz
musician)
mingy
min|gier
min|gi|est
Minho (river, Spain
and Portugal)
Mini +s (car) *Propr.*
mini +s (dress etc.)
mini|ate
mini|ates
mini|ated
mini|at|ing
mini|ature
mini|atures
mini|atured
mini|atur|ing
mini|atur|isa|tion
Br. +s (use
miniaturization)
mini|atur|ise *Br.*
(use miniaturize)
mini|atur|ises
mini|atur|ised
mini|atur|is|ing
mini|atur|ist +s
mini|atur|iza|tion
+s
mini|atur|ize
mini|atur|izes
mini|atur|ized
mini|atur|iz|ing
mini|bar +s
mini|bus
mini|buses

mini|cab +s
Mini|com +s *Propr.*
mini|com|puter +s
Mini|coy Is|lands
(now part of
Lakshadweep
Islands)
mini|dress
mini|dresses
min|ify
mini|fies
mini|fied
mini|fy|ing
mini|golf
mini|kin +s
minim +s
mini|ma
min|imal
min|im|al|ism
min|im|al|ist +s
min|im|al|ly
mini|max
mini|misa|tion *Br.*
+s (use
minimization)
min|im|ise *Br.* (use
minimize)
min|im|ises
min|im|ised
min|im|is|ing
min|im|iser *Br.* +s
(use minimizer)
mini|miza|tion +s
min|im|ize
min|im|izes
min|im|ized
min|im|iz|ing
min|im|izer +s
min|imum
plural min|ima *or*
min|imums
min|ion +s
mini|pill +s
min|is|cule (use
minuscule)
mini|ser|ies
plural mini|ser|ies
mini|skirt +s
min|is|ter +s +ed
+ing
min|is|ter|ial
min|is|teri|al|ist
+s
min|is|teri|al|ly
min|is|ter|ship +s
min|is|trable
min|is|trant +s
min|is|tra|tion +s
min|is|tra|tive
min|is|try
min|is|tries
min|iver +s

mink +s (stoatlike
animal. △minx)
minke +s (whale)
Min¦kow¦ski,
Her¦mann
(Russian-born
German
mathematician)
Minna
Min¦ne¦ap¦olis
(city, USA)
min¦ne¦sing¦er +s
Min¦ne¦sota (state,
USA)
Min¦nie
min¦now +s
Miño (Spanish
name for Minho)
Min¦oan +s
minor +s +ed +ing
(below legal age;
unimportant.
△mina, miner,
myna, mynah)
Min¦orca (Spanish
island)
Min¦or¦can +s
Mi¦nor¦ite +s
mi¦nor¦ity
mi¦nor¦ities
Minos (legendary
Cretan king)
Mi¦no¦taur +s
Minsk (capital of
Belarus)
min¦ster +s
min¦strel +s
min¦strelsy
min¦strel¦sies
mint +s +ed +ing
(plant; sweet;
place where
money is made.
△mince)
mint¦age +s
Min¦ton (pottery)
minty
mint¦ier
minti¦est
minu¦end +s
min¦uet +s +ed
+ing
minus
mi¦nuses
min¦us¦cu¦lar
min¦us¦cule
mi¦nute
mi¦nuter
minut¦est
(tiny)
min¦ute
min¦utes

min¦ute (cont.)
min¦uted
min¦ut¦ing
(60 seconds;
proceedings; to
record)
minute-gun +s
min¦ute hand +s
mi¦nute¦ly
Min¦ute¦man
Min¦ute¦men
mi¦nute¦ness
min¦ute steak +s
mi¦nu¦tia
mi¦nu¦tiae
minx
minxes
(girl. △minks)
minx¦ish
minx¦ish¦ly
Mio¦cene
mi¦osis
mi¦oses
(eye disorder.
△meiosis)
mi¦otic (to do with
miosis. △meiotic)
MIPS (= million
instructions per
second)
Mi¦que¦lon (in 'St.
Pierre and
Miquelon')
Mir (Soviet space
station)
Mira (star)
Mi¦ra¦beau,
Hon¦oré Gab¦riel
Ri¦queti, Comte
de (French
revolutionary)
Mira¦bel
mi¦ra¦belle +s
mira¦cid¦ium
mira¦cidia
mir¦acle +s
mi¦racu¦lous
mi¦racu¦lous¦ly
mi¦racu¦lous¦ness
mira¦dor +s
mir¦age +s
Mi¦randa (moon of
Saturn; name)
MIRAS
(= mortgage
interest relief at
source)
mire
mires
mired
mir¦ing

mire|poix
plural mire|poix
Mir¦iam
mirid +s
miri¦ness
mirk (use murk)
mirky (use murky)
Miró, Joan
(Spanish painter)
mir¦ror +s +ed
+ing
mir¦ror image +s
mir¦ror writ¦ing
mirth
mirth|ful
mirth|ful¦ly
mirth|ful|ness
mirth|less
mirth|less¦ly
mirth|less|ness
MIRV +s
(= multiple
independently-
targeted re-entry
vehicle)
miry
mis¦ad¦dress
mis¦ad¦dresses
mis¦ad¦dressed
mis¦ad¦dress|ing
mis¦ad¦ven¦ture +s
mis¦align +s +ed
+ing
mis¦align|ment +s
mis¦alli¦ance +s
mis¦ally
mis¦allies
mis¦allied
mis¦ally|ing
mis¦andry
mis¦an¦thrope +s
mis¦an¦throp¦ic
mis¦an¦throp¦ic¦al
mis¦an¦throp¦ic¦
al¦ly
mis¦an¦thro¦pise
Br. (use
misanthropize)
mis¦an¦thro¦pises
mis¦an¦thro¦pised
mis¦an¦thro¦
pis¦ing
mis¦an¦thro¦pist
+s
mis¦an¦thro¦pize
mis¦an¦thro¦pizes
mis¦an¦thro¦pized
mis¦an¦thro¦
piz¦ing
mis¦an¦thropy
mis¦ap¦pli¦ca¦tion
+s

mis¦ap¦ply
mis¦ap¦plies
mis¦ap¦plied
mis¦ap¦ply|ing
mis¦ap¦pre¦hend
+s +ed +ing
mis¦ap¦pre¦hen¦
sion +s
mis¦ap¦pre¦hen¦sive
mis¦ap¦pro¦pri¦ate
mis¦ap¦pro¦pri¦
ates
mis¦ap¦pro¦pri¦
ated
mis¦ap¦pro¦pri¦
at¦ing
mis¦ap¦pro¦pri¦
ation +s
mis¦be¦come
mis¦be¦comes
mis¦be¦came
mis¦be¦com¦ing
mis¦be¦got¦ten
mis¦be¦have
mis¦be¦haves
mis¦be¦haved
mis¦be¦hav¦ing
mis¦be¦haver +s
mis¦be¦hav¦ior Am.
mis¦be¦hav¦iour Br.
mis¦be¦lief +s
mis¦cal¦cu¦late
mis¦cal¦cu¦lates
mis¦cal¦cu¦lated
mis¦cal¦cu¦lat¦ing
mis¦cal¦cu¦la¦tion
+s
mis¦call +s +ed
+ing
mis¦car¦riage +s
mis¦carry
mis¦car¦ries
mis¦car¦ried
mis¦carry|ing
mis¦cast
mis¦casts
mis¦cast
mis¦cast|ing
mis¦ce¦gen¦ation
mis¦cel¦la¦nea
mis¦cel¦lan¦eous
mis¦cel¦
lan¦eous¦ly
mis¦cel¦lan¦eous¦
ness
mis¦cel¦lan¦ist +s
mis¦cel¦lany
mis¦cel¦lanies
mis¦chance +s
mis¦chief +s
mischief-maker
+s

mischief-making
mis|chiev|ous
mis|chiev|ous|ly
mis|chiev|ous|
         ness
misch metal +s
mis|ci|bil|ity
mis|cible
mis|con|ceive
mis|con|ceives
mis|con|ceived
mis|con|ceiv|ing
mis|con|ceiver +s
mis|con|cep|tion
  +s
mis|con|duct +s
  +ed +ing
mis|con|struc|tion
  +s
mis|con|strue
mis|con|strues
mis|con|strued
mis|con|stru|ing
mis|copy
mis|cop|ies
mis|cop|ied
mis|copy|ing
mis|count +s +ed
  +ing
mis|cre|ant +s
mis|cue
mis|cues
mis|cued
mis|cue|ing or
mis|cuing
mis|date
mis|dates
mis|dated
mis|dat|ing
mis|deal
mis|deals
mis|dealt
mis|deal|ing
mis|dec|lar|ation
  +s
mis|deed +s
mis|de|mean|ant
  +s
mis|de|meanor
  Am. +s
mis|de|mean|our
  Br. +s
mis|de|scribe
mis|de|scribes
mis|de|scribed
mis|de|scrib|ing
mis|de|scrip|tion
  +s
mis|diag|nose
mis|diag|noses
mis|diag|nosed
mis|diag|nos|ing

mis|diag|nosis
mis|diag|noses
mis|dial
mis|dials
mis|dialled Br.
mis|dialed Am.
mis|dial|ling Br.
mis|dial|ing Am.
mis|dir|ect +s +ed
  +ing
mis|dir|ec|tion +s
mis|doing +s
mis|doubt +s +ed
  +ing
mis|edu|cate
mis|edu|cates
mis|edu|cated
mis|edu|cat|ing
mis|edu|ca|tion
mise en scène
mises en scène
mis|em|ploy +s
  +ed +ing
mis|em|ploy|ment
  +s
miser +s
mis|er|able
mis|er|able|ness
mis|er|ably
mis|ère +s
mis|er|ere +s
mis|eri|cord +s
miser|li|ness
miser|ly
mis|ery
mis|er|ies
mis|feas|ance +s
mis|field +s +ed
  +ing
mis|fire
mis|fires
mis|fired
mis|fir|ing
mis|fit +s
mis|for|tune +s
mis|give
mis|gives
mis|gave
mis|giv|ing
mis|given
mis|giv|ing +s
mis|gov|ern +s
  +ed +ing
mis|gov|ern|ment
mis|guid|ance
mis|guide
mis|guides
mis|guided
mis|guid|ing
mis|guided|ly
mis|guided|ness
mis|handle
mis|handles

mis|handle (cont.)
mis|handled
mis|hand|ling
mis|hap +s
mis|hear
mis|hears
mis|heard
mis|hear|ing
mis|hit
mis|hits
mis|hit
mis|hit|ting
mish|mash
mish|mashes
Mish|nah
Mish|na|ic
mis|iden|ti|fi|
      ca|tion +s
mis|iden|tify
mis|iden|ti|fies
mis|iden|ti|fied
mis|iden|ti|fy|ing
mis|in|form +s
  +ed +ing
mis|in|for|ma|tion
mis|in|ter|pret +s
  +ed +ing
mis|in|ter|pret|
     ation +s
mis|in|ter|pret|er
  +s
mis|judge
mis|judges
mis|judged
mis|judg|ing
mis|judge|ment +s
mis|judg|ment +s
  (use
  misjudgement)
mis|key +s +ed
  +ing
mis|kick +s +ed
  +ing
Mis|kito
  plural Mis|kito or
  Mis|kitos
Mis|kolc (city,
  Hungary)
mis|lay
mis|lays
mis|laid
mis|lay|ing
mis|lead
mis|leads
mis|led
mis|lead|ing
mis|lead|er +s
mis|lead|ing
mis|lead|ing|ly
mis|lead|ing|ness
mis|like
mis|likes

mis|like (cont.)
mis|liked
mis|lik|ing
mis|man|age
mis|man|ages
mis|man|aged
mis|man|aging
mis|man|age|ment
  +s
mis|mar|riage +s
mis|match
mis|matches
mis|matched
mis|match|ing
mis|mated
mis|meas|ure
mis|meas|ures
mis|meas|ured
mis|meas|ur|ing
mis|meas|ure|
      ment
mis|name
mis|names
mis|named
mis|nam|ing
mis|nomer +s
miso
mis|og|am|ist +s
mis|og|amy
mis|ogyn|ist +s
mis|ogyn|is|tic
mis|ogyn|ous
mis|ogyny
mis|olo|gist +s
mis|ol|ogy
miso|ne|ism
miso|ne|ist +s
mis|pickel +s
mis|place
mis|places
mis|placed
mis|placing
mis|place|ment +s
mis|play +s +ed
  +ing
mis|print +s +ed
  +ing
mis|pri|sion +s
mis|prize
mis|prizes
mis|prized
mis|priz|ing
mis|pro|nounce
mis|pro|nounces
mis|pro|nounced
mis|pro|noun|
      cing
mis|pro|nun|ci|
     ation +s
mis|quo|ta|tion +s
mis|quote
mis|quotes

mis|quote (*cont.*)
  mis|quoted
  mis|quot|ing
mis|read
  mis|reads
  mis|read
  mis|read|ing
mis|re|mem|ber +s
  +ed +ing
mis|re|port +s +ed
  +ing
mis|rep|re|sent +s
  +ed +ing
mis|rep|re|sen|
      ta|tion +s
mis|rep|re|sen|
      ta|tive
mis|rule
  mis|rules
  mis|ruled
  mis|rul|ing
miss
  misses
  missed
  miss|ing
miss|able
mis|sal +s (book)
mis|sel thrush (use
  mistle thrush)
  mis|sel thrushes
mis|shape
  mis|shapes
  mis|shaped
  mis|shap|ing
mis|sha|pen
mis|sha|pen|ly
mis|sha|pen|ness
mis|sile +s
mis|sil|ery
  mis|sil|er|ies
mis|sion +s
mis|sion|ary
  mis|sion|ar|ies
mis|sion|er +s
mis|sis
miss|ish
Mis|sis|sauga
  (town, Canada)
Mis|sis|sippi (river,
  USA)
mis|sive +s
Mis|so|lon|ghi
  (city, Greece)
Mis|souri (river
  and state, USA)
mis|spell
  mis|spells
  mis|spelled *or*
  mis|spelt
  mis|spell|ing
mis|spell|ing +s

mis|spend
  mis|spends
  mis|spent
  mis|spend|ing
mis|state
  mis|stat|ing
mis|state|ment +s
mis|step +s
mis|sus
missy
  mis|sies
mist +s +ed +ing
  (condensed
  vapour etc.
  △ missed)
mis|tak|able
mis|tak|ably
mis|take
  mis|takes
  mis|took
  mis|tak|ing
  mis|taken
mis|taken|ly
mis|taken|ness
mis|teach
  mis|teaches
  mis|taught
  mis|teach|ing
mis|ter +s
mist|ful
mis|ti|gris
mist|ily
mis|time
  mis|times
  mis|timed
  mis|tim|ing
misti|ness
mis|title
  mis|titles
  mis|titled
  mis|tit|ling
mis|tle thrush
  mis|tle thrush|es
mistle|toe +s
mist|like
mis|took
mis|tral +s
mis|trans|late
  mis|trans|lates
  mis|trans|lated
  mis|trans|lat|ing
mis|trans|la|tion
  +s
mis|treat +s +ed
  +ing
mis|treat|ment +s
mis|tress
  mis|tresses
Mis|tress of the
  Robes
mis|trial +s

mis|trust +s +ed
  +ing
mis|trust|ful
mis|trust|ful|ly
mis|trust|ful|ness
misty
  mist|ier
  misti|est
mis|type
  mis|types
  mis|typed
  mis|typ|ing
mis|un|der|stand
  mis|un|der|stands
  mis|un|der|stood
  mis|un|der|stand|
      ing
mis|un|der|stand|
      ing +s
mis|us|age +s
mis|use
  mis|uses
  mis|used
  mis|us|ing
mis|user +s
Mi|tanni
  plural Mi|tanni
Mi|tan|nian +s
Mitch|ell, Joni
  (Canadian singer-
  songwriter)
Mitch|ell,
  Mar|ga|ret
  (American
  novelist)
Mitch|ell,
  Regi|nald
  Jo|seph (English
  aeronautical
  designer)
mite +s (arachnid;
  small amount.
  △ might)
miter *Am.* +s +ed
  +ing (*Br.* mitre)
miter block *Am.* +s
  (*Br.* mitre block)
miter box *Am.*
  miter boxes
  (*Br.* mitre box)
miter joint *Am.* +s
  (*Br.* mitre joint)
miter wheel *Am.*
  +s (*Br.* mitre
  wheel)
Mit|ford, Nancy
  (English writer)
Mith|ra|ic
Mith|ra|ism
Mith|ra|ist +s
Mith|ras *Persian*
  Mythology

Mith|ri|da|tes
  (king of Pontus)
mith|ri|dat|ic
mith|rida|tise *Br.*
  (use mithridatize)
  mith|rida|tises
  mith|rida|tised
  mith|rida|tis|ing
mith|ri|da|tism
mith|rida|tize
  mith|rida|tizes
  mith|rida|tized
  mith|rida|tiz|ing
miti|gable
miti|gate
  miti|gates
  miti|gated
  miti|gat|ing
miti|ga|tion +s
miti|ga|tor +s
miti|ga|tory
Miti|lini (Greek
  name for
  Mytilene)
Mitla (ancient city,
  Mexico)
mi|to|chon|drion
  mi|to|chon|dria
mi|tosis
  mi|toses
mi|tot|ic
mit|*rail*|*leuse* +s
mi|tral
mitre *Br.*
  mitres
  mitred
  mitr|ing
  (*Am.* miter)
mitre block *Br.* +s
  (*Am.* miter block)
mitre box *Br.*
  mitre boxes
  (*Am.* miter box)
mitre joint *Br.* +s
  (*Am.* miter joint)
mitre wheel *Br.* +s
  (*Am.* miter wheel)
Mit|siwa
  (= Massawa)
mitt +s
Mit|tel|land Canal
  (in Germany)
mit|ten +s
mit|tened
Mit|ter|rand,
  Fran|çois (French
  president)
mit|ti|mus
  mit|ti|muses
Mitty, Wal|ter
  Wal|ter Mittys

mitz|vah
  mitz|voth
mix
  mixes
  mixed
  mix|ing
mix|able
mixed|ness
mixed-up
  attributive
mixer +s
mixer tap +s
Mix|tec +s
mix|ture +s
mix-up +s *noun*
mizen +s (use
  mizzen)
Mi|zo|ram (state,
  India)
miz|zen +s
mizzen-mast +s
mizzen-sail +s
miz|zen yard +s
miz|zle
  miz|zles
  miz|zled
  miz|zling
miz|zly
M.Litt. (= Master
  of Letters)
Mlle +s
  (= Mademoiselle)
m'lud
Mma|batho (town,
  South Africa)
M'Nagh|ten rules
  (use McNaughten
  rules)
mne|mon|ic +s
mne|mon|ic|al|ly
mne|mon|ics
mne|mon|ist +s
Mne|mos|yne
  Greek Mythology
mo +s (= moment.
  △ mho, mow)
moa +s (bird.
  △ mower)
Moab|ite +s
moan +s +ed +ing
  (plaintive sound;
  make a moan;
  complain.
  △ mown)
moan|er +s
moan|ful
moan|ing|ly
moan|ing min|nie
  +s
moat +s +ed +ing
  (ditch. △ mote)

mob
  mobs
  mobbed
  mob|bing
mob|ber +s
mob|bish
mob cap +s
Mo|bile (city, USA)
mo|bile +s
mo|bil|iary
mo|bil|is|able *Br.*
  (use mobilizable)
mo|bil|isa|tion *Br.*
  +s (use
  mobilization)
mo|bil|ise *Br.* (use
  mobilize)
  mo|bil|ises
  mo|bil|ised
  mo|bil|is|ing
mo|bil|iser *Br.* +s
  (use mobilizer)
mo|bil|ity
mo|bil|iz|able
mo|bil|iza|tion +s
mo|bil|ize
  mo|bil|izes
  mo|bil|ized
  mo|bil|iz|ing
mo|bil|izer +s
Mö|bius strip
mob|oc|racy
mob|oc|ra|cies
mob|ster +s
Mo|butu Sese
  Seko, Lake (in
  Zaire)
Mo|butu (Sese
  Seko) (president
  of Zaire)
moc|ca|sin +s
Mocha +s (stone;
  butterfly; pottery)
mocha +s (coffee;
  leather. △ mocker)
Mo|chica
  plural Mo|chica
mock +s +ed +ing
mock|able
mock|er +s
  (person who mocks.
  △ mocha)
mock|ery
  mock|er|ies
mock-heroic +s
mock|ing|bird +s
mock|ing|ly
mock-up +s *noun*
mod +s
modal
mo|dal|ity
  mo|dal|ities

mo|dal|ly
mod cons
  (= modern
  conveniences)
mode +s
model
  models
  mod|elled *Br.*
  mod|eled *Am.*
  mod|el|ling *Br.*
  mod|el|ing *Am.*
mod|el|er *Am.* +s
mod|el|ler *Br.* +s
modem +s
Mod|ena (city,
  Italy)
mod|er|ate
  mod|er|ates
  mod|er|ated
  mod|er|at|ing
mod|er|ate|ly
mod|er|ate|ness
mod|er|ation +s
Mod|er|ations
  (examination)
mod|er|at|ism
mod|er|ato +s
mod|er|ator +s
mod|er|ator|ship
  +s
mod|ern +s
mod|ern|isa|tion
  Br. +s (use
  modernization)
mod|ern|ise *Br.*
  (use modernize)
  mod|ern|ises
  mod|ern|ised
  mod|ern|is|ing
mod|ern|iser *Br.*
  +s (use
  modernizer)
mod|ern|ism +s
mod|ern|ist +s
mod|ern|is|tic
mod|ern|is|tic|
  al|ly
mod|ern|ity
mod|ern|ities
mod|ern|iza|tion
  +s
mod|ern|ize
  mod|ern|izes
  mod|ern|ized
  mod|ern|iz|ing
mod|ern|izer +s
mod|ern|ly
mod|ern|ness
mod|est
mod|est|ly
mod|esty
modi|cum

modi|fi|able
modi|fi|ca|tion +s
modi|fi|ca|tory
modi|fier +s
mod|ify
  modi|fies
  modi|fied
  modi|fy|ing
Modi|gliani,
  Ame|deo (Italian
  painter)
mo|dil|lion +s
mod|ish
mod|ish|ly
mod|ish|ness
mod|iste +s
Mods
  (= Moderations)
modu|lar
modu|lar|ity
modu|late
  modu|lates
  modu|lated
  modu|lat|ing
modu|la|tion +s
modu|la|tor +s
mod|ule +s
mod|ulo
modu|lus
  mod|uli
modus op|er|andi
  modi op|er|andi
modus vi|vendi
  modi vi|vendi
Moe|sia (ancient
  country, modern
  Bulgaria and
  Serbia)
mo|fette +s
mog +s
Moga|di|shu
  (capital of
  Somalia)
Moga|don
  plural Moga|don
  or Moga|dons
  Propr.
mog|gie +s
moggy
  mog|gies
  (use moggie)
Mo|ghul +s (use
  Mogul)
Mo|gi|lev (Russian
  name for
  Mahilyow)
Mogul +s
  (Mongolian
  Muslim)
mogul +s
  (important
  person)

Mo¦hács (river port, Hungary)

mo¦hair +s

Mo¦ham|med (use Muhammad)

Mo¦ham|medan +s (prefer Muslim)

Mo¦ham|med|an|ism (prefer Islam)

Mo¦ham|merah (former name of Khorramshahr)

Mo¦have Des¦ert (use Mojave Desert)

Mo¦hawk +s

Mo¦he|gan +s (people)

Mohenjo-Daro (ancient city, Pakistan)

Mo¦hi|can +s (hairstyle; for people, prefer Mohegan)

Moho +s

Moholy-Nagy, László (Hungarian-born American artist)

Moho|ro|vi¦čić dis|con|tinu|ity

Mohs' scale

moi|dore +s

moi¦ety moi|eties

moil +s +ed +ing

Moira also Moyra

Moi¦rai (Greek name for the Fates)

moire +s (watered fabric; patterned; pattern)

moiré +s (watered)

Mois¦san, Fer¦di|nand Fréd¦éric Henri (French chemist)

moist +er +est

mois|ten +s +ed +ing

moist¦ly

moist|ness

mois|ture

mois|ture|less

mois¦tur|ise Br. (use moisturize)

mois¦tur|ises

mois¦tur|ised

mois¦tur|is|ing

mois¦tur|iser Br. +s (use moisturizer)

mois¦tur|ize

mois¦tur|izes

mois¦tur|ized

mois¦tur|iz|ing

mois¦tur|izer +s

Mo¦jave Des¦ert (in USA)

moke +s

moko +s

mok¦sha

mol (= mole, chemical unit)

molal

mol|al|ity

mol|al|ities

molar +s

mo|lar|ity

mo|lar|ities

mo|las¦ses

Mold (town, Wales)

mold Am. +s +ed +ing (Br. mould)

mold|able Am. (Br. mouldable)

Mol¦dau (German name for the Vltava)

Mol¦davia (alternative name for Moldova)

Mol|davian +s

mold-board Am. +s (Br. mould-board)

mold|er Am. +s (person who moulds. Br. moulder)

mold|er Am. +s +ed +ing (rot. Br. moulder)

mol|di|ness Am. (Br. mouldiness)

mold|ing Am. +s (Br. moulding)

Mol|dova

Mol|do|van +s

moldy Am. mold|ier mold|iest (Br. mouldy)

mole +s

mo|lecu|lar

mo|lecu|lar|ity

mo|lecu|lar|ly

mol|ecule +s

mole|hill +s

mole|skin +s

mo|lest +s +ed +ing

mo|lest|ation +s

mo|lest|er +s

Mol¦ière (French dramatist)

mo|line (Heraldry. △ malign)

Mo|lise (region, Italy)

moll +s

Mol¦lie also Molly

mol|li|fi|ca¦tion +s

mol|li|fier +s

mol|lify mol|li|fies mol|li|fied mol|li|fy|ing

mol|lusc +s

mol|lus|can

mol|lusc|oid

mol|lusc|ous

Molly also Mol¦lie (name)

molly mol|lies (fish)

molly|cod|dle molly|cod|dles molly|cod|dled molly|cod|dling

mol|ly|mawk +s

Mo|loch (god)

mo|loch +s (reptile)

mo|los|sus mo|lossi

Molo|tov (former name of Perm; cocktail)

Molo|tov, Vyache|slav Mikh¦ail|ovich (Soviet statesman)

molt Am. +s +ed +ing (Br. moult)

mol|ten

molto

Mol|lucca Is|lands (in Indonesia)

Mol|luc|cas (= Molucca Islands)

moly molies

mo|lyb|den|ite

mo|lyb|denum

mom +s

Mom|basa (city, Kenya)

mo|ment +s

mo|menta

mo|ment|ar|ily

mo|ment|ari|ness

mo|ment|ary

mo|ment|ly

mo|men|tous

mo|men|tous|ly

mo|men|tous|ness

mo|men|tum

mo|menta

momma +s

Mom|msen, Theo|dor (German historian)

mommy mom|mies

Momus Mo|muses or Momi

Mon plural Mon or Mons (person; language)

Mona (name)

mon|acal (monastic; use monachal. △ monocle)

Mon|acan +s

mon|achal (monastic. △ monocle)

mon|ach|ism (monasticism. △ monarchism)

Mon¦aco

monad +s

mona|del|phous

mo|nad¦ic

mon|ad|ism

mon|ad|nock +s

Mona|ghan (county and town, Republic of Ireland)

Mona Lisa

mo|nan|drous

mo|nan|dry

mon|arch +s

mo|nar|chal

mo|nar|chial

mo|nar|chic

mo|nar|chic|al

mo|nar|chic|al|ly

mon|arch|ism (government by monarchs. △ monarchism)

mon|arch|ist +s

mon|archy mon|arch|ies

Mon|ash, John
(Australian
general)
mon|as|tery
mon|as|ter|ies
mo|nas|tic
mo|nas|tic|al|ly
mo|nas|ti|cise Br.
(use monasticize)
mo|nas|ti|cises
mo|nas|ti|cised
mo|nas|ti|cis|ing
mo|nas|ti|cism
mo|nas|ti|cize
mo|nas|ti|cizes
mo|nas|ti|cized
mo|nas|ti|ciz|ing
Mon|as|tir (town,
Tunisia)
mon|atom|ic
mon|aural
mon|aural|ly
mona|zite
Mön|chen|
glad|bach (city,
Germany)
Monck, George
(Duke of
Albemarle, English
general)
mon|daine +s female
Mon|day +s
mon|dial
Mon|drian, Piet
(Dutch painter)
mon|ecious Am.
(Br. monoecious)
Moné|gasque +s
Monel Propr.
Monet, Claude
(French painter)
mon|et|ar|ily
mon|et|ar|ism
mon|et|ar|ist +s
mon|et|ary
mon|et|isa|tion Br.
(use
monetization)
mon|et|ise Br. (use
monetize)
mon|et|ises
mon|et|ised
mon|et|is|ing
mon|et|iza|tion
mon|et|ize
mon|et|izes
mon|et|ized
mon|et|iz|ing
money
plural moneys or
mon|ies

money bag +s (bag
for money)
money|bags
(person)
money box
money boxes
money chan|ger
+s
mon|eyed
mon|ey|er +s
money-grubber +s
money-grubbing
money|lend|er +s
money|lend|ing
money|less
money|maker +s
money|mak|ing
money mar|ket +s
money order +s
money spi|der +s
money-spinner +s
money-spinning
money's-worth
money|wort +s
mon|ger +s
mon|ger|ing
mongo
plural mongo or
mon|gos
Mon|gol +s
(member of Asian
people)
mon|gol +s
(offensive person
with Down's
syndrome)
Mon|go|lia
Mon|go|lian +s
mon|gol|ism
(offensive)
Mon|gol|oid +s
(characteristic of
Mongolians)
mon|gol|oid +s
(offensive; affected
with Down's
syndrome)
mon|goose +s
mon|grel +s
mon|grel|isa|tion
Br. +s (use
mongrelization)
mon|grel|ise Br.
(use mongrelize)
mon|grel|ises
mon|grel|ised
mon|grel|is|ing
mon|grel|ism
mon|grel|iza|tion
+s
mon|grel|ize
mon|grel|izes

mon|grel|ize
(cont.)
mon|grel|ized
mon|grel|iz|ing
mon|grel|ly
'mongst
(= amongst)
mo|nial +s
Mon|ica (N. African-
born saint; actual
name)
mon|icker +s
(slang word for
'name'; use
moniker)
mon|ies (plural of
money)
moni|ker +s
mo|nili|form
mon|ism +s
mon|ist +s
mo|nis|tic
mon|ition +s
moni|tor +s +ed
+ing
moni|tor|ial
moni|tor|ship +s
moni|tory
moni|tor|ies
Monk,
The|lo|nious
(American jazz
musician)
monk +s
monk|ery
mon|key +s +ed
+ing
mon|key|ish
monkey-jacket +s
monkey-nut +s
monkey-puzzle +s
mon|key|shine +s
mon|key|wrench
mon|key|
        wrenches
mon|key|
        wrenched
mon|key|wrench|
        ing
verb
mon|key wrench
mon|key
    wrenches
noun
monk|fish
plural monk|fish
Mon-Khmer
(group of
languages)
monk|ish
monks|hood +s
(plant)

Mon|mouth (town,
Wales)
Mon|mouth|shire
(former county,
Wales)
mon|nik|er +s (use
moniker)
mono +s
mono|acid
mono|basic
mono|car|pic
mono|car|pous
mono|caus|al
mono|ceph|al|ous
mono|chord +s
mono|chro|mat|ic
mono|chro|mat|ic|
        al|ly
mono|
    chro|ma|tism
mono|chrome +s
mono|chro|mic
mon|ocle +s
(eyeglass.
△ monachal)
mon|ocled
mono|cli|nal
mono|cline +s
mono|clin|ic
mono|clo|nal
mono|coque +s
mono|cot +s
(= monocoty-
ledon)
mono|coty|ledon
+s
mono|coty|ledon|
        ous
mon|oc|racy
mon|oc|ra|cies
mono|crat|ic
mono|crot|ic
mono|ocu|lar
mono|ocu|lar|ly
mono|cul|ture +s
mono|cycle +s
mono|cyte +s
mono|dac|tyl|ous
mon|od|ic
mon|od|ist +s
mono|drama +s
mon|ody
mon|odies
mon|oe|cious Br.
(Am. monoecious)
mono|fila|ment +s
mon|og|amist +s
mon|og|am|ous
mon|og|am|ous|ly
mon|og|amy
mono|gen|esis
mono|genet|ic

mon|ogeny
mono|glot +s
mono|gram +s
mono|gram|mat|ic
mono|grammed
mono|graph +s
    +ed +ing
mon|og|raph|er +s
mono|graph|ic
mon|og|raph|ist
    +s
mon|ogyn|ous
mon|ogyny
mono|hull +s
mono|hy|brid +s
mono|hyd|ric
mono|kini +s
mon|ol|atry
mono|layer +s
mono|lin|gual
mono|lith +s
mono|lith|ic
mono|logic
mono|logic|al
mon|olo|gise Br.
    (use monologize)
mon|olo|gises
mon|olo|gised
mon|olo|gis|ing
mon|olo|gist +s
mon|olo|gize
mon|olo|gizes
mon|olo|gized
mon|olo|giz|ing
mono|logue +s
mono|mania +s
mono|maniac +s
mono|mani|ac|al
mono|mark +s
mono|mer +s
mono|mer|ic
mono|met|al|lism
mono|mial +s
mono|mo|lecu|lar
mono|morph|ic
mono|morph|ism
    +s
mono|morph|ous
mono|nucle|osis
    mono|nucle|oses
mono|pet|al|ous
mono|phon|ic
mono|phon|ic|
    al|ly
mono|ph|thong +s
mono|ph|thong|al
mono|phy|let|ic
Mono|phy|site +s
mono|plane +s
mono|pod +s
mono|pole +s

mon|op|ol|isa|tion
    Br. +s (use
    monopolization)
mon|op|ol|ise Br.
    (use monopolize)
mon|op|ol|ises
mon|op|ol|ised
mon|op|ol|is|ing
mon|op|ol|iser Br.
    +s (use
    monopolizer)
mon|op|ol|ist +s
mon|op|ol|is|tic
mon|op|ol|iza|tion
    +s
mon|op|ol|ize
mon|op|ol|izes
mon|op|ol|ized
mon|op|ol|iz|ing
mon|op|ol|izer +s
Mon|op|oly (game)
    Propr.
mon|op|oly
    mon|op|olies
    (exclusive
    possession etc.)
mon|op|sony
    mon|op|so|nies
mono|psych|ism
mono|rail +s
mono|rhyme +s
mono|sac|char|ide
    +s
mono|so|dium
    glu|ta|mate
mono|sperm|ous
mo|nos|ti|chous
mono|stroph|ic
mono|syl|lab|ic
mono|syl|lab|ic|
    al|ly
mono|syl|lable +s
mono|the|ism
mono|the|ist +s
mono|the|is|tic
mono|the|is|tic|
    al|ly
Mon|oth|elite +s
mono|tint +s
mono|tone +s
mono|ton|ic
mono|ton|ic|al|ly
mon|ot|on|ise Br.
    (use monotonize)
mon|ot|on|ises
mon|ot|on|ised
mon|ot|on|is|ing
mon|ot|on|ize
mon|ot|on|izes
mon|ot|on|ized
mon|ot|on|iz|ing
mon|ot|on|ous

mon|ot|on|ous|ly
mon|ot|on|ous|
    ness
mon|ot|ony
mono|treme +s
Mono|type
    (machine) Propr.
mono|type +s
    (picture)
mono|typ|ic
mono|un|satu|rate
    +s
mono|un|satu|
    rated
mono|va|lence
mono|va|lency
mono|va|lent
mon|ox|ide +s
Mon|roe, James
    (American
    president;
    doctrine)
Mon|roe, Mari|lyn
    (American
    actress)
Mon|ro|via (capital
    of Liberia)
Mons (town,
    Belgian)
Mon|sei|gneur
    Mes|sei|gneurs
    (title of French
    prince, cardinal,
    etc.)
Mon|sieur
    Mes|sieurs
Mon|si|gnor
    Mon|si|gnori
    (Roman Catholic
    title)
mon|soon +s
mon|soon|al
mons pubis
    mon|tes pubis
mon|ster +s
mon|stera +s
    (plant)
mon|strance +s
mon|stros|ity
    mon|stros|ities
mon|strous
mon|strous|ly
mon|strous|ness
mons Ven|eris
    montes Ven|eris
mont|age +s
Mon|tagna,
    Bar|to|lom|meo
    Cin|cani (Italian
    painter)
Mon|ta|gue

Mon|tagu's
    har|rier +s
Mon|taigne,
    Mi|chel Ey|quem
    de (French writer)
Mon|tana (state,
    USA)
Mon|tana, Joe
    (American football
    player)
mon|tane
Mon|tan|ism
Mon|tan|ist +s
Mont Blanc
    (mountain, Alps)
mont|bre|tia +s
Mont|calm,
    Mar|quis de
    (French general)
monte (card game)
Monte Albán
    (ancient city,
    Mexico)
Monte Carlo
    (commune,
    Monaco)
Monte Cas|sino
    (hill and
    monastery site,
    Italy)
Mon|tego Bay
    (port, Jamaica)
Mon|te|neg|rin +s
Mon|te|negro
    (Balkan republic)
Mon|terey (city,
    USA)
Mon|ter|rey (city,
    Mexico)
Mon|te|span,
    Mar|quise de
    (mistress of Louis
    XIV)
Mon|tes|quieu,
    Baron de (French
    political
    philosopher)
Mon|tes|sori,
    Maria (Italian
    educationist)
Mon|te|verdi,
    Clau|dio (Italian
    composer)
Mon|te|video
    (capital of
    Uruguay)
Mon|tez, Lola
    (mistress of
    Ludwig I of
    Bavaria)
Mon|te|zuma
    (Aztec ruler)

Mon¦te¦zuma's
re¦venge
Mont¦fort, Simon
de (French
soldier, father of
Earl of Leicester)
Mont¦fort, Simon
de (Earl of
Leicester; English
soldier)
Mont¦gol¦fier,
Jo¦seph and
Jacques-Étienne
(French
balloonists)
Mont¦gom¦ery
(city, USA)
Mont¦gom¦ery,
Ber¦nard Law
('Monty')
(Viscount
Montgomery of
Alamein, British
field marshal)
Mont¦gom¦ery,
Lucy Maud
(Canadian
novelist)
Mont¦gom¦ery¦
shire (former
county, Wales)
month +s
month¦ly
month¦lies
mon¦ti¦cule +s
Mont¦martre
(district of Paris,
France)
mont¦mor¦il¦lon¦
ite +s
Mont¦par¦nasse
(district, Paris)
Mont Pelée
(mountain,
Martinique)
Mont¦pel¦ier (city,
USA)
Mont¦pel¦lier (city,
France)
Mon¦treal (city,
Canada)
Mon¦treux (town,
Switzerland)
Mon¦trose,
Mar¦quis of
(Scottish general)
Mont¦ser¦rat (in
West Indies)
Mont St Michel
(islet off
Normandy coast)
Monty

monu¦ment +s
monu¦men¦tal
monu¦men¦tal¦ise
Br. (use
monumentalize)
monu¦men¦tal¦
ises
monu¦men¦tal¦
ised
monu¦men¦tal¦
is¦ing
monu¦men¦tal¦ism
monu¦men¦tal¦ity
monu¦men¦tal¦ize
monu¦men¦tal¦
izes
monu¦men¦tal¦
ized
monu¦men¦tal¦
iz¦ing
monu¦men¦tal¦ly
monu¦men¦tal
mason +s
moo +s +ed +ing
(cattle sound.
△ moue)
mooch
mooches
mooched
mooch¦ing
mooch¦er +s
moo-cow +s
mood +s
mood¦ily
moodi¦ness
moody
mood¦ies
mood¦ier
moodi¦est
Moog +s
moo¦lah +s
mooli +s
moolvi +s
mool¦vie +s (use
moolvi)
Moon, Sun Myung
(Korean religious
leader)
moon +s +ed +ing
moon¦beam +s
moon boot +s
moon¦calf
moon¦calves
moon-face +s
moon-faced
moon¦fish
plural moon¦fish
or moon¦fishes
moon-flower +s
Moonie +s
(offensive)
moon¦less

moon¦light +s +ed
+ing
moon¦light¦er +s
moon¦lit
moon¦quake +s
moon¦rise +s
moon¦scape +s
moon¦set +s
moon¦shee +s
moon¦shine +s
moon¦shiner +s
moon¦shot +s
moon¦stone +s
moon¦struck
moony
moon¦ier
mooni¦est
Moor +s (N.
African people)
moor +s +ed +ing
(open land; tie up
boat. △ maw,
mor, more)
moor¦age +s
moor¦cock +s
Moore, Bobby
(English
footballer)
Moore, Fran¦cis
(physician and
originator of 'Old
Moore's
Almanac')
Moore, G. E.
(English
philosopher)
Moore, George
(Irish novelist)
Moore, Henry
(English sculptor)
Moore, John
(British general)
Moore, Thomas
(Irish songwriter)
moor¦fowl
plural moor¦fowl
or moor¦fowls
moor¦hen +s
moor¦ing +s
mooring-mast +s
mooring place +s
Moor¦ish (of
Moors)
moor¦ish
(resembling
moorland.
△ moreish)
Moor¦ish idol +s
(fish)
moor¦land +s
Moor¦man
Moor¦men

moory
moose
plural moose
Moose Jaw (town,
Canada)
moot +s +ed +ing
mop
mops
mopped
mop¦ping
mope
mopes
moped
mop¦ing
moped +s
moper +s
mop¦head +s
mopi¦ly
mopi¦ness
mop¦ish
mo¦poke +s
mop¦pet +s
moppy
Mopti (city, Mali)
mopy
mopi¦er
mopi¦est
mo¦quette +s
mor +s (humus.
△ maw, moor,
more)
Mora¦da¦bad (city,
India)
Morag
mo¦rainal
mo¦raine +s
mo¦rain¦ic
moral +s
(concerned with
acceptable
behaviour; lesson;
etc.)
mor¦ale +s (mental
attitude)
mor¦al¦isa¦tion Br.
+s (use
moralization)
mor¦al¦ise Br. (use
moralize)
mor¦al¦ises
mor¦al¦ised
mor¦al¦is¦ing
mor¦al¦iser Br. +s
(use moralizer)
mor¦al¦is¦ing¦ly Br.
(use
moralizingly)
mor¦al¦ism
mor¦al¦ist +s
mor¦al¦is¦tic
mor¦al¦is¦tic¦al¦ly

mor¦al¦ity
mor¦al¦ities
mor¦al¦iza¦tion +s
mor¦al¦ize
mor¦al¦izes
mor¦al¦ized
mor¦al¦iz¦ing
mor¦al¦izer +s
mor¦al¦iz¦ing¦ly
mor¦al¦ly
Morar (Loch;
Scotland)
mor¦ass
mor¦asses
mora¦tor¦ium
mora¦tor¦iums *or*
mora¦toria
Mor¦avia (region,
Czech Republic)
Mor¦avia, Al¦berto
(Italian writer)
Mor¦avian +s
Moray (former
county, Scotland)
moray +s (eel)
Moray Firth (in
Scotland)
mor¦bid
mor¦bid¦ity
mor¦bid¦ly
mor¦bid¦ness
mor¦bif¦ic
mor¦billi
mor¦da¦cious
mor¦da¦city
mor¦dancy
mor¦dant +s
(corrosive
substance)
mor¦dant¦ly
mor¦dent +s
(musical
ornament)
Mor¦dred *Arthurian
Legend*
Mord|vinia
(republic, Russia)
Mord|vin¦ian +s
More, Thomas
(English
statesman and
saint)
more (greater in
number etc.
△maw, mor,
moor)
More|cambe
(town, England)
More|cambe Bay
(in England)
mor¦een +s

more|ish (pleasant
to eat. △ moorish)
morel +s
Mor|elia (city,
Mexico)
mor|ello +s
Mor|elos (state,
Mexico)
more|over
more|pork +s
(owl)
mores (customs)
Mor|esco (use
Morisco)
Mor|es|cos *or*
Mor|es|coes
Mor|esque
(Moorish)
Mor¦gan, J. P.
(American
philanthropist)
**Mor¦gan, Thomas
Hunt** (American
zoologist)
mor¦ga¦nat¦ic
mor¦ga¦nat¦ic¦al¦ly
Mor¦gan le Fay
Arthurian Legend
mor¦gen +s
(measure of land)
morgue +s
mori¦bund
mori¦bun¦dity
morion +s
Mor|isco +s
mor¦ish (use
moreish)
Mori|sot, Berthe
(French painter)
Mor|land, George
(English painter)
**Mor¦ley, Ed¦ward
Wil|liams**
(American
chemist)
Mor¦ley, Thomas
(English
composer)
Mor¦mon +s
Mor¦mon|ism
morn +s
mor¦nay
morn|ing +s (time
of day.
△mourning)
morning-after pill
+s
morn|ing coat +s
morn|ing dress
morn|ing glory
morn|ing glor|ies

morn|ing paper +s
(newspaper.
△ mourning-
paper)
morn|ing room +s
morn|ing
sick|ness
morn|ing star +s
morn|ing watch
morn|ing
watches
Moro +s
Mo|roc|can +s
Mo|rocco
mo|rocco +s
(leather)
moron +s
Mor|oni (city,
Comoros Islands)
mor|on|ic
mo|ron|ic|al|ly
mor|on|ism
mor|ose
mor|ose|ly
mor|ose|ness
Mor|peth (town,
England)
morph +s
mor|pheme +s
mor|phem|ic
mor|phem|ic|al|ly
mor|phem|ics
Mor|pheus *Roman
Mythology*
mor|phia
mor|phine
morph|ing
mor|phin|ism
mor|pho|gen|esis
mor|pho|genet|ic
mor|pho|gen|ic
mor|pho|logic|al
mor|pho|
        logic¦al¦ly
morph|olo|gist +s
morph|ology
Mor|ris, Wil|liam
(English designer;
chair)
**Mor|ris, Wil|liam
Rich|ard** (Lord
Nuffield, British
car maker)
Mor|ris *also*
Maur|ice
mor|ris dance +s
mor|ris dan|cer +s
mor|ris dan|cing
Mor|ri|son, Toni
(American
novelist)

Mor|ri|son, Van
(Northern Irish
musician)
mor|row +s
Morse, Sam¦uel
(American
inventor)
Morse
Morses
Morsed
Mors|ing
(code)
morse +s (walrus;
clasp)
Morse code
mor|sel +s
mort +s
mor|ta|della
mor|ta|delle
mor|tal +s
mor|tal|ity
mor|tal|ities
mor|tal|ly
mor|tar +s +ed
+ing
mor|tar|board +s
mor|tar|less
mor|tary
mort|gage
mort|gages
mort|gaged
mort|ga|ging
mort|gage|able
mort|ga|gee +s
(creditor in
mortgage)
mort|ga|ger +s
(debtor in
mortgage)
mort|ga|gor +s
(use mortgager)
mor|tice (use
mortise)
mor|tices
mor|ticed
mor|ticing
mor|ti|cian +s
mor|ti|fi|ca|tion +s
mor|tify
mor|ti|fies
mor|ti|fied
mor|ti|fy|ing
mor|ti|fy|ing|ly
**Mor|ti|mer, Roger
de** (English noble)
Mor|ti|mer
mor|tise
mor|tises
mor|tised
mor|tis|ing
mor|tise lock +s

mort|main +s

Mor|ton, Jelly
Roll (American
jazz musician)

Mor|ton, John
(English
statesman)

Mor|ton's Fork

mor|tu|ary
mor|tu|ar|ies

mor|ula
mor|ulae

Mor|wenna

mor|wong +s

Mo|saic (of Moses)

mo|saic
mo|saics
mo|saicked
mo|saick|ing
(picture; pattern)

mo|sai|cist +s

Mos|an|der, Carl
Gus|tav (Swedish
chemist)

mosa|saur +s

mosa|saurus
mosa|sauri

mos|cha|tel +s
(plant.
△ muscatel)

Mos|cow (capital of
Russia)

Mosel +s (river, W.
Europe; wine)

Mose|ley, Henry
(English physicist)

Mo|selle +s
(French name for
the Mosel; wine)

Moses Bible

Moses, Grandma
(American
painter)

Moses bas|ket +s

Moses ben
Mai|mon
(Spanish-born
Jewish
philosopher)

mosey +s +ed
+ing

MOSFET +s
(= metal oxide
semiconductor
field-effect
transistor)

mosh
moshes
moshed
mosh|ing

mo|shav
mo|shav|im

mosh-pit +s

Mos|lem +s (use
Muslim)

Mos|ley, Os|wald
(English Fascist
leader)

Mo|sotho
Sotho

mosque +s

Mos|quito (Central
American people;
use Miskito)
plural Mos|quito
or Mos|qui|tos

mos|quito
mos|qui|toes
(insect)

mosquito-boat +s

Mos|quito Coast
(region, S.
America)

mos|quito net +s

Moss, Stir|ling
(English motor-
racing driver)

moss
mosses
mossed
moss|ing

Mos|sad (Israeli
intelligence
service)

Mos|sel Bay (port,
South Africa)

moss-grown

moss-hag +s

mos|sie +s
(= mosquito)

mos|si|ness

moss|like

mosso Music

moss stitch

moss|troop|er +s

mossy
moss|ier
mossi|est
(covered with
moss)

most

Mos|tar
(city, Bosnia–
Herzegovina)

most|ly

Mosul (city, Iraq)

mot +s

mote +s (speck of
dust. △ moat)

motel +s

motet +s Music

moth +s

moth|ball +s +ed
+ing

moth-eaten

mother +s +ed
+ing

mother|board +s

Mother Carey's
chicken +s

mother coun|try
mother coun|tries

mother|craft

mother-figure +s

mother|fuck|er +s
(coarse slang)

mother|fuck|ing
(coarse slang)

mother god|dess
mother
god|desses

mother|hood

Mother|ing
Sun|day +s

mother-in-law
mothers-in-law

mother-in-law's
tongue

mother|land +s

mother|less

mother|less|ness

mother|like

mother|li|ness

mother-lode +s

mother|ly

mother-naked

mother-of-pearl

Mother's Day

mother-to-be
mothers-to-be

mother tongue +s

moth|proof

mothy
moth|ier
moth|iest

motif +s

mo|tile

mo|til|ity

mo|tion +s +ed
+ing

mo|tion|al

mo|tion|less

mo|tion|less|ly

mo|tion pic|ture
+s

mo|tiv|ate
mo|tiv|ates
mo|tiv|ated
mo|tiv|at|ing

mo|tiv|ation +s

mo|tiv|ation|al

mo|tiv|ation|al|ly

mo|tiv|ator +s

mo|tive
mo|tives
mo|tived
mo|tiv|ing

mo|tive|less

mo|tive|less|ly

mo|tive|less|ness

mo|tiv|ity

mot juste
mots justes

mot|ley
mot|leys
mot|lier
mot|li|est

mot|mot +s

moto|cross

moto per|petuo
Music

motor +s +ed +ing

motor|able

motor bi|cycle +s

motor|bike +s

motor boat +s

motor|cade +s

motor car +s

motor|cycle +s

motor|cyc|ling

motor|cyc|list +s

motor|home +s

motor|ial

motor|isa|tion Br.
(use
motorization)

motor|ise Br. (use
motorize)
motor|ises
motor|ised
motor|is|ing

motor|ist +s

motor|iza|tion

motor|ize
motor|izes
motor|ized
motor|iz|ing

motor|man
motor|men

motor|mouth +s

motor mower +s

motor ra|cing

motor scoot|er +s

motor sport +s

motor ve|hicle +s

motor|way +s

mo|tory

motor yacht +s

Mo|town
(= Detroit, USA)

motte +s

mot|tle
mot|tles
mot|tled
mot|tling

motto
mot|toes

moue +s (pout.
△ moo)

mouf|flon +s (use moufflon)

mouf|flon +s

mouillé

mou|jik +s (use muzhik)

Mou|lay Id|riss (Muslim holy town, Morocco)

mould *Br.* +s +ed +ing (*Am.* mold)

mould|able *Br.* (*Am.* moldable)

mould-board *Br.* +s (*Am.* mold-board)

mould|er *Br.* +s (person who moulds. *Am.* molder)

moul|der *Br.* +s +ed +ing (rot. *Am.* molder)

mouldi|ness *Br.* (*Am.* moldiness)

mould|ing *Br.* +s (*Am.* molding)

mouldy *Br.* mould|ier mouldi|est (*Am.* moldy)

mou|lin +s

Mou|lin Rouge (in Paris, France)

Moul|mein (port, Burma)

moult +s +ed +ing

moult|er +s

mound +s +ed +ing

mount +s +ed +ing

mount|able

moun|tain +s

moun|tain avens *plural* moun|tain avens

moun|tain bike +s

moun|tain chain +s

moun|tain climb|er +s

moun|tain climb|ing

moun|tain|eer +s +ed +ing

moun|tain|ous

moun|tain range +s

moun|tain|side +s

moun|tain top +s

moun|tainy

Mount|bat|ten, Louis (Earl Mountbatten of Burma, British admiral)

moun|te|bank +s

moun|te|bank|ery

mount|er +s

Moun|tie +s (Canadian police)

mount|ing +s

mount|ing block +s

Mount Isa (town, Australia)

Mount Ver|non (home of George Washington)

mourn +s +ed +ing

Mourne Moun|tains (in Northern Ireland)

mourn|er +s

mourn|ful

mourn|ful|ly

mourn|ful|ness

mourning-band +s

mourn|ing dove +s

mourning-paper (black-edged notepaper. △ morning paper)

mourn|ing ring +s

mou|saka +s (use moussaka)

Mou|salla, Mount (use Mount Musala)

mouse mice *noun*

mouse mouses moused mous|ing *verb*

mouse-colored *Am.*

mouse-coloured *Br.*

mouse deer *plural* mouse deer

mouse hare +s

mouse|like

mouser +s

mouse|trap +s

mousey (use mousy)

mous|ily

mousi|ness

mous|saka +s

mousse +s

mous|se|line +s

Mous|sorg|sky, Mo|dest (use Mussorgsky)

mous|tache *Br.* +s (*Am.* mustache)

mous|tache cup *Br.* +s (*Am.* mustache cup)

mous|tached *Br.* (*Am.* mustached)

mous|tachio *Br.* +s (*Am.* mustachio)

mous|tachi|oed *Br.* (*Am.* mustachioed)

Mous|ter|ian +s

mousy mous|ier mousi|est

mouth +s +ed +ing

mouth|brood|er +s

mouth|er +s

mouth|ful +s

mouth|less

mouth organ +s

mouth|part +s

mouth|piece +s

mouth-to-mouth

mouth|wash mouth|washes

mouth-watering

mouthy mouth|ier mouthi|est

mov|abil|ity

mov|able

movable-doh

mov|able|ness

mov|ably

move moves moved mov|ing

move|able (use movable)

move|ment +s

mover +s

movie +s

movie-goer +s

movie house +s

movie-maker +s

movie-making

moving-coil *attributive*

mov|ing|ly

mow mows mowed mow|ing mowed *or* mown (cut grass etc. △ mho, mo)

mow|able

mow|burnt

mower +s (grasscutter. △ moa)

mow|ing +s

mown (past participle of mow. △ moan)

moxa +s

moxi|bus|tion

moxie +s

Moya

Moyra *also* Moira

Mo|zam|bi|can +s

Mo|zam|bique (in southern Africa)

Moz|arab +s

Moz|arab|ic

Moz|art, Wolf|gang Ama|deus (Austrian composer)

Moz|art|ian +s

mozz

moz|za|rella +s

moz|zie +s (use mossie)

moz|zle

M.Phil. (= Master of Philosophy)

mpingo +s

Mr Messrs (man's title)

Mrs *plural* Mrs *or* Mes|dames (title of married woman)

Ms (woman's title)

M.Tech. (= Master of Technology)

mu +s (Greek letter. △ meu, mew)

Mu|ba|rak, Hosni (Egyptian president)

much

Mucha, Al|phonse (Czech artist)

Mu|chinga Moun|tains (in Zambia)

much¦ly
much|ness
muci|lage +s
muci|lagi|nous
muck +s +ed +ing
muck¦er +s
muck¦er|ish
mucki|ness
muckle +s
muck¦rake
  muck|rakes
  muck|raked
  muck|rak¦ing
muck¦raker +s
muck-spread¦er
  +s
muck sweat
muck|worm +s
mucky
  muck¦ier
  mucki|est
muco|poly|
  sac¦char|ide +s
mu¦cosa
  mu¦cosae
mu¦cos|ity
mu¦cous *adjective*
mucro
  mu¦cro¦nes
mu¦cron|ate
mucus *noun*
mud +s
mud|bank +s
mud|bath +s
mud|brick +s
mud¦dily
mud¦di|ness
mud¦dle
  mud¦dles
  mud¦dled
  mud¦dling
muddle-headed
muddle-
  headed¦ness
mud|dler +s
mud¦dling¦ly
muddy
  mud¦dies
  mud¦died
  muddy|ing
  mud¦dier
  mud¦di|est
Mu|dé¦jar
  Mu|dé¦jares
mud|fish
  plural mud|fish *or*
  mud|fishes
mud|flap +s
mud|flat +s
mud|flow +s
mud|guard +s
mud|lark +s

mud pack +s
mud pie +s
mud puppy
  mud pup|pies
mud|skip¦per +s
mud-sling¦er +s
mud-slinging
mud|stone +s
mud vol|cano
muesli +s
muez|zin +s
muff +s +ed +ing
muf|fetee +s
muf|fin +s
muf|fin¦eer +s
muffin-man
  muffin-men
muff¦ish
muf¦fle
  muf¦fles
  muf¦fled
  muf¦fling
muf¦fler +s
mufti +s
mug
  mugs
  mugged
  mug|ging
Mu¦gabe, Rob¦ert
  (president of
  Zimbabwe)
Mu|ganda
  Ba|ganda
mug¦ful +s
mug¦ger +s
mug¦gi|ness
mug¦ging +s
mug|gins
  plural mug|gins *or*
  mug|ginses
muggy
  mug|gier
  mug|gi|est
Mug|hal +s
mug|shot +s
mug|wort +s
mug|wump +s
Mu¦ham|mad
  (founder of Islam)
Mu¦ham|mad
  Ahmad
  (Sudanese Mahdi)
Mu¦ham|mad Ali
  (pasha of Egypt)
Mu¦ham|mad Ali
  (American boxer)
Mu¦ham|madan
  +s (prefer
  Muslim)
Mu¦ham|mad¦an|
  ism (prefer Islam)

Muir, Edwin
  (Scottish poet)
mu¦ja|hed¦din (use
  mujahedin)
mu¦ja|he¦deen (use
  mujahedin)
mu¦ja|he¦din
mu¦ja|hi¦deen (use
  mujahedin)
mu¦ja|hi¦din (use
  mujahedin)
Mu¦ji|bur
  Rah¦man
  (Bangladeshi
  president)
Mu|kalla (port,
  Yemen)
Muk¦den (former
  name of
  Shenyang)
mu|latto
  mu|lattos *or*
  mu|lat|toes
mul|berry
  mul|berries
mulch
  mulches
  mulched
  mulch|ing
mulct +s +ed +ing
Mul|doon, Rob¦ert
  (New Zealand
  prime minister)
mule +s (animal;
  slipper. △ mewl)
mule|teer +s
mulga +s
Mul|ha|cén
  (mountain, Spain)
Mül|heim (city,
  Germany)
Mul|house (city,
  France)
muli +s (use mooli)
muli|eb¦rity
mul¦ish
mul|ish|ly
mul|ish|ness
Mull (Scottish
  island)
mull +s +ed +ing
  (ponder; to warm;
  promontory;
  humus; fabric)
mul|lah +s
  (Muslim scholar.
  △ muller)
mul|lein +s
Mul¦ler, Her|mann
  Jo¦seph
  (American
  geneticist)

Mül¦ler, Fried|rich
  Max (German
  philologist)
Mül¦ler,
  Jo¦han¦nes Peter
  (German biologist)
Mül¦ler, Paul
  Her|mann (Swiss
  chemist)
mul¦ler +s
  (grinding stone.
  △ mullah)
Mül¦ler|ian
mul|let +s
mul|li¦ga|tawny +s
mul|li¦grubs
Mul|lin¦gar (town,
  Republic of
  Ireland)
mul|lion +s
mul|lioned
mul|lock +s
Mull of Kin|tyre
  (tip of Kintyre
  peninsula,
  Scotland)
mul¦lo|way +s
Mul|ro|ney, Brian
  (Canadian prime
  minister)
Mul¦tan (city,
  Pakistan)
mult|angu|lar
multi-access
multi|axial
multi|cel¦lu|lar
multi|chan¦nel
multi|color *Am.*
multi|col¦ored *Am.*
multi|col¦our *Br.*
multi|col¦oured *Br.*
multi|cul¦tural
multi|cul¦tural|
  ism
multi|cul¦tural|ist
  +s
multi|cul¦tur¦al|ly
multi|di¦men|
  sion|al
multi|di¦men|sion|
  al¦ity
multi|di¦men|sion|
  al¦ly
multi|dir¦ec¦tion|al
multi-ethnic
multi|fa¦cet|ed
multi|fari¦ous
multi|fari¦ous|ly
multi|fari¦ous|ness
multi|fid
multi|foil +s
multi|form

multi|form|ity
multi|func|tion
multi|func|tion|al
multi|grade +s
multi|hull +s
multi|lat|eral
multi|lat|eral|ism
multi|lat|eral|ist +s
multi|lat|eral|ly
multi-layered
multi|level
multi|lin|gual
multi|lin|gual|ism
multi|lin|gual|ly
multi|media
multi|mil|lion +s
multi|mil|lion|aire +s
multi|nation|al +s
multi|nation|al|ly
multi|nomial +s
mul|tip|ar|ous
multi|par|tite
multi-party
multi|phase
mul|tiple +s
multiple-choice
adjective
multi|plex
multi|plexes
multi|plexed
multi|plex|ing
multi|plex|er +s
multi|plex|or +s
(use multiplexer)
multi|pli|able
multi|plic|able
multi|pli|cand +s
multi|pli|ca|tion +s
multi|plica|tive
multi|pli|city
multi|pli|ci|ties
multi|plier +s
multi|ply
multi|plies
multi|plied
multi|ply|ing
multi|polar
multi|pro|cess|ing
multi|pro|ces|sor +s
multi|pro|gram|ming
multi-purpose
multi|racial
multi|racial|ly
multi-role
attributive
multi-stage
attributive

multi-storey +s
noun and attributive
multi|task +s +ed +ing
multi|tude +s
multi|tu|di|nous
multi|tu|di|nous|ly
multi|tu|di|nous|ness
multi-user
attributive
multi|va|lency
multi|va|lent
multi|valve +s
multi|vari|ate
multi|ver|sity
multi|ver|sities
multi|vocal
multi-way
mul|ture +s
mum
mums
mummed
mum|ming
mum|ble
mum|bles
mum|bled
mum|bling
mum|bler +s
mum|bling +s
mum|bling|ly
mumbo-jumbo
mu-meson +s
mum|mer +s
mum|mers' play +s
mum|mery
mum|mer|ies
mum|mi|fi|ca|tion
mum|mify
mum|mi|fies
mum|mi|fied
mum|mi|fy|ing
mummy
mum|mies
mummy's boy +s
mummy's girl +s
mump|ish
mumps
mumsy
Munch, Ed|vard
(Norwegian painter)
munch
munches
munched
munch|ing
Munch|ausen, Baron (fictional hero)

Munch|ausen's syn|drome
Mün|chen (German name for Munich)
Munda +s
mun|dane
mun|dane|ly
mun|dane|ness
mun|dan|ity
mun|dan|ities
mung (beans)
Mungo (name)
mungo +s (fibre)
Mun|ich (city, Germany)
mu|ni|ci|pal
mu|ni|ci|pal|isa|tion *Br.* (use municipalization)
mu|ni|ci|pal|ise *Br.* (use municipalize)
mu|ni|ci|pal|ises
mu|ni|ci|pal|ised
mu|ni|ci|pal|is|ing
mu|ni|ci|pal|ity
mu|ni|ci|pal|ities
mu|ni|ci|pal|iza|tion
mu|ni|ci|pal|ize
mu|ni|ci|pal|izes
mu|ni|ci|pal|ized
mu|ni|ci|pal|iz|ing
mu|ni|ci|pal|ly
mu|nifi|cence
mu|nifi|cent
mu|nifi|cent|ly
mu|ni|ment +s
mu|ni|tion +s +ed +ing
mu|ni|tion|er +s
mun|nion +s
Munro, Hec|tor Hugh (real name of British writer Saki)
mun|shi +s (use moonshee)
Mun|ster (province, Republic of Ireland)
Mün|ster (city, Germany)
munt +s (*offensive*)
munt|jac +s
munt|jak +s (use muntjac)
Muntz metal
muon +s

muon|ic
Muq|disho (alternative name for Mogadishu)
mur|age +s
mural +s
mural|ist +s
Murat, Joa|chim (French general, king of Naples)
Mur|chi|son Falls (in Malawi)
Mur|cia (city and region, Spain)
mur|der +s +ed +ing
mur|der|er +s
mur|der|ess
mur|der|esses
mur|der|ous
mur|der|ous|ly
mur|der|ous|ness
Mur|doch, Iris (English writer)
Mur|doch, Ru|pert (Australian-born American publisher)
mure
mures
mured
mur|ing
murex
muri|ces *or* mur|exes
muri|ate +s
muri|at|ic
Mur|iel
Mu|rillo, Bar|to|lomé Este|ban (Spanish painter)
mur|ine
murk +s
murk|ily
murki|ness
murky
murk|ier
murki|est
Mur|mansk (port, Russia)
mur|mur +s +ed +ing
mur|mur|er +s
mur|mur|ing|ly
mur|mur|ous
mur|phy
mur|phies
Mur|phy's Law
mur|rain +s
Mur|ray (name)

Mur¦ray, Gil¦bert (British classical scholar)
Mur¦ray, James (Scottish-born lexicographer)
Mur¦ray River (in Australia)
murre +s (bird. △ myrrh)
mur¦re¦let +s
mur¦rey
mur¦rhine +s
Mur¦rum¦bidgee (river, Australia)
mur¦ther +s +ed +ing
Muru¦roa (atoll, French Polynesia)
Mu¦sala, Mount (in Bulgaria)
Mus.B. (= Bachelor of Music)
mus¦ca¦del +s
Mus¦ca¦det +s (wine)
mus¦ca¦dine +s (grape)
mus¦car¦ine +s
Mus¦cat (capital of Oman)
mus¦cat +s (grape; wine)
mus¦ca¦tel +s (grape; wine; raisin. △ moschatel)
muscle muscles muscled muscl¦ing (Anatomy. △ mussel)
muscle-bound
muscle¦less
muscle-man muscle-men
muscly
musc¦olo¦gist +s
musc¦ology
mus¦co¦vado +s
Mus¦co¦vite +s (citizen of Moscow)
mus¦co¦vite (mica)
Mus¦covy (former principality, Russia; duck)
mus¦cu¦lar
mus¦cu¦lar¦ity
mus¦cu¦lar¦ly
mus¦cu¦la¦ture +s

mus¦cu¦lo¦ skel¦etal
Mus.D. (= Doctor of Music)
Muse +s Greek and Roman Mythology
muse muses mused mus¦ing (ponder; inspiration. △ mews)
mu¦seol¦ogy
mu¦sette +s
mu¦seum +s
mu¦seum piece +s
mush mushes mushed mush¦ing
mush¦ily
mushi¦ness
mush¦room +s +ed +ing
mush¦roomy
mushy mush¦ier mushi¦est
music +s
mu¦sic¦al +s
musi¦cale +s
mu¦sic¦al¦ise Br. (use musicalize)
mu¦sic¦al¦ises
mu¦sic¦al¦ised
mu¦sic¦al¦is¦ing
mu¦sic¦al¦ity
mu¦sic¦al¦ize mu¦sic¦al¦izes mu¦sic¦al¦ized mu¦sic¦al¦iz¦ing
mu¦sic¦al¦ly
mu¦sic¦al¦ness
music box music boxes
music centre +s
music drama +s
music hall +s noun
music-hall attributive
mu¦si¦cian +s
mu¦si¦cian¦ly
mu¦si¦cian¦ship
music lover +s
mu¦sico¦logic¦al
mu¦sic¦olo¦gist +s
mu¦sic¦ology
music paper
music stand +s
music stool +s

Musil, Rob¦ert (Austrian novelist)
mus¦ing +s
mus¦ing¦ly
mu¦sique con¦crète
musk +s
mus¦keg +s
mus¦kel¦lunge +s
mus¦ket +s
mus¦ket¦eer +s
mus¦ket¦oon +s
mus¦ket¦ry
mus¦ket shot +s
muski¦ness
Mus¦ko¦gean +s
musk¦rat +s
musk-rose +s
musk this¦tle +s
musk tree +s
musk¦wood
musky musk¦ier muski¦est
Mus¦lim +s
mus¦lin +s
mus¦lined
mus¦mon +s
muso +s
mus¦quash plural mus¦quash
muss musses mussed muss¦ing
mus¦sel +s (mollusc. △ muscle)
Mus¦so¦lini, Ben¦ito (Italian Fascist prime minister)
Mus¦sorg¦sky, Mo¦dest (Russian composer)
Mus¦sul¦man Mus¦sul¦mans or Mus¦sul¦men (prefer Muslim)
mussy
must +s
mus¦tache Am. +s (Br. moustache)
mus¦tache cup Am. +s (Br. moustache cup)
mus¦tached Am. (Br. moustached)
mus¦tachio Am. +s (Br. moustachio)

mus¦tachi¦oed Am. (Br. moustachioed)
mus¦tang +s
mus¦tard +s
mus¦tard gas mus¦tard gases
mus¦tard seed +s
mus¦te¦lid +s
mus¦ter +s +ed +ing
muster-book +s
mus¦ter¦er +s
muster-roll +s
musth (use must)
must¦ily
musti¦ness
Mus¦tique (island, Caribbean)
mustn't (= must not)
musty must¦ier musti¦est
Mut Egyptian Mythology
mut¦abil¦ity
mut¦able
muta¦gen +s
muta¦gen¦esis
muta¦gen¦ic
mu¦tant +s
Mu¦tare (town, Zimbabwe)
mu¦tate mu¦tates mu¦tated mu¦tat¦ing
mu¦ta¦tion +s
mu¦ta¦tion¦al
mu¦ta¦tion¦al¦ly
mu¦ta¦tis mu¦tan¦dis
mutch mutches
mute mutes muted mut¦ing
mute¦ly
mute¦ness
mu¦ti¦late mu¦ti¦lates mu¦ti¦lated mu¦ti¦lat¦ing
mu¦ti¦la¦tion +s
mu¦ti¦la¦tive
mu¦ti¦la¦tor +s
mu¦tin¦eer +s
mu¦tin¦ous
mu¦tin¦ous¦ly

mu|tiny
  mu|tin|ies
  mu|tin|ied
  mu|tiny|ing
mut|ism
muton +s
Mut|su|hito
  (original name of
  Meiji Tenno)
mutt +s
mut|ter +s +ed
  +ing
mut|terer +s
mut|ter|ing +s
mut|ter|ing|ly
mut|ton +s
mutton-bird +s
mut|ton chop +s
mutton-head +s
mutton-headed
mut|tony
mu|tual (reciprocal.
  ⚠ mutuel)
mu|tu|al|ism
mu|tu|al|ist +s
mu|tu|al|is|tic
mu|tu|al|is|tic|
      al|ly
mu|tu|al|ity
  mu|tu|al|ities
mu|tu|al|ly
mu|tuel +s
  (totalizator.
  ⚠ mutual)
mut|ule +s
muu-muu +s
Muzaf|fara|bad
  (town, Pakistan)
muzak Propr.
mu|zhik +s
Muz|tag (mountain,
  China)
muz|zily
muz|zi|ness
muz|zle
  muz|zles
  muz|zled
  muz|zling
muzzle-loader +s
muz|zler +s
muzzy
  muz|zier
  muz|zi|est
my
my|al|gia
my|al|gic
my|al|ism
myall +s (tree.
  ⚠ mile)
Myan|mar (official
  name of Burma)

Myan|mar|ese
  plural
  Myan|mar|ese
my|as|the|nia
my|ce|lial
my|ce|lium
  my|ce|lia
My|ce|nae (city of
  ancient Greece)
My|ce|naean +s
myco|logic|al
myco|logic|al|ly
my|colo|gist +s
my|col|ogy
myco|plasma
  myco|plas|mas or
  myco|plas|mata
myco|pro|tein
mycor|rhiza
  mycor|rhizae
  mycor|rhizal
my|co|sis
  my|co|ses
my|cot|ic
myco|toxin +s
my|cot|ro|phy
my|dria|sis
mye|lin +s
mye|lin|ation
mye|li|tis
mye|loid
mye|loma
  mye|lo|mas or
  mye|lo|mata
My|fanwy
Myko|layiv (city,
  Ukraine)
Myk|onos (Greek
  island)
Myles also Miles
my|lo|don +s
My|men|singh
  (port, Bangladesh)
myna +s (bird; use
  mynah. ⚠ miner,
  minor)
mynah +s (bird.
  ⚠ miner, minor)
myo|car|dial
myo|car|di|tis
myo|car|dium
  myo|car|dia
myo|fib|ril +s
myo|gen|ic
myo|glo|bin +s
my|ol|ogy
myope +s
my|opia
my|opic
my|opic|al|ly
my|osin

my|osis (use
  miosis.
  ⚠ meiosis)
myo|sote +s
myo|so|tis
  myo|so|tises
myo|tonia
myo|ton|ic
Myra
myr|iad +s
myr|ia|pod +s
myr|me|co|logic|al
myr|me|colo|gist
  +s
myr|me|col|ogy
myr|mi|don +s
Myrna
my|robalan +s
Myron (Greek
  sculptor)
myrrh +s (resin,
  incense. ⚠ murre)
myr|rhic
myr|rhy
myr|ta|ceous
Myr|tle (name)
myr|tle +s (shrub)
my|self
Mysia (ancient
  name for part of
  NW Asia Minor)
Mys|ian +s
My|sore (city,
  India; former
  name of
  Karnataka)
mys|ta|go|gic
mys|ta|go|gic|al
mys|ta|gogue +s
mys|teri|ous
mys|teri|ous|ly
mys|teri|ous|ness
mys|tery
  mys|ter|ies
mys|tic +s
mys|tic|al
mys|tic|al|ly
mys|ti|cism
mys|ti|fi|ca|tion +s
mys|tify
  mys|ti|fies
  mys|ti|fied
  mys|ti|fy|ing
  mys|ti|fy|ing|ly
mys|tique +s
myth +s
mythi
myth|ic
myth|ic|al
myth|ic|al|ly
mythi|cise Br. (use
  mythicize)

mythi|cise (cont.)
  mythi|cises
  mythi|cised
  mythi|cis|ing
mythi|cism
mythi|cist +s
mythi|cize
  mythi|cizes
  mythi|cized
  mythi|ciz|ing
myth-maker +s
myth-making
mytho|gen|esis
myth|og|raph|er
  +s
myth|og|raphy
myth|olo|ger +s
mytho|logic
mytho|logic|al
mytho|logic|al|ly
myth|olo|gise Br.
  (use mythologize)
  myth|olo|gises
  myth|olo|gised
  myth|olo|gis|ing
myth|ol|ogiser Br.
  +s (use
  mythologizer)
myth|olo|gist +s
myth|olo|gize
  myth|olo|gizes
  myth|olo|gized
  myth|olo|giz|ing
myth|olo|gizer +s
myth|ology
  myth|olo|gies
mytho|mania +s
mytho|maniac +s
mytho|poeia +s
mytho|poeic
my|thos
my|thoi
  (myth; narrative
  theme)
my|thus
mythi
  (myth)
Myti|lene (town,
  Lesbos)
myx|edema Am.
myx|oe|dema Br.
myx|oma
  myx|omas or
  myx|omata
myxo|ma|tosis
myxo|my|cete +s
myxo|virus
  myxo|viruses

Nn

....

'n (= and)

na (= not)

NAAFI (= Navy,
Army, and Air
Force Institutes;
canteen)

naan +s (use nan)

Naas (town,
Republic of
Ireland)

nab
nabs
nabbed
nab|bing

Naba|taean +s

Na|beul (city,
Tunisia)

Nabi +s

Nab|lus (town,
West Bank)

nabob +s

Nab|okov,
Vlad|imir
(Russian writer)

Na|cala (port,
Mozambique)

nac|arat

na|celle +s

nacho +s

NACODS
(= National
Association of
Colliery Overmen,
Deputies, and
Shotfirers)

nacre (mother-of-
pearl. △ naker)

nacred

nac|re|ous

nac|rous

Nader, Ralph
(American
campaigner)

Nadia

Na|dine

nadir +s

naev|oid Br. (Am.
nevoid)

naevus Br.
naevi
(Am. nevus)

naff +s +ed +ing
+er +est

Naffy

NAFTA (= North
American Free
Trade Agreement.
△ naphtha)

nag
nags
nagged
nag|ging

Naga +s (tribe in
India and Burma;
language)

naga +s Hinduism

Naga|land (state,
India)

na|gana

Naga|saki (city,
Japan)

nag|ger +s

nag|ging|ly

Nagorno-
Karabakh
(region,
Azerbaijan)

Na|goya (city,
Japan)

Nag|pur (city,
India)

Nagy, Imre
(Hungarian
statesman)

Naha (port, Japan)

Na|huatl +s

Na|huat|lan

Nahum Bible

naiad
naiads or
nai|ades

naif +s

nail +s +ed +ing

nail-biting

nail brush
nail brushes

nail enamel +s

nail|er +s

nail|ery
nail|er|ies

nail file +s

nail head +s

nail|less

nail pol|ish
nail pol|ishes

nail punch
nail punches

nail scis|sors

nail set +s

nail var|nish
nail var|nishes

nain|sook +s

Nai|paul, V. S.
(West Indian
writer)

naira +s

Nairn|shire (former
county, Scotland)

Nai|robi (capital of
Kenya)

naive

naive|ly

naive|ness

naïv|eté +s
(use naivety)

naiv|ety
naiv|eties

Najaf (city, Iraq)

naked

naked|ly

naked|ness

naker +s (drum.
△ nacre)

Na|khi|che|van
(Russian name for
Naxçivan)

Na|khon Sawan
(port, Thailand)

Na|kuru (city,
Kenya)

Nal|chik (capital of
Kabardino-
Balkaria)

NALGO (= National
and Local
Government
Officers'
Association)

Nam (= Vietnam)

Nama
plural Nama or
Namas

Nam|an|gan (city,
Uzbekistan)

Na|ma|qua|land
(homeland, South
Africa and
Namibia)

namby-pamby
namby-pambies

name
names
named
nam|ing

name|able

name-calling

name-child
name-children

name-day +s

name-drop
name-drops
name-dropped
name-dropping
name-dropper +s

name|less

name|less|ly

name|less|ness

name|ly

Namen (Flemish
name for Namur)

name part +s

name|plate +s

name|sake +s

name tag +s

name-tape +s

Namib Des|ert (in
SW Africa)

Na|mibia

Na|mib|ian +s

namma +s (use
gnamma)

Namur (province
and city, Belgium)

Nan (name)

nan +s
(grandmother;
Indian bread)

nana +s

Na|naimo (port,
Canada)

Nanak, Guru
(Indian founder of
Sikhism)

nance +s (offensive)

Nan|chang (city,
China)

Nancy (city,
France; name)

nancy
nan|cies
(offensive)

Nanda Devi
(mountain, India)

Nandi Hinduism

Nan|ette

Nanga Par|bat
(mountain, India)

Nan|jing (city,
China)

nan|keen +s

Nan|king
(= Nanjing)

nanna +s

Nan|ning (city,
China)

nanny
nan|nies
nan|nied
nanny|ing

nanny-goat +s

nano|gram +s

nano|meter Am. +s

nano|metre Br. +s

nano|sec|ond +s

nano|tech|nol|ogy

Nan|sen, Fridt|jof
(Norwegian
explorer and
statesman)

Nantes (city,
France)

Nan|tucket (island,
USA)

Naomi

naos
naoi
nap
naps
napped
nap|ping
(short sleep; pile
on textiles; card
game; tip as
winner. △ knap,
nappe)
napa +s (leather;
use nappa.
△ knapper,
napper)
na|palm +s +ed
+ing
nape +s
nap|ery
nap hand +s
Naph|tali *Bible*
naph|tha +s (oil.
△ NAFTA)
naph|tha|lene +s
naph|thal|ic
naph|thene +s
naph|then|ic
Na|pier (port, New
Zealand)
Na|pier, John
(Scottish
mathematician)
Na|pier|ian
Na|pier's bones
nap|kin +s
Na|ples (city, Italy)
Na|po|leon (three
rulers of France)
na|po|leon +s
(coin; game)
Na|po|leon|ic
nappa +s (leather.
△ knapper,
napper)
nappe +s (*Geology*.
△ knap, nap)
nap|per +s (head.
△ knapper,
nappa)
nappy
nap|pies
nappy rash
Nara (city, Japan)
Na|ra|yan, R. K.
(Indian writer)
Nar|ayan|ganj
(port, Bangladesh)
Nar|bonne (city,
France)
narc +s (narcotics
agent. △ nark)
nar|ceine

nar|cis|sism
nar|cis|sist +s
nar|cis|sis|tic
nar|cis|sis|tic|al|ly
Nar|cis|sus *Greek
Mythology*
nar|cis|sus
plural nar|cis|sus
or nar|cissi *or*
nar|cis|suses
nar|co|lepsy
nar|co|lep|tic +s
nar|co|sis
nar|co|ses
narco|ter|ror|ism
narco|ter|ror|ist +s
nar|cot|ic +s
nar|cot|ic|al|ly
nar|co|tisa|tion *Br.*
(use
narcotization)
nar|co|tise *Br.* (use
narcotize)
nar|co|tises
nar|co|tised
nar|co|tis|ing
nar|co|tism
nar|co|tiza|tion
nar|co|tize
nar|co|tizes
nar|co|tized
nar|co|tiz|ing
nard +s
nar|doo +s
nares (nostrils)
nar|ghile +s
nark +s +ed +ing
(informer;
annoying person;
annoy. △ narc)
narky
nark|ier
nark|iest
Nar|mada (river,
India)
Nar|nia (fictional
land)
Narra|gan|sett
plural
Narra|gan|sett
nar|rat|able
nar|rate
nar|rates
nar|rated
nar|rat|ing
nar|ra|tion +s
nar|ra|tion|al
nar|ra|tive +s
nar|ra|tive|ly
nar|rato|logic|al
nar|ra|tolo|gist +s
nar|ra|tol|ogy

nar|ra|tor +s
nar|row +s +ed
+ing +er +est
nar|row boat +s
nar|row|cast
nar|row|casts
nar|row|cast
nar|row|cast|ing
nar|row|cast|er +s
narrow-gauge
adjective
nar|row|ish
nar|row|ly
narrow-minded
narrow-minded|ly
narrow-
minded|ness
nar|row|ness
nar|thex
nar|thexes
Nar|vik (port,
Norway)
nar|whal +s
nary
NASA (= National
Aeronautics and
Space
Administration)
nasal
na|sal|isa|tion *Br.*
(use nasalization)
na|sal|ise *Br.* (use
nasalize)
na|sal|ises
na|sal|ised
na|sal|is|ing
na|sal|ity
na|sal|iza|tion
na|sal|ize
na|sal|izes
na|sal|ized
na|sal|iz|ing
nas|al|ly
nas|cency
nas|cent
nase|berry
nase|berries
Naseby (battle site,
England)
Nash, Beau
(English dandy)
Nash, John
(English architect)
Nash, Ogden
(American writer)
Nash, Paul
(English artist)
Nashe, Thomas
(English writer)
Nash|ville (city,
USA)
Nasik (city, India)

Nas|myth, James
(British engineer)
naso-frontal
naso|gas|tric
Nas|sau (capital of
the Bahamas)
Nas|ser, Gamal
Abdel (Egyptian
statesman)
Nas|tase, Ilie
(Romanian-born
tennis player)
nas|tic
nas|tily
nas|ti|ness
na|stur|tium +s
nasty
nas|tier
nas|ti|est
Natal (former
province, South
Africa; port,
Brazil)
natal
Nat|alie
na|tal|ity
na|tal|ities
Na|ta|sha
na|ta|tion
nata|tor|ial
na|ta|tor|ium +s
na|ta|tory
natch (= naturally)
nates (buttocks)
NATFHE
(= National
Association of
Teachers in
Further and
Higher Education)
Nath|alie
Na|than
Na|than|iel
nath|less
na|tion +s
na|tion|al +s
na|tion|al|isa|tion
Br. (use
nationalization)
na|tion|al|ise *Br.*
(use nationalize)
na|tion|al|ises
na|tion|al|ised
na|tion|al|is|ing
na|tion|al|iser *Br.*
+s (use
nationalizer)
na|tion|al|ism +s
na|tion|al|ist +s
na|tion|al|is|tic
na|tion|al|is|tic|
al|ly

na¦tion|al¦ity
na¦tion|al¦ities
na¦tion|al¦iza¦tion
na¦tion|al¦ize
na¦tion|al¦izes
na¦tion|al¦ized
na¦tion|al¦iz¦ing
na¦tion|al¦izer +s
na¦tion|al¦ly
na¦tion|hood +s
na¦tion state +s
na¦tion|wide
na¦tive +s
na¦tive|ly
na¦tive|ness
na¦tive speak¦er +s
na¦tiv|ism
na¦tiv|ist +s
na¦tiv|ity
na¦tiv|ities
NATO (= North
Atlantic Treaty
Organization)
Nat¦ron, Lake (in
Tanzania)
nat¦ron
NATSOPA (former
British trade
union)
nat¦ter +s +ed
+ing
nat¦ter|er +s
nat¦ter|jack +s
nat¦tier blue *noun
and adjective*
nattier-blue
attributive
nat¦tily
nat¦ti|ness
natty
nat¦tier
nat¦ti|est
Na¦tu|fian +s
nat¦ural +s
natural-born
nat¦ur|al|isa¦tion
Br. (use
naturalization)
nat¦ur|al|ise *Br.*
(use naturalize)
nat¦ur|al|ises
nat¦ur|al|ised
nat¦ur|al|is¦ing
nat¦ur|al|ism
nat¦ur|al|ist +s
nat¦ur|al|is¦tic
nat¦ur|al|is¦tic|
al¦ly
nat¦ur|al|iza¦tion
nat¦ur|al|ize
nat¦ur|al|izes

nat¦ur|al|ize *(cont.)*
nat¦ur|al|ized
nat¦ur|al|iz¦ing
nat¦ur|al|ly
nat¦ur|al|ness
na¦ture +s
na¦tured
na¦ture lover +s
nature-loving
na¦ture print|ing
na¦tur|ism
na¦tur|ist +s
na¦turo|path +s
na¦turo|path|ic
na¦tur|op|athy
naught (nothing.
△ nought)
naugh|tily
naugh|ti|ness
naugh|ti|nesses
naughty
naugh|tier
naugh|ti|est
ńau|plius
nau|plii
Nauru (in SW
Pacific)
Nau|ru|an +s
nau|sea +s
nau|se|ate
nau|se|ates
nau|se|ated
nau|se|at|ing
nau|se|at|ing|ly
nau|se|ous
nau|se|ous|ly
nau|se|ous|ness
nautch
nautches
nautch girl +s
naut|ical
naut|ical|ly
Naut|ilus
(submarine)
naut|ilus
naut|iluses *or*
naut|ili
Nav¦aho (use
Navajo)
plural Nav¦aho *or*
Nav¦ahos
Nav¦ajo
plural Nav¦ajo *or*
Nav¦ajos
naval (of navies.
△ navel)
na¦val|ly
Navan (town,
Republic of
Ireland)

Nava|nagar
(former state,
India)
nav|arin +s
Nava|rino (battle)
Na|varre (in Spain)
nave +s (part of
church or wheel.
△ knave)
navel +s *(Anatomy.*
△ naval)
navel-gazing
navel or|ange +s
na¦vel|wort +s
na¦vicu|lar +s
nav|ig|abil|ity
nav|ig|able
navi|gate
navi|gates
navi|gated
navi|gat|ing
navi|ga¦tion +s
navi|ga|tion|al
navi|ga¦tor +s
**Nav¦ra|ti¦lova,
Mar|tina** (Czech-
born American
tennis player)
navvy
nav|vies
nav|vied
navvy|ing
navy
na¦vies
navy blue +s *noun
and adjective*
navy-blue
attributive
navy yard +s
nawab +s
Nax¦çi|van
(republic, S. Asia;
its capital)
Naxos (island,
Greece)
nay +s (no. △ né,
née, neigh)
Naya|rit (state,
Mexico)
nay|say
nay|says
nay|said
nay|say|ing
nay|say|er +s
Naz¦ar|ene +s
Naz¦ar|eth (town,
Israel)
Naz¦ar|ite +s
Nazca Lines
Nazi +s
Nazi|dom
Nazi|fi|ca|tion

Nazify
Nazi|fies
Nazi|fied
Nazi|fy|ing
Nazi|ism
Naz¦ir|ite (use
Nazarite)
Nazism
Nde|bele
plural Nde|bele *or*
In|de|bele *or*
Nde|beles
N'Dja|mena
(capital of Chad)
Ndola (city,
Zambia)
né (before man's
previous name.
△ nay, née,
neigh)
Neagh, Lough (in
Northern Ireland)
Neal *also* **Neil**
Ne¦an|der|thal +s
neap +s +ed +ing
(tide. △ neep)
Nea|pol|itan +s
neap tide +s
near +s +ed +ing
+er +est
near-by
near-certain
Ne¦arc|tic
near-death
(experience)
Near East|ern
near|ish
near|ly
near miss
near misses
near-monopoly
near-monopolies
near|ness
near-perfect
near|side +s
near sight
near-sighted
near-sighted|ly
near-sighted|ness
neat
plural neat *or*
neats
neat|er
neat|est
neat|en +s +ed
+ing
Neath (town,
Wales)
neath (beneath)
neat|ly
neat|ness
neat's-foot oil

neb|bish
  neb|bishes
Neb|lina, Pico da
  (mountain, Brazil)
Neb|raska (state,
  USA)
Ne|bu|chad|
  nez|zar (king of
  Babylon)
ne|bu|chad|
  nez|zar +s (wine
  bottle)
neb|ula
  nebu|lae *or*
  nebu|las
  noun
nebu|lar
  adjective
nebu|lise *Br.* (use
  nebulize)
  nebu|lises
  nebu|lised
  nebu|lis|ing
nebu|liser *Br.* +s
  (use nebulizer)
nebu|lize
  nebu|lizes
  nebu|lized
  nebu|liz|ing
nebu|lizer +s
nebu|los|ity
nebu|lous
nebu|lous|ly
nebu|lous|ness
neb|uly *Heraldry*
ne|ces|sar|ian +s
ne|ces|sar|ian|ism
ne|ces|sar|ily
ne|ces|sary
  ne|ces|sar|ies
ne|ces|si|tar|ian +s
ne|ces|si|tar|ian|
  ism
ne|ces|si|tate
  ne|ces|si|tates
  ne|ces|si|tated
  ne|ces|si|tat|ing
ne|ces|si|tous
ne|ces|sity
  ne|ces|sities
Nech|tans|mere
  (battlefield)
neck +s +ed +ing
  (part of body,
  clothing, violin,
  etc.; impudence;
  kiss. ⚠ nek)
Neckar (river,
  Germany)
neck|band +s
neck|cloth +s

Necker, Jacques
  (Swiss banker)
neck|er|chief +s
neck|lace
  neck|laces
  neck|laced
  neck|lacing
neck|let +s
neck|line +s
neck|tie +s
neck|wear
necro|bi|osis
  necro|bi|oses
necro|bi|ot|ic
necro|gen|ic
ne|crol|atry
necro|logic|al
ne|crol|ogy
  ne|crolo|gies
necro|man|cer +s
necro|mancy
  necro|man|cies
necro|man|tic +s
ne|cropha|gous
necro|phil +s
necro|phile +s
necro|philia
necro|phil|iac +s
necro|phil|ic
ne|croph|il|ism
ne|croph|il|ist +s
ne|croph|ily
necro|phobe
necro|pho|bia
necro|pho|bic
ne|crop|olis
  ne|crop|olises
nec|ropsy
necro|scop|ic
ne|rosc|opy
  ne|crosc|op|ies
ne|cro|sis
  ne|cro|ses
nec|rot|ic
nec|ro|tise *Br.* (use
  necrotize)
  nec|ro|tises
  nec|ro|tised
  nec|ro|tis|ing
nec|ro|tize
  nec|ro|tizes
  nec|ro|tized
  nec|ró|tiz|ing
nec|tar +s
nec|tar|ean
nec|tared
nec|tar|eous
nec|tar|if|er|ous
nec|tar|ine +s
nec|tar|ous

nec|tary
  nec|tar|ies
Ned
NEDC (= National
  Economic
  Development
  Council)
Neddy (National
  Economic
  Development
  Council)
neddy
  ned|dies
  (= donkey)
née *Br.* (before
  woman's maiden
  name. ⚠ nay, né,
  neigh. *Am.* nee)
need +s +ed +ing
  (require. ⚠ knead)
need|ful
need|ful|ly
need|ful|ness
needi|ness
nee|dle
  nee|dles
  nee|dled
  need|ling
needle|cord
needle|craft
needle|fish
  plural needle|fish
  or needle|fishes
needle|ful +s
needle|point +s
Nee|dles (rocks,
  England)
need|less
need|less|ly
need|less|ness
needle|woman
  needle|women
needle|work
needn't
needy
  need|ier
  needi|est
neem +s
neep +s (turnip.
  ⚠ neap)
ne'er
ne'er-do-well +s
ne|fari|ous
ne|fari|ous|ly
ne|fari|ous|ness
Nef|er|titi
  (Egyptian queen)
neg +s (= negative)
neg|ate
  neg|ates
  neg|ated
  neg|at|ing

neg|ation +s
neg|ation|ist +s
nega|tive +s
nega|tive|ly
nega|tive|ness
nega|tiv|ism
nega|tiv|ist +s
nega|tiv|is|tic
nega|tiv|ity
neg|ator +s
neg|atory
Negev (desert,
  Israel)
neg|lect +s +ed
  +ing
neg|lect|ful
neg|lect|ful|ly
neg|lect|ful|ness
nég|ligé +s (use
  negligee)
neg|li|gee +s
neg|li|gence
neg|li|gent
neg|li|gent|ly
neg|ligi|bil|ity
neg|li|gible
neg|li|gibly
Ne|gombo (port,
  Sri Lanka)
ne|go|ti|abil|ity
ne|go|ti|able
ne|go|ti|ant +s
ne|go|ti|ate
  ne|go|ti|ates
  ne|go|ti|ated
  ne|go|ti|at|ing
ne|go|ti|ation +s
ne|go|ti|ator +s
Ne|gress
  Ne|gresses
  (*may cause offence*;
  prefer black)
Neg|rillo +s (tribe,
  Africa)
Negri Sem|bilan
  (state, Malaysia)
Neg|rito +s
Neg|ri|tude
Negro
  Ne|groes
  (*may cause offence*;
  prefer black)
Negro, Rio (river,
  S. America)
Ne|groid +s
Ne|gro|ism
Ne|gro|pho|bia
Ne|gro|pho|bic
Neg|ros (island,
  Philippines)
Negus (title of ruler
  of Ethiopia)

negus
ne¦guses
(drink)
Ne¦he¦miah *Bible*
Nehru, Pan¦dit
Jawa¦har¦lal
(Indian statesman)
neigh +s +ed +ing
(of a horse. △ nay,
né, née)
neigh¦bor *Am.* +s
+ed +ing
neigh¦bor¦hood
Am. +s
neigh¦bor¦li¦ness
Am.
neigh¦bor¦ly *Am.*
neigh¦bour *Br.* +s
+ed +ing
neigh¦bour¦hood
Br. +s
neigh¦bour¦li¦ness
Br.
neigh¦bour¦ly *Br.*
Neil *also* Neal
Neill, Alex¦an¦der
(Scottish-born
educationist)
Nei¦sse (rivers,
German-Polish
border and S.
Poland)
nei¦ther
Nejd (region, Saudi
Arabia)
nek +s (mountain
col. △ neck)
nek¦ton +s
Nell
Nell¦lore (city,
India)
nelly
nel¦lies
Nel¦son (port, New
Zealand)
Nel¦son, Ho¦ra¦tio
(British admiral)
nel¦son +s
Nel¦spruit (town,
South Africa)
ne¦lumbo +s
Neman (river, E.
Europe)
nem¦at¦ic +s
nem¦ato¦cyst +s
nema¦tode +s
Nem¦butal *Propr.*
nem. con.
(= nemine
contradicente,
without
dissension)

nem¦er¦tean
nem¦er¦tine
nem¦esia
Nem¦esis *Greek*
Mythology
nem¦esis
nem¦eses
Nemu¦nas
(alternative name
for the Neman)
nene +s
Nen¦nius (Welsh
writer)
nenu¦phar +s
neo-Cambrian
neo¦clas¦sic
neo¦clas¦sic¦al
neo¦clas¦si¦cism
neo¦clas¦si¦cist +s
neo¦co¦lo¦nial¦ism
neo¦co¦lo¦nial¦ist
+s
Neo-Darwin¦ian
+s
neo¦dym¦ium
neo-fascism
neo-fascist +s
neo-Georgian
neo-Gothic
neo-Hellen¦ism
neo-
impres¦sion¦ism
neo-
impres¦sion¦ist
+s
neo¦lith¦ic
Archaeology
neo¦lo¦gian +s
neo¦lo¦gise *Br.* (use
neologize)
neo¦lo¦gises
neo¦lo¦gised
neo¦lo¦gis¦ing
neo¦lo¦gism +s
neo¦lo¦gist +s
neo¦lo¦gize
neo¦lo¦gizes
neo¦lo¦gized
neo¦lo¦giz¦ing
neol¦ogy
neolo¦gies
neo-Marxist
neo¦my¦cin +s
neon +s
neo¦natal
neo¦nate +s
neo-Nazi +s
neo-Nazism
neon¦tolo¦gist +s
neon¦tol¦ogy
neo¦pen¦tane
neo¦pho¦bia

neo¦pho¦bic
neo¦phron +s
neo¦phyte +s
neo¦plasm +s
neo¦plas¦tic
neo-plasti¦cism *Art*
Neo¦pla¦ton¦ic
Neo¦pla¦ton¦ism
Neo¦pla¦ton¦ist +s
neo¦prene +s
Neop¦tole¦mus
Greek Mythology
neo-realism
neo-realist +s
neo¦ten¦ic
neot¦enous
neot¦eny
neot¦enies
neo¦ter¦ic
neo¦trop¦ic¦al
Neo¦zo¦ic *Geology*
Nepal
Nep¦al¦ese
plural Nep¦al¦ese
Nep¦ali
plural Nep¦ali *or*
Nep¦alis
ne¦pen¦the
ne¦pen¦thes
plural ne¦pen¦thes
neph¦el¦om¦eter
+s
neph¦elo¦met¦ric
neph¦el¦om¦etry
nephew +s
neph¦ol¦ogy
neph¦rec¦tomy
neph¦rec¦to¦mies
neph¦rite +s
neph¦rit¦ic
neph¦ritis
neph¦rol¦ogy
neph¦rop¦athy
neph¦rot¦omy
neph¦roto¦mies
Nepia, George
(New Zealand
rugby player)
ne plus ultra
nepo¦tism
nepo¦tist +s
nepo¦tis¦tic
Nep¦tune (*Roman*
Mythology; planet)
Nep¦tun¦ian
Geology
Nep¦tun¦ist +s
nep¦tun¦ium
nerd +s
nerdy
nerd¦ier
nerdi¦est

Ner¦eid (moon of
Neptune)
ner¦eid +s *Greek*
Mythology
Ner¦eus *Greek*
Mythology
ner¦ine +s
Ner¦issa
nerka +s
Nernst, Her¦mann
Wal¦ther
(German chemist)
Nero (Clau¦dius
Cae¦sar) (Roman
emperor)
ner¦oli
Nero¦nian
Ne¦ruda, Pablo
(Chilean poet and
diplomat)
Nerva, Mar¦cus
Coc¦ceius
(Roman emperor)
ner¦vate
nerv¦ation +s
nerve
nerves
nerved
nerv¦ing
nerve-cell +s
nerve cen¦ter *Am.*
+s
nerve cen¦tre *Br.*
+s
nerve gas
nerve gases
nerve¦less
nerve¦less¦ly
nerve¦less¦ness
nerve-racking
Nervi, Pier Luigi
(Italian engineer)
ner¦vily
ner¦vine +s
nervi¦ness
ner¦vous
ner¦vous¦ly
ner¦vous¦ness
nerv¦ure +s
nervy
ner¦vier
ner¦vi¦est
Nerys
Nes¦bit, Edith
(English writer)
nes¦ci¦ence
nes¦ci¦ent
ness
nesses
Nessa
nest +s +ed +ing
Nesta

nest box
  nest boxes
nest egg+s
nest|ful+s
nes|tle
  nes|tles
  nes|tled
  nest|ling
nest|like
nest|ling+s
Nes|tor *Greek*
  Mythology
Nes|tor|ian
Nes|tor|ian|ism
net
  nets
  net|ted
  net|ting
net|ball+s
net|ful+s
nether
Neth|er|land|er+s
Neth|er|land|ish
Neth|er|lands, the
Neth|er|lands
  An|til|les
neth|er|most
net|suke
  plural net|suke *or*
  net|sukes
nett (use net)
net|tle
  net|tles
  net|tled
  net|tling
nettle-rash
nettle|some
net|work+s +ed
  +ing
net|work|er+s
Neu|châ|tel, Lake
  (in Switzerland)
neum+s (use
  neume)
Neu|mann, John
  von (Hungarian-
  born
  mathematician)
neume+s
neur|al
neur|al|gia
neur|al|gic
neur|al|ly
neur|as|the|nia
neur|as|the|nic
neur|it|ic
neur|itis
neuro|ana|tom|
      ic|al
neuro|anat|omy
neuro|bio|logic|al
neuro|biol|ogy

neuro|gen|esis
neuro|gen|eses
neuro|gen|ic
neur|oglia
neuro|hor|mone
  +s
neuro|lin|guis|tic
neuro|lin|guis|tics
neuro|logic|al
neuro|logic|al|ly
neurolo|gist+s
neurol|ogy
neur|oma
  neur|omas *or*
  neur|omata
neuro|mus|cu|lar
neuron+s
neuron|al
neur|one+s
neur|on|ic
neuro|path+s
neuro|path|ic
neuro|
  path|olo|gist+s
neuro|path|ol|ogy
neur|opathy
neuro|physio|
      logic|al
neuro|
  physi|olo|gist+s
neuro|physi|ology
neuro|
  psycho|logic|al
neuro|psycho|logy
neur|op|teran+s
neur|op|ter|ous
neuro|sci|ence+s
neuro|sci|en|tist
  +s
neur|osis
  neur|oses
neuro|sur|geon+s
neuro|sur|gery
neuro|sur|gi|cal
neur|ot|ic+s
neur|ot|ic|al|ly
neur|oti|cism
neur|ot|omy
neur|oto|mies
neuro|toxin+s
neuro|trans|mit|
      ter+s
Neu|sied|ler See
  (lake, Austria and
  Hungary)
neu|ter+s +ed
  +ing
neu|tral+s
neu|tral|isa|tion
  Br. +s (use
  neutralization)

neu|tral|ise *Br.*
  (use neutralize)
neu|tral|ises
neu|tral|ised
neu|tral|is|ing
neu|tral|iser *Br.* +s
  (use neutralizer)
neu|tra|lism
neu|tra|list+s
neu|tral|ity
neu|tral|iza|tion
  +s
neu|tral|ize
neu|tral|izes
neu|tral|ized
neu|tral|iz|ing
neu|tral|izer+s
neu|tral|ly
neu|trino+s
neu|tron+s
neu|tro|phil+s
Neva (river, Russia)
Nev|ada (state,
  USA)
névé+s
never
never-ending
never|more
Never-Never
  (Australian
  outback)
never-never (hire
  purchase)
Never-Never
  Coun|try
  (alternative name
  for Never-Never
  Land)
Never-Never Land
  (region, N.
  Australia)
never-never land
  (imaginary
  utopian place)
Ne|vers (city,
  France)
never|the|less
Nev|ille
Nev|ille, Rich|ard
  (Earl of Warwick,
  English
  statesman)
Nevis (island, West
  Indies)
Nevis, Ben
  (mountain,
  Scotland)
nev|oid *Am.* (*Br.*
  naevoid)
Nev|sky,
  Alex|an|der
  (Russian hero)

nevus *Am.*
  nevi
  (*Br.* naevus)
new+er +est
  (recent; unused.
  ⚠ knew, nu)
New|ark (city,
  USA; town,
  England)
new|born+s
New Cale|donia
  (island, S. Pacific)
New|cas|tle (port,
  Australia)
Newcastle-under-
  Lyme (town,
  England)
Newcastle-upon-
  Tyne (city,
  England)
New|comen,
  Thomas (English
  metal-worker)
new|comer+s
newel+s
new|fan|gled
New|found|land
  (island, Canada)
New|found|
      land|er+s
New|gate (former
  prison, London)
Ne Win (Burmese
  statesman)
new|ish
new-laid
New|lands, John
  (English industrial
  chemist)
new-look *attributive*
newly
newly-appoint|ed
newly-elected
newly-formed
newly-wed+s
New|man, Bar|nett
  (American
  painter)
New|man, John
  Henry (English
  churchman)
New|man, Paul
  (American actor)
New|mar|ket
  (town, England)
new|ness
New Or|leans
  (port, USA)
New|port (port,
  Wales; etc.)
New|port News
  (city, USA)

Newry (port, Northern Ireland)

news

news agency
news agen|cies

news|agent +s

news|boy +s

news|brief +s

news|cast +s

news|cast|er +s

news|deal|er +s

news|flash
news|flashes

news-gather|er +s

news-gather|ing

news|girl +s

news hound +s

news|less

news|let|ter +s

news|man
news|men

news|mon|ger +s

news|paper +s

news|paper|man
news|paper|men

New|speak

news|print

news|read|er +s

news|reel +s

news|room +s

news-sheet +s

news-stand +s

new-style
attributive

news-vendor +s

news|worthi|ness

news|worthy

newsy
news|ier
news|est

newt +s

New Testa|ment
*Bible noun and
attributive*

New|ton, Isaac
(English
mathematician
and physicist)

new|ton +s (unit)

New|ton Abbot
(town, England)

New|ton|ian

New|town|abbey
(town, Northern
Ireland)

New World (*noun
and attributive* the
Americas)

New Zea|land

New Zea|land|er
+s

next

next-best

next door
*adverbial, adjective,
and noun*

next-door
attributive

nexus
nexuses

Ney, Mi|chel
(French soldier)

ngaio +s

Ngali|ema, Mount
(Zairean name for
Mount Stanley)

Ngami|land
(region,
Botswana)

**Ngata, Api|rana
Tar|upa** (Maori
leader and
politician)

Ng|bandi

Ngoro|ngoro
(crater, Tanzania)

Nguni
plural Nguni

Nhu|lun|buy
(town, Australia)

nia|cin

Ni|ag|ara (river and
Falls, Canada)

Niall

Nia|mey (capital of
Niger)

nib
nibs
nibbed
nib|bing

nib|ble
nib|bles
nib|bled
nib|bling

nib|bler +s

Nibel|ung
Nibel|ungs *or*
Nibel|ungen
*Germanic
Mythology*

Nibel|ung|en|lied
(poem)

nib|let +s

nib|lick +s

nicad +s

Ni|caea (ancient
city, Asia Minor)

Nicam *Propr.*

Nic|ar|agua (in
Central America)

Nic|ar|agua, Lake
(in Nicaragua)

Nic|ar|aguan +s

Nice (city, France)

nice
nicer
nicest
(pleasant)

nice|ish (use
nicish)

nice|ly

Ni|cene

nice|ness

ni|cety
ni|ceties

niche
niches
niched
nich|ing *or*
niche|ing

Nich|iren

Nich|olas *also*
Nico|las

Nich|olas (patron
saint of children)

Nich|ol|son, Ben
(English artist)

Nich|ol|son, Jack
(American actor)

Ni|chrome *Propr.*

nicish

Nick (name)

nick +s +ed +ing
(notch; prison;
steal; etc.)

nickel
nickels
nick|elled *Br.*
nick|eled *Am.*
nickel|ling *Br.*
nickel|ing *Am.*
(element. △ nicol)

nickel brass

nick|el|ic

nick|el|odeon +s

nick|el|ous

nickel-plated

nickel-plating

nick|er +s (tool;
person who nicks.
△ knicker,
knickers)

nicker
plural nicker
(pound in money.
△ knicker)

Nick|laus, Jack
(American golfer)

nick-nack +s (use
knick-knack)

nick|name
nick|names
nick|named
nick|nam|ing

Nicky

Nico|bar Is|lands
(off India)

nicol +s (prism.
△ nickel)

Nic|ola

Ni|cole

Ni|col|ette

Nico|sia (capital of
Cyprus)

ni|coti|ana
plural ni|coti|ana

nico|tina|mide

nico|tine

nico|tin|ic

nico|tin|ise *Br.* (use
nicotinize)

nico|tin|ises

nico|tin|ised

nico|tin|is|ing

nico|tin|ism

nico|tin|ize

nico|tin|izes

nico|tin|ized

nico|tin|iz|ing

nic|ti|tate

nic|ti|tates

nic|ti|tated

nic|ti|tat|ing

nic|ti|ta|tion

ni|da|men|tal

nide +s

nid|ifi|cate

nid|ifi|cates

nid|ifi|cated

nid|ifi|cat|ing

nidi|fi|ca|tion

nid|ify

nid|ifies

nid|ified

nid|ify|ing

nidus
nidi *or* nid|uses

niece +s

ni|ello
ni|elli *or* ni|ellos

ni|el|loed

niels|bohr|ium

Niel|sen, Carl
(Danish
composer)

Nie|meyer, Oscar
(Brazilian
architect)

**Nie|möller,
Mar|tin** (German
Lutheran pastor)

Ni|er|steiner
(German wine)

**Nietz|sche,
Fried|rich
Wil|helm**

Nietz|sche (*cont.*)
(German
philosopher)
Nietz|sche|an
niff +s +ed +ing
niffy
niff|ier
nif|fi|est
Nifl|heim
*Scandinavian
Mythology*
nif|tily
nif|ti|ness
nifty
nif|tier
nif|ti|est
Nigel
Ni|gella (name)
ni|gella +s (plant)
Niger (river and
country, Africa)
Niger-Congo
(group of
languages)
Ni|geria
Ni|ger|ian +s (of
Nigeria)
Ni|ger|ien +s (of
Niger)
nig|gard +s
nig|gard|li|ness
nig|gard|ly
nig|ger +s
(*offensive*)
nig|gle
nig|gles
nig|gled
nig|gling
nig|gling|ly
nig|gly
nig|glier
nig|gli|est
nigh (near. △ nye)
night +s (period of
darkness.
△ knight)
night|bird +s
night-blindness
night|cap +s
night|clothes
night|club +s
night|dress
night|dresses
night|fall
night fight|er +s
night fly|ing
night|gown +s
night|hawk +s
nightie +s
**Night|in|gale,
Flor|ence**
(English nurse)

night|in|gale +s
night|jar +s
night|life
night light +s
night-long
night|ly (in the
night; every night.
△ knightly)
night|mare +s
night|mar|ish
night|mar|ish|ly
night nurse +s
night-owl +s
night safe +s
night school +s
night|shade +s
night shift +s
night|shirt +s
night-soil +s
night|spot +s
night|stick +s
night-time +s
night|watch|man
night|watch|men
night|wear
night work
night work|er +s
nig|res|cence +s
nig|res|cent
nig|ri|tude
ni|hil|ism
ni|hil|ist +s
ni|hil|is|tic
ni|hil|ity
ni|hil|ities
ni|hilo (in '*ex nihilo*')
nihil ob|stat
Nii|gata (port,
Japan)
**Ni|jin|sky, Vas|lav
Fom|ich** (Russian
ballet dancer)
Nij|megen (town,
the Netherlands)
Nike *Greek
Mythology*
Nik|kei index
Niko|laev (Russian
name for
Mykolayiv)
nil
**nil
des|per|an|dum**
Nile (river, Africa)
Nile blue +s *noun
and adjective*
Nile-blue *attributive*
Nile green +s *noun
and adjective*

Nile-green
attributive
nil|gai +s
Nil|giri Hills (in
India)
Nil|giris (= Nilgiri
Hills)
Nil|ot|ic
Nils|son, Bir|git
(Swedish soprano)
nim
nim|ble
nim|bler
nim|blest
nim|ble|ness
nim|bly
nimbo|stratus
nimbo|strati
nim|bus
nimbi *or*
nim|buses
nim|bused
Nimby +s
Nîmes (city,
France)
niminy-piminy
Nim|rod *Bible*
Nim|rud (ancient
Mesopotamian
city)
Nina
nin|com|poop +s
nine +s
**nine days'
won|der**
nine|fold
nine-iron +s
nine|pence +s
nine|penny
nine|pen|nies
nine|pin +s
nine|teen +s
nine|teenth +s
nine|ti|eth +s
nine-to-five
ninety
nine|ties
**ninety-first,
ninety-second,**
etc.
ninety|fold
**ninety-one, ninety-
two,** etc.
Nin|eveh (city,
Assyria)
Ning|sia
(= Ningxia)
Ning|xia (region,
China)
Nin|ian (Scottish
saint)
ninja +s

nin|jutsu +s
ninny
nin|nies
ninon +s
ninth +s
ninth|ly
Niobe *Greek
Mythology*
nio|bic
nio|bium
nio|bous
Nip +s (*offensive
Japanese*)
nip
nips
nipped
nip|ping
(pinch; drink; etc.)
nipa +s (tree)
nip|per +s (tool;
claw; child)
nip|pily
nip|ple +s
nipple|wort +s
Nip|pon|ese
plural Nip|pon|ese
nippy
nip|pier
nip|pi|est
NIREX (≃ Nuclear
Industry
Radioactive Waste
Executive)
Niro, Rob|ert De
(American actor)
nir|vana +s
Niš (town, Serbia)
Nisan (Jewish
month)
nisei +s
Nish (use Niš)
nisi
Nis|sen, Peter
(British engineer)
Nis|sen hut +s
nit +s (louse; stupid
person. △ knit)
nite +s (in
commercial
language = night)
niter *Am.* (*Br.* nitre)
Ni|te|rói (port,
Brazil)
nitid
nit|inol
nit-pick +s +ed
+ing
nit-picker +s
ni|trate
ni|trates
ni|trated
ni|trat|ing

ni|tra|tion +s
nitre *Br.* (*Am.* niter)
ni|tric
ni|tride +s
ni|tri|fi|able
ni|tri|fi|ca|tion +s
ni|trify
  ni|tri|fies
  ni|tri|fied
  ni|tri|fy|ing
ni|trile +s
ni|trite +s
nitro|ben|zene
nitro|cel|lu|lose
ni|tro|gen
ni|tro|gen|ous
nitro|gly|cerin (use
  nitroglycerine)
nitro|gly|cer|ine
ni|tro|sa|mine +s
ni|trous
nitty-gritty
nit|wit +s
nit|wit|ted
nit|wit|ted|ness
nit|wit|tery
Niue (island, S.
  Pacific)
Ni|ver|nais (former
  province, France)
nix
  nixes
  nixed
  nix|ing
Nixon, Rich|ard
  Mil|hous
  (American
  president)
Niz|ari +s
Nizhni Nov|go|rod
  (former name of
  Gorky)
Nizhni Tagil (city,
  Russia)
Nkomo, Joshua
  (Zimbabwean
  statesman)
Nkru|mah,
  Kwame
  (Ghanaian
  statesman)
No (Japanese
  drama; use Noh.
  △ know, no)
no
  noes
  (negative.
  △ know, Noh)
no-account +s
  adjective and noun
Noah *Bible*
Noah's ark

nob +s (upper-class
  person; head.
  △ knob)
no-ball +s +ed
  +ing
nob|ble
  nob|bles
  nob|bled
  nob|bling
  (tamper with.
  △ knobble)
nob|bler +s
Nobel, Al|fred
  (Swedish chemist
  and engineer)
No|bel|ist +s
no|bel|ium
no|bil|iary
  no|bil|iar|ies
no|bil|ity
  no|bil|ities
noble +s
  no|bler
  nob|lest
noble|man
  noble|men
noble|ness
no|blesse
no|blesse ob|lige
noble|woman
  noble|women
nobly
no|body
  no|bodies
nock +s +ed +ing
  (notch. △ knock)
no-claim *attributive*
no-claims
  attributive
no-confidence
  attributive
noc|tam|bu|lism
noc|tam|bu|list +s
noc|tiv|agant
noc|tiv|agous
noc|tuid +s
noc|tule +s
noc|turn +s (part of
  matins.
  △ nocturne)
noc|tur|nal
noc|tur|nal|ly
noc|turne +s (piece
  of music; painting.
  △ nocturn)
nocu|lous
nod
  nods
  nod|ded
  nod|ding
nodal

nod|dle
  nod|dles
  nod|dled
  nod|dling
Noddy (children's
  character)
noddy
  nod|dies
  (simpleton; bird)
node +s
nodi (plural of
  nodus)
nod|ic|al
nod|ose
nod|os|ity
nodu|lar
nodu|lated
nodu|la|tion
nod|ule +s
nodu|lose
nodu|lous
nodus
  nodi
Noel (Christmas;
  name. △ Nowell)
Noelle
Noe|ther, Emmy
  (German
  mathematician)
no|etic
no-fault *attributive*
no-fly zone +s
Nof|re|tete
  (alternative name
  for Nefertiti)
no-frills *attributive*
nog
  nogs
  nogged
  nog|ging
nog|gin +s
nog|ging +s
no-go area +s
no-good +s *noun*
  and attributive
Noh (Japanese
  drama. △ know,
  no)
no-hitter +s
no-hoper +s
nohow (in no way.
  △ know-how)
noil +s
noise
  noises
  noised
  nois|ing
noise|less
noise|less|ly
noise|less|ness
noise-maker +s
nois|ette +s

nois|ily
noisi|ness
noi|some
noi|some|ness
noisy
  nois|ier
  noisi|est
Nok (ancient
  Nigerian
  civilization)
Nolan, Sid|ney
  (Australian
  painter)
no|lens vo|lens
nolle pro|sequi
nomad +s
no|mad|ic
no|mad|ic|al|ly
no|mad|ise *Br.* (use
  nomadize)
  no|mad|ises
  no|mad|ised
  no|mad|is|ing
no|mad|ism
no|mad|ize
  no|mad|izes
  no|mad|ized
  no|mad|iz|ing
no man's land
nom|bril +s
nom de guerre
  noms de guerre
nom de plume
  noms de plume
nomen
  nom|ina
no|men|cla|tive
no|men|cla|tural
no|men|clat|ure
  +s
nom|ina
nom|in|al
nom|in|al|isa|tion
  Br. +s (use
  nominalization)
nom|in|al|ise *Br.*
  (use nominalize)
  nom|in|al|ises
  nom|in|al|ised
  nom|in|al|is|ing
nom|in|al|ism
nom|in|al|ist +s
nom|in|al|is|tic
nom|in|al|iza|tion
  +s
nom|in|al|ize
  nom|in|al|izes
  nom|in|al|ized
  nom|in|al|iz|ing
nom|in|al|ly
nom|in|ate
  nom|in|ates

nom|in|ate (*cont.*)
  nom|in|ated
  nom|in|at|ing
nom|in|ation +s
nom|ina|tival
nom|ina|tive +s
nom|in|ator +s
nom|inee +s
nomo|gram +s
nomo|graph +s
nomo|graph|ic
nomo|graph|ic|
    al|ly
nom|og|raphy
nomo|thet|ic
non-abstain|er +s
non-academ|ic
non-accept|ance
non-access
non-addict|ive
non|age +s
nona|gen|ar|ian +s
non-aggres|sion
non-aggres|sive
non|agon +s
non-alcohol|ic
non-aligned
non-alignment
non-allergic
non-ambigu|ous
non-appear|ance
non-art
non|ary
  non|ar|ies
non-Aryan +s
non-attached
non-attend|ance
non-attrib|ut|able
non-attrib|ut|ably
non-availabil|ity
non-believer +s
non-belliger|ency
non-belliger|ent
non-biologic|al
non-black +s
non-breakable
non-breeding
  attributive
non-capital
non-Cathol|ic +s
nonce +s
nonce-word +s
non|cha|lance
non|cha|lant
non|cha|lant|ly
non-Christian +s
non-citizen +s
non-classi|fied
non-cleric|al
non-collegi|ate
non-com +s

non-combat|ant
  +s
non-commer|cial
non-
    commis|sioned
non-commit|tal
non-commit|tal|ly
non-
    communi|cant
    +s
non-
    communi|cat|ing
non-Commun|ist
  +s (not a
    Communist Party
    member)
non-commun|ist
  +s (not practising
    communism)
non-competi|tive
non-compli|ance
non com|pos
  (men|tis)
non-conduct|ing
non-conduct|or +s
non-confiden|tial
non-
    confiden|tial|ly
Non|con|form|ism
  Religion
non|con|form|ism
  (general)
Non|con|form|ist
  +s *Religion*
non|con|form|ist
  +s (general)
non|con|form|ity
non-consen|sual
non-contagious
non-content +s
non-conten|tious
non-contribu|tory
non-
    contro|ver|sial
non-cooper|ation
non-custodial
nonda +s
non-delivery
non-
    denomin|ation|al
non|de|script +s
non|de|script|ly
non|de|script|ness
non-destruc|tive
non-domestic
non-drinker +s
non-driver +s
none (not any.
  △ nun)
none +s (canonical
  hour of prayer.
  △ known)

non-earning
non-econom|ic
non-effect|ive
non-ego +s
non-emergency
  attributive
non-English
non|en|tity
  non|en|tities
nones
  plural nones
  (Roman calendar)
none-so-pretty
  (plant)
non-essential +s
none|such (use
  nonsuch)
none|suches
nonet +s
none|the|less
non-Euclid|ean
non-European +s
non-event +s
non-executive
non-existence
non-existent
non-explosive +s
non-fatal
non-fatten|ing
non|feas|ance +s
non-ferrous
non-fiction
non-fiction|al
non-financial
non-flam (= non-
  flammable)
non-flammable
non-fulfil|ment
non-function|al
nong +s
non-
    govern|men|tal
non-human +s
non-infectious
non-inflationary
non-inflect|ed
non-interfer|ence
non-interven|tion
non-
    interven|tion|ist
    +s
non-intoxi|cat|ing
non-invasive
non-iron
non-Jewish
non|join|der +s
non|jur|ing
non|juror +s
non-jury
non-league *Soccer*
non-linear
non-linguis|tic

non-literary
non-living
  attributive
non-logical
non-logical|ly
non-magnet|ic
non-manual
non-material
non-medical
non-member +s
non-member|ship
non-metal
non-metallic
non-militant
non-military
non-minister|ial
non-moral
non-morally
non-Muslim +s
non-native +s
non-natural
non-negoti|able
non-net
non-nuclear
no-no
  no-noes
non-object|ive
non-observance
non-oil (*attributive*
  of trade)
no-nonsense
  attributive
non-operation|al
non-organic
non|par|eil +s
non-
    partici|pat|ing
non-partisan
non-party
  non-parties
non-payer +s
non-payment +s
non-penetra|tive
non-perform|ing
non-person +s
non-person|al
non-physic|al
non-physical|ly
non placet +s
non-playing
non|plus
  non|plusses
  non|plussed
  non|plus|sing
non-poison|ous
non-political
non-porous
non poss|umus
non-product|ive
non-
    product|ive|ly
non-profes|sion|al

non-profit
non-profit-making
non-prolifer|ation
  attributive
non-qualify|ing
  attributive
non-racial
non-reader +s
non-refund|able
non-religious
non-renewable
non-reproduc|tive
non-residence
non-resident +s
non-residen|tial
non-resistance
non-return
  attributive
non-return|able
non-rigid
non-scientif|ic
non-scientist +s
non-sectar|ian
non-select|ive
non|sense +s
non|sens|ical
non|sens|ical|ity
  non|sens|
    ical|ities
non|sens|ical|ly
non sequi|tur +s
non-sexist
  attributive
non-sexual
non-sexual|ly
non-skid
non-slip
non-smoker +s
non-smoking
non-soluble
non-special|ist +s
non-specif|ic
non-standard
non-starter +s
non-statutory
non-stick
non-stop
non-subscriber +s
non|such
  non|suches
non|suit +s
non-surgical
non-swimmer +s
non-taxable
non-taxpay|er +s
non-teaching
  attributive
non-technical
non-threaten|ing
non-toxic
non-tradition|al
non-transfer|able

non-U
non-uniform
non-union
non-urgent
non-usage
non-use
non-user +s
non-verbal
non-verbal|ly
non-vintage
non-violence
non-violent
non-volatile
non-voter +s
non-voting
non-Western
non-white +s
non-word +s
non-working
noo|dle +s
nook +s
nookie (use nooky)
nooky
noon +s
noon|day +s
no one
noon|tide +s
noon|time
Noord|hinder
  (light vessel,
  North Sea)
noose
  attributive
nooses
noosed
noos|ing
Nootka
  plural Nootka *or*
  Noot|kas
noo|trop|ic +s
nopal +s
nope
nor
nor' (= north)
Nora *also* Norah
nor|adren|alin
nor|adren|aline
  (use
  noradrenalin)
Norah *also* Nora
Nor|bert
Nor|dic +s
Nord|kapp
  (Norwegian name
  for North Cape)
Nord|kyn
  (promontory,
  Norway)
Nord-Pas-de-
  Calais (region,
  France)
Nor|een
nor|epin|eph|rine

Nor|folk (county,
  England)
Nor|folk Broads,
  the (region,
  England)
Nor|folk Is|land (in
  SW Pacific)
Nori|ega, Ma|nuel
  (Panamanian
  general and
  statesman)
nork +s
nor|land +s
norm +s
Norma
nor|mal +s
nor|malcy
nor|mal|cies
nor|mal|isa|tion
  Br. +s (use
  normalization)
nor|mal|ise *Br.*
  (use **normalize**)
nor|mal|ises
nor|mal|ised
nor|mal|is|ing
nor|mal|iser *Br.* +s
  (use normalizer)
nor|mal|ity
nor|mal|ities
nor|mal|iza|tion
  +s
nor|mal|ize
nor|mal|izes
nor|mal|ized
nor|mal|iz|ing
nor|mal|izer *Am.*
  +s
nor|mal|ly
Nor|man +s (of
  Normandy; name)
Nor|man, Greg
  (Australian golfer)
Nor|man, Jes|sye
  (American
  soprano)
Nor|mandy
  (region, France)
Nor|man|esque
  Architecture
Nor|man|ise *Br.*
  (use Normanize)
Nor|man|ises
Nor|man|ised
Nor|man|is|ing
Nor|man|ism +s
Nor|man|ize
Nor|man|izes
Nor|man|ized
Nor|man|iz|ing
nor|ma|tive
nor|ma|tive|ly

nor|ma|tive|ness
Norn +s
  Scandinavian
  Mythology
Nor|ris
Nor|r|kö|ping (port,
  Sweden)
Nor|roy *Heraldry*
Norse
Norse|man
  Norse|men
North, the (part of
  country etc.;
  Arctic)
north +s (point;
  direction)
North|al|ler|ton
  (town, England)
North|amp|ton
  (town, England)
North|amp|ton
  shire (county,
  England)
North|ants
  (= Northampton-
  shire)
north|bound
North|cliffe, Lord
  (British newspaper
  proprietor)
North Coun|try
  (region, England)
north-
  country|man
north-
  country|men
North-East, the
  (part of country
  etc.)
north-east (point;
  direction)
north|east|er +s
north-easter|ly
north-easter|lies
north-eastern
north-east
  pas|sage (seaway
  north of Europe
  and Asia)
north-eastward
north-eastwards
norther +s
north|er|ly
north|er|lies
north|ern
North|ern Cir|cars
  (former region,
  India)
North|ern Cross
  (constellation;
  = Cygnus)
north|ern|er +s

north|ern|most
north|ing +s
North|land
North|man
  North|men
north-north-east
north-north-west
North Rhine-
  Westphalia
  (state, Germany)
north-south
  attributive
North|um|ber|land
  (county, England)
North|um|bria
  (region, England)
North|um|brian +s
north|ward
north|wards
North-West, the
  (part of country
  etc.)
north-west (point;
  direction)
north|wester +s
north-wester|ly
  north-wester|lies
north-western
North-West
  Front|ier
  Pro|vince (in NW
  Pakistan)
north-west
  pas|sage (seaway
  north of America)
North-West
  Prov|ince (in
  South Africa)
North|west
  Ter|ri|tor|ies (in
  Canada)
North|west
  Ter|ri|tory
  (region, USA)
north-westward
north-westwards
Nor|way
Nor|we|gian +s
nor'|wester +s
Nor|wich (city,
  England)
no-score draw +s
nose
  noses
  nosed
  nos|ing
nose|bag +s
nose|band +s
nose|bleed +s
nose cap +s
nose-cone +s

nose|dive
  nose|dives
  nose|dived
  nose|div|ing
no-see-em +s
no-see-um +s (use
  no-see-em)
nose flute +s
nose|gay +s
nose|less
nose-piece +s
nose|pipe +s
nose-rag +s
nose|ring +s
nose-to-tail
nose wheel +s
nosey (use nosy)
  nosi|er
  nosi|est
nosh
  noshes
  noshed
  nosh|ing
nosh|ery
  nosh|er|ies
no-show +s
nosh-up +s
nosi|ly
nosi|ness
nos|ing +s
nos|og|raphy
noso|logic|al
nos|ology
nos|tal|gia +s
nos|tal|gic
nos|tal|gic|al|ly
nos|toc +s
Nos|tra|da|mus
  (Provençal
  astrologer)
no-strike *attributive*
nos|tril +s
nos|triled *Am.*
nos|trilled *Br.*
nos|trum
  nos|trums *or*
  nos|tra
nosy
  nosi|er
  nosi|est
Nosy Par|ker +s
not (negative word.
  △ knot)
nota bene
not|abil|ity
  not|abil|ities
not|able +s
not|able|ness
not|ably
Notam +s
no|tar|ial
no|tari|al|ly

no|tar|ise *Br.* (use
  notarize)
no|tar|ises
no|tar|ised
no|tar|is|ing
no|tar|ize
no|tar|izes
no|tar|ized
no|tar|iz|ing
no|tary
  no|tar|ies
no|tate
  no|tates
  no|tated
  no|tat|ing
no|ta|tion +s
nota|tion|al
notch
  notches
  notched
  notch|ing
notcher +s
notchy
  notch|ier
  notchi|est
note
  notes
  noted
  not|ing
note|book +s
note|case +s
note|less
note|let +s
note|pad +s
note|paper +s
note-row +s
note-taking
note|worthi|ness
note|worthy
noth|ing +s
noth|ing|ness
no|tice
  no|tices
  no|ticed
  no|ticing
no|tice|able
no|tice|ably
no|tice|board +s
no|ti|fi|able
no|ti|fi|ca|tion +s
no|tify
  no|ti|fies
  no|ti|fied
  no|ti|fy|ing
no|tion +s
no|tion|al
no|tion|al|ist +s
no|tion|al|ly
no|to|chord +s
no|tori|ety
no|tori|ous
no|tori|ous|ly

no|tor|nis
Notre Dame
  (university, USA)
Notre-Dame
  (cathedral, Paris)
no-trumper +s
no trumps
Not|ting|ham (city,
  England)
Not|ting|ham|
  shire (county,
  England)
Not|ting Hill
  (district, London)
Notts.
  (= Nottingham-
  shire)
not|with|stand|ing
Nou|ad|hi|bou
  (port, Mauritania)
Nou|ak|chott
  (capital of
  Mauritania)
nou|gat +s
nought +s (the
  digit 0; zero.
  △ naught)
noughts and
  crosses
Nouméa (capital of
  New Caledonia)
nou|menal
nou|men|al|ly
nou|menon
  nou|mena
noun +s
noun|al
nour|ish
  nour|ishes
  nour|ished
  nour|ish|ing
nour|ish|er +s
nour|ish|ing|ly
nour|ish|ment +s
nous (common
  sense)
nouse (use nous)
nou|veau riche
  nou|veaux riches
nou|veau roman
  nou|veaux romans
Nou|velle
  Calé|do|nie
  (French name for
  New Caledonia)
nou|velle cuis|ine
  nou|velles
  cuis|ines
nou|velle vague
  nou|velles vagues
nova
  novae *or* novas

Nova Lis|boa
(former name of
Huambo)
Nova Sco|tia
(province,
Canada)
Nova Sco|tian +s
Nov|aya Zemlya
(islands, Arctic
Ocean)
novel +s
nov|el|ese
nov|el|esque
nov|el|ette +s
nov|el|et|tish
nov|el|isa|tion *Br.*
+s (use
novelization)
nov|el|ise *Br.* (use
novelize)
nov|el|ises
nov|el|ised
nov|el|is|ing
nov|el|ist +s
nov|el|is|tic
nov|el|iza|tion +s
nov|el|ize
nov|el|izes
nov|el|ized
nov|el|iz|ing
nov|ella +s
Nov|ello, Ivor
(Welsh actor,
composer, and
playwright)
nov|elty
nov|el|ties
No|vem|ber +s
nov|ena +s
**No|verre, Jean-
Georges** (French
choreographer
and dancer)
Nov|go|rod (city,
Russia)
nov|ice +s
novi|ci|ate +s
Novi Sad (city,
Serbia)
Novo|caine *Propr.*
No|vo|kuz|netsk
(city, Siberia)
Novo|si|birsk (city,
Russia)
no-vote +s
**No|votný,
Anto|nín**
(Czechoslovak
Communist
statesman)
now
now|aday

now|adays
noway
Nowel +s
(*interjection*; use
Nowell.
Christmas; use
Noel)
No|well +s
(*interjection*.
△ Noel)
no|where
no-win
no|wise
nowt (nothing.
△ knout)
nox|ious
nox|ious|ly
nox|ious|ness
noyau
noy|aux
noz|zle +s
nth
nu +s (Greek letter.
△ knew, new)
Nuala
nu|ance
nu|ances
nu|anced
nu|an|cing
nub +s
nub|ble +s
nub|bly
nub|blier
nub|bli|est
nubby
nub|bier
nub|bi|est
Nubia (region of
Egypt and Sudan)
Nu|bian +s
nu|bile
nu|bil|ity
nu|chal
nucif|er|ous
nuciv|or|ous
nu|clear
nuclear-free
nuclear-powered
nu|cle|ase +s
nu|cle|ate
nu|cle|ates
nu|cle|ated
nu|cle|at|ing
nu|cle|ation +s
nu|clei
nu|cle|ic
nu|cle|olar
nu|cle|olus
nu|cle|oli
nu|cleon +s
nu|cle|on|ic

nu|cle|on|ics
nu|cleo|pro|tein +s
nu|cleo|side +s
nu|cleo|syn|thesis
nu|cle|ot|ide +s
nu|cleus
nu|clei
nu|clide +s
nu|clid|ic
nuddy
nude +s
nudge
nudges
nudged
nudg|ing
nudger +s
nudi|branch +s
nud|ism
nud|ist +s
nud|ity
nud|ities
nuée ar|dente
nuées ar|dentes
Nuer
plural **Nuer**
(people; language)
Nuevo León (state,
Mexico)
Nuf|field, Lord
(British car maker)
nu|ga|tory
nug|get +s
nuis|ance +s
nuke
nukes
nuked
nuk|ing
Nu|ku'alofa
(capital of Tonga)
null +s
nulla +s (= nulla-
nulla)
null|lah +s (dry
river bed)
nulla-nulla +s
(Australian
Aboriginal club)
Null|ar|bor Plain
(plain, Australia)
nul|li|fi|ca|tion +s
nul|li|fid|ian +s
nul|li|fier +s
null|ify
null|lifies
null|li|fied
null|li|fy|ing
null|lipara +s
null|lipar|ous
null|li|pore +s
null|ity
null|lities

Numa Pom|pil|ius
(legendary Roman
king)
numb
num|bat +s
num|ber +s +ed
+ing
num|ber crunch|er
+s
**num|ber
crunch|ing**
num|ber|less
num|ber plate +s
Num|ber Ten
(Downing Street,
London)
numb-fish
plural numb-fish
or numb-fishes
numb|ing|ly
num|bles
numb|ly
numb|ness
numb|skull +s (use
numskull)
num|dah +s
numen
nu|mina
nu|mer|able
nu|mer|ably
nu|mer|acy
nu|meral +s
nu|mer|ate
nu|mer|ates
nu|mer|ated
nu|mer|at|ing
nu|mer|ation
nu|mer|ator +s
nu|mer|ic
nu|mer|ic|al
nu|mer|ic|al|ly
nu|mero|logic|al
nu|mer|olo|gist +s
nu|mer|ology
nu|mer|ous
nu|mer|ous|ly
nu|mer|ous|ness
Nu|midia (ancient
kingdom, Africa)
Nu|mid|ian +s
nu|mina
nu|min|ous
nu|mis|mat|ic
**nu|mis|mat|ic|
al|ly**
nu|mis|mat|ics
nu|mis|ma|tist +s
nu|mis|mat|ology
num|mu|lite +s
num|nah +s
num|skull +s

nun +s (member of religious community. △ none)

nun|atak +s

nun-buoy +s

Nunc Di|mit|tis

nun|ci|ature +s

nun|cio +s

nun|cu|pate
nun|cu|pates
nun|cu|pated
nun|cu|pat|ing

nun|cu|pa|tion +s

nun|cu|pa|tive

Nun|eaton (town, England)

nun|hood +s

nun|like

nun|nery
nun|ner|ies

nun|nish

NUPE (= National Union of Public Employees)

nup|tial +s

nurd +s (use nerd)

Nur|em|berg (city, Germany)

Nur|eyev, Ru|dolf (Russian ballet dancer)

Nuri|stan (region, Afghanistan)

nurse
nurses
nursed
nurs|ing

nurse|ling +s (use nursling)

nurse|maid +s +ed +ing

nur|sery
nur|ser|ies

nur|sery|man
nur|sery|men

nurs|ling +s

nur|ture
nur|tures
nur|tured
nur|tur|ing

nur|turer +s

Nut *Egyptian Mythology*

nut
nuts
nut|ted
nut|ting

nu|tant

nu|ta|tion +s

nut brown +s *noun and adjective*

nut-brown
attributive

nut-butter +s

nut|case +s

nut|crack|er +s

nut|gall +s

nut|hatch
nut|hatches

nut|house +s

nut|let +s

nut|like

nut-meat +s

nut|meg +s

nutmeg-apple +s

nut oil +s

nu|tria +s

nu|tri|ent +s

nu|tri|ment +s

nu|tri|men|tal

nu|tri|tion

nu|tri|tion|al

nu|tri|tion|al|ly

nu|tri|tion|ist +s

nu|tri|tious

nu|tri|tious|ly

nu|tri|tious|ness

nu|tri|tive

nut|shell +s

nut|ter +s

nut|ti|ness

nut tree +s

nutty
nut|tier
nut|ti|est

Nuu-chah-nulth
plural Nuu-chah-nulth
(= Nootka)

Nuuk (capital of Greenland)

nux vom|ica +s

nuz|zle
nuz|zles
nuz|zled
nuz|zling

nyala
plural nyala *or* nyalas

Nyanja
plural Nyanja *or* Nyan|jas

Nyasa, Lake (in Africa)

Ny|asa|land (former name of Malawi)

nyc|tal|opia

nyc|ti|trop|ic

nye +s (*archaic* = nide. △ nigh)

Nye|rere, Ju|lius (African statesman)

nyl|ghau +s

nylon +s

nymph +s

nym|phae

nymph|al

nym|phalid +s

nymph|ean

nymph|et +s

nymph|like

nym|pho +s

nym|pho|lepsy
nym|pho|lep|sies

nym|pho|lept +s

nym|pho|lep|tic

nym|pho|mania

nym|pho|maniac +s

Ny|norsk

Nys|lott (Swedish name for Savonlinna)

nys|tag|mic

nys|tag|mus

ny|sta|tin

Nyun|gar

Nyx *Greek Mythology*

Oo

O (used before a name, as in 'O God'. △ oh, owe)

O' (prefix of Irish surnames)

o' (= of; on)

oaf +s

oaf|ish

oaf|ish|ly

oaf|ish|ness

Oahu (island, Hawaii)

oak +s

oak-apple +s

oaken

oak-gall +s

Oak|ham (town, England)

Oak|land (city, USA)

Oak|ley, Annie (American markswoman)

oakum

OAPEC (= Organization of Arab Petroleum Exporting Countries)

oar +s (for rowing. △ or, ore)

oared

oar|fish
plural oar|fish *or* oar|fishes

oar|less

oar|lock +s

oars|man
oars|men

oars|man|ship

oars|woman
oars|women

oar|weed

oasis
oases

oast +s

oast house +s

oat +s

oat|cake +s

oaten

Oates, Titus (Protestant clergyman)

oat-grass
oat-grasses

oath +s

oat|meal

oaty

Oax|aca (state and city, Mexico)

Ob (river, Siberia)

Oba|diah *Bible*

Oban (port, Scotland)

ob|bli|gato
  ob|bli|gatos *or*
  ob|bli|gati

ob|con|ic

ob|con|ic|al

ob|cor|date

ob|dur|acy

ob|dur|ate

ob|dur|ate|ly

ob|dur|ate|ness

obeah

ob|eche +s

obedi|ence +s

obedi|ent

obedi|ent|ly

obei|sance +s

obei|sant

obei|sant|ly

obeli

ob|el|ise *Br.* (use obelize)
  ob|el|ises
  ob|el|ised
  ob|el|is|ing

ob|el|isk +s

ob|el|ize
  ob|el|izes
  ob|el|ized
  ob|el|iz|ing

ob|elus
  obeli

Ober|am|mer|gau (village, Germany)

Ober|hau|sen (city, Germany)

Ob|eron (character in Shakespeare; moon of Uranus)

obese

obese|ness

obes|ity

obey +s +ed +ing

obey|er +s

ob|fus|cate
  ob|fus|cates
  ob|fus|cated
  ob|fus|cat|ing

ob|fus|ca|tion +s

ob|fus|ca|tory

obi +s

obit +s

ob|iter dic|tum
  ob|iter dicta

ob|itu|ar|ial

ob|itu|ar|ist +s

ob|itu|ary
  ob|itu|ar|ies

ob|ject +s +ed +ing

object-ball +s

object-glass
  object-glasses

ob|ject|ifi|ca|tion +s

ob|ject|ify
  ob|jecti|fies
  ob|jecti|fied
  ob|jecti|fy|ing

ob|jec|tion +s

ob|jec|tion|able

ob|jec|tion|able| ness

ob|jec|tion|ably

ob|ject|ival

ob|ject|ive +s

ob|ject|ive|ly

ob|ject|ive|ness

ob|ject|iv|isa|tion *Br.* (use objectivization)

ob|jec|tiv|ise *Br.* (use objectivize)
  ob|jec|tiv|ises
  ob|jec|tiv|ised
  ob|jec|tiv|is|ing

ob|ject|iv|ism

ob|ject|iv|ist +s

ob|ject|iv|is|tic

ob|ject|iv|ity

ob|ject|iv|iza|tion

ob|ject|iv|ize
  ob|ject|iv|izes
  ob|ject|iv|ized
  ob|ject|iv|iz|ing

ob|ject|less

object lesson +s

object|or +s

object-orient|ed

objet d'art
  ob|jets d'art

ob|jur|gate
  ob|jur|gates
  ob|jur|gated
  ob|jur|gat|ing

ob|jur|ga|tion +s

ob|jur|ga|tory

ob|lan|ceo|late

ob|last +s

ob|late +s

ob|la|tion +s

ob|la|tion|al

ob|la|tory

ob|li|gate
  ob|li|gates
  ob|li|gated
  ob|li|gat|ing

ob|li|ga|tion +s

ob|li|ga|tor +s

ob|liga|tor|ily

ob|liga|tory

ob|lige
  ob|liges
  ob|liged
  ob|li|ging

ob|li|gee +s

ob|li|ger +s (generally)

ob|li|ging|ly

ob|li|ging|ness

ob|li|gor +s *Law*

ob|lique
  ob|liques
  ob|liqued
  ob|li|quing

ob|lique|ly

ob|lique|ness

ob|li|quity
  ob|li|qui|ties

ob|lit|er|ate
  ob|lit|er|ates
  ob|lit|er|ated
  ob|lit|er|at|ing

ob|lit|er|ation +s

ob|lit|era|tive

ob|lit|er|ator +s

ob|liv|ion +s

ob|livi|ous

ob|livi|ous|ly

ob|livi|ous|ness

ob|long +s

ob|lo|quy
  ob|lo|quies

ob|nox|ious

ob|nox|ious|ly

ob|nox|ious|ness

oboe +s

oboe d'amore
  oboes d'amore

obo|ist +s

obol +s

Obote, Mil|ton (Ugandan statesman)

ob|ov|ate

O'Brien, Edna (Irish writer)

O'Brien, Flann (Irish writer)

ob|scene

ob|scene|ly

ob|scene|ness

ob|scen|ity
  ob|scen|ities

ob|scur|ant +s

ob|scur|ant|ism

ob|scur|ant|ist +s

ob|scur|ation +s

ob|scure
  ob|scures

ob|scure (*cont.*)
  ob|scured
  ob|scur|ing

ob|scure|ly

ob|scur|ity
  ob|scur|ities

ob|se|cra|tion +s

ob|se|quial

ob|se|quies

ob|se|qui|ous

ob|se|qui|ous|ly

ob|se|qui|ous|ness

ob|serv|able +s

ob|serv|ably

ob|ser|vance +s

ob|ser|vant

ob|ser|vant|ly

ob|ser|va|tion +s

ob|ser|va|tion|al

ob|ser|va|tion| al|ly

ob|ser|va|tory
  ob|ser|va|tor|ies

ob|serve
  ob|serves
  ob|served
  ob|serv|ing

ob|ser|ver +s

ob|sess
  ob|sesses
  ob|sessed
  ob|sess|ing

ob|ses|sion +s

ob|ses|sion|al

ob|ses|sion|al|ism

ob|ses|sion|al|ly

ob|ses|sive +s

ob|ses|sive|ly

ob|ses|sive|ness

ob|sid|ian +s

ob|soles|cence

ob|soles|cent

ob|so|lete

ob|so|lete|ly

ob|so|lete|ness

ob|so|let|ism

obs|tacle +s

obs|tacle race +s

ob|stat (in '*nihil obstat*')

ob|stet|ric

ob|stet|ric|al

ob|stet|ric|al|ly

ob|stet|ri|cian +s

ob|stet|rics

ob|stin|acy

ob|stin|ate

ob|stin|ate|ly

ob|strep|er|ous

ob|strep|er|ous|ly

ob|strep|er|ous| ness

ob|struct +s +ed
+ing
ob|struc|tion +s
ob|struc|tion|ism
ob|struc|tion|ist
+s
ob|struct|ive
ob|struct|ive|ly
ob|struct|ive|ness
ob|struct|or +s
ob|stu|pe|fac|tion
ob|stu|pefy
ob|stu|pe|fies
ob|stu|pe|fied
ob|stu|pe|fy|ing
ob|tain +s +ed
+ing
ob|tain|abil|ity
ob|tain|able
ob|tain|er +s
ob|tain|ment +s
ob|ten|tion +s
ob|trude
ob|trudes
ob|truded
ob|trud|ing
ob|truder +s
ob|tru|sion +s
ob|tru|sive
ob|tru|sive|ly
ob|tru|sive|ness
ob|tund +s +ed
+ing
ob|tur|ate
ob|tur|ates
ob|tur|ated
ob|tur|at|ing
ob|tur|ation
ob|tur|ator +s
ob|tuse
ob|tuse|ly
ob|tuse|ness
ob|tus|ity
ob|verse
ob|verse|ly
ob|ver|sion +s
ob|vert +s +ed
+ing
ob|vi|ate
ob|vi|ates
ob|vi|ated
ob|vi|at|ing
ob|vi|ation
ob|vi|ous
ob|vi|ous|ly
ob|vi|ous|ness
oca|rina +s
O'Casey, Sean
(Irish playwright)
Occam, Wil|liam
of (English
philosopher)

Occam's razor
oc|ca|sion +s +ed
+ing
oc|ca|sion|al
oc|ca|sion|al|ism
oc|ca|sion|al|ist +s
oc|ca|sion|al|ity
oc|ca|sion|al|ly
Oc|ci|dent, the
Oc|ci|den|tal +s
(person)
oc|ci|den|tal
adjective (western)
oc|ci|den|tal|ise
Br. (use
occidentalize)
oc|ci|den|tal|ises
oc|ci|den|tal|ised
oc|ci|den|tal|
is|ing
oc|ci|den|tal|ism
oc|ci|den|tal|ist +s
oc|ci|den|tal|ize
oc|ci|den|tal|izes
oc|ci|den|tal|ized
oc|ci|den|tal|
iz|ing
oc|ci|den|tal|ly
oc|ci|pi|tal +s
oc|ci|put +s
Oc|ci|tan
Oc|ci|tan|ian +s
oc|clude
oc|cludes
oc|cluded
oc|clud|ing
oc|clu|sion +s
oc|clu|sive
oc|cult +s +ed
+ing
oc|cult|ation
oc|cult|ism
oc|cult|ist +s
oc|cult|ly
oc|cult|ness
oc|cu|pancy
oc|cu|pan|cies
oc|cu|pant +s
oc|cu|pa|tion +s
oc|cu|pa|tion|al
oc|cu|pa|tion|al|ly
oc|cu|pier +s
oc|cupy
oc|cu|pies
oc|cu|pied
oc|cu|py|ing
occur
oc|curs
oc|curred
oc|cur|ring
oc|cur|rence +s
oc|cur|rent

ocean +s
ocean|arium
ocean|ariums or
ocean|aria
ocean-going
Ocea|nia (Pacific
and nearby
islands)
Ocean|ian +s
Ocean|ic (of
Oceania)
ocean|ic (of the
ocean)
Ocean|id
Oce|an|ids or
Oce|ani|des
ocean|og|raph|er
+s
oceano|graph|ic
oceano|graph|ic|al
ocean|og|raphy
Ocea|nus Greek
Mythology
ocean|ward
ocel|lar
ocel|late
ocel|lated
ocel|lus
ocelli
oce|lot +s
och interjection
oche +s (in darts)
ocher Am. +s (Br.
ochre)
och|loc|racy
och|loc|ra|cies
och|lo|crat +s
och|lo|crat|ic
och|one
ochre Br. +s (Am.
ocher)
ochre|ish
ochre|ous
och|rous
ochry
ocker +s
Ock|ham,
Wil|liam of (use
Occam)
Ock|ham's razor
(use Occam's
razor)
o'clock
O'Con|nell,
Dan|iel (Irish
nationalist and
social reformer)
oco|tillo +s
octa|chord +s
octad +s
octa|gon +s
oc|tag|on|al

oc|tag|on|al|ly
octa|he|dral
octa|he|dron
octa|he|dra or
octa|he|drons
octal +s
oc|tam|er|ous
oc|tam|eter +s
oc|tane +s
oc|tant +s
oc|tarchy
oc|tarch|ies
octa|roon +s (use
octoroon)
octa|style +s
Octa|teuch
octa|va|lent
oct|ave +s
Oc|ta|via
Oc|ta|vian (Roman
emperor)
oc|tavo +s
oc|ten|nial
octet +s
oc|tette +s
(use octet)
Oc|to|ber +s
Oc|to|brist +s
octo|cen|ten|ary
octo|cen|ten|
ar|ies
octo|decimo +s
octo|gen|ar|ian +s
octo|nar|ian +s
octo|nar|ius
octo|narii
octo|nary
octo|nar|ies
octo|pod +s
octo|pus
octo|puses
octo|roon +s
octo|syl|lab|ic
octo|syl|lable +s
oc|troi +s
OCTU (= Officer
Cadets Training
Unit)
oc|tu|ple
oc|tu|ples
oc|tu|pled
oc|tu|pling
ocu|lar +s
ocu|lar|ist +s
ocu|lar|ly
ocu|late
ocu|list +s
ocu|lis|tic
oculo|nasal
OD
OD's

OD (cont.)
OD'd
OD'ing
(= overdose)
od (hypothetical
force; also = God.
⚠ odd)
odal +s
odal|isque +s
odd +s +er +est
(strange; not
even; etc. ⚠ od)
odd|ball +s
Odd|fel|low +s
odd|ish
odd|ity
odd|ities
odd job +s
odd job|ber +s
odd-job man
odd-job men
oddly
odd|ment +s
odd|ness
odds-on
ode +s
Odense (port,
Denmark)
Oder (river, central
Europe)
Odessa (city and
port, Ukraine)
Odets, Clif|ford
(American
dramatist)
Odette
odeum
odeums or odea
(theatre.
⚠ odium)
Odile
Odin Scandinavian
Mythology
odi|ous
odi|ous|ly
odi|ous|ness
odium (dislike.
⚠ odeum)
odom|eter +s
odom|etry
Odon|ata
odon|ate +s
odon|to|glos|sum
+s
odont|oid
odon|to|logic|al
odon|tolo|gist +s
odon|tol|ogy
odon|to|rhynch|
ous
odor Am. +s (Br.
odour)

odor|ifer|ous
odor|ifer|ous|ly
odor|less Am. (Br.
odourless)
odor|ous
odor|ous|ly
odour Br. +s (Am.
odor)
odour|less Br. (Am.
odorless)
Odys|sean (of
Odysseus)
Odys|seus Greek
Mythology
Odys|sey (epic
poem)
odys|sey +s
(journey)
Oea (ancient name
for Tripoli, Libya)
oe|cist +s
oe|dema Br.
oe|de|mata or
oe|de|mas
(Am. edema)
oe|dema|tous Br.
(Am. edematous)
Oedi|pal
Oedi|pus Greek
Mythology
oeno|logic|al Br.
(Am. enological)
oen|olo|gist Br. +s
(Am. enologist)
oen|ology Br. (Am.
enology)
Oe|none Greek
Mythology
oeno|phile Br. +s
(Am. enophile)
oen|oph|il|ist Br.
+s (Am.
enophilist)
o'er (= over)
Oer|sted, Hans
Chris|tian
(Danish physicist)
oer|sted +s (unit)
oe|sopha|geal Br.
(Am. esophageal)
oe|sopha|gus Br.
oe|soph|agi or
oe|sopha|guses
(Am. esophagus)
oes|tra|diol
oes|tral Br. (Am.
estral)
oes|tro|gen Br. +s
(Am. estrogen)
oes|tro|gen|ic Br.
(Am. estrogenic)

oes|tro|gen|ic|al|ly
Br. (Am.
estrogenically)
oes|trous Br.
adjective (Am.
estrous)
oes|trum Br. (Am.
estrum)
oes|trus Br. noun
(Am. estrus)
oeuvre +s
of (belonging to
etc.)
ofay +s (offensive
white person.
⚠ au fait)
off +s +ed +ing
(away; not on;
gone bad; etc.)
Offa (king of
Mercia)
off-air attributive
offal +s
Of|faly (county,
Republic of
Ireland)
Offa's Dyke
(earthworks,
England and
Wales)
off bal|ance
off|beat +s noun
and adjective
off-break +s
off-center Am.
off-centre Br.
off chance
off-color Am.
off-colour Br.
off|cut +s
off day +s
off-drive
off-drives
off-drove
off-driving
off-driven
off duty
off-duty attributive
Of|fen|bach,
Jacques (German-
born French
composer)
of|fence Br. +s
(Am. offense)
of|fence|less Br.
(Am. offenseless)
of|fend +s +ed
+ing
of|fend|ed|ly
of|fend|er +s
of|fense Am. +s
(Br. offence)

of|fense|less Am.
(Br. offenceless)
of|fen|sive +s
of|fen|sive|ly
of|fen|sive|ness
OFFER (= Office of
Electricity
Regulation)
offer +s +ed +ing
of|fer|er +s
(generally)
of|fer|ing +s
of|fer|or +s Law
and Finance
of|fer|tory
off guard
off|hand
off|hand|ed
off|hand|ed|ly
off|hand|ed|ness
of|fice +s
office-bearer +s
of|fi|cer +s
of|fi|cial +s
of|fi|cial|dom
of|fi|cial|ese
of|fi|cial|ism
of|fi|cial|ly
of|fi|ci|ant +s
of|fi|ci|ate
of|fi|ci|ates
of|fi|ci|ated
of|fi|ci|at|ing
of|fi|ci|ation
of|fi|ci|ator +s
of|fi|cin|al
of|fi|cin|al|ly
of|fi|cious
of|fi|cious|ly
of|fi|cious|ness
off|ing
off|ish
off|ish|ly
off|ish|ness
off-key
off-licence Br. +s
off-limits
off-line
off|load +s +ed
+ing
off-peak
off-piste
off-price
off|print +s
off-putting
off-putting|ly
off-road attributive
off-roader +s
off-roading
off-screen
off-season +s
off|set
off|sets

off|set (*cont.*)
off|set
off|set|ting
off|shoot +s
off|shore
off|side +s
  (*Football etc.*; of
  vehicle)
off side *Cricket*
off|sider +s
off|spring
  plural off|spring
off-stage *attributive*
off-street *attributive*
off-the-cuff
  attributive
off-the-shelf
  attributive
off-the-shoulder
  attributive
off-the-wall
  attributive
off-time +s (slack
  period. △ oft-
  times)
off-white +s
Ofgas (= Office of
  Gas Supply)
OFSTED (= Office
  for Standards in
  Education)
oft
Oftel (= Office of
  Telecommuni-
  cations)
often +er +est
often|times
oft-quoted
oft-repeat|ed
oft-times (often.
  △ off-times)
Ofwat (= Office of
  Water Services)
Oga|den (region,
  Ethiopia)
ogam +s (use
  ogham)
og|doad +s
ogee +s
ogee'd
ogham +s
ogival
ogive +s
ogle
  ogles
  ogled
  og|ling
ogler +s
OGPU (USSR
  counter-
  revolutionary
  organization)

ogre +s
ogre|ish
ogress
  ogresses
ogrish (use
  ogreish)
Ogy|gian
oh (expression of
  surprise, pain, etc.;
  zero. △ O)
O'Hig|gins,
  Ber|nardo
  (Chilean
  revolutionary
  leader)
Ohio (state, USA)
Ohm, Georg
  (German
  physicist)
ohm +s (unit.
  △ om)
ohm|age
ohmic
ohm|meter +s
Ohm's law
oho
ohone (use
  ochone)
Ohrid, Lake (in SE
  Europe)
oi
oi|dium
  oidia
oik +s
oil +s +ed +ing
oil-based
oil-bird +s
oil|cake +s
oil can +s
oil|cloth +s
oil color *Am.* +s
oil col|our *Br.* +s
oil drum +s
oiler +s
oil|field +s
oil-fired
oil gauge +s
oil gland +s
oil|ily
oili|ness
oil lamp +s
oil|less
oil|man
  oil|men
oil-meal
oil paint +s
oil paint|ing +s
oil-palm +s
oil pan +s
oil-paper
oil plat|form +s

oil-press
  oil-presses
oil-producing
oil rig +s
oil-sand
oil|seed +s
oil-shale +s
oil|skin +s
oil slick +s
oil|stone +s
oil tank|er +s
oil well +s
oily
  oili|er
  oili|est
oink +s +ed +ing
oint|ment +s
Oire|ach|tas
  (Irish legislature)
Oisin (Irish name
  for Ossian)
Ojibwa
  plural Ojibwa *or*
  Ojib|was
OK +s *noun*
OK
  OK's
  OK'd
  OK'ing
  verb
okapi
  plural okapi *or*
  oka|pis
Okara (city, India)
Oka|vango (river,
  Africa)
okay +s +ed +ing
  (use OK)
Oka|yama (city,
  Japan)
Okee|cho|bee,
  Lake (in USA)
O'Keeffe, Geor|gia
  (American
  painter)
Oke|fe|no|kee
  Swamp (in USA)
okey-doke
okey-dokey
Ok|hotsk, Sea of
  (inlet, NW Pacific)
Oki|nawa (region
  and island, Japan)
Okla|homa (state,
  USA)
Okla|homa City
  (city, USA)
okra +s
okta
  plural okta *or*
  oktas

Olaf (Norwegian
  kings)
Öland (island,
  Baltic Sea)
Ol|bers' para|dox
old +er +est
old age *noun*
old-age *attributive*
Old Bailey (law
  court, London)
olden
olde worlde (old
  and quaint.
  △ old-world)
old-fashioned
Old|ham (town,
  England)
oldie +s
old|ish
old-maidish
old|ness
Old Sarum (hill
  and former town,
  England)
old|ster +s
Old Style (dates)
old-style (*attributive*
  in a former style)
Old Testa|ment
  noun and
  attributive
old-time *attributive*
old-timer +s
Ol|du|vai Gorge
  (in Tanzania)
Old Vic (theatre,
  London)
old-womanish
Old World (*noun*
  and attributive
  Europe, Asia, and
  Africa)
old-world (of old
  times. △ olde
  worlde)
ole|aceous
ole|agin|ous
ole|an|der +s
ole|as|ter +s
ole|ate +s
olec|ra|non +s
ole|fin +s
ole|fine +s (use
  olefin)
oleic
ole|if|er|ous
oleo|graph +s
oleo|mar|gar|ine
  +s
ole|om|eter +s
oleo|resin +s
oleum

O level +s
ol¦fac¦tion
ol¦fac¦tive
ol¦fac¦tory
Olga
olib¦anum
oli¦garch +s
oli¦garch¦ic
oli¦garch¦ic¦al
oli¦garch¦ic¦al¦ly
oli¦garchy
  oli¦garch¦ies
oligo¦carp¦ous
Oligo¦cene *Geology*
oligo¦chaete +s
oligo¦dendro¦cyte
  +s
oligo¦mer +s
oli¦gop¦ol¦ist +s
oli¦gop¦ol¦is¦tic
oli¦gop¦oly
  oli¦gop¦olies
oligo¦sac¦char¦ide
  +s
oligo¦troph¦ic
oli¦got¦rophy
olio +s
oliv¦aceous
oliv¦ary
Olive (name)
olive +s (tree; fruit)
olive drab +s *noun*
  and adjective
olive-drab
  attributive
olive green +s
  noun and adjective
olive-green
  attributive
Oli¦ver (in the
  Chanson de
  Roland; name)
Olives, Mount of
  (in Israel)
Olivia
Oliv¦ier, Laur¦ence
  (Lord Olivier,
  English actor and
  director)
oliv¦ine +s
olla pod¦rida +s
Ollie
olm +s
Olmec
  plural Olmec
Olmos (town, Peru)
Olo¦mouc (city,
  Czech Republic)
ol¦or¦oso +s
Ol¦sztyn (city,
  Poland)
Olwen

Olym¦pia (site of
  pan-Hellenic
  Olympic Games;
  city, USA)
Olym¦piad +s
Olym¦pian +s
Olym¦pic
Olym¦pus, Mount
  (in Greece)
om (mantra.
  ⚠ ohm)
Omagh (town,
  Northern Ireland)
Omaha
  plural Omaha *or*
  Oma¦has
  (American Indian)
Omaha (city, USA;
  D-Day beach)
Oman
Oman, Gulf of
  (inlet of Arabian
  Sea)
Omani +s
Omar (Muslim
  caliph)
Omar Khay¦yám
  (Persian poet,
  mathematician,
  and astronomer)
oma¦sum
  omasa
Omay¦yad +s (use
  Umayyad)
ombre (card game)
ombré (shaded)
om¦brogen¦ous
om¦brol¦ogy
om¦brom¦eter +s
om¦buds¦man
  om¦buds¦men
Om¦dur¦man (city,
  Sudan)
omega +s
om¦elet +s (use
  omelette)
om¦elette +s
omen +s +ed +ing
omen¦tal
omen¦tum
  omenta
om¦ertà
omi¦cron +s
om¦in¦ous
om¦in¦ous¦ly
om¦in¦ous¦ness
omis¦sible
omis¦sion +s
omis¦sive
omit
  omits

omit (*cont.*)
  omit¦ted
  omit¦ting
om¦ma¦tid¦ium
  om¦ma¦tidia
omni¦bus
  omni¦buses
omni¦com¦pe¦
              tence
omni¦com¦pe¦tent
omni¦dir¦ec¦tion¦al
omni¦fari¦ous
om¦nif¦ic
om¦nigen¦ous
om¦nipo¦tence
om¦nipo¦tent
om¦nipo¦tent¦ly
omni¦pres¦ence
omni¦pres¦ent
om¦nis¦ci¦ence
om¦nis¦ci¦ent
om¦nis¦ci¦ent¦ly
om¦nium
  gath¦erum
omni¦vore +s
om¦niv¦or¦ous
om¦niv¦or¦ous¦ly
om¦niv¦or¦ous¦
              ness
om¦pha¦los
om¦phal¦ot¦omy
  om¦phal¦oto¦mies
Omsk (city, Russia)
on
on¦ager +s
onan¦ism
onan¦ist +s
onan¦is¦tic
Onas¦sis,
  Aris¦totle (Greek
  shipping magnate
  and tycoon)
Onas¦sis, Jackie
  (US First Lady)
on board *adverbial*
  and preposition
on-board *attributive*
once
once-over +s
oncer +s
on¦cho¦cer¦cia¦sis
onco¦gene +s
onco¦gen¦ic
on¦cogen¦ous
on¦colo¦gist +s
on¦col¦ogy
on¦com¦ing +s
on¦cost +s
ondes mar¦tenot
  plural ondes
  mar¦tenot
on dit +s

one +s (single;
  number; a person.
  ⚠ won)
one-armed
one¦fold
Onega, Lake (in
  Russia)
one-horse
  attributive
On¦eida
  plural On¦eida *or*
  On¦eidas
O'Neill, Eu¦gene
  (American
  playwright)
oneir¦ic
oneiro¦crit¦ic +s
oneir¦olo¦gist +s
oneir¦ology
oneiro¦man¦cer +s
oneiro¦mancy
one-iron +s
one-liner +s
one-man
  attributive
one¦ness
one-night stand
  +s
one-off +s
one-piece +s
oner +s (£1;
  remarkable person
  or thing)
oner¦ous
oner¦ous¦ly
oner¦ous¦ness
one¦self
one-sided
one-sidedly
one-sidedness
one-step
  one-steps
one-stop *attributive*
one-time *attributive*
one-to-one
one-two +s
one-up *adjective*
one-upmanship
one-way *adjective*
on¦flow +s
on¦glaze
on¦going
on¦going¦ness
onion +s
onion-skin +s
  (paper)
on¦iony
onkus
on-line
on¦look¦er +s
on¦look¦ing
only

only-begotten
on-off *adjective*
ono|mas|tic
ono|mas|tics
ono|mato|poeia
ono|mato|poe|ic
ono|mato|poeic|
　　　　al|ly
ono|mato|po|et|ic
On|on|daga
　plural On|on|daga
　or On|on|da|gas
on|rush
　on|rushes
on-screen
onset +s *noun*
　(beginning)
on-set *adjective and*
　adverb (on a film
　set)
on|shore
on|side *Football etc.*
on side *Cricket*
on-site *attributive*
on|slaught +s
on-stage *attributive*
on-street *attributive*
On|tario (province,
　Canada)
On|tario, Lake (in
　N. America)
on-the-spot
　attributive
onto (use on to
　unless sense is 'to
　a position on' and
　is otherwise
　unclear)
on to
onto|gen|esis
onto|gen|et|ic
onto|gen|et|ic|
　　　　al|ly
onto|gen|ic
onto|gen|ic|al|ly
on|togeny
onto|logic|al
onto|logic|al|ly
on|tolo|gist +s
ontol|ogy
onus
　onuses
on|ward
on|wards
ony|choph|oran
　+s
onym|ous
onyx
　onyxes
oo|cyte +s
oo|dles

oof
oofi|ness
oofy
　oof|ier
　oofi|est
oog|am|ous
oog|amy
oo|gen|esis
oo|gen|et|ic
ooh +s +ed +ing
oo|lite +s
oo|lith +s
oo|lit|ic
oo|logic|al
oolo|gist +s
ool|ogy
oo|long
oo|miak +s (use
　umiak)
oom|pah +s
oomph
Oona *also* Oo|nagh
oo|phor|ec|tomy
oo|phor|
　　　　ec|to|mies
oops
oops-a-daisy
Oort, Jan
　Hen|drik (Dutch
　astronomer;
　cloud)
ooze
　oozes
　oozed
　ooz|ing
ooz|ily
oozi|ness
oozy
　ooz|ier
　oozi|est
op (= operation)
op. (= opus;
　operator)
opa|ci|fier +s
opa|cify
　opaci|fies
　opaci|fied
　opaci|fy|ing
opa|city
opah +s
opal +s
opal|esce
　opal|esces
　opal|esced
　opal|es|cing
opal|es|cence
opal|es|cent
opal|ine
opaque
opaque|ly
opaque|ness

op art
op. cit. (= opere
　citato)
OPEC
　(= Organization of
　Petroleum
　Exporting
　Countries)
Opel, Wil|helm
　von (German car
　maker)
open +s +ed +ing
open|able
open air *noun*
open-air *adjective*
open-armed
open|cast
open-door *adjective*
open-ended
open|er +s
open-eyed
open-faced
open-handed
open-handed|ly
open-handed|ness
open-hearted
open-hearted|ness
open-hearth
　pro|cess
open-heart
　sur|gery
open house
open|ing +s
open|ing time +s
open|ly
open-minded
open-minded|ly
open-minded|ness
open-mouthed
open-necked
　attributive
open|ness
open-plan
open pri|son +s
open-reel
open-side
　attributive
open-top
open-topped
open|work
opera +s (dramatic
　musical work)
opera (plural of
　opus)
op|er|abil|ity
op|er|able
opera buffa
　opera buffas *or*
　opere buffe
opéra com|ique
　op|éras com|iques

opera glasses
opera hat +s
opera house +s
op|er|and +s
opera seria
　opera serias *or*
　opere serie
op|er|ate
　op|er|ates
　op|er|ated
　op|er|at|ing
op|er|at|ic
op|er|at|ic|al|ly
op|er|at|ics
op|er|ation +s
op|er|ation|al
op|er|ation|al|ise
　Br. (use
　operationalize)
　op|er|ation|al|ises
　op|er|ation|al|
　　　　　　ised
　op|er|ation|al|
　　　　　　is|ing
op|er|ation|al|ize
　op|er|ation|al|izes
　op|er|ation|al|
　　　　　　ized
　op|er|ation|al|
　　　　　　iz|ing
op|er|ation|al|ly
op|era|tive +s
op|era|tive|ly
op|era|tive|ness
op|er|ator +s
oper|cu|lar
oper|cu|late
oper|cu|lum
　oper|cula
op|er|etta +s
op|eron +s
Ophe|lia
ophi|cleide +s
ophid|ian +s
ophi|ol|atry
ophi|olo|gist +s
ophi|ology
Ophir (*Bible* region)
oph|ite +s
oph|it|ic
Ophiu|chus
　(constellation)
oph|thal|mia
oph|thal|mic
oph|thal|mitis
oph|thal|mo|
　　　　　logic|al
oph|thal|molo|gist
　+s
oph|thal|mol|ogy
oph|thal|mo|scope
　+s

oph|thal|mo|
    scop|ic
oph|thal|mo|
    scop|ic|al|ly
oph|thal|
    mos|copy
opi|ate
  opi|ates
  opi|ated
  opi|at|ing
Opie, John
  (English painter)
opine
  opines
  opined
  opin|ing
opin|ion +s
opin|ion|ated
opin|ion|ated|ly
opin|ion|ated|ness
opin|ion|ative
opi|oid +s
opi|som|eter +s
opis|tho|graph +s
opis|thog|raphy
opium
opium|ise Br. (use
  opiumize)
  opium|ises
  opium|ised
  opium|is|ing
opium|ize
  opium|izes
  opium|ized
  opium|iz|ing
opop|anax
Oporto (city,
  Portugal)
opos|sum +s
Op|pen|heimer,
  Ju|lius Rob|ert
  (American
  physicist)
op|pi|dan +s
oppo +s
op|pon|ency
op|pon|ent +s
op|por|tune
op|por|tune|ly
op|por|tune|ness
op|por|tun|ism
op|por|tun|ist +s
op|por|tun|is|tic
op|por|tun|is|tic|
  al|ly
op|por|tun|ity
  op|por|tun|ities
op|pos|able
op|pose
  op|poses
  op|posed
  op|pos|ing

op|poser +s
op|pos|ite +s
op|pos|ite|ly
op|pos|ite|ness
Op|pos|ition
  (party)
op|pos|ition +s
op|pos|ition|al
op|posi|tive
op|press
  op|presses
  op|pressed
  op|press|ing
op|pres|sion +s
op|pres|sive
op|pres|sive|ly
op|pres|sive|ness
op|press|or +s
op|pro|bri|ous
op|pro|bri|ous|ly
op|pro|brium
  op|pro|bria
op|pugn +s +ed
  +ing
op|pug|nance
op|pug|nancy
op|pug|nant
op|pug|na|tion
op|pugn|er +s
opsi|math +s
op|sim|athy
op|son|ic
op|so|nin +s
opt +s +ed +ing
opt|ant +s
opta|tive
opta|tive|ly
optic +s (measure
  for spirits) Propr.
optic (of the eye)
op|tic|al +s
op|tic|al|ly
op|ti|cian +s
op|tics
op|tima
op|ti|mal
op|ti|mal|ly
op|ti|misa|tion Br.
  (use
  optimization)
op|ti|mise Br. (use
  optimize)
  op|ti|mises
  op|ti|mised
  op|ti|mis|ing
op|ti|mism
op|ti|mist +s
op|ti|mis|tic
op|ti|mis|tic|al|ly
op|ti|miza|tion
op|ti|mize
  op|ti|mizes

op|ti|mize (cont.)
  op|ti|mized
  op|ti|miz|ing
op|ti|mum
  op|tima or
  op|ti|mums
op|tion +s
op|tion|al
op|tion|al|ity
op|tion|al|ly
opto|elec|tron|ics
op|tom|eter +s
opto|met|ric
op|tom|etrist +s
op|tom|etry
opto|phone +s
opt-out +s noun
  and attributive
opu|lence
opu|lent
opu|lent|ly
opun|tia +s
opus
  opuses or opera
opus|cule +s
opus|cu|lum
  opus|cula
Opus Dei
  (organization)
opus dei (worship)
or (conjunction;
  Heraldry gold.
  ⚠ oar, ore)
orach +s (use
  orache)
or|ache +s
or|acle +s
or|acu|lar
or|acu|lar|ity
or|acu|lar|ly
oracy
Ora|dea (city,
  Romania)
oral +s (of or
  pertaining to the
  mouth. ⚠ aural)
oral|ism
oral|ist +s
oral|ity
or|al|ly
Oran (port, Algeria)
Or|ange (town,
  France)
Or|ange (Dutch
  royal house)
or|ange +s
or|ange|ade
Or|ange Free
  State (province,
  South Africa)
Or|ange|ism

Or|ange|man
  Or|ange|men
Or|ange Order (in
  Northern Ireland)
Or|ange River (in
  South Africa)
or|an|gery
  or|an|ger|ies
or|ange stick +s
orange-wood
orang-outang +s
  (use orang-utan)
orang-utan +s
Or|anje|stad
  (capital of Aruba)
Ora|şul Sta|lin
  (former name of
  Braşov)
orate
  orates
  orated
  orat|ing
ora|tion +s
ora|tor +s
ora|tor|ial
ora|tor|ian +s
ora|tor|ic|al
ora|torio +s
ora|tory
  ora|tor|ies
orb +s
or|bicu|lar
or|bicu|lar|ity
or|bicu|lar|ly
or|bicu|late
Or|bi|son, Roy
  (American singer)
orbit +s +ed +ing
or|bit|al +s
or|bit|er +s
orc +s (monster.
  ⚠ auk)
orca +s
Or|ca|dian +s
Or|cagna (Italian
  painter)
orch|ard +s
orch|ard|ing
orch|ard|ist +s
orch|ard|man
  orch|ard|men
or|ches|tic
or|ches|tra +s
or|ches|tral
or|ches|tral|ly
or|ches|trate
  or|ches|trates
  or|ches|trated
  or|ches|trat|ing
or|ches|tra|tion +s
or|ches|tra|tor +s
or|ches|trina +s

or¦chid+s
or¦chid¦aceous
or¦chid¦ist+s
or¦chid¦ology
or¦chil+s
or¦chilla+s
or¦chis
  or¦chises
or¦chi¦tis
orcin
or¦cinol
Orczy, Baron¦ess
  (Hungarian-born
  British writer)
or¦dain+s +ed
  +ing
or¦dain¦er+s
or¦dain¦ment+s
or¦deal+s
order+s +ed +ing
order book+s
or¦der¦er+s
order form+s
or¦der¦ing+s
or¦der¦li¦ness
or¦der¦ly
  or¦der¦lies
order paper+s
or¦din¦aire (in 'vin
  ordinaire')
or¦din¦al+s
or¦din¦ance+s
  (decree; rite.
  △ ordnance,
  ordonnance)
or¦din¦and+s
or¦din¦ar¦ily
or¦din¦ari¦ness
or¦din¦ary
  or¦din¦ar¦ies
or¦din¦ate+s
  Mathematics
or¦din¦ation+s
ord¦nance (guns.
  △ ordinance,
  ordonnance)
or¦don¦nance+s
  (arrangement of
  literary work etc.
  △ ordinance,
  ordnance)
Or¦do¦vi¦cian
  Geology
ord¦ure+s
Ord¦zho¦ni¦kidze
  (former name of
  Vladikavkaz)
ore +s (mineral.
  △ oar, or)
øre
  plural øre

øre (cont.)
  (Danish or
  Norwegian
  currency)
öre
  plural öre
  (Swedish
  currency)
oread+s
Öre¦bro (city,
  Sweden)
or¦ec¦tic
ore¦gano
Ore¦gon (state,
  USA)
Orel (city, Russia)
Ore Moun¦tains
  (English name for
  the Erzgebirge)
Oren¦burg (city,
  Russia)
Oreo+s Propr.
ore¦og¦raphy (use
  orography)
Ores¦tes Greek
  Mythology
Øre¦sund (channel
  between Sweden
  and Zealand)
ore¦weed (use
  oarweed)
orfe +s (fish)
Orff, Carl (German
  composer)
organ+s
organ-blower+s
or¦gan¦die Br. +s
or¦gandy Am.
  or¦gan¦dies
or¦gan¦elle+s
organ-grinder+s
or¦gan¦ic
or¦gan¦ic¦al¦ly
or¦gan¦is¦able Br.
  (use organizable)
or¦gan¦isa¦tion Br.
  +s (use
  organization)
or¦gan¦isa¦tion¦al
  Br. (use
  organizational)
or¦gan¦isa¦tion¦
  al¦ly Br. (use
  organizationally)
or¦gan¦ise Br. (use
  organize)
or¦gan¦ises
or¦gan¦ised
or¦gan¦is¦ing
or¦gan¦iser Br. +s
  (use organizer)
or¦gan¦ism +s

or¦gan¦ist+s
or¦gan¦iz¦able
or¦gan¦iza¦tion+s
or¦gan¦iza¦tion¦al
or¦gan¦iza¦tion¦
  al¦ly
or¦gan¦ize
or¦gan¦izes
or¦gan¦ized
or¦gan¦iz¦ing
or¦gan¦izer+s
organ loft+s
or¦gano¦chlor¦ine
  +s
or¦gano¦lep¦tic
or¦gano¦met¦al¦lic
or¦ga¦non+s
or¦gano¦
      phos¦phate+s
or¦gano¦
      phos¦phorus
or¦gano¦sul¦fur Am.
or¦gano¦sul¦phur Br.
or¦gano¦ther¦apy
organ pipe+s
organ-screen+s
organ stop+s
or¦ganum
  or¦gana
or¦ganza+s
or¦gan¦zine+s
or¦gasm+s
or¦gas¦mic
or¦gas¦mic¦al¦ly
or¦gas¦tic
or¦gas¦tic¦al¦ly
or¦geat+s
or¦gi¦as¦tic
or¦gi¦as¦tic¦al¦ly
or¦gu¦lous
orgy
  or¦gies
oribi
  plural oribi or
  ori¦bis
oriel+s
Ori¦ent, the (the
  East)
ori¦ent +s +ed
  +ing (to place or
  direct)
Orien¦tal+s (of the
  East; person)
orien¦tal (eastern)
orien¦tal¦ise Br.
  (use orientalize)
orien¦tal¦ises
orien¦tal¦ised
orien¦tal¦is¦ing
orien¦tal¦ism
orien¦tal¦ist +s

orien¦tal¦ize
orien¦tal¦izes
orien¦tal¦ized
orien¦tal¦iz¦ing
orien¦tal¦ly
orien¦tate
orien¦tates
orien¦tated
orien¦tat¦ing
orien¦ta¦tion+s
orien¦ta¦tion¦al
orien¦teer+s +ing
ori¦fice+s
ori¦flamme+s
ori¦gami
ori¦gan+s
ori¦ganum+s
Ori¦gen (early
  Christian scholar)
ori¦gin+s
ori¦gin¦al+s
ori¦gin¦al¦ity
ori¦gin¦al¦ly
ori¦gin¦ate
ori¦gin¦ates
ori¦gin¦ated
ori¦gin¦at¦ing
ori¦gin¦ation+s
ori¦gina¦tive
ori¦gin¦ator+s
Ori¦mul¦sion Propr.
ori¦nasal
O-ring+s
Ori¦noco (river, S.
  America)
ori¦ole+s
Orion (Greek
  Mythology;
  constellation)
ori¦son+s
Orissa (state, India)
Oriya
  Ori¦yas
ork+s (monster;
  use orc. △ auk)
Ork¦ney (= Orkney
  Islands)
Ork¦ney Is¦lands
  (off Scotland)
Ork¦neys
  (= Orkney
  Islands)
Or¦lando (city,
  USA)
orle +s (Heraldry
  border. △ all, awl)
Or¦lé¦an¦ais
  plural Or¦lé¦an¦ais
Or¦lean¦ist +s
Or¦leans (English
  name for Orléans)

Or|léans (city, France)

Orlon *Propr.*

orlop +s

Or|mazd (alternative name for Ahura Mazda)

ormer +s

or|molu

Ormuz (alternative name for Hormuz)

or|na|ment +s +ed +ing

or|na|men|tal +s

or|na|men|tal|ism

or|na|men|tal|ist +s

or|na|men|tal|ly

or|na|men|ta|tion +s

or|nate

or|nate|ly

or|nate|ness

or|neri|ness

or|nery

or|nith|ic

or|ni|this|chian +s

or|ni|tho|logic|al

or|ni|tho|logic| al|ly

or|ni|tholo|gist +s

or|ni|thol|ogy

or|ni|tho|mancy

or|ni|tho|pod +s

or|ni|tho| rhyn|chus

or|ni|tho| rhyn|chuses

or|ni|thos|copy

oro|gen|esis

oro|gen|et|ic

oro|gen|ic

or|ogeny

oro|graph|ic

oro|graph|ic|al

or|og|raphy

oro|ide +s

oro|logic|al

or|olo|gist +s

or|ol|ogy

Oron|tes (river, Asia)

oro|tund

orphan +s +ed +ing

or|phan|age +s

or|phan|hood

or|phan|ise *Br.* (use orphanize)

or|phan|ises

or|phan|ise (*cont.*)

or|phan|ised

or|phan|is|ing

or|phan|ize

or|phan|izes

or|phan|ized

or|phan|iz|ing

Orph|ean

Orph|eus *Greek Mythology*

Orph|ic

Orph|ism (ancient mystic religion; art movement)

or|phrey +s

or|pi|ment

orpin +s (use orpine)

or|pine +s

orra

or|rery

or|rer|ies

orris

or|rises

orris-powder

orris root

Orsk (city, Russia)

Orson

or|tan|ique +s

Or|tega, Dan|iel (Nicaraguan president)

ortho|ceph|al|ic

ortho|chro|mat|ic

ortho|clase +s

ortho|don|tia

ortho|don|tic

ortho|don|tics

ortho|don|tist +s

ortho|dox

ortho|dox|ly

ortho|doxy

ortho|dox|ies

ortho|ep|ic

ortho|ep|ist +s

ortho|epy

ortho|gen|esis

ortho|gen|et|ic

ortho|gen|et|ic| al|ly

orth|og|nath|ous

orth|og|on|al +s

orth|og|on|al|ly

orth|og|raph|er +s

ortho|graph|ic

ortho|graph|ic|al

ortho|graph|ic| al|ly

orth|og|raphy

ortho-hydrogen

ortho|paed|ic *Br.*

ortho|paed|ics *Br.*

ortho|paed|ist *Br.* +s

ortho|ped|ic *Am.*

ortho|ped|ics *Am.*

ortho|ped|ist *Am.* +s

orth|op|teran +s

orth|op|ter|ous

orth|op|tic

orth|op|tics

orth|op|tist +s

ortho|rhom|bic

ortho|tone +s

or|to|lan +s

Orton, Ar|thur (English butcher, the 'Tichborne claimant')

Orton, Joe (English playwright)

Oruro (city, Bolivia)

Or|vi|eto (town, Italy)

Or|well, George (English writer)

Or|well|ian

oryx

  plural oryx

Osage or|ange

Osaka (city, Japan)

Os|bert

Os|borne, John (English dramatist)

Oscan

Oscar +s (film award; name)

os|cil|late

os|cil|lates

os|cil|lated

os|cil|lat|ing

os|cil|la|tion +s

os|cil|la|tor +s

os|cil|la|tory

os|cil|lo|gram +s

os|cil|lo|graph +s

os|cil|lo|graph|ic

os|cil|log|raphy

os|cil|lo|scope +s

os|cil|lo|scop|ic

os|cine

os|cin|ine

os|ci|ta|tion +s

os|cula (plural of osculum)

os|cu|lant

os|cu|lar *adjective*

os|cu|late

os|cu|lates

os|cu|lated

os|cu|lat|ing

os|cu|la|tion +s

os|cu|la|tory

os|cu|lum

os|cula

Osh (city, Kyrgyzstan)

Osh|awa (city, Canada)

osier +s

osier bed +s

Osi|jek (city, Croatia)

Os|iris *Egyptian Mythology*

Osler, Wil|liam (Canadian-born physician and classical scholar)

Oslo (capital of Norway)

Osman (founder of Turkish Ottoman or Osmanli dynasty)

Os|manli +s

osmic

os|mic|al|ly

os|mium

osmo|regu|la|tion

os|mo|sis

os|mo|ses

os|mot|ic

os|mot|ic|al|ly

os|mund +s

os|munda +s

Os|na|brück (city, Germany)

os|prey +s

Ossa, Mount (in Greece or Tasmania)

os|sein

os|se|ous

Os|sete +s

Os|se|tia, North and South (regions, Russia and Georgia)

Os|se|tian +s

ossia

Os|sian (legendary Irish warrior)

Os|si|an|ic

os|sicle +s

Ossie (name)

Ossie +s (Australian; use Aussie)

os|sif|ic

os|si|fi|ca|tion +s

os|si|frage +s

os¦sify
  os¦si¦fies
  os¦si¦fied
  os¦si¦fy¦ing
osso bucco
os¦su¦ary
  os¦su¦ar¦ies
Ost¦ade, Adri¦aen
  van (Dutch
  painter)
os¦te¦itis
Ost¦end (port,
  Belgium)
os¦ten¦sible
os¦ten¦sibly
os¦ten¦sive
os¦ten¦sive¦ly
os¦ten¦sive¦ness
os¦ten¦sory
  os¦ten¦sor¦ies
os¦ten¦ta¦tion
os¦ten¦ta¦tious
os¦ten¦ta¦tious¦ly
osteo¦arth¦rit¦ic
osteo¦arth¦ritis
osteo¦gen¦esis
osteo¦gen¦et¦ic
oste¦ogeny
oste¦og¦raphy
osteo¦logic¦al
osteo¦logic¦al¦ly
oste¦olo¦gist +s
oste¦ology
osteo¦mal¦acia
osteo¦mal¦acic
osteo¦mye¦litis
osteo¦path +s
osteo¦path¦ic
oste¦op¦athy
osteo¦phyte +s
osteo¦por¦osis
Ostia (ancient city,
  Italy)
os¦tin¦ato +s
ost¦ium
  ostia
ost¦ler +s
Ost¦mark +s
  (former East
  German currency)
Ost¦poli¦tik
os¦tra¦cise Br. (use
  ostracize)
  os¦tra¦cises
  os¦tra¦cised
  os¦tra¦cis¦ing
os¦tra¦cism
os¦tra¦cize
  os¦tra¦cizes
  os¦tra¦cized
  os¦tra¦ciz¦ing

os¦tra¦con
  os¦traca
Ost¦rava (city,
  Czech Republic)
os¦trich
  os¦triches
Os¦tro¦goth +s
Os¦tro¦goth¦ic
Ost¦wald,
  Fried¦rich
  Wil¦helm
  (German chemist)
Os¦wald (English
  saint; name)
Os¦wald, Lee
  Har¦vey
  (American alleged
  assassin of John F.
  Kennedy)
Oś¦wię¦cim (Polish
  name for
  Auschwitz)
Otago (region, New
  Zealand)
otary
  otar¦ies
other +s
other-direct¦ed
other¦ness
other¦where
other¦wise
other-worldli¦ness
other-worldly
Oth¦man
  (alternative name
  for Osman)
Otho, Mar¦cus
  Sal¦vius (Roman
  emperor)
otic
oti¦ose
oti¦ose¦ly
oti¦ose¦ness
Otis, Eli¦sha
  Graves
  (American
  inventor)
ot¦itis
oto¦laryn¦go¦
            logic¦al
oto¦laryn¦golo¦gist
  +s
oto¦laryn¦gol¦ogy
oto¦lith +s
oto¦lith¦ic
oto¦logic¦al
ot¦olo¦gist +s
otol¦ogy
Otomi
  plural Otomi
oto¦rhino¦laryn¦
              gol¦ogy

oto¦scope +s
oto¦scop¦ic
Ot¦ranto, Strait of
  (in Mediterranean)
ot¦tava rima
Ot¦tawa (capital of
  Canada)
otter +s
otter-board +s
otter-dog +s
Otto (German king)
Otto, Niko¦laus
  Au¦gust (German
  engineer)
otto (essential oil)
Otto¦line
Ot¦to¦man +s
  (dynasty of
  Osman; Turkish
  person)
ot¦to¦man +s (seat)
Ot¦to¦man Porte,
  the
Otway, Thomas
  (English
  playwright)
oua¦bain
Ouaga¦dou¦gou
  (capital of
  Burkina)
ou¦bli¦ette +s
ouch
Ouden¦arde (town
  and battle site,
  Belgium)
Oudh (region,
  India)
ought (auxiliary
  verb; nought.
  △ aught)
oughtn't (= ought
  not)
ou¦giya +s (use
  ouguiya)
ou¦guiya +s
Ouida (English
  novelist)
Ouija (board) Propr.
Oulu (province,
  Finland)
ounce +s
our (belonging to
  us. △ hour)
ours (the one(s)
  belonging to us.
  △ hours)
our¦self (prefer
  ourselves)
our¦selves
Ouse (rivers,
  England)
ousel +s (use
  ouzel)

oust +s +ed +ing
oust¦er +s
out +s +ed +ing
  (not in etc. △ owt)
out¦act +s +ed
  +ing
out¦age +s
out and out
out-and-outer +s
out¦back +s
out¦back¦er +s
out¦bal¦ance
  out¦bal¦ances
  out¦bal¦anced
  out¦bal¦an¦cing
out¦bid
  out¦bids
  out¦bid
  out¦bid¦ding
out¦bid¦der +s
out¦blaze
  out¦blazes
  out¦blazed
  out¦blaz¦ing
out¦board +s
out¦bound
out¦brave
  out¦braves
  out¦braved
  out¦brav¦ing
out¦break +s
out¦breed
  out¦breeds
  out¦bred
  out¦breed¦ing
out¦build¦ing +s
out¦burst +s
out¦cast +s (person
  cast out)
out¦caste +s
  (Indian without
  caste)
out¦class
  out¦classes
  out¦classed
  out¦class¦ing
out¦come +s
out¦com¦pete
  out¦com¦petes
  out¦com¦peted
  out¦com¦pet¦ing
out¦crop
  out¦crops
  out¦cropped
  out¦crop¦ping
out¦cry
  out¦cries
out¦dance
  out¦dances
  out¦danced
  out¦dan¦cing

out|dare
 out|dares
 out|dared
 out|dar|ing
out|dated
out|dated|ness
out|dis|tance
 out|dis|tances
 out|dis|tanced
 out|dis|tan|cing
outdo
 out|does
 out|did
 out|do|ing
 out|done
out|door
out|doors
outer +s
outer|most
outer space
outer|wear
out|face
 out|faces
 out|faced
 out|facing
out|fall +s
out|field +s +ed
 +ing
out|field|er +s
out|fight
 out|fights
 out|fought
 out|fight|ing
out|fit
 out|fits
 out|fit|ted
 out|fit|ting
out|fit|ter +s
out|flank +s +ed
 +ing
out|flow +s
out|flung
out|fly
 out|flies
 out|flew
 out|fly|ing
 out|flown
out|fox
 out|foxes
 out|foxed
 out|fox|ing
out|gas
 out|gasses
 out|gassed
 out|gas|sing
out|gen|eral
 out|gen|er|als
 out|gen|er|alled
 Br.
 out|gen|er|aled
 Am.
 out|gen|er|al|ling

out|gen|eral (*cont.*)
 Br.
 out|gen|er|al|ing
 Am.
outgo
 out|goes
 out|went
 out|going
 out|gone
out|going +s
out|grow
 out|grows
 out|grew
 out|grow|ing
 out|grown
out|growth +s
out|guess
 out|guesses
 out|guessed
 out|guess|ing
out|gun
 out|guns
 out|gunned
 out|gun|ning
out|house +s
out|ing +s
out|jockey +s +ed
 +ing
out|jump +s +ed
 +ing
out|land|er +s
out|land|ish
out|land|ish|ly
out|land|ish|ness
out|last +s +ed
 +ing
out|law +s +ed
 +ing
out|law|ry
out|lay +s
out|let +s
out|lier +s
out|line
 out|lines
 out|lined
 out|lin|ing
out|live
 out|lives
 out|lived
 out|liv|ing
out|look +s
out|ly|ing
out|man|euver
 Am. +s +ed +ing
out|man|oeuvre
 Br.
 out|man|oeuvres
 out|man|oeuvred
 out|
  man|oeuv|ring
out|match
 out|matches

out|match (*cont.*)
 out|matched
 out|match|ing
out|meas|ure
 out|meas|ures
 out|meas|ured
 out|meas|ur|ing
out|moded
out|moded|ly
out|moded|ness
out|most
out|num|ber +s
 +ed +ing
out-of-body
 attributive
out of bounds
out-of-court
 attributive
out of date
 adjective
out-of-date
 attributive
out of doors
out-of-pocket
 attributive
out-of-school
 attributive
out-of-season
 attributive
out-of-the-way
 attributive
out-of-town
 attributive
out of work
 adjective
out-of-work
 attributive
out|pace
 out|paces
 out|paced
 out|pacing
out|pa|tient +s
out|per|form +s
 +ed +ing
out|per|form|ance
 +s
out|place|ment +s
out|play +s +ed
 +ing
out|point +s +ed
 +ing
out|port +s
out|post +s
out|pour|ing +s
out|psych +s +ed
 +ing
out|put
 out|puts
 out|put *or*
 out|put|ted
 out|put|ting

out|rage
 out|rages
 out|raged
 out|raging
out|ra|geous
out|ra|geous|ly
out|ra|geous|ness
out|ran
out|range
 out|ranges
 out|ranged
 out|ran|ging
out|rank +s +ed
 +ing
outré
out|reach
 out|reaches
 out|reached
 out|reach|ing
out-relief
out|ride
 out|rides
 out|rode
 out|rid|ing
 out|rid|den
out|rider +s
out|rigged
out|rig|ger +s
out|right
out|right|ness
out|rival
 out|rivals
 out|rivalled *Br.*
 out|rivaled *Am.*
 out|rival|ling *Br.*
 out|rival|ing *Am.*
outro +s
out|rode
out|run
 out|runs
 out|ran
 out|run|ning
 out|run
out|rush
 out|rushes
out|sail +s +ed
 +ing
out|sat
out|sell
 out|sells
 out|sold
 out|sell|ing
out|set +s
out|shine
 out|shines
 out|shone
 out|shin|ing
out|shoot
 out|shoots
 out|shot
 out|shoot|ing
out|side +s

out|sider +s
out|sit
  out|sits
  out|sat
  out|sit|ting
out|size +s
out|size|ness
out|skirts
out|smart +s +ed
  +ing
out|sold
out|source
  out|sources
  out|sourced
  out|sour|cing
out|span
  out|spans
  out|spanned
  out|span|ning
out|spend
  out|spends
  out|spent
  out|spend|ing
out|spoken
out|spoken|ly
out|spoken|ness
out|spread
  out|spreads
  out|spread
  out|spread|ing
out|stand|ing
out|stand|ing|ly
out|stare
  out|stares
  out|stared
  out|star|ing
out|sta|tion +s
out|stay +s +ed
  +ing
out|step
  out|steps
  out|stepped
  out|step|ping
out|stretch
  out|stretches
  out|stretched
  out|stretch|ing
out|strip
  out|strips
  out|stripped
  out|strip|ping
out-swinger +s
out-take +s
out-talk +s +ed
  +ing
out-think
  out-thinks
  out-thought
  out-thinking
out-thrust
  out-thrusts

out-thrust (*cont.*)
  out-thrust
  out-thrust|ing
out-top
  out-tops
  out-topped
  out-topping
out-tray +s
out-turn +s
out|value
  out|values
  out|valued
  out|valu|ing
out|vote
  out|votes
  out|voted
  out|vot|ing
out|walk +s +ed
  +ing
out|ward
outward-looking
out|ward|ly
out|ward|ness
out|wards
out|wash
  out|washes
out|watch
  out|watches
  out|watched
  out|watch|ing
out|wear
  out|wears
  out|wore
  out|wear|ing
  out|worn
out|weigh +s +ed
  +ing
out|went
out|wit
  out|wits
  out|wit|ted
  out|wit|ting
out|with
out|wore
out|work +s
out|work|er +s
out|work|ing
out|worn
ouzel +s
ouzo +s
ova (plural of
  ovum. △ over)
oval +s
oval|ity
oval|ly
oval|ness
Ov|ambo
  plural Ov|ambo or
  Ov|am|bos
Ov|ambo|land
  (homeland,
  Namibia)

ovar|ian
ovari|ec|tomy
  ovari|ec|to|mies
ovari|ot|omy
  ovari|oto|mies
ovar|itis
ovary
  ovar|ies
ovate
ova|tion +s
ova|tion|al
oven +s
oven|bird +s
oven|proof
oven-ready
oven|ware
over +s (across;
  past; above; etc.;
  Cricket. △ ova)
over-abundance
  +s
over-abundant
over-abundant|ly
over|achieve
  over|achieves
  over|achieved
  over|achiev|ing
over|achieve|ment
  +s
over|achiever +s
over|act +s +ed
  +ing
over|active
over|activ|ity
over|age +s
  (surplus)
over-age (*attributive*
  above age limit)
over|all +s
over|alled
over|am|bi|tion
over|am|bi|tious
over|
  am|bi|tious|ly
over-anxiety
over-anxious
over-anxious|ly
over|arch
  over|arches
  over|arched
  over|arch|ing
over|arm
over|ate (past tense
  of *overeat*.
  △ overrate)
over|awe
  over|awes
  over|awed
  over|aw|ing
over|bal|ance
  over|bal|ances

over|bal|ance
  (*cont.*)
  over|bal|anced
  over|bal|an|cing
over|bear
  over|bears
  over|bore
  over|bear|ing
  over|borne
over|bear|ing|ly
over|bear|ing|ness
over|bid
  over|bids
  over|bid
  over|bid|ding
over|bid|der +s
over|bite
over|blouse +s
over|blow
  over|blows
  over|blew
  over|blow|ing
  over|blown
over|board
over|bold
over|book +s +ed
  +ing
over|boot +s
over|bore
over|borne
over-borrow +s
  +ed +ing
over|bought
over|breed
  over|breeds
  over|bred
  over|breed|ing
over|brim
  over|brims
  over|brimmed
  over|brim|ming
over|build
  over|builds
  over|built
  over|build|ing
over|bur|den +s
  +ed +ing
over|bur|den|
      some
Over|bury,
  Thomas (English
  poet and courtier)
over|busy
over|buy
  over|buys
  over|bought
  over|buy|ing
over|call +s +ed
  +ing
over|came
over|cap|acity

over|cap|it|al|ised
  Br. (use
  overcapitalized)
over|cap|it|al|ized
over|care|ful
over|care|ful|ly
over|cast
  over|casts
  over|cast
  over|cast|ing
over|cau|tion
over|cau|tious
over|cau|tious|ly
over|cau|tious|
         ness
over|charge
  over|charges
  over|charged
  over|char|ging
over|check +s
over|cloud +s +ed
  +ing
over|coat +s
over|come
  over|comes
  over|came
  over|com|ing
  over|come
over|com|mit
  over|com|mits
  over|com|mit|ted
  over|com|mit|
        ting
over|com|pen|sate
  over|com|pen|
        sates
  over|com|pen|
        sated
  over|com|pen|
        sat|ing
over|com|pen|
        sa|tion
over|com|pen|
        sa|tory
over|con|fi|dence
over|con|fi|dent
over|con|fi|dent|ly
over|cook +s +ed
  +ing
over|crit|ic|al
over|crop
  over|crops
  over|cropped
  over|crop|ping
over|crowd +s +ed
  +ing
over-curios|ity
over-curious
over-curious|ly
over-delicacy
over-delicate

over|de|ter|min|
        ation
over|de|ter|mine
  over|de|ter|mines
  over|de|ter|mined
  over|
    de|ter|min|ing
over|de|velop +s
  +ed +ing
over|do
  over|does
  over|did
  over|do|ing
  over|done
over|dos|age +s
over|dose
  over|doses
  over|dosed
  over|dos|ing
over|draft +s
over|drama|tise
  Br. (use
  overdramatize)
  over|drama|tises
  over|drama|tised
  over|drama|
        tis|ing
over|drama|tize
  over|drama|tizes
  over|drama|tized
  over|drama|
        tiz|ing
over|draw
  over|draws
  over|drew
  over|draw|ing
  over|drawn
over|draw|er +s
over|dress
  over|dresses
  over|dressed
  over|dress|ing
over|drink
  over|drinks
  over|drank
  over|drink|ing
  over|drunk
over|drive +s
over|dub
  over|dubs
  over|dubbed
  over|dub|bing
over|due
over|eager
over|eager|ly
over|eager|ness
over|eat
  over|eats
  over|ate
  over|eat|ing
over-elabor|ate
over-elabor|ate|ly

over-elabor|ation
over-emotion|al
over-
  emotion|al|ly
over|empha|sis
over|empha|sise
  Br. (use
  overemphasize)
  over|empha|sises
  over|empha|sised
  over|
      empha|sis|ing
over|empha|size
  over|empha|sizes
  over|empha|sized
  over|
      empha|siz|ing
over|enthu|si|asm
over|enthu|si|
        as|tic
over|enthu|si|
      as|tic|al|ly
over|esti|mate
  over|esti|mates
  over|esti|mated
  over|esti|mat|ing
over|esti|mation
  +s
over|ex|cite
  over|ex|cites
  over|ex|cited
  over|ex|cit|ing
over|ex|cite|ment
over-exercise
  over-exercises
  over-exercised
  over-exercis|ing
over|ex|ert +s +ed
  +ing
over|ex|er|tion +s
over|ex|pose
  over|ex|poses
  over|ex|posed
  over|ex|pos|ing
over|ex|pos|ure +s
over|ex|tend +s
  +ed +ing
over|fall +s
over|fa|mil|iar
over|fa|mil|iar|ity
over|fa|tigue
over|feed
  over|feeds
  over|fed
  over|feed|ing
over|fill +s +ed
  +ing
over|fine
over|fish
  over|fishes
  over|fished
  over|fish|ing

over|flight +s
over|flow +s +ed
  +ing
over|fly
  over|flies
  over|flew
  over|flown
  over|fly|ing
over|fold +s
over|fond
over|fond|ly
over|fond|ness
over|ful|fil Br.
  over|ful|fils
  over|ful|filled
  over|ful|fil|ling
over|ful|fill Am.
  over|ful|fills
  over|ful|filled
  over|ful|fill|ing
over|ful|fill|ment
  Am.
over|ful|fil|ment
  Br.
over|full
over|gar|ment +s
over|gen|er|al|
    isa|tion Br. +s
  (use overgeneral-
  ization)
over|gen|er|al|ise
  Br. (use
  overgeneralize)
  over|gen|er|al|
        ises
  over|gen|er|al|
        ised
  over|gen|er|al|
        is|ing
over|gen|er|al|
    iza|tion +s
over|gen|er|al|ize
  over|gen|er|al|
        izes
  over|gen|er|al|
        ized
  over|gen|er|al|
        iz|ing
over|gen|er|ous
over|gen|er|ous|ly
over|glaze
  over|glazes
  over|glazed
  over|glaz|ing
over|graze
  over|grazes
  over|grazed
  over|graz|ing
over|ground
over|grow
  over|grows
  over|grew

over|grow (*cont.*)
  over|grow|ing
  over|grown
over|growth +s
over|hand
over|hang
  over|hangs
  over|hung
  over|hang|ing
over|haste
over|hasti|ly
over|hasty
over|haul +s +ed
  +ing
over|head +s
over|hear
  over|hears
  over|heard
  over|hear|ing
over|heat +s +ed
  +ing
over|hung
Over|ijs|sel
  (province, the
  Netherlands)
over-indulge
  over-indulges
  over-indulged
  over-indulging
over-indulgence
  +s
over-indulgent
over-inflated
over-insurance
over-insure
  over-insures
  over-insured
  over-insuring
over|issue
  over|issues
  over|issued
  over|issu|ing
over|joyed
over|kill +s +ed
  +ing
over|laden
over|laid
over|lain
over|land
over|land|er +s
over|lap
  over|laps
  over|lapped
  over|lap|ping
over-large
over|lay
  over|lays
  over|laid
  over|lay|ing
over|leaf
over|leap
  over|leaps

over|leap (*cont.*)
  over|leaped *or*
  over|leapt
  over|leap|ing
over|lie
  over|lies
  over|lay
  over|ly|ing
  over|lain
over|load +s +ed
  +ing
over|long
over|look +s +ed
  +ing
over|look|er +s
over|lord +s
over|lord|ship +s
over|ly
over|ly|ing
over|man
  over|mans
  over|manned
  over|man|ning
over|man|tel +s
over-many
over|mas|ter +s
  +ed +ing
over|mas|tery
over|match
  over|matches
  over|matched
  over|match|ing
over|meas|ure
  over|meas|ures
  over|meas|ured
  over|meas|ur|ing
over-mighty
over|much
over|nice
over|nice|ness
over|nicety
over|night
over|night|er +s
over-optimis|tic
over|paid
over|paint +s +ed
  +ing
over|part|ed
over-particu|lar
over|pass
  over|passes
  over|passed
  over|pass|ing
over|pay
  over|pays
  over|paid
  over|pay|ing
over|pay|ment +s
over|per|suade
  over|per|suades
  over|per|suaded
  over|per|suad|ing

over|pitch
  over|pitches
  over|pitched
  over|pitch|ing
over|play +s +ed
  +ing
over|plus
  over|pluses
over|popu|lated
over|popu|la|tion
over|power +s +ed
  +ing
over|power|ing|ly
over|praise
  over|praises
  over|praised
  over|prais|ing
over-prescribe
  over-prescribes
  over-prescribed
  over-prescrib|ing
over|price
  over|prices
  over|priced
  over|pricing
over|print +s +ed
  +ing
over|pro|duce
  over|pro|duces
  over|pro|duced
  over|pro|du|cing
over|pro|duc|tion
  +s
over|proof
over|pro|tect +s
  +ed +ing
over|pro|tec|tion
over|pro|tect|ive
over|quali|fied
over|ran
over|rate
  over|rates
  over|rated
  over|rat|ing
over|reach
  over|reaches
  over|reached
  over|reach|ing
over|react +s +ed
  +ing
over|reac|tion +s
over-refine
  over-refines
  over-refined
  over-refining
over-refine|ment
  +s
over|ride
  over|rides
  over|rode
  over|rid|ing
  over|rid|den

over|rider +s
over|ripe
over|ruff +s +ed
  +ing
over|rule
  over|rules
  over|ruled
  over|rul|ing
over|run
  over|runs
  over|ran
  over|run
  over|run|ning
over|sail|ing
over|saw
over|scru|pu|lous
over|sea (abroad)
over|seas (abroad)
over|see
  over|sees
  over|saw
  over|seen
  over|see|ing
  (supervise)
over|seer +s
over|sell
  over|sells
  over|sold
  over|sell|ing
over|sen|si|tive
over|sen|si|tive|
            ness
over|sen|si|tiv|ity
over|set
  over|sets
  over|set
  over|set|ting
over|sew +s +ed
  +ing
over|sexed
over|shadow +s
  +ed +ing
over|shoe +s
over|shoot
  over|shoots
  over|shot
  over|shoot|ing
over|side
over|sight +s
over|sim|pli|fi|
         ca|tion
over|sim|plify
  over|sim|pli|fies
  over|sim|pli|fied
  over|sim|pli|fy|
           ing
over|size
over|sized
over|skirt +s
over|slaugh +s
  +ed +ing

over|sleep
  over|sleeps
  over|slept
  over|sleep|ing
over|sleeve +s
over|sold
over|so|lici|tous
over|so|lici|tude
over|soul
over|spe|cial|
  isa|tion *Br.*
  (use overspecial-
  ization)
over|spe|cial|ise
  Br. (use
  overspecialize)
  over|spe|cial|ises
  over|spe|cial|ised
  over|spe|cial|
    is|ing
over|spe|cial|
    iza|tion
over|spe|cial|ize
  over|spe|cial|izes
  over|spe|cial|ized
  over|spe|cial|
    iz|ing
over|spend
  over|spends
  over|spent
  over|spend|ing
over|spill +s
over|spread
  over|spreads
  over|spread
  over|spread|ing
over|staff +s +ed
  +ing
over|state
  over|states
  over|stated
  over|stat|ing
over|state|ment
  +s
over|stay +s +ed
  +ing
over|steer +s +ed
  +ing
over|step
  over|steps
  over|stepped
  over|step|ping
over|stitch
  over|stitches
  over|stitched
  over|stitch|ing
over|stock +s +ed
  +ing
over|strain +s +ed
  +ing
over|stress
  over|stresses

over|stress (*cont.*)
  over|stressed
  over|stress|ing
over|stretch
  over|stretches
  over|stretched
  over|stretch|ing
over|strong
over|strung
over|study
  over|studies
  over|studied
  over|study|ing
over|stuff +s +ed
  +ing
over|sub|scribe
  over|sub|scribes
  over|sub|scribed
  over|
    sub|scrib|ing
over|subtle
over|sup|ply
  over|sup|plies
  over|sup|plied
  over|sup|ply|ing
over|sus|cep|tible
overt
over|take
  over|takes
  over|took
  over|tak|ing
  over|taken
over|task +s +ed
  +ing
over|tax
  over|taxes
  over|taxed
  over|tax|ing
over-the-counter
  attributive
over-the-top
  attributive
over|throw
  over|throws
  over|threw
  over|throw|ing
  over|thrown
over|thrust +s
over|time
over|tire
  over|tires
  over|tired
  over|tir|ing
overt|ly
overt|ness
over|tone +s
over|took
over|top
  over|tops
  over|topped
  over|top|ping

over|train +s +ed
  +ing
over|trick +s
over|trump +s +ed
  +ing
over|ture +s
over|turn +s +ed
  +ing
over|use
  over|uses
  over|used
  over|us|ing
over|valu|ation +s
over|value
  over|values
  over|valued
  over|valu|ing
over|view +s
over|water +s +ed
  +ing
over|ween|ing
over|ween|ing|ly
over|ween|ing|
    ness
over|weight
over|whelm +s
  +ed +ing
over|whelm|ing|ly
over|whelm|ing|
    ness
over|wind
  over|winds
  over|wound
  over|wind|ing
over|win|ter +s
  +ed +ing
over|work +s +ed
  +ing
over|wound
over|write
  over|writes
  over|wrote
  over|writ|ing
  over|writ|ten
over|wrought
over|zeal|ous
ovi|bov|ine +s
ovi|cide
Ovid (Roman poet)
ovi|ducal
ovi|duct +s
ovi|duct|al
Ovi|edo (city,
  Spain)
ovi|form
ovine
ovi|par|ity
ovip|ar|ous
ovip|ar|ous|ly
ovi|posit +s +ed
  +ing
ovi|pos|ition

ovi|posi|tor +s
ovoid
ovolo
ovoli
ovo|tes|tis
  ovo|tes|tes
ovo|vivi|par|ity
ovo|vi|vip|ar|ous
ovu|lar
ovu|late
  ovu|lates
  ovu|lated
  ovu|lat|ing
ovu|la|tion +s
ovu|la|tory
ovule +s
ovum
ova
ow *interjection*
owe
  owes
  owed
  owing
  (be in debt etc.
  ⚠ O, oh)
Owen (name)
Owen, David
  (Lord Owen,
  British statesman)
Owen, Rich|ard
  (English
  anatomist)
Owen, Rob|ert
  (British socialist
  and
  philanthropist)
Owen, Wil|fred
  (English poet)
Owens, Jesse
  (American athlete)
owl +s
owl|ery
  owl|er|ies
owlet +s
owl|ish
owl|ish|ly
owl|ish|ness
owl-light
owl-like
owl mon|key +s
own +s +ed +ing
own brand +s *noun*
own-brand
  attributive
owner +s
own|er|less
owner-occupied
owner-occupier
  +s
own|er|ship +s
owt (anything.
  ⚠ out)

ox
oxen
ox|al|ate +s
ox|al|ic
ox|alis
oxbow +s
Ox|bridge (Oxford and Cambridge universities)
oxen
oxer +s
ox-eye +s
ox-eyed
Oxfam (= Oxford Committee for Famine Relief)
ox-fence +s
Ox|ford (city, England)
Ox|ford|shire (county, England)
ox|herd +s
ox|hide +s
oxi|dant +s
oxi|date
oxi|dates
oxi|dated
oxi|dat|ing
oxi|da|tion +s
oxi|da|tion|al
oxi|da|tive
oxide +s
oxi|dis|able Br. (use oxidizable)
oxi|disa|tion Br. +s (use oxidization)
oxi|dise Br. (use oxidize)
oxi|dises
oxi|dised
oxi|dis|ing
oxi|diser Br. +s (use oxidizer)
oxi|diz|able
oxi|diza|tion +s
oxi|dize
oxi|dizes
oxi|dized
oxi|diz|ing
oxi|dizer +s
oxlip +s
Oxon (= Oxfordshire)
Ox|on|ian +s
ox-pecker +s
ox|tail +s
oxter +s
ox-tongue +s
Oxus (ancient name of Amu Darya)
oxy|acet|yl|ene

oxy|acid +s
oxy|carp|ous
oxy|gen
oxy|gen|ate
oxy|gen|ates
oxy|gen|ated
oxy|gen|at|ing
oxy|gen|ation
oxy|gen|ator +s
oxy|gen|ise Br. (use oxygenize)
oxy|gen|ises
oxy|gen|ised
oxy|gen|is|ing
oxy|gen|ize
oxy|gen|izes
oxy|gen|ized
oxy|gen|iz|ing
oxy|gen|ous
oxy|haemo|glo|bin
oxy-hydrogen
oxy|moron +s
oxy|opia
oxy-salt +s
oxy|tetra|cyc|line
oxy|to|cin +s
oxy|tone +s
oyes (use oyez)
oyez
oys|ter +s
oys|ter bank +s
oys|ter bed +s
oys|ter|catch|er +s
oyster-farm +s
oyster-plant +s
oys|ter white +s
  noun and adjective
oyster-white
  attributive
Oz (= Australia)
Ozark Moun|tains (in USA)
Oz|arks (= Ozark Mountains)
Ozawa, Seiji (Japanese conductor)
ozo|cer|ite
ozone
ozone-deplet|ing
  attributive
ozone de|ple|tion
ozone-friend|ly
ozon|ic
ozon|isa|tion Br. (use ozonization)
ozon|ise Br. (use ozonize)
ozon|ises
ozon|ised
ozon|is|ing
ozon|iza|tion

ozon|ize
ozon|izes
ozon|ized
ozon|iz|ing
Ozzie +s (use Aussie)

Pp

pa +s (father. △ pah, par)
pa'anga +s
Paarl (town, South Africa)
pabu|lum
PAC +s (= political action committee)
paca +s (rodent. △ packer)
pace
paces
paced
pa|cing
  (step)
pace (with due deference to)
pace|maker +s
pace|mak|ing
pace|man
pace|men
pacer +s
pace-setter +s
pace-setting
pacey (use pacy)
paci|er
paci|est
pacha +s (use pasha)
Pach|el|bel, Jo|hann (German composer)
pa|chinko
pa|chisi
Pa|chuca (de Soto) (city, Mexico)
pachy|derm +s
pachy|der|mal
pachy|der|ma|tous
pachy|tene
Pa|cif|ic (Ocean)
pa|cif|ic (peaceful)
pacif|ic|al|ly
paci|fi|ca|tion
paci|fi|ca|tory
paci|fier +s
paci|fism
paci|fist +s
pacify
paci|fies
paci|fied
paci|fy|ing
pack +s +ed +ing
pack|able
pack|age
pack|ages
pack|aged
pack|aging

pack|ager +s
pack ani|mal +s
pack drill
Pack|er, Kerry
  (Australian media
  entrepreneur)
pack|er +s (person
  who packs.
  △ paca)
packet +s +ed
  +ing
packet switch|ing
pack|horse +s
pack ice
pack|ing +s
pack|ing case +s
pack rat +s
pack|sad|dle +s
pack|thread
pact +s
  (agreement.
  △ packed)
pacy
  paci|er
  paci|est
pad
  pads
  pad|ded
  pad|ding
Pa|dang (city,
  Indonesia)
Pad|ding|ton
  (railway station,
  London)
pad|dle
  pad|dles
  pad|dled
  pad|dling
pad|dle boat +s
pad|dler +s
pad|dle steam|er
  +s
pad|dle wheel +s
pad|dock +s +ed
  +ing
Paddy
  Pad|dies
  (offensive
  Irishman; name)
paddy
  pad|dies
  (rage; rice field)
paddy field +s
paddy|whack +s
pade|melon +s
Pade|rew|ski,
  Ig|nacy Jan
  (Polish pianist and
  prime minister)
pad|lock +s +ed
  +ing

Padma (river,
  Bangladesh)
pa|douk +s
padre +s
pad|saw +s
Padua (city, Italy)
Pad|uan +s
paean Br. +s (Am.
  pean. song of
  praise. △ paeon,
  peon)
paed|er|ast Br. +s
  (use pederast)
paed|er|as|tic Br.
  (use pederastic)
paed|er|asty Br.
  (use pederasty)
paedi|at|ric Br.
  (Am. pediatric)
paedi|at|ri|cian Br.
  +s (Am.
  pediatrician)
paedi|at|rics Br.
  (Am. pediatrics)
paedi|at|rist Br. +s
  (Am. pediatrist)
paedo|morph|osis
paedo|phile Br. +s
  (Am. pedophile)
paedo|philia Br.
  (Am. pedophilia)
paedo|phil|iac Br.
  +s (Am.
  pedophiliac)
pa|ella +s
paeon +s (metrical
  foot. △ paean,
  pean, peon)
pae|on|ic
pae|ony (use
  peony)
pae|onies
Pa|galu (former
  name of
  Annobón)
Pagan (town,
  Burma)
pagan +s
Paga|nini,
  Nic|colò (Italian
  violinist)
pa|gan|ise Br. (use
  paganize)
pa|gan|ises
pa|gan|ised
pa|gan|is|ing
pa|gan|ish
pa|gan|ism
pa|gan|ize
pa|gan|izes
pa|gan|ized
pa|gan|iz|ing

Page, Fred|erick
  Hand|ley
  (English aircraft
  designer)
page
  pages
  paged
  pa|ging
pa|geant +s
pa|geant|ry
  pa|geant|ries
page-boy +s
pager +s
pa|ginal
pa|gin|ary
pa|gin|ate
  pa|gin|ates
  pa|gin|ated
  pa|gin|at|ing
pa|gin|ation
pa|goda +s
pa|goda tree +s
pah (interjection.
  △ pa, par)
Pa|hang (state,
  Malaysia)
Pah|lavi (language;
  member of Iranian
  dynasty)
Pah|lavi,
  Mu|ham|mad
  Reza (shah of
  Iran, 1941–79)
Pah|lavi, Reza
  (shah of Iran,
  1925–41)
pa|hoe|hoe
paid
paid-up attributive
Paign|ton (resort,
  England)
pail +s (bucket.
  △ pale)
pail|ful +s
Pai|lin (town,
  Cambodia)
pail|lasse +s (use
  palliasse)
pail|lette +s
pain +s +ed +ing
  (hurt. △ pane)
Paine, Thomas
  (English political
  writer)
Paine Towers
  (peaks, Chile)
pain|ful
pain|ful|ly
pain|ful|ness
pain|kill|er +s
pain|kill|ing
pain|less

pain|less|ly
pain|less|ness
pains|tak|ing
pains|tak|ing|ly
pains|tak|ing|ness
paint +s +ed +ing
paint|able
paint|ball
paint|box
  paint|boxes
paint|brush
  paint|brushes
paint|er +s
paint|er|li|ness
paint|er|ly
paint|ing +s
paint shop +s
paint|stick +s
paint|work
painty
pair +s +ed +ing
  (two. △ pare,
  pear, père)
pair|ing +s
  (forming pair.
  △ paring)
pair|work
paisa
paise
Pais|ley +s
  (pattern; garment)
Pais|ley (town,
  Scotland)
Pais|ley, Ian
  (Northern Irish
  politician)
Pais|ley|ite +s
Pai|ute
  plural Pai|ute or
  Pai|utes
pa|jama Am.
  attributive (Br.
  pyjama)
pa|ja|mas Am. (Br.
  pyjamas)
paka|poo
pak|apu (use
  pakapoo)
pa|keha +s
Pakh|tun +s
  (= Pathan)
Paki +s (offensive)
Paki|stan
Paki|stani +s
pa|kora +s
Pakse (town, Laos)
pal
  pals
  palled
  pal|ling
pal|ace +s
pal|adin +s

Palae|arc|tic *Br.*
(*Am.* Palearctic)
palaeo|an|thro|po|
logic|al *Br.* (*Am.*
paleoanthropo-
logical)
palaeo|
an|thro|polo|gist
Br. +s (*Am.* paleo-
anthropologist)
palaeo|an|thro|
pol|ogy *Br.* (*Am.*
paleoanthropol-
ogy)
palaeo|bot|any *Br.*
(*Am.*
paleobotany)
Palaeo|cene *Br.*
(*Am.* Paleocene)
palaeo|cli|mat|
ology *Br.* (*Am.*
paleoclimato-
logy)
palaeo|eco|logic|al
Br. (*Am.*
paleoecological)
palaeo|ecolo|gist
Br. +s (*Am.*
paleoecologist)
palaeo|ecol|ogy *Br.*
(*Am.*
paleoecology)
palaeo|
geog|raph|er *Br.*
+s (*Am.*
paleogeographer)
palaeo|geog|raphy
Br. (*Am.*
paleogeography)
palae|og|raph|er
Br. +s (*Am.*
paleographer)
palaeo|graph|ic *Br.*
(*Am.*
paleographic)
palaeo|graph|ic|al
Br. (*Am.*
paleographical)
palaeo|graph|ic|
al|ly *Br.* (*Am.*
paleographically)
palae|og|raphy *Br.*
(*Am.*
paleography)
palaeo|lith|ic *Br.*
(*Am.* paleolithic)
palaeo|mag|net|
ism *Br.* (*Am.*
paleomagnetism)
palae|onto|logic|al
Br. (*Am.*
paleontological)

palae|on|tolo|gist
Br. +s (*Am.*
paleontologist)
palae|on|tology *Br.*
(*Am.*
paleontology)
Palaeo|zo|ic *Br.*
(*Am.* Paleozoic)
pal|aes|tra +s
pal|ais
plural pal|ais
pal|an|keen +s
(use palanquin)
pal|an|quin +s
pal|at|abil|ity
pal|at|able
pal|at|able|ness
pal|at|ably
pal|atal +s
pal|at|al|isa|tion
Br. (use
palatalization)
pal|at|al|ise *Br.*
(use palatalize)
pal|at|al|ises
pal|at|al|ised
pal|at|al|is|ing
pal|at|al|iza|tion
pal|at|al|ize
pal|at|al|izes
pal|at|al|ized
pal|at|al|iz|ing
pal|at|al|ly
pal|ate +s (part of
mouth. △ palette,
pallet)
pa|la|tial
pa|la|tial|ly
pa|lat|in|ate +s
pal|at|ine
Palau (island group,
W. Pacific)
pa|la|ver +s +ed
+ing
Pa|la|wan (island,
Philippines)
pale
pales
paled
pal|ing
paler
pal|est
(lacking colour;
become pale.
△ pail)
palea
pa|leae
Pale|arc|tic *Am.*
(*Br.* Palaearctic)
pale|face +s
pale-faced

pale|ly (in a pale
way. △ paly)
Palem|bang (city,
Indonesia)
pale|ness
Pa|len|que (ancient
city, Mexico)
paleo|an|thro|po|
logic|al *Am.* (*Br.*
palaeoanthropo-
logical)
paleo|an|thro|polo|
gist *Am.* +s (*Br.*
palaeoanthropolo-
gist)
paleo|an|thro|
pol|ogy *Am.* (*Br.*
palaeoanthropol-
ogy)
paleo|bot|any *Am.*
(*Br.*
palaeobotany)
Paleo|cene *Am.* (*Br.*
Palaeocene)
paleo|cli|mat|
ology *Am.* (*Br.*
palaeoclimat-
ology)
paleo|eco|logic|al
Am. (*Br.*
palaeoecological)
paleo|ecolo|gist
Am. +s (*Br.*
palaeoecologist)
paleo|ecol|ogy *Am.*
(*Br.*
palaeoecology)
paleo|
geog|raph|er *Am.*
+s (*Br.* palaeo-
geographer)
paleo|geog|raphy
Am. (*Br.* palaeo-
geography)
pale|og|raph|er
Am. +s (*Br.*
palaeographer)
paleo|graph|ic *Am.*
(*Br.*
palaeographic)
paleo|graph|ic|al
Am. (*Br.*
palaeographical)
paleo|graph|ic|
al|ly *Am.* (*Br.*
palaeographic-
ally)
pale|og|raphy *Am.*
(*Br.*
palaeography)
paleo|lith|ic *Am.*
(*Br.* palaeolithic)

paleo|mag|net|ism
Am. (*Br.* palaeo-
magnetism)
pale|onto|logic|al
Am. (*Br.*
palaeontological)
pale|on|tolo|gist
Am. +s (*Br.*
palaeontologist)
pale|on|tology *Am.*
(*Br.*
palaeontology)
Paleo|zo|ic *Am.*
(*Br.* Palaeozoic)
Pa|lermo (capital of
Sicily)
Pal|es|tine
Pal|es|tin|ian +s
pa|les|tra +s (use
palaestra)
Pal|es|trina,
Gio|vanni
Pier|luigi da
(Italian composer)
pale|tot +s
pal|ette +s (in
painting. △ palate,
pallet)
palette-knife
palette-knives
pal|frey +s
Pali (language.
△ parley)
pali|mony
pal|imp|sest +s
pal|in|drome +s
pal|in|drom|ic
pal|in|drom|ist +s
pal|ing +s
pal|in|gen|esis
pal|in|gen|et|ic
pal|in|ode +s
pal|is|ade
pal|is|ades
pal|is|aded
pal|is|ad|ing
Pal|is|ades, the
(district of New
Jersey, USA)
pal|ish
Pa|lissy, Ber|nard
(French potter)
Palk Strait
(between India
and Sri Lanka)
pall +s +ed +ing
(covering; become
uninteresting.
△ pawl)
Pal|la|dian +s
Pal|la|dian|ism

Pal|ladio, An|drea
(Italian architect)

pal|la|dium

pal|la|dia

Pal|las (Greek
Mythology;
asteroid)

pall-bearer +s

pal|let +s
(mattress;
platform.
△ palate, palette)

pal|let|isa|tion Br.
(use
palletization)

pal|let|ise Br. (use
palletize)

pal|let|ises

pal|let|ised

pal|let|is|ing

pal|let|iza|tion

pal|let|ize

pal|let|izes

pal|let|ized

pal|let|iz|ing

pal|lia (plural of
pallium.
△ pallier)

pal|lial

pal|li|asse +s

pal|li|ate

pal|li|ates

pal|li|ated

pal|li|at|ing

pal|li|ation

pal|lia|tive +s

pal|lia|tive|ly

pal|li|ator +s

pal|lid

pal|lid|ity

pal|lid|ly

pal|lid|ness

pal|lium

pal|liums or

pal|lia

Pall Mall (street,
London)

pall-mall (game)

pal|lor

pally

pal|lier

pal|li|est

palm +s +ed +ing

Palma (city,
Majorca. △ La
Palma, Parma)

pal|ma|ceous

pal|mar +s

Pal|mas (town,
Brazil)

pal|mate

Palme, Olof
(Swedish prime
minister)

Pal|mer, Ar|nold
(American golfer)

pal|mer +s

**Pal|mer|ston,
Henry** (British
prime minister)

**Pal|mer|ston
North** (city, New
Zealand)

pal|mette +s

pal|metto +s

palm|ful +s

pal|mier +s

palmi|ped +s

palmi|pede +s

palm|ist +s

palm|is|try

palmi|tate +s

palm|it|ic

Palm Springs
(desert resort,
USA)

Palm Sun|day +s

palm|top +s

palm tree +s

palmy

palm|ier

palm|iest

Pal|myra (ancient
city, Syria)

pal|myra +s (tree)

pa|lolo +s

Palo|mar, Mount
(California, USA)

palo|mino +s

palo|verde +s

palp +s

palp|abil|ity

palp|able

palp|ably

palp|al

palp|ate

pal|pates

pal|pated

pal|pat|ing

pal|pa|tion

pal|pe|bral

pal|pi|tant

pal|pi|tate

pal|pi|tates

pal|pi|tated

pal|pi|tat|ing

pal|pi|ta|tion +s

pal|pus

palpi

pals|grave +s

pal|stave +s

palsy

pal|sies

palsy (cont.)

pal|sied

palsy|ing

pal|ter +s +ed
+ing

pal|ter|er +s

pal|tri|ness

pal|try

pal|trier

pal|tri|est

pal|udal

pal|ud|ism

paly (striped.
△ palely)

palyno|logic|al

paly|nolo|gist +s

paly|nol|ogy

Pam

Pam|ela

Pamir Moun|tains
(in central Asia)

Pa|mirs (= Pamir
Mountains)

pam|pas

pam|pas grass

pam|pas grasses

pam|per +s +ed
+ing

pam|per|er +s

pam|pero +s

pamph|let +s +ed
+ing

pamph|let|eer

pamph|let|eers

pamph|let|eered

pamph|let|eer|ing

Pam|phylia
(ancient region,
Turkey)

Pam|phyl|ian +s

Pam|plona (city,
Spain)

Pan Greek
Mythology

pan

pans

panned

pan|ning

(vessel; leaf;
swing camera.
△ panne)

pana|cea +s

pana|cean

pan|ache +s

pan|ada

pan-African

pan-African|ism

**Pan-African|ist
Con|gress (of
Azania)** (South
African political
movement)

Pa|naji (city, India)

Pan|ama (in
Central America)

pan|ama +s (hat)

Pan|ama Canal (in
Central America)

Pan|ama City
(capital of
Panama)

Pana|ma|nian +s

pan-American

pan-Anglican

pana|tella +s

Panay (island,
Philippines)

pan|cake

pan|cakes

pan|caked

pan|cak|ing

Pan|cake Day +s

pan|chayat +s

Pan|chen lama +s

pan|chro|mat|ic

pan|cos|mism

pan|creas

pan|creases

pan|cre|at|ic

pan|crea|tin

pan|crea|titis

panda +s (animal.
△ pander)

pan|da|nus
plural pan|da|nus

Pan|darus Greek
Mythology

pan|dean +s

pan|dect +s

pan|dem|ic

pan|de|mon|ium

pan|der +s +ed
+ing (indulge; go-
between.
△ panda)

Pan|dit, Vi|jaya
(Indian politician
and diplomat)

pan|dit +s (use
pundit)

Pan|dora Greek
Mythology

Pan|dora's box

pane +s (in window
etc. △ pain)

pan|egyr|ic +s

pan|egyric|al

pan|egyr|ise Br.
(use panegyrize)

pan|egyr|ises

pan|egyr|ised

pan|egyr|is|ing

pan|egyr|ist +s

pan|egyr|ize
pan|egyr|izes
pan|egyr|ized
pan|egyr|iz|ing
panel
panels
pan|elled *Br.*
pan|eled *Am.*
pan|el|ling *Br.*
pan|el|ing *Am.*
panel beat|er +s
pan|el|ist *Am.* +s
pan|el|list *Br.* +s
pan|et|tone
pan|et|toni
pan-European
pan|forte
pan-fry
pan-fries
pan-fried
pan-frying
pan|ful +s
pang +s
panga +s
Pan|gaea
(continent)
pan|go|lin +s
pan|han|dle
pan|han|dles
pan|han|dled
pan|hand|ling
pan|hand|ler +s
pan-Hellen|ic
pan-Hellen|ism
panic
panics
pan|icked
pan|ick|ing
pan|icky
pan|icle +s
pan|icled
panic|mon|ger +s
panic-stricken
panic-struck
Pa|nini (Indian
grammarian)
Pan|jabi +s (use
Punjabi)
pan|jan|drum +s
Pan|jim (= Panaji)
Panj|shir
(mountain range,
Afghanistan)
Pank|hurst,
Em|me|line,
Chris|ta|bel, and
Syl|via (English
suffragettes)
pan|like
Pan|mun|jom
(village, Korea)
pan|nage

panne (velvet.
△ pan)
pan|ner +s
pan|nier +s
pan|ni|kin +s
Pan|no|nia (ancient
country, SE
Europe)
pan|op|lied
pan|oply
pan|op|lies
pan|op|tic
pan|or|ama +s
pan|or|am|ic
pan|or|am|ic|al|ly
pan pipes
pansy
pan|sies
pant +s +ed +ing
pan|ta|lets
pan|ta|lettes (use
pantalets)
Pan|ta|loon (Italian
commedia dell'arte
character)
pan|ta|loons
(breeches; baggy
trousers)
Pan|ta|nal (swamp
region, Brazil)
pan|tech|nicon +s
Pan|tel|le|ria
(island,
Mediterranean)
Pan|tha|lassa
(ocean)
pan|the|ism
pan|the|ist +s
pan|the|is|tic
pan|the|is|tic|al
pan|the|is|tic|al|ly
Pan|theon (in
Rome)
pan|theon +s
(generally)
pan|ther +s
pantie-girdle +s
pan|ties
panti|hose (use
pantyhose)
pan|tile +s
pan|tiled
pant|ing|ly
panto +s
panto|graph +s
panto|graph|ic
panto|logic
pan|tol|ogy
panto|mime
panto|mimes
panto|mimed
panto|mim|ing

panto|mim|ic
panto|mim|ist
panto|morph|ic
panto|scop|ic
panto|then|ic
pan|try
pan|tries
pan|try|man
pan|try|men
pants
pants suit +s
pant suit +s (use
pants suit)
panty|hose
panty line +s
panty liner +s
pan|zer +s
Pao|lozzi,
Ed|uardo
(Scottish artist)
pap +s
papa +s
papa|bile
pap|acy
pap|acies
pa|pain
papal
pap|al|ism
pap|al|ist +s
pap|al|ly
Papal States (in
central Italy)
Pap|an|dreou,
An|dreas (Greek
prime minister)
pap|ar|azzo
pap|ar|azzi
pa|pa|ver|aceous
pa|pa|ver|ous
papaw +s (use
pawpaw)
pa|paya +s
Pa|pe|ete (capital
of French
Polynesia)
paper +s +ed +ing
paper|back +s
paper boy +s
pa|per|chase +s
paper clip +s
pa|per|er +s
paper girl +s
paper|hanger +s
paper|knife
pa|per|knives
paper|less
paper|maker +s
paper|mak|ing
paper mill +s
paper round +s
paper tape +s
paper-thin

paper|weight +s
paper|work
pa|pery
Paph|la|gonia
(ancient region,
Asia Minor)
Paph|la|gon|ian +s
pa|pier mâché
pa|pil|ion|aceous
pa|pilla
pa|pil|lae
pap|il|lary
pap|il|late
pap|il|loma
pap|il|lo|mas *or*
pap|il|lo|mata
pap|il|lon +s
pap|il|lose
Papi|neau, Louis
Jo|seph (French-
Canadian
politician)
pap|ism
pap|ist +s
pap|is|tic
pap|is|tic|al
pap|is|try
pa|poose +s (child)
pap|par|delle
pap|pose (of a
pappus)
Pap|pus (Greek
mathematician)
pap|pus
pappi
(hairs on thistle
etc.)
pappy
pap|pier
pap|pi|est
pap|rika +s
pap test +s
Papua (part of
Papua New
Guinea)
Pap|uan +s
pap|ula
pap|ulae *or*
pap|ulas
papu|lar
pap|ule +s
papu|lose
papu|lous
papyr|aceous
papyro|logic|al
pa|pyr|olo|gist
pa|pyr|ology
pa|pyrus
pa|pyri
par +s (average;
equality; *Golf;*
, *Stock Exchange;*

Para 390 parathyroid

par (*cont.*)
 paragraph. △pa,
 pah)
Pará (state, Brazil)
para +s
 (= paratrooper;
 paragraph)
para|basis
 para|bases
para|bi|osis
 para|bi|oses
para|bi|ot|ic
par|able +s
para|bola +s
para|bol|ic
para|bol|ic|al
para|bol|ic|al|ly
para|bol|oid +s
para|bol|oid|al
Para|cel Is|lands
 (in South China
 Sea)
Para|cel|sus (Swiss
 physician)
para|ceta|mol +s
para|chron|ism +s
para|chute
 para|chutes
 para|chuted
 para|chut|ing
para|chut|ist +s
Para|clete
par|ade
 par|ades
 par|aded
 par|ad|ing
par|ade ground +s
par|ader +s
para|di|chloro|
 ben|zene
para|did|dle +s
para|digm +s
para|dig|mat|ic
para|dig|mat|ic|
 al|ly
para|disa|ical
para|disal
para|dise +s
para|dis|iacal
para|dis|ical
para|dor +s
para|dos
 para|doses
para|dox
 para|doxes
para|dox|ical
para|dox|ic|al|ly
para|dox|ure +s
par|aes|the|sia *Br.*
 (*Am.* paresthesia)
par|af|fin +s
para|glide

para|glider +s
para|glid|ing
para|goge +s
para|gogic
para|gon +s
 (model of
 excellence.
 △parergon)
para|graph +s
para|graph|ic
para|graph|ist +s
Para|guay
Para|guay|an +s
para|hy|dro|gen
Para|íba (state,
 Brazil)
para|keet +s
para|lan|guage
par|al|de|hyde
para|legal +s
para|leip|om|ena
 (use
 paralipomena)
para|leip|sis (use
 paralipsis)
 para|leip|ses
para|lin|guis|tic
para|lip|om|ena
para|lip|sis
 para|lip|ses
par|al|lac|tic
par|al|lax
par|al|lel +s +ed
 +ing
par|al|lel|epi|ped
 +s
par|al|lel|ism +s
par|al|lelo|gram
 +s
par|alo|gise *Br.*
 (use paralogize)
 par|alo|gises
 par|alo|gised
 par|alo|gis|ing
par|alo|gism +s
par|alo|gist +s
par|alo|gize
 par|alo|gizes
 par|alo|gized
 par|alo|giz|ing
Para|lym|pic
Para|lym|pics
para|lysa|tion *Br.*
para|lyse *Br.*
 para|lyses
 para|lysed
 para|lys|ing
para|lys|ing|ly *Br.*
par|aly|sis
 par|aly|ses
para|lyt|ic +s
para|lyt|ic|al|ly

para|lyza|tion *Am.*
para|lyze *Am.*
 para|lyzes
 para|lyzed
 para|lyz|ing
para|lyz|ing|ly *Am.*
para|mag|net|ic
para|mag|net|ism
Para|ma|ribo
 (capital of
 Suriname)
para|matta (use
 parramatta)
para|me|cium
 para|me|cia *or*
 para|me|ciums
para|med|ic +s
para|med|ic|al
par|am|eter +s
para|met|ric
par|am|et|rise *Br.*
 (use parametrize)
 par|am|et|rises
 par|am|et|rised
 par|am|et|ris|ing
par|am|et|rize
 par|am|et|rizes
 par|am|et|rized
 par|am|et|riz|ing
para|mili|tary
 para|mili|tar|ies
par|am|nesia
par|amo +s
para|moe|cium
 (use
 paramecium)
 para|moe|cia *or*
 para|moe|ciums
Para|mount
 (American film
 company)
para|mount
 (supreme)
para|mount|cy
para|mount|ly
par|amour +s
Par|aná (river, S.
 America; city,
 Argentina; state,
 Brazil)
par|ang +s
para|noia
para|noiac +s
para|noi|ac|al|ly
para|no|ic
para|no|ic|al|ly
para|noid +s
para|nor|mal
para|nor|mal|ly
Par|an|thro|pus
para|pet +s
para|pet|ed

par|aph +s
para|pher|na|lia
para|phrase
 para|phrases
 para|phrased
 para|phras|ing
para|phras|tic
para|ple|gia
para|ple|gic +s
para|psycho|
 logic|al
para|
 psych|olo|gist +s
para|psych|ology
para|quat
para|sail +s
para|sail|er +s
para|sail|ing
para|sail|or +s
 (use parasailer)
par|as|cend +s
 +ed +ing
par|as|cend|er +s
para|se|lene
 para|se|lenes *or*
 para|se|lenae
para|site +s
para|sit|ic
para|sit|ic|al
para|sit|ic|al|ly
para|siti|cide
para|sit|isa|tion
 Br. (use
 parasitization)
para|sit|ise *Br.* (use
 parasitize)
 para|sit|ises
 para|sit|ised
 para|sit|is|ing
para|sit|ism
para|sit|iza|tion
para|sit|ize
 para|sit|izes
 para|sit|ized
 para|sit|iz|ing
para|sit|oid +s
para|sit|olo|gist +s
para|sit|ology
para|sol +s
para|statal +s
para|sui|cide +s
para|sym|pa|
 thet|ic
para|syn|thesis
 para|syn|theses
para|syn|thet|ic
para|tac|tic
para|tac|tic|al|ly
para|taxis
par|atha +s
para|thion
para|thy|roid +s

para¦troop +s
para¦troop¦er +s
para¦ty¦phoid
para¦vane +s
par avion
par¦boil +s +ed
+ing
par¦buckle
  par¦buckles
  par¦buckled
  par¦buck¦ling
Par¦cae *Roman
  Mythology*
par¦cel
  par¦cels
  par¦celled *Br.*
  par¦celed *Am.*
  par¦cel¦ling *Br.*
  par¦cel¦ing *Am.*
parch
  parches
  parched
  parch¦ing
parch¦ment +s
par¦close +s
pard +s
par¦da¦lote +s
pard¦ner +s
par¦don +s +ed
+ing
par¦don¦able
par¦don¦ably
par¦don¦er +s
pare
  pares
  pared
  par¦ing
  (trim; peel. △ pair,
  pear, *père*)
par¦egor¦ic +s
par¦eira
paren +s
  (= parenthesis)
par¦en¦chyma
par¦en¦chy¦mal
par¦en¦chy¦mat¦
    ous
par¦ent +s +ed
+ing
par¦ent¦age
par¦en¦tal
par¦en¦tal¦ly
par¦en¦teral
par¦en¦teral¦ly
par¦en¦theses
par¦en¦the¦sise *Br.*
  (use
  parenthesize)
  par¦en¦the¦sises
  par¦en¦the¦sised
  par¦en¦the¦sis¦ing

par¦en¦the¦size
  par¦en¦the¦sizes
  par¦en¦the¦sized
  par¦en¦the¦siz¦ing
par¦en¦thet¦ic
par¦en¦thet¦ic¦al
par¦en¦thet¦ic¦al¦ly
par¦ent¦hood
parer +s
par¦er¦gon
par¦erga
  (subsidiary work.
  △ paragon)
par¦esis
  par¦eses
par¦es¦the¦sia *Am.*
  (*Br.* paraesthesia)
par¦et¦ic
par ex¦cel¦lence
par¦fait +s
par¦gana +s
par¦get +s +ed
+ing
par¦he¦li¦acal
par¦he¦lic
par¦he¦lion
  par¦he¦lia
par¦iah +s
par¦iah dog +s
Par¦ian +s
par¦ietal
pari-mutuel
par¦ing +s (piece
  cut off. △ pairing)
pari passu
Paris (capital of
  France; in *Greek
  Mythology*)
Paris, Mat¦thew
  (English
  chronicler)
par¦ish
  par¦ishes
pa¦rish¦ion¦er +s
Paris¦ian +s
pari¦son +s
pari¦syl¦lab¦ic
par¦ity
  par¦ities
Park, Mungo
  (Scottish explorer)
park +s +ed +ing
parka +s (jacket.
  △ parker)
park-and-ride +s
Park Chung Hee
  (South Korean
  president)
Par¦ker, Char¦lie
  (American
  saxophonist)

Par¦ker, Doro¦thy
  (American
  humorist)
park¦er +s (person
  who parks;
  parking light.
  △ parka)
par¦kin
park¦ing light +s
park¦ing lot +s
park¦ing meter +s
park¦ing ticket +s
Par¦kin¦son¦ism
Par¦kin¦son's
  dis¦ease
Par¦kin¦son's law
park¦land +s
park¦way +s
parky
  park¦ier
  park¦iest
par¦lance
par¦lay +s +ed
  +ing (bet)
par¦ley +s +ed
  +ing (conference.
  △ Pali)
par¦lia¦ment +s
par¦lia¦men¦tar¦ian
  +s
par¦lia¦men¦tary
par¦lor *Am.* +s
par¦lor¦maid *Am.* +s
par¦lour *Br.* +s
par¦lour¦maid *Br.* +s
par¦lous
par¦lous¦ly
par¦lous¦ness
Parma (province
  and city, Italy;
  ham. △ Palma)
Par¦meni¦des
  (Greek
  philosopher)
Par¦mesan
Par¦mi¦gian¦ino
  (Italian painter)
Par¦mi¦giano
  (= Parmigianino)
Par¦nas¦sian +s
Par¦nas¦sus,
  Mount (in
  Greece)
Par¦nell, Charles
  (Irish nationalist)
pa¦ro¦chial
pa¦ro¦chial¦ism
pa¦ro¦chi¦al¦ity
pa¦ro¦chi¦al¦ly
par¦od¦ic
par¦od¦ist +s

par¦ody
  par¦odies
  par¦odied
  par¦ody¦ing
parol +s (oral;
  declaration)
par¦ole
  par¦oles
  par¦oled
  par¦ol¦ing
  (release)
par¦ole Linguistics
par¦olee +s
par¦ono¦masia
paro¦nym +s
par¦onym¦ous
Paros (Greek
  island)
par¦otid +s
parot¦itis
Par¦ou¦sia *Theology*
par¦ox¦ysm +s
par¦ox¦ys¦mal
par¦oxy¦tone +s
par¦pen +s
par¦quet +s +ed
+ing
par¦quet¦ry
Parr, Cath¦er¦ine
  (wife of Henry
  VIII of England)
parr
  plural parr or
  parrs
  (salmon)
parra¦matta
parri¦cidal
parri¦cide +s
par¦rot +s +ed
+ing
parrot-fashion
par¦rot¦fish
  plural par¦rot¦fish
  or par¦rot¦fishes
Parry, Hu¦bert
  (English
  composer)
parry
  par¦ries
  par¦ried
  parry¦ing
parse
  parses
  parsed
  pars¦ing
par¦sec +s
Par¦see +s
Par¦see¦ism
parser +s
Par¦si¦fal
  (alternative name
  for Perceval)

par|si|mo|ni|ous
par|si|mo|ni|ous|ly
par|si|mo|ni|ous|
      ness
par|si|mony
pars|ley
parsley-piert +s
pars|nip +s
par|son +s
par|son|age +s
par|son|ical
Par|sons, Charles
  (English engineer)
par|son's nose +s
part +s +ed +ing
  (portion;
  component; role;
  to divide; etc.
  △ pâte)
par|tak|able
par|take
  par|takes
  par|took
  par|tak|ing
  par|taken
  par|taker +s
par|tan +s
par|terre +s
part ex|change +s
  noun
part-exchange
  part-exchanges
  part-exchanged
  part-exchan|ging
  verb
par|theno|gen|esis
par|theno|
      gen|et|ic
par|theno|
    gen|et|ic|al|ly
Par|thenon
  (temple, Athens)
Par|thian +s
par|tial +s
par|ti|al|ity
  par|ti|al|ities
par|tial|ly
par|tial|ness
part|ible
par|tici|pant +s
par|tici|pate
  par|tici|pates
  par|tici|pated
  par|tici|pat|ing
par|tici|pa|tion +s
par|tici|pa|tive
par|tici|pa|tor +s
par|tici|pa|tory
par|ti|ci|pial
par|ti|ci|pi|al|ly
par|ti|ciple +s
par|ticle +s

parti|col|ored *Am.*
parti|col|oured *Br.*
par|ticu|lar +s
par|ticu|lar|
  isa|tion *Br.* (use
  particularization)
par|ticu|lar|ise *Br.*
  (use
  particularize)
  par|ticu|lar|ises
  par|ticu|lar|ised
  par|ticu|lar|is|ing
par|ticu|lar|ism
par|ticu|lar|ist +s
par|ticu|lar|ity
  par|ticu|lar|ities
par|ticu|lar|
      iza|tion
par|ticu|lar|ize
  par|ticu|lar|izes
  par|ticu|lar|ized
  par|ticu|lar|iz|ing
par|ticu|lar|ly
par|ticu|late +s
part|ing +s
parti pris
  partis pris
par|ti|san +s
par|ti|san|ship
par|tita +s
par|tite
par|ti|tion +s +ed
  +ing
par|ti|tion|er +s
par|ti|tion|ist +s
par|ti|tive +s
par|ti|tive|ly
par|ti|zan +s (use
  partisan)
part|ly
part|ner +s +ed
  +ing
part|ner|less
part|ner|ship +s
part of speech
  parts of speech
Par|ton, Dolly
  (American singer)
par|took
par|tridge +s
part-song +s
part-time
part-timer +s
par|turi|ent
par|tur|ition
party
  par|ties
  par|tied
  party|ing
party-goer +s

party line +s
party pol|it|ical +s
party pol|it|ics
party-poop +s
party-pooper +s
party-pooping
party pop|per +s
party wall +s
par|ure +s
Par|vati *Hinduism*
par|venu +s *male*
par|venue +s
  female
par|vis
  par|vises
par|vise +s (use
  parvis)
parvo|virus
  parvo|viruses
pas
  plural pas
Pasa|dena (city,
  USA)
Pas|cal (computer
  language)
Pas|cal, Blaise
  (French
  mathematician
  and physicist)
pas|cal +s (unit)
pas|chal (Easter)
pas de chat
  plural pas de chat
pas de deux
  plural pas de deux
pas glissé +s
pash
  pashes
pasha +s
pash|al|ic +s
pashm
Pashto
Pash|tun +s
  (= Pathan)
Pašić, Ni|kola
  (Serbian prime
  minister)
Pas|ion|aria, La
  (Dolores Ibarruri
  Gomez, Spanish
  Communist
  politician)
Pa|siphaë *Greek*
  Mythology
pas|kha
paso doble +s
pasque flower +s
pas|quin|ade +s
pass
  passes
  passed
  pass|ing

pass (*cont.*)
  (move; go past; be
  accepted; etc.;
  passage between
  mountains.
  △ past)
pass|able
  (adequate;
  unobstructed.
  △ passible)
pass|able|ness
pass|ably
pas|sa|caglia +s
pas|sage
  pas|sages
  pas|saged
  pas|sa|ging
pas|sage|way +s
pas|sant
pass|band +s
pass|book +s
Pas|schen|daele
  (battle site,
  Belgium)
passé
passed pawn +s
passe|ment|erie
pas|sen|ger +s
passenger-mile +s
pas|sen|ger
  pi|geon +s
passe|par|tout +s
passe|pied +s
pass|er +s
passer-by
  passers-by
pas|ser|ine +s
pas seul +s
pass|ibil|ity
pass|ible (capable
  of suffering.
  △ passable)
Pas|si|formes
pas|sim
pass|ing +s
pass|ing|ly
passing-out *noun*
  and attributive
Pas|sion (of Christ)
pas|sion +s
pas|sion|al +s
pas|sion|ate
pas|sion|ate|ly
pas|sion|ate|ness
pas|sion flower +s
pas|sion fruit +s
Pas|sion|ist +s
pas|sion|less
pas|sion play +s
Pas|sion Sun|day
Pas|sion|tide
Pas|sion Week

pas|siv|ate
  pas|siv|ates
  pas|siv|ated
  pas|siv|at|ing
pas|siv|ation
pas|sive +s
pas|sive|ly
pas|sive|ness
pas|siv|ity
pass-key +s
pass-mark +s
Pass|over (Jewish
  festival)
pass|port +s
pass|word +s
past +s (gone by in
  time; former time;
  beyond; so as to
  pass. △ passed)
pasta +s
paste
  pastes
  pasted
  past|ing
paste|board +s
pas|tel +s (colour.
  △ pastille)
pas|tel|ist +s Am.
pas|tel|list +s Br.
pas|tern +s
Pas|ter|nak, Boris
  (Russian writer)
paste-up +s noun
Pas|teur, Louis
  (French chemist)
pas|teur|isa|tion
  Br. (use
  pasteurization)
pas|teur|ise Br.
  (use pasteurize)
  pas|teur|ises
  pas|teur|ised
  pas|teur|is|ing
pas|teur|iser Br. +s
  (use pasteurizer)
pas|teur|iza|tion
pas|teur|ize
  pas|teur|izes
  pas|teur|ized
  pas|teur|iz|ing
pas|teur|izer +s
pas|tic|cio +s
pas|tiche +s
pas|tille +s
  (lozenge.
  △ pastel)
pastille-burner +s
past|ily
pas|time +s
pasti|ness

pas|tis
  plural pas|tis
past master +s
pas|tor +s +ed
  +ing
pas|tor|al +s
  (adjective; poem
  etc.; letter from
  bishop)
pas|tor|ale
  pas|tor|ales or
  pas|tor|ali
  (music; musical
  play)
pas|tor|al|ism
pas|tor|al|ist +s
pas|tor|al|ity
pas|tor|al|ly
pas|tor|ate +s
pas|tor|ship +s
past per|fect +s
pas|trami
pas|try
  pas|tries
pastry-cook +s
pas|tur|age
pas|ture
  pas|tures
  pas|tured
  pas|tur|ing
pas|ture|land +s
pasty
  pas|ties
  pasti|er
  pasti|est
Pat +s (name; often
  offensive Irishman)
pat
  pats
  pat|ted
  pat|ting
  (strike gently;
  gentle stroke; glib)
pat-a-cake
pa|ta|gium
  pa|ta|gia
Pata|gonia (region,
  S. America)
Pata|gon|ian +s
Pa|tali|putra
  (ancient name of
  Patna)
Pata|vin|ity
Pa|ta|vium (Latin
  name for Padua)
pat|ball
patch
  patches
  patched
  patch|ing
patch|board +s
patch cord +s

patch|er +s
patch|ily
patchi|ness
patch|ouli
patch panel +s
patch|work +s
patchy
  patch|ier
  patchi|est
pate +s (head)
pâte +s (paste for
  making porcelain.
  △ part)
pâté +s (meat etc.
  paste. △ pattée)
pâté de foie gras
  (goose liver paste)
pa|tella
  pa|tel|lae
pa|tel|lar
pa|tel|late
paten +s (shallow
  dish. △ patten,
  pattern)
pa|tency
pa|tent +s +ed
  +ing
pa|tent|able
pa|tent|ee +s
pa|tent|ly
pa|tent|or +s
Pater, Wal|ter
  (English essayist
  and critic)
pater +s
pater|famil|ias
pa|ter|nal
pa|ter|nal|ism
pa|ter|nal|ist +s
pa|ter|nal|is|tic
pa|ter|nal|is|tic|
      al|ly
pa|ter|nal|ly
pa|ter|nity
  pa|ter|nities
pater|nos|ter +s
path +s
Pa|than +s
Pathé, Charles
  (French film
  pioneer)
path|et|ic
path|et|ic|al|ly
path|find|er +s
path|less
patho|gen +s
patho|gen|esis
patho|gen|et|ic
patho|gen|ic
path|ogen|ous
path|ogeny

path|og|no|mon|ic
  +s
path|og|nomy
patho|logic|al
patho|logic|al|ly
path|olo|gist +s
path|ology
  path|olo|gies
pathos
path|way +s
Pa|tience (name)
pa|tience (calm
  endurance)
pa|tient +s
pa|tient|ly
pat|ina +s
pat|in|ated
pat|in|ation
pat|in|ous
patio +s
pa|tis|serie +s
patly
Pat|more,
  Cov|en|try
  (English poet)
Pat|mos (Greek
  island)
Patna (city, India)
pat|ness
pat|ois
  plural pat|ois
Paton, Alan (South
  African writer)
Pa|tras (port,
  Greece)
pat|rial +s
pat|ri|al|ity
patri|arch +s
patri|arch|al
pat|ri|arch|al|ly
patri|arch|ate +s
patri|arch|ism
patri|archy
  patri|arch|ies
Pa|tri|cia
pa|tri|cian +s
pa|trici|ate +s
patri|cidal
patri|cide +s
Pat|rick (patron
  saint of Ireland;
  name)
patri|lin|eal
patri|mo|nial
patri|mony
  patri|monies
pat|riot +s
pat|ri|ot|ic
pat|ri|ot|ic|al|ly
pat|ri|ot|ism
pa|tris|tic
pa|tris|tics

Pa¦troc¦lus *Greek Mythology*
pa¦trol
  pa¦trols
  pa¦trolled
  pa¦trol¦ling
pa¦trol¦ler +s
pa¦trol¦man
  pa¦trol¦men
patro¦logic¦al
pa¦trolo¦gist +s
pa¦trol¦ogy
  pa¦trolo¦gies
pat¦ron +s
pat¦ron¦age +s
pat¦ron¦al
pat¦ron¦ess
  pat¦ron¦esses
pat¦ron¦isa¦tion *Br.* (use patronization)
pat¦ron¦ise *Br.* (use patronize)
  pat¦ron¦ises
  pat¦ron¦ised
  pat¦ron¦is¦ing
pat¦ron¦iser *Br.* +s (use patronizer)
pat¦ron¦is¦ing¦ly *Br.* (use patronizingly)
pat¦ron¦iza¦tion
pat¦ron¦ize
  pat¦ron¦izes
  pat¦ron¦ized
  pat¦ron¦iz¦ing
pat¦ron¦izer +s
pat¦ron¦iz¦ing¦ly
patro¦nym¦ic +s
pa¦troon +s
Patsy (name)
patsy
  pat¦sies
  (person easily ridiculed, blamed etc.)
Pat¦taya (resort, Thailand)
pat¦tée (type of cross. △ pâté)
pat¦ten +s (shoe. △ paten, pattern)
pat¦ter +s +ed +ing
pat¦tern +s +ed +ing (design; model. △ paten, patten)
pat¦tern¦ing +s
Patty (name)

patty
  pat¦ties
  (pie; cake)
patty¦pan +s
patu¦lous
patu¦lous¦ly
patu¦lous¦ness
pat¦zer +s
paua +s (shellfish. △ power)
pau¦city
  pau¦ci¦ties
Paul (saint; name)
Paul, Les (American jazz guitarist)
Paula
Paul¦ette
Pauli, Wolf¦gang (Austrian-born American physicist)
Paul¦ine (of St Paul; name)
Paul¦ing, Linus (American chemist)
Paul Jones (dance)
paul¦ow¦nia +s
Paul Pry (inquisitive person)
paunch
  paunches
  paunched
  paunch¦ing
paunchi¦ness
paunchy
  paunch¦ier
  paunchi¦est
pau¦per +s
pau¦per¦dom
pau¦per¦isa¦tion *Br.* (use pauperization)
pau¦per¦ise *Br.* (use pauperize)
  pau¦per¦ises
  pau¦per¦ised
  pau¦per¦is¦ing
pau¦per¦ism
pau¦per¦iza¦tion
pau¦per¦ize
  pau¦per¦izes
  pau¦per¦ized
  pau¦per¦iz¦ing
Pau¦san¦ias (Greek geographer and historian)
pause
  pauses

pause *(cont.)*
  paused
  paus¦ing
pav¦age
pavan +s (use pavane)
pav¦ane +s
Pava¦rotti, Lu¦ciano (Italian tenor)
pave
  paves
  paved
  pav¦ing
pavé +s
pave¦ment +s
paver +s
Pa¦vese, Ce¦sare (Italian writer)
pa¦vil¦ion +s +ed +ing
pav¦ing +s
pav¦ing stone +s
pa¦vior +s
pa¦viour +s (use pavior)
Pav¦lov, Ivan Pet¦ro¦vich (Russian physiologist)
Pav¦lova, Anna (Russian dancer)
pav¦lova +s (cake)
Pav¦lov¦ian
pav¦on¦ine
paw +s +ed +ing (animal's foot. △ poor, pore, pour)
pawk¦ily
pawki¦ness
pawky
  pawk¦ier
  pawki¦est
  (drily humorous; shrewd. △ porky)
pawl +s (lever etc. △ pall)
pawn +s +ed +ing (chess piece, deposit as security for loan. △ porn)
pawn¦broker +s
pawn¦brok¦ing
pawn¦shop +s
paw¦paw +s
pax (peace)
Pax¦ton, Jo¦seph (English gardener and architect)
pay
  pays

pay *(cont.)*
  paid
  pay¦ing
pay¦able +s
pay-as-you-earn
pay-as-you-go
pay¦back +s
pay-bed +s
pay claim +s
pay day +s
pay dirt
payee +s
pay en¦vel¦ope +s
payer +s
pay¦load +s
pay¦mas¦ter +s
Pay¦mas¦ter Gen¦eral
Pay¦mas¦ters Gen¦eral
pay¦ment +s
pay¦nim +s
pay-off +s *noun*
pay¦ola +s
pay-out +s *noun*
pay packet +s
pay¦phone +s
pay¦roll +s
pays¦age +s
pays¦agist +s
Pays de la Loire (region, France)
pay¦slip +s
pay sta¦tion +s
Paz, Octa¦vio (Mexican poet and essayist)
P-Celtic
pea +s (vegetable; plant. △ pee)
pea-brain +s
peace (quiet; freedom from war. △ piece)
peace¦able
peace¦able¦ness
peace¦ably
Peace Corps
peace¦ful
peace¦ful¦ly
peace¦ful¦ness
peace¦keep¦er +s
peace¦keep¦ing
peace¦maker +s
peace¦mak¦ing
peace¦nik +s
peace-offering +s
peace pipe +s
peace stud¦ies
peace¦time
peach
  peaches

peach (*cont.*)
  peached
  peach|ing
peach-bloom
peach-blow
pea-chick +s
peachi|ness
peach Melba +s
peachy
  peach|ier
  peachi|est
Pea|cock, Thomas
  Love (English
  writer)
pea|cock +s
pea|cock blue +s
  noun and adjective
peacock-blue
  attributive
pea|cock|ery
pea|fowl
  plural pea|fowl
pea green +s *noun*
  and adjective
pea-green
  attributive
pea|hen +s
pea-jacket +s
peak +s +ed +ing
  (summit; reach
  highest value.
  △ peek, peke,
  pique)
Peak Dis|trict
  (in N. England)
Peake, Mer|vyn
  (British writer)
peak hour +s *noun*
peak-hour
  attributive
peaki|ness
peak|ish
peak load +s *noun*
peak-load
  attributive
peaky
  peak|ier
  peaki|est
peal +s +ed +ing
  (ring; fish. △ peel)
pean *Am.* +s (song
  of praise. *Br.*
  paean. △ paeon,
  peon)
pean (fur. △ peen)
pea|nut +s
pea|nut but|ter
pear +s (fruit.
  △ pair, pare, *père*)
pear drop +s

Pearl (name)
pearl +s +ed +ing
  (gem. △ purl)
pearl-diver +s
pearl|er +s (pearl-
  fisher. △ purler)
pearl|es|cent
pearl-fisher +s
Pearl Har|bor (in
  Hawaii)
pearli|ness
pearl|ised *Br.* (use
  pearlized)
pearl|ite (use
  perlite)
pearl|ized
pearl-oyster +s
Pearl River (in
  China)
pearl|ware
pearl|wort +s
pearly
  pearl|ies
  pearl|ier
  pearli|est
pear|main +s
Pear|son, Karl
  (English
  mathematician)
Pear|son, Les|ter
  (Canadian prime
  minister)
peart +er +est
  (cheerful. △ pert)
Peary, Rob|ert
  (American
  explorer)
Peary Land
  (region,
  Greenland)
peas|ant +s
peas|ant|ry
peas|anty
pease (*archaic*
  peas)
pease pud|ding
pea-shooter +s
pea-souper +s
pea stick +s
peat +s
peat|bog +s
peat|land +s
peat|moss
  peat|mosses
peaty
  peat|ier
  peati|est
peau-de-soie
peb|ble
  peb|bles
  peb|bled
  peb|bling

pebble-dash
pebble-dashed
pebbly
  peb|blier
  peb|bli|est
pecan +s (nut.
  △ pekan)
pecca|bil|ity
pec|cable
pecca|dillo
  pecca|dil|loes *or*
  pecca|dil|los
pec|cancy
pec|cant
pec|cary
  pec|car|ies
pec|cavi +s
pêche Melba +s
Pech|enga (region,
  Russia)
Pe|chora (river,
  Russia)
Peck, Greg|ory
  (American actor)
peck +s +ed +ing
peck|er +s
peck|ing order +s
peck|ish
peck order +s
pec|or|ino +s
Pécs (city,
  Hungary)
pec|ten
  pec|tens *or*
  pec|tines
  Zoology
pec|tic
pec|tin +s
  Biochemistry
pec|tin|ate
pec|tin|ated
pec|tin|ation
pec|toral +s
pec|tose
pecu|late
  pecu|lates
  pecu|lated
  pecu|lat|ing
pecu|la|tion
pecu|la|tor +s
pe|cu|liar +s
pe|cu|li|ar|ity
  pe|cu|li|ar|ities
pe|cu|li|ar|ly
pe|cu|ni|ar|ily
pe|cu|ni|ary
peda|gogic
peda|gogic|al
peda|gogic|al|ly
peda|gogics
peda|gog|ism
peda|gogue +s

peda|goguism (use
  pedagogism)
peda|gogy
pedal
  pedals
  ped|alled *Br.*
  ped|aled *Am.*
  ped|al|ling *Br.*
  ped|al|ing *Am.*
  (foot lever; to
  rotate a pedal.
  △ peddle)
ped|al|er *Am.* +s
  (person who
  pedals. △ peddler,
  pedlar)
ped|al|ler *Br.* +s
  (person who
  pedals. △ peddler,
  pedlar)
ped|alo
  ped|alos *or*
  ped|aloes
pedal-pusher +s
ped|ant +s
pe|dan|tic
pe|dan|tic|al|ly
ped|ant|ry
  ped|ant|ries
ped|ate
ped|dle
  ped|dles
  ped|dled
  ped|dling
  (sell; promote.
  △ pedal)
ped|dler +s *Am.*
  (hawker. *Br.*
  pedlar. △ pedaler,
  pedaller)
ped|dler +s (drug
  pusher. △ pedaler,
  pedaller, pedlar)
ped|er|ast +s
ped|er|as|tic
ped|er|asty
ped|es|tal
  ped|es|tals
  ped|es|talled *Br.*
  ped|es|taled *Am.*
  ped|es|tal|ling *Br.*
  ped|es|tal|ling *Am.*
ped|es|trian +s
ped|es|tri|an|
  isa|tion *Br.* (use
  pedestrian-
  ization)
ped|es|tri|an|ise
  Br. (use
  pedestrianize)
ped|es|tri|an|ises
ped|es|tri|an|ised

ped¦es¦tri¦an¦ise
(cont.)
  ped¦es¦tri¦an¦
                 is¦ing
ped¦es¦tri¦an¦ism
ped¦es¦tri¦an¦
                iza¦tion
  ped¦es¦tri¦an¦izes
  ped¦es¦tri¦an¦ized
  ped¦es¦tri¦an¦
                 iz¦ing
pedi¦at¦ric _Am._ (_Br._
  paediatric)
pedi¦at¦ri¦cian _Am._
  +s (_Br._
  paediatrician)
pedi¦at¦rics _Am._
  (_Br._ paediatrics)
pedi¦at¦rist _Am._ +s
  (_Br._ paediatrist)
pedi¦cab +s
pedi¦cel +s
pedi¦cel¦late
ped¦icle +s
pe¦dicu¦lar
pe¦dicu¦late
pe¦dicu¦losis
pe¦dicu¦lous
pedi¦cure
  pedi¦cures
  pedi¦cured
  pedi¦cur¦ing
pedi¦gree +s
pedi¦greed
pedi¦ment +s
pedi¦men¦tal
pedi¦ment¦ed
ped¦lar _Br._ +s (_Am._
  peddler. hawker.
  △ pedaler,
  pedaller, peddler)
ped¦lary
pedo|logic¦al
ped|olo|gist +s
ped|ology
ped|ometer +s
pedo|phile _Am._ +s
  (_Br._ paedophile)
pedo|philia _Am._
  (_Br._ paedophilia)
pedo|phil¦iac _Am._
  +s (_Br._
  paedophiliac)
ped|uncle +s
ped|un|cu|lar
ped|un|cu|late
ped¦way +s
pee
  pees
  peed
  pee¦ing

pee (_cont._)
  (urine; urinate.
  △ pea)
Peebles|shire
  (former county,
  Scotland)
peek +s +ed +ing
  (peep. △ peak,
  peke, pique)
peek|aboo
Peel, Rob¦ert
  (British prime
  minister)
peel +s +ed +ing
  (skin, rind, etc.;
  shovel; tower.
  △ peal)
peel¦er +s
peel¦ing +s
Peel¦ite +s
peen +s +ed +ing
  (part of hammer.
  △ pean)
Peene|munde
  (rocket site,
  Germany)
peep +s +ed +ing
peep-bo
peep¦er +s
peep|hole +s
peep|ing Tom +s
peep-show +s
peep-sight +s
peep-toe
peep-toed
pee¦pul +s (bo tree.
  △ people)
peer +s +ed +ing
  (look; noble;
  equal. △ pier)
peer¦age +s
peer|ess
  peer|esses
peer group +s _noun_
peer|less
peeve
  peeves
  peeved
  peev¦ing
peev¦ish
peev¦ish¦ly
peev¦ish|ness
pee¦wee +s
  (lapwing; magpie
  lark. △ pewee)
pee¦wit +s
peg
  pegs
  pegged
  peg|ging
Pega|sean
Pega|sus _Greek
  Mythology_

peg|board +s
Peggy
peg-leg +s
peg¦mat|ite
peg|top +s
Pegu (city, Burma)
Peh|levi
  (= Pahlavi)
Pei, I. M.
  (American
  architect)
Pei¦gan
  plural Pei¦gan or
  Pei¦gans
pei|gnoir +s
Peirce, C. S.
  (American
  philosopher.
  △ Pierce)
Pei¦sis|tra¦tus (use
  Pisistratus)
pe¦jora|tive +s
pe¦jora|tive¦ly
pekan (animal.
  △ pecan)
peke +s (dog.
  △ peak, peek,
  pique)
Pe¦kin|ese
  plural Pe¦kin|ese
  (dog)
Pe¦king (= Beijing)
Pe¦king|ese
  plural Pe¦king|ese
  (inhabitant of
  Peking)
Pe¦king man
pekoe
pel¦age +s
Pe¦la|gian +s (of
  Pelagius)
pe¦la|gian +s (of
  the sea)
Pe¦la¦gian|ism
pe¦la|gic
Pe¦la|gius (British
  or Irish monk)
pel¦ar|go|nium +s
Pe¦las|gian +s
Pe¦las|gic
Pelé (Brazilian
  footballer)
pele +s (tower; use
  peel. △ peal)
pel¦er|ine +s
Pel¦eus _Greek
  Mythology_
pelf
Pel¦ham, Henry
  (British prime
  minister)
pel¦ham +s
peli|can +s

Pel¦ion (mountain,
  Greece)
pe|lisse +s
pel¦ite +s
pel|lagra
pel|lag|rous
pel¦let +s +ed +ing
Pel¦le|tier, Pierre-
  Joseph (French
  chemist)
pel¦let|ise _Br._ (use
  pelletize)
  pel¦let|ises
  pel¦let|ised
  pel¦let|is¦ing
pel¦let|ize
  pel¦let|izes
  pel¦let|ized
  pel¦let|iz¦ing
pel¦licle +s
pel¦licu|lar
pel|li¦tory
  pel|li|tor¦ies
pell-mell
pel|lu¦cid
pel|lu¦cid|ity
pel|lu¦cid¦ly
Pel¦man|ise _Br._
  (use Pelmanize)
  Pel¦man|ises
  Pel¦man|ised
  Pel¦man|is¦ing
Pel¦man|ism
Pel¦man|ize
  Pel¦man|izes
  Pel¦man|ized
  Pel¦man|iz¦ing
pel¦met +s
Pelo|pon|nese
  (peninsula,
  Greece)
Pelo|pon|nes¦ian
  +s
Pe¦lops _Greek
  Mythology_
pe|lorus
pe|lota +s
pelt +s +ed +ing
pelta
  pel¦tae
pel|tate
pelt¦ry
pel¦vic
pel¦vis
  pel|vises or
  pel|ves
Pemba (port,
  Mozambique)
Pem|broke (town,
  Wales)

Pem¦broke¦shire
(former county,
Wales)
pem¦mican
pem¦phig¦oid
pem¦phig¦ous
pem¦phigus
PEN
(= International
Association of
Poets,
Playwrights,
Editors, Essayists,
and Novelists)
pen
pens
penned
pen¦ning
penal
pen¦al¦isa¦tion *Br.*
(use penalization)
pen¦al¦ise *Br.* (use
penalize)
pen¦al¦ises
pen¦al¦ised
pen¦al¦is¦ing
pen¦al¦iza¦tion
pen¦al¦ize
pen¦al¦izes
pen¦al¦ized
pen¦al¦iz¦ing
pen¦al¦ly
pen¦alty
pen¦al¦ties
pen¦ance
pen¦ances
pen¦anced
pen¦an¦cing
pen and ink *noun*
pen-and-ink
adjective
Pen¦ang (island and
state, Malaysia)
pen¦an¦nu¦lar
pe¦na¦tes
pence
pen¦chant +s
pen¦cil
pen¦cils
pen¦cilled *Br.*
pen¦ciled *Am.*
pen¦cil¦ling *Br.*
pen¦cil¦ing *Am.*
pen¦cil box
pen¦cil boxes
pen¦cil case +s
pen¦cil¦er *Am.* +s
pen¦cil¦ler *Br.* +s
pencil-pusher +s
pencil-pushing
pen¦cil sharp¦en¦er
+s

pen¦dant +s *noun*
pen¦dency
pen¦dent *adjective*
pen¦dente lite
pen¦dent¦ive +s
Pen¦de¦recki,
  Krzysz¦tof
  (Polish composer)
pend¦ing
pend¦ing tray +s
pen¦dragon
pen¦du¦late
pen¦du¦lates
pen¦du¦lated
pen¦du¦lat¦ing
pen¦du¦line
pen¦du¦lous
pen¦du¦lous¦ly
pen¦du¦lum +s
Pe¦nel¦ope (*Greek
  Mythology*; name)
pe¦ne¦plain +s
pene¦tra¦bil¦ity
pene¦trable
pene¦tra¦lia
pene¦trant +s
pene¦trate
  pene¦trates
  pene¦trated
  pene¦trat¦ing
pene¦trat¦ing¦ly
pene¦tra¦tion +s
pene¦tra¦tive
pene¦tra¦tor +s
pen-feather +s
pen¦friend +s
pen¦guin +s
pen hold¦er +s
peni¦cil¦late
peni¦cil¦lin +s
pen¦ile
pen¦ill¦ion
pen¦in¦sula +s
  noun
pen¦in¦su¦lar
  adjective
penis
  pen¦ises
peni¦tence +s
peni¦tent +s
peni¦ten¦tial +s
peni¦ten¦tial¦ly
peni¦ten¦tiary
  peni¦ten¦tiar¦ies
peni¦tent¦ly
pen¦knife
  pen¦knives
pen¦light +s
pen¦man
  pen¦men
pen¦man¦ship

Penn, Wil¦liam
(English Quaker,
founder of
Pennsylvania)
pen-name +s
pen¦nant +s
penne (pasta)
penni
  pen¦niä
  (Finnish currency.
  △ penny)
pen¦nies
pen¦ni¦less
pen¦ni¦less¦ly
pen¦ni¦less¦ness
pen¦nill
  pen¦ill¦ion
Pen¦nine Hills (in
  England)
Pen¦nines
  (= Pennine Hills)
pen¦non +s
pen¦noned
penn'orth
Penn¦syl¦va¦nia
  (state, USA)
Penn¦syl¦va¦nian
  +s
Penny (name)
penny
  pen¦nies *or* pence
  (British currency;
  US cent. △ penni)
penny-a-liner +s
penny black +s
penny dread¦ful
  +s
penny-farthing +s
  (bicycle)
penny-in-the-slot
penny-pincher +s
penny-pinching
penny¦royal
penny¦weight +s
penny whis¦tle +s
penny wise
penny¦wort +s
penny¦worth +s
peno¦logic¦al
pen¦olo¦gist +s
pen¦ology
pen pal +s
pen-pusher +s
pen-pushing
pen¦sée +s
pen¦sile
pen¦sion +s +ed
  +ing (payment)
pen¦sion +s
  (boarding house)
pen¦sion¦abil¦ity
pen¦sion¦able

pen¦sion¦ary
  pen¦sion¦ar¦ies
pen¦sion¦er +s
pen¦sion¦less
pen¦sive
pen¦sive¦ly
pen¦sive¦ness
pen¦ste¦mon +s
pen¦stock +s
pent
penta¦chord +s
pent¦acle +s
pent¦tad +s
penta¦dac¦tyl +s
Penta¦gon (US
  defence HQ)
penta¦gon +s (five-
  sided figure)
pen¦tagon¦al
penta¦gram +s
pent¦agyn¦ous
penta¦he¦dral
penta¦he¦dron
  penta¦he¦dra *or*
  penta¦he¦drons
pen¦tam¦er¦ous
pen¦tam¦eter +s
pen¦tan¦drous
pen¦tane +s
pent¦angle +s
penta¦no¦ic
penta¦prism +s
Penta¦teuch
Penta¦teuchal
pent¦ath¦lete +s
pent¦ath¦lon +s
penta¦tonic
penta¦va¦lent
Pente¦cost
Pente¦cos¦tal +s
Pente¦cos¦tal¦ism
Pente¦cos¦tal¦ist
  +s
Pen¦the¦si¦lea
  Greek Mythology
pent¦house +s
penti¦mento
  penti¦menti
Pent¦land Firth
  (off Scotland)
pento¦bar¦bital
pento¦bar¦bit¦one
pen¦tode +s
pen¦tose +s
Pento¦thal
pent roof +s
pent¦ste¦mon +s
  (use penstemon)
pen¦tyl
pen¦ult
pen¦ul¦ti¦mate

pen|um|bra
pen|um|brae
pen|um|bral
pen|uri|ous
pen|uri|ous|ly
pen|uri|ous|ness
pen|ury
Penza (city, Russia)
Pen|zance (town,
England)
peon +s (labourer.
△ paean, paeon,
pean)
pe|on|age
peony
peon|ies
people
peoples
peopled
peop|ling
(persons. △ peepul)
people's
dem|oc|racy
people's
dem|oc|ra|cies
Pe|oria (city, USA)
PEP (= Personal
Equity Plan)
pep
peps
pepped
pep|ping
(vigour; enliven)
pep|er|ino
pep|er|oni +s (use
pepperoni)
pep|lum +s
pepo +s
pep|per +s +ed
+ing
pep|per|box
pep|per|boxes
pep|per|corn +s
pep|peri|ness
pep|per mill +s
pep|per|mint +s
pep|per|minty
pep|per|oni
pep|per pot +s
pep|per|wort +s
pep|pery
pep pill +s
pep|pily
pep|pi|ness
peppy
pep|pier
pep|pi|est
Pepsi(-Cola) +s
Propr.
pep|sin
pep talk +s
pep|tic
pep|tide +s

pep|tone +s
pep|ton|ise *Br.* (use
peptonize)
pep|ton|ises
pep|ton|ised
pep|ton|is|ing
pep|ton|ize
pep|ton|izes
pep|ton|ized
pep|ton|iz|ing
Pepys, Sam|uel
(English diarist)
per
per|ad|ven|ture
Perak (state,
Malaysia)
per|am|bu|late
per|am|bu|lates
per|am|bu|lated
per|am|bu|lat|ing
per|am|bu|la|tion
per|am|bu|la|tor
+s
per|am|bu|la|tory
per annum
per|cale
per cap|ita
per caput
per|ceiv|able
per|ceive
per|ceives
per|ceived
per|ceiv|ing
per|ceiver +s
per|cent *Am.*
per cent *Br.*
per|cent|age +s
per|cent|ile +s
per|cept +s
per|cep|ti|bil|ity
per|cep|tible
per|cep|tibly
per|cep|tion +s
per|cep|tion|al
per|cep|tive
per|cep|tive|ly
per|cep|tive|ness
per|cep|tiv|ity
per|cep|tual
per|cep|tual|ly
Per|ce|val
(legendary hero.
△ Percival)
Per|ce|val,
Spen|cer (British
prime minister)
perch
perches
perched
perch|ing
(branch; measure)
perch
plural perch *or*

perch (*cont.*)
perches
(fish)
per|chance
perch|er +s
per|cheron +s
per|chlor|ate +s
per|chlor|ic
per|chloro|ethyl|
ene
per|cipi|ence
per|cipi|ent +s
per|cipi|ent|ly
Per|ci|val (name.
△ Perceval)
per|co|late
per|co|lates
per|co|lated
per|co|lat|ing
per|co|la|tion
per|co|la|tor +s
per con|tra
per|cuss
per|cusses
per|cussed
per|cuss|ing
per|cus|sion +s
per|cus|sion|ist +s
per|cus|sive
per|cus|sive|ly
per|cus|sive|ness
per|cu|tan|eous
Percy (name)
Percy, Henry
('Harry Hotspur',
English soldier)
per diem
per|di|tion
per|dur|abil|ity
per|dur|able
per|dur|ably
père +s (father.
△ pair, pare,
pear)
Père David's deer
plural Père
David's deer
pere|grin|ate
pere|grin|ates
pere|grin|ated
pere|grin|at|ing
pere|grin|ation +s
pere|grin|ator +s
Pere|grine (name)
pere|grine +s
(falcon)
Perel|man,
Sid|ney Jo|seph
(American writer)
per|emp|tor|ily
per|emp|tori|ness
per|emp|tory

per|en|nial +s
per|en|ni|al|ity
per|en|ni|al|ly
Peres, Shi|mon
(Israeli prime
minister)
pere|stroika
Pérez de Cuél|lar,
Ja|vier (Peruvian
Secretary-General
of the UN)
per|fect +s +ed
+ing
per|fecta +s (type
of bet.
△ perfecter,
perfector)
per|fect|er +s
(person or thing
that perfects.
△ perfecta,
perfector)
per|fect|ibil|ity
per|fect|ible
per|fec|tion +s
per|fec|tion|ism
per|fec|tion|ist +s
per|fect|ive +s
per|fect|ly
per|fect|ness
per|fecto +s
per|fect|or +s
(printing machine.
△ perfecta,
perfecter)
per|fer|vid
per|fer|vid|ly
per|fer|vid|ness
per|fidi|ous
per|fidi|ous|ly
per|fidy
per|fid|ies
per|fin +s
per|fo|li|ate
per|for|ate
per|for|ates
per|for|ated
per|for|at|ing
per|for|ation +s
per|fora|tive
per|for|ator +s
per|force
per|forin
per|form +s +ed
+ing
per|form|abil|ity
per|form|able
per|form|ance +s
per|forma|tive +s
per|forma|tory
per|forma|tor|ies
per|form|er +s

per|fume
  per|fumes
  per|fumed
  per|fum|ing
per|fumer +s
per|fumery
  per|fumer|ies
per|fumy
per|func|tor|ily
per|func|tori|ness
per|func|tory
per|fuse
  per|fuses
  per|fused
  per|fus|ing
per|fu|sion +s
per|fu|sive
Per|ga|mene +s
Per|ga|mum
  (ancient city)
per|gana +s (use
  pargana)
per|gola +s
per|gun|nah +s
  (use pargana)
per|haps
peri +s
peri|anth +s
peri|apt +s
peri|car|diac
peri|car|dial
peri|card|itis
peri|car|dium
  peri|car|dia
peri|carp +s
peri|chon|drium
  peri|chon|dria
peri|clase
Peri|cles (Athenian
  statesman)
peri|clinal
peri|cope +s
peri|cra|nium +s
peri|dot +s
peri|gean
peri|gee +s
peri|gla|cial
Péri|gord (district,
  France)
per|igyn|ous
peri|he|lion
  peri|he|lia
peril
  perils
  per|illed Br.
  per|iled Am.
  per|il|ling Br.
  per|il|ing Am.
per|il|ous
per|il|ous|ly
per|il|ous|ness
peri|lune

peri|lymph
per|im|eter +s
peri|met|ric
peri|natal
peri|neal
peri|neum +s
period +s
peri|od|ate +s
peri|od|ic
peri|od|ic|al +s
peri|od|ic|al|ly
peri|od|icity
peri|od|isa|tion Br.
  (use
  periodization)
peri|od|ise Br. (use
  periodize)
peri|od|ises
peri|od|ised
peri|od|is|ing
peri|od|iza|tion
peri|od|ize
peri|od|izes
peri|od|ized
peri|od|iz|ing
peri|odon|tal
peri|odon|tics
peri|odon|tist +s
peri|odon|tol|ogy
peri|opera|tive
peri|os|teal
peri|os|teum
  peri|os|tea
peri|ost|itis
peri|pat|et|ic
peri|pat|et|ic|al|ly
peri|pat|eti|cism
peri|pet|eia
per|iph|eral +s
per|iph|er|al|ly
per|iph|ery
  per|iph|er|ies
peri|phrasis
  peri|phrases
peri|phras|tic
peri|phras|tic|al|ly
per|ip|teral
per|ique
peri|scope +s
peri|scop|ic
peri|scop|ic|al|ly
per|ish
  per|ishes
  per|ished
  per|ish|ing
per|ish|abil|ity
per|ish|able +s
per|ish|able|ness
per|ish|er +s
per|ish|ing
per|ish|ing|ly
per|ish|less

peri|sperm +s
peri|isso|dac|tyl +s
peri|ista|lith +s
peri|stal|sis
peri|stal|tic
peri|stal|tic|al|ly
peri|stome +s
peri|style +s
peri|ton|eal
peri|ton|eum
  peri|ton|eums or
  peri|tonea
peri|ton|itis
peri|wig +s
peri|wigged
peri|win|kle +s
per|jure
  per|jures
  per|jured
  per|jur|ing
per|jurer +s
per|juri|ous
per|jury
  per|jur|ies
perk +s +ed +ing
perk|ily
Per|kin, Wil|liam
  Henry (English
  chemist)
perki|ness
perky
  perk|ier
  perki|est
Per|lis (state,
  Malaysia)
perl|ite
Perm (city, Russia)
perm +s +ed +ing
perma|cul|ture
perma|frost
perm|al|loy
per|man|ence
per|man|ency
per|man|ent
per|man|ent|ise
  Br. (use
  permanentize)
per|man|ent|ises
per|man|ent|ised
per|man|ent|
      is|ing
per|man|ent|izes
per|man|ent|ized
per|man|ent|
      iz|ing
per|man|ent|ly
per|man|gan|ate
  +s
per|man|gan|ic
per|mea|bil|ity
  per|mea|bil|ities

per|me|able
per|me|ance
per|me|ant
per|me|ate
  per|me|ates
  per|me|ated
  per|me|ating
per|me|ation
per|me|ator +s
per|meth|rin
Per|mian
per mil
per mille
per|mis|si|bil|ity
per|mis|sible
per|mis|sibly
per|mis|sion +s
per|mis|sive
per|mis|sive|ly
per|mis|sive|ness
per|mit
  per|mits
  per|mit|ted
  per|mit|ting
per|mit|tee +s
per|mit|ter +s
per|mit|tiv|ity
per|mu|tate
  per|mu|tates
  per|mu|tated
  per|mu|tat|ing
per|mu|ta|tion +s
per|mu|ta|tion|al
per|mute
  per|mutes
  per|muted
  per|mut|ing
Per|mu|tit Propr.
Per|nam|buco
  (state, Brazil;
  former name of
  Recife)
per|ni|cious
per|ni|cious|ly
per|ni|cious|ness
per|nick|ety
per|noc|tate
  per|noc|tates
  per|noc|tated
  per|noc|tat|ing
per|noc|ta|tion
Per|nod +s Propr.
Perón, Evita
  (Argentinian
  politician)
Perón, Juan
  Dom|ingo
  (Argentinian
  president)
pero|neal
Peron|ism
Peron|ist +s

per|or|ate
  per|or|ates
  per|or|ated
  per|or|at|ing
per|or|ation +s
per|ox|id|ase +s
per|ox|ide
  per|ox|ides
  per|ox|ided
  per|ox|id|ing
per|pend +s +ed +ing
Per|pen|dicu|lar Architecture
per|pen|dicu|lar +s
per|pen|dicu|lar|ity
per|pen|dicu|lar|ly
per|pet|rable
per|pet|rate
  per|pet|rates
  per|pet|rated
  per|pet|rat|ing
per|pet|ra|tion
per|pet|ra|tor +s
per|pet|ual
per|petu|al|ism
per|petu|al|ly
per|petu|ance
per|petu|ate
  per|petu|ates
  per|petu|ated
  per|petu|at|ing
per|petu|ation
per|petu|ator +s
per|petu|ity
  per|petu|ities
per|petuum mo|bile +s
Per|pignan (city, France)
per|plex
  per|plexes
  per|plexed
  per|plex|ing
per|plex|ed|ly
per|plex|ing|ly
per|plex|ity
  per|plex|ities
per pro.
per|quis|ite +s
Per|rault, Charles (French writer)
Per|rier +s Propr.
Per|rin, Jean Bap|tiste (French physical chemist)
per|ron +s
Perry (name)
Perry, Fred (English lawn

Perry (cont.)
  tennis and table tennis player)
perry
  per|ries (drink)
per se
per|se|cute
  per|se|cutes
  per|se|cuted
  per|se|cut|ing
per|se|cu|tion +s
per|se|cu|tor +s
per|se|cu|tory
Per|seids (meteor shower)
Per|seph|one Greek Mythology
Per|sep|olis (city, ancient Persia)
Per|seus Greek Mythology
per|se|ver|ance
per|sev|er|ate
  per|sev|er|ates
  per|sev|er|ated
  per|sev|er|at|ing
per|sev|er|ation
per|se|vere
  per|se|veres
  per|se|vered
  per|se|ver|ing
Per|shing (missile)
persh|merga
  plural
  persh|merga or
  persh|mer|gas
Per|sia
Per|sian +s
Per|sian Gulf
per|si|ennes
per|si|flage
per|sim|mon +s
per|sist +s +ed +ing
per|sist|ence
per|sist|ency
per|sist|ent
per|sist|ent|ly
per|snick|ety
per|son
  plural per|sons or
  people
per|sona
  per|so|nae or
  per|so|nas
per|son|able
per|son|able|ness
per|son|ably
per|son|age +s
per|sona grata

per|son|al (private. △ personnel)
per|son|al|isa|tion Br. (use personalization)
per|son|al|ise Br. (use personalize)
  per|son|al|ises
  per|son|al|ised
  per|son|al|is|ing
per|son|al|ity
  per|son|al|ities
per|son|al|iza|tion
per|son|al|ize
  per|son|al|izes
  per|son|al|ized
  per|son|al|iz|ing
per|son|al|ly
per|son|alty
  per|son|al|ties
per|sona non grata
per|son|ate
  per|son|ates
  per|son|ated
  per|son|at|ing
per|son|ation
per|son|ator +s
per|son|hood
per|soni|fi|ca|tion +s
per|son|ifier +s
per|son|ify
  per|soni|fies
  per|soni|fied
  per|soni|fy|ing
per|son|nel (employees. △ personal)
person-to-person
per|spec|tival
per|spec|tive +s
per|spec|tive|ly
per|spex Propr.
per|spi|ca|cious
per|spi|ca|cious|ly
per|spi|ca|cious|ness
per|spi|ca|city
per|spi|cu|ity
per|spicu|ous
per|spicu|ous|ly
per|spicu|ous|ness
per|spir|ation
per|spira|tory
per|spire
  per|spires
  per|spired
  per|spir|ing
per|suad|abil|ity
per|suad|able
per|suade
  per|suades

per|suade (cont.)
  per|suaded
  per|suad|ing
per|suader +s
per|sua|sible
per|sua|sion +s
per|sua|sive
per|sua|sive|ly
per|sua|sive|ness
PERT (= programme evaluation and review technique)
pert +er +est (impudent. △ peart)
per|tain +s +ed +ing
Perth (town, Scotland; city, Australia)
Perthes, Jacques Bou|cher de (French archaeologist)
Perth|shire (former county, Scotland)
per|tin|acious
per|tin|acious|ly
per|tin|acious|ness
per|tin|acity
per|tin|ence
per|tin|ency
per|tin|ent
per|tin|ent|ly
pert|ly
pert|ness
per|turb +s +ed +ing
per|turb|able
per|turb|ation +s
per|turb|ative
per|turb|ing|ly
per|tus|sis
Peru
Peru|gia (city, Italy)
per|uke +s
per|usal +s
per|use
  per|uses
  per|used
  per|us|ing
per|user +s
Peru|vian +s
perv +s (use perve)
per|vade
  per|vades
  per|vaded
  per|vad|ing
per|va|sion

per|va|sive
per|va|sive|ly
per|va|sive|ness
perve
  perves
  perved
  perv|ing
per|verse
per|verse|ly
per|verse|ness
per|ver|sion+s
per|vers|ity
  per|vers|ities
per|ver|sive
per|vert+s +ed
  +ing
per|vert|ed|ly
per|vert|er+s
per|vi|ous
per|vi|ous|ness
Pe|sach
pe|seta+s
pe|sewa+s
Pe|sha|war (city,
  Pakistan)
Pe|shitta
pesh|merga
  plural pesh|merga
  or pesh|mer|gas
pesk|ily
peski|ness
pesky
  pesk|ier
  peski|est
peso+s
pes|sary
  pes|sar|ies
pes|sim|ism
pes|sim|ist+s
pes|sim|is|tic
pes|sim|is|tic|al|ly
pest+s
Pesta|lozzi,
  Jo|hann
  Hein|rich (Swiss
  educationalist)
pes|ter+s +ed
  +ing
pes|ter|er+s
pest-house+s
pesti|cidal
pesti|cide+s
pest|ifer|ous
pesti|lence+s
pesti|lent
pesti|len|tial
pesti|len|tial|ly
pesti|lent|ly
pes|tle
  pes|tles
  pes|tled
  pest|ling

pesto
pesto|logic|al
pest|olo|gist+s
pest|ology
pet
  pets
  pet|ted
  pet|ting
  (animal; favourite;
  fondle; temper)
Peta (woman's
  name. △ Peter)
Pé|tain, Henri
  Phil|ippe (French
  general)
petal+s
pet|aled Am.
petal|ine
pet|alled Br.
petal-like
petal|oid
pet|alon
peta|meter Am. +s
peta|metre Br. +s
pé|tanque
pe|tard+s
peta|sus
pe|taur|ist+s
Pete
pe|techia
  pe|techiae
pe|tech|ial
Peter (Apostle and
  saint; man's name.
  △ Peta)
peter+s +ed +ing
  (diminish; prison
  cell)
Peter|bor|ough
  (city, England)
peter|man
  peter|men
Peter Pan (boy
  hero of play)
Peter Prin|ciple
peter|sham+s
Peter|son, Oscar
  (Canadian jazz
  musician)
Peter's pence
Peters pro|jec|tion
peth|id|ine
peti|olar
peti|ol|ate
peti|ole+s
Pe|tipa, Mar|ius
  (French
  choreographer)
petit (Law minor.
  △ petty)
petit bour|geois
  petits bour|geois

pe|tite female
pe|tite
  bour|geoisie
petit four
  petits fours
pe|ti|tion+s +ed
  +ing
pe|ti|tion|able
pe|ti|tion|ary
  pe|ti|tion|ar|ies
pe|ti|tion|er+s
pe|ti|tio prin|cipii
petit jury (use
  petty jury)
  petit jur|ies
petit-maître+s
petit mal
petit point
pe|tits pois
pet name+s
Petra (ancient city,
  SW Asia; name)
Pet|rarch (Italian
  poet)
Pet|rarch|an
pet|rel+s (bird.
  △ petrol)
Petri dish
  Petri dishes
Pe|trie, Flin|ders
  (English
  archaeologist)
petri|fac|tion
pet|rify
  petri|fies
  petri|fied
  petri|fy|ing
petro|chem|ical+s
petro|chem|is|try
petro|dol|lar+s
petro|gen|esis
petro|glyph+s
Petro|grad (former
  name of St
  Petersburg)
pet|rog|raph|er+s
petro|graph|ic
petro|graph|ic|al
pet|rog|raphy
pet|rol+s (fuel.
  △ petrel)
pet|rol|atum
pet|rol|eum+s
pet|rol|ic
petro|logic
petro|logic|al
pet|rolo|gist+s
pet|rology
pet|ronel+s
Pe|tro|nius, Gaius
  (Roman writer)

Petro|pav|lovsk in
  full Petropavlovsk-
  Kamchat|sky
  (port, Russia)
pet|rous
Petro|za|vodsk
  (city, Russia)
Pet|samo (former
  name of
  Pechenga)
pet|ter+s
petti|coat+s
petti|coat|ed
petti|coat|less
petti|fog
  petti|fogs
  petti|fogged
  petti|fog|ging
petti|fog|ger+s
petti|fog|gery
pet|tily
petti|ness
pet|tish
pet|tish|ly
pet|tish|ness
petti|toe+s
petty
  pet|tier
  pet|ti|est
  (trivial; mean.
  △ petit)
petty bour|geois
  (use petit
  bourgeois)
  plural petty
  bour|geois
petty bour|geoisie
  (use petite
  bourgeoisie)
petty jury
  petty jur|ies
petu|lance
petu|lant
petu|lant|ly
pe|tu|nia+s
pe|tun|tse
Pevs|ner, An|toine
  (Russian-born
  French artist)
pew+s +ed +ing
  (bench. △ più)
pew|age
pewee+s
  (flycatcher.
  △ peewee)
pewit+s (use
  peewit)
pew|less
pew|ter+s
pew|ter|er+s
pey|ote+s
pey|ot|ism

pfen|nig +s
Phae|acian +s
Phae|dra *Greek Mythology*
Phae|thon *Greek Mythology*
phae|ton +s (carriage; car)
phage +s
pha|ged|aena
pha|ged|aen|ic
phago|cyte +s
phago|cyt|ic
phago|cyt|ise *Br.* (use phagocytize)
phago|cyt|ises
phago|cyt|ised
phago|cyt|is|ing
phago|cyt|ize
phago|cyt|izes
phago|cyt|ized
phago|cyt|iz|ing
phago|cyt|ose
phago|cyt|oses
phago|cyt|osed
phago|cyt|os|ing
phago|cyt|osis
Phai|stos (town, Crete)
Phal|ange (Lebanese activist party. △ Falange)
phal|ange +s (bone)
pha|lan|geal
pha|lan|ger +s
Pha|lan|gist +s
phal|an|ster|ian
phal|an|stery
phal|an|ster|ies
phal|anx
phal|anxes *or* pha|lan|ges
phala|rope +s
phalli
phal|lic
phal|lic|al|ly
phalli|cism
phal|lism
phallo|cen|tric
phal|lo|cen|tri|city
phal|lo|cen|trism
phal|lus
phalli *or* phal|luses
phan|ariot +s
phan|ero|gam +s
phan|ero|gam|ic
phan|er|og|am|ous
phan|ta|sise *Br.* (use fantasize)
phan|ta|sises

phan|ta|sise (*cont.*)
phan|ta|sised
phan|ta|sis|ing
phan|ta|size (use fantasize)
phan|ta|sizes
phan|ta|sized
phan|ta|siz|ing
phan|tasm +s
phan|tas|ma|goria +s
phan|tas|ma|gor|ic
phan|tas|ma| gor|ic|al
phan|tas|mal
phan|tas|mic
phan|tast +s (use fantast)
phan|tasy (use fantasy)
phan|ta|sies
phantom +s
Phar|aoh +s
Phar|aoh's ant +s
Phar|aoh's ser|pent +s
Phar|aon|ic
Phari|sa|ic
Phari|saic|al
Phari|sa|ism
Phari|see +s
pharma|ceut|ical +s
pharma|ceut|ic| al|ly
pharma|ceut|ics
pharma|cist +s
pharma|cog|nosy
pharma|co|logic|al
pharma|co|logic| al|ly
pharma|colo|gist +s
pharma|col|ogy
pharma|co|poeia +s
pharma|co|poeial
phar|macy
phar|ma|cies
Pharos (island and ancient lighthouse off Egypt)
pharos
phar|oses (any lighthouse)
pha|ryn|gal
pha|ryn|geal
pha|ryn|gitis
pha|ryn|go|scope +s

pha|ryn|got|omy
pha|ryn| goto|mies
phar|ynx
pha|ryn|ges
phase
phases
phased
phas|ing (stage. △ faze)
phas|ic
phat|ic
phea|sant +s
phea|sant|ry
phea|sant|ries
Phei|dip|pi|des (Athenian messenger)
phen|acetin
phen|cyc|lid|ine
pheno|bar|bital
pheno|bar|bit|one
pheno|cryst +s
phe|nol +s
phen|ol|ic
pheno|logic|al
phen|olo|gist +s
phen|ology
phe|nol|phthal|ein
phe|nom +s
phe|nom|ena (plural of phenomenon)
phe|nom|enal
phe|nom|en|al|ise *Br.* (use phenomenalize)
phe|nom|en|al| ises
phe|nom|en|al| ised
phe|nom|en|al| is|ing
phe|nom|en|al|ism
phe|nom|en|al|ist +s
phe|nom|en|al| is|tic
phe|nom|en|al|ize
phe|nom|en|al| izes
phe|nom|en|al| ized
phe|nom|en|al| iz|ing
phe|nom|en|al|ly
phe|nom|eno| logic|al
phe|nom|eno|logic| al|ly
phe|nom|en| olo|gist +s

phe|nom|en|ology
phe|nom|enon
phe|nom|ena
pheno|type +s
pheno|typ|ic
pheno|typ|ic|al
pheno|typ|ic|al|ly
phenyl (chemical radical. △ fennel)
phenyl|alan|ine
phenyl|ke|ton|uria
phero|monal
phero|mone +s
phew (*interjection*. △ few)
phi +s (Greek letter. △ fie)
phial +s (small bottle. △ file)
Phi Beta Kappa +s
Phid|ias (Athenian sculptor)
Phil
phila|beg +s (use filibeg)
Phila|delphia (city, USA)
phila|delphus
phil|an|der +s +ed +ing
phil|an|der|er +s
phil|an|thrope +s
phil|an|throp|ic
phil|an|throp|ic| al|ly
Br. (use philanthropize)
phil|an|thro|pises
phil|an|thro|pised
phil|an|thro| pis|ing
phil|an|throp|ism
phil|an|throp|ist +s
phil|an|thro|pize
phil|an|thro|pizes
phil|an|thro|pized
phil|an|thro| piz|ing
phil|an|thropy
phila|tel|ic
phila|tel|ic|al|ly
phil|atel|ist +s
phil|ately
Philby, Kim (British Soviet spy)
Phi|le|mon *Greek Mythology*
phil|har|mon|ic
phil|hel|lene +s

phil|hel|len|ic
phil|hel|len|ism
phil|hel|len|ist +s
Philip (Prince,
  Duke of
  Edinburgh;
  Apostle and saint;
  Macedonian,
  French, and
  Spanish kings)
Philip also Phil|lip
  (name)
Phil|ippa
Phil|ippi (city,
  ancient
  Macedonia)
Phil|ip|pian +s
phil|ip|pic +s
phil|ip|pina +s
Phil|ip|pine
Phil|ip|pines
  (archipelago)
Phil|ip|popo|lis
  (ancient Greek
  name for **Plovdiv**)
Phil|is|tine +s
  (member of
  ancient people)
phil|is|tine +s
  (uncultured
  person)
phil|is|tin|ism
Phil|lida also
  Phyl|lida
Phil|lip also Philip
  (name)
Phil|lips (screw;
  screwdriver)
  Propr.
Phil|lips curve +s
phil|lu|men|ist +s
phil|lu|meny
Philly
  (= Philadelphia)
philo|den|dron
  philo|den|drons
  or philo|den|dra
phil|ogy|nist +s
Philo Ju|daeus
  (Jewish
  philosopher)
phil|olo|ger +s
philo|lo|gian +s
philo|logic|al
philo|logic|al|ly
phil|olo|gise *Br.*
  (use philologize)
  phil|olo|gises
  phil|olo|gised
  phil|olo|gis|ing
phil|olo|gist +s

phil|olo|gize
  phil|olo|gizes
  phil|olo|gized
  phil|olo|giz|ing
phil|ology
Philo|mel *Greek*
  Mythology
Philo|mela
  (= Philomel)
Philo|mena
philo|pro|geni|tive
philo|soph|as|ter
  +s
phil|oso|pher +s
phil|oso|phers'
  stone
philo|soph|ic
philo|soph|ic|al
philo|soph|ic|al|ly
phil|oso|phise *Br.*
  (use
  philosophize)
  phil|oso|phises
  phil|oso|phised
  phil|oso|phis|ing
phil|oso|phiser *Br.*
  +s (use
  philosophizer)
phil|oso|phize
  phil|oso|phizes
  phil|oso|phized
  phil|oso|phiz|ing
phil|oso|phizer +s
phil|oso|phy
  phil|oso|phies
phil|ter *Am.* +s (love
  potion. △ filter)
phil|tre *Br.* +s (love
  potion. △ filter)
phi|mo|sis
  phi|mo|ses
phi|mot|ic
Phin|eas
phiz (face. △ fizz)
phizog +s
phle|bit|ic
phle|bitis
phle|bot|om|ise *Br.*
  (use
  phlebotomize)
  phle|bot|om|ises
  phle|bot|om|ised
  phle|bot|om|
        is|ing
phle|bot|om|ist +s
phle|bot|om|ize
  phle|bot|om|izes
  phle|bot|om|ized
  phle|bot|om|
        iz|ing

phle|bot|omy
  phle|boto|mies
phlegm
phleg|mat|ic
phleg|mat|ic|al|ly
phlegmy
phloem
phlo|gis|tic
phlo|gis|ton
phlox
  phloxes
Phnom Penh
  (capital of
  Cambodia)
pho|bia +s
pho|bic +s
Pho|bos (*Greek*
  Mythology; moon
  of Mars)
Phoebe (*Greek*
  Mythology; moon
  of Saturn; name)
phoebe +s (bird)
Phoe|bus *Greek*
  Mythology
Phoe|ni|cia
  (ancient country,
  Near East)
Phoen|ician +s
Phoe|nix (city,
  USA)
phoe|nix
  phoe|nixes
  (mythical bird;
  unique person or
  thing)
Phoe|nix Is|lands
  (in W. Pacific)
pho|las
  pho|lases
phon +s
phon|ate
  phon|ates
  phon|ated
  phon|at|ing
phon|ation
phon|atory
phon|auto|graph
  +s
phone
  phones
  phoned
  phon|ing
phone book +s
phone|card +s
phone-in +s *noun*
  and adjective
phon|eme +s
phon|em|ic
phon|em|ics
phon|endo|scope
  +s

phon|et|ic
phon|et|ic|al|ly
phon|et|ician +s
phon|eti|cise *Br.*
  (use phoneticize)
  phon|eti|cises
  phon|eti|cised
  phon|eti|cis|ing
phon|eti|cism
phon|eti|cist +s
phon|eti|cize
  phon|eti|cizes
  phon|eti|cized
  phon|eti|ciz|ing
phon|et|ics
phon|et|ist +s
pho|ney
  pho|neys
  pho|nier
  pho|ni|est
phon|ic
phon|ic|al|ly
phon|ics
pho|nily
pho|ni|ness
phono *attributive*
phono|gram +s
phono|graph +s
phono|graph|ic
phon|og|raphy
phono|lite +s
phono|logic|al
phono|lo|gic|al|ly
phon|olo|gist +s
phon|ology
  phon|olo|gies
phon|ometer +s
pho|non +s
phono|scope +s
phony (use
  phoney)
  pho|nies
  pho|nier
  pho|ni|est
phooey
phor|esy
phor|et|ic
phor|mium
phos|gene
phos|phat|ase +s
phos|phate +s
phos|phat|ic
phos|phene
  (sensation in eye.
  △ phosphine)
phos|phide +s
phos|phine (gas.
  △ phosphene)
phos|phin|ic
phos|phite +s
phos|pho|lipid +s
phos|phor +s

phos¦phor¦ate
  phos¦phor¦ates
  phos¦phor¦ated
  phos¦phor¦at¦ing
phos¦phor¦esce
  phos¦phor¦esces
  phos¦phor¦esced
  phos¦phor¦es¦cing
phos¦phor¦
       es¦cence
phos¦phor¦es¦cent
phos¦phor¦ic
phos¦phor¦ite
phos¦phor¦ous
  adjective
phos¦phorus *noun*
phos¦phor¦yl¦ate
  phos¦phor¦yl¦ates
  phos¦phor¦yl¦ated
  phos¦phor¦yl¦
       at¦ing
phos¦phor¦yl¦ation
phossy jaw
phot +s
phot¦ic
phot¦ism +s
Pho¦tius (Byzantine
  scholar)
photo +s *noun*
photo
  pho¦toes
  pho¦toed
  photo¦ing
  verb
photo¦biol¦ogy
photo booth +s
photo¦call +s
photo¦cell +s
photo¦chem¦ical
photo¦chem¦is¦try
photo¦chro¦mic
photo¦com¦
      pos¦ition
photo¦
    con¦duct¦ive
photo¦con¦duct¦
      iv¦ity
photo¦con¦duct¦or
  +s
photo¦copi¦able
photo¦copier +s
photo¦copy
  photo¦cop¦ies
  photo¦cop¦ied
  photo¦copy¦ing
photo¦degrad¦able
photo¦diode +s
photo¦elec¦tric
photo¦elec¦tri¦city
photo¦elec¦tron +s
photo¦emis¦sion
photo¦emit¦ter +s

photo¦engrav¦ing
photo fin¦ish
photo¦fit +s
photo¦gen¦ic
photo¦gen¦ic¦al¦ly
photo¦gram +s
photo¦gram¦
    met¦rist +s
photo¦gram¦metry
photo¦graph +s
  +ed +ing
photo¦graph¦able
pho¦tog¦raph¦er +s
photo¦graph¦ic
photo¦graph¦ic¦
      al¦ly
pho¦tog¦raphy
photo¦grav¦ure
photo¦jour¦nal¦ism
photo¦jour¦nal¦ist
  +s
photo¦lith¦
    og¦raph¦er +s
photo¦litho¦
      graph¦ic
photo¦litho¦
    graph¦ic¦al¦ly
photo¦lith¦
      og¦raphy
photo¦lyse
  photo¦lyses
  photo¦lysed
  photo¦lys¦ing
pho¦toly¦sis
photo¦lyt¦ic
photo¦
    mech¦an¦ical
photo¦mech¦an¦ic¦
      al¦ly
pho¦tometer +s
pho¦tom¦et¦ric
pho¦tom¦etry
photo¦micro¦graph
  +s
photo¦
    microg¦raphy
photo¦mon¦tage
  +s
photo¦multi¦plier
  +s
pho¦ton +s
pho¦ton¦ics
photo¦novel +s
photo-offset
photo
  op¦por¦tun¦ity
photo
  op¦por¦tun¦ities
photo¦period +s
photo¦peri¦od¦ic
photo¦period¦ism
photo¦pho¦bia

photo¦pho¦bic
photo¦real¦ism
photo¦recep¦tor +s
photo¦sensi¦tive
photo¦sensi¦tiv¦ity
photo¦set
  photo¦sets
  photo¦set
  photo¦set¦ting
photo¦set¦ter +s
photo shoot +s
photo¦sphere +s
photo¦spher¦ic
photo¦stat +s *noun*
  Propr.
photo¦stat
  photo¦stats
  photo¦stat¦ted
  photo¦stat¦ting
  verb
photo¦stat¦ic
photo¦syn¦thesis
photo¦syn¦the¦sise
  Br. (use
  photosynthesize)
photo¦
    syn¦the¦sises
photo¦
    syn¦the¦sised
photo¦
    syn¦the¦sis¦ing
photo¦syn¦the¦size
photo¦
    syn¦the¦sizes
photo¦
    syn¦the¦sized
photo¦
    syn¦the¦siz¦ing
photo¦syn¦thet¦ic
photo¦syn¦thet¦ic¦
      al¦ly
photo¦tran¦sis¦tor
  +s
photo¦trop¦ic
photo¦trop¦ism
photo¦type¦set
photo¦type¦set¦ter
  +s
photo¦type¦set¦
      ting
photo¦vol¦ta¦ic
phrasal
phrase
  phrases
  phrased
  phras¦ing
phrase book +s
phraseo¦gram +s
phraseo¦logic¦al
phrase¦ology
  phraseolo¦gies
phras¦ing +s

phre¦at¦ic
phren¦et¦ic
  (use frenetic)
phren¦et¦ic¦al¦ly
  (use frenetically)
phren¦ic
phreno¦logic¦al
phren¦olo¦gist +s
phren¦ology
Phry¦gia (ancient
  region, Asia
  Minor)
Phry¦gian +s
phthal¦ate +s
phthal¦ic
phthi¦sic
phthi¦sic¦al
phthi¦sis
Phu¦ket (island and
  port, Thailand)
phut
phyco¦logic¦al
phy¦colo¦gist +s
phy¦cology
phyco¦my¦cete +s
phyla (plural of
  phylum. △ filer)
phyl¦ac¦tery
  phyl¦ac¦ter¦ies
phy¦let¦ic
phy¦let¦ic¦al¦ly
Phyl¦lida *also*
  Phil¦lida
Phyl¦lis
phyllo (use filo)
phyl¦lode +s
phyl¦lopha¦gous
phyl¦lo¦quin¦one
phyl¦lo¦tac¦tic
phyl¦lo¦taxis
phyl¦lo¦taxy
phyl¦lox¦era
phylo¦gen¦esis
phylo¦gen¦et¦ic
phylo¦gen¦et¦ic¦
      al¦ly
phylo¦gen¦ic
phyl¦ogeny
  phyl¦ogen¦ies
phy¦lum
  phyla
phy¦salis
physic
  phys¦ics
  phys¦icked
  phys¦ick¦ing
phys¦ic¦al +s
phys¦ic¦al¦ism
phys¦ic¦al¦ist +s
phys¦ic¦al¦is¦tic
phys¦ic¦al¦ity
phys¦ic¦al¦ly

phys|ic|al|ness
phys|ician +s
physi|cist +s
phys|icky
physico-chemical
phys|ics
physio +s
physi|ocracy
  physi|ocra|cies
physio|crat +s
physio|crat|ic
physio|gnom|ic
physio|gnom|ic|al
physio|gnom|ic|
  al|ly
physi|ognom|ist
  +s
physi|ognomy
  physi|ogno|mies
physi|og|raph|er
  +s
physio|graph|ic
physio|graph|ic|al
physio|graph|ic|
  al|ly
physi|og|raphy
physio|logic|al
physio|lo|gic|al|ly
physi|olo|gist +s
physi|ology
  physi|olo|gies
physio|ther|ap|ist
  +s
physio|ther|apy
phys|ique +s
phyto|chem|ical
phyto|chem|ist +s
phyto|chem|is|try
phyto|chrome +s
phyto|gen|esis
phy|togeny
phyto|geog|raphy
phy|tog|raphy
phyto|path|ology
phy|topha|gous
phyto|plank|ton
phyt|ot|omy
phyto|toxic
phyto|toxin +s
pi +s (Greek letter;
  pious. △ pie)
pi Am.
  pies
  pied
  piing or pie|ing
  (Br. pie. muddle.
  △ pie)
pi|acu|lar
Piaf, Edith (French
  singer)
pi|affe
  pi|affes

pi|affe (cont.)
  pi|affed
  pi|aff|ing
pi|aff|er
Pia|get, Jean
  (Swiss
  psychologist)
pia mater
piani
pi|an|ism
pi|an|is|simo +s
pi|an|ist +s
pi|an|is|tic
pi|an|is|tic|al|ly
piano +s
  (instrument)
piano
  pi|anos or piani
  (soft passage)
piano ac|cor|dion
  +s
pi|ano|forte +s
pi|an|ola +s Propr.
piano no|bile
piano organ +s
piano play|er +s
piano-tuner +s
pi|as|sava +s
pi|aster Am. +s
pi|astre Br. +s
Piat +s (anti-tank
  weapon)
Piauí (state, Brazil)
pi|azza +s
pi|broch +s
PIBS (= permanent
  interest-bearing
  share)
pic +s (picture.
  △ pick)
pica +s (printing
  measure; eating
  non-food. △ pika,
  piker)
pica|dor +s
pica|ninny Am.
  (use pickaninny)
  pica|nin|nies
Pic|ardy (region,
  France)
pic|ar|esque
pic|ar|oon +s
Pi|casso, Pablo
  (Spanish painter)
pic|ay|une +s
Pic|ca|dilly (street,
  London)
pic|ca|lilli +s
pic|ca|ninny Br.
  pic|ca|nin|nies

pic|ca|ninny (cont.)
  (often offensive;
  Am. pickaninny)
pic|colo +s
pich|ici|ago +s
pick +s +ed +ing
  (choose; pluck;
  tool. △ pic)
pick|aback
pick|able
picka|ninny Am.
  picka|nin|nies
  (often offensive; Br.
  piccaninny)
pickax Am.
  pick|axes
  pick|axed
  pick|ax|ing
pick|axe Br.
  pick|axes
  pick|axed
  pick|ax|ing
pick|el|haube +s
pick|er +s
pick|erel
  plural pick|erel or
  pick|erels
**Pick|er|ing,
  Wil|liam
  Hay|ward** (New
  Zealand-born
  American rocket
  engineer)
picket +s +ed +ing
  (sentry; person
  supporting strike;
  stake. △ piquet)
pick|et|er +s
picket line +s
Pick|ford, Mary
  (Canadian-born
  American actress)
picki|ness
pick|ing +s
pickle
  pickles
  pickled
  pick|ling
pick|ler +s
pick|lock +s
pick-me-up +s
pick|pocket +s
pick|pock|et|ing
pick-up +s adjective
  and noun
Pick|wick|ian +s
picky
  pick|ier
  picki|est
pick-your-own +s
  adjective and noun

pic|nic
pic|nics
pic|nicked
pic|nick|ing
  (meal. △ pyknic)
pic|nick|er +s
pic|nicky
Pico da Neb|lina
  (mountain, Brazil)
Pico de Ori|zaba
  (Spanish name for
  Citlaltépetl)
pico|meter Am. +s
pico|metre Br. +s
pico|sec|ond +s
picot +s
pi|cotee +s
picquet +s (sentry
  etc.; use picket
  △ piquet)
pic|rate +s
pic|ric
Pict +s
Pict|ish
picto|gram +s
picto|graph +s
picto|graph|ic
pic|tog|raphy
pic|tor|ial +s
pic|tori|al|ly
pic|ture
  pic|tures
  pic|tured
  pic|tur|ing
pic|ture book +s
pic|ture card +s
pic|ture frame +s
pic|ture gal|lery
  pic|ture
  gal|ler|ies
pic|ture|goer +s
pic|ture hat +s
picture-moulding
  +s
pic|ture pal|ace +s
pic|ture post|card
  +s
pic|tur|esque
pic|tur|esque|ly
pic|tur|esque|ness
pic|ture win|dow
  +s
picture-writing
pid|dle
  pid|dles
  pid|dled
  pid|dling
pid|dler +s
pid|dock +s
pidgin +s
  (language.
  △ pigeon)

pi-dog +s (use pye-
dog)
pie +s (food;
magpie; former
Indian currency.
△ pi)
pie *Br.*
pies
pied
pie¦ing
(*Am.* pi. muddle.
△ pi)
pie¦bald +s
piece
pieces
pieced
piecing
(part, coin, etc.;
to join. △ peace)
pièce de
ré¦sist¦ance
pièces de
ré¦sist¦ance
piece-goods
piece¦meal
piecer +s
piece-rate +s
piece¦work
pie chart +s
pie¦crust +s
pied
pied-à-terre
pieds-à-terre
Pied¦mont (region,
Italy)
pied¦mont +s
(slope)
pie-dog +s (use
pye-dog)
pie-eater +s
pie-eyed
Pie¦gan (use
Peigan)
plural Pie¦gan *or*
Pie¦gans
pie in the sky
pie¦man
pie¦men
pier +s (at seaside;
pillar. △ peer)
Pierce, Frank¦lin
(American
president.
△ Peirce)
pierce
pierces
pierced
pier¦cing
pier¦cer +s
pier¦cing¦ly
pier glass
pier glasses
Pi¦er¦ian

Piero della
Fran¦cesca
(Italian painter)
Pierre (city, USA)
Pier¦rette +s *female*
Pier¦rot +s *male*
Piers (name)
pietà +s
(sculpture etc.)
pietas (respect for
an ancestor)
Pieter¦maritz¦burg
(city, South
Africa)
Pie¦ters¦burg
(town, South
Africa)
Piet¦ism
(movement)
piet¦ism
(sentiment)
piet¦ist +s
piet¦is¦tic
piet¦is¦tic¦al
piety
piet¦ies
piezo¦elec¦tric
piezo¦elec¦tric¦
al¦ly
piezo¦elec¦tri¦city
pi¦ez¦ometer +s
pif¦fle
pif¦fles
pif¦fled
pif¦fling
pif¦fler +s
pig
pigs
pigged
pig¦ging
pi¦geon +s (bird.
△ pidgin)
pigeon-breast +s
pigeon-breast¦ed
pigeon-chest +s
pigeon-chested
pi¦geon fan¦cier +s
pigeon-fancying
pigeon-hawk +s
pigeon-hearted
pigeon-hole
pigeon-holes
pigeon-holed
pigeon-holing
pi¦geon pair +s
pi¦geon¦ry
pi¦geon¦ries
pigeon-toed
pig¦gery
pig¦ger¦ies
pig¦gish
pig¦gish¦ly

pig¦gish¦ness
Pig¦gott, Les¦ter
(English jockey)
piggy
pig¦gies
pig¦gier
pig¦gi¦est
pig¦gy¦back +s
+ed +ing
piggy bank +s
piggy in the
mid¦dle
pig-headed
pig-headed¦ly
pig-headed¦ness
pigh¦tle +s
pig-ignorant
pig in the mid¦dle
pig-iron
Pig Is¦land (New
Zealand)
pig-jump +s +ed
+ing
pig Latin
pig¦let +s
pig¦like
pig¦ling +s
pig¦maean (use
pygmaean)
pig¦mean (use
pygmaean)
pig meat
pig¦ment +s +ed
+ing
pig¦men¦tal
pig¦men¦tary
pig¦men¦ta¦tion +s
pigmy (use pygmy)
pig¦mies
pig¦nut +s
pig¦pen +s
pig¦skin +s
pig-sticker +s
pig¦stick¦ing
pig¦sty
pig¦sties
pig's wash
pig¦swill
pig¦tail +s
pig¦tailed
pig¦wash
pig¦weed +s
pi jaw +s
pika +s (animal.
△ pica, piker)
pike
pikes
piked
pik¦ing
(weapon; hilltop;
toll; dive)

pike
plural pike *or*
pikes
(fish)
pike¦let +s
pike¦man
pike¦men
pike¦perch
plural pike¦perch
piker +s (person.
△ pica, pika)
pike¦staff +s
Pik Po¦bedy
(mountain,
Kyrgyzstan)
pilaf +s
pi¦laff +s (use pilaf)
pi¦las¦ter +s
pi¦las¦tered
Pi¦late, Pon¦tius
(Roman
procurator of
Judaea)
pilau +s
pilaw +s (use
pilau)
pilch
pilches
pil¦chard +s
pile
piles
piled
pil¦ing
pil¦eate
pil¦eated
pile¦driver +s
pile¦driv¦ing
pile-dwelling +s
piles
pile-up +s *noun*
pi¦leus
pilei
pile¦wort +s
pil¦fer +s +ed +ing
pil¦fer¦age
pil¦fer¦er +s
pil¦grim +s +ed
+ing
pil¦grim¦age
pil¦grim¦ages
pil¦grim¦aged
pil¦grim¦aging
pil¦grim¦ise *Br.*
(use pilgrimize)
pil¦grim¦ises
pil¦grim¦ised
pil¦grim¦is¦ing
pil¦grim¦ize
pil¦grim¦izes
pil¦grim¦ized
pil¦grim¦iz¦ing
pi¦lif¦er¦ous

pi¦li¦form
pil¦ing +s
Pili¦pino
pill +s +ed +ing
pil¦lage
  pil¦lages
  pil¦laged
  pil¦laging
pil¦la¦ger +s
pil¦lar +s
pil¦lar box
  pil¦lar boxes
pillar-box red
pil¦lared
pil¦laret +s
pill¦box
  pill¦boxes
pil¦lion +s
pil¦li¦winks
pil¦lock +s
pil¦lory
  pil¦lor¦ies
  pil¦lor¦ied
  pil¦lory¦ing
pil¦low +s +ed
  +ing
pil¦low¦case +s
pillow-fight +s
pil¦low lace
pil¦low lava
pil¦low¦slip +s
pil¦low talk
pil¦lowy
pill-popper +s
pill-pusher +s
pil¦lule +s (use
  pilule)
pill¦wort +s
pil¦ose
pil¦os¦ity
pilot +s +ed +ing
pi¦lot¦age
pilot bal¦loon +s
pilot-bird +s
pilot chute +s
pilot-cloth +s
pilot fish
  plural pilot fish
pilot house +s
pilot-jacket +s
pi¦lot¦less
pilot light +s
pil¦ous
Pil¦sen (city, Czech
  Republic)
Pil¦sen¦er +s (use
  Pilsner)
Pils¦ner +s
Pilt¦down man
pilu¦lar
pil¦ule +s
pilu¦lous

pi¦mento +s
pi-meson +s
pi¦miento
  pi¦mien¦tos *or*
  pi¦mien¦toes
pimp +s +ed +ing
pim¦per¦nel +s
pim¦ple +s
pim¦pled
pim¦ply
  pim¦plier
  pim¦pli¦est
PIN (= personal
  identification
  number)
pin
  pins
  pinned
  pin¦ning
  (for sewing; etc.)
pina co¦lada +s
pina¦fore +s
Pin¦ang (use
  Penang)
pin¦as¦ter +s
Pina¦tubo, Mount
  (in the
  Philippines)
pin¦ball
PINC (= property
  income certificate)
pince-nez
  plural pince-nez
pin¦cer +s +ed
  +ing
pin¦cette +s
pinch
  pinches
  pinched
  pinch¦ing
pinch¦beck +s
pinch-hit
  pinch-hits
  pinch-hit
  pinch-hitting
pinch-hitter +s
pinch¦penny
  pinch¦pen¦nies
pinch-run
  pinch-runs
  pinch-ran
  pinch-running
pinch-runner +s
pin¦cush¦ion +s
Pin¦dar (Greek lyric
  poet)
Pin¦dar¦ic
pin-down *noun and*
  attributive
Pin¦dus
  Moun¦tains (in
  Greece)

pine
  pines
  pined
  pin¦ing
pin¦eal
pine¦apple +s
pine cone +s
pine mar¦ten +s
pine nee¦dle +s
pine nut +s
Pin¦ero, Ar¦thur
  Wing (English
  dramatist)
pin¦ery
  pin¦eries
pine tree +s
pin¦etum
  pin¦eta
Pine¦wood (film
  studios, England)
pine¦wood (timber)
pine wood +s
  (forest)
piney
pin-feather +s
pin¦fold +s +ed
  +ing
ping +s +ed +ing
ping¦er +s
pingo +s
ping-pong
pin¦guid
pin¦guin +s
pin¦head +s
pin¦head¦ed
pin¦head¦ed¦ness
pin-high
pin¦hole +s
pin¦ion +s +ed
  +ing
pink +s +ed +ing
  +er +est
pink-collar
  attributive
Pink¦er¦ton, Allan
  (Scottish-born
  American
  detective)
pink-eye
Pink Floyd
  (English rock
  group)
pinkie +s (little
  finger; wine; white
  person. △ pinky)
pink¦ish
pink¦ly
pink¦ness
pinko
  pinkos *or*
  pink¦oes

Pink¦ster
  (Whitsuntide)
pink¦ster flower
  +s
pinky
  pink¦ier
  pinki¦est
  (slightly pink.
  △ pinkie)
pin money
pinna
  pin¦nae *or* pin¦nas
pin¦nace +s
pin¦na¦cle
  pin¦na¦cles
  pin¦na¦cled
  pin¦na¦cling
pin¦nate
pin¦nated
pin¦nate¦ly
pin¦na¦tion
pinni¦grade
pinni¦ped +s
pin¦nu¦lar
pin¦nule +s
PIN num¦ber +s
pinny
  pin¦nies
Pino¦chet,
  Au¦gusto
  (Chilean
  president)
pin¦ochle
pino¦cyt¦osis
pin¦ole
piñon +s
Pinot Blanc +s
Pinot Noir +s
pin¦point +s +ed
  +ing
pin¦prick +s
pin¦stripe +s
pin¦striped
pint +s
pinta +s (= a pint
  of milk)
pin-table +s
pin¦tado +s
pin¦tail +s
Pin¦ter, Har¦old
  (English
  dramatist)
pin¦tle +s
pinto +s
pint pot +s
pint-sized
pin-tuck +s
pin-tucked
pin-up +s *noun and*
  attributive
pin¦wheel +s +ed
  +ing

pin|worm +s
piny
Pin|yin
pin|yon +s (use piñon)
pio|let +s
pion +s
Pi|on|eer
(American space probes)
pi|on|eer +s +ed +ing
pi|onic
pious
pi|ous|ly
pi|ous|ness
Pip (name)
pip
pips
pipped
pip|ping
(seed; remove pips; high-pitched sound; defeat; etc.)
pipa +s (toad)
pipal +s (= bo tree; use peepul. △ people)
pipe
pipes
piped
pip|ing
pipe|clay +s +ed +ing
pipe-cleaner +s
pipe dream +s
pipe|fish
plural pipe|fish
pipe|ful +s
pipe|less
pipe-light +s
pipe|line
pipe|lines
pipe|lined
pipe|lin|ing
pipe major +s
pip emma (= p.m.)
pipe organ +s
Piper, John
(English painter)
piper +s
pipe-rack +s
Piper Alpha
pi|pera|zine
pi|peri|dine
pipe roll +s
pipe-stem +s
pipe-stone
pip|ette
pip|ettes

pip|ette (cont.)
pip|et|ted
pip|et|ting
pipe|work
pip|ing hot
pipi|strelle +s
pipit +s
pip|kin +s
pip|less
Pippa
pip|pin +s
pippy
pip|squeak +s
pipy
pi|quancy
pi|quant
pi|quant|ly
pique
piques
piqued
piquing
(resentment; irritate; in card games. △ peak, peek, peke)
piqué +s
pi|quet (game. △ picket)
pir|acy
pir|acies
Pi|raeus (port, Greece)
pi|ra|gua +s
Piran|dello, Luigi
(Italian writer)
Pira|nesi, Gio|vanni Bat|tista (Italian engraver)
pi|ranha +s
pir|ate
pir|ates
pir|ated
pir|at|ing
pir|at|ic
pir|at|ic|al
pir|at|ic|al|ly
pi|raya +s
piri|piri +s
pi|rogue +s
pirou|ette
pirou|ettes
pirou|et|ted
pirou|et|ting
Pisa (city, Italy)
pis aller
Pisan, Chris|tine de (Italian-born writer)
Pi|sano, An|drea, Gio|vanni,

Pi|sano (cont.)
Ni|cola, and Nino
(Italian sculptors)
pis|cary
pisca|tor|ial
pisca|tori|al|ly
pisca|tory
Pis|cean +s
Pis|ces
(constellation; sign of zodiac)
pisci|cul|tural
pisci|cul|ture
pisci|cul|tur|ist +s
pis|cina
pis|ci|nae or pis|ci|nas
pis|cine +s
pis|civ|or|ous
pish
Pish|pek (former name of Bishkek)
Pi|sidia (ancient region, Asia Minor)
Pi|sid|ian +s
pisi|form
Pi|sis|tra|tus
(tyrant of Athens)
pis|mire +s
piss
pisses
pissed
piss|ing
(coarse slang)
Pis|sarro, Cam|ille
(French artist)
piss art|ist +s
(coarse slang)
pis|soir +s
piss|pot +s (coarse slang)
piss-take +s
piss-taker +s
(coarse slang)
piss-taking (coarse slang)
piss-up +s noun
(coarse slang)
pis|ta|chio +s
piste +s
pis|teur +s
pis|til +s (of flower. △ pistol)
pis|til|lary
pis|til|late
pis|til|lif|er|ous
pis|til|line
pis|tol
pis|tols
pis|tolled Br.
pis|toled Am.

pis|tol (cont.)
pis|tol|ling Br.
pis|tol|ing Am.
(gun. △ pistil)
pis|tole +s (coin)
pis|tol|eer +s
pis|tol grip +s
pis|tol shot +s
pistol-whip
pistol-whips
pistol-whipped
pistol-whipping
pis|ton +s
piston-engined
attributive
pit
pits
pit|ted
pit|ting
pita +s (use pitta)
pit-a-pat
pit bull +s
pit bull ter|rier +s
Pit|cairn Is|lands
(in S. Pacific)
pitch
pitches
pitched
pitch|ing
pitch-and-toss
pitch black noun and adjective
pitch-black
attributive
pitch|blende
pitch|er +s
pitch|er|ful +s
pitcher-plant +s
pitch|fork +s +ed +ing
pitch pine
pitch-pipe +s
pitch|stone
pitchy
pitch|ier
pitchi|est
pit|eous
pit|eous|ly
pit|eous|ness
pit|fall +s
pith
pit|head +s
Pithe|can|thro|pus
pithe|coid +s
pith hel|met +s
pith|ily
pithi|ness
pith|less
pithos
pithoi

pithy
pith|ier
pithi|est
piti|able
piti|able|ness
piti|ably
piti|ful
piti|ful|ly
piti|ful|ness
piti|less
piti|less|ly
piti|less|ness
Pit|man, Isaac
(English shorthand
inventor)
pit|man
pit|men
(miner)
pit|man +s
(connecting rod)
piton +s (spike)
Pi|tons, the (two
mountains, St
Lucia)
Pitot tube +s
pit|pan +s
pit pony
pit po|nies
pit prop +s
pit-saw +s
pit stop +s
Pitt, Wil|liam
(British prime
ministers)
pitta +s
pit|tance +s
pitter-patter
Pitti (art gallery and
museum, Italy)
Pitt Is|land (one of
the Chatham
Islands)
pitto|sporum +s
Pitt-Rivers,
Au|gus|tus
(English
archaeologist)
Pitts|burgh (city,
USA)
pi|tu|it|ary
pi|tu|it|ar|ies
pit|uri
pity
pit|ies
pit|ied
pity|ing
pity|ing|ly
pityr|ia|sis
pityr|ia|ses
più (*Music* more.
△ pew)
Pius (popes)

pivot +s +ed +ing
piv|ot|abil|ity
piv|ot|able
piv|otal
pix (= pictures.
△ pyx)
pixel +s
pix|el|ate
pix|el|ates
pix|el|ated
pix|el|at|ing
(display as or
divide into pixels)
pixie +s (elf.
△ pyxes)
pix|il|ated (crazy;
drunk)
pix|il|lated (use
pixilated)
pixy (use pixie)
pixies
Pizan, Chris|tine
de (use Pisan)
Pi|zarro,
Fran|cisco
(Spanish
conquistador)
pi|zazz (use
pizzazz)
pizza +s
piz|zazz
piz|zeria +s
pizzi|cato
pizzi|ca|tos *or*
pizzi|cati
piz|zle +s
plac|abil|ity
plac|able
plac|ably
plac|ard +s +ed
+ing
pla|cate
pla|cates
pla|cated
pla|cat|ing
pla|cat|ing|ly
pla|ca|tion
pla|ca|tory
place
places
placed
pla|cing
(position.
△ plaice)
place-bet +s
pla|cebo +s
place brick +s
place card +s
place-kick +s
place-kicker +s
place|less

place|man
place|men
place mat +s
place|ment +s
place name +s
pla|centa
pla|cen|tae *or*
pla|cen|tas
pla|cen|tal +s
pla|cer +s
place set|ting +s
pla|cet +s (vote)
pla|cid
pla|cid|ity
pla|cid|ly
pla|cid|ness
pla|cing +s
placket +s
(opening in
garment.
△ plaquette)
placky bag +s
plac|oid +s
pla|fond +s
pla|gal
plage +s (beach;
part of sun)
pla|giar|ise *Br.* (use
plagiarize)
pla|giar|ises
pla|giar|ised
pla|giar|is|ing
pla|giar|iser *Br.* +s
(use plagiarizer)
pla|giar|ism +s
pla|giar|ist +s
pla|giar|is|tic
pla|giar|ize
pla|giar|izes
pla|giar|ized
pla|giar|iz|ing
pla|giar|izer +s
plagio|ceph|al|ic
plagio|clase +s
plagio|clas|tic
plagio|stome +s
plague
plagues
plagued
pla|guing
(disease etc.)
plague|some
pla|guy
plaice
plural plaice
(fish. △ place)
plaid +s
Plaid Cymru
(Welsh Nationalist
Party)
plaid|ed

plain +s +er +est
(flat land; simple;
not milk
(chocolate); not
self-raising (flour);
not a court card;
not trumps.
△ plane)
plain|chant +s
plain clothes
plain-clothes
attributive
plain cook +s
plain|ly
plain|ness
plain sail|ing
(straightforward;
uncomplicated.
△ plane sailing)
Plains In|dian +s
plains|man
plains|men
Plains of
Abra|ham (in
Canada)
plain|song
plain-spoken
plaint +s
plain|tiff +s
plain|tive
plain|tive|ly
plain|tive|ness
plait +s +ed +ing
(interlace hair etc.
△ plat)
plan
plans
planned
plan|ning
pla|nar
(*Mathematics.*
△ planer)
plan|ar|ian +s
plan|chet +s (coin-
blank)
plan|chette +s
(board at seance)
Planck, Max
(German
physicist)
plane
planes
planed
plan|ing
(aircraft; flat
surface; tool; tree;
skim; shave.
△ plain)
plane chart +s
plane|load +s
plane|maker +s
plane|mak|ing

planer +s (tool.
△ planar)
plane sail|ing
(position-finding.
△ plain sailing)
planet +s
plane-table +s
plan|et|arium +s
plan|et|ary
plan|et|esimal +s
plan|et|oid +s
plan|et|ology
plane tree +s
plan|gency
plan|gent
plan|gent|ly
plan|im|eter +s
plani|met|ric
plani|met|ric|al
plan|im|etry
plan|ish
plan|ishes
plan|ished
plan|ish|ing
plan|ish|er +s
plani|sphere +s
plani|spher|ic
plank +s +ed +ing
plank|ton
plank|ton|ic
plan|ner +s
plano|con|cave
plano|con|vex
plano|graph|ic
plan|og|raphy
plan|om|eter +s
plant +s +ed +ing
plant|able
Plan|tagenet +s
plan|tain +s
plan|tar (of the sole
of the foot)
plan|ta|tion +s
plant|er +s
(person;
container)
planti|grade +s
Plan|tin,
Chris|tophe
(Belgian printer;
typeface)
plant|ing +s
plant|let +s
plant life
plant|like
plant-louse
plant-lice
plants|man
plants|men
plants|woman
plants|women
plaque +s

pla|quette +s
(small plaque.
△ placket)
plash
plashes
plashed
plash|ing
plasm +s
plasma +s
plas|mat|ic
plas|mic
plas|mid +s
plasmo|desma
plasmo|des|mata
plas|mo|dial
plas|mo|dium
plas|modia
plasmo|lyse Br.
plasmo|lyses
plasmo|lysed
plasmo|lys|ing
plas|moly|sis
plasmo|lyze Am.
plasmo|lyzes
plasmo|lyzed
plasmo|lyz|ing
Plas|sey (battle
site, India)
plas|teel
plas|ter +s +ed
+ing
plas|ter|board +s
plas|ter cast +s
plas|ter|er +s
plas|ter of Paris
plas|ter|work
plas|tery
plas|tic +s
plas|tic|al|ly
plas|ti|cine Propr.
plas|ti|cisa|tion Br.
(use
plasticization)
plas|ti|cise Br. (use
plasticize)
plas|ti|cises
plas|ti|cised
plas|ti|cis|ing
plas|ti|ciser Br. +s
(use plasticizer)
plas|ti|city
plas|ti|ciza|tion
plas|ti|cize
plas|ti|cizes
plas|ti|cized
plas|ti|ciz|ing
plas|ti|cizer +s
plas|ticky
plas|tid +s
plas|tron +s
plat +s (land.
△ plait)

Pla|taea (battle site,
Greece)
platan +s (tree.
△ platen)
plat du jour
plats du jour
Plate, River
(estuary, S.
America)
plate
plates
plated
plat|ing
plat|eau
plat|eaux or
plat|eaus
plate|ful +s
plate glass noun
plate-glass
adjective
plate|lay|er +s
plate|less
plate|let +s
plate|maker +s
plate-mark +s
platen +s (plate;
roller. △ platan)
plater +s
plate rack +s
plat|er|esque
plat|form +s
Plath, Syl|via
(American poet)
plat|ing +s
pla|tin|ic
plat|in|isa|tion Br.
(use
platinization)
plat|in|ise Br. (use
platinize)
plat|in|ises
plat|in|ised
plat|in|is|ing
plat|in|iza|tion
plat|in|ize
plat|in|izes
plat|in|ized
plat|in|iz|ing
plat|in|oid +s
plat|ino|type +s
plat|inum
platinum-black
plat|inum blonde
+s
plati|tude +s
plati|tud|in|ar|ian
+s
plati|tud|in|ise Br.
(use
platitudinize)
plati|tud|in|ises

plati|tud|in|ise
(cont.)
plati|tud|in|ised
plati|tud|in|is|ing
plati|tud|in|ize
plati|tud|in|izes
plati|tud|in|ized
plati|tud|in|iz|ing
plati|tud|in|ous
Plato (Greek
philosopher)
Pla|ton|ic (of Plato)
pla|ton|ic (not
sexual;
theoretical)
Pla|ton|ic|al|ly (in
a Platonic way)
pla|ton|ic|al|ly (in
a platonic way)
Pla|ton|ism
Pla|ton|ist +s
pla|toon +s
Platt|deutsch
platte|land
platte|land|er +s
plat|ter +s
platy|hel|minth +s
platy|pus
platy|puses
platyr|rhine +s
plau|dit +s
plausi|bil|ity
plausi|bil|ities
plaus|ible
plaus|ibly
Plau|tus, Titus
Mac|cius (Roman
dramatist)
play +s +ed +ing
playa +s
play|abil|ity
play|able
play-act +s +ed
+ing
play-actor +s
play|back +s
play|bill +s
play|boy +s
Play|er, Gary
(South African
golfer)
play|er +s
player-manager
+s
player-piano +s
Play|fair, John
(Scottish
mathematician
and geologist)
play|fel|low +s
play|ful
play|ful|ly

play|ful|ness
play|girl +s
play|goer +s
play|ground +s
play|group +s
play|house +s
play|ing card +s
play|ing field +s
play|ing time
play|let +s
play|list +s
play|maker +s
play|mate +s
play-off +s *noun*
play|pen +s
play-reading +s
play|room +s
play|school +s
play|suit +s
play|thing +s
play|time +s
play|wright +s
play|writ|ing
plaza +s
plea +s
plea bar|gain +s
plea bar|gain|ing
pleach
  pleaches
  pleached
  pleach|ing
plead
  pleads
  pleaded
  pled *Am.*
  plead|ing
plead|able
plead|er +s
plead|ing +s
plead|ing|ly
pleas|ance +s
pleas|ant +er +est
pleas|ant|ly
pleas|ant|ness
pleas|ant|ry
  pleas|ant|ries
please
  pleases
  pleased
  pleas|ing
pleas|ing|ly
pleas|ur|able
pleas|ur|able|ness
pleas|ur|ably
pleas|ure
  pleas|ures
  pleas|ured
  pleas|ur|ing
pleat +s +ed +ing
pleb +s
plebby
ple|beian +s

ple|beian|ism
ple|bis|cit|ary
pleb|is|cite +s
plec|trum
  plec|trums *or*
  plec|tra
pled
pledge
  pledges
  pledged
  pledg|ing
pledge|able
pledgee +s
pledger +s
  (generally)
pledget +s
pledgor +s (*Law*)
pleiad +s
Plei|ades (star
  cluster)
plein-air
plein-airist +s
pleio|trop|ic
plei|otrop|ism
plei|otropy
Pleis|to|cene
plen|ary
  plen|ar|ies
pleni|po|ten|tiary
  pleni|po|ten|
        tiar|ies
pleni|tude
plent|eous
plent|eous|ly
plent|eous|ness
plen|ti|ful
plen|ti|ful|ly
plen|ti|ful|ness
plenty
ple|num +s
pleo|chro|ic
pleo|chro|ism
pleo|morph|ic
pleo|morph|ism
ple|on|asm +s
ple|on|as|tic
ple|on|as|tic|al|ly
ple|sio|saur +s
ple|sio|saurus
  ple|sio|sauri
ples|sor +s
pleth|ora
pleth|or|ic
pleth|or|ic|al|ly
pleura
  pleurae
pleural
pleur|isy
pleur|it|ic
pleuro|dynia
pleuron
  pleura

pleuro|
    pneu|mo|nia
Plé|ven (town,
  Bulgaria)
plexi|form
plexi|glas *Propr.*
plexor +s
plexus
  plural plexus *or*
  plex|uses
pli|abil|ity
pli|able
pli|able|ness
pli|ably
pli|ancy
pli|ant
pli|ant|ly
pli|cate
pli|cated
pli|ca|tion +s
plié +s
pli|ers
plight +s +ed +ing
plim|sole +s (use
  plimsoll)
plim|soll +s
Plim|soll line +s
Plim|soll mark +s
plinth +s
Pliny ('the Elder',
  Roman scholar)
Pliny ('the
  Younger', Roman
  writer)
Plio|cene
plio|saur +s
plio|saurus
  plio|saur|uses
plissé
plod
  plods
  plod|ded
  plod|ding
plod|der +s
plod|ding|ly
ploidy
  ploi|dies
Ploi|eşti (city,
  Romania)
plonk +s +ed +ing
plonk|er +s
plonko +s
plot
  plots
  plot|ted
  plot|ting

Plo|tinus (Roman
  philosopher)
plot|less
plot|less|ness
plot|ter +s
Plough
  (constellation)
plough *Br.* +s +ed
  +ing (*Am.* plow)
plough|able *Br.*
  (*Am.* plowable)
plough|er *Br.* +s
  (*Am.* plower)
plough|land *Br.* +s
  (*Am.* plowland)
plough|man *Br.*
  plough|men
  (*Am.* plowman)
plough|man's
  lunch
  plough|man's
  lunches
plough|man's
  spike|nard
Plough Mon|day
  +s
plough|share *Br.*
  +s (*Am.*
  plowshare)
Plov|div (city,
  Bulgaria)
plover +s
plow *Am.* +s +ed
  +ing (*Br.* plough)
plow|able *Am.* (*Br.*
  ploughable)
plow|er *Am.* +s (*Br.*
  plougher)
plow|land *Am.* +s
  (*Br.* ploughland)
plow|man *Am.*
  plow|men
  (*Br.* ploughman)
plow|share *Am.* +s
  (*Br.* ploughshare)
ploy +s
pluck +s +ed +ing
pluck|er +s
pluck|ily
plucki|ness
pluck|less
plucky
  plucki|er
  plucki|est
plug
  plugs
  plugged
  plug|ging
plug|ger +s
plug|hole +s
plug-in *adjective*
plug|ola +s

plug-ugly
  plug-uglies
plum +s (fruit.
  ⚠ plumb)
plum|age
plum|aged
plu|mas|sier +s
plumb +s +ed +ing
  (measure depth;
  vertical; exactly;
  fit pipes. ⚠ plum)
plum|bagin|ous
plum|bago +s
plum|bate +s
plum|be|ous
plumb|er +s
plum|bic
plum|bif|er|ous
plum|bism
plumb|less
plumb line +s
plum|bous
plumb rule +s
plume
  plumes
  plumed
  plum|ing
plume|less
plume|like
plu|mery
plum|met +s +ed
  +ing
plummy
  plum|mier
  plum|mi|est
plum|ose
plump +s +ed +ing
  +er +est
plump|ish
plump|ly
plump|ness
plumpy
plumul|aceous
plumu|lar
plum|ule +s
plumy
  plu|mier
  plu|mi|est
plun|der +s +ed
  +ing
plun|der|er +s
plun|der|ing +s
plunge
  plunges
  plunged
  plun|ging
plun|ger +s
plunk +s +ed +ing
plu|per|fect
plural +s

plur|al|isa|tion *Br.*
  (use
  pluralization)
plur|al|ise *Br.* (use
  pluralize)
plur|al|ises
plur|al|ised
plur|al|is|ing
plur|al|ism
plur|al|ist +s
plur|al|is|tic
plur|al|is|tic|al|ly
plur|al|ity
plur|al|iza|tion
plur|al|ize
  plur|al|izes
  plur|al|ized
  plur|al|iz|ing
plur|al|ly
pluri|po|ten|tial
pluri|pres|ence
plurry
plus
  pluses
plus ça change
plus fours
plush +er +est
plushi|ness
plush|ly
plush|ness
plushy
  plushi|er
  plushi|est
Plu|tarch (Greek
  biographer)
plu|tarchy
  plu|tarch|ies
Pluto (*Greek
  Mythology*; planet;
  = pipeline under
  the ocean)
plu|toc|racy
  plu|toc|ra|cies
plu|to|crat +s
plu|to|crat|ic
plu|to|crat|ic|al|ly
plu|tol|atry
plu|ton +s
Plu|to|nian
Plu|ton|ic (theory;
  infernal)
plu|ton|ic (rock)
Plu|to|nism
Plu|to|nist +s
plu|to|nium
plu|vial +s
pluvi|om|eter +s
pluvio|met|ric
pluvio|met|ric|al
pluvio|met|ric|
          al|ly
plu|vi|ous

ply
  plies
  plied
  ply|ing
Ply|mouth (port,
  England; town,
  USA; capital of
  Montserrat, West
  Indies)
ply|wood +s
pneu|mat|ic
pneu|mat|ic|al|ly
pneuma|ti|city
pneu|mat|ics
pneum|ato|cyst +s
pneum|ato|logic|al
pneuma|tol|ogy
pneu|mato|phore
  +s
pneumo|coc|cus
  pneumo|cocci
pneumo|coni|osis
pneumo|cystis
  (car|inii
  pneu|mo|nia)
pneumo|gas|tric
pneu|mon|ec|tomy
  pneu|mon|
      ec|to|mies
pneu|mo|nia +s
pneu|mon|ic
pneu|mon|itis
pneumo|thorax
Po (river, Italy)
po +s (chamber
  pot)
poach
  poaches
  poached
  poach|ing
poach|er +s
Poca|hon|tas
  (American Indian
  princess)
po|chard
  plural po|chard *or*
  po|chards
po|chette +s
pock +s +ed +ing
pocket +s +ed
  +ing
pock|et|able
pocket battle|ship
  +s
pock|et|book +s
pocket bor|ough
  +s
pock|et|ful +s
pocket go|pher +s
pocket knife
  pocket knives
pock|et|less

pocket money
pocket watch
  pocket watches
pock|ety
pock|mark +s
pock-marked
pocky
poco
pod
  pods
  pod|ded
  pod|ding
pod|agra
pod|ag|ral
pod|ag|ric
pod|ag|rous
poddy
  pod|dies
po|destà
podgi|ness
Pod|gorica (capital
  of Montenegro)
podgy
  podgi|er
  podgi|est
po|dia|trist +s
po|dia|try
po|dium
  po|di|ums *or*
  podia
Pod|olsk (city,
  Russia)
podo|phyl|lin
pod|sol +s (use
  podzol)
pod|zol +s
pod|zol|isa|tion
  Br. (use
  podzolization)
pod|zol|ise *Br.* (use
  podzolize)
pod|zol|ises
pod|zol|ised
pod|zol|is|ing
pod|zol|iza|tion
pod|zol|ize
  pod|zol|izes
  pod|zol|ized
  pod|zol|iz|ing
Poe, Edgar Allan
  (American writer)
poem +s
poesy
poet +s
poet|as|ter +s
poet|ess
  poet|esses
poet|ic
poet|ic|al
poet|ic|al|ly
poeti|cise *Br.* (use
  poeticize)

poeti|cise (cont.)
  poeti|cises
  poeti|cised
  poeti|cis|ing
poeti|cize
  poeti|cizes
  poeti|cized
  poeti|ciz|ing
poet|ics
poet|ise Br. (use
  poetize)
  poet|ises
  poet|ised
  poet|is|ing
poet|ize
  poet|izes
  poet|ized
  poet|iz|ing
Poet Laure|ate +s
poet|ry
  poet|ries
Poets' Cor|ner (in
  Westminster
  Abbey)
po-faced
pogo +s noun
pogo
  po|goes
  po|goed
  pogo|ing
  verb
pog|rom +s
Po Hai (= Bo Hai)
poign|ance
poign|ancy
poign|ant
poign|ant|ly
poi|kilo|therm +s
poi|kilo|ther|mal
poi|kilo|ther|mia
poi|kilo|ther|mic
poi|kilo|thermy
poilu +s
Poin|caré, Jules-
  Henri (French
  mathematician)
poin|ci|ana +s
poind +s +ed +ing
poin|set|tia +s
point +s +ed +ing
point-blank
point duty
Pointe-à-Pitre
  (port,
  Guadeloupe)
point|ed|ly
point|ed|ness
Pointe-Noire (port,
  the Congo)
point|er +s
Point|ers (two stars
  in the Plough or
  Southern Cross)

poin|til|lism
poin|til|list +s
poin|til|lis|tic
point|less
point|less|ly
point|less|ness
point of sale noun
point-of-sale
  attributive
point-scoring
points|man
  points|men
point-to-point +s
point-to-pointer
  +s
point-to-pointing
pointy
  point|ier
  pointi|est
Poirot, Her|cule
  (fictional
  detective)
poise
  poises
  poised
  pois|ing
poi|sha
  plural poi|sha
poi|son +s +ed
  +ing
poi|son|er +s
poi|son|ing +s
poi|son|ous
poi|son|ous|ly
poi|son pen let|ter
  +s
Pois|son, Siméon-
  Denis (French
  mathematical
  physicist;
  distribution)
Poi|tiers (city,
  France)
Poi|tou (former
  province, France)
Poitou-Charentes
  (region, France)
poke
  pokes
  poked
  pok|ing
poker +s
poker dice
poker-face +s
poker-faced
poker play|er +s
poker|work
poke|weed +s
pokey (prison.
  △ poky)
poki|ly

po|ki|ness
poky
  poki|er
  poki|est
  (small. △ pokey)
pol|lacca +s (dance.
  △ polacre)
pol|lack +s offensive
pol|lacre +s (sailing
  vessel. △ polacca)
Pol|and
Pol|an|ski, Roman
  (film director of
  Polish descent)
polar
po|lar|im|eter +s
po|lari|met|ric
po|lar|im|etry
Po|laris (North
  Star)
po|lar|is|able Br.
  (use polarizable)
po|lar|isa|tion Br.
  +s (use
  polarization)
po|lari|scope +s
po|lari|scop|ic
po|lar|ise Br. (use
  polarize)
  po|lar|ises
  po|lar|ised
  po|lar|is|ing
po|lar|iser Br. +s
  (use polarizer)
po|lar|ity
  po|lar|ities
po|lar|iz|able
po|lar|iza|tion +s
po|lar|ize
  po|lar|izes
  po|lar|ized
  po|lar|iz|ing
po|lar|izer +s
po|lar|ly
po|laro|graph|ic
po|lar|og|raphy
Po|lar|oid +s Propr.
pola|touche +s
pol|der +s
Pole +s (Polish
  person)
pole
  poles
  poled
  pol|ing
  (piece of wood.
  △ poll)
pole|ax Am.
  pole|axes
  pole|axed
  pole|ax|ing

pole-axe Br.
  pole-axes
  pole-axed
  pole-axing
pole|cat +s
po|lem|ic +s
po|lem|ic|al
po|lem|ic|al|ly
po|lemi|cise Br.
  (use polemicize)
  po|lemi|cises
  po|lemi|cised
  po|lemi|cis|ing
po|lemi|cist +s
po|lemi|cize
  po|lemi|cizes
  po|lemi|cized
  po|lemi|ciz|ing
po|lem|ics
po|lenta
pole vault +s noun
pole-vault +s +ed
  +ing verb
pole-vaulter +s
pole|ward
pole|wards
po|lice
  po|lices
  po|liced
  po|licing
po|lice|man
  po|lice|men
po|lice|woman
  po|lice|women
poli|clinic +s (use
  polyclinic)
pol|icy
  pol|icies
pol|icy|hold|er +s
polio
polio|my|el|itis
polis (= police)
Poli|sario
Pol|ish
  plural Pol|ish
  (of Poland;
  person)
pol|ish
  pol|ishes
  pol|ished
  pol|ish|ing
  (make shiny;
  substance)
pol|ish|able
pol|ish|er +s
pol|it|buro +s
po|lite
  po|liter
  po|litest
po|lite|ly
po|lite|ness
  po|lite|nesses

poli|tesse
pol|it|ic
  pol|it|ics
  pol|it|icked
  pol|it|ick|ing
pol|it|ical+s
pol|it|ic|al|ly (in a political way.
  △ politicly)
pol|it|ician+s
pol|iti|cisa|tion *Br.* (use politicization)
pol|iti|cise *Br.* (use politicize)
  pol|iti|cises
  pol|iti|cised
  pol|iti|cis|ing
pol|iti|ciza|tion
pol|iti|cize
  pol|iti|cizes
  pol|iti|cized
  pol|iti|ciz|ing
pol|it|ic|ly (judiciously.
  △ politically)
pol|it|ico+s
politico-
  econom|ical
pol|it|ics
pol|ity
  pol|ities
Polk, James Knox (American president)
polka
  pol|kas
  pol|kaed *or* polka'd
  pol|ka|ing
polka dot +s *noun*
polka-dot
  attributive
poll +s +ed +ing (vote. △ pole)
pol|lack
  plural pol|lack *or* pol|lacks
Pol|lai|uolo, An|tonio and Piero (Italian artists)
pol|lan
  plural pol|lan (fish. △ pollen)
pol|lard +s +ed +ing
poll|ee +s (person questioned in a poll)

pol|len +s (grains in flower.
  △ pollan)
pol|len|less
pol|lex
  pol|li|ces
pol|li|ci|ta|tion
pol|lie +s (use polly)
pol|lin|ate
  pol|lin|ates
  pol|lin|ated
  pol|lin|at|ing
pol|lin|ation
pol|lin|ator+s
poll|ing booth+s
poll|ing day+s
poll|ing sta|tion +s
pol|linic
pol|lin|ifer|ous
polli|wog +s
Pol|lock, Jack|son (American painter)
pol|lock
  plural pol|lock *or* pol|locks
  (use pollack)
poll par|rot +s
poll|ster+s
poll tax
pol|lu|tant +s
pol|lute
  pol|lutes
  pol|luted
  pol|lut|ing
pol|luter+s
pol|lu|tion +s
Pol|lux (*Greek Mythology*; star)
Polly (name)
polly
  pol|lies
  (Apollinaris water; politician. △ poly)
Polly|anna+s
Polly|anna|ish
Polly|anna|ism
polly|wog +s (use polliwog)
Polo, Marco (Italian traveller)
polo +s
polo|crosse
pol|on|aise +s
polo neck +s *noun*
polo-neck
  attributive
po|lo|nium
Po|lon|na|ruwa (town, Sri Lanka)

po|lony
  po|lo|nies
polo play|er+s
polo stick+s
Pol Pot (Cambodian prime minister)
Pol|tava (city, Ukraine)
pol|ter|geist+s
Pol|tor|atsk (former name of Ashgabat)
pol|troon+s
pol|troon|ery
poly+s (= polytechnic.
  △ polly)
poly|adelph|ous
poly|amide+s
poly|an|drous
poly|an|dry
poly|an|thus
  poly|an|thuses
poly|atom|ic
poly|basic
Po|lyb|ius (Greek historian)
poly|car|bon|ate +s
Poly|carp (Greek saint)
poly|chaetan
poly|chaete +s
poly|chaet|ous
poly|chlor|in|ated
poly|chro|mat|ic
poly|chro|ma|tism
poly|chrome +s
poly|chro|mic
poly|chro|mous
poly|chromy
poly|clinic +s
Poly|cli|tus (Greek sculptor)
poly|cot|ton +s
poly|crys|tal +s
poly|crys|tal|line
poly|cyc|lic +s
poly|dac|tyl +s
poly|dae|mon|ism
Poly|deu|ces (*Greek Mythology*; alternative name for Pollux)
poly|es|ter +s
poly|eth|ene +s (= polythene)
poly|ethyl|ene
poly|gam|ic
pol|yg|am|ist +s
pol|yg|am|ous

pol|yg|am|ous|ly
pol|yg|amy
poly|gene +s
poly|gen|esis
poly|gen|et|ic
poly|gen|ic
poly|gen|ism
poly|gen|ist +s
pol|ygeny
poly|glot+s
poly|glot|tal
poly|glot|tic
poly|glot|tism
poly|gon+s
pol|yg|on|al
pol|yg|onum+s
poly|graph+s
pol|ygyn|ous
pol|ygyny
poly|he|dral
poly|he|dric
poly|he|dron
  poly|he|dra *or* poly|he|drons
poly|his|tor+s
Poly|hym|nia (*Greek and Roman Mythology*)
poly|math +s
poly|math|ic
poly|ym|athy
poly|mer+s
poly|mer|ase +s
poly|mer|ic
poly|mer|isa|tion *Br.* (use polymerization)
poly|mer|ise *Br.* (use polymerize)
  poly|mer|ises
  poly|mer|ised
  poly|mer|is|ing
poly|mer|ism
poly|mer|iza|tion
poly|mer|ize
  poly|mer|izes
  poly|mer|ized
  poly|mer|iz|ing
poly|mer|ous
poly|morph|ic
poly|morph|ism
poly|morph|ous
Poly|nesia (region, Pacific Ocean)
Poly|nes|ian +s
poly|neur|it|ic
poly|neur|itis
poly|no|mial +s
po|lynya +s
poly|opia
polyp +s

polyp|ary
  polyp|ar¦ies
poly|pep¦tide +s
pol¦ypha|gous
poly|phase
Poly|phe¦mus
  Greek Mythology
poly|phone +s
poly|phon¦ic
poly|phon¦ic|al¦ly
pol¦yph¦on|ous
pol¦yph¦ony
  pol¦yph¦on¦ies
poly|phos¦phate
  +s
poly|phyl¦et¦ic
polypi
poly|ploid +s
poly|ploidy
poly|pod +s
poly|pody
  poly|pod¦ies
polyp|oid
polyp|ous
poly|pro¦pene +s
poly|pro¦pyl|ene
  +s
polyp|tych +s
poly|pus
  polypi
poly|rhythm +s
poly|sac¦char|ide
  +s
poly|sem¦ic
poly|sem¦ous
poly|semy
poly|styr¦ene +s
poly|syl¦lab¦ic
poly|syl¦lab¦ic|
      al¦ly
poly|syl¦lable +s
poly|syn¦thet¦ic
poly|tech¦nic +s
poly|tetra|fluoro|
     ethyl|ene
poly|the¦ism
poly|the¦ist +s
poly|the¦is¦tic
poly|thene +s
poly|tonal
poly|ton¦al|ity
poly|un¦sat¦ur|ate
  +s
poly|un¦sat¦ur|
     ated
poly|ur¦eth¦ane
  poly|ur¦eth¦anes
  poly|ur¦eth¦aned
  poly|ur¦eth¦an¦ing
poly|va¦lence
poly|va¦lent
poly|vi¦nyl +s

poly|zoan +s
Pom +s (dog;
  offensive Briton)
pom¦ace
po|made
  po|mades
  po|maded
  po|mad¦ing
po|man|der +s
po|ma|tum +s +ed
  +ing
pombe
pome +s
pom¦egran|ate +s
pom¦elo +s
Pom¦er|ania
  (region, N.
  Europe)
Pom¦er|anian +s
pom¦fret +s
pomfret-cake +s
pomi¦cul¦ture
pom¦ifer¦ous
pom¦mel +s (knob)
pom¦mel (use
  pummel)
  pom¦mels
  pom¦melled *Br.*
  pom¦meled *Am.*
  pom¦mel¦ling *Br.*
  pom¦mel¦ing *Am.*
pom¦mel horse +s
Pom¦mie +s (use
  Pommy)
Pommy
  Pom¦mies
  (*offensive*)
pomo|logic¦al
pom¦olo¦gist +s
pom¦ology
pomp +s
Pom¦pa|dour,
  Ma¦dame de
  (French
  noblewoman)
pom¦pa|dour +s
pom¦pano +s
Pom¦peii (ancient
  city, Italy)
Pom¦pey (Roman
  general;
  = Portsmouth,
  England)
Pom¦pi¦dou,
  Georges (French
  president)
pom¦pom +s
  (use pompon)
pom-pom +s (gun)
pom¦pon +s
  (ornament)
pom¦pos¦ity
  pom¦pos¦ities

pom¦pous
pom¦pous|ly
pom¦pous|ness
'pon (= upon)
ponce
  ponces
  ponced
  pon|cing
pon|ceau +s
Ponce de León,
  Juan (Spanish
  explorer)
poncey
  pon|cier
  pon|ci|est
pon¦cho +s
poncy
  pon|cier
  pon|ci|est
  (use poncey)
pond +s +ed +ing
pond|age
pon¦der +s +ed
  +ing
pon¦der|abil¦ity
pon¦der|able
pon¦der|ation
pon¦der|ing +s
pon¦der|osa +s
pon¦der|os¦ity
pon¦der|ous
pon¦der|ous|ly
pon¦der|ous|ness
Pondi|cherry (city
  and territory,
  India)
pond life
pond-skater +s
pond|weed +s
pone +s
pong +s +ed +ing
pon¦gal
pon¦gee +s
pon¦gid +s
pongo +s (*offensive*
  in sense
  'Englishman')
pongy
  pong|ier
  pongi|est
pon¦iard +s
pons
  pon¦tes
pons as¦in|orum
  pon¦tes
  as¦in|orum
pons Var|olii
  pon¦tes Var|olii
pont +s
Ponte, Lor¦enzo
  Da (Italian
  librettist and poet)

Pontefract-cake
  +s
pon¦tes
Ponti¦anak (port,
  Indonesia)
pon¦ti¦fex
  pon|tifi¦ces
pon¦tiff +s
pon¦tif¦ic¦al
pon¦tifi|calia
pon¦tif¦ic|al¦ly
pon¦tifi|cate
  pon|tifi|cates
  pon|tifi|cated
  pon|tifi|cat¦ing
pon|tifi¦ces
Pon¦tine Marshes
  (in Italy)
pon|toon +s +ed
  +ing
Pon|tormo,
  Ja¦copo da
  (Italian painter)
Pon¦tus (ancient
  region, Asia
  Minor)
pony
  po|nies
pony|tail +s
pony-trekker +s
pony-trekking
poo +s (excrement.
  △ pooh)
pooch
  pooches
poo|dle +s
poof +s (*offensive*
  male homosexual;
  interjection.
  △ pouffe)
poof|ter +s
  (*offensive*)
poofy
  poof|ier
  poofi|est
  (*offensive*)
Pooh, Win¦nie the
  (bear)
pooh +s
  (*interjection.*
  △ poo)
Pooh-Bah +s
pooh-pooh +s +ed
  +ing (dismiss.
  △ poo-poo)
pooja +s (use
  puja)
poo|jah +s (use
  puja)
pooka +s

pool +s +ed +ing
(body of water;
common supply;
share etc. △ pul)
Poole (town,
England)
pool hall +s
pool room +s
pool|side
poon +s
Poona (city, India)
poon oil
poop +s +ed +ing
pooper scoop|er
+s
poo-poo +s
(excrement.
△ pooh-pooh)
poop scoop +s
poor +er +est (not
rich. △ paw, pore,
pour)
poor box
poor boxes
Poor Clare +s
(nun)
poor|house +s
poor|ly
poor man's
weather-glass
poor|ness
poor rate +s
poor-spirit|ed
poo|tle
poo|tles
poo|tled
poot|ling
poove +s (*offensive*)
pop
pops
popped
pop|ping
popa|dam +s (use
poppadom)
popa|dom +s (use
poppadom)
pop|corn
Pope, Alex|an|der
(English poet)
pope +s (head of
Roman Catholic
Church; Orthodox
parish priest)
pope|dom
Pope Joan
(legendary female
pope)
pope|less
Pope|mo|bile +s
popery
pope's eye +s
(gland in sheep)

pop-eyed
pop|gun +s
pop|in|jay +s
pop|ish
pop|ish|ly
Pop|ish Plot
English history
pop|lar +s
pop|lin
pop|lit|eal
Popo|caté|petl
(volcano, Mexico)
poppa +s (father.
△ popper)
pop|pa|dom +s
pop|pa|dum +s
(use poppadom)
Pop|per, Karl
(Austrian-born
British
philosopher)
pop|per +s (press-
stud; person or
thing that pops;
vial. △ poppa)
pop|pet +s
poppet-head +s
poppet-valve +s
pop|pied
pop|ping crease
+s
pop|ple
pop|ples
pop|pled
pop|pling
pop|ply
Poppy (name)
poppy
pop|pies
(flower)
poppy|cock
Poppy Day +s
poppy-head +s
pop-shop +s
Pop|sicle +s *Propr.*
popsy
pop|sies
popu|lace (the
masses.
△ populous)
popu|lar
popu|lar|isa|tion
Br. (use
popularization)
popu|lar|ise *Br.*
(use popularize)
popu|lar|ises
popu|lar|ised
popu|lar|is|ing
popu|lar|iser *Br.*
+s (use
popularizer)

popu|lar|ism
popu|lar|ity
popu|lar|iza|tion
popu|lar|ize
popu|lar|izes
popu|lar|ized
popu|lar|iz|ing
popu|lar|izer +s
popu|lar|ly
popu|late
popu|lates
popu|lated
popu|lat|ing
popu|la|tion +s
popu|lism
popu|list +s
popu|lis|tic
popu|lous (densely
populated.
△ populace)
popu|lous|ly
popu|lous|ness
pop-up *adjective*
por|bea|gle +s
por|cel|ain +s
porcelain-shell +s
por|cel|lan|eous
por|cel|lan|ous
porch
porches
porched
porch|less
por|cine
por|cu|pine +s
por|cu|pine fish
plural por|cu|pine
fish
por|cu|pin|ish
por|cu|piny
pore
pores
pored
por|ing
(tiny opening;
study intently.
△ paw, poor,
pour)
porgy
por|gies
Pori (port, Finland)
pori|fer +s
por|if|er|an +s
por|ism +s
por|is|mat|ic
pork
pork bar|rel *noun*
pork-barrel
attributive
pork butch|er +s
porker +s
pork|ling +s
pork pie +s

pork-pie hat +s
porky
pork|ies
pork|ier
porki|est
(fat; like pork; a
lie. △ pawky)
porky-pie
porky-pies
porn
(= pornography.
△ pawn)
porno
porn|og|raph|er +s
porno|graph|ic
porno|graph|ic|
al|ly
porn|og|raphy
poro|plas|tic
por|os|ity
por|os|ities
por|ous
por|ous|ly
por|ous|ness
por|phy|ria
por|phy|rin +s
por|phy|rit|ic
por|phyro|gen|ite
+s
Por|phyry (ancient
philosopher)
por|phyry
por|phy|ries
por|poise +s
por|rect +s +ed
+ing
por|ridge
por|ridgy
por|rin|ger +s
Porsche,
Fer|di|nand
(Austrian car
designer)
Por|senna, Lars
(legendary
Etruscan chieftain)
port +s +ed +ing
(harbour; town;
wine; left;
opening)
port|abil|ity
port|able +s
port|able|ness
port|ably
port|age
port|ages
port|aged
port|aging
Porta|kabin +s
Propr.
por|tal +s

por|ta|mento
  por|ta|menti *or*
  por|ta|men|tos
porta|tive
Port-au-Prince
  (capital of Haiti)
Port Blair (capital
  of the Andaman
  and Nicobar
  Islands)
Port|cul|lis
  Heraldry
port|cul|lis
  port|cul|lises
  port|cul|lised
Porte (Ottoman
  court at
  Constantinople)
porte co|chère +s
Port Eliza|beth
  (port, South
  Africa)
por|tend +s +ed
  +ing
por|tent +s
por|tent|ous
por|tent|ous|ly
por|tent|ous|ness
Por|ter, Cole
  (American
  composer and
  lyricist)
Por|ter,
  Kath|er|ine Anne
  (American writer)
Por|ter, Peter
  (Australian poet)
por|ter +s +ed
  +ing
por|ter|age
por|ter|house +s
por|ter|house
  steak +s
Port Éti|enne
  (former name of
  Nouadhibou)
port|fire +s
port|folio +s
Port-Gentil (port,
  Gabon)
Port Har|court
  (port, Algeria)
Port Hed|land
  (port, Australia)
port|hole +s
Por|tia
por|tico
  por|ti|coes *or*
  por|ti|cos
por|ti|coed
por|ti|ère +s

por|tion +s +ed
  +ing
por|tion|less
Port|land (port,
  USA; shipping
  area, English
  Channel; cement;
  stone; vase)
Port|land, Isle of
  (peninsula,
  England)
Port|laoighise (use
  Portlaoise)
Port|laoise (town,
  Republic of
  Ireland)
port|li|ness
Port Louis (capital
  of Mauritius)
port|ly
  port|lier
  port|li|est
Port Mahon
  (alternative name
  for Mahón)
port|man|teau
  port|man|teaus *or*
  port|man|teaux
Port Moresby
  (capital of Papua
  New Guinea)
Porto (Portuguese
  name for Oporto)
Pôrto Alegre (city,
  Brazil)
Port-of-Spain
  (capital of
  Trinidad and
  Tobago)
por|to|lan +s
por|to|lano +s
Porto Novo
  (capital of Benin)
Pôrto Velho (town,
  Brazil)
Port Pet|rovsk
  (former name of
  Makhachkala)
Port Pirie (port,
  Australia)
por|trait +s
por|trait|ist +s
por|trait|ure +s
por|tray +s +ed
  +ing
por|tray|able
por|tray|al +s
por|tray|er +s
Port Said (port,
  Egypt)
Port Salut (cheese)

Ports|mouth (port,
  England)
Port Stan|ley (port,
  Falkland Islands)
Port Sudan (port,
  Sudan)
Por|tu|gal
Por|tu|guese
  plural
  Por|tu|guese
Port Vila (capital of
  Vanuatu)
pose
  poses
  posed
  pos|ing
Po|sei|don *Greek
  Mythology*
poser +s (problem)
pos|eur +s (*male
  person who poses*)
pos|euse +s (*female
  person who poses*)
posey (pretentious.
  △ posy)
posh +er +est
posh|ly
posh|ness
posit +s +ed +ing
pos|ition +s +ed
  +ing
pos|ition|al
pos|ition|al|ly
pos|ition|er +s
posi|tive +s
posi|tive|ly
posi|tive|ness
posi|tiv|ism
posi|tiv|ist +s
posi|tiv|is|tic
posi|tiv|is|tic|al|ly
posi|tiv|ity
posi|tron +s
posi|tron|ic
posi|tro|nium
poso|logic|al
pos|ology
posse +s
posse comi|ta|tus
pos|sess
  pos|sesses
  pos|sessed
  pos|sess|ing
pos|ses|sion +s
pos|ses|sion|less
pos|ses|sive +s
pos|ses|sive|ly
pos|ses|sive|ness
pos|ses|sor +s
pos|ses|sory
pos|set +s

pos|si|bil|ity
  pos|si|bil|ities
pos|sible +s
pos|sibly
pos|sum +s
post +s +ed +ing
post|age
pos|tal +s
pos|tal code +s
pos|tal|ly
post|bag +s
post|box
  post|boxes
post-boy +s
post|card +s
post-chaise +s
post-classic|al
post|code +s
post-coital
post-coital|ly
post-colonial
post-date
  post-dates
  post-dated
  post-dating
post|doc|tor|al
post-entry
pos|ter +s
poste rest|ante
pos|ter|ior +s
pos|ter|ior|ity
pos|ter|ior|ly
pos|ter|ity
pos|tern +s
pos|ter paint +s
post ex|change +s
post|face +s
post-feminism
post-feminist +s
post|fix
  post|fixes
  post|fixed
  post|fix|ing
post-free
post|gla|cial
post|grad +s
post|gradu|ate +s
post-haste
post-horn +s
post|hu|mous
post|hu|mous|ly
pos|tiche +s
pos|tie +s
pos|til +s
pos|til|ion +s
post-
  Impres|sion|ism
post-
  Impres|sion|ist
  +s
post-industrial
post|ing +s

post|lim|iny
post|lude +s
post|man
  post|men
post|man's knock
post|mark +s +ed
  +ing
post|mas|ter +s
post|mas|ter
  gen|eral
  post|mas|ters
  gen|eral
post-mill +s
post-millen|nial
post-
  millen|nial|ism
post-
  millen|nial|ist +s
post|mis|tress
  post|mis|tresses
post|mod|ern
post|mod|ern|ism
post|mod|ern|ist
  +s
post|mod|ern|ity
post-mortem +s
post-natal
post-natally
post-nuptial
post-obit +s
Post Of|fice +s
  (organization)
post of|fice +s
  (individual office)
post of|fice box
  post of|fice boxes
post-operative
post-paid
post-partum
post|pon|able
post|pone
  post|pones
  post|poned
  post|pon|ing
post|pone|ment +s
post|poner +s
post|pos|ition +s
post|pos|ition|al
post|posi|tive +s
post|posi|tive|ly
post|pran|dial
post-produc|tion
post-
  revolu|tion|ary
post room +s
post|script +s
post-
  structur|al|ism
post-
  structur|al|ist +s
post-tax
post town +s

post-traumat|ic
  stress dis|order
pos|tu|lant +s
pos|tu|late
  pos|tu|lates
  pos|tu|lated
  pos|tu|lat|ing
pos|tu|la|tion +s
pos|tu|la|tor +s
pos|tural
pos|ture
  pos|tures
  pos|tured
  pos|tur|ing
pos|turer +s
pos|tur|ing +s
post-war
post|woman
  post|women
Posy (name)
posy
  po|sies
  (flowers. △ posey)
posy ring +s
pot
  pots
  pot|ted
  pot|ting
pot|abil|ity
pot|able
pot|age
pota|ger +s
pot|am|ic
pot|am|ology
pot|ash
po|tas|sic
po|tas|sium
potassium–argon
  dat|ing
po|ta|tion +s
po|tato
  po|ta|toes
pot|atory
pot-au-feu
pot-bellied
pot-belly
  pot-bellies
pot|boil|er +s
pot-bound
potch
  potches
pot cheese
po|teen +s
Po|tem|kin
  (Russian
  battleship)
po|tence
po|tency
  po|ten|cies
po|tent
po|ten|tate +s
po|ten|tial +s

po|ten|ti|al|ity
  po|ten|ti|al|ities
po|ten|tial|ly
po|tenti|ate
  po|tenti|ates
  po|tenti|ated
  po|tenti|at|ing
po|ten|tilla +s
po|tenti|om|eter
  +s
po|tentio|met|ric
po|tenti|om|etry
po|tent|isa|tion Br.
  (use
  potentization)
po|tent|ise Br. (use
  potentize)
  po|tent|ises
  po|tent|ised
  po|tent|is|ing
po|tent|iza|tion
po|tent|ize
  po|tent|izes
  po|tent|ized
  po|tent|iz|ing
po|tent|ly
Po|tenza (town,
  Italy)
pot|ful +s
pot|head +s
po|theen +s (use
  poteen)
pother +s +ed
  +ing
pot-herb +s
pot|hole
  pot|holes
  pot|holed
  pot|hol|ing
pot|holer +s
pot-hook +s
pot-hunter +s
po|tion +s
Poti|phar Bible
pot|latch
  pot|latches
pot|latch|ing
pot|luck
Poto|mac (river,
  USA)
poto|roo +s
Pot|osi (city,
  Bolivia)
pot plant +s
pot-pourri +s
po|trero +s
pot roast +s noun
pot-roast +s +ed
  +ing verb
Pots|dam (city,
  Germany)
pot|sherd +s

pot-shot +s
pot|stone
pot|tage +s
Pot|ter, Bea|trix
  (English writer)
pot|ter +s +ed
  +ing
pot|ter|er +s
Pot|ter|ies, the
  (district, England)
pot|ter's field +s
pot|ter's wheel +s
pot|tery
  pot|ter|ies
pot|ti|ness
pot|tle +s
potto +s
Pott's frac|ture +s
potty
  pot|ties
  pot|tier
  pot|ti|est
potty-train
  potty-trains
  potty-trained
  potty-training
pot-valiant
pot-valour
pouch
  pouches
  pouched
  pouch|ing
pouchy
  pouch|ier
  pouchi|est
pouf +s (cushion;
  use pouffe.
  △ poof)
pouffe +s (cushion.
  △ poof)
poul|ard +s
Pou|lenc, Fran|cis
  (French
  composer)
poult +s
poult-de-soie
poult|er|er +s
poult|ice
  poult|ices
  poult|iced
  poult|icing
poult|ry
pounce
  pounces
  pounced
  poun|cing
poun|cer +s
pouncet-box
  pouncet-boxes
Pound, Ezra
  (American poet)
pound +s +ed +ing

pound|age +s
pound|al +s
pound|er +s
pour +s +ed +ing
(flow; rain.
△ paw, poor,
pore)
pour|able
pour|boire +s
pour|er +s
pous|sette
pous|settes
pous|set|ted
pous|set|ting
Pous|sin, Nico|las
(French painter)
pous|sin +s
pout +s +ed +ing
pout|er +s
pout|ing|ly
pouty
pout|ier
pouti|est
pov|erty
poverty-stricken
pow
powan
plural powans *or*
powan
pow|der +s +ed
+ing
pow|der blue +s
noun and adjective
powder-blue
attributive
pow|der flask +s
pow|der keg +s
pow|der mon|key
+s
pow|der puff +s
pow|der room +s
pow|dery
Pow|ell, An|thony
(English novelist)
Pow|ell, Enoch
(English politician)
power +s +ed +ing
(energy; ability;
etc. △ paua)
power-assist|ed
power base +s
power block +s
power|boat +s
power-broker +s
power-broking
power-crazed
power cut +s
power-dive
power-dives
power-dived
power-diving
power|ful

power|ful|ly
power|ful|ness
power|house +s
power-hungry
power|less
power|less|ly
power|less|ness
power line +s
power pack +s
power plant +s
power play +s
power point +s
power pol|it|ics
power-sharing
power sta|tion +s
power sup|ply
power tool +s
power train +s
Powis (Lord; castle,
Wales)
pow|wow +s +ed
+ing
Powys (county,
Wales)
pox
poxy
pox|ier
poxi|est
Pozi|driv
(screwdriver)
Propr.
Poz|nań (city,
Poland)
poz|zo|lana
praam +s (use
pram)
prac|tic|abil|ity
prac|tic|able
prac|tic|able|ness
prac|tic|ably
prac|tical +s
prac|ti|cal|ity
prac|ti|cal|ities
prac|tic|al|ly
prac|tic|al|ness
prac|tice +s *noun*
prac|tice *Am.*
prac|tices
prac|ticed
prac|ticing
(*verb. Br.* practise)
prac|ticer *Am.* +s
(*Br.* practiser)
prac|ti|cian +s
prac|tise *Br.*
prac|tises
prac|tised
prac|tis|ing
(*verb. Am.*
practice)
prac|tiser *Br.* +s
(*Am.* practicer)

prac|ti|tion|er +s
prad +s
Prado (art gallery,
Madrid)
prae|cipe +s
prae|co|cial (use
precocial)
prae|dial (use
predial)
prae|mu|nire
prae|no|men +s
prae|pos|tor +s
Prae|sepe (cluster
of stars)
prae|sid|ium +s
(use presidium)
prae|tor +s
prae|tor|ial
prae|tor|ian +s
prae|tor|ship +s
prag|mat|ic
prag|mat|ic|al
prag|mat|ic|al|ity
prag|mat|ic|al|ly
prag|mat|ics
prag|ma|tise *Br.*
(use pragmatize)
prag|ma|tises
prag|ma|tised
prag|ma|tis|ing
prag|ma|tism
prag|ma|tist +s
prag|ma|tis|tic
prag|ma|tize
prag|ma|tizes
prag|ma|tized
prag|ma|tiz|ing
Prague (capital of
the Czech
Republic)
prahu +s
Praia (port, São
Tiago, Cape Verde
Islands)
prairie +s
praise
praises
praised
prais|ing
(approval.
△ prase)
praise|ful
praiser +s
praise|wor|thily
praise|worthi|ness
praise|worthy
Prak|rit
pra|line +s
prall|trill|er +s
pram +s
prana

prance
pran|ces
pranced
pran|cing
pran|cer +s
pran|dial
Prandtl, Lud|wig
(German
physicist)
prang +s +ed +ing
prank +s
prank|ful
prank|ish
prank|some
prank|ster +s
prase (quartz.
△ praise)
praseo|dym|ium
prat +s
prate
prates
prated
prat|ing
prater +s
prat|fall +s
pra|tie +s
prat|in|cole +s
prat|ique +s
Prato (city, Italy)
prat|tle
prat|tles
prat|tled
prat|tling
prat|tler +s
prau +s
Pravda (Russian
newspaper)
prawn +s +ed +ing
praxis
Prax|it|eles
(Athenian
sculptor)
pray +s +ed +ing
(say prayers.
△ prey)
pray|er +s (request
etc. to god; person
who prays.
△ preyer)
pray|er book +s
pray|er|ful
pray|er|ful|ly
pray|er|ful|ness
pray|er|less
pray|er mat +s
pray|er wheel +s
pray|ing man|tis
preach
preaches
preached
preach|ing
preach|able

preach|er +s
preach|ify
  preachi|fies
  preachi|fied
  preachi|fy|ing
preachi|ness
preach|ing +s
preach|ment +s
preachy
pre-adolescence
pre-adolescent +s
pre|amble +s
pre|ambu|lar
pre|amp +s
  (= preamplifier)
pre|amp|li|fied
pre|amp|li|fier +s
pre-arrange
  pre-arranges
  pre-arranged
  pre-arranging
pre-arrange|ment
pre|atom|ic
preb|end +s
preb|endal
preb|end|ary
  preb|end|ar|ies
preb|end|ary|ship
  +s
pre-book +s +ed
  +ing
pre-bookable
Pre|cam|brian
pre|can|cer|ous
pre|car|ious
pre|car|ious|ly
pre|car|ious|ness
pre-cast
preca|tive +s
preca|tory
pre|cau|tion +s
pre|cau|tion|ary
pre|cede
  pre|cedes
  pre|ceded
  pre|ced|ing
  (go before.
  △ proceed)
pre|ce|dence
pre|ce|dency
  pre|ce|den|cies
pre|ce|dent +s
pre|ce|dented
pre|ce|dent|ly
pre|cent +s +ed
  +ing
pre|cent|or +s
pre|cen|tor|ship +s
pre|cen|trix
  pre|cen|tri|ces
  female
pre|cept +s

pre|cep|tive
pre|cept|or +s
pre|cep|tor|ial
pre|cep|tor|ship +s
pre|cep|tress
  pre|cep|tresses
pre|ces|sion (of the
  equinoxes etc.
  △ procession)
pre|ces|sion|al (of
  precession.
  △ processional)
pre-Christian +s
pre-Christmas
pre|cinct +s
pre|ci|os|ity
pre|cious
pre|cious|ly
pre|cious|ness
preci|pice +s
pre|cipit|abil|ity
pre|cipit|able
pre|cipi|tance
pre|cipi|tancy
pre|cipi|tant +s
pre|cipi|tate
  pre|cipi|tates
  pre|cipi|tated
  pre|cipi|tat|ing
pre|cipi|tate|ly
pre|cipi|tate|ness
pre|cipi|ta|tion
pre|cipi|ta|tor +s
pre|cipit|ous
pre|cipit|ous|ly
pre|cipit|ous|ness
pré|cis
  plural pré|cis
  noun
pré|cis
  pré|cises
  pré|cised
  pré|cis|ing
  verb
pre|cise
pre|cise|ly
pre|cise|ness
pre|ci|sian +s
  (precise person.
  △ precision)
pre|ci|sian|ism
  (the practice of a
  precisian.
  △ precisionism)
pre|ci|sion
  (accuracy.
  △ precisian)
pre|ci|sion|ism
  (the practice of a
  precisionist.
  △ precisianism)
pre|ci|sion|ist +s

pre|clas|sic|al
pre|clin|ic|al
pre|clude
  pre|cludes
  pre|cluded
  pre|clud|ing
pre|clu|sion
pre|clu|sive
pre|co|cial +s
pre|co|cious
pre|co|cious|ly
pre|co|cious|ness
pre|co|city
pre|cog|ni|tion
pre|cog|ni|tive
pre-coital
pre-coital|ly
pre-Columbian
pre|con|ceive
  pre|con|ceives
  pre|con|ceived
  pre|con|ceiv|ing
pre|con|cep|tion
  +s
pre|con|cert +s
  +ed +ing
pre|con|di|tion +s
  +ed +ing
pre|con|isa|tion *Br.*
  (use
  preconization)
pre|con|ise *Br.* (use
  preconize)
  pre|con|ises
  pre|con|ised
  pre|con|is|ing
pre|con|iza|tion
pre|con|ize
  pre|con|izes
  pre|con|ized
  pre|con|iz|ing
pre|con|scious
pre|con|scious|
           ness
pre-cook +s +ed
  +ing
pre-cool +s +ed
  +ing
pre|cor|dial
pre|cos|tal
pre|cur|sive
pre|cur|sor +s
pre|cur|sory
pre-cut
  pre-cuts
  pre-cut
  pre-cutting
pre|da|cious
pre|da|cious|ness
pre|da|city
pre|date
  pre|dates

pre|date (*cont.*)
  pre|dated
  pre|dat|ing
  (prey on)
pre-date
  pre-dates
  pre-dated
  pre-dating
  (be earlier than)
pre|da|tion
preda|tor +s
preda|tor|ily
preda|tori|ness
preda|tory
pre-dawn
pre|de|cease
  pre|de|ceases
  pre|de|ceased
  pre|de|ceas|ing
pre|de|ces|sor +s
pre-decimal
pre|della +s
pre|des|tin|ar|ian
  +s
pre|des|tin|ate
  pre|des|tin|ates
  pre|des|tin|ated
  pre|des|tin|at|ing
pre|des|tin|ation
pre|des|tine
  pre|des|tines
  pre|des|tined
  pre|des|tin|ing
pre|de|ter|min|
           able
pre|de|ter|min|ate
pre|de|ter|min|
           ation
pre|de|ter|mine
  pre|de|ter|mines
  pre|de|ter|mined
  pre|de|ter|min|ing
pre|de|ter|miner
  +s
pre|dial +s (rural;
  slave)
pred|ic|abil|ity
pred|ic|able +s
pre|dica|ment +s
predi|cant +s
predi|cate
  predi|cates
  predi|cated
  predi|cat|ing
predi|ca|tion +s
pre|dica|tive +s
pre|dica|tive|ly
predi|ca|tor +s
predi|ca|tory
pre|dict +s +ed
  +ing

pre|dict|abil|ity
  pre|dict|abil|ities
pre|dict|able
pre|dict|ably
pre|dic|tion +s
pre|dict|ive
pre|dict|ive|ly
pre|dict|or +s
pre|digest +s +ed
  +ing
pre|di|ges|tion
predi|kant +s
pre|di|lec|tion +s
pre|dis|pose
  pre|dis|poses
  pre|dis|posed
  pre|dis|pos|ing
pre|dis|pos|ition
  +s
pred|nis|one
pre|dom|in|ance
pre|dom|in|ant
pre|dom|in|ant|ly
pre|dom|in|ate
  pre|dom|in|ates
  pre|dom|in|ated
  pre|dom|in|at|ing
pre|dom|in|ate|ly
pre|doom +s +ed
  +ing
pre|dor|sal
pre|dyn|as|tic
pre-echo
  pre-echoes
  pre-echoed
  pre-echoing
pre-eclamp|sia
pre-eclamp|tic
pre-elect +s +ed
  +ing
pre-election +s
pre-embryo +s
pre-embryon|ic
pre-eminence
pre-eminent
pre-eminent|ly
pre-empt +s +ed
  +ing
pre-emption
pre-emptive
pre-emptive|ly
pre-emptor +s
pre-emptory
preen +s +ed +ing
preen|er +s
pre-engage
  pre-engages
  pre-engaged
  pre-engaging
pre-engage|ment
pre-establish
  pre-establishes

pre-establish
  (*cont.*)
  pre-established
  pre-establish|ing
pre-exist +s +ed
  +ing
pre-existence
pre-existent
pre|fab +s
  (= prefabricated
  building)
pre|fab|ri|cate
  pre|fab|ri|cates
  pre|fab|ri|cated
  pre|fab|ri|cat|ing
pre|fab|ri|ca|tion
pref|ace
  pref|aces
  pref|aced
  pref|acing
prefa|tor|ial
prefa|tory
pre|fect +s
pre|fect|oral
pre|fect|orial
pre|fec|tural
pre|fec|ture +s
pre|fer
  pre|fers
  pre|ferred
  pre|fer|ring
pref|er|abil|ity
pref|er|able
pref|er|ably
pref|er|ence +s
pref|er|en|tial
pref|er|en|tial|ly
pre|fer|ment
pre|fig|ur|ation
pre|fig|ura|tive
pre|fig|ure
  pre|fig|ures
  pre|fig|ured
  pre|fig|ur|ing
pre|fig|ure|ment
pre|fix
  pre|fixes
  pre|fixed
  pre|fix|ing
pre|fix|ation
pre|fix|ion
pre|fix|ture
pre-flight
pre|form +s +ed
  +ing
pre|form|ation
pre|form|ation|ist
  +s
pre|forma|tive +s
pre-format|ted
pre|front|al
pre|gla|cial

preg|nable
preg|nancy
  preg|nan|cies
preg|nant
preg|nant|ly
pre|heat +s +ed
  +ing
pre|hen|sile
pre|hen|sil|ity
pre|hen|sion
pre|his|tor|ian +s
pre|his|toric
pre|his|tor|ic|al|ly
pre|his|tory
pre-human
pre-ignition
pre-industrial
pre|judge
  pre|judges
  pre|judged
  pre|judg|ing
pre|judge|ment +s
pre|judg|ment +s
  (use
  prejudgement)
preju|dice
  preju|dices
  preju|diced
  preju|dicing
preju|di|cial
preju|di|cial|ly
prel|acy
  prel|acies
pre|lap|sar|ian +s
prel|ate +s
prel|at|ic
prel|at|ic|al
prel|at|ure +s
pre-launch
pre|lect +s +ed
  +ing
pre|lec|tion +s
pre|lec|tor +s
pre|li|ba|tion +s
pre|lim +s
pre|lim|in|ar|ily
pre|lim|in|ary
  pre|lim|in|ar|ies
pre-linguis|tic
pre|lit|er|ate +s
prel|ude
  prel|udes
  prel|uded
  prel|ud|ing
prel|ud|ial
pre|mar|ital
pre|mar|it|al|ly
pre|ma|ture
pre|ma|ture|ly
pre|ma|ture|ness
pre|ma|tur|ity
pre|max|il|lary

pre|med +s
  (premedical
  studies; student)
pre-med +s (pre-
  medication)
pre|med|ical
pre-medica|tion
pre|medi|tate
  pre|medi|tates
  pre|medi|tated
  pre|medi|tat|ing
pre|medi|ta|tion
pre|men|strual
pre|men|stru|al|ly
pre|mia (plural of
  premium)
prem|ier +s (first in
  importance etc.;
  prime minister)
premi|ère
  premi|ères
  premi|èred
  premi|èr|ing
  (first performance)
prem|ier|ship +s
pre|mil|len|nial
pre|mil|len|nial|
        ism
pre|mil|len|nial|ist
  +s
prem|ise +s
  (buildings etc.)
prem|ise
  prem|ises
  prem|ised
  prem|is|ing
  verb
prem|iss
  prem|isses
  (statement)
pre|mium
  pre|miums *or*
  pre|mia
Pre|mium Bond +s
pre|molar +s
pre|mon|ition +s
pre|moni|tor +s
pre|moni|tory
Pre|mon|stra|
      ten|sian +s
pre|morse
pre|mo|tion
  (*Theology.*
  △ promotion)
pre|natal
pre|natal|ly
pren|tice
  pren|tices
  pren|ticed
  pren|ticing
pren|tice|ship +s
pre|nup|tial

pre|occu|pa|tion +s

pre|occupy
  pre|occu|pies
  pre|occu|pied
  pre|occu|py|ing
pre|ocu|lar
pre|or|dain +s +ed +ing
pre-owned
prep
  preps
  prepped
  prep|ping
pre-pack +s +ed +ing
pre-package
  pre-packages
  pre-packaged
  pre-packaging
prep|ar|ation +s
pre|para|tive
pre|para|tive|ly
pre|para|tor|ily
pre|para|tory
pre|pare
  pre|pares
  pre|pared
  pre|par|ing
pre|pared|ness
pre|parer +s
pre|pay
  pre|pays
  pre|paid
  pre|pay|ing
pre|pay|able
pre|pay|ment +s
pre|pense
pre|pense|ly
pre-plan
  pre-plans
  pre-planned
  pre-planning
pre|pon|der|ance
pre|pon|der|ant
pre|pon|der|ant|ly
pre|pon|der|ate
  pre|pon|der|ates
  pre|pon|der|ated
  pre|pon|der|at|ing
pre|pone
  pre|pones
  pre|poned
  pre|pon|ing
pre|pose
  pre|poses
  pre|posed
  pre|pos|ing
prep|os|ition +s
  (word)

pre-position +s +ed +ing (put in place beforehand)
prep|os|ition|al
prep|os|ition|al|ly
pre|posi|tive
pre|pos|sess
  pre|pos|sesses
  pre|pos|sessed
  pre|pos|sess|ing
pre|pos|ses|sion +s
pre|pos|ter|ous
pre|pos|ter|ous|ly
pre|pos|ter|ous|ness
pre|pos|tor +s (use praepostor)
pre|po|tence
pre|po|tency
pre|po|tent
prep|pie +s (use preppy)
preppy
  prep|pies
  prep|pier
  prep|pi|est
pre-prandial
pre-prefer|ence
pre|print +s noun
pre-print +s +ed +ing verb
pre-process
  pre-processes
  pre-processed
  pre-process|ing
pre-proces|sor +s
pre-produc|tion
pre-program
  pre-programs
  pre-programmed
  pre-program|ming (Computing)
pre-pubertal
pre-puberty
pre-pubescence
pre-pubescent +s
pre-publica|tion
pre|puce +s
pre|pu|tial
pre-qualifier +s
pre-qualify
  pre-qualifies
  pre-qualified
  pre-qualify|ing
pre|quel +s
Pre-Raphael
Pre-Raphael|ism
Pre-Raphael|ite +s
Pre-Raphael|it|ism

pre-record +s +ed +ing
pre|requis|ite +s
pre-revolu|tion|ary
pre|roga|tive +s
pres|age
  pres|ages
  pres|aged
  pres|aging
pres|ager +s
pres|by|opia
pres|by|op|ic
pres|by|ter +s
pres|by|ter|al
pres|by|ter|ate +s
pres|by|ter|ial
Pres|by|ter|ian +s (Church)
Pres|by|ter|ian|ism
pres|by|ter|ship +s
pres|by|tery
  pres|by|ter|ies
pre-school
pre-schooler +s
pres|ci|ence
pres|ci|ent
pres|ci|ent|ly
pre|scind +s +ed +ing
pre|scribe
  pre|scribes
  pre|scribed
  pre|scrib|ing (advise use of medicine etc.; impose.
  △ proscribe)
pre|scriber +s
pre|script +s
pre|scrip|tion +s (prescribing; doctor's instruction; medicine.
  △ proscription)
pre|scrip|tive (prescribing.
  △ proscriptive)
pre|scrip|tive|ly
pre|scrip|tive|ness
pre|scrip|tiv|ism
pre|scrip|tiv|ist +s
pre-season
pre-select +s +ed +ing
pre-selection +s
pre-select|ive
pre-select|or +s
pres|ence +s

pre|sent +s +ed +ing (introduce etc.)
pres|ent +s (not absent; current; time now passing; gift)
pre|sent|abil|ity
pre|sent|able
pre|sent|able|ness
pre|sent|ably
pre|sen|ta|tion +s
pre|sen|ta|tion|al
pre|sen|ta|tion|al|ly
pre|sen|ta|tion|ism
pre|sen|ta|tion|ist +s
pre|senta|tive
present-day attributive
pre|sent|ee +s
pre|sent|er +s
pre|sen|tient
pre|sen|ti|ment +s (foreboding)
pres|ent|ly
pre|sent|ment +s (presentation; statement)
pre|serv|able
pre|ser|va|tion
pre|ser|va|tion|ist +s
pre|ser|va|tive +s
pre|serve
  pre|serves
  pre|served
  pre|serv|ing
pre|server +s
pre-set
  pre-sets
  pre-set
  pre-setting
pre-shrink
  pre-shrinks
  pre-shrunk
  pre-shrink|ing
pre|side
  pre|sides
  pre|sided
  pre|sid|ing
presi|dency
  presi|den|cies
presi|dent +s
president-elect
  presidents-elect
presi|den|tial
presi|den|tial|ly
presi|dent|ship +s
pre|sidi|ary
pre|sidio +s

pre|sid|ium +s
Pres|ley, Elvis
(American pop
singer)
pre|soc|rat|ic
press
  presses
  pressed
  press|ing
press agent
press box
  press boxes
Press|burg
(German name for
Bratislava)
press-button +s
press cut|ting +s
press-gang +s +ed
  +ing
pres|sie +s (use
  prezzie)
press|ing +s
press|ing|ly
press|man
  press|men
press|mark +s
press-on *adjective*
press stud +s
press-up +s *noun*
pres|sure
  pres|sures
  pres|sured
  pres|sur|ing
pressure-cook
  pressure-cooks
  pressure-cooked
  pressure-cooking
pres|sure cook|er
  +s
pres|sur|isa|tion
  Br. (use
  pressurization)
pres|sur|ise *Br.*
  (use pressurize)
  pres|sur|ises
  pres|sur|ised
  pres|sur|is|ing
pres|sur|iza|tion
pres|sur|ize
  pres|sur|izes
  pres|sur|ized
  pres|sur|iz|ing
pressurized-water
  re|ac|tor +s
Pres|tel *Propr.*
Pres|ter John
(legendary king)
pres|ti|digi|ta|tion
pres|ti|digi|ta|tor
  +s
pres|tige
pres|tige|ful

pres|ti|gious
pres|ti|gious|ly
pres|ti|gious|ness
pres|tis|simo +s
presto +s (*Music*; in
  'hey presto!')
Pres|ton (city,
  England)
Pres|ton|pans
  (town and battle
  site, Scotland)
pre|stressed
Prest|wick (airport,
  Scotland)
pre|sum|able
pre|sum|ably
pre|sume
  pre|sumes
  pre|sumed
  pre|sum|ing
pre|sumed|ly
pre|sum|ing|ly
pre|sum|ing|ness
pre|sump|tion +s
pre|sump|tive
pre|sump|tive|ly
pre|sump|tu|ous
pre|sump|tu|
          ous|ly
pre|sump|tu|ous|
             ness
pre|sup|pose
  pre|sup|poses
  pre|sup|posed
  pre|sup|pos|ing
pre|sup|pos|ition
  +s
pre-tax
pre-teen +s
pre|tence *Br.* +s
  (*Am.* pretense)
pre|tend +s +ed
  +ing
pre|tend|er +s
pre|tense *Am.* +s
  (*Br.* pretence)
pre|ten|sion +s
  (claim)
pre-tension +s
  +ed +ing
  (tension
  beforehand)
pre-tension|er +s
pre|ten|tious
pre|ten|tious|ly
pre|ten|tious|ness
pre|ter|hu|man
pret|erit *Am.* +s
pret|er|ite *Br.* +s
pret|er|ition +s
pre-term
pre|ter|mis|sion

pre|ter|mit
pre|ter|mits
pre|ter|mit|ted
pre|ter|mit|ting
pre|ter|nat|ural
pre|ter|nat|ur|al|
            ism +s
pre|ter|nat|ur|al|ly
pre|text +s
pre|tone +s
pre|ton|ic +s
pre|tor +s (use
  praetor)
Pre|toria
  (administrative
  capital of South
  Africa)
pre|tor|ial (use
  praetorial)
pre|tor|ian +s (use
  praetorian)
pre|tor|ship +s
  (use praetorship)
pre|treat +s +ed
  +ing
pre|treat|ment +s
pre-trial
pret|ti|fi|ca|tion +s
pret|ti|fier +s
pret|tify
  pret|ti|fies
  pret|ti|fied
  pret|ti|fy|ing
pret|tily
pret|ti|ness
pretty
  pret|ties
  pret|tied
  pretty|ing
  pret|tier
  pret|ti|est
pret|ty|ish
pret|ty|ism
pretty-pretty
pret|zel +s
pre|vail +s +ed
  +ing
pre|vail|ing|ly
preva|lence
preva|lent
preva|lent|ly
pre|vari|cate
  pre|vari|cates
  pre|vari|cated
  pre|vari|cat|ing
pre|vari|ca|tion +s
pre|vari|ca|tor +s
pre|veni|ent
pre|vent +s +ed
  +ing
pre|vent|abil|ity
pre|vent|able

pre|venta|tive +s
pre|venta|tive|ly
pre|vent|er +s
pre|ven|tion +s
pre|vent|ive +s
pre|vent|ive|ly
pre|view +s +ed
  +ing
Pre|vin, André
(German-born
  American
  conductor)
pre|vi|ous
pre|vi|ous|ly
pre|vi|ous|ness
pre|vise
  pre|vises
  pre|vised
  pre|vis|ing
pre|vi|sion +s
  (foresight.
  △ provision)
pre|vi|sion|al (of
  foresight.
  △ provisional)
pre-vocation|al
Pré|vost d'Exiles,
  Antoine-
  François (French
  novelist)
pre|vue *Am.* +s (*Br.*
  preview)
pre-war
pre-wash
  pre-washes
  pre-washed
  pre-washing
prex
  prexes
prexy
  prex|ies
prey +s +ed +ing
  (food. △ pray)
prey|er +s (feeder.
  △ prayer)
Prez, Jos|quin des
  (Flemish
  composer)
prez|zie +s
Priam *Greek
  Mythology*
pri|ap|ic
pri|ap|ism
Pria|pus *Greek
  Mythology*
Pri|bi|lof Is|lands
  (off Alaska)
Price, Vin|cent
  (American actor)
price
  prices

price (cont.)
priced
pri|cing
price-fixing
price|less
price|less|ly
price list +s
pricer +s
price ring +s
price-sensitive
price tag +s
price war +s
pricey
prici|er
prici|est
pri|ci|ness
prick +s +ed +ing
prick|er +s
pricket +s
prickle
prickles
prickled
prick|ling
prick|li|ness
prick|ly
prick|lier
prick|li|est
pricy
prici|er
prici|est
(use pricey)
pride
prides
prided
prid|ing
pride|ful
pride|ful|ly
pride|less
Pride's Purge
prie-dieu
prie-dieux
priest +s +ed +ing
priest|craft
priest|ess
priest|esses
priest|hood
priest-in-charge
priests-in-charge
priest|less
Priest|ley, J. B.
(English writer)
Priest|ley, Jo|seph
(English chemist)
priest|like
priest|li|ness
priest|ling +s
priest|ly
priest|lier
priest|li|est
prig +s
prig|gery
prig|gish

prig|gish|ly
prig|gish|ness
prig|gism
prim
prims
primmed
prim|ming
prim|mer
prim|mest
prima bal|ler|ina
+s
pri|macy
pri|ma|cies
prima donna +s
prima donna-ish
prim|aeval (use
primeval)
prima facie
prima inter pares
female (male
primus inter pares)
primal
pri|mal|ly
pri|mar|ily
pri|mary
pri|mar|ies
Pri|mate +s (title of
archbishop)
pri|mate +s
(individual animal;
archbishop)
Pri|mates (order of
mammals)
pri|ma|tial
pri|mat|olo|gist +s
pri|mat|ology
pri|ma|vera +s
prime
primes
primed
prim|ing
prime|ness
primer +s
prime time *noun*
prime-time
attributive
pri|meval
pri|mev|al|ly
primi|grav|ida
primi|grav|idae
prim|ipara
prim|iparae
prim|ipar|ous
primi|tive +s
primi|tive|ly
primi|tive|ness
primi|tiv|ism
primi|tiv|ist +s
prim|ly
prim|ness
primo +s

Primo de Ri|vera,
Mi|guel (Spanish
general and
statesman)
primo|geni|tal
primo|geni|tary
primo|geni|tor +s
primo|geni|ture
prim|or|dial
prim|or|di|al|ity
prim|or|di|al|ly
prim|or|dium
prim|or|dia
Pri|mor|sky Krai
(territory, Russia)
primp +s +ed +ing
Prim|rose (name)
prim|rose +s
(flower)
prim|ula +s
pri|mum mo|bile +s
Pri|mus
Pri|muses
(stove) *Propr.*
pri|mus
pri|muses
(bishop)
pri|mus inter pares
male (female prima
inter pares)
prince +s
prince con|sort +s
prince|dom +s
Prince Ed|ward
Is|land (province,
Canada)
prince|like
prince|li|ness
prince|ling +s
prince|ly
Prince Ru|pert's
Land (= Rupert's
Land)
prince's fea|ther
+s (plant)
prince|ship +s
prince's metal
prin|cess
prin|cesses
Prince|ton
(university, USA)
prin|ci|pal +s
(chief.
△ principle)
prin|ci|pal|ity
prin|ci|pal|ities
prin|ci|pal|ly
prin|ci|pal|ship +s
prin|ci|pate +s
Prin|cipe (island,
Gulf of Guinea)

prin|ciple +s
(fundamental truth
etc. △ principal)
prin|cipled
prink +s +ed +ing
print +s +ed +ing
print|abil|ity
print|able
print|er +s
print|er's devil +s
print|er's mark +s
print|er's pie
print|ery
print|er|ies
print|head +s
print|ing +s
print|ing press
print|ing presses
print|less
print|maker +s
print|mak|ing
print|out +s
print|works
prion +s
prior +s
pri|or|ate +s
pri|or|ess
pri|or|esses
pri|ori|tisa|tion *Br.*
(use
prioritization)
pri|ori|tise *Br.* (use
prioritize)
pri|ori|tises
pri|ori|tised
pri|ori|tis|ing
pri|ori|tiza|tion
pri|ori|tize
pri|ori|tizes
pri|ori|tized
pri|ori|tiz|ing
pri|or|ity
pri|or|ities
prior|ship +s
pri|ory
pri|or|ies
Pri|pyat (river, E.
Europe)
Pris|cian
(Byzantine
grammarian)
Pris|cilla
prise *Br.*
prises
prised
pris|ing
(force. *Am.* prize)
prism +s
pris|mal
pris|mat|ic
pris|mat|ic|al|ly
pris|moid +s

pris|moid|al
prison +s +ed +ing
prison-breaking
prison camp +s
pris|on|er +s
pris|on|er of war
  pris|on|ers of war
prisoner-of-war
  attributive
pris|on|er's base
pris|sily
pris|si|ness
prissy
  pris|sier
  pris|si|est
Priš|tina (city,
  Serbia)
pris|tine
Prit|chett, V. S.
  (English writer)
pri|thee
priv|acy
  priv|acies
pri|vate +s
pri|vat|eer +s
pri|vat|eer|ing
pri|vat|eers|man
  pri|vat|eers|men
pri|vate first class
  pri|vates first
  class
pri|vate|ly
pri|vate
  mem|ber's bill
  +s
pri|va|tion +s
pri|vat|isa|tion *Br.*
  +s (use
  privatization)
pri|vat|ise *Br.* (use
  privatize)
  pri|vat|ises
  pri|vat|ised
  pri|vat|is|ing
pri|vat|iser +s (use
  privatizer)
priv|ative
priv|ative|ly
pri|vat|iza|tion +s
pri|vat|ize
  pri|vat|izes
  pri|vat|ized
  pri|vat|iz|ing
pri|vat|izer +s
privet +s
priv|il|ege
  priv|il|eges
  priv|il|eged
  priv|il|eging
priv|ily
priv|ity
  priv|ities

privy
  priv|ies
Privy Coun|cil
Privy Coun|cil|lor
  +s (use Privy
  Counsellor)
Privy Coun|sel|lor
  +s
privy seal +s
Prix Gon|court
  plural Prix
  Gon|court
prize
  prizes
  prized
  priz|ing
  (award. △ prise)
prize *Am.*
  prizes
  prized
  priz|ing
  (force. *Br.* prise)
prize court +s
prize|fight +s
prize|fight|er +s
prize|fight|ing
prize-giving +s
prize|man
  prize|men
prize-money
prize ring +s
prize|win|ner +s
prize|win|ning
pro +s
proa +s
pro|action
pro|active
pro|active|ly
pro|activ|ity
pro-am +s
prob +s
prob|abil|ism
prob|abil|ist +s
prob|abil|is|tic
prob|abil|ity
  prob|abil|ities
prob|able +s
prob|ably
pro|band +s
pro|bang +s
pro|bate
  pro|bates
  pro|bated
  pro|bat|ing
pro|ba|tion
pro|ba|tion|al
pro|ba|tion|ary
pro|ba|tion|er +s
pro|ba|tion|er|ship
  +s
pro|ba|tive

probe
  probes
  probed
  prob|ing
probe|able
prober +s
prob|ing +s
prob|ing|ly
pro|bit +s
prob|ity
prob|lem +s
prob|lem|at|ic
prob|lem|at|ic|al
prob|lem|at|ic|
  al|ly
prob|lem|atisa|
  tion *Br.* (use
  problematiza-
  tion)
prob|lem|atise *Br.*
  (use
  problematize)
  prob|lem|atises
  prob|lem|atised
  prob|lem|atis|ing
prob|lem|atiza|
  tion
prob|lem|atize
  prob|lem|atizes
  prob|lem|atized
  prob|lem|atiz|ing
problem-solving
pro bono
pro|bos|cid|ean +s
pro|bos|cid|ian +s
  (use
  proboscidean)
pro|bos|cid|ifer|
  ous
pro|bos|cidi|form
pro|bos|cis
  pro|bos|ces *or*
  pro|bos|cides *or*
  pro|bos|cises
pro|cain (use
  procaine)
pro|caine
pro|cary|ote +s
  (use prokaryote)
pro|cary|ot|ic (use
  prokaryotic)
pro|ced|ural
pro|ced|ur|al|ly
pro|ced|ure +s
pro|ceed +s +ed
  +ing (go forward.
  △ precede)
pro|ceed|ing +s
  (action.
  △ preceding)
pro|ceeds (money)

pro|cess
  pro|cesses
  pro|cessed
  pro|cess|ing
pro|cess|able
pro|ces|sion +s
  (movement of
  people or vehicles.
  △ precession)
pro|ces|sion|al +s
  (relating to
  processions; book
  of processional
  hymns.
  △ precessional)
pro|ces|sion|ary
pro|ces|sion|ist +s
pro|ces|sor +s
procès-verbal
  procès-verbaux
pro-choice
pro|chron|ism +s
pro|claim +s +ed
  +ing
pro|claim|er +s
proc|lam|ation +s
pro|clama|tory
pro|clit|ic +s
pro|clit|ic|al|ly
pro|cliv|ity
  pro|cliv|ities
Procne *Greek
  Mythology*
pro|con|sul +s
pro|con|su|lar
pro|con|su|late +s
pro|con|sul|ship
  +s
Pro|co|pius
  (Byzantine
  historian)
pro|cras|tin|ate
  pro|cras|tin|ates
  pro|cras|tin|ated
  pro|cras|tin|at|ing
pro|cras|tin|ation
  +s
pro|cras|tina|tive
pro|cras|tin|ator
  +s
pro|cras|tin|atory
pro|cre|ant +s
pro|cre|ate
  pro|cre|ates
  pro|cre|ated
  pro|cre|at|ing
pro|cre|ation
pro|cre|ative
pro|cre|ator +s
Pro|crus|tean
Pro|crus|tes *Greek
  Mythology*

proctological
proctologist +s
proctology
proctor +s
proctorial
proctorship +s
proctoscope +s
procumbent
procurable
procural
procurance
procuration +s
procurator +s
procurator fiscal
    procurators
    fiscal
procuratorial
procuratorship
    +s
procuratory
procure
    procures
    procured
    procuring
procurement +s
procurer +s
procuress
    procuresses
Procyon (star)
Prod +s (offensive)
prod
    prods
    prodded
    prodding
prodder +s
Proddie +s
    (offensive)
Proddy
    Proddies
    (offensive)
pro-democracy
prodigal +s
prodigalise Br.
    (use prodigalize)
    prodigalises
    prodigalised
    prodigalising
prodigality
    prodigalities
prodigalize
    prodigalizes
    prodigalized
    prodigalizing
prodigally
prodigious
prodigiously
prodigiousness
prodigy
    prodigies
prodromal
prodrome +s
prodromic

produce
    produces
    produced
    producing
producer +s
producibility
producible
product +s
production +s
productional
productive
productively
productiveness
productivity
    productivities
proem +s
proemial
prof +s
profanation +s
profane
    profanes
    profaned
    profaning
profanely
profaneness
profaner +s
profanity
    profanities
profess
    professes
    professed
    professing
professedly
profession +s
professional +s
professional-
    isation Br. (use
    professionaliza-
    tion)
professionalise
    Br. (use
    professionalize)
    professional-
        ises
    professional-
        ised
    professional-
        ising
professionalism
professional-
        ization
professionalize
    professional-
        izes
    professional-
        ized
    professional-
        izing
professionally
professionless
professor +s
professorate +s

professorial
professorially
professoriate +s
professorship +s
proffer +s +ed
    +ing
proficiency
    proficiencies
proficient
proficiently
profile
    profiles
    profiled
    profiling
profiler +s
profilist +s
profit +s +ed +ing
    (gain. △ prophet)
profitability
    profitabilities
profitable
profitableness
profitably
profiteer +s +ed
    +ing
profiterole +s
profitless
profit-making
profit-related
profit-sharing
profit-taking
profligacy
profligate +s
profligately
pro forma +s noun
pro-forma
    attributive
profound +er +est
profoundly
profoundness
Profumo, John
    (British politician)
profundity
    profundities
profuse
profusely
profuseness
profusion +s
prog +s
    (= programme)
progenitive
progenitor +s
progenitorial
progenitorship
progenitress
    progenitresses
progenitrix
    progenitrices
    female
progeniture
progeny
    progenies

progesterone
progestogen +s
proglottid +s
proglottis
    proglottides
prognathic
prognathism
prognathous
prognosis
    prognoses
prognostic
prognosticable
prognostically
prognosticate
    prognosticates
    prognosticated
    prognosti|
        cating
prognostication
    +s
prognosticative
prognosticator
    +s
prognosticatory
program +s (for
    computer.
    △ programme)
    noun
program Br.
    programs
    programmed
    programming
    (in computing.
    △ programme)
    verb
program Am.
    programs
    programmed
    programming
    (verb. Br.
    programme)
program|
    mability
programmable
programmatic
programmatic|
    ally
programme Br.
    programmes
    programmed
    programming
    (Am. program. all
    senses except
    computing.
    △ program)
programmer +s
progress
    progresses
    progressed
    progressing
progress-chaser
    +s

pro|gres|sion +s
pro|gres|sion|al
pro|gres|sion|ist
  +s
pro|gres|sive +s
pro|gres|sive|ly
pro|gres|sive|ness
pro|gres|siv|ism
pro|gres|siv|ist +s
pro hac vice
pro|hibit +s +ed
  +ing
pro|hib|it|er +s
pro|hib|ition +s
pro|hib|ition|ary
pro|hib|ition|ist +s
pro|hibi|tive
pro|hibi|tive|ly
pro|hibi|tive|ness
pro|hibi|tor +s
pro|hibi|tory
pro|ject +s +ed
  +ing
pro|ject|ile +s
pro|jec|tion +s
pro|jec|tion|ist +s
pro|ject|ive
pro|ject|ive|ly
pro|ject|or +s
pro|kary|ote +s
pro|kary|ot|ic
Pro|kof|iev,
  Ser|gei (Russian
  composer)
Pro|kop|evsk (city,
  Russia)
pro|lac|tin
pro|lapse
  pro|lapses
  pro|lapsed
  pro|laps|ing
pro|lap|sus
pro|late
pro|late|ly
pro|la|tive
prole +s
pro|leg +s
pro|leg|om|en|ary
pro|leg|om|enon
  pro|leg|om|ena
pro|leg|om|en|ous
pro|lep|sis
  pro|lep|ses
pro|lep|tic
pro|le|tar|ian +s
pro|le|tar|ian|
  isa|tion *Br.* (use
  proletarianiza-
  tion)
pro|le|tar|ian|ise
  Br. (use
  proletarianize)

pro|le|tar|ian|ise
  (*cont.*)
  pro|le|tar|ian|ises
  pro|le|tar|ian|ised
  pro|le|tar|ian|
    is|ing
pro|le|tar|ian|ism
pro|le|tar|ian|
  iza|tion
pro|le|tar|ian|ize
  pro|le|tar|ian|izes
  pro|le|tar|ian|ized
  pro|le|tar|ian|
    iz|ing
pro|le|tar|iat +s
pro-life
pro|lif|er|ate
  pro|lif|er|ates
  pro|lif|er|ated
  pro|lif|er|at|ing
pro|lif|er|ation
pro|lif|era|tive
pro|lif|er|ator +s
pro|lif|er|ous
pro|lif|ic
pro|lif|ic|acy
pro|lif|ic|al|ly
pro|li|fi|city
pro|lif|ic|ness
pro|line +s
pro|lix
pro|lix|ity
pro|lix|ly
pro|locu|tor +s
pro|locu|tor|ship
  +s
Pro|log *Computing*
pro|log|ise *Br.* (use
  prologize)
  pro|log|ises
  pro|log|ised
  pro|log|is|ing
pro|log|ize
  pro|log|izes
  pro|log|ized
  pro|log|iz|ing
pro|logue
  pro|logues
  pro|logued
  pro|loguing
pro|long +s +ed
  +ing
pro|longa|tion +s
pro|long|ed|ly
pro|long|er +s
pro|lu|sion +s
pro|lu|sory
prom +s
  (= promenade;
  promenade
  concert)

prom|en|ade
prom|en|ades
prom|en|aded
prom|en|ad|ing
prom|en|ader +s
pro|meth|az|ine
Pro|me|thean
Pro|me|theus *Greek
  Mythology*
pro|me|thium
prom|in|ence +s
prom|in|ency
prom|in|ent +s
prom|in|enti
prom|in|ent|ly
prom|is|cu|ity
  prom|is|cu|ities
pro|mis|cu|ous
pro|mis|cu|ous|ly
pro|mis|cu|ous|
      ness
prom|ise
  prom|ises
  prom|ised
  prom|is|ing
prom|isee +s
prom|iser +s
  (generally.
  △ promisor)
prom|is|ing|ly
prom|isor +s (*Law.*
  △ promiser)
prom|is|sory
prom|mer +s
promo +s
prom|on|tory
  prom|on|tor|ies
pro|mot|abil|ity
pro|mot|able
pro|mote
  pro|motes
  pro|moted
  pro|mot|ing
pro|moter +s
pro|mo|tion +s
  (advancement etc.
  △ premotion)
pro|mo|tion|al
pro|mo|tive
prompt +s +ed
  +ing
prompt book +s
prompt-box
  prompt-boxes
prompt|er +s
prompt|ing +s
prompti|tude
prompt|ly
prompt|ness
prompt-note +s
prompt side

pro|mul|gate
  pro|mul|gates
  pro|mul|gated
  pro|mul|gat|ing
pro|mul|ga|tion
pro|mul|ga|tor +s
pro|mulge
  pro|mulges
  pro|mulged
  pro|mul|ging
pro|naos
pro|naoi
pro|nate
pro|nates
pro|nated
pro|nat|ing
pro|na|tion
pro|na|tor +s
prone
prone|ly
prone|ness
pron|eur +s
prong +s +ed +ing
prong|horn +s
prong-horned
  ante|lope +s
pro|nom|inal
pro|nom|in|al|ise
  Br. (use
  pronominalize)
pro|nom|in|al|
      ises
pro|nom|in|al|
      ised
pro|nom|in|al|
      is|ing
pro|nom|in|al|ize
pro|nom|in|al|
      izes
pro|nom|in|al|
      ized
pro|nom|in|al|
      iz|ing
pro|nom|in|al|ly
pro|noun +s
pro|nounce
  pro|nounces
  pro|nounced
  pro|noun|cing
pro|nounce|able
pro|nounced|ly
pro|nounce|ment
  +s
pro|noun|cer +s
pronto
pro|nun|cia|mento
  +s
pro|nun|ci|ation
  +s
pro-nuncio +s
proof +s +ed +ing
proof|less

proof-plane +s
proof-read
  proof-reads
  proof-read
  proof-reading
proof-reader +s
proof-sheet +s
prop
  props
  propped
  prop|ping
pro|pae|deutic +s
pro|pae|deut|ic|al
propa|ganda
propa|gand|ise Br.
  (use
  propagandize)
  propa|gand|ises
  propa|gand|ised
  propa|gand|is|ing
propa|gand|ism
propa|gand|ist +s
propa|gand|is|tic
propa|gand|is|tic|
      al|ly
propa|gand|ize
  propa|gand|izes
  propa|gand|ized
  propa|gand|iz|ing
propa|gate
  propa|gates
  propa|gated
  propa|gat|ing
propa|ga|tion +s
propa|ga|tive
prop|aga|tor +s
pro|pane
pro|pan|oic
pro|pan|one
pro|par|oxy|tone
  +s
pro|pel
  pro|pels
  pro|pelled
  pro|pel|ling
pro|pel|lant +s
  noun
pro|pel|lent
  adjective
pro|pel|ler +s
pro|pene
pro|pen|sity
  pro|pen|sities
proper +s
pro|peri|
      spo|menon
  pro|peri|
      spo|mena
prop|er|ly
prop|er|ness
prop|er|tied

Pro|per|tius,
  Sex|tus (Roman
  poet)
prop|erty
  prop|er|ties
pro|phase +s
proph|ecy
  proph|ecies
  noun
proph|esier +s
proph|esy
  proph|es|ies
  proph|es|ied
  proph|esy|ing
Prophet, the
  (Muhammad;
  Joseph Smith)
prophet +s
  (foreteller.
  ⚠ profit)
proph|et|ess
  proph|et|esses
proph|et|hood
proph|et|ic
proph|et|ic|al
proph|et|ic|al|ly
proph|eti|cism +s
proph|et|ism
proph|et|ship
prophy|lac|tic +s
prophy|laxis
  prophy|laxes
pro|pin|quity
  pro|pin|qui|ties
pro|pi|on|ate +s
pro|pi|on|ic
pro|piti|ate
  pro|piti|ates
  pro|piti|ated
  pro|piti|at|ing
pro|piti|ation
pro|piti|ator +s
pro|piti|ator|ily
pro|piti|atory
pro|pi|tious
pro|pi|tious|ly
pro|pi|tious|ness
prop-jet +s
prop|olis
pro|pon|ent +s
Pro|pon|tis
  (ancient name for
  the Sea of
  Marmara)
pro|por|tion +s
  +ed +ing
pro|por|tion|able
pro|por|tion|ably
pro|por|tion|al
pro|por|tion|al|ist
  +s

pro|por|tion|al|ity
pro|por|tion|al|
      ities
pro|por|tion|al|ly
pro|por|tion|ate
pro|por|tion|ate|ly
pro|por|tion|less
pro|por|tion|ment
pro|posal +s
pro|pose
  pro|poses
  pro|posed
  pro|pos|ing
pro|poser +s
prop|os|ition +s
  +ed +ing
prop|os|ition|al
pro|pound +s +ed
  +ing
pro|pound|er +s
pro|prae|tor +s
pro|pri|etary
  pro|pri|etar|ies
pro|pri|etor +s
pro|pri|etor|ial
pro|pri|etori|al|ly
pro|pri|etor|ship
  +s
pro|pri|etress
  pro|pri|et|resses
pro|pri|ety
  pro|pri|eties
pro|prio|cep|tion
pro|prio|cep|tive
pro-proctor +s
prop|tosis
  prop|toses
pro|pul|sion
pro|pul|sive
pro|pul|sor +s
pro|pyl
propy|laeum
  propy|laea
pro|pyl|ene
pro|pylon
  pro|pylons or
  pro|pyla
pro rata
pro|rate
  pro|rates
  pro|rated
  pro|rat|ing
pro|ra|tion
pro|roga|tion +s
pro|rogue
  pro|rogues
  pro|rogued
  pro|roguing
pro|sa|ic
pro|saic|al|ly
pro|saic|ness
pro|sa|ism +s

pro|sa|ist +s
pro|scen|ium
  pro|scen|iums or
  pro|scenia
pro|sciutto +s
pro|scribe
  pro|scribes
  pro|scribed
  pro|scrib|ing
  (banish;
  denounce.
  ⚠ prescribe)
pro|scrip|tion +s
  (banishment;
  denouncement
  etc.
  ⚠ prescription)
pro|scrip|tive
  (proscribing.
  ⚠ prescriptive)
prose
  proses
  prosed
  pros|ing
pro|sec|tor +s
pros|ecut|able
pros|ecute
  pros|ecutes
  pros|ecuted
  pros|ecut|ing
pros|ecu|tion +s
pros|ecu|tor +s
pros|ecu|tor|ial
pros|ecu|trix
  pros|ecu|tri|ces
  female
pros|elyte +s
pros|elyt|ise Br.
  (use proselytize)
  pros|elyt|ises
  pros|elyt|ised
  pros|elyt|is|ing
pros|elyt|iser Br.
  +s (use
  proselytizer)
pros|elyt|ism
pros|elyt|ize
  pros|elyt|izes
  pros|elyt|ized
  pros|elyt|iz|ing
pros|elyt|izer +s
pros|en|ceph|alon
  +s
pros|en|chyma
pros|en|chy|mal
pros|en|chy|ma|
      tous
prose poem +s
prose poet|ry
proser +s
Pro|ser|pina (use
  Proserpine)

Pro|ser|pine
(Roman name for
Persephone)
pros|ify
  prosi|fies
  prosi|fied
  prosi|fy|ing
prosi|ly
pro|sim|ian +s
pro|si|ness
pro|sit
pros|od|ic
pros|od|ist +s
pros|ody
  pros|od|ies
pros|op|og|raph|er
  +s
pros|opo|graph|ic
pros|opo|
      graph|ic|al
pros|op|og|raphy
  pros|op|
     og|raph|ies
pros|opo|poeia
pro|spect +s +ed
  +ing
pro|spect|ive
pro|spect|ive|ly
pro|spect|ive|ness
pro|spect|less
pro|spect|or +s
pro|spec|tus
  pro|spec|tuses
pros|per +s +ed
  +ing
pros|per|ity
  pros|per|ities
pros|per|ous
pros|per|ous|ly
pros|per|ous|ness
Prost, Alain
  (French motor-
  racing driver)
prost
pros|ta|glandin +s
pro|state +s
pro|stat|ic
pros|thesis
  pros|theses
pros|thet|ic
pros|thet|ic|al|ly
pros|thet|ics
pros|ti|tute
  pros|ti|tutes
  pros|ti|tuted
  pros|ti|tut|ing
pros|ti|tu|tion
pros|ti|tu|tion|al
pros|ti|tu|tor +s
pros|trate
  pros|trates

pros|trate (*cont.*)
  pros|trated
  pros|trat|ing
pros|tra|tion +s
pro|style +s
prosy
  prosi|er
  prosi|est
prot|ac|tin|ium
prot|ag|on|ist +s
prot|am|ine +s
prot|asis
  prot|ases
pro|tat|ic
pro|tea +s
pro|tean
pro|te|ase +s
pro|tect +s +ed
  +ing
pro|tec|tion +s
pro|tec|tion|ism
  +s
pro|tec|tion|ist +s
pro|tect|ive +s
pro|tect|ive|ly
pro|tect|ive|ness
pro|tect|or +s
pro|tect|or|al
pro|tect|or|ate +s
pro|tect|or|ship
pro|tec|tress
  pro|tec|tresses
pro|tégé +s *male*
pro|té|gée +s
  female
pro|tei|form
pro|tein +s
pro|tein|aceous
pro|tein|ic
pro|tein|ous
pro tem
pro tem|pore
pro|te|oly|sis
  pro|te|oly|ses
pro|teo|lyt|ic
Pro|tero|zo|ic
pro|test +s +ed
  +ing
Prot|est|ant +s
  (Christian)
prot|est|ant +s
  (generally)
Prot|est|ant|ise *Br.*
  (use
  Protestantize)
  Prot|est|ant|ises
  Prot|est|ant|ised
  Prot|est|ant|is|ing
Prot|est|ant|ism
Prot|est|ant|ize
  Prot|est|ant|izes
  Prot|est|ant|ized

Prot|est|ant|ize
  (*cont.*)
  Prot|est|ant|
      iz|ing
prot|est|ation +s
pro|test|er +s
pro|test|ing|ly
pro|test|or +s (use
  protester)
Pro|teus (*Greek
  Mythology*; moon
  of Neptune)
pro|teus
  pro|tei *or*
  pro|teuses
  (bacterium)
pro|tha|lam|ion
  (use
  prothalamium)
pro|tha|lamia
pro|tha|lam|ium
  pro|tha|lamia
pro|thal|lium
  pro|thal|lia
pro|thal|lus
  pro|thalli
pro|thesis
  pro|theses
pro|thet|ic
pro|tho|not|ary
  pro|tho|not|ar|ies
pro|tist +s
pro|tist|ology
pro|tium
proto|col
  proto|cols
  proto|colled
  proto|col|ling
**Proto-Indo-
  European**
proto|mar|tyr +s
pro|ton +s
pro|ton|ic
proto|not|ary
  proto|not|ar|ies
proto|pec|tin +s
proto|phyte +s
proto|plasm
proto|plas|mal
proto|plas|mat|ic
proto|plas|mic
proto|plast +s
proto|plas|tic
proto|theria
proto|ther|ian +s
proto|typal
proto|type
  proto|types
  proto|typed
  proto|typ|ing
proto|typ|ic
proto|typ|ic|al

proto|typ|ic|al|ly
proto|zoal
proto|zoan +s
proto|zo|ic
proto|zo|ology
proto|zoon
  proto|zoa
pro|tract +s +ed
  +ing
pro|tract|ed|ly
pro|tract|ed|ness
pro|tract|ile
pro|trac|tion
pro|tract|or +s
pro|trude
  pro|trudes
  pro|truded
  pro|trud|ing
pro|tru|dent
pro|tru|sible
pro|tru|sile
pro|tru|sion +s
pro|tru|sive
pro|tu|ber|ance +s
pro|tu|ber|ant
proud +er +est
proud-hearted
**Proud|hon, Pierre
  Jo|seph** (French
  social
  philosopher)
proud|ly
proud|ness
**Proust, Jo|seph
  Louis** (French
  analytical chemist)
Proust, Mar|cel
  (French writer)
Prout, Wil|liam
  (English chemist
  and biochemist)
prov|abil|ity
prov|able
prov|ably
prove
  proves
  proved
  prov|ing
  proved *or* proven
prov|en|ance +s
prov|en|anced
Pro|ven|çal +s
Pro|vence (former
  province, France)
Provence–Alpes–
  Côte d'Azur
  (region, France)
prov|en|der +s
  +ed +ing
pro|veni|ence +s
prov|erb +s
pro|verb|ial +s

pro|verbi|al|ity
pro|verbi|al|ly
pro|vide
  pro|vides
  pro|vided
  pro|vid|ing
Provi|dence (city, USA; God)
provi|dence (care; foresight)
provi|dent
provi|den|tial
provi|den|tial|ly
provi|dent|ly
pro|vider +s
Pro|vie +s
prov|ince +s
pro|vin|cial +s
pro|vin|cial|ise *Br.* (use provincialize)
pro|vin|cial|ises
pro|vin|cial|ised
pro|vin|cial|is|ing
pro|vin|cial|ism
pro|vin|cial|ist +s
pro|vin|ci|al|ity
pro|vin|cial|ize
pro|vin|cial|izes
pro|vin|cial|ized
pro|vin|cial|iz|ing
pro|vin|cial|ly
pro|vi|sion +s +ed +ing (providing; food; etc.
  △ prevision)
Pro|vi|sion|al +s (of IRA)
pro|vi|sion|al +s (temporary.
  △ previsional)
pro|vi|sion|al|ity
pro|vi|sion|al|ly
pro|vi|sion|al|ness
pro|vi|sion|er +s
pro|vi|sion|less
pro|vi|sion|ment
pro|viso +s
pro|visor +s
pro|visor|ily
pro|vi|sory
Provo +s
provo|ca|tion +s
pro|voca|tive
pro|voca|tive|ly
pro|voca|tive|ness
pro|vok|able
pro|voke
  pro|vokes
  pro|voked
  pro|vok|ing
pro|voker +s

pro|vok|ing|ly
prov|ost +s
prov|ost|ship +s
prow +s
prow|ess
prowl +s +ed +ing
prowl|er +s
prox. (= proximo)
prox|em|ics
Prox|ima
  Cen|tauri (star)
prox|imal
prox|im|al|ly
prox|im|ate
prox|im|ate|ly
prox|ime ac|ces|sit
prox|im|ity
  prox|im|ities
prox|imo
proxy
  prox|ies
Pru *also* Prue
prude +s
Pru|dence (name)
pru|dence (care; discretion)
pru|dent
pru|den|tial +s
pru|den|tial|ism
pru|den|tial|ist +s
pru|den|tial|ly
pru|dent|ly
prud|ery
Prud|hoe Bay (on coast of Alaska)
prud|ish
prud|ish|ly
prud|ish|ness
Prue *also* Pru
pru|in|ose
prune
  prunes
  pruned
  prun|ing
Pru|nella (name)
pru|nella +s (plant; fabric)
pruner +s
prun|ing hook +s
pruri|ence
pruri|ency
pruri|ent
pruri|ent|ly
pruri|gin|ous
prur|igo
prur|it|ic
prur|itus
Prus|sia (former German state)
Prus|sian +s
Prus|sian blue +s
  noun and adjective

Prussian-blue
  attributive
prus|sic
Prut (river, SE Europe)
pry
  pries
  pried
  pry|ing
pry|ing|ly
psalm +s +ed +ing
psalm-book +s
psalm|ic
psalm|ist +s
psalm|od|ic
psalm|od|ise *Br.* (use psalmodize)
  psalm|od|ises
  psalm|od|ised
  psalm|od|is|ing
psalm|od|ist +s
psalm|od|ize
  psalm|od|izes
  psalm|od|ized
  psalm|od|iz|ing
psalm|ody
psal|ter +s
psal|ter|ium +s
psal|tery
  psal|ter|ies
psepho|logic|al
psepho|logic|al|ly
pseph|olo|gist +s
pseph|ology
pseud +s
pseud|epig|rapha
pseud|
  epig|raph|al
pseud|
  epi|graph|ic
pseud|epi|graph|
  ic|al
pseudo +s
pseudo|carp +s
pseudo|graph +s
pseudo|morph +s
pseudo|morph|ic
pseudo|morph|
  ism
pseudo|morph|
  ous
pseudo|nym +s
pseudo|nym|ity
pseud|onym|ous
pseud|onym|
  ous|ly
pseudo|pod +s
pseudo|po|dium
  pseudo|po|dia
pseudo-science
pseudo-scientif|ic
pshaw

psi +s (Greek letter)
psil|an|throp|ic
psil|an|throp|ism
psil|an|throp|ist +s
psilo|cybin +s
psil|osis
  psil|oses
psit|ta|cine
psit|ta|cism +s
psit|ta|cosis
  psit|ta|coses
psoas
  plural psoas muscles
psor|ia|sis
  psor|ia|ses
psori|at|ic
psst
psych +s +ed +ing
Psy|che *Greek Mythology*
psy|che +s (the soul; the mind)
psy|che|delia
psy|che|del|ic +s
psy|che|del|ic|
  al|ly
psy|chi|atric
psy|chi|atric|al
psy|chi|atric|al|ly
psych|iatrist +s
psych|iatry
psy|chic +s
psych|ic|al
psych|ic|al|ly
psy|chi|cism
psy|chi|cist +s
psy|cho +s
psy|cho|active
psy|cho|ana|lyse *Br.*
  psy|cho|ana|lyses
  psy|cho|
  ana|lysed
  psy|cho|
  ana|lys|ing
psy|cho|analy|sis
psy|cho|ana|lyst +s
psy|cho|ana|lyt|ic
psy|cho|ana|lyt|
  ic|al
psy|cho|ana|lyt|ic|
  al|ly
psy|cho|ana|lyze *Am.*
  psy|cho|ana|lyzes
  psy|cho|
  ana|lyzed
  psy|cho|
  ana|lyz|ing
psy|cho|bab|ble

psy|cho|
   bio|logic|al
psy|cho|biolo|gist
  +s
psy|cho|biol|ogy
psy|cho|drama +s
psy|cho|dynam|ic
psy|cho|dynam|ic|
   al|ly
psy|cho|
   dynam|ics
psy|cho|gen|esis
psy|cho|graph +s
psy|cho|graph|ic
psy|cho|graph|ics
psy|cho|kin|esis
psy|cho|kin|et|ic
psy|cho|lin|guist
  +s
psy|cho|
   lin|guis|tic
psy|cho|
   lin|guis|tics
psy|cho|logic|al
psy|cho|logic|al|ly
psych|olo|gise Br.
  (use
  psychologize)
psych|olo|gises
psych|olo|gised
psych|olo|gis|ing
psych|olo|gist +s
psych|olo|gize
psych|olo|gizes
psych|olo|gized
psych|olo|giz|ing
psych|ology
psych|olo|gies
psy|cho|met|ric
psy|cho|met|ric|
   al|ly
psy|cho|met|rics
psych|om|etrist +s
psych|om|etry
psy|cho|motor
psy|cho|neur|osis
psy|cho|
   neur|oses
psy|cho|neur|ot|ic
psy|cho|path +s
psy|cho|path|ic
psy|cho|path|ic|
   al|ly
psy|cho|patho|
   logic|al
psy|cho|
   path|ology
psych|op|athy
psy|cho|phys|ic|al
psy|cho|phys|ics
psy|cho|
   physio|logic|al

psy|cho|
   physi|ology
psy|cho|sex|ual
psy|cho|sexu|al|ly
psych|osis
psych|oses
  (mental disorder.
  △ sycosis)
psy|cho|social
psy|cho|social|ly
psy|cho|somat|ic
psy|cho|somat|ic|
   al|ly
psy|cho|sur|gery
psy|cho|sur|gi|cal
psy|cho|
   thera|peut|ic
psy|cho|ther|ap|ist
  +s
psy|cho|ther|apy
psych|ot|ic +s
psych|otic|al|ly
psy|cho|trop|ic
psy|chrom|eter +s
Ptah Egyptian
  Mythology
ptar|migan +s
PT boat +s
pter|ano|don +s
pter|ido|logic|al
pter|id|olo|gist +s
pter|id|ology
pter|ido|phyte +s
ptero|dac|tyl +s
ptero|pod +s
ptero|saur +s
pteroyl|glut|am|ic
pteryg|oid
pti|san +s
  (nourishing drink,
  esp. barley water.
  △ tisane)
Ptol|em|aic
Ptol|emy
  Ptol|emies
  (Egyptian kings)
Ptol|emy (Greek
  astronomer and
  geographer)
pto|maine +s
pto|sis
  pto|ses
ptot|ic
ptya|lin
pub +s
pub crawl +s noun
pub-crawl
  pub-crawls
  pub-crawled
  pub-crawling
  verb
pu|ber|tal

pu|berty
pubes
  plural pubes
  (part of abdomen)
pubes (plural of
  pubis)
pu|bes|cence
pu|bes|cent
pubic
pubis
  pubes
  (bone)
pub|lic +s
pub|lican +s
pub|li|ca|tion +s
pub|lic house +s
pub|li|cise Br. (use
  publicize)
  pub|li|cises
  pub|li|cised
  pub|li|cis|ing
pub|li|cism
pub|li|cist +s
pub|li|cis|tic
pub|li|city
pub|li|cize
  pub|li|cizes
  pub|li|cized
  pub|li|ciz|ing
pub|lic|ly
public-spirit|ed
public-spirit|ed|ly
public-
  spirit|ed|ness
pub|lish
  pub|lishes
  pub|lished
  pub|lish|ing
pub|lish|able
pub|lish|er +s
Puc|cini,
  Gia|como (Italian
  composer)
puc|coon +s
puce
Puck (mischievous
  sprite, 'Robin
  Goodfellow')
puck +s (sprite
  generally; child;
  disc in ice hockey)
pucka (good;
  genuine; use
  pukka)
puck|er +s +ed
  +ing (wrinkle.
  △ pukka)
puck|ery
puck|ish
puck|ish|ly
puck|ish|ness
puck|like

pud +s
pud|ding +s
pud|ding basin +s
pud|ding cloth +s
pud|ding face +s
pudding-head +s
pudding-stone
pud|dingy
pud|dle
  pud|dles
  pud|dled
  pud|dling
pud|dler +s
pud|dly
pu|dency
pu|den|dal
pu|den|dum
  pu|denda
pudge +s
pudg|ily
pudgi|ness
pudgy
  pudgi|er
  pudgi|est
pudic
Pue|bla (city and
  state, Mexico)
Pue|blo +s
  (American Indian)
pue|blo +s (village)
pu|er|ile
pu|er|ile|ly
pu|er|il|ity
pu|er|peral
Puerto Cor|tés
  (port, Honduras)
Puerto Limón
  (alternative name
  for Limón)
Puerto Plata
  (resort town,
  Dominican
  Republic)
Puerto Rican +s
Puerto Rico
  (island, West
  Indies)
puff +s +ed +ing
puff-adder +s
puff|ball +s
puff|er +s
puff|er fish
  plural puff|er fish
puff|ery
puff|ily
puf|fin +s
puf|fi|ness
puff-puff +s
puffy
  puff|ier
  puffi|est

pug
pugs
pugged
pug¦ging
pug-dog +s
pug-faced
pug¦garee +s
pug¦gish
puggy
pu¦gil¦ism
pu¦gil¦ist +s
pu¦gil¦is¦tic
Pugin, Au¦gus¦tus
(English architect)
Pu¦glia (Italian
name for **Apulia**)
pug-mill +s
pug¦na¦cious
pug¦na¦cious¦ly
pug¦na¦cious¦ness
pug¦na¦city
pug-nose +s
pug-nosed
puisne (*Law*.
△ **puny**)
puis¦sance
puis¦sant
puis¦sant¦ly
puja +s
puke
pukes
puked
puk¦ing
pu¦keko +s
pukey
pukka (good;
genuine.
△ **pucker**)
puk¦kah (use
pukka)
puku +s
pul
puls *or* puli
(Afghan currency.
△ **pool**)
pula +s
(Botswanan
currency.
△ **puller**)
pulao +s (use
pilau)
Pulau Ser¦ibu
(Indonesian name
for the **Thousand
Islands**)
pul¦chri¦tude
pul¦chri¦tud¦in¦ous
pule
pules
puled
pul¦ing
(whimper)

Pul¦it¦zer, Jo¦seph
(Hungarian-born
American
newspaper
proprietor)
Pul¦it¦zer prize +s
pull +s +ed +ing
pull-back +s *noun*
pull-down +s
adjective and noun
pull¦er +s (person
or thing that pulls.
△ **pula**)
pul¦let +s
pul¦ley +s
pull-in +s *noun*
Pull¦man +s
pull-off +s *noun*
pull-on +s *adjective
and noun*
pull-out +s
adjective and noun
pull¦over +s
pul¦lu¦lant
pul¦lu¦late
pul¦lu¦lates
pul¦lu¦lated
pul¦lu¦lat¦ing
pul¦lu¦la¦tion +s
pull-up +s
pul¦mon¦ary
pul¦mon¦ate
pul¦mon¦ic
pulp +s +ed +ing
pulp¦er +s
pulpi¦ness
pul¦pit +s
pul¦pit¦eer +s +ed
+ing
pulp¦less
pulp¦ous
pulp¦wood
pulpy
pulp¦ier
pulpi¦est
pul¦que
pul¦sar +s
pul¦sate
pul¦sates
pul¦sated
pul¦sat¦ing
pul¦sa¦tile
pul¦satilla +s
pul¦sa¦tion +s
pul¦sa¦tor +s
pul¦sa¦tory
pulse
pulses
pulsed
puls¦ing
pulse¦less
puls¦im¦eter +s

Pulu (alternative
name for **Tiglath-
pileser III**)
pul¦ver¦is¦able *Br*.
(use **pulverizable**)
pul¦ver¦isa¦tion *Br*.
(use
pulverization)
pul¦ver¦isa¦tor *Br*.
+s (use
pulverizator)
pul¦ver¦ise *Br*. (use
pulverize)
pul¦ver¦ises
pul¦ver¦ised
pul¦ver¦is¦ing
pul¦ver¦iser *Br*. +s
(use **pulverizer**)
pul¦ver¦iz¦able
pul¦ver¦iza¦tion
pul¦ver¦iza¦tor +s
pul¦ver¦ize
pul¦ver¦izes
pul¦ver¦ized
pul¦ver¦iz¦ing
pul¦ver¦izer +s
pul¦veru¦lent
pul¦vin¦ate
pul¦vin¦ated
puma +s
pum¦ice
pum¦ices
pum¦iced
pum¦icing
pu¦mi¦ceous
pum¦ice stone +s
pum¦mel
pum¦mels
pum¦melled *Br*.
pum¦meled *Am*.
pum¦mel¦ling *Br*.
pum¦mel¦ing *Am*.
(hit. △ **pommel**)
pump +s +ed +ing
pump-action
pump-brake +s
pum¦per¦nickel
pump-handle
pump-handles
pump-handled
pump-handling
pump¦kin +s
pump¦kin¦seed +s
pump-priming
pump room +s
pun
puns
punned
pun¦ning
puna +s (plateau;
mountain
sickness)

punch
punches
punched
punch¦ing
**Punch and Judy
show** +s
punch¦bag +s
punch¦ball +s
punch¦bowl +s
punch¦card +s
punch-drunk
pun¦cheon +s
punch¦er +s
punch¦ily
Pun¦chin¦ello +s
punchi¦ness
punch¦ing bag +s
punch¦line +s
punch-up +s
punchy
punch¦ier
punchi¦est
puncta
punc¦tate
punc¦ta¦tion
punc¦tilio +s
punc¦tili¦ous
punc¦tili¦ous¦ly
punc¦tili¦ous¦ness
punc¦tual
punc¦tu¦al¦ity
punc¦tu¦al¦ly
punc¦tu¦ate
punc¦tu¦ates
punc¦tu¦ated
punc¦tu¦at¦ing
punc¦tu¦ation +s
punc¦tum
puncta
punc¦ture
punc¦tures
punc¦tured
punc¦tur¦ing
pun¦dit +s
pun¦dit¦ry
Pune (use **Poona**)
pun¦gency
pun¦gent
pun¦gent¦ly
Punic
puni¦ly
pu¦ni¦ness
pun¦ish
pun¦ishes
pun¦ished
pun¦ish¦ing
pun¦ish¦able
pun¦ish¦er +s
pun¦ish¦ing¦ly
pun¦ish¦ment +s
pu¦ni¦tive
pu¦ni¦tive¦ly

pu|ni|tory
Pun|jab
Pun|jabi +s
punk +s
pun|kah +s
punkah-wallah +s
punk|ish
punky
  punk|ier
  punki|est
pun|ner +s
pun|net +s
pun|ning|ly
pun|ster +s
punt +s +ed +ing
Punta Arenas
  (port, Chile)
punt|er +s
puny
  puni|er
  puni|est
  (weak. △ puisne)
pup
  pups
  pupped
  pup|ping
pupa
  pupae
pupal
pu|pate
  pu|pates
  pu|pated
  pu|pat|ing
pu|pa|tion
pupil +s
pu|pil|age +s (use
  pupillage)
pu|pilar (use
  pupillar)
pu|pil|ar|ity (use
  pupillarity)
pu|pil|ary (use
  pupillary)
pu|pil|lage +s
pu|pil|lar
pu|pil|lar|ity
pu|pil|lary
pu|pip|ar|ous
pup|pet +s
pup|pet|eer +s
pup|pet|eer|ing
pup|pet|ry
pup|pet state +s
puppy
  pup|pies
puppy fat
puppy|hood
puppy|ish
puppy love
Pur|ana +s
Pur|an|ic

Pur|beck, Isle of
  (peninsula,
  England; marble)
pur|blind
pur|blind|ness
Pur|cell, Henry
  (English
  composer)
pur|chas|able
pur|chase
  pur|chases
  pur|chased
  pur|chas|ing
pur|chaser +s
pur|chase tax
  pur|chase taxes
pur|dah +s
pure
  purer
  purest
pure-bred
purée
  pur|ées
  pur|éed
  pur|ée|ing
pure|ly
pure|ness
pur|fle
  pur|fles
  pur|fled
  pur|fling
pur|ga|tion
pur|ga|tive +s
pur|ga|tor|ial
pur|ga|tory
  pur|ga|tor|ies
purge
  purges
  purged
  pur|ging
pur|ger +s
puri|fi|ca|tion +s
puri|fi|ca|tor +s
puri|fi|ca|tory
puri|fier +s
puri|fy
  puri|fies
  puri|fied
  puri|fy|ing
Purim
pur|ine +s
Pur|ism (in 20th-
  century painting)
pur|ism (generally)
pur|ist +s
pur|is|tic
Pur|itan +s
  (English
  Protestant)
pur|itan +s
  (generally)
pur|it|an|ic

pur|it|an|ic|al
pur|it|an|ic|al|ly
Pur|itan|ism (of
  Puritans)
pur|itan|ism
  (generally)
pur|ity
  pur|ities
purl +s +ed +ing
  (stitch; babble.
  △ pearl)
pur|ler +s (fall.
  △ pearler)
pur|lieu +s
pur|lin +s
pur|loin +s +ed
  +ing
pur|loin|er +s
pur|ple
  pur|ples
  pur|pled
  purp|ling
Pur|ple Heart +s
  (medal)
pur|ple heart +s
  (drug)
purple|ness
purp|lish
pur|ply
pur|port +s +ed
  +ing
pur|port|ed|ly
pur|pose
  pur|poses
  pur|posed
  pur|pos|ing
purpose-built
pur|pose|ful
pur|pose|ful|ly
pur|pose|ful|ness
pur|pose|less
pur|pose|less|ly
pur|pose|less|ness
pur|pose|ly
purpose-made
pur|pos|ive
pur|pos|ive|ly
pur|pos|ive|ness
pur|pura
pur|pure
pur|pur|ic
pur|purin
purr +s +ed +ing
purse
  purses
  pursed
  purs|ing
pur|ser +s
pur|ser|ship
purse seine +s
  noun

purse-seine
  attributive
purse-seiner +s
purse strings
pursi|ness
purs|lane +s
pur|su|able
pur|su|ance
pur|su|ant
pur|su|ant|ly
pur|sue
  pur|sues
  pur|sued
  pur|su|ing
pur|suer +s
pur|suit +s
pur|sui|vant +s
pursy
  purs|ier
  pursi|est
puru|lence
puru|lency
puru|lent
puru|lent|ly
pur|vey +s +ed
  +ing
pur|vey|ance
pur|vey|or +s
pur|view +s
pus (matter.
  △ puss)
Pusan (city, South
  Korea)
Pusey, Ed|ward
  Bou|verie
  (English
  theologian)
push
  pushes
  pushed
  push|ing
push-bike +s
push-button +s
push|cart +s
push|chair +s
push|er +s
push|ful
push|ful|ly
push|ily
pushi|ness
push|ing|ly
Push|kin,
  Alek|sandr
  (Russian writer)
push|over +s
push-pull
push|rod +s
push-start +s
Pushtu
push-up +s

pushy
push|ier
pushi|est
pu|sil|lan|im|ity
pu|sil|lan|im|ous
pu|sil|lan|im|
    ous|ly
Pus|kas, Fer|enc
    (Hungarian
    footballer)
puss
    pusses
    (cat. △ pus)
puss moth +s
pussy
    puss|ies
pussy cat +s
pussy|foot +s +ed
    +ing
pussy|foot|er +s
pussy wil|low +s
pus|tu|lar
pus|tu|late
    pus|tu|lates
    pus|tu|lated
    pus|tu|lat|ing
pus|tu|la|tion
pus|tule +s
pus|tu|lous
put
    puts
    put
    put|ting
    (place. △ putt)
pu|ta|tive
pu|ta|tive|ly
put-down +s
put-in +s
put|lock +s
put|log +s
put-on +s
put-put
    put-puts
    put-putted
    put-putting
pu|tre|fa|cient
pu|tre|fac|tion
pu|tre|fac|tive
pu|trefy
    pu|tre|fies
    pu|tre|fied
    pu|tre|fy|ing
pu|tres|cence
pu|tres|cent
pu|tres|cible
pu|trid
pu|trid|ity
pu|trid|ly
pu|trid|ness
putsch
    putsches

putt +s +ed +ing
    (Golf. △ put)
put|tee +s (leg-
    cloth)
putt|er +s +ed
    +ing
putt|ing green +s
putto
    putti
    (cherub)
putty
    put|ties
    put|tied
    putty|ing
    (cement)
put-up attributive
put-upon attributive
put-you-up +s
    noun and
    attributive
puy +s
puz|zle
    puz|zles
    puz|zled
    puz|zling
puzzle|ment +s
puz|zler +s
puz|zling|ly
puz|zo|lana
pya +s
py|aemia Br. (Am.
    pyemia)
py|aem|ic Br. (Am.
    pyemic)
pyc|nic +s (stocky;
    use pyknic.
    △ picnic)
pye-dog +s
py|el|itis
py|elo|gram +s
py|emia Am. (Br.
    pyaemia)
py|emic Am. (Br.
    pyaemic)
pyg|maean
Pyg|ma|lion (kings
    of Tyre and
    Cyprus)
pyg|mean (use
    pygmaean)
pygmy
    pyg|mies
py|jama Br.
    attributive (Am.
    pajama)
py|ja|mas Br. (Am.
    pajamas)
pyk|nic +s (stocky.
    △ picnic)
pylon +s
pyl|or|ic

pyl|orus
    pyl|ori
Pyong|yang
    (capital of North
    Korea)
pyor|rhea Am.
pyor|rhoea Br.
pyra|can|tha +s
pyra|lid +s
pyra|mid +s
pyr|am|ida!
pyr|am|id|al|ly
pyra|mid|ic
pyra|mid|ic|al|ly
pyra|mid|wise
Pyra|mus Roman
    Mythology
pyre +s
Pyr|en|ean
Pyr|en|ees
    (mountains, SW
    Europe)
pyr|eth|rin +s
pyr|eth|roid +s
pyr|eth|rum +s
pyr|et|ic
Pyrex Propr.
pyr|exia
pyr|exial
pyr|ex|ic
pyr|exic|al
pyr|heli|om|eter
    +s
pyri|dine
pyr|id|ox|ine
pyr|imi|dine +s
pyr|ite
pyr|ites
pyr|it|ic
pyr|it|ifer|ous
pyr|it|ise Br. (use
    pyritize)
    pyr|it|ises
    pyr|it|ised
    pyr|it|is|ing
pyr|it|ize
    pyr|it|izes
    pyr|it|ized
    pyr|it|iz|ing
pyr|it|ous
pyro (= pyrogallic
    acid)
pyro|clast +s
pyro|clas|tic +s
pyro|elec|tric
pyro|elec|tri|city
pyro|gal|lic
pyro|gal|lol
pyro|gen|ic
pyr|ogen|ous (use
    pyrogenic)
pyr|og|raphy

pyr|ol|atry
pyro|lig|neous
pyro|lyse Br.
    pyro|lyses
    pyro|lysed
    pyro|lys|ing
pyr|oly|sis
pyro|lyt|ic
pyro|lyze Am.
    pyro|lyzes
    pyro|lyzed
    pyro|lyz|ing
pyro|mancy
pyro|mania
pyro|maniac +s
pyr|om|eter +s
pyro|met|ric
pyro|met|ric|al|ly
pyr|om|etry
pyr|ope +s
pyro|phor|ic
pyr|osis
pyro|tech|nic
pyro|tech|nic|al
pyro|tech|nics
pyro|tech|nist +s
pyro|techny
pyr|ox|ene +s
pyr|oxy|lin
Pyr|rha Greek
    Mythology
pyr|rhic +s
Pyr|rho (Greek
    philosopher)
Pyr|rho|nian
Pyr|rhon|ic
Pyr|rhon|ism
Pyr|rhon|ist +s
Pyr|rhus (king of
    Epirus)
pyr|role
pyr|roli|dine
pyru|vate +s
pyru|vic
Py|thag|oras
    (Greek
    philosopher)
Py|thag|oras'
    the|orem
Py|thag|or|ean +s
Pythia (Greek
    priestess)
Pyth|ian +s
Pyth|ian games
Pyth|ias (friend of
    Damon)
py|thon +s
Py|thon|esque
py|thon|ess
    py|thon|esses
py|thon|ic
py|uria

Qq

pyx
  pyxes
  (box. △ pix)
pyx|id|ium
  pyx|idia
pyxis
  pyx|ides
pzazz (use
  pizzazz)

Qabis (use Gabès)
Qad|dafi,
  Mu'am|mer
  Mu'ham|mad al
  (use Gaddafi)
Qaf|sah (use
  Gafsa)
Qara|ghandy (city,
  Kazakhstan)
Qatar (sheikhdom,
  Middle East)
Qa|tari +s
Qat|tara
  De|pres|sion
  (desert basin,
  Libyan desert)
Q-boat +s
Q fever
qibla (use kiblah)
Qin (Chinese
  dynasty)
Qin|dao (port,
  China)
Qing (Chinese
  dynasty)
Qing|hai (province,
  China)
Qiqi|har (city,
  China)
Qom (city, Iran)
Q-ship +s
Qua
  plural Qua
  (person; language;
  use Kwa)
qua (in the capacity
  of)
quack +s +ed +ing
quack|ery
  quack|eries
quack|ish
quad +s
  (= quadrangle;
  quadruplet;
  Printing;
  quadraphony;
  quadraphonic.
  △ quod)
quadra|gen|ar|ian
  +s
Quadra|ges|ima
  +s
quadra|gesi|mal
quad|ran|gle +s
quad|ran|gu|lar
quad|rant +s
quad|rantal

Quad|ran|tids
  (meteor shower)
quadra|phon|ic
quadra|phon|ic|
      al|ly
quadra|phon|ics
quadra|raph|ony
quad|rat +s (area
  of ground)
quad|rate
  quad|rates
  quad|rated
  quad|rat|ing
  (square; bone;
  muscle; make
  square)
quad|rat|ic +s
quad|ra|ture +s
quad|ren|nial
quad|ren|ni|al|ly
quad|ren|nium
  quad|ren|niums
  or quad|ren|nia
quad|ric +s
quad|ri|ceps
  plural
  quad|ri|ceps
quad|ri|fid
quad|riga
  quad|rigae
quad|ri|lat|eral +s
quad|ri|lin|gual
quad|rille +s
quad|ril|lion
  plural
  quad|ril|lion *or*
  quad|ril|lions
quadri|nomial +s
quadri|par|tite
quadri|ple|gia
quadri|ple|gic +s
quadri|reme +s
quadri|syl|lab|ic
quadri|syl|lable
  +s
quadri|va|lent
quad|riv|ium
  quad|riv|ia
quad|roon +s
quadro|phon|ic
  (use
  quadraphonic)
quadro|phon|ic|
  al|ly (use quadra-
  phonically)
quadro|phon|ics
  (use
  quadraphonics)
quad|ro|ph|ony
  (use
  quadraphony)
quad|ru|man|ous

quad|ru|ped +s
quad|ru|pedal
quad|ru|ple
  quad|ru|ples
  quad|ru|pled
  quad|ru|pling
quad|ru|plet +s
quad|ru|pli|cate
  quad|ru|pli|cates
  quad|ru|pli|cated
  quad|ru|pli|
        cat|ing
quad|ru|pli|ca|tion
  +s
quad|ru|pli|city
quad|ruply
quad|ru|pole +s
quaes|tor +s
quaes|tor|ial
quaes|tor|ship +s
quaff +s +ed +ing
quaff|able
quaff|er +s
quag +s
quagga +s
quaggy
  quag|gier
  quag|gi|est
quag|mire +s
qua|haug *Am.* +s
qua|hog *Br.* +s
quaich +s
Quai d'Orsay
  (street, Paris)
quail +s +ed +ing
  (flinch)
quail
  plural quail *or*
  quails
  (bird)
quail|ery
  quail|eries
quaint +er +est
quaint|ly
quaint|ness
quake
  quakes
  quaked
  quak|ing
Quaker +s
Quaker|ish
Quaker|ism +s
Quaker|ly
quaking-grass
  quaking-grasses
quaky
  quaki|er
  quaki|est
quali|fi|able
quali|fi|ca|tion +s
quali|fi|ca|tory
quali|fier +s

qual|ify
  quali|fies
  quali|fied
  quali|fy|ing
quali|ta|tive
quali|ta|tive|ly
qual|ity
  qual|ities
qualm +s
qualm|ish
quan|dary
  quan|dar|ies
quand même
quango +s
Quant, Mary
  (English fashion
  designer)
quant +s +ed +ing
  (pole)
quanta
quant|al
quant|al|ly
quant|ic +s
quan|ti|fi|abil|ity
quan|ti|fi|able
quan|ti|fi|ca|tion
  +s
quan|ti|fier +s
quan|tify
  quan|ti|fies
  quan|ti|fied
  quan|ti|fy|ing
quant|isa|tion *Br.*
  +s (use
  quantization)
quant|ise *Br.* (use
  quantize)
  quant|ises
  quant|ised
  quant|is|ing
quan|ti|ta|tive
quan|ti|ta|tive|ly
quan|ti|tive
quanti|tive|ly
quan|tity
  quan|tities
quant|iza|tion +s
quant|ize
  quant|izes
  quant|ized
  quant|iz|ing
quan|tum
  quanta
quantum-
  mechan|ic|al
quantum-
  mechan|ic|al|ly
quan|tum
  mech|anics
qua|qua|versal
quar|an|tine
  quar|an|tines

quar|an|tine (*cont.*)
  quar|an|tined
  quar|an|tin|ing
quark +s
quar|rel
  quar|rels
  quar|relled *Br.*
  quar|reled *Am.*
  quar|rel|ling *Br.*
  quar|rel|ing *Am.*
quar|rel|er *Am.* +s
quar|rel|ler +s
quar|rel|some
quar|rel|some|ly
quar|rel|some|
        ness
quar|rian +s
quar|rion +s (use
  quarrian)
quarry
  quar|ries
  quar|ried
  quarry|ing
quar|ry|man
  quar|ry|men
quart +s (liquid
  measure)
quart (*Fencing.*
  △cart , kart , khat)
quar|tan
quar|ta|tion +s
quarte (*Fencing*;
  use quart · △cart ,
  kart , khat)
quar|ter +s +ed
  +ing
quar|ter|age +s
quar|ter|back +s
quarter-binding
  +s
quar|ter day +s
quar|ter|deck +s
quarter-final +s
quarter-hour +s
quar|ter|ing +s
quarter-light +s
quarter-line +s
quar|ter|ly
  quar|ter|lies
quar|ter|mas|ter
  +s
**Quar|ter|mas|ter
Gen|eral +s**
quar|ter|mas|ter
  ser|geant +s
quar|tern +s
quar|ter note +s
quarter-plate +s
quarter-pounder
  +s
quar|ter ses|sions

quar|ter|staff
  quar|ter|staves
quarter-tone +s
quar|tet +s
quar|tic +s
quar|tile +s
quarto +s
quartz
  quartzes
quartz|ite +s
qua|sar +s
quash
  quashes
  quashed
  quash|ing
quasi
**Quasi|modo,
Sal|va|tore**
  (Italian poet)
quas|sia +s
quat|er|cen|ten|
        ary
quat|er|cen|ten|
        ar|ies
Qua|ter|nary
  Geology
qua|ter|nary
  qua|ter|nar|ies
  (fourth; *Chemistry*)
qua|ter|nion +s
qua|tern|ity
  qua|tern|ities
quat|orz|ain +s
quat|orze +s
quat|rain +s
quatre|foil +s
quat|tro|cent|ist
  +s
quat|tro|cento *Art*
qua|ver +s +ed
  +ing
qua|veri|ness
qua|ver|ing|ly
qua|very
quay +s (landing
  place. △key)
quay|age +s
quay|side +s
quean +s
  (impudent
  woman. △queen)
queas|ily
queasi|ness
queasy
  queas|ier
  queasi|est
Que|bec (province
  and city, Canada)
Que|bec|er +s (use
  Quebecker)
Que|beck|er +s

Que|bec|ois
  plural Que|bec|ois
que|bra|cho +s
Que|chua
  plural Que|chua
Que|chuan
Queen, El|lery
  (two American
  writers)
queen +s +ed +ing
  (sovereign etc.
  △quean)
**Queen Anne's
Bounty**
  (charitable fund)
**Queen Anne's
lace** (plant)
queen bee +s
queen cake +s
**Queen Char|lotte
Is|lands** (off
  Canada)
queen con|sort +s
queen|dom +s
queen dow|ager
  +s
queen|hood +s
Queenie (name)
queenie +s (*slang*
  queen)
queen|less
queen|like
queen|li|ness
queen|ly
Queen Maud Land
  (in Antarctica)
queen mother +s
queen post +s
Queens (borough,
  New York City)
**Queens|berry
Rules**
Queen's County
  (former name of
  Laois)
queen|ship +s
queen-size
queen-sized
Queens|land
  (state, Australia)
Queens|land|er +s
queen's-ware
  (ceramics)
queer +s +ed +ing
  +er +est
queer|ish
queer|ly
queer|ness
quell
  quells
  quelled
  quell|ing

quell¦er +s

quench

  quenches

  quenched

  quench¦ing

quench¦able

quench¦er +s

quench¦less

que¦nelle +s

Quen¦tin

Quer¦cia, Ja¦copo

  della (Italian

  sculptor)

Que¦rétaro (city

  and state, Mexico)

quer¦ist +s

quern +s   *J*

quern-stone +s

queru¦lous

queru¦lous¦ly

queru¦lous¦ness

query

  quer¦ies

  quer¦ied

  query¦ing

quest +s +ed +ing

quest¦er +s

quest¦ing¦ly

ques¦tion +s +ed

  +ing

ques¦tion¦abil¦ity

ques¦tion¦able

ques¦tion¦able¦

          ness

ques¦tion¦ably

ques¦tion¦ary

  ques¦tion¦ar¦ies

ques¦tion¦er +s

ques¦tion¦ing +s

ques¦tion¦ing¦ly

ques¦tion¦less

ques¦tion mark +s

question-master

  +s

ques¦tion¦naire +s

ques¦tion time +s

quest¦or +s (use

  quester)

Quetta (city,

  Pakistan)

quet¦zal +s

Quet¦zal¦có¦atl

  (Toltec and Aztec

  god)

queue

  queues

  queued

  queu¦ing *or*

  queue¦ing

  (line of people.

  △cue)

queue-jump +s

  +ed +ing

Que¦vedo y

  Ville¦gas,

  Fran¦cisco

  Gómez de

  (Spanish writer)

Que¦zon City (city,

  Philippines)

Qufu (town, China)

quib¦ble

  quib¦bles

  quib¦bled

  quib¦bling

quib¦bler +s

quib¦bling¦ly

quiche +s

Qui¦chua

  (= Quechua)

quick +s +er +est

quick-drying

quick¦en +s +ed

  +ing

quick-fire

quick-freeze

  quick-freezes

  quick-froze

  quick-freezing

  quick-frozen

quick-growing

quickie +s

quick¦lime +s

quick¦ly

quick march

quick¦ness

quick¦sand +s

quick¦set +s

quick¦sil¦ver +s

quick¦step

  quick¦steps

  quick¦stepped

  quick¦step¦ping

  (dance)

quick step (march)

quick-tempered

quick-thinking

  attributive

quick¦thorn +s

quick time

quick-witted

quick-witted¦ness

quid

  plural quid *or*

  quids

quid¦dity

  quid¦dities

quid¦nunc +s

quid pro quo +s

qui¦es¦cence

qui¦es¦cency

qui¦es¦cent

qui¦es¦cent¦ly

quiet +s +ed +ing

  +er +est (silent

  etc.)

quiet¦en +s +ed

  +ing

quiet¦ism

quiet¦ist +s

quiet¦is¦tic

quiet¦ly

quiet¦ness

quiet-spoken

quiet¦ude

qui¦etus

quiff +s

quill +s +ed +ing

quill-coverts

Quiller-Couch,

  Ar¦thur (British

  novelist)

quilt +s +ed +ing

quilt¦er +s

quim +s (*coarse*

  slang)

quin +s

  (= quintuplets)

quina¦crine

quin¦ary

quin¦ate

quince +s

quin¦cen¦ten¦ary

  quin¦cen¦ten¦

           ar¦ies

quin¦cen¦ten¦nial

Quin¦cey, Thomas

  De (English

  writer)

quin¦cun¦cial

quin¦cun¦cial¦ly

quin¦cunx

  quin¦cunxes

Quine, Wil¦lard

  Van Orman

  (American

  philosopher)

quin¦ella +s

quin¦ine

quinol

quin¦oline +s

quin¦one +s

quin¦qua¦

  gen¦ar¦ian +s

quin¦qua¦gen¦ary

  quin¦qua¦

      gen¦ar¦ies

Quin¦qua¦ges¦ima

quin¦que¦cen¦ten¦

          nial

quin¦que¦nial

quin¦quen¦ni¦al¦ly

quin¦quen¦nium

  quin¦quen¦niums

  or quin¦quen¦nia

quin¦que¦reme +s

quin¦que¦va¦lent

quin¦sied

quinsy

  quin¦sies

quint +s (five

  cards; quintuplet)

quinta +s

quin¦tain +s

quin¦tal +s

quin¦tan

Quin¦tana Roo

  (state, Mexico)

quinte +s *Fencing*

quint¦es¦sence +s

quint¦es¦sen¦tial

quint¦es¦sen¦

          tial¦ly

quin¦tet +s

Quin¦til¦ian

  (Roman

  rhetorician)

quin¦til¦lion

  plural quin¦til¦lion

  or quin¦til¦lions

quin¦til¦lionth

Quin¦tin

quint major +s

Quin¦ton *also*

  Quen¦tin,

  Quin¦tin

quin¦tu¦ple

  quin¦tu¦ples

  quin¦tu¦pled

  quin¦tu¦pling

quin¦tu¦plet +s

quin¦tu¦pli¦cate

  quin¦tu¦pli¦cates

  quin¦tu¦pli¦cated

  quin¦tu¦pli¦cat¦ing

quin¦tu¦pli¦ca¦tion

  +s

quin¦tuply

quip

  quips

  quipped

  quip¦ping

quip¦ster +s

quipu +s

quire +s (paper.

  △choir)

quirk +s

quirk¦ily

quirki¦ness

quirk¦ish

quirky

  quirk¦ier

  quirki¦est

quirt +s +ed +ing

quis¦ling +s

quis¦ling¦ite +s

quit

  quits

quit (*cont.*)
quit|ted *or* quit
quit|ting
quitch
quitches
quit|claim +s +ed
+ing
quite (completely;
rather; definitely)
Quito (capital of
Ecuador)
quit|rent +s
quit|tance +s
quit|ter +s
quiver +s +ed +ing
quiver|ful +s
quiver|ing +s
quiver|ing|ly
quivery
qui vive (in 'on the
qui vive')
Quix|ote, Don
(fictional hero)
quix|ot|ic
quix|ot|ic|al|ly
quix|ot|ise *Br.* (use
quixotize)
quix|ot|ises
quix|ot|ised
quix|ot|is|ing
quix|ot|ism
quix|ot|ize
quix|ot|izes
quix|ot|ized
quix|ot|iz|ing
quix|otry
quiz
quiz|zes
quizzed
quiz|zing
quiz|master +s
quiz|zer +s
quiz|zical
quiz|zi|cal|ity
quiz|zi|cal|ly
quiz|zi|cal|ness
Qum (use Qom)
Qum|ran (region,
Israel)
quod +s (prison.
△ quad)
quod erat
dem|on|
stran|dum
quod|libet +s
quod|libet|arian
+s
quod|libet|ic|al
quod|libet|ic|al|ly
quod vide
quoin +s +ed +ing
(angle of building;

quoin (*cont.*)
cornerstone.
△ coin, coign)
quoit +s +ed +ing
quokka +s
quon|dam
Quon|set +s *Propr.*
quor|ate
Quorn *Propr.*
quorum +s
quota +s (share.
△ quoter)
quot|able
quota|tion +s
quota|tion mark
+s
quota|tive
quote
quotes
quoted
quot|ing
quoter +s (person
who quotes.
△ quota)
quoth
quo|tid|ian +s
quo|tient +s
Quran (use Koran)
Qu|ran|ic (use
Koranic)
Qwa|qwa (former
homeland, South
Africa)
qwerty

Rr

Ra *Egyptian*
Mythology
Rabat (capital of
Morocco)
Ra|baul (port, New
Britain, Papua
New Guinea)
rab|bet +s +ed
+ing (groove in
wood. △ rabbit)
rabbi +s
rab|bin
plural rab|bin *or*
rab|bins
rab|bin|ate +s
rab|bin|ic
rab|bin|ic|al
rab|bin|ic|al|ly
rab|bin|ism
rab|bin|ist +s
rab|bit +s +ed
+ing (animal; to
chatter; in 'Welsh
rabbit'. △ rabbet)
rab|bity
rab|ble +s
rabble-rouser +s
rabble-rousing
Rabe|lais,
Fran|çois (French
satirist)
Rabe|lais|ian
rabi +s
rabid
ra|bid|ity
ra|bid|ly
ra|bid|ness
ra|bies
Rabin, Yit|zhak
(Israeli prime
minister)
rac|coon +s (use
racoon)
race
races
raced
ra|cing
race|card +s
race|course +s
race|goer +s
race|going
race|horse +s
ra|cem|ate +s
Chemistry
ra|ceme +s
ra|cemic
ra|cem|ise *Br.* (use
racemize)

ra|cem|ise (*cont.*)
ra|cem|ises
ra|cem|ised
ra|cem|is|ing
ra|cem|ize
ra|cem|izes
ra|cem|ized
ra|cem|iz|ing
ra|cem|ose
racer +s
race|track +s
race|way +s
Ra|chael *also*
Ra|chel
Ra|chel *also*
Ra|chael
(name)
ra|chel +s (colour)
ra|chid|ial
ra|chis
ra|chi|des
rach|it|ic
rach|itis
Rach|man|inov,
Ser|gei (Russian
composer)
Rach|man|ism
ra|cial
ra|cial|ism
ra|cial|ist +s
ra|cial|ly
raci|ly
Ra|cine, Jean
(French dramatist)
raci|ness
ra|cing car +s
ra|cing driver +s
ra|cism
ra|cist +s
rack +s +ed +ing
(framework;
instrument of
torture;
destruction; joint
of meat; draw off
wine or beer;
clouds; horse's
gait; to torture;
put on rack.
△ wrack)
rack-and-pinion
attributive
racket +s +ed +ing
rack|et|eer +s
rack|et|eer|ing
rack|ets (game)
racket-tail +s
rack|ety
rack rail|way +s
rack-rent +s +ed
+ing
rack-renter +s

rack-wheel +s
ra¦clette +s
racon +s
ra¦con¦teur +s *male*
ra¦con¦teuse +s
female
ra¦coon +s
rac¦quet +s (use
racket)
racy
raci¦er
raci¦est
rad +s
RADA (= Royal
Academy of
Dramatic Art)
radar +s
Rad¦cliffe, Mrs
Ann Ward
(English novelist)
rad¦dle
rad¦dles
rad¦dled
rad¦dling
Radha *Hinduism*
Radha¦krish¦nan,
Sar¦ve¦palli
(Indian
philosopher and
president)
ra¦dial +s
ra¦di¦al¦ly
ra¦dian +s
ra¦di¦ance +s
ra¦di¦ancy
ra¦di¦an¦cies
ra¦di¦ant +s
ra¦di¦ant¦ly
ra¦di¦ate
ra¦di¦ates
ra¦di¦ated
ra¦di¦at¦ing
ra¦di¦ate¦ly
ra¦di¦ation +s
ra¦di¦ation¦al
ra¦di¦ation¦al¦ly
ra¦dia¦tive
ra¦di¦ator +s
rad¦ical +s (of the
root;
revolutionary.
△ radicle)
rad¦ic¦al¦isa¦tion
Br. (use
radicalization)
rad¦ic¦al¦ise *Br.*
(use radicalize)
rad¦ic¦al¦ises
rad¦ic¦al¦ised
rad¦ic¦al¦is¦ing
rad¦ic¦al¦ism
rad¦ic¦al¦iza¦tion

rad¦ic¦al¦ize
rad¦ic¦al¦izes
rad¦ic¦al¦ized
rad¦ic¦al¦iz¦ing
rad¦ic¦al¦ly
rad¦ic¦al¦ness
rad¦ical sign +s
rad¦icchio +s
rad¦ices
rad¦icle +s (rootlet;
subdivision of
vein. △ radical)
ra¦dicu¦lar
radii
radio +s *noun*
radio
ra¦dioes
ra¦dioed
radio¦ing
verb
radio¦active
radio¦active¦ly
radio¦activ¦ity
radio-assay +s
radio as¦tron¦omy
radio¦bio¦logic¦al
radio¦bio¦logic¦
al¦ly
radio¦biolo¦gist +s
radio¦biol¦ogy
radio-caesium
radio¦car¦bon +s
radio-carpal +s
radio cas¦sette
play¦er +s
radio¦chem¦ical
radio¦chem¦ist +s
radio¦chem¦is¦try
radio-cobalt
radio-controlled
radio-element +s
radio¦gen¦ic
radio¦gen¦ic¦al¦ly
radio-goniom¦eter
+s
radio¦gram +s
radio¦graph +s
+ed +ing
radi¦og¦raph¦er +s
radio¦graph¦ic
radio¦graph¦ic¦
al¦ly
radi¦og¦raphy
radio¦im¦mun¦
ology
radio¦iso¦tope +s
radio¦iso¦top¦ic
radio¦iso¦top¦ic¦
al¦ly
radio¦lar¦ian +s
radio¦loca¦tion +s
radio¦logic

radio¦logic¦al
radi¦olo¦gist +s
radi¦ology
radi¦om¦eter +s
radio¦met¦ric
radi¦om¦etry
radi¦on¦ics
radio¦nuclide +s
radio-opaque (use
radiopaque)
radi¦opa¦city
radi¦opaque
radio¦phon¦ic
radio¦scop¦ic
radi¦os¦copy
radio¦sonde +s
radio-telegram +s
radio-telegraph +s
radio-telegraphy
radio-telephone
+s
radio-telephon¦ic
radio-telepho¦ny
radio tele¦scope
+s
radio¦telex
radio¦telexes
radio¦thera¦peut¦ic
radio¦thera¦pist +s
radio¦ther¦apy
rad¦ish
rad¦ishes
ra¦dium
ra¦dius
radii
ra¦diused
radix
ra¦di¦ces
Rad¦nor¦shire
(former county,
Wales)
Radom (city,
Poland)
ra¦dome +s
radon
rad¦ula
radu¦lae
radu¦lar
Rae¦burn, Henry
(Scottish painter)
RAF (= Royal Air
Force)
Raf¦fer¦ty's rules
raf¦fia +s
raf¦fin¦ate +s
raff¦ish
raff¦ish¦ly
raff¦ish¦ness
raf¦fle
raf¦fles
raf¦fled
raf¦fling

Raf¦fles, Stam¦ford
(British colonial
administrator)
Raf¦san¦jani, Ali
Akbar Hash¦emi
(Iranian president)
raft +s +ed +ing
raft¦er +s (person
who rafts)
raf¦ter +s (beam)
raf¦tered
rafts¦man
rafts¦men
rag
rags
ragged
rag¦ging
raga +s (Indian
musical piece or
pattern)
raga¦muf¦fin +s
rag-and-bone man
rag-and-bone
men
rag¦bag +s
rag bolt +s
rag book +s
Rag¦doll +s (cat)
rag doll +s (doll)
rage
rages
raged
ra¦ging
ragee (cereal)
ragga (style of
popular music)
rag¦ged (torn,
frayed)
rag¦ged¦ly
rag¦ged¦ness
rag¦ged robin +s
rag¦gedy
rag¦gee (use ragee)
raggle-taggle
rag¦lan +s
rag¦man
rag¦men
Rag¦na¦rök
*Scandinavian
Mythology*
ra¦gout +s +ed
+ing
rag paper +s
rag¦pick¦er +s
rag¦stone +s
rags-to-riches
rag¦tag
rag¦tail
rag¦time
rag¦uly *Heraldry*

Ra¦gusa (former
name of
Dubrovnik)
rag|weed +s
rag-wheel +s
rag|worm +s
rag|wort +s
rah
Rah¦man, Tunku
Abdul (Malayan
and Malaysian
prime minister)
rah-rah +s
rai (Music. △ rye,
wry)
raid +s +ed +ing
raid¦er +s
rail +s +ed +ing
rail|age +s
rail|car +s
rail|card +s
rail¦er +s
rail gun +s
rail|head +s
rail|ing +s
rail|lery
rail|ler¦ies
rail|less
rail|man
rail|men
rail|road +s +ed
+ing
rail|way +s
rail|way|man
rail|way|men
rail|way yard +s
rai|ment +s
rain +s +ed +ing
(water. △ reign,
rein)
rain|bird +s
rain|bow +s
rain check +s
rain cloud +s
rain|coat +s
rain dance +s
rain|drop +s
rain|fall +s
rain|for¦est +s
rain gauge +s
Rai¦nier, Mount
(volcanic peak,
USA)
rain|ily
raini|ness
rain|less
rain|maker +s
rain|mak¦ing
rain|out +s
rain|proof
rain shadow +s
rain-soaked

rain|storm +s
rain|swept
rain-wash
rain|water
rain|wear
rain-worm +s
rainy
rain|ier
raini|est
Rai¦pur (city, India)
rais|able
raise
raises
raised
rais|ing
(lift. △ raze)
rai¦sin +s
rai|siny
rai¦son d'être
rai¦sons d'être
raita
Raj
raja +s
rajah +s (use raja)
ra¦jah|ship +s (use
rajaship)
raja|ship +s
Ra¦jas|than (state,
India)
Ra¦jas|thani +s
raja yoga
Raj¦kot (city, India)
Raj|neesh,
Bhag|wan Shree
(Indian guru)
Raj¦poot +s (use
Rajput)
Raj¦put +s
Raj¦pu|tana (in
India)
Raj¦shahi (port,
Bangladesh)
rake
rakes
raked
rak¦ing
rake-off +s noun
raker +s
raki +s
rak¦ish
rak¦ish¦ly
rak¦ish|ness
Rá¦kosi, Mát¦yás
(Hungarian
Communist prime
minister)
raku
rale +s
Ra|leigh (city, USA)
Ra|leigh, Wal¦ter
(English explorer)
rall. (= rallentando)

ral¦len|tando +s
Music
ralli car +s (horse-
drawn vehicle.
△ rally car)
ral|lier +s
ral|line
rally
ral|lies
ral|lied
rally|ing
rally car +s (motor
vehicle. △ ralli
car)
rally|cross
Ralph
RAM +s (= random-
access memory)
Ram, the
(constellation;
sign of zodiac)
ram
rams
rammed
ram|ming
Rama Hinduism
Ram|adan Islam
Ram|adhan (use
Ramadan)
Rama|krishna,
Gad|adhar
Chat|terji (Indian
Hindu mystic)
ramal
Raman,
Chan|dra|
sekh|ara
Ven|kata (Indian
physicist)
Raman ef¦fect
Physics
Ra¦manu|jan,
Srini|vasa
Aai|yan|gar
(Indian
mathematician)
Rama|yana
(Sanskrit epic)
Ram|bert, Marie
(Polish-born
British ballet
dancer)
ram¦ble
ram|bles
ram|bled
ram|bling
ram|bler +s
ram|bling +s
ram|bling¦ly
Rambo (fictional
hero)
rambo +s (apple)

ram|bunc¦tious
ram|bunc¦tious|ly
ram|bunc¦tious|
ness
ram|bu¦tan +s
Ram|eau, Jean-
Philippe (French
composer)
ram|ekin +s
ramen
Ram|eses
(= Ramses)
ramie +s
ram|ifi|ca¦tion +s
ram|ify
rami|fies
rami|fied
rami|fy|ing
Ram|il|lies (battle
site, Belgium)
ramin +s
ram|jet +s
ram¦mer +s
rammy
ram|mies
Ramón y Cajal,
San|tiago
(Spanish
histologist)
ram|ose
ramp +s +ed +ing
ram|page
ram|pages
ram|paged
ram|paging
ram|pageous
ram|pager +s
ram|pancy
ram|pant
ram|pant¦ly
ram|part +s +ed
+ing
ram|pion +s
Ram|pur (city,
India)
ram-raid +s +ed
+ing
ram|rod +s
Ram¦say, Allan
(Scottish portrait
painter)
Ram¦say, Wil|liam
(Scottish chemist)
Ram¦ses
(pharaohs)
ram|shackle
ram's-horn snail
+s
ram|sons
ran
ranch
ranches

ranch (cont.)
ranched
ranch|ing
ranch|er +s
ranch|ero +s
Ran|chi (city, India)
ran|cid
ran|cid|ity
ran|cid|ness
ran|cor Am. +s (Br.
rancour.
bitterness.
△ ranker)
ran|cor|ous
ran|cor|ous|ly
ran|cour Br. +s
(Am. rancor.
bitterness.
△ ranker)
Rand, the
(= Witwaters-
rand)
rand +s (South
African or
Namibian
currency; ridge;
part of shoe)
ran|dan +s
Rand|ers (port,
Denmark)
ran|dily
ran|di|ness
Ran|dolf also
Ran|dolph
Ran|dolph also
Ran|dolf
ran|dom
random-access
adjective
ran|dom error +s
ran|dom|isa|tion
Br. (use
randomization)
ran|dom|ise Br.
(use randomize)
ran|dom|ises
ran|dom|ised
ran|dom|is|ing
ran|dom|iza|tion
ran|dom|ize
ran|dom|izes
ran|dom|ized
ran|dom|iz|ing
ran|dom|ly
ran|dom|ness
Rand|stad
(conurbation, the
Netherlands)
Randy (name)
randy
ran|dier

randy (cont.)
ran|di|est
(lustful)
ranee +s
rang
ran|ga|tira +s
range
ranges
ranged
ran|ging
rangé male
ran|gée female
range|find|er +s
Ran|ger (former
name for a
Ranger Guide)
ran|ger +s (forest
warden etc.;
soldier)
Ran|ger Guide +s
(senior Guide)
ran|ger|ship +s
ranging-pole +s
Ran|goon (capital
of Burma)
rangy
ran|gier
ran|gi|est
rani +s (use ranee)
Ran|jit Singh (Sikh
ruler)
Ran|jit|sinhji
Vi|bhaji (Indian
cricketer and
statesman)
Rank, J. Ar|thur
(English film
executive)
rank +s +ed +ing
rank-and-file
attributive
rank|er +s (soldier.
△ rancor,
rancour)
rank|ing +s
ran|kle
ran|kles
ran|kled
rank|ling
rank|ly
rank|ness
Rann of Kutch
(salt marsh, India
and Pakistan)
ran|sack +s +ed
+ing
ran|sack|er +s
ran|som +s +ed
+ing
Ran|some, Ar|thur
(English writer)
ran|somer +s

rant +s +ed +ing
Rant|er +s
(member of
Christian sect)
rant|er +s (person
who rants)
rant|ing +s
rant|ing|ly
ranti|pole
ranti|poles
ranti|poled
ranti|pol|ing
Ran|ulf
ra|nun|cul|aceous
ra|nun|cu|lus
ra|nun|cu|luses or
ra|nun|culi
Rao, P. V.
Nara|simha
(Indian prime
minister)
rap
raps
rapped
rap|ping
(knock. △ rapt.
wrap)
ra|pa|cious
ra|pa|cious|ly
ra|pa|cious|ness
rap|acity
rape
rapes
raped
rap|ing
rape-cake +s
rape-oil +s
raper +s
rape|seed +s
Raph|ael Bible
Raph|ael (Italian
painter)
raphia +s (use
raffia)
raph|ide +s
rapid +s +er +est
rapid eye-
movement +s
rapid-fire attributive
rap|id|ity
rap|id|ly
rap|id|ness
ra|pier +s
ra|pine +s
rap|ist +s
rap|paree +s
rap|pee +s
rap|pel
rap|pels
rap|pelled Br.
rap|peled Am.

rap|pel (cont.)
rap|pel|ling Br.
rap|pel|ing Am.
rap|per +s
rap|port +s
rap|por|teur +s
rap|proche|ment
+s
rap|scal|lion +s
rapt (absorbed.
△ rapped.
wrapped)
rapt|ly
rapt|ness
rap|tor +s
rap|tor|ial
rap|ture +s
rap|tured
rap|tur|ous
rap|tur|ous|ly
rap|tur|ous|ness
Ra|quel
rara avis
rarae aves
rare
rarer
rar|est
rare|bit +s (in
'Welsh rarebit';
use rabbit)
raree-show +s
rar|efac|tion +s
rar|efac|tive
rar|efi|ca|tion +s
rar|efy
rar|efies
rar|efied
rar|efy|ing
rare|ly
rare|ness
rar|ify (use rarefy)
rari|fies
rari|fied
rari|fy|ing
rar|ing
rar|ity
rar|ities
Raro|tonga (island,
S. Pacific)
Raro|tongan +s
Ras al Khai|mah
(state and city,
UAE)
ras|cal +s
ras|cal|dom
ras|cal|ism
ras|cal|ity
ras|cal|ities
ras|cal|ly
raschel +s
rase (use raze.
destroy; erase.

rase (cont.)
△ **raise**)
rases
rased
ras¦ing
rash
rashes
rash¦er
rash¦est
rasher +s *noun*
rash¦ly
rash¦ness
rasp +s +ed +ing
rasp¦atory
rasp¦ator¦ies
rasp¦berry
rasp¦berries
rasp¦berry cane +s
rasp¦er +s
rasp¦ing¦ly
**Ras¦pu¦tin,
Gri¦gori
Efimo¦vich**
(Russian monk)
raspy
Rasta
(= Rastafarian.
△ **raster**)
Ras¦ta¦fari
plural **Ras¦ta¦fari**
or **Ras¦ta¦faris**
Ras¦ta¦far¦ian +s
Ras¦ta¦far¦ian¦ism
ras¦ter +s
(*Electronics*.
△ **Rasta**)
ras¦ter¦isa¦tion *Br.*
(use
rasterization)
ras¦ter¦ise *Br.* (use
rasterize)
ras¦ter¦ises
ras¦ter¦ised
ras¦ter¦is¦ing
ras¦ter¦iser *Br.* +s
(use **rasterizer**)
ras¦ter¦iza¦tion
ras¦ter¦ize
ras¦ter¦izes
ras¦ter¦ized
ras¦ter¦iz¦ing
ras¦ter¦izer +s
Ras¦tya¦pino
(former name of
Dzerzhinsk)
rat
rats
rat¦ted
rat¦ting
rata +s
ratabil¦ity (use
rateability)

rat¦able (use
rateable)
rat¦ably (use
rateably)
rata¦fia +s
ratan +s (use
rattan)
**Ra¦tana,
Ta¦hu¦po¦tiki
Wi¦remu** (Maori
leader)
rata¦plan
rata¦plans
rata¦planned
rata¦plan¦ning
rat-arsed
rata¦tat +s
rata¦touille +s
rat¦bag +s
rat-catcher +s
ratch
ratches
ratchet +s +ed
+ing
rate
rates
rated
rat¦ing
rate¦abil¦ity
rate¦able
rate¦ably
rate-capped
rate-capping
ratel +s
rate¦pay¦er +s
rat¦fink +s
rathe
ra¦ther
rathe-ripe
Rath¦lin Is¦land
(off Ireland)
rat-hole +s
raths¦keller +s
rati¦fi¦able
rati¦fi¦ca¦tion +s
rati¦fier +s
rat¦ify
rati¦fies
rati¦fied
rati¦fy¦ing
rat¦ing +s
ratio +s
rati¦ocin¦ate
rati¦ocin¦ates
rati¦ocin¦ated
rati¦ocin¦at¦ing
rati¦ocin¦ation +s
rati¦ocina¦tive
rati¦ocin¦ator +s
ra¦tion +s +ed
+ing
ra¦tion¦al

ra¦tion¦ale +s
ra¦tion¦al¦isa¦tion
Br. +s (use
rationalization)
ra¦tion¦al¦ise *Br.*
(use **rationalize**)
ra¦tion¦al¦ises
ra¦tion¦al¦ised
ra¦tion¦al¦is¦ing
ra¦tion¦al¦iser *Br.*
+s (use
rationalizer)
ra¦tion¦al¦ism
ra¦tion¦al¦ist +s
ra¦tion¦al¦is¦tic
**ra¦tion¦al¦is¦tic¦
al¦ly**
ra¦tion¦al¦ity
ra¦tion¦al¦iza¦tion
+s
ra¦tion¦al¦ize
ra¦tion¦al¦izes
ra¦tion¦al¦ized
ra¦tion¦al¦iz¦ing
ra¦tion¦al¦izer +s
ra¦tion¦al¦ly
ra¦tion book +s
rat¦ite +s
rat kan¦ga¦roo +s
rat¦line +s
ra¦toon +s +ed
+ing
rat race +s
rat-run +s
rats¦bane +s
rat's tail +s
rat-tail +s (fish;
horse; spoon)
rat¦tan +s
rat-tat +s
rat¦ter +s
**Ratti¦gan,
Ter¦ence** (English
dramatist)
rat¦tily
rat¦ti¦ness
Rat¦tle, Simon
(English
conductor)
rat¦tle
rat¦tles
rat¦tled
rat¦tling
rattle¦box
rattle¦boxes
rat¦tler +s
rattle¦snake +s
rattle¦trap +s
rat¦tling +s
rat¦tly

ratty
rat¦tier
rat¦ti¦est
rau¦cous
rau¦cous¦ly
rau¦cous¦ness
raunch¦ily
raunchi¦ness
raunchy
raunch¦ier
raunchi¦est
rav¦age
rav¦ages
rav¦aged
rav¦aging
rav¦ager +s
rave
raves
raved
rav¦ing
Ravel, Maur¦ice
(French
composer)
ravel
ravels
rav¦elled *Br.*
rav¦eled *Am.*
rav¦el¦ling *Br.*
rav¦el¦ing *Am.*
rav¦elin +s
raven +s +ed +ing
Rav¦enna (city,
Italy)
rav¦en¦ous
rav¦en¦ous¦ly
rav¦en¦ous¦ness
raver +s
rave-up +s *noun*
Ravi (river, India
and Pakistan)
ravin +s
rav¦ine +s
rav¦ined
rav¦ing +s
rav¦ing¦ly
ravi¦oli
rav¦ish
rav¦ishes
rav¦ished
rav¦ish¦ing
rav¦ish¦er +s
rav¦ish¦ing¦ly
rav¦ish¦ment +s
raw
rawer
raw¦est
(uncooked etc.
△ **roar**)
Rawal¦pindi (city,
Pakistan)
raw-boned
raw¦hide +s

raw|ish
Rawl|plug +s
  Propr.
Rawls, John
  (American
  philosopher)
rawly
raw|ness
Raw|son (city,
  Argentina)
Ray, John (English
  naturalist)
Ray, Man
  (American
  painter)
Ray, Sat|ya|jit
  (Indian film
  director)
ray +s +ed +ing
  (beam of light etc.;
  fish; *Music*)
rayah +s
ray gun +s
Ray|leigh, Lord
  (English physicist;
  scattering)
ray|less
ray|let +s
Ray|mond
rayon +s
raze
  razes
  razed
  raz|ing
  (destroy; erase.
  △ raise)
razoo +s
razor +s +ed +ing
razor|back +s
razor|bill +s
razor blade +s
razor cut
  razor cuts
  razor cut
  razor cut|ting
razor edge +s
razor-edged
razor-fish
  plural razor-fish *or*
  razor-fishes
razor's edge
razor-sharp
razor-shell +s
razor wire
razz
  razzes
  razzed
  razz|ing
raz|za|ma|tazz
  (use razzmatazz)
raz|zia +s
raz|zle +s

razzle-dazzle +s
razz|ma|tazz
Re (*Egyptian
  Mythology*; use
  Ra)
re (concerning)
re (*Music*; use ray)
re|absorb +s +ed
  +ing
re|absorp|tion +s
re|accept +s +ed
  +ing
re|accept|ance +s
re|accus|tom +s
  +ed +ing
reach
  reaches
  reached
  reach|ing
reach|able
reach|er +s
reach-me-down
  +s
re|acquaint +s +ed
  +ing
re|acquaint|ance
  +s
re|acquire
  re|acquires
  re|acquired
  re|acquir|ing
re|acqui|si|tion +s
react +s +ed +ing
  (respond to)
re-act +s +ed +ing
  (act again)
react|ance +s
react|ant +s
re|ac|tion +s
re|ac|tion|ary
  re|ac|tion|ar|ies
re|ac|tion|ist +s
re|acti|vate
  re|acti|vates
  re|acti|vated
  re|acti|vat|ing
re|acti|va|tion +s
re|act|ive
re|activ|ity
re|act|or +s
read
  reads
  read
  read|ing
  (interpret writing.
  △ reed, red, rede,
  redd)
read|abil|ity
read|able
read|able|ness
read|ably

re|adapt +s +ed
  +ing
re|adap|ta|tion +s
re|address
  re|addresses
  re|addressed
  re|address|ing
Reade, Charles
  (English writer)
read|er +s
read|er|ship +s
read|ily
read-in +s *noun*
readi|ness
Read|ing (town,
  England)
read|ing +s
  (interpreting
  writing.
  △ reeding)
re|adjust +s +ed
  +ing
re|adjust|ment +s
re|admis|sion +s
re|admit
  re|admits
  re|admit|ted
  re|admit|ting
re|admit|tance
read-only
  mem|ory
  read-only
  mem|or|ies
re|adopt +s +ed
  +ing
re|adop|tion +s
read-out +s *noun*
re-advertise
  re-advertises
  re-advertised
  re-advertis|ing
re-advertise|ment
  +s
read-write *adjective*
ready
  read|ies
  read|ied
  ready|ing
  read|ier
  readi|est
  (prepared etc.
  △ reddy)
ready-made +s
ready-mix
  ready-mixes
ready-mixed
ready money
ready reck|on|er
  +s
ready-to-wear
re|affirm +s +ed
  +ing

re|affirm|ation +s
re|affor|est +s +ed
  +ing
re|affor|est|ation
  +s
Rea|gan, Ron|ald
  (American
  president)
re|agency
  re|agen|cies
re|agent +s
real (genuine.
  △ reel)
real +s (Brazilian
  and former
  Spanish currency)
re|algar
re|align +s +ed
  +ing
re|align|ment +s
real|is|abil|ity *Br.*
  (use realizability)
real|is|abil|ities
real|is|able *Br.* (use
  realizable)
real|isa|tion *Br.* +s
  (use realization)
real|ise *Br.* (use
  realize)
  real|ises
  real|ised
  real|is|ing
real|iser *Br.* +s (use
  realizer)
real|ism
real|ist +s
real|is|tic
real|is|tic|al|ly
real|ity
  real|ities
real|iz|abil|ity
  real|iz|abil|ities
real|iz|able
real|iza|tion +s
real|ize
  real|izes
  real|ized
  real|iz|ing
real|izer +s
real life
  real lives
  noun (not fiction,
  drama, etc.)
real-life *attributive*
  (not fictional)
real live *attributive*
  (not pretended or
  simulated)
re|allo|cate
  re|allo|cates
  re|allo|cated
  re|allo|cat|ing
re|allo|ca|tion +s

re|allot
  re|allots
  re|allot|ted
  re|allot|ting
re|allot|ment +s
real¦ly
realm +s
real|ness
Real|poli¦tik
real-time *attributive*
real|tor +s
realty
ream +s +ed +ing
ream¦er +s
re|ana¦lyse *Br.*
  re|ana¦lyses
  re|ana¦lysed
  re|ana¦lys¦ing
re|analy¦sis
re|ana¦lyze *Am.*
  re|ana¦lyzes
  re|ana¦lyzed
  re|ana¦lyz¦ing
re|ani¦mate
  re|ani¦mates
  re|ani¦mated
  re|ani¦mat¦ing
re|ani¦ma¦tion +s
reap +s +ed +ing
reap¦er +s
re|appear +s +ed
  +ing
re|appear|ance +s
re|appli|ca¦tion +s
re|apply
  re|applies
  re|applied
  re|apply|ing
re|appoint +s +ed
  +ing
re|appoint|ment
  +s
re|appor¦tion +s
  +ed +ing
re|appor¦tion|
    ment +s
re|appraisal +s
re|appraise
  re|appraises
  re|appraised
  re|apprais¦ing
rear +s +ed +ing
  (back; raise.
  △ rhea, ria)
rear ad|miral +s
rear-arch
  rear-arches
rear-end +s +ed
  +ing *verb*
rear¦er +s
rear-facing
rear|guard +s

rear lamp +s
rear light +s
rearm +s +ed +ing
re|arma¦ment +s
rear¦most
re|arrange
  re|arranges
  re|arranged
  re|arran¦ging
re|arrange|ment
  +s
re|arrest +s +ed
  +ing
rear-view mir¦ror
  +s
rear|ward +s
rear-wheel drive
re|ascend +s +ed
  +ing
re|ascen|sion +s
rea¦son +s +ed
  +ing
rea¦son|able
rea¦son|able|ness
rea¦son|ably
rea¦son¦er +s
rea¦son|ing +s
rea¦son|less
re|assem¦ble
  re|assem¦bles
  re|assem¦bled
  re|assem¦bling
re|assem¦bly
re|assert +s +ed
  +ing
re|asser¦tion +s
re|assess
  re|assesses
  re|assessed
  re|assess|ing
re|assess|ment +s
re|assign +s +ed
  +ing
re|assign|ment +s
re|assume
  re|assumes
  re|assumed
  re|assum¦ing
re|assump¦tion +s
re|assur¦ance +s
re|assure
  re|assures
  re|assured
  re|assur¦ing
re|assurer +s
re|assur¦ing¦ly
re|attach
  re|attaches
  re|attached
  re|attach|ing
re|attach|ment +s

re|attain +s +ed
  +ing
re|attain|ment +s
re|attempt +s +ed
  +ing
Ré|au|mur, René
  An|toine
  Fer|chault de
  (French naturalist;
  temperature scale)
reave
  reaves
  reft
  reav|ing
  (deprive of; carry
  off. △ reeve,
  reive)
re|awaken +s +ed
  +ing
re|badge
  re|badges
  re|badged
  re|badg¦ing
re|bal¦ance
  re|bal¦ances
  re|bal¦anced
  re|bal¦an¦cing
re|bap¦tise *Br.* (use
  rebaptize)
  re|bap¦tises
  re|bap¦tised
  re|bap¦tis¦ing
re|bap¦tize
  re|bap¦tizes
  re|bap¦tized
  re|bap¦tiz¦ing
re|bar¦ba|tive
re|base
  re|bases
  re|based
  re|bas¦ing
re|bat¦able
re|bate
  re|bates
  re|bated
  re|bat¦ing
re|bater +s
rebec +s
Re|becca (*Bible*;
  name)
re|beck +s (use
  rebec)
rebel +s *noun*
rebel
  re|bels
  re|belled
  re|bel|ling
  verb
re|bel¦lion +s
re|bel¦li|ous
re|bel¦li|ous¦ly
re|bel¦li|ous¦ness

rebid
  re|bids
  rebid
  re|bid|ding
re|bind
  re|binds
  re|bound
  re|bind|ing
re|birth +s +ed
  +ing
re|birth¦er +s
re|birth|ing +s
re|boot +s +ed
re|bore
  re|bores
  re|bored
  re|bor¦ing
re|born
re|bound +s +ed
  +ing
re|bound¦er +s
re|broad|cast
  re|broad|casts
  re|broad|cast *or*
  re|broad|cast¦ed
  re|broad|cast|ing
re|buff +s +ed
  +ing
re|build
  re|builds
  re|built
  re|build|ing
re|build¦er +s
re|build|ing +s
re|buke
  re|bukes
  re|buked
  re|buk|ing
re|buker +s
re|buk¦ing|ly
re|burial +s
re|bury
  re|buries
  re|buried
  re|bury|ing
rebus
  re|buses
rebut
  re|buts
  re|but|ted
  re|but|ting
re|but|ment +s
re|but|table
re|but|tal +s
re|but|ter +s
rec +s (= recreation
  ground. △ reck,
  wreck)
re|cal¦ci|trance
re|cal¦ci|trant +s
re|cal¦ci|trant¦ly

re|cal|cu|late
  re|cal|cu|lates
  re|cal|cu|lated
  re|cal|cu|lat|ing
re|cal|cu|la|tion +s
re|cal|esce
  re|cal|esces
  re|cal|esced
  re|cal|es|cing
re|cal|es|cence
re|call +s +ed +ing
re|call|able
re|cant +s +ed
  +ing
re|can|ta|tion +s
re|cant|er +s
recap
  re|caps
  re|capped
  re|cap|ping
re|cap|it|al|
  isa|tion *Br.* (use
  recapitalization)
re|cap|it|al|ise *Br.*
  (use recapitalize)
  re|cap|it|al|ises
  re|cap|it|al|ised
  re|cap|it|al|is|ing
re|cap|it|al|
       iza|tion
re|cap|it|al|ize
  re|cap|it|al|izes
  re|cap|it|al|ized
  re|cap|it|al|iz|ing
re|cap|itu|late
  re|cap|itu|lates
  re|cap|itu|lated
  re|cap|itu|lat|ing
re|cap|itu|la|tion
  +s
re|cap|itu|la|tive
re|cap|itu|la|tory
re|cap|ture
  re|cap|tures
  re|cap|tured
  re|cap|tur|ing
re|cast
  re|casts
  re|cast
  re|cast|ing
recce
  rec|ces
  rec|ced
  recce|ing
re|cede
  re|cedes
  re|ceded
  re|ced|ing
  (go or shrink
  back)
re-cede
  re-cedes

re-cede (*cont.*)
  re-ceded
  re-ceding
  (cede back)
re|ceipt +s +ed
  +ing
re|ceiv|able
re|ceive
  re|ceives
  re|ceived
  re|ceiv|ing
re|ceiver +s
re|ceiv|er|ship +s
re|ceiv|ing order
  +s
re|cency
re|cen|sion +s
re|cent
re|cent|ly
re|cent|ness
recep
  plural recep or
  receps
  (= reception
  room)
re|cep|tacle +s
re|cep|tion +s
re|cep|tion|ist +s
re|cep|tive
re|cep|tive|ly
re|cep|tive|ness
re|cep|tiv|ity
re|cep|tor +s
re|cess
  re|cesses
  re|cessed
  re|cess|ing
re|ces|sion +s
re|ces|sion|al
re|ces|sion|ary
re|ces|sive
re|ces|sive|ly
re|ces|sive|ness
Rech|ab|ite +s
re|charge
  re|charges
  re|charged
  re|char|ging
re|charge|able
re|char|ger +s
ré|*chauffé* +s
re|check +s +ed
  +ing
re|cher|ché
re|chris|ten +s +ed
  +ing
re|cid|iv|ism
re|cid|iv|ist +s
re|cid|iv|is|tic
Re|cife (port,
  Brazil)
re|cipe +s

re|cipi|ency
re|cipi|ent +s
re|cip|ro|cal +s
re|cip|ro|cal|ity
  re|cip|ro|cal|ities
re|cip|ro|cal|ly
re|cip|ro|cate
  re|cip|ro|cates
  re|cip|ro|cated
  re|cip|ro|cat|ing
re|cip|ro|ca|tion +s
re|cip|ro|ca|tor +s
reci|procity
  reci|proci|ties
re|cir|cu|late
  re|cir|cu|lates
  re|cir|cu|lated
  re|cir|cu|lat|ing
re|cir|cu|la|tion +s
re|cital +s
re|cital|ist +s
reci|ta|tion +s
reci|ta|tive +s
re|cite
  re|cites
  re|cited
  re|cit|ing
re|citer +s
reck +s +ed +ing
  (pay heed to.
  ⚠ rec, wreck)
reck|less
reck|less|ly
reck|less|ness
reckon +s +ed
  +ing
reck|on|er +s
reck|on|ing +s
re|claim +s +ed
  +ing
re|claim|able
re|claim|er +s
rec|lam|ation +s
re|clas|si|fi|ca|tion
  +s
re|clas|sify
  re|clas|si|fies
  re|clas|si|fied
  re|clas|si|fy|ing
re|clin|able
rec|lin|ate
re|cline
  re|clines
  re|clined
  re|clin|ing
re|cliner +s
re|clothe
  re|clothes
  re|clothed
  re|cloth|ing
re|cluse +s
re|clu|sion

re|clu|sive
re|clu|sive|ness
re|code
  re|codes
  re|coded
  re|cod|ing
rec|og|nis|abil|ity
  Br. (use
  recognizability)
rec|og|nis|able *Br.*
  (use
  recognizable)
rec|og|nis|ably *Br.*
  (use
  recognizably)
re|cog|ni|sance *Br.*
  +s (use
  recognizance)
re|cog|ni|sant *Br.*
  (use recognizant)
rec|og|nise *Br.* (use
  recognize)
  rec|og|nises
  rec|og|nised
  rec|og|nis|ing
rec|og|niser *Br.* +s
  (use recognizer)
rec|og|ni|tion +s
re|cog|ni|tory
rec|og|niz|abil|ity
rec|og|niz|able
rec|og|niz|ably
re|cog|ni|zance +s
re|cog|ni|zant
rec|og|nize
  rec|og|nizes
  rec|og|nized
  rec|og|niz|ing
rec|og|nizer +s
re|coil +s +ed +ing
re|coil|less
re|coin +s +ed
  +ing
rec|ol|lect +s +ed
  +ing (remember)
re-collect +s +ed
  +ing (collect
  again)
rec|ol|lec|tion +s
rec|ol|lect|ive
re|col|on|isa|tion
  Br. +s (use
  recolonization)
re|col|on|ise *Br.*
  (use recolonize)
  re|col|on|ises
  re|col|on|ised
  re|col|on|is|ing
re|col|on|iza|tion
  +s
re|col|on|ize
  re|col|on|izes

re|col|on|ize (*cont.*)
  re|col|on|ized
  re|col|on|iz|ing
re|color *Am.* +s
  +ed +ing
re|col|our *Br.* +s
  +ed +ing
re|com|bin|ant +s
re|com|bin|ation
  +s
re|com|bine
  re|com|bines
  re|com|bined
  re|com|bin|ing
re|com|mence
  re|com|mences
  re|com|menced
  re|com|men|cing
re|com|mence|
        ment +s
rec|om|mend +s
  +ed +ing
rec|om|mend|able
rec|om|
    men|da|tion +s
rec|om|
      men|da|tory
re|com|mend|er
  +s
re|com|mis|sion
  +s +ed +ing
re|com|mit
  re|com|mits
  re|com|mit|ted
  re|com|mit|ting
re|com|mit|ment
  +s
re|com|mit|tal +s
rec|om|pense
  rec|om|penses
  rec|om|pensed
  rec|om|pens|ing
re|com|pose
  re|com|poses
  re|com|posed
  re|com|pos|ing
recon (= reconnaiss-
  ance)
rec|on|cil|abil|ity
rec|on|cil|able
rec|on|cile
  rec|on|ciles
  rec|on|ciled
  rec|on|cil|ing
rec|on|cile|ment
  +s
rec|on|ciler +s
rec|on|cili|ation +s
rec|on|cili|atory
rec|on|dite
rec|on|dite|ly
rec|on|dite|ness

re|con|di|tion +s
  +ed +ing
re|con|di|tion|er
  +s
re|con|fig|ur|ation
  +s
re|con|fig|ure
  re|con|fig|ures
  re|con|fig|ured
  re|con|fig|ur|ing
re|con|firm +s +ed
  +ing
re|con|firm|ation
  +s
re|con|nais|sance
  +s
re|con|nect +s +ed
  +ing
re|con|nec|tion +s
rec|on|noiter *Am.*
  +s +ed +ing
rec|on|noitre *Br.*
  rec|on|noitres
  rec|on|noitred
  rec|on|noi|tring
re|con|quer +s +ed
  +ing
re|con|quest +s
re|con|se|crate
  re|con|se|crates
  re|con|se|crated
  re|con|se|crat|ing
re|con|se|cra|tion
re|con|sider +s
  +ed +ing
re|con|sid|er|ation
  +s
re|con|sign +s +ed
  +ing
re|con|sign|ment
  +s
re|con|soli|date
  re|con|soli|dates
  re|con|soli|dated
  re|con|soli|
        dat|ing
re|con|soli|da|tion
  +s
re|con|sti|tute
  re|con|sti|tutes
  re|con|sti|tuted
  re|con|sti|tut|ing
re|con|sti|tu|tion
  +s
re|con|struct +s
  +ed +ing
re|con|struct|able
re|con|struc|tion
  +s
re|con|struct|ive
re|con|struct|or +s

re|con|vene
  re|con|venes
  re|con|vened
  re|con|ven|ing
re|con|ver|sion +s
re|con|vert +s +ed
  +ing
re|cord +s +ed
  +ing
re|cord|able
record-breaking
re|cord|er +s
re|cord|er|ship +s
rec|ord hold|er +s
re|cord|ing +s
re|cord|ist +s
rec|ord play|er +s
re|count +s +ed
  +ing (narrate)
re-count +s +ed
  +ing (count again)
re|coup +s +ed
  +ing
re|coup|able
re|coup|ment +s
re|course +s
re|cover +s +ed
  +ing (reclaim; etc.)
re-cover +s +ed
  +ing (cover again)
re|cov|er|abil|ity
re|cov|er|
        abil|ities
re|cov|er|able
re|cov|er|er +s
re|cov|ery
  re|cov|er|ies
rec|re|ancy
rec|re|ant +s
rec|re|ant|ly
re|cre|ate
  re|cre|ates
  re|cre|ated
  re|cre|at|ing
  (create again)
rec|re|ate
  rec|re|ates
  rec|re|ated
  rec|re|at|ing
  (take recreation)
rec|re|ation +s
  (entertainment)
re-creation +s
  (creation of
  something again)
rec|re|ation|al
rec|re|ation|al|ly
rec|re|ation
  ground +s
rec|re|ative
re|crim|in|ate
  re|crim|in|ates

re|crim|in|ate
  (*cont.*)
  re|crim|in|ated
  re|crim|in|at|ing
re|crim|in|ation +s
re|crim|ina|tive
re|crim|in|atory
re|cross
  re|crosses
  re|crossed
  re|cross|ing
re|cru|desce
  re|cru|desces
  re|cru|desced
  re|cru|des|cing
re|cru|des|cence
  +s
re|cru|des|cent
re|cruit +s +ed
  +ing
re|cruit|able
re|cruit|al +s
re|cruit|er +s
re|cruit|ment +s
re|crys|tal|lisa|
  tion *Br.* +s (use
  recrystallization)
re|crys|tal|lise *Br.*
  (use recrystallize)
  re|crys|tal|lises
  re|crys|tal|lised
  re|crys|tal|lis|ing
re|crys|tal|liza|
        tion +s
re|crys|tal|lize
  re|crys|tal|lizes
  re|crys|tal|lized
  re|crys|tal|liz|ing
recta (plural of
  rectum △ rector)
rec|tal
rec|tal|ly
rect|angle +s
rect|angu|lar
rect|angu|lar|ity
rect|angu|lar|ly
recti
rec|ti|fi|able
rec|ti|fi|ca|tion +s
rec|ti|fier +s
rect|ify
  rec|ti|fies
  rec|ti|fied
  rec|ti|fy|ing
rec|ti|lin|eal
rec|ti|lin|ear
rec|ti|lin|ear|ity
rec|ti|lin|ear|ly
rec|ti|tude
recto +s
rec|tor +s (priest.
  △ recta)

rec|tor|ate +s
rec|tor|ial
rec|tor|ship +s
rec|tory
  rec|tor|ies
rec|trix
  rec|tri|ces
rec|tum
  rec|tums or recta
rec|tus
  recti
re|cum|bency
re|cum|bent
re|cum|bent|ly
re|cu|per|able
re|cu|per|ate
  re|cu|per|ates
  re|cu|per|ated
  re|cu|per|at|ing
re|cu|per|ation +s
re|cu|pera|tive
re|cu|per|ator +s
recur
  re|curs
  re|curred
  re|cur|ring
re|cur|rence +s
re|cur|rent
re|cur|rent|ly
re|cur|sion +s
re|cur|sive
re|cur|sive|ly
re|cur|vate
re|cur|vat|ure +s
re|curve
  re|curves
  re|curved
  re|curv|ing
recu|sance
recu|sancy
recu|sant +s
re|cyc|lable
re|cycle
  re|cycles
  re|cycled
  re|cyc|ling
re|cyc|ler +s
Red +s
  (Communist)
red
  reds
  red|der
  red|dest
  (colour. △ redd,
  read)
re|dact +s +ed
  +ing
re|dac|tion +s
re|dac|tion|al
re|dact|or +s
redan +s
red-back +s

red bark +s (tree)
red-blooded
red-blooded|ness
red|breast +s
red-brick *attributive*
red|bud +s
red|cap +s
red|coat +s
red|cur|rant +s
redd
  redds
  redd
  redd|ing
  (clear up; arrange.
  △ red, read)
red|den +s +ed
  +ing
red|dish
Red|ditch (town,
  England)
red|dle +s
reddy (reddish.
  △ ready)
rede
  redes
  reded
  red|ing
  (advise; advice.
  △ read, reed)
re|dec|or|ate
  re|dec|or|ates
  re|dec|or|ated
  re|dec|or|at|ing
re|dec|or|ation +s
re|dedi|cate
  re|dedi|cates
  re|dedi|cated
  re|dedi|cat|ing
re|dedi|ca|tion
re|deem +s +ed
  +ing
re|deem|able
re|deem|er +s
re|define
  re|defines
  re|defined
  re|defin|ing
re|def|in|ition +s
re|demp|tion +s
re|demp|tive
Re|demp|tor|ist +s
re|deploy +s +ed
  +ing
re|deploy|ment +s
re|des|cend +s +ed
  +ing
re|design +s +ed
  +ing
re|des|ig|nate
  re|des|ig|nates
  re|des|ig|nated
  re|des|ig|nat|ing

re|des|ig|na|tion
re|de|ter|min|ation
  +s
re|de|ter|mine
  re|de|ter|mines
  re|de|ter|mined
  re|de|ter|min|ing
re|develop +s +ed
  +ing
re|devel|oper +s
re|devel|op|ment
  +s
red-eye +s (fish;
  effect in
  photograph)
red-faced
red|fish
  plural red|fish *or*
  red|fishes
Red|ford, Rob|ert
  (American actor)
Red|grave,
  Mi|chael,
  Van|essa, Corin,
  and Lynn (family
  of English actors)
red-handed
red|head +s
red-headed
red-hot
re|dial
  re|dials
  re|dialled *Br.*
  re|dialed *Am.*
  re|dial|ling *Br.*
  re|dial|ing *Am.*
redid
re|dif|fu|sion +s
Red In|dian +s
  (*offensive*)
red|in|gote +s
red|in|te|grate
  red|in|te|grates
  red|in|te|grated
  red|in|te|grat|ing
red|in|te|gra|tion
  +s
red|in|te|gra|tive
re|dir|ect +s +ed
  +ing
re|dir|ec|tion
re|dis|cover +s
  +ed +ing
re|dis|cov|er|er +s
re|dis|cov|ery
  re|dis|cov|er|ies
re|dis|so|lu|tion +s
re|dis|solve
  re|dis|solves
  re|dis|solved
  re|dis|solv|ing

re|dis|trib|ute
  re|dis|trib|utes
  re|dis|trib|uted
  re|dis|trib|ut|ing
re|dis|tri|bu|tion
  +s
re|dis|tribu|tive
re|div|ide
  re|div|ides
  re|div|ided
  re|div|id|ing
re|div|ision +s
redi|vivus
red-letter day +s
red-light dis|trict
  +s
redly
Red|mond, John
  Ed|ward (Irish
  statesman)
red|neck +s
red|ness
redo
  re|does
  redid
  re|do|ing
  re|done
redo|lence
redo|lent
redo|lent|ly
Redon, Odi|lon
  (French painter)
re|double
  re|doubles
  re|doubled
  re|doub|ling
re|doubt +s
re|doubt|able
re|doubt|ably
re|dound +s +ed
  +ing
redox
red|poll +s
re|draft +s +ed
  +ing
re|draw
  re|draws
  re|drew
  re|draw|ing
  re|drawn
re|dress
  re|dresses
  re|dressed
  re|dress|ing
  (remedy; readjust)
re-dress
  re-dresses
  re-dressed
  re-dressing
  (dress again)
re|dress|able
re|dress|al +s

re|dress|er +s
re|dress|ment +s
red|shank +s
red shift +s
  Astronomy
red-shifted
red|skin +s
  (*offensive*)
red spi|der +s
  (mite)
red|start +s
re|duce
  re|duces
  re|duced
  re|du|cing
re|du|cer +s
re|du|ci|bil|ity
  re|du|ci|bil|ities
re|du|cible
re|du|cing agent
  +s
re|duc|tio ad
  ab|sur|dum
re|duc|tion +s
re|duc|tion|ism
re|duc|tion|ist +s
re|duc|tion|is|tic
re|duc|tive
re|dun|dance
re|dun|dancy
  re|dun|dan|cies
re|dun|dant
re|dun|dant|ly
re|dupli|cate
  re|du|pli|cates
  re|du|pli|cated
  re|du|pli|cat|ing
re|dupli|ca|tion +s
re|dupli|ca|tive
red|water
red|wing +s
red|wood +s
redye
  re|dyes
  re|dyed
  re|dye|ing
ree|bok +s
re-echo
  re-echoes
  re-echoed
  re-echoing
Reed, Carol
  (English film
  director)
Reed, Wal|ter
  (American
  physician)
reed +s +ed +ing
  (grass; thatch with
  reed. △ read,
  rede)
reed-bed +s

reed|buck +s
reed bunt|ing +s
reedi|ness
reed|ing +s
  (architectural
  moulding.
  △ reading)
re-edit +s +ed
  +ing
re-edition +s
reed|ling +s
reed mace
reed-organ +s
reed pipe +s
reed-stop +s
re-educate
  re-educates
  re-educated
  re-educat|ing
re-education
reed warb|ler +s
reedy
  reed|ier
  reedi|est
reef +s +ed +ing
reef|er +s
reefing-jacket +s
reef knot +s
reef|point +s
reek +s +ed +ing
  (smell. △ wreak)
reeky
  reek|ier
  reeki|est
reel +s +ed +ing
  (winding device;
  dance; wind in,
  up, etc.; stagger.
  △ real)
re-elect +s +ed
  +ing
re-election +s
reel|er +s
re-eligible
re-embark +s +ed
  +ing
re-embark|ation
  +s
re-emerge
  re-emerges
  re-emerged
  re-emerging
re-emergence +s
re-emergent
re-emphasis
  re-emphases
re-emphasise *Br.*
  (use re-
  emphasize)
  re-emphasises
  re-emphasised
  re-emphasis|ing

re-emphasize
  re-emphasizes
  re-emphasized
  re-emphasiz|ing
re-employ +s +ed
  +ing
re-employ|ment
re-enact +s +ed
  +ing
re-enactment +s
re-enforce
  re-enforces
  re-enforced
  re-enforcing
  (enforce again.
  △ reinforce)
re-enforce|ment
  (act of re-enforcing.
  △ reinforcement)
re-engineer +s
  +ed +ing
re-enlist +s +ed
  +ing
re-enlist|er +s
re-enter +s +ed
  +ing
re-entrance +s
re-entrant +s
re-entry
  re-entries
re-equip
  re-equips
  re-equipped
  re-equipping
re-erect +s +ed
  +ing
re-erection
re-establish
  re-establishes
  re-established
  re-establish|ing
re-establish|ment
re-evaluate
  re-evaluates
  re-evaluated
  re-evaluat|ing
re-evaluation +s
reeve
  reeves
  rove *or* reeved
  reev|ing
  (magistrate; bird;
  to thread.
  △ reave, reive)
re-examin|ation
  +s
re-examine
  re-examines
  re-examined
  re-examin|ing
re-export +s +ed
  +ing

re-export|ation +s
re-export|er +s
ref
  refs
  reffed
  ref|fing
  (= referee)
re|face
  re|faces
  re|faced
  re|fa|cing
re|fash|ion +s +ed
  +ing
re|fec|tion +s
re|fec|tory
  re|fec|tor|ies
refer
  re|fers
  re|ferred
  re|fer|ring
re|fer|able
ref|er|ee
  ref|er|ees
  ref|er|eed
  ref|er|ee|ing
ref|er|ence
  ref|er|ences
  ref|er|enced
  ref|er|en|cing
ref|er|en|dum
  ref|er|en|dums *or*
  ref|er|enda
ref|er|ent +s
ref|er|en|tial
ref|er|en|ti|al|ity
ref|er|en|tial|ly
re|fer|ral +s
re|fer|rer +s
re|fill +s +ed +ing
re|fill|able
re|fin|able
re|fi|nance
  re|fi|nances
  re|fi|nanced
  re|fi|nan|cing
re|fine
  re|fines
  re|fined
  re|fin|ing
re|fine|ment +s
re|finer +s
re|finery
  re|finer|ies
re|fin|ish
  re|fin|ishes
  re|fin|ished
  re|fin|ish|ing
refit
  re|fits
  re|fit|ted
  re|fit|ting
re|fit|ment +s

re|flag
re|flags
re|flagged
re|flag|ging
re|flate
re|flates
re|flated
re|flat|ing
re|fla|tion +s
re|fla|tion|ary
re|flect +s +ed
+ing
re|flect|ance +s
re|flec|tion +s
re|flec|tion|al
re|flect|ive
re|flect|ive|ly
re|flect|ive|ness
re|flect|iv|ity
re|flect|iv|ities
re|flect|or +s
re|flet +s
re|flex
re|flexes
re|flexed
re|flex|ibil|ity
re|flex|ible
re|flex|ion +s (use
reflection)
re|flex|ive
re|flex|ive|ly
re|flex|ive|ness
re|flex|iv|ity
re|flex|ly
re|flex|olo|gist +s
re|flex|ology
re|float +s +ed
+ing
ref|lu|ence +s
ref|lu|ent
re|flux
re|fluxes
re|focus
re|focuses or
re|focus|ses
re|focused or
re|focussed
re|focus|ing or
re|focus|sing
re|fold +s +ed
+ing
re|for|est +s +ed
+ing
re|for|est|ation
re|forge
re|forges
re|forged
re|for|ging
re|form +s +ed
+ing (correct,
improve)

re-form +s +ed
+ing (form again)
re|form|able
re|format
re|formats
re|format|ted
re|format|ting
ref|or|ma|tion +s
re-formation +s
(act or process of
forming again)
re|forma|tive
re|forma|tory
re|forma|tor|ies
re|form|er +s
re|form|ism
re|form|ist +s
re|for|mu|late
re|for|mu|lates
re|for|mu|lated
re|for|mu|lat|ing
re|for|mu|la|tion
+s
re|fract +s +ed
+ing
re|frac|tion +s
re|fract|ive
re|fract|om|eter +s
re|fracto|met|ric
re|fract|om|etry
re|frac|tor +s
re|frac|tor|ily
re|frac|tori|ness
re|frac|tory
re|fract|or|ies
re|frain +s +ed
+ing
re|frain|ment +s
re|fran|gi|bil|ity
re|fran|gible
re|freeze
re|freezes
re|froze
re|freez|ing
re|frozen
re|fresh
re|freshes
re|freshed
re|fresh|ing
re|fresh|er +s
re|fresh|er course
+s
re|fresh|ing|ly
re|fresh|ment +s
re|friger|ant +s
re|friger|ate
re|friger|ates
re|friger|ated
re|friger|at|ing
re|friger|ation
re|frigera|tive
re|frigera|tor +s

re|frigera|tory
re|fri|gera|tor|ies
re|frin|gent
re|froze
re|frozen
reft
re|fuel
re|fuels
re|fuelled *Br.*
re|fueled *Am.*
re|fuel|ling *Br.*
re|fuel|ing *Am.*
ref|uge +s
refu|gee +s
re|fu|gium
re|fu|gia
re|ful|gence
re|ful|gent
re|ful|gent|ly
re|fund +s +ed
+ing (pay back)
re-fund +s +ed
+ing (fund again)
re|fund|able
re|fund|er +s
re|fund|ment +s
re|fur|bish
re|fur|bishes
re|fur|bished
re|fur|bish|ing
re|fur|bish|ment
+s
re|furn|ish
re|furn|ishes
re|furn|ished
re|furn|ish|ing
re|fus|able
re|fusal +s
re|fuse
re|fuses
re|fused
re|fus|ing
(withhold consent
etc.)
ref|use (rubbish)
re-fuse
re-fuses
re-fused
re-fusing
(fuse again)
re|fuse|nik +s
re|fuser +s
re|fut|able
re|futal +s
refu|ta|tion +s
re|fute
re|futes
re|futed
re|fut|ing
re|futer +s
Reg (name)

reg +s
(= registration
mark or
regulation)
re|gain +s +ed
+ing
regal
re|gale
re|gales
re|galed
re|gal|ing
re|gale|ment +s
re|galia
re|gal|ism
re|gal|ity
re|gal|ities
re|gal|ly
re|gard +s +ed
+ing
re|gard|ant
Heraldry
re|gard|ful
re|gard|less
re|gard|less|ly
re|gard|less|ness
re|gather +s +ed
+ing
re|gatta +s
re|gel|ate
re|gel|ates
re|gel|ated
re|gel|at|ing
re|gel|ation +s
re|gency
re|gen|cies
re|gen|er|ate
re|gen|er|ates
re|gen|er|ated
re|gen|er|at|ing
re|gen|er|ation +s
re|gen|era|tive
re|gen|era|tive|ly
re|gen|er|ator +s
re|gen|esis
re|gen|eses
re|gent +s
regent-bird +s
re|ger|min|ate
re|ger|min|ates
re|ger|min|ated
re|ger|min|at|ing
re|ger|min|ation
+s
reg|gae +s
Reg|gio di
Ca|lab|ria (port,
Italy)
regi|cidal
regi|cide +s
re|gild +s +ed +ing
re|gime +s
regi|men +s

regi|ment +s +ed
+ing
regi|men|tal +s
regi|men|tal|ly
regi|men|ta|tion
Re|gina (city,
Canada; name)
Re|gina (queen)
Regi|nald
Regio|mon|ta|nus,
Jo|han|nes
(German
astronomer and
mathematician)
re|gion +s
re|gion|al +s
re|gion|ali|sa|tion
Br. (use
regionalization)
re|gion|al|ise Br.
(use regionalize)
re|gion|al|ises
re|gion|al|ised
re|gion|al|is|ing
re|gion|al|ism +s
re|gion|al|ist +s
re|gion|ali|za|tion
re|gion|al|ize
re|gion|al|izes
re|gion|al|ized
re|gion|al|iz|ing
re|gion|al|ly
regis|seur +s
regis|ter +s +ed
+ing
regis|trable
regis|trar +s
Regis|trar
Gen|eral +s
regis|trar|ship +s
regis|trary
regis|trar|ies
regis|tra|tion +s
regis|tra|tion
mark +s
regis|try
regis|tries
Re|gius (professor)
re|glaze
re|glazes
re|glazed
re|glaz|ing
reg|let +s
reg|nal
reg|nant
rego +s
rego|lith +s
re|gorge
re|gorges
re|gorged
re|gor|ging

re|grade
re|grades
re|graded
re|grad|ing
re|grate
re|grates
re|grated
re|grat|ing
re|green +s +ed
+ing
re|gress
re|gresses
re|gressed
re|gress|ing
re|gres|sion +s
re|gres|sive
re|gres|sive|ly
re|gres|sive|ness
re|gret
re|grets
re|gret|ted
re|gret|ting
re|gret|ful
re|gret|ful|ly
re|gret|ful|ness
re|gret|table
re|gret|tably
re|group +s +ed
+ing
re|group|ment +s
re|grow
re|grows
re|grew
re|grow|ing
re|grown
re|growth +s
regu|lable
regu|lar +s
regu|lari|sa|tion
Br. (use
regularization)
regu|lar|ise Br. (use
regularize)
regu|lar|ises
regu|lar|ised
regu|lar|is|ing
re|gu|lar|ity
re|gu|lar|ities
regu|lari|za|tion
regu|lar|ize
regu|lar|izes
regu|lar|ized
regu|lar|iz|ing
regu|lar|ly
regu|late
regu|lates
regu|lated
regu|lat|ing
regu|la|tion +s
regu|la|tive
regu|la|tor +s
regu|la|tory

regu|line
reg|ulo +s
Regu|lus (star)
regu|lus
regu|luses or
reg|uli
(metallic
substance)
re|gur|gi|tate
re|gur|gi|tates
re|gur|gi|tated
re|gur|gi|tat|ing
re|gur|gi|ta|tion +s
rehab
(= rehabilitation)
re|habili|tate
re|habili|tates
re|habili|tated
re|habili|tat|ing
re|habili|ta|tion +s
re|habili|ta|tive
re|han|dle
re|han|dles
re|han|dled
re|hand|ling
re|hang
re|hangs
re|hung
re|hang|ing
re|hash
re|hashes
re|hashed
re|hash|ing
re|hear
re|hears
re|heard
re|hear|ing
re|hearsal +s
re|hearse
re|hearses
re|hearsed
re|hears|ing
re|hearser +s
re|heat +s +ed
+ing
re|heat|er +s
re|heel +s +ed
+ing
Re|ho|boam (king
of Israel)
re|ho|boam +s
(wine bottle)
re|home
re|homes
re|homed
re|hom|ing
re|house
re|houses
re|housed
re|hous|ing
re|hung
re|hy|drat|able

re|hy|drate
re|hy|drates
re|hy|drated
re|hy|drat|ing
re|hy|dra|tion
Reich +s (German
state)
Reich, Steve
(American
composer)
Reichs|tag
(German
parliament)
re|ifi|ca|tion +s
re|ifi|ca|tory
reify
re|ifies
re|ified
re|ify|ing
Rei|gate (town,
England)
reign +s +ed +ing
(rule. △ rain, rein)
re|ignite
re|ignites
re|ignited
re|ignit|ing
Reilly (in 'the life of
Reilly'; use Riley)
re|im|burs|able
re|im|burse
re|im|burses
re|im|bursed
re|im|burs|ing
re|im|burse|ment
+s
re|im|burser +s
re|im|port +s +ed
+ing
re|im|port|ation
re|im|pose
re|im|poses
re|im|posed
re|im|pos|ing
re|im|pos|ition
Reims (city,
France)
rein +s +ed +ing
(control-strap;
restrain. △ rain,
reign)
re|incar|nate
re|incar|nates
re|incar|nated
re|incar|nat|ing
re|incar|na|tion +s
re|incor|por|ate
re|incor|por|ates
re|incor|por|ated
re|incor|por|
at|ing
re|incor|por|ation

rein|deer
   plural rein|deer *or*
   rein|deers
re|in|dus|trial|
   isa|tion *Br.* (use
   reindustrializa-
   tion)
re|in|dus|trial|ise
   Br. (use
   reindustrialize)
re|in|dus|trial|ises
re|in|dus|trial|
       ised
re|in|dus|trial|
       is|ing
re|in|dus|trial|
       iza|tion
re|in|dus|trial|ize
re|in|dus|trial|
       izes
re|in|dus|trial|
       ized
re|in|dus|trial|
       iz|ing
re|infect +s +ed
   +ing
re|infec|tion +s
re|inforce
   re|inforces
   re|inforced
   re|infor|cing
   (strengthen. △re-
   enforce)
re|inforce|ment +s
   (act of reinforcing;
   troops. △re-
   enforcement)
re|infor|cer +s
Rein|hardt,
   Django (Belgian
   jazz guitarist)
Rein|hardt, Max
   (Austrian theatre
   director)
re|inject +s +ed
   +ing
rein|less
re|insert +s +ed
   +ing
re|inser|tion +s
re|inspect +s +ed
   +ing
re|inspec|tion +s
re|instal (use
   reinstall)
   re|instals
   re|installed
   re|instal|ling
re|install +s +ed
   +ing
re|instate
   re|instates

re|instate (*cont.*)
   re|instated
   re|instat|ing
re|instate|ment +s
re|insti|tute
   re|insti|tutes
   re|insti|tuted
   re|insti|tut|ing
re|insti|tu|tion
re|insur|ance
re|insure
   re|insures
   re|insured
   re|insur|ing
re|insurer +s
re|inte|grate
   re|inte|grates
   re|inte|grated
   re|inte|grat|ing
re|inte|gra|tion
re|inter
   re|inters
   re|interred
   re|inter|ring
re|inter|ment +s
re|inter|pret +s
   +ed +ing
re|inter|pret|ation
   +s
re|intro|duce
   re|intro|duces
   re|intro|duced
   re|intro|du|cing
re|intro|duc|tion
   +s
re|invent +s +ed
   +ing
re|inven|tion
re|invest +s +ed
   +ing
re|inves|ti|gate
   re|inves|ti|gates
   re|inves|ti|gated
   re|inves|ti|gat|ing
re|inves|ti|ga|tion
   +s
re|invest|ment +s
re|invig|or|ate
   re|invig|or|ates
   re|invig|or|ated
   re|invig|or|at|ing
re|invig|or|ation
re|issue
   re|issues
   re|issued
   re|issu|ing
re|iter|ate
   re|iter|ates
   re|iter|ated
   re|iter|at|ing
re|iter|ation +s
re|itera|tive

Reith, John
   (director-general
   of the BBC)
reive
   reives
   reived
   reiv|ing
   (go plundering.
   △reave, reeve)
reiver +s
re|ject +s +ed +ing
re|ject|able
re|jec|ta|menta
re|ject|er +s
   (person who
   rejects.
   △rejector)
re|jec|tion +s
re|jec|tion|ist +s
re|ject|ive
re|ject|or +s
   (electronic circuit.
   △rejecter)
rejig
   re|jigs
   re|jigged
   re|jig|ging
re|joice
   re|joices
   re|joiced
   re|joi|cing
re|joi|cer +s
re|joi|cing +s
re|joi|cing|ly
re|join +s +ed +ing
re|join|der +s
re|ju|ven|ate
   re|ju|ven|ates
   re|ju|ven|ated
   re|ju|ven|at|ing
re|ju|ven|ation
re|ju|ven|ator +s
re|ju|ven|esce
   re|ju|ven|esces
   re|ju|ven|esced
   re|ju|ven|es|cing
re|ju|ven|es|cence
re|ju|ven|es|cent
rekey +s +ed +ing
re|kin|dle
   re|kin|dles
   re|kin|dled
   re|kind|ling
re|label
   re|labelled *Br.*
   re|labeled *Am.*
   re|label|ling *Br.*
   re|label|ing *Am.*
re|laid (past tense
   and past participle
   of relay.
   △relayed)

re|lapse
   re|lapses
   re|lapsed
   re|laps|ing
re|lapser +s
re|lat|able
re|late
   re|lates
   re|lated
   re|lat|ing
re|lated|ness
re|later +s (person
   who relates
   something.
   △relator)
re|la|tion +s
re|la|tion|al
re|la|tion|al|ly
re|la|tion|ism
re|la|tion|ist +s
re|la|tion|ship +s
rela|tival
rela|tive +s
rela|tive|ly
rela|tive|ness
rela|tiv|isa|tion *Br.*
   (use
   relativization)
rela|tiv|ise *Br.* (use
   relativize)
   rela|tiv|ises
   rela|tiv|ised
   rela|tiv|is|ing
rela|tiv|ism
rela|tiv|ist +s
rela|tiv|is|tic
rela|tiv|is|tic|al|ly
rela|tiv|ity
rela|tiv|ities
rela|tiv|iza|tion
rela|tiv|ize
   rela|tiv|izes
   rela|tiv|ized
   rela|tiv|iz|ing
re|la|tor +s (*Law.*
   △relater)
re|launch
   re|launches
   re|launched
   re|launch|ing
relax
   re|laxes
   re|laxed
   re|lax|ing
re|lax|ant +s
re|lax|ation +s
re|lax|ed|ly
re|lax|ed|ness
re|lax|er +s
relay +s +ed +ing
   (pass on)

relay
re|lays
re|laid
re|lay|ing
(lay again)
re|learn +s +ed
+ing
re|leas|able
re|lease
re|leases
re|leased
re|leas|ing
re|leasee +s
re|leaser +s
(person who
releases
something)
re|leasor +s Law
rele|gable
rele|gate
rele|gates
rele|gated
rele|gat|ing
rele|ga|tion +s
re|lent +s +ed +ing
re|lent|less
re|lent|less|ly
re|lent|less|ness
relet
re|lets
relet
re|let|ting
rele|vance
rele|vancy
rele|van|cies
rele|vant
rele|vant|ly
re|li|abil|ity
re|li|able
re|li|able|ness
re|li|ably
re|li|ance
re|li|ant
relic +s
rel|ict +s
re|lief +s
re|liev|able
re|lieve
re|lieves
re|lieved
re|liev|ing
re|lieved|ly
re|liever +s
re|lievo +s
re|light +s +ed
+ing
re|li|gion +s
re|li|gion|er +s
re|li|gion|ism
re|li|gion|ist +s
re|li|gion|less
religio-political

re|ligi|ose
re|ligi|os|ity
re|li|gious
re|li|gious|ly
re|li|gious|ness
re|line
re|lines
re|lined
re|lin|ing
re|lin|quish
re|lin|quishes
re|lin|quished
re|lin|quish|ing
re|lin|quish|ment
+s
reli|quary
reli|quar|ies
re|liquiae
rel|ish
rel|ishes
rel|ished
rel|ish|ing
rel|ish|able
re|live
re|lives
re|lived
re|liv|ing
re|load +s +ed
+ing
re|locate
re|locates
re|located
re|locat|ing
re|loca|tion +s
re|lucent
re|luc|tance
re|luc|tant
re|luc|tant|ly
rely
re|lies
re|lied
rely|ing
REM (= rapid eye-
movement)
rem
plural rem or rems
(unit of radiation)
re|made
re|main +s +ed
+ing
re|main|der +s
+ed +ing
re|mains
re|make
re|makes
re|made
re|mak|ing
reman
re|mans
re|manned
re|man|ning

re|mand +s +ed
+ing
rem|an|ence +s
rem|an|ent
(remaining,
residual.
△ remnant)
re|mark +s +ed
+ing
re|mark|able
re|mark|able|ness
re|mark|ably
re|mar|riage +s
re|marry
re|mar|ries
re|mar|ried
re|marry|ing
re|mas|ter +s +ed
+ing
re|match
re|matches
Rem|brandt
(Har|mensz van
Rijn) (Dutch
painter)
REME (= Royal
Electrical and
Mechanical
Engineers)
re|meas|ure
re|meas|ures
re|meas|ured
re|meas|ur|ing
re|meas|ure|ment
+s
re|medi|able
re|med|ial
re|medi|al|ly
rem|edy
rem|ed|ies
rem|ed|ied
rem|edy|ing
re|mem|ber +s
+ed +ing
re|mem|ber|able
re|mem|ber|er +s
re|mem|brance +s
re|mem|bran|cer
+s
remex
remi|ges
re|mind +s +ed
+ing
re|mind|er +s
re|mind|ful
rem|in|isce
rem|in|isces
rem|in|isced
rem|in|is|cing
rem|in|is|cence +s
rem|in|is|cent
rem|in|is|cen|tial

rem|in|is|cent|ly
rem|in|is|cer +s
re|mint +s +ed
+ing
re|mise
re|mises
re|mised
re|mis|ing
re|miss
re|mis|sible
re|mis|sion +s
re|mis|sive
re|miss|ly
re|miss|ness
remit
re|mits
re|mit|ted
re|mit|ting
re|mit|table
re|mit|tal +s
re|mit|tance +s
re|mit|tee +s
re|mit|tent
re|mit|ter +s
remix
re|mixes
re|mixed
re|mix|ing
re|mix|er +s
rem|nant +s (small
remaining
quantity.
△ remanent)
re|model
re|models
re|mod|elled Br.
re|mod|eled Am.
re|mod|el|ling Br.
re|mod|el|ing Am.
re|modi|fi|ca|tion
+s
re|mod|ify
re|modi|fies
re|modi|fied
re|modi|fy|ing
re|mold Am. +s
+ed +ing (Br.
remould)
re|mon|et|isa|tion
Br. (use
remonetization)
re|mon|et|ise Br.
(use remonetize)
re|mon|et|ises
re|mon|et|ised
re|mon|et|is|ing
re|mon|et|iza|tion
re|mon|et|ize
re|mon|et|izes
re|mon|et|ized
re|mon|et|iz|ing
rem|on|strance +s

Re|mon|strant +s
(Dutch protestant)

re|mon|strant
(remonstrating)

rem|on|strate
rem|on|strates
rem|on|strated
rem|on|strat|ing

rem|on|stra|tion
+s

rem|on|stra|tive

rem|on|stra|tor +s

re|mon|tant +s

rem|ora +s

re|morse

re|morse|ful

re|morse|ful|ly

re|morse|less

re|morse|less|ly

re|morse|less|ness

re|mort|gage
re|mort|gages
re|mort|gaged
re|mort|ga|ging

re|mote
re|moter
re|mot|est

re|mote con|trol

remote-controlled

re|mote|ly

re|mote|ness

re|mould *Br.* +s
+ed +ing (*Am.*
remold)

re|mount +s +ed
+ing

re|mov|abil|ity

re|mov|able

re|moval +s

re|move
re|moves
re|moved
re|mov|ing

re|move|able (use
removable)

re|mover +s

re|mu|ner|ate
re|mu|ner|ates
re|mu|ner|ated
re|mu|ner|at|ing

re|mu|ner|ation +s

re|mu|nera|tive

re|mu|nera|tory

Remus *Roman
Mythology*

re|nais|sance

renal

re|name
re|names
re|named
re|nam|ing

Re|namo (guerilla
movement,
Mozambique)

Renan, Er|nest
(French historian)

re|nas|cence

re|nas|cent

re|nation|al|
isa|tion *Br.* (use
renationaliza-
tion)

re|nation|al|ise *Br.*
(use
renationalize)
re|nation|al|ises
re|nation|al|ised
re|nation|al|is|ing

re|nation|al|
iza|tion

re|nation|al|ize
re|nation|al|izes
re|nation|al|ized
re|nation|al|iz|ing

Ren|ault, Louis
(French car
maker)

Ren|ault, Mary
(British novelist)

ren|contre +s

ren|coun|ter +s
+ed +ing

rend
rends
rent
rend|ing

Ren|dell, Ruth
(English writer)

ren|der +s +ed
+ing

ren|der|er +s

ren|der|ing +s

render-set
render-sets
render-set
render-setting

ren|dez|vous
ren|dez|vouses
ren|dez|voused
ren|dez|vous|ing

ren|di|tion +s

ren|dzina

Renée

rene|gade
rene|gades
rene|gaded
rene|gad|ing

rene|gado
rene|gadoes

re|nege
re|neges
re|neged
re|neg|ing

re|neg|er +s

re|nego|ti|able

re|nego|ti|ate
re|nego|ti|ates
re|nego|ti|ated
re|nego|ti|at|ing

re|nego|ti|ation +s

re|negue (use
renege)
re|negues
re|negued
re|neguing

re|neguer +s (use
reneger)

renew +s +ed +ing

re|new|abil|ity

re|new|able +s

re|newal +s

re|new|er +s

Ren|frew|shire
(former county,
Scotland)

reni|form

reni|tence

reni|tency

reni|tent

Rennes (city,
France)

ren|net +s

Ren|nie, John
(Scottish civil
engineer)

ren|nin +s

Reno (city, USA)

Ren|oir, Jean
(French film
director)

**Ren|oir, Pierre
Au|guste** (French
painter)

re|nomin|ate
re|nomin|ates
re|nomin|ated
re|nomin|at|ing

re|nomin|ation +s

re|nounce
re|nounces
re|nounced
re|noun|cing

re|nounce|able

re|nounce|ment +s

re|noun|cer +s

reno|vate
reno|vates
reno|vated
reno|vat|ing

reno|va|tion +s

reno|va|tive

reno|va|tor +s

re|nown

re|nowned

rent +s +ed +ing

rent|abil|ity

rent|able

ren|tal +s

rent boy +s

rent|er +s

rent-free

ren|tier +s

rent roll +s

re|num|ber +s +ed
+ing

re|nun|ci|ant +s

re|nun|ci|ation +s

re|nun|cia|tive

re|nun|ci|atory

ren|voi +s

re|occu|pa|tion

re|occupy
re|occu|pies
re|occu|pied
re|occu|py|ing

re|occur
re|occurs
re|occurred
re|occur|ring

re|occur|rence +s

re|offend +s +ed
+ing

re|open +s +ed
+ing

re|open|ing +s

re|order +s +ed
+ing

re|organ|isa|tion
Br. +s (use
reorganization)

re|organ|ise *Br.*
(use reorganize)
re|organ|ises
re|organ|ised
re|organ|is|ing

re|organ|iser *Br.*
+s (use
reorganizer)

re|organ|iza|tion
+s

re|organ|ize
re|organ|izes
re|organ|ized
re|organ|iz|ing

re|organ|izer +s

re|ori|ent +s +ed
+ing

re|orien|tate
re|orien|tates
re|orien|tated
re|orien|tat|ing

re|orien|ta|tion +s

rep
reps
repped
rep|ping

re¦pack+s +ed
  +ing
re¦pack¦age
  re¦pack¦ages
  re¦pack¦aged
  re¦pack¦aging
re¦pagin¦ate
  re¦pagin¦ates
  re¦pagin¦ated
  re¦pagin¦at¦ing
re¦pagin¦ation+s
re¦paid
re¦paint+s +ed
  +ing
re¦pair+s +ed
  +ing
re¦pair¦able
  (capable of being
  repaired.
  △ reparable)
re¦pair¦er+s
re¦pair¦man
  re¦pair¦men
re¦pand
re¦paper+s +ed
  +ing
rep¦ar¦abil¦ity
rep¦ar¦able (of a
  loss etc., that can
  be made good.
  △ repairable)
rep¦ar¦ably
rep¦ar¦ation+s
rep¦ara¦tive
rep¦ar¦tee+s
re¦par¦ti¦tion+s
  +ed +ing
re¦pass
  re¦passes
  re¦passed
  re¦pass¦ing
re¦past+s
repat+s
  (= repatriate)
re¦pat¦ri¦ate
  re¦pat¦ri¦ates
  re¦pat¦ri¦ated
  re¦pat¦ri¦at¦ing
re¦pat¦ri¦ation+s
repay
  re¦pays
  re¦paid
  re¦pay¦ing
re¦pay¦able
re¦pay¦ment+s
re¦peal+s +ed
  +ing
re¦peal¦able
re¦peat+s +ed
  +ing
re¦peat¦abil¦ity
re¦peat¦able

re¦peat¦ed¦ly
re¦peat¦er+s
re¦pêch¦age+s
repel
  re¦pels
  re¦pelled
  re¦pel¦ling
re¦pel¦lence
re¦pel¦lency
re¦pel¦lent+s
re¦pel¦lent¦ly
re¦pel¦ler+s
re¦pent+s +ed
  +ing
re¦pent¦ance
re¦pent¦ant
re¦pent¦er+s
re¦people
  re¦peoples
  re¦peopled
  re¦peop¦ling
re¦per¦cus¦sion+s
re¦per¦cus¦sive
rep¦er¦toire+s
rep¦er¦tory
  rep¦er¦tor¦ies
rep¦er¦tory
  com¦pany
  rep¦er¦tory
  com¦panies
rep¦et¦end+s
ré¦péti¦teur+s
repe¦ti¦tion+s
repe¦ti¦tion¦al
repe¦ti¦tion¦ary
repe¦ti¦tious
repe¦ti¦tious¦ly
repe¦ti¦tious¦ness
re¦peti¦tive
re¦peti¦tive¦ly
re¦peti¦tive¦ness
re¦phrase
  re¦phrases
  re¦phrased
  re¦phras¦ing
re¦pine
  re¦pines
  re¦pined
  re¦pin¦ing
re¦pique
  re¦piques
  re¦piqued
  re¦piquing
re¦place
  re¦places
  re¦placed
  re¦placing
re¦place¦able
re¦place¦ment+s
re¦placer+s
re¦plan
  re¦plans

re¦plan (cont.)
  re¦planned
  re¦plan¦ning
re¦plant+s +ed
  +ing
re¦play+s +ed
  +ing
re¦plen¦ish
  re¦plen¦ishes
  re¦plen¦ished
  re¦plen¦ish¦ing
re¦plen¦ish¦er+s
re¦plen¦ish¦ment
  +s
re¦plete
re¦plete¦ness
re¦ple¦tion+s
re¦plevin+s
re¦plevy
  re¦plev¦ies
  re¦plev¦ied
  re¦plevy¦ing
rep¦lica+s
rep¦lic¦abil¦ity
rep¦lic¦able
rep¦li¦cate
  rep¦li¦cates
  rep¦li¦cated
  rep¦li¦cat¦ing
rep¦li¦ca¦tion+s
rep¦li¦ca¦tive
rep¦li¦ca¦tor+s
re¦plier+s
reply
  re¦plies
  re¦plied
  re¦ply¦ing
reply-paid
repo+s
re¦point+s +ed
  +ing
re¦pol¦ish
  re¦pol¦ishes
  re¦pol¦ished
  re¦pol¦ish¦ing
re¦popu¦late
  re¦popu¦lates
  re¦popu¦lated
  re¦popu¦lat¦ing
re¦popu¦la¦tion
re¦port+s +ed
  +ing
re¦port¦able
rep¦or¦tage+s
re¦port¦ed¦ly
re¦port¦er+s
rep¦or¦tor¦ial
re¦por¦tori¦al¦ly
re¦posal+s
re¦pose
  re¦poses

re¦pose (cont.)
  re¦posed
  re¦pos¦ing
re¦pose¦ful
re¦pose¦ful¦ly
re¦pose¦ful¦ness
re¦pos¦ition+s +ed
  +ing
re¦posi¦tory
  re¦posi¦tor¦ies
re¦pos¦sess
  re¦pos¦sesses
  re¦pos¦sessed
  re¦pos¦sess¦ing
re¦pos¦ses¦sion+s
re¦pos¦ses¦sor+s
repot
  re¦pots
  re¦pot¦ted
  re¦pot¦ting
re¦poussé+s
repp (use rep)
rep¦re¦hend+s
  +ed +ing
rep¦re¦hen¦si¦
          bil¦ity
rep¦re¦hen¦sible
rep¦re¦hen¦sibly
rep¦re¦hen¦sion+s
rep¦re¦sent+s +ed
  +ing (stand for)
re-present+s +ed
  +ing (present
  again)
rep¦re¦sent¦abil¦ity
rep¦re¦sent¦able
rep¦re¦sen¦ta¦tion
  +s (representing
  something)
re-presen¦ta¦tion
  (presenting
  something again)
rep¦re¦sen¦
          ta¦tion¦al
rep¦re¦sen¦
          ta¦tion¦al¦ism
rep¦re¦sen¦
          ta¦tion¦al¦ist+s
rep¦re¦sen¦ta¦tion¦
                ism
rep¦re¦sen¦ta¦tion¦
                ist+s
rep¦re¦sen¦ta¦tive
  +s
rep¦re¦sen¦
          ta¦tive¦ly
rep¦re¦sen¦ta¦tive¦
                ness
re¦press
  re¦presses
  re¦pressed
  re¦press¦ing

re|press|er +s (use
  repressor)
re|press|ible
re|pres|sion +s
re|pres|sive
re|pres|sive|ly
re|pres|sive|ness
re|pres|sor +s
re|pres|sur|isa|
  tion *Br.* (use
  repressurization)
re|pres|sur|ise *Br.*
  (use repressurize)
re|pres|sur|ises
re|pres|sur|ised
re|pres|sur|is|ing
re|pres|sur|iza|
        tion
re|pres|sur|ize
re|pres|sur|izes
re|pres|sur|ized
re|pres|sur|iz|ing
re|price
re|prices
re|priced
re|pricing
re|prieve
re|prieves
re|prieved
re|priev|ing
rep|ri|mand +s
  +ed +ing
re|print +s +ed
  +ing
re|print|er +s
re|print|ing +s
re|prisal +s
re|prise +s
repro +s
  (= reproduction)
re|proach
re|proaches
re|proached
re|proach|ing
re|proach|able
re|proach|er +s
re|proach|ful
re|proach|ful|ly
re|proach|ful|ness
re|proach|ing|ly
rep|ro|bate
rep|ro|bates
rep|ro|bated
rep|ro|bat|ing
rep|ro|ba|tion
re|pro|cess
re|pro|cesses
re|pro|cessed
re|pro|cess|ing
re|pro|duce
re|pro|duces

re|pro|duce (*cont.*)
re|pro|duced
re|pro|du|cing
re|pro|du|cer +s
re|pro|du|ci|bil|ity
re|pro|du|cible
re|pro|du|cibly
re|pro|duc|tion +s
re|pro|duct|ive +s
re|pro|duc|tive|ly
re|pro|duc|tive|
        ness
re|pro|gram *Br.*
re|pro|grams
re|pro|grammed
re|pro|gram|ming
  (in computing)
re|pro|gram *Am.*
re|pro|grams
re|pro|grammed
re|pro|gram|ming
  (generally)
re|pro|gram|
       ma|bil|ity
re|pro|gram|mable
re|pro|gramme *Br.*
re|pro|grammes
re|pro|grammed
re|pro|gram|ming
  (generally)
rep|rog|raph|er +s
repro|graph|ic
repro|graph|ic|
      al|ly
repro|graph|ics
rep|rog|raphy
re|proof +s +ed
  +ing
re|prov|able
re|prove
re|proves
re|proved
re|prov|ing
re|prover +s
re|prov|ing|ly
re|pro|vi|sion +s
  +ed +ing
rep|tant
rep|tile +s
Rep|tilia
rep|til|ian +s
Rep|ton,
  Hum|phry
  (English landscape
  gardener)
re|pub|lic +s
Re|pub|li|can +s
  (of US Republican
  Party)
re|pub|lic|an +s
  (generally)

re|pub|lic|an|ism
re|pub|li|ca|tion
re|pub|lish
re|pub|lishes
re|pub|lished
re|pub|lish|ing
re|pudi|able
re|pudi|ate
re|pudi|ates
re|pudi|ated
re|pudi|at|ing
re|pudi|ation +s
re|pudi|ator +s
re|pug|nance
re|pug|nant
re|pug|nant|ly
re|pulse
re|pulses
re|pulsed
re|puls|ing
re|pul|sion +s
re|pul|sive
re|pul|sive|ly
re|pul|sive|ness
re|pur|chase
re|pur|chases
re|pur|chased
re|pur|chas|ing
re|puri|fi|ca|tion
  +s
re|pur|ify
re|puri|fies
re|puri|fied
re|puri|fy|ing
rep|ut|able
rep|ut|ably
repu|ta|tion +s
re|pute
re|putes
re|puted
re|put|ing
re|puted|ly
re|quest +s +ed
  +ing
re|quest|er +s
re|quick|en +s +ed
  +ing
re|quiem +s
requi|escat +s
re|quire
re|quires
re|quired
re|quir|ing
re|quire|ment +s
re|quirer +s
requis|ite +s
requis|ite|ly
requi|si|tion +s
  +ed +ing
requi|si|tion|er +s
requi|si|tion|ist +s
re|quital +s

re|quite
re|quites
re|quited
re|quit|ing
reran
re|rate
re|rates
re|rated
re|rat|ing
re|read
re|reads
re|read
re|read|ing
re-readable
re-record +s +ed
  +ing
rere|dos
rere|doses
re-release
re-releases
re-released
re-releas|ing
re-roof +s +ed
  +ing
re-route
re-routes
re-routed
re-routing *or* re-
  routeing
rerun
re|runs
reran
re|run|ning
rerun
re|sal|able (use
  resaleable)
re|sale +s
re|sale|able
resat
re|sched|ule
re|sched|ules
re|sched|uled
re|sched|ul|ing
re|scind +s +ed
  +ing
re|scind|able
re|scind|ment +s
re|scis|sion +s
re|script +s +ed
  +ing
res|cu|able
res|cue
res|cues
res|cued
res|cu|ing
res|cuer +s
re|seal +s +ed
  +ing
re|seal|able
re|search
re|searches

re|search (*cont.*)
  re|searched
  re|search|ing
re|search|able
re|search|er +s
re|seat +s +ed
  +ing
re|sect +s +ed
  +ing
re|sec|tion +s
re|sec|tion|al
re|sec|tion|ist +s
res|eda +s
re|seed +s +ed
  +ing
re|se|lect +s +ed
  +ing
re|se|lec|tion +s
re|sell
  re|sells
  re|sold
  re|sell|ing
re|sell|er +s
re|sem|blance +s
re|sem|blant
re|sem|ble
  re|sem|bles
  re|sem|bled
  re|sem|bling
re|sem|bler +s
re|sent +s +ed
  +ing
re|sent|ful
re|sent|ful|ly
re|sent|ful|ness
re|sent|ment +s
re|ser|pine +s
re|serv|able
res|er|va|tion +s
re|serve
  re|serves
  re|served
  re|serv|ing
  (put aside)
re-serve
  re-serves
  re-served
  re-serving
  (serve again)
re|served|ly
re|serv|ed|ness
re|server +s
re|serv|ist +s
res|er|voir +s
reset
  re|sets
  reset
  re|set|ting
re|set|tabil|ity
re|set|table
re|set|tle
  re|set|tles

re|set|tle (*cont.*)
  re|set|tled
  re|set|tling
re|settle|ment +s
re|shape
  re|shapes
  re|shaped
  re|shap|ing
re|ship
  re|ships
  re|shipped
  re|ship|ping
re|shuf|fle
  re|shuf|fles
  re|shuf|fled
  re|shuf|fling
res|ide
  res|ides
  res|ided
  res|id|ing
resi|dence +s
resi|dency
  resi|den|cies
resi|dent +s
resi|den|tial
resi|den|tial|ly
resi|den|tiary
  resi|den|tiar|ies
resi|dent|ship +s
re|sidua
re|sidual +s
re|sidu|al|ly
re|sidu|ary
resi|due +s
re|siduum
  re|sidua
re|sign +s +ed
  +ing (give up
  employment etc.)
re-sign +s +ed
  +ing (sign again)
re|sig|nal
  re|sig|nals
  re|sig|nalled *Br.*
  re|sig|naled *Am.*
  re|sig|nal|ling *Br.*
  re|sig|nal|ing *Am.*
res|ig|na|tion +s
re|sign|ed|ly
re|sign|ed|ness
re|sign|er +s
re|sile
  re|siles
  re|siled
  re|sil|ing
re|sili|ence
re|sili|ency
re|sili|ent
re|sili|ent|ly
re-silver +s +ed
  +ing
resin +s +ed +ing

res|in|ate
  res|in|ates
  res|in|ated
  res|in|at|ing
  (treat with resin.
  △ resonate)
res|in|ifer|ous
res|ini|fi|ca|tion
res|ini|form
res|in|ify
  res|ini|fies
  res|ini|fied
  res|ini|fy|ing
res|in|oid +s
res|in|ous
re|sist +s +ed +ing
re|sist|ance +s
re|sist|ant
re|sist|er +s
  (person who
  resists. △ resistor)
re|sist|ibil|ity
re|sist|ible
re|sist|ive
re|sist|iv|ity
re|sist|less
re|sist|less|ly
re|sis|tor +s
  (electrical device.
  △ resister)
resit
  re|sits
  resat
  re|sit|ting
re|site
  re|sites
  re|sited
  re|sit|ing
re|size
  re|sizes
  re|sized
  re|siz|ing
re|skill +s +ed
  +ing
Res|nais, Alain
  (French film
  director)
re|sold
re|sole
  re|soles
  re|soled
  re|sol|ing
re|sol|uble (that
  can be resolved)
re-soluble (that
  can be dissolved
  again)
reso|lute
reso|lute|ly
reso|lute|ness
reso|lution +s
reso|lu|tive

re|solv|abil|ity
re|solv|able
re|solve
  re|solves
  re|solved
  re|solv|ing
re|solved|ly
re|solv|ed|ness
re|solv|ent +s
re|solver +s
res|on|ance +s
res|on|ant
res|on|ant|ly
res|on|ate
  res|on|ates
  res|on|ated
  res|on|at|ing
  (produce or show
  resonance.
  △ resinate)
res|on|ator +s
re|sorb +s +ed
  +ing
re|sorb|ence
re|sorb|ent
re|sor|cin
re|sor|cinol
re|sorp|tion +s
re|sorp|tive
re|sort +s +ed
  +ing (seaside
  resort etc.;
  recourse; turn to)
re-sort +s +ed
  +ing (sort again)
re|sort|er +s
re|sound +s +ed
  +ing
re|sound|ing|ly
re|source
  re|sources
  re|sourced
  re|sour|cing
re|source|ful
re|source|ful|ly
re|source|ful|ness
re|source|less
re|source|less|
             ness
re|spect +s +ed
  +ing
re|spect|abil|ity
re|spect|able
re|spect|ably
re|spect|er +s
re|spect|ful
re|spect|ful|ly
re|spect|ful|ness
re|spect|ive
re|spect|ive|ly
re|spell
  re|spells

re|spell (*cont.*)
re|spelled *or*
re|spelt
re|spell|ing
Res|pighi,
   Otto|rino (Italian
   composer)
res|pir|able
res|pir|ate
   res|pir|ates
   res|pir|ated
   res|pir|at|ing
res|pir|ation +s
res|pir|ator +s
re|spira|tory
re|spire
   re|spires
   re|spired
   re|spir|ing
res|pite
   res|pites
   res|pited
   res|pit|ing
re|splen|dence
re|splen|dency
re|splen|dent
re|splen|dent|ly
re|spond +s +ed
   +ing
re|spond|ence +s
re|spond|ency
re|spond|ent +s
re|spond|er +s
re|sponse +s
re|spon|si|bil|ity
   re|spon|si|bil|ities
re|spon|sible
re|spon|sible|ness
re|spon|sibly
re|spon|sive
re|spon|sive|ly
re|spon|sive|ness
re|spon|sor|ial
re|spon|sory
   re|spon|sor|ies
re|spray +s +ed
   +ing
rest +s +ed +ing
   (repose;
   remainder.
   △ wrest)
re|stage
   re|stages
   re|staged
   re|staging
re|start +s +ed
   +ing
re|state
   re|states
   re|stated
   re|stat|ing
re|state|ment +s

res|taur|ant +s
res|taur|ant car +s
res|taura|teur +s
rest-balk +s
rest-cure +s
rest day +s
rest|ful
rest|ful|ly
rest|ful|ness
rest-harrow +s
rest home +s
rest house +s
rest|ing place +s
res|ti|tu|tion +s
res|titu|tive
rest|ive
rest|ive|ly
rest|ive|ness
rest|less
rest|less|ly
rest|less|ness
rest mass
   rest masses
re|stock +s +ed
   +ing
re|stor|able
res|tor|ation +s
res|tor|ation|ism
res|tor|ation|ist +s
re|stora|tive +s
res|tora|tive|ly
re|store
   re|stores
   re|stored
   re|stor|ing
re|storer +s
re|strain +s +ed
   +ing (control etc.)
re-strain +s +ed
   +ing (strain again)
re|strain|able
re|strain|ed|ly
re|strain|er +s
re|straint +s
re|strict +s +ed
   +ing
re|strict|ed|ly
re|strict|ed|ness
re|stric|tion +s
re|stric|tion|ist +s
re|strict|ive
re|strict|ive|ly
re|strict|ive|ness
re|string
   re|strings
   re|strung
   re|string|ing
rest|room +s
re|struc|ture
   re|struc|tures
   re|struc|tured
   re|struc|tur|ing

re|struc|tur|ing +s
re|study
   re|stud|ies
   re|stud|ied
   re|study|ing
re|style
   re|styles
   re|styled
   re|styl|ing
re|sub|mit
   re|sub|mits
   re|sub|mit|ted
   re|sub|mit|ting
re|sult +s +ed +ing
re|sult|ant +s
re|sult|ful
re|sult|less
re|sum|able
re|sume
   re|sumes
   re|sumed
   re|sum|ing
   (begin again; get
   back; etc.)
ré|sumé +s
   (summary;
   curriculum vitae)
re|sump|tion +s
re|sump|tive
re|su|pin|ate
re|sup|ply
   re|sup|plies
   re|sup|plied
   re|sup|ply|ing
re|sur|face
   re|sur|faces
   re|sur|faced
   re|sur|facing
re|sur|gence +s
re|sur|gent
res|ur|rect +s +ed
   +ing
res|ur|rec|tion +s
res|ur|rec|tion|al
re|sur|vey +s +ed
   +ing
re|sus|ci|tate
   re|sus|ci|tates
   re|sus|ci|tated
   re|sus|ci|tat|ing
re|sus|ci|ta|tion +s
re|sus|ci|ta|tive
re|sus|ci|ta|tor +s
ret
   rets
   ret|ted
   ret|ting
re|table +s
re|tail +s +ed +ing
re|tail|er +s
re|tain +s +ed
   +ing

re|tain|abil|ity
re|tain|able
re|tain|er +s
re|tain|ment +s
re|take
   re|takes
   re|took
   re|tak|ing
   re|taken
re|tali|ate
   re|tali|ates
   re|tali|ated
   re|tali|at|ing
re|tali|ation +s
re|talia|tive
re|tali|ator +s
re|tali|atory
re|tard +s +ed
   +ing
re|tard|ant +s
re|tard|ate +s
re|tard|ation +s
re|tarda|tive
re|tarda|tory
re|tard|er +s
re|tard|ment +s
retch
   retches
   retched
   retch|ing
   (vomit. △ wretch)
rete
   retia
re|teach
   re|teaches
   re|taught
   re|teach|ing
re|tell
   re|tells
   re|told
   re|tell|ing
re|ten|tion +s
re|ten|tive
re|ten|tive|ly
re|ten|tive|ness
re|tex|ture
   re|tex|tures
   re|tex|tured
   re|tex|tur|ing
re|think
   re|thinks
   re|thought
   re|think|ing
Rethym|non (port,
   Crete)
retia
reti|ar|ius
   reti|arii
re|tiary
   re|tiar|ies
reti|cence
reti|cent

reti|cent|ly
ret|icle +s
re|ticula (plural of reticulum)
re|ticu|lar (of the reticulum)
re|ticu|late
  re|ticu|lates
  re|ticu|lated
  re|ticu|lat|ing
re|ticu|late|ly
re|ticu|la|tion +s
reti|cule +s
re|ticu|lo|cyte +s
re|ticu|lose
re|ticu|lum
  re|tic|ula
retie
  re|ties
  re|tied
  re|tying
reti|form
re-time
  re-times
  re-timed
  re-timing
ret|ina
  ret|inas or
  ret|inae
ret|inal
ret|in|itis
ret|in|itis
  pig|ment|osa
ret|inol
ret|inue +s
re|tir|acy
re|tiral +s
re|tire
  re|tires
  re|tired
  re|tir|ing
re|tired|ness
re|tiree +s
re|tire|ment +s
re|tirer +s
re|tir|ing|ly
re|title
  re|titles
  re|titled
  re|tit|ling
re|told
re|took
re|tool +s +ed
  +ing
re|tort +s +ed +ing
re|tor|tion +s
re|touch
  re|touches
  re|touched
  re|touch|ing
re|touch|er +s

re|trace
  re|traces
  re|traced
  re|tracing
re|tract +s +ed
  +ing
re|tract|able
re|tract|ation +s
  (further treatment
  and corrections.
  △ retraction)
re|tract|ile
re|tract|il|ity
re|trac|tion +s
  (revocation,
  withdrawal.
  △ retractation)
re|trac|tive
re|tract|or +s
re|train +s +ed
  +ing
ret|ral
re|trans|late
  re|trans|lates
  re|trans|lated
  re|trans|lat|ing
re|trans|la|tion +s
re|trans|mis|sion
  +s
re|trans|mit
  re|trans|mits
  re|trans|mit|ted
  re|trans|mit|ting
re|tread
  re|treads
  re|trod
  re|tread|ing
  re|trod|den
  (tread again)
re|tread +s +ed
  +ing (tyre; put
  fresh tread on)
re|treat +s +ed
  +ing
re|trench
  re|trenches
  re|trenched
  re|trench|ing
re|trench|ment +s
re|trial +s
ret|ri|bu|tion
re|tribu|tive
re|tribu|tory
re|triev|able
re|trieval +s
re|trieve
  re|trieves
  re|trieved
  re|triev|ing
re|triever +s
re|trim
  re|trims

re|trim (cont.)
  re|trimmed
  re|trim|ming
retro +s
retro|act +s +ed
  +ing
retro|action +s
retro|active
retro|active|ly
retro|activ|ity
retro|cede
  retro|cedes
  retro|ceded
  retro|ced|ing
retro|ced|ence
retro|ced|ent
retro|ces|sion
retro|ces|sive
retro|choir +s
retro|trod
retro|trod|den
retro|fit
  retro|fits
  retro|fit|ted
  retro|fit|ting
retro|flex
retro|flexed
retro|flex|ion +s
retro|grad|ation
  +s
retro|grade
  retro|grades
  retro|graded
  retro|grad|ing
retro|grade|ly
retro|gress
  retro|gresses
  retro|gressed
  retro|gress|ing
retro|gres|sion
retro|gres|sive
retro|gres|sive|ly
retro|ject +s +ed
  +ing
retro-rocket +s
ret|rorse
ret|rorse|ly
retro|spect +s
retro|spec|tion +s
retro|spect|ive +s
retro|spect|ive|ly
retro|sternal
re|troussé
retro|ver|sion
retro|vert +s +ed
  +ing
retro|virus
  retro|viruses
retry
  re|tries
  re|tried
  re|try|ing

ret|sina +s
ret|tery
ret|ter|ies
re|tune
  re|tunes
  re|tuned
  re|tun|ing
re|turf +s +ed +ing
re|turn +s +ed
  +ing
re|turn|able
re|turn|ee +s
re|turn|er +s
re|turn|less
re|tuse
re|tying (present participle of retie)
re|type
  re|types
  re|typed
  re|typ|ing
Reu|ben Bible
re|uni|fi|ca|tion
re|unify
  re|uni|fies
  re|uni|fied
  re|uni|fy|ing
Ré|union (island, Indian Ocean)
re|union +s
re|unite
  re|unites
  re|united
  re|unit|ing
re|uphol|ster +s
  +ed +ing
re|uphol|stery
re|urge
  re|urges
  re|urged
  re|ur|ging
re|usable
reuse
  re|uses
  re|used
  re|us|ing
re|use|able (use reusable)
Reu|ter, Paul Ju|lius von (German founder of Reuters)
Reu|ters (international news agency)
re|util|isa|tion Br. (use reutilization)
re|util|ise Br. (use reutilize)
  re|util|ises
  re|util|ised
  re|util|is|ing

re|util|iza|tion
re|util|ize
re|util|izes
re|util|ized
re|util|iz|ing
rev
revs
revved
rev|ving
re|vac|cin|ate
re|vac|cin|ates
re|vac|cin|ated
re|vac|cin|at|ing
re|vac|cin|ation +s
re|val|or|isa|tion
Br. +s (use
revalorization)
re|val|or|ise Br.
(use revalorize)
re|val|or|ises
re|val|or|ised
re|val|or|is|ing
re|val|or|iza|tion
+s
re|val|or|ize
re|val|or|izes
re|val|or|ized
re|val|or|iz|ing
re|valu|ation +s
re|value
re|values
re|valued
re|valu|ing
re|vamp +s +ed
+ing
re|vanch|ism
re|vanch|ist +s
re|var|nish
re|var|nishes
re|var|nished
re|var|nish|ing
re|veal +s +ed
+ing
re|veal|able
re|veal|er +s
re|veal|ing
re|veal|ing|ly
re|vege|tate
re|vege|tates
re|vege|tated
re|vege|tat|ing
re|vege|ta|tion
revel
revels
rev|elled Br.
rev|eled Am.
rev|el|ling Br.
rev|el|ing Am.
reve|la|tion +s
reve|la|tion|al
reve|la|tion|ist +s

rev|ela|tory
rev|el|er Am. +s
rev|el|ler Br. +s
rev|el|ry
rev|el|ries
rev|enant +s
re|ven|di|ca|tion
+s
re|venge
re|venges
re|venged
re|ven|ging
re|venge|ful
re|venge|ful|ly
re|venge|ful|ness
re|ven|ger +s
rev|enue +s
re|verb +s
(= reverberation)
re|ver|ber|ant
re|ver|ber|ant|ly
re|ver|ber|ate
re|ver|ber|ates
re|ver|ber|ated
re|ver|ber|at|ing
re|ver|ber|ation +s
re|ver|bera|tive
re|ver|ber|ator +s
re|ver|ber|atory
Re|vere, Paul
(American patriot)
re|vere
re|veres
re|vered
re|ver|ing
(venerate.
△ revers)
rev|er|ence
rev|er|ences
rev|er|enced
rev|er|en|cing
rev|er|end +s
(deserving
reverence)
rev|er|ent (feeling
or showing
reverence)
rev|er|en|tial
rev|er|en|tial|ly
rev|er|ent|ly
rev|erie +s
re|vers
plural re|vers
(on garment.
△ revere)
re|ver|sal +s
re|verse
re|verses
re|versed
re|vers|ing
reverse-charge
attributive

re|verse|ly
re|verser +s
re|vers|ibil|ity
re|vers|ible
re|vers|ibly
re|ver|sion +s
re|ver|sion|al
re|ver|sion|ary
re|ver|sion|er +s
re|vert +s +ed
+ing
re|vert|er +s
re|vert|ible
revet
re|vets
re|vet|ted
re|vet|ting
(face with
masonry. △ rivet)
re|vet|ment +s
re|victual
re|victuals
re|victualled Br.
re|victualed Am.
re|victual|ling Br.
re|victual|ing Am.
re|view +s +ed
+ing (assess; (as
noun) assessment.
△ revue)
re|view|able
re|view|al +s
re|view|er +s
re|vile
re|viles
re|viled
re|vil|ing
re|vile|ment +s
re|viler +s
re|vil|ing +s
re|vis|able
re|visal +s
re|vise
re|vises
re|vised
re|vis|ing
re|viser +s
re|vi|sion +s
re|vi|sion|ary
re|vi|sion|ism
re|vi|sion|ist +s
re|visit +s +ed
+ing
re|vis|ory
re|vit|al|isa|tion
Br. (use
revitalization)
re|vit|al|ise Br.
(use revitalize)
re|vit|al|ises
re|vit|al|ised
re|vit|al|is|ing

re|vit|al|iza|tion
re|vit|al|ize
re|vit|al|izes
re|vit|al|ized
re|vit|al|iz|ing
re|viv|able
re|vival +s
re|vival|ism
re|vival|ist +s
re|vival|is|tic
re|vive
re|vives
re|vived
re|viv|ing
re|viver +s
re|vivi|fi|ca|tion
re|viv|ify
re|vivi|fies
re|vivi|fied
re|vivi|fy|ing
re|viv|is|cence
re|viv|is|cent
rev|oc|abil|ity
rev|oc|able
revo|ca|tion +s
revo|ca|tory
re|voke
re|vokes
re|voked
re|vok|ing
re|voker +s
re|volt +s +ed
+ing
re|volt|ing|ly
revo|lute
revo|lu|tion +s
revo|lu|tion|ary
revo|lu|tion|ar|ies
revo|lu|tion|ise Br.
(use
revolutionize)
revo|lu|tion|ises
revo|lu|tion|ised
revo|lu|tion|is|ing
revo|lu|tion|ism
revo|lu|tion|ist +s
revo|lu|tion|ize
revo|lu|tion|izes
revo|lu|tion|ized
revo|lu|tion|iz|ing
re|volv|able
re|volve
re|volves
re|volved
re|volv|ing
re|volver +s
revue +s (theatrical
entertainment.
△ review)
re|vul|sion
re|vul|sive

re¦ward +s +ed
  +ing
re¦ward¦ing¦ly
re¦ward¦less
rewa¦rewa +s
re¦wash
  re¦washes
  re¦washed
  re¦wash¦ing
re¦weigh +s +ed
  +ing
re¦wind
  re¦winds
  re¦wound
  re¦wind¦ing
re¦wind¦er +s
re¦wir¦able
re¦wire
  re¦wires
  re¦wired
  re¦wir¦ing
re¦word +s +ed
  +ing
re¦work +s +ed
  +ing
re¦work¦ing +s
re¦wound
re¦wrap
  re¦wraps
  re¦wrapped
  re¦wrap¦ping
re¦write
  re¦writes
  re¦wrote
  re¦writ¦ing
  re¦writ¦ten
Rex (name)
Rex (reigning king;
  in lawsuits)
Rex¦ine *Propr.*
Rey¦kja¦vik (capital
  of Iceland)
Rey¦nard +s
Rey¦nolds, Joshua
  (English painter)
Rey¦nolds
  num¦ber +s
Reza Shah (ruler of
  Iran)
rhab¦do¦mancy
Rhada¦man¦thine
Rhada¦man¦thus
  Greek Mythology
Rhae¦tian +s
Rhae¦tic +s
Rhaeto-Romance
Rhaeto-Romanic
Rha¦kine (state,
  Burma)
rhap¦sode +s
rhap¦sodic
rhap¦sodic¦al

rhap¦sod¦ise *Br.*
  (use rhapsodize)
  rhap¦sod¦ises
  rhap¦sod¦ised
  rhap¦sod¦is¦ing
rhap¦sod¦ist +s
rhap¦sod¦ize
  rhap¦sod¦izes
  rhap¦sod¦ized
  rhap¦sod¦iz¦ing
rhap¦sody
  rhap¦sod¦ies
rhat¦any
  rhat¦anies
Rhea (*Greek
  Mythology*; moon
  of Saturn)
rhea +s (bird.
  ⚠ rear, ria)
rhe¦bok +s (use
  reebok)
Rheims (use
  Reims)
Rheinland-Pfalz
  (German name for
  Rhineland-
  Palatinate)
Rhem¦ish
Rhen¦ish
rhe¦nium
rheo¦logic¦al
rhe¦olo¦gist +s
rhe¦ology
rheo¦stat +s
rheo¦stat¦ic
rheo¦trop¦ic
rheo¦trop¦ism
rhe¦sus
rhesus-negative
rhesus-positive
rhe¦tor +s
rhet¦oric
rhet¦oric¦al
rhet¦oric¦al¦ly
rhet¦or¦ician +s
rheum +s (watery
  discharge.
  ⚠ room)
rheum¦at¦ic +s
rheum¦atic¦al¦ly
rheum¦aticky
rheum¦atics
rheuma¦tism
rheuma¦toid
rheum¦ato¦logic¦al
rheum¦ato¦logi¦st
  +s
rheuma¦tol¦ogy
rheumy (full of
  rheum. ⚠ roomie,
  roomy)
rhinal

Rhine (river, W.
  Europe)
Rhine¦land (region,
  Germany)
Rhineland-
  Palatin¦ate (state,
  Germany)
rhine¦stone +s
rhin¦itis
rhino +s
  (= rhinoceros)
rhi¦noceros
  plural rhi¦noceros
  or rhi¦nocer¦oses
rhi¦nocer¦ot¦ic
rhino¦pharyn¦geal
rhino¦plas¦tic
rhino¦plasty
  rhino¦plas¦ties
rhino¦scope +s
rhi¦zo¦bium
  rhi¦zo¦bia
rhizo¦carp +s
rhi¦zoid
rhi¦zome +s
rhizo¦pod +s
rho +s (Greek
  letter. ⚠ roe, row)
Rhoda
rhoda¦mine +s
Rhode Is¦land
  (state, USA)
Rhodes (Greek
  island)
Rhodes, Cecil
  (British-born
  South African
  statesman;
  scholarship)
Rhodes, Wil¦fred
  (English cricketer)
Rho¦desia (in
  former names of
  Zambia and
  Zimbabwe)
Rho¦desian +s
Rho¦dian +s
rho¦dium
rhodo¦chros¦ite
rhodo¦den¦dron +s
Rho¦dope
  Moun¦tains (in
  SE Europe)
rhod¦op¦sin
rho¦dora +s
rhomb +s
rhomb¦
  en¦ceph¦alon +s
rhombi
rhom¦bic
rhombo¦he¦dral
rhombo¦he¦dron
  rhombo¦he¦dra *or*
  rhombo¦he¦drons

rhom¦boid +s
rhom¦boid¦al
rhom¦boid¦al¦ly
rhom¦boid¦eus
  rhom¦boidei
rhom¦bus
  rhom¦buses *or*
  rhombi
Rhona *also* Rona
Rhon¦dda (district,
  Wales)
Rhône (river, W.
  Europe)
Rhône-Alpes
  (region, France)
rho¦tic
rhu¦barb +s
Rhum (Scottish
  island)
rhumb +s (on
  compass. ⚠ rum)
rhumba (use
  rumba)
rhum¦bas
rhum¦baed *or*
rhum¦ba'd
rhumba¦ing
rhumb-line +s
rhyme
  rhymes
  rhymed
  rhym¦ing
  (in poetry.
  ⚠ rime)
rhyme¦less
rhymer +s
rhyme¦ster +s
rhym¦ist +s
rhyo¦lite +s
Rhys, Jean (British
  writer)
rhythm +s
rhythm and blues
  noun
rhythm-and-blues
  attributive
rhyth¦mic
rhyth¦mic¦al
rhyth¦mic¦al¦ly
rhyth¦mi¦city
rhyth¦mist +s
rhythm¦less
ria +s (narrow inlet.
  ⚠ rear, rhea)
rial +s (gold coin;
  Iranian or Omani
  currency. ⚠ riyal)
Ri¦alto (island,
  Venice; Bridge)
rib
  ribs

rib (*cont.*)
ribbed
rib|bing
rib|ald +s
rib|ald¦ry
rib¦ald|ries
rib|and +s
Riba|tejo
(province,
Portugal)
Rib¦ben|trop,
Joa|chim von
(German Nazi
politician)
rib¦ber +s
rib|bing +s
rib|bon +s
rib|boned
rib|bon|fish
plural rib¦bon|fish
or rib¦bon|fishes
rib|bon worm +s
rib|cage +s
Ri¦bera, José
(Spanish painter)
rib|less
ribo|fla¦vin
ribo|fla¦vine
ribo|nucle¦ic
rib|ose +s
ribo|so¦mal
ribo|some +s
rib-tickler +s
rib|wort +s
Ric¦ard|ian +s
rice
rices
riced
ri¦cing
rice-bowl +s (rice-
producing area)
rice-paper +s
ricer +s
ri¦cer|car +s
ri¦cer|care +s
rich +er +est
Rich|ard (English
kings)
Rich|ard, Cliff
(British pop
singer)
Rich|ards,
Gor¦don (English
jockey)
Rich|ards, Viv
(West Indian
cricketer)
Rich¦ard|son,
Sam¦uel (English
novelist)
Riche|lieu,
Ar¦mand Jean

Riche|lieu (*cont.*)
du Ples|sis
(French cardinal)
rich|en +s +ed
+ing
riches
Richie
rich¦ly
Rich|mond (towns,
England; city,
USA)
rich|ness
Rich|ter, Jo¦hann
Fried|rich
(German novelist)
Rich|ter scale
ricin
Rick (name)
rick +s +ed +ing
(haystack; sprain)
rick¦eti|ness
rick|ets
rick¦ett|sia
rick¦ett|siae
rick¦ett|sial
rick|ety
rickey +s
rick|rack (use
ricrac)
rick|sha +s (use
rickshaw)
rick|shaw +s
rico|chet
rico|chets
rico|cheted *or*
rico¦chet|ted
rico¦chet|ing *or*
rico¦chet|ting
ri|cotta +s
ric¦rac +s
ric¦tal
ric¦tus
ric|tuses
rid
rids
rid
rid|ding
rid¦able (use
rideable)
rid|dance
rid|den
rid¦dle
rid¦dles
rid¦dled
rid|dling
rid|dler +s
rid|dling¦ly
ride
rides
rode
rid¦ing
rid|den

ride|able
ride-off +s *noun*
ride-on +s *adjective
and noun*
rider +s
rider|less
ridge
ridges
ridged
ridg¦ing
ridge piece +s
ridge pole +s
ridge tile +s
ridge tree +s
ridge|way +s
ridgy
ridgi¦er
ridgi|est
ridi|cule
ridi|cules
ridi|culed
ridi|cul¦ing
ri¦dicu|lous
ri¦dicu|lous¦ly
ri¦dicu|lous|ness
rid¦ing +s
rid¦ing light +s
rid¦ing school +s
Rid¦ley, Nich|olas
(English
Protestant martyr)
Rief¦en|stahl, Leni
(German film-
maker)
Riel, Louis
(Canadian political
leader)
Rie|mann,
Bern|hard
(German
mathematician)
Rie|mann|ian
Ries|ling +s
rife
rife|ness
riff +s +ed +ing
rif¦fle
rif¦fles
rif¦fled
rif|fling
riff-raff
rifle
ri¦fles
ri¦fled
rif|ling
rifle bird +s
rifle|man
rifle|men
rifle range +s
rifle|scope +s
rifle shot +s
rifi|ing +s

Rif Moun|tains (in
Morocco)
rift +s +ed +ing
rift|less
rift val¦ley +s
rifty
rift|ier
rifti|est
rig
rigs
rigged
rig|ging
Riga (capital of
Latvia)
riga|doon +s
riga|toni
Rigel (star)
rig¦ger +s (person
who rigs. △ rigor,
rigour)
rig|ging +s
Right *Politics*
right +s +ed +ing
+er +est (just;
correct; not left;
entitlement;
immediately;
completely;
restore. △ rite,
wright, write)
right|able
right angle +s
right-angled
right-back +s *Sport*
right|en +s +ed
+ing
right|eous
right|eous¦ly
right|eous|ness
right|er +s
(comparative of
right; in 'animal-
righter' etc.
△ writer)
right-footed
right|ful
right|ful¦ly
right|ful|ness
right hand +s *noun*
right-hand
attributive
right-handed
right-handed¦ly
right-handed|ness
right-hander +s
right|ish
right|ism
right|ist +s
right|less
right|less|ness
right¦ly
right-minded

right|most

right|ness

righto

right of search
  rights of search

right of visit
  rights of visit

right of way
  rights of way

right|ward

right|wards

right whale +s

right wing +s *noun*

right-wing *adjective*

right-winger +s

rigid

ri¦gid|ify
  ri¦gidi|fies
  ri¦gidi|fied
  ri¦gidi|fy|ing

ri¦gid|ity
  ri¦gid|ities

ri¦gid|ly

ri¦gid|ness

rig|mar|ole +s

rigor +s (feeling of
  cold; rigidity.
  △ rigger, rigour)

rigor *Am.* +s
  (severity. *Br.*
  rigour. △ rigger)

rig|or|ism

rigor mor|tis

rig|or|ous

rig|or|ous|ly

rig|or|ous|ness

rig|our *Br.* +s (*Am.*
  rigor. severity.
  △ rigger, rigor)

rig-out +s *noun*

Rig-veda *Hinduism*

Rij|eka (port,
  Croatia)

Rijks|mu¦seum (art
  gallery, the
  Netherlands)

Riks|mål

Rila Moun|tains
  (in Bulgaria)

rile
  riles
  riled
  ril¦ing

Riley (in 'the life of
  Riley')

Riley, Brid¦get
  (English painter)

ri|lievo +s (use
  relievo)

Rilke, Rai¦ner
  Maria (German
  poet)

rill +s (small
  stream)

rille +s (valley on
  moon)

rim
  rims
  rimmed
  rim|ming

Rim|baud, Ar¦thur
  (French poet)

rim-brake +s

rime
  rimes
  rimed
  rim¦ing
  (frost; also *archaic*
  = rhyme)

Rim¦ini (resort,
  Italy)

rim|less

Rim¦mon (ancient
  deity)

rim¦ose

rim¦ous

Rimsky-Korsakov,
  Niko|lai (Russian
  composer)

rimu +s

rimy
  rimi¦er
  rimi¦est

rind +s +ed +ing

rin|der|pest

rind|less

ring +s +ed +ing
  (circle etc.
  △ wring)

ring
  rings
  rang
  ring|ing
  rung
  (sound. △ wring)

ring|bark +s +ed
  +ing

ring-binder +s

ring|bolt +s

ring-dove +s

rin|gent

ringer +s

ring|ette

ring-fence
  ring-fences
  ring-fenced
  ring-fencing

ring fin¦ger +s

ring|hals (use
  rinkhals)
  ring|halses

ring|ing|ly

ring|ing tone +s

ring|lead¦er +s

ring|less

ring|let +s

ring¦let|ed *Am.*

ring¦let|ted *Br.*

ring|lety

ring|mas¦ter +s

ring-neck +s

ring-necked

ring-pull +s

ring road +s

ring|side +s

ring|sider +s

ring|ster +s

ring|tail +s

ring-tailed

ring-wall +s

ring|worm

rink +s

rink|hals
  rink|halse

rinse
  rinses
  rinsed
  rins¦ing

rinser +s

Rio Branco (city,
  Brazil)

Rio de Ja¦neiro
  (city, Brazil)

Rio de Oro (region,
  NW Africa)

Rio Grande (river,
  N. America)

Rio Grande do
  Norte (state,
  Brazil)

Rio Grande do Sul
  (state, Brazil)

Rioja, La (region,
  Spain)

Rio Muni (region,
  Equatorial Guinea)

Rio Negro (river, S.
  America)

riot +s +ed +ing
  (disturbance.
  △ ryot)

riot¦er +s

riot|less

riot|ous

riot¦ous¦ly

riot¦ous|ness

rip
  rips
  ripped
  rip|ping

ri|par|ian +s

rip|cord +s

ripe
  riper
  rip¦est
  ripe¦ly

ripen +s +ed +ing

ripe|ness

ri¦pi|eno
  ri¦pi|enos *or*
  ri¦pi|eni

rip-off +s

ri|poste
  ri|postes
  ri|posted
  ri|post|ing

rip¦per +s

rip|ping¦ly

rip¦ple
  rip¦ples
  rip¦pled
  rip|pling

rip|plet +s

rip¦ply
  rip|plier
  rip|pli|est

rip¦rap

rip-roaring

rip-roaring¦ly

rip¦saw +s

rip|snort¦er +s

rip|snort¦ing

rip|snort|ing¦ly

rip|stop

Ripu|arian +s

Rip Van Win¦kle
  (fictional
  character)

RISC (*Computing*.
  △ risk)

rise
  rises
  rose
  risen
  ris¦ing

riser +s

rishi +s

risi|bil¦ity

ris|ible

ris|ibly

ris¦ing +s

risk +s +ed +ing
  (chance. △ RISC)

risk-free

risk|ily

riski|ness

risk-taker +s

risk-taking

risky
  risk¦ier
  riski¦est

Ri¦sor¦gi|mento

ris|otto +s

ris¦qué

ris|sole +s

rit. (= ritardando.
  △ writ)

Rita

rit|ar|dando
  rit|ar|dandos *or*
  rit|ar|dandi
rite +s (ritual.
  △ right, wright,
  write)
rite|less
rit|en|uto
  rit|en|utos *or*
  rit|en|uti
rit|orn|ello
  rit|orn|el|los *or*
  rit|orn|elli
rit|ual +s
ritu|al|isa|tion *Br.*
  (use ritualization)
ritu|al|ise *Br.* (use
  ritualize)
  ritu|al|ises
  ritu|al|ised
  ritu|al|is|ing
ritu|al|ism
ritu|al|ist +s
ritu|al|is|tic
ritu|al|is|tic|al|ly
ritu|al|iza|tion
ritu|al|ize
  ritu|al|izes
  ritu|al|ized
  ritu|al|iz|ing
ritu|al|ly
ritz|ily
ritzi|ness
ritzy
  ritz|ier
  ritzi|est
rival
  ri|vals
  ri|valled *Br.*
  ri|valed *Am.*
  ri|val|ling *Br.*
  ri|val|ing *Am.*
ri|val|ry
  ri|val|ries
rive
  rives
  rived
  riv|ing
  riven
river +s
Ri|vera, Diego
  (Mexican painter)
river|ain +s
river bank +s
river bed +s
river|boat +s
riv|ered
river-head +s
river|ine
river|less
River|side (city,
  USA)

river|side +s
rivet +s +ed +ing
  (nail or bolt;
  fasten with rivets.
  △ revet)
riv|et|er +s
Rivi|era
  (Mediterranean
  coastal region)
rivi|era +s (similar
  region)
rivi|ère +s
  (necklace)
Rivne (city,
  Ukraine)
rivu|let +s
Riy|adh (capital of
  Saudi Arabia)
riyal +s (Saudi
  Arabian, Qatari, or
  Yemeni currency.
  △ rial)
roach
  plural roach
  (fish)
roach
  roaches
  (cockroach;
  marijuana
  cigarette butt;
  curve on sail)
road +s +ed +ing
  (street; highway;
  track game birds
  by scent. △ rode,
  roed, rowed)
road|bed +s
road|block +s
road fund li|cence
  +s
road hog +s
road-holding
road|house +s
roadie +s
road|less
road|man
  road|men
road map +s
road metal
road-pricing
road|roll|er +s
road|run|ner +s
road|show +s
road|side +s
road sign +s
road|stead +s
road|ster +s
road sweep|er +s
road tax
  road taxes
road test +s *noun*

road-test +s +ed
  +ing
  verb
Road Town
  (capital of the
  British Virgin
  Islands)
road train +s (lorry
  pulling trailer)
road user +s
road|way +s
road|work +s
road|worthi|ness
road|worthy
roam +s +ed +ing
roam|er +s
  (wanderer.
  △ romer)
roan +s (colour;
  animal. △ rone)
roar +s +ed +ing
  (sound of lion; etc.
  △ raw)
roar|er +s
roar|ing +s
roar|ing|ly
roast +s +ed +ing
roast|er +s
roast|ing +s
Rob (name)
rob
  robs
  robbed
  rob|bing
  (steal)
Robbe-Grillet,
  Alain (French
  novelist)
Rob|ben Is|land
  (off South Africa)
rob|ber +s
rob|ber baron +s
rob|bery
  rob|ber|ies
Rob|bia, Luca
  della (Italian
  sculptor and
  ceramicist)
Rob|bie
Rob|bins, Je|rome
  (American
  choreographer)
robe
  robes
  robed
  rob|ing
Rob|ert (Scottish
  kings; name)
Rob|erta
Rob|erts,
  Fred|erick Sleigh
  (Lord Roberts of

Rob|erts (*cont.*)
  Kandahar, British
  field marshal)
Rob|ert the Bruce
  (Scottish king)
Robe|son, Paul
  (American singer)
Robes|pierre,
  Max|imil|ian
  (French
  revolutionary)
Robey, George
  (British comedian)
Robin (name)
robin +s (bird)
Rob|ina
Robin
  Good|fel|low
  (another name for
  Puck)
Robin Hood (semi-
  legendary English
  outlaw)
rob|inia +s (tree)
Robin|son,
  Ed|ward G.
  (Romanian-born
  American actor)
Robin|son, Sugar
  Ray (American
  boxer)
Robin|son Cru|soe
  (fictional
  character)
ro|bor|ant +s
robot +s
ro|bot|ic
ro|bot|ic|al|ly
ro|bot|ics
ro|bot|isa|tion *Br.*
  (use robotization)
ro|bot|ise *Br.* (use
  robotize)
  ro|bot|ises
  ro|bot|ised
  ro|bot|is|ing
ro|bot|iza|tion
ro|bot|ize
  ro|bot|izes
  ro|bot|ized
  ro|bot|iz|ing
Rob Roy (Scottish
  outlaw)
Rob|sart, Amy
  (wife of Robert
  Dudley)
Rob|son, Flora
  (English actress)
ro|bust +er +est
  (sturdy)
ro|busta +s
  (coffee)

ro¦bus¦tious
ro¦bust¦ly
ro¦bust¦ness
roc +s (legendary
    bird. △ rock)
ro¦caille
roc¦am¦bole +s
Roch¦dale (town,
    England)
roche
    mou¦ton¦née
    roches
    mou¦ton¦nées
    Geology
Ro¦ches¦ter (town,
    England; city,
    USA)
Ro¦ches¦ter, Earl
    of (English poet)
rochet +s
rock +s +ed +ing
    (stone;
    confectionery;
    move to and fro;
    music. △ roc)
rocka¦billy *Music*
Rock¦all (islet and
    shipping area, N.
    Atlantic)
rock and roll
rock and roll¦er +s
rock-bed +s
rock-bottom
rock-bound
rock¦burst +s
rock cake +s
rock candy
rock-climber +s
rock-climbing
rock crys¦tal
rock-dove +s
Rocke¦fel¦ler,
    John Davi¦son
    (American
    industrialist)
rock¦er +s
rock¦ery
    rock¦er¦ies
rocket +s +ed +ing
rock¦et¦eer +s
rocket launch¦er
    +s
rocket-propelled
rock¦et¦ry
rock face +s
rock¦fall +s
rock¦fish
    plural rock¦fish *or*
    rock¦fishes
rock gar¦den +s
Rock¦hamp¦ton
    (town, Australia)

rock¦hop¦per +s
Rock¦ies (= Rocky
    Mountains)
rock¦ily
rocki¦ness
rock¦ing chair +s
rock¦ing horse +s
rocking-stone +s
rock¦less
rock¦let +s
rock¦like
rock¦ling
    plural rock¦ling
rock'n'roll (use
    rock and roll)
rock'n'roll¦er +s
    (use rock and
    roller)
rock-pigeon +s
rock pipit +s
rock plant +s
rock pool +s
rock rab¦bit +s
rock sal¦mon
    plural rock
    sal¦mon
rock salt
rock-shaft +s
rock-solid
rock-steady
rocku¦men¦tary
    rocku¦men¦tar¦ies
rock-wool
rocky
    rock¦ier
    rocki¦est
Rocky Moun¦tains
    (in N. America)
ro¦coco
rod +s
Rod¦den¦berry,
    Gene (American
    television
    producer)
rode
    rodes
    roded
    rod¦ing
    (past tense of
    ride; to fly.
    △ road, roed,
    rowed)
ro¦dent +s
ro¦den¦tial
ro¦den¦ti¦cide +s
rodeo +s
Rod¦er¦ick
Rodger *also* Roger
Rodg¦ers, Rich¦ard
    (American
    composer)
rod¦ham +s

Rodin, Au¦guste
    (French sculptor)
rod¦less
rod¦let +s
rod¦like
Rod¦ney
rodo¦mon¦tade
    rodo¦mon¦tades
    rodo¦mon¦taded
    rodo¦mon¦tad¦ing
roe +s (fish eggs or
    milt. △ ro, row)
roe
    plural roe *or* roes
    (deer. △ rho, row)
roe¦buck +s
roed (having roe.
    △ road, rode,
    rowed)
Roe¦dean (school,
    England)
roe-deer
    plural roe-deer
Roeg, Nich¦olas
    (English film
    director)
roent¦gen +s
roent¦gen¦
        og¦raphy
roent¦gen¦ology
Roese¦lare (town,
    Belgium)
roe-stone +s (rock)
ro¦ga¦tion +s
ro¦ga¦tion¦al
Ro¦ga¦tion¦tide
Roger (name)
roger +s +ed +ing
    (on radio etc.; also
    coarse slang)
Rogers, Gin¦ger
    (American actress
    and dancer)
Rogers, Rich¦ard
    (British architect)
Roget, Peter Mark
    (English scholar)
rogue
    rogues
    rogued
    roguing
roguery
    roguer¦ies
rogues' gal¦lery
    rogues' gal¦ler¦ies
roguish
roguish¦ly
roguish¦ness
roil +s +ed +ing
rois¦ter +s +ed
    +ing
rois¦ter¦er +s

rois¦ter¦ing +s
rois¦ter¦ous
Ro¦land (paladin of
    Charlemagne)
Ro¦land *also*
    Row¦land
    (name)
role +s (part in play
    etc. △ roll)
role-play
role-playing
role re¦ver¦sal +s
roll +s +ed +ing
    (turn over;
    cylinder; list;
    bread. △ role)
roll¦able
Rol¦land, Ro¦main
    (French writer)
roll¦away +s
roll-back +s *noun*
roll bar +s
roll-call +s
roll¦er +s
roll¦er¦ball +s
Roll¦er¦blade +s
    Propr.
roll¦er¦blade
    roll¦er¦blades
    roll¦er¦bladed
    roll¦er¦blad¦ing
roll¦er¦blader +s
roller-coast +s
    +ed +ing
roll¦er coast¦er +s
    noun
roller-coaster +s
    +ed +ing *verb and*
    attributive
roll¦er skate
    roll¦er skates
    roll¦er skated
    roll¦er skat¦ing
roll¦er skater +s
roll¦er towel +s
rol¦lick +s +ed
    +ing
roll¦ing mill +s
roll¦ing pin +s
roll¦ing stock
Roll¦ing Stones,
    the (English rock
    group)
roll¦mop +s
roll-neck +s
roll-on +s *adjective*
    and noun
roll-on roll-off
    adjective
roll-out +s *noun*
roll-over +s *noun*
    and attributive

Rolls, Charles Stew|art (English motoring and aviation pioneer)
Rolls-Royce +s
Propr.
roll-top +s
roll-top desk +s
roll-up +s
roly-poly
roly-polies
ROM +s (= read-only memory)
Rom
Roma
(male gypsy)
Ro|maic
ro|maine
ro|maji
Roman
roman (typeface)
roman-à-clef
romans-à-clef
Ro|mance
(languages)
ro|mance
ro|man|ces
ro|manced
ro|man|cing
(romantic atmosphere; love affair; story; exaggerate)
ro|man|cer +s
Roman de la rose
Ro|manes (the Romany language)
Ro|man|esque
roman-fleuve
romans-fleuves
Ro|mania
Ro|ma|nian +s
Ro|man|ic
ro|man|isa|tion *Br.*
(use romanization)
ro|man|ise *Br.* (use romanize)
ro|man|ises
ro|man|ised
ro|man|is|ing
Ro|man|ish
Ro|man|ism
Ro|man|ist +s
ro|man|iza|tion
ro|man|ize
ro|man|izes
ro|man|ized
ro|man|iz|ing
Ro|mano +s
Romano-British

Rom|anov (Russian dynasty)
Ro|mansh (dialects)
ro|man|tic +s
ro|man|tic|al|ly
ro|man|ti|cisa|tion *Br.* (use romanticization)
ro|man|ti|cise *Br.* (use romanticize)
ro|man|ti|cises
ro|man|ti|cised
ro|man|ti|cis|ing
ro|man|ti|cism
ro|man|ti|cist +s
ro|man|ti|ciza|tion
ro|man|ti|cize
ro|man|ti|cizes
ro|man|ti|cized
ro|man|ti|ciz|ing
Rom|any
Rom|anies
Rom|berg, Sig|mund (Hungarian-born American composer)
Rome (capital of Italy)
Romeo +s (in *Romeo and Juliet*; male lover)
romer +s (map-reading device.
△ roamer)
Rom|ish
Rom|mel, Erwin (German field marshal)
Rom|ney, George (English portrait painter)
rom|neya +s
romp +s +ed +ing
romp|er +s
romp|ing|ly
rompy
romp|ier
rompi|est
Rom|ulus *Roman Mythology*
Ron
Rona *also* Rhona
Ron|ald
Ronces|valles *also* Ronce|vaux (battle site, Spain)
ron|davel +s
ronde +s (dance)

ron|deau
ron|deaux
(poem. △ rondo)
ron|del +s
rondo +s (music.
△ rondeau)
Ron|dônia (state, Brazil)
rone +s (gutter.
△ roan)
roneo
ro|neoes
ro|neoed
ro|neo|ing
ronin +s
Rönt|gen, Wil|helm Con|rad (German physicist)
rönt|gen +s (use roentgen)
rönt|gen|og|raphy (use roentgenography)
rönt|gen|ology (use roentgenology)
roo +s (= kangaroo.
△ roux, rue)
rood +s (crucifix.
△ rude)
rood-loft +s
rood-screen +s
roof
roofs (*or* rooves) *noun*
roof +s +ed +ing *verb*
roof|age +s
roof|er +s
roof gar|den +s
roof|less
roof light +s
roof-rack +s
roof|scape +s
roof space +s
roof tile +s
roof|top +s
roof-tree +s (in roof)
rooi|bos
rooi|nek +s (*offensive*)
rook +s +ed +ing
rook|ery
rook|er|ies
rookie +s
rook|let +s
rook|ling +s
room +s +ed +ing (space; enclosed

room (*cont.*)
part of building; to lodge. △ rheum)
room|er +s
room|ette +s
room|ful +s
roomie +s (room-mate. △ rheumy, roomy)
room|ily
roomi|ness
room|ing house +s
room|mate *Am.* +s
room-mate *Br.* +s
room ser|vice
roomy
room|ier
roomi|est
(spacious.
△ rheumy, roomie)
Roose|velt, Elea|nor (American humanitarian)
Roose|velt, Frank|lin D. (American president)
Roose|velt, Theo|dore ('Teddy') (American president)
roost +s +ed +ing
roost|er +s
root +s +ed +ing (part of plant; basis; grow roots.
△ route)
root|age +s
root beer +s
root canal +s
root|ed|ness
root|er +s (supporter.
△ router)
roo|tle
roo|tles
roo|tled
root|ling
root|less
root|let +s
root|like
root-mean-square +s
root sign +s
root|stock +s
rootsy
root|sier
root|si|est

rooty
root|ier
rooti|est
rooves (use
roofs)
rope
ropes
roped
rop|ing
rope|able
rope lad¦der +s
rope¦man|ship
rope-moulding +s
rope's end +s
rope-walk +s
rope-walker +s
rope-walking
rope|way +s
ropey (use ropy)
rope-yard +s
rope-yarn +s
ropi¦ly
ropi|ness
rop|ing +s
ropy
ropi¦er
ropi|est
roque
Roque|fort
(cheese) *Propr.*
roque|laure +s
ro|quet +s +ed
+ing (croquet)
ro|*quette* (= rocket,
the herb)
Ror|aima (state,
(Brazil; mountain,
S. America)
ro-ro (= roll-on roll-
off)
ror|qual +s
Ror|schach test +s
rort +s (trick.
△ **wrought**)
rorty
rort|ier
rorti|est
Rory
Ros *also* Roz
Rosa, Sal|va¦tor
(Italian painter)
Rosa
ros¦ace +s
ros|aceous
Rosa|leen
Rosa|lie
Rosa|lind
rosa|line +s
Rosa|lyn
Rosa|mond *also*
Rosa|mund

Rosa|mund *also*
Rosa|mond
ros|an¦il|line +s
Ros¦anna
Ros¦anne *also*
Rose|anne
ros¦ar|ian +s
Ros¦ario (port,
Argentina)
ros¦ar|ium
ros¦ar|iums *or*
ros|aria
ros¦ary
ros¦ar|ies
(devotion; beads.
△ **rosery**)
Ros|cian
Ros|cius (Roman
actor)
ros¦coe +s
Ros|com|mon
(county and town,
Republic of
Ireland)
Rose (name)
rose +s (flower;
past tense of **rise**)
rosé +s (wine)
Rose|anne *also*
Ros¦anne
rose-apple +s
ros¦eate
Ros¦eau (capital of
Dominica, West
Indies)
rose|bay +s
Rose|bery, Lord
(British prime
minister)
rose|bowl +s
rose|bud +s
rose bush
rose bushes
rose-chafer +s
(beetle)
rose color *Am.*
rose-colored *Am.*
rose colour *Br.*
rose-coloured *Br.*
rose comb +s
rose-cut
rose dia|mond +s
rose-engine +s
rose-fish
plural rose-fish *or*
rose-fishes
rose-hip +s
rose leaf
rose leaves
rose|less
rose|like
ro|sella +s

rose mad¦der
rose|mal¦ing
rose-mallow +s
Rose|mary (name)
rose|mary (herb)
rose nail +s
ros|eola (rash;
disease)
ros|eo|lar
ros|eo|lous
rose pink +s *noun*
and adjective
rose-pink *attributive*
rose-point +s
rose quartz
rose red +s *noun*
and adjective
rose-red *attributive*
rose-root +s
(plant)
ros¦ery
ros|er|ies
(rose garden.
△ **rosary**)
rose-tinted
rose tree +s
Ros|etta Stone
ros|ette +s
ros|et¦ted
rose-water +s
rose-window +s
rose|wood +s
Rosh Hash|ana
Rosh Hash|anah
(use Rosh
Hashana)
Roshi +s
Rosi|cru¦cian +s
Rosi|cru¦cian|ism
Rosie
rosi¦ly
rosin +s +ed +ing
(resin, esp. the
type obtained
from turpentine.
△ **resin**)
Ros|in|ante (horse)
rosi|ness
ros¦iny
Ros|kilde (port,
Denmark)
ro|soglio +s (use
rosolio)
ro|solio +s
RoSPA (= Royal
Society for the
Prevention of
Accidents)
Ross, Diana
(American pop
singer)

Ross, James Clark
(British explorer)
Ross, John (British
explorer)
Ross, Ron|ald
(British physician)
Ross and
Crom|arty
(former county,
Scotland)
Ross
De¦pend|ency (in
Antarctica)
Ros|sel|lini,
Rob|erto (Italian
film director)
Ros|setti,
Chris|tina
(English poet)
Ros|setti, Dante
Gab|riel (English
painter)
Ros|sini,
Gioacch|ino
(Italian composer)
Ross|lare (port,
Republic of
Ireland)
Ross Sea (off
Antarctica)
Ross-shire (former
county, Scotland)
Ros|tand,
Ed¦mond (French
playwright)
ros|ter +s +ed
+ing
Ros|tock (port,
Germany)
Rostov-on-Don
(city, Russia)
ros¦tra
ros¦tral
ros|tral¦ly
ros|trate
ros|trated
ros|trif|er|ous
ros|tri|form
ros|trum
ros|trums *or*
ros¦tra
rosy
rosi¦er
rosi|est
rot
rots
rot¦ted
rot|ting
(decay. △ **wrot**)
rota +s (list; roster.
△ **rotor**)
Ro¦tar|ian +s

Ro¦tary (society)
ro¦tary
ro¦tar¦ies
Ro¦tary club +s
rotary-wing
  adjective
ro¦tat¦able
ro¦tate
  ro¦tates
  ro¦tated
  ro¦tat¦ing
ro¦ta¦tion +s
ro¦ta¦tion¦al
ro¦ta¦tion¦al¦ly
ro¦ta¦tive
ro¦ta¦tor +s
ro¦ta¦tory
ro¦ta¦vate
  ro¦ta¦vates
  ro¦ta¦vated
  ro¦ta¦vat¦ing
Ro¦ta¦va¦tor +s
  Propr.
rote +s (repetition.
  △ wrote)
rote learn¦ing
rote¦none
rot-gut
Roth, Philip
  (American
  novelist)
Rother¦ham (town,
  England)
Rothko, Mark
  (American
  painter)
Roths¦child,
  Meyer Am¦schel
  (German
  financier)
Roths¦child
  (banking-house)
ro¦ti¦fer +s
ro¦tis¦serie +s
ro¦to¦grav¦ure
rotor +s (rotating
  part. △ rota)
Ro¦to¦rua (resort,
  New Zealand)
roto¦till +s +ed
  +ing
Ro¦to¦va¦tor +s
  (alternative
  spelling of
  Rotavator) *Propr.*
rot-proof
rot¦ten
  rot¦tener
  rot¦ten¦est
rot¦ten¦ly
rot¦ten¦ness
rotten-stone

rot¦ter +s
Rot¦ter¦dam (city,
  the Netherlands)
Rott¦weiler +s
ro¦tund
ro¦tunda +s
ro¦tund¦ity
ro¦tund¦ly
Rou¦ault, Georges
  (French painter)
rou¦ble +s
rou¦cou +s
roué +s
Rouen (port,
  France)
rouge
  rouges
  rouged
  rou¦ging
rouge-et-noir
rough +s +ed +ing
  +er +est (coarse;
  treat roughly.
  △ ruff, ruffe)
rough¦age
rough-and-ready
rough-and-tumble
rough¦cast
  rough¦casts
  rough¦cast
  rough¦cast¦ing
rough-dry
  rough-dries
  rough-dried
  rough-drying
rough¦en +s +ed
  +ing
rough-handle
  rough-handles
  rough-handled
  rough-handling
rough-hew
  rough-hews
  rough-hewed
  rough-hewing
  rough-hewed *or*
  rough-hewn
rough hound +s
  (dogfish)
rough-house
  rough-houses
  rough-housed
  rough-housing
roughie +s
  (hooligan;
  outsider in horse
  race; unfair act.
  △ roughy)
rough¦ish
rough¦ly
rough¦neck +s
rough¦ness

rough-rider +s
rough¦shod
roughy
  rough¦ies
  (fish. △ roughie)
roul¦ade +s
roul¦eau
  roul¦eaux
Roul¦ers (French
  name for
  Roeselare)
roul¦ette +s
roul¦et¦ted
Rou¦mania (use
  Romania)
Rou¦ma¦nian (use
  Romanian)
Rou¦melia (use
  Rumelia)
round +s +ed +ing
round¦about +s
round-arm
  adjective
roundel +s
round¦elay +s
round¦er +s
Round¦head +s
round¦house +s
round¦ish
round¦ly
round¦ness
round-shouldered
rounds¦man
  rounds¦men
Round Tabler +s
round-the-clock
round-the-world
round-up +s *noun*
round¦worm +s
roup +s +ed +ing
roupy
rous¦able
rouse
  rouses
  roused
  rous¦ing
rouse¦about +s
rouser +s
rous¦ing¦ly
Rousse (use Ruse)
Rous¦seau, Henri
  (French painter)
Rous¦seau, Jean-
  Jacques (French
  philosopher)
Rous¦seau,
  Théo¦dore
  (French landscape
  painter)
Rous¦sil¦lon +s
  (wine; former
  French province)

roust +s +ed +ing
roust¦about +s
rout +s +ed +ing
  (defeat; riot; cut a
  groove)
route
  routes
  routed
  route¦ing
  (way taken.
  △ root)
router +s (tool.
  △ rooter)
rou¦tine
  rou¦tines
  rou¦tined
  rou¦tin¦ing
rou¦tine¦ly
rou¦tin¦isa¦tion *Br.*
  (use
  routinization)
rou¦tin¦ise *Br.* (use
  routinize)
  rou¦tin¦ises
  rou¦tin¦ised
  rou¦tin¦is¦ing
rou¦tin¦ism
rou¦tin¦ist +s
rou¦tin¦iza¦tion
rou¦tin¦ize
  rou¦tin¦izes
  rou¦tin¦ized
  rou¦tin¦iz¦ing
roux
  plural roux
  (sauce. △ roo,
  rue)
Ro¦van¦iemi (town,
  Finnish Lapland)
rove
  roves
  roved
  rov¦ing
rove bee¦tle +s
rover +s
Rovno (Russian
  name for Rivne)
row +s +ed +ing
  (series; propel
  boat; noise;
  quarrel; etc.
  △ rho, roe)
Rowan (name)
rowan +s (tree.
  △ rowen)
rowan-berry
  rowan-berries
row¦boat +s
row¦dily
row¦di¦ness
rowdy
  row¦dies

rowdy (*cont.*)
 row|dier
 row|di|est
rowdy|ism
Rowe, Nich|olas
 (English
 dramatist)
rowel
 rowels
 row|elled *Br.*
 row|eled *Am.*
 row|el|ling *Br.*
 ro|wel|ing *Am.*
rowen +s (second
 growth of grass.
 △ rowan)
Row|ena
rower +s
row house +s
row|ing boat +s
row|ing ma|chine
 +s
Row|land *also*
 Ro|land
**Row|land|son,
 Thomas** (English
 artist)
row|lock +s
Rown|tree (family
 of English
 entrepreneurs and
 philanthropists)
Row|ton house +s
Rox|burgh|shire
 (former county,
 Scotland)
Roy
royal +s
royal blue +s *noun
 and adjective*
royal-blue
 attributive
roy|al|ism
roy|al|ist +s
roy|al|is|tic
roy|al|ly
roy|alty
 roy|al|ties
Royce, Henry
 (English engine
 designer)
Roy|ston (town,
 England)
Roz *also* Ros
roz|zer +s
rub
 rubs
 rubbed
 rub|bing
rub-a-dub
 rub-a-dubs

rub-a-dub (*cont.*)
 rub-a-dubbed
 rub-a-dubbing
ru|bato
 ru|ba|tos *or*
 ru|bati
Rub'al Khali
 (desert, Arabian
 Peninsula)
rub|ber +s
rub|beri|ness
rub|ber|ise *Br.* (use
 rubberize)
 rub|ber|ises
 rub|ber|ised
 rub|ber|is|ing
rub|ber|ize
 rub|ber|izes
 rub|ber|ized
 rub|ber|iz|ing
rubber-like
rub|ber|neck +s
 +ed +ing
rub|ber plant +s
rub|ber stamp +s
 noun
rubber-stamp +s
 +ed +ing *verb*
rub|ber tree +s
rub|bery
rub|bing +s
rub|bish
 rub|bishes
 rub|bished
 rub|bish|ing
rub|bishy
rub|bity
rubbity-dub
rub|ble
rub|bly
Rub|bra, Ed|mund
 (English
 composer)
rub-down +s *noun*
rube +s
ru|be|fa|cient +s
ru|be|fac|tion
ru|befy
 ru|be|fies
 ru|be|fied
 ru|be|fy|ing
ru|bella (virus;
 German measles.
 △ rubeola)
ru|bel|lite +s
**Ru|bens, Peter
 Paul** (Flemish
 painter)
ru|beola (measles.
 △ rubella)
Ru|bi|con (stream,
 Italy)

ru|bi|con +s (in
 piquet)
ru|bi|cund
ru|bi|cund|ity
ru|bid|ium
ru|bify (use rubefy)
 ru|bi|fies
 ru|bi|fied
 ru|bi|fy|ing
ru|bigin|ous
Rubik's cube +s
 Propr.
**Rub|in|stein,
 Anton** (Russian
 composer)
**Rub|in|stein,
 Artur** (Polish-
 born American
 pianist)
**Rub|in|stein,
 Hel|ena**
 (American
 beautician)
ruble +s (use
 rouble)
ru|bric +s
ru|bric|al
ru|bri|cate
 ru|bri|cates
 ru|bri|cated
 ru|bri|cat|ing
 ru|bri|ca|tion
 ru|bri|ca|tor** +s
ru|bri|cian +s
ru|bri|cism
ru|bri|cist +s
rub-up +s
Ruby (name)
ruby
 ru|bies
 ru|bied
 ruby|ing
 (precious stone;
 dye ruby-colour)
ruby-tail +s
ruche
 ruches
 ruched
 ruch|ing
ruck +s +ed +ing
ruckle
 ruckles
 ruckled
 ruck|ling
ruck|sack +s
ruckus
 ruck|uses
ruc|tion +s
ru|da|ceous
rud|beckia +s
rudd
 plural rudd

rud|der +s
rud|der|less
rud|dily
rud|di|ness
rud|dle
 rud|dles
 rud|dled
 rud|dling
rud|dock +s
ruddy
 rud|dies
 rud|died
 ruddy|ing
 rud|dier
 rud|di|est
rude
 ruder
 rud|est
rude|ly
rude|ness
ru|deral +s
rudery
 ruder|ies
ru|di|ment +s
ru|di|men|tar|ily
**ru|di|men|tari|
 ness**
ru|di|men|tary
rud|ish
Ru|dolf *also*
 Ru|dolph
Ru|dolf, Lake
 (former name of
 Lake Turkana)
Ru|dolph *also*
 Ru|dolf
Rudra
Rud|ras
rue
 rues
 rued
 rue|ing *or* ruing
 (shrub; regret.
 △ roo, roux)
rue|ful
rue|ful|ly
rue|ful|ness
ruf|es|cence
ruf|es|cent
ruff +s +ed +ing
 (collar; bird;
 trump at cards.
 △ rough, ruffe)
ruffe +s (fish.
 △ rough, ruff)
ruf|fian +s
ruf|fian|ism
ruf|fian|ly
ruf|fle
 ruf|fles
 ruf|fled
 ruf|fling

ruff|like

rufi|yaa
  plural rufi|yaa

ruf|ous

Rufus (name)

Rufus, Wil|liam
  (William II of
  England)

rug +s

Rug|beian +s

Rugby (town and
  school, England)

rugby (football)

Rugby League

rugby play|er +s

Rugby Union

Rügen (island,
  Baltic Sea)

rug|ged

rug|ged|isa|tion
  (use
  ruggedization)

rug|ged|ise (use
  ruggedize)

rug|ged|ises

rug|ged|ised

rug|ged|is|ing

rug|ged|iza|tion

rug|ged|ize

rug|ged|izes

rug|ged|ized

rug|ged|iz|ing

rug|ged|ly

rug|ged|ness

rug|ger

ru|gosa +s

ru|gose

ru|gose|ly

ru|gos|ity

Ruhr (river and
  region, Germany)

ruin +s +ed +ing

ruin|ation

ruin|ous

ruin|ous|ly

ruin|ous|ness

Ruis|dael, Jacob
  van (Dutch
  painter)

Ruiz de Alar|cón y
  Men|doza, Juan
  (Spanish
  playwright)

rule

rules

ruled

rul|ing

rule book +s

rule-governed

rule|less

ruler +s

ruler|ship +s

rul|ing +s

rum

rums

rum|mer

rum|mest

Ru|mania (use
  Romania)

Ru|ma|nian +s
  (use Romanian)

Ru|mansh (use
  Romansh)

rumba

rum|bas

rum|baed *or*
  rumba'd

rumba|ing

rum baba +s

rum|ble

rum|bles

rum|bled

rum|bling

rum|bler +s

rum|bling +s

rum|bus|tious

rum|bus|tious|ly

rum|bus|tious|
  ness

Ru|melia (former
  region, S.E.
  Europe)

rumen

ru|mens *or*
  ru|mina

Rumi (Persian
  Islamic poet)

ru|min|ant +s

ru|min|ate

ru|min|ates

ru|min|ated

ru|min|at|ing

ru|min|ation +s

ru|mina|tive

ru|mina|tive|ly

ru|min|ator +s

rumly

rum|mage

rum|mages

rum|maged

rum|ma|ging

rum|ma|ger +s

rum|mer +s

rummy

rum|mier

rum|mi|est

rum|ness

rumor *Am.* +s +ed
  +ing

ru|mor|mon|ger
  Am. +s

ru|mor|mon|ger|
  ing *Am.*

ru|mour *Br.* +s +ed
  +ing

rumour-monger
  Br. +s

rumour-
  mongering *Br.*

rump +s

rum|ple

rum|ples

rum|pled

rum|pling

rump|less

rum|ply

rum|pus

rum|puses

rumpy

rum|pies

rumpy-pumpy

run

runs

ran

run|ning

run

run|about +s

run-around +s
  noun

run|away +s

run|cible spoon +s

run|cin|ate

Run|corn (town,
  England)

run|dale +s

run|down +s *noun*

run-down *adjective*

rune +s

rune-staff +s

rung +s (of ladder;
  past participle of
  ring. △ wrung)

runged

rung|less

runic

run-in +s *noun*

run|let +s

run|nable

run|nel +s

run|ner +s

runner-up
  runners-up

running-board +s

run|ning race +s

run|ning shoe +s

runny

run|nier

run|ni|est

Runny|mede (site
  of signing of
  Magna Carta,
  England)

run-off +s *noun and
  attributive*

run-of-the-mill

run-out +s *noun*

runt +s

run-through +s
  noun

runty

run-up +s *noun*

run|way +s

Run|yon, Damon
  (American writer)

rupee +s

Ru|pert (name)

Ru|pert, Prince
  (English Royalist
  general)

Ru|pert's Land (in
  Canada)

ru|pes|trian

ru|piah +s

rup|tur|able

rup|ture

rup|tures

rup|tured

rup|tur|ing

rural

rur|al|isa|tion *Br.*
  (use ruralization)

rur|al|ise *Br.* (use
  ruralize)

rur|al|ises

rur|al|ised

rur|al|is|ing

rur|al|ism

rur|al|ist +s

rur|al|ity

rur|al|ities

rur|al|iza|tion

rur|al|ize

rur|al|izes

rur|al|ized

rur|al|iz|ing

rur|al|ly

ruri|decan|al

Rurik +s (Russian
  dynasty)

Ruri|ta|nia

Ruri|ta|nian +s

rusa +s

Ruse (city,
  Bulgaria)

ruse +s (trick)

rush

rushes

rushed

rush|ing

Rush|die, Sal|man
  (Indian-born
  British novelist)

rush|er +s

rush hour +s *noun*

rush-hour *adjective*

rush|ing|ly

rush|light

rush|like
Rush|more,
 Mount (in USA)
rushy
 rush|ier
 rushi|est
rusk +s
Rus|kin, John
 (English art and
 social critic)
Russ
Rus|sell (name)
Rus|sell, Ber|trand
 (3rd Earl Russell,
 British
 philosopher)
Rus|sell, George
 Wil|liam (Irish
 poet)
Rus|sell, Henry
 Nor|ris (American
 astronomer)
Rus|sell, John (1st
 Earl Russell,
 British prime
 minister)
rus|set +s
rus|sety
Rus|sia +s
Rus|sian +s
Rus|sian|isa|tion
 Br. (use
 Russianization)
Rus|sian|ise Br.
 (use Russianize)
Rus|sian|ises
Rus|sian|ised
Rus|sian|is|ing
Rus|sian|iza|tion
Rus|sian|ize
Rus|sian|izes
Rus|sian|ized
Rus|sian|iz|ing
Rus|sian|ness
Rus|si|fi|ca|tion
Rus|sify
 Rus|si|fies
 Rus|si|fied
 Rus|si|fy|ing
Russki +s (often
 offensive)
Russo-Japanese
Russo|phile +s
Russo|phobe +s
Russo|pho|bia
rust +s +ed +ing
Rust Belt (region,
 USA)
rust belt
 (generally)
rus|tic +s
rus|tic|al|ly

rus|ti|cate
 rus|ti|cates
 rus|ti|cated
 rus|ti|cat|ing
 rus|ti|ca|tion +s
rus|ti|city
rust|ily
rusti|ness
rus|tle
 rus|tles
 rus|tled
 rust|ling
rust|ler +s
rust|less
rust|ling +s
rust|proof +s +ed
 +ing
rustre +s Heraldry
rusty
 rust|ier
 rusti|est
rut
 ruts
 rut|ted
 rut|ting
ru|ta|baga +s
Ruth (Bible; name)
Ruth, Babe
 (American
 baseball player)
Ru|the|nia (region,
 Ukraine)
ru|the|nium
Ruth|er|ford,
 Er|nest (New
 Zealand physicist)
Ruth|er|ford,
 Mar|ga|ret
 (English actress)
ruth|er|ford|ium
ruth|less
ruth|less|ly
ruth|less|ness
ru|tile +s
Rut|land (former
 county, England)
rut|tish
rutty
 rut|tier
 rut|ti|est
Ru|wen|zori
 (national park,
 Uganda)
Ruys|dael, Jacob
 van (use
 Ruisdael)
Rwanda
Rwan|dan +s
Rwan|dese
 plural Rwan|dese
Ryan

Rya|zan (city,
 Russia)
Ry|binsk (city,
 Russia)
Ryder, Sue
 (English
 philanthropist)
Ryder Cup +s (golf
 tournament)
rye +s (grain. △ rai,
 wry)
rye|grass
 rye|grasses
Ryle, Gil|bert
 (English
 philosopher)
Ryle, Mar|tin
 (English
 astronomer)
ry|okan +s
ryot +s (Indian
 peasant. △ riot)
Rysy (mountain,
 Poland)
Ryu|kyu Is|lands
 (in W. Pacific)
Ryurik +s (use
 Rurik)

Ss

Saadi (use Sadi)
Saale (river,
 Germany)
Saar (river, France
 and Germany)
Saar|brücken (city,
 Germany)
Saar|land (state,
 Germany)
sab
 sabs
 sabbed
 sab|bing
Saba (island,
 Netherlands
 Antilles)
saba|dilla +s
Sa|baean +s (of
 ancient Yemen.
 △ Sabian)
Sabah (state,
 Malaysia)
Saba|ism
Saba|oth
Sab|ba|tar|ian +s
Sab|ba|tar|ian|ism
sab|bath +s
sab|bat|ic +s
sab|bat|ic|al +s
sab|bat|ic|al|ly
sab|ba|tisa|tion Br.
 (use
 sabbatization)
sab|ba|tise Br. (use
 sabbatize)
 sab|ba|tises
 sab|ba|tised
 sab|ba|tis|ing
sab|ba|tiza|tion
sab|ba|tize
 sab|ba|tizes
 sab|ba|tized
 sab|ba|tiz|ing
Sa|bel|lian +s
saber Am. +s +ed
 +ing (Br. sabre)
saber-bill Am. +s
 (Br. sabre-bill)
saber-cut Am. +s
 (Br. sabre-cut)
saber-rattling Am.
 +s (Br. sabre-
 rattling)
saber|tooth Am. +s
 (Br. sabretooth)
saber-toothed Am.
 (Br. sabre-
 toothed)

Sa¦bian +s (of
ancient religious
sect. △Sabaean)
sab¦icu +s
Sabin, Al¦bert
Bruce (Russian-
born American
microbiologist;
vaccine)
Sab¦ina
Sab¦ine +s
sable +s
sabled
sably
sabot +s
sabo|tage
sabo|tages
sabo|taged
sabo|ta¦ging
sab|oted
sabo|teur +s
sabra +s
Sab|rata
(= Sabratha)
Sab|ra¦tha (ancient
city, Libya)
sabre Br.
sabres
sabred
sab¦ring
(Am. saber)
sabre-bill Br. +s
(Am. saber-bill)
sabre-cut Br. +s
(Am. saber-cut)
sabre-rattling Br.
+s (Am. saber-
rattling)
sabre|tache +s
sabre|tooth Br. +s
(Am. sabertooth)
sabre-toothed Br.
(Am. saber-
toothed)
sab|reur +s
sabre|wing +s
Sab¦rina
sac +s (baglike
cavity. △sack)
sac|cade +s
sac|cad¦ic
sac|cate
sac|char|ide +s
sac|char|im¦eter
+s
sac|char|im¦etry
sac|charin +s noun
sac|char¦ine
adjective
sac|charo|gen¦ic
sac|char|om¦eter
+s

sac|char|om¦etry
sac|char|ose
sac|ci|form
sac|cu|lar
sac|cu|late
sac|cu|lated
sac|cu|la¦tion +s
sac|cule +s
sacer|dot¦age
sacer|dotal
sacer|dot¦al|ism
sacer|dot¦al|ist +s
sacer|dot¦al|ly
Sacha also Sasha
sa¦chem +s
Sach¦er|torte
Sach¦er|tor¦ten
sa¦chet +s
Sa¦chev¦er|ell
Sachs, Hans
(German poet)
sack +s +ed +ing
(large bag; wine;
dismiss; plunder.
△sac)
sack|able
sack|but +s
sack|cloth +s
sack¦er +s
sack|ful +s
sack|ing +s
sack|less
sack|like
Sackville-West,
Vita (English
novelist)
sacra
sac¦ral
sac¦ra|ment +s
sac|ra|men¦tal
sac|ra|men|tal|ism
sac|ra|men|tal|ist
+s
sac|ra|men|tal|ity
sac|ra|men|tal|ly
sac|ra|ment|arian
+s
Sac¦ra|mento (city,
USA)
sac|rar¦ium
sac|raria
sac¦red
sac|red|ly
sac|red|ness
sac|ri|fice
sac|ri|fices
sac|ri|ficed
sac|ri|ficing
sac|ri|fi¦cial
sac|ri|fi¦cial|ly
sac|ri|lege +s
sac|ri|le¦gious

sac|ri|le¦gious|ly
sac¦ring
sac|rist +s
sac|ris|tan +s
sac|risty
sac|ris|ties
sacro|iliac
sacro|sanct
sacro|sanct|ity
sac¦rum
sacra
sad
sad¦der
sad|dest
Sadat, Anwar al-
(Egyptian
president)
Sad¦dam Hus|sein
(Iraqi president)
sad¦den +s +ed
+ing
sad|dish
sad¦dle
sad¦dles
sad¦dled
sad¦dling
saddle|back +s
saddle|backed
saddle|bag +s
sad¦dle bow +s
saddle-cloth +s
saddle-horse +s
saddle|less
sad¦dler +s
sad¦dlery
sad¦dler|ies
saddle-sore
sad¦dle stitch noun
sad¦dle tree +s
(saddle frame;
tree)
Sad¦du|cean
Sad¦du|cee +s
Sad¦du|cee|ism
Sade, Mar|quis de
(French writer)
sadhu +s
Sadi (Persian poet)
Sadie (name)
sad-iron +s
sad|ism
sad¦ist +s
sad|is¦tic
sad|is|tic|al|ly
Sad¦ler's Wells
(theatre, London)
sadly
sad|ness
sad|nesses
sado|maso¦chism
sado|maso¦chist
+s

sado|maso¦chis¦tic
sae¦ter +s (pasture.
△setter)
Safa|qis
(alternative name
for Sfax)
sa¦fari +s
Safa|vid +s
safe
safes
safer
saf¦est
safe-blower +s
safe-breaker +s
safe-cracker +s
safe|guard +s +ed
+ing
safe keep|ing
safe|ly
safe|ness
safety
safe|ties
safety belt +s
safety catch
safety catches
safety net +s
safety pin +s
safety valve +s
saf|flower +s
saf|fron +s
saf|froned
saf|frony
saf|ranin +s
saf|ran|ine +s
sag
sags
sagged
sag|ging
saga +s
sal|ga¦cious
sal|ga|cious|ly
sal|ga¦city
saga|more +s
Sagan, Fran|çoise
(French writer)
sage +s
sage|brush
sage green +s noun
and adjective
sage-green
attributive
sage grouse
plural sage grouse
sage|ly
sage|ness
sage|ship +s
sag|gar +s
sag|ger +s (use
saggar)
saggy
sag|gier
sag|gi|est

sag|itta +s
sag|it|tal
Sag|it|tar|ian +s
Sag|it|tar|ius
(constellation;
sign of zodiac)
sag|it|tate
sago +s
sa|guaro +s
Sa|guia el Hamra
(river and region,
Western Sahara)
sagy
Saha, Megh|nad
(Indian physicist)
Sa|hara (desert,
Africa)
Sa|haran +s
Sahel (savannah
region, W. Africa)
Sa|hel|ian (of or
pertaining to this
region)
sahib +s
sa|huaro +s (use
saguaro)
Said, Ed|ward W.
(American critic)
said (past tense and
past participle of
say)
Saida (Arabic name
for Sidon)
saiga +s
Sai|gon (city,
Vietnam)
sail +s +ed +ing
(on boat; travel on
the sea; move
easily. △ sale)
sail|able
sail-arm +s
sail|bag +s
sail|board +s
sail|board|er +s
sail|board|ing
sail|boat +s
sail|cloth +s
sail|er +s (ship.
△ sailor)
sail|fish
    plural sail|fish
sail-fluke +s
sail|ing +s
sail|ing boat +s
sail|ing mas|ter +s
sail|ing ship +s
sail|ing yacht +s
sail|less
sail|maker +s
sail|or +s (seaman.
△ sailer)

sail|or|ing
sail|or|less
sail|or|ly
sailor-man
    sailor-men
sail|plane +s
(glider)
Sai|maa Canal (in
Finland)
sain|foin +s
Sains|bury, John
James (English
grocer)
saint +s +ed +ing
St Al|bans (city,
England)
St An|drews (town,
Scotland)
St An|drew's cross
St An|thony cross
St An|thony's
cross
St An|thony's fire
St Anton (ski
resort, Austria)
St Ber|nard +s
(dog)
St Ber|nard Pass
('Great' and
'Little', in the
European Alps)
St Chris|to|pher
and Nevis, The
Fed|er|ation of
(official name of
St Kitts and
Nevis)
St Croix (island, US
Virgin Islands)
St David's (city,
Wales)
Saint-Denis
(suburb, Paris;
capital of
Réunion)
saint|dom +s
Sainte-Beuve,
Charles
Au|gus|tin
(French critic)
St Elmo's fire
St Émil|ion +s
(wine)
St-Étienne (city,
France)
St Eu|sta|tius
(Caribbean island)
St George's
(capital of
Grenada, West
Indies)

St George's
Chan|nel
(between Wales
and Ireland)
St Got|thard Pass
(in Switzerland)
St Hel|ena (island,
S. Atlantic)
St Hel|ens (town,
England)
St Hel|ens, Mount
(volcano, USA)
St Hel|ier (town,
Jersey, Channel
Islands)
saint|hood +s
St James's, Court
of (British royal
court)
St James's Pal|ace
(in London)
St John (island, US
Virgin Islands)
St John
Am|bu|lance
(first-aid
organization)
St John's (cities,
Canada and
Antigua)
St John's wort
St Kilda (group of
Scottish islands)
St Kitts and Nevis
(islands, West
Indies)
Saint Laur|ent,
Yves (French
couturier)
St Law|rence
River (in N.
America)
St Law|rence
Sea|way
St Leger (horse
race)
saint|like
saint|li|ness
saint|ling +s
St Louis (city, USA)
St Lucia (island,
West Indies)
saint|ly
    saint|lier
    saint|li|est
St Malo (port,
France)
St Mar|tin (island,
Caribbean Sea)
St Mor|itz (winter-
sports resort,
Switzerland)

St-Nazaire (port,
France)
Saint Nico|las
(town, Belgium)
St Pan|cras
(railway station,
London)
St Paul (city, USA)
saint|paulia +s
St Peter Port
(capital of
Guernsey)
St Peters|burg
(city, Russia)
St Pierre and
Mique|lon (island
group off
Newfoundland)
St Pöl|ten (city,
Austria)
Saint-Saëns,
Cam|ille (French
composer)
saint|ship +s
Saint-Simon,
Claude-Henri de
Rouv|roy, Comte
de (French social
reformer)
Saint-Simon,
Louis de
Rouv|roy, Duc
de (French writer)
St So|phia
(museum,
Istanbul)
St Ste|phens
(House of
Commons)
St Thomas (island,
US Virgin Islands)
St Trin|ian's
(fictional school)
St-Tropez (resort,
France)
St Vin|cent (island,
West Indies)
St Vin|cent, Cape
(in Portugal)
St Vitus's dance
Sai|pan (island, W.
Pacific)
saith (*archaic*
= says)
saithe
    plural saithe
(fish)
Sa|jama (mountain,
Bolivia)
Sakai (city, Japan)
sake +s (in 'for my
sake' etc.;

sake (*cont.*)
Japanese drink.
△ saki)
saker +s
sa¦keret +s
**Sakha, Re¦pub¦lic
of** (official name
of **Yakutia**)
Sakh¦alin (island,
Sea of Okhotsk)
**Sakh¦arov,
An¦drei** (Russian
nuclear physicist)
Saki (British writer)
saki +s (monkey.
△ **sake**)
Sakta +s
Sakti
Sakt¦ism
sal +s
sa¦laam +s +ed
+ing
sal¦able (use
saleable)
sal¦acious
sal¦acious¦ly
sal¦acious¦ness
sal¦acity
salad +s (food)
salad dress¦ing +s
sal¦ade +s (helmet)
Sala¦din (sultan of
Egypt and Syria)
Salam, Abdus
(Pakistani
physicist)
Sala¦manca (city,
Spain)
sala¦man¦der +s
sala¦man¦drian
sala¦man¦drine
sala¦man¦droid +s
sa¦lami +s
Sala¦mis (island,
Saronic Gulf,
Greece)
sal am¦mo¦niac
sal¦an¦gane
Sa¦lang Pass
(Afghanistan)
sal¦ar¦iat +s
sal¦ar¦ied
sal¦ary
sal¦ar¦ies
sal¦ary¦man
sal¦ary¦men
**Sala¦zar, An¦tonio
de Oli¦veira**
(Portuguese prime
minister)
sal¦bu¦ta¦mol

sal¦chow +s
sale +s (selling.
△ **sail**)
sale¦abil¦ity
sale¦able
Salem (cities, USA
and India)
salep +s
sal¦er¦atus
sale ring +s
Sal¦erno (port,
Italy)
sale¦room +s
sales force +s
sales¦girl +s
Sal¦es¦ian +s
sales¦lady
sales¦ladies
sales¦man
sales¦men
sales¦man¦ship
sales¦per¦son
sales¦per¦sons *or*
sales¦people
sales¦room +s
sales¦woman
sales¦women
Sal¦ford (city,
England)
Sa¦lian +s
Salic +s
sali¦cet +s
sali¦cin
sali¦cine
sal¦icional +s
sa¦li¦cyl¦ate +s
sali¦cyl¦ic
sa¦li¦ence
sa¦li¦ency
sa¦li¦ent +s
sa¦li¦en¦tian +s
sa¦li¦ent¦ly
Sali¦eri, An¦tonio
(Italian composer)
sal¦ifer¦ous
sal¦ina +s
sa¦line +s
Sal¦in¦ger, J. D.
(American writer)
salin¦isa¦tion *Br.*
(use **salinization**)
sal¦in¦ity
salin¦iza¦tion
salin¦om¦eter +s
Salis¦bury (city,
England; former
name of **Harare**)
Salis¦bury, Lord
(British prime
minister)
Sa¦lish
plural Sa¦lish

sal¦iva +s
sal¦iv¦ary
sali¦vate
sali¦vates
sali¦vated
sali¦vat¦ing
sali¦va¦tion
Salk vac¦cine
sal¦lee +s (tree.
△ **sally**)
sal¦len¦ders
sal¦let +s
sal¦low +s +ed
+ing
sal¦low¦ish
sal¦low¦ness
sal¦lowy
Sal¦lust (Roman
historian)
Sally (name)
sally
sal¦lies
sal¦lied
sally¦ing
(sortie etc.; part of
bell-rope)
sally-hole +s
Sally Lunn +s
sally-port +s
sal¦ma¦gundi +s
sal¦ma¦nazar +s
salmi +s
sal¦mon
plural sal¦mon *or*
sal¦mons
sal¦mon¦ella
sal¦mon¦el¦lae
sal¦mon¦el¦losis
sal¦monid +s
salmon-ladder +s
sal¦mon¦oid +s
sal¦mon pink
noun and adjective
salmon-pink
attributive
sal¦mon trout
plural sal¦mon
trout *or* sal¦mon
trouts
sal¦mony
Sal¦ome *Bible*
Salon, the (French
art exhibition)
salon +s (room)
Sal¦on¦ica
(alternative name
for **Thessaloníki**)
sal¦oon +s
saloon-keeper +s
Salop (alternative
name for
Shropshire)

sal¦op¦ette +s
Sal¦op¦ian +s
sal¦pi¦glos¦sis
sal¦pin¦gec¦tomy
sal¦pin¦
gec¦to¦mies
sal¦pin¦gitis
salsa +s
sal¦sify
sal¦si¦fies
SALT (= Strategic
Arms Limitation
Talks)
salt +s +ed +ing
salt-and-pepper
attributive
sal¦tar¦ello
sal¦tar¦el¦los *or*
sal¦tar¦elli
sal¦ta¦tion +s
sal¦ta¦tor¦ial
sal¦ta¦tory
salt¦bush
salt¦bushes
salt-cat +s
salt cellar +s
salt¦er +s
salt¦ern +s
salt-glaze
salt-glazes
salt-glazed
salt-glazing
salt grass
salt grasses
sal¦ti¦grade +s
Sal¦tillo (city,
Mexico)
salti¦ness
salt¦ing +s
sal¦tire +s *Heraldry*
sal¦tire¦wise
salt¦ish
Salt Lake City
(city, USA)
salt¦less
salt lick +s
salt¦ly
salt marsh
salt marshes
salt mine +s
salt¦ness
salt pan +s
salt¦peter *Am.*
salt¦petre *Br.*
salt shaker +s
salt spoon +s
sal¦tus
plural sal¦tus
salt water *noun*
salt-water
attributive
salt well +s

salt works
  plural **salt works**
salt|wort +s
salty
  salt|ier
  salti|est
sa|lu|bri|ous
sa|lu|bri|ous|ly
sa|lu|bri|ous|ness
sa|lu|brity
sa|luki +s
salu|tar|ily
salu|tary
sa|lu|ta|tion +s
sa|lu|ta|tion|al
sa|lu|ta|tor|ian +s
sa|lu|ta|tory
sa|lute
  sa|lutes
  sa|luted
  sa|lut|ing
sa|luter +s
sa|lut|ing base +s
salv|able
Sal|va|dor (port, Brazil)
Sal|va|dor, El (in Central America)
Sal|va|dor|ean +s
sal|vage
  sal|vages
  sal|vaged
  sal|va|ging
sal|vage|able
sal|va|ger +s
sal|va|tion
sal|va|tion|ism
sal|va|tion|ist +s
salve
  salves
  salved
  salv|ing
  (ointment; soothe)
sal|ver +s (tray.
  △ salvor)
sal|via +s
Salvo +s (member of Salvation Army)
salvo
  · salvos *or* sal|voes
  (gunfire)
salvo +s (saving clause; excuse)
sal vola|tile
sal|vor +s
  (salvager.
  △ salver)
Sal|ween (river, SE Asia)
Sal|yut +s (Soviet space stations)

Salz|burg (state and city, Austria)
Salz|git|ter (city, Germany)
Salz|kam|mer|gut (area, Austria)
SAM (= surface-to-air missile)
Sam (name)
sam|adhi
Sam|an|tha
Samar (island, Philippines)
Sam|ara (city, Russia)
sam|ara +s (winged seed)
Sam|aria (ancient Hebrew city and surrounding region)
Sam|ar|inda (city, Indonesia)
Sa|mar|itan +s
Sa|mar|it|an|ism
sa|mar|ium
Sam|ar|kand (city, central Asia)
Sam|arra (city, Iraq)
Sama-veda *Hinduism*
samba
  sam|bas
  sam|baed *or* samba'd
  samba|ing
  (dance)
sam|bar +s (large deer)
sam|bhar +s (use sambar)
Sambo
  Sam|bos *or* Sam|boes
  (*offensive*)
Sam Browne +s
sam|bur +s (use sambar)
same
samel
same|ness
samey
samey|ness
samfu +s
Sam|hain +s
Sami (Lapps; Lappish)
Sa|mian +s
sami|sen +s
sam|ite +s
sam|iz|dat +s

sam|let +s
Sammy
Sam|nite +s
Samoa (group of Polynesian islands)
Sa|moan +s
Samos (island, Aegean Sea)
sa|mosa +s
samo|var +s
Sam|oyed +s
Sam|oy|ed|ic
samp
sam|pan +s
sam|phire +s
sam|ple
  sam|ples
  sam|pled
  sam|pling
sam|pler +s
sam|pling +s
sam|sara
sam|sar|ic
sam|skara +s
Sam|son *Bible*
Sam|son post +s
Sam|son's post +s (use Samson post)
Sam|uel (*Bible*; name)
sam|urai
  plural **sam|urai**
San
  plural **San**
  (African aboriginal Bushman)
san +s
  (= sanatorium)
Sa|na'a (capital of Yemen)
San An|dreas fault (in California)
San An|drés (island, Caribbean Sea)
San An|tonio (city, USA)
sana|tive
sana|tor|ium
  sana|tor|iums *or* sana|toria
sana|tory (healing.
  △ sanitary)
san|ben|ito +s
San Car|los de Bari|loche (ski resort, Argentina)
San|chi (site of Buddhist shrines, India)

San|cho Panza (fictional character)
sanc|ti|fi|ca|tion
sanc|ti|fier +s
sanc|tify
  sanc|ti|fies
  sanc|ti|fied
  sanc|ti|fy|ing
sanc|ti|mo|ni|ous
sanc|ti|mo|ni| ous|ly
sanc|ti|mo|ni|ous| ness
sanc|ti|mony
sanc|tion +s +ed +ing
sanc|tion|able
sanc|ti|tude
sanc|tity
  sanc|tities
sanc|tu|ary
  sanc|tu|ar|ies
sanc|tum +s
sanc|tum
sanc|torum
  sancta
  sanc|torum *or* sanc|tum
  sanc|tor|ums
sanc|tus
Sand, George (French novelist)
sand +s +ed +ing (grains etc.
  △ sans)
san|dal
  san|dals
  san|dalled *Br.*
  san|daled *Am.*
  san|dal|ling *Br.*
  san|dal|ing *Am.*
san|dal tree +s
san|dal|wood +s
San|dal|wood Is|land (alternative name for Sumba)
san|darac
san|dar|ach (use sandarac)
sand|bag
  sand|bags
  sand|bagged
  sand|bag|ging
sand|bag|ger +s
sand|bank +s
sand|bar +s
sand-bath +s
sand-bed +s
sand|blast +s +ed +ing

sand|blast|er +s
sand|box
  sand|boxes
sand|boy +s
sand|cas|tle +s
sand cloud +s
sand-crack +s
sand dune +s
sand|er +s (person
  or thing that
  sands)
san|der|ling +s
san|ders
  plural san|ders
  (tree)
sand flea +s
sand|fly
  sand|flies
sand-glass
  sand-glasses
  (hourglass)
sand-groper +s
sand|grouse
  plural
  sand|grouse
san|dhi
sand|hill +s
sand|hog +s
sand-hopper +s
Sand|hurst (Royal
  Military Academy,
  England)
San Diego (city,
  USA)
sandi|ness
San|di|nista +s
san|di|ver
sand|like
sand|lot +s
sand|man
  sand|men
sand mar|tin +s
sand|paper +s +ed
  +ing
sand|piper +s
sand|pit +s
San|dra
San|dring|ham
  House (royal
  residence,
  England)
sand-shoe +s
sand-skipper +s
sand|soap +s
sand|stock
sand|stone +s
sand|storm +s
Sand|wich (town,
  England)
sand|wich
  sand|wiches
  sand|wiched

sand|wich (*cont.*)
  sand|wich|ing
  (food)
sandwich-board
  +s
Sand|wich
  Is|lands (former
  name of Hawaii)
sandwich-man
  sandwich-men
Sand|wich tern +s
sand|wort +s
Sandy (name)
sandy
  sand|ier
  sandi|est
  (like or having
  much sand)
sand yacht +s
sandy|ish
sane
  saner
  san|est
  (not mad. △ seine,
  seiner)
sane|ly
sane|ness
San|for|ised (use
  Sanforized)
San|for|ized *Propr.*
San Fran|cisco
  (city, USA)
sang
sanga +s (use
  sangar)
san|gar +s
  (stone breastwork.
  △ sangha)
san|garee +s
sang-de-boeuf
Sang|er,
  Mar|ga|ret
  (American birth-
  control
  campaigner)
sang-froid
sangha +s
  (Buddhist
  monastic order.
  △ sangar)
Sango
san|grail
san|gria +s
san|gui|fi|ca|tion
san|guin|ar|ily
san|guin|ari|ness
san|guin|ary
san|guine +s
san|guine|ly
san|guine|ness
san|guin|eous

San|hed|rim
  (= Sanhedrin)
San|hed|rin
san|icle +s
san|ify
  sani|fies
  sani|fied
  sani|fy|ing
sani|tar|ian +s
sani|tar|ily
sani|tari|ness
sani|tar|ium
  sani|tar|iums *or*
  sani|taria
sani|tary (healthy,
  hygienic.
  △ sanatory)
sani|tate
  sani|tates
  sani|tated
  sani|tat|ing
sani|ta|tion
sani|ta|tion|ist +s
sani|tisa|tion *Br.*
  (use sanitization)
sani|tise *Br.* (use
  sanitize)
  sani|tises
  sani|tised
  sani|tis|ing
sani|tiser *Br.* +s
  (use sanitizer)
sani|tiza|tion
sani|tize
  sani|tizes
  sani|tized
  sani|tiz|ing
sani|tizer +s
san|ity
San Jose (city,
  USA)
San José (capital of
  Costa Rica)
San Juan (capital
  of Puerto Rico)
sank
San Luis Pot|osí
  (state, Mexico)
San Mar|ino
  (republic)
San Mar|tín, José
  de (Argentinian
  soldier)
san|nyasi
  plural san|nyasi *or*
  san|nya|sis
San Pedro Sula
  (city, Honduras)
san|pro (= sanitary
  protection)
sans (without.
  △ sand)

San Sal|va|dor
  (capital of El
  Salvador)
sans-culotte +s
sans-culott|ism
San Se|bas|tián
  (port, Spain)
san|serif (use sans
  serif)
San|skrit
San|skrit|ic
San|skrit|ist +s
San|so|vino,
  Ja|copo Tatti
  (Italian sculptor)
sans serif +s
Santa +s (= Santa
  Claus)
Santa Ana (city, El
  Salvador)
Santa Bar|bara
  (city, USA)
Santa Cata|rina
  (state, Brazil)
Santa Claus
  Santa Clauses
Santa Cruz (city,
  Bolivia)
Santa Fe (cities,
  USA and
  Argentina)
Santa Mon|ica
  (city, USA)
San|tan|der (port,
  Spain)
Santa So|phia
  (= St Sophia)
San|tiago (capital
  of Chile)
San|tiago de
  Com|po|stela
  (city, Spain)
San|tiago de Cuba
  (city, Cuba)
Santo Dom|ingo
  (capital of the
  Dominican
  Republic)
san|to|lina +s
san|ton|ica +s
san|tonin
San|tor|ini
  (alternative name
  for Thera)
San|tos (port,
  Brazil)
san|yasi
  plural san|yasi *or*
  san|ya|sis
  (use sannyasi)
São Fran|cisco
  (river, Brazil)

São Luís (port,
  Brazil)
Saône (river,
  France)
São Paulo (city and
  state, Brazil)
São Tomé (capital
  of São Tomé and
  Príncipe)
São Tomé and
  Prin|cipe (islands,
  Gulf of Guinea)
sap
  saps
  sapped
  sap|ping
sapa|jou +s
sapan|wood (use
  sappanwood)
sa|pele +s
sap|ful
sap green +s noun
  and adjective
sap-green
  attributive
sapid
sa|pid|ity
sapi|ence
sapi|ens (in 'Homo
  sapiens')
sapi|ent
sa|pi|en|tial
sa|pi|ent|ly
Sapir, Ed|ward
  (German-born
  American
  linguistics scholar)
sap|less
sap|ling +s
sapo|dilla +s
sap|on|aceous
sa|poni|fi|able
sa|poni|fi|ca|tion
sa|pon|ify
  sa|poni|fies
  sa|poni|fied
  sa|poni|fy|ing
sap|onin +s
sapor +s
sap|pan|wood
sap|per +s
Sap|phic +s (of
  Sappho or her
  poetry; lesbian)
sap|phic +s (verse)
sap|phire +s
sap|phire blue +s
  noun and adjective
sapphire-blue
  attributive
sap|phir|ine
Sap|phism

Sap|pho (Greek
  lyric poet)
sap|pily
sap|pi|ness
Sap|poro (city,
  Japan)
sappy
  sap|pier
  sap|pi|est
sapro|gen|ic
sap|ropha|gous
sapro|phile +s
sap|roph|il|ous
sapro|phyte +s
sapro|phyt|ic
sap|suck|er +s
sap|wood
Saq|qara
  (necropolis,
  ancient Memphis)
Sara also Sarah
sara|band +s
Sara|cen +s
Sara|cen|ic
Sara|gossa (city,
  Spain)
Sarah Bible
Sarah also Sara
  (name)
Sara|jevo (capital
  of
  Bosnia–Herzegovina)
sar|angi +s
Sar|ansk (city,
  Russia)
sar|ape +s (use
  serape)
Sara|toga (city,
  USA)
Sara|tov (city,
  Russia)
Sara|wak (state,
  Malaysia)
sar|casm +s
sar|cas|tic
sar|cas|tic|al|ly
sar|celle +s
sar|cenet +s (use
  sarsenet)
sar|coma
  sar|co|mas or
  sar|co|mata
sar|coma|tosis
sar|coma|tous
sar|copha|gus
  sar|coph|agi
sarco|plasm
sar|cous
Sard +s
  (= Sardinian)
sard +s
Sar|da|na|pa|lian

Sar|da|napa|lus
  (Assyrian king)
sar|dar +s
sar|delle +s
sar|dine +s
Sar|dinia (island,
  Mediterranean)
Sar|din|ian +s
Sar|dis (ancient
  city, Asia Minor)
sar|dius
sar|don|ic
sar|don|ic|al|ly
sar|doni|cism +s
sard|onyx
saree +s (use sari)
sar|gasso +s
Sar|gasso Sea (part
  of W. Atlantic)
sarge (= sergeant)
Sar|gent, John
  Sing|er (American
  painter)
Sar|gent,
  Mal|colm
  (English
  conductor)
Sar|godha (city,
  Pakistan)
Sar|gon (founder of
  Akkad)
Sar|gon II
  (Assyrian king)
sari +s
sarin
Sark (Channel
  Island)
sark +s (garment)
sar|kar +s
sark|ily
sarki|ness
sark|ing
sarky
  sark|ier
  sark|iest
Sar|ma|tia (ancient
  region, E. Europe)
Sar|ma|tian +s
sar|men|tose
sar|men|tous
sar|nie +s
  (= sandwich)
sar|ong +s
Sar|on|ic Gulf (on
  coast of Greece)
saros
Sarre (French name
  for the Saar)
sar|ruso|phone +s
sar|sa|par|illa +s
sar|sen +s
sar|senet +s

Sarto, An|drea del
  (Italian painter)
sar|tor|ial
sar|tori|al|ly
sar|tor|ius
  plural sar|tor|ius
  muscles
Sartre, Jean-Paul
  (French
  philosopher)
Sar|trean +s
Sarum (former
  name of
  Salisbury,
  England; in 'Old
  Sarum')
sash
  sashes
Sasha also Sacha
sashay +s +ed
  +ing
sash cord +s
sashed
sash|imi +s
sash tool +s
sash weight +s
sash win|dow +s
sasin +s (gazelle)
sas|ine +s Law
Sas|katch|ewan
  (province and
  river, Canada)
Sas|ka|toon (city,
  Canada)
Sas|kia
Sas|quatch
  Sas|quatches
sass
  sasses
  sassed
  sass|ing
sas|saby
  sas|sa|bies
sas|sa|fras
Sas|sa|nian +s
Sas|sanid +s
Sas|sen|ach +s
  (may cause offence)
sas|si|ly
sas|si|ness,
Sas|soon,
  Sieg|fried
  (English writer)
Sas|soon, Vidal
  (English
  hairstylist)
sassy
  sas|sier
  sas|si|est
sas|trugi
SAT +s (= standard
  assessment task)

sat (past tense and
past participle of
sit)
satai +s (use satay)
Satan
sat¦ang
  plural sat¦ang or
  sat¦angs
sa¦tan¦ic
sa¦tan¦ic¦al¦ly
Sa¦tan¦ise Br. (use
  Satanize)
  Sa¦tan¦ises
  Sa¦tan¦ised
  Sa¦tan¦is¦ing
Sa¦tan¦ism
Sa¦tan¦ist +s
Sa¦tan¦ize
  Sa¦tan¦izes
  Sa¦tan¦ized
  Sa¦tan¦iz¦ing
Sa¦tan¦ology
satay +s
satchel +s
sate
  sates
  sated
  sat¦ing
  (gratify; surfeit)
saté +s (food; use
  satay)
sat¦een +s
sate¦less
sat¦el¦lite +s
sat¦el¦lit¦ic
sat¦el¦lit¦ism
Sati (wife of Siva)
sati +s (widow who
  immolates herself;
  such self-
  immolation; use
  suttee)
sa¦tiable
sa¦ti¦ate
  sa¦ti¦ates
  sa¦ti¦ated
  sa¦ti¦at¦ing
sa¦ti¦ation
Satie, Erik (French
  composer)
sa¦ti¦ety
satin +s +ed +ing
sat¦inet +s (use
  satinette)
satin¦ette +s
satin¦flower +s
satin¦ised Br. (use
  satinized)
satin¦ized
satin stitch
satin-stitched

satin white +s
  noun and adjective
satin-white
  attributive
satin¦wood +s
sat¦iny
sat¦ire +s
sa¦tir¦ic
sa¦tir¦ic¦al
sa¦tir¦ic¦al¦ly
sat¦ir¦isa¦tion Br.
  (use satirization)
sat¦ir¦ise Br. (use
  satirize)
  sat¦ir¦ises
  sat¦ir¦ised
  sat¦ir¦is¦ing
sat¦ir¦ist +s
sat¦ir¦iza¦tion
sat¦ir¦ize
  sat¦ir¦izes
  sat¦ir¦ized
  sat¦ir¦iz¦ing
sat¦is¦fac¦tion +s
sat¦is¦fac¦tor¦ily
sat¦is¦fac¦tori¦ness
sat¦is¦fac¦tory
sat¦is¦fi¦abil¦ity
sat¦is¦fi¦able
sat¦is¦fied¦ly
sat¦isfy
  sat¦is¦fies
  sat¦is¦fied
  sat¦is¦fy¦ing
  sat¦is¦fy¦ing¦ly
sat¦nav (= satellite
  navigation)
sa¦tori
sat¦ranji +s
sat¦rap +s
sat¦rapy
  sat¦rap¦ies
Sat¦suma (former
  province, Japan;
  pottery)
sat¦suma +s (fruit)
sat¦ur¦able
sat¦ur¦ant +s
sat¦ur¦ate
  sat¦ur¦ates
  sat¦ur¦ated
  sat¦ur¦at¦ing
sat¦ur¦ation +s
sat¦ur¦ation point
  +s
Sat¦ur¦day +s
Sat¦urn (Roman
  Mythology; planet)
Sat¦ur¦na¦lia
  (Roman festival)
sat¦ur¦na¦lia +s
  (orgy)

Sat¦ur¦na¦lian (of
  Saturnalia)
sat¦ur¦na¦lian
  (orgiastic)
Sat¦urn¦ian
sat¦urn¦ic
sat¦urni¦id +s
sat¦ur¦nine
sat¦ur¦nine¦ly
sat¦urn¦ism
sat¦ya¦graha +s
satyr +s
satyr¦ia¦sis
sa¦tyr¦ic
sa¦tyrid +s
sauce
  sauces
  sauced
  sau¦cing
sauce-boat +s
sauce¦box
  sauce¦boxes
sauce¦less
sauce¦pan +s
sauce¦pan¦ful +s
sau¦cer +s
sau¦cer¦ful +s
sau¦cer¦less
sau¦cily
sau¦ci¦ness
saucy
  sau¦cier
  sau¦ci¦est
Saudi +s
Saudi Ara¦bia
Saudi Ara¦bian +s
sauer¦kraut +s
sau¦ger +s
Saul Bible
Sault Sainte Marie
  (cities, USA and
  Canada)
Sau¦mur +s (town,
  France; wine)
sauna +s
saun¦ders
saun¦ter +s +ed
  +ing
saun¦ter¦er +s
saur¦ian +s
saur¦is¦chian +s
sauro¦pod +s
saury
  saur¦ies
saus¦age +s
Saus¦sure,
  Fer¦di¦nand de
  (Swiss linguistics
  scholar)
sauté +s +ed +ing
Sau¦ternes
  plural Sau¦ternes

Sau¦ternes (cont.)
  (district, France;
  wine)
Sauve¦ter¦rian +s
Sau¦vi¦gnon +s
sav¦able
Sav¦age, Mi¦chael
  (New Zealand
  prime minister)
sav¦age
  sav¦ages
  sav¦aged
  sav¦aging
sav¦age¦dom
sav¦age¦ly
sav¦age¦ness
sav¦agery
  sav¦ager¦ies
Sav¦ai'i (island,
  Western Samoa)
sa¦vanna +s (use
  savannah)
Sa¦van¦nah (port
  and river, USA)
sa¦van¦nah +s
  (grassy plain)
Sa¦van¦na¦khet
  (town, Laos)
sav¦ant +s male
sav¦ante +s female
sa¦vate (form of
  boxing)
save
  saves
  saved
  sav¦ing
save-all +s
sav¦eloy +s
saver +s
Sav¦ery, Thomas
  (English engineer)
savin +s
sav¦ine +s (use
  savin)
sav¦ing +s
sa¦vior Am. +s
sa¦viour Br. +s
sav¦oir faire
sav¦oir vivre
Sav¦ona¦rola,
  Gir¦ol¦amo
  (Italian preacher)
Sav¦on¦linna
  (town, Finland)
Sav¦on¦nerie +s
savor Am. +s +ed
  +ing (Br. savour)
sa¦vor¦ily Am. (Br.
  savourily)
sa¦vori¦ness Am.
  (Br. savouriness)

sa¦vor|less *Am.* (*Br.*
  savourless)
sa¦vory
  sa¦vor|ies
  (herb. △ savoury)
sa¦vory *Am.*
  sa¦vor|ies
  (not sweet; dish.
  △ savoury)
sa¦vour *Br.* +s +ed
  +ing (*Am.* savor)
sa¦vour|ily *Br.* (*Am.*
  savorily)
sa¦vouri|ness *Br.*
  (*Am.* savoriness)
sa¦vour|less *Br.*
  (*Am.* savorless)
sa¦voury *Br.*
  sa¦vour|ies
  (*Am.* savory. not
  sweet; dish.
  △ savory)
Savoy (region,
  France)
savoy +s (cabbage)
Sa¦voy|ard
Savu Sea (part of
  Indian Ocean)
savvy
  sav|vies
  sav|vied
  savvy|ing
saw
  saws
  sawed
  saw¦ing
  sawn *or* sawed
  (tool; cut;
  proverb; past
  tense of see.
  △ soar, sore)
saw|bench
  saw|benches
saw|bill +s
saw|bones
  plural saw|bones
saw|buck +s
saw¦cut +s
saw-doctor +s
saw|dust
saw-edged
sawed-off
  attributive
saw|fish
  plural saw|fish *or*
  saw|fishes
saw¦fly
  saw|flies
saw frame +s
saw-gate +s
saw-gin +s

saw|grass
  saw|grasses
saw|horse +s
saw|like
saw|mill +s
sawn
sawn-off *attributive*
saw-pit +s
saw-set +s
saw|tooth
saw|toothed
saw-wort +s
saw¦yer +s
sax
  saxes
  (saxophone; tool.
  △ saxe)
saxa|tile
sax|board +s
saxe +s (colour.
  △ sax)
saxe blue +s *noun*
  and adjective
saxe-blue
  attributive
Saxe-Coburg-
  Gotha (former
  name of royal
  house of Windsor)
sax|horn +s
sax|icol|ine
sax|ico|lous
saxi|frage +s
sax¦ist +s
Saxon +s
Saxon blue
Saxon|dom
Saxon|ise *Br.* (use
  Saxonize)
  Saxon|ises
  Saxon|ised
  Saxon|is|ing
Saxon|ism
Saxon|ist +s
Saxon|ize
  Saxon|izes
  Saxon|ized
  Saxon|iz|ing
Sax¦ony (state,
  Germany)
sax¦ony
  sax¦on|ies
  (wool; cloth)
Saxony-Anhalt
  (state, Germany)
saxo|phone +s
saxo|phon¦ic
sax|opho|nist +s
say
  says
  said

say (*cont.*)
  say¦ing
  (utter. △ sei)
say|able
sayer +s
Say¦ers, Doro|thy
  L. (English writer)
say¦ing +s
say-so
S-bend +s
scab
  scabs
  scabbed
  scab|bing
scab|bard +s
scabbard-fish
  plural scabbard-
  fish *or* scabbard-
  fishes
scab|bi|ness
scabby
  scab|bier
  scab|bi|est
sca|bies
sca|bi|ous
  plural sca|bi|ous
scab|like
scab|rous
scab|rous¦ly
scab|rous|ness
scad +s
Sca|fell Pike (peak,
  England)
scaf|fold +s +ed
  +ing
scaf|fold¦er +s
scaf¦fold|ing +s
scag +s (use skag)
scagli|ola
scal|abil|ity
scal|able
sca¦lar +s
  (*Mathematics.*
  △ scaler)
sca|lari|form
scala|wag +s (use
  scallywag)
scald +s +ed +ing
  (burn with liquid
  or steam. △ skald)
scald¦er +s
scald-head +s
scale
  scales
  scaled
  scal¦ing
scale armor *Am.*
scale ar¦mour *Br.*
scale-board +s
scale-bug +s
scale-fern +s

scale-leaf
  scale-leaves
scale|less
scale|like
scale-moss
  scale-mosses
scal|ene +s
sca|lenus
  sca|leni
scale-pan +s
scaler +s (person
  or thing that
  scales. △ scalar)
Scales, the
  (constellation;
  sign of zodiac)
scale-winged
scale work
Scali|ger, Jo|seph
  Justus (French
  scholar of ancient
  chronology)
Scali|ger, Ju|lius
  Cae|sar (Italian-
  born French
  classical scholar
  and physician)
scali|ness
scaling-ladder +s
scalla|wag +s (use
  scallywag)
scal|lion +s
scal|lop +s +ed
  +ing
scal|lop¦er +s
scally|wag +s
scalp +s +ed +ing
scal|pel +s
scalp¦er +s
scalp|less
scal|pri|form
scaly
  scali¦er
  scali|est
scam +s
scam|mony
  scam|monies
scamp +s +ed
  +ing
scam|per +s +ed
  +ing
scampi
scamp|ish
scan
  scans
  scanned
  scan|ning
scan|dal +s
scan¦dal|ise *Br.*
  (use scandalize)
  scan¦dal|ises

scan|dal|ise (*cont.*)
  scan|dal|ised
  scan|dal|is|ing
scan|dal|ize
  scan|dal|izes
  scan|dal|ized
  scan|dal|iz|ing
scan|dal|mon|ger
  +s
scan|dal|ous
scan|dal|ous|ly
scan|dal|ous|ness
Scan|di|navia
  (peninsula, NW
  Europe; or wider
  region)
Scan|di|navian +s
scan|dium
scan|nable
scan|ner +s
scan|sion
scan|sor|ial
scant +s +ed +ing
scant|ies
scant|ily
scanti|ness
scant|ling +s
scant|ly
scant|ness
scanty
  scant|ier
  scanti|est
Scapa Flow (strait
  in the Orkney
  Islands)
scape +s
scape|goat +s +ed
  +ing
scape|goat|er +s
scape|grace +s
scaph|oid +s
scap|ula
  scapu|lae *or*
  scapu|las
  (shoulder blade)
scapu|lar +s (of the
  shoulder; cloak;
  bandage; feather)
scapu|lary
  scapu|lar|ies
scar
  scars
  scarred
  scar|ring
  (mark on skin etc.;
  outcrop. △ ska)
scarab +s
scara|baeid +s
scara|mouch
  scara|mouches
Scar|bor|ough
  (town, England)

scarce
  scar|cer
  scar|cest
scarce|ly
scarce|ness
scar|city
  scar|ci|ties
scare
  scares
  scared
  scar|ing
scare|crow +s
scaredy-cat +s
scare|mon|ger +s
scare|monger|ing
  +s
scarer +s
scarf
  scarves *or* scarfs
  (piece of material
  worn around
  neck)
scarf +s +ed +ing
  (join ends; cut
  whale blubber; eat
  or drink greedily)
scarfed (wearing a
  scarf)
scarf pin +s
scarf ring +s
scarf-skin
scarf-wise
scari|fi|ca|tion +s
scari|fi|ca|tor +s
scari|fier +s
scari|fy
  scari|fies
  scari|fied
  scari|fy|ing
scari|ly
scari|ness
scari|ous
scar|lat|ina (scarlet
  fever)
Scar|latti,
  Do|men|ico
  (Italian composer)
Scar|latti,
  Ales|san|dro
  (Italian composer)
scar|less
scar|let +s (colour)
Scar|lett (name)
scar|oid +s
scarp +s +ed +ing
scar|per +s +ed
  +ing
Scart (*Video.*
  △ skat)
scarus
  scari
  scarves

scary
  scari|er
  scari|est
scat
  scats
  scat|ted
  scat|ting
scathe
  scathes
  scathed
  scath|ing
scathe|less
scath|ing|ly
scato|logic|al
scat|ology
scat|opha|gous
scat|ter +s +ed
  +ing
scat|ter|brain +s
scat|ter|brained
scat|ter|er +s
scatter-gun +s
scat|ter|shot
scat|tily
scat|ti|ness
scatty
  scat|tier
  scat|ti|est
scaup +s
scaup|er +s
scaur +s +ed +ing
  (outcrop. △ score)
scav|enge
  scav|enges
  scav|enged
  scav|en|ging
scav|en|ger +s
scav|en|gery
sca|zon +s
scena +s
scen|ario +s
scen|ar|ist +s
scend +s +ed +ing
scene +s (place;
  view; part of play.
  △ seen)
scene-dock +s
scen|ery
scene-shifter +s
scene-shifting
scenic
scen|ic|al|ly
scen|og|raph|er +s
scen|og|raphy
scent +s +ed +ing
  (smell; perfume.
  △ cent, sent)
scent-bag +s
scent gland +s
scent|less
scep|sis *Br.* (*Am.*
  skepsis)

scep|ter *Am.* (*Br.*
  sceptre.
  sovereign's rod.
  △ septa)
scep|tered *Am.* (*Br.*
  sceptred)
scep|tic *Br.* +s (*Am.*
  skeptic)
scep|tic|al *Br.* (*Am.*
  skeptical)
scep|tic|al|ly *Br.*
  (*Am.* skeptically)
scep|ti|cism *Br.* +s
  (*Am.* skepticism)
sceptre *Br.* +s (*Am.*
  scepter.
  sovereign's rod.
  △ septa)
sceptred *Br.* (*Am.*
  sceptered)
schad|en|*freude*
Schaff|hausen
  (town and canton,
  Switzerland)
schappe +s
sched|ule
  sched|ules
  sched|uled
  sched|ul|ing
sched|uler +s
Scheele, Carl
  Wil|helm
  (Swedish chemist)
scheel|ite +s
Sche|hera|zade (in
  the *Arabian Nights*)
Scheldt (river in
  France, Belgium,
  the Netherlands)
Schel|ling,
  Fried|rich
  Wil|helm
  Jo|seph von
  (German
  philosopher)
schema
  sche|mata *or*
  sche|mas
  (plan etc.
  △ schemer)
sche|mat|ic +s
sche|mat|ic|al|ly
sche|ma|tisa|tion
  Br. (use
  schematization)
sche|ma|tise *Br.*
  (use schematize)
  sche|ma|tises
  sche|ma|tised
  sche|ma|tis|ing
sche|ma|tism +s
sche|ma|tiza|tion

sche|ma|tize
sche|ma|tizes
sche|ma|tized
sche|ma|tiz|ing
scheme
schemes
schemed
schem|ing
schemer +s
schem|ing +s
schem|ing|ly
sche|moz|zle +s
(use shemozzle)
scherz|ando
scherz|an|dos or
scherz|andi
scherzo +s
Schia|pa|relli, Elsa
(Italian-born
French fashion
designer)
Schia|pa|relli,
Gio|vanni
Vir|gi|nio (Italian
astronomer)
Schie|dam (port,
the Netherlands)
Schiele, Egon
(Austrian painter)
Schil|ler,
Fried|rich von
(German writer)
schil|ling +s
(Austrian
currency.
△ shilling)
Schind|ler, Oskar
(German rescuer
of Jews)
schip|perke +s
schism +s
schis|mat|ic +s
schis|mat|ic|al
schis|mat|ic|al|ly
schis|ma|tise Br.
(use schismatize)
schis|ma|tises
schis|ma|tised
schis|ma|tis|ing
schis|ma|tize
schis|ma|tizes
schis|ma|tized
schis|ma|tiz|ing
schist +s
schis|tose
schis|to|some +s
schis|to|som|ia|sis
schis|to|
som|ia|ses
schiz|an|thus
schiz|an|thuses
schizo +s

schizo|carp +s
schizo|car|pic
schizo|car|pous
schiz|oid +s
schizo|my|cete +s
schizo|phre|nia
schizo|phren|ic +s
schizo|thy|mia
schizo|thy|mic
Schle|gel, Au|gust
Wil|helm von
(German
translator of
Shakespeare)
Schle|gel,
Fried|rich von
(German
philosopher)
schle|miel +s
schlep
schleps
schlepped
schlep|ping
schlepp +s +ed
+ing (use schlep)
Schles|wig (former
duchy, N. Europe)
Schleswig-
Holstein (state,
Germany)
Schlie|mann,
Hein|rich
(German
archaeologist)
schlier|en +s
schlock
schlump +s
schmaltz
schmaltzy
schmaltz|ier
schmaltzi|est
Schmidt
(telescope;
camera)
Schmidt–Cassegrain
(telescope)
schmooze
schmoozes
schmoozed
schmooz|ing
schmuck +s
schnapps
plural schnapps
schnau|zer +s
Schnei|der,
Jacques (French
flying enthusiast)
schnit|zel +s
schnook +s
schnor|kel +s (use
snorkel)
schnor|rer +s

Schoen|berg,
Ar|nold (Austrian-
born American
composer)
scholar +s
schol|ar|li|ness
schol|ar|ly
schol|ar|ship +s
scho|las|tic +s
scho|las|tic|al|ly
scho|las|ti|cism
scho|li|ast +s
scho|li|as|tic
scho|lium
scho|lia
school +s +ed
+ing
school|able
school age noun
school-age
attributive
school-aged
school book +s
school|boy +s
school|child
school|chil|dren
school day, the
school|days
school|fel|low +s
school friend +s
school|girl +s
school|house +s
schoolie +s
school in|spect|or
+s
school|kid +s
school leav|er +s
school-leaving
age +s
school-ma'm +s
(use school-
marm)
school|man
school|men
school-marm +s
school-marmish
school|mas|ter +s
school|mas|ter|ing
school|mas|ter|ly
school|mate +s
school|mis|tress
school|
mis|tresses
school|mis|tressy
school|room +s
school-ship +s
school|teach|er +s
school|teach|ing
school time +s
school work
school|yard +s
schooner +s

Schop|en|hauer,
Ar|thur (German
philosopher)
schorl +s (mineral.
△ shawl)
schot|tische +s
Schottky ef|fect
Schrei|ner, Olive
(South African
novelist)
Schröd|inger,
Erwin (Austrian
physicist;
equation)
Schu|bert, Franz
(Austrian
composer)
Schu|bert|ian +s
Schulz, Charles
(American
cartoonist)
Schu|macher, E.
F. (German
economist and
conservationist)
Schu|mann,
Rob|ert (German
composer)
schuss
schusses
schussed
schuss|ing
Schütz, Hein|rich
(German
composer)
schwa +s
Schwäb|isch
Gmünd (city,
Germany)
Schwann,
Theo|dor
(German
physiologist)
Schwarz|kopf,
Elisa|beth
(German soprano)
Schwarz|wald
(German name for
the Black Forest)
Schwein|furt (city,
Germany)
Schweit|zer,
Al|bert (German
theologian)
Schwerin (city,
Germany)
Schwyz (city and
canton,
Switzerland)
scia|gram +s
scia|graph +s +ed
+ing

scia|graph|ic
sci|ag|raphy
sci|am|achy
sci|at|ic
sci|at|ica
sci|at|ic|al|ly
sci|ence +s
sci|en|ter
sci|en|tial +s
sci|en|tif|ic
sci|en|tif|ic|ally
sci|en|tism +s
sci|en|tist +s
sci|en|tis|tic
Sci|en|tolo|gist +s
Sci|en|tol|ogy
   Propr.
sci-fi (= science
   fiction)
scili|cet
scilla +s (plant.
   △ Scylla)
Scil|lies (= Scilly
   Isles)
Scil|lo|nian +s (of
   the Scilly Isles)
Scilly Isles (off
   England)
scimi|tar +s
scin|ti|gram +s
scin|tig|raphy
scin|tilla +s
scin|til|lant
scin|til|late
   scin|til|lates
   scin|til|lated
   scin|til|lat|ing
scin|til|lat|ing|ly
scin|til|la|tion +s
scin|ti|scan +s
sci|ol|ism
sci|ol|ist +s
sci|ol|is|tic
scion +s
Scipio
   Ae|mili|anus
   (Roman general)
Scipio Af|ri|canus
   (Roman general)
scire fa|cias
sci|rocco +s (use
   sirocco)
scir|rhoid
scir|rhos|ity
scir|rhous (of a
   scirrhus. △ cirrous)
scir|rhus
   scir|rhi
   (carcinoma.
   △ cirrus)
scis|sel (metal
   clippings)

scis|sile (able to be
   cut)
scis|sion +s
scis|sor +s +ed
   +ing
scissor-bill +s
scissor-bird +s
scis|sor|wise
sci|ur|ine
sci|ur|oid
sclera +s
scleral
scler|en|chyma
scler|ite +s
scler|itis
sclero|derma
scler|oid
scler|oma
   scler|omata
scler|om|eter +s
sclero|phyll +s
scler|ophyl|lous
sclero|pro|tein +s
scler|osed
scler|osis
   scler|oses
scler|ot|ic +s
sclero|titis
scler|otomy
   scler|oto|mies
scler|ous
scoff +s +ed +ing
scoff|er +s
scoff|ing|ly
scold +s +ed +ing
scold|er +s
scold|ing +s
sco|lex
   sco|le|ces
scoli|osis
   scoli|oses
scoli|ot|ic
scol|lop +s (use
   scallop)
scolo|pen|drium
   scolo|pen|dri|ums
   or scolo|pen|dria
scom|ber +s
scom|brid +s
scom|broid +s
sconce
   sconces
   sconced
   scon|cing
Scone (village,
   Scotland)
scone +s (cake)
scoop +s +ed +ing
scoop|er +s
scoop|ful +s
scoop neck +s
scoop-net +s

scoot +s +ed +ing
   (run away.
   △ scute)
scoot|er +s +ed
   +ing (vehicle.
   △ scuta)
scoot|er|ist +s
scopa
   sco|pae
scope +s
sco|pol|am|ine +s
scop|ula
   scopu|lae
scor|bu|tic +s
scor|bu|tic|al|ly
scorch
   scorches
   scorched
   scorch|ing
scorch|er +s
scorch|ing|ly
score
   scores
   scored
   scor|ing
   (number of points;
   music; groove.
   △ scaur)
score|board +s
score|book +s
score|card +s
score|less
score|line +s
scorer +s
score sheet +s
scoria
   scor|iae
scori|aceous
scori|fi|ca|tion
scori|fier
scor|ify
   scori|fies
   scori|fied
   scori|fy|ing
scorn +s +ed +ing
scorn|er +s
scorn|ful
scorn|ful|ly
scorn|ful|ness
scorp|er +s
Scor|pian +s
   (pertaining to
   Scorpio or
   Scorpius; person.
   △ scorpion)
Scor|pio (sign of
   zodiac)
scor|pi|oid +s
scor|pion +s
   (arachnid.
   △ Scorpian)
Scor|pius
   (constellation)

Scor|sese, Mar|tin
   (American film
   director)
scor|zon|era +s
Scot +s (person
   from Scotland.
   △ Scott)
scot +s (tax)
Scotch
   Scotches
   (whisky; Scottish)
scotch
   scotches
   scotched
   scotch|ing
   (put an end to)
Scotch|man
   Scotch|men
Scotch|woman
   Scotch|women
sco|ter
   plural sco|ter *or*
   sco|ters
scot-free
sco|tia +s
Scoti|cise *Br.* (use
   Scotticize)
   Scoti|cises
   Scoti|cised
   Scoti|cis|ing
Scoti|cism +s (use
   Scotticism)
Scoti|cize (use
   Scotticize)
   Scoti|cizes
   Scoti|cized
   Scoti|ciz|ing
Scot|ism +s
Scot|ist +s
Scot|land
scot|oma
   scot|omata
Scots (Scottish;
   Scots people)
Scots|man
   Scots|men
Scots|woman
   Scots|women
Scott (name.
   △ Scot)
Scott, Gil|bert
   (English architect)
Scott, Peter
   (English
   naturalist)
Scott, Rob|ert
   (English explorer)
Scott, Wal|ter
   (Scottish writer)
Scot|ti|cise *Br.* (use
   Scotticize)
   Scot|ti|cises

Scot|ti|cise (*cont.*)
  Scot|ti|cised
  Scot|ti|cis|ing
Scot|ti|cism +s
Scot|ti|cize
  Scot|ti|cizes
  Scot|ti|cized
  Scot|ti|ciz|ing
Scot|tie +s (Scotch
  terrier; a Scot)
Scot|tish
Scot|tish|ness
scoun|drel +s
scoun|drel|dom
scoun|drel|ism
scoun|drel|ly
scour +s +ed +ing
scour|er +s
scourge
  scourges
  scourged
  scour|ging
scour|ger +s
scouring-rush
  scouring-rushes
  (plant)
Scouse +s
  (Liverpudlian)
scouse +s (food)
Scouser +s
Scout +s (member
  of Scout
  Association)
scout +s +ed +ing
Scout
  As|so|ci|ation
Scout|er +s (adult
  member of Scout
  Association)
scout|er +s (person
  who scouts)
Scout|mas|ter +s
scow +s
scowl +s +ed +ing
scowl|er +s
Scrab|ble (game)
  Propr.
scrab|ble
  scrab|bles
  scrab|bled
  scrab|bling
  (scratch; grope)
Scrab|bler +s
scrag
  scrags
  scragged
  scrag|ging
scrag|gily
scrag|gi|ness
scrag|gly

scraggy
  scrag|gier
  scrag|gi|est
scram
  scrams
  scrammed
  scram|ming
scram|ble
  scram|bles
  scram|bled
  scram|bling
scram|bler +s
scran
Scran|ton (city,
  USA)
scrap
  scraps
  scrapped
  scrap|ping
scrap|book +s
scrape
  scrapes
  scraped
  scrap|ing
scraper +s
scraper|board +s
scrap heap +s
scra|pie
scrap|ing +s
scrap|per +s
scrap|pily
scrap|pi|ness
scrappy
  scrap|pier
  scrap|pi|est
scrap|yard +s
scratch
  scratches
  scratched
  scratch|ing
scratch|board +s
scratch|er +s
scratch|ily
scratchi|ness
scratch|ing +s
scratchy
  scratchi|er
  scratchi|est
scrawl
  scrawls
  scrawled
  scrawl|ing
scrawly
scrawni|ness
scrawny
  scrawn|ier
  scrawni|est
scream +s +ed
  +ing
scream|er +s
scream|ing|ly
scree +s

screech
  screeches
  screeched
  screech|ing
screech|er +s
screech owl +s
screechy
  screechi|er
  screechi|est
screed +s +ed
  +ing
screen +s +ed
  +ing
screen|able
screen|er +s
screen|ing +s
screen|play +s
screen print +s
  noun
screen-print +s
  +ed +ing *verb*
screen print|er +s
screen print|ing
  noun
screen test +s
screen|writer +s
screen|writ|ing
screw +s +ed +ing
screw|able
screw|ball +s
screw cap +s *noun*
screw-cap *adjective*
screw-coupling +s
screw|driver +s
screw|driv|ing
screw|er +s
screw-hole +s
screwi|ness
screw-jack +s
screw-plate +s
screw-tap +s
screw top +s *noun*
screw-top *adjective*
screw-up +s
screwy
  screwi|er
  screwi|est
Scria|bin,
  Alek|sandr
  (Russian
  composer)
scribal
scrib|ble
  scrib|bles
  scrib|bled
  scrib|bling
scrib|bler +s
scrib|bling +s
scrib|bly
scribe
  scribes

scribe (*cont.*)
  scribed
  scrib|ing
scriber +s
scrim +s
scrim|mage
  scrim|mages
  scrim|maged
  scrim|ma|ging
scrim|ma|ger +s
scrimp +s +ed
  +ing
scrimpy
  scrimp|ier
  scrimpi|est
scrim|shander +s
  +ed +ing
scrim|shank +s
  +ed +ing
scrim|shank|er +s
scrim|shaw +s
  +ed +ing
scrip +s
script +s +ed +ing
scrip|tor|ial
scrip|tor|ium
  scrip|tor|iums *or*
  scrip|toria
script|ory
  script|or|ies
scrip|tural
scrip|tur|al|ism
scrip|tur|al|ist +s
scrip|tur|al|ly
Scrip|ture +s (of a
  particular religion)
scrip|ture +s
  (generally)
script|writer +s
script|writ|ing
scriv|en|er +s
scro|bicu|late
scrod +s
scrof|ula
  scrofu|las *or*
  scrofu|lae
scrofu|lous
scroll +s +ed +ing
scroll|er +s
scroll-head +s
scroll-lathe +s
scroll saw +s
scroll|work
Scrooge +s
scro|tal
scrot|itis
scro|tum
  scro|tums *or*
  scrota
scrounge
  scrounges
  scrounged
  scroun|ging

scroun|ger +s
scrub
  scrubs
  scrubbed
  scrub|bing
scrub|ber +s
scrubbing-brush
  scrubbing-
  brushes
scrub-brush
  scrub-brushes
scrubby
  scrub|bier
  scrub|bi|est
scrub|land +s
scruff +s
scruff|ily
scruffi|ness
scruffy
  scruff|ier
  scruffi|est
scrum +s
scrum-half
  scrum-halves
scrum|mage
  scrum|mages
  scrum|maged
  scrum|ma|ging
scrum|ma|ger +s
scrummy
  scrum|mier
  scrum|mi|est
scrump +s +ed
  +ing
scrum|ple
  scrum|ples
  scrum|pled
  scrump|ling
scrump|tious
scrump|tious|ly
scrump|tious|ness
scrumpy
  scrump|ies
scrunch
  scrunches
  scrunched
  scrunch|ing
scrunch-dry
  scrunch-dries
  scrunch-dried
  scrunch-drying
scrunchie +s (use
  scrunchy)
scrunchy
  scrunch|ies
scru|ple
  scru|ples
  scru|pled
  scrup|ling
scru|pu|los|ity
scru|pu|lous
scru|pu|lous|ly

scru|pu|lous|ness
scru|ta|tor +s
scru|tin|eer +s
scru|tin|isa|tion
  Br. (use
  scrutinization)
scru|tin|ise *Br.* (use
  scrutinize)
  scru|tin|ises
  scru|tin|ised
  scru|tin|is|ing
scru|tin|iser *Br.* +s
  (use scrutinizer)
scru|tin|iza|tion
scru|tin|ize
  scru|tin|izes
  scru|tin|ized
  scru|tin|iz|ing
scru|tin|izer +s
scru|tiny
  scru|tin|ies
scry
  scries
  scried
  scry|ing
scry|er +s
scuba +s
scuba-dive
  scuba-dives
  scuba-dived
  .scuba-diving
scuba-diver +s
Scud +s (missile)
scud
  scuds
  scud|ded
  scud|ding
  (move fast)
scuff +s +ed +ing
scuf|fle
  scuf|fles
  scuf|fled
  scuf|fling
scul|dug|gery (use
  skulduggery)
scull +s +ed +ing
  (oar. △ skull)
scull|er +s
scull|ery
  scull|er|ies
scul|lion +s
sculp +s +ed +ing
sculpt +s +ed +ing
sculp|tor +s
  (person who
  sculpts.
  △ sculpture)
sculp|tress
  sculp|tresses
sculp|tural
sculp|tur|al|ly

sculp|ture
  sculp|tures
  sculp|tured
  sculp|tur|ing
  (art form.
  △ sculptor)
sculp|tur|esque
scum
  scums
  scummed
  scum|ming
scum|bag +s
scum|ble
  scum|bles
  scum|bled
  scum|bling
scummy
  scum|mier
  scum|mi|est
scun|cheon +s
scunge +s
scungy
  scun|gier
  scun|gi|est
scun|ner +s +ed
  +ing
Scun|thorpe (town,
  England)
scup
  scups
  scupped
  scup|ping
scup|per +s +ed
  +ing
scurf
scurfy
  scurf|ier
  scurfi|est
scur|ril|ity
  scur|ril|ities
scur|ril|ous
scur|ril|ous|ly
scur|ril|ous|ness
scurry
  scur|ries
  scur|ried
  scurry|ing
scur|vied
scur|vily
scurvy
  scur|vier
  scur|vi|est
scut +s
scuta (plural of
  scutum.
  △ scooter)
scut|age +s
scu|tal
Scu|tari (Italian
  name for
  Shkodër)

Scu|tari (former
  name of Üsküdar)
scu|tate
scutch
  scutches
  scutched
  scutch|ing
scutch|eon +s
scutch|er +s
scute +s (bony
  plate. △ scoot)
scu|tel|late
scu|tel|la|tion +s
scu|tel|lum
  scu|tella
scu|ti|form
scut|ter +s +ed
  +ing
scut|tle
  scut|tles
  scut|tled
  scut|tling
scuttle|butt +s
  (water-butt)
scu|tum
  scuta
scuzzy
  scuzz|ier
  scuzz|zi|est
Scylla (*Greek
  Mythology.*
  △ scilla)
scyphi|form
scy|phose
scy|pho|zoan +s
scy|phus
  scy|phi
scythe
  scythes
  scythed
  scyth|ing
Scythia (ancient
  region, SE Europe
  and Asia)
Scyth|ian +s
sea +s (ocean.
  △ see, si)
sea-angel +s
sea|bed +s
sea|bird +s
sea|board +s
sea-boat +s
sea|boot +s
Sea|borg, Glenn
  (American nuclear
  chemist)
sea|borg|ium
sea|borne
sea bot|tom
sea change +s
sea-chest +s
sea coast +s

sea|cock +s
Sea Dyak +s
(alternative name
for the Iban)
sea-ear +s
sea|farer +s
sea|far|ing
sea fish
plural sea fish or
sea fishes
sea floor +s
sea|food +s
sea|front +s
sea-girt
sea|going
sea green +s noun
and adjective
sea-green
attributive
sea|gull +s
sea horse +s
sea-island cot|ton
+s
sea|jack +s +ed
+ing
sea|jack|er +s
sea|kale
seal +s +ed +ing
(sea mammal;
fasten; fastening.
△ ceiling, seel)
seal|able
seal|ant +s
sealed-beam
attributive
sea legs
seal|er +s
(something used
for sealing joints;
hunter; ship.
△ selah)
seal|ery
seal|er|ies
sea level +s
sea-level attributive
seal|ing wax
seal|ing waxes
sea lion +s
seal|point +s
seal|skin +s
seal|stone +s
Sealy|ham +s
seam +s +ed +ing
(line; join with a
seam. △ seem)
sea mam|mal +s
sea|man
sea|men
(sailor. △ semen)
sea|man|like
sea|man|ly
sea|man|ship

sea|mark +s
seam|er +s
seami|ness
seam|less
seam|less|ly
seam|stress
seam|stresses
Sea|mus
seamy
seam|ier
seami|est
Sean also Shaun
Seanad (upper
House in Irish
Parliament)
se|ance +s
sea|plane +s
sea|port +s
SEAQ (= Stock
Exchange
Automated
Quotations)
sea|quake +s
sear +s +ed +ing
(scorch. △ cere,
seer, sere)
search
searches
searched
search|ing
search|able
search|er +s
search|ing +s
search|ing|ly
search|less
search|light +s
search party
search par|ties
sear|ing|ly
Sears Tower
(skyscraper,
Chicago, USA)
sea|scape +s
sea shanty
sea shan|ties
sea|shell +s
sea|shore +s
sea|sick
sea|sick|ness
sea|side +s
sea|son +s +ed
+ing
sea|son|able
sea|son|able|ness
sea|son|ably
sea|son|al
sea|son|al|ity
sea|son|al|ly
sea|son|er +s
sea|son|ing +s
sea|son|less
sea|son ticket +s

seat +s +ed +ing
seat belt +s
-seater +s (in
'single-seater' etc.)
seat|ing +s
seat|less
SEATO (= South-
East Asia Treaty
Organization)
Se|attle (city, USA)
sea ur|chin +s
sea|ward
sea|wards
sea water
sea|way +s
sea|weed +s
sea-wife
sea-wives
sea-wind +s
sea|worthi|ness
sea|worthy
sea-wrack +s
se|ba|ceous
Se|bas|tian
(Roman saint;
name)
Se|bas|to|pol
(naval base,
Ukraine)
Sebat (Jewish
month)
se|bes|ten +s
seb|or|rhea Am.
seb|or|rhe|ic Am.
seb|or|rhoea Br.
seb|or|rhoe|ic Br.
sebum
sec (dry)
sec +s (= secant;
second)
se|cant +s
seca|teurs
secco +s
se|cede
se|cedes
se|ceded
se|ced|ing
se|ceder +s
se|ces|sion +s
se|ces|sion|al
se|ces|sion|ism
se|ces|sion|ist +s
Se|chuana (use
Setswana)
se|clude
se|cludes
se|cluded
se|clud|ing
se|clu|sion +s
se|clu|sion|ist +s
se|clu|sive

sec|ond +s +ed
+ing (unit of time;
next after first;
support)
se|cond +s +ed
+ing (transfer.
△ seconde)
sec|ond|ar|ily
sec|ond|ari|ness
sec|ond|ary
sec|ond|ar|ies
second-best
second-class
adjective and
adverb
second-degree
adjective
se|conde +s (in
fencing.
△ second)
se|cond|ee +s
(person
transferred)
sec|ond|er +s
(person seconding
a motion)
second-floor
adjective
second-
generation
adjective
second-guess
second-guesses
second-guessed
second-guessing
sec|ond hand (on
clock; in 'at
second hand')
second-hand
adjective and
adverb
sec|ond|ly
se|cond|ment +s
se|condo
se|condi
Music
second-rate
adjective
second-rater +s
second-sighted
se|crecy
se|cret +s
sec|re|taire +s
sec|re|tar|ial
sec|re|tar|iat +s
sec|re|tary
sec|re|tar|ies
(in office.
△ secretory)
Secretary-General
+s

Sec|re|tary of
State
Sec|re|tar|ies of
State
sec|re|tary|ship +s
se|crete
se|cretes
se|creted
se|cret|ing
se|cre|tion +s
se|cret|ive
se|cret|ive|ly
se|cret|ive|ness
se|cret|ly
se|cre|tor +s
se|cre|tory
(producing by
secretion.
△ secretary)
sect +s (religious
group. △ Sekt)
sect|ar|ian +s
sect|ar|ian|ise Br.
(use sectarianize)
sect|ar|ian|ises
sect|ar|ian|ised
sect|ar|ian|is|ing
sect|ar|ian|ism
sect|ar|ian|ize
sect|ar|ian|izes
sect|ar|ian|ized
sect|ar|ian|iz|ing
sect|ary
sect|ar|ies
sec|tion +s +ed
+ing
sec|tion|al
sec|tion|al|ise Br.
(use sectionalize)
sec|tion|al|ises
sec|tion|al|ised
sec|tion|al|is|ing
sec|tion|al|ism
sec|tion|al|ist +s
sec|tion|al|ize
sec|tion|al|izes
sec|tion|al|ized
sec|tion|al|iz|ing
sec|tion|al|ly
section-mark +s
sec|tor +s
sec|tor|al
sec|tor|ial
secu|lar +s
secu|lar|isa|tion
Br. (use
secularization)
secu|lar|ise Br. (use
secularize)
secu|lar|ises
secu|lar|ised
secu|lar|is|ing

secu|lar|ism
secu|lar|ist +s
secu|lar|ity
secu|lar|iza|tion
secu|lar|ize
secu|lar|izes
secu|lar|ized
secu|lar|iz|ing
secu|lar|ly
se|cund
Se|cun|dera|bad
(town, India)
se|cund|ly
se|cur|able
se|cure
se|cures
se|cured
se|cur|ing
se|cure|ly
se|cure|ment +s
Se|curi|tate
(former Romanian
internal security
force)
se|curi|tisa|tion Br.
(use
securitization)
se|curi|tise Br. (use
securitize)
se|curi|tises
se|curi|tised
se|curi|tis|ing
se|curi|tiza|tion
se|curi|tize
se|curi|tizes
se|curi|tized
se|curi|tiz|ing
se|cur|ity
se|cur|ities
Sedan (battle site,
France)
sedan +s (chair)
sedan chair +s
sed|ate
sed|ates
sed|ated
sed|at|ing
sed|ate|ly
sed|ate|ness
sed|ation
seda|tive +s
sed|en|tar|ily
sed|en|tari|ness
sed|en|tary
Seder +s (Jewish
ritual)
se|der|unt +s
sedge +s
Sedge|moor (battle
site, England)
sedge warb|ler +s

Sedg|wick, Adam
(English geologist)
sedgy
se|dile
se|dilia
sedi|ment +s +ed
+ing
sedi|ment|ary
sedi|men|ta|tion
+s
se|di|tion +s
se|di|tion|ary
se|di|tion|ar|ies
se|di|tion|ist +s
se|di|tious
se|di|tious|ly
se|duce
se|duces
se|duced
se|du|cing
se|du|cer +s
se|du|cible
se|duc|tion +s
se|duc|tive
se|duc|tive|ly
se|duc|tive|ness
se|duc|tress
se|duc|tresses
se|du|lity
sedu|lous
sedu|lous|ly
sedu|lous|ness
sedum +s
see
sees
saw
see|ing
seen
(discern with the
eyes; diocese;
archdiocese.
△ sea, si)
see|able
seed +s +ed +ing
(of plant; sow or
remove seeds; in
sports
competition.
△ cede)
seed|bed +s
seed cake +s
seed-coat +s
seed|corn +s
seed-eater +s
seed|er +s (person
or thing that
seeds. △ cedar)
seed-fish
plural seed-fish
seed-head +s
seed|ily
seedi|ness

seed-leaf
seed-leaves
seed|less
seed|ling +s
seed-lip +s
seed|pearl +s
seed-plot +s
seed po|tato
seed po|ta|toes
seeds|man
seeds|men
seed-time +s
seed ves|sel +s
seedy
seed|ier
seedi|est
See|ger, Pete
(American
musician)
see|ing +s
seek
seeks
sought
seek|ing
(look for. △ Sikh)
seek|er +s (person
who seeks. △ sika,
caeca)
seel +s +ed +ing
(close a person's
eyes. △ seal)
seem +s +ed +ing
(appear to be.
△ seam)
seem|ing +s
seem|ing|ly
seem|li|ness
seem|ly
seem|lier
seem|li|est
seen (past participle
of see. △ scene)
seep +s +ed +ing
seep|age +s
seer +s (prophet;
measure. △ cere,
sear, sere)
seer|sucker +s
see-saw +s +ed
+ing
seethe
seethes
seethed
seeth|ing
seeth|ing|ly
see-through +s
adjective and noun
Se|feris, George
(Greek poet)
seg|ment +s +ed
+ing
seg|men|tal

seg|men|tal|
  isa|tion *Br.* (use
  segmentaliza-
  tion)
seg|men|tal|ise *Br.*
  (use
  segmentalize)
seg|men|tal|ises
seg|men|tal|ised
seg|men|tal|is|ing
seg|men|tal|
  iza|tion
seg|men|tal|ize
seg|men|tal|izes
seg|men|tal|ized
seg|men|tal|iz|ing
seg|men|tal|ly
seg|men|tary
seg|men|ta|tion +s
sego +s
Sego|via (city,
  Spain)
Sego|via, An|drés
  (Spanish guitarist)
seg|reg|able
seg|re|gate
seg|re|gates
seg|re|gated
seg|re|gat|ing
seg|re|ga|tion
seg|re|ga|tion|al
seg|re|ga|tion|ist
  +s
seg|re|ga|tive
segue
segues
segued
segue|ing
segui|dilla +s
Sehn|sucht
sei +s (whale.
  △ say)
sei|cent|ist +s
sei|cento (artistic
  and literary style)
sei|cento|ist +s
seiche +s
Seid|litz pow|der
  +s
seif +s
sei|gneur +s
sei|gneur|ial
sei|gneury (use
  seigniory)
sei|gneur|ies
sei|gnior +s (use
  seigneur)
sei|gnior|age +s
sei|gnior|ial (use
  seigneurial)
sei|gniory
  sei|gnor|ies

sei|gnor|age +s
  (use seigniorage)
Sei|kan Tun|nel (in
  Japan)
Seine (river,
  France)
seine
seines
seined
sein|ing
  (fishing net; fish or
  catch with a seine.
  △ sane)
seiner +s
  (fisherman; boat.
  △ saner)
seise (use seize)
seises
seised
seis|ing
sei|sin +s
seis|mal
seis|mic
seis|mic|al
seis|mic|al|ly
seis|mi|city
seis|mo|gram +s
seis|mo|graph +s
seis|mog|raph|er
  +s
seis|mo|graph|ic
seis|mo|
      graph|ic|al
seis|mog|raphy
seis|mo|logic|al
seis|mo|logic|al|ly
seis|molo|gist +s
seis|mol|ogy
seis|mom|eter +s
seis|mo|met|ric
seis|mo|met|ric|al
seis|mom|etry
seis|mo|scope +s
seis|mo|scop|ic
sei whale +s
seiz|able
seize
seizes
seized
seiz|ing
seizer +s
sei|zin +s (use
  seisin)
seiz|ing +s
seiz|ure +s
se|jant
Sekh|met *Egyptian*
  Mythology
Sekt +s (wine.
  △ sect)
se|lach|ian +s
se|la|dang +s

selah (in Psalms.
  △ sealer)
Se|langor (state,
  Malaysia)
Sel|craig,
  Alex|an|der
  (alternative name
  for Alexander
  Selkirk)
sel|dom
se|lect +s +ed +ing
se|lect|able
se|lect|ee +s
se|lec|tion +s
se|lec|tion|al
se|lec|tion|al|ly
se|lect|ive
se|lect|ive|ly
se|lect|ive|ness
se|lect|iv|ity
se|lect|man
  se|lect|men
se|lect|ness
se|lect|or +s
Sel|ena *also* Sel|ina
sel|en|ate +s
Sel|ene *Greek*
  Mythology
sel|en|ic
sel|en|ide +s
sel|eni|ous
sel|en|ite
sel|en|it|ic
sel|en|ium
sel|eno|cen|tric
sel|eno|dont +s
sel|en|og|raph|er
  +s
sel|eno|graph|ic
sel|en|og|raphy
sel|en|olo|gist +s
sel|en|ology
Se|leu|cid +s
self
  selves
  (individual)
self +s (flower)
self-abandon
self-abandoned
self-
  abandon|ment
self-abasement
self-abhorrence
self-abnegation
self-absorbed
self-absorp|tion
self-abuse
self-accusa|tion
self-accusa|tory
self-acting
self-action
self-activity

self-addressed
self-adhesive
self-adjust|ing
self-adjust|ment
self-admiration
self-advance|ment
self-
  advertise|ment
self-advertiser +s
self-affirm|ation
self-aggrand|ise|
  ment *Br.* (use self-
  aggrandizement)
self-aggrand|is|ing
  Br. (use self-
  aggrandizing)
self-aggrand|ize|
        ment
self-
  aggrand|iz|ing
self-analys|ing
self-analysis
self-appoint|ed
self-appreci|ation
self-approba|tion
self-approval
self-assembly
self-assert|ing
self-assertion
self-assert|ive
self-
  assert|ive|ness
self-assurance
self-assured
self-assured|ly
self-aware
self-awareness
self-begotten
self-betray|al
self-binder +s
self-born
self-catering
self-censor|ship
self-centred
self-centred|ly
self-centred|ness
self-certifi|ca|tion
self-certify
  self-certifies
  self-certified
  self-certify|ing
self-cleaning
self-closing
self-cocking
self-collect|ed
self-colored *Am.*
self-coloured *Br.*
self-command
self-commun|ion
self-conceit
self-conceit|ed

self-
    condemǃnaǃtion
self-condemned
self-confessed
self-confidence
self-confident
self-confidentǃly
self-
    congratuǃlaǃtion
self-
    congratuǃlaǃtory
self-conquest
self-conscious
self-consciousǃly
self-
    consciousǃness
self-consistǃency
self-consistǃent
self-constituted
self-contained
self-containǃment
self-contempt
self-
    contempǃtuǃous
self-content
self-contentǃed
self-contraǃdicǃtion
    +s
self-
    contraǃdictǃory
self-control
self-controlled
self-convictǃed
self-correctǃing
self-created
self-creation
self-critical
self-criticism
self-deceit
self-deceiver +s
self-deceivǃing
self-deception +s
self-deceptive
self-defeatǃing
self-defence
self-defensive
self-delight
self-delusion +s
self-denial
self-denying
self-dependǃence
self-dependǃent
self-deprecatǃing
self-
    deprecatǃingǃly
self-deprecaǃtion
self-depreciǃation
self-depreciaǃtory
self-despair
self-destroyǃing
self-destruct +s
    +ed +ing

self-destrucǃtion
self-destrucǃtive
self-
    destrucǃtiveǃly
self-
    determinǃation
self-determined
self-determinǃing
self-developǃment
self-devotion
self-discipǃline
self-discipǃlined
self-discovǃery
self-disgust
self-doubt
self-drive
self-educated
self-education
self-effaceǃment
self-effacing
self-effacingǃly
self-elective
self-employed
self-employǃment
self-esteem
self-evidence
self-evident
self-evidentǃly
self-examinǃation
self-executǃing
self-existent
self-explanaǃtory
self-expresǃsion
self-expresǃsive
self-faced
self-feeder +s
self-feeding
self-fertile
self-fertilǃisaǃtion
    Br. (use self-
    fertilization)
self-fertilǃised Br.
    (use self-
    fertilized)
self-fertilǃisǃing Br.
    (use self-
    fertilizing)
self-fertilǃity
self-fertilǃizaǃtion
self-fertilǃized
self-fertilǃizǃing
self-finance
self-finances
self-financed
self-financing
self-flagelǃlaǃtion
self-flatterǃing
self-flattery
self-forgetǃful
self-
    forgetǃfulǃness
self-fulfilǃling

self-fulfillǃment
    Am.
self-fulfilǃment Br.
self-generatǃing
self-glorifiǃcaǃtion
self-governed
self-governǃing
self-governǃment
self-gratifiǃcaǃtion
self-gratifyǃing
self-hate
self-hatred
self-heal +s
self-help
selfǃhood
self-image +s
self-immolatǃing
self-immolaǃtion
self-importǃance
self-importǃant
self-importǃantǃly
self-imposed
self-improveǃment
self-induced
self-inductǃance
self-induction
self-inductǃive
self-indulgence +s
self-indulgent
self-indulgentǃly
self-inflictǃed
self-interest +s
self-interestǃed
self-involved
self-involveǃment
selfǃish
selfǃishǃly
selfǃishǃness
self-justifiǃcaǃtion
self-justifyǃing
self-knowledge
selfǃless
selfǃlessǃly
selfǃlessǃness
self-loader +s
self-loading
self-locking
self-love
self-made
self-mastery
selfǃmate +s Chess
self-mocking
self-motion
self-motivated
self-motivaǃtion
self-moving
self-murder
self-murderǃer +s
self-mutilaǃtion +s
self-neglect
selfǃness
self-obsessed

self-opinion
self-opinionǃated
self-parody
self-parodyǃing
self-perpetuǃatǃing
self-perpetuǃation
self-pity
self-pitying
self-pityingǃly
self-pollinǃated
self-pollinǃatǃing
self-pollinǃation
self-pollinǃator +s
self-portrait +s
self-possessed
self-possesǃsion
self-praise
self-preserǃvaǃtion
self-proclaimed
self-propagatǃing
self-propelled
self-propelǃling
self-protecǃtion
self-protectǃive
self-raising
self-realisaǃtion
    Br. (use self-
    realization)
self-realizaǃtion
self-recordǃing
self-referenǃtial
self-regard
self-regardǃing
self-registerǃing
self-regulatǃing
self-regulaǃtion
self-regulaǃtory
self-reliance
self-reliant
self-reliantǃly
self-renewal
self-renunciǃation
self-reproach
self-reproachǃful
self-respect
self-respectǃing
self-restrained
self-restraint
self-revealǃing
self-revelaǃtion
Selfǃridge, Harry
    Gorǃdon
    (American-born
    British
    businessman)
self-righteous
self-righteousǃly
self-
    righteousǃness
self-righting
self-rising
self-rule
self-sacrifice

self-sacrifi|cing
self|same
self-satisfac|tion
self-satisfied
self-satisfied|ly
self-sealing
self-seed +s +ed
+ing
self-seeker +s
self-seeking
self-select|ing
self-selection
self-service
self-serving
self-slaugh|ter
self-sown
self-starter +s
self-sterile
self-steril|ity
self-styled
self-sufficiency
self-sufficient
self-sufficient|ly
self-sufficing
self-sugges|tion
self-support
self-support|ing
self-surren|der
self-sustained
self-sustain|ing
self-tanning
self-tapping
self-taught
self-torture
self-
    understand|ing
self-will
self-willed
self-winding
self-worth
Sel|ima
Sel|ina *also* Sel|ena
Sel|juk +s
Sel|juk|ian +s
Sel|kirk,
    Alex|an|der
    (Scottish sailor)
Sel|kirk|shire
    (former county,
    Scotland)
sell
    sells
    sold
    sell|ing
    (dispose of for
    money. △ cell)
sell|able
Sel|la|field (nuclear
    installation,
    England)
sell-by date +s

sell|er +s (person
    who sells.
    △ cellar)
Sel|lers, Peter
    (English comic
    actor)
sell|ing point +s
sell|ing race +s
sell-off +s *noun*
Sel|lo|tape *noun
    Propr.*
sel|lo|tape
    sel|lo|tapes
    sel|lo|taped
    sel|lo|tap|ing
    verb
sell-out +s *noun
    and attributive*
sell-through *noun
    and attributive*
Selma
Se|lous, Fred|erick
    Court|enay
    (English explorer)
selt|zer +s
selv|age +s (use
    selvedge)
selv|edge +s
selves
Sel|wyn
Selye, Hans Hugo
    Bruno (Austrian-
    born Canadian
    physician)
Selz|nick, David
    O. (American film
    producer)
se|man|teme +s
se|man|tic
se|man|tic|al|ly
se|man|ti|cian +s
se|man|ti|cist +s
se|man|tics
sema|phore
    sema|phores
    sema|phored
    sema|phor|ing
sema|phor|ic
sema|phor|ic|al|ly
Se|mar|ang (port,
    Indonesia)
se|masio|logic|al
se|masi|ology
se|mat|ic
sem|blable +s
semb|lance +s
semé (*Heraldry.*
    △ semi)
semée (use semé)
Semei (city,
    Kazakhstan)

semei|ology (use
    semiology)
semei|ot|ics (use
    semiotics)
Sem|ele *Greek
    Mythology*
sem|eme +s
semen (sperm.
    △ seaman)
se|mes|ter +s
Semey (use Semei)
semi +s (house;
    semi-final; semi-
    trailer. △ semé)
semi-annual
semi-annual|ly
semi|aquat|ic
semi-automat|ic
semi-
    autono|mous
semi-basement +s
semi-bold
semi|breve +s
semi|circle +s
semi|cir|cu|lar
semi-civilised *Br.*
    (use semi-
    civilized)
semi-civilized
semi|colon +s
semi|con|duct|ing
semi|con|duct|or
    +s
semi-conscious
semi|cyl|in|der +s
semi|cyl|in|drical
semi-darkness
semi|demi|semi|
        quaver +s
semi-deponent
semi-derelict
semi-detached +s
semi|diam|eter +s
semi-
    documen|tary
semi-
    documen|tar|ies
semi-dome +s
semi-double
semi-final +s
semi-finalist +s
semi-finished
semi-fitted
semi-fluid +s
semi-
    independ|ent
semi-infinite
semi-invalid +s
semi-liquid +s
semi-literacy
semi-literate
Sé|mil|lon +s

semi-lunar
semi-metal +s
semi-metallic
semi-monthly
sem|inal
sem|in|al|ly
sem|inar +s
sem|in|ar|ian +s
sem|in|ar|ist +s
sem|in|ary
sem|in|ar|ies
sem|in|ifer|ous
Sem|in|ole
    plural Sem|in|ole
    or Sem|in|oles
semi-official
semi-official|ly
semio|logic|al
semi|olo|gist +s
semi|ology
semi-opaque
semi|ot|ic
semi|ot|ic|al
semi|ot|ic|al|ly
semi|oti|cian +s
semi|ot|ics
Semi|pa|la|tinsk
    (former name of
    Semei)
semi|palm|ated
semi-perman|ent
semi-permeable
semi-plume +s
semi-precious
semi-pro +s
semi-
    profes|sion|al +s
semi|quaver +s
Se|mira|mis *Greek
    Mythology*
semi-retired
semi-retire|ment
semi-rigid
semi-skilled
semi-skimmed
semi-smile +s
semi-solid
semi-sweet
semi-synthet|ic
Sem|ite +s
Sem|it|ic
Sem|it|isa|tion *Br.*
    (use
    Semitization)
Sem|it|ise *Br.* (use
    Semitize)
Sem|it|ises
Sem|it|ised
Sem|it|is|ing
Sem|it|ism
Sem|it|ist +s
Sem|it|iza|tion

Sem¦it¦ize
  Sem¦it¦izes
  Sem¦it¦ized
  Sem¦it¦iz¦ing
semi¦tone +s
semi-trailer +s
semi-transpar¦ent
semi-tropic¦al
semi-tropics
semi-uncial +s
semi¦vowel +s
semi-weekly
Sem¦mel¦weis,
  Ignaz Phil¦ipp
  (Austro-Hungarian
  obstetrician)
sem¦mit +s
semo¦lina
sem¦per¦vivum +s
sem¦pi¦ter¦nal
sem¦pi¦ter¦nal¦ly
sem¦pi¦ter¦nity
sem¦plice
sem¦pre
semp¦stress (use
  seamstress)
  semp¦stresses
Sem¦tex *Propr.*
Sena¦nay¦ake,
  Don Ste¦phen
  (Ceylonese prime
  minister)
sen¦ar¦ius
  sen¦arii
sen¦ary
sen¦ate +s
  (legislative body.
  △ sennet, sennit)
sen¦ator +s
sen¦at¦or¦ial
sen¦at¦or¦ship +s
send
  sends
  sent
  send¦ing
send¦able
Sen¦dai (city,
  Japan)
sen¦dal +s
send¦er +s
sending-off
  sendings-off
send-off +s
send-up +s
Sen¦eca
  plural Sen¦eca *or*
  Sen¦ecas
  (American Indian)
Sen¦eca, Lu¦cius
  An¦naeus ('the
  Younger', Roman

Sen¦eca (*cont.*)
  statesman,
  philosopher, and
  dramatist)
Sen¦eca, Mar¦cus
  An¦naeus ('the
  Elder', Roman
  rhetorician)
se¦necio +s
Sene¦gal
Sene¦gal¦ese
  plural
  Sen¦egal¦ese
Sene¦gam¦bia
  (region, W. Africa)
sen¦esce
  sen¦esces
  sen¦esced
  sen¦es¦cing
sen¦es¦cence
sen¦es¦cent
sene¦schal +s
senhor +s
  (Portuguese or
  Brazilian man.
  △ señor)
senhora +s
  (Portuguese
  woman; Brazilian
  married woman.
  △ señora)
senhor¦ita +s
  (Brazilian
  unmarried
  woman.
  △ señorita)
se¦nile +s
sen¦il¦ity
se¦nior +s
se¦ni¦or¦ity
sen¦iti
  plural sen¦iti
Senna, Ayr¦ton
  (Brazilian motor-
  racing driver)
senna +s
Sen¦nach¦erib
  (Assyrian king)
sen¦net +s
  (trumpet call.
  △ senate, sennit)
sen¦night (week)
sen¦nit (plaited
  straw; in sense
  'braided cordage',
  use sinnet.
  △ senate, sennet)
señor
  se¦ñores
  (Spanish-speaking
  man. △ senhor)

se¦ñora +s (Spanish-
  speaking married
  woman.
  △ senhora)
se¦ñor¦ita +s
  (Spanish-speaking
  unmarried
  woman.
  △ senhorita)
sen¦sate
sen¦sa¦tion +s
sen¦sa¦tion¦al
sen¦sa¦tion¦al¦ise
  Br. (use
  sensationalize)
  sen¦sa¦tion¦al¦ises
  sen¦sa¦tion¦al¦
    ised
  sen¦sa¦tion¦al¦
    is¦ing
sen¦sa¦tion¦al¦ism
sen¦sa¦tion¦al¦ist
  +s
sen¦sa¦tion¦al¦
    is¦tic
sen¦sa¦tion¦al¦ize
  sen¦sa¦tion¦al¦izes
  sen¦sa¦tion¦al¦
    ized
  sen¦sa¦tion¦al¦
    iz¦ing
sen¦sa¦tion¦al¦ly
sense
  senses
  sensed
  sens¦ing
sense-datum
  sense-data
sense-experi¦ence
  +s
sense¦less
sense¦less¦ly
sense¦less¦ness
sense-organ +s
sens¦ibil¦ity
  sens¦ibil¦ities
sens¦ible
sens¦ible¦ness
sens¦ibly
sen¦si¦tisa¦tion *Br.*
  (use
  sensitization)
sen¦si¦tise *Br.* (use
  sensitize)
  sen¦si¦tises
  sen¦si¦tised
  sen¦si¦tis¦ing
sen¦si¦tiser *Br.* +s
  (use sensitizer)
sen¦si¦tive
sen¦si¦tive¦ly
sen¦si¦tive¦ness

sen¦si¦tiv¦ity
  sen¦si¦tiv¦ities
sen¦si¦tiza¦tion
sen¦si¦tize
  sen¦si¦tizes
  sen¦si¦tized
  sen¦si¦tiz¦ing
sen¦si¦tizer +s
sen¦si¦tom¦eter +s
sen¦sor +s
  (detecting or
  measuring device.
  △ censer, censor)
sen¦sor¦ial
sen¦sori¦al¦ly
sen¦sor¦ily
sen¦sor¦ium
  sen¦sor¦iums *or*
  sen¦soria
sens¦ory
sens¦ual
sens¦ual¦ise *Br.*
  (use sensualize)
  sens¦ual¦ises
  sens¦ual¦ised
  sens¦ual¦is¦ing
sens¦ual¦ism
sens¦ual¦ist +s
sens¦su¦al¦ity
sens¦ual¦ize
  sens¦ual¦izes
  sens¦ual¦ized
  sens¦ual¦iz¦ing
sen¦su¦al¦ly
sen¦sum
  sensa
sen¦su¦ous
sen¦su¦ous¦ly
sen¦su¦ous¦ness
sensu stricto
sent +s (past tense
  and past participle
  of send; Estonian
  currency. △ cent,
  scent)
sente
  li¦sente
sen¦tence
  sen¦tences
  sen¦tenced
  sen¦ten¦cing
sen¦ten¦tial
sen¦ten¦tious
sen¦ten¦tious¦ly
sen¦ten¦tious¦ness
sen¦tience
sen¦tiency
sen¦tient
sen¦tient¦ly
sen¦ti¦ment +s
sen¦ti¦men¦tal

sen|ti|men|tal|
isa|tion Br. (use
sentimentaliza-
tion)
sen|ti|men|tal|ise
Br. (use
sentimentalize)
sen|ti|men|tal|
ises
sen|ti|men|tal|
ised
sen|ti|men|tal|
is|ing
sen|ti|men|tal|ism
sen|ti|men|tal|ist
+s
sen|ti|men|tal|ity
sen|ti|men|tal|
iza|tion
sen|ti|men|tal|ize
sen|ti|men|tal|
izes
sen|ti|men|tal|
ized
sen|ti|men|tal|
iz|ing
sen|ti|men|tal|ly
sen|ti|nel
sen|ti|nels Br.
sen|ti|nelled Br.
sen|ti|neled Am.
sen|ti|nel|ling Br.
sen|ti|nel|ing Am.
sen|try
sen|tries
sen|try box
sen|try boxes
sentry-go
Se|nussi
plural Se|nussi
Seoul (capital of
South Korea)
sepal +s
sep|ar|abil|ity
sep|ar|able
sep|ar|able|ness
sep|ar|ably
sep|ar|ate
sep|ar|ates
sep|ar|ated
sep|ar|at|ing
sep|ar|ate|ly
sep|ar|ate|ness
sep|ar|ation +s
sep|ar|at|ism
sep|ar|at|ist +s
sep|ara|tive
sep|ar|ator +s
sep|ar|atory
Seph|ardi
Seph|ar|dim
Seph|ar|dic

sepia +s
sepoy +s
sep|puku
sep|sis
sep|ses
sept +s
septa (plural of
septum.
△ scepter,
sceptre)
sep|tal
sept|ate
sept|ation
septa|va|lent
sept|cen|ten|ary
sept|cen|ten|
ar|ies
Sep|tem|ber +s
sep|ten|ar|ius
sep|ten|arii
sep|ten|ary
sep|ten|ar|ies
sep|ten|ate
sep|ten|nial
sep|ten|nium
sep|ten|niums _or_
sep|ten|nia
sep|tet +s
sept|foil +s
sep|tic
septi|cae|mia Br.
septi|caem|ic Br.
sep|tic|al|ly
septi|cemia Am.
septi|cem|ic Am.
sep|ti|city
septi|lat|eral
sep|til|lion
plural sep|til|lion
sep|timal
sep|time +s
Sep|tim|ius
Se|verus (Roman
emperor)
septi|va|lent
sep|tua|gen|ar|ian
+s
sep|tua|gen|ary
sep|tua|gen|ar|ies
Sep|tua|ges|ima
Sep|tua|gint
sep|tum
septa
sep|tu|ple
sep|tu|ples
sep|tu|pled
sep|tu|pling
sep|tu|plet +s
sep|ul|cher Am. +s
+ed +ing
se|pul|chral
se|pul|chral|ly

sep|ul|chre Br.
sep|ul|chres
sep|ul|chred
sep|ul|chring
sep|ul|ture +s
se|qua|cious
se|qua|cious|ly
se|qua|city
se|quel +s
se|quela
se|que|lae
se|quence
se|quences
se|quenced
se|quen|cing
se|quen|cer +s
se|quent
se|quen|tial
se|quen|ti|al|ity
se|quen|tial|ly
se|quent|ly
se|ques|ter +s +ed
+ing
se|ques|trable
se|ques|tral
se|ques|trate
se|ques|trates
se|ques|trated
se|ques|trat|ing
se|ques|tra|tion
se|ques|tra|tor +s
se|ques|trot|omy
se|ques|
troto|mies
se|ques|trum
se|ques|tra
se|quin +s
se|quined Am.
se|quinned Br.
sequi|tur (in 'non
sequitur')
se|quoia +s
sera
serac +s
se|ra|glio +s
serai +s
Se|raing (town,
Belgium)
Seram Sea (use
Ceram Sea)
se|rang +s
se|rape +s
ser|aph
ser|aph|im _or_
ser|aphs
ser|aph|ic
ser|aph|ic|al|ly
Sera|pis _Egyptian
Mythology_
ser|as|kier +s
Serb +s
Ser|bia

Ser|bian +s
Serbo-Croat +s
Serbo-Croatian +s
SERC (= Science
and Engineering
Research Council)
sere +s (of gun;
sequence of
animal or plant
communities.
△ cere, sear, seer)
se|_rein_ (fine rain)
Ser|em|ban (city,
Malaysia)
Ser|ena
ser|en|ade
ser|en|ades
ser|en|aded
ser|en|ad|ing
ser|en|ader +s
ser|en|ata +s
ser|en|dip|it|ous
ser|en|dip|it|ous|ly
ser|en|dip|ity
se|rene
se|rener
se|ren|est
(calm. △ serine)
se|rene|ly
se|rene|ness
Ser|en|geti (plain,
Tanzania)
Se|ren|ity
Se|ren|ities
(title)
se|ren|ity
se|ren|ities
(tranquillity)
serf +s (labourer.
△ surf)
serf|age
serf|dom +s
serf|hood
serge +s (cloth.
△ surge)
ser|geancy
ser|gean|cies
ser|geant +s (army,
air force, or police
officer,
△ serjeant)
Ser|geant Baker
+s (fish)
sergeant-fish
plural sergeant-
fish _or_ sergeant-
fishes
ser|geant major
+s
ser|geant|ship +s
Ser|gipe (state,
Brazil)

Ser|gius (Russian
saint)
ser|ial +s (story in
episodes; forming
a series. ⚠ cereal)
seri|al|isa|tion Br.
+s (use
serialization)
seri|al|ise Br. (use
serialize)
seri|al|ises
seri|al|ised
seri|al|is|ing
seri|al|ism
seri|al|ist +s
seri|al|ity
seri|al|iza|tion +s
seri|al|ize
seri|al|izes
seri|al|ized
seri|al|iz|ing
ser|ial kill|er +s
seri|al|ly
ser|ial num|ber +s
ser|ial rights
seri|ate
seri|ates
seri|ated
seri|at|ing
seri|atim
seri|ation +s
Seric
se|ri|ceous
seri|cul|tural
seri|cul|ture
seri|cul|tur|ist +s
seri|ema +s
ser|ies
    plural ser|ies
serif +s
ser|iffed
seri|graph +s
ser|ig|raph|er +s
ser|ig|raphy
serin +s
ser|ine (amino acid.
    ⚠ serene)
ser|in|ette +s
ser|inga +s
serio-comic
serio-comical|ly
ser|ious
ser|ious|ly
ser|ious|ness
ser|jeant +s
    (barrister; army
    sergeant in official
    lists. ⚠ sergeant)
serjeant-at-arms
    serjeants-at-arms
serjeant-at-law
    serjeants-at-law

ser|jeant|ship +s
ser|mon +s
ser|mon|ette +s
ser|mon|ise Br.
    (use sermonize)
ser|mon|ises
ser|mon|ised
ser|mon|is|ing
ser|mon|iser Br. +s
    (use sermonizer)
ser|mon|ize
ser|mon|izes
ser|mon|ized
ser|mon|iz|ing
ser|mon|izer +s
sero|logic|al
sero|olo|gist +s
ser|ology
sero|nega|tive
sero|posi|tive
ser|osa +s
ser|os|ity
sero|tine +s
sero|tonin +s
ser|ous
serow +s
Ser|pens
    (constellation)
ser|pent +s
ser|pen|ti|form
ser|pen|tine
ser|pen|tines
ser|pen|tined
ser|pen|tin|ing
ser|pigin|ous
SERPS (= state
    earnings-related
    pension scheme)
ser|pula
ser|pullae
serra
ser|rae
ser|ra|dilla +s
ser|ran +s
ser|ranid +s
ser|rate
ser|rates
ser|rated
ser|rat|ing
ser|ra|tion +s
ser|ried
ser|ru|late
ser|ru|la|tion +s
serum
    sera or ser|ums
ser|val +s
ser|vant +s
serve
    serves
    served
    serv|ing
ser|ver +s

serv|ery
    serv|er|ies
Ser|vian +s
    (archaic variant of
    Serbian)
Ser|vian (of Servius
    Tullius, Roman
    king)
ser|vice
    ser|vices
    ser|viced
    ser|vicing
ser|vice|abil|ity
ser|vice|able
ser|vice|able|ness
ser|vice|ably
service-berry
    service-berries
ser|vice book +s
ser|vice|man
    ser|vice|men
ser|vice|woman
    ser|vice|women
ser|vi|ette +s
ser|vile
ser|vile|ly
ser|vil|ity
serv|ing +s
Ser|vite +s
ser|vi|tor +s
ser|vi|tor|ship +s
ser|vi|tude
servo +s
servo-mechan|ism
    +s
servo-motor +s
ses|ame +s
ses|am|oid
Se|so|tho
ses|qui|cen|ten|
                    ary
ses|qui|cen|ten|
                    ar|ies
ses|qui|cen|ten|
                    nial +s
ses|qui|ped|alian
    +s
sess (use cess)
ses|sile
ses|sion +s
    (meeting; bout.
    ⚠ cession)
ses|sion|al
ses|terce +s
ses|ter|tium
ses|ter|tia
ses|ter|tius
ses|ter|tii
ses|tet +s
ses|tina +s
Set (= Seth)

set
sets
set
set|ting
    (all senses except
    badger's burrow
    and paving block;
    for these, use sett)
seta
    setae
se|ta|ceous
set-aside +s noun
    and attributive
set|back +s
se-tenant
Seth (Egyptian
    Mythology; name)
SETI (= Search for
    Extraterrestrial
    Intelligence)
se|tif|er|ous
se|tiger|ous
set-off +s noun
seton +s
se|tose
set piece +s noun
set-piece attributive
set square +s
Set|swana
    (language)
sett +s (badger's
    burrow; paving-
    block. ⚠ set)
set|tee +s
set|ter +s (dog;
    person or thing
    that sets.
    ⚠ saeter)
set|ter|wort
set|ting +s
set|tle
    set|tles
    set|tled
    set|tling
settle|able
settle|ment +s
set|tler +s (person
    who settles in a
    new place)
set|tlor +s Law
set-to +s noun
Setú|bal (port,
    Portugal)
set-up +s noun
set|wall +s
Seu|rat, Georges
    Pierre (French
    painter)
Se|vas|to|pol
    (Russian name for
    Sebastopol)
seven +s

seven|fold
seven-iron+s
seven|teen+s
seven|teenth+s
sev|enth+s
Seventh-Day
  Ad|vent|ist+s
sev|enth|ly
seven|ti|eth+s
sev|enty
  sev|en|ties
seventy-first,
  seventy-second,
  etc.
sev|enty|fold
seventy-one,
  seventy-two,
  etc.
sever+s +ed +ing
sev|er|able
sev|eral+s
sev|er|al|ly
sev|er|al|ty
  sev|er|al|ties
sev|er|ance+s
se|vere
  se|verer
  se|ver|est
se|vere|ly
se|ver|ity
  se|ver|ities
Sev|ern (river,
  England and
  Wales)
Se|ver|naya
  Zem|lya (island
  group, north of
  Russia)
Sev|er|od|vinsk
  (port, Russia)
Se|verus (Roman
  emperor)
sev|ery
  sev|er|ies
se|viche
Sev|ille (city, Spain;
  orange)
Sèvres (town,
  France; porcelain)
sew
  sews
  sewed
  sew|ing
  sewn
  (stitch. △ so, soh,
  sow)
sew|age
se|wel|lel+s
sewen+s (use
  sewin)
sewer+s
sew|er|age

sewin+s
sew|ing ma|chine
  +s
sewn (past
  participle of sew.
  △ sown)
sex
  sexes
  sexed
  sex|ing
sexa|gen|ar|ian+s
sexa|gen|ary
  sexa|gen|ar|ies
Sexa|ges|ima
  (church calendar)
sexa|ges|imal+s
sexa|ges|im|al|ly
sex|angu|lar
sexa|va|lent
sex|cen|ten|ary
  sex|cen|ten|ar|ies
sex|digi|tate
sex|en|nial
sexer+s
sex|foil+s
sex|ily
sexi|ness
sex|ism
sex|ist+s
sexi|syl|lab|ic
sexi|syl|lable+s
sexi|va|lent
sex|less
sex|less|ly
sex|less|ness
sex-linked
sexo|logic|al
sex|olo|gist+s
sex|ology
sex|par|tite
sex|ploit|ation
sex|pot+s
sex-starved
sext+s
sex|tain+s
sex|tant+s
sex|tet+s
sex|til|lion
  plural sex|til|lion
  or sex|til|lions
sex|til|lionth+s
sexto+s
sexto|decimo+s
sex|ton+s
sex|tu|ple
  sex|tu|ples
  sex|tu|pled
  sex|tu|pling
sex|tu|plet+s
sex|tu|ply
sex|ual

sexu|al|ise Br. (use
  sexualize)
sexu|al|ises
sexu|al|ised
sexu|al|is|ing
sexu|al|ist+s
sexu|al|ity
sexu|al|ities
sexu|al|ize
sexu|al|izes
sexu|al|ized
sexu|al|iz|ing
sexu|al|ly
sex|va|lent
sexy
  sex|ier
  sexi|est
Sey|chelles
  (islands, Indian
  Ocean)
Sey|chel|lois
  plural
  Sey|chel|lois
  male
Sey|chel|loise+s
  female
Sey|mour, Jane
  (wife of Henry
  VIII of England)
Sey|mour, Lynn
  (Canadian ballet
  dancer)
sez (= says)
Sfax (port, Tunisia)
sforz|ando
  sforz|an|dos or
  sforz|andi
sforz|ato
sfu|mato
  sfu|mati
sgraf|fito
  sgraf|fiti
's-Gravenhage
  (= The Hague, the
  Netherlands)
sh
Shaanxi (province,
  China)
Shaba (region,
  Zaire)
Sha|baka (pharaoh)
shab|bily
shab|bi|ness
shabby
  shab|bier
  shab|bi|est
shab|by|ish
shab|rack+s
shack+s +ed +ing
shackle
  shackles

shackle (cont.)
  shackled
  shack|ling
shackle-bolt+s
Shackle|ton,
  Er|nest (Irish
  explorer)
shad
  plural shad or
  shads
shad|dock+s
shade
  shades
  shaded
  shad|ing
shade|less
shadi|ly
shadi|ness
shad|ing+s
sha|doof+s
shadow+s +ed
  +ing
shadow-boxing
shad|ow|er+s
shad|ow|graph+s
shad|ow|iness
shad|ow|less
shad|owy
shady
  shadi|er
  shadi|est
shaft+s +ed +ing
Shaftes|bury, Lord
  (English social
  reformer)
shag
  shags
  shagged
  shag|ging
  (hair etc.; carpet
  pile; tobacco; bird;
  also coarse slang)
shag|ger+s (coarse
  slang)
shag|gily
shag|gi|ness
shaggy
  shag|gier
  shag|gi|est
shag pile+s
sha|green+s
shah+s
Shah Alam (city,
  Malaysia)
shah|dom+s
shaikh+s (use
  sheikh △ shake)
Shaka (Zulu chief)
shake
  shakes
  shook
  shak|ing

shake (*cont.*)
  shaken
  (agitate. △ **sheikh**)
shake|able
shake|down +s
shake-out +s *noun*
Shaker +s
  (religious sect
  member)
shaker +s (person
  or thing that
  shakes)
Shaker|ess
Shaker|esses
Shaker|ism
Shake|speare,
  Wil|liam (English
  dramatist)
Shake|spear|ean
  +s
Shake|speare|ana
Shake|spear|ian
  +s (use
  Shakespearean)
Shake|speari|ana
  (use
  Shakespeareana)
shake-up +s *noun*
Shakhty (city,
  Russia)
shaki|ly
shaki|ness
shako +s
shaku|hachi +s
shaky
  shaki|er
  shaki|est
shale +s
shall
shall|loon +s
shal|lop +s
shal|lot +s (plant.
  △ **Shalott**)
shal|low +er +est
shal|low|ly
shal|low|ness
Shal|man|eser
  (Assyrian kings)
sha|lom +s
Sha|lott (in *'The
  Lady of Shalott'*.
  △ **shallot**)
shalt
shal|war
shaly
  shali|er
  shali|est
sham
  shams
  shammed
  sham|ming
shaman +s

sha|man|ic
sham|an|ism
sham|an|ist +s
sham|an|is|tic
shama|teur +s
shama|teur|ism
sham|ble
  sham|bles
  sham|bled
  sham|bling
  (walk or run
  awkwardly)
sham|bles (mess;
  slaughterhouse;
  scene of carnage)
sham|bol|ic
shame
  shames
  shamed
  sham|ing
shame|faced
shame|faced|ly
shame|faced|ness
shame|ful
shame|ful|ly
shame|ful|ness
shame|less
shame|less|ly
shame|less|ness
sham|ing|ly
Sha|mir, Yit|zhak
  (Israeli prime
  minister)
sham|mer +s
shammy
  sham|mies
sham|poo +s +ed
  +ing
sham|rock +s
sha|mus
  sha|muses
Shand|ean +s
Shan|dong
  (province, China)
shan|dry|dan +s
shandy
  shan|dies
shandy|gaff +s
Shang (Chinese
  dynasty)
Shan|gaan
  plural Shan|gaan
  or Shan|gaans
Shang|hai (city,
  China)
shang|hai +s +ed
  +ing (trick into
  joining ship's
  crew; shoot with
  catapult)
Shangri-La +s
  (fictional utopia)

shank +s
Shan|kar, Ravi
  (Indian musician)
shanked
shanks's mare
shanks's pony
Shan|non (river
  and airport,
  Republic of
  Ireland; shipping
  area, NE Atlantic)
Shan|non, Claude
  El|wood
  (American
  engineer)
shanny
  shan|nies
Shansi (= Shanxi)
shan't (= shall not)
Shan|tou (port,
  China)
Shan|tung
  (= Shandong)
shan|tung +s (silk)
shanty
  shan|ties
shanty|man
  shanty|men
shanty town +s
Shanxi (province,
  China)
shap|able
SHAPE (= Supreme
  Headquarters
  Allied Powers in
  Europe)
shape
  shapes
  shaped
  shap|ing
shape|able (use
  shapable)
shape|chan|ger +s
shape|chan|ging
shape|less
shape|less|ly
shape|less|ness
shape|li|ness
shape|ly
  shape|lier
  shape|li|est
shaper +s
shap|ing +s
Shap|ley, Har|low
  (American
  astronomer)
shard +s
share
  shares
  shared
  shar|ing
share|able

share|crop
  share|crops
  share|cropped
  share|crop|ping
share|crop|per +s
share-farmer +s
share|hold|er +s
share|hold|ing +s
share-out +s *noun*
sharer +s
share|ware
sha|ria
sha|riah (use
  sharia)
sha|rif +s
Shar|jah (city state,
  UAE)
shark +s
shark|skin +s
Sharma, Shan|kar
  Dayal (Indian
  president)
Sharon (coastal
  plain, Israel)
Sharon *also*
  Shar|ron
  (name)
sharon fruit +s
Sharp, Cecil
  (English collector
  of folk-songs and
  folk dances)
sharp +s +ed +ing
  +er +est
shar-pei +s
sharp|en +s +ed
  +ing
sharp|en|er +s
sharp|en|ing +s
sharp|er +s
Sharpe|ville
  (township, South
  Africa)
sharp-eyed
sharp|ish
sharp|ly
sharp|ness
sharp-set
sharp|shoot|er +s
sharp|shoot|ing
sharp-tongued
sharp-witted
sharp-witted|ly
sharp-witted|ness
Shar|ron *also*
  Sharon
shash|lik +s
Shasta +s (daisy)
Shas|tra
shat (*coarse slang*)
Shatt al-Arab
  (river, Iraq)

shat|ter +s +ed
+ing
shat|ter|er +s
shat|ter|ing|ly
shatter-proof
Shaun *also* Sean
shave
 shaves
 shaved
 shav|ing
shave|ling +s
shaven
shaven-headed
shaver +s
Sha|vian +s
shav|ing +s
Sha|vuot (use
 Shavuoth)
Sha|vu|oth (Jewish
 Pentecost)
Shaw, George
 Ber|nard (Irish
 playwright)
shaw +s (vegetable
 stalks and leaves.
 △ shore, sure)
shawl +s (garment.
 △ schorl)
shawled
shawlie +s
 (working-class
 woman. △ surely)
shawm +s
Shaw|nee
 plural Shaw|nee *or*
 Shaw|nees
Shcher|ba|kov
 (former name of
 Rybinsk)
shchi +s (soup)
she
s/he (= she or he)
shea +s (tree)
shea-butter +s
shead|ing +s
 (administrative
 division, Isle of
 Man)
sheaf
 sheaves
 noun
sheaf +s +ed +ing
 verb
sheal|ing +s (use
 shieling)
shear
 shears
 sheared
 shear|ing
 sheared *or* shorn
 (cut with shears.
 △ sheer)

shear|bill +s
Shear|er, Moira
 (Scottish ballet
 dancer)
shear|er +s (person
 who shears sheep)
shear|ing +s
shear|ling +s
shear|tail +s
shear|water +s
sheath +s
sheathe
 sheathes
 sheathed
 sheath|ing
sheath|ing +s
sheath|less
sheath-like
sheave
 sheaves
 sheaved
 sheav|ing
sheaves (plural of
 sheaf)
Sheba (ancient
 country)
she|bang +s
She|bat (use Sebat)
she|been +s
She|chi|nah (use
 Shekinah)
shed
 sheds
 shed
 shed|ding
 (building; throw
 off, spill, separate,
 etc.)
shed
 sheds
 shed|ded
 shed|ding
 (keep in shed)
she'd (= she had;
 she would)
shed|der +s
she-devil +s
shed|hand +s
Shee|lagh *also*
 Sheila, She|lagh
Sheela-na-gig +s
sheen +s +ed +ing
Sheena
Sheene, Barry
 (English racing
 motorcyclist)
sheeny
 sheen|ier
 sheeni|est
sheep
 plural sheep
sheep-dip +s

sheep|dog +s
sheep farm|er +s
sheep farm|ing
sheep|fold +s
sheep|ish
sheep|ish|ly
sheep|ish|ness
sheep|like
sheep|meat
sheep-run +s
sheep's-bit +s
 (plant)
sheep|shank +s
 (knot)
sheep|skin +s
sheep|walk +s
sheep-worrying
sheer +s +ed +ing
 +est (swerve;
 shape of ship;
 mere; unqualified;
 steep; thin.
 △ shear)
sheer|legs
 plural sheer|legs
sheer|ly
Sheer|ness (port,
 England)
sheer|ness
sheet +s +ed +ing
sheet|ing
Shef|field (city,
 England)
sheik +s (use
 sheikh. △ shake)
sheik|dom +s (use
 sheikhdom)
sheikh +s (Arab
 chief; Muslim
 leader. △ shake)
sheikh|dom +s
Sheila *also*
 Shee|lagh,
 She|lagh (name)
sheila +s
 (young woman)
shekel +s
She|ki|nah
She|lagh *also*
 Shee|lagh, Sheila
shell|drake +s
shelf
 shelves
 (ledge)
shelf +s +ed +ing
 (inform; informer.
 △ shelve)
shelf|ful +s
shelf-life
 shelf-lives
shelf-like

shelf mark +s
shelf-room
shell +s +ed +ing
 (case of mollusc,
 egg, etc.)
she'll (= she will;
 she shall. △ shill)
shell|lac
 shell|lacs
 shell|lacked
 shell|lack|ing
shell|back +s
shell-bit +s
Shell|ey (name)
Shell|ey, Mary
 Woll|stone|craft
 (English writer)
Shell|ey, Percy
 Bysshe (English
 poet)
shell|fire
shell|fish
 plural shell|fish *or*
 shell|fishes
shell-heap +s
shell-jacket +s
shell-keep +s
shell-less
shell-like
shell-lime
shell-money
shell-out +s *noun*
shell pink +s *noun
and attributive*
shell-pink
 attributive
shell|proof
shell-shock
shell-shocked
shell suit +s
shell-work
shelly
Shelta (language)
shel|ter +s +ed
 +ing (protection;
 protect)
shel|ter belt +s
shel|ter|er +s
shel|ter|less
shel|tie +s
shelve
 shelves
 shelved
 shelv|ing
shelver +s
shelves (plural of
 shelf)
Shem *Bible*
Shema +s
she|moz|zle +s
Shen|an|doah
 (river and

Shen|an|doah
(cont.)
National Park,
USA)
she|nani|gan +s
Shensi (= Shaanxi)
Shen|yang (city,
China)
Shen|zhen (city,
China)
Sheol
shep|herd +s +ed
+ing
shep|herd|ess
shep|herd|esses
shep|herd's purse
+s
Shep|pey, Isle of
(in England)
sher|ard|ise Br.
(use sherardize)
she|rard|ises
sher|ard|ised
sher|ard|is|ing
sher|ard|ize
sher|ard|izes
sher|ard|ized
sher|ard|iz|ing
Shera|ton (style of
furniture)
sher|bet +s
sherd +s
she|reef +s (use
sharif)
Sheri|dan,
Rich|ard
Brins|ley (Irish
dramatist)
Sheri|dan
she|rif +s (Islam;
use sharif)
sher|iff +s (civil or
law officer)
sher|iff|alty
sher|iff|al|ties
sheriff-depute +s
sher|iff|dom +s
sher|iff|hood +s
sher|iff|ship +s
Sher|lock +s
Sher|man,
Wil|liam
(American
general)
Sherpa
plural Sherpa or
Sher|pas
Sher|rill (man's
name. △ Sheryl)
Sher|ring|ton,
Charles Scott

Sher|ring|ton
(cont.)
(English
physiologist)
Sherry (name)
sherry
sher|ries
(drink)
sherry glass
sherry glasses
's-Hertogenbosch
(city, the
Netherlands)
Sheryl (woman's
name. △ Sherrill)
she's (= she is; she
has)
Shet|land (region,
Scotland)
Shet|land|er +s
Shet|land Is|lands
(in Scotland)
Shet|lands
(= Shetland
Islands)
sheva +s (use
schwa)
Shev|ard|nadze,
Ed|uard
(Georgian
statesman)
She|vat (use Sebat)
shew
shews
shewed
shew|ing
shewn or shewed
(archaic; use
show)
shew|bread
Shia +s (branch of
Islam; Shi'ite)
shi|atsu (Japanese
therapy. △ shih-
tzu)
shib|bo|leth +s
shicer +s
shick|er
shick|ered
shield +s +ed +ing
shield bug +s
shield|less
shiel|ing +s
shier (comparative
of shy)
shiest (superlative
of shy)
shift +s +ed +ing
shift|able
shift|er +s
shift|ily
shifti|ness

shift|less
shift|less|ly
shift|less|ness
shift work
shifty
shift|ier
shifti|est
shi|gella +s
shih-tzu +s (dog.
△ shiatsu)
Shi'|ism
shii|take +s
Shi'|ite +s
Shi|jiaz|huang
(city, China)
shi|kar +s
shi|kara +s
shi|kari +s
Shi|koku (island,
Japan)
shiksa +s (often
offensive)
shill +s (person
who drums up
business. △ she'll)
shil|le|lagh +s
shil|ling +s
(Kenyan,
Tanzanian,
Ugandan, and
former British
currency.
△ schilling)
shilling-mark +s
shil|lings|worth +s
Shil|long (city,
India)
shilly-shallier +s
(use shilly-
shallyer)
shilly-shally
shilly-shallies
shilly-shallied
shilly-shally|ing
shilly-shally|er +s
shim
shims
shimmed
shim|ming
shim|mer +s +ed
+ing
shim|mer|ing|ly
shim|mery
shimmy
shim|mies
shim|mied
shimmy|ing
shin
shins
shinned
shin|ning
shin bone +s

shin|dig +s
shindy
shin|dies
shine
shines
shined or shone
shin|ing
shiner +s
shin|gle
shin|gles
shin|gled
shin|gling
shin|gly
shin-guard +s
shini|ly
shini|ness
shin|ing|ly
Shin|kan|sen
plural
Shin|kan|sen
shinny
shin|nies
shin|nied
shinny|ing
shin-pad +s
Shinto
Shin|to|ism
Shin|to|ist +s
shinty
shin|ties
shiny
shini|er
shini|est
ship
ships
shipped
ship|ping
ship|board
ship-breaker +s
ship|broker +s
ship|build|er +s
ship|build|ing
ship canal +s
ship-fever
ship|lap
ship|laps
ship|lapped
ship|lap|ping
ship|less
ship|load +s
ship|mas|ter +s
ship|mate +s
ship|ment +s
ship money
ship|owner +s
ship|pable
ship|per +s
ship|ping agent +s
shipping-articles
shipping-bill +s
shipping-master
+s

shipping-office +s
ship-rigged
ship|shape
ship-to-shore +s
ship|worm +s
ship|wreck +s +ed +ing
ship|wright +s
ship|yard +s
shira|lee +s
Shi|raz
  Shi|razes
  (city, Iran; grape;
  wine)
shire +s (county.
  ⚠ shyer)
shire-horse +s
shire-moot +s
shirk +s +ed +ing
shirk|er +s
Shir|ley
shirr +s +ed +ing
shirt +s
shirt-dress
  shirt-dresses
shirt|ed
shirt-front +s
shirt|ily
shirti|ness
shirt|ing +s
shirt|less
shirt|sleeve +s
shirt-sleeved
shirt-tail +s
shirt|waist +s
shirt|waist|er +s
shirty
  shirt|ier
  shirti|est
shish kebab +s
shit
  shits
  shit|ted or shit or
  shat
  shit|ting
  (coarse slang)
shit|bag +s (coarse
  slang)
shit creek (coarse
  slang)
shite +s (coarse
  slang)
shit|house +s
  (coarse slang)
shit|less (coarse
  slang)
shit-scared (coarse
  slang)
shitty
  shit|tier

shitty (cont.)
  shit|ti|est
  (coarse slang)
Shiva (use Siva)
Shi|vaji (Indian
  raja)
shiva|ree +s
shiver +s +ed +ing
shiv|er|er +s
shiv|er|ing|ly
shiv|ery
shi|voo +s
Shizu|oka (city,
  Japan)
Shko|dër (city,
  Albania)
shoal +s +ed +ing
shoaly
shoat +s
shock +s +ed +ing
shock|abil|ity
shock|able
shock-brigade +s
shock cord +s
shock|er +s
shock|ing|ly
shock|ing|ness
shock|ing pink
Shock|ley,
  Wil|liam
  (American
  physicist)
shock|proof
shock wave +s
shock-worker +s
shod
shod|dily
shod|di|ness
shoddy
  shod|dier
  shod|di|est
shoe
  shoes
  shod
  shoe|ing
  (footwear; on
  horse. ⚠ choux,
  shoo)
shoe|bill +s
shoe|black +s
shoe|box
  shoe|boxes
shoe-buckle +s
shoe|horn +s +ed
  +ing
shoe|lace +s
shoe lea|ther +s
shoe|less
shoe|maker +s
Shoemaker–Levy
  9 (comet)
shoe|mak|ing

shoe|shine
shoe|string +s
shoe-tree +s
sho|far
  shof|roth
  (ram's-horn
  trumpet.
  ⚠ chauffeur)
sho|gun +s
sho|gun|ate +s
Sho|la|pur (city,
  India)
Sholo|khov,
  Mikh|ail (Russian
  writer)
Shona
  plural Shona or
  Sho|nas
  (group of Bantu
  peoples; any of
  their languages;
  name)
shone
shonky
  shonk|ier
  shonki|est
shoo +s +ed +ing
shoo-in +s noun
shook +s
shoot
  shoots
  shot
  shoot|ing
  (fire gun etc.; act
  of shooting.
  ⚠ chute)
shoot|able
shoot|er +s
shoot|ing +s
shoot|ing box
  shoot|ing boxes
shoot|ing brake +s
shoot|ing coat +s
shoot|ing gal|lery
  shoot|ing
  gal|ler|ies
shoot|ing iron +s
shoot|ing match
shoot|ing range +s
shoot|ing stick +s
shoot-out +s noun
shop
  shops
  shopped
  shop|ping
shop|ahol|ic +s
shop-bought
shop boy +s
shop|fit|ter +s
shop|fit|ting
shop floor +s noun

shop-floor
  attributive
shop|front +s
shop girl +s
shop|keep|er +s
shop|keep|ing
shop|less
shop|lift +s +ed
  +ing
shop|lift|er +s
shop|man
  shop|men
shop owner +s
shop|per +s
shoppy
shop-soiled
shop talk
shop|walk|er +s
shop win|dow +s
shop|work|er +s
shop|worn
shoran
shore
  shores
  shored
  shor|ing
  (coast; prop.
  ⚠ shaw, sure)
shore-based
shore|bird +s
shore|less
shore|line +s
shore|ward
shore|wards
shore|weed +s
shorn
short +s +ed +ing
  +er +est
short|age +s
short-arm adjective
short|bread +s
short|cake +s
short-change
  short-changes
  short-changed
  short-changing
  verb
short-circuit +s
  +ed +ing verb
short|com|ing +s
short|crust
short cut +s
short-dated
short-day adjective
short-eared owl
  +s
short|en +s +ed
  +ing
short|en|ing +s
short|fall +s
short|hair +s
short-haired

short|hand
short-handed
short-haul
  attributive
short-head +s +ed
  +ing *verb*
short|hold
short|horn +s
shortie +s (use
  shorty)
short|ish
short|list +s +ed
  +ing
short-lived
short|ly
short|ness
short-order
  attributive
short-pitched
short-range
  adjective
short-sighted
short-sighted|ly
short-sighted|ness
short-sleeved
short-staffed
short|stop +s
short-tempered
short-term
  adjective
short-termism
short-winded
shorty
  short|ies
Sho|shone
  plural Sho|shone
  or Sho|shones
Sho|shon|ean
Shosta|ko|vich,
  Dmi|tri (Russian
  composer)
shot +s
shot-blasting +s
shot-firer +s
shot|gun +s
shot|proof
shot-put +s
shot-putter +s
shot|ten
shot-tower +s
should
shoul|der +s +ed
  +ing
shoul|der bag +s
shoulder-belt +s
shoul|der blade +s
shoulder-high
shoul|der hol|ster
  +s
shoulder-knot +s
shoulder-length
shoul|der note +s
shoul|der pad +s

shoul|der strap +s
shouldn't
  (= should not)
shout +s +ed +ing
shout|er +s
shout-up +s *noun*
shove
  shoves
  shoved
  shov|ing
shove-halfpenny
shovel
  shovels
  shov|elled *Br.*
  shov|eled *Am.*
  shov|el|ling *Br.*
  shov|el|ing *Am.*
shovel|board
shov|el|er *Am.* +s
  (*Br.* shoveller)
shovel|ful +s
shovel|head +s
shov|el|ler *Br.* +s
  (*Am.* shoveler)
show
  shows
  showed
  show|ing
  shown *or* showed
show|band +s
show|biz
show|boat +s
show|card +s
show|case
  show|cases
  show|cased
  show|cas|ing
show|down +s
shower +s +ed
  +ing
shower|proof +s
  +ed +ing
show|ery
show flat +s
show|girl +s
show|ground +s
show home +s
show house +s
show|ily
show|iness
show|ing +s
show|jump +s +ed
  +ing
show|jump|er +s
show|man
  show|men
show|man|ship
shown
show-off +s *noun*
show|piece +s
show|place +s
show|room +s
show-stopper +s

show-stopping
show|time
show-window +s
showy
  show|ier
  show|iest
shoyu
shrank
shrap|nel +s
shred
  shreds
  shred|ded
  shred|ding
shred|der +s
Shreve|port (city,
  USA)
shrew +s
shrewd +er +est
shrewd|ly
shrewd|ness
shrew|ish
shrew|ish|ly
shrew|ish|ness
Shrews|bury
  (town, England)
shriek +s +ed +ing
shriek|er +s
shrieval
shriev|al|ty
  shriev|al|ties
shrift +s
shrike +s
shrill +s +ed +ing
shrill|ness
shrilly
shrimp +s +ed
  +ing
shrimp|er +s
shrine
  shrines
  shrined
  shrin|ing
shrink
  shrinks
  shrank
  shrink|ing
  shrunk
shrink|able
shrink|age +s
shrink|er +s
shrink|ing|ly
shrink-proof
shrink-resist|ant
shrink-wrap
  shrink-wraps
  shrink-wrapped
  shrink-wrapping
shrive
  shrives
  shrove
  shriv|ing
  shriven

shrivel
  shrivels
  shriv|elled *Br.*
  shriv|eled *Am.*
  shriv|el|ling *Br.*
  shriv|el|ing *Am.*
Shrop|shire
  (county, England)
shroud +s +ed
  +ing
shroud-laid
shroud|less
shrove
Shrove|tide +s
Shrove Tues|day
  +s
shrub +s
shrub|bery
  shrub|ber|ies
shrubby
  shrub|bier
  shrub|bi|est
shrug
  shrugs
  shrugged
  shrug|ging
shrunk
shrunk|en
shtick +s
shtook
shu|bun|kin +s
shuck +s +ed +ing
shuck|er +s
shucks
shud|der +s +ed
  +ing
shud|der|ing|ly
shud|dery
shuf|fle
  shuf|fles
  shuf|fled
  shuf|fling
shuffle-board
shuf|fler +s
shuf|fling +s
shufti +s
shul +s
Shula
Shula|mit *also*
  Shula|mith
shule +s (use *shul*)
Shu|men (city,
  Bulgaria)
shun
  shuns
  shunned
  shun|ning
shunt +s +ed +ing
shunt|er +s
shush
  shushes

shush (*cont.*)
  shushed
  shush|ing
shut
  shuts
  shut
  shut|ting
shut|down +s
Shute, Nevil
  (English novelist)
shut-eye
shut-in +s *adjective*
  and noun
shut-off +s *noun*
  and attributive
shut|out +s
  adjective and noun
shut-out bid +s
shut|ter +s +ed
  +ing
shut|ter|less
shut|tle
  shut|tles
  shut|tled
  shut|tling
shuttle|cock +s
shy
  shies
  shied
  shy|ing
  shyer
  shy|est
shyer +s (horse etc.
  that shies.
  △ shire)
Shy|lock (character
  in Shakespeare)
shyly
shy|ness
shy|ster +s
si (*Music*. △ sea,
  see)
Sia|chen Gla|cier
  (in India)
sial
siala|gogue +s (use
  sialogogue)
Si|al|kot (city,
  Pakistan)
sialo|gogue +s
Siam (former name
  of Thailand)
Siam, Gulf of
  (former name of
  the Gulf of
  Thailand)
sia|mang +s
Siam|ese
  plural Siam|ese
Siân
sib +s

Si|bel|ius, Jean
  (Finnish
  composer)
Ši|benik (port,
  Croatia)
Si|ber|ia
Si|ber|ian +s
sibi|lance
sibi|lancy
sibi|lant +s
sibi|late
  sibi|lates
  sibi|lated
  sibi|lat|ing
sibi|la|tion +s
Sibiu (city,
  Romania)
sib|ling +s
sib|ship +s
Sibyl *also* Sybil
  (name)
sibyl +s
  (prophetess)
sibyl|line (of a
  sibyl; prophetic)
Sibyl|line books
  (Roman oracles)
sic (correct thus.
  △ sick)
sic|ca|tive +s
sice +s (the six on
  dice. △ syce)
Si|chuan (province,
  China)
Si|cil|ian +s
si|cili|ana +s
si|cili|ano +s
Si|cily
sick +s +ed +ing
  +er +est (ill.
  △ sic)
sick bag +s
sick|bay +s
sick|bed +s
sick bene|fit +s
sick call +s
sick|en +s +ed
  +ing
sick|en|er +s
sick|en|ing|ly
**Sick|ert, Wal|ter
  Rich|ard** (British
  painter)
sick flag +s
sickie +s
sick|ish
sickle +s
sick leave
sickle-bill +s
sickle-cell +s
sickle-feather +s
sick|li|ness

sick list +s
sick|ly
  sick|lier
  sick|li|est
sick-making
sick|ness
  sick|nesses
sicko +s
sick pay
sick|room +s
si|dal|cea +s
**Sid|dhar|tha
  Gau|tama**
  (founder of
  Buddhism)
Sid|dons, Sarah
  (English actress)
side
  sides
  sided
  sid|ing
side|arm *Baseball*
side arm +s
  (weapon)
side band +s
side-bet +s
side|board +s
side-bone +s
side|burn +s
side|car +s
side chapel +s
side dish
  side dishes
sided|ness
side door +s
side drum +s
side ef|fect +s
side glance +s
side-handled
side|hill +s
side issue +s
side|kick +s
side|lamp +s
side|less
side|light +s
side|line
  side|lines
  side|lined
  side|lin|ing
side|long
side note +s
side-on *adverb*
si|der|eal
sid|er|ite +s
side road +s
sid|ero|stat +s
side-saddle +s
side-screen +s
side seat +s
side shoot +s
side|show +s

side-slip
  side-slips
  side-slipped
  side-slipping
sides|man
  sides|men
side-splitting
side|step
  side|steps
  side|stepped
  side|step|ping
side|step|per +s
side street +s
side|stroke +s
side|swipe
  side|wipes
  side|swiped
  side|swip|ing
side table +s
side|track +s +ed
  +ing
side trip +s
side view +s
side|walk +s
side|ward
side|wards
side|ways
side-wheeler +s
side-whiskers
side wind +s
side|wind|er +s
side|wise
Sidi bel Abbès
  (town, Algeria)
sid|ing +s
sidle
  sidles
  sidled
  sid|ling
Sid|ney *also*
  Syd|ney
  (name)
Sid|ney, Philip
  (English poet)
Sidon (city,
  Lebanon)
Sidra, Gulf of (off
  Libya)
Sie|ben|ge|birge
  (hills, Germany)
siege +s
siege gun +s
Sieg|fried (hero of
  Nibelungenlied)
Sieg|fried Line
  (German
  defences)
**Sie|mens, Ernst
  Wer|ner von**
  (German electrical
  engineer)
sie|mens (unit)
  plural sie|mens

Siena (city, Italy)
Sien|ese
  plural Sien|ese
Sien|kie|wicz,
  Hen|ryk (Polish
  novelist)
si|enna +s
  (pigment)
si|erra +s
Si|erra Leone (in
  West Africa)
Si|erra Leon|ian
  +s
Si|erra Madre
  (mountain range,
  Mexico)
Si|erra Nev|ada
  (mountain range,
  Spain)
si|esta +s
sieve
  sieves
  sieved
  siev|ing
sieve|like
sie|vert +s
si|faka +s
sif|fleur +s *male*
sif|fleuse +s *female*
sift +s +ed +ing
sift|er +s
sigh +s +ed +ing
sight +s +ed +ing
  (vision; see;
  observe. △ cite,
  site)
sight|er +s
sight-glass
  sight-glasses
sight|ing +s
sight|less
sight|less|ly
sight|less|ness
sight line +s
sight|li|ness
sight|ly
  sight|lier
  sight|li|est
sight-read
  sight-reads
  sight-read
  sight-reading
sight-reader +s
sight-screen +s
sight|see
  sight|sees
  sight|saw
  sight|see|ing
sight|seer +s
sight-sing
  sight-sings

sight-sing (*cont.*)
  sight-sang
  sight-singing
sight|worthy
sigil|late
SIGINT (= signals
  intelligence)
sig|lum
  sigla
sigma +s
sig|mate
sig|moid +s
sign +s +ed +ing
  (signal. △ sine,
  syne)
sign|able
Si|gnac, Paul
  (French painter)
sign|age
sig|nal
  sig|nals
  sig|nalled *Br.*
  sig|naled *Am.*
  sig|nal|ling *Br.*
  sig|nal|ing *Am.*
signal-book +s
sig|nal box
  sig|nal boxes
sig|nal|ise *Br.* (use
  signalize)
  sig|nal|ises
  sig|nal|ised
  sig|nal|is|ing
sig|nal|ize
  sig|nal|izes
  sig|nal|ized
  sig|nal|iz|ing
sig|nal|ler +s
sig|nal|ly
sig|nal|man
  sig|nal|men
sig|nal tower +s
sig|nary
  sig|nar|ies
  (list of signs.
  △ signory)
sig|na|tory
  sig|na|tor|ies
sig|na|ture +s
sign|board +s
sign|ee +s
sign|er +s
sig|net +s (seal
  used as
  authentication.
  △ cygnet)
sig|net ring +s
sig|nifi|cance +s
sig|nifi|cancy
sig|nifi|cant
sig|nifi|cant|ly
sig|ni|fi|ca|tion +s

sig|nifi|ca|tive
sig|ni|fied +s
sig|ni|fier +s
sig|nify
  sig|ni|fies
  sig|ni|fied
  sig|ni|fy|ing
sign|ing +s
sign-off +s *noun*
si|gnor
  si|gnori
  male
si|gnora +s *female*
si|gnor|ina +s
  female
si|gnory (governing
  body. △ signary)
  si|gnor|ies
sign-painter +s
sign-painting
sign|post +s +ed
  +ing
sign|writer +s
sign|writ|ing
Sig|urd *Norse Legend*
Siha|nouk, Prince
  Noro|dom
  (Cambodian ruler)
Siha|nouk|ville
  (former name of
  Kampong Som)
sika +s (deer.
  △ caeca, seeker)
Sikh +s (adherent
  of Sikhism.
  △ seek)
Sikh|ism
Si|king (former
  name of Xian)
Sik|kim (state,
  India)
Sik|kim|ese
  plural Sik|kim|ese
Si|kor|sky, Igor
  (Russian-born
  American aircraft
  designer)
Sik|sika
sil|age
  sil|ages
  sil|aged
  sil|aging
Silas
Sil|bury Hill
  (neolithic site,
  England)
Sil|ches|ter
  (village, England)
sild
  plural sild
si|lence
  si|lences

si|lence (*cont.*)
  si|lenced
  si|len|cing
si|len|cer +s
si|lent
si|lent|ly
Si|lenus (*Greek
  Mythology*; teacher
  of Dionysus)
si|lenus
  si|leni
  (*Greek Mythology*;
  woodland spirit
  generally)
Si|le|sia (region of
  central Europe)
Si|le|sian +s
silex
sil|hou|ette
  sil|hou|ettes
  sil|hou|et|ted
  sil|hou|et|ting
sil|ica (silicon
  dioxide. △ siliqua)
sili|cate +s
si|li|ceous
si|li|cic
sili|cif|er|ous
si|lici|fi|ca|tion
si|licify
  si|lici|fies
  si|lici|fied
  si|lici|fy|ing
sil|icon (element)
sili|cone
  sili|cones
  sili|coned
  sili|con|ing
  (compound; treat
  with silicone)
Sili|con Val|ley
  (industrial region,
  USA)
sili|cosis
  sili|coses
sili|cot|ic
sili|qua
  sili|quae
  (seed pod.
  △ silica)
si|lique +s
sili|quose
sili|quous
silk +s
silk|en
silk-fowl
  plural silk-fowl
silk-gland +s
silk|ily
silki|ness
silk|like

silk-screen +s +ed +ing
silk|worm +s
silky
  silk|ier
  silki|est
sill +s
sil|la|bub +s (use syllabub)
sil|lily
sil|li|man|ite +s
sil|li|ness
Sil|li|toe, Alan (English writer)
silly
  sil|lies
  sil|lier
  sil|li|est
silo +s *noun*
silo
  si|loes
  si|loed
  silo|ing
  verb
Si|loam *Bible*
silt +s +ed +ing
silt|ation +s
silt|stone +s
silty
  silt|ier
  silti|est
Si|lur|ian +s
  Geology
silva +s (use sylva ⚠ silver)
sil|van (use sylvan)
Sil|vanus *Roman Mythology*
sil|ver +s +ed +ing (precious metal; colour. ⚠ sylva)
sil|ver|back +s
sil|ver|fish
  plural sil|ver|fish or sil|ver|fishes
silver-grey +s
sil|veri|ness
sil|ver leaf (thin silver)
silver-leaf (disease of fruit trees)
sil|ver mine +s
sil|vern (made of or coloured like silver. ⚠ sylvan)
sil|ver plate *noun*
silver-plate
  silver-plates
  silver-plated
  silver-plating
  verb

silver-point
sil|ver|side +s
sil|ver|smith +s
sil|ver|smith|ing
Sil|ver|stone (motor-racing circuit, England)
sil|ver|ware
sil|ver|weed +s
sil|very
silvi|cul|tural
silvi|cul|ture
silvi|cul|tur|ist +s
sima
Sim|birsk (city, Russia)
Sime|non, Georges (Belgian-born French novelist)
Sim|eon (*Bible*; name)
Sim|eon Sty|lites (Syrian saint)
Sim|fero|pol (city, Russia)
sim|ian +s (ape)
simi|lar +s
simi|lar|ity
  simi|lar|ities
simi|lar|ly
sim|ile +s
si|mili|tude +s
Simla (city, India)
sim|mer +s +ed +ing
Sim|nel, Lam|bert (English claimant to the throne)
sim|nel cake +s
Simon (Apostle and saint ('the Zealot'); name)
Simon, Neil (American playwright)
Simon, Paul (American singer-songwriter)
Sim|one
simo|niac +s
si|mo|ni|ac|al
si|mo|ni|ac|al|ly
Si|moni|des (Greek lyric poet)
simon-pure
si|mony
si|moom +s
si|moon +s
simp +s (= simpleton)

sim|pat|ico
sim|per +s +ed +ing
sim|per|ing|ly
sim|ple
  sim|pler
  sim|plest
simple-minded
simple-minded|ly
simple-minded|ness
simple|ness
simple|ton +s
sim|plex
  sim|plexes
sim|pli|city
  sim|pli|ci|ties
sim|pli|fi|ca|tion +s
sim|plify
  sim|pli|fies
  sim|pli|fied
  sim|pli|fy|ing
sim|plism
sim|plis|tic
sim|plis|tic|al|ly
Sim|plon (Alpine pass, Switzerland)
sim|ply
Simp|son, James Young (Scottish surgeon)
Simp|son, Wal|lis (American wife of Edward VIII)
Simp|son Des|ert (in Australia)
simu|lac|rum
  simu|lacra
simu|late
  simu|lates
  simu|lated
  simu|lat|ing
simu|la|tion +s
simu|la|tive
simu|la|tor +s
sim|ul|cast +s
sim|ul|tan|eity
sim|ul|tan|eous
sim|ul|tan|eous|ly
sim|ul|tan|eous|ness
sim|urg +s
sin
  sins
  sinned
  sin|ning
Sinai (peninsula, Egypt)
Sina|it|ic
Sina iti|cus (in 'Codex Sinaiticus')

Sina|loa (state, Mexico)
Sin|an|thro|pus
sin|ap|ism
Sin|atra, Frank (American singer)
Sin|bad the Sailor (in the *Arabian Nights*)
since
sin|cere
  sin|cerer
  sin|cerest
sin|cere|ly
sin|cere|ness
sin|cer|ity
  sin|cer|ities
sin|cipi|tal
sin|ci|put +s
Sin|clair, Clive (English electronics engineer)
Sind (province, Pakistan)
Sind|bad the Sailor (use Sinbad the Sailor)
Sin|de|bele
Sindhi +s
sin|don|ology
Sindy *also* Cindy
sine +s (trigonometric function. ⚠ sign, syne)
Sin|ead
sine|cure +s
sine|cur|ism
sine|cur|ist +s
sine die
sine qua non
sinew +s +ed +ing
sin|ew|less
sinewy
sin|fonia +s
sin|foni|etta +s
sin|ful
sin|ful|ly
sin|ful|ness
sing
  sings
  sang
  sing|ing
  sung
sing|able
sing|along +s
Singa|pore
Singa|por|ean +s
singe
  singes

singe (cont.)
singed
singe|ing
Sing|er, Isaac
Bash|evis (Polish-
born American
novelist)
Sing|er, Isaac
Mer|rit
(American
inventor)
sing|er +s
singer-songwriter
+s
Singh (Sikh
adopted name)
Sing|hal|ese (use
Sinhalese)
plural Sing|hal|ese
sing|ing|ly
sin|gle
sin|gles
sin|gled
sin|gling
single-acting
single-breast|ed
single-decker +s
sin|gle file
single-handed
single-handed|ly
single-lens re|flex
single-lens
re|flexes
single-line
attributive
single-minded
single-minded|ly
single-
minded|ness
single|ness
single-seater +s
sing|let +s
single|ton +s
single|tree +s
sin|gly
Sing Sing (prison,
USA)
sing-song +s +ed
+ing
sin|gu|lar +s
sin|gu|lar|isa|tion
Br. (use
singularization)
sin|gu|lar|ise Br.
(use singularize)
sin|gu|lar|ises
sin|gu|lar|ised
sin|gu|lar|is|ing
sin|gu|lar|ity
sin|gu|lar|ities
sin|gu|lar|iza|tion

sin|gu|lar|ize
sin|gu|lar|izes
sin|gu|lar|ized
sin|gu|lar|iz|ing
sin|gu|lar|ly
sinh (= hyperbolic
sine)
Sin|hala
Sin|hal|ese
plural Sin|hal|ese
Si|ning (= Xining)
sin|is|ter
sin|is|ter|ly
sin|is|ter|ness
sin|is|tral +s
sin|is|tral|ity
sin|is|tral|ly
sin|is|trorse
sink
sinks
sank or sunk
sink|ing
sunk
(fall; founder.
△ cinque)
sink|able
sink|age
sink|er +s
sink-hole +s
Sin|kiang
(= Xinjiang)
sink|ing +s
sin|less
sin|less|ly
sin|less|ness
sin|ner +s
sin|net
Sinn Fein (Irish
political
movement and
party)
Sinn Fein|er +s
Sino-British
Sino-Japanese
sino|logic|al
sin|olo|gist +s
sino|logue +s
sin|ology
Sino|mania
Sino|phile +s
Sino|phobe +s
Sino|pho|bia
Sino-Soviet
Sino-Tibetan +s
Sino-US
sin|ter +s +ed +ing
Sint-Niklaas
(town, Belgium)
Sin|tra (town,
Portugal)
sinu|ate

Sin|uiju (port,
North Korea)
sinu|os|ity
sinu|os|ities
sinu|ous
sinu|ous|ly
sinu|ous|ness
sinus
si|nuses
si|nus|itis
si|nus|oid +s
si|nus|oid|al
si|nus|oid|al|ly
Sio|bhan
Sion (use Zion)
Siouan +s
Sioux
plural Sioux
sip
sips
sipped
sip|ping
sipe +s
si|phon Am. +s +ed
+ing (pipe for
transferring liquid;
cause to flow. Br.
syphon)
si|phon +s (of
mollusc)
si|phon|age Am.
(Br. syphonage)
si|phon|al
si|phon|ic Am.
(pertaining to a
pipe for siphoning.
Br. syphonic)
si|phon|ic
(pertaining to a
mollusc's siphon)
si|phono|phore +s
siph|uncle +s
sip|per +s
sip|pet +s
sir +s
Sira|cusa (Italian
name for
Syracuse, Italy)
sir|dar +s
Sir|daryo (river,
central Asia)
sire
sires
sired
sir|ing
siren +s
si|ren|ian +s
sir|gang +s
Sir|ius (star)
sir|loin +s
si|rocco +s
sir|rah +s

sir|ree
Sirte, Gulf of
(= Gulf of Sidra)
sirup Am. +s (Br.
syrup)
sis (= sister)
sisal +s
sis|kin +s
Sis|ley, Al|fred
(French painter)
sis|si|fied
sis|si|ness
sis|soo
sissy
sis|sies
sis|sier
sis|si|est
sissy|ish
sis|ter +s
sis|ter|hood +s
sister-in-law
sisters-in-law
sis|ter|less
sis|ter|li|ness
sis|ter|ly
Sis|tine (of popes
called Sixtus, esp.
Sixtus IV.
△ cystine)
Sis|tine Chapel (in
the Vatican.
△ cystine)
sis|trum
sis|tra
Sisy|phean
Sisy|phus Greek
Mythology
sit
sits
sat
sit|ting
Sita Hinduism
sitar +s
sitar|ist +s
sita|tunga
plural sita|tunga
or sita|tungas
sit|com +s
(= situation
comedy)
sit-down +s
adjective and noun
site
sites
sited
sit|ing
(of building etc.;
locate. △ cite,
sight)
sit-fast +s
sit-in +s adjective
and noun
Sitka +s

sito|pho|bia
sit|rep +s
  (= situation
  report)
sit|ringee
sits vac
  (= situations
  vacant)
Sit|tang (river,
  Burma)
sit|ter +s
sitter-in
  sitters-in
sit|ting +s
Sit|ting Bull (Sioux
  chief)
sit|ting room +s
situ (in 'in situ')
situ|ate
  situ|ates
  situ|ated
  situ|at|ing
situ|ation +s
situ|ation|al
situ|ation|al|ly
situ|ation|ism
situ|ation|ist +s
sit-up +s
sit-upon +s noun
Sit|well, Edith
  (English poet)
sitz-bath +s
Siva Hinduism
Siva|ism
Siva|ite +s
Sivaji (use Shivaji)
Sivan (Jewish
  month)
Si|walik Hills (in
  India and Nepal)
six
  sixes
six|ain +s
Six Day War
sixer +s
six|fold
six-gun +s
six-iron +s
six-pack +s
six|pence +s
six|penny
  six|pen|nies
six-shooter +s
sixte +s Fencing
six|teen +s (16.
  △ Sixtine)
six|teenmo +s
six|teenth +s
sixth +s
sixth-form
  col|lege +s
sixth-former +s

sixth|ly
six|ti|eth +s
Six|tine (= Sistine.
  △ sixteen)
sixty
  six|ties
sixty-first, sixty-
  second, etc.
six|ty|fold
sixty-fourmo +s
sixty-one, sixty-
  two, etc.
siz|able (use
  sizeable)
sizar +s (college
  grant. △ sizer)
siz|ar|ship +s
size
  sizes
  sized
  siz|ing
size|able
size|ably
sizer +s (person
  who assesses size.
  △ sizar)
size-stick +s
Size|well (nuclear
  power station,
  England)
sizy
siz|zle
  siz|zles
  siz|zled
  siz|zling
siz|zler +s
sjam|bok +s +ed
  +ing (whip)
ska (Music. △ scar)
skag +s
Skag|er|rak (strait
  linking Baltic and
  North Seas)
skald +s (bard.
  △ scald)
skald|ic
Skanda Hinduism
Skara Brae
  (neolithic
  settlement,
  Orkney)
skat (card game.
  △ Scart)
skate
  skates
  skated
  skat|ing
skate|board +s
  +ed +ing
skate|board|er +s
skate|park +s
skater +s

skat|ing rink +s
skean +s (dagger)
skean-dhu +s
sked
  skeds
  sked|ded
  sked|ding
ske|dad|dle
  ske|dad|dles
  ske|dad|dled
  ske|dad|dling
skeet (shooting
  sport)
skeet|er +s
  (mosquito)
skeg +s
skein +s (bundle of
  yarn; flock of
  geese)
skel|etal
skel|et|al|ly
skel|eton +s
Skel|eton Coast
  (in Namibia)
skel|et|on|ise Br.
  (use skeletonize)
  skel|et|on|ises
  skel|et|on|ised
  skel|et|on|is|ing
skel|et|on|ize
  skel|et|on|izes
  skel|et|on|ized
  skel|et|on|iz|ing
skelf +s
Skel|ton, John
  (English poet)
skep +s
skep|sis Am. (Br.
  scepsis)
skep|tic Am. (Br.
  sceptic)
skep|tic|al Am. (Br.
  sceptical)
skep|tic|al|ly Am.
  (Br. sceptically)
skep|ti|cism Am.
  +s (Br.
  scepticism)
sker|rick +s
skerry
  sker|ries
sketch
  sketches
  sketched
  sketch|ing
sketch|book +s
sketch|er +s
sketch|ily
sketchi|ness
sketch map +s
sketch pad +s

sketchy
  sketch|ier
  sketchi|est
skeuo|morph +s
skeuo|morph|ic
skew +s +ed +ing
skew|back +s
skew|bald +s
skew|er +s +ed
  +ing (spike.
  △ skua)
skew-eyed
skew|ness
skew-whiff
ski
  skis
  skied
  ski|ing
ski|able
ski|ag|raphy
ski|am|achy
Ski|athos (Greek
  island)
ski-bob
  ski-bobs
  ski-bobbed
  ski-bobbing
ski-bobber +s
skid
  skids
  skid|ded
  skid|ding
skid|doo +s (use
  skidoo)
skid-lid +s
ski|doo +s (vehicle)
  Propr.
ski'doo +s +ed
  +ing (ride on
  skidoo; go away)
skid-pan +s
skier +s (person
  who skis. △ skyer)
skiff +s
skif|fle
ski-jorer +s
ski-joring
ski jump +s
ski jump|er +s
ski jump|ing
skil|ful Br. (Am.
  skillful)
skil|ful|ly
skil|ful|ness
ski lift +s
skill +s
skil|let +s
skill|ful Am. (Br.
  skilful)
skill-less
skilly
  skil|lies

skim
  skims
  skimmed
  skim|ming
skim|mer +s
skim|mia +s
skimp +s +ed +ing
skimp|ily
skimpi|ness
skimpy
  skimp|ier
  skimpi|est
skin
  skins
  skinned
  skin|ning
skin|care
skin-deep
skin diver +s
skin div|ing
skin-flick +s
skin|flint +s
skin-food +s
skin|ful +s
skin graft +s
skin|head +s
skink +s
skin|less
skin|like
Skin|ner, B. F.
  (American
  psychologist)
skin|ner +s
skin|ni|ness
skinny
  skin|nier
  skin|ni|est
skinny-dipping
skint
skin|tight
skip
  skips
  skipped
  skip|ping
skip|jack +s
ski-plane +s
skip|per +s +ed
  +ing
skip|pet +s
skip|ping rope +s
skirl +s +ed +ing
skir|mish
  skir|mishes
  skir|mished
  skir|mish|ing
skir|mish|er +s
skirr +s +ed +ing
skir|ret +s
skirt +s +ed +ing
skirt-dance +s
skirt|ing +s
skirt|ing board +s

skirt|less
ski run +s
ski slope +s
skit +s
skite
  skites
  skited
  skit|ing
skit|ter +s +ed
  +ing
skit|tery
skit|tish
  skit|tish|ly
  skit|tish|ness
skit|tle
  skit|tles
  skit|tled
  skit|tling
skive
  skives
  skived
  skiv|ing
skiver +s
skivvy
  skiv|vies
  skiv|vied
  skivvy|ing
ski|wear
skol
Skopje (city,
  Macedonia)
Skrya|bin,
  Alek|sandr (use
  Scriabin)
skua +s (bird.
  △ skewer)
skul|dug|gery
skulk +s +ed +ing
skulk|er +s
skull +s +ed +ing
  (bone. △ scull)
skull|cap +s
skunk +s +ed +ing
skunk-bear +s
skunk-cabbage +s
sky
  skies
  skied
  sky|ing
sky blue +s noun
  and adjective
sky-blue *attributive*
sky-blue pink
sky-clad
sky|dive
  sky|dives
  sky|dived
  sky|dove *Am.*
  sky|div|ing
sky|diver +s
Skye (Scottish
  island; terrier)

skyer +s (*Cricket.*
  △ skier)
skyey
sky-high
sky|jack +s +ed
  +ing
sky|jack|er +s
Sky|lab (American
  space laboratory)
sky|lark +s +ed
  +ing
sky|less
sky|light +s
sky|line +s
sky|rocket +s +ed
  +ing
sky|sail +s
sky|scape +s
sky|scraper +s
sky-shouting
sky-sign +s
sky|walk +s
sky|ward
sky|wards
sky|watch
  sky|watches
sky|way +s
sky-writing
slab
  slabs
  slabbed
  slab|bing
slack +s +ed +ing
slack|en +s +ed
  +ing
slack|er +s
slack|ly
slack|ness
slag
  slags
  slagged
  slag|ging
slaggy
  slag|gier
  slag|gi|est
slag heap +s
slag-wool +s
slain
slainte
slake
  slakes
  slaked
  slak|ing
sla|lom +s
slam
  slams
  slammed
  slam|ming
slam|bang
slam dunk +s noun
slam-dunk +s +ed
  +ing *verb*

slam|mer +s
slan|der +s +ed
  +ing
slan|der|er +s
slan|der|ous
slan|der|ous|ly
slang +s +ed +ing
slang|ily
slangi|ness
slang|ing match
  slang|ing
  matches
slangy
  slang|ier
  slangi|est
slant +s +ed +ing
slant-eyed
slant|ways
slant|wise
slap
  slaps
  slapped
  slap|ping
slap bang
slap|dash
slap-happy
slap|head +s
  (*offensive*)
slap|jack +s
slap|per +s
slap|stick +s
slap-up *adjective*
slash
  slashes
  slashed
  slash|ing
slash-and-burn
slash|er +s
slat
  slats
  slat|ted
  slat|ting
slate
  slates
  slated
  slat|ing
slate blue +s noun
  and adjective
slate-blue
  attributive
slate color *Am.*
slate-colored *Am.*
slate col|our *Br.*
slate-coloured *Br.*
slate grey +s noun
  and adjective
slate-grey
  attributive
slate-pencil +s
slater +s
slather +s +ed
  +ing

slat|ing +s
slat|tern +s
slat|tern|li|ness
slat|tern|ly
slaty
  slati|er
  slati|est
slaugh|ter +s +ed +ing
slaugh|ter|er +s
slaugh|ter|house +s
slaugh|ter|ing +s
slaugh|ter|ous
Slav +s
slave
  slaves
  slaved
  slav|ing
slave-bangle +s
slave-born
slave-bracelet +s
slave-drive
  slave-drives
  slave-drove
  slave-driving
  slave-driven
slave-driver +s
slaver +s +ed +ing
slav|ery
Slave State +s (in USA)
slave trade
slave trader +s
slavey
Slav|ic
slav|ish
slav|ish|ly
slav|ish|ness
Slav|ism
Sla|vo|nian +s
Sla|von|ic
Slavo|phile +s
Slavo|phobe +s
slaw +s
slay
  slays
  slew
  slay|ing
  slain
  (kill. △ sleigh, sley)
slay|er +s
slay|ing +s
Slea|ford (town, England)
sleaze
  sleazes
  sleazed
  sleaz|ing
sleaze|bag +s
sleaze|ball +s

sleaz|ily
sleazi|ness
sleaz|oid +s
sleazy
  sleaz|ier
  sleazi|est
sled
  sleds
  sled|ded
  sled|ding
sledge
  sledges
  sledged
  sledg|ing
sledge|ham|mer +s
sleek +s +ed +ing
  +er +est
sleek|ly
sleek|ness
sleeky
sleep
  sleeps
  slept
  sleep|ing
sleep|er +s
sleep|ily
sleep-in +s noun and adjective
sleepi|ness
sleep|ing bag +s
sleep|ing car +s
sleep|ing draught +s
sleep|ing pill +s
sleep|ing suit +s
sleep-learning
sleep|less
sleep|less|ly
sleep|less|ness
sleep-out +s
  adjective and noun
sleep|over +s
sleep|walk +s +ed +ing
sleep|walk|er +s
sleepy
  sleepi|er
  sleepi|est
sleepy|head +s
sleet +s +ed +ing
sleety
  sleet|ier
  sleeti|est
sleeve +s
sleeve board +s
sleeve-coupling +s
sleeved
sleeve|less
sleeve link +s
sleeve note +s
sleeve-nut +s

sleeve-valve +s
sleev|ing +s
sleigh +s +ed +ing
  (sledge; travel on a sledge. △ slay, sley)
sleigh-bell +s
sleight +s
  (dexterity. △ slight)
slen|der +er +est
slen|der|ise Br.
  (use slenderize)
slen|der|ises
slen|der|ised
slen|der|is|ing
slen|der|ize
slen|der|izes
slen|der|ized
slen|der|iz|ing
slen|der|ly
slen|der|ness
slept
sleuth +s +ed +ing
sleuth-hound +s
slew +s +ed +ing
sley +s (weaver's reed. △ slay, sleigh)
slice
  slices
  sliced
  sli|cing
slice|able
slicer +s
slick +s +ed +ing
  +er +est
slick|er +s
slick|ly
slick|ness
slid|able
slid|ably
slide
  slides
  slid
  slid|ing
slider +s
slide rule +s
slide-valve +s
slide|way +s
slight +s +ed +ing
  +er +est
  (inconsiderable; slender; be disrespectful towards; instance of slighting. △ sleight)
slight|ing|ly
slight|ish
slight|ly
slight|ness

Sligo (county and town, Republic of Ireland)
slily (use slyly)
slim
  slims
  slimmed
  slim|ming
slim|mer
slim|mest
slime
  slimes
  slimed
  slim|ing
slimi|ly
slimi|ness
slim|line
slim|ly
slim|mer +s
slim|mish
slim|ness
slimy
  slimi|er
  slimi|est
sling
  slings
  slung
  sling|ing
sling-back +s
sling-bag +s
sling|er +s
sling|shot +s
slink
  slinks
  slunk
  slink|ing
  (go stealthily)
slink +s +ed +ing
  (produce young prematurely)
slink|ily
slinki|ness
slink|weed
slinky
  slink|ier
  slinki|est
slip
  slips
  slipped
  slip|ping
slip-carriage +s
slip case +s
slip-coach
  slip-coaches
slip cover +s
slip-hook +s
slip-knot +s
slip-on +s adjective and noun
slip|over +s noun
slip-over adjective
slip|page +s

slip|per +s +ed
+ing
slip|per|ily
slip|peri|ness
slip|per|wort +s
slip|pery
slip|pi|ness
slippy
  slip|pier
  slip|pi|est
slip ring +s
slip road +s
slip-rope +s
slip|shod
slip stitch
  slip stitches
  noun
slip-stitch
  slip-stitches
  slip-stitched
  slip-stitch|ing
  verb
slip|stream +s +ed
+ing
slip-up +s *noun*
slip|ware
slip|way +s
slit
  slits
  slit
  slit|ting
  (see also slitted)
slit-eyed
slither +s +ed +ing
slith|ery
slit pocket +s
slit|ted *adjective*
slit|ter +s
slitty
  slit|tier
  slit|ti|est
Sliven (city,
  Bulgaria)
sliver +s +ed +ing
slivo|vitz (plum
  brandy)
Sloane +s
  (= Sloane Ranger)
Sloane, Hans
  (English
  physician)
Sloaney
slob +s
slob|ber +s +ed
+ing
slob|bery
slob|bish
sloe +s (fruit.
  △ slow)
sloe-eyed
sloe gin +s

slog
  slogs
  slogged
  slog|ging
slo|gan +s
slog|ger +s
sloid +s
sloop +s
sloop-rigged
sloosh
  slooshes
  slooshed
  sloosh|ing
sloot +s
slop
  slops
  slopped
  slop|ping
slop basin +s
slope
  slopes
  sloped
  slop|ing
slope|wise
slop pail +s
slop|pily
slop|pi|ness
sloppy
  slop|pier
  slop|pi|est
slosh
  sloshes
  sloshed
  slosh|ing
sloshy
  sloshi|er
  sloshi|est
slot
  slots
  slot|ted
  slot|ting
sloth +s
sloth|ful
sloth|ful|ly
sloth|ful|ness
slot ma|chine +s
slouch
  slouches
  slouched
  slouch|ing
slouchy
  slouch|ier
  slouchi|est
Slough (town,
  England)
slough +s +ed
+ing
sloughy
  slough|ier
  sloughi|est
Slo|vak +s
Slo|vakia

Slo|vak|ian +s
sloven +s
Slo|vene +s
Slo|venia
Slo|ven|ian +s
slov|en|li|ness
slov|en|ly
slow +s +ed +ing
  +er +est (not fast;
  reduce speed.
  △ sloe)
slow|coach
  slow|coaches
slow|down +s
slow-growing
slow|ish
slow|ly
slow-moving
slow|ness
slow|poke +s
slow-witted
slow-worm +s
slub
  slubs
  slubbed
  slub|bing
sludge +s
sludgy
  sludgi|er
  sludgi|est
slue (use slew)
  slues
  slued
  slu|ing
slug
  slugs
  slugged
  slug|ging
slug|abed +s
slug|gard +s
slug|gard|li|ness
slug|gard|ly
slug|ger +s
slug|gish
slug|gish|ly
slug|gish|ness
sluice
  sluices
  sluiced
  slui|cing
sluice-gate +s
sluit +s (use sloot)
slum
  slums
  slummed
  slum|ming
slum|ber +s +ed
+ing
slum|ber|er +s
slum|ber|ous
slum|ber|wear
slum|brous

slum|gul|lion +s
slum|mi|ness
slummy
  slum|mier
  slum|mi|est
slump +s +ed +ing
slung
slunk
slur
  slurs
  slurred
  slur|ring
slurp +s +ed +ing
slurry
  slur|ries
slush
  slushes
  slushed
  slush|ing
slushi|ness
slushy
  slush|ier
  slushi|est
slut +s
slut|tish
slut|tish|ness
sly
  slyer
  sly|est
sly|boots
slyly
sly|ness
slype +s
smack +s +ed
+ing
smack-dab
smack|er +s
smack|eroo +s
small +s +er +est
small|lage +s
small-bore
  adjective
small|goods
  (delicatessen
  meats)
small|hold|er +s
small|hold|ing +s
small|ish
small-minded
small-minded|ly
small-
  minded|ness
small|ness
small|pox
small-scale
small-sword +s
  (light tapering
  sword)
small talk
small-time
small-timer +s

small-town
  adjective
small|wares
smalt +s
smarm +s +ed
  +ing
smarm|ily
smarmi|ness
smarmy
  smarm|ier
  smarmi|est
smart +s +ed +ing
  +er +est
smart alec +s
smart aleck +s
  (use smart alec)
smart-alecky
smart alick +s (use
  smart alec)
smart-arse +s
smart card +s
smart|en +s +ed
  +ing
smart|ing|ly
smart|ish
smart|ly
smart|ness
smart|weed
smarty
  smart|ies
smarty-boots
smarty-pants
smash
  smashes
  smashed
  smash|ing
smash-and-grab
  +s
smash|er +s
smash|ing|ly
smash-up +s *noun*
smat|ter +s
smat|ter|er +s
smat|ter|ing +s
smear +s +ed +ing
smear|er +s
smeari|ness
smeary
smec|tic +s
smegma +s
smeg|mat|ic
smell
  smells
  smelled *or* smelt
  smell|ing
smell|able
smell|er +s
smelli|ness
smell|ing bot|tle
  +s
smell|ing salts
smell-less

smelly
  smell|ier
  smelli|est
smelt +s +ed +ing
smelt|er +s
smelt|ery
  smelt|er|ies
Smersh (Russian
  counter-espionage
  organization)
**Smet|ana,
  Bed|řich** (Czech
  composer)
smew +s
smidgen +s
smidg|eon +s (use
  smidgen)
smidgin +s (use
  smidgen)
smi|lax
smile
  smiles
  smiled
  smil|ing
smile|less
smiler +s
smiley
smil|ing|ly
smirch
  smirches
  smirched
  smirch|ing
smirk +s +ed +ing
smirk|er +s
smirk|ily
smirk|ing|ly
smirky
smit (*archaic*
  smitten)
smite
  smites
  smote
  smit|ing
  smit|ten
smiter +s
Smith, Adam
  (Scottish
  economist)
Smith, Bes|sie
  (American singer)
Smith, Ian
  (Rhodesian prime
  minister)
Smith, Jo|seph
  (American
  founder of the
  Mormon Church)
Smith, Stevie
  (English poet)
Smith, Syd|ney
  (English
  churchman)

Smith, Wil|liam
  (English geologist)
smith +s +ed +ing
smith|er|eens
smith|ers
smith|ery
  smith|er|ies
Smith|field
  (market, London)
**Smith|son|ian
  In|sti|tu|tion**
  (American
  foundation)
smithy
  smith|ies
smit|ten
smock +s +ed
  +ing
smock-mill +s
smog +s
smoggy
  smog|gier
  smog|gi|est
smok|able
smoke
  smokes
  smoked
  smok|ing
smoke|able (use
  smokable)
smoke-ball +s
smoke bomb +s
smoke box
  smoke boxes
smoke bush
  smoke bushes
smoke-dried
smoke-free
smoke-ho +s
smoke|less
smoke-plant +s
smoker +s
smoke ring +s
smoke-room +s
smoke|screen +s
smoke|stack +s
smoke-stone +s
smoke-tunnel +s
smoki|ly
smoki|ness
smok|ing jacket
  +s
smok|ing room +s
smoko +s
smoky
  smoki|er
  smoki|est
smol|der *Am.* +s
  +ed +ing (*Br.*
  smoulder)

smol|der|ing|ly
  Am. (*Br.*
  smoulderingly)
Smo|lensk (city,
  Russia)
Smol|lett, To|bias
  (Scottish novelist)
smolt +s
smooch
  smooches
  smooched
  smooch|ing
smooch|er +s
smoochy
  smooch|ier
  smoochi|est
smoodge
  smoodges
  smoodged
  smoodg|ing
smooth +s +ed
  +ing +er +est
smooth|able
smooth-bore +s
smoothe (use
  smooth)
  smoothes
  smoothed
  smooth|ing
smoother +s
smooth-faced
smoothie +s
smooth|ing iron
  +s
smooth|ing plane
  +s
smooth|ish
smooth|ly
smooth|ness
smooth-talk +s
  +ed +ing *verb*
smooth-tongued
smor|gas|bord +s
smorz|ando
smorz|an|dos *or*
smorz|andi
smote
smother +s +ed
  +ing
smoth|ery
smoul|der *Br.* +s
  +ed +ing (*Am.*
  smolder)
smoul|der|ing|ly
  Br. (*Am.*
  smolderingly)
smriti
smudge
  smudges
  smudged
  smudg|ing
smudge|less

smudge pot +s
smudgi|ly
smudgi|ness
smudgy
  smudgi|er
  smudgi|est
smug
  smug|ger
  smug|gest
smug|gle
  smug|gles
  smug|gled
  smug|gling
smug|gler +s
smug|ly
smug|ness
smut
  smuts
  smut|ted
  smut|ting
smut-ball +s
smut-mill +s
Smuts, Jan
  Chris|tiaan
  (South African
  prime minister)
smut|tily
smut|ti|ness
smutty
  smut|tier
  smut|ti|est
Smyrna (former
  name of Izmir)
Smyth, Ethel
  (English
  composer)
snack +s +ed +ing
snack bar +s
snaf|fle
  snaf|fles
  snaf|fled
  snaf|fling
snafu
snag
  snags
  snagged
  snag|ging
snaggle-tooth
  snaggle-teeth
snaggle-toothed
snaggy
snail +s
snail-like
snail mail
snail's pace
snake
  snakes
  snaked
  snak|ing
snake|bite +s
snake-charmer +s
snake|like

snake-pit +s
snake|root +s
snake|skin +s
snaki|ly
snaki|ness
snaky
  snaki|er
  snaki|est
snap
  snaps
  snapped
  snap|ping
snap-bolt +s
snap-brim
snap|dragon +s
snap-fasten|er +s
snap-hook +s
snap-lock +s
snap|pable
snap|per +s
snap|pily
snap|pi|ness
snap|ping|ly
snap|pish
snap|pish|ly
snap|pish|ness
snappy
  snap|pier
  snap|pi|est
snap|shot +s
snare
  snares
  snared
  snar|ing
snarer +s
snark +s
snarl +s +ed +ing
snarl|er +s
snarl|ing|ly
snarl-up +s noun
snarly
  snarl|ier
  snarli|est
snatch
  snatches
  snatched
  snatch|ing
snatch|er +s
snatchy
snavel
  snavels
  snav|elled
  snav|el|ling
snaz|zily
snaz|zi|ness
snazzy
  snaz|zier
  snaz|zi|est
sneak
  sneaks
  sneaked

sneak (cont.)
  snuck Am.
  sneak|ing
sneak|er +s
sneak|ily
sneaki|ness
sneak|ing|ly
sneak-thief
  sneak-thieves
sneaky
  sneak|ier
  sneaki|est
sneck +s +ed +ing
Sneek (town, the
  Netherlands)
sneer +s +ed +ing
sneer|er +s
sneer|ing|ly
sneeze
  sneezes
  sneezed
  sneez|ing
sneezer +s
sneeze|wort +s
sneezy
Snell's law
snib
  snibs
  snibbed
  snib|bing
snick +s +ed +ing
snicker +s +ed
  +ing
snick|er|ing|ly
snicket +s
snide +s
snide|ly
snide|ness
sniff +s +ed +ing
sniff|able
sniff|er +s
sniff|er dog +s
sniff|ily
sniffi|ness
sniff|ing|ly
snif|fle
  snif|fles
  snif|fled
  snif|fling
snif|fler +s
sniffly
sniffy
  sniffi|ier
  sniffi|est
snif|ter +s
snifter-valve +s
snig
  snigs
  snigged
  snig|ging
snig|ger +s +ed
  +ing

snig|ger|er +s
snig|ger|ing|ly
snig|gery
snig|ging chain +s
snig|gle
  snig|gles
  snig|gled
  snig|gling
snip
  snips
  snipped
  snip|ping
snipe
  plural snipe or
  snipes
  (bird)
snipe
  snipes
  sniped
  snip|ing
  (shoot)
snipe fish
  plural snipe fish
sniper +s
snip|pet +s
snip|pety
snip|pily
snip|pi|ness
snip|ping +s
snippy
  snip|pier
  snip|pi|est
snit +s
snitch
  snitches
  snitched
  snitch|ing
snivel
  snivels
  sniv|elled Br.
  sniv|eled Am.
  sniv|el|ling Br.
  sniv|el|ing Am.
  sniv|el|er Am. +s
  sniv|el|ler Br. +s
  sniv|el|ling|ly Br.
snob +s
snob|bery
  snob|ber|ies
snob|bish
snob|bish|ly
snob|bish|ness
snobby
  snob|bier
  snob|bi|est
SNOBOL
  Computing
snoek +s (fish.
  △ snook)
snog
  snogs

snog (*cont.*)
snogged
snog|ging
snood +s
snook +s (gesture.
  ⚠ snoek)
snook|er +s +ed
  +ing
snook|er play|er
  +s
snoop +s +ed +ing
snoop|er +s
snoop|er|scope +s
snoopy
snoot +s
snoot|ily
snooti|ness
snooty
  snoot|ier
  snooti|est
snooze
  snoozes
  snoozed
  snooz|ing
snoozer +s
snoozy
  snooz|ier
  snoozi|est
snore
  snores
  snored
  snor|ing
snorer +s
snor|ing|ly
Snor|kel +s (fire-
  fighting platform)
  Propr.
snor|kel
  snor|kels
  snor|kelled *Br.*
  snor|keled *Am.*
  snor|kel|ling *Br.*
  snor|kel|ing *Am.*
  (tube for swimmer
  or submarine)
snor|kel|er *Am.* +s
snor|kel|ler *Br.* +s
Snorri Stur|lu|son
  (Icelandic
  historian)
snort +s +ed +ing
snort|er +s
snot +s
snot-rag +s
snot|tily
snot|ti|ness
snotty
  snot|tier
  snot|ti|est
snotty-nosed
snout +s
snout-beetle +s

snout|ed
snout|like
snouty
Snow, C. P.
  (English novelist)
snow +s +ed +ing
snow|ball +s +ed
  +ing
snow|ball tree +s
snow|berry
  snow|berries
snow-blind
snow-blindness
snow-blink
snow|blow|er +s
snow|board +s
snow|board|er +s
snow|board|ing
snow boot +s
snow|bound
snow-broth
snow|cap +s
snow-capped
snow-covered
Snow|don
  (mountain, Wales)
Snow|donia
  (region, Wales)
snow|drift +s
snow|drop +s
snow|fall +s
snow|field +s
snow|flake +s
snow goose
  snow geese
snow-ice
snow|ily
snowi|ness
snow job +s *noun*
snow-job
  snow-jobs
  snow-jobbed
  snow-jobbing
  verb
snow|less
snow|like
snow|line +s
snow|mak|ing
snow|man
  snow|men
snow|mobile +s
snow|plough *Br.* +s
snow|plow *Am.* +s
snow|scape +s
snow|shoe +s
snow|shoer +s
snow ski|ing
snow-slip +s
snow|storm +s
snow white +s
  noun and adjective
snow-white
  attributive

snowy
  snow|ier
  snowi|est
snub
  snubs
  snubbed
  snub|bing
snub|ber +s
snub|bing|ly
snub-nosed
snuck
snuff +s +ed +ing
snuff|box
  snuff|boxes
snuff-colored *Am.*
snuff-coloured *Br.*
snuff|er +s
snuf|fle
  snuf|fles
  snuf|fled
  snuf|fling
snuff|ler +s
snuffly
snuffy
  snuff|ier
  snuffi|est
snug
  snugs
snug|ger
snug|gest
snug|gery
  snug|ger|ies
snug|gle
  snug|gles
  snug|gled
  snug|gling
snug|ly
snug|ness
so (*adverb and
  conjunction.*
  ⚠ sew, soh, sow)
soak +s +ed +ing
  (drench; drink;
  drinker. ⚠ soke)
soak|age
soak|away +s
soak|er +s
  (drinker; heavy
  rain; on roof.
  ⚠ soca)
soak|ing +s
so-and-so +s
Soane, John
  (English architect)
soap +s +ed +ing
soap|bark +s
soap|berry
  soap|berries
soap|box
  soap|boxes
soap|ily
soapi|ness

soap|less
soap|like
soap opera +s
soap|stone +s
soap|suds
soap|wort +s
soapy
  soap|ier
  soapi|est
soar +s +ed +ing
  (rise. ⚠ saw, sore)
soar|er +s (person
  or thing that soars.
  ⚠ sora)
soar|ing|ly
sob
  sobs
  sobbed
  sob|bing
sob|ber +s
sob|bing|ly
sober +s +ed +ing
  +er +est
sober|ing|ly
sober|ly
So|bers, Gar|field
  ('Gary') (West
  Indian cricketer)
Sob|ieski, John
  (Polish king)
so|bri|ety
so|bri|quet +s
sob-stuff
soca (music.
  ⚠ soaker)
soc|age +s
so-called
soc|cer
  (= Association
  Football)
soc|cer play|er +s
Sochi (port, Russia)
so|ci|abil|ity
so|ci|able
so|ci|able|ness
so|ci|ably
so|cial +s
so|cial|isa|tion *Br.*
  (use
  socialization)
so|cial|ise *Br.* (use
  socialize)
so|cial|ises
so|cial|ised
so|cial|is|ing
so|cial|ism
so|cial|ist +s
so|cial|is|tic
so|cial|is|tic|al|ly
so|cial|ite +s
so|ci|al|ity
so|cial|iza|tion

so|cial|ize
  so|cial|izes
  so|cial|ized
  so|cial|iz|ing
so|cial|ly
so|ci|etal
so|ci|et|al|ly
so|ci|ety
  so|ci|eties
So|ci|ety Is|lands
  (in S. Pacific)
So|cin|ian +s
socio|bio|logic|al
socio|bio|logic|
  al|ly
socio|biolo|gist +s
socio|biol|ogy
socio|cul|tural
socio|cul|tur|al|ly
socio-econom|ic
socio-
  economic|al|ly
socio|lin|guist +s
socio|lin|guis|tic
socio|lin|guis|tic|
  al|ly
socio|lin|guis|tics
socio|logic|al
socio|logic|al|ly
soci|olo|gist +s
soci|ology
socio|met|ric
socio|met|ric|al|ly
soci|om|et|rist +s
soci|om|etry
socio-politic|al
sock +s +ed +ing
socket +s +ed
  +ing
sock|eye +s
sock|less
socle +s
So|cotra (island,
  Arabian Sea)
Soc|ra|tes (Greek
  philosopher)
So|crat|ic
So|crat|ic|al|ly
sod
  sods
  sod|ded
  sod|ding
  (*coarse slang*
  except in sense of
  'turf, ground')
soda +s
so|dal|ity
  so|dal|ities
sod|den
sod|den|ly
sod|den|ness

Soddy, Fred|erick
  (English physicist)
sodic
so|dium
sodium-vapor *Am.*
  attributive
sodium-vapour *Br.*
  attributive
Sodom (town,
  ancient Palestine)
sod|om|ise *Br.* (use
  sodomize)
  sod|om|ises
  sod|om|ised
  sod|om|is|ing
sod|om|ite +s
sod|om|ize
  sod|om|izes
  sod|om|ized
  sod|om|iz|ing
sod|omy
Sodor (medieval
  diocese, Hebrides
  and Isle of Man)
Sod's Law
so|ever
sofa +s
sofa bed +s
So|fala (province,
  Mozambique)
Sofar (= sound
  fixing and ranging)
sof|fit +s
Sofia (capital of
  Bulgaria)
soft +er +est (not
  hard; etc.)
softa +s (Muslim
  student of law and
  theology)
soft|ball (game)
soft-boiled
soft-centred
soft|en +s +ed
  +ing
soft|en|er +s
soft-headed
soft-headed|ness
soft-hearted
soft-hearted|ness
softie +s
soft|ish
soft-land +s +ed
  +ing
soft|ly
softly-softly
soft|ness
soft-paste *adjective*
soft-pedal
  soft-pedals
  soft-pedalled *Br.*
  soft-pedaled *Am.*

soft-pedal (*cont.*)
  soft-pedalling *Br.*
  soft-pedaling *Am.*
soft-sell
  soft-sells
  soft-sold
  soft-selling
soft-soap +s +ed
  +ing
soft-spoken
soft-top +s (car;
  roof)
soft|ware
soft|wood +s
softy (use softie)
  soft|ies
SOGAT (= Society
  of Graphical and
  Allied Trades)
sog|gily
sog|gi|ness
soggy
  sog|gier
  sog|gi|est
Sogne Fiord (in
  Norway)
soh (*Music.* △sew,
  so, sow)
Soho (district,
  London)
soi-disant
soi|gné male
soi|gnée female
soil +s +ed +ing
soil-less
soily
soirée +s
soixante-neuf
so|journ +s +ed
  +ing
so|journ|er +s
Soka Gak|kai
  (Japanese
  organization)
soke +s (district.
  △soak)
Sol *Roman
  Mythology*
sol (*Music*; = soh)
sol +s *Chemistry*
sola +s (plant.
  △solar)
sola *female* (alone;
  male solus.
  △solar)
sol|ace
  sol|aces
  sol|aced
  sol|acing
solan +s
so|lan|aceous
sol|an|der +s

solar +s (of the sun.
  △sola)
so|lar|isa|tion *Br.*
  (use solarization)
so|lar|ise *Br.* (use
  solarize)
  so|lar|ises
  so|lar|ised
  so|lar|is|ing
sol|ar|ism
so|lar|ist +s
sol|ar|ium
  sol|ar|iums *or*
  sol|aria
so|lar|iza|tion
so|lar|ize
  so|lar|izes
  so|lar|ized
  so|lar|iz|ing
so|la|tium
  so|la|tia
sola topi +s
sold (past tense and
  past participle of
  sell. △soled)
sol|dan|ella +s
sol|der +s +ed
  +ing
sol|der|able
sol|der|er +s
sol|der|ing iron +s
sol|dier +s +ed
  +ing
soldier-like
sol|dier|ly
sol|dier|ship
sol|diery
  sol|dier|ies
Sole (shipping area,
  NE Atlantic)
sole
  soles
  soled
  sol|ing
  (of foot or shoe;
  fish; single.
  △soul)
sol|ecism +s
sol|ecist +s
sol|ecis|tic
sole|ly (only.
  △soli)
sol|emn
sol|em|ness
sol|em|nisa|tion
  Br. (use
  solemnization)
sol|em|nise *Br.*
  (use solemnize)
  sol|em|nises
  sol|em|nised
  sol|em|nis|ing

so¦lem¦nity
  so¦lem¦nities
sol¦em¦niza¦tion
sol¦em¦nize
  sol¦em¦nizes
  sol¦em¦nized
  sol¦em¦niz¦ing
sol¦emn¦ly
Sol¦emn Mass
  Sol¦emn Masses
solen +s
so¦leno¦don +s
so¦len¦oid +s
so¦len¦oid¦al
So¦lent (channel,
  England)
sole-plate +s
sol-fa +s +ed +ing
  Music
sol¦fa¦tara +s
sol¦feg¦gio
  sol¦feggi
soli (plural of solo
  △ solely)
so¦licit +s +ed
  +ing
so¦lici¦ta¦tion +s
so¦lici¦tor +s
solicitor-advocate
  +s
Solicitor-General
  Solicitors-
  General
so¦lici¦tous
so¦lici¦tous¦ly
so¦lici¦tous¦ness
so¦lici¦tude
solid +s +er +est
Soli¦dar¦ity (Polish
  trade-union
  movement)
soli¦dar¦ity
  soli¦dar¦ities
solid-drawn
sol¦idi
so¦lidi¦fi¦ca¦tion
so¦lidi¦fier +s
so¦lid¦ify
  so¦lidi¦fies
  so¦lidi¦fied
  so¦lidi¦fy¦ing
so¦lid¦ity
sol¦id¦ly
sol¦id¦ness
solid-state *adjective*
solid¦un¦gu¦late +s
sol¦idus
  sol¦idi
sol¦ifid¦ian +s
soli¦fluc¦tion
Soli¦hull (town,
  England)

so¦lilo¦quise *Br.*
  (use soliloquize)
  so¦lilo¦quises
  so¦lilo¦quised
  so¦lilo¦quis¦ing
so¦lilo¦quist +s
so¦lilo¦quize
  so¦lilo¦quizes
  so¦lilo¦quized
  so¦lilo¦quiz¦ing
so¦lilo¦quy
  so¦lilo¦quies
Soli¦man
  (= Suleiman)
soli¦ped +s
sol¦ip¦sism
sol¦ip¦sist +s
sol¦ip¦sis¦tic
sol¦ip¦sis¦tic¦al¦ly
soli¦taire +s
soli¦tar¦ily
soli¦tari¦ness
soli¦tary
  soli¦tar¦ies
soli¦tude +s
sol¦miz¦ate
  sol¦miz¦ates
  sol¦miz¦ated
  sol¦miz¦at¦ing
sol¦miza¦tion
solo
  plural solos *or* soli
  Music; Dancing
solo +s (flight; card
  game; etc.)
solo
  so¦loes
  so¦loed
  solo¦ing
  verb
solo¦ist +s
Solo¦mon (king of
  Israel; name)
Solo¦mon¦ic
Solo¦mon Is¦lands
  (in S. Pacific)
Solo¦mon's seal
  (plant)
Solon (Athenian
  statesman)
So¦lo¦thurn (town
  and canton,
  Switzerland)
sol¦stice +s
sol¦sti¦tial
solu¦bil¦isa¦tion *Br.*
  (use
  solubilization)
solu¦bil¦ise *Br.* (use
  solubilize)
  solu¦bil¦ises

solu¦bil¦ise (*cont.*)
  solu¦bil¦ised
  solu¦bil¦is¦ing
solu¦bil¦ity
solu¦bil¦iza¦tion
solu¦bil¦ize
  solu¦bil¦izes
  solu¦bil¦ized
  solu¦bil¦iz¦ing
sol¦uble
solus *male (female*
  sola)
sol¦ute +s
so¦lu¦tion +s
So¦lu¦trean +s
solv¦able
solv¦ate
  solv¦ates
  solv¦ated
  solv¦at¦ing
solv¦ation +s
Sol¦vay pro¦cess
solve
  solves
  solved
  solv¦ing
solv¦ency
solv¦ent +s
solv¦er +s
Sol¦way Firth
  (inlet, Irish Sea)
Soly¦man
  (= Suleiman)
Sol¦zhen¦it¦syn,
  Alek¦sandr
  (Russian novelist)
soma +s
So¦mali
  plural So¦mali *or*
  So¦malis
So¦ma¦lia (country,
  NE Africa)
So¦ma¦lian +s
So¦ma¦li¦land
  (former
  protectorates, NE
  Africa)
som¦at¦ic
som¦at¦ic¦al¦ly
som¦ato¦gen¦ic
soma¦tol¦ogy
som¦ato¦tonic
som¦ato¦troph¦in
  +s
som¦ato¦type +s
som¦ber *Am.*
sombre *Br.*
sombre¦ly
sombre¦ness
som¦brero +s
som¦brous

some (unspecified
  amount or
  number. △ sum)
some¦body
  some¦bodies
some day *adverbial*
some¦how
some¦one
some¦place
som¦er¦sault +s
  +ed +ing
Som¦er¦set (county,
  England)
some¦thing +s
some¦time (at
  some point in
  time)
some time (a
  certain amount of
  time)
some¦times
some¦what
some¦when
some¦where
so¦mite +s
so¦mit¦ic
Somme (river and
  battle site, France)
som¦mel¦ier +s
som¦nam¦bu¦lant
som¦nam¦bu¦
          lant¦ly
som¦nam¦bu¦lism
som¦nam¦bu¦list
  +s
som¦nam¦bu¦lis¦tic
som¦nam¦bu¦lis¦tic¦
          al¦ly
som¦nif¦er¦ous
som¦no¦lence
som¦no¦lency
som¦no¦lent
som¦no¦lent¦ly
Som¦oza,
  Ana¦sta¦sio
  (Nicaraguan
  president)
son +s (male child.
  △ sun, sunn)
son¦ancy
son¦ant +s
sonar +s
son¦ata +s
sona¦tina +s
sonde +s
Sond¦heim,
  Ste¦phen
  (American
  composer)
sone +s (unit.
  △ sewn, sown)

son et lu|mi|ère
+s
Song (Chinese
dynasty; = Sung)
song +s
song|bird +s
song|book +s
song|ful
song|ful|ly
song|less
song|smith
song|ster +s
song|stress
song|stresses
song|writer +s
song|writ|ing
Sonia also Sonya
sonic
son|ic|al|ly
son-in-law
sons-in-law
son|less
son|net +s +ed
+ing
son|net|eer +s
sonny
son|nies
(form of address.
△ sunny)
sono|buoy +s
son of a bitch
sons of bitches
son of a gun
sons of guns
sono|gram +s
son|om|eter +s
Son|ora (state,
Mexico; Desert)
son|or|ity
son|or|ities
son|or|ous
son|or|ous|ly
son|or|ous|ness
son|ship
son|sie (use sonsy)
son|sier
son|si|est
sonsy
son|sier
son|si|est
Son|tag, Susan
(American critic)
Sonya also Sonia
Soo|chow
(= Suzhou)
sook +s (coward;
calf. △ souk)
sool +s +ed +ing
sool|er +s
soon +er +est
soon|ish
soot +s +ed +ing

soot|er|kin +s
sooth +s (truth)
soothe
soothes
soothed
sooth|ing
(calm; ease pain)
sooth|er +s
sooth|ing|ly
sooth|say
sooth|says
sooth|said
sooth|say|ing
sooth|say|er +s
soot|ily
sooti|ness
sooty
soot|ier
sooti|est
sop
sops
sopped
sop|ping
So|phia (in 'St
Sophia'; name.
△ Sofia)
So|phie (name.
△ Sophy)
soph|ism +s
soph|ist +s
soph|ist|er +s
so|phis|tic
so|phis|tic|al
so|phis|tic|al|ly
so|phis|ti|cate
so|phis|ti|cates
so|phis|ti|cated
so|phis|ti|cat|ing
so|phis|ti|cated|ly
so|phis|ti|ca|tion
+s
soph|is|try
soph|is|tries
Sopho|clean
Sopho|cles (Greek
dramatist)
sopho|more +s
sopho|mor|ic
Sophy
So|phies
(Persian ruler.
△ Sophie)
sop|or|ifer|ous
sop|or|if|ic
sop|or|if|ic|al|ly
sop|pily
sop|pi|ness
sop|ping
soppy
sop|pier
sop|pi|est
sop|ra|nino +s

sop|ran|ist +s
sop|rano +s
Sop|with, Thomas
(English aircraft
designer)
sora +s (bird.
△ soarer)
Sorb +s (person)
sorb +s (tree; fruit)
sor|be|fa|cient +s
sor|bet +s
Sorb|ian +s
sorb|itol
Sorbo (rubber)
Propr.
Sor|bonne
(University of
Paris)
sor|cer|er +s
sor|cer|ess
sor|cer|esses
sor|cer|ous
sor|cery
sor|cer|ies
sor|did
sor|did|ly
sor|did|ness
sor|dino
sor|dini
sor|dor +s
sore
sores
sorer
sor|est
(painful; vexed;
painful place.
△ saw, soar)
sore|head +s
sorel +s (deer.
△ sorrel)
sore|ly
sore|ness
sor|ghum +s
sori (plural of
sorus)
sor|ites
plural so|rites
sor|iti|cal
Sor|op|ti|mist +s
sor|ori|cidal
sor|ori|cide +s
sor|or|ity
sor|or|ities
sor|osis
sor|oses
(fruit. △ cirrhosis)
sorp|tion
sor|rel +s (herb;
colour. △ sorel)
Sor|rento (town,
Italy)
sor|rily

sor|ri|ness
sor|row +s +ed
+ing
sor|row|er +s
sor|row|ful
sor|row|ful|ly
sor|row|ful|ness
sorry
sor|rier
sor|ri|est
sort +s +ed +ing
(class of things;
piece of printing;
type; arrange.
△ sought)
sort|able
sort|er +s
sor|tie
sor|ties
sor|tied
sor|tie|ing
sor|ti|lege +s
sor|ti|tion +s
sort-out +s *noun*
sorus
sori
Sos|no|wiec (town,
Poland)
so-so
sos|ten|uto +s
sot
sots
sot|ted
sot|ting
so|terio|logic|al
so|teri|ology
So|thic
Sotho
plural Sotho or
So|thos or
Ba|sotho
(people; language)
sot|tish
sotto voce
sou +s (former
French coin; very
small amount of
money. △ sue, xu)
sou|brette +s
sou|bri|quet +s
(use sobriquet)
sou|chong +s
souf|fle +s
(murmur in body)
souf|flé +s (food)
Sou|frière
(volcanoes,
Guadeloupe and
St Vincent)
sough +s +ed +ing
(moan; whistle.
△ sow)

sought (past tense
  and past participle
  of **seek**. △ **sort**)
sought after
  adjective
sought-after
  attributive
souk +s (market.
  △ **sook**)
sou|kous
soul +s (spirit.
  △ **sole**)
soul-destroy|ing
soul|ful
soul|ful|ly
soul|ful|ness
soul|less
soul|less|ly
soul|less|ness
soul|mate +s
soul-searching +s
sound +s +ed +ing
  +er +est
sound|alike +s
sound|bite +s
sound|board +s
sound|box
  sound|boxes
sound|check +s
sound|er +s
sound|hole +s
sound|ing +s
sounding-balloon
  +s
sound|ing board
  +s
sound|ing line +s
sound|ing rod +s
sound|less
sound|less|ly
sound|less|ness
sound|ly
sound|ness
sound post +s
sound|proof +s
  +ed +ing
sound|track +s
sound wave +s
soup +s +ed +ing
soup|çon +s
souped-up *adjective*
soup|ily
soupi|ness
soup kitchen +s
soup plate +s
soup spoon +s
soupy
  soup|ier
  soupi|est
sour +s +ed +ing
  +er +est

source
  sources
  sourced
  sour|cing
source|book +s
source-criticism
  +s
sour|dough +s
sour|ish
sour|ly
sour|ness
sour|puss
  sour|pusses
sour|sop +s
Sousa, John
  Philip (American
  composer)
sousa|phone +s
sousa|phon|ist +s
souse
  souses
  soused
  sous|ing
sous|lik +s
Sousse (port,
  Tunisia)
sou|tache +s
sou|tane +s
sou|ten|eur +s
souter +s
  (shoemaker.
  △ **suiter, suitor**)
sou|ter|rain +s
South, the (part of
  country etc.)
south +s +ed +ing
  (point; direction;
  move southwards)
South|amp|ton
  (port, England)
south|bound
South|down +s
  (sheep)
South Downs
  (hills, England)
South-East, the
  (part of country
  etc.)
south-east (point;
  direction)
south|easter +s
south-easter|ly
  south-easter|lies
south-eastern
south-eastern|er
  +s
South-East
  Ice|land (shipping
  area)
south-eastward
south-eastwards

Southend-on-Sea
  (resort, England)
souther +s
south|er|ly
  south|er|lies
south|ern
south|ern|er +s
south|ern|most
south|ern|wood
  +s
Southey, Rob|ert
  (English poet)
south-facing
South Geor|gia
  (island, S.
  Atlantic)
South
  Gla|mor|gan
  (county, Wales)
south|ing +s
South Orkney
  Is|lands (in S.
  Atlantic)
south|paw +s
South|port (town,
  England)
South Sand|wich
  Is|lands (in S.
  Atlantic)
South Shet|land
  Is|lands (in S.
  Atlantic)
south-south-east
south-south-west
south|ward
south|wards
South-West, the
  (part of country
  etc.)
south-west (point;
  direction)
south|wester +s
  (wind.
  △ **sou'wester**)
south-wester|ly
  south-wester|lies
south-western
south-western|er
  +s
south-westward
south-westwards
Sou|tine, Chaim
  (French painter)
sou|venir +s +ed
  +ing
souv|la|ki
  souv|la|kia or
  souv|la|kis
sou'|wester +s
  (hat.
  △ **southwester**)

sov +s
  (= sovereign)
sov|er|eign +s
sov|er|eign|ly
sov|er|eign|ty
  sov|er|eign|ties
So|viet +s (of the
  Soviet Union;
  citizen)
so|viet +s (council)
So|viet|isa|tion *Br.*
  (use
  Sovietization)
So|viet|ise *Br.* (use
  Sovietize)
  So|viet|ises
  So|viet|ised
  So|viet|is|ing
So|viet|iza|tion
So|viet|ize
  So|viet|izes
  So|viet|ized
  So|viet|iz|ing
so|viet|olo|gist +s
sow
  sows
  sowed
  sow|ing
  sown *or* **sowed**
  (plant seed etc.
  △ **sew, so, soh**)
sow +s (female pig.
  △ **sough**)
sow|back +s
sow|bread +s
sower +s (person
  who sows.
  △ **sewer**)
So|wetan +s
So|weto (township,
  South Africa)
sow|ing +s
  (planting seed etc.
  △ **sewing**)
sown (past
  participle of **sow**.
  △ **sewn**)
sow|this|tle +s
Sox (in name of
  baseball teams)
sox (clothing; use
  socks)
soy (sauce)
soya (plant)
soya bean +s
soy|bean +s
Soy|inka, Wole
  (Nigerian writer)
soy sauce +s
Soyuz (Soviet
  spacecraft)
soz|zled

Spa (town,
Belgium)
spa +s (spring.
△ spar)
space
spaces
spaced
spa¦cing
space-age
space bar +s
space¦craft +s
space¦man
space¦men
spa¦cer +s
space-saving
space¦ship +s
space¦suit +s
space-time
space¦woman
space¦women
spacey
spaci¦er
spaci¦est
spa¦cial (use
spatial)
spa¦cing +s
spa¦cious
spa¦cious¦ly
spa¦cious¦ness
spacy (use spacey)
spaci¦er
spaci¦est
spade
spades
spaded
spad¦ing
spade¦ful +s
spade¦work
spa¦di¦ceous
spadi¦cose
spa¦dille +s
spa¦dix
spa¦di¦ces
spado +s
spae
spaes
spaed
spae¦ing
(foretell. △ spay)
spae¦wife
spae¦wives
spag bol
(= spaghetti
Bolognese)
spa¦ghetti +s
spahi +s
Spain
spake
spall +s +ed +ing
Spal¦lan¦zani,
Laz¦zaro (Italian
biologist)

spal¦la¦tion +s
spal¦peen +s
spam *Propr.*
span
spans
spanned
span¦ning
Span¦dex *Propr.*
span¦drel +s
spang
span¦gle
span¦gles
span¦gled
span¦gling
span¦gly
span¦glier
span¦gli¦est
Span¦iard +s
span¦iel +s
Span¦ish
Spanish-American
+s
Span¦ish¦ness
spank +s +ed +ing
spank¦er +s
spank¦ing +s
span¦ner +s
span¦sule +s *Propr.*
span-worm +s
spar
spars
sparred
spar¦ring
(fight; dispute;
pole; mineral.
△ spa)
spar¦able +s (nail)
spa¦raxis
spa¦raxes
(plant)
spar-buoy +s
spar-deck +s
spare
spares
spared
spar¦ing
sparer
spar¦est
spare¦ly
spare¦ness
sparer +s
spare-rib +s (food)
spare time *noun*
spare-time
attributive
sparge
sparges
sparged
spar¦ging
spar¦ger +s
sparid +s
spar¦ing¦ly

spar¦ing¦ness
Spark, Mur¦iel
(Scottish novelist)
spark +s +ed +ing
spark-gap +s
spark¦ing plug +s
spark¦ish
spar¦kle
spar¦kles
spar¦kled
spark¦ling
spark¦ler +s
spark¦less
spark¦ling¦ly
sparkly
spark plug +s
sparky
spark¦ier
spark¦iest
spar¦ling
plural spar¦ling or
spar¦lings
spar¦oid +s
spar¦row +s
sparrow-grass
spar¦row¦hawk +s
sparry
sparse
sparse¦ly
sparse¦ness
spars¦ity
Sparta (city,
Greece)
Spar¦ta¦cist +s
Spar¦ta¦cus
(Thracian
gladiator)
Spar¦tan +s
spar¦tina +s
spasm +s +ed +ing
spas¦mod¦ic
spas¦mod¦ic¦al¦ly
spas¦tic +s
(*offensive as term of
abuse*)
spas¦tic¦al¦ly
spas¦ti¦city
spat
spats
spat¦ted
spat¦ting
spatch¦cock +s
+ed +ing
spate +s
spa¦tha¦ceous
spathe +s
spath¦ic
spath¦ose
spa¦tial
spa¦tial¦ise *Br.* (use
spatialize)
spa¦tial¦ises

spa¦tial¦ise (*cont.*)
spa¦tial¦ised
spa¦tial¦is¦ing
spa¦ti¦al¦ity
spa¦tial¦ize
spa¦tial¦izes
spa¦tial¦ized
spa¦tial¦iz¦ing
spa¦tial¦ly
spatio-temporal
spatio-
tempor¦al¦ly
Spät¦lese
Spät¦lesen or
Spät¦leses
spat¦ter +s +ed
+ing
spat¦ter¦dash
spat¦ter¦dashes
spat¦ula +s
spatu¦late
Spätzle
spavin +s
spav¦ined
spawn +s +ed
+ing
spawn¦er +s
spawn¦ing +s
spay +s +ed +ing
(sterilize. △ spae)
speak
speaks
spoke
speak¦ing
spoken
speak¦able
speak¦easy
speak¦easies
speak¦er +s
speak¦er¦phone +s
speak¦er¦ship +s
speaking-trumpet
+s
speaking-tube +s
spear +s +ed +ing
spear-carrier +s
spear¦gun +s
spear¦head +s +ed
+ing
spear¦man
spear¦men
spear¦mint +s
spear¦wort +s
spec +s
(= speculation;
specification;
(*specs*) spectacles.
△ speck)
spe¦cial +s
spe¦cial¦isa¦tion
Br. +s (use
specialization)

spe¦cial¦ise Br. (use
  specialize)
spe¦cial¦ises
spe¦cial¦ised
spe¦cial¦is¦ing
spe¦cial¦ism+s
spe¦cial¦ist+s
spe¦cial¦is¦tic
spe¦ci¦al¦ity
spe¦ci¦al¦ities
spe¦cial¦iza¦tion
  +s
spe¦cial¦ize
spe¦cial¦izes
spe¦cial¦ized
spe¦cial¦iz¦ing
spe¦cial¦ly
spe¦cial¦ness
spe¦cialty
spe¦cial¦ties
spe¦cial¦ty
spe¦cial¦ties
  Law
spe¦ci¦ation+s
spe¦cie (coins)
spe¦cies
  plural spe¦cies
  (category of
  animals or plants)
spe¦cies¦ism
spe¦cies¦ist+s
spe¦ci¦fi¦able
spe¦cif¦ic+s
spe¦cif¦ic¦al¦ly
spe¦ci¦fi¦ca¦tion+s
spe¦ci¦fi¦city
spe¦cif¦ic¦ness
spe¦ci¦fier+s
spe¦cify
spe¦ci¦fies
spe¦ci¦fied
spe¦ci¦fy¦ing
spe¦ci¦men+s
spe¦cio¦logic¦al
spe¦ci¦ology
spe¦ci¦os¦ity
spe¦cious
spe¦cious¦ly
spe¦cious¦ness
speck +s +ed +ing
  (spot. △ spec)
speckle
  speckles
  speckled
  speck¦ling
speck¦less
specs
  (= spectacles)
spec¦tacle+s
spec¦tacled
spec¦tacle frame
  +s

spec¦tacu¦lar+s
spec¦tacu¦lar¦ly
spec¦tate
  spec¦tates
  spec¦tated
  spec¦tat¦ing
spec¦ta¦tor+s
spec¦ta¦tor¦ial
spec¦ter Am. +s
  (Br. spectre)
Spec¦tor, Phil
  (American record
  producer and
  songwriter)
spec¦tra
spec¦tral
spec¦tral¦ly
spectre Br. +s (Am.
  specter)
spec¦tro¦
    chem¦is¦try
spec¦tro¦gram+s
spec¦tro¦graph+s
spec¦tro¦graph¦ic
spec¦tro¦graph¦ic¦
    al¦ly
spec¦trog¦raphy
spec¦tro¦helio¦
    graph+s
spec¦tro¦helio¦
    scope+s
spec¦trom¦eter+s
spec¦tro¦met¦ric
spec¦trom¦etry
spec¦tro¦
    pho¦tom¦eter+s
spec¦tro¦photo¦
    met¦ric
spec¦tro¦
    pho¦tom¦etry
spec¦tro¦scope+s
spec¦tro¦scop¦ic
spec¦tro¦scop¦ic¦al
spec¦tros¦co¦pist
  +s
spec¦tros¦copy
spec¦trum
  spec¦tra
spec¦ula (plural of
  speculum)
specu¦lar (of a
  speculum)
specu¦late
  specu¦lates
  specu¦lated
  specu¦lat¦ing
specu¦la¦tion+s
specu¦la¦tive
specu¦la¦tive¦ly
specu¦la¦tive¦ness
specu¦la¦tor+s

specu¦lum
  spec¦ula
speculum-metal
  +s
sped
speech
  speeches
speech¦ful
speech¦ifi¦ca¦tion
speechi¦fier+s
speech¦ify
  speechi¦fies
  speechi¦fied
  speechi¦fy¦ing
speech¦less
speech¦less¦ly
speech¦less¦ness
speech-reading
speech-writer+s
speed +s +ed +ing
  (travel at illegal or
  dangerous speed;
  regulate speed of)
speed
  speeds
  sped
  speed¦ing
  (other senses)
speed¦ball
speed¦boat+s
speed¦er+s
speed¦ily
speedi¦ness
speedo+s
speed¦om¦eter+s
speed¦ster+s
speed-up+s noun
speed¦way+s
speed¦well+s
speedy
  speed¦ier
  speedi¦est
speiss (metallic
  compound.
  △ spice)
Speke, John
  Han¦ning
  (English explorer)
speleo¦logic¦al
spele¦olo¦gist+s
spele¦ology
spell
  spells
  spelt or spelled
  spell¦ing
spell¦able
spell¦bind
  spell¦binds
  spell¦bound
  spell¦bind¦ing
spell¦bind¦er+s
spell¦bind¦ing¦ly

spell-check+s +ed
  +ing
spell-checker+s
spell¦er+s
spelli¦can+s
spell¦ing+s
spelling-bee+s
spelling-checker
  +s
spelt
spell¦ter
spe¦lunk¦er+s
spe¦lunk¦ing
Spence, Basil
  (British architect)
spence+s
Spen¦cer, Her¦bert
  (English
  philosopher.
  △ Spenser)
Spen¦cer, Stan¦ley
  (English painter.
  △ Spenser)
spen¦cer+s
Spen¦cer¦ian+s (of
  Herbert Spencer;
  handwriting.
  △ Spenserian)
spend
  spends
  spent
  spend¦ing
spend¦able
Spend¦er,
  Ste¦phen (English
  poet)
spend¦er+s
spend¦thrift+s
Spen¦gler,
  Os¦wald (German
  philosopher)
Spen¦ser,
  Ed¦mund
  (English poet.
  △ Spencer)
Spen¦ser¦ian+s (of
  Spenser.
  △ Spencerian)
spent
sperm
  plural sperm or
  sperms
sperma¦ceti
sperma¦cet¦ic
sperm¦ary
  sperm¦ar¦ies
sperm¦at¦ic
sperm¦atid+s
sperm¦at¦id¦al
sperm¦ato¦blast+s
sperm¦ato¦cyte+s

sperm|ato|gen|esis
sperm|ato|
     gen|et|ic
sperm|ato|
     gon|ium
sperm|ato|gonia
sperm|ato|phore
+s
sperm|ato|phor|ic
sperm|ato|phyte
+s
sperm|ato|zoal
sperm|ato|zoan
  adjective
sperm|ato|zo|ic
sperm|ato|zoid +s
sperm|ato|zoon
  sperm|ato|zoa
  noun
spermi|cidal
spermi|cide +s
spermo|blast +s
spermo|cyte +s
spermo|gen|esis
spermo|gon|ium
  spermo|gonia
spermo|phore +s
spermo|phyte +s
spermo|zoid +s
spermo|zoon
  spermo|zoa
spew +s +ed +ing
spew|er +s
Spey (river,
  Scotland)
sphag|num
  sphagna
sphal|er|ite +s
sphen|oid +s
sphen|oid|al
spheral
sphere
  spheres
  sphered
  spher|ing
spher|ic
spher|ic|al
spher|ic|al|ly
spher|icity
spher|oid +s
spher|oid|al
spher|oid|icity
spher|om|eter +s
spher|ular
spher|ule +s
spher|ul|ite +s
spher|ul|it|ic
sphinc|ter +s
sphinc|ter|al
sphinc|tered
sphinc|ter|ial
sphinc|ter|ic

sphin|gid +s
sphinx
  sphinxes
sphra|gis|tics
sphyg|mo|gram +s
sphyg|mo|graph
+s
sphyg|mo|graph|ic
sphyg|mo|graph|ic|
     al|ly
sphyg|mog|raphy
sphyg|mo|logic|al
sphyg|mol|ogy
sphyg|mo|
  man|om|eter +s
sphyg|mo|mano|
     met|ric
spic +s (offensive
  Mexican etc.
  △ spick and
  span)
Spica (star)
spica +s (spike;
  bandage)
spi|cate
spi|cated
spic|cato +s
spice
  spices
  spiced
  spi|cing
  (flavouring etc.
  △ speiss)
spice|bush
  spice|bushes
Spice Is|lands
  (former name of
  the Moluccas)
spicery
  spicer|ies
spicey (use spicy)
  spici|er
  spici|est
spici|ly
spici|ness
spick and span
spick|nel +s
spicu|lar
spicu|late
spic|ule +s
spicy
  spici|er
  spici|est
spider +s +ed +ing
spider|ish
spider|man
  spider|men
spider|wort +s
spi|dery
spie|gel|eisen
spiel +s +ed +ing

Spiel|berg,
  Ste|ven
  (American film
  director)
spiel|er +s
spiff +s +ed +ing
spiff|ily
spiffy
  spiff|ier
  spiff|est
spif|li|cate
  spif|li|cates
  spif|li|cated
  spif|li|cat|ing
spif|li|ca|tion
spig|nel +s
spigot +s
spike
  spikes
  spiked
  spik|ing
spike|let +s
spike|nard +s
spiki|ly
spiki|ness
spiky
  spiki|er
  spiki|est
spile
  spiles
  spiled
  spil|ing
spill
  spills
  spilled or spilt
  spill|ing
spill|age +s
spill|er +s
spilli|kin +s
spill|over +s
spill|way +s
spilt
spilth +s
spin
  spins
  spun or span
  spin|ning
spina bif|ida
spin|aceous
spin|ach
  spin|aches
spin|achy
spinal
spinal|ly
spin|dle
  spin|dles
  spin|dled
  spind|ling
spindle-berry
  spindle-berries
spindle-shanked
spindle-shanks

spindly
  spind|lier
  spind|li|est
spin doc|tor +s
spin-drier +s (use
  spin-dryer)
spin|drift +s
spin-dry
  spin-dries
  spin-dried
  spin-drying
spin-dryer +s
spine +s
spine-chiller +s
spine-chilling
spined
spi|nel +s
spine|less
spine|less|ly
spine|less|ness
spi|net +s
spine-tingling
spini|fex
  spini|fexes
spini|ness
spin|naker +s
spin|ner +s
spin|neret +s
spin|ney +s
spin|ning noun
spin|ning jenny
  spin|ning jen|nies
spin|ning
  ma|chine +s
spin|ning mule +s
spin|ning top +s
spin|ning wheel
  +s
spin-off +s noun
  and attributive
spin|ose
spin|ous
Spin|oza, Bar|uch
  de (Dutch
  philosopher)
Spin|oz|ism
Spin|oz|ist +s
Spin|oz|is|tic
spin|ster +s
spin|ster|hood +s
spin|ster|ish
spin|ster|ish|ness
spin|thari|scope
+s
spin|ule +s
spinu|lose
spinu|lous
spiny
  spini|er
  spini|est
spir|acle +s
spir|acu|lar

spir¦acu¦lum
  spir¦acula
spir¦aea *Br.* +s
  (*Am.* spirea)
spiral
  spir¦als
  spir¦alled *Br.*
  spir¦aled *Am.*
  spiral¦ling *Br.*
  spiral¦ing *Am.*
spiral¦ity
spir¦al¦ly
spir¦ant +s
spire
  spires
  spired
  spir¦ing
spirea *Am.* +s (*Br.*
  spiraea)
spir¦il¦lum
  spir¦illa
spirit +s +ed +ing
spir¦it¦ed¦ly
spir¦it¦ed¦ness
spir¦it¦ism
spir¦it¦ist +s
spirit lamp +s
spir¦it¦less
spir¦it¦less¦ly
spir¦it¦less¦ness
spirit level +s
spir¦it¦ous
spir¦it¦ual +s
spir¦itu¦al¦isa¦tion
  Br. (use
  spiritualization)
spir¦itu¦al¦ise *Br.*
  (use spiritualize)
  spir¦itu¦al¦ises
  spir¦itu¦al¦ised
  spir¦itu¦al¦is¦ing
spir¦itu¦al¦ism
spir¦itu¦al¦ist +s
spir¦itu¦al¦is¦tic
spir¦itu¦al¦ity
  spir¦itu¦al¦ities
spir¦itu¦al¦iza¦tion
spir¦itu¦al¦ize
  spir¦itu¦al¦izes
  spir¦itu¦al¦ized
  spir¦itu¦al¦iz¦ing
spir¦itu¦al¦ly
spir¦itu¦al¦ness
spiri¦tuel *male*
spiri¦tu¦elle *female*
spir¦itu¦ous
spir¦itu¦ous¦ness
spir¦ket¦ting
spiro¦chaete *Br.* +s
spiro¦chete *Am.* +s
spiro¦graph +s
spiro¦graph¦ic

spiro¦graph¦ic¦
  al¦ly
spiro¦gyra +s
spir¦om¦eter +s
spirt +s +ed +ing
  (use spurt)
spiry
spit
  spits
  spat *or* spit
  spit¦ting
  (eject saliva etc.;
  spatter; rain
  lightly)
spit
  spits
  spit¦ted
  spit¦ting
  (skewer; cook on
  spit)
spit
  plural spit *or* spits
  (spade-depth)
spit¦ball +s +ed
  +ing
spit¦ball¦er +s
spitch¦cock +s
  +ed +ing
spite
  spites
  spited
  spit¦ing
spite¦ful
spite¦ful¦ly
spite¦ful¦ness
spit¦fire +s
Spit¦head (channel
  off S. England)
spit-roast +s +ed
  +ing
Spits¦ber¦gen
  (island, Arctic
  Ocean)
spit¦ter +s
spit¦tle
spit¦tly
spit¦toon +s
spitty
Spitz, Mark
  (American
  swimmer)
spitz
  spitzes
spiv +s
spiv¦very
spiv¦vish
spivvy
splake +s
splanch¦nic
splanch¦nol¦ogy

splanch¦not¦omy
  splanch¦
        noto¦mies
splash
  splashes
  splashed
  splash¦ing
splash¦back +s
splash-board +s
splash¦down +s
splash¦ily
splashy
  splash¦ier
  splashi¦est
splat
  splats
  splat¦ted
  splat¦ting
splat¦ter +s +ed
  +ing
splay +s +ed +ing
splay-foot
  splay-feet
splay-footed
spleen +s
spleen¦ful
spleen¦wort +s
spleeny
  spleen¦ier
  spleeni¦est
splen¦dent
splen¦did
splen¦did¦ly
splen¦did¦ness
splen¦dif¦er¦ous
splen¦dif¦er¦ous¦ly
splen¦dif¦er¦ous¦
        ness
splen¦dor *Am.* +s
splen¦dour *Br.* +s
splen¦ec¦tomy
  splen¦ec¦to¦mies
splen¦et¦ic
splen¦et¦ic¦al¦ly
sple¦nial
splen¦ic
splen¦itis
sple¦nius
  sple¦nii
splen¦oid
splen¦ology
spleno¦meg¦aly
  spleno¦meg¦alies
splen¦ot¦omy
  splen¦oto¦mies
splice
  splices
  spliced
  spli¦cing
spli¦cer +s
splif +s (use spliff)
spliff +s

spline
  splines
  splined
  splin¦ing
splint +s +ed +ing
splint-bone +s
splint-coal +s
splin¦ter +s +ed
  +ing
splinter-bar +s
splinter-proof +s
  +ed +ing
splin¦tery
Split (port, Croatia)
split
  splits
  split
  split¦ting
  (divide; break)
split-level *adjective*
split-screen +s
split-second
  adjective
split¦ter +s
splodge
  splodges
  splodged
  splodg¦ing
splodgy
  splodgi¦er
  splodgi¦est
sploosh
  splooshes
  splooshed
  sploosh¦ing
splosh
  sploshes
  sploshed
  splosh¦ing
splotch
  splotches
  splotched
  splotch¦ing
splotchy
  splotch¦ier
  splotchi¦est
splurge
  splurges
  splurged
  splur¦ging
splut¦ter +s +ed
  +ing
splut¦ter¦er +s
splut¦ter¦ing¦ly
splut¦tery
Spock, Dr
  Benja¦min
  (American
  paediatrician)
Spode (pottery)
spoil
  spoils

spoil (*cont.*)
  spoilt *or* spoiled
  spoil|ing
spoil|age +s
spoil|er +s
spoils|man
  spoils|men
spoil|sport +s
spoilt
Spo|kane (city and river, USA)
spoke
  spokes
  spoked
  spok|ing
spoken
spoke|shave +s
spokes|man
  spokes|men
spokes|per|son
  spokes|per|sons
  or spokes|people
spokes|woman
  spokes|women
spoke|wise
Spo|leto (town, Italy)
spoli|ation +s
spoli|ator +s
spoli|atory
spon|da|ic
spon|dee +s
spon|du|licks
spon|dyl|itis
sponge
  sponges
  sponged
  spon|ging *or*
  sponge|ing
sponge|able
sponge|like
spon|ger +s
spongi|form
spon|gily
spon|gi|ness
spongy
  spon|gier
  spon|gi|est
spon|sion +s
spon|son +s
spon|sor +s +ed +ing
spon|sor|ial
spon|sor|ship +s
spon|tan|eity
spon|tan|eous
spon|tan|eous|ly
spon|tan|eous|ness
spon|toon +s
spoof +s +ed +ing
spoof|er +s

spoof|ery
spook +s +ed +ing
spook|ily
spooki|ness
spooky
  spook|ier
  spooki|est
spool +s +ed +ing
spoon +s +ed +ing
spoon|beak +s
spoon|bill +s
spoon-bread +s
spoon|er +s
spoon|er|ism +s
spoon-feed
  spoon-feeds
  spoon-fed
  spoon-feeding
spoon|ful +s
spoon|ily
spooni|ness
spoony
  spoon|ies
  spoon|ier
  spooni|est
spoor +s +ed +ing
spoor|er +s
Spora|des (two groups of Greek islands)
spor|ad|ic
spor|ad|ic|al|ly
spor|an|gial
spor|an|gium
  spor|an|gia
spore +s
spore case +s
sporo|cyst +s
sporo|gen|esis
spor|ogen|ous
spor|ogony
sporo|phore +s
sporo|phyll +s
sporo|phyte +s
sporo|phyt|ic
sporo|phyt|ic|al|ly
sporo|zo|ite +s
spor|ran +s
sport +s +ed +ing
sport|er +s
sportif
sport|ily
sporti|ness
sport|ing|ly
sport|ive
sport|ive|ly
sport|ive|ness
sports car +s
sports|cast +s
sports|cast|er +s
sports ground +s

sports|man
  sports|men
sports|man|like
sports|man|ly
sports|man|ship
sports|per|son
  sports|people *or*
  sports|per|sons
sports|wear
sports|woman
  sports|women
sports writer +s
sporty
  sport|ier
  sporti|est
spor|ular
spor|ule +s
spot
  spots
  spot|ted
  spot|ting
spot check +s *noun*
spot-check +s +ed +ing *verb*
spot|lamp +s
spot|less
spot|less|ly
spot|less|ness
spot|light
  spot|lights
  spot|light|ed *or* spot|lit
  spot|light|ing
spot on
spot|ted|ness
spot|ter +s
spot|tily
spot|ti|ness
spotty
  spot|tier
  spot|ti|est
spot weld +s *noun*
spot-weld +s +ed +ing *verb*
spot-welder +s
spou|sal
spouse +s
spout +s +ed +ing
spout|er +s
spout|less
sprad|dle
  sprad|dles
  sprad|dled
  sprad|dling
sprag +s
sprain +s +ed +ing
spraint
  plural spraint
sprang
sprat
  sprats

sprat (*cont.*)
  sprat|ted
  sprat|ting
Spratly Is|lands (in South China Sea)
sprat|ter +s
sprauncy
spraun|cier
spraun|ci|est
sprawl +s +ed +ing
sprawl|er +s
sprawl|ing|ly
spray +s +ed +ing
spray|able
spray-dry
  spray-dries
  spray-dried
  spray-drying
spray|er +s
sprayey
spray-gun +s
spray-paint +s +ed +ing
spread
  spreads
  spread
  spread|ing
spread|able
spread|eagle
  spread|eagles
  spread|eagled
  spread|eag|ling *verb*
spread eagle +s *noun*
spread-eagle *adjective*
spread|er +s
spread|sheet +s
Sprech|ge|sang
Sprech|stimme
spree
  sprees
  spreed
  spree|ing
sprig
  sprigs
  sprigged
  sprig|ging
spriggy
  sprig|gier
  sprig|gi|est
spright|li|ness
spright|ly
  spright|lier
  spright|li|est
spring
  springs
  sprang

spring (*cont.*)
spring|ing
spring
spring|board +s
spring|bok +s
spring-clean +s
+ed +ing
springe +s
spring|er +s
Spring|field (city, USA)
spring|ily
springi|ness
spring|less
spring|let +s
spring|like
spring-loaded
Spring|steen, Bruce (American rock musician)
spring|tail +s
spring|tide (springtime)
spring tide +s (tide of greatest range)
spring|time +s
springy
spring|ier
springi|est
sprin|kle
sprin|kles
sprin|kled
sprin|kling
sprink|ler +s
sprink|ling +s
sprint +s +ed +ing
sprint|er +s
sprit +s
sprite +s
sprite|ly
sprite|lier
sprite|li|est
(use sprightly)
sprit|sail +s
spritz
spritzes
spritzed
spritz|ing
spritz|er +s
sprocket +s
sprog +s
sprout +s +ed +ing
spruce
spruces
spruced
spru|cing
spruce|ly
spruce|ness
spru|cer +s
sprue +s

spruik +s +ed +ing
spruik|er +s
spruit +s
sprung
spry +er +est
spry|ly
spry|ness
spud
spuds
spud|ded
spud|ding
spud-bashing
spue (use spew)
spues
spued
spu|ing
spu|mante +s
spume
spumes
spumed
spum|ing
spu|moni +s
spu|mous
spumy
spumi|er
spumi|est
spun
spunk
spunk|ily
spunki|ness
spunky
spunk|ier
spunki|est
spur
spurs
spurred
spur|ring
spurge +s
spur-gear +s
spuri|ous
spuri|ous|ly
spuri|ous|ness
spur|less
spurn +s +ed +ing
spurn|er +s
spur-of-the-moment *adjective*
spur|rey +s
spur|rier +s
spurry (use spurrey)
spur|ries
spurt +s +ed +ing
spur-wheel +s
spur|wort +s
sput|nik +s
sput|ter +s +ed +ing
sput|ter|er +s
spu|tum
sputa

spy
spies
spied
spy|ing
spy|glass
spy|glasses
spy|hole +s
spy|mas|ter +s
squab +s
squab|ble
squab|bles
squab|bled
squab|bling
squab|bler +s
squabby
squab-chick +s
squacco +s
squad +s
squad|die +s
squad|ron +s
squail +s
squail-board +s
squalid
squal|id|ity
squal|id|ly
squal|id|ness
squall +s +ed +ing
squally
squa|loid +s
squalor +s
squama
squa|mae
squa|mate
squa|mose
squa|mous
squa|mule +s
squan|der +s +ed +ing
squan|der|er +s
square
squares
squared
squar|ing
squarer
squar|est
square-bashing *noun*
square-built
square-eyed
square|ly
square|ness
squarer +s
square-rigged
square-shouldered
square-toed
squar|ial +s *Propr.*
squar|ish
squar|rose
squash
squashes
squashed

squash (*cont.*)
squash|ing
(crush; game)
squash
plural squash or squashes
(vegetable)
squash court +s
squash|ily
squashi|ness
squash play|er +s
squashy
squash|ier
squashi|est
squat
squats
squat|ted
squat|ting
squat|ter
squat|test
squat|ly
squat|ness
squat|ter +s
squaw +s
(*offensive*)
squawk +s +ed +ing
squawk-box
squawk-boxes
squawk|er +s
squaw-man
squaw-men
(*offensive*)
squeak +s +ed +ing
squeak|er +s
squeak|ily
squeaki|ness
squeaky
squeak|ier
squeaki|est
squeal +s +ed +ing
squeal|er +s
squeam|ish
squeam|ish|ly
squeam|ish|ness
squee|gee
squee|gees
squee|geed
squee|gee|ing
squeez|able
squeeze
squeezes
squeezed
squeez|ing
squeeze-box
squeeze-boxes
squeezer +s
squeezy
squelch
squelches

squelch (*cont.*)
squelched
squelch|ing
squelch|er +s
squelchy
squelch|ier
squelchi|est
squib
squibs
squibbed
squib|bing
SQUID +s (= super-
conducting
quantum
interference
device)
squid
plural squid *or*
squids
noun
squid
squids
squid|ded
squid|ding
squidgy
squidgi|er
squidgi|est
squiffed
squiffy
squif|fier
squif|fi|est
squig|gle
squig|gles
squig|gled
squig|gling
squig|gly
squill +s
squil|lion +s
squinch
squinches
squint +s +ed +ing
squint|er +s
squint-eyed
squinty
squire
squires
squired
squir|ing
squire|arch +s
squire|arch|ical
squire|archy
squire|arch|ies
squire|dom +s
squir|een +s
squire|hood +s
squire|let +s
squire|ling +s
squire|ly
squire|ship +s
squirl +s
squirm +s +ed
+ing

squirm|er +s
squirmy
squir|rel
squir|rels
squir|relled *Br.*
squir|reled *Am.*
squir|rel|ling *Br.*
squir|rel|ing *Am.*
squir|rel|ly
squirrel-monkey
+s
squirt +s +ed +ing
squirt|er +s
squirt gun +s
squish
squishes
squished
squish|ing
squishy
squish|ier
squishi|est
squit +s
squitch
squitches
squit|ters
squiz
Sri Lanka
Sri Lankan +s
Sri|nagar (city,
India)
stab
stabs
stabbed
stab|bing
stab|ber +s
stab|bing +s
sta|bil|ator +s
sta|bile +s
sta|bil|isa|tion *Br.*
(use stabilization)
sta|bil|ise *Br.* (use
stabilize)
sta|bil|ises
sta|bil|ised
sta|bil|is|ing
sta|bil|iser *Br.* +s
(use stabilizer)
sta|bil|ity
sta|bil|iza|tion
sta|bil|ize
sta|bil|izes
sta|bil|ized
sta|bil|iz|ing
sta|bil|izer +s
stable
stables
stabled
stab|ling
stabler
stab|lest
stable boy +s

stable
com|pan|ion +s
stable|ful +s
stable girl +s
stable lad +s
stable|man
stable|men
stable|mate +s
stable|ness
stab|lish
stab|lishes
stab|lished
stab|lish|ing
sta|bly
stac|cato +s
Sta|cey
stack +s +ed +ing
stack|able
stack|er +s
stack-yard +s
stacte +s
stad|dle +s
staddle-stone +s
sta|dium
sta|diums *or*
sta|dia
stadt|hold|er +s
stadt|hold|er|ship
+s
Staël, Mme de
(French writer)
staff +s +ed +ing
(personnel;
provide with staff)
staff
staffs *or* staves
Music
Staffa (Scottish
island)
staff|age
staff|er +s
Staf|ford (town,
England)
Staf|ford|shire
(county, England)
staff|room +s
Staffs.
(= Staffordshire)
stag
stags
stagged
stag|ging
stage
stages
staged
sta|ging
stage|abil|ity
stage|able
stage|coach
stage|coaches
stage|craft

stage fright
stage|hand +s
stage-manage
stage-manages
stage-managed
stage-managing
stage
man|age|ment
stage man|ager +s
stager +s
stage-struck
stagey (use stagy)
sta|gier
stagi|est
stag|fla|tion
stag|ger +s +ed
+ing
stag|ger|er +s
stag|ger|ing|ly
stag|gers
stag-horn +s
stag|hound +s
stagi|ly
stagi|ness
sta|ging +s
stag|nancy
stag|nant
stag|nant|ly
stag|nate
stag|nates
stag|nated
stag|nat|ing
stag|na|tion
stag-night +s
stagy
stagi|er
stagi|est
staid +er +est
staid|ly
staid|ness
stain +s +ed +ing
stain|able
stained glass *noun*
stained-glass
attributive
Stain|er, John
(English
composer)
stain|er +s
stain|less
stair +s (in
building. △ stare)
stair|case +s
stair|head +s
stair|lift +s
stair-rod +s
stair|way +s
stair|well +s
staithe +s
stake
stakes

stake (*cont.*)
  staked
  stak¦ing
  (stick; bet.
   ⚠ steak)
stake-boat +s
stake-body
  stake-bodies
stake¦build¦ing
stake¦hold¦er +s
stake-net +s
stake-out +s *noun*
staker +s
Stakh¦an¦ov¦ism
Stakh¦an¦ov¦ist +s
Stakh¦an¦ov¦ite +s
stal¦ac¦tic
stal¦ac¦ti¦form
stal¦ac¦tite +s
stal¦ac¦tit¦ic
Stalag +s
stal¦ag¦mite +s
stal¦ag¦mit¦ic
stale
  stales
  staled
  stal¦ing
  staler
  stal¦est
stale¦ly
stale¦mate
  stale¦mates
  stale¦mated
  stale¦mat¦ing
stale¦ness
Sta¦lin (former
  name of Donetsk)
Sta¦lin, Jo¦seph
  (Soviet leader)
Sta¦lin¦abad
  (former name of
  Dushanbe)
Sta¦lin¦grad
  (former name of
  Volgograd)
Sta¦lin¦ism
Sta¦lin¦ist +s
Sta¦lino (former
  name of Donetsk)
stalk +s +ed +ing
  (stem of plant etc.;
  pursue stealthily.
  ⚠ stork)
stalk¦er +s
stalk-eyed
stalking-horse +s
stalk¦less
stalk¦let +s
stalk¦like
stalky
stall +s +ed +ing
stall¦age +s

stall-feed
  stall-feeds
  stall-fed
  stall-feeding
stall¦hold¦er +s
stal¦lion +s
stal¦wart +s
stal¦wart¦ly
stal¦wart¦ness
Stam¦boul (former
  name of Istanbul)
sta¦men +s
stam¦ina
stam¦inal
stam¦in¦ate
stam¦in¦ifer¦ous
stam¦mer +s +ed
  +ing
stam¦mer¦er +s
stam¦mer¦ing¦ly
stamp +s +ed +ing
stamp col¦lect¦ing
stamp col¦lect¦or
  +s
stamp duty
  stamp duties
stam¦pede
  stam¦pedes
  stam¦peded
  stam¦ped¦ing
stam¦peder +s
stamp¦er +s
stamp hinge +s
stamp¦ing ground
  +s
stamp ma¦chine
  +s
stamp-mill +s
stamp of¦fice +s
stamp paper
stance +s
stanch (use
  staunch)
  stanches
  stanched
  stanch¦ing
stan¦chion +s +ed
  +ing
stand
  stands
  stood
  stand¦ing
stand-alone
  adjective
stand¦ard +s
standard-bearer
  +s
Stand¦ard¦bred +s
stand¦ard¦is¦able
  Br. (use
  standardizable)

stand¦ard¦isa¦tion
  Br. +s (use
  standardization)
stand¦ard¦ise *Br.*
  (use standardize)
  stand¦ard¦ises
  stand¦ard¦ised
  stand¦ard¦is¦ing
stand¦ard¦iser *Br.*
  +s (use
  standardizer)
stand¦ard¦iz¦able
stand¦ard¦iza¦tion
  +s
stand¦ard¦ize
  stand¦ard¦izes
  stand¦ard¦ized
  stand¦ard¦iz¦ing
stand¦ard¦izer +s
stand¦by +s
stand¦ee +s
stand¦er +s
stand-in +s *noun*
  and attributive
stand¦ing +s
stand¦ing room
stand-off +s *noun*
  and attributive
stand-offish
stand-offish¦ly
stand-offish¦ness
stand¦out +s
stand¦pipe +s
stand¦point +s
stand¦still +s
stand-to *noun*
stand-up +s
  adjective and noun
Stan¦ford
  (university, USA)
Stan¦ford, Charles
  Vil¦liers (British
  composer)
Stan¦hope, Lady
  Hes¦ter Lucy
  (English traveller)
stan¦hope +s
stan¦iel +s
Stan¦ier, Wil¦liam
  (English railway
  engineer)
Stan¦is¦laus
  (patron saint of
  Poland)
Stan¦is¦lav¦sky,
  Kon¦stan¦tin
  (Russian theatre
  director)
stank
Stan¦ley, Henry
  Mor¦ton (Welsh
  explorer)

Stan¦ley, Mount
  (in central Africa)
Stan¦ley, Port
  (town, Falkland
  Islands)
Stan¦ley knife
  Stan¦ley knives
  Propr.
Stan¦ley¦ville
  (former name of
  Kisangani)
stan¦nary
  stan¦nar¦ies
stan¦nate
stan¦nic
stan¦nite +s
stan¦nous
Stan¦sted (airport,
  England)
stanza +s
stan¦za'd
stan¦zaed (use
  stanza'd)
stan¦za¦ic
sta¦pelia +s
stapes
  plural stapes
staphylo¦coc¦cal
staphylo¦coc¦cus
  staphylo¦cocci
staple
  staples
  stapled
  stapl¦ing
staple gun +s
stapler +s
star
  stars
  starred
  star¦ring
star-apple +s
Stara Za¦gora (city,
  Bulgaria)
star¦board +s
star¦burst +s
starch
  starches
  starched
  starch¦ing
starch¦er +s
starch¦ily
starchi¦ness
starch-reduced
starchy
  starch¦ier
  starchi¦est
star-crossed
star¦dom
star¦dust
stare
  stares
  stared

stare (cont.)
star|ing
(gaze fixedly.
⚠ stair)
starer +s
star|fish
plural star|fish or
star|fishes
star fruit
plural star fruit
star|gaze
star|gazes
star|gazed
star|gaz|ing
star|gazer +s
stark +er +est
Stark ef|fect
stark|ers
stark|ly
stark|ness
star|less
star|let +s
star|light
star|like
Star|ling, Er|nest
Henry (English
physiologist)
star|ling +s
star|lit
star|rily
star|ri|ness
starry
star|rier
star|ri|est
starry-eyed
star|ship +s
star-spangled
star-struck
star-studded
START (= Strategic
Arms Reduction
Talks)
start +s +ed +ing
start|er +s
start|ing block +s
start|ing gate +s
starting-handle +s
start|ing point +s
star|tle
star|tles
star|tled
start|ling
start|ler +s
start|ling|ly
start-up +s
attributive and
noun
star|va|tion
starve
starves
starved
starv|ing

starve|ling +s
star|wort +s
stash
stashes
stashed
stash|ing
Stasi +s (security
police of German
Democratic
Republic)
sta|sis
sta|ses
(inactivity)
stat +s
(= thermostat;
(stats) statistics)
stat|able
statal
state
states
stated
stat|ing
state|craft
stated|ly
state|hood
state house +s
state|less
state|less|ness
state|let +s
state|li|ness
state|ly
state|lier
state|li|est
state|ment +s +ed
+ing
Staten Is|land (in
New York)
sta|ter +s (coin.
⚠ stator)
state|room +s
state's evi|dence
state|side
states|man
states|men
states|man|like
states|man|ly
states|man|ship
states|per|son +s
states' rights
states|woman
states|women
State trial +s
state|wide
static
stat|ic|al
stat|ic|al|ly
stat|ice +s
stat|ics
sta|tion +s +ed
+ing
sta|tion|ari|ness

sta|tion|ary (not
moving.
⚠ stationery)
station-bill +s
sta|tion|er +s
Sta|tion|ers' Hall
(in London)
sta|tion|ery (paper
etc. ⚠ stationary)
station-keeping
sta|tion|mas|ter +s
sta|tion wagon +s
stat|ism
stat|ist +s
stat|is|tic +s
stat|is|tic|al
stat|is|tic|al|ly
stat|is|ti|cian +s
stat|is|tics
Sta|tius, Pub|lius
Pap|in|ius
(Roman poet)
sta|tor +s (in
electric motor etc.
⚠ stater)
stato|scope +s
stats (= statistics)
statu|ary
statu|ar|ies
statue +s
stat|ued
statu|esque
statu|esque|ly
statu|esque|ness
statu|ette +s
stat|ure +s
stat|ured
sta|tus
sta|tuses
sta|tus quo
sta|tus quo ante
stat|ut|able
stat|ut|ably
stat|ute +s
statute-barred
statute-book +s
statute-roll +s
statu|tor|ily
statu|tory
staunch
staunches
staunched
staunch|ing
staunch|er
staunch|est
staunch|ly
staunch|ness
Sta|vanger (port,
Norway)
stave
staves

stave (cont.)
staved or stove
stav|ing
staves|acre +s
Stav|ro|pol (city
and territory,
Russia)
stay +s +ed +ing
stay-at-home +s
adjective and noun
stay-bar +s
stay|er +s
stay-in strike +s
stay-rod +s
stay|sail +s
stay-up +s noun
stead +s
stead|fast
stead|fast|ly
stead|fast|ness
stead|ier +s
stead|ily
steadi|ness
stead|ing +s
steady
stead|ies
stead|ied
steady|ing
stead|ier
steadi|est
steady-going
steak +s (meat.
⚠ stake)
steak|house +s
steak knife
steak knives
steal
steals
stole
steal|ing
stolen
(rob; a bargain.
⚠ steel, stele)
steal|er +s (thief.
⚠ stela, stelar)
stealth
stealth|ily
stealth|iness
stealthy
stealth|ier
stealthi|est
steam +s +ed +ing
steam|boat +s
steam en|gine +s
steam|er +s
steam-heat
steam|ily
steami|ness
steam|ing +s
steam-jacket +s
steam|roll +s +ed
+ing

steam|roll|er +s
+ed +ing
steam|ship +s
steam-tight
steamy
steam|ier
steami|est
stear|ate +s
ste|aric
stearin +s
stea|tite +s
stea|tit|ic
steato|pygia
stea|topy|gous
steed +s
steel +s +ed +ing
(metal; make
resolute. △ steal,
stele)
steel-clad
Steele, Rich|ard
(Irish writer)
steel|head +s (fish)
steeli|ness
steel-making
steel|work (steel
articles)
steel|work|er +s
steel|works
plural steel|works
(factory)
steely
steel|ier
steeli|est
(like steel.
△ stelae, stele)
steel|yard +s
steen|bok
plural steen|bok
steen|kirk +s
steep +s +ed +ing
+er +est
steep|en +s +ed
+ing
steep|ish
steeple +s
steeple|chase +s
steeple|chaser +s
steeple|chas|ing
steeple-crowned
steepled
steeple|jack +s
steep|ly
steep|ness
steer +s +ed +ing
(guide or direct;
guidance; animal.
△ stere)
steer|able
steer|age
steerage-way
steer|er +s

steer|ing col|umn
+s
steer|ing wheel +s
steers|man
steers|men
steeve
steeves
steeved
steev|ing
stego|saur +s
stego|saurus
stego|saur|uses
Stein, Ger|trude
(American writer)
stein +s
Stein|beck, John
(American
novelist)
stein|bock
plural stein|bock
Steiner, Ru|dolf
(Austrian founder
of anthroposophy)
Stein|way, Henry
(German piano-
builder)
stela
ste|lae
(pillar. △ stealer,
stelar)
ste|lar (pertaining to
a stele. △ stealer,
stela)
stele +s (plant
tissue. △ steal,
steel, steely)
Stella (name)
Stella, Frank
(American
painter)
stel|lar (of stars)
stel|late
stel|lated
Stel|len|bosch
(town, South
Africa)
Stel|ler's sea cow
+s
stelli|form
stel|lini
stel|lu|lar
stem
stems
stemmed
stem|ming
stem|less
stem|let +s
stem|like
stemma
stem|mata
stem|ple +s
stem turn +s

stem|ware
stem-winder +s
stench
stenches
sten|cil
sten|cils
sten|cilled *Br.*
sten|ciled *Am.*
sten|cil|ling *Br.*
sten|cil|ing *Am.*
Stend|hal (French
novelist)
Sten gun +s
Steno, Nico|laus
(Danish geologist)
steno +s
(= stenographer)
sten|og|raph|er +s
steno|graph|ic
sten|og|raphy
sten|osis
sten|oses
sten|ot|ic
steno|type +s
steno|typ|ist +s
Sten|tor +s
sten|tor|ian
step
steps
stepped
step|ping
(pace; stair.
△ steppe)
Step|ana|kert
(Russian name for
Xankändi)
step|brother +s
step|child
step|chil|dren
step-cut
step-cuts
step-cut
step-cutting
step|dad +s
step|daugh|ter +s
step|fam|ily
step|fam|ilies
step|father +s
step-grand|child
step-
grand|chil|dren
step-
grand|daugh|ter
+s
step-grand|father
+s
step-
grand|mother +s
step-
grand|par|ent +s
step-grand|son +s
Steph|anie

steph|an|otis
steph|an|otises
Ste|phen *also*
Ste|ven (name)
Ste|phen (English
king; early saint;
patron saint of
Hungary)
Ste|phens (in 'even
Stephens')
Ste|phen|son,
George (English
engineer)
step-in +s *adjective
and noun*
step|lad|der +s
step|like
step|mother +s
step|mum +s
step-parent +s
steppe +s (grassy
plain. △ step)
step|ping stone +s
step|sis|ter +s
step|son +s
step-up +s *noun
and attributive*
step|wise
ster|adian +s
ster|cor|aceous
ster|coral
stere +s (unit.
△ steer)
stereo +s
stereo|bate +s
stereo|chem|is|try
stereo|graph +s
ster|eog|raphy
stereo|iso|mer +s
stere|om|etry
stereo|phon|ic
stereo|phon|ic|
al|ly
stere|oph|ony
stere|op|sis
stere|op|tic
stere|op|ticon +s
stereo|scope +s
stereo|scop|ic
stereo|scop|ic|
al|ly
stere|os|copy
stereo|spe|cif|ic
stereo|spe|cif|ic|
al|ly
stereo|speci|fi|city
stereo|tac|tic
stereo|taxic
stereo|taxis
stereo|taxy
stereo|type
stereo|types

stereo|type (*cont.*)
stereo|typed
stereo|typ|ing
stereo|typ|ic
stereo|typ|ical
stereo|typ|ic|al|ly
stereo|typy
steric
ster|ile
ster|ile|ly
ster|il|is|able *Br.*
(use sterilizable)
ster|il|isa|tion *Br.*
+s (use
sterilization)
ster|il|ise *Br.* (use
sterilize)
ster|il|ises
ster|il|ised
ster|il|is|ing
ster|il|iser *Br.* +s
(use sterilizer)
ster|il|ity
ster|il|iz|able
ster|il|iza|tion +s
ster|il|ize
ster|il|izes
ster|il|ized
ster|il|iz|ing
ster|il|izer +s
ster|let +s
ster|ling +s
ster|ling|ness
Ster|lita|mak (city,
Russia)
stern +s +er +est
ster|nal
Stern|berg,
Jo|seph von
(Austrian-born
American film
director)
Sterne, Laur|ence
(Irish novelist)
Stern Gang
(Zionist group)
stern|ly
stern|most
stern|ness
stern|post +s
ster|num
ster|nums *or*
sterna
ster|nu|ta|tion +s
ster|nu|ta|tor +s
ster|nu|ta|tory
stern|ward
stern|wards
stern|way +s
stern|wheel|er +s
ster|oid +s
ster|oid|al

sterol +s
ster|tor|ous
ster|tor|ous|ly
ster|tor|ous|ness
stet
stets
stet|ted
stet|ting
stetho|scope +s
stetho|scop|ic
stetho|scop|ic|
al|ly
steth|os|co|pist +s
steth|os|copy
stet|son +s
Stet|tin (German
name for
Szczecin)
steve|dore
steve|dores
steve|dored
steve|dor|ing
Ste|ven *also*
Ste|phen
Ste|ven|age (town,
England)
ste|ven|graph +s
Ste|vens, Wal|lace
(American poet)
Ste|ven|son,
Rob|ert Louis
(Scottish novelist)
stew +s +ed +ing
stew|ard +s +ed
+ing
stew|ard|ess
stew|ard|esses
stew|ard|ship +s
Stew|art *also*
Stuart
(name)
Stew|art, Jackie
(British motor-
racing driver.
△ Stuart)
Stew|art, James
(American actor.
△ Stuart)
Stew|art Is|land
(off New Zealand)
stew|pot +s
sthen|ic
sticho|mythia
stick
sticks
stuck
stick|ing
stick|abil|ity
stick|er +s
stick|ily
sticki|ness

stick|ing plas|ter
+s
stick|ing point +s
stick in|sect +s
stick-in-the-mud
+s
stick|jaw +s
stickle|back +s
stick|ler +s
stick|less
stick|like
stick|pin +s
stick-up +s
stick|weed +s
sticky
stick|ier
sticki|est
sticky|beak +s +ed
+ing
Stieg|litz, Al|fred
(American
photographer)
stiff +s +er +est
stiff|en +s +ed
+ing
stiff|en|er +s
stiff|en|ing +s
stiff|ish
stiff|ly
stiff-necked
stiff|ness
stiffy
stiff|ies
stifle
stifles
stifled
stif|ling
stifle-bone
stifler +s
stif|ling|ly
stigma
stig|mas *or*
stig|mata
stig|mat|ic +s
stig|mat|ic|al|ly
stig|ma|tisa|tion
Br. (use
stigmatization)
stig|ma|tise *Br.*
(use stigmatize)
stig|ma|tises
stig|ma|tised
stig|ma|tis|ing
stig|ma|tist +s
stig|ma|tiza|tion
stig|ma|tize
stig|ma|tizes
stig|ma|tized
stig|ma|tiz|ing
Stijl, De (Dutch art
movement)
stilb +s

stil|bene
stil|bes|trol *Am.*
stil|boes|trol *Br.*
stile +s (steps over
fence; part of
door. △ style)
stil|etto +s
still +s +ed +ing
+er +est
still|age +s
still|birth +s
still|born
stilli|cide +s
still life +s *noun*
still-life *attributive*
still|ness
still|nesses
still room +s
Still|son +s
stilly
stilt +s
stilt|ed
stilt|ed|ly
stilt|ed|ness
stilt|less
Stil|ton +s (village,
England; cheese)
Propr.
stimu|lant +s
stimu|late
stimu|lates
stimu|lated
stimu|lat|ing
stimu|lat|ing|ly
stimu|la|tion +s
stimu|la|tive
stimu|la|tor +s
stimu|la|tory
stimu|lus
stim|uli
stimy (use stymie)
sti|mies
sti|mied
stimy|ing
sting
stings
stung
sting|ing
sting|aree +s
sting|er +s
stin|gily
stingi|ness
sting|ing|ly
sting|ing net|tle
+s
sting|less
sting|like
sting|ray +s
stingy
stin|gier
stin|gi|est

stink
  stinks
  stank *or* stunk
  stink|ing
  stunk
stink|ard +s
stink|er +s
stink|horn +s
stink|ing|ly
stinko
stink|pot +s
stink|weed +s
stink|wood +s
stinky
  stink|ier
  stinki|est
stint +s +ed +ing
stint|er +s
stint|less
stipe +s
sti|pel +s
sti|pel|late
sti|pend +s
sti|pen|diary
  sti|pen|diar|ies
sti|pes
  stipi|tes
stipi|form
stipi|tate
sti|piti|form
stip|ple
  stip|ples
  stip|pled
  stip|pling
stip|pler +s
stipu|lar
stipu|late
  stipu|lates
  stipu|lated
  stipu|lat|ing
stipu|la|tion +s
stipu|la|tor +s
stip|ule +s
stir
  stirs
  stirred
  stir|ring
stir-crazy
stir-fry
  stir-fries
  stir-fried
  stir-frying
stirk +s
stir|less
Stir|ling (city,
  Scotland)
Stir|ling, James
  (Scottish
  mathematician)
Stir|ling, Rob|ert
  (Scottish
  engineer)

stir|pi|cul|ture
stirps
  stir|pes
stir|rer +s
stir|ring +s
stir|ring|ly
stir|rup +s
stir|rup cup +s
stir|rup iron +s
stir|rup lea|ther +s
stir|rup pump +s
stitch
  stitches
  stitched
  stitch|ing
stitch|er +s
stitch|ery
stitch|less
stitch-up +s
stitch|wort +s
sti|ver +s
Stoa, the (Stoic
  school of
  philosophy)
stoa +s *Architecture*
stoat +s
sto|chas|tic
sto|chas|tic|al|ly
stock +s +ed +ing
stock|ade
  stock|ades
  stock|aded
  stock|ad|ing
stock-book +s
stock|breed|er +s
stock|breed|ing
stock|broker +s
stock|broker|age
stock|brok|ing
stock car +s
stock|er +s
stock|fish
  plural stock|fish
Stock|hausen,
  Karl|heinz
  (German
  composer)
stock|hold|er +s-
stock|hold|ing +s
Stock|holm
  (capital of
  Sweden)
stock|ily
stocki|ness
stock|inet
stock|in|ette (use
  stockinet)
stock|ing +s
stock|inged
stocking-filler +s
stock|ing|less
stock|ing stitch

stock-in-trade
stock|ist +s
stock|job|ber +s
stock|job|bing
stock|less
stock|list +s
stock|man
  stock|men
stock mar|ket +s
stock|out +s
stock|pile
  stock|piles
  stock|piled
  stock|pil|ing
stock|piler +s
Stock|port (town,
  England)
stock|pot +s
stock|room +s
stock-still
stock|take +s
stock|tak|ing
Stockton-on-Tees
  (town, England)
stocky
  stock|ier
  stocki|est
stock|yard +s
stodge
  stodges
  stodged
  stodg|ing
stodgi|ly
stodgi|ness
stodgy
  stodgi|er
  stodgi|est
stoep +s (veranda.
  ⚠ stoop, stoup)
sto|gie +s (use
  stogy)
stogy
  sto|gies
  (cigar)
Stoic +s *Philosophy*
stoic +s (stoical
  person)
sto|ic|al
sto|ic|al|ly
stoi|chio|met|ric
stoi|chi|om|etry
Sto|icism
  (philosophy of the
  Stoics)
sto|icism (stoical
  attitude)
stoke
  stokes
  stoked
  stok|ing
stoke|hold +s
stoke|hole +s

Stoke-on-Trent
  (city, England)
Stoker, Bram (Irish
  novelist)
stoker +s
stokes
  plural stokes
Sto|kow|ski,
  Leo|pold (British-
  born American
  conductor)
STOL (= short take-
  off and landing)
stola
  sto|lae
stole +s
stolen
stolid
stol|id|ity
stol|id|ly
stol|id|ness
stollen +s
sto|lon +s
sto|lon|ate
sto|lon|ifer|ous
stoma
  stomas *or*
  sto|mata
stom|ach +s +ed
  +ing
stomach-ache +s
stom|ach|er +s
stom|ach|ful +s
stom|ach|ic
stom|ach|less
stom|ach pump +s
stom|ach tube +s
sto|mal
sto|mata
sto|ma|tal
sto|ma|titis
sto|mato|logic|al
sto|ma|tolo|gist +s
sto|ma|tol|ogy
stomp +s +ed +ing
stomp|er +s
stone
  stones
  stoned
  ston|ing
Stone Age
  (prehistoric
  period)
stone|chat +s
stone-coal +s
stone-cold
stone-cold sober
stone|crop +s
stone|cut|ter +s
stone-dead
stone-deaf

stone|fish
  plural stone|fish *or*
  stone|fishes
stone|fly
  stone|flies
stone fruit +s
stone|ground
stone|hatch
  stone|hatches
Stone|henge
  (megalithic
  monument,
  England)
stone|less
stone|mason +s
stone|mason¦ry
stone-pit +s
stoner +s
stone|wall +s +ed
  +ing
stone|wall¦er +s
stone|ware
stone|washed
stone|weed +s
stone|work
stone|work¦er +s
stone|wort +s
stoni¦ly
stoni|ness
stonk¦er +s +ed
  +ing
stonk|ing
stony
  stoni|er
  stoni|est
stony-broke
stony-hearted
stood
stooge
  stooges
  stooged
  stoo¦ging
stook +s +ed +ing
stool +s +ed +ing
stool|ball
stoolie +s
stool-pigeon +s
stoop +s +ed +ing
  (bend forward;
  stooping posture;
  swoop onto prey.
  △ stoep, stoup)
stop
  stops
  stopped
  stop|ping
stop|bank +s
stop|cock +s
stop-drill +s
stope +s
Stopes, Marie
  (Scottish birth-

Stopes (*cont.*)
  control
  campaigner)
stop|gap +s
stop-go +s
stop-knob +s
stop|less
stop|off +s
stop|over +s
stop|pable
stop|page +s
Stop|pard, Tom
  (British
  playwright)
stop|per +s +ed
  +ing
stop|ping +s
stop|ping place +s
stop|ple
  stop|ples
  stop|pled
  stop|pling
stop-start *adjective*
stop-volley +s
stop|watch
  stop|watches
stor|able
stor|age
storax
  stor|axes
store
  stores
  stored
  stor|ing
store|front +s
store|house +s
store|keep¦er +s
store|man
  store|men
storer +s
store|room +s
storey +s (floor of
  building. △ story)
stor¦eyed (divided
  into storeys, in
  'three-storeyed'
  etc. △ storied)
stori|ated
stori|ation +s
stor|ied (celebrated
  in stories.
  △ storeyed)
stork +s (bird.
  △ stalk)
stork's-bill +s
  (plant)
storm +s +ed +ing
storm-bird +s
storm|bound
storm-cock +s
storm-collar +s
storm cone +s

storm-door +s
storm¦er +s
storm-finch
  storm-finches
storm-glass
  storm-glasses
storm|ily
stormi|ness
storming-party
  storming-parties
storm lan|tern +s
storm|less
Stor|mont (castle,
  Northern Ireland)
storm pet¦rel +s
storm|proof
storm-sail +s
storm-signal +s
storm troop¦er +s
storm troops
stormy
  storm|ier
  stormi|est
Stor|no|way (port,
  Scotland)
story
  stor|ies
  (tale; plot; fib.
  △ storey)
story|board +s
story book +s
story|line +s
story|tell¦er +s
story|tell¦ing
sto|tinka
  sto|tinki
stoup +s (holy-
  water basin;
  flagon. △ stoep,
  stoop)
Stour (rivers,
  England)
stoush
  stoushes
  stoushed
  stoush|ing
stout +er +est
stout-hearted
stout-hearted¦ly
stout-
  hearted¦ness
stout|ish
stout¦ly
stout|ness
stove
  stoves
  stoved
  stov¦ing
stove-enamel
  stove-enamels
  stove-enamelled

stove-enamel
  (*cont.*)
  stove-
  enamel¦ling
stove-pipe +s
stow +s +ed +ing
stow|age +s
stow|away +s
Stowe, Har|riet
  Bee|cher
  (American
  novelist)
Stra|bane (county,
  Northern Ireland)
stra¦bis|mal
stra¦bis|mic
stra¦bis|mus
Strabo (geographer
  of Greek descent)
Stra|chey, Lyt|ton
  (English
  biographer)
Strad +s
  (= Stradivarius)
strad|dle
  strad|dles
  strad|dled
  strad|dling
strad|dler +s
Stradi|vari,
  An|tonio (Italian
  violin maker)
Stradi|var¦ius
strafe
  strafes
  strafed
  straf¦ing
strag¦gie
  strag|gles
  strag¦gled
  strag|gling
strag|gler +s
strag|gly
  strag|glier
  strag|gli|est
straight +s +er
  +est (not bent
  etc.; straight part;
  heterosexual;
  direct. △ strait)
straight|away
straight-bred
straight-cut
straight-edge +s
straight-eight +s
straight|en +s +ed
  +ing (make or
  become straight.
  △ straiten)
straight|en¦er +s
straight-faced
straight|for¦ward

straight|
    for|ward|ly
straight|for|ward|
      ness
straight|ish
straight|jacket
  (use straitjacket)
  +s +ed +ing
straight-laced (use
  strait-laced)
straight|ly
straight|ness
  (quality of being
  straight.
  △ straitness)
straight-out
straight-up
straight|way
strain +s +ed +ing
strain|able
strain|er +s
strait +s (water
  connecting seas;
  narrow; trouble.
  △ straight)
strait|en +s +ed
  +ing (restrict.
  △ straighten)
strait|jacket +s
  +ed +ing
strait-laced
strait|ly
strait|ness
  (severity;
  hardship.
  △ straightness)
Straits
  Settle|ments
  (former British
  colony, SE Asia)
strake +s
Stral|sund (town,
  Germany)
stra|mo|nium
strand +s +ed
  +ing
strand|ing +s
strange
  stran|ger
  stran|gest
strange|ly
strange|ness
stran|ger +s
stran|gle
  stran|gles
  stran|gled
  stran|gling
strangle|hold +s
stran|gler +s
stran|gling +s
stran|gu|late
  stran|gu|lates

stran|gu|late
  (cont.)
  stran|gu|lated
  stran|gu|lat|ing
stran|gu|la|tion
stran|guri|ous
stran|gury
  stran|gur|ies
Stran|raer (port,
  Scotland)
strap
  straps
  strapped
  strap|ping
strap-hang
  strap-hangs
  strap-hung
  strap-hanging
strap|hang|er +s
strap|less
strap|pado +s
strap|per +s
strappy
strap-work
Stras|berg, Lee
  (American actor
  and drama
  teacher)
Stras|bourg (city,
  France)
strata (plural of
  stratum)
strata|gem +s
stratal
stra|tegic
stra|tegic|al
stra|tegic|al|ly
stra|tegics
strat|egist +s
strat|egy
  strat|egies
Stratford-upon-
  Avon (town,
  England)
strath +s
Strath|clyde (in
  Scotland)
strath|spey +s
strati
stra|ticu|late
strati|fi|ca|tion +s
strati|fi|ca|tion|al
strat|ify
  strati|fies
  strati|fied
  strati|fy|ing
strati|graph|ic
strati|graph|ic|al
stra|tig|raphy
strato|cir|rus
stra|toc|racy
  stra|toc|ra|cies

strato|cumu|lus
strato|pause
strato|sphere
strato|spher|ic
stra|tum
  strata
stra|tus
  strati
Strauss, Jo|hann
  (father and son,
  Austrian
  composers)
Strauss, Rich|ard
  (German
  composer)
Stra|vin|sky, Igor
  (Russian-born
  American
  composer)
straw +s
straw|berry
  straw|berries
straw|berry tree
  +s
straw|board +s
straw color Am. +s
straw-colored Am.
straw colour Br.
  +s
straw-coloured Br.
straw-worm +s
strawy
stray +s +ed +ing
stray|er +s
streak +s +ed +ing
streak|er +s
streak|ily
streaki|ness
streaky
  streak|ier
  streaki|est
stream +s +ed
  +ing
stream-anchor +s
stream|er +s
stream|less
stream|let +s
stream|line
  stream|lines
  stream|lined
  stream|lin|ing
Streep, Meryl
  (American
  actress)
street +s
street|car +s
street|ed
street lamp +s
street light +s
street light|ing
street trader +s
street|walk|er +s

street|walk|ing
street|ward
street|wise
Strei|sand,
  Bar|bra
  (American singer)
stre|litzia +s
strength +s
strength|en +s
  +ed +ing
strength|en|er +s
strength|less
strenu|ous
strenu|ous|ly
strenu|ous|ness
strep
  (= streptococcus)
strepto|car|pus
strepto|coc|cal
strepto|coc|cus
  strepto|cocci
strepto|kin|ase
strepto|mycin
Strep|yan
stress
  stresses
  stressed
  stress|ing
stress|ful
stress|ful|ly
stress|ful|ness
stress|less
stretch
  stretches
  stretched
  stretch|ing
stretch|abil|ity
stretch|able
stretch|er +s
stretcher-bearer
  +s
stretchi|ness
stretch mark +s
stretchy
  stretch|ier
  stretchi|est
stretta
  strette or stret|tas
stretto
  stretti or stret|tos
strew
  strews
  strewn or strewed
  strew|ing
strew|er +s
strewth
stria
  striae
stri|ate
  stri|ates
  stri|ated
  stri|at|ing

stri|ation +s
stricken
strickle +s
strict +er +est
strict|ly
strict|ness
stric|ture +s
stric|tured
stride
 strides
 strode
 strid|ing
 strid|den
stri|dency
stri|dent
stri|dent|ly
strider +s
stridu|lant
stridu|late
 stridu|lates
 stridu|lated
 stridu|lat|ing
stridu|la|tion +s
strife +s
stri|gil +s
stri|gose
strik|able
strike
 strikes
 struck *or*
 strick|en
 strik|ing
strike-bound
strike-breaker +s
strike-breaking
strike call +s
strike force +s
strike-measure +s
strike-out +s
striker +s
strike rate +s
strike-slip fault +s
striking-circle +s
strik|ing force +s
strik|ing|ly
strik|ing|ness
strim|mer +s *Propr.*
Strind|berg,
 Au|gust (Swedish
 writer)
Strine
string
 strings
 strung
 string|ing
string|board +s
string-course +s
strin|gency
 strin|gen|cies
strin|gendo
strin|gent

strin|gent|ly
string|er +s
string|halt +s
string|ily
stringi|ness
string|less
string|like
string-piece +s
string play|er +s
stringy
 string|ier
 stringi|est
stringy-bark +s
strip
 strips
 stripped
 strip|ping
strip|agram +s
stripe
 stripes
 striped
 strip|ing
strip farm|ing
strip light +s
strip|ling +s
strip-mining
strip|pa|gram +s
 (use stripagram)
strip|per +s
strip|per|gram +s
 (use stripagram)
strip-search
 strip-searches
 strip-searched
 strip-search|ing
strip|tease
 strip|teases
 strip|teased
 strip|teas|ing
strip|teaser +s
stripy
 stripi|er
 stripi|est
strive
 strives
 strove *or* strived
 striv|ing
 striven *or* strived
striver +s
strobe
 strobes
 strobed
 strob|ing
stro|bila
 stro|bilae
stro|bile +s
stro|bilus
 stro|bili
strobo|scope +s
strobo|scop|ic
strobo|scop|ic|al

strobo|scop|ic|
 al|ly
strode
Strog|an|off +s
stroke
 strokes
 stroked
 strok|ing
stroke|play
stroll +s +ed +ing
stroll|er +s
stroma
 stro|mata
stro|mat|ic
stro|mato|lite +s
Strom|boli
 (volcano off Italy)
strong +er +est
strong-arm
 attributive
strong|box
 strong|boxes
strong|hold +s
strong|ish
strong|ly
strong|man
 strong|men
 (forceful leader;
 circus performer)
strong-minded
strong-
 minded|ness
strong|room +s
stron|tia
stron|tium
strontium-90
strop
 strops
 stropped
 strop|ping
stro|phan|thin
strophe +s
stroph|ic
strop|pily
strop|pi|ness
stroppy
 strop|pier
 strop|pi|est
strove
strow
 strows
 strowed
 strow|ing
 strowed *or*
 strown
struck
struc|tural
struc|tur|al|ism
struc|tur|al|ist +s
struc|tur|al|ly

struc|ture
 struc|tures
 struc|tured
 struc|tur|ing
struc|ture|less
stru|del +s
strug|gle
 strug|gles
 strug|gled
 strug|gling
strug|gler +s
strum
 strums
 strummed
 strum|ming
struma
 stru|mae
strum|mer +s
stru|mose
stru|mous
strum|pet +s
strung
strut
 struts
 strut|ted
 strut|ting
struth (use
 strewth)
stru|thi|ous
strut|ter +s
strut|ting|ly
Struve, Otto
 (Russian-born
 American
 astronomer)
Struw|wel|peter
 (fictional
 character)
strych|nic
strych|nine
strych|nin|ism
strych|nism
Stu|art *also*
 Stew|art
 (name)
Stu|art +s (royal
 house of Scotland
 and later England)
Stu|art, Charles
 Ed|ward ('Bonnie
 Prince Charlie',
 'Young Pretender'
 to the British
 throne)
Stu|art, James
 ('Old Pretender' to
 the British throne)
Stu|art, John
 McDou|all
 (Scottish explorer.
 △ Stewart)

stub
  stubs
  stubbed
  stub|bing
stub-axle +s
stub|bily
stub|bi|ness
stub|ble
stub|bled
stub|bly
stub|born
stub|born|ly
stub|born|ness
Stubbs, George
  (English painter)
Stubbs, Wil|liam
  (English historian)
stubby
  stub|bier
  stub|bi|est
stucco
  stuc|coes
  stuc|coed
  stucco|ing
stuck
stuck-up *adjective*
stud
  studs
  stud|ded
  stud|ding
stud-book +s
stud|ding +s
studding-sail +s
stu|dent +s
stu|dent|ship +s
stud farm +s
stud-horse +s
stud|ied|ly
stud|ied|ness
stu|dio +s
stu|di|ous
stu|di|ous|ly
stu|di|ous|ness
stud poker
study
  stud|ies
  stud|ied
  study|ing
study-bedroom +s
stuff +s +ed +ing
stuff|er +s
stuff|ily
stuffi|ness
stuff|ing +s
stuff|ing box
  stuff|ing boxes
stuffy
  stuff|ier
  stuffi|est
stul|ti|fi|ca|tion
stul|ti|fier +s

stul|tify
  stul|ti|fies
  stul|ti|fied
  stul|ti|fy|ing
stum
  stums
  stummed
  stum|ming
stum|ble
  stum|bles
  stum|bled
  stum|bling
stumble|bum +s
stum|bler +s
stum|bling block
  +s
stum|bling|ly
stu|mer +s
stump +s +ed +ing
stump|er +s
stump|ily
stumpi|ness
stumpy
  stump|ier
  stumpi|est
stun
  stuns
  stunned
  stun|ning
stung
stun gun +s
stunk
stun|ner +s
stun|ning|ly
stun|sail +s
stunt +s +ed +ing
stunt|ed|ness
stunt|er +s
stunt|man
  stunt|men
stupa +s (shrine.
  △ stupor)
stupe
  stupes
  stuped
  stup|ing
stu|pe|fa|cient +s
stu|pe|fac|tion
stu|pe|fac|tive
stu|pe|fier +s
stupefy
  stu|pe|fies
  stu|pe|fied
  stu|pe|fy|ing
stu|pe|fy|ing|ly
stu|pen|dous
stu|pen|dous|ly
stu|pen|dous|ness
stu|pid +er +est
stu|pid|ity
  stu|pid|ities
stu|pid|ly

stu|por +s (dazed
  state. △ stupa)
stu|por|ous
stur|died
stur|dily
stur|di|ness
sturdy
  stur|dier
  stur|di|est
stur|geon +s
Sturm|ab|teil|ung
Sturm und Drang
Sturt, Charles
  (English explorer)
stut|ter +s +ed
  +ing
stut|ter|er +s
stut|ter|ing|ly
Stutt|gart (city,
  Germany)
sty
  sties
  stied
  sty|ing
stye +s (use sty)
Sty|gian
style
  styles
  styled
  styl|ing
  (fashion; writing
  implement; part of
  flower. △ stile)
style|less
style|less|ness
styler +s
sty|let +s
styli
styl|isa|tion *Br.*
  (use stylization)
styl|ise *Br.* (use
  stylize)
  styl|ises
  styl|ised
  styl|is|ing
styl|ish
styl|ish|ly
styl|ish|ness
styl|ist +s
styl|is|tic
styl|is|tic|al|ly
styl|is|tics
styl|ite +s
styl|iza|tion
stylize
  styl|izes
  styl|ized
  styl|iz|ing
stylo +s
stylo|bate +s
stylo|graph +s
stylo|graph|ic

styl|oid +s
sty|lus
  styli *or* sty|luses
sty|mie
  sty|mies
  sty|mied
  sty|mie|ing *or*
  sty|mying
styp|tic +s
sty|rax
  sty|raxes
styr|ene
Styria (state,
  Austria)
styro|foam
Styx (river in
  Hades)
Su *also* Sue
  (name)
su|abil|ity
su|able
sua|sion
sua|sive
suave
suave|ly
suave|ness
suav|ity
  suav|ities
sub
  subs
  subbed
  sub|bing
sub|abdom|inal
sub|acid
sub|acid|ity
sub|acute
sub|adult +s
sub|agency
  sub|agen|cies
sub|agent +s
su|bah|dar +s
sub|alpine
sub|al|tern +s
sub|ant|arc|tic
sub-aqua
sub|aqua|tic
sub|aque|ous
sub|arc|tic
sub|astral
sub|atom|ic
sub|audi|tion
sub|axil|lary
sub-basement +s
sub-branch
  sub-branches
sub-breed +s
sub|cat|egor|isa|
  tion *Br.* +s (use
  subcategoriza-
  tion)
sub|cat|egor|ise
  Br. (use

sub|cat|egor|ise
  (cont.)
  subcategorize)
sub|cat|egor|ises
sub|cat|egor|ised
sub|cat|egor|
    is|ing
sub|cat|egor|iza|
    tion +s
sub|cat|egor|ize
sub|cat|egor|izes
sub|cat|egor|ized
sub|cat|egor|
    iz|ing
sub|cat|egory
sub|cat|egor|ies
sub|caudal
sub|class
  sub|classes
sub-clause +s
sub|clavian +s
sub|clin|ical
sub|com|mis|
    sioner +s
sub|com|mit|tee
    +s
sub|con|ic|al
sub|con|scious
sub|con|scious|ly
sub|con|scious|
    ness
sub|con|tin|ent +s
sub|con|tin|en|tal
sub|con|tract +s
    +ed +ing
sub|con|tract|or
    +s
sub|con|trary
  sub|con|trar|ies
sub|cord|ate
sub|cort|ical
sub|cos|tal
sub|cra|nial
sub|crit|ic|al
sub|cul|tural
sub|cul|ture +s
sub|cuta|ne|ous
sub|cuta|ne|ous|ly
sub|cuticu|lar
sub|deacon +s
sub|dean +s
sub|dean|ery
  sub|dean|er|ies
sub|decan|al
sub|deliri|ous
sub|delir|ium
sub|diac|on|ate +s
sub|div|ide
  sub|div|ides

sub|div|ide (cont.)
  sub|div|ided
  sub|div|id|ing
sub|div|ision +s
sub|dom|in|ant +s
sub|du|able
sub|dual +s
sub|duct +s +ed
    +ing
sub|duc|tion
sub|due
  sub|dues
  sub|dued
  sub|du|ing
sub|dural
sub-edit +s +ed
    +ing
sub-editor +s
sub-editor|ial
sub|erect
su|ber|eous
su|ber|ic
su|ber|ose
sub|fam|ily
  sub|fam|ilies
sub|floor +s
sub|form +s
sub-frame +s
sub|fusc
sub|gen|er|ic
sub|genus
  sub|gen|era
sub|gla|cial
sub|group +s
  Mathematics
sub-group +s
  (generally)
sub-head +s
sub-heading +s
sub|human
sub|jacent
sub|ject +s +ed
    +ing
subject-heading
    +s
sub|jec|tion +s
sub|ject|ive +s
sub|ject|ive|ly
sub|ject|ive|ness
sub|ject|iv|ism
sub|ject|iv|ist +s
sub|ject|iv|ity
  sub|ject|iv|ities
sub|ject|less
sub|ject mat|ter
    +s
sub|join +s +ed
    +ing
sub|joint +s
sub ju|dice
sub|jug|able

sub|ju|gate
  sub|ju|gates
  sub|ju|gated
  sub|ju|gat|ing
sub|ju|ga|tion
sub|ju|ga|tor +s
sub|junct|ive +s
sub|junct|ive|ly
sub|king|dom +s
sub|lap|sar|ian +s
sub-lease
  sub-leases
  sub-leased
  sub-leasing
sub-lessee +s
sub-lessor +s
sub-let
  sub-lets
  sub-let
  sub-letting
sub-licence +s
  noun
sub-license
  sub-licenses
  sub-licensed
  sub-licensing
  verb
sub-licensee +s
sub-licensor +s
sub lieu|ten|ant +s
sub|lim|ate
  sub|lim|ates
  sub|lim|ated
  sub|lim|at|ing
sub|lim|ation +s
sub|lime
  sub|limes
  sub|limed
  sub|lim|ing
  sub|limer
  sub|lim|est
sub|lime|ly
Sub|lime Porte,
  the
sub|lim|inal
sub|lim|in|al|ly
sub|lim|ity
  sub|lim|ities
sub|lin|gual
sub|lit|toral
sub|lun|ary
sub|lux|ation +s
sub-machine gun
    +s
sub|man
  sub|men
sub|mar|gin|al
sub|mar|ine +s
sub|mari|ner +s
sub|mas|ter +s
sub|max|il|lary

sub|medi|ant +s
  Music
sub|men|tal
sub|merge
  sub|merges
  sub|merged
  sub|mer|ging
sub|mer|gence
sub|mer|gible
sub|merse
  sub|merses
  sub|mersed
  sub|mers|ing
sub|mers|ible +s
sub|mer|sion +s
sub|micro|scop|ic
sub|mini|ature
sub|mis|sion +s
sub|mis|sive
sub|mis|sive|ly
sub|mis|sive|ness
sub|mit
  sub|mits
  sub|mit|ted
  sub|mit|ting
sub|mit|tal +s
sub|mit|ter +s
sub|mul|tiple +s
sub|nor|mal
sub|nor|mal|ity
sub-nuclear
sub|ocu|lar
sub|opti|mal
sub-orbital
sub|order +s
sub|or|dinal
sub|or|din|ary
  sub|or|din|ar|ies
sub|or|din|ate
  sub|or|din|ates
  sub|or|din|ated
  sub|or|din|at|ing
sub|or|din|ate|ly
sub|or|din|ation
sub|or|dina|tive
sub|orn +s +ed
    +ing
sub|orn|ation +s
sub|orn|er +s
sub|oxide +s
sub-paragraph +s
sub|phy|lum
  sub|phyla
sub-plot +s
sub|poena
  sub|poenas
  sub|poenaed *or*
  sub|poena'd
  sub|poena|ing
sub-postmas|ter
    +s

sub-postmis|tress
sub-
postmis|tresses
sub-post of|fice +s
sub|prior +s
sub|pro|cess
sub|pro|cesses
sub|pro|gram +s
sub|region +s
sub|region|al
sub|rep|tion +s
sub|ro|gate
sub|ro|gates
sub|ro|gated
sub|ro|gat|ing
sub|ro|ga|tion +s
sub rosa
sub|rou|tine +s
sub-Saharan
sub|scribe
sub|scribes
sub|scribed
sub|scrib|ing
sub|scriber +s
sub|script +s
sub|scrip|tion +s
sub|sec|tion +s
sub-sector +s
sub|sel|lium
sub|sel|lia
sub|se|quence +s
(consequence)
sub-sequence +s
(part of larger
sequence)
sub|se|quent
sub|se|quent|ly
sub|serve
sub|serves
sub|served
sub|serv|ing
sub|ser|vi|ence
sub|ser|vi|ency
sub|ser|vi|ent
sub|ser|vi|ent|ly
sub|set +s
sub|shrub +s
sub|side
sub|sides
sub|sided
sub|sid|ing
sub|sid|ence
sub|sidi|ar|ily
sub|sidi|ar|ity
sub|sid|iary
sub|sid|iar|ies
sub|sid|isa|tion Br.
(use
subsidization)
sub|sid|ise Br. (use
subsidize)
sub|sid|ises

sub|sid|ise (cont.)
sub|sid|ised
sub|sid|is|ing
sub|sid|iser Br. +s
(use subsidizer)
sub|sid|iza|tion
sub|sid|ize
sub|sid|izes
sub|sid|ized
sub|sid|iz|ing
sub|sid|izer +s
sub|sidy
sub|sid|ies
sub|sist +s +ed
+ing
sub|sist|ence
sub|sist|ent
sub|soil +s
sub|son|ic
sub|son|ic|al|ly
sub|spe|cies
plural
sub|spe|cies
sub|spe|cif|ic
sub|stance +s
sub-standard
sub|stan|tial
sub|stan|tial|ise
Br. (use
substantialize)
sub|stan|tial|ises
sub|stan|tial|ised
sub|stan|tial|
is|ing
sub|stan|tial|ism
sub|stan|tial|ist +s
sub|stan|ti|al|ity
sub|stan|tial|ize
sub|stan|tial|izes
sub|stan|tial|ized
sub|stan|tial|
iz|ing
sub|stan|tial|ly
sub|stan|ti|ate
sub|stan|ti|ates
sub|stan|ti|ated
sub|stan|ti|at|ing
sub|stan|ti|ation
sub|stan|tival
sub|stan|tiv|al|ly
sub|stan|tive +s
sub|stan|tive|ly
sub-station +s
sub|stitu|ent +s
sub|sti|tut|abil|ity
sub|sti|tut|able
sub|sti|tute
sub|sti|tutes
sub|sti|tuted
sub|sti|tut|ing
sub|sti|tu|tion +s
sub|sti|tu|tion|al

sub|sti|tu|tion|ary
sub|sti|tu|tive
sub|strate +s
sub|stra|tum
sub|strata
sub|struc|tural
sub|struc|ture +s
sub|sum|able
sub|sume
sub|sumes
sub|sumed
sub|sum|ing
sub|sump|tion +s
sub|sur|face +s
sub|sys|tem +s
sub|ten|ancy
sub|ten|an|cies
sub|ten|ant +s
sub|tend +s +ed
+ing
sub|ter|fuge +s
sub|ter|minal
sub|ter|ra|nean +s
sub|ter|ra|ne|
ous|ly
sub|text +s
sub|til|isa|tion Br.
(use subtilization)
sub|til|ise Br. (use
subtilize)
sub|til|ises
sub|til|ised
sub|til|is|ing
sub|til|iza|tion
sub|til|ize
sub|til|izes
sub|til|ized
sub|til|iz|ing
sub|title
sub|titles
sub|titled
sub|titling
sub|tle
sub|tler
sub|tlest
(mysterious; faint;
clever; etc.
△ sutler)
subtle|ness
subtle|ty
subtle|ties
subtly
sub|tonic +s Music
sub|topia +s
sub|topian
sub|total +s
sub|tract +s +ed
+ing
sub|tract|er +s
(person or thing
that subtracts)
sub|trac|tion +s

sub|tract|ive
sub|tract|or +s
Electronics
sub|tra|hend +s
sub|trop|ic|al
sub|trop|ics
sub-type +s
subu|late
sub|unit +s
sub|urb +s
sub|ur|ban
sub|ur|ban|
isa|tion Br. (use
suburbanization)
sub|ur|ban|ise Br.
(use suburbanize)
sub|ur|ban|ises
sub|ur|ban|ised
sub|ur|ban|is|ing
sub|ur|ban|ite +s
sub|ur|ban|
iza|tion
sub|ur|ban|ize
sub|ur|ban|izes
sub|ur|ban|ized
sub|ur|ban|iz|ing
sub|ur|bia
sub|ven|tion +s
sub|ver|sion +s
sub|ver|sive +s
sub|ver|sive|ly
sub|ver|sive|ness
sub|vert +s +ed
+ing
sub|vert|er +s
sub|way +s
sub|woof|er +s
sub-zero
suc|ced|an|eous
suc|ced|an|eum
suc|ced|anea
suc|ceed +s +ed
+ing
suc|ceed|er +s
suc|cen|tor +s
suc|cen|tor|ship
+s
suc|cès de
scan|dale
suc|cess
suc|cesses
suc|cess|ful
suc|cess|ful|ly
suc|cess|ful|ness
suc|ces|sion +s
suc|ces|sion|al
suc|ces|sive
suc|ces|sive|ly
suc|ces|sive|ness
suc|ces|sor +s
suc|cin|ate +s
suc|cinct

suc|cinct|ly
suc|cinct|ness
suc|cin|ic
suc|cor *Am.* +s +ed
  +ing (*Br.* succour.
  help. △ sucker)
suc|cor|less *Am.*
  (*Br.* succourless)
suc|cory
  suc|cor|ies
suc|co|tash
Suc|coth (Jewish
  festival)
suc|cour *Br.* +s
  +ed +ing (*Am.*
  succor. help.
  △ sucker)
suc|cour|less *Br.*
  (*Am.* succorless)
suc|cuba
  suc|cu|bae
suc|cu|bus
  suc|cubi
suc|cu|lence
suc|cu|lent +s
suc|cu|lent|ly
suc|cumb +s +ed
  +ing
suc|cur|sal
suc|cuss
  suc|cusses
  suc|cussed
  suc|cuss|ing
suc|cus|sion +s
such
such|like
Su|chou
  (= Suzhou)
Su|chow
  (= Xuzhou)
suck +s +ed +ing
suck|er +s (person
  or thing that
  sucks; gullible or
  susceptible
  person; attaching-
  device; plant
  shoot. △ succor,
  succour)
suck|ered
sucking-disc +s
sucking-fish
  plural sucking-fish
  or sucking-fishes
suckle
  suckles
  suckled
  suck|ling
suck|ler +s
Suck|ling, John
  (English poet)
suck|ling +s

Sucre (city, Bolivia)
Sucre, An|tonio
  José de
  (president of
  Bolivia)
su|crose
suc|tion
suc|tion pump +s
suc|tor|ial
suc|tor|ian +s
Sudan
Su|dan|ese
  plural Su|dan|ese
su|dar|ium
  su|daria
suda|tor|ium
  suda|toria
suda|tory
  suda|tor|ies
Sud|bury (city,
  Canada)
sudd +s (floating
  vegetation.
  △ suds)
sud|den
sud|den|ly
sud|den|ness
Su|deten|land
  (region, Czech
  Republic)
su|dor|ifer|ous
su|dor|if|ic +s
Sudra +s *Hinduism*
suds
  sudses
  sudsed
  suds|ing
  (lather. △ sudd)
sudsy
  suds|ier
  sudsi|est
Sue *also* Su
  (name)
sue
  sues
  sued
  suing
  (take legal
  proceedings;
  entreat etc. △ sou,
  xu)
suede +s
suer +s (person
  who sues.
  △ sewer)
suet
Sueto|nius (Roman
  biographer)
suety
Suez (port, Egypt)
Suez, Isth|mus of
  (in Egypt)

Suez Canal (in
  Egypt)
suf|fer +s +ed +ing
suf|fer|able
suf|fer|ance
suf|fer|er +s
suf|fer|ing +s
suf|fice
  suf|fices
  suf|ficed
  suf|ficing
suf|fi|ciency
  suf|fi|cien|cies
suf|fi|cient
suf|fi|cient|ly
suf|fix
  suf|fixes
suf|fix|ation
suf|fixed
suf|fo|cate
  suf|fo|cates
  suf|fo|cated
  suf|fo|cat|ing
  suf|fo|cat|ing|ly
suf|fo|ca|tion +s
Suf|folk (county,
  England)
suf|fra|gan +s
suf|fra|gan|ship +s
suf|frage +s
suf|fra|gette +s
suf|fra|gism
suf|fra|gist +s
suf|fuse
  suf|fuses
  suf|fused
  suf|fus|ing
suf|fu|sion +s
Sufi +s
Sufic
Suf|ism
sugar +s +ed +ing
sugar beet
sugar-candy
  sugar-candies
sugar cane +s
sugar-coated
sugar daddy
  sugar dad|dies
sugar-gum +s
  (tree)
sug|ari|ness
sugar|less
Sugar Loaf
  Moun|tain (near
  Rio de Janeiro,
  Brazil)
sugar maple +s
sugar pea +s
sugar|plum +s
sug|ary

sug|gest +s +ed
  +ing
sug|gest|er +s
sug|gest|ibil|ity
sug|gest|ible
sug|ges|tion +s
sug|gest|ive
sug|gest|ive|ly
sug|gest|ive|ness
Sui (Chinese
  dynasty)
sui|cidal
sui|cid|al|ly
sui|cide
  sui|cides
  sui|cided
  sui|cid|ing
sui gen|eris
sui juris
su|il|line
suint
suit +s +ed +ing
suit|abil|ity
suit|able
suit|able|ness
suit|ably
suit|case +s
suit|case|ful +s
suite +s (set of
  things. △ sweet)
suit|er +s (bag.
  △ souter, suitor)
suit|ing +s
suitor +s (wooer;
  plaintiff. △ souter,
  suiter)
suk +s (market; use
  souk. △ sook)
Su|karno,
  Ach|mad
  (Indonesian
  president)
sukh +s (market;
  use souk. △ sook)
Sukho|tai (town,
  Thailand)
suki|yaki +s
Suk|kur (city,
  Pakistan)
Su|lai|man|iya (use
  Sulaymaniyah)
Sula|wesi (island,
  Indonesia)
Su|lay|man|iyah
  in full
  As Su|lay|man|iyah
  (town, Iraq)
sul|cate
sul|cus
  sulci

Su┊lei┊man I (sultan
of Ottoman
empire)
sulfa *Am.* (*Br.*
sulpha. class of
drugs. △ sulfur)
sulfa┊dimi┊dine
Am. (*Br.*
sulphadimidine)
sulfa┊mate *Am.* +s
(*Br.* sulphamate)
sul┊fam┊ic *Am.* (*Br.*
sulphamic)
sulf┊anila┊mide
Am. (*Br.*
sulphanilamide)
sul┊fate *Am.* (*Br.*
sulphate)
sul┊fide *Am.* +s (*Br.*
sulp`ide)
sul┊fite *Am.* +s (*Br.*
sulphite)
sul┊fona┊mide *Am.*
+s (*Br.*
sulphonamide)
sul┊fon┊ate *Am.*
sul┊fon┊ates
sul┊fon┊ated
sul┊fon┊at┊ing
(*Br.* sulphonate)
sul┊fon┊ation *Am.*
(*Br.*
sulphonation)
sul┊fone *Am.* +s
(*Br.* sulphone)
sul┊fon┊ic *Am.* (*Br.*
sulphonic)
sul┊fur *Am.* +s +ed
+ing (*Br.* sulphur.
chemical element.
△ sulfa)
sul┊fur┊ate *Am.*
sul┊fur┊ates
sul┊fur┊ated
sul┊fur┊at┊ing
(*Br.* sulphurate)
sul┊fur┊ation *Am.*
(*Br.* sulphuration)
sul┊fur┊ator *Am.* +s
(*Br.* sulphurator)
sul┊fur┊eous *Am.*
(*Br.* sulphureous)
sul┊fur┊et┊ed *Am.*
(*Br.* sulphuretted)
sul┊fur┊ic *Am.* (*Br.*
sulphuric)
sul┊fur┊iza┊tion
Am. (*Br.*
sulphurization)
sul┊fur┊ize *Am.*
sul┊fur┊izes
sul┊fur┊ized

sul┊fur┊ize (*cont.*)
sul┊fur┊iz┊ing
(*Br.* sulphurize)
sul┊fur┊ous *Am.* (*Br.*
sulphurous)
sul┊fury *Am.* (*Br.*
sulphury)
sulk +s +ed +ing
sulk┊er +s
sulk┊ily
sulki┊ness
sulky
sulk┊ier
sulki┊est
Sulla (Roman
general)
sul┊lage
sul┊len
sul┊len┊ly
sul┊len┊ness
Sulli┊van, Ar┊thur
(English
composer)
sully
sul┊lies
sul┊lied
sully┊ing
sulpha *Br.* +s (*Am.*
sulfa. class of
drugs. △ sulphur)
sulpha┊dimi┊dine
Br. (*Am.*
sulfadimidine)
sulpha┊mate *Br.* +s
(*Am.* sulfamate)
sul┊pham┊ic *Br.*
(*Am.* sulfamic)
sulph┊anila┊mide
Br. (*Am.*
sulfanilamide)
sul┊phate *Br.* +s
(*Am.* sulfate)
sul┊phide *Br.* +s
(*Am.* sulfide)
sul┊phite *Br.* +s
(*Am.* sulfite)
sul┊phona┊mide *Br.*
+s (*Am.*
sulfonamide)
sul┊phon┊ate *Br.*
sul┊phon┊ates
sul┊phon┊ated
sul┊phon┊at┊ing
(*Am.* sulfonate)
sul┊phon┊ation *Br.*
(*Am.* sulfonation)
sul┊phone *Br.* +s
(*Am.* sulfone)
sul┊phon┊ic *Br.*
(*Am.* sulfonic)
sul┊phur *Br.* +s
+ed +ing (*Am.*

sul┊phur (*cont.*)
sulfur. chemical
element.
△ sulpha)
sul┊phur┊ate *Br.*
sul┊phur┊ates
sul┊phur┊ated
sul┊phur┊at┊ing
(*Am.* sulfurate)
sul┊phur┊ation *Br.*
(*Am.* sulfuration)
sul┊phur┊ator *Br.*
+s (*Am.*
sulfurator)
sul┊phur┊eous *Br.*
(*Am.* sulfureous)
sul┊phur┊et┊ted *Br.*
(*Am.* sulfureted)
sul┊phur┊ic *Br.* (*Am.*
sulfuric)
sul┊phur┊isa┊tion
Br. (use
sulphurization)
sul┊phur┊ise *Br.*
(use sulphurize)
sul┊phur┊ises
sul┊phur┊ised
sul┊phur┊is┊ing
sul┊phur┊iza┊tion
Br. (use
sulphurization)
sul┊phur┊ize
sul┊phur┊izes
sul┊phur┊ized
sul┊phur┊iz┊ing
sul┊phur┊ous *Br.*
(*Am.* sulfurous)
sul┊phury *Br.* (*Am.*
sulfury)
sul┊tan +s
sul┊tana +s
sul┊tan┊ate +s
sul┊trily
sul┊tri┊ness
sul┊try
sul┊trier
sul┊tri┊est
Sulu Sea (in SE
Asia)
sum
sums
summed
sum┊ming
(total; arithmetical
problem. △ some)
sumac +s
su┊mach +s (use
sumac)
Su┊ma┊tra (island,
Indonesia)
Su┊ma┊tran +s
Sumba (island,
Indonesia)

Sum┊bawa (island,
Indonesia)
Sum┊burgh
(weather station
off Shetland
Islands)
Sum┊burgh Head
(Shetland Islands)
Sumer (ancient
region, Iraq)
Su┊mer┊ian +s
Sum┊gait (Russian
name for
Sumqayit)
summa
sum┊mae
summa cum laude
sum┊mar┊ily
sum┊mari┊ness
sum┊mar┊is┊able
Br. (use
summarizable)
sum┊mar┊isa┊tion
Br. (use
summarization)
sum┊mar┊ise *Br.*
(use summarize)
sum┊mar┊ises
sum┊mar┊ised
sum┊mar┊is┊ing
sum┊mar┊iser *Br.*
+s (use
summarizer)
sum┊mar┊ist +s
sum┊mar┊iz┊able
sum┊mar┊iza┊tion
sum┊mar┊ize
sum┊mar┊izes
sum┊mar┊ized
sum┊mar┊iz┊ing
sum┊mar┊izer +s
sum┊mary
sum┊mar┊ies
(brief account;
without
formalities.
△ summery)
sum┊ma┊tion +s
sum┊ma┊tion┊al
sum┊mer +s +ed
+ing
sum┊mer house +s
sum┊mer┊less
sum┊mer┊ly
sum┊mer┊sault +s
+ed +ing (use
somersault)
sum┊mer┊time
(period of
summer)
sum┊mer time
(time advanced

sum|mer time
(*cont.*)
during summer;
but **British
Summer Time**)
summer-weight
adjective
sum|mery
(characteristic of
summer.
△ summary)
summing-up
summings-up
noun
sum|mit +s
sum|mit|eer +s
sum|mit|less
sum|mit|ry
sum|mon +s +ed
+ing
sum|mon|able
sum|mon|er +s
sum|mons
summonses
summoned
summonsing
sum|mum bonum
sumo +s
sump +s
sump|ter +s
sump|tu|ary
sump|tu|os|ity
sump|tu|ous
sump|tu|ous|ly
sump|tu|ous|ness
Sum|qa|yit (city,
Azerbaijan)
Sumy (city,
Ukraine)
sun
suns
sunned
sun|ning
(star. △ son,
sunn)
sun-baked
sun-bath +s
sun|bathe
sun|bathes
sun|bathed
sun|bath|ing
sun|bather +s
sun|beam +s
sun|bed +s
sun|belt +s
sun|bird +s
sun|blind +s
sun|block +s
sun-bonnet +s
sun|bow +s
sun-bronzed

sun|burn
sun|burns
sun|burnt *or*
sun|burned
sun|burn|ing
sun|burst +s
Sun City (resort,
South Africa)
sun cream +s
sun|dae +s (ice-
cream dish.
△ Sunday)
Sunda Is|lands (in
Malay
Archipelago)
sun-dance +s
Sun|dan|ese
plural Sun|dan|ese
Sun|dar|bans
(swamp,
Bangladesh)
Sun|day +s (day of
the week.
△ sundae)
sun deck +s
sun|der +s +ed
+ing
Sun|der|land (city,
England)
sun|dew +s
sun|dial +s
sun-disc +s
sun-dog +s
sun|down +s
sun|down|er +s
sun|dress
sun|dresses
sun-dried
sun|dries|man
sun|dries|men
sun|dry
sun|dries
sun|fast
sun|fish
plural sun|fish *or*
sun|fishes
sun|flower +s
Sung (Chinese
dynasty)
sung (past
participle of *sing*)
sun|glasses
sun-god +s
sun|hat +s
sun-helmet +s
sunk
sunk|en
sun-kissed
sun|lamp +s
sun|less
sun|less|ness
sun|light

sun|like
sun|lit
sun|loun|ger +s
sun-lover +s
sunn (fibre. △ son,
sun)
Sunna (Islamic
customs and
practices)
Sunni
plural Sunni *or*
Sun|nis
(branch of Islam)
sun|nily
sun|ni|ness
Sun|nite +s
sunny
sun|nier
sun|ni|est
(bright with
sunlight. △ sonny)
sun|proof
sun|ray +s
sun|rise
sun|roof +s
sun|room +s
sun|screen +s
sun|set +s
sun|shade +s
sun|shine
sun|shiny
sun|spot +s
sun|star +s
sun|stone +s
sun|stroke
sun|suit +s
sun|tan
sun|tans
sun|tanned
sun|tan|ning
sun|trap +s
sunup
sun|ward
sun|wards
Sun Yat-sen
(Chinese
statesman)
sup
sups
supped
sup|ping
Supa|driv
(screwdriver)
Propr.
super +s
super|able
super|abound +s
+ed +ing
super|abun|dance
super|abun|dant
super|
abun|dant|ly

super|add +s +ed
+ing
super|add|ition +s
super|altar +s
super|annu|able
super|annu|ate
super|annu|ates
super|annu|ated
super|annu|at|ing
super|annu|ated
super|annu|ation
super|aqueous
su|perb
su|perb|ly
su|perb|ness
Super Bowl +s
Propr.
super|cal|en|der
+s +ed +ing
super|cargo
super|car|goes
super|cede (use
supersede)
super|cedes
super|ceded
super|ced|ing
super|celes|tial
super|charge
super|charges
super|charged
super|char|ging
super|char|ger +s
super|cil|iary
super|cili|ous
super|cili|ous|ly
super|cili|ous|ness
super|class
super|classes
super|co|lum|nar
super|co|lum|ni|
ation
super|com|puter
+s
super|com|put|ing
super|con|duct|ing
super|con|duct|ive
super|con|duct|
iv|ity
super|con|duct|or
+s
super|con|scious
super|
con|scious|ly
super|con|scious|
ness
super|con|tin|ent
+s
super|cool
super|crit|ical
super-duper
super|ego +s

super|eleva|tion
+s
super|emi|nence
+s
super|emi|nent
super|emi|nent|ly
super|eroga|tion
super|eroga|tory
super|ex|cel|lence
super|ex|cel|lent
super|
    ex|cel|lent|ly
super|fam|ily
 super|fam|ilies
super|fat|ted
super|fec|und|
    ation +s
super|feta|tion +s
super|fi|cial
super|fici|al|ity
 super|fici|al|ities
super|fi|cial|ly
super|fi|cial|ness
super|fi|cies
 plural super|fi|cies
super|fine
super|fluid +s
super|flu|id|ity
super|flu|ity
 super|flu|ities
su|per|flu|ous
su|per|flu|ous|ly
su|per|flu|ous|ness
super|giant +s
super|glue
 super|glues
 super|glued
 super|glu|ing *or*
 super|glue|ing
super|grass
 super|grasses
super|gun +s
super|heat +s +ed
 +ing
super|heat|er +s
super|hero
 super|heroes
super|het +s
super|het|ero|
    dyne +s
super|high|way +s
super|human +s
super|human|ly
super|humeral +s
super|im|pose
 super|im|poses
 super|im|posed
 super|im|pos|ing
super|im|pos|ition
 +s
super|in|cum|bent

super|in|duce
 super|in|duces
 super|in|duced
 super|in|du|cing
super|in|tend +s
 +ed +ing
super|in|tend|ence
super|in|tend|ency
super|in|tend|ent
 +s
Su|per|ior, Lake
 (in N. America)
su|per|ior +s
su|per|ior|ess
 su|per|ior|esses
su|per|ior|ity
 su|per|ior|ities
su|per|ior|ly
super|jacent
su|per|la|tive +s
su|per|la|tive|ly
su|per|la|tive|ness
super|lumi|nal
super|lun|ary
Super|man
 (American cartoon
 character)
super|man
 super|men
 (man of
 exceptional
 strength or ability)
super|mar|ket +s
super|mini +s
super|model +s
super|mun|dane
super|nacu|lar
super|nacu|lum
su|per|nal
su|per|nal|ly
super|natant +s
super|nat|ural
super|nat|ur|al|ise
 Br. (use
 supernaturalize)
super|nat|ur|al|
    ises
super|nat|ur|al|
    ised
super|nat|ur|al|
    is|ing
super|nat|ur|al|
    ism
super|nat|ur|al|ist
 +s
super|nat|ur|al|ize
 super|nat|ur|al|
    izes
 super|nat|ur|al|
    ized
 super|nat|ur|al|
    iz|ing

super|nat|ur|al|ly
super|nat|ur|al|
    ness
super|nor|mal
super|nor|mal|ity
super|nova
 super|novae
super|numer|ary
 super|numer|
    ar|ies
super|order +s
super|ordinal
super|ordin|ate +s
super|phos|phate
 +s
super|phys|ic|al
super|pose
 super|poses
 super|posed
 super|pos|ing
super|pos|ition +s
super|power +s
super|sat|ur|ate
 super|sat|ur|ates
 super|sat|ur|ated
 super|sat|ur|
    at|ing
super|sat|ur|ation
super|scribe
 super|scribes
 super|scribed
 super|scrib|ing
super|script +s
super|scrip|tion +s
super|sede
 super|sedes
 super|seded
 super|sed|ing
super|sedence
super|sedure
super|ses|sion
super|sonic
super|son|ic|al|ly
super|son|ics
super|star +s
super|star|dom
super|state +s
super|sti|tion +s
super|sti|tious
super|sti|tious|ly
super|sti|tious|
    ness
super|store +s
super|stra|tum
 super|strata
super|string +s
super|struc|tural
super|struc|ture
 +s
super|subtle
super|subtle|ty
 super|subtle|ties

super|sym|met|ric
super|sym|metry
super|tank|er +s
super|tax
 super|taxes
super|tem|poral
super|ter|rene
super|ter|res|trial
super|title +s
super|tonic +s
super|vene
 super|venes
 super|vened
 super|ven|ing
super|ven|ient
super|ven|tion +s
super|vise
 super|vises
 super|vised
 super|vis|ing
super|vi|sion
super|visor +s
super|vis|ory
super|woman
 super|women
su|pin|ate
 su|pin|ates
 su|pin|ated
 su|pin|at|ing
su|pin|ation
su|pin|ator +s
su|pine
su|pine|ly
su|pine|ness
sup|per +s
sup|per|less
sup|per|time +s
sup|plant +s +ed
 +ing
sup|plant|er +s
sup|ple
 sup|ples
 sup|pled
 sup|pling
 sup|pler
 sup|plest
supple|jack +s
sup|ple|ly (use
 supply)
sup|ple|ment +s
 +ed +ing
sup|ple|men|tal
sup|ple|men|tal|ly
sup|ple|men|
    tar|ily
sup|ple|men|tary
sup|ple|men|
    tar|ies
sup|ple|men|
    ta|tion
supple|ness
sup|ple|tion +s
sup|ple|tive

sup|pli|ant +s
sup|pli'ant|ly
sup|pli|cant +s
sup|pli|cate
  sup|pli|cates
  sup|pli|cated
  sup|pli|cat|ing
sup|pli|ca|tion +s
sup|pli|ca|tory
sup|plier +s
sup|ply
  sup|plies
  sup|plied
  sup|ply|ing
supply-side
sup|port +s +ed
  +ing
sup|port|abil|ity
sup|port|able
sup|port|ably
sup|port|er +s
sup|port|ing|ly
sup|port|ive
sup|port|ive|ly
sup|port|ive|ness
sup|port|less
sup|pos|able
sup|pose
  sup|poses
  sup|posed
  sup|pos|ing
sup|posed|ly
sup|pos|ition +s
sup|pos|ition|al
sup|pos|itious
sup|pos|itious|ly
sup|pos|itious|
    ness
sup|posi|ti|tious
sup|posi|ti|tious|ly
sup|posi|ti|tious|
    ness
sup|posi|tory
  sup|posi|tor|ies
sup|press
  sup|presses
  sup|pressed
  sup|press|ing
sup|pres|sant +s
sup|press|ible
sup|pres|sion +s
sup|pres|sive
sup|pres|sor +s
sup|pur|ate
  sup|pur|ates
  sup|pur|ated
  sup|pur|at|ing
sup|pur|ation +s
sup|pura|tive
supra
supra|lap|sar|ian
  +s

supra|max|il|lary
supra|mund|ane
supra|nation|al
supra|nation|al|
    ism
supra|nation|al|ity
supra|orbit|al
supra|renal
supra|seg|men|tal
su|prema|cism
su|prema|cist +s
su|prem|acy
  su|prem|acies
su|prema|tism
su|preme +s
su|prême +s
  Cookery
su|preme|ly
su|preme|ness
Su|premes, the
  (American pop
  group)
su|premo +s
suq +s (market; use
  souk. △ sook)
sura +s (section of
  Koran. △ surah)
Sura|baya (port,
  Indonesia)
surah +s (fabric.
  △ sura)
sural
Surat (port, India)
sur|cease
  sur|ceases
  sur|ceased
  sur|ceas|ing
sur|charge
  sur|charges
  sur|charged
  sur|char|ging
sur|cin|gle +s
sur|coat +s
surd +s
sure
  surer
  sur|est
  (certain. △ shaw,
  shore)
sure-fire
sure-footed
sure-footed|ly
sure-footed|ness
sure|ly (with
  certainty.
  △ shawlie)
sure|ness
surety
  sure|ties
surety|ship

surf +s +ed +ing
  (breaking waves;
  go surfing. △ serf)
sur|face
  sur|faces
  sur|faced
  sur|facing
surface-active
sur|facer +s
surface-to-air
  (missile)
surface-to-surface
  (missile)
sur|fac|tant +s
surf|bird +s
surf|board +s
surf-casting
sur|feit +s +ed
  +ing
surf|er +s
sur|fi|cial
sur|fi|cial|ly
surfie +s (surfer.
  △ surfy)
surf-riding
surfy
  surf|ier
  surfi|est
  (having much surf.
  △ surfie)
surge
  surges
  surged
  sur|ging
  (swell; increase.
  △ serge)
sur|geon +s
sur|geon gen|eral
  sur|geons
  gen|eral
sur|gery
  sur|ger|ies
sur|gi|cal
sur|gi|cal|ly
suri|cate +s
Suri|nam (use
  Suriname)
Suri|name (in S.
  America)
Suri|nam|er +s
Suri|nam|ese
  plural
  Suri|nam|ese
sur|lily
sur|li|ness
surly
  sur|lier
  sur|li|est
sur|mise
  sur|mises
  sur|mised
  sur|mis|ing

sur|mount +s +ed
  +ing
sur|mount|able
sur|mul|let
  plural sur|mul|let
  or sur|mul|lets
sur|name
  sur|names
  sur|named
  sur|nam|ing
sur|pass
  sur|passes
  sur|passed
  sur|pass|ing
sur|pass|ing|ly
sur|plice +s
  (vestment)
sur|pliced
sur|plus
  sur|pluses
  (amount left over)
sur|plus|age +s
sur|prise
  sur|prises
  sur|prised
  sur|pris|ing
sur|prised|ly
sur|pris|ing|ly
sur|pris|ing|ness
surra
sur|real
sur|real|ism
sur|real|ist +s
sur|real|is|tic
sur|real|is|tic|al|ly
sur|real|ity
sur|real|ly
sur|rebut|ter +s
sur|rejoin|der +s
sur|ren|der +s +ed
  +ing
sur|rep|ti|tious
sur|rep|ti|tious|ly
sur|rep|ti|tious|
    ness
Sur|rey (county,
  England)
sur|rey +s
  (carriage)
sur|ro|gacy
sur|ro|gate +s
sur|ro|gate|ship +s
sur|round +s +ed
  +ing
sur|round|ings
sur|tax
  sur|taxes
Sur|tees, Rob|ert
  Smith (English
  writer)
sur|title +s
sur|tout +s

Surt|sey (island off Iceland)
sur|veil|lance
sur|vey +s +ed +ing
sur|vey|or +s
sur|vey|or|ship +s
sur|viv|abil|ity
sur|viv|able
sur|vival +s
sur|viv|al|ism
sur|viv|al|ist +s
sur|vive
  sur|vives
  sur|vived
  sur|viv|ing
sur|vivor +s
Surya *Hinduism*
sus (use **suss**)
  susses
  sussed
  suss|ing
Susa (ancient city, SW Asia; alternative name for Sousse)
Susah (alternative name for Sousse)
Susan
Su|sanna *also* **Su|san|nah, Su|zanna**
Su|sanna *Apocrypha*
Su|san|nah *also* **Su|sanna, Su|zanna**
Su|sanne *also* **Su|zanne**
sus|cep|ti|bil|ity
  sus|cep|ti|bil|ities
sus|cep|tible
sus|cep|tibly
sus|cep|tive
sushi
Susie *also* **Suzie, Suzy**
sus|lik +s (use **souslik**)
sus|pect +s +ed +ing
sus|pend +s +ed +ing
sus|pend|er +s
sus|pense
sus|pense|ful
sus|pen|sible
sus|pen|sion +s
sus|pen|sive
sus|pen|sive|ly
sus|pen|sive|ness
sus|pen|sory

sus|pi|cion +s
sus|pi|cious
sus|pi|cious|ly
sus|pi|cious|ness
sus|pir|ation +s
sus|pire
  sus|pires
  sus|pired
  sus|pir|ing
Sus|que|hanna (river, USA)
suss
  susses
  sussed
  suss|ing
Sus|sex, East and **West** (counties, England)
sus|tain +s +ed +ing
sus|tain|abil|ity
sus|tain|able
sus|tain|ably
sus|tain|ed|ly
sus|tain|er +s
sus|tain|ment +s
sus|ten|ance
sus|ten|ta|tion
su|sur|ra|tion +s
su|sur|rus
Suth|er|land, Gra|ham (English painter)
Suth|er|land, Joan (Australian soprano)
Sut|lej (river, S. Asia)
sut|ler +s (army provisioner. △ subtler)
Sutra +s
sut|tee +s
Sut|ton Cold|field (town, England)
Sut|ton Hoo (archaeological site, England)
su|tural
su|ture
  su|tures
  su|tured
  su|tur|ing
Suva (capital of Fiji)
Su|wan|nee (river, USA. △ Swanee)
Su|zanna *also* **Su|sanna, Su|san|nah**
Su|zanne *also* **Su|sanne**

su|zer|ain +s
su|zer|ainty
Su|zette (in 'crêpe Suzette')
Su|zhou (city, China)
Suzie *also* **Susie, Suzy**
Suz|man, Helen (South African politician)
Sval|bard (island group, Arctic Ocean)
svelte
Sven (= Sweyn)
Sven|gali +s
Sverd|lovsk (former name of Yekaterinburg)
Svet|am|bara +s
swab
  swabs
  swabbed
  swab|bing
Swabia (former German duchy)
Swab|ian +s
swad|dle
  swad|dles
  swad|dled
  swad|dling
swaddling-clothes
swaddy
  swad|dies
swag
  swags
  swagged
  swag|ging
swage
  swages
  swaged
  swa|ging
swage-block +s
swag|ger +s +ed +ing
swag|ger|er +s
swag|ger|ing|ly
swag|gie +s
swag|man
  swag|men
Swa|hili
  plural **Swa|hili**
swain +s
swal|low +s +ed +ing
swal|low|able
swallow-dive
  swallow-dives
  swallow-dived
  swallow-diving
swal|low|er +s

swallow-hole +s
swal|low|tail +s
swallow-tailed
swam
swami +s
Swam|mer|dam, Jan (Dutch naturalist)
swamp +s +ed +ing
swamp|land +s
swampy
  swamp|ier
  swampi|est
Swan, Jo|seph Wil|son (English scientist)
swan
  swans
  swanned
  swan|ning
swan-dive +s
Swanee (in 'down the Swanee'. △ Suwannee)
swank +s +ed +ing
swank|ily
swanki|ness
swank|pot +s
swanky
  swank|ier
  swanki|est
swan|like
swan-neck +s
swan|nery
  swan|ner|ies
swans|down
Swan|sea (city, Wales)
Swan|son, Gloria (American actress)
swan|song +s
swan-upping
swap
  swaps
  swapped
  swap|ping
Swapo (= South West Africa People's Organization)
swap|per +s
Swa|raj
Swa|raj|ist +s
sward +s
sward|ed
sware (*archaic* = swore)
swarf

swarm +s +ed
 +ing
swart
swar|thily
swar|thi|ness
swar|thy
 swar|thier
 swar|thi|est
swash
 swashes
 swashed
 swash|ing
swash|buck|ler +s
swash|buck|ling
swash-plate +s
swas|tika +s
swat
 swats
 swat|ted
 swat|ting
 (hit sharply.
 △ swot)
swatch
 swatches
swath +s
swathe
 swathes
 swathed
 swath|ing
Swa|tow (former
 name of Shantou)
swat|ter +s
sway +s +ed +ing
sway-back +s
sway-backed
Swazi
 plural Swazi *or*
 Swa|zis
Swa|zi|land
swear
 swears
 swore
 swear|ing
 sworn
swear|er +s
swear word +s
sweat +s +ed +ing
sweat|band +s
sweat|er +s
sweat|ily
sweati|ness
sweating-sickness
sweat|pants
sweat|shirt +s
sweat|shop +s
sweat|suit +s
sweaty
 sweat|ier
 sweati|est
Swede +s (Swedish
 person)
swede +s (turnip)

Swe|den
**Swe|den|borg,
 Eman|uel**
 (Swedish scientist)
Swed|ish
Swee|ney, the
 (flying squad)
sweep
 sweeps
 swept
 sweep|ing
sweep|back +s
sweep|er +s
sweep|ing +s
sweep|ing|ly
sweep|ing|ness
sweep|stake +s
sweet +s +er +est
 (confectionery;
 not bitter. △ suite)
sweet and sour
sweet|bread +s
sweet-brier +s
sweet|corn
sweet|en +s +ed
 +ing
sweet|en|er +s
sweet|en|ing +s
sweet gale
sweet|heart +s
sweetie +s
sweetie-pie +s
sweet|ing +s
sweet|ish
sweet|ly
sweet|meal +s
sweet|meat +s
sweet|ness
sweet|shop +s
sweet-smelling
sweet|sop +s
sweet-talk
 sweet-talks
 sweet-talked
 sweet-talking
sweet-tempered
swell
 swells
 swelled
 swell|ing
 swol|len
swell-box
 swell-boxes
swell|ing +s
swell|ish
swell-organ +s
swel|ter +s +ed
 +ing
swel|ter|ing|ly
swept
swept-back
 adjective

swept-up *adjective*
swept-wing
 adjective
swerve
 swerves
 swerved
 swerv|ing
swerve|less
swerver +s
Sweyn (Danish
 king)
Swift, Jona|than
 (Irish writer)
swift +s +er +est
swiftie +s
swift|let +s
swift|ly
swift|ness
swig
 swigs
 swigged
 swig|ging
swig|ger +s
swill +s +ed +ing
swill|er +s
swim
 swims
 swam
 swim|ming
 swum
swim-bladder +s
swim|mable
swim|mer +s
swim|meret +s
swim|ming bath
 +s
**swim|ming
 cos|tume** +s
swim|ming|ly
swim|ming pool
 +s
swim|ming trunks
swim|suit +s
swim|suit|ed
swim|wear
**Swin|burne,
 Alger|non
 Charles** (English
 poet)
swin|dle
 swin|dles
 swin|dled
 swind|ling
swind|ler +s
Swin|don (town,
 England)
swine
 plural swine
swine|herd +s
swin|ery
 swin|eries

swing
 swings
 swung
 swing|ing
swing|bin +s
swing|boat +s
swing-bridge +s
swing-door +s
swinge
 swinges
 swinged
 swinge|ing
swinge|ing|ly
swing|er +s
swing|ing|ly
swin|gle
 swin|gles
 swin|gled
 swin|gling
swingle|tree +s
swing|om|eter +s
swing-wing +s
swingy
 swing|ier
 swingi|est
swin|ish
swin|ish|ly
swin|ish|ness
swipe
 swipes
 swiped
 swip|ing
swiper +s
swip|ple +s
swirl +s +ed +ing
swirly
 swirl|ier
 swirli|est
swish
 swishes
 swished
 swish|ing
swishy
 swish|ier
 swishi|est
Swiss
 plural Swiss
switch
 switches
 switched
 switch|ing
switch|able
switch|back +s
switch|blade +s
switch|board +s
switched-on
 adjective
switch|er +s
switch|gear
switch-over +s
 noun

swither +s +ed
+ing
Swithin (English
saint)
Swithun (use
Swithin)
Switz¦er¦land
swivel
swivels
swiv¦elled Br.
swiv¦eled Am.
swiv¦el¦ling Br.
swiv¦el¦ling Am.
swivet
swiz (use swizz)
swizzes
swizz
swizzes
swiz¦zle
swiz¦zles
swiz¦zled
swiz¦zling
swizzle-stick +s
swob (use swab)
swobs
swobbed
swob¦bing
swol¦len
swoon +s +ed
+ing
swoop +s +ed
+ing
swoosh
swooshes
swooshed
swoosh¦ing
swop (use swap)
swops
swopped
swop¦ping
sword +s
sword-bearer +s
sword¦bill +s
sword¦fish
plural sword¦fish
or sword¦fishes
sword¦like
sword¦play
swords¦man
swords¦men
swords¦man¦ship
sword¦stick +s
sword-swallow¦er
+s
sword¦tail +s
swore
sworn
swot
swots
swot¦ted
swot¦ting

swot (cont.)
(study hard.
△ swat)
swum
swung
swy +s
syb¦ar¦ite +s
syb¦ar¦it¦ic
syb¦ar¦it¦ic¦al
syb¦ar¦it¦ic¦al¦ly
syb¦ar¦it¦ism
Sybil also Sibyl
(name. △ sibyl)
syca¦mine +s
syca¦more +s
syce +s (groom.
△ sice)
syco¦more +s (use
sycamore)
sy¦co¦nium
sy¦co¦nia
syco¦phancy
syco¦phant +s
syco¦phan¦tic
syco¦phan¦tic¦al¦ly
sy¦cosis
sy¦coses
(skin disease.
△ psychosis)
Syd¦en¦ham,
Thomas (English
physician)
Syd¦en¦ham's
cho¦rea
Syd¦ney (city,
Australia)
Syd¦ney also
Sid¦ney
(name)
sy¦en¦ite +s
sy¦en¦it¦ic
Syk¦tyv¦kar (city,
Russia)
syl¦lab¦ary
syl¦lab¦ar¦ies
syl¦labi
syl¦lab¦ic
syl¦lab¦ic¦al¦ly
syl¦labi¦ca¦tion
syl¦lab¦icity
syl¦labi¦fi¦ca¦tion
syl¦lab¦ify
syl¦labi¦fies
syl¦labi¦fied
syl¦labi¦fy¦ing
syl¦lab¦ise Br. (use
syllabize)
syl¦lab¦ises
syl¦lab¦ised
syl¦lab¦is¦ing
syl¦lab¦ize
syl¦lab¦izes

syl¦lab¦ize (cont.)
syl¦lab¦ized
syl¦lab¦iz¦ing
syl¦lable
syl¦lables
syl¦labled
syl¦lab¦ling
syl¦la¦bub +s
syl¦la¦bus
syl¦la¦buses or
syl¦labi
syl¦lep¦sis
syl¦lep¦ses
syl¦lep¦tic
syl¦lep¦tic¦al¦ly
syl¦lo¦gise Br. (use
syllogize)
syl¦lo¦gises
syl¦lo¦gised
syl¦lo¦gis¦ing
syl¦lo¦gism +s
syl¦lo¦gis¦tic
syl¦lo¦gis¦tic¦al¦ly
syl¦lo¦gize
syl¦lo¦gizes
syl¦lo¦gized
syl¦lo¦giz¦ing
sylph +s
sylph¦like
sylva
syl¦vas or syl¦vae
(trees of a region
etc.; list of such
trees. △ silver)
syl¦van (of woods;
wooded.
△ silvern)
Syl¦via
syl¦vi¦cul¦ture (use
silviculture)
Syl¦vie
sym¦biont +s
sym¦bi¦osis
sym¦bi¦oses
sym¦bi¦ot¦ic
sym¦bi¦ot¦ic¦al¦ly
sym¦bol
sym¦bols
sym¦bolled Br.
sym¦boled Am.
sym¦bol¦ling Br.
sym¦bol¦ling Am.
(sign. △ cymbal)
sym¦bol¦ic
sym¦bol¦ic¦al
sym¦bol¦ic¦al¦ly
sym¦bol¦ics
sym¦bol¦isa¦tion
Br. (use
symbolization)
sym¦bol¦ise Br.
(use symbolize)

sym¦bol¦ise (cont.)
sym¦bol¦ises
sym¦bol¦ised
sym¦bol¦is¦ing
sym¦bol¦ism +s
sym¦bol¦ist +s
(adherent of
symbolism etc.
△ cymbalist)
sym¦bol¦is¦tic
sym¦bol¦iza¦tion
sym¦bol¦ize
sym¦bol¦izes
sym¦bol¦ized
sym¦bol¦iz¦ing
sym¦bol¦ogy
sym¦bol¦ology
sym¦met¦ric
sym¦met¦ric¦al
sym¦met¦ric¦al¦ly
sym¦met¦rise Br.
(use symmetrize)
sym¦met¦rises
sym¦met¦rised
sym¦met¦ris¦ing
sym¦met¦rize
sym¦met¦rizes
sym¦met¦rized
sym¦met¦riz¦ing
sym¦met¦ro¦
pho¦bia
sym¦metry
sym¦met¦ries
Sy¦mons, Ju¦lian
(English writer)
sym¦path¦ec¦tomy
sym¦path¦
ec¦to¦mies
sym¦pa¦thet¦ic
sym¦pa¦thet¦ic¦
al¦ly
sym¦pa¦thise Br.
(use sympathize)
sym¦pa¦thises
sym¦pa¦thised
sym¦pa¦this¦ing
sym¦pa¦thiser Br.
+s (use
sympathizer)
sym¦pa¦thize
sym¦pa¦thizes
sym¦pa¦thized
sym¦pa¦thiz¦ing
sym¦pa¦thizer +s
sym¦pathy
sym¦pa¦thies
sym¦pat¦ric
sym¦pet¦al¦ous
sym¦phon¦ic
sym¦phon¦ic¦al¦ly
sym¦pho¦ni¦ous
sym¦phon¦ist +s

sym|phony
  sym|phon|ies
sym|phyl|lous
sym|phys|eal
sym|phys|ial
sym|phy|sis
  sym|phy|ses
sym|po|dial
sym|po|di|al|ly
sym|po|dium
  sym|po|dia
sym|po|siac+s
sym|po|sial
sym|po|si|arch+s
sym|po|si|ast+s
sym|po|sium
  sym|po|sia or
  sym|po|siums
symp|tom+s
symp|tom|at|ic
symp|tom|at|ic|
      al|ly
symp|tom|
    atol|ogy
symp|tom|less
syn|aer|esis
  syn|aer|eses
syn|aes|the|sia Br.
  (Am. synesthesia)
syn|aes|thet|ic Br.
  (Am. synesthetic)
syna|gogal
syna|gogic|al
syna|gogue+s
syn|al|lag|mat|ic
syn|an|ther|ous
syn|an|thous
syn|apse+s
syn|ap|sis
  synap|ses
syn|ap|tic
syn|ap|tic|al|ly
syn|arth|rosis
  syn|arth|roses
sync+s+ed+ing
  (= synchronize;
  synchronization)
syn|carp+s
syn|carp|ous
synch+s+ed+ing
  (use sync)
syn|chon|drosis
  syn|chon|droses
syn|chro|cyclo|
      tron+s
syn|chro|mesh
  syn|chro|meshes
syn|chron|ic
syn|chron|ic|al|ly
syn|chron|icity

syn|chron|isa|tion
  Br. (use
  synchronization)
syn|chron|ise Br.
  (use synchronize)
syn|chron|ises
syn|chron|ised
syn|chron|is|ing
syn|chron|iser Br.
  +s (use
  synchronizer)
syn|chron|ism
syn|chron|is|tic
syn|chron|is|tic|
      al|ly
syn|chron|iza|tion
syn|chron|ize
syn|chron|izes
syn|chron|ized
syn|chron|iz|ing
syn|chron|izer+s
syn|chron|ous
syn|chron|ous|ly
syn|chrony
  syn|chron|ies
syn|chro|tron+s
syn|clinal
syn|cline+s
syn|co|pal
syn|co|pate
syn|co|pates
syn|co|pated
syn|co|pat|ing
syn|co|pa|tion+s
syn|co|pa|tor+s
syn|cope+s
syn|cre|tic
syn|cre|tise Br.
  (use syncretize)
syn|cre|tises
syn|cre|tised
syn|cre|tis|ing
syn|cre|tism
syn|cre|tist+s
syn|cre|tis|tic
syn|cre|tize
syn|cre|tizes
syn|cre|tized
syn|cre|tiz|ing
syn|cyt|ial
syn|cyt|ium
  syn|cytia
syn|dac|tyl
syn|dac|tyl|ism
syn|dac|tyl|ous
syn|dac|tyly
syn|desis
  syn|deses
syn|des|mosis
  syn|des|moses
syn|det|ic
syn|dic+s

syn|dic|al
syn|dic|al|ism
syn|dic|al|ist+s
syn|di|cate
syn|di|cates
syn|di|cated
syn|di|cat|ing
syn|di|ca|tion+s
syn|drome+s
syn|drom|ic
syne (since. △ sine,
  sign)
syn|ec|doche+s
syn|ec|doch|ic
syn|ecious Am. (Br.
  synoecious)
syn|eco|logic|al
syn|ecolo|gist+s
syn|ecol|ogy
syn|ere|sis Am. (Br.
  synaeresis)
syn|er|get|ic
syn|er|gic
syn|er|gism+s
syn|er|gist+s
syn|er|gis|tic
syn|er|gis|tic|al|ly
syn|ergy
  syn|er|gies
syn|es|the|sia Am.
  (Br. synaesthesia)
syn|es|thet|ic Am.
  (Br. synaesthetic)
syn|gam|ous
syn|gamy
Synge, J. M. (Irish
  playwright)
syn|gen|esis
syn|gnath|ous
syn|iz|esis
  syn|iz|eses
synod+s
syn|od|al
syn|od|ic
syn|od|ic|al
syn|oe|cious Br.
  (Am. synecious)
syno|nym+s
syno|nym|ic
syno|nym|ity
syn|onym|ous
syn|onym|ous|ly
syn|onym|ous|
      ness
syn|onymy
  syn|ony|mies
syn|op|sis
  syn|op|ses
syn|op|sise Br. (use
  synopsize)
syn|op|sises

syn|op|sise(cont.)
  syn|op|sised
  syn|op|sis|ing
syn|op|size
  syn|op|sizes
  syn|op|sized
  syn|op|siz|ing
syn|op|tic+s
syn|op|tic|al
syn|op|tic|al|ly
syn|op|tist+s
syn|os|tosis
syn|ovia
syn|ovial
syno|vitis
syn|tac|tic
syn|tac|tic|al
syn|tac|tic|al|ly
syn|tagma
  syn|tag|mas or
  syn|tag|mata
syn|tag|mat|ic
syn|tag|mic
syn|tax
synth+s
  (= synthesizer)
syn|the|sis
  syn|the|ses
syn|the|sise Br.
  (use synthesize)
syn|the|sises
syn|the|sised
syn|the|sis|ing
syn|the|siser Br. +s
  (use synthesizer)
syn|the|sist+s
syn|the|size
syn|the|sizes
syn|the|sized
syn|the|siz|ing
syn|the|sizer+s
syn|thet|ic+s
syn|thet|ic|al
syn|thet|ic|al|ly
syn|the|tise Br.
  (use synthetize)
syn|the|tises
syn|the|tised
syn|the|tis|ing
syn|the|tize
syn|the|tizes
syn|the|tized
syn|the|tiz|ing
syph|ilis
syph|il|ise Br. (use
  syphilize)
syph|il|ises
syph|il|ised
syph|il|is|ing
syph|il|it|ic
syph|il|ize
syph|il|izes

syph¦il¦ize (*cont.*)
  syph¦il¦ized
  syph¦il¦iz¦ing
syph¦il¦oid
sy¦phon *Br.* +s +ed
  +ing (pipe for
  transferring liquid.
  Am. siphon.
  ⚠ siphon)
sy¦phon¦age *Br.*
  (*Am.* siphonage)
sy¦phon¦ic *Br.*
  (pertaining to a
  syphon. *Am.*
  siphonic.
  ⚠ siphonic)
Syra¦cuse (port,
  Italy; city, USA)
Syr Darya (Russian
  name for the
  Sirdaryo)
syren +s (use
  siren)
Syria
Syr¦iac (language)
Syr¦ian +s (of
  Syria)
syr¦inga +s
syr¦inge
  syr¦inges
  syr¦inged
  syr¦in¦ging
syr¦in¦geal
syr¦inx
  syr¦inxes *or*
  syr¦inges
Syro-Phoenician
  +s
syr¦phid +s
syrup *Br.* +s (*Am.*
  sirup)
syr¦upy
SYSOP (= system
  operator)
sys¦sar¦cosis
  sys¦sar¦coses
sys¦tal¦tic
sys¦tem +s
sys¦tem¦at¦ic
sys¦tem¦at¦ic¦al¦ly
sys¦tem¦at¦ics
sys¦tem¦atisa¦tion
  Br. (use
  systematization)
sys¦tem¦atise *Br.*
  (use systematize)
  sys¦tem¦atises
  sys¦tem¦atised
  sys¦tem¦atis¦ing
sys¦tem¦atiser *Br.*
  +s (use
  systematizer)

sys¦tem¦atism
sys¦tem¦atist +s
sys¦tem¦atiza¦tion
sys¦tem¦atize
  sys¦tem¦atizes
  sys¦tem¦atized
  sys¦tem¦atiz¦ing
  sys¦tem¦atizer +s
sys¦tem¦ic
sys¦tem¦ic¦al¦ly
sys¦tem¦isa¦tion
  Br. (use
  systemization)
sys¦tem¦ise *Br.* (use
  systemize)
  sys¦tem¦ises
  sys¦tem¦ised
  sys¦tem¦is¦ing
sys¦tem¦iser *Br.* +s
  (use systemizer)
sys¦tem¦iza¦tion
sys¦tem¦ize
  sys¦tem¦izes
  sys¦tem¦ized
  sys¦tem¦iz¦ing
  sys¦tem¦izer +s
sys¦tem¦less
sys¦tole +s
sys¦tol¦ic
syzygy
  syzy¦gies
Szcze¦cin (port,
  Poland)
Sze¦chuan
  (= Sichuan)
Sze¦chwan
  (= Sichuan)
Sze¦ged (city,
  Hungary)
Szi¦lard, Leo
  (Hungarian-born
  American
  physicist)

Tt

'**t** (= it)
ta (= thank you.
  ⚠ tahr, tar)
taal, the
  (Afrikaans)
TAB (= typhoid-
  paratyphoid A
  and B vaccine)
tab
  tabs
  tabbed
  tab¦bing
  (flap, bill, etc.; also
  = tabulator)
tab¦ard +s
tab¦aret +s
Tab¦asco (state,
  Mexico)
Tab¦asco (sauce)
  Propr.
tab¦asco +s
  (pepper)
tab¦bou¦leh +s
tabby
  tab¦bies
tab¦er¦nacle +s
tab¦er¦nacled
tabes
tab¦et¦ic
tab¦inet +s
Tab¦itha
tabla +s
tab¦la¦ture +s
table
  tables
  tabled
  tab¦ling
tab¦leau
  tab¦leaux
tab¦leau viv¦ant
  tab¦leaux viv¦ants
table¦cloth +s
table d'hôte
  tables d'hôte
table¦ful +s
table lamp +s
table¦land +s
table-mat +s
Table Moun¦tain
  (in South Africa)
table¦spoon +s
table¦spoon¦ful +s
tab¦let +s +ed
  +ing
table ten¦nis
table top +s *noun*
table-top *attributive*
table¦ware

tab¦lier +s
tab¦loid +s
taboo +s +ed +ing
tabor +s
tab¦oret *Am.* +s
  (*Br.* tabouret)
tab¦ouret *Br.* +s
  (*Am.* taboret)
Ta¦briz (city, Iran)
tabu +s +ed +ing
  (use taboo)
tabu¦lar
tab¦ula rasa
  tabu¦lae rasae
tabu¦lar¦ly
tabu¦late
  tabu¦lates
  tabu¦lated
  tabu¦lat¦ing
tabu¦la¦tion +s
tabu¦la¦tor +s
tabun
taca¦ma¦hac +s
tac-au-tac +s
tacet (*Music.*
  ⚠ tacit)
tach +s
  (= tachometer.
  ⚠ tack)
tache +s (use tash)
Ta¦ching
  (= Daqing)
tach¦ism
tach¦isme (use
  tachism)
tach¦is¦to¦scope +s
tach¦is¦to¦scop¦ic
tacho +s
  (= tachograph,
  tachometer.
  ⚠ taco)
tacho¦graph +s
tach¦om¦eter +s
tachy¦car¦dia
tachy¦graph¦er +s
tachy¦graph¦ic
tachy¦graph¦ic¦al
tach¦yg¦raphy
tach¦ym¦eter +s
tach¦ym¦etry
tachy¦on +s
tacit (understood or
  implied. ⚠ tacet)
Tacit¦ean
tacit¦ly
taci¦turn
taci¦turn¦ity
taci¦turn¦ly
Taci¦tus (Roman
  historian)
tack +s +ed +ing
  (senses except

tack (*cont.*)
 'tachometer'.
 △ tach)
tack|er +s
tack|ily
tacki|ness
tackle
 tackles
 tackled
 tack|ling
tackle-block +s
tackle-fall +s
tack|ler +s
tack room +s
tacky
 tack|ier
 tacki|est
taco +s (food.
 △ tacho)
tact
tact|ful
tact|ful|ly
tact|ful|ness
tac|tic +s
tac|tic|al
tac|tic|al|ly
tac|ti|cian +s
tac|tics
tact|ile
tac|til|ity
tact|less
tact|less|ly
tact|less|ness
tac|tual
tad +s
Ta|djik (use Tajik)
 plural Ta|djik *or*
 Ta|djiks
Ta|djiki|stan (use
 Tajikistan)
Tad|mur (modern
 name for
 Palmyra)
tad|pole +s
Ta|dzhik (use
 Tajik)
 plural Ta|dzhik *or*
 Ta|dzhiks
Ta|dzhiki|stan
 (use Tajikistan)
tae|dium vitae
Taegu (city, South
 Korea)
Tae|jon (city, South
 Korea)
tae kwon do
tae|nia *Br.*
 tae|niae *or*
 tae|nias
 (*Am.* tenia)
tae|ni|oid *Br.*
 (*Am.* tenioid)

Taff +s (*often
 offensive*)
taf|feta +s
taff|rail +s
Taffy
 Taf|fies
 (*often offensive
 Welsh person*)
taffy
 taf|fies
 (confection;
 insincere flattery)
tafia +s
Taft, Wil|liam
 How|ard
 (American
 president)
tag
 tags
 tagged
 tag|ging
Taga|log +s
Tag|an|rog (port,
 Russia)
ta|getes
taglia|telle
tag line +s
tag|meme +s
tag|mem|ics
Tag|ore,
 Rab|in|dra|nath
 (Indian writer)
Tagus (river, Spain
 and Portugal)
Ta|hiti (island, S.
 Pacific)
Ta|hi|tian +s
tahr +s (animal.
 △ ta, tar)
tah|sil +s
tah|sil|dar +s
Tai'an (city, China)
t'ai chi (ch'uan)
Tai|chung (city,
 China)
Ta'if (city, Saudi
 Arabia)
Taig +s (*offensive*)
taiga +s (forest.
 △ tiger)
tail +s +ed +ing (of
 animal; end;
 follow. △ tale)
tail|back +s
tail|board +s
tail|coat +s
tail-end +s
tail-ender +s
tail fea|ther +s
tail fin +s
tail|gate +s
 tail|gated
 tail|gat|ing

tail|gater +s
tailie +s
tail|ing +s
tail lamp +s
Taille|ferre,
 Ger|maine
 (French
 composer)
tail|less
tail light +s
tail-off +s *noun*
tailor +s +ed +ing
tailor-bird +s
tail|or|ess
tailor-made
tail|piece +s
tail|pipe +s
tail|plane +s
tail-race +s
tail-skid +s
tail|spin
 tail|spins
 tail|spun
 tail|spin|ning
tail|stock +s
tail|wheel +s
tail|wind +s
Tai|myr
 Pen|in|sula (in
 Siberia)
Tai|nan (city,
 Taiwan)
taint +s +ed +ing
taint|less
tai|pan +s
Tai|pei (capital of
 Taiwan)
Tai|ping
 Re|bel|lion (in
 China)
Tai|wan
Tai|wan|ese
 plural Tai|wan|ese
Tai|yuan (city,
 China)
Tai Yue Shan
 (Chinese name for
 Lantau)
Ta'iz (city, Yemen)
taj +s
Tajik
 plural Tajik *or*
 Ta|jiks
Ta|jiki|stan
Taj Mahal
 (mausoleum,
 India)
taka
 plural taka
 (Bangladeshi
 currency)
tak|able

tak|ahe +s
take
 takes
 took
 tak|ing
 taken
take|away +s
take-home
 attributive
take-in +s *noun*
take-off +s *noun*
 and attributive
take-out +s
 *attributive and
 noun*
take|over +s
taker +s
take-up +s *noun*
 and attributive
takin +s
tak|ing|ly
tak|ing|ness
tak|ings
Tak|li|ma|kan
 Des|ert (in NW
 China)
Tako|radi (port,
 Ghana)
tala +s (*Music.*
 △ thaler)
tala
 plural tala *or* talas
 (Western Samoan
 currency.
 △ thaler)
Ta|laing
 plural Ta|laing *or*
 Ta|laings
tala|poin +s
tal|aria
Tal|bot, Wil|liam
 Henry Fox
 (English
 photography
 pioneer)
tal|bot +s
talc
 talcs
 talced *or* talcked
 talc|ing
talc|ose
talc|ous
tal|cum +s +ed
 +ing
talcy
tale +s (story.
 △ tail)
tale|bearer +s
tale|bear|ing
tal|ent +s
tal|ent|ed
tal|ent|less

talent-spot
  talent-spots
  talent-spotted
  talent-spotting
talent-spotter +s
tales (writ for
  summoning
  substitute jurors)
ta¦les|man
  ta¦les|men
  (*Law.* △talisman)
tale|tell¦er +s
tali (plural of talus)
tal¦ion +s
tali|pes
tali|pot +s
tal¦is|man +s
  (lucky charm.
  △talesman)
tal¦is|man¦ic
talk +s +ed +ing
  (speak. △torc,
  torque)
talka|thon +s
talka|tive
talka|tive¦ly
talka|tive|ness
talk|back +s
talk¦er +s
talk|fest +s
talkie +s (film.
  △torquey)
talk|ing point +s
talk|ing shop +s
talking-to
  talkings-to
tall +er +est
tall|age +s
Tal¦la|has¦see
  (city, Florida)
tall|boy +s
**Tal¦ley|rand,
  Charles
  Maur¦ice de** *in
  full* Talleyrand-
  Périgord
  (French
  statesman)
Tal|linn (capital of
  Estonia)
Tal¦lis, Thomas
  (English
  composer)
tall|ish
tall|lith
  tall|lith¦im
tall|ness
**tal¦low +s +ed
  +ing**
tal¦low|ish
tal¦low tree +s
tal|lowy

tally
  tal|lies
  tal|lied
  tally|ing
tally-ho +s *noun*
tally-ho
  tally-hoes
  tally-hoed
  tally-hoing
  verb
tally|man
  tally|men
Tal¦mud
Tal¦mud|ic
Tal¦mud|ic¦al
Tal¦mud|ist +s
talon +s
tal|oned
talus
  tali
  (ankle-bone)
talus
  tal|uses
  (slope of wall etc.)
TAM (= television
  audience
  measurement)
tam +s (= tam-o'-
  shanter)
tam¦able (use
  tameable)
tam¦ale +s
tam¦an|dua +s
tam¦an|oir +s
Tamar (river,
  England)
Tam¦ara (name)
tam¦ar|ack +s
tam¦ar|illo +s
tam¦arin +s
  (marmoset)
tam¦ar|ind +s
  (fruit; tree)
tam¦ar|isk +s
Tamau|lipas (state,
  Mexico)
Tambo, Oli¦ver
  (South African
  politician)
**tam|bour +s +ed
  +ing**
tam|boura +s
tam|bourin +s
  (drum; dance;
  music for this)
tam¦bour|ine +s
  (jingling
  percussion
  instrument)
tam¦bour|in|ist +s
Tam¦bov (city,
  Russia)

Tam¦bur|laine
  (alternative name
  of Tamerlane)
tame
  tames
  tamed
  tam|ing
  tamer
  tam¦est
tame|abil¦ity
tame|able
tame|able|ness
tame¦ly
tame|ness
tamer +s
Tam|er¦lane
  (Mongol ruler)
Tamil +s
Ta¦mil|ian
Tamil Nadu (state,
  India)
Tamla Mo¦town
  (record company)
  Propr.
Tam|many
  (benevolent
  society, New York
  City)
Tam¦muz
  *Babylonian and
  Assyrian Mythology*
Tam¦muz (Jewish
  month; use
  Thammuz)
tammy
  tam|mies
tam-o'-shanter +s
tam|oxi|fen
tamp +s +ed +ing
Tampa (port, USA)
tam|pan +s
**tam|per +s +ed
  +ing**
Tam|pere (city,
  Finland)
tam|per¦er +s
tam|per|ing +s
tamper-proof
Tam|pico (port,
  Mexico)
tam|pion +s
**tam|pon +s +ed
  +ing**
tam¦pon|ade +s
tam¦pon|age +s
Tam|sin
tam-tam +s
Tam|worth +s
  (town, England;
  pig)
tan
  tans

tan (*cont.*)
  tanned
  tan|ning
  (colour; make
  leather; become
  brown; also
  = tangent)
Tana, Lake (in
  Ethiopia)
tan|ager +s
Tan|agra +s
Tanak
Tana¦na|rive
  (former name of
  Antananarivo)
tan|bark +s
tan|dem +s
tan|door +s
tan|doori +s
Tang (Chinese
  dynasty)
tang +s +ed +ing
Tanga (port,
  Tanzania)
tanga +s
Tan|gan|yika
  (former name of
  Tanzania)
**Tan|gan|yika,
  Lake** (in E. Africa)
Tan|gan|yi¦kan +s
Tange, Kenzo
  (Japanese
  architect)
tan|gelo +s
tan|gency
  tan|gen|cies
tan|gent +s
tan|gen|tial
tan|gen|tial¦ly
tan|ger|ine +s
tan|ghin +s
tan|gi|bil¦ity
tan|gible +s
tan|gible|ness
tan|gibly
Tan|gier (port,
  Morocco)
Tan|giers (older
  form of Tangier)
tangi|ness
tan|gle
  tan|gles
  tan|gled
  tan|gling
tan|gly
  tan|glier
  tan|gli¦est
tango +s (dance
  (*noun*); colour)
tango
  tan|goes

tango (*cont.*)
tan|goed
tango|ing
verb
tan|gram +s
Tang|shan (city, China)
tangy
tangi|er
tangi|est
tanh (= hyperbolic tangent)
Tania *also* Tanya
tan|ist +s
tan|ist|ry
Tan|jung|ka|rang (city, Indonesia)
tank +s +ed +ing
tanka +s (Japanese poem. △tanker)
tank|age +s
tank|ard +s
tank|er +s +ed +ing (ship; aircraft; vehicle. △tanka)
tank-farming
tank|ful +s
tank|less
tank top +s
tan|nable
tan|nage +s
tan|nate +s
tan|ner +s
tan|nery
tan|ner|ies
Tann|häuser (German poet)
tan|nic
tan|nin +s
tan|nish
tan|noy (public-address system)
Propr.
Tannu-Tuva (former name of Tuva)
tan|rec +s
Tan|sen (Indian musician)
tansy
tan|sies
tan|tal|ic (of or pertaining to tantalus)
tan|tal|isa|tion *Br.* (use tantalization)
tan|tal|ise *Br.* (use tantalize)
tan|tal|ises

tan|tal|ise (*cont.*)
tan|tal|ised
tan|tal|is|ing
tan|tal|iser *Br.* +s (use tantalizer)
tan|tal|is|ing|ly *Br.* (use tantalizingly)
tan|tal|ite
tan|tal|iza|tion
tan|tal|ize
tan|tal|izes
tan|tal|ized
tan|tal|iz|ing
tan|tal|izer +s
tan|tal|iz|ing|ly
tan|ta|lum
Tan|ta|lus *Greek Mythology*
tan|ta|lus
tan|ta|luses
tan|ta|mount
tan|tivy
tan|tivies
tant mieux
tant pis
tan|tra +s
tan|tric
tan|trism
tan|trist +s
tan|trum +s
Tanya *also* Tania
Tan|za|nia
Tan|za|nian +s
Tao +s
Taoi|seach (Irish prime minister)
Tao|ism
Tao|ist +s
Tao|is|tic
Taor|mina (resort, Sicily)
Tao-te-Ching
tap
  taps
  tapped
  tap|ping
tapa +s (bark; cloth. △tapper)
tapas (Spanish bar snacks)
tap-dance
  tap-dances
  tap-danced
  tap-dancing
tap-dancer +s
tape
  tapes
  taped
  tap|ing
tape|able
tape|less
tape|like

tape-measure +s
taper +s +ed +ing (thin candle; make or become thinner. △tapir)
tape-record
  tape-records
  tape-record|ed
  tape-record|ing
verb
tape re|cord|er +s
tape re|cord|ing +s *noun*
taper|er +s
tap|es|tried
tap|es|try
tap|es|tries
tap|etum
  tap|eta *or*
  tap|etums
tape|worm +s
tapho|nom|ic
taph|ono|mist +s
taph|onomy
tap-in +s *noun*
tapi|oca
tapir +s (animal. △taper)
tapir|oid +s
tapis
  plural tapis
tap|less
tapote|ment
tap|pable
tap|per +s (person or thing that taps. △tapa)
tap|pet +s
tap|ping +s
tap|room +s
tap root +s
tap|ster +s
tap-tap +s
tapu
tap water
tar
  tars
  tarred
  tar|ring (liquid; sailor. △ta, tahr)
Tara (hill, Republic of Ireland; name)
ta-ra (goodbye)
tara|did|dle +s
tara|kihi
  plural tara|kihi
tara|ma|sa|lata
Tara|naki (region, New Zealand)
tar|an|tass
tar|an|tasses

tar|an|tella +s
tar|ant|ism
Tar|anto (port, Italy)
tar|an|tula +s
Tar|awa (atoll, S. Pacific)
tar|axa|cum +s
tar|boosh
  tar|booshes
tar-brush
  tar-brushes
Tar|den|ois|ian
tar|di|grade +s
tar|dily
tar|di|ness
tardy
  tar|dier
  tar|di|est
tare +s (weed; unladen weight. △tear)
tare and tret
targa +s
targe +s
tar|get +s +ed +ing
tar|get|able
Tar|gum +s
Tar|gum|ist +s
tar|iff +s +ed +ing
Tarim (river, China)
tar|latan +s
tar|mac (*noun*)
Propr.
tar|mac
  tar|macs
  tar|macked
  tar|mack|ing
verb
tar|mac|adam
Tarn (river, France)
tarn +s (lake)
tar|na|tion
interjection
tar|nish
  tar|nishes
  tar|nished
  tar|nish|ing
tar|nish|able
Tar|nów (city, Poland)
taro +s (plant)
tarot +s (cards)
tarp (= tarpaulin)
tar|pan +s (horse)
tar|paulin +s
Tar|peia (Roman Vestal Virgin)
Tar|peian Rock (cliff, Rome)

tar¦pon +s (fish)
Tar¦quin (= either
  Tarquinius)
Tar¦quin¦ius
  Pris¦cus (king of
  Rome)
Tar¦quin¦ius
  Su¦perb¦us (king
  of Rome)
tar¦ra¦did¦dle +s
  (use taradiddle)
tar¦ra¦gon
Tar¦ra¦gona (town
  and province,
  Spain)
tar¦ras
Tar¦rasa (city,
  Spain)
tar¦rier +s (person
  who tarries)
tar¦ri¦ness (of tar)
tarry
  tar¦rier
  tar¦ri¦est
  (of tar)
tarry
  tar¦ries
  tar¦ried
  tarry¦ing
  (linger)
tar¦sal +s
tarsi
tar¦sia (= intarsia)
tar¦sier +s (animal)
Tar¦sus (city,
  Turkey)
tar¦sus
  tarsi
tart +s +ed +ing
tar¦tan +s
Tar¦tar +s (Turkic
  people)
tar¦tar +s (deposit
  on teeth etc.;
  violent-tempered
  person; in 'cream
  of tartar'.
  △ tartare, ta-ta)
tar¦tare (sauce.
  △ tartar, ta-ta)
Tar¦tar¦ean (of
  Tartarus)
Tar¦tar¦ian (of
  Tartars)
tar¦tar¦ic
tar¦tar¦ise Br. (use
  tartarize)
  tar¦tar¦ises
  tar¦tar¦ised
  tar¦tar¦is¦ing
tar¦tar¦ize
  tar¦tar¦izes

tar¦tar¦ize (cont.)
  tar¦tar¦ized
  tar¦tar¦iz¦ing
Tar¦tarus Greek
  Mythology
Tar¦tary (historical
  region, Asia and E.
  Europe)
tart¦ily
tarti¦ness
tart¦let +s
tart¦ly
tart¦ness
  (sharpness,
  acidity)
tar¦trate +s
tar¦tra¦zine
tarty
  tart¦ier
  tarti¦est
Tar¦zan +s
  (fictional hero;
  strong or agile
  man)
tash
  tashes
  (= moustache)
Tashi lama +s
Tash¦kent (capital
  of Uzbekistan)
task +s +ed +ing
task force +s
task¦mas¦ter +s
task¦mis¦tress
  task¦mis¦tresses
Tas¦man, Abel
  Jans¦zoon (Dutch
  navigator)
Tas¦mania (island
  and state,
  Australia)
Tas¦man¦ian +s
Tas¦man Sea
  (between Australia
  and New Zealand)
Tass (Soviet news
  agency; now
  ITAR-Tass)
tass
  tasses
  (cup)
tas¦sel
  tas¦sels
  tas¦selled Br.
  tas¦seled Am.
  tas¦sel¦ling Br.
  tas¦sel¦ing Am.
tas¦sie +s
Tasso, Tor¦quato
  (Italian poet and
  dramatist)

taste
  tastes
  tasted
  tast¦ing
taste¦able
taste bud +s
taste¦ful
taste¦ful¦ly
taste¦ful¦ness
taste¦less
taste¦less¦ly
taste¦less¦ness
taster +s
tasti¦ly
tasti¦ness
tast¦ing +s
tasty
  tasti¦er
  tasti¦est
tat
  tats
  tat¦ted
  tat¦ting
ta-ta (goodbye.
  △ tartar, tartare)
tat¦ami +s
Tatar +s (use
  Tartar)
Tatar¦stan
  (republic, Russia)
Tate, Nahum (Irish
  dramatist)
Tate Gal¦lery (in
  London)
tater +s (= potato)
Tati, Jacques
  (French film
  director)
Tati¦ana
tat¦ler +s (archaic;
  = tattler)
tatou +s
Tatra Moun¦tains
  (in E. Europe)
Tat¦ras (= Tatra
  Mountains)
tat¦ter +s
tat¦ter¦de¦ma¦lion
  +s
tat¦tered
Tat¦ter¦sall,
  Rich¦ard (English
  horseman)
tat¦ter¦sall +s
  (fabric)
Tat¦ter¦salls
  (English horse
  auctioneers)
tat¦tery
tat¦tie +s (= potato.
  △ tatty)
tat¦tily

tat¦ti¦ness
tat¦ting (lace)
tat¦tle
  tat¦tles
  tat¦tled
  tat¦tling
tat¦tler +s
tattle-tale +s
tat¦too +s +ed
  +ing
tat¦too¦er +s
tat¦too¦ist +s
tatty
  tat¦tier
  tat¦ti¦est
  (tattered; tawdry.
  △ tattie)
Tatum, Art
  (American jazz
  pianist)
tau +s (Greek
  letter. △ taw, tor,
  tore, torr)
tau cross
  tau crosses
taught (past tense
  and past participle
  of teach. △ taut,
  tort, torte)
taunt +s +ed +ing
taunt¦er +s
taunt¦ing¦ly
Taun¦ton (town,
  England)
tau par¦ticle +s
taupe +s (colour.
  △ tope)
Taupo (town, New
  Zealand)
Taupo, Lake (in
  New Zealand)
Tau¦ranga (port,
  New Zealand)
Taur¦ean +s
taur¦ine
taur¦om¦achy
  taur¦om¦achies
Taurus
  (constellation;
  sign of zodiac;
  Stock Exchange.
  △ torus)
Taurus
  Moun¦tains (in
  Turkey)
taut +er +est (tight.
  △ taught, tort,
  torte)
taut¦en +s +ed
  +ing
taut¦ly
taut¦ness

tau|tog +s
tauto|logic
tauto|logic|al
tauto|logic|al|ly
tau|tolo|gise *Br.*
(use tautologize)
tau|tolo|gises
tau|tolo|gised
tau|tolo|gis|ing
tau|tolo|gist +s
tau|tolo|gize
tau|tolo|gizes
tau|tolo|gized
tau|tolo|giz|ing
tau|tolo|gous
tau|tol|ogy
tau|tolo|gies
tauto|mer +s
tauto|mer|ic
tau|to|mer|ism
tau|toph|ony
tau|toph|onies
tav|ern +s
tav|erna +s
Tav|ern|ers (in
'Lord's
Taverners')
taw +s +ed +ing
(make into
leather; marble.
△ tau, tor, tore,
torr)
taw|drily
taw|dri|ness
taw|dry
taw|drier
taw|dri|est
tawer +s
taw|ni|ness
tawny
taw|nier
taw|ni|est
taws
plural taws
(use tawse)
tawse +s
tax
taxes
taxed
tax|ing
taxa (plural of
taxon. △ taxer)
tax|abil|ity
tax|able
tax|ation
tax col|lect|or +s
tax-deduct|ible
tax-efficient
taxer +s (person
who levies a tax.
△ taxa)
tax-exempt

tax-free
taxi +s *noun*
taxi
tax|ies
tax|ied
taxi|ing *or*
taxy|ing
verb
taxi|cab +s
taxi|der|mal
taxi|der|mic
taxi|der|mist +s
taxi|dermy
taxi driver +s
taxi man
taxi men
taxi|meter +s
tax|ing|ly
taxis (plural of taxi)
taxis
taxes
*Surgery; Biology;
Grammar*
taxi|way +s
tax|less
tax|man
tax|men
taxon
taxa
taxo|nom|ic
taxo|nom|ic|al
taxo|nom|ic|al|ly
tax|ono|mist +s
tax|onomy
tax|ono|mies
tax|pay|er +s
tax|pay|ing
tax-saving
Tay (river,
Scotland)
Tay, Firth of
(estuary,
Scotland)
tay|berry
tay|berries
Tay|lor, Eliza|beth
(American
actress)
Tay|lor, Jer|emy
(English
churchman)
Tay|lor, Zach|ary
(American
president)
Tay|myr
Pen|in|sula (use
Taimyr
Peninsula)
Tay–Sachs
dis|ease
Tay|side (region,
Scotland)

tazza +s
T-bar +s
Tbil|isi (capital of
Georgia)
T-bone +s
T-cell +s
Tchai|kov|sky,
Pyotr (Russian
composer)
te (*Music.* △ tea,
tee, ti)
tea
teas
teaed *or* tea'd
tea|ing
(drink; take tea.
△ te, tee, ti)
tea bag +s
tea-ball +s
tea-bread +s
tea break +s
tea|cake +s
teach
teaches
taught
teach|ing
teach|abil|ity
teach|able
teach|able|ness
teach|er +s
teach|er|ly
tea chest +s
teach-in +s
teach|ing +s
Teachta Dála
Teachti Dála
(member of Irish
parliament)
tea clip|per +s
tea cosy
tea cos|ies
tea|cup +s
tea|cup|ful +s
teak +s
teal
plural teal *or* teals
tea leaf
tea leaves
team +s +ed +ing
(group; form a
team. △ teem)
team-mate +s
team play|er +s
team|ster +s
team-teaching
team|work
tea party
tea par|ties
tea plant|er +s
tea|pot +s

tea|poy +s
tear
tears
tore
tear|ing
torn
(rip; pull; rush;
etc. △ tare)
tear +s (fluid in
eyes. △ tier)
tear|able
tear|away +s
tear|drop +s
tear duct +s
tear|er +s
tear|ful
tear|ful|ly
tear|ful|ness
tear gas
tear gases
noun
tear-gas
tear-gasses
tear-gassed
tear-gassing
attributive and verb
tear-jerker +s
tear-jerking
tear|less
tear|less|ly
tear|less|ness
tear|like
tear-off *adjective*
tea|room +s
tea rose +s
tear sheet +s
tear-stained
teary
tease
teases
teased
teas|ing
tea|sel +s +ed
+ing
tea|sel|er +s
teaser +s
tea|set +s
tea shop +s
teas|ing|ly
tea|spoon +s
tea|spoon|ful +s
tea-strainer +s
teat +s
tea|time +s
tea towel +s
tea tray +s
tea-tree +s (shrub.
△ ti-tree)
tea|zel +s +ed
+ing (use teasel)

tea|zle (use teasel)
tea|zles
tea|zled
teaz|ling
Tebet (Jewish
  month)
tec +s (= detective;
  technical college)
tech +s (= technical
  college;
  technology)
techie +s
  (technology
  enthusiast.
  ⚠ tetchy)
tech|ne|tium
tech|nic +s
tech|nical +s
tech|ni|cal|ity
  tech|ni|cal|ities
tech|nic|al|ly
tech|nic|al|ness
tech|ni|cian +s
tech|ni|cist +s
Tech|ni|color
  (cinematographic
  process) *Propr.*
tech|ni|color *Am.*
  (vivid colour;
  artificial brilliance;
  Br. technicolour)
tech|ni|colored
  Am.
tech|ni|col|our *Br.*
tech|ni|col|oured
  Br.
tech|nique +s
techno
tech|no|bab|ble
tech|noc|racy
  tech|noc|ra|cies
tech|no|crat +s
tech|no|crat|ic
tech|no|crat|ic|
    al|ly
tech|no|logic|al|ly
tech|no|logic|al|ly
tech|nolo|gist +s
tech|nol|ogy
  tech|nolo|gies
tech|no|phile +s
tech|no|phobe +s
tech|no|pho|bia
tech|no|pho|bic
techy (technology
  enthusiast; use
  techie)
  tech|ies
techy (irritable; use
  tetchy)
  techi|er
  techi|est

tec|ton|ic
tec|ton|ic|al|ly
tec|ton|ics
tec|tor|ial
tec|trix
  tec|tri|ces
Ted +s (= Teddy
  boy; name)
ted
  teds
  ted|ded
  ted|ding
  (turn hay etc.)
ted|der +s
Teddy (name)
teddy
  ted|dies
  (teddy bear;
  garment)
teddy bear +s
Teddy boy +s
Te Deum +s
  (hymn. ⚠ tedium)
te|di|ous
te|di|ous|ly
te|di|ous|ness
te|dium (boredom.
  ⚠ Te Deum)
tee
  tees
  teed
  tee|ing
  (in golf etc. ⚠ te,
  tea, ti)
tee-hee
  tee-hees
  tee-heed
  tee-heeing
teem +s +ed +ing
  (be full; flow
  copiously.
  ⚠ team)
teen +s
teen|age
teen|aged
teen|ager +s
teens
teensy
  teen|sier
  teen|si|est
teensy-weensy
teeny
  teen|ier
  teeni|est
teeny-bop
teeny-bopper +s
teeny-weeny
tee|pee +s (use
  tepee)
Tees (river,
  England)

tee shirt +s (use T-
  shirt)
Tees|side (region,
  England)
tee|ter +s +ed +ing
teeth (plural of
  tooth)
teethe
  teethes
  teethed
  teeth|ing
  verb
teeth|ing ring +s
tee|total
tee|total|er *Am.* +s
tee|total|ism
tee|total|ler *Br.* +s
tee|total|ly
tee|totum +s
teff +s
TEFL (= teaching of
  English as a
  foreign language)
Tef|lon *Propr.*
teg +s
Tegu|ci|galpa (city,
  Honduras)
tegu|lar
tegu|lar|ly
tegu|ment +s
tegu|men|tal
tegu|men|tary
te-hee (use tee-
  hee)
  te-hees
  te-heed
  te-heeing
Teh|ran (capital of
  Iran)
**Teil|hard de
Char|din, Pierre**
  (French Jesuit
  philosopher)
Te Kan|awa, Kiri
  (New Zealand
  soprano)
tek|nonym|ous
tek|nonymy
tek|tite +s
tel|aes|the|sia *Br.*
  (*Am.* telesthesia)
tel|aes|thet|ic *Br.*
  (*Am.* telesthetic)
tela|mon
  tela|mo|nes
Tel Aviv (city,
  Israel)
telco +s
tele-ad +s
tele|bank|ing
tele|cam|era +s

tele|cast
  tele|casts
  tele|cast
  tele|cast|ing
tele|cast|er +s
tele|cine
tele|comms
  (= telecommunica-
  tions)
tele|com|mu|ni|
    ca|tion +s
tele|com|mute
  tele|com|mutes
  tele|com|muted
  tele|com|mut|ing
tele|com|muter +s
tele|coms
  (= telecommunica-
  tions)
tele|con|fer|ence
  +s
tele|con|fer|
    en|cing
tele|cot|tage +s
tele|cot|ta|ging
tel|edu +s (badger)
tele-evangel|ism
  (use
  televangelism)
tele-evangel|ist +s
  (use
  televangelist)
tele|fac|sim|ile +s
tele|fax
  tele|faxes
  Propr.
tele|fax
  tele|faxes
  tele|faxed
  tele|fax|ing
tele|film +s
tele|gen|ic
tele|gon|ic
tel|egony
tele|gram +s
tele|graph +s +ed
  +ing
tel|eg|raph|er +s
tele|graph|ese
tele|graph|ic
tele|graph|ic|al|ly
tel|eg|raph|ist +s
tel|eg|raphy
Tel|egu (use
  Telugu)
  plural Tel|egu or
  Tel|egus
tele|kin|esis
  tele|kin|eses
tele|kin|et|ic
Tel|ema|chus
  Greek Mythology

Tele|mann, Georg
  Phil|ipp (German
  composer)
tele|mark +s +ed
  +ing
tele|mar¦ket¦er +s
tele|mar¦ket|ing
tele|mes¦sage +s
tel|em¦eter +s +ed
  +ing
tele|met¦ric
tel|em¦etry
teleo|logic
teleo|logic|al
teleo|logic|al¦ly
tele|olo¦gism
tele|olo¦gist +s
tele|ology
  tele|olo¦gies
tele|ost +s
tele|path +s
tele|path¦ic
tele|path¦ic|al¦ly
tel¦ep¦ath|ise Br.
  (use telepathize)
tel¦ep¦ath|ises
tel¦ep¦ath|ised
tel¦ep¦ath|is¦ing
tel¦ep¦ath|ist +s
tel¦ep¦ath|ize
tel¦ep¦ath|izes
tel¦ep¦ath|ized
tel¦ep¦ath|iz¦ing
tel¦ep¦athy
tele|phone
  tele|phones
  tele|phoned
  tele|phon¦ing
tele|phoner +s
tele|phon¦ic
tele|phon¦ic|al¦ly
tel¦eph|on|ist +s
tel¦eph|ony
tele|photo +s
tele|photo|
              graph¦ic
tele|photo|
       graph¦ic|al¦ly
tele|pho¦tog¦raphy
tele|point +s
tele|port +s +ed
  +ing
tele|por¦ta¦tion
tele|pres¦ence
tele|print¦er +s
tele|prompt¦er +s
tele|re¦cord +s +ed
  +ing
tele|re¦cord|ing +s
tel|ergy
tele|sales

tele|scope
tele|scopes
tele|scoped
tele|scop¦ing
tele|scop¦ic
tele|scop¦ic|al¦ly
tele|shop¦ping
tele|soft¦ware
tel|es¦the¦sia Am.
  (Br. telaesthesia)
tel|es¦thet¦ic Am.
  (Br. telaesthetic)
tele|tex
  tele|texes
  (electronic text
  transmission)
  Propr.
tele|text (text and
  graphics
  transmitted to
  televisions)
Tele|text Ltd
  (teletext service
  on British
  Independent
  Television) Propr.
tele|thon +s
tele|type +s Propr.
tele|type|writer +s
tele|van¦gel|ism
tele|van¦gel|ist +s
tele|view +s +ed
  +ing
tele|view¦er +s
tele|vis|able
tele|vise
  tele|vises
  tele|vised
  tele|vis¦ing
tele|vi¦sion +s
tele|visor +s
tele|vis¦ual
tele|visu¦al¦ly
tele|work +s +ed
  +ing
tele|work¦er +s
telex
  tel|exes
  tel|exed
  tel¦ex|ing
Tel|ford (town,
  England)
Tel|ford, Thomas
  (Scottish civil
  engineer)
Tell, Wil|liam
  (legendary Swiss
  hero)
tell
  tells
  told
  tell|ing

tell|able
Tell el-Amarna
  (site of Akhetaten,
  Egypt)
Tel¦ler, Ed¦ward
  (Hungarian-born
  American
  physicist)
tell¦er +s
tell¦er|ship +s
tell¦ing¦ly
telling-off
  tellings-off
tell-tale +s
tel¦lur|ate +s
tel¦lur|ian +s
tel¦lur|ic
tel¦lur|ide +s
tel¦lur|ite +s
tel¦lur|ium
tel¦lur|ous
telly
  tel|lies
telo|phase +s
tel|pher +s
tel|pher|age
tel|son +s
Tel|star
Tel|ugu
  plural Tel¦ugu or
  Tel¦ugus
tem|blor +s
tem|er|ari¦ous
tem|er¦ity
Temne
  plural Temne or
  Tem¦nes
temp +s +ed +ing
tem|peh
tem|per +s +ed
  +ing
tem|pera
tem|per|able
tem|pera|ment +s
tem|pera|men¦tal
tem|pera|
          men¦tal¦ly
tem|per|ance
tem|per|ate
tem|per|ate¦ly
tem|per|ate|ness
tem|pera|tive
tem|pera|ture +s
tem|pered¦ly
tem|per¦er +s
tem|per|some
Tem|pest, Marie
  (English actress)
tem|pest +s
tem|pes¦tu|ous
tem|pes¦tu|ous¦ly

tem|pes¦tu|ous|
                 ness
tempi
Tem|plar +s (Law.
  △ Knight
  Templar)
tem|plate +s
Tem|ple, Shir|ley
  (American actress
  and diplomat)
tem|ple +s
tem|plet +s (use
  template)
tempo
  tem|pos or tempi
tem|pora (in 'O
  tempora, O
  mores'.
  △ tempura)
tem|poral
tem|por|al|ity
  tem|por|al|ities
tem|por|al¦ly
tem|por|ar¦ily
tem|por|ari|ness
tem|por|ary
  tem|po|rar¦ies
tem|por|isa|tion
  Br. (use
  temporization)
tem|por|ise Br.
  (use temporize)
  tem|por|ises
  tem|por|ised
  tem|por|is¦ing
tem|por|iser Br. +s
  (use temporizer)
tem|por|iza|tion
tem|por|ize
  tem|por|izes
  tem|por|ized
  tem|por|iz¦ing
tem|por|izer +s
tempt +s +ed +ing
tempt|abil¦ity
tempt|able
temp|ta¦tion +s
tempt¦er +s
tempt|ing¦ly
temp|tress
  temp|tresses
tem|pura
  (Japanese dish.
  △ tempora)
ten +s
ten|abil¦ity
ten|able
ten|able|ness
ten|ace +s
ten|acious
ten|acious¦ly
ten|acious|ness

ten|acity
ten|acu|lum
  ten|acula
ten|ancy
  ten|an|cies
  (status or period
  of being a tenant.
  △ tenancy)
ten|ant +s +ed
  +ing
ten|ant|able
ten|ant|less
ten|ant|ry
tench
  plural tench
tend +s +ed +ing
ten|dance
ten|dency
  ten|den|cies
ten|den|tious
ten|den|tious|ly
ten|den|tious|ness
ten|der +s +ed
  +ing +er +est
ten|der|er +s
tender-eyed
ten|der|foot +s
tender-hearted
tender-
  hearted|ness
ten|der|ise *Br.* (use
  tenderize)
  ten|der|ises
  ten|der|ised
  ten|der|is|ing
ten|der|iser *Br.* +s
  (use tenderizer)
ten|der|ize
  ten|der|izes
  ten|der|ized
  ten|der|iz|ing
ten|der|izer +s
ten|der|loin +s
ten|der|ly
ten|der|ness
ten|din|itis
ten|din|ous
ten|don +s
ten|don|itis (use
  tendinitis)
ten|dril +s
Tene|brae
tene|brous
tene|ment +s
tene|men|tal
tene|men|tary
tene|ment house
  +s
ten|ency
  ten|en|cies
  (in 'locum

ten|ency (*cont.*)
  tenency'.
  △ tenancy)
Ten|er|ife (Canary
  Islands)
ten|es|mus
tenet +s
ten|fold
ten-gallon hat +s
Teng Hsiao-p'ing
  (= Deng
  Xiaoping)
tenia *Am.* +s (*Br.*
  taenia)
Ten|iers, David
  (Flemish painter)
teni|oid *Am.* (*Br.*
  taenioid)
ten-iron +s
Ten|nant Creek
  (town, Australia)
tenné
ten|ner +s
  (banknote.
  △ tenor)
Ten|nes|see (river
  and state, USA)
Ten|niel, John
  (English
  illustrator)
ten|nis
ten|nis play|er +s
tenno +s
tenny (use tenné)
Ten|ny|son,
  Al|fred, Lord
  (English poet)
Ten|ny|son|ian
Ten|och|ti|tlán
  (ancient city,
  Mexico)
tenon +s +ed +ing
ten|on|er +s
tenon saw +s
tenor +s (singer.
  △ tenner)
ten|or|ist +s
teno|syno|vitis
ten|ot|omy
  ten|oto|mies
ten|pence +s
ten|penny
  ten|pen|nies
ten|pin +s
ten|rec +s
tense
  tenses
  tensed
  tens|ing
  tenser
  tens|est
tense|less

tense|ly
tense|ness
ten|sile
ten|sil|ity
ten|sim|eter +s
ten|sion +s +ed
  +ing
ten|sion|al
ten|sion|al|ly
ten|sion|er +s
ten|sion|less
ten|sity
ten|son +s
ten|sor +s
ten|sor|ial
tent +s +ed +ing
ten|tacle +s
ten|tac|led
ten|tacu|lar
ten|tacu|late
tent|age
ten|ta|tive +s
ten|ta|tive|ly
ten|ta|tive|ness
tent-bed +s
ten|ter +s
ten|ter|hook +s
tent-fly
  tent-flies
tenth +s
tenth|ly
tenth-rate
tent-like
tent peg +s
tent-pegging
tent stitch
  tent stitches
ten|uis
  ten|ues
tenu|ity
tenu|ous
tenu|ous|ly
tenu|ous|ness
ten|ure +s
ten|ured
ten|ur|ial
ten|uri|al|ly
ten|uto +s
ten-week stock +s
  (plant)
Ten|zing Nor|gay
  (Sherpa
  mountaineer)
ten|zon +s
teo|calli +s
teo|sinte
Teo|ti|hua|cán
  (ancient city,
  Mexico)
tepal +s
tepee +s
tephra +s

Tepic (city,
  Mexico)
tepid
tep|id|arium
  tep|id|ar|iums *or*
  tep|id|aria
tep|id|ity
tep|id|ly
tep|id|ness
te|quila +s
tera|flop +s
terai +s
tera|kihi
  plural tera|kihi
tera|metre +s
ter|aph
  ter|aph|im
ter|ato|gen +s
tera|to|gen|ic
tera|togeny
tera|to|logic|al
tera|tolo|gist +s
tera|tol|ogy
  tera|tolo|gies
tera|toma
  tera|to|mas *or*
  tera|to|mata
tera|watt +s
ter|bium
terce +s (time for
  prayer. △ terse)
ter|cel +s
ter|cen|ten|ary
  ter|cen|ten|ar|ies
ter|cen|ten|nial +s
ter|cet +s
tere|bene
tere|binth +s
tere|binth|ine
tere|bra
  plural tere|bras *or*
  tere|brae
tere|brant +s
ter|edo +s
Ter|ence (name)
Ter|ence (Roman
  comic dramatist)
Ter|eng|ganu (use
  Trengganu)
ter|eph|thal|ate +s
ter|eph|thal|ic
Ter|esa *also*
  Ther|esa
  (name)
Ter|esa, Mother
  (nun and
  missionary in
  India)
Ter|esa of Ávila
  (Spanish saint)
Ter|esa of Lis|ieux
  (French saint)

Ter|esh|kova,
Val|en|tina
(Russian
cosmonaut)
Tere|sina (port,
Brazil)
ter|ete
ter|gal
ter|gi|ver|sate
  ter|gi|ver|sates
  ter|gi|ver|sated
  ter|gi|ver|sat|ing
ter|gi|ver|sa|tion
  +s
ter|gi|ver|sa|tor +s
teri|yaki
term +s +ed +ing
Ter|ma|gant +s
  (imaginary deity)
ter|ma|gant +s
  (virago)
ter|min|able
ter|min|able|ness
ter|min|al +s
ter|min|al|ly
ter|min|ate
  ter|min|ates
  ter|min|ated
  ter|min|at|ing
ter|min|ation +s
ter|min|ation|al
ter|min|ator +s
ter|min|er (in 'oyer
  and terminer')
ter|mini
ter|min|ism
ter|min|ist +s
ter|mino|logic|al
ter|mino|logic|
  al|ly
ter|min|olo|gist +s
ter|min|ology
  ter|min|olo|gies
ter|minus
  ter|mini
ter|minus ad quem
*ter|minus ante
  quem*
ter|minus a quo
ter|mit|arium
  ter|mit|aria
ter|mit|ary
  ter|mit|ar|ies
ter|mite +s
term|less
term|ly
ter|mor +s
term-time *noun
  and attributive*
tern +s (bird.
  △ terne, turn)
tern|ary

tern|ate
tern|ate|ly
terne (metal.
  △ tern, turn)
terne-plate
tero|tech|nol|ogy
ter|pene +s
Terp|sich|ore
  *Greek and Roman
  Mythology*
Terp|sich|or|ean
terra alba
ter|race
  ter|races
  ter|raced
  ter|ra|cing
terra|cotta +s
terra firma
terra|form +s +ed
  +ing
ter|rain +s
terra in|cog|nita
terra|mara
  terra|mare
terra|mare +s
Terra|pin +s
  (prefabricated
  building) *Propr.*
terra|pin +s (turtle)
ter|raque|ous
ter|rar|ium
  ter|raria
terra sigil|lata
Ter|rassa (use
  Tarrasa)
ter|razzo +s
Terre Haute (city,
  USA)
ter|rene (of the
  earth; earthly,
  worldly.
  △ terrine)
terre|plein +s
ter|res|trial +s
ter|res|tri|al|ly
ter|ret +s
terre-verte +s
ter|rible
ter|rible|ness
ter|ribly
ter|rico|lous
Ter|rier +s
  (member of the
  Territorial Army)
ter|rier +s (dog)
ter|rif|ic
ter|rif|ic|al|ly
ter|ri|fier +s
ter|rify
  ter|ri|fies
  ter|ri|fied
  ter|ri|fy|ing

ter|ri|fy|ing|ly
ter|ri|gen|ous
ter|rine +s (coarse
  pâté; earthenware
  dish. △ terrene)
ter|rit +s (use
  terret)
ter|ri|tor|ial +s
ter|ri|tori|al|
  isa|tion *Br.* (use
  territorialization)
ter|ri|tori|al|ise *Br.*
  (use territorialize)
  ter|ri|tori|al|ises
  ter|ri|tori|al|ised
  ter|ri|tori|al|is|ing
ter|ri|tori|al|ism
ter|ri|tori|al|ity
ter|ri|tori|al|
  iza|tion
ter|ri|tori|al|ize
  ter|ri|tori|al|izes
  ter|ri|tori|al|ized
  ter|ri|tori|al|iz|ing
ter|ri|tori|al|ly
ter|ri|tory
  ter|ri|tor|ies
ter|ror +s
ter|ror|isa|tion *Br.*
  (use
  terrorization)
ter|ror|ise *Br.* (use
  terrorize)
  ter|ror|ises
  ter|ror|ised
  ter|ror|is|ing
ter|ror|iser *Br.* +s
  (use terrorizer)
ter|ror|ism
ter|ror|ist +s
ter|ror|is|tic
ter|ror|is|tic|al|ly
ter|ror|iza|tion
ter|ror|ize
  ter|ror|izes
  ter|ror|ized
  ter|ror|iz|ing
ter|ror|izer +s
terror-stricken
Terry (name)
Terry, Ellen
  (English actress)
terry
  ter|ries
  (fabric)
terse
  terser
  ters|est
  (brief; curt.
  △ terce)
terse|ly
terse|ness

ter|tian
Ter|tiary *Geology*
ter|tiary
  ter|tiar|ies
  (third; monk)
ter|tium quid
Ter|tul|lian
  (Carthaginian
  theologian)
ter|va|lent
Tery|lene *Propr.*
terza rima
ter|zetto
  ter|zet|tos *or*
  ter|zetti
TESL (= teaching of
  English as a
  second language)
Tesla, Ni|kola
  (Croatian-born
  American
  electrical
  engineer; coil)
tesla +s (unit)
TESOL (= teaching
  of English to
  speakers of other
  languages)
Tess
TESSA +s (= tax
  exempt special
  savings account)
Tessa (name)
tes|sel|late
  tes|sel|lates
  tes|sel|lated
  tes|sel|lat|ing
tes|sel|la|tion +s
tes|sera
  tes|serae
tes|seral
Tes|sin (French
  and German name
  for Ticino)
tes|si|tura +s
test +s +ed +ing
testa
  tes|tae
  (seed-coat.
  △ tester)
test|abil|ity
test|able
test|aceous
Test Act +s
tes|tacy
  tes|ta|cies
tes|ta|ment +s
tes|ta|ment|ary
tes|tate +s
tes|ta|tor +s *male*

tes|ta|trix
tes|ta|tri|ces
female
Test-Ban Treaty
test bed +s
test case +s
test drive +s *noun*
test-drive
  test-drives
  test-drove
  test-driven
  test-driving
  verb
test|ee +s
test|er +s (person
  or thing that tests;
  sample; canopy.
  △ testa)
tes|tes (plural of
  testis)
test flight +s
test-fly
  test-flies
  test-flew
  test-flying
  test-flown
tes|ticle +s
tes|ticu|lar
tes|ticu|late
tes|ti|fier +s
test|ify
  testi|fies
  testi|fied
  testi|fy|ing
test|ily
tes|ti|mo|nial +s
tes|ti|mony
  tes|ti|monies
testi|ness
test|ing ground +s
tes|tis
  tes|tes
tes|tos|ter|one
test piece +s
test pilot +s
test tube +s *noun*
test-tube *attributive*
tes|tu|din|al
tes|tudo
  tes|tu|dos *or*
  tes|tu|di|nes
testy
  test|ier
  testi|est
tet|an|ic
tet|an|ic|al|ly
tet|an|ise *Br.* (use
  tetanize)
  tet|an|ises
  tet|an|ised
  tet|an|is|ing

tet|an|ize
tet|an|izes
tet|an|ized
tet|an|iz|ing
tet|an|oid
tet|anus
tet|any
tetch|ily
tetchi|ness
tetchy
  tetch|ier
  tetchi|est
  (irritable.
  △ techie)
tête-à-tête +s
tête-bêche
tether +s +ed +ing
Te|thys (*Greek
  Mythology*; moon
  of Saturn; former
  ocean)
Tet Of|fen|sive (in
  Vietnam War)
Té|touan (city,
  Morocco)
tetra +s
tetra|chlor|ide
tetra|chloro|
       ethyl|ene
tetra|chord +s
tetra|cyc|lic
tetra|cyc|line +s
tet|rad +s
tetra|dac|tyl +s
tetra|dac|tyl|ous
tetra|ethyl
tetra|gon +s
tet|rag|on|al
tet|rag|on|al|ly
tetra|gram +s
Tetra|gram|ma|
       ton
tet|ragyn|ous
tetra|he|dral
tetra|he|dron
  tetra|he|dra
tetra|hydro|
     canna|binol
tet|ralogy
  tet|ralo|gies
tet|ram|er|ous
tet|ram|eter +s
tetra|morph +s
tet|ran|drous
tetra|plegia
tetra|plegic +s
tetra|ploid +s
tetra|pod +s
tet|rapod|ous
tet|rap|ter|ous
tet|rarch +s
tet|rarch|ate +s

tet|rarch|ic|al
tet|rarchy
  tet|rarch|ies
tetra|stich +s
tetra|style +s
tetra|syl|lab|ic
tetra|syl|lable +s
tet|rath|lon +s
tetra|tom|ic
tetra|va|lent
tet|rode +s
tet|rox|ide
tet|ter +s
Teuton +s
Teut|on|ic
Teut|oni|cism
Tevet (use Tebet)
Texan +s
Texas (state, USA)
Tex-Mex
text +s
text|book +s
text|book|ish
tex|tile +s
text|less
text|ual
text|ual|ism
text|ual|ist
textu|al|ity
text|ual|ly
tex|tural
tex|tur|al|ly
tex|ture
  tex|tures
  tex|tured
  tex|tur|ing
tex|ture|less
tex|tur|ise *Br.* (use
  texturize)
  tex|tur|ises
  tex|tur|ised
  tex|tur|is|ing
tex|tur|ize
  tex|tur|izes
  tex|tur|ized
  tex|tur|iz|ing
Thack|eray,
  Wil|liam
  Make|peace
  (British novelist)
Thad|daeus
  (Apostle)
Thai
  plural **Thai** *or*
  Thais
Thai|land
Thai|land, Gulf of
  (inlet of South
  China Sea)
Thai|land|er +s
thal|am|ic

thal|amus
thal|ami
thal|as|sae|mia *Br.*
thal|as|semia *Am.*
thal|as|sic
thal|as|so|
       ther|apy
thaler +s (German
  coin. △ tala)
Tha|les (Greek
  philosopher)
Tha|lia (*Greek and
  Roman Mythology*;
  name)
thal|ido|mide
thalli
thal|lic
thal|lium
thal|lo|gen
thal|loid
thal|lo|phyte +s
thal|lous
thal|lus
  thalli
thal|weg +s
Thames (river,
  England; shipping
  area, North Sea)
Tham|muz
  (Jewish month.
  △ Tammuz)
than
than|age +s
thana|tol|ogy
Thana|tos
thane +s (English
  or Scottish
  landholder.
  △ thegn)
thane|dom +s
thane|ship +s
thank +s +ed +ing
thank|ful
thank|ful|ly
thank|ful|ness
thank|less
thank|less|ly
thank|less|ness
thank-offering +s
thanks|giv|ing +s
thank you (actual
  utterance)
thank-you +s
  (instance of saying
  'thank you')
thar +s (use tahr.
  animal. △ ta, tar)
Thar Des|ert (in
  India and Pakistan)
that
  those
thatch
  thatches

thatch (cont.)
  thatched
  thatch|ing
Thatch|er,
  Mar|ga|ret
  (British prime
  minister)
thatch|er +s
Thatch|er|ism
Thatch|er|ite +s
thauma|trope +s
thauma|turge +s
thauma|tur|gic
thauma|tur|gic|al
thauma|tur|gist +s
thauma|turgy
thaw +s +ed +ing
thaw|less
the (definite article.
  △ thee)
the|an|dric
the|an|throp|ic
the|archy
  the|arch|ies
the|ater Am. +s
theater|goer Am.
  +s
theater|going Am.
theater-in-the-
  round Am.
the|atre Br. +s
theatre|goer Br. +s
theatre|going Br.
theatre-in-the-
  round Br.
the|at|ric +s
the|at|ri|cal +s
the|at|ri|cal|
  isa|tion Br. (use
  theatricalization)
the|at|ri|cal|ise Br.
  (use theatricalize)
  the|at|ri|cal|ises
  the|at|ri|cal|ised
  the|at|ri|cal|is|ing
the|at|ri|cal|ism
the|at|ri|cal|ity
the|at|ri|cal|
    iza|tion
the|at|ri|cal|ize
  the|at|ri|cal|izes
  the|at|ri|cal|ized
  the|at|ri|cal|iz|ing
the|at|ri|cal|ly
Theban +s
thebe
  plural thebe
  (Botswanan
  currency)
Thebes (cities,
  ancient Egypt and
  Greece)

theca
  the|cae
the|cate
thé dan|sant
  thés dan|sants
thee (archaic = you.
  △ the)
theft +s
thegn +s (English
  landholder.
  △ thane)
theine (caffeine)
their (of or
  belonging to them.
  △ there, they're)
theirs (the one(s)
  belonging to them.
  △ there's)
their|selves (dialect
  or nonstandard;
  use themselves)
the|ism
the|ist +s
the|is|tic
the|is|tic|al
the|ist|ic|al|ly
Thelma
them
the|mat|ic
the|mat|ic|al|ly
the|mat|ics
theme
  themes
  themed
  them|ing
theme park +s
The|mis Greek
  Mythology
The|mis|to|cles
  (Athenian
  statesman)
them|self prefer
  themselves)
them|selves
then
the|nar +s
thence
thence|forth
thence|for|ward
Theo
Theo|bald
theo|bro|mine
theo|cen|tric
The|oc|racy, the
  (Jewish
  commonwealth)
the|oc|racy
  the|oc|ra|cies
  (divine
  government)
the|oc|rasy
  (mingling of
  deities into one;

the|oc|rasy (cont.)
  union of the soul
  with God)
theo|crat +s
theo|crat|ic
theo|crat|ic|al|ly
The|oc|ri|tus
  (Greek poet)
theo|di|cean
the|odicy
  the|odi|cies
the|odo|lite +s
the|odo|lit|ic
Theo|dora
  (Byzantine
  empress; name)
Theo|dor|akis,
  Mikis (Greek
  composer)
Theo|dore
Theo|dor|ic (king
  of the Ostrogoths)
Theo|dos|ius
  (Roman emperor)
the|ogo|nist +s
the|ogony
  the|ogo|nies
theo|lo|gian +s
theo|logic|al
theo|logic|al|ly
the|olo|gise Br.
  (use theologize)
  the|olo|gises
  the|olo|gised
  the|olo|gis|ing
the|olo|gist +s
the|olo|gize
  the|olo|gizes
  the|olo|gized
  the|olo|giz|ing
the|ology
  the|olo|gies
the|om|achy
  the|om|achies
theo|mania
the|ophany
  the|opha|nies
theo|phor|ic
Theo|phras|tus
  (Greek
  philosopher)
theo|phyl|line
the|op|neust
the|or|bist +s
the|orbo +s
the|orem +s
the|or|em|at|ic
the|or|et|ic
the|or|et|ic|al
the|or|et|ic|al|ly
the|or|et|ician +s

the|or|isa|tion Br.
  (use theorization)
the|or|ise Br. (use
  theorize)
  the|or|ises
  the|or|ised
  the|or|is|ing
the|or|iser Br. +s
  (use theorizer)
the|or|ist +s
the|or|iza|tion
the|or|ize
  the|or|izes
  the|or|ized
  the|or|iz|ing
the|or|izer +s
the|ory
  the|or|ies
theo|soph +s
the|oso|pher +s
theo|soph|ic
theo|soph|ic|al
theo|soph|ic|al|ly
the|oso|phise Br.
  (use theosophize)
  the|oso|phises
  the|oso|phised
  the|oso|phis|ing
the|oso|phist +s
the|oso|phize
  the|oso|phizes
  the|oso|phized
  the|oso|phiz|ing
the|oso|phy
  the|oso|phies
Thera (Greek
  island)
Theran
thera|peut|ic
thera|peut|ic|al
thera|peut|ic|al|ly
thera|peut|ics
thera|peut|ist +s
ther|ap|ist +s
ther|ap|sid +s
ther|apy
  ther|ap|ies
Thera|vada
  Buddhism
there (in that place
  etc. △ their,
  they're)
there|about
there|abouts
there|after
there|anent
there|at
there|by
there|for (archaic
  for that purpose)
there|fore (for that
  reason)

there|from
there|in
there|in|after
there|in|before
there|in|to
there|of
there|on
there|out
there's (= there is.
△ theirs)
Ther|esa *also*
Ter|esa
(name)
Ther|esa, Mother
(use Teresa)
Thérèse of
Lis|ieux
(= Teresa of
Lisieux)
there|through
there|to
there|to|fore
there|under
there|unto
there|upon
there|with
there|with|al
ther|iac +s
theri|an|throp|ic
therio|morph|ic
therm +s
ther|mae
ther|mal +s
ther|mal|isa|tion
Br. (use
thermalization)
ther|mal|ise *Br.*
(use thermalize)
ther|mal|ises
ther|mal|ised
ther|mal|is|ing
ther|mal|iza|tion
ther|mal|ize
ther|mal|izes
ther|mal|ized
ther|mal|iz|ing
ther|mal|ly
ther|mic
thermi|dor
ther|mion +s
thermi|on|ic
ther|mi|on|ics
ther|mis|tor +s
ther|mit
ther|mite
thermo|chem|ical
thermo|
chem|is|try
thermo|cline +s
thermo|couple +s
thermo|dynam|ic

thermo|dynam|
ic|al
thermo|dynam|ic|
al|ly
thermo|dynami|
cist +s
thermo|dynam|ics
thermo|elec|tric
thermo|elec|tric|
al|ly
thermo|
elec|tri|city
thermo|gen|esis
thermo|gram +s
thermo|graph +s
thermo|graph|ic
therm|og|raphy
thermo|labile
thermo|lumin|
es|cence
thermo|lumin|
es|cent
thermo|ly|sis
thermo|lyt|ic
therm|om|eter +s
thermo|met|ric
thermo|met|ric|al
thermo|met|ric|
al|ly
therm|om|etry
thermo|nuclear
thermo|phile +s
thermo|phil|ic
thermo|pile +s
thermo|plas|tic +s
Therm|opy|lae
(coastal pass and
battle, Greece)
therm|mos
ther|moses
Propr.
thermo|set
thermo|set|ting
thermo|sphere +s
thermo|stable
thermo|stat +s
thermo|stat|ic
thermo|stat|ic|
al|ly
thermo|tac|tic
thermo|tax|ic
thermo|taxis
thermo|trop|ic
thermo|trop|ism
thero|pod +s
the|saurus
the|sauri *or*
the|saur|uses
these
The|seus *Greek
Mythology*

thesis
theses
thesp +s
thes|pian +s
Thes|pis (Greek
poet)
Thes|sal|ian +s
Thes|sa|lon|ian +s
Thes|sa|lon|ica
(Latin name for
Thessaloníki)
Thes|sa|lon|iki
(port, Greece)
Thes|saly (region,
Greece)
theta +s
The|tis *Greek
Mythology*
the|ur|gic
the|ur|gic|al
the|ur|gist +s
the|urgy
thew +s
they
they'd (= they had;
they would)
they'll (= they will;
they shall)
they're (= they are.
△ their, there)
they've (= they
have)
thia|min (use
thiamine)
thia|mine
thia|zide +s
thick +er +est
thick|en +s +ed
+ing
thick|en|er +s
thick|en|ing +s
thicket +s
thick|head +s
thick|head|ed
thick|head|ed|
ness
thick|ish
thick-knee +s
thick|ly
thick|ness
thick|nesses
thick|nessed
thick|ness|ing
thick|ness|er +s
thicko +s
thick|set +s
thick-skinned
thick-skulled
thief
thieves
thieve
thieves

thieve (*cont.*)
thieved
thiev|ing
thiev|ery
thieves (plural of
thief)
thiev|ish
thiev|ish|ly
thiev|ish|ness
thigh +s
thigh bone +s
thig|mo|trop|ic
thig|mo|trop|ism
thill +s
thill|er +s
thill-horse +s
thim|ble +s
thimble|ful +s
thimble|rig
thimble|rig|ger +s
Thim|phu (capital
of Bhutan)
thin
thins
thinned
thin|ning
thin|ner
thin|nest
thine
thing +s
thing|ama|bob +s
thing|ama|jig +s
thing|am|bob +s
thing|amy (use
thingummy)
thing|amies
thingum +s
thing|uma|jig +s
(use thingamajig)
thing|ummy
thing|um|mies
thingy
thing|ies
think
thinks
thought
think|ing
think|able
think|er +s
think-tank +s
thin|ly
thin|ner +s
thin|ness
thin|ning +s
thin|nish
thin-skinned
thio-acid
thiol +s
thio|pen|tone
thio|sul|phate
thio|urea

Thíra (Greek name for **Thera**)

third +s

third-best

third-class *adjective*

third¦ly

third-party *attributive*

third-rate *adjective*

thirst +s +ed +ing

thirst¦ily

thirsti¦ness

thirst¦less

thirsty
thirst¦ier
thirsti¦est

thir¦teen +s

thir¦teenth +s

thir¦ti¦eth +s

thirty
thir¦ties

thirty-first, thirty-second, etc.

thirty¦fold

thirty-one, thirty-two, etc.

thirty-second note +s

thirty-something +s

thirty-two-mo

Thirty Years War

this
these

Thisbe *Roman Mythology*

this¦tle +s

thistle¦down

this¦tly

thither

thixo¦trop¦ic

thix¦otropy

tho' (use **though**)

thole
tholes
tholes
tholed
thol¦ing

thole-pin +s

tho¦los
tho¦loi

Thomas (Apostle and saint; name)

Thomas, Dylan (Welsh poet)

Thomas, Ed¦ward (English poet)

Thomas à Kem¦pis (German theologian)

Thomas Aqui¦nas (Italian saint)

Thom¦ism

Thom¦ist +s

Thom¦is¦tic

Thom¦is¦tic¦al

Thomp¦son, Daley (English athlete)

Thomp¦son, Fran¦cis (English poet)

Thom¦son, James (two Scottish poets)

Thom¦son, Jo¦seph John (English physicist)

Thom¦son, Wil¦liam (Lord Kelvin)

thong +s +ed +ing

Thor *Scandinavian Mythology*

thor¦ac¦al

thor¦acic

thorax
thora¦ces *or*
thor¦axes

Thor¦eau, Henry David (American writer)

thoria

thor¦ium

thorn +s

thorn apple +s

thorn¦back +s

thorn¦bill +s

thorn¦bush
thorn¦bushes

Thorn¦dike, Sybil (English actress)

thorn¦ily

thorni¦ness

thorn¦less

thorn¦proof

thorn¦tail +s

thorny
thorn¦ier
thorni¦est

thor¦ough

thor¦ough¦bred +s

thor¦ough¦fare +s

thor¦ough¦going

thor¦ough¦ly

thor¦ough¦ness

thorough-paced

thorough-wax (use **thorow-wax**)

thorow-wax

thorp +s

thorpe +s (use **thorp**)

Thors¦havn (use **Tórshavn**)

Thor¦vald¦sen, Ber¦tel (Danish sculptor)

those

Thoth *Egyptian Mythology*

thou (*archaic* you)

thou
plural thou *or* thous
(thousandth of an inch)

though

thought +s

thought¦ful

thought¦ful¦ly

thought¦ful¦ness

thought¦less

thought¦less¦ly

thought¦less¦ness

thought-provok¦ing

thought-reader +s

thought-reading

thought-wave +s

thou¦sand +s

thou¦sand¦fold

Thou¦sand Is¦land (mayonnaise)

Thou¦sand Is¦lands (in St Lawrence River, N. America; in Indonesia)

thou¦sandth +s

Thrace (ancient country, part of E. Balkan Peninsula; region, Greece)

Thra¦cian +s

thral¦dom +s

thrall +s

thrash
thrashes
thrashed
thrash¦ing

thrash¦er +s

thrash¦ing +s

thras¦on¦ical

thras¦on¦ic¦al¦ly

thrawn

thread +s +ed +ing

thread¦bare

thread¦er +s

thread¦fin +s

thread¦fish
plural thread¦fish *or* thread¦fishes

thread-like

Thread¦nee¦dle Street (in London)

thread¦worm +s

thready
thread¦ier
threadi¦est

threat +s

threat¦en +s +ed +ing

threat¦en¦er +s

threat¦en¦ing +s

threat¦en¦ing¦ly

three +s

three-cornered

three-decker +s

three-dimension¦al

three¦fold

three-handed

three-iron +s

three-legged race +s

three-line whip +s

Three Mile Is¦land (site of nuclear power station, USA)

three¦ness

three¦pence +s

three¦penny
three¦pen¦nies

three-phase

three-piece

three-ply

three-point

three-pronged

three-quarter +s

three¦score

three¦some +s

three-way

three-wheeler +s

threm¦ma¦tol¦ogy

thren¦ode +s

thren¦odial

thren¦od¦ic

thren¦od¦ist +s

thren¦ody
thren¦odies

threo¦nine

thresh
threshes
threshed
thresh¦ing

thresh¦er +s

thresh¦ing floor +s

thresh¦ing ma¦chine +s

thresh¦old +s

threw (past tense of **throw**.
△ **through**)

thrice
thrift+s
thrift|ily
thrifti|ness
thrift|less
thrift|less|ly
thrift|less|ness
thrifty
  thrift|ier
  thrifti|est
thrill+s +ed +ing
thrill|er+s
thrill|ing|ly
thrips
  plural thrips
thrive
  thrives
  thrived *or* throve
  thriv|ing
  thriven
thro' (use through)
throat+s
throat|ily
throati|ness
throaty
  throat|ier
  throati|est
throb
  throbs
  throbbed
  throb|bing
throe+s (pang;
  anguish. △ throw)
thrombi
throm|bin+s
thrombo|cyte+s
thrombo|cyto|
      penia
throm|bose
  throm|boses
  throm|bosed
  throm|bos|ing
throm|bosis
  throm|boses
throm|bot|ic
throm|bus
  thrombi
throne
  thrones
  throned
  thron|ing
  (chair of state;
  sovereign power.
  △ thrown)
throne|less
throng+s +ed
  +ing
thros|tle+s
thros|tle frame+s
throt|tle
  throt|tles

throt|tle (*cont.*)
  throt|tled
  throt|tling
throt|tler+s
through (from
  beginning to end
  etc. △ threw)
through|out
through|put+s
through|way *Br.*
  +s (*Am.* thruway)
throve
throw
  throws
  threw
  throw|ing
  thrown
  (propel etc.
  △ throe)
throw|able
throw|away+s
throw|back+s
throw|er+s
throw-in+s *noun*
thrown (past
  participle of
  throw. △ throne)
throw-off+s *noun*
throw-out+s *noun*
throw-over+s
  noun
throw|ster+s
thru *Am.* (use
  through *Br.*
  through)
thrum
  thrums
  thrummed
  thrum|ming
thrum|mer+s
thrummy
  thrum|mier
  thrum|mi|est
thrush
  thrushes
thrust
  thrusts
  thrust
  thrust|ing
thrust bear|ing+s
thrust block+s
thrust|er+s
thru|way *Am.* +s
  (*Br.* throughway)
Thu|cydi|des
  (Greek historian)
thud
  thuds
  thud|ded
  thud|ding
thud|ding|ly

Thug+s (member
  of Indian group)
thug+s (generally)
thug|gee
thug|gery
thug|gish
thug|gish|ly
thug|gish|ness
thug|gism
thuja+s
Thule (ancient
  northern land;
  Eskimo culture;
  settlement,
  Greenland)
thu|lium
thumb+s +ed
  +ing
thumb hole+s
thumb index
  thumb in|dexes
  noun
thumb-index
  thumb-indexes
  thumb-indexed
  thumb-indexing
  verb
thumb|less
thumb|nail+s
thumb nut+s
thumb|print+s
thumb|screw+s
thumb|tack+s
thump
  thumps
  thumped
  thump|ing
thump|er+s
thun|der+s +ed
  +ing
Thun|der Bay
  (city, Canada)
thun|der|bird+s
thun|der|bolt+s
thun|der|box
  thun|der|boxes
thun|der|bug+s
thun|der|clap+s
thun|der|cloud+s
thun|der|er+s
thun|der|flash
  thun|der|flashes
thun|der|fly
  thun|der|flies
thun|der|head+s
thun|der|ing+s
thun|der|ing|ly
thun|der|less
thun|der|ous
thun|der|ous|ly
thun|der|ous|ness
thun|der|storm+s

thun|der|struck
thun|dery
thunk+s +ed +ing
Thur|ber, James
  (American
  humorist)
Thur|gau (canton,
  Switzerland)
thur|ible+s
thuri|fer+s
thur|ifer|ous
thur|ifi|ca|tion
Thur|in|gia (state,
  Germany)
Thur|in|gian+s
Thurs|day+s
Thurso (port,
  Scotland)
thus
thus|ly
thuya+s
  (use thuja)
thwack+s +ed
  +ing
thwaite+s
thwart+s +ed
  +ing
thy
Thy|es|tean
Thy|es|tes *Greek*
  Mythology
thy|la|cine+s
thyme+s (herb.
  △ time)
thymi
thy|mi|dine
thy|mine
thy|mol
thy|mus
  thymi
thymy (like thyme)
thy|ris|tor+s
thy|roid+s
thy|rox|ine
thyr|sus
  thyrsi
thy|self
ti+s (tree. △ te,
  tea, tee)
ti (*Music*; use te
  △ tea, tee)
Tia|mat *Babylonian*
  Mythology
Tian|an|men
  Square (in
  Beijing, China)
Tian|jin (city,
  China)
Tian Shan (= Tien
  Shan)
tiara+s
tiara'd (use
  tiaraed)

tiaraed

Tiber (river, Italy)

Ti¦ber¦ias, Lake
(alternative name
for the Sea of
Galilee)

Ti¦ber¦ius (Roman
emperor)

Ti¦besti
Moun¦tains (in N.
Africa)

Tibet

Ti¦bet¦an +s

tibia
tib¦iae

tib¦ial

tibio¦tar¦sus
tibio¦tarsi

Tib¦ul¦lus (Roman
poet)

tic +s (twitch.
△ tick)

tic dou¦lour¦eux

tice +s

Tich¦borne
(claimant)

Ti¦cino (canton,
Switzerland)

tick +s +ed +ing
(click; moment;
mark; animal;
credit; mattress
cover. △ tic)

tick-bird +s

tick¦er +s (heart;
watch; tape
machine. △ tikka)

tick¦er tape +s

ticker-tape
attributive

ticket +s +ed +ing

ticket col¦lect¦or
+s

ticket-day +s

ticket-holder +s

ticket¦less

ticket-of-leave
man

ticket-of-leave
men

tickety-boo

tick¦ing +s

tickle
tickles
tickled
tick¦ling

tick¦ler +s

tick¦less

tick¦lish

tick¦lish¦ly

tick¦lish¦ness

tickly
tick¦lier
tick¦li¦est

tick-over noun

tick-tack
tick¦tack¦toe

tick-tock

tic-tac (use tick-
tack)

tic-tac-toe (use
ticktacktoe)

tidal

tid¦al¦ly

tid¦bit Am. +s (Br.
titbit)

tiddle¦dy¦wink Am.
+s (use
tiddlywink Br.
tiddlywink)

tid¦dler +s

tid¦dly
tid¦dlier
tiddli¦est

tiddly¦wink +s

tide
tides
tided
tid¦ing
(of sea; trend etc.
△ tied)

tide¦land +s

tide¦less

tide¦line +s

tide¦mark +s

tide mill +s

tide-rip +s

tide table +s

tide¦wait¦er +s

tide¦water +s

tide¦wave +s

tide¦way +s

tidi¦ly

tidi¦ness

tid¦ings

tidy
tidies
tidied
tidy¦ing
tidi¦er
tidi¦est

tie
ties
tied
tying

tie-back +s noun

tie-bar +s

tie-beam +s

tie-break +s

tie-breaker +s

tie-breaking

tie-clip +s

tie-dye
tie-dyes
tie-dyed
tie-dyeing

tie-in +s noun and
attributive

tie¦less

tie line +s

Tien Shan
(mountain range,
China)

Tien¦tsin
(= Tianjin)

tie¦pin +s

Tiep¦olo,
Gio¦vanni
Bat¦tista (Italian
painter)

tier +s (layer.
△ tear)

tierce +s

tierced

tier¦cel +s

tier¦cet +s

tiered

tier¦ing +s

Tierra del Fuego
(island off S.
America)

tie-up +s

tiff
tiffs
tiffed
tiff¦ing

Tif¦fany (name)

Tif¦fany, Louis
Com¦fort
(American
glassmaker)

tif¦fany
tif¦fa¦nies
(muslin)

tif¦fin +s +ed +ing

Tif¦lis (former
name of Tbilisi)

tig +s

tiger +s (animal.
△ taiga)

tiger-cat +s

tiger-eye +s
(stone; use tiger's-
eye)

tiger¦ish

tiger¦ish¦ly

tiger lily
tiger lil¦ies

Ti¦gers (Tamil
military
organization)

tiger's-eye +s
(stone)

tiger¦skin +s

tiger-wood

tight +s +er +est

tight¦en +s +ed
+ing

tight-fisted

tight-fitting

tight-knit

tight-lipped

tight¦ly

tightly-knit

tight¦ness

tight¦rope +s

tights

tight¦wad +s

Tiglath-pileser
(Assyrian kings)

tigon +s

Ti¦gray (province,
Ethiopia)

Ti¦gray¦an +s

Tigre (province,
Ethiopia; use
Tigray)

Tigre (Semitic
language)

Ti¦gre¦an +s (use
Tigrayan)

tig¦ress
tig¦resses

Tig¦rinya

Ti¦gris (river,
Mesopotamia)

Tihwa (former
name of Urumqi)

Ti¦juana (town,
Mexico)

Tikal (ancient city,
Guatemala)

tike +s (use tyke)

tiki +s

tikka +s (food.
△ ticker)

'til (use till)

til¦apia
plural til¦apia or
til¦apias

Til¦burg (city, the
Netherlands)

Til¦bury (port,
England)

til¦bury
til¦bur¦ies
(carriage)

Tilda (name)

tilde +s (accent)

tile
tiles
tiled
til¦ing

tiler +s

til¦ing +s

till
  tills
  tilled
  till|ing
till|able
till|age
till|er +s +ed +ing
til|ley lamp +s
  Propr.
Til|lich, Paul
  Jo|han|nes
  (German-born
  American
  theologian)
Tilly
til|t +s +ed +ing
tilt|er +s
tilth
tilt-hammer +s
tilt-yard +s
Tim
Tim|aru (port, New
  Zealand)
tim|bal +s (drum)
tim|bale +s (dish)
tim|ber +s +ed
  +ing
timber-frame
  adjective
timber-framed
timber-getter +s
tim|ber|land +s
tim|ber|line +s
tim|ber|man
  tim|ber|men
timbre +s
tim|brel +s
Tim|buc|too (use
  Timbuktu)
Tim|buktu (town,
  Mali; any remote
  place)
time
  times
  timed
  tim|ing
  (progress of
  events; etc.
  △ thyme)
time-and-motion
time bomb +s
time clock +s
time-consum|ing
time-frame +s
time-fuse +s
time-honored *Am.*
time-honoured *Br.*
time|keep|er +s
time|keep|ing
time lag +s
time-lapse
  attributive
time|less

time|less|ly
time|less|ness
time limit +s
time|li|ness
time lock +s
time-locked
time|ly
  time|lier
  time|li|est
time-out +s
time|piece +s
timer +s
time|scale +s
time-served
time-server +s
time-serving
time|share +s
time-sharing
time-shift
  time-shifts
  time-shifted
  time-shifting
time-span +s
time switch
  time switches
time|table
  time|tables
  time|tabled
  time|tab|ling
time travel
time trav|el|er *Am.*
  +s
time trav|el|ler *Br.*
  +s
time trial +s
time value +s
time warp +s
time-waster +s
time-wasting
time-work
time-worn
time zone +s
timid +er +est
tim|id|ity
tim|id|ly
tim|id|ness
tim|ing +s
Timi|şoara (city,
  Romania)
tim|oc|racy
  tim|oc|ra|cies
timo|crat|ic
Timor (island,
  Indonesia)
Ti|mor|ese
  plural Ti|mor|ese
tim|or|ous
tim|or|ous|ly
tim|or|ous|ness
Timor Sea
  (between Timor
  and Australia)

Tim|othy (early
  saint; name)
tim|othy
  tim|othies
  (grass; brothel)
tim|pani
tim|pan|ist +s
tin
  tins
  tinned
  tin|ning
tina|mou +s
Tin|ber|gen, Jan
  (Dutch economist)
Tin|ber|gen,
  Niko|laas (Dutch
  zoologist)
tinc|tor|ial
tinc|ture
  tinc|tures
  tinc|tured
  tinc|tur|ing
tin|dal +s
tin|der
tin|der|box
  tin|der|boxes
tin|dery
tine +s
tinea
tined
tin|foil
ting +s +ed +ing
  (bell-like sound;
  make this sound)
tinge
  tinges
  tinged
  tinge|ing *or*
  tin|ging
  (colour or affect
  slightly; slight
  trace)
tin-glaze +s
tin|gle
  tin|gles
  tin|gled
  tin|gling
tin|gly
  tin|glier
  tin|gli|est
tin|horn +s
tini|ly
tini|ness
tin|ker +s +ed
  +ing
tin|ker|er +s
tin|ker|ing +s
tin|kle
  tin|kles
  tin|kled
  tink|ling
tink|ling +s
tin|kly
tin|ner +s

tin|nily
tin|ni|ness
tin|nitus
tinny
  tin|nier
  tin|ni|est
tin-opener +s
tin plate *noun*
tin-plate
  tin-plates
  tin-plated
  tin-plating
  verb
tin|pot
tin|sel
  tin|sels
  tin|selled *Br.*
  tin|seled *Am.*
  tin|sel|ling *Br.*
  tin|sel|ing *Am.*
tin|sel|ly
Tin|sel|town
  (= Hollywood)
tin|smith +s
tin|snips
tin|stone
tint +s +ed +ing
tin-tack +s
Tin|tagel (village,
  England)
tint|er +s
tin|tin|nabu|lar
tin|tin|nabu|lary
tin|tin|nabu|
  la|tion +s
tin|tin|nabu|lous
tin|tin|nabu|lum
  tin|tin|nab|ula
Tin|tor|etto (Italian
  painter)
tin|ware
tiny
  tinies
  tini|er
  tini|est
tip
  tips
  tipped
  tip|ping
tip-and-run
tip|cat +s
tipi +s (use tepee)
tip|less
tip-off +s *noun*
tip|per +s
Tip|per|ary
  (county, Republic
  of Ireland)
tip|pet +s
Tip|pett, Mi|chael
  (English
  composer)

Tipp-Ex noun
Propr.
Tipp-Ex
Tipp-Exes
Tipp-Exed
Tipp-Exing
, verb
tip|ple
tip|ples
tip|pled
tip|pling
tip|pler +s
tippy
tip|pier
tip|pi|est
tip|sily
tip|si|ness
tip|staff
tip|staffs or
tip|staves
tip|ster +s
tipsy
tip|sier
tip|si|est
tipsy-cake +s
tip|toe
tip|toes
tip|toed
tip|toe|ing
tip-top
tip-up +s adjective
and noun
tir|ade +s
tir|ail|leur +s
tira|misu +s
Tir|ana (use
Tiranë)
Tir|anë (capital of
Albania)
tire
tires
tired
tir|ing
(grow weary etc.
△ tyre)
tire Am. (on
vehicle; Br. tyre)
tired +er +est
tired|ly
tired|ness
Tiree (Scottish
island; weather
station)
tire gauge Am. +s
(Br. tyre gauge)
tire|less
tire|less|ly
tire|less|ness
Tir|esias Greek
Mythology
tire|some
tire|some|ly

tire|some|ness
Tîrgu Mureş (city,
Romania)
Tir|ich Mir
(mountain,
Pakistan)
Tir-nan-Og Irish
Mythology
tiro +s (use tyro)
Tirol (German
name for Tyrol)
Tiru|chi|ra|palli
(city, India)
'tis (archaic = it is)
Tisa (Serbian name
for the Tisza)
tis|ane +s (infusion
of dried herbs etc.
△ ptisan)
Tishri (Jewish
month)
Tis|iph|one Greek
Mythology
Tisri (use Tishri)
tis|sue +s
tis|sue paper +s
Tisza (river, E.
Europe)
tit +s
Titan (Greek
Mythology; moon
of Saturn)
titan +s (person of
great strength,
intellect, etc.)
ti|tan|ate +s (salt
of titanic acid)
Ti|tan|ess
Ti|tan|esses
Greek Mythology
Tit|ania (fairy
queen; moon of
Uranus)
ti|tan|ic (of
titanium; gigantic)
Ti|tan|ic (ship)
ti|tan|ic|al|ly
ti|tan|ium
tit|bit Br. +s (Am.
tidbit)
titch
titches
titchy
titch|ier
titchi|est
titer Am. +s (Br.
titre)
tit|fer +s
tit-for-tat
tith|able
tithe
tithes

tithe (cont.)
tithed
tith|ing
tith|ing +s
Tith|onus Greek
Mythology
titi +s (monkey.
△ titty)
Ti|tian (Italian
painter)
Titi|caca, Lake (in
Peru and Bolivia)
tit|il|late
tit|il|lates
tit|il|lated
tit|il|lat|ing
tit|il|lat|ing|ly
tit|il|la|tion +s
titi|vate
titi|vates
titi|vated
titi|vat|ing
titi|va|tion +s
tit|lark +s
title
titles
titled
tit|ling
title deed +s
title-holder +s
title-page +s
tit|ling +s
tit|mouse
tit|mice
Tito born Josip
Broz
(Yugoslav
president)
Tito|grad (former
name of
Podgorica)
Tito|ism
Tito|ist +s
ti|trat|able
ti|trate
ti|trates
ti|trated
ti|trat|ing
ti|tra|tion +s
titre Br. +s (Am.
titer)
ti-tree +s (cabbage
tree. △ tea-tree)
tit|ter +s +ed +ing
tit|ter|er +s
tit|ter|ing|ly
tit|ti|vate (use
titivate)
tit|ti|vates
tit|ti|vated
tit|ti|vat|ing
tit|tle +s

tittle|bat +s
tittle-tattle
tittle-tattles
tittle-tattled
tittle-tattling
tit|tup
tit|tups
tit|tuped or
tit|tupped
tit|tup|ing or
tit|tup|ping
tit|tuppy
titty
tit|ties
(nipple; breast.
△ titi)
titu|ba|tion
titu|lar
titu|lar|ly
Titus (Roman
emperor; Greek
saint)
Tiv|oli (town, Italy)
tiz (use tizz)
tizzes
tizz
tizzes
tizzy
tiz|zies
T-joint +s
T-junction +s
Tlax|cala (city and
state, Mexico)
Tlem|cen (city,
Algeria)
Tlin|git
plural Tlin|git or
Tlin|gits
T-lympho|cyte +s
tme|sis
tme|ses
to (preposition in 'to
London' etc.; with
verb infinitives,
e.g. 'to go'. △ too,
two)
toad +s
toad-eater +s
toad|fish
plural toad|fish or
toad|fishes
toad|flax
toad-in-the-hole
+s
toad|ish
toad|let +s
toad|like
toad|stone +s
toad|stool +s
toady
toad|ies
toad|ied

toady (*cont.*)
toady|ing
(sycophant; to
fawn. △ tody)
toady|ish
toady|ism
toast +s +ed +ing
toast|er +s
toastie +s (toasted
sandwich.
△ toasty)
toasting-fork +s
toast|mas|ter +s
toast|mis|tress
toast|mis|tresses
toast rack +s
toasty (like toast)
to|bacco +s
to|bac|con|ist +s
tobacco-stopper
+s
To|bagan +s
To|bago (island,
West Indies)
Toba|go|nian +s
To|bias
Tobit *Bible*
to|bog|gan +s +ed
+ing
to|bog|gan|er +s
to|bog|gan|ist +s
To|bruk (port,
Libya)
Toby
toby jug +s
Toc|an|tins (river
and state, Brazil)
toc|cata +s
Toc H (Christian
society)
Toch|ar|ian +s
toco|pherol +s
toc|sin +s (alarm.
△ toxin)
tod
today +s
Todd, Mark
James (New
Zealand
equestrian)
tod|dle
tod|dles
tod|dled
tod|dling
tod|dler +s
toddler|hood
toddy
tod|dies
to-do +s
tody
todies
(bird. △ toady)

toe
toes
toed
toe|ing
(on foot. △ tow)
toe|cap +s
toe clip +s
toe|hold +s
toe-in
toe|less
toe|nail +s
toe-rag +s
toey
toff +s +ed +ing
tof|fee +s
tof|fee apple +s
tof|fee|ish
toffee-nosed
toft +s
tofu
tog
togs
togged
tog|ging
toga +s
toga'd
togaed (use toga'd)
to|gether
to|gether|ness
tog|gery
tog|gle
tog|gles
tog|gled
tog|gling
Togli|atti (city,
Russia)
Togo (in W. Africa)
Togo|land (former
region, W. Africa)
Togo|lese
plural Togo|lese
To|hoku (region,
Japan)
toil +s +ed +ing
(work)
toile +s (cloth)
toil|er +s
toi|let +s +ed +ing
toi|let roll +s
toi|let|ry
toi|let|ries
toi|lette +s
toilet-train +s +ed
+ing
toil|some
toil|some|ly
toil|some|ness
toil-worn
toing and fro|ing
to|ings and
fro|ings

Tojo, Hi|deki
(Japanese prime
minister)
toka|mak +s
Tokay +s (wine)
tokay +s (gecko)
Tok|elau (island
group, W. Pacific)
token +s
token|ism
token|ist
token|is|tic
Toku|gawa
Tokyo (capital of
Japan)
toll|booth +s (use
toll-booth)
Tol|bu|khin
(former name of
Dobrich)
told (past tense and
past participle of
tell △ tolled)
To|ledo (cities,
Spain and USA)
tol|er|abil|ity
tol|er|able
tol|er|able|ness
tol|er|ably
tol|er|ance +s
tol|er|ant
tol|er|ant|ly
tol|er|ate
tol|er|ates
tol|er|ated
tol|er|at|ing
tol|er|ation +s
tol|er|ator +s
To|lima (volcano,
Colombia)
Tol|kien, J. R. R.
(British novelist)
toll +s +ed +ing
(charge; cost; ring.
△ told)
toll-booth +s
toll bridge +s
toll gate +s
toll-house +s
toll|road +s
Tol|lund Man
Tol|pud|dle
mar|tyrs
Tol|stoy, Leo
(Russian writer)
Tol|tec
plural Tol|tec *or*
Tol|tecs
Tol|tec|an +s
tolu
To|luca (de Lerdo)
(city, Mexico)

tolu|ene
tol|uic
tol|uol
Tol|yatti (Russian
name for
Togliatti)
Tom (name)
tom +s (male
animal)
toma|hawk +s +ed
+ing
to|mal|ley +s
toma|tillo +s
to|mato
to|ma|toes
to|ma|toey
tomb +s
tom|bac
Tom|baugh, Clyde
Wil|liam
(American
astronomer)
tom|bola +s
tom|bolo +s
Tom|bouc|tou
(French name for
Timbuktu)
tom|boy +s
tom|boy|ish
tom|boy|ish|ness
tomb|stone +s
tom-cat +s
Tom Col|lins
Tom Col|linses
(drink)
tome +s
to|men|tose
to|men|tous
to|men|tum
to|menta
tom|fool +s
tom|fool|ery
tom|fool|er|ies
Tomis (ancient
name for
Constanţa)
Tommy
Tom|mies
(British soldier;
name)
tommy bar +s
tommy-gun +s
tommy|rot
tommy ruff +s
tomo|gram +s
tomo|graph +s
tomo|graph|ic
tom|og|raphy
Tomor, Mount (in
Albania)
to|mor|row +s

Tom|pion,
  Thomas (English
  clockmaker)
tom|pion +s
tom|pot +s
tom|pot blenny
  tom|pot blen|nies
Tomsk (city,
  Siberia)
tom|tit +s
tom-tom +s
ton +s (various
  units of weight;
  100. △ tonne,
  tun)
ton +s (fashion)
tonal
ton|al|ity
  ton|al|ities
ton|al|ly
Ton|bridge (town,
  England.
  △ Tunbridge
  Wells)
tondo
  tondi
tone
  tones
  toned
  ton|ing
tone arm +s
tone|burst +s
tone-deaf
tone-deafness
tone|less
tone|less|ly
ton|eme +s
ton|em|ic
tone|pad +s
tone poem +s
toner +s
tone-row +s
tong +s +ed +ing
Tonga (in S.
  Pacific)
Tonga
  plural Tonga or
  Ton|gas
  (member of
  African people;
  their language)
tonga +s (horse-
  drawn vehicle)
Ton|gan +s (of
  Tonga; person;
  language)
Tonga|riro, Mount
  (in New Zealand)
tong|kang +s
tongs
Tong|shan (former
  name of Xuzhou)

tongue
tongues
tongued
tonguing
  (in mouth etc.
  △ tung)
tongue-and-
  groove attributive
tongue-in-cheek
tongue-lashing +s
tongue|less
tongue-tie +s
tongue-tied
tongue-twister +s
Toni (woman's
  name. △ Tony)
Tonia also Tonya
tonic +s
ton|ic|al|ly
ton|icity
tonic sol-fa
to|night
ton|ish
tonka bean +s
Ton|kin, Gulf of
  (between Vietnam
  and China)
Tonlé Sap (lake,
  Cambodia)
ton-mile +s
ton|nage +s
tonne +s (1000 kg.
  △ ton, tun)
ton|neau +s
ton|om|eter +s
ton|sil +s
ton|sil|lar
ton|sil|lec|tomy
  ton|sil|lec|to|mies
ton|sil|litis
ton|sor|ial
ton|sure
  ton|sures
  ton|sured
  ton|sur|ing
ton|tine +s
Ton|ton Ma|coute
  Ton|tons
  Ma|coutes
ton-up +s
Tony (man's name.
  △ Toni)
Tony
  Tonies
  (American theatre
  award)
tony
  toni|er
  toni|est
  (stylish)
Tonya also Tonia

too (adverb, in 'too
  much' etc. △ to,
  two)
toodle-oo
took
tool +s +ed +ing
tool bag +s
tool|box
  tool|boxes
tool|er +s
tool hold|er +s
tool kit +s
tool|maker +s
tool|mak|ing
tool-pusher +s
tool shed +s
toot +s +ed +ing
toot|er +s
tooth
  teeth
tooth|ache +s
tooth-billed
tooth|brush
  tooth|brushes
tooth|comb +s
toothed
tooth-glass
  tooth-glasses
tooth|ily
toothi|ness
tooth|ing
tooth|less
tooth|like
tooth-mug +s
tooth|paste +s
tooth|pick +s
tooth|some
tooth|some|ly
tooth|some|ness
tooth|wort +s
toothy
  tooth|ier
  toothi|est
too|tle
  too|tles
  too|tled
  toot|ling
toot|ler +s
too-too (extreme,
  excessive;
  excessively.
  △ tutu)
tootsy
  toot|sies
  (toe. △ Tutsi)
Too|woomba
  (town, Australia)
top
  tops
  topped
  top|ping

topaz
  to|pazes
top|azo|lite +s
top-boot +s
top|coat +s
top-down
top-drawer
  adjective
top dress
  top dresses
  top dressed
  top dress|ing
tope
  topes
  toped
  top|ing
  (drink; grove;
  Buddhist shrine;
  fish. △ taupe)
topee +s (use topi)
To|peka (city,
  USA)
toper +s
top-flight
top|gal|lant +s
top-hamper +s
top-hatted
top-heavily
top-heaviness
top-heavy
To|phet Bible
top-hole
to|phus
  tophi
topi +s
topi|ar|ian +s
topi|ar|ist +s
topi|ary
  topi|ar|ies
topic +s
top|ic|al
top|ic|al|ity
top|ic|al|ly
Top|kapi Pal|ace
  (in Istanbul)
top|knot +s
top|less
top|less|ness
top-level adjective
top-line adjective
top|lofty
top|man
  top|men
top|mast +s
top|most
top-notch
top-notcher +s
top|og|raph|er +s
topo|graph|ic
topo|graph|ic|al
topo|graph|ic|al|ly

top¦og¦raphy
  top¦og¦raph¦ies
topoi (plural of topos)
topo¦logic¦al
topo¦logic¦al¦ly
top¦olo¦gist +s
top¦ology
topo¦nym +s
topo¦nym¦ic
top¦onymy
topos
  topoi
top¦per +s
top¦ping +s
top¦ple
  top¦ples
  top¦pled
  top¦pling
top¦sail +s
top-sawyer +s
top se¦cret
top-shell +s
top¦side +s
top¦slice (in tennis etc.)
top-slicing *Tax*
top¦soil +s
top¦spin +s
top¦stitch
  top¦stitches
  top¦stitched
  top¦stitch¦ing
topsy-turvily
topsy-turviness
topsy-turvy
top-up +s *noun and attributive*
toque +s
to¦quilla +s
tor +s (hill. △ tau, taw, tore, torr)
Torah
Tor¦bay (resort, England)
torc +s (necklace. △ talk, torque)
torch
  torches
  torched
  torch¦ing
torch-bearer +s
tor¦chère +s
torch-fishing
torch¦light
torch¦lit
tor¦chon +s
torch race +s
torch-thistle +s
tore +s (past tense of tear; *Architecture*;

tore (*cont.*)
  Geometry. △ tau, taw, tor, torr)
torea¦dor +s
tor¦ero +s
tor¦eut¦ic
tor¦eut¦ics
tor¦goch
  plural tor¦goch
tori (plural of torus. △ Tory)
toric
torii
  plural torii
tor¦ment +s +ed +ing
tor¦ment¦ed¦ly
tor¦men¦til +s
tor¦ment¦ing¦ly
tor¦ment¦or +s
torn
tor¦nad¦ic
tor¦nado
  tor¦na¦does *or*
  tor¦na¦dos
Torne Älv (Swedish name for the Tornio)
Tor¦nio (river, Scandinavia)
tor¦oid
tor¦oid¦al
tor¦oid¦al¦ly
To¦ronto (city, Canada)
tor¦ose
tor¦pedo
  tor¦pe¦does
  tor¦pe¦doed
  tor¦pe¦do¦ing
tor¦pedo boat +s
tor¦pedo bomb¦er +s
torpedo-like
torpedo-net +s
torpedo-netting
tor¦pefy
  tor¦pe¦fies
  tor¦pe¦fied
  tor¦pe¦fying
tor¦pid
tor¦pid¦ity
tor¦pid¦ly
tor¦pid¦ness
tor¦por +s
tor¦por¦if¦ic
tor¦quate
Tor¦quay (resort, England)
torque
  torques
  torqued

torque (*cont.*)
  tor¦quing
  (turning force. △ talk, torc)
Tor¦que¦mada, Tomás de (Inquisitor-General of Spain)
tor¦quey (producing much torque. △ talkie)
torr
  plural torr
  (unit of pressure. △ tau, taw, tor, tore)
tor¦re¦fac¦tion
tor¦refy
  tor¦re¦fies
  tor¦re¦fied
  tor¦re¦fying
tor¦rent +s
tor¦ren¦tial
tor¦ren¦tial¦ly
Tor¦res Strait (N. of Australia)
Tor¦ri¦celli, Evan¦ge¦lista (Italian physicist)
Tor¦ri¦cel¦lian
tor¦rid
tor¦rid¦ity
tor¦rid¦ly
tor¦rid¦ness
torse +s
tor¦sel +s
Tórs¦havn (capital of the Faeroe Islands)
tor¦sion
tor¦sion¦al
tor¦sion¦al¦ly
tor¦sion¦less
torsk +s
torso +s
tort +s (*Law.* △ taught, taut, torte)
torte
  tort¦en *or* tortes (cake. △ taught, taut, tort)
Tor¦tel¦ier, Paul (French cellist)
tor¦telli
tor¦tel¦lini
tort¦fea¦sor +s
tor¦ti¦col¦lis
tor¦tilla +s
tor¦tious
tor¦tious¦ly
tor¦toise +s

tortoise-like
tor¦toise¦shell +s
Tor¦tola (island, British Virgin Islands)
tor¦trix
  tor¦tri¦ces
tor¦tu¦os¦ity
tor¦tu¦ous
tor¦tu¦ous¦ly
tor¦tu¦ous¦ness
tor¦tur¦able
tor¦ture
  tor¦tures
  tor¦tured
  tor¦tur¦ing
tor¦turer +s
tor¦tur¦ous
tor¦tur¦ous¦ly
tor¦ula
  toru¦lae
Toruń (city, Poland)
torus
  tori *or* tor¦uses (*Architecture; Botany; Anatomy; Geometry.* △ Taurus)
Tor¦vill, Jayne (English ice-skater)
Tory
  Tor¦ies (Conservative. △ tori)
Tory¦ism
tosa +s
Tos¦ca¦nini, Ar¦turo (Italian conductor)
tosh
Tosk
  plural Tosk *or* Tosks
toss
  tosses
  tossed
  toss¦ing
toss¦er +s (*coarse slang*)
toss-up +s
tot
  tots
  totted
  tot¦ting
total
  to¦tals
  to¦talled *Br.*
  to¦taled *Am.*
  to¦tal¦ling *Br.*
  to¦tal¦ing *Am.*

to¦tal¦isa¦tion *Br.*
 (use totalization)
to¦tal¦isa¦tor *Br.*
 (use totalizator)
to¦tal¦ise *Br.* (use
 totalize)
to¦tal¦ises
to¦tal¦ised
to¦tal¦is¦ing
to¦tal¦iser *Br.* +s
 (use totalizer)
to¦tali¦tar¦ian +s
to¦tali¦tar¦ian¦ism
to¦tal¦ity
 to¦tal¦ities
to¦tal¦iza¦tion
to¦tal¦iza¦tor +s
to¦tal¦ize
 to¦tal¦izes
 to¦tal¦ized
 to¦tal¦iz¦ing
 to¦tal¦izer +s
to¦tal¦ly
tote
 totes
 toted
 tot¦ing
 (carry; totalizator;
 lottery)
tote bag +s
totem +s
to¦tem¦ic
to¦tem¦ism
to¦tem¦ist +s
to¦tem¦is¦tic
totem pole +s
toter +s
tother (= the other)
tot¦ter +s +ed +ing
tot¦ter¦er +s
tot¦tery
totting-up
 tottings-up
totty
tou¦can +s
touch
 touches
 touched
 touch¦ing
touch¦able
touch-and-go
touch¦back +s
touch¦down +s
tou¦ché
touch¦er +s
touch-hole +s
touch¦ily
touchi¦ness
touch¦ing +s
touch¦ing¦ly
touch¦ing¦ness
touch-in-goal +s

touch judge +s
touch¦line +s
touch-mark +s
touch-me-not +s
 (plant)
touch-needle +s
touch¦paper +s
touch screen +s
touch¦stone +s
touch-type
 touch-typing
touch-typing
touch-typist +s
touch-up +s *noun
 and attributive*
touch¦wood +s
touchy
 touch¦ier
 . touchi¦est
tough +s +er +est
 (durable; hardy;
 severe; etc. △ tuff)
tough¦en +s +ed
 +ing
tough¦en¦er +s
toughie +s
tough¦ish
tough¦ly
tough-minded
tough-
 minded¦ness
tough¦ness
Tou¦lon (port,
 France)
Tou¦louse (city,
 France)
Toulouse-Lautrec,
 Henri de (French
 artist)
tou¦pee +s
tour +s +ed +ing
tour¦aco +s
tour de force
 tours de force
Tour de France
 (cycle race)
tour¦er +s
Tour¦ette's
 syn¦drome
tour¦ism
tour¦ist +s
tour¦ist¦ed
tour¦is¦tic
tour¦is¦tic¦al¦ly
tour¦isty
tour¦ma¦line +s
Tour¦nai (town,
 Belgium)
tour¦na¦ment +s
tour¦ne¦dos
 plural tour¦ne¦dos

tour¦ney +s +ed
 +ing
tour¦ni¦quet +s
Tours (city, France)
tou¦sle
 tou¦sles
 tou¦sled
 tous¦ling
tousle-haired
tous-les-mois
 *plural tous-les-
 mois*
Tous¦saint
 L'Ouver¦ture,
 Pierre (Haitian
 revolutionary)
tout +s +ed +ing
tout-court
tout de suite
tout¦er +s
to¦var¦ich (use
 tovarish)
to¦var¦iches
to¦var¦ish
 to¦var¦ishes
tow +s +ed +ing
 (pull; fibres.
 △ toe)
tow¦able
tow¦age
to¦ward
to¦ward¦ness
to¦wards
tow bar +s
towel
 towels
 tow¦elled *Br.*
 tow¦eled *Am.*
 tow¦el¦ling *Br.*
 tow¦el¦ing *Am.*
towel-horse +s
tow¦el¦ling *Am.* +s
tow¦el¦ling *Br.* +s
tower +s +ed +ing
tower block +s
tow¦ery
tow-head +s
tow-headed
tow¦hee +s
towing-path +s
towing-rope +s
tow¦line +s
town +s
townee +s (use
 townie)
Townes, Charles
 Hard (American
 physicist)
tow-net +s
town house +s
townie +s
town¦ish

town¦less
town¦let +s
town-major +s
town¦scape +s
towns¦folk
town¦ship +s
towns¦man
towns¦men
towns¦people
Towns¦ville (port,
 Australia)
towns¦woman
towns¦women
Towns¦women's
 Guild +s
town¦ward
town¦wards
tow¦path +s
tow¦plane +s
tow rope +s
towy
tox¦ae¦mia *Br.*
tox¦aem¦ic *Br.*
tox¦emia *Am.*
tox¦em¦ic *Am.*
toxic +s
tox¦ic¦al¦ly
toxi¦cant +s
tox¦icity
 toxi¦ci¦ties
toxi¦co¦logic¦al
toxi¦colo¦gist +s
toxi¦col¦ogy
toxi¦co¦mania
toxin +s (poison.
 △ tocsin)
toxo¦cara
toxo¦caria¦sis
tox¦oph¦il¦ite +s
tox¦oph¦ily
toxo¦plas¦mo¦sis
toy +s +ed +ing
toy-box
 toy-boxes
toy¦boy +s
toy¦like
toy¦maker +s
Toyn¦bee, Ar¦nold
 Jo¦seph (English
 historian)
toy¦shop +s
toy¦town
T-piece +s
trab¦eate
trabea¦tion
trab¦ecula
 trab¦ecu¦lae
trab¦ecu¦lar
trab¦ecu¦late
Trab¦zon (city,
 Turkey)
trac¦as¦serie +s

trace
  traces
  traced
  tra|cing
trace|abil|ity
trace|able
trace-horse +s
trace|less
tracer +s
tra|cer|ied
tra|cery
  tra|cer|ies
Tra|cey also Tracy
trachea
  trach|eae
trach|eal
trach|eate
trache|os|tomy
  trache|os|to|mies
trache|ot|omy
  trache|oto|mies
trach|oma
trach|oma|tous
trach|yte +s
trach|yt|ic
tra|cing +s
tra|cing paper +s
track +s +ed +ing
track|age
track|ball +s
track|bed +s
track|er +s
track|lay|er +s
track-laying
trackle|ment +s
track|less
track|man
  track|men
track|side
track|suit +s
track|way +s
tract +s
tract|abil|ity
tract|able
tract|able|ness
tract|ably
Tract|arian +s
Tract|ar|ian|ism
trac|tate +s
trac|tion +s
trac|tion|al
trac|tion en|gine
  +s
trac|tion wheel +s
trac|tive
trac|tor +s
Tracy, Spen|cer
  (American actor)
Tracy also Tra|cey
trad (= traditional
  jazz; traditional)
trad|able

trade
  trades
  traded
  trad|ing
trade|able
trade-in +s noun
  and attributive
trade-last +s
trade|mark +s +ed
  +ing verb
trade mark +s
  noun
trade name +s
trade-off +s noun
trader +s
trad|es|can|tia +s
trades|man
  trades|men
trades|people
trades union +s
trades union|ism
trades union|ist
  +s
trade union +s
trade union|ism
trade union|ist +s
trade-weight|ed
trad|ing stamp +s
trad|ing sta|tion
  +s
trad|ition +s
trad|ition|al
trad|ition|al|ism
trad|ition|al|ist +s
trad|ition|al|ly
trad|ition|ary
trad|ition|ist +s
trad|ition|less
tradi|tor
  tradi|tors or
  tradi|tor|es
tra|duce
  tra|duces
  tra|duced
  tra|du|cing
tra|duce|ment +s
tra|ducer +s
tra|du|cian +s
tra|du|cian|ism
tra|du|cian|ist +s
Tra|fal|gar (naval
  battle; shipping
  area)
traf|fic
  traf|fics
  traf|ficked
  traf|fick|ing
traf|fic|ator +s
traf|fic calm|ing
traf|fick|er +s
traf|fic|less

traf|fic light +s
traga|canth +s
tra|gedian +s
  (writer of or male
  actor in tragedies)
tra|gedi|enne +s
  (actress in
  tragedies)
tra|gedy
  tra|ged|ies
tra|gic
tra|gic|al
tra|gic|al|ly
tragi|com|edy
  tragi|com|ed|ies
tragi|com|ic
tragi|com|ic|al|ly
trago|pan +s
Tra|herne,
  Thomas (English
  writer)
trahi|son des clercs
trail +s +ed +ing
trail|blazer +s
trail|blaz|ing
trail|er +s +ed
  +ing
trail-net +s
train +s +ed +ing
train|abil|ity
train|able
train|band +s
train-bearer +s
train driver +s
train|ee +s
trainee|ship +s
train|er +s
train ferry
  train fer|ries
train|less
train|load +s
train|man
  train|men
train-mile +s
train-oil
train set +s
train-shed +s
train|sick
train|sick|ness
train-spotter +s
train-spotting
traipse
  traipses
  traipsed
  traips|ing
trait +s
  (characteristic.
  △ tray, trey)
trai|tor +s
trai|tor|ous
trai|tor|ous|ly

trai|tress
  trai|tresses
Tra|jan (Roman
  emperor)
tra|jec|tory
  tra|jec|tor|ies
tra-la
Tra|lee (town,
  Republic of
  Ireland)
tram +s
tram|car +s
Tra|miner +s
tram|line +s
tram|mel
  tram|mels
  tram|melled Br.
  tram|meled Am.
  tram|mel|ling Br.
  tram|mel|ing Am.
tram|mie +s
tra|mon|tana +s
tra|mon|tane +s
tramp +s +ed +ing
tramp|er +s
tramp|ish
tram|ple
  tram|ples
  tram|pled
  tramp|ling
tramp|ler +s
tramp-like
tram|po|line
  tram|po|lines
  tram|po|lined
  tram|po|lin|ing
tram|po|lin|ist +s
tram road +s
tram|way +s
trance
  trances
  tranced
  tran|cing
trance-like
tranche +s
tranny
  tran|nies
tran|quil
tran|quil|isa|tion
  Br.
  tranquillization
  Am.
  tranquillization)
tran|quil|ise Br.
  (use tranquillize)
  tran|quil|ises
  tran|quil|ised
  tran|quil|is|ing
  (Am. tranquilize)
tran|quil|liser Br.
  +s (use

tran¦quil¦liser
(cont.)
tranquillizer . Am.
tranquilizer)
tran¦quil¦lity (use
tranquillity)
tran¦quil¦liza¦tion
Am. (Br.
tranquillization)
tran¦quil¦lize Am.
tran¦quil¦lizes
tran¦quil¦lized
tran¦quil¦liz¦ing
(Br. tranquillize)
tran¦quil¦lizer Am.
+s (Am.
tranquilizer)
tran¦quil¦lisa¦tion
Br. (use
tranquillization .
Am.
tranquilization)
tran¦quil¦lise Br.
(use tranquillize)
tran¦quil¦lises
tran¦quil¦lised
tran¦quil¦lis¦ing
(Am. tranquilize)
tran¦quil¦liser Br.
+s (use
tranquillizer . Am.
tranquilizer)
tran¦quil¦lity
tran¦quil¦liza¦tion
Br. (Am.
tranquilization)
tran¦quil¦lize Br.
tran¦quil¦lizes
tran¦quil¦lized
tran¦quil¦liz¦ing
(Am. tranquilize)
tran¦quil¦lizer Br.
+s (Am.
tranquilizer)
tran¦quil¦ly
trans¦act +s +ed
+ing
trans¦ac¦tion +s
trans¦ac¦tion¦al
trans¦ac¦tion¦al¦ly
trans¦act¦or +s
trans¦alpine
trans¦at¦lan¦tic
Trans¦cau¦ca¦sia
Trans¦cau¦ca¦sian
trans¦ceiver +s
tran¦scend +s +ed
+ing
tran¦scend¦ence
tran¦scend¦ency
tran¦scend¦en¦
    cies

tran¦scend¦ent +s
tran¦scen¦den¦tal
**tran¦scen¦den¦tal¦
ise** Br. (use
transcendental-
ize)
tran¦scen¦den¦tal¦
    ises
tran¦scen¦den¦tal¦
    ised
tran¦scen¦den¦tal¦
    is¦ing
**tran¦scen¦den¦tal¦
ism**
**tran¦scen¦den¦tal¦
ist** +s
**tran¦scen¦den¦tal¦
ize**
tran¦scen¦den¦tal¦
    izes
tran¦scen¦den¦tal¦
    ized
tran¦scen¦den¦tal¦
    iz¦ing
**tran¦scen¦
den¦tal¦ly** (in a
visionary, abstract
manner)
**Tran¦scen¦den¦tal
Medi¦ta¦tion**
tran¦scend¦ent¦ly
(pre-eminently)
trans¦code
trans¦codes
trans¦coded
trans¦cod¦ing
**trans¦con¦tin¦
en¦tal**
**trans¦con¦tin¦
en¦tal¦ly**
tran¦scribe
tran¦scribes
tran¦scribed
tran¦scrib¦ing
tran¦scriber +s
tran¦script +s
tran¦scrip¦tion +s
tran¦scrip¦tion¦al
tran¦scrip¦tive
**Trans¦dan¦ub¦ian
High¦lands** (in
Hungary)
trans¦duce
trans¦duces
trans¦duced
trans¦du¦cing
trans¦ducer +s
trans¦duc¦tion
tran¦sect +s +ed
+ing
tran¦sec¦tion +s
tran¦sept +s

tran¦sep¦tal
tran¦sex¦ual +s
(use transsexual)
tran¦sexu¦al¦ism
(use
transsexualism)
trans¦fer
trans¦fers
trans¦ferred
trans¦fer¦ring
trans¦fer¦abil¦ity
trans¦fer¦able
transfer-book +s
trans¦fer¦ee +s
trans¦fer¦ence
trans¦fer¦or +s
(generally)
transfer-paper +s
trans¦fer¦ral +s
trans¦fer¦rer +s
Law
trans¦fer¦rin
trans¦fer RNA
trans¦fig¦ur¦ation
+s
trans¦fig¦ure
trans¦fig¦ures
trans¦fig¦ured
trans¦fig¦ur¦ing
trans¦finite
trans¦fix
trans¦fixes
trans¦fixed
trans¦fix¦ing
trans¦fix¦ion
trans¦form +s +ed
+ing
trans¦form¦able
trans¦form¦ation
+s
**trans¦form¦
ation¦al**
**trans¦form¦ation¦
al¦ly**
trans¦forma¦tive
trans¦form¦er +s
trans¦fuse
trans¦fuses
trans¦fused
trans¦fus¦ing
trans¦fu¦sion +s
trans¦gen¦ic
trans¦gress
trans¦gresses
trans¦gressed
trans¦gress¦ing
trans¦gres¦sion +s
trans¦gres¦sion¦al
trans¦gres¦sive
trans¦gres¦sor +s
tran¦ship (use
trans-ship)
tran¦ships

tran¦ship (cont.)
tran¦shipped
tran¦ship¦ping
tran¦ship¦ment +s
(use trans-
shipment)
trans¦hu¦mance
tran¦si¦ence
tran¦si¦ency
tran¦si¦ent +s
tran¦si¦ent¦ly
trans¦illu¦min¦ate
trans¦illu¦min¦
    ates
trans¦illu¦min¦
    ated
trans¦illu¦min¦
    at¦ing
**trans¦illu¦min¦
ation**
tran¦sire +s
tran¦sis¦tor +s
**tran¦sis¦tor¦
isa¦tion** Br. (use
transistorization)
tran¦sis¦tor¦ise Br.
(use
transistorize)
tran¦sis¦tor¦ises
tran¦sis¦tor¦ised
tran¦sis¦tor¦is¦ing
**tran¦sis¦tor¦
iza¦tion**
tran¦sis¦tor¦ize
tran¦sis¦tor¦izes
tran¦sis¦tor¦ized
tran¦sis¦tor¦iz¦ing
tran¦sit +s +ed
+ing
transit-circle +s
transit-compass
transit-
  compasses
transit-duty
transit-duties
transit-
  instru¦ment +s
tran¦si¦tion +s
tran¦si¦tion¦al
tran¦si¦tion¦al¦ly
tran¦si¦tion¦ary
tran¦si¦tive +s
tran¦si¦tive¦ly
tran¦si¦tive¦ness
tran¦si¦tiv¦ity
tran¦si¦tor¦ily
tran¦si¦tori¦ness
tran¦si¦tory
transit-theodo¦lite
+s
Trans¦jor¦dan
(region, Jordan)

Trans|jor|dan|ian +s
Trans|kei (former homeland, South Africa)
trans|lata|bil|ity
trans|lat|able
trans|late
trans|lates
trans|lated
trans|lat|ing
trans|la|tion +s
trans|la|tion|al
trans|la|tion|al|ly
trans|la|tor +s
trans|lit|er|ate
trans|lit|er|ates
trans|lit|er|ated
trans|lit|er|at|ing
trans|lit|er|ation +s
trans|lit|er|ator +s
trans|lo|cate
trans|lo|cates
trans|lo|cated
trans|lo|cat|ing
trans|loca|tion +s
trans|lu|cence
trans|lu|cency
trans|lu|cent
trans|lu|cent|ly
trans|lunar
trans|lun|ary
trans|mar|ine
trans|mi|grant +s
trans|mi|grate
trans|mi|grates
trans|mi|grated
trans|mi|grat|ing
trans|mi|gra|tion +s
trans|mi|gra|tor +s
trans|mi|gra|tory
trans|mis|sible
trans|mis|sion +s
trans|mis|sive
trans|mit
trans|mits
trans|mit|ted
trans|mit|ting
trans|mit|table
trans|mit|tal +s
trans|mit|tance
trans|mit|ter +s
trans|mog|ri|fi|ca|tion
trans|mog|rify
trans|mog|ri|fies
trans|mog|ri|fied
trans|mog|ri|fy|ing
trans|mon|tane

trans|mut|abil|ity
trans|mut|able
trans|mu|ta|tion +s
trans|mu|ta|tion|al
trans|mu|ta|tion|ist +s
trans|mu|ta|tive
trans|mute
trans|mutes
trans|muted
trans|mut|ing
trans|muter +s
trans|nation|al +s
trans|ocean|ic
tran|som +s
tran|somed
tran|sonic
trans|pa|cif|ic
trans|pad|ane
trans|par|ence
trans|par|ency
trans|par|en|cies
trans|par|ent
trans|par|ent|ly
trans|par|ent|ness
trans-Pennine
trans|per|son|al
trans|pierce
trans|pierces
trans|pierced
trans|pier|cing
tran|spir|able
tran|spir|ation
tran|spira|tory
tran|spire
tran|spires
tran|spired
tran|spir|ing
trans|plant +s +ed +ing
trans|plant|able
trans|plant|ation
trans|plant|er +s
tran|spon|der +s
trans|pon|tine
trans|port +s +ed +ing
trans|port|abil|ity
trans|port|able
trans|por|ta|tion
trans|port|er +s
trans|pos|able
trans|posal
trans|pose
trans|poses
trans|posed
trans|pos|ing
trans|poser +s
trans|pos|ition +s
trans|pos|ition|al
trans|posi|tive

trans|puter +s
trans|sex|ual +s
trans|sex|ual|ism
trans-ship
trans-ships
trans-shipped
trans-shipping
trans-shipment +s
trans-Siberian
trans-sonic
tran|sub|stan|ti|ate
tran|sub|stan|ti|ated
tran|sub|stan|ti|at|ing
tran|sub|stan|ti|ation
tran|su|da|tion
tran|su|da|tory
tran|sude
tran|sudes
tran|suded
tran|sud|ing
trans|uran|ic
Trans|vaal (former province, South Africa)
trans|ver|sal +s
trans|ver|sal|ity
trans|ver|sal|ly
trans|verse
trans|verse|ly
trans|vest +s +ed +ing
trans|vest|ism
trans|vest|ist +s
trans|vest|ite +s
Tran|syl|va|nia (region, Romania)
Tran|syl|va|nian
trant|er +s
trap
traps
trapped
trap|ping
trap-ball
trap|door +s
trapes (use traipse)
trapeses
trapesed
trapes|ing
trap|eze +s
tra|pez|ium
tra|pezia or
tra|pez|iums
tra|pez|ius
tra|pezii
trap|ez|oid +s
trap|ez|oid|al

trap|like
trap|pean
trap|per +s
trap|pings
Trap|pist +s
Trap|pist|ine
trap-rock +s
trap-shooter +s
trap-shooting
trash
trashes
trashed
trash|ing
trash|ery
trash|er|ies
trash-ice
trash|ily
trashi|ness
trashy
trash|ier
trashi|est
Trás-os-Montes (region, Portugal)
trass
trat|toria +s
trauma +s
trau|mat|ic
trau|mat|ic|al|ly
trau|ma|tisa|tion Br. (use traumatization)
trau|ma|tise Br. (use traumatize)
trau|ma|tises
trau|ma|tised
trau|ma|tis|ing
trau|ma|tism
trau|ma|tiza|tion
trau|ma|tize
trau|ma|tizes
trau|ma|tized
trau|ma|tiz|ing
trav|ail +s +ed +ing
travel
travels
trav|elled Br.
trav|eled Am.
trav|el|ling Br.
trav|el|ing Am.
trav|el|er Am. +s
trav|el|er's check Am. +s
trav|el|ling bag Am. +s
trav|el|ling rug Am. +s
trav|el|ler Br. +s
trav|el|ler's cheque Br. +s
trav|el|ling bag Br. +s

trav¦el¦ling rug *Br.*
+s
trav¦el¦ogue +s
travel-sick
travel-sickness
trav¦ers¦able
tra¦vers¦al
tra¦verse
  tra¦verses
  tra¦versed
  tra¦vers¦ing
tra¦ver¦ser +s
trav¦er¦tine +s
trav¦esty
  trav¦es¦ties
  trav¦es¦tied
  trav¦esty¦ing
tra¦vois
  plural tra¦vois
trawl +s +ed +ing
trawl¦er +s
trawler|man
  trawler|men
trawl net +s
tray +s (for
  carrying plates
  etc. ⚠ trait, trey)
tray|ful +s
treach¦er¦ous
treach¦er¦ous¦ly
treach¦er¦ous¦ness
treach|ery
  treach¦er¦ies
trea¦cle +s
trea¦cly
tread
  treads
  trod
  tread¦ing
  trod|den
tread¦ed (having
  tread)
tread¦er +s
treadle
  treadles
  treadled
  tread¦ling
tread|mill +s
tread|wheel +s
trea¦son +s
trea¦son|able
trea¦son|ably
trea¦son|ous
treas|ure
  treas|ures
  treas|ured
  treas|ur|ing
treas|urer +s
treas|urer|ship +s
treas|ury
  treas|ur|ies
treat +s +ed +ing

treat|able
treat|er +s
trea|tise +s
  (written work)
treat|ment +s
treaty
  treat|ies
  (agreement)
Trebi|zond (former
  name of Trabzon)
treble
  trebles
  trebled
  treb|ling
Treb|linka
  (concentration
  camp, Poland)
trebly
trebu|chet +s
tre|cent|ist +s
tre|cento
tree
  trees
  treed
  tree|ing
tree|creep¦er +s
tree fern +s
tree house +s
tree|less
tree|less|ness
tree-like
treen
tree|nail +s
tree stump +s
tree|top +s
tree trunk +s
trefa
tref|oil +s
tref|oiled
trek
  treks
  trekked
  trek|king
trek|ker +s
Trek|kie +s
trel|lis
  trel|lises
  trel|lised
  trel|lis|ing
trellis-work +s
trema|tode +s
trem|ble
  trem|bles
  trem|bled
  trem|bling
trem|bler +s
trem|bling +s
trem|bling¦ly
trem|bly
  trem|blier
  trem|bli¦est
tre|men|dous

tre|men¦dous¦ly
tre|men¦dous|ness
trem|olo +s
tremor +s +ed
  +ing
tremu|lous
tremu|lous¦ly
tremu|lous|ness
tren|ail +s (use
  treenail)
trench
  trenches
  trenched
  trench|ing
tren|chancy
tren|chant
tren|chant¦ly
trench coat +s
trench|er +s
trench|er|man
  trench|er|men
trend +s +ed +ing
trend|ify
  trendi|fies
  trendi|fied
  trendi|fy|ing
trend|ily
trendi|ness
trend|set|ter +s
trend|set|ting
trendy
  trend|ies
  trend|ier
  trendi|est
Treng|ganu (state,
  Malaysia; also in
  'Kuala
  Trengganu')
Trent (river,
  England)
Trent, Coun|cil of
tren|tal +s
trente-et-quarante
Trentino-Alto
  Adige (region,
  Italy)
Trento (city, Italy)
Tren|ton (city,
  USA)
tre|pan
  tre|pans
  tre|panned
  tre|pan|ning
trep|an|ation +s
tre|pang +s
treph|in|ation +s
tre|phine
  tre|phines
  tre|phined
  tre|phin|ing
trepi|da|tion

tres|pass
  tres|passes
  tres|passed
  tres|pass|ing
tres|pass|er +s
tress
  tresses
  tressed
  tress|ing
tres|sure +s
tressy
tres|tle +s
trestle-tree +s
tret +s
Tret¦ya|kov
  Gal|lery (art
  gallery, Moscow)
tre|vally
  tre|val|lies
Tre|vith|ick,
  Rich|ard (English
  engineer)
Trevor
trews
trey +s (three dice
  . or cards. ⚠ trait,
  tray)
tri|able
tri|acet|ate +s
tri|acid +s
Triad +s (Chinese
  secret society)
triad +s (three)
tri|adel|phous
tri|ad|ic
tri|ad|ic|al|ly
tri|age
trial
  trials
  trialled *Br.*
  trialed *Am.*
  trial|ling *Br.*
  trial|ing *Am.*
trial|ist +s
trial|list +s (use
  trialist)
tri|an¦drous
tri|angle +s
tri|angu|lar
tri|angu|lar|ity
tri|angu|lar|ly
tri|angu|late
  tri|angu|lates
  tri|angu|lated
  tri|angu|lat|ing
tri|angu|late|ly
tri|angu|la|tion +s
Tria|non (palaces,
  France)
tri|an|te|lope +s
Trias

Tri|as|sic
tri|ath|lete +s
tri|ath|lon +s
tri|atom|ic
tri|axial
trib|ade +s
trib|ad|ism
tri|bal +s
tri|bal|ism
tri|bal|ist +s
tri|bal|is|tic
tri|bal|ly
tri|basic
tribe +s
tribes|man
uribes|men
tribes|people
tribes|woman
tribes|women
trib|let +s
tribo|elec|tri|city
trib|olo|gist +s
trib|ology
tribo|lumin|
  escence
tribo|lumin|escent
trib|om|eter +s
tri|brach +s
tri|brach|ic
tribu|la|tion +s
tri|bu|nal +s
trib|un|ate +s
trib|une +s
trib|une|ship +s
trib|un|icial
trib|un|ician +s
trib|un|itial
tribu|tar|ily
tribu|tari|ness
tribu|tary
  tribu|tar|ies
trib|ute +s
tri|car +s
trice
  trices
  triced
  tri|cing
tri|cen|ten|ary
  tri|cen|ten|ar|ies
tri|ceps
tri|cera|tops
trich|ia|sis
trich|ina
  trich|inae
Trichi|nop|oly
  (former name of
  Tiruchirapalli)
trich|in|osis
trich|in|ous
tri|chlor|ide +s
tri|chloro|eth|ane
trich|ogen|ous

tricho|logic|al
trich|olo|gist +s
trich|ology
trich|ome +s
tricho|monad +s
tricho|mon|ia|sis
tricho|path|ic
trich|op|athy
tri|chord +s
tricho|tom|ic
trich|ot|om|ise Br.
  (use
  trichotomize)
  trich|ot|om|ises
  trich|ot|om|ised
  trich|ot|om|is|ing
trich|ot|om|ize
  trich|ot|om|izes
  trich|ot|om|ized
  trich|ot|om|iz|ing
trich|ot|om|ous
trich|ot|omy
  trich|oto|mies
tri|chro|ic
tri|chro|ism
tri|chro|mat|ic
tri|chro|ma|tism
Tricia also Trisha
trick +s +ed +ing
trick|er +s
trick|ery
  trick|er|ies
trick|ily
tricki|ness
trick|ish
trickle
  trickles
  trickled
  trick|ling
trick|ler +s (thing
  that trickles.
  △ tricolor,
  tricolour)
trick|less
trick|ly
trick|sily
trick|si|ness
trick|ster +s
tricksy
  trick|ier
  tricki|est
tri|clin|ic
tri|clin|ium
  tri|clinia
tri|color Am. +s
tri|col|ored Am.
tri|col|our Br. +s
  (flag etc.
  △ trickler)
tri|col|oured Br.

tri|corn +s (use
  tricorne)
tri|corne +s
tri|cot +s
tri|coty|ledon|ous
tri|crot|ic
tri|cus|pid +s
tri|cycle
  tri|cyc|les
  tri|cyc|led
  tri|cyc|ling
tri|cyc|lic +s
tri|cyc|list +s
tri|dac|tyl
tri|dac|tyl|ous
tri|dent +s
tri|den|tate
Tri|den|tine +s
tri|digi|tate
tri|dimen|sion|al
trid|uum
tridy|mite +s
tri|ecious Am. (Br.
  trioecious)
tried
tri|en|nial
tri|en|ni|al|ly
tri|en|nium
  tri|en|ni|ums or
  tri|en|nia
Trier (city,
  Germany)
trier +s (person
  who tries)
trier|archy
  trier|arch|ies
Tri|este (city, Italy)
tri|facial
tri|fecta +s
trif|fid +s (fictional
  plant)
tri|fid (in three
  parts)
trifle
  trifles
  trifled
  trif|ling
trifler +s
trif|ling|ly
tri|focal +s
tri|foli|ate
tri|for|ium
  tri|foria
tri|form
tri|fur|cate
  tri|fur|cates
  tri|fur|cated
  tri|fur|cat|ing
trig
  trigs
  trigged
  trig|ging

trig (cont.)
  (wedge, tidy, etc.;
  trigonometry)
trig|am|ist +s
trig|am|ous
trig|amy
tri|gem|in|al
tri|gem|inus
  tri|gem|ini
trig|ger +s +ed
  +ing
trig|ger|fish
  plural trig|ger|fish
  or trig|ger|fishes
trigger-happy
Trig|lav (mountain,
  Slovenia)
tri|gly|cer|ide +s
tri|glyph +s
tri|glyph|ic
tri|glyph|ic|al
tri|gon +s
tri|gon|al
tri|gon|al|ly
tri|gon|eut|ic
trig|ono|met|ric
trig|ono|met|ric|al
trig|onom|etry
tri|gram +s
tri|graph +s
tri|gyn|ous
tri|he|dral
tri|he|dron
  tri|he|dra or
  tri|he|drons
tri|hy|dric
trike
  trikes
  triked
  trik|ing
tri|labi|ate
tri|lam|in|ar
tri|lat|eral +s
tril|bied
trilby
  tril|bies
tri|lemma +s
tri|lin|ear
tri|lin|gual
tri|lin|gual|ism
tri|lit|eral
tri|lith +s
tri|lith|ic
tri|lithon +s
trill +s +ed +ing
tril|lion
  plural tril|lion or
  tril|lions
tril|lionth +s
tril|lium +s
tri|lob|ate
tri|lo|bite +s

tri|locu|lar
tril|ogy
  trilo|gies
Trim (town, Republic of Ireland)
trim
  trims
  trimmed
  trim|ming
  trim|mer
  trim|mest
tri|maran +s
tri|mer +s
tri|mer|ic
tri|mer|ous
tri|mes|ter +s
tri|mes|tral
trim|eter +s
tri|met|ric
tri|met|ric|al
trim|ly
trim|mer +s
trim|ming +s
trim|ness
Tri|mon|tium
  (Roman name for Plovdiv)
tri|morph|ic
tri|morph|ism
tri|morph|ous
Tri|murti
tri|nal
Trinco|ma|lee
  (port, Sri Lanka)
trine +s
Trin|ian (in 'St Trinian's')
Trini|dad (island, West Indies)
Trini|dad and To|bago (country, West Indies)
Trini|dad|ian +s
Trini|tar|ian +s
Trini|tar|ian|ism
tri|nitro|tolu|ene
tri|nitro|toluol
trin|ity
  trin|ities
trin|ket +s
trin|ket|ry
tri|nomial
tri|nomi|al|ism
trio +s
tri|ode +s
tri|oe|cious *Br.*
  (*Am.* triecious)
trio|let +s
tri|ox|ide
trip
  trips

trip (*cont.*)
  tripped
  trip|ping
trip|par|tite
trip|par|tite|ly
trip|par|ti|tion
tripe +s
tri|pet|al|ous
trip-hammer +s
tri|phibi|ous
tri|phos|phate +s
triph|thong +s
triph|thong|al
triph|yl|lous
tri|pin|nate
Tri|pit|aka
tri|plane +s
triple
  triples
  tripled
  trip|ling
trip|let +s
Trip|lex (glass) *Propr.*
trip|lex (triple)
trip|li|cate
  trip|li|cates
  trip|li|cated
  trip|li|cat|ing
trip|li|ca|tion +s
trip|li|city
  trip|li|ci|ties
trip|loid +s
trip|loidy
triply
trip|meter +s
tri|pod +s
tri|pod|al
Trip|oli (capital of Libya; port, Lebanon)
trip|oli +s (stone; powder)
Trip|oli|tania (coastal region, Libya)
Trip|oli|tan|ian +s
tri|pos
  tri|poses
trip|per +s
trip|pery
trippy
trip|tych +s (set of three hinged pictures, writing tablets etc. △ tryptic)
trip|tyque +s
Trip|ura (state, India)
trip|wire +s

tri|quetra
  tri|quet|rae
tri|quet|ral
tri|quet|rous
tri|reme +s
tri|sac|char|ide +s
Tris|agion +s
tri|sect +s +ed +ing
tri|sec|tion +s
tri|sect|or +s
Trish
Trisha *also* **Tricia**
tri|shaw +s
tris|kai|deka|
        pho|bia
tri|skel|ion +s
tris|mus
tri|somy
trisomy-21
Tris|tan
Tris|tan da Cunha (island, S. Atlantic)
triste
trist|esse
tri|stich|ous
tri|stig|mat|ic
Tris|tram
tri|styl|ous
tri|sul|cate
tri|syl|lab|ic
tri|syl|lable +s
tri|tag|on|ist +s
trite
  triter
  trit|est
trite|ly
trite|ness
tri|tern|ate
tri|the|ism
tri|the|ist +s
triti|ate
  triti|ates
  triti|ated
  triti|at|ing
triti|ation
trit|ium
Tri|ton (*Greek Mythology*; moon of Neptune)
tri|ton +s (mollusc; newt; nucleus)
tri|tone +s (musical interval)
trit|ur|able
trit|ur|ate
  trit|ur|ates
  trit|ur|ated
  trit|ur|at|ing
trit|ur|ation
trit|ur|ator +s

tri|umph +s +ed +ing
tri|umph|al
tri|umph|al|ism
tri|umph|al|ist
tri|umph|al|ly
tri|umph|ant
tri|umph|ant|ly
tri|um|vir
  tri|um|virs *or* tri|um|viri
tri|um|vir|al
tri|um|vir|ate +s
tri|une
tri|un|ity
  tri|un|ities
tri|va|lency
  tri|va|len|cies
tri|va|lent
Tri|van|drum (city, India)
trivet +s
trivia
triv|ial
trivi|al|isa|tion *Br.* (use trivialization)
trivi|al|ise *Br.* (use trivialize)
  trivi|al|ises
  trivi|al|ised
  trivi|al|is|ing
trivi|al|ity
  trivi|al|ities
trivi|al|iza|tion
trivi|al|ize
  trivi|al|izes
  trivi|al|ized
  trivi|al|iz|ing
trivi|al|ly
trivi|al|ness
triv|ium
  trivia
tri-weekly
Trixie
Troad (ancient region, NW Asia Minor)
Tro|bri|and Is|lands (in SW Pacific)
tro|car +s
tro|cha|ic
tro|chal
tro|chan|ter +s
troche +s (tablet)
tro|chee +s (metric foot)
troch|lea
  troch|leae
  noun
troch|lear *adjective*

troch|oid +s
troch|oid|al
tro|chus
  tro|chi *or*
  tro|chuses
trod
trod|den
trog +s
trog|lo|dyte +s
trog|lo|dyt|ic
trog|lo|dyt|ic|al
trog|lo|dyt|ism
tro|gon +s
troika +s
troil|ism
Troi|lus *Greek Mythology*
Tro|jan +s
troll +s +ed +ing
troll|er +s
trol|ley +s
trol|ley|bus
  trol|ley|buses
trolley-car +s
trol|lop +s
Trol|lope, An|thony
  (English novelist)
trol|lop|ish
trol|lopy
trom|bone +s
trom|bon|ist +s
trom|mel +s
trom|om|eter +s
tromo|met|ric
trompe +s
trompe l'œil +s
Tromsø (port, Norway)
Trond|heim (port, Norway)
Troon (town, Scotland)
troop +s +ed +ing
  (assemblage; soldiers; to assemble or move in large numbers.
  △troupe)
troop car|rier +s
troop|er +s
  (soldier; police officer; troopship.
  △trouper)
troop|ship +s
tro|pae|olum +s
trope +s
troph|ic
tro|phied
tropho|blast +s
tropho|neur|osis
  tropho|neur|oses

trophy
  tro|phies
trop|ic +s (of Cancer or Capricorn)
trop|ic|al +s
trop|ic|al|ly
Trop|ics (region)
trop|ism +s
tropo|logic|al
trop|ology
  trop|olo|gies
tropo|pause +s
tropo|sphere +s
tropo|spher|ic
troppo
Tros|sachs, the
  (valley, Scotland)
Trot +s
  (= Trotskyist)
trot
  trots
  trot|ted
  trot|ting
  (run etc.)
troth +s
Trot|sky, Leon
  (Russian revolutionary)
Trot|sky|ism
Trot|sky|ist +s
Trot|sky|ite +s
trot|ter +s
trot|ting race +s
tro|tyl +s
trou|ba|dour +s
trouble
  troubles
  troubled
  troub|ling
trouble|maker +s
trouble-making
troub|ler +s
trouble|shoot
  trouble|shoots
  trouble|shot
  trouble|shoot|ing
  trouble|shoot|er +s
trouble|some
trouble|some|ly
trouble|some|ness
trouble spot +s
troub|lous
trough +s +ed +ing
trounce
  trounces
  trounced
  troun|cing
troun|cer +s

troupe +s
  (company of actors etc.
  △troop)
trouper +s
  (member of troupe; staunch colleague.
  △trooper)
trou|ser *attributive*
trouser-clip +s
trou|sered
trou|ser leg +s
trouser|less
trou|ser press
  trou|ser presses
trou|sers
trou|ser suit +s
trous|seau
  trous|seaus *or*
  trous|seaux
trout
  plural trout *or*
  trouts
trout|let +s
trout|ling +s
trouty
trou|vaille +s
trou|vère +s
trove +s
trover +s
trow +s +ed +ing
Trow|bridge
  (town, England)
trowel
  trowels
  trow|elled *Br.*
  trow|eled *Am.*
  trow|el|ling *Br.*
  trow|el|ing *Am.*
Troy (ancient city, Turkey)
troy (weight)
Troyes (town, France)
Troyes, Chré|tien de (French poet)
tru|ancy
tru|ant +s +ed +ing
truce +s
truce|less
tru|cial
Tru|cial States
  (former name of the United Arab Emirates)
truck +s +ed +ing
truck|age
truck|er +s
truckie +s

truckle
  truckles
  truckled
  truck|ling
truck|ler +s
truck|load +s
trucu|lence
trucu|lency
trucu|lent
trucu|lent|ly
Tru|deau, Pierre
  (Canadian prime minister)
trudge
  trudges
  trudged
  trudg|ing
trudgen
trudger +s
Trudi *also* Trudy
Trudy *also* Trudi
true
  trues
  trued
  tru|ing *or* true|ing
  truer
  tru|est
true-blue +s
true-born
true-bred
true-hearted
true|ish
true love +s
true-love knot +s
True|man, Fred|die (English cricketer)
true|ness
Truf|faut, Fran|çois (French film director)
truf|fle +s
trug +s
tru|ism +s
tru|is|tic
Tru|jillo (city, Peru; in 'Ciudad Trujillo')
Tru|jillo, Raf|ael (Dominican president)
Truk Is|lands (in W. Pacific)
trull +s
truly
Tru|man, Harry S. (American president)
tru|meau
  tru|meaux
trump +s +ed +ing

trump|ery
  trump|er|ies
trum|pet +s +ed
  +ing
trum|pet blast +s
trum|pet call +s
trum|pet|er +s
trum|pet|ing +s
trum|pet|less
trum|pet play|er
  +s
trun|cal
trun|cate
  trun|cates
  trun|cated
  trun|cat|ing
trun|cate|ly
trun|ca|tion +s
trun|cheon +s
trun|dle
  trun|dles
  trun|dled
  trund|ling
trundle-bed +s
trunk +s
trunk|ful +s
trunk|ing +s
trunk|less
trunk|like
trunk line +s
trunk road +s
trun|nion +s
Truro (city,
  England)
truss
  trusses
  trussed
  truss|ing
truss|er +s
trust +s +ed +ing
trust|able
trust|bust|er +s
trust|bust|ing
trust|ee +s
  (administrator of
  trust. △trustie,
  trusty)
trustee|ship +s
trust|er +s
trust|ful
trust|ful|ly
trust|ful|ness
trust fund +s
trustie +s
  (prisoner; use
  trusty. △trustee)
trust|ily
trusti|ness
trust|ing|ly
trust|ing|ness
trust|wor|thily
trust|worthi|ness

trust|worthy
trusty
  trust|ies
  trust|ier
  trusti|est
  (trustworthy;
  prisoner.
  △trustee)
truth +s
truth|ful
truth|ful|ly
truth|ful|ness
truth|less
try
  tries
  tried
  try|ing
try|ing|ly
trying-plane +s
try-on +s noun
try-out +s noun
tryp|ano|some +s
tryp|ano|
    som|ia|sis
tryp|sin
tryp|sino|gen
tryp|tic (of or
  pertaining to
  trypsin.
  △triptych)
tryp|to|phan +s
try|sail +s
try-scorer +s
try-scoring noun
  and attributive
try-square +s
tryst +s +ed +ing
tryst|er +s
Tsao-chuang
  (= Zaozhuan)
tsar +s
tsar|dom +s
tsar|ev|ich
  tsar|ev|iches
tsar|evna +s
tsar|ina +s
tsar|ism
tsar|ist +s
Tsar|it|syn (former
  name of
  Volgograd)
Tsavo Na|tion|al
  Park (in Kenya)
tses|sebi +s
tse|tse +s
T-shirt +s
Tsi|nan (= Jinan)
Tsing|hai
  (= Qinghai)
Tsiol|kov|sky,
  Kon|stan|tin
  (Russian

Tsiol|kov|sky
  (cont.)
  aeronautical
  engineer)
Tsi|tsi|kamma
  For|est (in South
  Africa)
Tskhin|vali (capital
  of South Ossetia,
  Russia)
Tsonga
  plural Tsonga or
  Tson|gas
T-square +s
tsu|nami +s
Tsu|shima
  (Japanese island,
  Korea Strait)
Tswana +s
Tua|motu
  Archi|pe|lago (in
  French Polynesia)
Tua|reg
  plural Tua|reg or
  Tua|regs
tua|tara +s
Tua|tha Dé
  Dan|aan
  (legendary Irish
  people)
tub
  tubs
  tubbed
  tub|bing
tuba +s
tubal
tub|bable
tub|bi|ness
tub|bish
tubby
  tub|bier
  tub|bi|est
tubby|ish
tube
  tubes
  tubed
  tub|ing
tub|ec|tomy
  tub|ec|to|mies
tube|less
tube|like
tuber +s
tu|ber|cle +s
tu|ber|cu|lar +s
tu|ber|cu|late
tu|ber|cu|la|tion +s
tu|ber|cu|lin
tuberculin-tested
tu|ber|cu|losis
tu|ber|cu|lous
tu|ber|ose +s
tu|ber|os|ity

tu|ber|ous
tube worm +s
tub|ful +s
tu|bico|lous
tu|bi|corn +s
tu|bi|fex
tu|bi|fex worm +s
tu|bi|form
tu|bi|lin|gual
tub|ing +s
tub-sized
tub-thumper +s
tub-thumping
Tu|buai Is|lands
  (in S. Pacific)
tu|bu|lar
tu|bule +s
tu|bu|lous
tuck +s +ed +ing
tuck-box
  tuck-boxes
tuck|er +s +ed
  +ing
tucker-bag +s
tucket +s
tuck-in +s adjective
  and noun
tuck-net +s
tuck shop +s
Tuc|son (city, USA)
Tudor +s (English
  royal house)
Tudor|bethan
Tudor|esque
Tues|day +s
tufa +s
tu|fa|ceous
tuff (rock. △tough)
tuff|aceous
tuf|fet +s
tuft +s +ed +ing
tufty
  tuft|ier
  tufti|est
Tu Fu (Chinese
  poet)
tug
  tugs
  tugged
  tug|ging
tug|boat +s
tug|ger +s
tug of love
  tug-of-war
  tugs-of-war
tu|grik +s
tui
  plural tui or tuis
Tuil|er|ies
  (Gar|dens) (in
  Paris)
tu|ition

tu|ition|al
tu|ition|ary
Tula (city, Russia;
  ancient city,
  Mexico)
tu|lar|ae|mia *Br.*
tu|lar|aem|ic *Br.*
tu|lar|emia *Am.*
tu|lar|em|ic *Am.*
tul|chan +s
tulip +s
tulip-root +s
tulip tree +s
tulip|wood +s
Tull, Jethro
  (English
  agriculturalist)
Tul|la|more (town,
  Republic of
  Ireland)
tulle (net)
Tulsa (port, USA)
Tul|si|das (Indian
  poet)
tul|war +s
tum +s (= tummy)
tum|ble
  tum|bles
  tum|bled
  tum|bling
tumble|down
tumble-drier +s
  (use tumble-
  dryer)
tumble-dry
  tumble-dries
  tumble-dried
  tumble-drying
tumble-dryer +s
tum|bler +s
tum|bler|ful +s
tumble|weed +s
tumbling-barrel
  +s
tumbling-bay +s
tum|brel +s (use
  tumbril)
tum|bril +s
tu|me|fa|cient
tu|me|fac|tion
tu|mefy
  tu|me|fies
  tu|me|fied
  tu|me|fy|ing
tu|mes|cence
tu|mes|cent
tu|mes|cent|ly
tumid
tu|mid|ity
tu|mid|ly
tu|mid|ness

tummy
  tum|mies
tummy ache +s
tummy bug +s
tummy but|ton +s
tumor *Am.* +s
tu|mor|ous
tu|mour *Br.* +s
tump +s
tum|tum +s
tu|mu|lar
tu|mult +s
tu|mul|tu|ary
tu|mul|tu|ous
tu|mul|tu|ous|ly
tu|mul|tu|ous|ness
tu|mu|lus
  tu|muli
tun
  tuns
  tunned
  tun|ning
  (cask. △ton,
  tonne)
tuna
  plural tuna *or*
  tunas
  (fish. △tuner)
tun|able
tuna fish
  plural tuna fish
Tunb Is|lands (in
  Persian Gulf)
Tun|bridge Wells
  (officially Royal
  Tunbridge Wells;
  spa town,
  England.
  △Tonbridge)
tun|dish
  tun|dishes
tun|dra +s
tune
  tunes
  tuned
  tun|ing
tune|able
tune|ful
tune|ful|ly
tune|ful|ness
tune|less
tune|less|ly
tune|less|ness
tuner +s (person
  who tunes
  instruments; part
  of radio. △tuna)
tung +s (tree; oil.
  △tongue)
tung|state +s
tung|sten
tung|stic

Tun|gus
  plural Tun|gus
Tun|gus|ian +s
Tun|gus|ic
Tun|guska (two
  rivers, Russia)
tunic +s
tu|nica
  tu|nicae
tu|ni|cate +s
tu|nicle +s
tun|ing +s
Tunis (capital of
  Tunisia)
Tu|nisia
Tu|nis|ian +s
tun|nel
  tun|nels
  tun|nelled *Br.*
  tun|neled *Am.*
  tun|nel|ling *Br.*
  tun|nel|ing *Am.*
tun|nel|er *Am.* +s
tunnel-kiln +s
tun|nel|ler *Br.* +s
tunnel-net +s
tun|nel vi|sion
tunny
  tun|nies
tup
  tups
  tupped
  tup|ping
Tupa|maro +s
Tup|elo (city, USA)
tu|pelo +s
Tupi
  plural Tupi *or*
  Tupis
Tupi-Guarani
  plural
  Tupi-Guarani *or*
  Tupi-Guara|nis
tup|pence +s
tup|penny
  tup|pen|nies
**tuppenny-
ha'penny**
Tup|per|ware
  Propr.
tuque +s
tur|aco +s
Tur|an|ian +s
tur|ban +s
tur|baned
tur|bary
  tur|bar|ies
tur|bel|lar|ian +s
tur|bid
tur|bid|ity
tur|bid|ly
tur|bid|ness

tur|bin|al
tur|bin|ate
tur|bin|ation
tur|bine +s
tur|bit +s (pigeon.
  △turbot)
turbo +s
turbo|charge
  turbo|charges
  turbo|charged
  turbo|char|ging
turbo|char|ger +s
turbo-diesel +s
turbo|fan +s
turbo|jet +s
turbo|prop +s
turbo|shaft +s
turbo|super|
      char|ger +s
tur|bot
  plural tur|bot *or*
  tur|bots
  (fish. △turbit)
tur|bu|lence
tur|bu|lent
tur|bu|lent|ly
Turco +s
Turco|man +s (use
  Turkoman)
Turco|phile +s
Turco|phobe +s
turd +s (*coarse
  slang*)
turd|oid
tur|een +s
turf
  turfs *or* turves
  noun
turf +s +ed +ing
  verb
**Tur|fan
De|pres|sion**
  (area, China)
turf|man
  turf|men
turfy
Tur|genev, Ivan
  (Russian writer)
tur|ges|cence
tur|ges|cent
tur|gid
tur|gid|es|cence
tur|gid|es|cent
tur|gid|ity
tur|gid|ly
tur|gid|ness
tur|gor
Turin (city, Italy)
Tur|ing, Alan
  (English
  mathematician;
  test; machine)

tur¦ion+s

Turk+s

Tur¦kana
plural Tur¦kana
(person; language)

Tur¦kana, Lake(in
Kenya)

Turk¦estan(region,
central Asia)

Tur¦key(country)

tur¦key+s (bird;
flop; stupid
person)

tur¦key¦cock+s

Turki+s
(languages;
person)

Turk¦ic

Turk¦ish

Turki¦stan(use
Turkestan)

Turk¦men
plural Turk¦men
or Turk¦mens

Turk¦meni¦stan

Turko¦man+s

Turks and Cai¦cos
Is¦lands(in West
Indies)

Turku(port,
Finland)

tur¦meric

tur¦moil+s

turn+s +ed +ing
(rotate; change;
etc. △ tern, terne)

turn¦about+s

turn¦around+s

turn¦back+s

turn-bench

turn-benches

turn-buckle+s

turn-cap+s

turn¦coat+s

turn¦cock+s

turn¦down+s

Turn¦er, Jo¦seph
Mal¦lord
Wil¦liam(English
painter)

turn¦er+s

turn¦ery

turn¦er¦ies

turn-in+s *noun*

turn¦ing+s

turn¦ing circle+s

turn¦ing point+s

tur¦nip+s

turnip-top+s

tur¦nipy

turn¦key+s

turn-off+s *noun*

turn-on+s *noun*

turn¦out+s

turn¦over+s

turn¦pike+s

turn¦round+s

turn¦sick

turn¦side

turn¦sole+s

turn¦spit+s

turn¦stile+s

turn¦stone+s

turn¦table+s

turn-up+s *noun
and adjective*

tur¦pen¦tine

tur¦pen¦tines

tur¦pen¦tined

tur¦pen¦tin¦ing

tur¦peth+s

Tur¦pin, Dick
(English
highwayman)

tur¦pi¦tude

turps(= turpentine)

tur¦quoise+s

tur¦ret+s

tur¦ret¦ed

tur¦tle+s

turtle-dove+s

turtle¦neck+s

turtle¦shell
adjective

tur¦tle shell+s
noun

turves

Tus¦can+s

Tus¦cany(region,
Italy)

Tus¦ca¦rora
plural Tus¦ca¦rora
or Tus¦ca¦roras

tush

tushes

tusk+s +ed +ing

tusk¦er+s

tusky

tus¦sah*Am.* (*Br.*
tussore)

Tus¦saud,
Ma¦dame Marie
(wax-modeller)

Tus¦saud's,
Ma¦dame
(waxworks)

tus¦ser(use
tussore)

tus¦sive

tus¦sle

tus¦sles

tus¦sled

tus¦sling

tus¦sock+s

tus¦socky

tus¦sore+s

tut

tuts

tut¦ted

tut¦ting

Tu¦tan¦kha¦men
(pharaoh)

Tu¦tan¦kha¦mun
(use
Tutankhamen)

tutee+s

tu¦tel¦age

tu¦tel¦ar

tu¦tel¦ary

tu¦tenag

Tuth¦mo¦sis
(pharaoh)

tutor+s +ed +ing

tu¦tor¦age

tu¦tor¦ess

tu¦tor¦esses

tu¦tor¦ial+s

tu¦tori¦al¦ly

tu¦tor¦ship+s

tut¦san+s

Tutsi
plural Tutsi *or*
Tut¦sis
(person. △ tootsy)

tutti+s *Music*

tutti-frutti+s

tut-tut

tut-tuts

tut-tutted

tut-tutting

tutty(polishing
powder)

Tutu, Des¦mond
(South African
archbishop)

tutu+s (dancer's
skirt; plant. △ too-
too)

Tuva(republic,
Russia)

Tu¦valu

Tu¦va¦lu¦an+s

tu-whit, tu-whoo
+s

tux

tuxes
(= tuxedo)

tux¦edo+s

Tux¦tla Gu¦tiér¦rez
(city, Mexico)

tuy¦ère+s (?)

Tuzla(town,
Bosnia)

Tver(port, Russia)

Twa
plural Twa *or*
Twas *or* Batwa

twad¦dle

twad¦dles

twad¦dled

twad¦dling

twad¦dler+s

twad¦dly

Twain, Mark
(American writer)

twain

twang+s +ed +ing

twan¦gle

twan¦gles

twan¦gled

twan¦gling

twangy

'twas(= it was)

twat+s (*coarse
slang*)

tway¦blade+s

tweak+s +ed +ing

twee

tweer

tweest

Tweed(river,
Scotland and
England)

tweed+s (cloth;
clothes)

tweed¦ily

,tweedi¦ness

Tweedle¦dum and
Tweedle¦dee

tweedy

twee¦ly

'tween(= between)

'tween-decks

twee¦ness

tweeny

tween¦ies

tweet+s +ed +ing

tweet¦er+s

tweez¦er+s +ed
+ing

twelfth+s

twelfth¦ly

twelve+s

twelve-bore+s

twelve¦fold

twelvemo

twelve¦month+s

twelve-note
adjective

twen¦ti¦eth+s

twenty

twen¦ties

twenty¦fold

twenty-fourmo

twenty¦
some¦thing+s

twenty-twenty

'twere(= it were)

twerp+s

Twi
 plural **Twi** *or* **Twis**
twi|bill +s
twice
twicer +s
Twick|en|ham
 (district, London;
 rugby ground)
twid|dle
 twid|dles
 twid|dled
 twid|dling
twid|dler +s
twid|dly
twig
 twigs
 twigged
 twig|ging
twiggy
twi|light +s
twi|lit
twill +s +ed +ing
'twill (= it will)
twin
 twins
 twinned
 twin|ning
twin-cam
twine
 twines
 twined
 twin|ing
twin-engined
twiner +s
twinge
 twinges
 twinged
 twin|ging *or*
 twinge|ing
twink +s
twin|kle
 twin|kles
 twin|kled
 twink|ling
twink|ler +s
twin|kly
twin|ning +s
Twins, the
 (constellation;
 sign of zodiac)
twin-screw
twin|set +s
twirl +s +ed +ing
twirl|er +s
twirly
twirp +s (use
 twerp)
twist +s +ed +ing
twist|able
twist|er +s
twist|ing +s

twisty
 twist|ier
 twisti|est
twit
 twits
 twit|ted
 twit|ting
twitch
 twitches
 twitched
 twitch|ing
twitch|er +s
twitch|ily
twitchi|ness
twitchy
 twitch|ier
 twitchi|est
twite +s
twit|ter +s +ed
 +ing
twit|ter|er +s
twit|tery
twit|tish
'twixt (= betwixt)
twiz|zle
 twiz|zles
 twiz|zled
 twiz|zling
two +s (number.
 ⚠ to, too)
two-bit
two-by-four +s
two-dimension|al
two-edged
two-faced
two|fold
two-handed
two-iron +s
two|ness
two|pence +s
two|penn'orth
two|penny
 two|pen|nies
**twopenny-
 halfpenny**
two|penny|worth
two-piece +s
two-ply +s
two-seater +s
two-sided
two|some +s
two-step +s
two-stroke +s
two-time
 two-times
 two-timed
 two-timing
two-timer +s
two-tone
'twould (= it
 would)
two-up

two-way
two -wheeler +s
twyer +s
Ty|burn (former
 site of public
 hangings, London)
tych|ism
tych|ist +s
Ty|cho|nian +s
Tych|on|ic
ty|coon +s
tying
tyke +s (may cause
 offence in
 Australia and New
 Zealand)
Tyler, John
 (American
 president)
Tyler, Wat
 (English
 revolutionary)
ty|lo|pod +s
ty|lopo|dous
tym|pan +s
tym|pana
tym|pani
 (kettledrums; use
 timpani)
tym|pan|ic
tym|pan|ites
 (swelling of
 abdomen)
tym|pan|it|ic
tym|pan|itis
 (inflammation of
 eardrum)
tym|pa|num
 tym|pa|nums *or*
 tym|pana
tym|pany
 (= tympanites)
**Tyn|dale,
 Wil|liam** (English
 translator of Bible)
Tyn|dall, John
 (Irish physicist)
Tyne (river,
 England; shipping
 area)
Tyne and Wear
 (metropolitan
 county, England)
Tyne|side (region,
 England)
Tyne|sider +s
Tyn|wald
 (legislative
 assembly, Isle of
 Man)
typal
type
 types

type (*cont.*)
 typed
 typ|ing
type|cast
 type|casts
 type|cast
 type|cast|ing
type|face +s
type found|er +s
type foun|dry
 type foun|dries
type metal
type|script +s
type|set
 type|sets
 type|set
 type|set|ting
type|set|ter +s
type site +s
type size +s
type|writer +s
type|writ|ing
type|writ|ten
typh|lit|ic
typh|litis
ty|phoid
ty|phoid|al
ty|phon|ic
ty|phoon +s
typh|ous *adjective*
ty|phus *noun*
typ|ical
typ|ic|al|ity
typ|ic|al|ly
typi|fi|ca|tion +s
typi|fier +s
typ|ify
 typi|fies
 typi|fied
 typi|fy|ing
typ|ist +s
typo +s
typ|og|raph|er +s
typo|graph|ic
typo|graph|ic|al
typo|graph|ic|al|ly
typ|og|raphy
 typ|og|raph|ies
typo|logic|al
typ|olo|gist +s
typ|ology
 typ|olo|gies
typo|nym +s
Tyr *Scandinavian
 Mythology*
tyr|am|ine
tyr|an|nic|al
tyr|an|nic|al|ly
tyr|an|ni|cidal
tyr|an|ni|cide +s
tyr|an|nise *Br.* (use
 tyrannize)

tyr¦an¦nise *(cont.)*
  tyr¦an¦nises
  tyr¦an¦nised
  tyr¦an¦nis¦ing
tyr¦an¦nize
  tyr¦an¦nizes
  tyr¦an¦nized
  tyr¦an¦niz¦ing
tyr¦an¦no¦saur +s
tyr¦an¦no¦saurus
  tyr¦an¦no¦
  saur¦uses *or*
  tyr¦an¦no¦sauri
Tyr¦an¦no¦saurus
  Rex
tyr¦an¦nous
tyr¦an¦nous¦ly
tyr¦anny
  tyr¦an¦nies
tyr¦ant +s
Tyre (port,
  Lebanon)
tyre *Br.* +s (on
  wheel. *Am.* tire
  △ tire)
tyre gauge *Br.* +s
  (*Am.* tire gauge)
Tyr¦ian +s
tyro +s
Tyrol (state,
  Austria)
Tyr¦ol¦ean +s
Tyr¦ol¦ese
  plural Tyr¦ol¦ese
Tyr¦one (county,
  Northern Ireland;
  name)
tyro¦sine
Tyr¦rhene +s
Tyr¦rhen¦ian +s
Tyr¦rhen¦ian Sea
Tyu¦men (city,
  Russia)
tzar +s (use tsar)
Tzara, Tris¦tan
  (Romanian-born
  French poet)
tzar¦ina +s (use
  tsarina)
tzar¦ist +s (use
  tsarist)
tza¦tziki +s
tzi¦gane +s
Tzu-po (= Zibo)

Uu

Ubaid
Ubanghi Shari
  (former name of
  the Central
  African Republic)
Über¦mensch
  Über¦mensch¦en
ubi¦ety
  ubi¦eties
ubi¦qui¦tar¦ian +s
ubi¦qui¦tar¦ian¦ism
ubi¦qui¦tous
ubi¦qui¦tous¦ly
ubi¦qui¦tous¦ness
ubi¦quity
U-boat +s
UCATT (= Union of
  Construction,
  Allied Trades, and
  Technicians)
UCCA
  (= Universities
  Central Council on
  Admissions)
Uc¦cello, Paolo
  (Italian painter)
udal +s
udal¦ler +s
udal¦man
  udal¦men
udder +s
ud¦dered
Ud¦mur¦tia
  (republic, Russia)
udom¦eter +s
UEFA (= Union of
  European Football
  Associations)
U-ey +s
Ufa (city, Russia)
Uf¦fizi (art gallery,
  Florence, Italy)
UFO +s
  (= unidentified
  flying object)
ufolo¦gist +s
ufol¦ogy
Uganda
Ugan¦dan +s
Ugarit (ancient
  port, Syria)
Ugar¦it¦ic
ugh
ug¦li¦fi¦ca¦tion
ugli fruit
  plural ugli fruit
  (fruit. △ ugly)
  Propr.

uglify
  ugli¦fies
  ugli¦fied
  ugli¦fy¦ing
ug¦lily
ugli¦ness
ugly
  ug¦lier
  ugli¦est
  (hideous etc.
  △ ugli fruit)
Ugrian +s
Ugric +s
uh-huh
uhlan +s
Ui¦ghur +s
Uigur +s (use
  Uighur)
Uist, North and
  South +s
  (Scottish islands)
Uit¦land¦er +s
uja¦maa
Uji¦ya¦mada
  (former name of
  Ise)
Uj¦jain (city, India)
Ujung Pan¦dang
  (port, Indonesia)
ukase +s
ukiyo-e
Ukraine
Ukrain¦ian +s
uku¦lele +s
Ulala (former name
  of Gorno-Altaisk)
Ulan Bator (capital
  of Mongolia)
Ulan¦ova, Gal¦ina
  (Russian ballet
  dancer)
Ulan-Ude (city,
  Russia)
ulcer +s
ul¦cer¦able
ul¦cer¦ate
  ul¦cer¦ates
  ul¦cer¦ated
  ul¦cer¦at¦ing
ul¦cer¦ation +s
ul¦cera¦tive
ul¦cered
ul¦cer¦ous
Uleå¦borg (Swedish
  name for Oulu)
ulema +s
Ul¦fi¦las (bishop
  and translator)
Ul¦has¦nagar (city,
  India)
uligin¦ose
uligin¦ous

ull¦age
Ulm (city,
  Germany)
ulna
  ulnae
  noun
ulnar *adjective*
ulot¦ri¦chan +s
ulot¦ri¦chous
Ul¦pian (Roman
  jurist)
Ulsan (port, South
  Korea)
Ul¦ster (former
  province,
  Northern Ireland)
ul¦ster +s (coat)
Ul¦ster¦man
  Ul¦ster¦men
Ul¦ster¦woman
  Ul¦ster¦women
ul¦ter¦ior
ul¦ter¦ior¦ly
ul¦tima +s
ul¦tim¦acy
ul¦ti¦mata
ul¦tim¦ate +s
ul¦tim¦ate¦ly
ul¦tim¦ate¦ness
ul¦tima Thule
ul¦ti¦matum
  ul¦ti¦matums *or*
  ul¦ti¦mata
ul¦timo
ul¦ti¦mo¦geni¦ture
  +s
ultra +s
ultra¦cen¦tri¦fuge
  +s
ul¦tra¦dian
ultra¦fil¦tra¦tion
ultra-high
ultra¦ism
ultra¦ist +s
ultra-left
ultra¦mar¦ine +s
ultra¦micro¦scope
  +s
ultra¦micro¦
         scop¦ic
ultra¦mon¦tane +s
ultra¦mon¦tan¦ism
ultra¦mon¦tan¦ist
  +s
ultra¦mun¦dane
ultra-right
ultra¦son¦ic
ultra¦son¦ic¦al¦ly
ultra¦son¦ics
ultra¦sound
ultra¦struc¦ture +s
ultra¦vio¦let

ultra vires
ulu|lant
ulu|late
  ulu|lates
  ulu|lated
  ulu|lat¦ing
ulu|la¦tion +s
Ul¦undi (town,
  South Africa)
Uluru (Aboriginal
  name for Ayers
  Rock)
Ul¦ya|nov (original
  surname of Lenin)
Ul¦yan|ovsk
  (former name of
  Simbirsk)
Ulys|ses (Roman
  name for
  Odysseus;
  European space
  probe)
um
Umay|yad +s
umbel +s
um¦bel|lar
um¦bel|late
um¦bel|lif¦er +s
um¦bel|lif¦er|ous
um¦bel|lule +s
umber +s
um¦bil|ical +s
um¦bil|ic|al¦ly
um¦bil|icate
um¦bil|icus
  um¦bil|ici *or*
  um¦bil|ic|uses
um¦bles
umbo
  umbos *or*
  umbo|nes
umbo|nal
umbo|nate
umbra
  um¦bras *or*
  um¦brae
um¦brage +s
um¦bra|geous
um¦bral
um¦brella +s
umbrella-like
um¦brette +s
Um¦bria (region,
  Italy)
Um¦brian +s
Um¦briel (moon of
  Uranus)
um¦brif¦er|ous
Umeå (city,
  Sweden)
umiak +s

um¦laut +s +ed
  +ing
Umm al Qai|wain
  (state and city,
  UAE)
ump +s
um|pir¦age +s
um¦pire
  um|pires
  um|pired
  um|pir¦ing
um¦pire|ship +s
ump|teen
ump|teenth
umpty
umpty-doo
Um¦tali (former
  name of Mutare)
'un (= one, as in
  'young 'un')
Una *also* Oona,
  Oo|nagh
un|abashed
un|abashed¦ly
un|abated
un|abated¦ly
un|able
un|abridged
un|absorbed
un|aca|dem¦ic
un|accent¦ed
un|accept|abil¦ity
un|accept|able
un|accept|able|
       ness
un|accept|ably
un|accept¦ed
un|acclaimed
un|accom|
      mo|dated
un|accom|
      mo|dat¦ing
un|accom|pan|ied
un|accom|plished
un|account|
      abil¦ity
un|account|able
un|account|able|
      ness
un|account|ably
un|account¦ed
un|accus¦tomed
un|accus¦tomed|ly
un|achiev|able
un|acknow|ledged
un|acquaint¦ed
un|adapt¦able
un|adapt¦ed
un|ad|dressed
un|adja|cent
un|adjust¦ed
un|ad|mit¦ted

un|adopt¦ed
un|adorned
un|adul¦ter|ated
un|ad¦ven¦tur|ous
un|ad¦ven¦tur|
      ous¦ly
un|ad¦ver|tised
un|ad¦vis|able
un|ad¦vised
un|ad¦vised|ly
un|ad¦vised|ness
un|aes¦thet¦ic *Br.*
  (*Am.* unesthetic)
un|affect¦ed
un|affect¦ed|ly
un|affect¦ed|ness
un|affec¦tion|ate
un|affili¦ated
un|afford|able
un|afraid
un|aggres¦sive
un|aid¦ed
un|alarmed
un|alien¦able
un|alien¦ated
un|aligned
un|alike
un|alive
un|allevi¦ated
un|allied
un|allo¦cated
un|allow¦able
un|alloyed
un|alter¦able
un|alter¦able|ness
un|alter¦ably
un|altered
un|alter¦ing
un|amazed
un|am¦bi|gu¦ity
un|am¦bigu¦ous
un|am¦bigu¦ous|ly
un|am¦bi¦tious
un|am¦bi¦tious|ly
un|am¦bi¦tious|
      ness
un|am¦biva|lent
un|am¦biva|lent|ly
un|amen¦able
un|amend¦ed
un-American
un-American¦ism
un|ami¦able
un|amp|li¦fied
un|amused
un|amus¦ing
un|ana¦lys|able
un|ana¦lysed
un|aneled
unan¦im|ity
unani|mous
unani|mous¦ly

unani|mous|ness
un|announced
un|answer|able
un|answer|able|
      ness
un|answer|ably
un|answered
un|antici¦pated
un|apolo|get¦ic
un|apolo|get¦ic|
      al¦ly
un|ap¦os¦tol¦ic
un|appar¦ent
un|appeal|able
un|appeal|ing
un|appeal|ing¦ly
un|appeas|able
un|appeased
un|appe¦tis|ing *Br.*
  (use
  unappetizing)
un|appe¦tis|ing¦ly
  Br. (use
  unappetizingly)
un|appe¦tiz|ing
un|appe¦tiz|ing¦ly
un|applied
un|appre¦ci¦ated
un|appre¦cia|tive
un|appre¦hend¦ed
un|approach|
      abil¦ity
un|approach|able
un|approach|able|
      ness
un|approach|ably
un|appro¦pri¦ated
un|approved
unapt
un|apt¦ly
un|apt|ness
un|argu¦able
un|argu¦ably
un|argued
unarm +s +ed
  +ing
un|arrest|ing
un|arrest|ing¦ly
un|articu¦lated
un|artis¦tic
un|artis¦tic|al¦ly
un|ascer¦tain|able
un|ascer¦tain|ably
un|ascer¦tained
un|ashamed
un|ashamed¦ly
un|ashamed|ness
un|asked
unasked-for
un|assail|abil¦ity
un|assail|able

un|assail|able|
      ness
un|assail|ably
un|assert|ive
un|assert|ive|ly
un|assert|ive|ness
un|assign|able
un|assigned
un|assim|il|able
un|assim|il|ated
un|assist|ed
un|associ|ated
un|assuage|able
un|assuaged
un|assum|ing
un|assum|ing|ly
un|assum|ing|ness
un|atoned
un|attached
un|attack|able
un|attain|able
un|attain|able|
      ness
un|attain|ably
un|attempt|ed
un|attend|ed
un|attest|ed
un|attract|ive
un|attract|ive|ly
un|attract|ive|ness
un|attrib|ut|able
un|attrib|ut|ably
un|attrib|uted
unau +s
un|audit|ed
un|authen|tic
un|authen|tic|al|ly
un|authen|ti|cated
un|author|ised *Br.*
  (use
  unauthorized)
un|author|ized
un|avail|abil|ity
un|avail|able
un|avail|able|ness
un|avail|ing
un|avail|ing|ly
un|avoid|abil|ity
un|avoid|able
un|avoid|able|
      ness
un|avoid|ably
un|avowed
un|awakened
un|aware
un|aware|ness
un|awares
un|awed
un|back|able
un|backed
un|baked

un|bal|ance
un|bal|ances
un|bal|anced
un|bal|an|cing
unban
un|bans
un|banned
un|ban|ning
un|bap|tised *Br.*
  (use unbaptized)
un|bap|tized
unbar
un|bars
un|barred
un|bar|ring
un|bear|able
un|bear|able|ness
un|bear|ably
un|beat|able
un|beat|ably
un|beat|en
un|beau|ti|ful
un|beau|ti|ful|ly
un|be|com|ing
un|be|com|ing|ly
un|be|com|ing|
      ness
un|be|fit|ting
un|be|fit|ting|ly
un|be|fit|ting|ness
un|be|friend|ed
un|be|got|ten
un|be|hold|en
un|be|known
un|be|knownst
un|belief
un|believ|abil|ity
un|believ|able
un|believ|able|
      ness
un|believ|ably
un|believed
un|believer +s
un|believ|ing
un|believ|ing|ly
un|believ|ing|ness
un|be|loved
un|belt +s +ed
  +ing
un|bend
un|bends
un|bent
un|bend|ing
un|bend|ing|ly
un|bend|ing|ness
un|biased
un|bib|li|cal
un|bid|dable
un|bid|den
un|bind
un|binds

un|bind (*cont.*)
  un|bound
  un|bind|ing
un|birth|day +s
un|bleached
un|blem|ished
un|blend|ed
un|blessed
un|blest (use
  unblessed)
un|blink|ing
un|blink|ing|ly
un|block +s +ed
  +ing
un|bloody
un|blown
un|blush|ing
un|blush|ing|ly
un|bolt +s +ed
  +ing
un|bon|net +s +ed
  +ing
un|book|ish
un|boot +s +ed
  +ing
un|born
un|bosom +s +ed
  +ing
un|bothered
un|bound
un|bound|ed
un|bound|ed|ly
un|bound|ed|ness
un|bowed
un|brace
un|braces
un|braced
un|bracing
un|brand|ed
un|breach|able
un|break|able
un|break|ably
un|breath|able
un|brib|able
un|bridge|able
un|bridle
un|bridles
un|bridled
un|brid|ling
un-British
un|broken
un|broken|ly
un|broken|ness
un|brother|ly
un|bruised
un|brushed
un|buckle
un|buckles
un|buckled
un|buck|ling
un|build
un|builds

un|build (*cont.*)
  un|built
  un|build|ing
un|bun|dle
un|bun|dles
un|bun|dled
un|bund|ling
un|bund|ler +s
un|bur|den +s +ed
  +ing
un|bur|ied
un|burned (use
  unburnt)
un|burnt
un|bury
un|buries
un|buried
un|bury|ing
un|busi|ness|like
un|but|ton +s +ed
  +ing
un|cage
un|cages
un|caged
un|caging
un|cal|cu|lat|ing
un|called
uncalled-for
un|can|did
un|can|nily
un|can|ni|ness
un|canny
un|can|nier
un|canni|est
un|can|on|ic|al
un|can|on|ic|al|ly
uncap
un|caps
un|capped
un|cap|ping
uncared for
uncared-for
  attributive
un|car|ing
un|car|pet|ed
un|case
un|cases
un|cased
un|cas|ing
un|cashed
un|catch|able
un|cat|egor|is|able
  Br. (use
  uncategorizable)
un|cat|egor|iz|able
un|caught
un|caused
un|ceas|ing
un|ceas|ing|ly
un|cele|brated
un|cen|sored
  (uncut)

un|cen|sured
(uncriticized)
un|cere|mo|ni|ous
un|cere|mo|ni|
        ous|ly
un|cere|mo|ni|ous|
        ness
un|cer|tain
un|cer|tain|ly
un|cer|tainty
 un|cer|tain|ties
un|cer|tifi|cated
un|cer|ti|fied
un|chain +s +ed
 +ing
un|chal|lenge|able
un|chal|lenge|ably
un|chal|lenged
un|chal|len|ging
un|change|abil|ity
un|change|able
un|change|able|
        ness
un|change|ably
un|changed
un|chan|ging
un|chan|ging|ly
un|chan|ging|ness
un|chap|er|oned
un|char|ac|ter|
        is|tic
un|char|ac|ter|
        is|tic|al|ly
un|charged
un|char|is|mat|ic
un|char|it|able
un|char|it|able|
        ness
un|char|it|ably
un|charm|ing
un|chart|ed
un|char|tered
un|chaste
un|chaste|ly
un|chas|tened
un|chaste|ness
un|chas|tity
un|checked
un|chiv|al|rous
un|chiv|al|rous|ly
un|chosen
un|chris|tian
un|chris|tian|ly
un|church
 un|churches
 un|churched
 un|church|ing
un|cial
un|ci|form
un|cin|ate
un|cir|cum|cised
un|cir|cum|ci|sion

un|civil
un|civ|il|ised *Br.*
 (use uncivilized)
un|civ|il|ized
un|civ|il|ly
un|clad
un|claimed
un|clasp +s +ed
 +ing
un|clas|si|fi|able
un|clas|si|fied
uncle +s
un|clean
un|cleaned
un|clean|li|ness
un|clean|ly
un|clean|ness
un|cleansed
un|clear
un|cleared
un|clear|ly
un|clear|ness
uncle-in-law +s
un|clench
 un|clenches
 un|clenched
 un|clench|ing
un|climb|able
un|climbed
un|clinch
 un|clinches
 un|clinched
 un|clinch|ing
un|clip
 un|clips
 un|clipped
 un|clip|ping
un|cloak +s +ed
 +ing
un|clog
 un|clogs
 un|clogged
 un|clog|ging
un|close
 un|closes
 un|closed
 un|clos|ing
un|clothe
 un|clothes
 un|clothed
 un|cloth|ing
un|cloud|ed
un|clut|tered
unco +s
un|coded
un|coil +s +ed
 +ing
un|col|lect|ed
un|col|ored *Am.*
un|col|oured *Br.*
un|combed
uncome-at-able
un|come|ly

un|com|fort|able
un|com|fort|able|
        ness
un|com|fort|ably
un|com|mer|cial
un|
  com|mer|cial|ly
un|
  com|mis|sioned
un|com|mit|ted
un|com|mon
un|com|mon|ly
un|com|mon|ness
un|com|mu|ni|
        ca|tive
un|com|mu|ni|
        ca|tive|ly
un|com|mu|ni|
        ca|tive|ness
un|com|pan|ion|
        able
un|com|pen|sated
un|com|peti|tive
un|com|peti|tive|
        ness
un|com|plain|ing
un|com|plain|
        ing|ly
un|com|pleted
un|com|pli|cated
un|com|pli|
        men|tary
un|com|pound|ed
un|com|pre|
        hend|ed
un|com|pre|hend|
        ing
un|com|pre|hend|
        ing|ly
un|com|pre|hen|
        sion
un|com|prom|
        is|ing
un|com|prom|
        is|ing|ly
un|com|prom|
        is|ing|ness
un|con|cealed
un|con|cern
un|con|cerned
un|con|cern|ed|ly
un|con|cluded
un|con|di|tion|al
un|con|di|tion|
        al|ity
un|con|di|tion|
        al|ly
un|con|di|tioned
un|con|fi|dent
un|con|fined
un|con|firmed
un|con|form|able

un|con|form|able|
        ness
un|con|form|ably
un|con|form|ity
un|con|gen|ial
un|con|geni|al|ly
un|con|gest|ed
un|con|jec|tur|able
un|con|nect|ed
un|con|nect|ed|ly
un|con|nect|ed|
        ness
un|con|quer|able
un|con|quer|able|
        ness
un|con|quer|ably
un|con|quered
un|con|scion|able
un|con|scion|able|
        ness
un|con|scion|ably
un|con|scious
un|con|scious|ly
un|con|scious|
        ness
un|con|se|crated
un|con|sent|ing
un|con|sid|ered
un|con|sol|able
un|con|sol|ably
un|con|soli|dated
un|con|sti|
        tu|tion|al
un|con|sti|tu|tion|
        al|ity
un|con|sti|tu|tion|
        al|ly
un|con|strained
un|con|strain|
        ed|ly
un|con|straint
un|con|strict|ed
un|con|struct|ive
un|con|sult|ed
un|con|sumed
un|con|sum|mated
un|con|tact|able
un|con|tain|able
un|con|tam|in|
        ated
un|con|ten|tious
un|
  con|ten|tious|ly
un|con|test|ed
un|con|test|ed|ly
un|con|tra|dict|ed
un|con|trived
un|con|trol|lable
un|con|trol|lable|
        ness
un|con|trol|lably
un|con|trolled

un|con|trolled|ly
un|con|tro|ver|sial
un|con|tro|
    ver|sial|ly
un|con|tro|vert|ed
un|con|tro|vert|
    ible
un|con|ven|tion|al
un|con|ven|tion|al|
    ism
un|con|ven|tion|
    al|ity
un|con|ven|tion|
    al|ly
un|con|vert|ed
un|con|vert|ible
un|con|vict|ed
un|con|vinced
un|con|vin|cing
un|con|vin|cing|ly
un|cooked
un|cool
un|co|opera|tive
un|co|opera|
    tive|ly
un|co|opera|tive|
    ness
un|co|or|din|ated
un|copi|able
un|cord +s +ed
    +ing
un|cor|dial
un|cork +s +ed
    +ing
un|cor|rect|ed
un|cor|rel|ated
un|cor|rob|or|ated
un|cor|rupt|ed
un|cor|set|ed
un|count|abil|ity
un|count|able
un|count|ably
un|count|ed
un|count noun +s
un|couple
un|couples
un|coupled
un|coup|ling
un|court|ly
un|couth
un|couth|ly
un|couth|ness
un|cov|en|ant|ed
un|cover +s +ed
    +ing
un|crack|able
un|cracked
un|creased
un|cre|ate
un|cre|ates
un|cre|ated
un|cre|at|ing

un|crea|tive
un|cred|it|ed
un|crit|ic|al
un|crit|ic|al|ly
un|cropped
un|cross
un|crosses
un|crossed
un|cross|ing
un|cross|able
un|crowd|ed
un|crown +s +ed
    +ing
un|crum|pled
un|crush|able
un|crushed
UNCTAD (= United
    Nations
    Conference on
    Trade and
    Development)
unc|tion +s
unc|tu|ous
unc|tu|ous|ly
unc|tu|ous|ness
un|culled
un|culti|vated
un|cul|tured
un|curb +s +ed
    +ing
un|cured
un|curl +s +ed
    +ing
un|cur|tailed
un|cur|tained
un|cus|tomed
uncut
un|dam|aged
un|damped
un|dated
un|daunt|ed
un|daunt|ed|ly
un|daunt|ed|ness
un|dead
un|dealt
un|deca|gon +s
un|deceive
un|deceives
un|deceived
un|deceiv|ing
un|decid|abil|ity
un|decid|able
un|decided
un|decided|ly
un|de|cipher|able
un|de|ciphered
un|declared
un|de|cod|able
un|dec|or|ated
un|defeat|ed
un|defend|ed
un|defiled

un|defin|able
un|defin|ably
un|defined
un|deflect|ed
un|deformed
un|deliv|ered
un|demand|ing
un|demand|ing|
    ness
un|demo|crat|ic
un|demo|crat|ic|
    al|ly
un|dem|on|strable
un|dem|on|
    stra|ted
un|demon|stra|
    tive
un|demon|stra|
    tive|ly
un|
   demon|stra|tive|
    ness
un|deni|able
un|deni|able|ness
un|deni|ably
un|denied
un|denom|in|
    ation|al
un|dent|ed
un|depend|able
under
under|achieve
   under|achieves
   under|achieved
   under|achiev|ing
under|achieve|
    ment
under|achiever +s
under|act +s +ed
    +ing
under-age
   attributive
under|appre|ci|
    ated
under|arm +s
under|belly
   under|bel|lies
under|bid
   under|bids
   under|bid
   under|bid|ding
under|bid|der +s
under|blan|ket +s
under|body
   under|bodies
under|bred
under|brush
under|cap|acity
under|cap|it|al|ise
   Br. (use
   undercapitalize)

under|cap|it|al|ise
   (*cont.*)
   under|cap|it|al|
     ises
   under|cap|it|al|
     ised
   under|cap|it|al|
     is|ing
under|cap|it|al|ize
   under|cap|it|al|
     izes
   under|cap|it|al|
     ized
   under|cap|it|al|
     iz|ing
under|car|riage +s
under|cart +s
under|charge
under|charges
under|charged
under|char|ging
under|class
   under|classes
under|clay +s
under|cliff +s
under|clothes
under|cloth|ing
under|coat +s +ed
    +ing
under|
   con|sump|tion
under|
   con|sump|tion|
     ist +s
under|cook +s +ed
    +ing
under|cover
under|croft +s
under|cur|rent +s
under|cut
   under|cuts
   under|cut
   under|cut|ting
under|devel|oped
under|devel|op|
    ment
under|do
   under|does
   under|did
   under|do|ing
   under|done
under|dog +s
under|drain|age
under|drawers
under|draw|ing
under|dress
   under|dresses
   under|dressed
   under|dress|ing
under|edu|cated
under|empha|sis
   under|empha|ses

under|empha|sise
Br. (use
underemphasize)
under|
    empha|sises
under|
    empha|sised
under|
    empha|sis|ing
under|empha|size
under|
    empha|sizes
under|
    empha|sized
under|
    empha|siz|ing
under|employed
under|
    employ|ment
under|equipped
under|esti|mate
under|esti|mates
under|esti|mated
under|
    esti|mat|ing
under|esti|ma|tion
under|exploit|ed
under|expose
under|exposes
under|exposed
under|expos|ing
under|expos|ure
under|fed
under|felt +s
under|financed
under|finan|cing
under-fives
under|floor
under|flow +s
under|foot
under|frame +s
under|fund +s +ed
  +ing
under|fur
under-garden|er
  +s
under|gar|ment +s
under|gird +s +ed
  +ing
under|glaze
under|go
under|goes
under|went
under|go|ing
under|gone
under|grad +s
under|gradu|ate
  +s
under|ground
under|growth
under|hand
under|hand|ed

under|heat|ed
under|hung
under|lay
under|lays
under|laid
under|lay|ing
under|lease
under|leases
under|leased
under|leas|ing
under|let
under|lets
under|let
under|let|ting
under|lie
under|lies
under|lay
under|lain
under|lying
under|line
under|lines
under|lined
under|lin|ing
under|linen
under|ling +s
under|lip +s
under|lit
under-manager +s
under|manned
under|man|ning
under|men|tioned
under|mine
under|mines
under|mined
under|min|ing
under|miner +s
under|min|ing|ly
under|most
under|neath
under|nour|ished
under|nour|ish|
    ment
under-occupancy
under-occupy
under-occupies
under-occupied
under-occupy|ing
under|paid
under|paint|ing
under|pants
under|part +s
under|pass
under|passes
under|pay
under|pays
under|paid
under|pay|ing
under|pay|ment
  +s
under|per|form +s
  +ed +ing

under|per|form|
    ance
under|pin
under|pins
under|pinned
under|pin|ning
under|pin|ning +s
under|plant +s
  +ed +ing
under|play +s +ed
  +ing
under|plot +s
under|popu|lated
under|pow|ered
under-prepared
under|price
under|prices
under|priced
under|pricing
under|priv|il|eged
under|
    pro|duc|tion
under|proof
under|prop
under|props
under|propped
under|prop|ping
under-provision
under|quote
under|quotes
under|quoted
under|quot|ing
under|rate
under|rates
under|rated
under|rat|ing
under-read
under-reads
under-read
under-reading
under-rehearsed
under-report +s
  +ed +ing
under-represent
  +s +ed +ing
under-resourced
under|ripe
under|score
under|scores
under|scored
under|scor|ing
under|sea
under|seal
under-secretary
under-
  secretar|ies
under|sell
under|sells
under|sold
under|sell|ing
under|set
under|sets

under|set (cont.)
under|set
under|set|ting
under|sexed
under|sheet +s
under-sheriff +s
under|shirt +s
under|shoot
under|shoots
under|shot
under|shoot|ing
under|shorts
under|shrub +s
under|side +s
under|signed
under|size
under|sized
under|skirt +s
under|slung
under|sold
under|sow
under|sows
under|sowed
under|sow|ing
under|sown
under|spend
under|spends
under|spent
under|spend|ing
under|staffed
under|staff|ing
under|stairs
under|stand
under|stands
under|stood
under|stand|ing
under|stand|
    abil|ity
under|stand|able
under|stand|ably
under|stand|er +s
under|stand|ing
  +s
under|stand|ing|ly
under|state
under|states
under|stated
under|stat|ing
under|state|ment
  +s
under|stater +s
under|steer +s +ed
  +ing
under|stood
under|storey +s
under|strap|per +s
under|strength
  attributive
under|study
under|stud|ies
under|stud|ied
under|study|ing

under|sub|scribed
under|sur|face +s
under|take
  under|takes
  under|took
  under|tak|ing
  under|taken
under|taker +s
under|tak|ing +s
under|ten|ancy
  under|ten|an|cies
under|ten|ant +s
under-the-counter
  attributive
under|things
under|tint +s
under|tone +s
under|took
under|tow +s
under|trained
under|trick +s
under|use
  under|uses
  under|used
  under|using
under|util|isa|tion
  Br. (use
  underutilization)
under|util|ise *Br.*
  (use underutilize)
  under|util|ises
  under|util|ised
  under|util|is|ing
under|util|iza|tion
under|util|ize
  under|util|izes
  under|util|ized
  under|util|iz|ing
under|valu|ation
  +s
under|value
  under|values
  under|valued
  under|valu|ing
under|vest +s
under|water
under way
under|wear
under|weight
under|went
under|whelm +s
  +ed +ing
under|wing +s
under|wired
under|wood +s
under|work +s
  +ed +ing
under|world +s
under|write
  under|writes
  under|wrote

under|write (*cont.*)
  under|writ|ing
  under|writ|ten
under|writer +s
un|des|cend|ed
un|described
un|deserved
un|deserved|ly
un|deserv|ing
un|deserv|ing|ly
un|des|ig|nated
un|designed
un|design|ed|ly
un|desir|abil|ity
un|desir|able +s
un|desir|able|ness
un|desir|ably
un|desired
un|desir|ous
un|detect|abil|ity
un|detect|able
un|detect|ably
un|detect|ed
un|deter|mined
un|deterred
un|devel|oped
un|devi|at|ing
un|devi|at|ing|ly
un|diag|nosed
undid
un|dies
un|dif|fer|en|
            ti|ated
un|digest|ed
un|dig|ni|fied
un|diluted
un|dimin|ished
un|dimmed
un|dine +s
un|dip|lo|mat|ic
un|dip|lo|mat|ic|
            al|ly
un|dir|ect|ed
un|dis|cern|ing
un|dis|charged
un|dis|cip|line
un|dis|cip|lined
un|dis|closed
un|dis|cov|er|able
un|dis|cov|ered
un|dis|crim|in|
            at|ing
un|dis|cussed
un|dis|guised
un|dis|guised|ly
un|dis|mayed
un|dis|puted
un|dis|solved
un|dis|tin|guish|
            able
un|dis|tin|guished
un|dis|tort|ed

un|dis|trib|uted
un|dis|turbed
un|div|ided
un|divulged
undo
  un|does
  undid
  un|do|ing
  un|done
un|dock +s +ed
  +ing
un|docu|ment|ed
un|dog|mat|ic
un|do|ing +s
un|domes|ti|cated
un|done
un|doubt|able
un|doubt|ably
un|doubt|ed
un|doubt|ed|ly
un|doubt|ing
un|drained
un|dram|at|ic
un|draped
undreamed-of
  attributive
undreamt-of (use
  undreamed-of)
un|dress
  un|dresses
  un|dressed
  un|dress|ing
un|drink|able
un|driv|able
un|drive|able (use
  undrivable)
UNDRO (= United
  Nations Disaster
  Relief Office)
undue
un|du|lant
un|du|late
  un|du|lates
  un|du|lated
  un|du|lat|ing
un|du|late|ly
un|du|la|tion +s
un|du|la|tory
un|duly
un|duti|ful
un|duti|ful|ly
un|duti|ful|ness
un|dyed
un|dying
un|dying|ly
un|dynam|ic
un|earned
un|earth +s +ed
  +ing
un|earth|li|ness
un|earth|ly
un|ease

un|eas|ily
un|easi|ness
un|easy
  un|eas|ier
  un|easi|est
un|eat|able
un|eat|en
un|eco|nom|ic
un|eco|nom|ic|al
un|eco|nom|ic|
            al|ly
un|edify|ing
un|edify|ing|ly
un|edit|ed
un|educ|able
un|edu|cated
un|elect|able
un|elect|ed
un|embar|rassed
un|embel|lished
un|em|bit|tered
un|emo|tion|al
un|emo|tion|al|ly
un|emphat|ic
un|emphat|ic|al|ly
un|employ|abil|ity
un|employ|able
un|employed
un|employ|ment
un|emp|tied
un|en|closed
un|en|cum|bered
un|en|dear|ing
un|end|ing
un|end|ing|ly
un|end|ing|ness
un|en|dowed
un|en|dur|able
un|en|dur|ably
un|en|force|able
un|en|forced
un|en|gaged
un-English
un|en|joy|able
un|en|light|ened
un|en|light|en|ing
un|enter|pris|ing
un|en|thu|si|as|tic
un|en|thu|si|as|tic|
            al|ly
un|envi|able
un|envi|ably
un|envied
un|en|vir|on|
            men|tal
UNEP (= United
  Nations
  Environment
  Programme)
un|equable
un|equal

un|equaled *Am.*
  (*Br.* unequalled)
un|equal|ise *Br.*
  (use unequalize)
un|equal|ises
un|equal|ised
un|equal|is|ing
un|equal|ize
un|equal|izes
un|equal|ized
un|equal|iz|ing
un|equalled *Br.*
  (*Am.* unequaled)
un|equal|ly
un|equipped
un|equivo|cal
un|equivo|cal|ly
un|equivo|cal|
        ness
un|err|ing
un|err|ing|ly
un|err|ing|ness
un|escap|able
UNESCO (= United
  Nations
  Educational,
  Scientific, and
  Cultural
  Organization)
un|escort|ed
un|essen|tial
un|estab|lished
un|esthet|ic *Am.*
  (*Br.* unaesthetic)
un|eth|ic|al
un|eth|ic|al|ly
un|evan|gel|ic|al
un|even
un|even|ly
un|even|ness
un|event|ful
un|event|ful|ly
un|event|ful|ness
un|exact|ing
un|exam|ined
un|exam|pled
un|ex|ca|vated
un|ex|cep|tion|
        able
un|ex|cep|tion|
     able|ness
un|ex|cep|tion|
        ably
un|ex|cep|tion|al
un|ex|cep|tion|
        al|ly
un|ex|cit|abil|ity
un|ex|cit|able
un|ex|cit|ing
un|ex|clu|sive
un|ex|ecuted
un|ex|haust|ed

un|ex|pect|ed
un|ex|pect|ed|ly
un|ex|pect|ed|ness
un|ex|pi|ated
un|ex|pired
un|ex|plain|able
un|ex|plain|ably
un|ex|plained
un|ex|ploded
un|ex|ploit|ed
un|ex|plored
un|ex|port|able
un|ex|posed
un|ex|pressed
un|ex|pur|gated
un|face|able
un|fad|ing
un|fad|ing|ly
un|fail|ing
un|fail|ing|ly
un|fail|ing|ness
un|fair
un|fair|ly
un|fair|ness
un|faith|ful
un|faith|ful|ly
un|faith|ful|ness
un|fal|ter|ing
un|fal|ter|ing|ly
un|famil|iar
un|famili|ar|ity
un|fan|cied
un|fash|ion|able
un|fash|ion|able|
        ness
un|fash|ion|ably
un|fash|ioned
un|fas|ten +s +ed
  +ing
un|fathered
un|father|li|ness
un|father|ly
un|fath|om|able
un|fath|om|able|
        ness
un|fath|om|ably
un|fath|omed
un|favor|able *Am.*
un|favor|able|ness
  Am.
un|favor|ably *Am.*
un|favor|ite *Am.*
un|favour|able *Br.*
un|favour|able|
        ness *Br.*
un|favour|ably *Br.*
un|favour|ite *Br.*
un|fazed (not
  disconcerted.
  ⚠ unphased)
un|feas|ibil|ity
un|feas|ible

un|feas|ibly
unfed
un|feel|ing
un|feel|ing|ly
un|feel|ing|ness
un|feigned
un|feign|ed|ly
un|felt
un|fem|in|ine
un|fem|in|in|ity
un|fenced
un|fer|ment|ed
un|fer|til|ised *Br.*
  (use unfertilized)
un|fer|til|ized
un|fet|ter +s +ed
  +ing
un|fil|ial
un|fili|al|ly
un|filled
un|fil|tered
un|finan|cial
un|fin|ished
unfit
un|fit|ly
un|fit|ness
un|fit|ted
un|fit|ting
un|fit|ting|ly
unfix
un|fixes
un|fixed
un|fix|ing
un|flag|ging
un|flag|ging|ly
un|flap|pabil|ity
un|flap|pable
un|flap|pably
un|flat|ter|ing
un|flat|ter|ing|ly
un|fla|vored *Am.*
un|fla|voured *Br.*
un|fledged
un|fleshed
un|flexed
un|flick|er|ing
un|flinch|ing
un|flinch|ing|ly
un|flur|ried
un|flus|tered
un|focused
un|focussed (use
  unfocused)
un|fold +s +ed
  +ing
un|fold|ment
un|forced
un|for|ced|ly
un|ford|able
un|fore|cast
un|fore|see|able
un|fore|seen

un|fore|told
un|for|get|table
un|for|get|tably
un|for|giv|able
un|for|giv|ably
un|for|given
un|for|giv|ing
un|for|giv|ing|ly
un|for|giv|ing|ness
un|for|got|ten
un|formed
un|for|mu|lated
un|forth|com|ing
un|for|ti|fied
un|for|tu|nate
un|for|tu|nate|ly
un|found|ed
un|found|ed|ly
un|found|ed|ness
un|framed
un|free
un|free|dom
un|freeze
un|freezes
un|froze
un|freez|ing
un|frozen
un|fre|quent|ed
un|friend|ed
un|friend|li|ness
un|friend|ly
un|friend|lier
un|friendli|est
un|fright|en|ing
un|frock +s +ed
  +ing
un|froze
un|frozen
un|fruit|ful
un|fruit|ful|ly
un|fruit|ful|ness
un|ful|fil|lable
un|ful|filled
un|ful|fill|ing
un|fund|ed
un|fun|nily
un|fun|ni|ness
un|funny
un|fun|nier
un|funni|est
un|furl +s +ed
  +ing
un|fur|nished
un|fuss|ily
un|fussy
un|gain|li|ness
un|gain|ly
un|gal|lant
un|gal|lant|ly
un|gen|er|ous
un|gen|er|ous|ly
un|gen|er|ous|ness

un|gen|ial
un|gen|tle
un|gentle|man|li|
    ness
un|gentle|man|ly
un|gentle|ness
un|gently
unget-at-able
un|gift|ed
un|gild|ed
un|gird +s +ed
  +ing
un|glam|ór|ous
un|glazed
un|gloved
un|god|li|ness
un|god|ly
un|gov|ern|abil|ity
un|gov|ern|able
un|gov|ern|ably
un|grace|ful
un|grace|ful|ly
un|grace|ful|ness
un|gra|cious
un|gra|cious|ly
un|gra|cious|ness
un|gram|mat|ical
un|gram|mat|ic|
    al|ity
un|gram|mat|ic|
    al|ly
un|gram|mat|ic|al|
    ness
un|grasp|able
un|grate|ful
un|grate|ful|ly
un|grate|ful|ness
un|green
un|ground|ed
un|grudg|ing
un|grudg|ing|ly
un|gual
un|guard +s +ed
  +ing
un|guard|ed|ly
un|guard|ed|ness
un|guent +s
un|guess|able
un|guicu|late
un|guided
un|guis
  un|gues
un|gula
  un|gu|lae
un|gu|late +s
ungum
  un|gums
  un|gummed
  un|gum|ming
un|hal|lowed
un|ham|pered

un|hand +s +ed
  +ing
un|hand|ily
un|handi|ness
un|hand|some
un|handy
un|hang
  un|hangs
  un|hung
  un|hang|ing
un|hap|pily
un|hap|pi|ness
un|happy
  un|hap|pier
  un|happi|est
un|har|bor *Am.* +s
  +ed +ing
un|har|bour *Br.* +s
  +ed +ing
un|harmed
un|harm|ful
un|har|mon|ious
un|har|ness
  un|har|nesses
  un|har|nessed
  un|har|ness|ing
un|har|vest|ed
un|hasp +s +ed
  +ing
un|hatched
un|healed
un|health|ful
un|health|ful|ness
un|health|ily
un|healthi|ness
un|healthy
  un|health|ier
  un|healthi|est
un|heard
unheard-of
un|heat|ed
un|hedged
un|heed|ed
un|heed|ful
un|heed|ing
un|heed|ing|ly
un|help|ful
un|help|ful|ly
un|help|ful|ness
un|her|ald|ed
un|hero|ic
un|hero|ic|al|ly
un|hesi|tat|ing
un|hesi|tat|ing|ly
un|hesi|tat|ing|
    ness
un|hid|den
un|hin|dered
un|hinge
  un|hinges
  un|hinged

un|hinge *(cont.)*
  un|hinge|ing *or*
  un|hin|ging
unhip
un|his|tor|ic
un|his|tor|ic|al
un|his|tor|ic|al|ly
un|hitch
  un|hitches
  un|hitched
  un|hitch|ing
un|holi|ness
un|holy
  un|holi|er
  un|holi|est
un|hon|ored *Am.*
un|hon|oured *Br.*
un|hood +s +ed
  +ing
un|hook +s +ed
  +ing
un|hoped
un|hope|ful
un|horse
  un|horses
  un|horsed
  un|hors|ing
un|house
  un|houses
  un|housed
  un|hous|ing
un|human
un|hung
un|hur|ried
un|hur|ried|ly
un|hurry|ing
un|hurt
un|husk +s +ed
  +ing
un|hygien|ic
un|hygien|ic|al|ly
un|hyphen|ated
uni +s
  (= university)
Uni|ate +s
uni|axial
uni|axial|ly
uni|cam|eral
UNICEF (= United
  Nations Children's
  Fund)
uni|cel|lu|lar
uni|color *Am.*
uni|col|ored *Am.*
uni|col|our *Br.*
uni|col|oured *Br.*
uni|corn +s
uni|cus|pid +s
uni|cycle +s
uni|cyc|list +s
un|idea'd
un|ideal
un|ideal|ised *Br.*
  (use unidealized)

un|ideal|ized
un|iden|ti|fi|able
un|iden|ti|fied
uni|di|men|sion|al
un|idiom|at|ic
uni|dir|ec|tion|al
uni|dir|ec|tion|
    al|ity
uni|dir|ec|tion|
    al|ly
UNIDO (= United
  Nations Industrial
  Development
  Organization)
uni|fi|able
uni|fi|ca|tion
uni|fi|ca|tory
uni|fier +s
uni|flow
uni|form +s +ed
  +ing
uni|formi|tar|ian
  +s
uni|formi|tar|ian|
    ism
uni|form|ity
  uni|form|ities
uni|form|ly
unify
  uni|fies
  uni|fied
  uni|fy|ing
uni|lat|eral
uni|lat|eral|ism
uni|lat|eral|ist +s
uni|lat|eral|ly
uni|lin|gual
uni|lin|gual|ly
uni|lit|eral
un|illu|min|ated
un|illu|min|at|ing
un|illus|trated
uni|locu|lar
un|imagin|able
un|imagin|ably
un|imagina|tive
un|imagina|tive|ly
un|imagina|tive|
    ness
un|imagined
un|im|paired
un|im|part|ed
un|im|pas|sioned
un|im|peach|able
un|im|peach|ably
un|im|peded
un|im|peded|ly
un|im|port|ance
un|im|port|ant
un|im|pos|ing
un|im|pos|ing|ly
un|im|pressed

un|im|pres|sion|
⠀⠀⠀⠀⠀able
un|im|pres|sive
un|im|pres|sive|ly
un|im|pres|sive|
⠀⠀⠀⠀⠀ness
un|im|proved
un|im|pugned
un|in|cor|por|ated
un|indexed
un|in|fect|ed
un|in|flamed
un|in|flam|mable
un|inflect|ed
un|influ|enced
un|influ|en|tial
un|in|forma|tive
un|in|formed
un|in|hab|it|able
un|in|hab|it|able|
⠀⠀⠀⠀⠀ness
un|in|hab|it|ed
un|in|hib|it|ed
un|in|hib|it|ed|ly
un|in|hib|it|ed|
⠀⠀⠀⠀⠀ness
un|initi|ated
un|in|jured
un|in|spired
un|in|spir|ing
un|in|spir|ing|ly
un|in|struct|ed
un|insu|lated
un|in|sur|able
un|in|sured
un|inte|grated
un|in|tel|lec|tual
un|in|tel|li|gent
un|in|tel|li|gent|ly
un|in|tel|li|gi|
⠀⠀⠀⠀⠀bil|ity
un|in|tel|li|gible
un|in|tel|li|gible|
⠀⠀⠀⠀⠀ness
un|in|tel|li|gibly
un|in|tend|ed
un|in|ten|tion|al
un|in|ten|tion|al|ly
un|inter|est|ed
un|inter|est|ed|ly
un|inter|est|ed|
⠀⠀⠀⠀⠀ness
un|inter|est|ing
un|inter|est|ing|ly
un|inter|est|ing|
⠀⠀⠀⠀⠀ness
un|in|ter|pret|able
un|in|ter|pret|ed
un|inter|rupt|ed
un|inter|rupt|ed|ly
un|inter|rupt|ed|
⠀⠀⠀⠀⠀ness

un|inter|rupt|ible
un|in|timi|dated
un|in|nucle|ate
un|in|vent|ed
un|in|vent|ive
un|in|vent|ive|ly
un|in|vent|ive|
⠀⠀⠀⠀⠀ness
un|in|vest|ed
un|in|ves|ti|gated
un|in|vited
un|in|vited|ly
un|in|vit|ing
un|in|vit|ing|ly
un|in|voked
un|in|volved
union +s
union-bashing
union|isa|tion *Br.*
⠀(use
⠀unionization)
union|ise *Br.* (bring
⠀under trade-union
⠀organization; use
⠀unionize)
union|ises
union|ised
union|is|ing
un-ionised *Br.* (not
⠀ionised; use un-
⠀ionized)
union|ism
union|ist +s
union|is|tic
union|iza|tion
union|ize
union|izes
union|ized
union|iz|ing
⠀(bring under trade-
⠀union
⠀organization)
un-ionized (not
⠀ionized)
unip|ar|ous
uni|part|ite
uni|ped +s
uni|per|son|al
uni|planar
uni|pod +s
uni|polar
uni|polar|ity
unique +s
unique|ly
unique|ness
un|ironed
uni|ser|ial
uni|sex
uni|sex|ual
uni|sexu|al|ity
uni|sexu|al|ly

UNISON (trade
⠀union)
uni|son +s (sound;
⠀agreement)
unis|on|ant
unis|on|ous
un|issued
unit +s
UNITA (Angolan
⠀nationalist
⠀movement)
UNITAR (= United
⠀Nations Institute
⠀for Training and
⠀Research)
Uni|tar|ian +s
Uni|tar|ian|ism
uni|tar|ily
uni|tar|ity
uni|tary
unite
unites
united
unit|ing
united|ly
unit|hold|er +s
uni|tive
uni|tive|ly
unit-linked
Unity (name)
unity
⠀uni|ties
⠀(oneness;
⠀harmony; etc.)
uni|va|lent +s
uni|valve +s
uni|ver|sal +s
uni|ver|sal|is|
⠀abil|ity *Br.* (use
⠀universalizabil-
⠀ity)
uni|ver|sal|isa|tion
⠀*Br.* (use
⠀universalization)
uni|ver|sal|ise *Br.*
⠀(use universalize)
uni|ver|sal|ises
uni|ver|sal|ised
uni|ver|sal|is|ing
uni|ver|sal|ism
uni|ver|sal|ist +s
uni|ver|sal|is|tic
uni|ver|sal|ity
uni|ver|sal|iz|
⠀⠀⠀⠀⠀abil|ity
uni|ver|sal|
⠀⠀⠀⠀⠀iza|tion
uni|ver|sal|ize
uni|ver|sal|izes
uni|ver|sal|ized
uni|ver|sal|iz|ing
uni|ver|sal|ly

uni|verse +s
uni|ver|sity
⠀uni|ver|sities
uni|vocal
uni|vocal|ity
uni|vocal|ly
Unix *Computing*
⠀⠀*Propr.*
un|jaun|diced
un|join +s +ed
⠀+ing
un|joint +s +ed
⠀+ing
un|just
un|jus|ti|fi|able
un|jus|ti|fi|ably
un|jus|ti|fied
un|just|ly
un|just|ness
un|kempt
un|kempt|ly
un|kempt|ness
un|kept
un|kill|able
un|kind +er +est
un|kind|ly
un|kind|ness
un|king +s +ed
⠀+ing
un|kink +s +ed
⠀+ing
un|kissed
un|knit
⠀un|knits
⠀un|knit|ted
⠀un|knit|ting
un|knot
⠀un|knots
⠀un|knot|ted
⠀un|knot|ting
un|know|able
un|know|ing
un|know|ing|ly
un|know|ing|ness
un|known +s
un|known|ness
un|labeled *Am.*
un|labelled *Br.*
un|labored *Am.*
un|laboured *Br.*
un|lace
⠀un|laces
⠀un|laced
⠀un|lacing
un|lade
⠀un|lades
⠀un|laded
⠀un|lad|ing
⠀(unload. △ unlaid)
un|laden
un|lady|like

un|laid (past tense
   and past participle
   of unlay .
   △unlade)
un|lam|ent|ed
un|lash
   un|lashes
   un|lashed
   un|lash|ing
un|latch
   un|latches
   un|latched
   un|latch|ing
un|law|ful
un|law|ful|ly
un|law|ful|ness
unlay
   un|lays
   un|laid
   un|lay|ing
un|lead|ed
un|learn
   un|learns
   un|learned or
   un|learnt
   un|learn|ing
   verb
un|learn|ed
   adjective
un|learn|ed|ly
un|leash
   un|leashes
   un|leashed
   un|leash|ing
un|leav|ened
un|less
unlet
un|let|tered
un|lib|er|ated
un|licensed
un|light|ed
un|like
un|like|able
un|like|li|hood
un|like|li|ness
un|like|ly
   un|like|lier
   un|likeli|est
un|like|ness
un|lim|ber +s +ed
   +ing
un|lim|it|ed
un|lim|it|ed|ly
un|lim|it|ed|ness
un|lined
un|link +s +ed
   +ing
un|liquid|ated
un|list|ed
un|lis|ten|able
unlit
un|lit|er|ary

un|liv|able
unlived-in
un|load +s +ed
   +ing
un|load|er +s
un|locat|able
un|located
un|lock +s +ed
   +ing
un|looked
unlooked-for
un|loose
   un|looses
   un|loosed
   un|loos|ing
un|loosen +s +ed
   +ing
un|lov|able
un|loved
un|love|li|ness
un|love|ly
un|lov|ing
un|lov|ing|ly
un|lov|ing|ness
un|luck|ily
un|lucki|ness
un|lucky
   un|luck|ier
   un|lucki|est
un|maid|en|ly
un|make
   un|makes
   un|made
   un|mak|ing
un|mal|le|able
unman
   un|mans
   un|manned
   un|man|ning
un|man|age|able
un|man|age|able|
             ness
un|man|age|ably
un|man|aged
un|man|eu|ver|
   able Am.
un|man|li|ness
un|man|ly
un|man|nered
un|man|ner|li|ness
un|man|ner|ly
un|man|oeuv|
   rable Br.
un|man|ured
un|mapped
un|marked
un|marked|ness
un|mar|ket|able
un|marred
un|mar|riage|able
un|mar|ried
un|mas|cu|line

un|mask +s +ed
   +ing
un|mask|er +s
un|match|able
un|match|ably
un|matched
un|mated
un|matured
un|mean|ing
un|mean|ing|ly
un|mean|ing|ness
un|meant
un|meas|ur|able
un|meas|ur|ably
un|meas|ured
un|me|di|ated
un|melo|di|ous
un|melo|di|ous|ly
un|melt|ed
un|mem|or|able
un|mem|or|ably
un|mend|ed
un|men|tion|
         abil|ity
un|men|tion|able
   +s
un|men|tion|able|
         ness
un|men|tion|ably
un|men|tioned
un|mer|chant|able
un|mer|ci|ful
un|mer|ci|ful|ly
un|mer|ci|ful|ness
un|mer|it|ed
un|meri|tori|ous
unmet
un|met|alled
un|meth|od|ical
un|meth|od|ic|al|ly
un|met|ric|al
un|mili|tary
un|mind|ful
un|mind|ful|ly
un|mind|ful|ness
un|miss|able
un|mis|tak|abil|ity
un|mis|tak|able
un|mis|tak|able|
         ness
un|mis|tak|ably
un|mis|take|
   abil|ity (use
   unmistakability)
un|mis|take|able
   (use
   unmistakable)
un|mis|take|able|
   ness (use
   unmistakable-
   ness)
un|mis|take|ably
   (use
   unmistakably)

un|mis|taken
un|miti|gated
un|miti|gated|ly
un|mixed
un|mod|ern|ised
   Br. (use
   unmodernized)
un|mod|ern|ized
un|modi|fied
un|modu|lated
un|mol|est|ed
un|moor +s +ed
   +ing
un|moral
un|mor|al|ity
un|mor|al|ly
un|mother|ly
un|moti|vated
un|mount|ed
un|mourned
un|mov|able
un|move|able
   (use unmovable)
un|moved
un|mov|ing
un|mown
un|muf|fle
   un|muf|fles
   un|muf|fled
   un|muf|fling
un|mur|mur|ing
un|mur|mur|ing|ly
un|music|al
un|music|al|ity
un|music|al|ly
un|music|al|ness
un|mutil|ated
un|muz|zle
   un|muz|zles
   un|muz|zled
   un|muz|zling
un|nail +s +ed
   +ing
un|name|able
un|named
un|nat|ural
un|nat|ur|al|ly
un|nat|ur|al|ness
un|nav|ig|abil|ity
un|nav|ig|able
un|neces|sar|ily
un|neces|sari|ness
un|neces|sary
un|need|ed
un|neigh|bor|li|
         ness Am.
un|neigh|bor|ly Am.
un|neigh|bour|li|
         ness Br.
un|neigh|bour|ly Br.
un|nerve |
   un|nerves

un|nerve (*cont.*)
un|nerved
un|nerv|ing
un|nerv|ing|ly
un|nil|pen|tium
un|nil|qua|dium
un|notice|able
un|notice|ably
un|noticed
un|num|bered
UNO (= United
Nations
Organization)
un|ob|jec|tion|able
un|ob|jec|tion|able|
ness
un|ob|jec|tion|ably
un|ob|li|ging
un|ob|scured
un|ob|serv|able
un|ob|ser|vant
un|ob|ser|vant|ly
un|ob|served
un|ob|served|ly
un|ob|struct|ed
un|ob|tain|able
un|ob|tain|ably
un|ob|tru|sive
un|ob|tru|sive|ly
un|ob|tru|sive|
ness
un|occu|pancy
un|occu|pied
un|offend|ed
un|offend|ing
un|offi|cial
un|offi|cial|ly
un|oiled
un|open|able
un|opened
un|opposed
un|ordained
un|ordin|ary
un|organ|ised *Br.*
(use
unorganized)
un|organ|ized
un|ori|gin|al
un|ori|gin|al|ity
un|ori|gin|al|ly
un|orna|men|tal
un|orna|ment|ed
un|ortho|dox
un|ortho|dox|ly
un|ortho|doxy
un|ortho|dox|ies
un|osten|ta|tious
un|
osten|ta|tious|ly
un|osten|ta|tious|
ness
un|owned

un|oxi|dised *Br.*
(use unoxidized)
un|oxi|dized
un|pack +s +ed
+ing
un|pack|er +s
un|pad|ded
un|paged
un|paid
un|paint|ed
un|paired
un|pal|at|abil|ity
un|pal|at|able
un|pal|at|able|
ness
un|pal|at|ably
un|par|al|leled
un|par|don|able
un|par|don|able|
ness
un|par|don|ably
un|par|lia|
men|tary
un|pas|teur|ised
Br. (use
unpasteurized)
un|pas|teur|ized
un|pat|ent|ed
un|pat|ri|ot|ic
un|pat|ri|ot|ic|
al|ly
un|pat|ron|is|ing
Br. (use
unpatronizing)
un|pat|ron|iz|ing
un|pat|terned
un|paved
un|peace|ful
un|peeled
unpeg
un|pegs
un|pegged
un|peg|ging
un|pen|al|ised *Br.*
(use unpenalized)
un|pen|al|ized
un|people
un|peoples
un|peopled
un|peop|ling
un|per|ceived
un|per|cep|tive
un|per|cep|tive|ly
un|per|cep|tive|
ness
un|per|fect|ed
un|per|for|ated
un|per|formed
un|per|fumed
un|per|son +s
un|per|suad|able
un|per|suad|ed

un|per|sua|sive
un|per|sua|sive|ly
un|per|turbed
un|per|turb|ed|ly
un|phased (not in
phases.
△ unfazed)
un|philo|soph|ic
un|philo|soph|ic|al
un|philo|soph|ic|
al|ly
un|physio|logic|al
un|physio|logic|
al|ly
un|pick +s +ed
+ing
un|pic|tur|esque
unpin
un|pins
un|pinned
un|pin|ning
un|pitied
un|pity|ing
un|pity|ing|ly
un|place|able
un|placed
un|planned
un|plant|ed
un|plas|tered
un|plas|ti|cised *Br.*
(use
unplasticized)
un|plas|ti|cized
un|plaus|ible
un|play|able
un|play|ably
un|played
un|pleas|ant
un|pleas|ant|ly
un|pleas|ant|ness
un|pleas|ant|ry
un|pleas|ant|ries
un|pleas|ing
un|pleas|ing|ly
un|pleas|ur|able
un|pledged
un|ploughed *Br.*
un|plowed *Am.*
un|plucked
un|plug
un|plugs
un|plugged
un|plug|ging
un|plumb|able
un|plumbed
un|poet|ic
un|poet|ic|al
un|poet|ic|al|ly
un|point|ed
un|polar|ised *Br.*
(use unpolarized)
un|polar|ized
un|pol|ished

un|pol|it|ic
un|pol|it|ic|al
un|pol|it|ic|al|ly
un|polled
un|pol|lin|ated
un|pol|luted
un|pom|pous
un|popu|lar
un|popu|lar|ity
un|popu|lar|ly
un|popu|lated
un|posed
un|pos|sessed
un|post|ed
un|pow|ered
un|prac|ti|cal
un|prac|ti|cal|ity
un|prac|ti|cal|ly
un|prac|tised
un|pre|ced|ent|ed
un|pre|ced|ent|
ed|ly
un|pre|dict|
abil|ity
un|pre|dict|able
un|pre|dict|able|
ness
un|pre|dict|ably
un|pre|dict|ed
un|pre|ju|diced
un|pre|medi|tated
un|pre|medi|
tated|ly
un|pre|pared
un|pre|pared|ly
un|pre|pared|ness
un|pre|pos|sess|
ing
un|pre|scribed
un|pre|sent|able
un|pressed
un|pres|sur|ised
Br. (use
unpressurized)
un|pres|sur|ized
un|pre|sum|ing
un|pre|sump|tu|
ous
un|pre|tend|ing
un|pre|tend|ing|ly
un|pre|tend|ing|
ness
un|pre|ten|tious
un|pre|ten|tious|ly
un|pre|ten|tious|
ness
un|pre|vent|able
un|priced
un|primed
un|prin|cipled
un|prin|cipled|
ness

un|print|able
un|print|ably
un|print|ed
un|priv|il|eged
un|prob|lem|at|ic
un|prob|lem|at|ic|
   al|ly
un|pro|cessed
un|pro|claimed
un|pro|cur|able
un|pro|duct|ive
un|pro|duct|ive|ly
un|pro|duct|ive|
   ness
un|pro|fes|sion|al
un|pro|fes|sion|al|
   ism
un|pro|fes|sion|
   al|ly
un|prof|it|able
un|prof|it|able|
   ness
un|prof|it|ably
Un|pro|for
  (= United Nations
  Protection Force)
un|pro|gres|sive
un|prom|is|ing
un|prom|is|ing|ly
un|prompt|ed
un|pro|nounce
   able
un|pro|nounce|
   ably
un|prop|er|tied
un|proph|et|ic
un|pro|pi|tious
un|pro|pi|tious|ly
un|pros|per|ous
un|pros|per|ous|ly
un|pro|tect|ed
un|pro|tec|ted|
   ness
un|pro|test|ing
un|pro|test|ing|ly
un|prov|abil|ity
un|prov|able
un|prov|able|ness
un|proved
un|proven
un|pro|vided
un|pro|voca|tive
un|pro|voked
un|pruned
un|pub|li|cised *Br.*
  (use
  unpublicized)
un|pub|li|cized
un|pub|lish|able
un|pub|lished
un|punc|tual
un|punc|tu|al|ity

un|punc|tu|al|ly
un|punc|tu|ated
un|pun|ish|able
un|pun|ished
un|puri|fied
un|put|down|able
un|quali|fied
un|quan|ti|fi|able
un|quan|ti|fied
un|quench|able
un|quench|ably
un|quenched
un|ques|tion|
   abil|ity
un|ques|tion|able
un|ques|tion|able|
   ness
un|ques|tion|ably
un|ques|tioned
un|ques|tion|ing
un|
   ques|tion|ing|ly
un|quiet
un|quiet|ly
un|quiet|ness
un|quot|able
un|quote
un|quoted
un|raced
un|ran|somed
un|rated
un|rati|fied
un|rationed
un|ravel
un|ravels
un|rav|elled *Br.*
un|rav|eled *Am.*
un|rav|el|ling *Br.*
un|rav|el|ing *Am.*
un|reach|able
un|reach|able|
   ness
un|reach|ably
un|reached
un|re|act|ive
un|read
un|read|abil|ity
un|read|able
un|read|ably
un|read|ily
un|readi|ness
un|ready
un|real (not real.
  △ unreel)
un|real|is|able *Br.*
  (use unrealizable)
un|real|ised *Br.*
  (use unrealized)
un|real|ism
un|real|is|tic
un|real|is|tic|al|ly
un|real|ity

un|real|iz|able
un|real|ized
un|real|ly
un|rea|son
un|rea|son|able
un|rea|son|able|
   ness
un|rea|son|ably
un|rea|soned
un|rea|son|ing
un|rea|son|ing|ly
un|re|bel|lious|
   ness
un|re|cep|tive
un|re|cip|ro|cated
un|reck|oned
un|re|claimed
un|rec|og|nis|able
  Br. (use
  unrecognizable)
un|rec|og|nis|able|
  ness *Br.* (use
  unrecognizable-
  ness)
un|rec|og|nis|ably
  Br. (use
  unrecognizably)
un|rec|og|nised *Br.*
  (use
  unrecognized)
un|rec|og|niz|able
un|rec|og|niz|able|
   ness
un|rec|og|niz|ably
un|rec|og|nized
un|rec|om|pensed
un|rec|on|cil|able
un|rec|on|ciled
un|re|con|
   struct|ed
un|re|cord|able
un|re|cord|ed
un|re|cov|ered
un|rec|ti|fied
un|re|deem|able
un|re|deem|ably
un|re|deemed
un|re|dressed
un|reel +s +ed
  +ing (unwind
  from a reel.
  △ unreal)
un|reeve
un|reeves
un|rove
un|reev|ing
un|re|fined
un|re|flect|ed
un|re|flect|ing
un|re|flect|ing|ly
un|re|flect|ing|
   ness

un|re|flect|ive
un|re|formed
un|re|futed
un|re|gard|ed
un|re|gen|er|acy
un|re|gen|er|ate
un|re|gen|er|ate|ly
un|regi|ment|ed
un|regis|tered
un|re|gret|ted
un|regu|lated
un|re|hearsed
un|rein +s +ed
   +ing
un|re|inforced
un|re|lated
un|re|lated|ness
un|re|laxed
un|re|leased
un|re|lent|ing
un|re|lent|ing|ly
un|re|lent|ing|ness
un|re|li|abil|ity
un|re|li|able
un|re|li|able|ness
un|re|li|ably
un|re|lieved
un|re|lieved|ly
un|re|li|gious
un|re|mark|able
un|re|mark|ably
un|re|marked
un|re|mem|bered
un|re|mit|ting
un|re|mit|ting|ly
un|re|mit|ting|
   ness
un|re|morse|ful
un|re|morse|ful|ly
un|re|mov|able
un|re|mu|nera|tive
un|re|mu|nera|
   tive|ly
un|re|mu|nera|tive|
   ness
un|re|new|able
un|re|newed
un|re|nounced
un|re|pair|able
un|re|paired
un|re|pealed
un|re|peat|abil|ity
un|re|peat|able
un|re|peat|ed
un|re|pent|ant
un|re|pent|ant|ly
un|re|pent|ed
un|re|port|ed
un|rep|re|sen|
   ta|tive
un|rep|re|sen|
   ta|tive|ness

un|rep|re|sent|ed
un|re|proved
un|re|quest|ed
un|re|quit|ed
un|re|quited|ly
un|re|quited|ness
un|re|searched
un|re|serve
un|re|served
un|re|served|ly
un|re|serv|ed|ness
un|re|sist|ed
un|re|sist|ed|ly
un|re|sist|ing
un|re|sist|ing|ly
un|re|sist|ing|ness
un|re|solv|able
un|re|solved
un|re|solved|ly
un|re|solved|ness
un|re|spon|sive
un|re|spon|sive|ly
un|re|spon|sive|
    ness
un|rest
un|rest|ed
un|rest|ful
un|rest|ful|ly
un|rest|ing
un|rest|ing|ly
un|re|stored
un|re|strain|able
un|re|strained
un|re|strain|ed|ly
un|re|strain|ed|
    ness
un|re|straint
un|re|strict|ed
un|re|strict|ed|ly
un|re|strict|ed|
    ness
un|re|turned
un|re|vealed
un|re|veal|ing
un|re|versed
un|re|vised
un|re|voked
un|revo|lu|tion|ary
un|re|ward|ed
un|re|ward|ing
un|re|ward|ing|ly
un|rhymed
un|rhyth|mic|al
un|rhyth|mic|al|ly
un|rid|able (use
  unrideable)
un|rid|den
un|rid|dle
  un|rid|dles
  un|rid|dled
  un|rid|dling
un|rid|dler+s

un|ride|able
unrig
  un|rigs
  un|rigged
  un|rig|ging
un|right|eous
un|right|eous|ly
un|right|eous|ness
unrip
  un|rips
  un|ripped
  un|rip|ping
un|ripe
un|rip|ened
un|ripe|ness
un|risen
un|rivaled *Am.*
un|rivalled *Br.*
un|rivet+s +ed
  +ing
un|road|worthy
un|roast|ed
un|robe
  un|robes
  un|robed
  un|rob|ing
un|roll+s +ed
  +ing
un|roman|tic
un|roman|tic|al|ly
un|roof+s +ed
  +ing
un|root+s +ed
  +ing
un|rope
  un|ropes
  un|roped
  un|rop|ing
un|round|ed
un|rove
un|royal
UNRRA(= United
  Nations Relief and
  Rehabilitation
  Administration.
  △ UNRWA)
un|ruf|fled
un|ruled
un|ru|li|ness
un|ruly
  un|ru|lier
  un|ruli|est
UNRWA(= United
  Nations Relief and
  Works Agency.
  △ UNRRA)
un|sack|able
un|sad|dle
  un|sad|dles
  un|sad|dled
  un|sad|dling
un|safe

un|safe|ly
un|safe|ness
un|said
un|sal|ar|ied
un|sale|abil|ity
un|sale|able
un|salt|ed
un|salu|bri|ous
un|sal|vage|able
un|sanc|ti|fied
un|sanc|tioned
un|sani|tary
un|sapped
un|sat|is|fac|tor|
    ily
un|sat|is|fac|tori|
    ness
un|sat|is|fac|tory
un|sat|is|fied
un|sat|is|fied|ness
un|sat|is|fy|ing
un|sat|is|fy|ing|ly
un|sat|ur|ated
un|sat|ur|ation
un|saved
un|savor|ily *Am.*
un|savori|ness *Am.*
un|savory *Am.*
un|savour|ily *Br.*
un|savouri|ness
  Br.
un|savoury *Br.*
unsay
  un|says
  un|said
  un|say|ing
un|say|able
un|scal|able
un|scaled
un|scarred
un|scathed
un|scent|ed
un|sched|uled
un|schol|ar|li|ness
un|schol|ar|ly
un|schooled
un|sci|en|tif|ic
un|sci|en|tif|ic|
    al|ly
un|scram|ble
  un|scram|bles
  un|scram|bled
  un|scram|bling
un|scram|bler+s
un|scratched
un|screened
un|screw+s +ed
  +ing
un|script|ed
un|scrip|tural
un|scrip|tur|al|ly
un|scru|pu|lous

un|scru|pu|lous|ly
un|scru|pu|lous|
    ness
un|seal+s +ed
  +ing
un|search|able
un|search|able|
    ness
un|search|ably
un|searched
un|sea|son|able
un|sea|son|able|
    ness
un|sea|son|ably
un|sea|son|al
un|sea|soned
un|seat+s +ed
  +ing
un|sea|worthi|
    ness
un|sea|worthy
un|sec|ond|ed
un|sect|ar|ian
un|secured
un|see|able
un|seed|ed
un|see|ing
un|see|ing|ly
un|seem|li|ness
un|seem|ly
  un|seem|lier
  un|seemli|est
un|seen
un|seg|re|gated
un|select
un|select|ed
un|select|ive
un|self|con|scious
un|self|
    con|scious|ly
un|self|con|scious|
    ness
un|self|ish
un|self|ish|ly
un|self|ish|ness
un|sell|able
un|sen|sa|tion|al
un|sen|sa|tion|
    al|ly
un|sent
un|sen|ti|men|tal
un|sen|ti|men|tal|
    ity
un|sen|ti|
    men|tal|ly
un|sep|ar|ated
un|seri|ous
un|ser|vice|abil|ity
un|ser|vice|able
unset
un|set|tle
  un|set|tles

un|set|tle (*cont.*)
  un|set|tled
  un|set|tling
un|settled|ness
un|settle|ment
un|sev|ered
un|sewn (not sewn.
  △unsown)
unsex
  un|sexes
  un|sexed
  un|sex|ing
un|sexy
un|shackle
  un|shackles
  un|shackled
  un|shack|ling
un|shaded
un|shak|abil|ity
  (use
  unshakeability)
un|shak|able (use
  unshakeable)
un|shak|ably (use
  unshakeably)
un|shake|abil|ity
un|shake|able
un|shake|ably
un|shaken
un|shaken|ly
un|shape|li|ness
un|shape|ly
un|shared
un|sharp
un|sharp|ened
un|sharp|ness
un|shaved
un|shaven
un|sheathe
  un|sheathes
  un|sheathed
  un|sheath|ing
un|shed
un|shell +s +ed
  +ing
un|shel|tered
un|shield|ed
un|shift|able
un|ship
  un|ships
  un|shipped
  un|ship|ping
un|shock|abil|ity
un|shock|able
un|shock|ably
un|shod
un|shorn
un|shrink|abil|ity
un|shrink|able
un|shrink|ing
un|shrink|ing|ly
un|shriven

un|shut|tered
un|sight +s +ed
  +ing
un|sight|li|ness
un|sight|ly
  un|sight|lier
  un|sightli|est
un|signed
un|sign|post|ed
un|silenced
un|sim|pli|fied
un|sink|abil|ity
un|sink|able
un|sized
un|skil|ful *Br.*
un|skil|ful|ly *Br.*
un|skil|ful|ness *Br.*
un|skilled
un|skill|ful *Am.*
un|skill|ful|ly *Am.*
un|skill|ful|ness
  Am.
un|skimmed
un|slak|able (use
  unslakeable)
un|slake|able
un|slaked
un|sleep|ing
un|sleep|ing|ly
un|sliced
un|sling
  un|slings
  un|slung
  un|sling|ing
un|smil|ing
un|smil|ing|ly
un|smil|ing|ness
un|smoked
un|smoothed
un|snap
  un|snaps
  un|snapped
  un|snap|ping
un|snarl +s +ed
  +ing
un|soaked
un|soci|abil|ity
un|soci|able
un|soci|able|ness
un|soci|ably
un|social
un|social|ist +s
un|social|ly
un|soft|ened
un|soiled
un|sold
un|sol|der +s +ed
  +ing
un|sol|dier|ly
un|soli|cit|ed
un|soli|cit|ed|ly
un|solv|abil|ity

un|solv|able
un|solv|able|ness
un|solved
un|sophis|ti|cated
un|sophis|ti|
        cated|ly
un|sophis|ti|cated|
         ness
un|sophis|ti|
       ca|tion
un|sort|ed
un|sought
un|sound
un|sound|ed
un|sound|ly
un|sound|ness
un|soured
un|sown (not sown.
  △unsewn)
un|spar|ing
un|spar|ing|ly
un|spar|ing|ness
un|speak|able
un|speak|able|
       ness
un|speak|ably
un|speak|ing
un|spe|cial
un|spe|cial|ised
  Br. (use
  unspecialized)
un|spe|cial|ized
un|spe|cif|ic
un|speci|fied
un|spec|tacu|lar
un|spec|tacu|lar|ly
un|spent
un|spilled
un|spilt
un|spir|it|ual
un|spir|itu|al|ity
un|spir|itu|al|ly
un|spir|it|ual|ness
un|spoiled *Am.*
un|spoilt *Br.*
un|spoken
un|spon|sored
un|spool +s +ed
  +ing
un|sport|ing
un|sport|ing|ly
un|sport|ing|ness
un|sports|man|
       like
un|spot|ted
un|sprayed
un|sprung
un|stable
un|stable|ness
un|stably
un|staffed
un|stained

un|stall +s +ed
  +ing
un|stamped
un|stan|dard|ised
  Br. (use
  unstandardized)
un|stan|dard|ized
un|starched
un|stat|able
un|stated
un|states|man|like
un|stat|ut|able
un|stat|ut|ably
un|stead|fast
un|stead|ily
un|steadi|ness
un|steady
un|ster|ile
un|ster|il|ised *Br.*
  (use unsterilized)
un|ster|il|ized
un|stick
  un|sticks
  un|stuck
  un|stick|ing
un|stifled
un|stimu|lated
un|stimu|lat|ing
un|stint|ed
un|stint|ed|ly
un|stint|ing
un|stint|ing|ly
un|stirred
un|stitch
  un|stitches
  un|stitched
  un|stitch|ing
un|stocked
un|stock|inged
un|stop
  un|stops
  un|stopped
  un|stop|ping
un|stop|pabil|ity
un|stop|pable
un|stop|pably
un|stop|per +s +ed
  +ing
un|strained
un|strap
  un|straps
  un|strapped
  un|strap|ping
un|strati|fied
un|streamed
un|stream|lined
un|strength|ened
un|stressed
un|stretched
un|string
  un|strings

un|string (*cont.*)
un|strung
un|string|ing
un|stripped
un|struc|tured
un|stuck
un|stud|ied
un|stud|ied|ly
un|stuffed
un|stuffy
un|styl|ish
un|sub|dued
un|sub|ju|gated
un|sub|scribed
un|sub|sid|ised *Br.*
(use
unsubsidized)
un|sub|sid|ized
un|sub|stan|tial
un|sub|stan|ti|al|
ity
un|sub|stan|tial|ly
un|sub|stan|ti|
ated
un|subtle
un|subtly
un|suc|cess
un|suc|cesses
un|suc|cess|ful
un|suc|cess|ful|ly
un|suc|cess|ful|
ness
un|sugared
un|sug|gest|ive
un|suit|abil|ity
un|suit|able
un|suit|able|ness
un|suit|ably
un|suit|ed
un|sul|lied
un|sum|moned
un|sung
un|super|vised
un|sup|plied
un|sup|port|able
un|sup|port|ably
un|sup|port|ed
un|sup|port|ed|ly
un|sup|port|ive
un|sup|pressed
un|sure
un|sure|ly
un|sure|ness
un|sur|faced
un|sur|mount|able
un|sur|pass|able
un|sur|pass|ably
un|sur|passed
un|sur|prised
un|sur|pris|ing
un|sur|pris|ing|ly
un|sur|veyed

un|sur|viv|able
un|sus|cep|ti|
bil|ity
un|sus|cep|tible
un|sus|pect|ed
un|sus|pect|ed|ly
un|sus|pect|ing
un|sus|pect|ing|ly
un|sus|pect|ing|
ness
un|sus|pi|cious
un|sus|pi|cious|ly
un|sus|pi|cious|
ness
un|sus|tain|able
un|sus|tain|ably
un|sus|tained
un|swal|lowed
un|swathe
un|swathes
un|swathed
un|swath|ing
un|swayed
un|sweet|ened
un|swept
un|swerv|ing
un|swerv|ing|ly
un|sworn
un|sym|met|ric|al
un|sym|met|ric|
al|ly
un|sym|pa|thet|ic
un|sym|pa|thet|ic|
al|ly
un|sys|tem|at|ic
un|sys|tem|at|ic|
al|ly
un|tack +s +ed
+ing
un|taint|ed
un|taken
un|tal|ent|ed
un|tame|able
un|tamed
un|tan|gle
un|tan|gles
un|tan|gled
un|tan|gling
un|tanned
un|tapped
un|tar|nished
un|tasted
un|taxed
un|teach
un|teaches
un|taught
un|teach|ing
un|teach|able
un|tear|able
un|tech|nic|al
un|tech|nic|al|ly
un|tem|pered

un|tempt|ed
un|ten|abil|ity
un|ten|able
un|ten|able|ness
un|ten|ably
un|ten|ant|ed
un|tend|ed
un|ten|ured
Un|ter|mensch
Un|ter|mensch|en
Un|ter|walden
(canton,
Switzerland)
un|test|able
un|test|ed
un|tether +s +ed
+ing
un|thanked
un|thank|ful
un|thank|ful|ly
un|thank|ful|ness
un|thatched
un|theo|logic|al
un|the|or|et|ic|al
un|the|or|ised *Br.*
(use untheorized)
un|the|or|ized
un|thick|ened
un|think
un|thinks
un|thought
un|think|ing
un|think|abil|ity
un|think|able
un|think|able|ness
un|think|ably
un|think|ing|ly
un|think|ing|ness
un|thought
un|thought|ful
un|thought|ful|ly
un|thought|ful|
ness
unthought-of
unthought-out
un|thread +s +ed
+ing
un|threat|ened
un|threat|en|ing
un|threshed
un|thrift|ily
un|thrifti|ness
un|thrifty
un|throne
un|thrones
un|throned
un|thron|ing
un|tidi|ly
un|tidi|ness
un|tidy
un|tidi|er
un|tidi|est

untie
un|ties
un|tied
un|tying
until
un|tilled
un|timed
un|time|li|ness
un|time|ly
un|tinged
un|tipped
un|tired
un|tir|ing
un|tir|ing|ly
un|titled
unto
un|toast|ed
un|told
un|touch|abil|ity
un|touch|able +s
un|touch|able|
ness
un|touched
un|to|ward
un|to|ward|ly
un|to|ward|ness
un|trace|able
un|trace|ably
un|traced
un|tracked
un|trad|ition|al
un|train|able
un|trained
un|tram|meled
Am.
un|tram|melled *Br.*
un|tram|pled
un|trans|fer|able
un|trans|formed
un|trans|
lat|abil|ity
un|trans|lat|able
un|trans|lat|ably
un|trans|lated
un|trans|mit|ted
un|trans|port|able
un|trav|eled *Am.*
un|trav|elled *Br.*
un|treat|able
un|treat|ed
un|trendy
un|tried
un|trimmed
un|trod|den
un|troubled
un|true
un|truly
un|truss
un|trusses
un|trussed
un|truss|ing
un|trust|ing

un|trust|worthi|ness
un|trust|worthy
un|truth +s
un|truth|ful
un|truth|ful|ly
un|truth|ful|ness
un|tuck +s +ed +ing
un|tun|able
un|tuned
un|tune|ful
un|tune|ful|ly
un|tune|ful|ness
un|turned
un|tutored
un|twine
un|twines
un|twined
un|twin|ing
un|twist +s +ed +ing
un|tying
un|typ|ical
un|typ|ic|al|ly
un|usable
un|use|able (use unusable)
un|used
un|usual
un|usual|ly
un|usual|ness
un|utter|able
un|utter|able|ness
un|utter|ably
un|uttered
un|vac|cin|ated
un|valued
un|van|dal|ised Br. (use unvandalized)
un|van|dal|ized
un|van|quished
un|var|ied
un|var|nished
un|vary|ing
un|vary|ing|ly
un|vary|ing|ness
un|veil +s +ed +ing
un|vent|ed
un|ven|til|ated
un|veri|fi|able
un|veri|fied
un|versed
un|viabil|ity
un|viable
un|vio|lated
un|visit|ed
un|viti|ated
un|voiced
un|waged

un|wak|ened
un|walled
un|want|ed
un|war|ily
un|wari|ness
un|war|like
un|warmed
un|warned
un|war|rant|able
un|war|rant|able|ness
un|war|rant|ably
un|war|rant|ed
un|wary
un|wari|er
un|wari|est
un|washed
un|watch|able
un|watched
un|watch|ful
un|watered
un|waver|ing
un|waver|ing|ly
un|waxed
un|weak|ened
un|weaned
un|wear|able
un|wear|ied
un|wear|ied|ly
un|wear|ied|ness
un|weary
un|weary|ing
un|weary|ing|ly
unwed
un|wed|ded
un|wed|ded|ness
un|weed|ed
un|weighed
un|weight +s +ed +ing
un|wel|come
un|wel|comed
un|wel|come|ly
un|wel|come|ness
un|wel|com|ing
un|well
un|wept
un|wet|ted
un|whipped
un|whitened
un|whole|some
un|whole|some|ly
un|whole|some|ness
un|wield|ily
un|wieldi|ness
un|wieldy
un|wield|ier
un|wieldi|est
un|will|ing
un|will|ing|ly
un|will|ing|ness

un|wind
un|winds
un|wound
un|wind|ing
un|wink|ing
un|wink|ing|ly
un|win|nable
un|wiped
un|wired
un|wis|dom
un|wise
un|wise|ly
un|wished
un|with|ered
un|wit|nessed
un|wit|ting
un|wit|ting|ly
un|wit|ting|ness
un|woman|li|ness
un|woman|ly
un|wont|ed
un|wont|ed|ly
un|wont|ed|ness
un|wood|ed
un|work|abil|ity
un|work|able
un|work|able|ness
un|work|ably
un|worked
un|work|man|like
un|world|li|ness
un|world|ly
un|worn
un|wor|ried
un|wor|shipped
un|worth|ily
un|worthi|ness
un|worthy
un|wor|thier
un|worthi|est
un|wound
un|wound|ed
un|woven
un|wrap
un|wraps
un|wrapped
un|wrap|ping
un|wrin|kled
un|writ|able
un|writ|ten
un|wrought
un|wrung
un|yield|ing
un|yield|ing|ly
un|yield|ing|ness
un|yoke
un|yokes
un|yoked
un|yok|ing
unzip
un|zips

unzip (cont.)
un|zipped
un|zip|ping
up
ups
upped
up|ping
up-anchor +s +ed +ing
up-and-coming
up-and-over
up and run|ning
up-and-under +s
Upani|shad +s
upas
upas tree +s
up|beat +s
up|braid +s +ed +ing
up|braid|ing +s
up|bring|ing +s
up|build
up|builds
up|built
up|build|ing
up|cast +s
up|chuck +s +ed +ing
up|com|ing
up-country
up|cur|rent +s
up|date
up|dates
up|dated
up|dat|ing
up|dater +s
Up|dike, John (American writer)
up|draft Am. +s
up|draught Br. +s
upend +s +ed +ing
up|field
up|flow
up|fold +s
up|front adjective
up front adverb
up|grade
up|grades
up|graded
up|grad|ing
up|grade|able
up|grader +s
up|grad|ing +s
up|growth
up|haul +s
up|heav|al +s
up|heave
up|heaves
up|heaved
up|heav|ing
up|hill

up|hold
up|holds
up|held
up|hold|ing
up|hold|er +s
up|hol|ster +s +ed
  +ing
up|hol|ster|er +s
up|hol|stery
up|keep
up|land +s
up|lift +s +ed +ing
up|lift|er +s
up|light|er +s
up|link +s +ed
  +ing
up|load +s +ed
  +ing
up|lying
up|mar|ket
up|most
upon
upper +s
upper case *noun*
upper-case
  attributive
upper-class
  adjective
upper|cut
  upper|cuts
  upper|cut
  upper|cut|ting
upper-middle-
  class *adjective*
upper|most
upper|part +s
Upper Volta
  (former name of
  Burkina)
up|pish
up|pish|ly
up|pish|ness
up|pity
Upp|sala (city,
  Sweden)
up|raise
  up|raises
  up|raised
  up|rais|ing
up|rate
  up|rates
  up|rated
  up|rat|ing
up|rat|ing +s
up|right +s +ed
  +ing
up|right|ly
up|right|ness
up|rise
  up|rises
  up|rose

up|rise *(cont.)*
  up|ris|ing
  up|risen
up|ris|ing +s
up|river
up|roar +s
up|roari|ous
up|roari|ous|ly
up|roari|ous|ness
up|root +s +ed
  +ing
up|root|er
up|rose
up|rush
  up|rushes
ups-a-daisy
up|scale
upset
  up|sets
  upset
  up|set|ting
up|set|ter +s
up|set|ting|ly
up|shift +s +ed
  +ing
up|shot +s
up|side down
  *adverb and
  adjective*
upside-down
  attributive
up|sides
up|si|lon +s
up|stage
  up|stages
  up|staged
  up|staging
up|stair
up|stairs
up|stand +s
up|stand|ing
up|start +s
up|state
up|stater +s
up|stream
up|stretched
up|stroke +s
up|surge +s
up|swept
up|swing +s
upsy-daisy
up|take +s
up-tempo
up|throw +s
up|thrust +s
up|tick +s
up|tight
up|tilt|ed
up|time
up to date *adverb
  and adjective*
up-to-date
  attributive

up-to-the-minute
up|town
up|town|er +s
up|turn +s +ed
  +ing
up|ward
up|ward|ly
up|wards
up|warp +s
up|well +s +ed
  +ing
up|wind
Ur (ancient city,
  Iraq)
ura|cil
ur|ae|mia *Br. (Am.*
  uremia)
ur|aem|ic *Br. (Am.*
  uremic)
ur|aeus
  uraei
Ural-Altaic +s
Ural|ic +s
Ural Moun|tains
  (in Russia)
Urals (= Ural
  Mountains)
Ur|ania *Greek and
  Roman Mythology*
ur|an|ic
ur|an|in|ite
ur|an|ism
ur|an|ium
uran|og|raph|er +s
urano|graph|ic
uran|og|raphy
uran|om|etry
uran|ous
  (of uranium)
Ura|nus *(Greek
  Mythology;* planet)
urate +s
urban
ur|bane
ur|bane|ly
ur|bane|ness
ur|ban|isa|tion *Br.*
  (use
  urbanization)
ur|ban|ise *Br.* (use
  urbanize)
  ur|ban|ises
  ur|ban|ised
  ur|ban|is|ing
ur|ban|ism
ur|ban|ist +s
ur|ban|ite +s
ur|ban|ity
  ur|ban|ities
ur|ban|iza|tion
ur|ban|ize
  ur|ban|izes

ur|ban|ize *(cont.)*
  ur|ban|ized
  ur|ban|iz|ing
ur|ceo|late
ur|chin +s
Urdu
urea
urea-
  formal|de|hyde
ureal
ur|emia *Am. (Br.*
  uraemia)
ur|emic *Am. (Br.*
  uraemic)
ur|eter +s
ur|eter|al
ur|eter|ic
ur|eter|itis
ur|eter|ot|omy
  ur|eter|oto|mies
ur|eth|ane
ur|ethra
  ur|eth|rae
ur|eth|ral
ur|eth|ritis
ur|eth|rot|omy
  ur|eth|roto|mies
Urey, Har|old
  Clay|ton
  (American
  chemist)
Urga (former name
  of Ulan Bator)
urge
  urges
  urged
  ur|ging
ur|gen|cy
  ur|gen|cies
ur|gent
ur|gent|ly
urger +s
ur|ging +s
Uriah *Bible*
uric
urim
ur|inal +s
urin|aly|sis
  urin|aly|ses
urin|ary
urin|ate
  urin|ates
  urin|ated
  urin|at|ing
urin|ation
urine +s
urin|ous
urn +s (vase; vessel
  for tea etc.
  △ earn, ern, erne)
urn|field +s
urn|ful +s

uro|chord +s
uro|chord|ate +s
uro|dele +s
uro|geni|tal
uro|lith|ia|sis
uro|logic
ur|olo|gist +s
ur|ology
uro|pygium
uro|pygia
uros|copy
Ursa Major
(constellation)
Ursa Minor
(constellation)
ur|sine
Ur|sula (legendary
British saint;
name)
Ur|su|line +s
ur|ti|caria
ur|ti|cate
ur|ti|cates
ur|ti|cated
ur|ti|cat|ing
ur|ti|ca|tion
Uru|guay
Uru|guay|an +s
Uruk (ancient city,
Mesopotamia)
Urum|chi
(= Urumqi)
Urumqi (city,
China)
urus
plural urus
us
us|abil|ity
us|able
us|able|ness
usage +s
us|ance +s
USDAW (= Union
of Shop,
Distributive, and
Allied Workers)
use
uses
used
using
(bring into service;
exploit. △ youse)
use|abil|ity (use
usability)
use|able (use
usable)
use|able|ness (use
usableness)
use-by date +s
use|ful
use|ful|ly
use|ful|ness

use|less
use|less|ly
use|less|ness
user +s
user-friendli|ness
user-friend|ly
ushabti +s
U-shaped
usher +s +ed +ing
ush|er|ette +s
ush|er|ship +s
Ushu|aia (port,
Tierra del Fuego)
Üskü|dar (suburb
of Istanbul,
Turkey)
Us|pa|llata Pass
(in Andes)
usque|baugh
Us|ta|ba|kan|skoe
(former name of
Abakan)
Usta|sha +s
(member of
Croatian
nationalist
movement)
Usta|she (these
collectively)
Us|ti|nov (former
name of Izhevsk)
Us|ti|nov, Peter
(British actor)
usual
usu|al|ly
usual|ness
usu|cap|tion
usu|fruct +s +ed
+ing
usu|fruc|tu|ary
usu|fruc|tu|ar|ies
Usum|bura (former
name of
Bujumbura)
us|urer +s
us|uri|ous
us|uri|ous|ly
usurp +s +ed +ing
usurp|ation
usurp|er +s
usury
Utah (state, USA; D-
Day beach)
Uta|maro,
Kita|gawa
(Japanese painter)
Ute
plural Ute *or* Utes
(American Indian)
ute +s (utility truck)
uten|sil +s
uter|ine

ut|er|itis
uterus
uteri
Uther Pen|dragon
Arthurian Legend
utile
util|is|able *Br.* (use
utilizable)
util|isa|tion *Br.*
(use utilization)
util|ise *Br.* (use
utilize)
util|ises
util|ised
util|is|ing
util|iser *Br.* +s (use
utilizer)
utili|tar|ian +s
utili|tar|ian|ism
util|ity
util|ities
util|ity pro|gram
+s
util|iz|able
util|iza|tion
util|ize
util|izes
util|ized
util|iz|ing
util|izer +s
ut|most
Uto|pia +s
Uto|pian +s
Uto|pian|ism
Ut|recht (city, the
Netherlands)
ut|ricle +s
ut|ricu|lar
Ut|rillo, Maur|ice
(French painter)
Ut|sire (island,
Norway)
Ut|sire, North and
South (shipping
areas, North Sea)
Uttar Pra|desh
(state, India)
utter +s +ed +ing
ut|ter|able
ut|ter|ance +s
ut|ter|er +s
ut|ter|ly
ut|ter|most
ut|ter|ness
Ut|tley, Ali|son
(English writer)
U-turn +s
U2 (Irish rock
group)
uvea +s

uvula
uvu|lae
(part of throat)
uvu|lar +s
(of the uvula;
consonant)
ux|or|ial
ux|ori|cidal
ux|ori|cide +s
ux|ori|ous
ux|ori|ous|ly
Uzbek +s
Uz|beki|stan
Uzi +s (gun)

Vv

Vaal (river, South Africa)

Vaasa (port, Finland. △Vasa, Vasa)

vac +s (= vacation; vacuum cleaner)

va¦cancy
va¦can|cies

va¦cant

va¦cant¦ly

vac|at|able

vac|ate
vac|ates
vac|ated
vac|at¦ing

vac|ation +s +ed +ing

vac|ation¦er +s

vac|ation|ist +s

vac|ation|land +s

vac|cinal

vac|cin|ate
vac|cin|ates
vac|cin|ated
vac|cin|at¦ing

vac|cin|ation +s

vac|cin|ator +s

vac|cine +s

vac|cinia +s

vacil|late
vacil|lates
vacil|lated
vacil|lat¦ing

vacil|la¦tion +s

vacil|la¦tor +s

vacua

vacu¦ity

vacu|olar

vacu|ol|ation +s

vacu|ole +s

vacu¦ous

vacu¦ous¦ly

vacu¦ous|ness

vac¦uum
vac¦uums *or* vacua
noun

vac¦uum +s +ed +ing *verb*

vacuum-clean +s +ed +ing

vac¦uum clean¦er +s

vacuum-packed

vade-mecum +s

Vado|dara (city and district, India)

Vaduz (capital of Liechtenstein)

vag
vags
vagged
vag|ging

vaga|bond +s +ed +ing

vaga|bond|age

vagal

va¦gari|ous

va¦gary
va¦gar|ies

vagi

va¦gina +s

va¦ginal

vagin|is|mus

vagin|itis

va|grancy

va|grant +s

va|grant¦ly

vague
vaguer
vaguest

vague¦ly

vague|ness

vaguish

vagus
vagi

vail +s +ed +ing (doff; yield. △vale, veil)

vain +er +est (conceited. △vane, vein)

vain|glori¦ous

vain|glori¦ous|ly

vain|glori¦ous|ness

vain|glory

vain¦ly

vain|ness

vair

Vaish|nava +s

Vai¦sya +s

Val

Val¦ais (canton, Switzerland)

val|ance +s (short curtain. △valence)

val|anced

Valda

vale +s (valley; farewell. △vail, veil)

val|edic|tion +s

val|edic|tor¦ian +s

val|edic|tory
val|edic|tor¦ies

val|lence +s (*Chemistry.* △valance)

Val¦en|cia (city and region, Spain)

Val¦en|cian

Val¦en|ci|ennes (lace)

va|lency
va|len|cies

Val¦en|tia (weather station off Ireland)

Val¦en|tine (Italian saint; name)

val¦en|tine +s

Val¦en|tino, Ru|dolph (Italian-born American actor)

Val¦era, Eamon de (Irish statesman)

val¦er|ate +s

Val¦er|ian (Roman emperor)

val¦er|ian +s (plant)

val¦er¦ic

Val|erie

Val¦éry, Paul (French writer)

valet +s +ed +ing

val¦eta +s (use veleta)

val¦etu|din|ar¦ian +s

val¦etu|din| ar¦ian|ism

val¦etu|din|ary
val¦etu|din|ar¦ies

val|gus
val|guses

Val|halla
Scandinavian Mythology

vali|ant

vali|ant¦ly

valid

val|id|ate
val|id|ates
val|id|ated
val|id|at¦ing

val|id|ation +s

val|id|ity

val|id¦ly

val|ine +s

val|ise +s

Val|ium *Propr.*

Val|kyrie +s
Scandinavian Mythology

Valla|do|lid (city, Spain)

val|lec¦ula
val|lecu|lae

val¦lecu|lar

val|lecu|late

Valle d'Aosta (region, Italy)

Val|letta (capital of Malta)

val¦ley +s (region between hills)

val¦lum
valli
(Roman rampart and stockade)

Val¦ois, Nin|ette de (Irish dancer and choreographer)

val|onia

valor *Am.* (*Br.* valour)

val|orem (in 'ad valorem')

val|or|isa¦tion *Br.* (use valorization)

val|or|ise *Br.* (use valorize)

val|or|ises

val|or|ised

val|or|is¦ing

val|or|iza¦tion

val|or|ize

val|or|izes

val|or|ized

val|or|iz¦ing

val|or¦ous

val¦our *Br.* (*Am.* valor)

Val|par|aíso (port, Chile)

valse +s

valu|able +s

valu|ably

valu|ate
valu|ates
valu|ated
valu|at¦ing

valu|ation +s

valu|ator +s

value
val¦ues
val¦ued
valu¦ing

value added *noun and adjective*

value-added (*attributive* except of tax)

value added tax

value-based

value-for-money *attributive*

value judge|ment
+s

value judg|ment
+s (use value
judgement)

value|less

value|less|ness

valuer +s

val|uta +s

valv|ate

valve +s

valved

valve gear

valve|less

valvu|lar

valv|ule +s

valv|ul|itis

vam|brace +s

vam|oose

vam|ooses

vam|oosed

vam|oos|ing

vamp +s +ed +ing

vam|pire +s

vam|pir|ic

vam|pir|ism

vamp|ish

vam|plate +s

vampy

vamp|ier

vampi|est

Van (name)

Van, Lake (in
Turkey)

van +s (vehicle)

van|ad|ate +s

van|ad|ic

van|adium

van|ad|ous

Van Allen (belt;
layer)

Van|brugh, John
(English architect)

Van Buren,
Mar|tin
(American
president)

Van|cou|ver (city,
Canada)

Van|cou|ver,
George (English
navigator)

Van|cou|ver
Is|land
(in Canada)

Vanda (Swedish
name for Vantaa)

Van|dal +s
(member of
Germanic people)

van|dal +s
(destructive
person)

Van|dal|ic

van|dal|ise Br. (use
vandalize)

van|dal|ises

van|dal|ised

van|dal|is|ing

van|dal|ism

van|dal|is|tic

van|dal|is|tic|al|ly

van|dal|ize

van|dal|izes

van|dal|ized

van|dal|iz|ing

van de Graaff
(generator)

Van|der|bijl|park
(city, South
Africa)

Van|der|bilt,
Cor|ne|lius
(American
shipping and
railway magnate)

Van der Post,
Laur|ens (South
African explorer)

van der Waals
(forces)

van de Velde,
Adri|aen (Dutch
painter)

van de Velde,
Henri (Belgian
architect)

van de Velde,
Wil|lem ('the
Elder' and 'the
Younger', Dutch
painters)

Van Die|men's
Land (former
name of
Tasmania)

Van Dyck,
An|thony
(Flemish painter)

Van|dyke,
An|thony (use
Van Dyck)

Van|dyke +s
(beard)

van|dyke +s (lace
point; cape or
collar)

Van|dyke brown
noun and adjective

Vandyke-brown
attributive

vane +s
(weathervane;
blade of propeller
etc.; sight on
instrument; part of
feather. △ vain,
vein)

vaned

vane|less (without
vanes. △ veinless)

Vän|ern (lake,
Switzerland)

Van|essa (name)

van|essa +s
(butterfly)

Van Eyck, Jan
(Flemish painter)

vang +s

Van Gogh,
Vin|cent (Dutch
painter)

van|guard +s

van|illa +s

van|il|lin

van|ish

van|ishes

van|ished

van|ish|ing

van|ish|ing point
+s

vani|tory

vani|tor|ies
Propr.

van|ity

van|ities

van Ley|den,
Lucas (Dutch
painter)

van|load +s

van|quish

van|quishes

van|quished

van|quish|ing

van|quish|able

van|quish|er +s

Van|taa (city,
Finland)

vant|age +s

vant|age point +s

Vanua Levu
(island, Fiji)

Vanu|atu (in S.
Pacific)

vapid

vap|id|ity

vap|id|ly

vap|id|ness

vapor Am. +s (Br.
vapour)

vapor-check Am.
attributive (Br.
vapour-check)

va|por|er Am. +s
(Br. vapourer)

vap|or|etto

vap|or|etti or
vap|or|ettos

va|por|if|ic

va|pori|form

va|por|im|eter +s

va|por|ing Am. +s
(Br. vapouring)

va|por|is|able Br.
(use vaporizable)

va|por|isa|tion Br.
(use
vaporization)

va|por|ise Br. (use
vaporize)

va|por|ises

va|por|ised

va|por|is|ing

va|por|iser Br. +s
(use vaporizer)

va|por|ish Am. (Br.
vapourish)

va|por|iz|able

va|por|iza|tion

va|por|ize

va|por|izes

va|por|ized

va|por|iz|ing

va|por|izer +s

va|por|ous

va|por|ous|ly

va|por|ous|ness

va|pory Am. (Br.
vapoury)

va|pour Br. +s +ed
+ing (Am. vapor)

vapour-check Br.
attributive (Am.
vapor-check)

va|pour|er Br. +s
(Am. vaporer)

va|pour|ing Br. +s
(Am. vaporing)

va|pour|ish Br.
(Am. vaporish)

va|poury Br. (Am.
vapory)

va|quero +s

var|ac|tor +s

Varah, Chad
(English founder
of the Samaritans)

Vara|nasi (city,
India)

Var|an|gian +s

varec

Var|ese (town,
Italy)

Var|èse, Ed|gard
(French-born

Var¦èse (*cont.*)
American
composer)
Var¦gas, Getú¦lio
Dor¦nel¦les
(Brazilian
president)
Var¦gas Llosa,
Mario (Peruvian
writer)
vari¦abil¦ity
vari¦abil¦ities
vari¦able +s
vari¦able¦ness
variable-rate
attributive
variable-speed
attributive
vari¦ably
vari¦ance +s
vari¦ant +s
vari¦ate +s
vari¦ation +s
vari¦ation¦al
vari¦cella
vari¦ces
vari¦co¦cele +s
vari¦col¦ored *Am.*
vari¦col¦oured *Br.*
vari¦cose
vari¦cosed
vari¦cos¦ity
var¦ied
var¦ied¦ly
varie¦gate
varie¦gates
varie¦gated
varie¦gat¦ing
varie¦ga¦tion +s
var¦ietal
var¦ietal¦ly
var¦iet¦ist +s
var¦iety
var¦ieties
vari¦focal +s
vari¦form
vari¦ola *noun*
vari¦olar *adjective*
vari¦ole +s
vari¦ol¦ite +s
vari¦ol¦it¦ic
vari¦ol¦oid +s
vari¦ol¦ous
vari¦om¦eter +s
vari¦orum +s
vari¦ous
vari¦ous¦ly
vari¦ous¦ness
var¦is¦tor +s
varix
vari¦ces
var¦let +s

var¦let¦ry
var¦mint +s
Varna (port,
Bulgaria)
varna +s *Hinduism*
Varne (lightvessel,
English Channel)
var¦nish
var¦nishes
var¦nished
var¦nish¦ing
var¦nish¦er +s
Varro, Mar¦cus
Ter¦en¦tius
(Roman scholar)
var¦sity
var¦sities
Var¦so¦vian +s
var¦so¦vi¦ana +s
var¦so¦vi¦enne +s
Var¦una (Hindu
god)
varus
var¦uses
varve +s
varved
vary
var¦ies
var¦ied
vary¦ing
vary¦ing¦ly
vas
vasa
Vasa (Swedish
dynasty. △Vaasa)
Vasa (ship.
△Vaasa)
vasal
Vas¦ar¦ely, Vik¦tor
(Hungarian-born
French painter)
Vas¦ari, Gior¦gio
(Italian painter
and biographer)
Vasco da Gama
(Portuguese
explorer)
vas¦cu¦lar
vas¦cu¦lar¦isa¦tion
Br. (use
vascularization)
vas¦cu¦lar¦ise *Br.*
(use vascularize)
vas¦cu¦lar¦ises
vas¦cu¦lar¦ised
vas¦cu¦lar¦is¦ing
vas¦cu¦lar¦ity
vas¦cu¦lar¦iza¦tion
vas¦cu¦lar¦ize
vas¦cu¦lar¦izes
vas¦cu¦lar¦ized
vas¦cu¦lar¦iz¦ing

vas¦cu¦lar¦ly
vas¦cu¦lum
vas¦cula
vas def¦er¦ens
vasa def¦er¦entia
vase +s
vas¦ec¦tom¦ise *Br.*
(use
vasectomize)
vas¦ec¦tom¦ises
vas¦ec¦tom¦ised
vas¦ec¦tom¦is¦ing
vas¦ec¦tom¦ize
vas¦ec¦tom¦izes
vas¦ec¦tom¦ized
vas¦ec¦tom¦iz¦ing
vas¦ec¦tomy
vas¦ec¦to¦mies
vase¦ful +s
Vas¦el¦ine *noun*
Propr.
vas¦el¦ine
vas¦el¦ines
vas¦el¦ined
vas¦el¦in¦ing
verb
vasi¦form
vaso¦active
vaso¦con¦stric¦tion
vaso¦con¦strict¦ive
vaso¦con¦strict¦or
+s
vaso¦dilat¦ing
vaso¦dila¦tion
vaso¦dila¦tor +s
vaso¦motor
vaso¦pres¦sin
vas¦sal +s
vas¦sal¦age +s
vast +er +est
Väs¦ter¦ås (port,
Sweden)
vast¦ly
vast¦ness
vast¦nesses
VAT (= value
added tax)
vat
vats
vat¦ted
vat¦ting
(tank)
VAT-free
vat¦ful +s
vatic
Vati¦can (pope's
palace)
Vati¦can City
(papal state,
Rome)
Vati¦can¦ism
Vati¦can¦ist +s

va¦ti¦cinal
va¦ti¦cin¦ate
va¦ti¦cin¦ates
va¦ti¦cin¦ated
va¦ti¦cin¦at¦ing
va¦ti¦cin¦ation +s
va¦ti¦cin¦ator +s
va¦ti¦cin¦atory
VAT¦man
VAT¦men
(tax officer)
vat-man
vat-men
(paper worker)
VAT-registered
Vät¦tern (lake,
Sweden)
Vaud (canton,
Switzerland)
vaude¦ville +s
vaude¦vil¦lian +s
Vaud¦ois
plural Vaud¦ois
Vaughan, Henry
(Welsh
metaphysical
poet)
Vaughan, Sarah
(American jazz
musician)
Vaughan
Wil¦liams, Ralph
(English
composer)
vault +s +ed +ing
(arch;
underground
chamber; jump.
△volt, volte)
vault¦er +s
vault¦ing horse +s
vaunt +s +ed +ing
vaunt¦er +s
vaunt¦ing¦ly
vava¦sory
vava¦sor¦ies
vava¦sour +s
Vav¦ilov, Niko¦lai
(Soviet plant
geneticist)
V-bomber +s
veal
vealy
Veb¦len,
Thor¦stein
(American
economist)
vec¦tor +s +ed
+ing
vec¦tor¦ial

vec|tor|isa|tion *Br.*
(use
vectorization)
vec|tor|ise *Br.* (use
vectorize)
vec|tor|ises
vec|tor|ised
vec|tor|is|ing
vec|tor|iza|tion
vec|tor|ize
vec|tor|izes
vec|tor|ized
vec|tor|iz|ing
Veda +s *Hinduism*
Ve|danta
Ve|dan|tic
Ve|dan|tist +s
Vedda +s (Sri
Lankan aboriginal)
ved|ette +s
Vedic
vee +s
veep +s
veer +s +ed +ing
veery
veer|ies
veg
plural veg
(= vegetable)
Vega (star)
Vega Car|pio,
Lope Felix de
(Spanish
dramatist)
vegan +s
Vege|bur|ger +s
(△ veggie burger)
Propr.
Vege|mite *Propr.*
vege|table +s
vege|tal
vege|tar|ian +s
vege|tar|ian|ism
vege|tate
vege|tates
vege|tated
vege|tat|ing
vege|ta|tion
vege|ta|tion|al
vege|ta|tive
vege|ta|tive|ly
vege|ta|tive|ness
veg|gie +s
veg|gie bur|ger +s
(△ Vegeburger)
vegie +s (use
veggie)
vehe|mence
vehe|ment
vehe|ment|ly
ve|hicle +s
ve|hicu|lar

veil +s +ed +ing
(cover. △ vail,
vale)
veil|ing +s
veil|less
vein +s +ed +ing
(blood vessel.
△ vain, vane)
vein|less (without
veins. △ vaneless)
vein|let +s
vein|like
vein|stone
veiny
vein|ier
veini|est
vela (plural of
velum. △ velar)
ve|la|men
ve|la|mina
velar (of a veil or
velum; *Phonetics.*
△ vela)
Ve|láz|quez, Diego
Rod|ríguez de
Silva y (Spanish
painter)
Ve|láz|quez de
Cué|llar, Diego
(Spanish
conquistador)
Vel|cro *Propr.*
Vel|croed
veld +s
Velde, van de (see
van de Velde)
veld|skoen
veld|skoens *or*
veld|skoene
vel|eta +s
veli|ger +s
veli|ta|tion +s
vel|le|ity
vel|le|ities
Vel|leius
Pat|er|cu|lus
(Roman historian)
vel|lum +s
(parchment etc.
△ velum)
Velma
velo|cim|eter +s
vel|oci|pede +s
vel|oci|ped|ist +s
vel|oci|rap|tor +s
vel|ocity
vel|oci|ties
velo|drome +s
vel|our +s
vel|ours *singular*
(use velour)
vel|outé +s

velum
vela
(membrane.
△ vellum)
velu|tin|ous
vel|vet +s
vel|vet|ed
vel|vet|een +s
vel|vety
vena cava
venae cavae
venal
ve|nal|ity
ve|nal|ly
ven|ation +s
ven|ation|al
vend +s +ed +ing
Venda +s (person;
language; former
homeland, South
Africa)
ven|dace
plural ven|dace
Ven|dée
(department,
France)
vend|ee +s (buyer)
vend|er +s (use
vendor)
ven|detta +s
vend|euse +s
vend|ible
vend|ing ma|chine
+s
vend|or +s
ven|due +s
ven|eer +s +ed
+ing
vene|punc|ture +s
ven|er|abil|ity
ven|er|able
ven|er|able|ness
ven|er|ably
ven|er|ate
ven|er|ates
ven|er|ated
ven|er|at|ing
ven|er|ation
ven|er|ator +s
ven|ereal
ven|ere|al|ly
ven|ereo|logic|al
ven|ere|olo|gist +s
ven|ere|ology
ven|ery
vene|sec|tion +s
Ven|etia (English
name for the
Veneto; name)
Ven|etian +s
ven|etianed

Ven|eto (region,
Italy)
Vene|zuela
Vene|zuelan +s
ven|geance
venge|ful
venge|ful|ly
venge|ful|ness
ve|nial
veni|al|ity
veni|al|ly
veni|al|ness
Ven|ice (city, Italy)
Ven|ing Mein|esz,
Felix An|dries
(Dutch
geophysicist)
veni|punc|ture +s
(use
venepuncture)
veni|sec|tion +s
(use venesection)
ven|ison
Ven|ite +s
Venn dia|gram +s
venom +s
ven|omed
ven|om|ous
ven|om|ous|ly
ven|om|ous|ness
ven|ose
ven|os|ity
ven|ous
ven|ous|ly
vent +s +ed +ing
vent-hole +s
venti|duct +s
venti|fact +s
ven|til +s
ven|ti|late
ven|ti|lates
ven|ti|lated
ven|ti|lat|ing
ven|ti|la|tion
ven|ti|la|tive
ven|ti|la|tor +s
vent|less
Ven|to|lin *Propr.*
ven|touse +s
ven|tral
ven|tral|ly
ventre à terre
ven|tricle +s
ven|tri|cose
ven|tricu|lar
ven|tri|lo|quial
ven|trilo|quise *Br.*
(use
ventriloquize)
ven|trilo|quises
ven|trilo|quised
ven|trilo|quis|ing

ven|trilo|quism
ven|trilo|quist +s
ven|trilo|quis|tic
ven|trilo|quize
ven|trilo|quizes
ven|trilo|quized
ven|trilo|quiz|ing
ven|trilo|quous
ven|trilo|quy
ven|ture
ven|tures
ven|tured
ven|tur|ing
ven|turer +s
Ven|ture Scout +s
ven|ture|some
ven|ture|some|ly
ven|ture|some|
    ness
'n|turi, Rob|ert
    (American
    architect)
ven| ri +s (tube)
venu +s
ven|ule +s
Venus (*Roman
    Mythology*; planet)
Venus de Milo
    (statue)
Venus fly|trap +s
Ven|us|ian +s
Venus's comb
Venus's looking-
    glass
Vera
ver|acious
ver|acious|ly
ver|acious|ness
ver|acity
Vera|cruz (city and
    state, Mexico)
ver|anda +s
ver|an|daed
ver|an|dah +s (use
    veranda)
vera|trine
verb +s
ver|bal
    ver|bals
    ver|balled
    ver|bal|ling
ver|bal|is|able *Br.*
    (use verbalizable)
ver|bal|isa|tion *Br.*
    +s (use
    verbalization)
ver|bal|ise *Br.* (use
    verbalize)
    ver|bal|ises
    ver|bal|ised
    ver|bal|is|ing

ver|bal|iser *Br.* +s
    (use verbalizer)
ver|bal|ism
ver|bal|ist +s
ver|bal|is|tic
ver|bal|iz|able
ver|bal|iza|tion +s
ver|bal|ize
    ver|bal|izes
    ver|bal|ized
    ver|bal|iz|ing
ver|bal|izer +s
ver|bal|ly
ver|bas|cum +s
ver|ba|tim
ver|bena +s
verb form +s
ver|bi|age
ver|bose
ver|bose|ly
ver|bose|ness
ver|bos|ity
ver|bo|ten
verb. sap.
ver|dancy
ver|dant
verd-antique
ver|dant|ly
ver|der|er +s
Verdi, Giu|seppe
    (Italian composer)
Verdi|an +s
ver|dict +s
ver|di|gris
ver|diter
Verdon-Roe,
    Al|li|ott (English
    engineer)
Ver|dun (town,
    France)
ver|dure
ver|dured
ver|dur|ous
Ver|eeni|ging (city,
    Transvaal)
Ver|ena *also*
    Ver|ina
verge
    verges
    verged
    ver|ging
ver|ger +s
ver|ger|ship +s
Ver|gil (Roman
    poet; use Virgil)
Ver|gil *also* Virgil
    (name)
ver|glas
ver|idi|cal
ver|idi|cal|ity
ver|idi|cal|ly
veri|est

veri|fi|able
veri|fi|ably
veri|fi|ca|tion
veri|fier
ver|ify
    veri|fies
    veri|fied
    veri|fy|ing
ver|ily
Ver|ina *also*
    Ver|ena
veri|sim|ilar
veri|sim|ili|tude
ver|ism
ver|ismo +s
ver|ist +s
ver|is|tic
ver|it|able
ver|it|ably
Ver|ity (name)
ver|ity
    ver|ities
    (truth)
ver|juice
Ver|khne|udinsk
    (former name of
    Ulan-Ude)
ver| krampte +s
Ver|laine, Paul
    (French poet)
ver| ligte +s
Ver|meer, Jan
    (Dutch painter)
ver|meil
ver|mian
vermi|celli
vermi|cide +s
ver|micu|lar
ver|micu|late
ver|micu|la|tion
    +s
ver|micu|lite
vermi|form
vermi|fuge +s
ver|mil|ion
ver|min
ver|min|ate
    ver|min|ates
    ver|min|ated
    ver|min|at|ing
ver|min|ation
ver|min|ous
ver|mivor|ous
Ver|mont (state,
    USA)
ver|mouth +s
ver|nacu|lar +s
ver|nacu|lar|ise *Br.*
    (use
    vernacularize)
ver|nacu|lar|ises
ver|nacu|lar|ised

ver|nacu|lar|ise
    (*cont.*)
ver|nacu|lar|
        is|ing
ver|nacu|lar|ism
ver|nacu|lar|ity
ver|nacu|lar|ize
    ver|nacu|lar|izes
    ver|nacu|lar|ized
    ver|nacu|lar|
        iz|ing
ver|nacu|lar|ly
ver|nal
ver|nal|isa|tion *Br.*
    (use
    vernalization)
ver|nal|ise *Br.* (use
    vernalize)
    ver|nal|ises
    ver|nal|ised
    ver|nal|is|ing
ver|nal|iza|tion
ver|nal|ize
    ver|nal|izes
    ver|nal|ized
    ver|nal|iz|ing
ver|nal|ly
ver|na|tion
Verne, Jules
    (French novelist)
vern|icle +s
ver|nier +s
Ver|non
Verny (former
    name of Almaty)
Ver|ona (city, Italy;
    name)
ver|onal (drug)
Vero|nese, Paolo
    (Italian painter)
Ver|on|ica (early
    saint; name)
ver|on|ica +s
    (plant)
Ver|ra|zano
    Nar|rows Bridge
    (in New York)
ver|ruca
ver|ru|cae
ver|ru|cose
ver|ru|cous
Ver|sailles (town
    and palace,
    France)
ver|sant +s
ver|sa|tile
ver|sa|tile|ly
ver|sa|til|ity
verse
    verses
    versed
    vers|ing

verse (cont.)
(poetry etc.
△ verst)
verse|let +s
ver|set +s
vers|icle +s
ver|si|col|ored Am.
ver|si|col|oured Br.
ver|sicu|lar
ver|si|fi|ca|tion
ver|si|fier +s
vers|ify
ver|si|fies
ver|si|fied
ver|si|fy|ing
ver|sin +s
ver|sine +s
ver|sion +s
ver|sion|al
vers libre
verso +s
verst +s (Russian
measure of length.
△ versed)
ver|sus
vert +s Heraldry
ver|te|bra
ver|te|brae
ver|te|bral
ver|te|bral|ly
ver|te|brate +s
ver|te|bra|tion
ver|tex
ver|ti|ces
ver|ti|cal
ver|ti|cal|ise Br.
(use verticalize)
ver|ti|cal|ises
ver|ti|cal|ised
ver|ti|cal|is|ing
ver|ti|cal|ity
ver|ti|cal|ize
ver|ti|cal|izes
ver|ti|cal|ized
ver|ti|cal|iz|ing
ver|ti|cal|ly
ver|ti|cil +s
ver|ticil|late
ver|tigin|ous
ver|tigin|ous|ly
ver|tigo +s
vertu (use virtu)
Veru|la|mium
(Roman city,
England)
ver|vain +s
verve
ver|vet +s
Ver|viers (town,
Belgium)
Ver|woerd,
Hen|drik (South

Ver|woerd (cont.)
African prime
minister)
Very (light; pistol)
very
veri|est
(extremely; real;
etc.)
Vesa|lius,
An|dreas
(Flemish
anatomist)
ves|ica +s
vesi|cal
vesi|cant +s
vesi|cate
vesi|cates
vesi|cated
vesi|cat|ing
vesi|ca|tion +s
vesi|ca|tory
ves|icle +s
ves|icu|lar
ves|icu|late
ves|icu|la|tion +s
Vespa +s (motor
scooter) Propr.
Ves|pa|sian
(Roman emperor)
ves|per +s
ves|per|tine
ves|pi|ary
ves|pi|ar|ies
ves|pine
Ves|pucci,
Amer|igo (Italian
explorer)
ves|sel +s
vest +s +ed +ing
Vesta (Roman
Mythology;
asteroid; name)
vesta +s (match)
Ves|tal +s (of
Vesta; Vestal
Virgin)
ves|tal +s (chaste;
chaste woman)
vest|ee +s
Ves|ter|ålen
(islands off
Norway)
ves|ti|ary
ves|ti|ar|ies
ves|tibu|lar
ves|ti|bule +s
ves|tige +s
ves|tigial
ves|tigial|ly
ves|ti|ture +s
vest|ment +s

vest-pocket
attributive
ves|tral
ves|try
ves|tries
vestry|man
vestry|men
ves|ture
ves|tures
ves|tured
ves|tur|ing
Vesu|vian
Vesu|vius
(volcano, Italy)
vet
vets
vet|ted
vet|ting
vetch
vetches
vetch|ling +s
vetchy
vet|eran +s
Vet|er|ans Day (11
November in
USA)
vet|er|in|ar|ian +s
vet|er|in|ary
vet|er|in|ar|ies
veti|ver +s
veto
ve|toes
ve|toed
veto|ing
veto|er +s
vex
vexes
vexed
vex|ing
vex|ation +s
vex|atious
vex|atious|ly
vex|atious|ness
vex|ed|ly
vexer +s
vex|il|lo|logic|al
vex|il|lolo|gist +s
vex|il|lol|ogy
vex|il|lum
vex|illa
vex|ing|ly
Vi (name)
via
Via Appia (Latin
name for the
Appian Way)
via|bil|ity
vi|able
vi|ably
via|duct +s

vial +s (glass
vessel. △ vile,
viol)
vial|ful +s
via media
viand +s
vi|ati|cum
vi|at|ica
vibes
vi|bracu|lar
adjective
vi|bracu|lum
vi|brac|ula
noun
vi|brancy
vi|brant
vi|brant|ly
vi|bra|phone +s
vi|bra|phon|ist +s
vi|brate
vi|brates
vi|brated
vi|brat|ing
vi|bra|tile
vi|bra|tion +s
vi|bra|tion|al
vi|bra|tive
vi|brato +s
vi|bra|tor +s
vi|bra|tory
vib|rio
vib|rios or
vibri|ones
vi|bris|sae
vi|bur|num +s
Vic
vicar +s
vic|ar|age +s
vicar-general
vicars-general
vic|ar|ial
vic|ari|ate +s
vic|ari|ous
vic|ari|ous|ly
vic|ari|ous|ness
vic|ar|ship +s
vice +s (depravity;
character defect;
vice-president
etc.; in the place
of; in succession
to. △ vise)
vice Br.
vices
viced
vi|cing
(clamp; Am. vise)
vice ad|miral +s
vice-captain +s
vice-captain|cy
vice-captain|cies
vice-chair +s

vice-chairman
vice-chairmen
vice-
chairman¦ship
+s
vice-chairwoman
vice-chairwomen
vice-chamber¦lain
+s
vice-chancel¦lor
+s
vice-consul +s
vice-direct¦or +s
vice|ger¦ency
vice|ger¦en¦cies
vice|ger¦ent +s
vice-govern¦or +s
vice|less
vice-like
Vice-Marshal +s
(in 'Air Vice-
Marshal')
vi¦cen¦nial
Vi¦cente, Gil
(Portuguese
dramatist)
Vi¦cenza (town,
Italy)
vice-premier +s
vice-presidency
vice-
presiden¦cies
vice-president +s
vice-presiden¦tial
vice-princi¦pal +s
vice-provost +s
vice|regal
vice|regal¦ly
vice|reine +s
vice|roy +s
vice|royal
vice|roy¦alty
vice|roy¦ship +s
vi¦cesi¦mal
vice versa
Vichy (town,
France; water)
vichys|soise +s
vicin|age +s
vi¦cinal
vicin|ity
vicin|ities
vi¦cious
vi¦cious¦ly
vi¦cious|ness
vi¦cis¦si¦tude +s
vi¦cis¦si¦tu¦din|ous
Vicki also Vickie,
Vicky
Vickie also Vicki,
Vicky

Vicks|burg (city,
USA)
Vicky also Vicki,
Vickie
Vico,
Giam|bat¦tista
(Italian
philosopher)
vic¦tim +s
vic¦tim|hood
vic¦tim|isa¦tion Br.
(use
victimization)
vic¦tim|ise Br. (use
victimize)
vic¦tim|ises
vic¦tim|ised
vic¦tim|is¦ing
vic¦tim|iser Br. +s
(use victimizer)
vic¦tim|iza¦tion
vic¦tim|ize
vic¦tim|izes
vic¦tim|ized
vic¦tim|iz¦ing
vic¦tim|izer +s
vic¦tim|less
Vic¦tor (name)
vic¦tor +s (winner)
Vic¦tor
Em¦man|uel
(Italian kings)
Vic|toria +s
(British queen;
name; carriage)
Vic|toria (state,
Australia; port,
Canada; capital of
Hong Kong or the
Seychelles;
railway station,
London)
Vic|toria, Tomás
Luis de (Spanish
composer)
Vic|toria and
Al¦bert Mu¦seum
(in London)
Vic|toria Falls (in
central Africa)
Vic|toria Is¦land
(in Canadian
Arctic)
Vic¦tor¦ian +s
Vic|tori|ana
Vic|toria Nile
(river, E. Africa)
Vic¦tor¦ian|ism +s
Vic|toria Peak
(mountain, Hong
Kong)
vic|tori|ous

vic|tori|ous¦ly
vic|tori|ous|ness
vic|tor lu|dorum
male
vic|tory
vic|tor|ies
vic|trix
vic|tri|ces
vic|trix lu|dorum
female
vict|ual
vict|uals
vict|ualled Br.
vict|ualed Am.
vict|ual|ling Br.
vict|ual|ing Am.
vict|ual¦er Am. +s
vict|ual|ler Br. +s
vict|ual|less
vi|cuña +s
Vic-Wells Bal¦let
vid +s (= video)
Vidal, Gore
(American writer)
vide
vi|de|licet
video +s *noun*
video
vid|eoes
vid|eoed
video|ing
verb
video|con¦fer|ence
+s
video|con¦fer|
en¦cing
video|disc +s
video|fit +s
video|phile +s
video|phone +s
video re|cord|er
+s
video re|cord|ing
+s
video|tape
video|tapes
video|taped
video|tap|ing
video|tape
re|cord|er +s
video|tape
re|cord|ing +s
video|tex
video|texes
video|text +s
vidi|mus
vidi|muses
vie
vies
vied
vying
vi|elle +s

Vi|enna (capital of
Austria)
Vi|enne (city,
France)
Vi|en|nese
plural Vi|en|nese
Vien|tiane (capital
of Laos)
Viet|cong
plural Viet|cong
Viet|minh
plural Viet|minh
Viet|nam
Viet|nam|ese
plural
Viet|nam|ese
vieux jeu
view +s +ed +ing
view|able
view|data
view|er +s
view|er|ship
view|find¦er +s
view|graph +s
view|ing +s
view|less
view|point +s
view|port +s
view|screen +s
Vigée-Lebrun,
Élisa|beth
(French painter)
vi|gesi|mal
vi|gesi|mal¦ly
vigil +s
vigi|lance
vigi|lant
vigi|lante +s
vigi|lant|ism
vigi|lant¦ly
vi|gneron +s
vi|gnette
vi|gnettes
vi|gnet|ted
vi|gnet|ting
vi|gnet|ter +s
vi|gnet|tist +s
Vi|gnola,
Gia|como
Bar|ozzi da
(Italian architect)
Vigny, Al¦fred,
Comte de
(French writer)
Vigo (port, Spain)
Vigo, Jean (French
film director)
vigor Am. (Br.
vigour)
vig|or¦ish
vig|or|less Am. (Br.
vigourless)

vig¦oro
vig¦or¦ous
vig¦or¦ous¦ly
vig¦or¦ous¦ness
vig¦our *Br.* (*Am.* vigor)
vig¦our¦less *Br.* (*Am.* vigorless)
vi¦hara +s
Vi¦jaya¦wada (city, India)
Vi¦king +s (Scandinavian people; American space probes; shipping area, North Sea)
Vila (capital of Vanuatu)
vil¦ayet +s
vile
viler
vil¦est (loathsome. △ vial, viol)
vile¦ly
vile¦ness
vili¦fi¦ca¦tion
vili¦fier +s
vil¦ify
vili¦fies
vili¦fied
vili¦fy¦ing
vill +s
Villa, Pan¦cho (Mexican revolutionary)
villa +s
vil¦lage +s
vil¦la¦ger +s
vil¦la¦gey
vil¦la¦gisa¦tion *Br.* (use villagization)
vil¦la¦giza¦tion
Vil¦la¦her¦mosa (city, Mexico)
vil¦lain +s (wicked person. △ villein)
vil¦lain¦ess
vil¦lain¦esses
vil¦lain¦ous
vil¦lain¦ous¦ly
vil¦lain¦ous¦ness
vil¦lainy
vil¦lain¦ies
Villa-Lobos, Hei¦tor (Brazilian composer)
vil¦lan¦elle +s
vil¦leggia¦tura
vil¦leggia¦ture

vil¦lein +s (serf. △ villain)
vil¦lein¦age
vil¦li¦form
Vil¦lon, Fran¦çois (French poet)
vil¦lose
vil¦los¦ity
vil¦lous *adjective*
vil¦lus
villi *noun*
Vil¦nius (capital of Lithuania)
vim
vim¦in¦eous
Vimy Ridge (battle site, France)
vina +s
vin¦aceous
vin¦ai¦grette +s
vinca +s
Vince
Vin¦cent
Vin¦cent de Paul (French saint)
Vin¦cen¦tian +s
Vinci, Leo¦nardo da (Italian painter and designer)
vin¦ci¦bil¦ity
vin¦cible
vin¦cu¦lum
vin¦cula
vin¦da¦loo +s
vin¦dic¦able
vin¦di¦cate
vin¦di¦cates
vin¦di¦cated
vin¦di¦cat¦ing
vin¦di¦ca¦tion +s
vin¦di¦ca¦tor +s
vin¦di¦ca¦tory
vin¦dic¦tive
vin¦dic¦tive¦ly
vin¦dic¦tive¦ness
Vine, Bar¦bara (pseudonym of Ruth Rendell)
vine +s
vine-dresser +s
vin¦egar +s
vin¦egared
vin¦egar¦ish
vin¦egary
vin¦ery
vin¦eries
vine¦stock +s
vine¦yard +s
vingt-et-un
vinho verde +s

vini¦cul¦tural
vini¦cul¦ture
vini¦cul¦tur¦ist +s
vini¦fi¦ca¦tion
vin¦ify
vini¦fies
vini¦fied
vini¦fy¦ing
vin¦ing
Vin¦land (region, N. America)
Vin¦ney +s (in 'Blue Vinney')
Vin¦nitsa (Russian name for Vinnytsya)
Vin¦nyt¦sya (city, Ukraine)
vino +s
vin or¦din¦aire
vins or¦din¦aires
vin¦os¦ity
vin¦ous
vin rosé
vins rosés
Vin¦son Mas¦sif (in Antarctica)
vint +s +ed +ing
vin¦tage +s
vin¦ta¦ger +s
vint¦ner +s
viny
vini¦er
vini¦est
vinyl +s
viol +s (musical instrument. △ vial, vile)
Viola (name)
viola +s (flower; musical instrument)
viol¦able
viol¦aceous
viola da brac¦cio +s
viola da gamba +s
viola d'amore
violas d'amore
viola play¦er +s
vio¦late
vio¦lates
vio¦lated
vio¦lat¦ing
vio¦la¦tion +s
vio¦la¦tor +s
vio¦lence +s
vio¦lent
vio¦lent¦ly
Vio¦let (name)
vio¦let +s
vio¦lin +s

vio¦lin¦ist +s
viol¦ist +s
vio¦lon¦cel¦list +s
vio¦lon¦cello +s
vio¦lone +s
viper +s
vi¦peri¦form
vi¦per¦ine
vi¦per¦ish
viper-like
vi¦per¦ous
viper's bu¦gloss
viper's grass
vir¦ago +s
viral
vir¦al¦ly
Vir¦chow, Ru¦dolf Karl (German physician)
vir¦elay +s
vire¦ment +s
vireo +s
vires (in 'ultra vires')
vir¦es¦cence
vir¦es¦cent
virga (evaporating rain)
vir¦gate +s
vir¦ger +s (use verger)
Vir¦gil (Roman poet)
Vir¦gil *also* Vergil
Vir¦gil¦ian
Vir¦gin, the (constellation; sign of zodiac)
vir¦gin +s
vir¦gin¦al
vir¦gin¦al¦ist +s
vir¦gin¦al¦ly
vir¦gin¦hood
Vir¦ginia (state, USA; tobacco; name)
Vir¦gin¦ian +s
Vir¦gin Is¦lands, Brit¦ish and US (in Caribbean)
vir¦gin¦ity
Virgo (constellation; sign of zodiac)
Vir¦go¦an +s
vir¦gule +s
viri¦des¦cence
viri¦des¦cent
vir¦id¦ian +s
vir¦id¦ity
vir¦ile
vir¦il¦ism
vir¦il¦ity

vir¦ino +s
vir¦ion +s
vir¦oid +s
viro|logic¦al
viro|logic¦al¦ly
vir|olo¦gist +s
vir|ology
virtu (knowledge of
fine arts; in 'object
of virtu'. △ virtue)
vir¦tual
vir¦tu|al¦ity
vir¦tu|al¦ly
vir¦tue +s (moral
excellence etc.
△ virtu)
vir¦tue|less
vir¦tu|osic
vir¦tu|os¦ity
vir¦tu|oso
vir¦tu|osi or
vir¦tu|osos
vir¦tu|oso|ship
vir¦tu|ous
vir¦tu|ous¦ly
vir¦tu|ous|ness
viru|lence
viru|lent
viru|lent¦ly
virus
vir¦uses
visa
visas
visaed or visa'd
visa|ing
vis¦age +s
vis¦aged
Visa¦kha¦pat¦nam
(port, India)
vis-à-vis
plural vis-à-vis
Visby (port,
Sweden)
vis¦cacha +s
vis¦cera
vis¦ceral
vis¦cer|al¦ly
vis¦cid
vis¦cid|ity
visc|om¦eter +s
visco|met¦ric
visco|met¦ric|al¦ly
visc|om¦etry
Vis¦conti,
Lu¦chino (Italian
film director)
vis¦cose
vis¦cos|im¦eter +s
vis¦cos|ity
vis¦cos|ities
vis¦count +s

vis¦count¦cy
vis¦count¦cies
vis¦count|ess
vis¦count|esses
vis¦count|ship
vis¦county
vis¦count¦ies
vis¦cous (sticky.
△ viscus)
vis¦cous¦ly
vis¦cous|ness
vis¦cus
vis¦cera
(internal organ.
△ viscous)
vise Am.
vises
vised
vis¦ing
(Br. vice; clamp.
△ vice)
Vishnu
Vishnu|ism
Vishnu|ite +s
visi|bil¦ity
vis¦ible
vis¦ible|ness
vis¦ibly
Visi|goth +s
Visi|goth¦ic
vi¦sion +s
vi¦sion¦al
vi¦sion¦ari¦ness
vi¦sion¦ary
vi¦sion|ar¦ies
vi¦sion|ist +s
vi¦sion|less
vi¦sion mixer +s
vi¦sion mix¦ing
visit +s +ed +ing
vis¦it|able
vis¦it|ant +s
vis¦it|ation +s
vis¦it|ator¦ial
vis¦it|ing +s
vis¦it|ing card +s
vis¦it|or +s
vis¦it|or¦ial
vis¦it|ors' book +s
visor +s
vi¦sored
vi¦sor|less
vista +s
vis¦taed
Vis|tula (river,
Poland)
vis¦ual +s
visu¦al¦is¦able Br.
(use visualizable)
visu¦al¦isa¦tion Br.
+s (use
visualization)

visu¦al¦ise Br. (use
visualize)
visu¦al¦ises
visu¦al¦ised
visu¦al¦is¦ing
visu¦al¦ity
visu¦al¦iz¦able
visu¦al¦iza¦tion +s
visu¦al¦ize
visu¦al¦izes
visu¦al¦ized
visu¦al¦iz¦ing
visu¦al¦ly
Vita
vital +s
vi¦tal¦isa¦tion Br.
(use vitalization)
vi¦tal¦ise Br. (use
vitalize)
vi¦tal¦ises
vi¦tal¦ised
vi¦tal¦is¦ing
vi¦tal¦ism
vi¦tal¦ist +s
vi¦tal¦is¦tic
vi¦tal¦ity
vi¦tal¦iza¦tion
vi¦tal¦ize
vi¦tal¦izes
vi¦tal¦ized
vi¦tal¦iz¦ing
vi¦tal¦ly
vita|min +s
vita|min¦ise Br.
(use vitaminize)
vita|min¦ises
vita|min¦ised
vita|min¦is¦ing
vita|min¦ize
vita|min¦izes
vita|min¦ized
vita|min¦iz¦ing
Vi|tebsk (Russian
name for
Vitsebsk)
vi¦tel|lary
vi¦telli
vi¦tel|lin (protein)
vi¦tel|line (of a
vitellus)
Vi¦tel|lius, Aulus
(Roman emperor)
vi¦tel|lus
vi¦telli
viti|ate
viti|ates
viti|ated
viti|at¦ing
viti|ation
viti|ator +s
viti|cul¦tural
viti|cul¦tur|al¦ly

viti|cul¦ture
viti|cul¦tur|ist +s
Viti Levu (island,
Fiji)
viti|ligo
Vi|toria (town,
Spain)
Vi|tória (port,
Brazil)
Vi|tosha (ski resort,
Bulgaria)
vit¦re|ous
vit¦re|ous|ness
vit¦res|cence
vit¦res|cent
vit¦ri|fac¦tion
vit¦ri|fi¦able
vit¦ri|fi|ca¦tion
vit¦ri|form
vit¦rify
vit¦ri|fies
vit¦ri|fied
vit¦ri|fy¦ing
vit¦riol
vit¦ri|ol¦ic
vitro (in 'in vitro')
Vit¦ru|vian
Vit¦ru|vius (Roman
architect)
Vit¦sebsk (city,
Belarus)
vitta
vit¦tae
vit¦tate
vi¦tu|per|ate
vi¦tu|per|ates
vi¦tu|per|ated
vi¦tu|per|at¦ing
vi¦tu|per|ation +s
vi¦tu|pera|tive
vi¦tu|per|ator +s
Vitus (early saint;
in 'St Vitus's
dance')
Viv
viva
vivas
viv¦aed or viva'd
viva|ing
(oral exam.
△ vivers)
viva +s (shout; long
live .... △ vivers)
viv¦ace
viv¦acious
viv¦acious¦ly
viv¦acious|ness
viv¦acity
Viv|aldi, An|tonio
(Italian composer)
viv¦ar¦ium
viv¦aria

vivat

viva voce +s *noun*

viva-voce
  viva-voces
  viva-voced
  viva-voceing
  verb

vivax

Viv|eka|nanda, Swami (Indian spiritual leader and reformer)

vi|ver|rid +s

vi|ver|rine

vi|vers (food.
  △viva, *viva*)

Viv|ian *also* Vyv|yan (man's name.
  △Vivien, Vivienne)

vivid

viv|id|ly

viv|id|ness

Viv|ien *also* Vivi|enne (woman's name.
  △Vivian, Vyvyan)

Vivi|enne *also* Viv|ien (woman's name.
  △Vivian, Vyvyan)

vivi|fi|ca|tion

vivi|fy
  vivi|fies
  vivi|fied
  vivi|fy|ing

vivip|ar|ity

viv|ip|ar|ous

viv|ip|ar|ous|ly

viv|ip|ar|ous|ness

vivi|sect +s +ed +ing

vivi|sec|tion

vivi|sec|tion|al

vivi|sec|tion|ist +s

vivi|sect|or +s

vivo (in *'in vivo'*)

vixen +s

vix|en|ish

vix|en|ly

Vi|yella (fabric)
  Propr.

viz.

viz|ard +s

viz|cacha +s (use viscacha)

viz|ier +s

viz|ier|ate +s

viz|ier|ial

viz|ier|ship +s

vizor +s (use visor)

Vlach +s

Vladi|kav|kaz (city, Russia)

Vlad|imir (city, Russia)

Vlad|imir ('the Great', Russian saint)

Vladi|vos|tok (city, Russia)

Vlam|inck, Maur|ice de (French painter)

vlei +s

Vlis|singen (port, the Netherlands)

Vlorë (port, Albania)

Vltava (river, Czech Republic)

V-neck +s

voc|able

vo|cabu|lary
  vo|cabu|lar|ies

vocal +s

vocal cords

vo|cal|ese (singing to instrumental music.
  △vocalise)

vo|cal|ic

vo|cal|isa|tion *Br.* +s (use vocalization)

vo|cal|ise +s (vocal music written with no words.
  △vocalese)

vo|cal|ise *Br.* (form sound; use vocalize)
  vo|cal|ises
  vo|cal|ised
  vo|cal|is|ing

vo|cal|iser *Br.* +s (use vocalizer)

vo|cal|ism +s

vo|cal|ist +s

vo|cal|ity

vo|cal|iza|tion +s

vo|cal|ize
  vo|cal|izes
  vo|cal|ized
  vo|cal|iz|ing

vo|cal|izer +s

vo|cal|ly

vo|ca|tion +s

vo|ca|tion|al

vo|ca|tion|al|ise *Br.* (use

vo|ca|tion|al|ise
(cont.)
  vocationalize)
  vo|ca|tion|al|ises
  vo|ca|tion|al|ised
  vo|ca|tion|al| is|ing

vo|ca|tion|al|ism

vo|ca|tion|al|ize
  vo|ca|tion|al|izes
  vo|ca|tion|al|ized
  vo|ca|tion|al| iz|ing

vo|ca|tion|al|ly

voca|tive +s

vo|cif|er|ance

vo|cif|er|ant +s

vo|cif|er|ate
  vo|cif|er|ates
  vo|cif|er|ated
  vo|cif|er|at|ing

vo|cif|er|ation

vo|cif|er|ator +s

vo|cif|er|ous

vo|cif|er|ous|ly

vo|cif|er|ous|ness

vo|coder +s

Voda|fone +s
  Propr.

vodka +s

voe +s

vogue
  vogues
  vogued
  vo|guing *or* vogue|ing

vogue word +s

vo|guish

voice
  voices
  voiced
  voi|cing

voice box
  voice boxes

voice|ful

voice|less

voice|less|ly

voice|less|ness

voice-over +s

voice|print +s

voicer +s

voi|cing +s

void +s +ed +ing

void|able

void|ance +s

void|ness

voile +s

Voj|vo|dina (province, Serbia)

vol|ant

volar

vola|tile +s

vola|tile|ness

vola|til|is|able *Br.* (use volatilizable)

vola|til|isa|tion *Br.* (use volatilization)

vola|til|ise *Br.* (use volatilize)
  vola|til|ises
  vola|til|ised
  vola|til|is|ing

vola|til|ity

vola|til|iz|able

vola|til|iza|tion

vola|til|ize
  vola|til|izes
  vola|til|ized
  vola|til|iz|ing

vol-au-vent +s

vol|can|ic +s

vol|can|ic|al|ly

vol|can|icity

vol|can|ism

vol|cano
  vol|ca|noes

vol|cano|logic|al

vol|can|olo|gist +s

vol|can|ology

vole +s

volet +s

Volga (river, E. Europe)

Vol|go|grad (city, Russia)

voli|tant

vol|ition

vol|ition|al

vol|ition|al|ly

voli|tive

volk (Afrikaners)

Volk (Germans, in Nazi ideology)

Völker| wan|der|ung

Völker| wan|der|ung|en

völk|isch

vol|ley +s +ed +ing

vol|ley|ball

vol|ley|er +s

Vol|ogda (city, Russia)

Volos (port, Greece)

vol|plane
  vol|planes
  vol|planed
  vol|plan|ing

Vol|scian +s

volt +s (*Electricity*.
  △vault, volte)

Volta(river, Ghana)
Volta,
  Ales|san|dro
  (Italian physicist)
volt|age+s
Vol|ta|ic(language)
vol|ta|ic*Electricity*
Vol|taire(French
  writer)
volt|ameter+s
  (measures electric
  charge.
  △ voltmeter)
volte+s (*Fencing*;
  movement by
  horse. △ vault,
  volt)
volte-face
  plural volte-face
volt|meter+s
  (measures electric
  potential in volts.
  △ voltameter)
volu|bil|ity
vol|uble
vol|uble|ness
vol|ubly
vol|ume+s
vol|umed
volu|met|ric
volu|met|ric|al|ly
vo|lu|min|os|ity
vo|lu|min|ous
vo|lu|min|ous|ly
vo|lu|min|ous|ness
vol|un|tar|ily
vol|un|tari|ness
vol|un|tar|ism
vol|un|tar|ist
vol|un|tary
  vol|un|tar|ies
voluntary-aided
voluntary-
  controlled
vol|un|tary|ism
vol|un|tary|ist+s
vol|un|teer+s +ed
  +ing
vol|un|teer|ism
vo|lup|tu|ary
  vo|lup|tu|ar|ies
vo|lup|tu|ous
vo|lup|tu|ous|ly
vo|lup|tu|ous|ness
vol|ute+s
vol|uted
volu|tion+s
vol|vox
  vol|voxes
Volzh|sky (city,
  Russia)
vomer+s

vomit+s +ed +ing
vom|it|er+s
vom|it|orium
vom|it|oria
vom|it|ory
  vom|it|or|ies
von Braun,
  Wern|her
  (German rocket
  designer)
V-1+s (German
  flying bomb)
Von|ne|gut, Kurt
  (American writer)
von Neu|mann,
  John(Hungarian-
  born American
  mathematician)
von Stern|berg,
  Josef(Austrian-
  born American
  film director)
voo|doo+s +ed
  +ing
voo|doo|ism
voo|doo|ist+s
Vopo+s
vor|acious
vor|acious|ly
vor|acious|ness
vor|acity
Vor|arl|berg (state,
  Austria)
Vor|on|ezh (city,
  Russia)
Voro|shi|lov|grad
  (former name of
  Lugansk)
Vor|ster, John
  (South African
  president.
  △ Forster)
vor|tex
  vor|texes *or*
  vor|ti|ces
vor|ti|cal
vor|ti|cal|ly
vor|ti|cella+s
vor|ti|cism
vor|ti|cist+s
vor|ti|city
vor|ti|cose
vor|ticu|lar
Vosges (mountains,
  France)
Vos|tok (Soviet
  spacecraft)
vot|able
vo|tar|ess
vo|tar|esses
vo|tar|ist+s

vo|tary
  vo|tar|ies
vote
votes
voted
vot|ing
vote|less
voter+s
vot|ing ma|chine
  +s
vot|ing paper+s
vo|tive+s
vouch
vouches
vouched
vouch|ing
vouch|er+s
vouch|safe
vouch|safes
vouch|safed
vouch|saf|ing
vous|soir+s
Vou|vray+s
  (village, France;
  wine)
vow+s +ed +ing
vowel+s
vow|eled*Am.* (*Br.*
  vowelled)
vow|el|ise*Br.* (use
  vowelize)
vow|el|ises
vow|el|ised
vow|el|is|ing
vow|el|ize
vow|el|izes
vow|el|ized
vow|el|iz|ing
vow|elled*Br.* (*Am.*
  voweled)
vow|el|less
vowel|ly
vowel-point+s
vox an|gel|ica
vox hu|mana
vox pop+s
vox pop|uli
voy|age
voy|ages
voy|aged
voy|aging
voy|age|able
Voy|ager
  (American space
  probe)
voy|ager+s
  (traveller)
voy|ageur+s
  (Canadian
  boatman)
voy|eur+s
voy|eur|ism

voy|eur|is|tic
voy|eur|is|tic|al|ly
vraic
vroom+s +ed
  +ing
V-sign+s
V/STOL(= vertical
  and short take-off
  and landing)
VTOL(= vertical
  take-off and
  landing)
V-2+s (German
  missile)
vug+s
vuggy
vugu|lar
Vuil|lard,
  Éd|ouard(French
  painter)
Vul|can*Roman
  Mythology*
Vul|can|ian+s
vul|can|ic
vul|can|is|able*Br.*
  (use
  vulcanizable)
vul|can|isa|tion*Br.*
  (use
  vulcanization)
vul|can|ise*Br.* (use
  vulcanize)
vul|can|ises
vul|can|ised
vul|can|is|ing
vul|can|iser*Br.* +s
  (use vulcanizer)
vul|can|ism
Vul|can|ist+s
vul|can|ite
vul|can|iz|able
vul|can|iza|tion
vul|can|ize
vul|can|izes
vul|can|ized
vul|can|iz|ing
vul|can|izer+s
Vul|cano (island off
  Italy)
vul|cano|logic|al
vul|can|olo|gist+s
vul|can|ology
vul|gar
vul|gar|ian+s
vul|gar|isa|tion*Br.*
  (use
  vulgarization)
vul|gar|ise*Br.* (use
  vulgarize)
vul|gar|ises
vul|gar|ised
vul|gar|is|ing

vul¦gar¦ism +s
vul¦gar¦ity
  vul¦gar¦ities
vul¦gar¦iza¦tion
vul¦gar¦ize
  vul¦gar¦izes
  vul¦gar¦ized
  vul¦gar¦iz¦ing
vul¦gar¦ly
Vul¦gate +s (bible)
vul¦gate +s (other text)
vul¦ner¦abil¦ity
  vul¦ner¦abil¦ities
vul¦ner¦able
vul¦ner¦able¦ness
vul¦ner¦ably
vul¦ner¦ary
  vul¦ner¦ar¦ies
vul¦pine
vul¦ture +s
vul¦tur¦ine
vul¦tur¦ish
vul¦tur¦ous
vulva +s *noun*
vul¦val
vul¦var *adjective*
vulv¦itis
Vyatka (town, Russia)
vying
Vyv¦yan *also* Viv¦ian (man's name. △ Vivien, Vivienne)

Ww

Waac +s (member of Women's Army Auxiliary Corps)
Waaf +s (member of Women's Auxiliary Air Force)
Waal (river, the Netherlands)
WAC (= Women's Army Corps)
wack +s (crazy person; familiar term of address. △ wacke, whack)
wacke +s (rock. △ wack, whack)
wack¦ily
wacki¦ness
wacko
  wackos *or* wack¦oes (crazy. △ whacko)
wacky
  wack¦ier
  wacki¦est
wad
  wads
  wad¦ded
  wad¦ding
wad¦able
wad¦ding +s
wad¦dle
  wad¦dles
  wad¦dled
  wad¦dling
wad¦dler +s
waddy
  wad¦dies (club. △ wadi)
Wade, George (English field marshal)
Wade, Vir¦ginia (English tennis player)
wade
  wades
  waded
  wad¦ing
Wade–Giles (system for transliterating Chinese)
wader +s
wadg¦ula +s

wadi +s (watercourse. △ waddy)
Wadi Halfa (town, Sudan)
wady
  wad¦ies (use wadi. watercourse. △ waddy)
WAF (= Women in the Air Force)
wafer +s +ed +ing
wafer-thin
wafery
waf¦fle
  waf¦fles
  waf¦fled
  waf¦fling
waffle-iron +s
waf¦fler +s
waf¦fly
waft +s +ed +ing
wag
  wags
  wagged
  wag¦ging
wage
  wages
  waged
  wa¦ging
wage bill +s
wage claim +s
wage cut +s
wage earn¦er +s
wage-earning
wager +s +ed +ing
Wagga Wagga (town, Australia)
wag¦gery
  wag¦ger¦ies
wag¦gish
wag¦gish¦ly
wag¦gish¦ness
wag¦gle
  wag¦gles
  wag¦gled
  wag¦gling
wag¦gly
wag¦gon +s (use wagon)
wag¦gon¦er +s
wag¦gon¦ette +s
wag¦gon¦ful +s (use wagonful)
wag¦gon¦load +s (use wagonload)
Wag¦ner, Rich¦ard (German composer)
Wag¦ner¦ian +s
wagon +s

wag¦on¦er +s
wag¦on¦ette +s
wag¦on¦ful +s
wagon-lit
  wagons-lits
wag¦on¦load +s
wagon-roof +s
wagon train +s
wag¦tail +s
Wa¦habi +s
Wah¦habi +s (use Wahabi)
wa¦hine +s
wahoo +s (tree; *interjection*)
wah-wah +s
waif +s
waif¦ish
waif-like
Wai¦kato (river, New Zealand)
Wai¦kiki (resort, Honolulu)
wail +s +ed +ing (cry. △ whale, wale)
wail¦er +s (person who wails. △ whaler)
wail¦ful
wail¦ing +s (crying. △ whaling)
wail¦ing¦ly
Wain, John (British writer. △ Wayne)
Wain, the (constellation)
wain +s (wagon. △ wane)
wains¦cot
  wains¦cots
  wains¦cot¦ed *or* wains¦cot¦ted
  wains¦cot¦ing *or* wains¦cot¦ting
wain¦wright +s
Waira¦rapa (region, New Zealand)
waist +s (part of body etc. △ waste)
waist¦band +s
waist-cloth +s
waist¦coat +s
waist-deep
waist¦ed (having a waist; in 'high-waisted' etc. △ wasted)
waist-high
waist¦less

waist|line +s
wait +s +ed +ing
(delay action; etc.
△ weight)
wait-a-bit (plant)
Wai|tangi (Day and
Treaty, New
Zealand)
wait|er +s
wait|ing list +s
wait|ing room +s
wait|per|son +s
wait|ress
wait|resses
wait|ress|ing
waive
waives
waived
waiv|ing
(forgo. △ wave)
waiver +s (act of
waiving. △ waver)
Wajda, An|drzej
(Polish film
director)
wake
wakes
wak|ing
woken
Wake|field (town,
England)
wake|ful
wake|ful|ly
wake|ful|ness
waken +s +ed
+ing
waker +s
wake-robin +s
wakey-wakey
Wa|khan Sali|ent
(strip of land,
Afghanistan)
Waks|man,
Sel|man
Abra|ham
(Russian-born
American
microbiologist)
Wal|ach +s (use
Vlach)
Wal|achia (use
Wallachia)
Wal|ach|ian (use
Wallachian)
Wal|den|ses
Wal|den|sian +s
Wald|heim, Kurt
(Austrian
president)
Waldo
wale
wales

wale (cont.)
waled
wal|ing
(ridge in fabric;
timber on ship etc.
△ wail, whale)
wale-knot +s
Wales (part of
United Kingdom)
Wał|ęsa, Lech
(Polish president)
Waleses, the
(Prince and
Princess)
Wal|ian +s (in
'North Walian'
and 'South
Walian')
walk +s +ed +ing
walk|able
walk|about +s
walk|athon +s
Walk|er, Alice
(American writer)
Walk|er, John
(New Zealand
athlete)
walk|er +s
walk|ies
walkie-talkie +s
walk-in +s adjective
and noun
walk|ing boot +s
walk|ing frame +s
walking-on part
+s
walk|ing shoe +s
walk|ing stick +s
walk|ing tour +s
Walk|man
Walk|mans or
Walk|men
Propr.
walk-on +s
adjective and noun
walk|out +s
walk|over +s
walk-up +s
adjective and noun
walk|way +s
wall +s +ed +ing
(structure.
△ waul, whorl)
wall|aby
wal|la|bies
Wal|lace (name)
Wal|lace, Al|fred
Rus|sel (English
naturalist)
Wal|lace, Edgar
(English writer)

Wal|lace, Wil|liam
(Scottish national
hero)
Wal|lace
Col|lec|tion
(museum,
London)
Wal|lace's line
Wal|lachia (former
principality,
Romania)
Wal|lach|ian +s
wal|lah +s
wal|la|roo +s
Wal|la|sey (town,
England)
wall-barley
wall|board +s
wall|chart +s
wall clock +s
wall|cover|ing +s
Wal|len|berg,
Raoul (Swedish
diplomat)
Wal|ler, Fats
(American jazz
musician)
wal|let +s
wall-eye +s
wall-eyed
wall fern +s
wall|flower +s
wall-fruit
wall hang|ing +s
wall-hung
Wal|lis, Barnes
(English inventor)
Wal|lis and
Fu|tuna Is|lands
(in Pacific Ocean)
wall-knot +s
wall-less
wall-mounted
Wal|loon +s
wal|lop +s +ed
+ing
wal|lop|er +s
wal|low +s +ed
+ing
wal|low|er +s
wall paint|ing +s
wall|paper +s +ed
+ing
wall|plan|ner +s
wall plaque +s
wall-plate +s
wall plug +s
wall rocket
wall space
Wall Street (in
New York)
wall tie +s

wall-to-ceiling
wall-to-wall
Wally (name)
wally
wal|lies
(foolish or inept
person)
wal|nut +s
Wal|pole, Hor|ace
(English writer)
Wal|pole, Hugh
(British novelist)
Wal|pole, Rob|ert
(British prime
minister)
Wal|pole, Rob|ert
Penn (American
poet)
Wal|pur|gis night
+s
wal|rus
wal|ruses
Wal|sall (town,
England)
Wal|sing|ham
(pilgrimage town,
England)
Wal|sing|ham,
Fran|cis (English
politician)
Wal|ter
Wal|ton, Er|nest
(Irish physicist)
Wal|ton, Izaak
(English writer)
Wal|ton, Wil|liam
(English
composer)
waltz
waltzes
waltzed
waltz|ing
waltz|er +s
Waltz|ing Ma|tilda
(Australian song)
Wal|vis Bay (port,
Namibia)
wam|pum
WAN (= wide area
network)
wan
wan|ner
wan|nest
(pale. △ won)
wand +s
Wanda (name)
wan|der +s +ed
+ing (go
aimlessly)
wan|der|er +s
wan|der|ing +s
wan|der|lust

wan|deroo +s
wan|der plug +s
wan|doo +s
wane
  wanes
  waned
  wan|ing
  (decline; decrease;
  defect in plank.
  △ wain)
waney
wang +s +ed +ing
  (use whang)
Wanga|nui (port,
  New Zealand)
wan|gle
  wan|gles
  wan|gled
  wan|gling
wan|gler +s
wank +s +ed +ing
  (coarse slang)
Wan|kel, Felix
  (German
  engineer)
wank|er +s (coarse
  slang)
Wankie (former
  name of Hwange)
wanky (coarse slang
  worthless)
wanly
wanna (= want to)
wan|nabe +s
wan|ness
want +s +ed +ing
want ad +s
want|er +s
wan|ton +s +ed
  +ing (motiveless.
  △ wonton)
wan|ton|ly
wan|ton|ness
wap|en|take +s
wap|iti +s
Wap|ping (district,
  London)
war
  wars
  warred
  war|ring
  (fighting. △ wore)
wara|tah +s
warb +s
War|beck, Per|kin
  (Flemish
  pretender to the
  English throne)
war|ble
  war|bles
  war|bled
  warb|ling

war|ble fly
  war|ble flies
warb|ler +s
War|burg, Aby
  (German art
  historian)
War|burg, Otto
  Hein|rich
  (German
  biochemist)
warby
war cloud +s
war cry
  war cries
Ward, Mrs
  Hum|phry
  (English writer)
ward +s +ed +ing
war|den +s
war|den|ship +s
war|der +s
ward-heeler +s
ward|ress
  ward|resses
ward|robe +s
ward|room +s
ward|ship +s
ware +s (articles
  for sale; aware;
  beware. △ wear,
  where)
ware|house
  ware|houses
  ware|housed
  ware|hous|ing
ware|house|man
  ware|house|men
war|fare
war|farin
war game +s
war gam|ing
war|head +s
War|hol, Andy
  (American artist)
war|horse +s
wari|ly
wari|ness
Warka (Arabic
  name for Uruk)
war|like
war|lock +s
war|lord +s
warm +s +ed +ing
  +er +est
warm-blooded
warm-
  blooded|ness
warmed-over
  attributive
warmed-up
  attributive
warm|er +s

warm-hearted
warm-hearted|ly
warm-
  hearted|ness
warming-pan +s
warm|ish
warm|ly
warm|ness
war|mon|ger +s
war|mon|ger|ing
warmth +s
warm-up +s noun
  and attributive
warn +s +ed +ing
  (inform;
  admonish.
  △ worn)
warn|er +s
War|ner Broth|ers
  (American film
  company)
warn|ing +s
warn|ing|ly
warp +s +ed +ing
  (bend; pervert;
  haul; rope; threads
  in loom; sediment.
  △ whaup)
warp|age
war|paint +s
war|path +s
warp|er +s
war|plane +s
war|ra|gal +s (use
  warrigal)
war|rant +s +ed
  +ing
war|rant|able
war|rant|able|ness
war|rant|ably
war|rant|ee +s
  (person.
  △ warranty)
war|rant|er +s
  (person giving an
  assurance.
  △ warrantor)
war|rant of|ficer
  +s
war|rant|or +s
  (Law person
  giving a warranty)
war|ranty
  war|ran|ties
  (undertaking.
  △ warrantee)
War|ren (name)
War|ren, Earl
  (American judge)
War|ren, Rob|ert
  Penn (American
  writer)

war|ren +s (rabbits'
  burrows)
war|ren|er +s
war|ri|gal +s
War|ring|ton
  (town, England)
war|rior +s
war|rior king +s
war|rior queen +s
War|saw (capital of
  Poland)
war|ship +s
wart +s
wart|hog +s
war|time
war-torn
warty
  wart|ier
  warti|est
war-weariness
war-weary
War|wick (town,
  England)
War|wick, Earl of
  ('the Kingmaker',
  English
  statesman)
War|wick|shire
  (county, England)
war-worn
war wound +s
war-wounded
wary
  wari|er
  wari|est
was
Wash, the (inlet,
  England)
wash
  washes
  washed
  wash|ing
wash|abil|ity
wash|able +s
wash-and-wear
wash|bag +s
wash|basin +s
wash|board +s
wash|day +s
washed-out
  attributive
wash|er +s
washer-drier +s
  (use washer-
  dryer)
washer-dryer +s
wash|er|man
  wash|er|men
washer-up
  washers-up
wash|er|woman
  wash|er|women

wash|ery
wash|er|ies
wash|et|eria +s
wash-hand basin +s
wash-hand stand +s
wash-house +s
wash|ily
washi|ness
wash|ing
  ma|chine +s
wash|ing pow|der +s
wash|ing soda +s
Wash|ing|ton
  (state and capital of the USA; town, England)
Wash|ing|ton, Booker T.
  (American educationist)
Wash|ing|ton, George
  (American president)
washing-up *noun and attributive*
wash|land +s
wash-leather +s
Washoe
  (chimpanzee)
wash|out +s
  Geology
wash-out +s
  (failure; gap in road etc. caused by flood)
wash|room +s
wash|stand +s
wash|tub +s
wash-up *noun and attributive*
wash/wipe
washy
  wash|ier
  washi|est
wasn't (= was not)
Wasp +s (*usually offensive*; White Anglo-Saxon Protestant)
wasp +s (insect)
waspie +s (corset. △ waspy)
Wasp|ish (*usually offensive*; of a Wasp)
wasp|ish (spiteful)
wasp|ish|ly
wasp|ish|ness

wasp|like
wasp-waist +s
wasp-waisted
Waspy (*usually offensive*; of a Wasp. △ waspie)
waspy (wasplike. △ waspie)
was|sail +s +ed +ing
wassail-bowl +s
wassail-cup +s
was|sail|er +s
Was|ser|mann
  (test)
wast
wast|able
wast|age
waste
  wastes
  wasted
  wast|ing
  (squander. △ waist)
waste|bas|ket +s
waste bin +s
waste|ful
waste|ful|ly
waste|ful|ness
waste ground
waste|land +s
waste|less
waste paper
waste-paper bas|ket +s
waste pipe +s
waster +s
wast|rel +s
watch
  watches
  watched
  watch|ing
watch|able
watch|band +s
watch-case +s
watch-chain +s
watch|dog +s
watch|er +s
watch face +s
watch|fire +s
watch|ful
watch|ful|ly
watch|ful|ness
watch-glass
  watch-glasses
watch|keep|er +s
watch|maker +s
watch|mak|ing
watch|man
  watch|men
watch-night +s
watch spring +s

watch strap +s
watch|tower +s
watch|word +s
water +s +ed +ing
water-bag +s
water-based
Water-bearer, the
  (constellation; sign of zodiac)
water|bed +s
water|bird +s
water bis|cuit +s
water-bloom
water-boatman
  water-boatmen
water-borne
water bot|tle +s
water|brash
water-buck +s
water buf|falo
  plural water buf|falo *or* water buf|fa|loes
water-butt +s
water-cannon +s
Water-carrier, the
  (constellation; sign of zodiac)
water chute +s
water-clock +s
water closet +s
water|color *Am.* +s
water|col|or|ist *Am.* +s
water|col|our *Br.* +s
water|col|our|ist *Br.* +s
water-cooled
water-cooler +s
water|course +s
water|cress
water-diviner +s
water|er +s
water|fall +s
Water|ford (town and county, Republic of Ireland; glass)
water|fowl
water|front +s
Water|gate (US political scandal)
water|gate +s
  (floodgate; gate to river etc.)
water glass
  water glasses
  (tumbler)
water-glass
  (substance)
water ham|mer +s

water heat|er +s
water hen +s
water|hole +s
water ice +s
wateri|ness
water|ing +s
water|ing can +s
water|ing hole +s
water|ing place +s
water jug +s
water|less
water level +s
water lily
  water lil|ies
water|line +s
water|logged
Water|loo (battle, Belgium; railway station, London)
water|man
  water|men
water|mark +s +ed +ing
water-meadow +s
water|melon +s
water|mill +s
water nymph +s
water-pepper +s
water pipe +s
water pis|tol +s
water polo
water-power
water|proof +s +ed +ing
water|proof|er +s
water|proof|ness
water rat +s
water rate +s
water-repellency
water-repellent
water-resist|ance
water-resist|ant
Waters, Muddy
  (American blues musician)
water scor|pion +s
water|shed +s
water|side +s
water-ski +s +ed +ing
water-skier +s
water slide +s
water snake +s
water soft|en|er +s
water-soluble
water-splash
  water-splashes
water sport +s
water|spout +s
water-sprite +s

water supply
  water sup|plies
water-table +s
water taxi +s
water|thrush
  water|thrushes
water|tight
water tower +s
water vole +s
water|way +s
water|weed +s
water|wheel +s
water wings
water|works
watery
Wat|ford (town,
  England)
Watha|wur|ung
wa|tjin +s
Wat|ling Street
  (Roman road,
  England)
Wat|son, Dr
  (companion of
  Sherlock Holmes)
**Wat|son, James
  D.** (American
  biologist)
Wat|son, John B.
  (American
  psychologist)
wat|sonia +s
  (plant)
**Watson-Watt,
  Rob|ert** (Scottish
  physicist)
Watt, James
  (Scottish
  engineer)
watt +s (unit.
  △ what, wot)
watt|age +s
**Wat|teau, Jean
  An|toine** (French
  painter)
watt-hour +s
wat|tle
  wat|tles
  wat|tled
  wat|tling
watt|meter +s
**Watts, George
  Fred|erick**
  (English artist)
Watts, Isaac
  (English hymn-
  writer)
Wa|tusi
  plural **Wa|tusi** or
  Wa|tu|sis
  (person)
Wa|tusi (dance)

Wa|tutsi
  plural **Wa|tutsi** or
  Wa|tut|sis
Waugh, Eve|lyn
  (English novelist)
waul +s +ed +ing
  (cry like cat.
  △ wall, whorl)
wave
  waves
  waved
  wav|ing
  (gesture; on
  water; curve.
  △ waive)
wave|band +s
wave|form +s
wave|front +s
wave|guide +s
wave|length +s
wave|less
wave|let +s
wave|like
wave mo|tion +s
waver +s +ed +ing
  (falter. △ waiver)
waver|er +s
waver|ing|ly
wav|ery
wave|top +s
wavi|ly
wavi|ness
wavy
  wavi|er
  wavi|est
wa-wa +s (use wah-
  wah)
wawl +s +ed +ing
  (cry like cat. use
  waul. △ wall,
  whorl)
wax
  waxes
  waxed
  wax|ing
wax|berry
  wax|berries
wax|bill +s
wax|cloth +s
waxen
waxer +s
wax|ily
waxi|ness
wax|ing +s
wax·light +s
wax-like
wax myr|tle +s
wax-painting +s
wax-pod +s
wax-tree +s
wax|wing +s
wax|work +s

waxy
  waxi|er
  waxi|est
way +s (road etc.;
  method. △ weigh,
  wey, whey)
way|back (outback)
way|bill +s
way|bread +s
way|farer +s
way|far|ing
way|far|ing tree
  +s
way in (entrance.
  △ weigh-in)
**Way|land the
  Smith** English
  Legend
way|lay
  way|lays
  way|laid
  way|lay|ing
way|lay|er +s
way-leave +s
way|mark +s +ed
  +ing
way|mark|er +s
Wayne (name)
Wayne, John
  (American actor.
  △ Wain)
way out (exit)
way-out adjective
way|point +s
way|side +s
way sta|tion +s
way|ward
way|ward|ly
way|ward|ness
way-worn
wayz|goose +s
we (plural of I.
  △ wee, whee)
weak +er +est
  (feeble. △ week)
weak|en +s +ed
  +ing
weak|en|er +s
weak|fish
  plural **weak|fish** or
  weak|fishes
weak|ish
weak-kneed
weak|li|ness
weak|ling +s
weak|ly
  weak|lier
  weak|li|est
  (feebly. △ weekly)
weak-minded
**weak-
  minded|ness**

weak|ness
  weak|nesses
weal +s +ed +ing
  (mark on skin;
  prosperity; in 'the
  common weal'.
  △ we'll, wheel)
Weald, the (region,
  SE England)
weald-clay +s
Weald|en
wealth
wealth|ily
wealthi|ness
wealthy
  wealth|ier
  wealthi|est
wean +s +ed +ing
  (accustom to food.
  △ ween)
wean|er +s
  (animal.
  △ wiener)
wean|ling +s
weapon +s
weap|oned
weapon|less
weapon|ry
  weap|on|ries
Wear (river,
  England; in 'Tyne
  and Wear')
wear
  wears
  wore
  wear|ing
  worn
  (have on (clothes
  etc.). △ ware,
  where)
wear|abil|ity
wear|able
wear|er +s
weari|less
weari|ly
weari|ness
wear|ing|ly
weari|some
weari|some|ly
weari|some|ness
Wear|side (region,
  England)
weary
  wear|ies
  wear|ied
  weary|ing
  weari|er
  weari|est
weary|ing|ly
weasel +s +ed
  +ing
weasel-faced

weas|el|ly
wea|ther +s +ed
+ing (atmospheric
conditions; expose
to weather;
survive. △ wether,
whether)
weather-beaten
wea|ther|board +s
+ed +ing
weather-bound
weather-chart +s
wea|ther|cock +s
wea|ther|girl +s
weather-glass
weather-glasses
wea|ther|li|ness
wea|ther|ly
wea|ther|man
wea|ther|men
wea|ther|most
wea|ther|proof +s
+ed +ing
wea|ther|strip
wea|ther|strips
wea|ther|stripped
wea|ther|strip|
ping
wea|ther|tight
weather-tiles
wea|ther|vane +s
weather-worn
weave
weaves
wove
weav|ing
woven or wove
(make fabric or
story. △ we've)
weave
weaves
weaved
weav|ing
(move; zigzag.
△ we've)
weaver +s (person
who weaves.
△ weever)
weav|ing +s
web
webs
webbed
web|bing
Webb, Bea|trice
and Sid|ney
(English
economists and
historians)
.Webb, Mary
(English novelist)
web|bing +s
webby

Weber, Carl Maria
von (German
composer)
Weber, Max
(German
sociologist)
weber +s (unit)
Web|ern, Anton
(Austrian
composer)
web-footed
Web|ster, John
(English
dramatist)
Web|ster, Noah
(American
lexicographer)
web-wheel +s
web|work +s
web|worm +s
wed
weds
wed|ded or wed
wed|ding
we'd (= we had; we
should; we would.
△ weed)
Wed|dell Sea
(off Antarctica)
wed|ding +s
Wede|kind, Frank
(German
dramatist)
wedge
wedges
wedged
wedg|ing
wedge|like
wedge-shaped
wedge|wise
wedgie +s
Wedg|wood,
Jo|siah (English
potter)
Wedg|wood
(pottery; colour)
Propr.
wed|lock
Wed|nes|day +s
wee
wees
weed
wee|ing
(urinate. △ we
whee)
wee
weer
weest
(tiny. △ we
whee)
weed +s +ed +ing
(plant. △ we'd)

weed|er +s
weed-grown
weedi|ness
weed|kill|er +s
weed|less
weedy
weed|ier
weedi|est
Wee Free +s
week +s (seven
days. △ weak)
week|day +s
week|end +s +ed
+ing
week|end|er +s
week-long
week|ly
week|lies
(once a week;
newspaper etc.
△ weakly)
ween +s +ed +ing
(think. △ wean)
weenie +s
(sausage; use
wienie)
weeny
ween|ier
weeni|est
(tiny. △ wienie)
weeny-bopper +s
weep
weeps
wept
weep|ing
weep|er +s
weepie +s (film etc.
△ weepy)
weep|ily
weepi|ness
weep|ing|ly
weepy
weep|ier
weepi|est
(tearful.
△ weepie)
weever +s (fish.
△ weaver)
wee|vil +s
wee|vily
wee-wee
wee-wees
wee-weed
wee-weeing
weft +s
Weg|en|er, Al|fred
Lothar (German
meteorologist)
Wehr|macht
Wei (Chinese
dynasties)

Wei|fang (city,
China)
wei|gela +s
weigh +s +ed +ing
(measure the
weight of. △ way,
wey, whey)
weigh|able
weigh|bridge +s
weigh|er +s
weigh-in +s (noun;
weighing of boxer.
△ way in)
weigh|ing
ma|chine +s
weight +s +ed
+ing (heaviness
etc. △ wait)
weight gain
weight|ily
weighti|ness
weight|ing +s
weight|less
weight|less|ly
weight|less|ness
weight|lift|er +s
weight|lift|ing
weight loss
weight train|ing
Weight Watch|er
+s (member of
Weight Watchers)
weight-watcher
+s (dieter)
Weight Watch|ers
(organization)
Propr.
weight-watching
weighty
weight|ier
weighti|est
Weih|sien (former
name of Weifang)
Weil, Sim|one
(French
philosopher)
Weill, Kurt
(German
composer)
Weil's dis|ease
Wei|mar (town,
Germany;
Republic)
Wei|mar|aner +s
weir +s (dam.
△ we're)
weird +er +est
weirdie +s
weird|ly
weird|ness
weirdo +s

**Weis|mann,
Au|gust
Fried|rich**
(German biologist)
Weis|mann|ism
**Weiss|mul|ler,
Johnny**
(American
swimmer and
actor)
**Weiz|mann,
Chaim** (Israeli
president)
weka +s
We|land
(= Wayland the
Smith)
Welch (in 'Royal
Welch Fusiliers'.
△ Welsh)
welch (default; use
welsh)
welches
welched
welch|ing
wel|come
wel|comes
wel|comed
wel|com|ing
wel|come|ly
wel|come|ness
wel|comer +s
wel|com|ing|ly
weld +s +ed +ing
weld|abil|ity
weld|able
weld|er +s
wel|fare
wel|far|ism
wel|far|ist +s
wel|kin
Wel|kom (town,
South Africa)
well
 bet|ter
 best
(satisfactorily etc.)
well +s +ed +ing
(shaft for water;
etc.)
well- (Unless given
below, phrases
beginning with
well, such as *well
aimed* and *well
balanced*, are
written as two
words when used
predicatively, i.e.
when they follow
a verb, as in *That
shot was well*

well- (*cont.*)
aimed, but with a
hyphen when used
attributively, i.e.
when they come
before a noun, as
in *That was a
well-aimed shot.*)
we'll (= we shall;
we will. △ weal,
wheel, will)
well ac|quaint|ed
well ad|vised
**Wel|land (Ship)
Canal** (in Canada)
well-being
well-conditioned
well deck +s
well-dressed
well-dressing +s
Welles, Orson
(American actor
and director)
**Wel|les|ley,
Ar|thur** (Duke of
Wellington)
well-found
well-head +s
well-heeled
wel|lie (use welly)
wel|lies
wel|lied
welly|ing
Wel|ling|ton
(capital of New
Zealand)
**Wel|ling|ton,
Duke of** (British
soldier and
prime minister)
wel|ling|ton +s
(boot)
well-knit
well-laid
well|ness
well-nigh
well pleased
Wells (town,
England)
Wells, H. G.
(English novelist)
**Wells, Fargo &
Co.** (American
transport
company)
well-spoken
well|spring +s
well-structured
well thought of
well-thought-of
attributive
well thought out

well-thought-out
attributive
well-to-do
well-traveled *Am.*
well-travelled *Br.*
well-trodden
well-wisher +s
well woman
welly
wel|lies
wel|lied
welly|ing
wels
plural wels
(fish)
**Wels|bach, Carl
Auer von**
(Austrian chemist)
Welsh (of Wales.
△ Welch)
welsh
welshes
welshed
welsh|ing
(default)
welsh|er +s
Welsh|man
Welsh|men
Welsh|ness
Welsh|pool (town,
Wales)
Welsh|woman
Welsh|women
welt +s +ed +ing
Welt|an|schau|ung
Welt|an|schau|
ung|en
wel|ter +s +ed
+ing
wel|ter|weight +s
Welt|schmerz
Welty, Eu|dora
(American writer)
Wemba-wemba
Wem|bley (district
and stadium,
London)
wen +s (runic
letter. △ when)
Wen|ces|las ('Good
King Wenceslas',
Czech saint)
Wen|ces|laus (king
of Bohemia and
Germany)
wench
wenches
wenched
wench|ing
wench|er +s
Wen-Chou
(= Wenzhou)

Wend +s (Slavic
people)
wend +s +ed +ing
(go)
Wenda
Wend|ic
Wend|ish
Wendy
Wendy house +s
Wens|ley|dale +s
(region, England;
cheese; sheep)
went
wentle|trap +s
Wen|zhou (city,
China)
wept
were (in 'we were'
etc. △ whirr)
we're (= we are)
weren't (= were
not)
were|wolf
were|wolves
**Wer|ner,
Abra|ham
Gott|lob** (German
geologist)
Wer|ner, Al|fred
(French-born
Swiss chemist)
wert (in 'thou wert'.
△ wort)
Weser (river,
Germany)
Wes|ker, Ar|nold
(English
playwright)
Wes|ley (name)
Wes|ley, John
(English founder
of Methodism)
Wes|ley|an +s
Wes|ley|an|ism
Wes|sex (region,
SW England)
West, Ben|ja|min
(American
painter)
West, Mae
(American
actress)
West, Re|becca
(British writer)
West, the (part of
country etc.;
European
civilization; non-
Communist states)
west (point;
direction)
west|about

west|bound

West Brom|wich
(town, England)

west|er|ing

west|er¦ly

west|er|lies

West|ern (of the
West)

west|ern +s (of or
in the west;
cowboy film etc.)

west|ern|er +s

west|ern|isa¦tion
Br. (use
westernization)

west|ern|ise Br.
(use westernize)

west|ern|ises

west|ern|ised

west|ern|is¦ing

west|ern|iser Br.
+s (use
westernizer)

west|ern|iza¦tion

west|ern|ize

west|ern|izes

west|ern|ized

west|ern|iz¦ing

west|ern|izer +s

west|ern|most

West In¦dian +s

west|ing +s

West|ing|house,
George
(American
engineer)

West Irian
(province,
Indonesia)

West|mann
Is¦lands (off
Iceland)

West|meath
(county, Republic
of Ireland)

West|min¦ster
(borough;
London)

West¦mor|land
(former county,
England)

west-north-west

Weston-super-
Mare (resort,
England)

West|pha¦lia
(former province,
Germany)

West|pha¦lian +s

west-south-west

west|ward

west|wards

wet

wets

wet|ted

wet|ting

wet¦ter

wet|test
(moist; make
moist. △ whet)

weta +s (insect)

wet-and-dry
attributive

wet|back +s

wether +s (sheep.
△ weather,
whether)

wet|land +s

wet-look attributive

wetly

wet|ness

wet-nurse

wet-nurses

wet-nursed

wet-nursing

wet|suit +s

wet|table

wet|ting +s

wet|tish

wet-weather
attributive

we've (= we have.
△ weave)

Wex|ford (town
and county,
Republic of
Ireland)

wey +s (unit.
△ way, weigh,
whey)

Wey¦den, Ro¦gier
van de (Flemish
painter)

Wey|mouth (town,
England)

whack +s +ed
+ing (strike.
△ wack, wacke)

whack¦er +s

whack|ing +s

whacko
(interjection.
△ wacko)

whacky

whack¦ier

whacki¦est
(use wacky)

whale

whales

whaled

whal¦ing
(sea mammal.
△ wail, wale)

whale|back +s

whale|boat +s

whale|bone

whale-headed
stork +s

whale oil

whaler +s (ship;
person who hunts
whales; shark;
tramp. △ wailer)

whale-watching

whaling-master
+s

wham

whams

whammed

wham|ming

whammy

wham|mies

whang +s +ed
+ing

Whanga|rei (port,
New Zealand)

whangee +s

whap (use whop)

whaps

whapped

whap|ping

whare +s (Maori
house)

wharf

wharves or
wharfs

wharf|age

wharfie +s

wharf|inger +s

Whar|ton, Edith
(American writer)

wharves

what (which; which
thing. △ watt,
wot)

what-d'you-call-it

what|e'er
(= whatever)

what|ever

what|not +s

what's-her-name

what's-his-name

whats|it +s

what's-its-name

what|so

what|so|e'er
(= whatsoever)

what|so|ever

whaup +s (curlew.
△ warp)

wheal +s +ed +ing
(use weal
△ we'll, wheel)

wheat +s

wheat belt +s

wheat|ear +s

wheat|en

wheat flour

wheat|germ

wheat|grass

wheat|meal

wheat|sheaf

wheat|sheaves

Wheat|stone,
Charles (English
inventor; bridge)

whee (interjection.
△ we, wee)

whee¦dle

whee¦dles

whee¦dled

wheed|ling

wheed|ler +s

wheed|ling¦ly

wheel +s +ed +ing
(on vehicle etc.
△ weal, we'll)

wheel arch

wheel arches

wheel-back

wheel|bar¦row +s

wheel|base +s

wheel|chair +s

wheel clamp +s
noun

wheel-clamp +s
+ed +ing verb

wheel¦er +s

wheeler-dealer +s

wheeler-dealing

wheel|house +s

wheelie +s

wheelie bin +s

wheel|ing +s

wheel|less

wheel lock +s

wheel|man

wheel|men

wheel|slip

wheels|man

wheels|men

wheel|spin

wheel|wright +s

wheely bin +s (use
wheelie bin)

wheeze

wheezes

wheezed

wheez|ing

wheezer +s

wheez|ily

wheezi|ness

wheez|ing¦ly

wheezy

wheez|ier

wheezi|est

whelk +s

whelm +s +ed
+ing
whelp +s +ed +ing
when (at what time.
△ wen)
whence
whence|so|ever
when|e'er
(= whenever)
when|ever
when|so|e'er
(= whensoever)
when|so|ever
where (what place
etc. △ ware,
wear)
where|abouts
where|after
where|as
where|at
where|by
wher|e'er
(= wherever)
where|fore +s
where|from
where|in
where|of
where|on
where|so|e'er
(= wheresoever)
where|so|ever
where|to
where|upon
wher|ever
where|with
where|withal
wherry
wher|ries
wherry|man
wherry|men
whet
whets
whet|ted
whet|ting
(sharpen;
stimulate. △ wet)
whether
(conjunction.
△ weather,
wether)
whet|stone +s
whet|ter +s
whew
whey (from milk.
△ way, weigh,
wey)
whey-faced
which (adjective and
pronoun. △ witch,
wych)
which|ever
which|so|ever

whicker +s +ed
+ing (noise of
horse. △ wicker)
whi|dah +s (bird;
use whydah.
△ wider)
whiff +s +ed +ing
whif|fle
whif|fles
whif|fled
whif|fling
whif|fler +s
whiffle|tree +s
whiffy
Whig +s (Politics.
△ wig)
Whig|gery
Whig|gish
Whig|gism
while
whiles
whiled
whil|ing
(period; during;
pass time. △ wile)
whi|lom
whilst
whim +s
whim|brel +s
whim|per +s +ed
+ing
whim|per|er +s
whim|per|ing +s
whim|per|ing|ly
whim|si|cal
whim|si|cal|ity
whim|si|cal|ities
whim|si|cal|ly
whim|si|cal|ness
whimsy
whim|sies
whim-wham +s
whin +s (gorse;
rock or stone.
△ win, wyn)
whin|chat +s
whine
whines
whined
whin|ing
(sound; complain.
△ wine)
whiner +s
whinge
whinges
whinged
whinge|ing or
whin|ging
whinge|ing|ly
whin|ger +s
whin|gey
whin|ging|ly (use
whingeingly)

whingy (use
whingey)
whin|ing|ly
whinny
whin|nies
whin|nied
whinny|ing
whin|sill +s
whin|stone +s
whiny
whi|nier
whini|est
(whining.
△ winey)
whip
whips
whipped
whip|ping
whip|bird +s
whip|cord +s
whip-cracking
whip-crane +s
whip-graft +s
whip hand
whip|lash
whip|lashes
whip|lashed
whip|lash|ing
whip|less
whip-like
whip|per +s
whipper-in
whippers-in
whip|per|snap|per
+s
whip|pet +s
whip|pi|ness
whip|ping +s
whip|ping boy +s
whip|ping cream
+s
whip|ping post +s
whipping-top +s
whipple|tree +s
whip|poor|will +s
whippy
whip|pier
whip|pi|est
whip-round +s
whip|saw +s
whip snake +s
whip|ster +s
whip stitch
whip stitches
whip|stock +s
whir (sound; use
whirr. △ were)
whirs
whirred
whir|ring

whirl +s +ed +ing
(swing round.
△ whorl)
whirl|er +s
whirli|gig +s
whirl|ing|ly
whirl|pool +s
whirl|wind +s
whirly|bird +s
whirr +s +ed +ing
(sound. △ were)
whisht
whisk +s +ed +ing
whis|ker +s
whis|kered
whis|kery
whis|key +s (Irish
and American)
whisky
whis|kies
(Scotch)
whis|per +s +ed
+ing
whis|per|er +s
whis|per|ing +s
whis|per|ing
gal|lery
whis|per|ing
gal|ler|ies
whist (game; hush.
△ wist)
whis|tle
whis|tles
whis|tled
whist|ling
whistle-blower +s
whistle-blowing
Whist|ler, James
Mc|Neill
(American artist)
whist|ler +s
Whist|ler|ian
whistle-stop
Whit (Whitsuntide.
△ wit)
whit (least possible
amount. △ wit)
Whitby (town,
England)
White, Gil|bert
(English
naturalist)
White, Pat|rick
(Australian
novelist)
white
whites
whited
whit|ing
whiter
whit|est

white (cont.)
(colour; person.
△ wight)
white|bait
plural white|bait
white|beam +s
white|board +s
white|cap +s
white-collar
attributive
white|cur|rant +s
white-eye +s
white|face
white|fish
plural white|fish
or white|fishes
(lake fish of trout
family)
white fish (plaice,
cod, etc.)
white|fly
white|flies
White|hall (street,
London)
**White|head,
Al|fred North**
(English
philosopher)
white|head +s
(pimple)
White|horse (city,
Canada)
white-hot
White House (in
Washington D.C.)
white-knuckle
attributive
white|ly
whiten +s +ed
+ing
whit|en|er +s
white|ness
whiten|ing
white-out +s noun
White Sea (inlet,
NW Russia)
white|smith +s
white|thorn +s
white|throat +s
white|wash
white|washes
white|washed
white|wash|ing
white|wash|er +s
white|wood +s
whitey +s (offensive
person. △ whity)
whither (to where.
△ wither)
whith|er|so|ever
whith|er|ward

whit|ing
plural whit|ing
(fish)
whit|ing +s
(substance)
whit|ish
Whit|lam, Gough
(Australian prime
minister)
whit|leather
whit|low +s
whitlow-grass
Whit|man, Walt
(American poet)
Whit|ney, Eli
(American
inventor)
Whit|ney, Mount
(in USA)
Whit|sun
Whit Sun|day +s
Whit|sun|tide
**Whit|tier, John
Green|leaf**
(American poet)
**Whit|ting|ton,
Dick** (Lord Mayor
of London)
Whit|tle, Frank
(English
aeronautical
engineer)
whit|tle
whit|tles
whit|tled
whit|tling
Whit|worth (screw
thread)
whity (whitish.
△ whitey)
whiz (use whizz)
whizzes
whizzed
whizz|ing
whiz-bang +s
whiz-kid +s (use
whizz-kid)
whizz
whizzes
whizzed
whizz|ing
whizz-bang +s
(use whiz-bang)
whiz|zer +s
whizz-kid +s
whizzo
Who, the (English
rock group)
who
whoa (stop. △ woe)
who'd (= who had;
who would)

who-does-what
attributive
who|dunit Am. +s
who|dun|nit Br. +s
who|e'er
(= whoever)
who|ever
whole +s (entire;
entirety. △ hole)
whole|food +s
whole|grain +s
whole|heart|ed
whole|heart|ed|ly
**whole|heart|ed|
ness**
whole-life
attributive
whole|ly (fully; use
wholly. △ holey,
Holi, holy)
whole|meal
whole|ness
whole|sale
whole|sales
whole|saled
whole|sal|ing
whole|saler +s
whole|some
whole|some|ly
whole|some|ness
whole-time
whole-tone scale
whole|wheat
whol|ism
whol|ly (fully.
△ holey, Holi,
holy)
whom
whom|ever
whom|so
whom|so|ever
whoop +s +ed
+ing (shout.
△ hoop)
whoo|pee
whoop|er +s
whoop|ing cough
whoops
whoosh
whooshes
whooshed
whoosh|ing
whop
whops
whopped
whop|ping
whop|per +s
whore
whores
whored
whor|ing

whore (cont.)
(prostitute.
△ haw, hoar)
who're (= who are)
whore|dom
whore|house +s
whore|mas|ter
whore|mon|ger +s
whorer +s
whore|son +s
whor|ish
whor|ish|ly
whor|ish|ness
whorl +s (ring.
△ wall,
waul, whirl)
whorled (having
whorls.
△ whirled)
whortle|berry
whortle|berries
who's (= who is)
whose (of or
belonging to
whom or which)
whose|so
whose|so|ever
whos|ever
whoso
who|so|ever
who's who
who've (= who
have)
whump +s +ed
+ing
why +s
Why|alla (town,
Australia)
why|dah +s (bird.
△ wider)
**Whym|per,
Ed|ward** (English
mountaineer)
wibbly-wobbly
Wicca
Wic|can +s
Wich|ita (city,
USA)
wick +s
wicked +er +est
wick|ed|ly
wick|ed|ness
wicker (basket
material. △ whicker)
wick|er|work
wicket +s
wicket|keep|er +s
wicket|keep|ing
wicket-taker +s
wicket-taking
wicki|up +s
Wick|low (town
and county,

Wick|low (*cont.*)
Republic of
Ireland)
wid|der|shins (use
withershins)
wide
wider
wid|est
wide-angle +s
(*noun* lens;
adjective)
wide|awake +s
(hat)
wide awake (fully
awake)
wide boy +s
wide-eyed
wide|ly
wide|ly ac|cept|ed
wide|ly based
wide|ly ex|pect|ed
wide|ly held
wide|ly known
widely-known
attributive
wide|ly read
widely-read
attributive
wide|ly
re|spect|ed
wide|ly scat|tered
wide|ly spaced
wide|ly used
widen +s +ed +ing
widen|er +s
wide|ness
widen|ing +s
wide open
wide-open
attributive (in
sense 'fully
opened')
wider (comparative
of wide
△ whydah)
wide-ranging
wide-screen
wide|spread
widg|eon +s
widget +s
widgie +s
wid|ish
Wid|nes (town,
England)
widow +s +ed
+ing
widow-bird +s
wid|ow|er +s
widow|hood
widow's cruse +s
widow's mite +s
widow's peak +s

widow's weeds
width +s
width|ways
width|wise
Wie|land,
Chris|toph
Mar|tin (German
writer)
wield +s +ed +ing
wield|er +s
wieldy
Wie|ner, Nor|bert
(American
mathematician)
wie|ner +s
(sausage.
△ weaner)
Wie|ner schnit|zel
+s
wie|nie +s (sausage.
△ weeny)
Wies|baden (city,
Germany)
Wie|sel, Elie
(Romanian-born
American
authority on the
Holocaust)
Wie|sen|thal,
Simon (Austrian
Jewish
investigator of
Nazi war crimes)
wife
wives
wife|hood
wife|less
wife|like
wife|li|ness
wife|ly
wife-swapping
wif|ish
wig
wigs
wigged
wig|ging
(hair; rebuke.
△ Whig)
Wigan (town,
England)
wi|geon +s (use
widgeon)
wig|ging +s
wig|gle
wig|gles
wig|gled
wig|gling
wig|gler +s
wig|gly
wig|glier
wig|gli|est

Wight (shipping
area, English
Channel)
Wight, Isle of (off
England)
wight +s (*archaic*
person. △ white)
Wight|man Cup
(tennis contest)
Wig|town|shire
(former county,
Scotland)
wig|wag
wig|wags
wig|wagged
wig|wag|ging
wig|wam +s
Wil|ber|force,
Wil|liam (English
social reformer)
Wil|bur
wilco
Wil|cox, Ella
Wheel|er
(American writer)
wild +s +er +est
wild card +s *noun*
wild-card
attributive
wild|cat +s
wild-caught
Wilde, Oscar (Irish
writer)
wilde|beest
plural wilde|beest
or wilde|beests
Wilder, Billy
(American film
director)
Wilder, Thorn|ton
(American writer)
wil|der +s +ed +ing
wil|der|ness
wil|der|nesses
wild|fire
wild flower +s
wild|fowl
plural wild|fowl
wild-goose chase
+s
wild|ing +s
wild|ish
wild|life
wild|ly
wild|ness
wild|wood +s
wile
wiles
wiled
wil|ing
(trick. △ while)

Wil|fred *also*
Wil|frid
Wil|frid *also*
Wil|fred
wil|ful *Br.* (*Am.*
willful)
wil|ful|ly *Br.* (*Am.*
willfully)
wil|ful|ness *Br.*
(*Am.* willfulness)
wilga +s
Wil|helm (German
emperors)
Wil|hel|mina
Wil|helms|haven
(port, Germany)
wili|ly
wili|ness
Wilkes Land (in
Antarctica)
Wil|kie, David
(Scottish painter)
Wil|kins, Maur|ice
(New Zealand-
born British
biochemist)
Will (name)
will (*auxiliary verb.*
△ we'll)
will +s +ed +ing
(wish; impel;
bequeath. △ we'll)
Willa (name)
Wil|lard, Emma
(American
educational
reformer)
Wil|lem|stad
(capital of the
Netherlands
Antilles)
will|er +s
will|let
plural will|let
will|ful *Am.* (*Br.*
wilful)
will|ful|ly *Am.* (*Br.*
wilfully)
will|ful|ness *Am.*
(*Br.* wilfulness)
Wil|liam (English
and British kings)
Wil|liam of
Occam (English
philosopher)
Wil|liam of
Orange (William
III of Great Britain
and Ireland)
Wil|liam Rufus
(William II of
England)

Wil|liams, John
(Australian
guitarist)
Wil|liams, J. P. R.
(Welsh Rugby
Union player)
**Wil|liams,
Ten|nes|see**
(American
dramatist)
**Wil|liams,
Wil|liam Car|los**
(American writer)
Wil|liams|burg
(city, USA)
wil|lie +s (penis;
use willy)
wil|lies, the
(unease)
will|ing
will|ing|ly
will|ing|ness
will-less
will-o'-the-wisp
+s
wil|low +s
wil|low|herb +s
wil|low tree +s
wil|low warb|ler
+s
wil|low wren +s
wil|lowy
will-power
**Wills, Wil|liam
John** (English
explorer)
willy
wil|lies
willy-nilly
willy wag|tail +s
willy-willy
willy-willies
Wilma
Wil|son, Angus
(English writer)
**Wil|son, Charles
Thom|son Rees**
(Scottish
physicist)
Wil|son, Ed|mund
(American writer)
**Wil|son, Ed|ward
Os|borne**
(American social
biologist)
Wil|son, Har|old
(British prime
minister)
**Wil|son, Thomas
Wood|row**
(American
president)

wilt +s +ed +ing
Wil|ton +s (carpet)
Wilts. (= Wiltshire)
Wilt|shire (county,
England)
wily
wili|er
wili|est
Wim|ble|don
(district, London;
tennis
championship)
wimp +s +ed +ing
wimp|ish
wimp|ish|ly
wimp|ish|ness
wim|ple
wim|ples
wim|pled
wimp|ling
Wimpy +s
(hamburger)
Propr.
wimpy
wimp|ier
wimpi|est
(feeble)
Wims|hurst
(machine)
win
wins
won
win|ning
(gain through
effort etc. △ whin,
wyn)
wince
winces
winced
win|cing
win|cer +s
win|cey +s
win|cey|ette
winch
winches
winched
winch|ing
winch|er +s
Win|ches|ter (city,
England)
Win|ches|ter +s
(rifle) *Propr.*
Win|ches|ter (disk;
drive)
win|ches|ter +s
(bottle)
win|cing|ly
**Winck|el|mann,
Jo|hann** (German
archaeologist)

wind +s +ed +ing
(moving air;
breath; scent; etc.)
wind
winds
wound
wind|ing
(coil. △ wynd)
wind|age
Win|daus, Adolf
(German organic
chemist)
wind|bag +s
wind-blown
wind|bound
wind|break +s
wind|break|er +s
wind|burn
wind|cheat|er +s
wind-chill
wind-cone +s
wind-down +s
noun
wind|er +s
Win|der|mere
(town, England)
**Win|der|mere,
Lake** (in England)
wind|fall +s
wind|farm +s
wind|flower +s
wind force +s
wind gap +s
wind-gauge +s
Wind|hoek (capital
of Namibia)
wind|hover +s
wind|ily
windi|ness
wind|ing +s
wind|ing en|gine
+s
winding-house +s
winding-sheet +s
wind|jam|mer +s
wind|lass
wind|lasses
wind|lassed
wind|lass|ing
(machine)
wind|less (without
wind)
windle|straw +s
wind ma|chine +s
wind|mill +s +ed
+ing
win|dow +s +ed
+ing
win|dow box
win|dow boxes
win|dow clean|er
+s

win|dow clean|ing
win|dow dress|ing
win|dow frame +s
win|dow ledge +s
win|dow|less
window-pane +s
win|dow seat +s
window-shop
window-shops
window-shopped
**window-
shopping**
window-shopper
+s
win|dow|sill +s
wind|pipe +s
wind-rose +s
wind|row +s
wind-sail +s
Wind|scale (former
name of
Sellafield)
wind|screen +s
wind shear +s
wind|shield +s
wind shift +s
wind-sleeve +s
wind|sock +s
Wind|sor (city,
Canada; town,
England)
Wind|sor +s
(British royal
house)
wind speed +s
wind|storm +s
wind|surf +s +ed
+ing
wind|surf|er +s
wind|swept
wind-tossed
wind tun|nel +s
wind-up +s
(*adjective and noun*
clock; conclusion;
provocation)
wind|ward
**Wind|ward
Is|lands** (in E.
Caribbean)
windy
wind|ier
windi|est
wine
wines
wined
win|ing
(drink. △ whine)
wine bar +s
wine|berry
wine|berries
wine|bib|ber +s

wine|bib|bing
wine box
  wine boxes
wine|glass
  wine|glasses
wine|glass|ful +s
wine-grower +s
wine-growing
wine|less
wine list +s
wine|maker +s
wine|mak|ing
wine|press
  wine|presses
wine red +s *noun*
  and adjective
wine-red *attributive*
win|ery
  win|eries
wine shop +s
wine|skin +s
wine taster +s
wine tast|ing +s
winey
  wini|er
  wini|est
  (like wine.
  ⚠ whiny)
wing +s +ed +ing
wing-beat +s
wing-case +s
wing chair +s
wing col|lar +s
wing
  com|mand|er +s
wing|ding +s
wing|er +s
wing for|ward +s
wing-game +s
wing-half
  wing-halves
wing|less
wing|let +s
wing|like
wing|man
  wing|men
wing nut +s
wing|span +s
wing|spread +s
wing-stroke +s
wing-tip +s
wing-walker +s
wing-walking
Wini|fred
wink +s +ed +ing
wink|er +s
win|kle
  win|kles
  win|kled
  wink|ling
winkle-picker +s
wink|ler +s

win|less
win|nable
win|ner +s
Win|nie
win|ning +s
win|ning|ly
win|ning|ness
win|ning post +s
Win|ni|peg (city,
  Canada)
Win|ni|peg, Lake
  (in Canada)
win|now +s +ed
  +ing
win|now|er +s
wino +s
Win|ona
win|some
win|some|ly
win|some|ness
Win|ston
win|ter +s +ed
  +ing
win|ter|er +s
win|ter|green +s
Win|ter|hal|ter,
  Franz Xav|ier
  (German painter)
win|ter|isa|tion *Br.*
  (use
  winterization)
win|ter|ise *Br.* (use
  winterize)
  win|ter|ises
  win|ter|ised
  win|ter|is|ing
win|ter|iza|tion
win|ter|ize
  win|ter|izes
  win|ter|ized
  win|ter|iz|ing
win|ter|less
win|ter|ly
win|ter sports
Win|ter|thur (town,
  Switzerland)
winter-tide
win|ter|time
winter-weight
  adjective
win|tery (use
  wintry)
win|trily
win|tri|ness
win|try
  win|trier
  win|tri|est
winy
  wini|er
  wini|est
  (like wine; use
  winey. ⚠ whiny)

wipe
  wipes
  wiped
  wip|ing
wipe|able
wipe-clean
  adjective
wipe-out +s *noun*
wiper +s
Wir|ad|huri
wire
  wires
  wired
  wir|ing
wire brush
  wire brushes
  noun
wire-brush
  wire-brushes
  wire-brushed
  wire-brushing
  verb
wire-cutter +s
wire|draw
  wire|draws
  wire|drew
  wire|draw|ing
  wire|drawn
wire-haired
wire|less
  wire|lesses
wire|man
  wire|men
wire|pull|er +s
wire|pull|ing
wirer +s
wire strip|per +s
wire-tap
  wire-taps
  wire-tapped
  wire-tapping
wire-tapper +s
wire-walker +s
wire|worm +s
wir|ily
wiri|ness
Wir|ral, the
  (peninsula, NW
  England)
wiry
  wiri|er
  wiri|est
Wis|con|sin (state,
  USA)
Wis|den, John
  (English cricketer)
wis|dom +s
wise
  wises
  wised
  wis|ing

wise (*cont.*)
  wiser
  wis|est
wise|acre +s
wise|crack +s +ed
  +ing
wise|crack|er +s
wise|ly
wis|ent +s
wish
  wishes
  wished
  wish|ing
wish|bone +s
wish|er +s
wish|ful
wish-fulfil|ling
wish-fulfill|ment
  Am.
wish-fulfil|ment
  Br.
wish|ful|ly
wish|ful|ness
wishing-well +s
wish-list +s
wish-wash
wishy-washy
wisp +s
wisp|ily
wispi|ness
wispy
  wisp|ier
  wispi|est
wist (*archaic* knew.
  ⚠ whist)
wis|taria +s (use
  wisteria)
wis|teria +s
wist|ful
wist|ful|ly
wist|ful|ness
wit +s (intelligence;
  humour; person;
  in 'to wit'. ⚠ whit,
  Whit)
witan +s
witch
  witches
  witched
  witch|ing
  (sorceress; charm;
  lure. ⚠ which)
witch alder +s
witch|craft
witch doc|tor +s
witch elm +s (use
  wych elm)
witch|ery
witches' broom +s
witches' sab|bath
  +s

witch|etty
  witch|et|ties
witch hazel +s
witch-hunt +s
witch-hunter +s
witch-hunting
witch|like
wit|ena|gemot +s
with (in the
  company of; etc.
  △ withe)
withal
with|draw
  with|draws
  with|drew
  with|draw|ing
  with|drawn
with|draw|al +s
with|draw|er +s
with|draw|ing
  room +s
withe +s (willow
  shoot. △ with)
wither +s +ed
  +ing (shrivel.
  △ whither)
wither|ing|ly
with|ers (on horse)
wither|shins
  adverb
with|hold
  with|holds
  with|held
  with|hold|ing
with|hold|er +s
with|in
with it adjective and
  adverb
with-it attributive
with|out
with-profits
with|stand
  with|stands
  with|stood
  with|stand|ing
with|stand|er
withy
  with|ies
wit|less
wit|less|ly
wit|less|ness
wit|ling +s
wit|loof +s
wit|ness
  wit|nesses
  wit|nessed
  wit|ness|ing
wit|ness box
  wit|ness boxes
witness-stand +s
Wit|ten|berg
  (town, Germany)

wit|ter +s +ed
  +ing
wit|ter|ing +s
Witt|gen|stein,
  Lud|wig
  (Austrian-born
  British
  philosopher)
wit|ti|cism +s
wit|tily
wit|ti|ness
wit|ting
wit|ting|ly
witty
  wit|tier
  wit|ti|est
Wit|waters|rand,
  the (region, South
  Africa)
wi|vern +s (use
  wyvern)
wives
wiz noun (use
  whizz)
  wizzes
wiz|ard +s
wiz|ard|ly
wiz|ard|ry
  wiz|ard|ries
wiz|ened
wizzo (use whizzo)
wo (stop; use
  whoa △ woe)
woad
wob|be|gong +s
wob|ble
  wob|bles
  wob|bled
  wob|bling
wobble-board +s
wob|bler +s
wob|bli|ness
wob|bly
  wob|blier
  wob|bli|est
Wode|house, P. G.
  (British-born
  American
  novelist)
Woden
  Scandinavian
  Mythology
wodge +s
woe +s (grief.
  △ whoa)
woe|be|gone
woe|ful
woe|ful|ly
woe|ful|ness
wog +s (offensive)
wog|gle +s

Wöhl|er,
  Fried|rich
  (German chemist)
wok +s
woke
woken
Wo|king (town,
  England)
wold +s
Wolf, Hugo
  (Austrian
  composer)
wolf
  wolves
  noun
wolf +s +ed +ing
  verb
Wolf Cub +s
  (former name for
  a Cub Scout)
wolf cub +s
  (animal)
Wolfe, James
  (British general.
  △ Woolf, Woolfe)
wolf-fish
  plural wolf-fish or
  wolf-fishes
  (fish)
wolf|hound +s
wolf|ish (wolf-like)
wolf|ish|ly
wolf-like
wolf-man
  wolf-men
wolf pack +s
wolf|ram
wolf|ram|ite
wolfs|bane
Wolfs|burg (town,
  Germany)
wolf|skin +s
wolf's-milk (plant)
Wolf|son, Isaac
  (British
  businessman)
wolf spi|der +s
wolf whis|tle +s
  noun
wolf-whistle
  wolf-whistles
  wolf-whistled
  wolf-whistling
  verb
Wol|las|ton,
  Wil|liam Hyde
  (English scientist)
Wol|lon|gong (city,
  Australia)
Woll|stone|craft,
  Mary (English
  writer)

Wolof
  plural Wolof or
  Wol|ofs
Wol|sey, Thomas
  (English
  churchman and
  statesman)
Wol|ver|hamp|ton
  (city, England)
wol|ver|ine +s
wolves
woman
  women
woman|hood
woman|ise Br. (use
  womanize)
  woman|ises
  woman|ised
  woman|is|ing
woman|iser Br. +s
  (use womanizer)
woman|ish
woman|ish|ly
woman|ish|ness
woman|ist +s
woman|ize
  woman|izes
  woman|ized
  woman|iz|ing
woman|izer +s
woman|kind
woman|less
woman|like
woman|li|ness
woman|ly
womb +s
wom|bat +s
womb-like
women (plural of
  woman)
women|folk
women|kind
  (use
  womankind)
Women's
  In|sti|tute +s
womens|wear
won
  plural won
  (North or South
  Korean currency.
  △ wan)
won (past tense
  and past participle
  of win. △ one)
Won|der, Stevie
  (American
  musician)
won|der +s +ed
  +ing
won|der|er +s
won|der|ful

won|der|ful|ly
won|der|ful|ness
won|der|ing +s
won|der|ing|ly
won|der|land +s
won|der|ment +s
|wonder-struck
wonder-worker +s
wonder-working
won|drous
won|drous|ly
won|drous|ness
wonk|ily
wonki|ness
wonky
  wonk|ier
  wonki|est
wont
  wonts *or* wont
  wont|ed *or* wont
  wont|ing
  (accustom(ed);
  habit)
won't (= will not)
won|ton +s
  (dumpling.
  △ wanton)
woo +s +ed +ing
woo|able
Wood, Henry
  (English
  conductor)
wood +s (timber;
  forest. △ would)
wood|bind +s
wood|bine +s
wood|block +s
wood|carver +s
wood|carv|ing +s
wood|chat +s
wood|chip +s
wood|chuck +s
wood|cock
  plural wood|cock
wood|craft +s
wood|cut +s
wood|cut|ter +s
wood|cut|ting
wood|ed
wood|en
wood en|graver +s
wood en|grav|ing
  +s
wooden-head +s
wooden-headed
wooden-
  headed|ness
wood|en|ly
wood|en|ness
wood fiber *Am.* +s
wood fibre *Br.* +s
wood grain

wood-grain
  attributive
wood|grouse
  plural
  wood|grouse
woodi|ness
wood|land +s
wood|land|er +s
wood|lark +s
wood|less
wood|louse
  wood|lice
wood|man
  wood|men
wood mouse
  wood mice
wood|note +s
wood nymph +s
wood|peck|er +s
wood|pie +s
wood pi|geon +s
wood|pile +s
wood pulp
wood rat +s
wood|ruff +s
wood|rush
  wood|rushes
**Woods, Lake of
  the** (in Canada
  and USA)
wood|screw +s
wood|shed +s
woods|man
  woods|men
wood|smoke
wood stain +s
Wood|stock (town,
  USA)
woodsy
wood|turn|er +s
wood|turn|ing
**Wood|ward,
  Rob|ert Burns**
  (American organic
  chemist)
wood|wasp +s
wood|wind +s
wood|work
wood|work|er +s
wood|work|ing
wood|worm +s
woody
  wood|ier
  woodi|est
wood|yard +s
wooer +s
woof +s +ed +ing
  (bark; weft)
woof|er +s
woof|ter +s
  (*offensive*)
wool +s

wool|en *Am.* +s
  (*Br.* woollen)
Woolf, Vir|ginia
  (English writer.
  △ Wolfe, Woulfe)
wool-fat
wool-fell +s
wool-gather|ing
wool-grower +s
wool|len *Br.* +s
  (*Am.* woolen)
**Wool|ley,
  Leon|ard** (English
  archaeologist)
wool-like
wool|li|ness
wool|ly
  wool|lies
  wool|lier
  wool|li|est
woolly-bear +s
  (caterpillar)
wool|man
  wool|men
wool-oil
wool|pack +s
Wool|sack (in
  House of Lords)
wool|shed +s
wool-skin +s
wool-sorters'
  dis|ease
wool-stapler +s
**Wool|worth,
  Frank Win|field**
  (American
  businessman)
Woo|mera (nuclear
  testing site,
  Australia)
woo|mera +s
  (Aboriginal stick
  or thrown club)
woop woop
woosh (use
  whoosh)
  wooshes
  wooshed
  woosh|ing
woozi|ly
woozi|ness
woozy
  wooz|ier
  woozi|est
wop +s (*offensive*
  Italian. △ whop)
Wor|ces|ter (city,
  England; sauce)
Wor|ces|ter|shire
  (former county,
  England)
word +s +ed +ing

word|age
word-blind
word-blindness
word|book +s
word-class
  word-classes
word-deaf
word-deafness
word div|ision +s
word end|ing +s
word|find|er +s
word game +s
word|ily
wordi|ness
word|ing +s
word|less
word|less|ly
word|less|ness
word list +s
word order +s
word-painting +s
word-perfect
word-picture +s
word|play
word-processed
word pro|cess|ing
word pro|ces|sor
  +s
word|search
  word|searches
word|smith +s
word-square +s
**Words|worth,
  Wil|liam** (English
  poet)
Words|worth|ian
  +s
wordy
  word|ier
  wordi|est
wore (past tense of
  wear △ war)
work +s +ed +ing
work|abil|ity
work|able
work|able|ness
work|ably
work|aday
work|ahol|ic +s
work-bag +s
work-basket +s
work|bench
  work|benches
work|boat +s
work|book +s
work|box
  work|boxes
work camp +s
work|day +s
work|er +s
work|er priest +s
work|fare

work|force +s
work group +s
work|horse +s
work|house +s
work-in +s *noun*
work|ing +s
work|ing class
  work|ing classes
working-class
  attributive
work|ing man
  work|ing men
working-out *noun*
work|ing party
  work|ing par|ties
Work|ing|ton
  (port, England)
work|less
work|load +s
work|man
  work|men
work|man|like
work|man|ship
Work|mate +s
  (workbench)
  Propr.
work|mate +s
  (person)
work|out +s
work|people
work|piece +s
work|place +s
work-rate +s
work|room +s
work|sheet +s
work|shop +s
work-shy
work|site +s
work|space +s
work|sta|tion +s
work sur|face +s
work table +s
work|top +s
work-to-rule +s
work-up +s *noun*
work|wear
work|woman
  work|women
work-worn
world +s
world-beater +s
world-class
worlde (in 'olde
  worlde')
world-famous
world-line +s
world|li|ness
world|ling +s
world|ly
  world|lier
  world|li|est
worldly-minded

worldly-wise
world order +s
world-shaking
World Trade
  Cen|ter
world-view +s
world-weariness
world-weary
world|wide
World Wide Fund
  for Nature
World Wide Web
worm +s +ed +ing
worm-cast +s
worm-eaten
worm|er +s
worm-fishing
worm-gear +s
worm|hole +s
wormi|ness
worm|like
Worms (town,
  Germany; Diet)
worm|seed +s
worm's-eye view
  +s
worm-wheel +s
worm|wood +s
wormy
  wormi|er
  wormi|est
worn (past
  participle of wear.
  △warn)
worn out *adjective*
worn-out *attributive*
wor|ried|ly
wor|rier +s
wor|ri|ment
wor|ri|some
wor|ri|some|ly
wor|rit +s +ed
  +ing
worry
  wor|ries
  wor|ried
  worry|ing
worry-guts
  plural worry-guts
worry|ing|ly
worse
worsen +s +ed
  +ing
wor|ship
  wor|ships
  wor|shipped Br.
  wor|shiped Am.
  wor|ship|ping Br.
  wor|ship|ing Am.
wor|ship|able
wor|ship|er Am. +s
  (Br. worshipper)

wor|ship|ful
wor|ship|ful|ly
wor|ship|ful|ness
wor|ship|per Br. +s
  (Am. worshiper)
worst +s +ed +ing
  (most bad; get the
  better of. △wurst)
worst|ed +s
wort +s (Brewing;
  plant. △wert)
Worth, Charles
  Fred|erick
  (English couturier)
worth +s
wor|thily
worthi|ness
Wor|thing (town,
  England)
worth|less
worth|less|ly
worth|less|ness
worth|while
worth|while|ness
worthy
  wor|thies
  wor|thier
  wor|thi|est
wot (= know, e.g. in
  'God wot'. △watt,
  what)
Wotan
  Scandinavian
  Mythology
wotcha (= what are
  you; what do you;
  what have you)
wotch|er (greeting)
would (auxiliary
  verb. △wood)
would-be *attributive*
wouldn't (= would
  not)
wouldst
Woulfe (bottle.
  △Wolfe, Woolf)
wound +s +ed
  +ing
Wound|ed Knee
  (battle site, USA)
wound|ed|ness
wound|ing +s
wound|ing|ly
wound|less
wound|wort +s
wove
woven
wow +s +ed +ing
wow|ser +s
WRAC (= Women's
  Royal Army
  Corps)

wrack +s +ed +ing
  (seaweed; a
  wreck. △rack)
WRAF (= Women's
  Royal Air Force)
wraggle-taggle
wraith +s
wraith|like
Wran|gel Is|land
  (in Arctic Ocean)
wran|gle
  wran|gles
  wran|gled
  wran|gling
wran|gler +s
wran|gling +s
wrap
  wraps
  wrapped
  wrap|ping
  (envelop. △rap,
  rapt)
wrap|around +s
wrap-over +s
  adjective and noun
wrap|page
wrap|per +s
wrap|ping +s
wrap|ping paper
  +s
wrap|round +s
wrasse +s
Wrath, Cape (in
  Scotland)
wrath (anger.
  △wroth)
wrath|ful
wrath|ful|ly
wrath|ful|ness
wrathy
wreak +s +ed +ing
  (inflict. △reek)
wreak|er +s
wreath +s
wreathe
  wreathes
  wreathed
  wreath|ing
wreck +s +ed +ing
  (destroy; ruin etc.
  △rec, reck)
wreck|age
wreck|er +s
wreck-master +s
Wren +s (member
  of Women's Royal
  Naval Service)
Wren,
  Chris|to|pher
  (English architect)
Wren, P. C.
  (English novelist)

wren +s (bird)
wrench
  wrenches
  wrenched
  wrench|ing
wrest +s +ed +ing
  (wrench away.
  △ rest)
wrest-block +s
wres|tle
  wres|tles
  wres|tled
  wrest|ling
wrest|ler +s
wrest|ling +s
wrest-pin +s
wretch
  wretches
  (wretched person.
  △ retch)
wretch|ed
wretch|ed|ly
wretch|ed|ness
Wrex|ham (town,
  Wales)
wrick +s +ed +ing
  (use rick)
wrig|gle
  wrig|gles
  wrig|gled
  wrig|gling
wrig|gler +s
wrig|gly
  wrig|glier
  wrig|gli|est
**Wright, Frank
Lloyd** (American
  architect)
Wright, Or|ville
and Wil|bur
  (American
  aviation pioneers)
wright +s (maker
  or builder. △ right,
  rite, write)
wrily (use wryly)
wring
  wrings
  wrung
  wring|ing
  (squeeze tightly.
  △ ring)
wring|er +s
wrin|kle
  wrin|kles
  wrin|kled
  wrink|ling
wrin|kli|ness
wrin|kly
  wrink|lies
  wrink|lier
  wrink|li|est

wrist +s
wrist|band +s
wrist-drop
wrist|let +s
wrist-pin +s
wrist|watch
  wrist|watches
wrist-work
wristy
writ +s (written
  command; archaic
  past participle of
  write. △ rit.)
writ|able
write
  writes
  wrote
  writ|ten
  writ|ing
  (put words on
  paper. △ right,
  rite, wright)
write-down +s
  noun
write-in +s *noun*
write-off +s *noun*
writer +s (person
  who writes.
  △ righter)
writer|ly
writer's block
writer's cramp
write-up +s *noun*
writhe
  writhes
  writhed
  with|ing
writh|ing +s
writ|ing +s
writ|ing desk +s
writ|ing pad +s
writ|ing paper +s
writ|ing room +s
writ|ten
WRNS (= Women's
  Royal Naval
  Service)
Wroc|ław (city,
  Poland)
wrong +s +ed +ing
  +er +est
wrong|doer +s
wrong|doing +s
wrong|er +s
wrong-foot +s +ed
  +ing
wrong|ful
wrong|ful|ly
wrong|ful|ness
wrong-headed
wrong-headed|ly

**wrong-
headed|ness**
wrong|ly
wrong|ness
wrong'un +s
wrot (wrought
  timber. △ rot)
wrote (past tense of
  write. △ rote)
wroth (angry.
  △ wrath)
wrought (worked.
  △ rort)
wrought iron
  noun
wrought-iron
  attributive
wrung (past tense
  and past participle
  of wring. △ rung)
wry
  wryer
  wry|est *or* wri|est
  (contorted;
  mocking. △ rai,
  rye)
wry|bill +s
wryly
wry-mouth +s
wry-mouthed
wry|neck +s
wry|ness
Wu (Chinese
  dialect)
Wuhan (port,
  China)
Wu-hsi (= Wuxi)
Wul|fila (=
  Ulfilas)
wun|der|kind +s
Wundt, Wil|helm
  (German
  psychologist)
Wup|per|tal (city,
  Germany)
Wur|litz|er +s *Propr.*
wurst +s (sausage.
  △ worst)
Würz|burg (city,
  Germany)
wuss
  wusses
wussy
  wus|sies
wu-wei
Wuxi (city, China)
Wy|an|dot
  plural Wy|an|dot
  or Wy|an|dots
  (person)

Wy|an|dotte
  plural
  Wy|an|dotte *or*
  Wy|an|dottes
  (fowl)
Wyatt, James
  (English architect)
Wyatt, Thomas
  (English poet)
wych elm +s
**Wych|er|ley,
Wil|liam** (English
  dramatist)
wych hazel +s
  (use witch hazel)
Wyc|lif, John
  (English religious
  reformer)
Wyc|liffe, John
  (use Wyclif)
Wye (river, England
  and Wales)
Wyke|ham|ist +s
wyn +s (runic
  letter. △ win,
  whin)
wynd +s (narrow
  street. △ wind)
Wynd|ham, John
  (English science
  fiction writer)
Wyo|ming (state,
  USA)
WYSIWYG (= what
  you see is what
  you get)
Wys|tan
wy|vern +s

Xx

Xan|kändi (capital
of Nagorno-
Karabakh)
xan|thate +s
Xan|the
Xan|thian
   Mar|bles
xan|thic
xan|thin
xan|thine
Xan|thippe (wife of
   Socrates)
xan|thoma
   xan|tho|mas or
   xan|tho|mata
xan|tho|phyll
Xan|tippe (use
   Xanthippe)
Xav|ier
Xav|ier, St
   Fran|cis (Spanish
   missionary)
x-axis
   x-axes
xebec +s
Xen|akis, Ian|nis
   (French composer
   of Greek descent)
xen|og|am|ous
xen|og|amy
xeno|graft +s
xeno|lith +s
xenon
Xen|opha|nes
   (Greek
   philosopher)
xeno|phobe +s
xeno|pho|bia
xeno|pho|bic
Xeno|phon (Greek
   historian)
xer|an|the|mum
   +s
xeric
xero|derma
xero|graph +s
xero|graph|ic
xero|graph|ic|al|ly
xer|og|raphy
xero|phile +s
xer|oph|il|ous
xero|phyte +s
Xerox
   Xer|oxes
   noun Propr.
xerox
   xer|oxes
   xer|oxed

xerox (cont.)
   xer|ox|ing
   verb
Xer|xes (king of
   Persia)
Xhosa
   plural Xhosa or
   Xho|sas
xi +s (Greek letter)
Xia|men (port,
   China)
Xian (city, China)
Xi|me|nes de
   Cis|neros (use
   Jiménez de
   Cisneros)
Xing|tai (city,
   China)
Xingú (river, S.
   America)
Xi|ning (city,
   China)
Xin|jiang (region,
   China)
Xiph|ias (old name
   for Dorado)
xiphi|ster|num
   xiphi|sterna or
   xiphi|ster|nums
xiph|oid
Xmas
   (= Christmas)
xoa|non
   xoana
X-rated
X-ray +s +ed +ing
xu
   plural xu
   (Vietnamese
   currency. △ sou,
   sue)
Xu|zhou (city,
   China)
xylem
xy|lene +s
xylo|carp +s
xylo|carp|ous
xylo|graph +s
xyl|og|raphy
Xy|lon|ite Propr.
xyl|opha|gous
xylo|phone +s
xylo|phon|ic
xyl|oph|on|ist +s
xys|tus
   xysti

Yy

yab|ber +s +ed
   +ing
yab|bie +s (use
   yabby)
yabby
   yab|bies
yacht +s +ed +ing
yacht club +s
yachtie +s
yacht ra|cing
yachts|man
   yachts|men
yack +s +ed +ing
   (use yak)
yacka (work; use
   yakka. △ yakker)
yacker (work; use
   yakka. △ yakker)
yackety-yack +s
   +ed +ing
yaf|fle +s
Ya|gara
yager +s (use
   jaeger)
Yagi +s
yah
yahoo +s
Yah|veh (use
   Yahweh)
Yah|vist +s (use
   Yahwist)
Yah|weh Bible
Yah|wist +s
Yajur-veda
yak
   yaks
   yakked
   yak|king
   (animal; chatter)
yaki|tori
yakka (work)
yak|ker +s
   (chatterer)
Yakut
   plural Yakut or
   Ya|kuts
Ya|ku|tia (republic,
   Russia)
Ya|kutsk (city,
   Russia)
ya|kuza
   plural ya|kuza
Yale +s (lock)
   Propr.
Yale (university,
   USA)
y'all (= you-all.
   △ yawl, you'll)

Yalta (port,
   Ukraine)
Yalu (river, E. Asia)
yam +s
Yama Hindu
   Mythology
Yama|moto,
   Iso|roku
   (Japanese
   admiral)
Yama|saki,
   Min|oru
   (American
   architect)
Yamato-e
   (Japanese
   painting style)
yam|mer +s +ed
   +ing
Yam|ous|sou|kro
   (capital of the
   Ivory Coast)
Ya|muna (river,
   India)
Yan|cheng (city,
   China)
yandy
   yan|dies
   yan|died
   yandy|ing
yang
Yan|gon (Burmese
   name for
   Rangoon)
Yang|shao (Chinese
   civilization)
Yang|tze (river,
   China)
Yank +s (may cause
   offence; American)
yank +s +ed +ing
   (tug)
Yan|kee +s (may
   cause offence)
Yan|kee Doo|dle
   +s
Yan|tai (port,
   China)
yan|tra +s
Ya|oundé (capital
   of Cameroon)
yap
   yaps
   yapped
   yap|ping
   (bark; talk noisily)
yapok +s
yapp +s
   Bookbinding
yap|per +s

yappy
  yap|pier
  yap|pi|est
yar|bor|ough+s
yard+s +ed +ing
yard|age+s
yard|arm+s
yard|bird+s
Yardie+s
yard|man
  yard|men
yard|stick+s
yar|mulka+s (use
  yarmulke)
yar|mulke+s
yarn+s +ed +ing
Yaro|slavl (port,
  Russia)
yar|ran+s
yar|row+s
yash|mak+s
Yas|min
yata|ghan+s
yat|ter+s +ed
  +ing
yaw+s +ed +ing
  (deviate. △ yore
  your, you're)
yawl+s (boat.
  △ y'all you'll)
yawn+s +ed +ing
yawn|er+s
yawn|ing|ly
yawp+s +ed +ing
yawp|er+s
yaws (disease.
  △ yours)
y-axis
  y-axes
Yayoi
yclept
ye
yea+s archaic
yeah+s colloquial
yean+s +ed +ing
yean|ling+s
year+s
year|book+s
year-end+s
year in, year out
year|ling+s
year-long
year|ly
yearn+s +ed +ing
yearn|er+s
yearn|ing+s
yearn|ing|ly
year-round
yeast+s
yeast|ily
yeasti|ness
yeast|less

yeast|like
yeasty
  yeast|ier
  yeasti|est
Yeats, W. B. (Irish
  writer)
Yeats|ian
yegg+s
Ye|kat|er|in|burg
  (city, Russia)
Ye|kat|er|ino|dar
  (former name of
  the city of
  Krasnodar)
Ye|kat|er|ino|slav
  (former name of
  Dnipropetrovsk)
Ye|liza|vet|pol
  (former Russian
  name for Gäncä)
yell+s +ed +ing
yel|low+s +ed
  +ing +er +est
yel|low|back+s
yellow-bellied
yellow-belly
  yellow-bellies
yellow-bill
yel|low|cake
yel|low|fin
  plural yel|low|fin
  or yel|low|fins
yel|low|ham|mer
  +s
yel|low|ish
Yel|low|knife (city,
  Canada)
yel|low|legs
  plural yel|low|legs
yel|low|ness
Yel|low|stone
  (national park,
  USA)
yel|lowy
yelp+s +ed +ing
yelp|er+s
Yelt|sin, Boris
  (Russian
  president)
Yemen (in Arabian
  peninsula)
Yem|eni+s
Yem|en|ite+s
yen
  plural yen
  (Japanese
  currency)
yen
  yens
  yenned
  yen|ning

yen (cont.)
  (longing; feel a
  longing)
Yen-cheng
  (= Yancheng)
Yeni|sei (river,
  Siberia)
Yen-tai (= Yantai)
yeo|man
  yeo|men
yeo|man|ly
yeo|man|ry
  yeo|man|ries
Yeo|vil (town,
  England)
yep
yerba maté
Yere|van (capital of
  Armenia)
yes
  yeses
yes-man
  yes-men
yes|ter|day+s
yes|ter|eve
yes|ter|morn
yes|ter|night
yes|ter|year
yet
yeti+s
Yev|tu|shenko,
  Yev|geni (Russian
  poet)
yew+s (tree.
  △ ewe you)
yew tree+s
Y-fronts Propr.
Ygg|dra|sil
Yi|chun (city,
  China)
Yid+s (offensive)
Yid|dish
Yid|dish|er+s
Yid|dish|ism+s
yield+s +ed +ing
yield|er+s
yield|ing|ly
yield|ing|ness
yikes
yin
Yin|chuan (city,
  China)
Yin|dji|barndi
yip
  yips
  yipped
  yip|ping
yip|pee
ylang-ylang+s
Ymir Scandinavian
  Mythology
yo

yob+s
yob|bish
yob|bish|ly
yob|bish|ness
yobbo
  yob|bos or
  yob|boes
yocto|meter Am.
  +s
yocto|metre Br. +s
yod+s
yodel
  yo|dels
  yo|delled Br.
  yo|deled Am.
  yo|del|ling Br.
  yo|del|ling Am.
yo|del|er+s Am.
yo|del|ler+s Br.
yoga
yogh+s
yog|hurt+s (use
  yogurt)
yogi+s
yogic
yo|gism
yog|urt+s
Yog|ya|karta (city,
  Java, Indonesia)
yo-heave-ho
yohi+s
yo-ho
yoicks
yoke
  yokes
  yoked
  yok|ing
  (neck-frame.
  △ yolk, yolked)
yokel+s
Yoko|hama (port,
  Japan)
Yo|landa
Yo|lande
yolk+s (part of
  egg; wool grease.
  △ yoke)
yolk-bag+s
yolked (having yolk.
  △ yoked)
yolk|less
yolk-sac+s
yolky
Yom Kip|pur
yomp+s +ed +ing
yon
yon|der
yoni+s
yonks
yoof (= youth)
yoo-hoo

yore (in 'of yore'.
△ yaw, your,
you're)
York (city,
England)
York, Cape (in
Australia)
York, Duke of
(Prince Andrew)
york +s +ed +ing
york¦er +s
York¦ist +s
**York¦shire, North,
West, and South**
(counties,
England)
York¦shire¦man
York¦shire¦men
York¦shire¦woman
York¦shire¦
women
York¦town (town,
USA)
Yor¦uba
plural **Yor¦uba**
Yor¦vik (Viking
name for **York**)
Yo¦sem¦ite
(national park,
USA)
Yoshkar-Ola (city,
Russia)
yotta¦meter *Am.*
+s
yotta¦metre *Br.* +s
you (*pronoun.*
△ ewe, yew)
you-all
you'd (= you had;
you would)
youi +s (use **yohi**)
you-know-what
+s
you-know-who
you'll (= you shall;
you will. △ Yule)
Young, Brig¦ham
(American
Mormon leader)
Young, Thomas
(English physicist)
young +er +est
young¦ish
young¦ling +s
Young's modu¦lus
Young's mod¦uli
young¦ster +s
young 'un +s
youn¦ker +s
your (belonging to
you. △ yaw, yore,
you're)

you're (= you are.
△ yaw, yore,
your)
yours (the one(s)
belonging to you.
△ yaws)
your¦self
your¦selves
youse (you *plural.*
△ use)
youth +s
youth¦ful
youth¦ful¦ly
youth¦ful¦ness
you've (= you
have)
yowl +s +ed +ing
yo-yo +s *noun*
Propr.
yo-yo
yo-yoes
yo-yoed
yo-yoing
verb
Ypres (town and
battle site,
Belgium)
yt¦ter¦bium
yt¦trium
Yuan (Chinese
dynasty)
yuan
plural **yuan**
(Chinese
currency)
Yuca¦tán (state and
peninsula,
Mexico)
yucca +s
yuck
yucki¦ness
yucky
yuck¦ier
yucki¦est
Yugo¦slav +s
Yugo¦slavia
Yugo¦slav¦ian +s
Yuit
plural **Yuit** or
Yuits
yuk (use **yuck**)
yukki¦ness (use
yuckiness)
yukky (use **yucky**)
Yukon (river, N.
America)
Yukon Ter¦ri¦tory
(in Canada)
Yule +s (Christmas.
△ you'll)
yule log +s
Yule¦tide +s

yummy
yum¦mier
yum¦mi¦est
yum-yum
Yun¦nan (province,
China)
yup
Yupik
yup¦pie +s
yup¦pie¦dom
yup¦pi¦fi¦ca¦tion
yup¦pify
yup¦pi¦fies
yup¦pi¦fied
yup¦pi¦fy¦ing
yuppy (use **yuppie**)
yup¦pies
yurt +s
Yu¦waa¦la¦raay
Yuz¦ovka (former
name of Donetsk)
Yv¦ette *also* **Ev¦ette**
Yv¦onne *also*
Ev¦onne

Zz

zaba¦gli¦one +s
Zabrze (city,
Poland)
Zaca¦tecas (city
and state, Mexico)
Zac¦chaeus *Bible*
Zach¦ary
Zack
zaf¦fer *Am.*
zaffre *Br.*
zag +s
Zaga¦zig (city,
Egypt)
Zag¦reb (capital of
Croatia)
**Zag¦ros
Moun¦tains** (in
Iran)
Zaire (country and
river)
zaire +s (Zairean
currency)
Za¦irean +s
Za¦irian +s (use
Zairean)
Zák¦in¦thos (Greek
name for
Zakynthos)
Zako¦pane (winter-
sports resort,
Poland)
Zak¦yn¦thos (Greek
island)
Zam¦besi (use
Zambezi)
Zam¦bezi (river, E.
Africa)
Zam¦bia
Zam¦bian +s
Zam¦bo¦anga (port,
Mindanao,
Philippines)
zam¦in¦dar +s
zan¦der
plural **zan¦der**
zani¦ly
zani¦ness
Zan¦skar (river and
mountain range,
India)
Zan¦skari +s
Zánte (alternative
name for
Zakynthos)
ZANU
(= Zimbabwe
African National
Union)

zany
zanies
zani¦er
zani¦est
Zan¦zi|bar (island, Tanzania)
Zan¦zi|bari +s
Zao|zhuang (city, China)
zap
zaps
zapped
zap|ping
Zap¦ata, Emili¦ano (Mexican revolutionary)
zapa|te|ado +s
Zapo|rizh¦zhya (city, Ukraine)
Zapo|rozhe (Russian name for Zaporizhzhya)
Zapo|tec
plural Zapo|tec *or* Zapo|tecs
Zappa, Frank (American rock musician)
zap¦per +s
zappy
zap|pier
zap|pi¦est
ZAPU (= Zimbabwe African People's Union)
Zaqa|ziq (use Zagazig)
Zara
Zara|goza (Spanish name for Saragossa)
zar¦ape +s (use serape)
Zara|thus¦tra (Avestan name for Zoroaster)
Zara|thus¦trian +s
zar¦eba +s (use zariba)
Zaria (city, Nigeria)
zar¦iba +s
Zarqa (city, Jordan)
zar|zuela +s
Zato|pek, Emil (Czechoslovak runner)
zax
zaxes
zeal
Zea|land (island, Denmark.
⚠ Zeeland)

Zealot +s (member of ancient Jewish sect)
zealot +s (fanatic)
zeal|ot¦ry
zeal¦ous
zeal¦ous¦ly
zeal¦ous|ness
zebec +s (use xebec)
ze¦beck +s (use xebec)
Zeb|edee
zebra
plural zebra *or* zebras
zeb|rine
zebu +s·
Zebu|lon (use Zebulun)
Zebu|lun *Bible*
Zech|ar¦iah *Bible*
zed +s
Zed|ekiah *Bible*
zedo|ary
zedo|ar¦ies
zee +s
Zee|brugge (port, Belgium)
Zee|land (province, the Netherlands.
⚠ Zealand)
Zee¦man ef¦fect
Zef¦fi|relli, Franco (Italian film and theatre director)
zein +s
Zeiss, Carl (German optical-instrument maker)
Zeit|geist
Zelda
zem|in|dar +s (use zamindar)
Zen
Zena
zen¦ana +s
Zend +s
Zend-Avesta
Zener (card; diode)
Zen¦ist +s
zen¦ith
zen|ith¦al
Zeno (two Greek philosophers)
Zen|obia (queen of Palmyra)
zeo|lite +s
zeo|lit¦ic
Zepha|niah *Bible*
zephyr +s
Zep|pelin, Fer¦di|nand,

Zep|pelin (*cont.*)
Count von (German aviation pioneer)
Zep|pelin +s (airship)
zepto|meter *Am.* +s
zepto|metre *Br.* +s
Zer|matt (ski resort, Switzerland)
zero +s *noun*
zero
zer¦oes
zer¦oed
zero|ing
verb
zero hour
zero rate *noun*
zero-rate
zero-rates
zero-rated
zero-rating
verb
zero-sum
zer¦oth
zest
zest¦er +s
zest|ful
zest|ful¦ly
zest|ful|ness
zesti|ness
zesty
zest|ier
zesti|est
Zeta (name)
zeta +s (Greek letter)
ze|tet¦ic
zetta|meter *Am.* +s
zetta|metre *Br.* +s
zeugma +s
zeug|mat¦ic
Zeus *Greek Mythology*
Zeuxis (Greek painter)
Zhang|jia¦kou (city, China)
Zhan|jiang (port, China)
Zhda|nov (former name of Mariupol)
Zhe|jiang (province, China)
Zheng|zhou (city, China)
Zhen|jiang (port, China)

Zhito|mir (Russian name for Zhytomyr)
zho (use dzo)
plural zho *or* zhos
Zhong|shan (city, China)
Zhou (Chinese dynasty)
Zhou Enlai (Chinese statesman)
Zhu¦kov, Georgi (Soviet military leader)
Zhyto|myr (city, Ukraine)
Zia ul-Haq, Mu¦ham|mad (Pakistani president)
Zibo (city, China)
zi¦dovu|dine
Zieg|feld, Flor|enz (American theatre manager)
ziff +s
zig
zigs
zigged
zig|ging
zig|gurat +s
zig¦zag
zig|zags
zig|zagged
zig|zag|ging
zig¦zag|ged¦ly
zilch
zil¦lah +s
zil|lion +s
zil|lionth +s
Zim|babwe
Zim|bab¦we|an +s
Zim¦mer frame +s
Propr.
zinc +s +ed +ing
zinc blende
zinco +s *noun*
zinco
zin|coes
zin|coed
zinco|ing
verb
zinco|graph +s
zinc|og¦raphy
zinco|type +s
zincy
zing +s +ed +ing
Zin|garo
Zin|gari
zing¦er +s

zingy
  zing|ier
  zingi|est
Zin|jan|thro|pus
zin|nia +s
Zion
Zion|ism
Zion|ist +s
zip
  zips
  zipped
  zip|ping
Zip code +s
zip fas|ten|er +s
zip|per +s +ed
  +ing
zip|pily
zip|pi|ness
zippy
  zip|pier
  zip|pi|est
zip-up *adjective*
zir|con +s
zir|co|nia
zir|co|nium
zit +s
zith|er +s
zith|er|ist +s
zizz
  zizzes
  zizzed
  zizz|ing
zloty
  plural zloty *or*
  zlotys *or* zlot|ies
zo|diac +s
zo|di|ac|al
Zoe *also* Zoë
Zoë *also* Zoe
zoe|trope +s
Zof|fany, Jo|hann
  (German painter)

Zog (Albanian king)
zoic
Zola (name)
Zola, Émile
  (French writer)
Zöll|ner's lines
zoll|ver|ein +s
zom|bie +s
zonal
zon|ary
zon|ate
zon|ation +s
zonda +s
zone
  zones
  zoned
  zon|ing
zonk +s +ed +ing
zoo +s
zoo|geo|graph|ic
zoo|
  geo|graph|ic|al
zoo|geo|graph|ic|
  al|ly
zoo|geog|raphy
zo|og|raphy
zooid +s
zo|oid|al
zoo|keep|er +s
zo|ol|atry
zoo|logic|al
zoo|logic|al|ly
zo|olo|gist +s
zo|ology
zoom +s +ed +ing
zoo|mancy
zoo|morph|ic
zoo|morph|ism
zoon|osis
  zoon|oses
zoo|phyte +s
zoo|phyt|ic

zoo|plank|ton
zoo|spore +s
zoo|spor|ic
zo|ot|omy
zoot suit +s
zori +s
zoril +s
zor|illa +s
Zoro|as|ter
  (Persian founder
  of Zoroast.ianism)
Zoro|as|trian +s
Zoro|as|trian|ism
Zou|ave +s
zouk
zounds
Zsig|mondy,
  Rich|ard
  Ad|olph (Austrian-
  born German
  chemist)
zuc|chetto +s
zuc|chini
  plural zuc|chini *or*
  zuc|chi|nis
Zug (city and
  canton,
  Switzerland)
zug|zwang +s
Zui|der Zee
  (former inlet, the
  Netherlands)
Zulu +s
Zulu|land (former
  name of
  KwaZulu)
Zur|ba|rán,
  Fran|cisco de
  (Spanish painter)
Zur|ich (city and
  canton,
  Switzerland)

Zür|ich (German
  name for Zurich)
Zwickau (city,
  Germany)
zwie|back
Zwingli, Ul|rich
  (Swiss Protestant
  reformer)
Zwing|li|an +s
zwit|ter|ion +s
Zwolle (town, the
  Netherlands)
Zwory|kin,
  Vlad|imir
  (Russian-born
  American
  physicist)
zy|deco
zygo|dac|tyl +s
zygo|dac|tyl|ous
zyg|oma
  zyg|omata *or*
  zyg|omas
zygo|mat|ic
zygo|morph|ic
zygo|morph|ous
zyg|osis
zygo|spore +s
zyg|ote +s
zyg|ot|ene
zyg|ot|ic
zyg|ot|ic|al|ly
zym|ase
zymo|logic|al
zym|olo|gist +s
zym|ology
zym|osis
zym|ot|ic
zym|urgy